PSYCHOLOGY, MENTAL HEALTH AND DISTRESS

PSYCHOLOGY, MENTAL HEALTH AND DISTRESS

John Cromby
University of Loughborough

David Harper
University of East London

and

Paula Reavey
London South Bank University

First published 2013 by
PALGRAVE

Red Globe Press in the UK is an imprint of Springer Nature Limited, registered in
England, company number 785998, of 4 Crinan Street, London N1 9XW.

Palgrave Macmillan in the US is a division of St Martin's Press LLC,
175 Fifth Avenue, New York, NY 10010.

Red Globe Press is a global imprint of the above companies and is represented
throughout the world.

Red Globe Press® is a registered trademark in the United States,
the United Kingdom, Europe and other countries

ISBN: 978–0–230–54955–5 hardback
ISBN: 978–0–230–54956–2 paperback

This book is printed on paper suitable for recycling and made from fully
managed and sustained forest sources. Logging, pulping and manufacturing
processes are expected to conform to the environmental regulations of the
country of origin.

A catalogue record for this book is available from the British Library.

A catalogue record for this book is available from the Library of Congress.

BRIEF CONTENTS

LONG CONTENTS

LIST OF ILLUSTRATIONS

TOUR OF THE BOOK

HISTORY

Michael's story

Michael is a middle-aged man who is married with children. One
work he sees something strange which he struggles to understar
figure in white approaching him. Later that day he hears a voice th
is hearing the voice of God and that he should give up his life ar

How might we understand this experience? As we will see i
one context for understanding such experiences is a cult
we might want to know what country the man lives i
xist – are religious visions and voices seen a
nd expected, even valued

Case story

Case stories at the beginning of each
chapter introduce that chapter's theme,
using a fictional individual's experiences
of mental health and distress.

**Learning outcomes and guiding
questions**

These outline what the chapter will focus
on to help organise your study. The
guiding questions will help to focus your
learning as you read the chapter.

Learning outcomes

After you have read this chapter, you will be able to:

1 identify some of the core assumptions underlying
   psychiatric diagnosis
2 explain how psychiatric diagnosis differs from most
   medical diagnosis
3 describe how issues of reli part of the chapter describes wha elevant
   to psychiatric diagn ation is, explains how it is used by clinical psych
   xplain what a fc d provides an evaluation of its benefits and limitations.

Guiding questions

Throughout this chapter, you should bear in mind these
two questions:

1 *How is psychiatric diagnosis similar to, and different
   from, diagnosis in general medicine?*
2 *How adequate is formulation as an alternative to
   psychiatric diagnosis?*

End of chapter questions

Each chapter ends with
questions to help test your
knowledge and understanding
by encouraging you to reflect
on the key issues discussed.

End of chapter questions

1 What different ways of understanding distress have there been
   and why is it currently seen as an issue of health?
2 To what extent has the dominance of particular models
   been a result of struggles between different institutions and
   professional groups?
3 To what extent are modern debates about the relationship
   between biology and the social environment related to earlier
   debates between competing kinds of causal explanations
   such as somatogenesis, psychogenesis and sociogenesis?

Find out more

1 www.studymore.org.uk/mhhtim.htm
   A very informative and detailed website about key historical
   events in the history of mental health.

Find out more

A helpful guide to point you in the
direction of further information, this
directs you to further academic reading,
fiction books and films related to the
chapter's themes.

Companion website

www.palgrave.com/psychology/Cromby
Go online to explore mental health and distress further
through multiple-choice questions, videos and more.

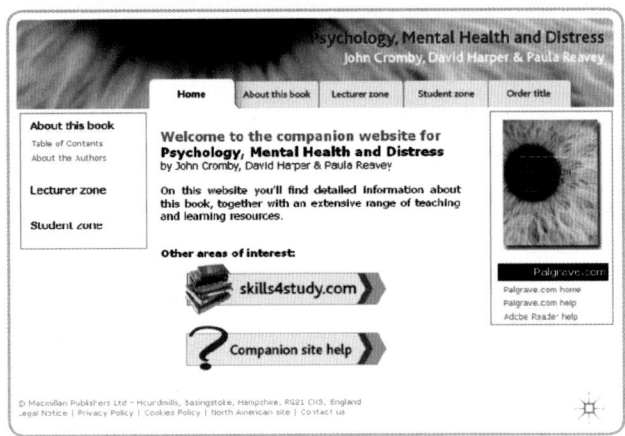

ABOUT THE AUTHORS

John Cromby is Senior Lecturer, Psychology Division, SSEHS, Loughborough University. Previously, he conducted research and teaching at the Universities of Nottingham and Bradford, and he has experience of working in mental health, drug addiction and learning disability settings. His work engages with the ways that bodies and social processes come together to produce experience, including experiences of distress. In recent years this has meant exploring topics such as paranoia, clinical sadness, emotion and fear of crime, and experimenting with methods of jointly analysing textual data and embodied activity. He is a former editor of the journal *Subjectivity*.

David Harper is Reader in Clinical Psychology at the University of East London (UEL). He trained as a clinical psychologist at the University of Liverpool and worked as a clinical psychologist in National Health Service mental health services in the north-west of the UK for nine years. For a number of years he combined work as a clinician with part-time study for a PhD at Manchester Metropolitan University. He has been at UEL since 2000 and his research interests are in applying critical psychology and social constructionist ideas to the understanding both of distress (particularly paranoia and unusual experiences and beliefs) and the work of mental health professions. He co-authored *Deconstructing Psychopathology* (1995) and co-edited *Qualitative Research Methods in Mental Health and Psychotherapy: An Introduction for Students and Practitioners* (2012).

Paula Reavey is Professor of Psychology at London South Bank University, where she delivers a module on the psychology of mental health and distress. She edited the volume *Visual Psychologies: Using and Interpreting Images in Qualitative Research* (2011) and also co-edited two volumes, *New Feminist Stories of Child Sexual Abuse: Sexual Scripts and Dangerous Dialogues* (with Sam Warner, 2003) and *Memory Matters: Contexts for Understanding Sexual Abuse Recollections* (with Janice Haaken, 2009). She is currently working on a co-authored book *Vital Memory: Ethics, Affect and Agency* (with Steven D. Brown, 2013) and has also published numerous articles on social remembering, child sexual abuse and sexuality, mental distress, and embodiment and space, using a variety of methodologies, including memory work, discourse analysis and visual methods.

A NOTE ON AUTHORSHIP

Out of the thirteen chapters of the book, eight are written solely by the lead authors (John Cromby, David Harper and Paula Reavey) but five are written by or with other contributors who, we felt, would introduce valuable perspectives. Where a chapter or section has been authored by one of our additional contributors we have indicated this by including their name at the start of the chapter or section. Where a chapter or section does not list an author, that indicates that it has been written by John Cromby, David Harper or Paula Reavey.

Lucy Johnstone (author of Chapter 5 and co-author of Chapter 6) is a clinical psychologist who has previously written about diagnosis and formulation.

In many textbooks, the words of those who experience mental distress are often heard only indirectly as case examples described by researchers and textbook authors. Rarely do we get the chance to hear the voices of those who have experienced distress more directly. Peter Campbell, Jacqui Dillon and Eleanor Longden have all had first hand experience of mental health services and have also written and presented extensively about mental health, so they were ideally placed to write Chapter 7. Jacqui and Eleanor have both had the experience of hearing voices (i.e. 'auditory hallucinations' in psychiatric terminology) and have been involved with the hearing voices movement for a number of years (Jacqui is Chair of the UK National Hearing Voices Network).

In Chapter 8, which concerns mental health interventions, Joanna Moncrieff wrote the section on medication. As a practising psychiatrist and researcher, Joanna has written about medication in a number of arenas. Paul Moloney (a counselling psychologist) and Paul Kelly (a clinical psychologist) wrote the section on psychological therapies, and they also have published on this topic. The section on community psychological interventions was written collaboratively by Paul Moloney and clinical psychologists Rachel Cox, Guy Holmes, Penny Priest and Mike Ridley-Dash. These authors have had considerable experience of using community psychological interventions, about which they've written widely.

Academic researcher and activist Allan Tyler wrote the section on 'gender, variance and distress' in Chapter 10.

Finally, Chapter 11 is co-authored by John Read and Richard Bentall. John and Richard are both clinical psychologists and researchers who have been researching and writing about madness for over twenty years.

ADDITIONAL CONTRIBUTOR BIOGRAPHIES

Richard Bentall is Professor of Clinical Psychology at the University of Liverpool. His research encompasses the psychological mechanisms underlying psychotic experiences (hallucinations and delusions), the role of social adversity in psychosis, and the development of novel psychological interventions for patients with psychosis. He is the author of *Madness Explained: Psychosis and Human Nature* (2003) and *Doctoring the Mind: Why Psychiatric Treatments Fail* (2009).

Peter Campbell is a mental health system survivor. He worked for many years with pre-school age children and children with special needs. Now he works as a freelance trainer and writer in the mental health field. He is also a poet and has published a collection of his poems titled *Brown Linoleum, Green Lawns*.

Rachel Cox is a consultant clinical psychologist working with adults with learning disabilities in Shropshire and Telford and Wrekin. Her main areas of interest include working with and developing services for parents with learning disabilities and in developing policy, services and training in the areas of personal relationships and sexuality of people with learning disabilities.

Jacqui Dillon is a campaigner, writer, international speaker and trainer and national Chair of the Hearing Voices Network in England. She is a co-editor of *Living with Voices: Fifty Stories of Recovery* (2009) and *Models of Madness* (2013).

Guy Holmes is a clinical psychologist who works in a Community Mental Health Team in Shropshire. His books include *This is Madness* (1999), *This is Madness, Too* (2001) and *Psychology in the Real World: Community-based Groupwork* (2010).

Lucy Johnstone is a clinical psychologist and former Programme Director of the Bristol Clinical Psychology Doctorate. She has spent many years working in adult mental health settings. She is the author of *Users and Abusers of Psychiatry* (2000), and co-editor of *Formulation in Psychology and Psychotherapy: Making Sense of People's Problems* (2013).

Paul Kelly is a clinical psychologist who trained in Birmingham, UK. He was involved in setting up the West Midlands Community and Critical Psychology Interest Group and the Midlands Psychology Group. Since returning to his home country of Ireland he has been working as a clinical psychologist at University College Dublin. His main interest is in understanding the links between oppressive forms of social organization and experiences of distress.

Eleanor Longden is a postgraduate researcher at the University of Leeds, co-ordinator of the Intervoice Scientific Committee, and a faculty member of the International Centre for Recovery Action in Practice, Education and Research (ICRA).

Paul Moloney is a counselling psychologist working in an NHS Adult Learning Disabilities Service. He is a member of the Midlands Psychology Group. Previously he worked in a Community Mental Health Team in Birmingham, as an alcohol counsellor in the voluntary sector, as a social and community worker, and also as an associate tutor with the Open University. As a psychologist, his main interest is in how well-being and distress are shaped by the world in which people live.

Joanna Moncrieff is a senior lecturer at University College London and an honorary consultant psychiatrist at the North East London Foundation Trust. She is the co-chairperson of the Critical Psychiatry Network, and author of *The Myth of the Chemical Cure* (2007), *A Straight Talking Introduction to Psychiatric Drugs* (2009), and many academic papers.

Penny Priest was brought up in Hull, studied psychology at Manchester University, and started work as a teacher in East London. She now lives and works in Shropshire, having trained as a clinical psychologist at Birmingham University.

John Read is Professor of Clinical Psychology at the University of Liverpool and Programme Director for the Doctorate of Clinical Psychology. He is editor of the journal *Psychosis: Psychological, Social and Integrative Approaches* and co-editor of *Models of Madness* (2013).

Mike Ridley-Dash is a clinical psychologist working at Northamptonshire Healthcare NHS Foundation Trust with individuals with diabetes. He has an enduring interest in critical community psychology, which began during his undergraduate degree at the University of Stirling, through Dr David Fryer's community psychology module (now, sadly, defunct). He keeps his interest in this area alive in part through lecturing within the Society and Context module on the Shropshire and Staffordshire Clinical Psychology Training Programme.

Allan Tyler is an academic advisor with PACE (a London-based charity promoting the mental health and emotional well-being of the lesbian, gay, bisexual and transgender community) for a national lottery-funded project studying issues of risk and resilience in mental health for British LGBT people. He has been an activist, organizer and performance artist in the queer community since 1995. His research interests include body image and sexuality, particularly focusing on gay, lesbian, bisexual and transgender cultures and politics.

FOREWORD

It is with considerable delight, and no small measure of relief, that I write this foreword to *Psychology, Mental Health and Distress*. The delight comes from the opportunity to recommend a beautifully written and thoughtfully constructed textbook, which will fire the interest of the next generation of students, enhancing their understanding of the various kinds of psychological suffering experienced by a sizeable minority of human beings living today. The relief is because this book at last solves a problem that has long troubled me as an academic clinical psychologist, and which I suspect must be a source of concern to many other psychologists working in universities around the globe.

Like most academic clinical psychologists, I not only carry out research and see patients, but teach students. Every year, therefore, I find myself facing a new class of young undergraduates eager to learn about the clinical applications of psychology. They are typically very bright, energetic and anxious to learn. Some wish to progress on to careers as clinical psychologists or psychotherapists. (Occasionally, one will be bold enough to say that she'd like my job when she gets older.) Very often, they came into psychology because of a fascination with clinical phenomena and the quirks of mental life. They may have experienced mental health difficulties themselves, or know friends and relatives who have been affected in this way. Some have endured lecture courses on related topics such as cognitive psychology or neuroscience solely in order to progress to the point at which they can begin to learn about psychiatric conditions. Typically, at the beginning of the first lecture in a module, there is an air of expectation. They want to know more about what my course will be covering, how it will be assessed ... and, of course, which textbook I will recommend.

There are numerous textbooks of 'abnormal psychology' or 'psychopathology' to choose from. Often they are expensive, heavy tomes, colourfully illustrated, and suggest a confidence about our understanding of these experiences that is, in my view, entirely unwarranted. Chapters organized around diagnostic categories such as 'schizophrenia' or 'depression' imply that steady progress has been achieved in understanding their causes, and in developing effective treatments for them. And, of course, this idea of steady and inevitable progress, facilitated by technological advances such as functional magnetic resonance imaging and gene sequencing, is widely accepted outside the field. In his highly cited Whig history of psychiatry, the historian Edward Shorter (1997) was moved to remark that 'If there is one central intellectual reality at the end of the twentieth century, it is that the biological approach to psychiatry – treating mental illness as a genetically influenced disorder of the brain chemistry – has been a smashing success'. If only that were true.

The reality is that evidence of progress, at least in the treatment of mental health difficulties, is sparse. As I have detailed elsewhere, there is no evidence that the long-term outcome for people diagnosed with severe mental illness has improved since

the Victorian era, and some evidence that people with severe mental health problems fare better in nonindustrial societies than in industrialized nations populated by expensively trained psychiatrists and psychologists (Bentall, 2009). In the developed nations, the proportion of people disabled by mental health problems has risen inexorably since the end of the Second World War (Whitaker, 2005), again, hardly evidence of the smashing success that Shorter would have us believe in. Recently, disquiet has been emerging about the effectiveness of widely used, and often coercively applied, medical remedies such as antidepressant (Kirsch, 2009) and antipsychotic drugs (Lepping, Sambhi, Whittington, Lane & Poole, 2011). Part of the problem seems to be the extraordinary steps pharmaceutical companies have taken, which have now been extensively documented, to massage the data from clinical trials (Healy, 2004; Turner, Matthews, Linardatos, Tell & Rosenthal, 2007), but which it is difficult to teach students about without sounding paranoid. Against this background, it is important that any textbook on mental health issues, especially one that is written for impressionable students at the start of their careers, should be critical and well-balanced.

Unfortunately, most of the existing textbooks have neither of these characteristics. For example, they often fail to acknowledge the role of culture and values in determining our decisions about what counts as a mental health problem in the first place. They take the classifications used in widely used diagnostic manuals as a given (often using them as chapter headings) when, in reality, these classifications are now widely recognized as having very limited clinical and scientific value. For example, researchers studying mental health problems are increasingly questioning the value of the 'schizophrenia' diagnosis (Craddock & Owen, 2005) and advocating alternative approaches, such as dimensional models (van Os & Kapur, 2009). Finally, in the discussion of the causes of mental health problems, traditional textbooks typically over-emphasize genetic and neurobiological causes of distress and neglect environmental factors. To take another example from my own field of psychosis, there is now compelling evidence that adverse experiences in childhood, for example various forms of abuse, play a causal role in the development of hallucinations and delusions (Read, van Os, Morrison & Ross, 2005; Varese et al., 2012, and see Chapter 11 in this volume) but this important fact is not mentioned in most textbooks. Overshadowing these limitations is the dead hand of the American Psychiatric Association's *Diagnostic and Statistical Manual* which, since its third edition (American Psychiatric Association, 1980), has promoted an American-centred, bio-bio-bio conception of psychiatric disorder (Sharfstein, 2005) and stifled debate about the best ways of thinking about and addressing human distress.

This textbook has been designed to specifically address these deficits. It has been, above all, designed to help students *think* about the nature of mental illness and mental health. I know (because I have watched the project progress over some years) that its construction has been a far from easy task. We should all be thankful that the efforts undertaken by the authors have yielded a helpful, accessible and useful book, which will guide future generations of students away from the narrow path prescribed by more traditional volumes.

Richard P. Bentall
Institute of Psychology, Health and Society
University of Liverpool

References

American Psychiatric Association (1980). *Diagnostic and Statistical Manual of Mental Disorders* (3rd edn). Washington DC: Author.

Bentall, R. P. (2009). *Doctoring the Mind: Why Psychiatric Treatments Fail.* London: Penguin.

Craddock, N. & Owen, M. J. (2005). The beginning of the end of the Kraepelinian dichotomy. *British Journal of Psychiatry*, 186, 364–66.

Healy, D. (2004). *Let Them Eat Prozac: The Unhealthy Relationship between the Pharmaceutical Industry and Depression.* New York: New York University Press.

Kirsch, I. (2009). T*he Emperor's New Drugs: Exploding the Antidepressant Myth.* London: Bodley Head.

Lepping, P., Sambhi, R. S., Whittington, R., Lane, S. & Poole, R. (2011). Clinical relevance of findings in trials of antipsychotics: Systematic Review. *British Journal of Psychiatry*, 198, 341–5.

Read, J., van Os, J., Morrison, A. P. & Ross, C. A. (2005). Childhood trauma, psychosis and schizophrenia: A literature review and clinical implications. *Acta Psychiatrica Scandinavica*, 112, 330–50.

Sharfstein, S. S. (2005). Big pharma and American psychiatry: The good, the bad, and the ugly. *Psychiatric News*, 40, 3.

Shorter, E. (1997). *A History of Psychiatry.* New York: Wiley.

Turner, E. H., Matthews, A. M., Linardatos, E., Tell, R. A. & Rosenthal, R. (2007). Selective publication of antidepressant trials and its influence on apparent efficacy. *The New England Journal of Medicine*, 358, 252–60.

van Os, J. & Kapur, S. (2009). Schizophrenia. *Lancet*, 374, 635–45.

Varese, F., Smeets, F., Drukker, M., Lieverse, R., Viechtbauer, W., Read, J., van Os, J. & Bentall, R. P. (2012). Childhood adversities increase the risk of psychosis: A meta-analysis of patient-control, prospective and cross-sectional cohort studies. *Schizophrenia Bulletin*, 38.

Whitaker, R. (2005). Anatomy of an epidemic: Psychiatric drugs and the astonishing rise of mental illness in America. *Ethical Human Psychology and Psychiatry*, 7, 23–35.

NOTE TO LECTURERS

In 2004, the three lead authors of this book – John Cromby, David Harper and Paula Reavey – were discussing mental health teaching for psychology undergraduates. Two of us, John and Paula, convene specialist mental health modules on UK psychology degrees, and also contribute to teaching and examining on clinical psychology training courses. Dave is a clinical psychologist who moved into research and clinical psychology education after nine years' practice in the UK's National Health Service (NHS).

We found that we shared some concerns about the way mental health was addressed in psychology teaching. A primary concern was that mental health did not seem to be taught in a consistently psychological manner. In most areas of psychology, phenomena are both defined and studied from a psychological perspective. In mental health teaching, however, the curriculum was frequently structured by diagnostic categories drawn from psychiatry. Rather than teaching about psychological phenomena, we were teaching about phenomena that had already been conceptualized in a particular way. This conceptualization came from a discipline – psychiatry – with quite different starting assumptions, training, traditions and functions to psychology.

We secured a small grant from the Higher Education Academy for Psychology, to survey mental health teaching to UK psychology undergraduates. We discovered that the great majority of this teaching – 82% of mental health modules on UK psychology degrees – were said to endorse more than one conceptual framework (Cromby, Harper & Reavey, 2008). These frameworks were described by lecturers as cognitive–behavioural, psychosocial, psychoanalytic, humanistic and family systems, as well as psychiatric or medical. Yet the overwhelming majority of textbooks being used on these modules were structured entirely around psychiatric diagnoses, usually those contained within the American Psychiatric Association's *Diagnostic and Statistical Manual* or DSM.

So the textbooks did not seem to really fit with the modules where they were being used. But it seemed to us that many had other shortcomings, too. Most of them:

- Assumed that dimensional models were less useful than categorical models, even though (in the UK, at least) most clinical psychologists use dimensional models in their practice
- Paid relatively little attention to influential recent research, mostly from the UK, which works with relatively homogeneous experiences (e.g. 'hearing voices') rather than diagnostic categories
- Tended to write as though serious critical debate in mental health had mostly stopped at the end of the 1960s – even though, in the forty years since, there have been many critiques of, and alternatives to, mainstream psychiatric approaches
- Described their approach as 'biopsychosocial' but did not explain what this means, nor seriously consider the difficulties (conceptual and empirical) of such an approach
- Largely ignored the views of mental health service users, and the important contributions that service user movements have recently made to clinical psychological understandings and practices.

We wanted there to be a textbook that addressed these shortcomings: a book that presented a coherent conceptual framework for thinking psychologically about mental health and illness; a book which recognized that knowledge of psychiatric diagnoses is necessary in clinical psychology, but which did not invoke them as explanations. This is the book you are now holding.

ACKNOWLEDGEMENTS

Authors' acknowledgements

We would all like to thank Mary Boyle, who kindly read a draft of nearly every chapter in this book, offering insightful, helpful comments that helped set the tone of the entire text. Our thanks also go to Annie Trapp and HEA Psychology, Jill Anderson and MHHE, Richard Bentall (for his generous foreword), our contributors (who patiently responded to our requests), and Paul Stevens, Jenny Hindley and the rest of the Palgrave Macmillan editorial and production team.

John: thanks to both Jay Joseph and Steven Rose for their invaluable help in preparing parts of this book. The Midlands Psychology Group (Bob Diamond, Paul Kelly, Paul Moloney, Penny Priest, Jan Soffe-Caswell and David Smail) continue to provide inspiration, guidance and support for my engagements with mental health and distress: together, they constitute an asylum in the proper sense of that word. More general intellectual sustenance comes from far too many people to name, but special mentions must go to my co-authors, and to my current and former students Darren Ellis, Leanne Franklin and Martin Willis. Fran Walsh, Julie Skinner, Colin Huggins and Jaz Singh continue to provide insights into the realms of experience beyond the academy; they help to keep me grounded. Mandy Dalglish drew the brains, and didn't laugh too much at my own feeble attempts. My much-loved twins, Naomi and Liam, make me proud, make me smile, and make excellent photographic models. And finally, I want to thank Rachel Fyson: for her love, her practical support, her editorial advice, her photographic skills, and generally for just being there.

Dave: In addition to my co-authors John and Paula I would like to thank the clinical psychology programme staff team at UEL for their support over the course of writing this book. Over the years a number of people have been a source of inspiration and insightful discussion: trainees and supervisees at UEL, Richard Bentall, Mary Boyle, Gary Brown, Anne Cooke, Jacqui Dillon, Darren Ellis, Lucy Johnstone, Ian Parker, Guy Shennan, Ian Tucker, Sam Warner, Carla Willig, members of the Psychology and Social Change research group, and those who attended Critical Mental Health Forum meetings in London (2001–05). I am very grateful to Andrew Roberts for providing the images of the Mental Patients' Union (p. 52), for permission to draw on his Mental Health Timeline (http://study more.org.uk/mhhtim.htm) for Tables 2.1 and 2.3 and for generously reviewing them for me. Any errors, of course, are my own. Finally, thanks to Andy Cullen, Matthew Jones Chesters and Dave Spellman for their help with some of the graphs and photographs.

Paula: There are various people I wish to thank for their input into my work generally and their reading of earlier drafts of this work, as well as the advice and expertise they have offered. Ava Kanyeredzi, Laura McGrath, Jeffrey Weeks and Meg Barker have all provided very valuable support and discussion on a number of aspects of the book. For that input, I am ever grateful. I thank also my undergraduate students on my final-year module on mental health and distress, at London South Bank University. The lively discussions we had in class contributed a great deal to my thinking on how to write about the topics included in the book. Their experience of life also made me think very hard about a number of issues and their humour in response to some of my wilder ideas remain firmly ingrained on my consciousness. My students have always challenged me and continue to do so, in an encouraging and positive way. Gawd bless 'em all I say!

Steve Brown has continued to be a much-valued presence in my life, in every way. His tireless contribution to my way of thinking is always appreciated, and our abnormal ways of working, a source of great joy.

Finally, I wish to add a personal note to my family, Alex, Oskar and Viktor, to whom I dedicate this book. My mental health has only ever been preserved by their love, understanding and presence in my life. The home we have created together is a haven from the many challenges the last few years have presented us with. I look forward to more comedy, TV-watching and general ridiculous behaviour. Long live silliness...

Publisher's acknowledgements

The publisher and authors would like to thank the organizations and people listed below for permission to reproduce material from their publications:

Rethink Mental Illness for permission to reproduce the images on pp. 7 and 47

Bridgeman Art Library for permission to reproduce the image on p. 30, *Philippe Pinel (1745-1826) releasing lunatics from their chains at the Salpetrière asylum in Paris* by Tony Robert-Fleury

Craig Kempf for permission to reproduce the image on p. 44

Andrew Roberts for the two Mental Patients' Union images (p. 52). The picture of a fish on a hook was drawn by Brian Douieb for the cover of the pamphlet *The Need for a Mental Patients' Union: Some Proposals*, 1973. The spider's web logo was drawn by John Walsh who adapted it from an image used by the homelessness charity Shelter.

Loren Kerns for permission to reproduce the image on p. 57

Robert Scoble for permission to reproduce the image on p. 64

iStockphoto for permission to reproduce the images on pp. 69 and 287

Nature Publishing Group for permission to reproduce the image on p. 105, from *Applications of real-time fMRI*, R. Christopher deCharms (2008), *Nature Reviews Neuroscience*

Jaume Plensa and Yorkshire Sculpture Park for permission to use photographs of Jaume Plensa's work in the images on pp. 110 and 205

Andy Cullen for permission to reproduce the images on pp. 142, 185 and 274

Mad Pride for permission to reproduce the Mad Pride logo on p. 150

The Equality Trust for permission to reproduce a graph from *The Spirit Level*, Wilkinson & Pickett (2009) on p. 132

National Hearing Voices Network for permission to reproduce the Hearing Voices Network logo on p. 153

Dave Spellman for permission to reproduce the image on p. 166

Alan Cleaver for permission to reproduce the image on p. 175

Figures 8.3 and 8.4 are reprinted with permission under the Open Government Licence http://www.nationalarchives.gov.uk/doc/open-government-licence/

The Royal College of Psychiatrists for permission to reproduce Figure 8.2, taken from Large, M. et al. (2008): Homicide due to mental disorder in England and Wales over 50 years. *British Journal of Psychiatry*, 193, 130–3, figure 2 on p. 131: Homicide rates in England and Wales 1946–2004 and for Figure 8.6 taken from Ilyas, S. & Moncrieff, J. (2012). Trends in prescriptions and costs of drugs for mental disorders in England, 1998–2010. *British Journal of Psychiatry*, 200, 393–98.

PCCS books for permission to reproduce Figure 8.1 and Box 8.2, from Moncrieff, J. (2009). *A Straight-talking Guide to Psychiatric Drugs*. Ross-on-Wye: PCCS Books.

Jessica Rone for permission to reproduce the image on p. 229

Peter Castelton for permission to reproduce the image on p. 238

Rachel Waddingham and Intervoice for permission to reproduce the Intervoice logo on p. 251

Jolanda van Hoej for permission to reproduce the photo of Sandra Escher and Marius Romme on p. 280

Judy Schreiber for the photo of Loren Mosher on p. 278

Lex Johan for permission for permission to reproduce the images on pp. 284, 292 and 302

Narrativeapproaches.com for permission to include a poem from the website in Box 12.3

Guilford Publications for permission to reproduce an excerpt from *Clinical Handbook of Psychological Disorders* (4th edn), David H. Barlow (2008) in Box 12.2

Maddy Smith and Asylum magazine for permission to reproduce the image on p. 317, originally printed as the cover to *Asylum* magazine (Volume 14, No.3)

Timothy Leary's estate for permission to reproduce the Interpersonal Circumplex from which Figure 13.1 is adapted

Bobby Baker and Wellcome Images for permission to reproduce the images on pp. 334 and 335, taken from *Diary Drawings*: Day 400 and Day 480

Every effort has been made to trace all copyright holders, but if any have been inadvertently overlooked, the publisher will be pleased to make the necessary arrangements at the first opportunity.

DEDICATION

To my mum and dad, Edna and Buddy, for all of the great things you do for everyone you know

– JC

For Jim Harper (1922–1987), Agnes Harper (1923–2001) and Tony, Carol, Ryan, Laura & Michael Harper

– DH

For Alex, Oskar & Viktor – my boys

– PR

PART **1**

CONCEPTS

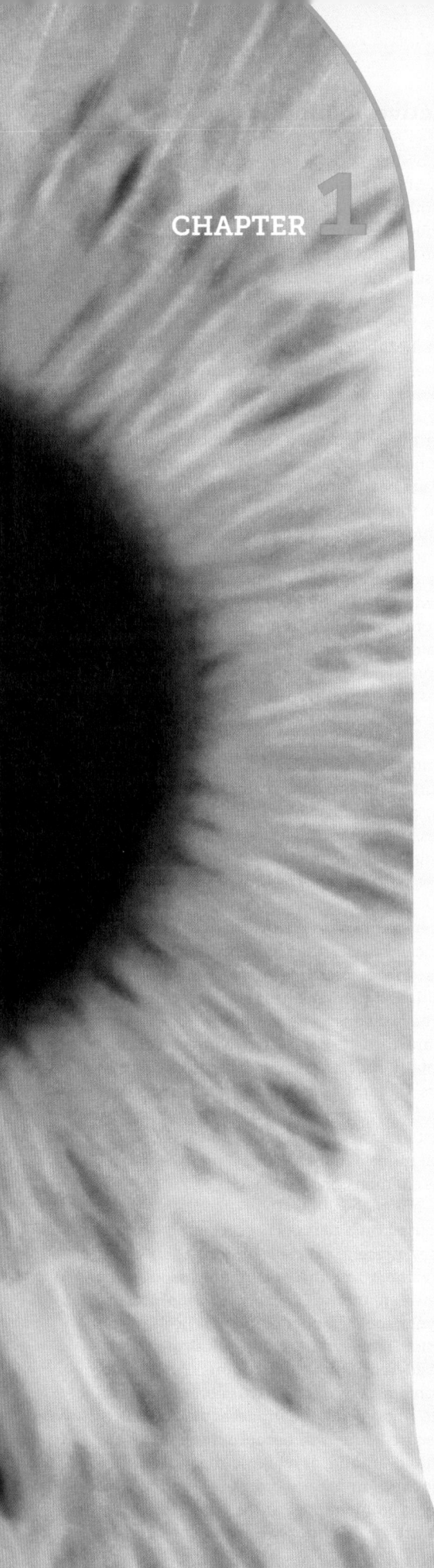

CHAPTER 1

FROM DISORDER TO EXPERIENCE

Bess's story

Bess is a 19 year old African Caribbean woman. She was referred to clinical psychology services after being admitted to a psychiatric hospital, because her medication had not lessened the voices she heard nor altered the unusual beliefs she held. Before her admission she had been living with her mother, brothers and sisters in a large industrial town.

Bess is the oldest of four children. Since the age of 9 she had been largely responsible for taking care of her siblings, whilst her mother worked long hours to support the family. Nevertheless, Bess did well at school, although she sometimes experienced racist bullying. Often, her father drank heavily and was physically and verbally abusive – towards his wife, but occasionally towards Bess. Then, when Bess was 12, her father came home drunk and pressured her for sex. He threatened to hurt her brothers and sisters if she didn't comply, and Bess reluctantly agreed. She hated the sexual contact, but relished the affection she received from him. After two years of this sexual abuse, Bess's father left to begin a new relationship. Bess was devastated. She deeply resented her mother's anguish at losing him, and their relationship deteriorated.

After her father left, Bess was confused. She resented the way he had treated her, and wondered why he didn't contact her. She continued to work hard at school and did extremely well in her exams. When she was 16, Bess noticed that although the bullying had mostly stopped she still felt like an outsider. She began finding it difficult to concentrate, and became preoccupied with the belief that one day she would meet someone who would take her away to a new life. Around this time she had a new boyfriend who wanted to turn their relationship into a sexual one, but Bess refused. When she eventually explained to him what had happened with her father, he ended the relationship. Bess felt that everyone she loved would abandon her. She was deeply shamed by what her father had done to her, judging it to be her own fault.

Bess began to spend more time alone, praying. She believed she was receiving messages from God, and began listening to loud music to block out the voices she increasingly heard. She drank large quantities of alcohol, and slowly became convinced she had a personal relationship – with sexual overtones – with one of the pop stars she listened to. This made her feel ashamed, but the pop star told her that one day he would take her to heaven where she would find peace. She heard his voice often, especially when she felt lonely and miserable. Increasingly, though, she also heard her father's voice, commenting critically on her actions and morals.

Eventually, Bess told her mother about these experiences. Her mother became angry and contacted a doctor, who referred Bess to psychiatric services. This led to a violent confrontation between Bess and her mother; Bess was then forcibly admitted to hospital.

After you have read this chapter, you will be able to:

1 Explain why terminology is especially important in relation to mental health
2 Explain what is meant in this book by 'distress'
3 Describe some of the problems associated with everyday definitions of normality
4 Explain the problem of thresholds in relation to psychiatric diagnosis
5 Define key terms, including: service user, distress, madness, psychosis, neurosis, hallucination and delusion

Introduction

This book is about people like Bess. People distressed by life, their relationships, and their position in the social world. It is clear from Bess's story that her distress is far from straightforward. Do her difficulties arise from her unstable relationships, from the way she thinks about the world, or the ways in which she has learned to cope? Whilst there are no easy answers to these questions, we hope that this book will provide some ways of thinking psychologically about the kinds of issues facing Bess and others who have had experiences like hers.

In this chapter, we first of all explain what is distinctive about this book and why we approached this topic in the way that we did. We discuss the importance of terminology and describe why language is important: both because it provides the concepts we use when thinking, and because of its links to stigma and discrimination. We explain how in this book we will focus on **distress** (which for now you can simply read as meaning 'mental illness' or 'psychopathology'), and how we will treat distress as a form of **experience** – something that happens within the life and the subjective awareness of a person – rather than as a form of illness.

Then we give some of the reasons why we decided not to call this a book about 'abnormal psychology'. Approaches to mental health and illness that do not endorse simple notions of abnormality are often described as **anti-psychiatry**: this is the collective term for a set of disparate work, published mostly in the 1960s, which rejected the view that mental health problems are illnesses or diseases. We explain why we do not call our approach anti-psychiatry; consider the issues raised by a focus on distress as something that is perhaps 'in the mind'; and briefly describe some of the ways in which mental health professionals have modelled and conceptualized their field.

These discussions are followed by a short overview of the rest of the book, and a guide explaining how to get the most out of reading it.

Guiding questions

As you read this chapter, you should bear in mind these two questions:

1 *Why might we question the notion of abnormal psychology?*
2 *What are the implications of rejecting psychiatric diagnoses in mental health?*

What is distinctive about this book?

The approach taken by this book is somewhat different from those of other books in this area. One very obvious difference is that, unlike many others, we do not use the term 'abnormal psychology' to describe what our book is about (later, we offer a detailed explanation for this). But in fact this book has several distinctive features, so it will be useful to emphasize some of them here.

First, in this book we take a *consistently psychological* approach to mental health. Usually, psychology books on mental health are already pre-structured in terms of psychiatric diagnostic manuals such as the Diagnostic and Statistical Manual of the American Psychiatric Association – the **DSM** (see Box 1.1). Chapter titles are usually based upon diagnostic labels, and explanations are typically directed at ideas of mental illness that have already been formulated within psychiatry or medicine. Instead, in this book we offer a perspective that is more suitable for students from non-medical backgrounds who might want to train as (for example) clinical psychologists, social workers or CBT practitioners. We have already suggested that we will do this by starting with experience rather than notions of disorder, and there is more discussion of what this means later in the chapter.

Second, most other books of this kind pay relatively little attention to recent psychological research – much of it from the UK – which has focused on particular kinds of experience, such as 'hearing voices', rather than diagnostic categories, such as schizophrenia. This research has shown that it is possible to make significant progress in understanding and responding to people's difficulties without having to endorse psychiatric diagnoses. Of course, this does not mean that we don't consider psychiatric diagnoses in this book – just that we don't treat them as necessarily explaining people's mental health difficulties.

Third, many other textbooks claim that **dimensional models** are less clinically useful than psychiatric diagnoses. Dimensional models do not presume a sharp dividing line between mental health and mental illness, and recognize that all of us, sometimes, have distressing and unusual experiences in our lives. They are usually contrasted with **categorical models**, where mental illness is clearly distinguished from mental health and is thought to fall into specific, separate categories: psychiatric diagnosis exemplifies this approach. But in the UK, at least, the vast majority of clinical psychologists use dimensional models in their clinical practice, so this book frequently takes a dimensional approach.

Fourth, most other mental health textbooks contain a series of chapters, each focused on a particular psychiatric diagnosis. But although they present extensive information about each diagnosis, they rarely try to explain the associations and connections between them. Typically, textbooks claim to promote a **biopsychosocial model** of mental health – an approach within which biological, psychological and social influences are all considered or modelled together. But because they don't usually contain very much discussion of the links between 'bio', 'psycho' and 'social', the model actually tends to remain relatively obscure. Moreover, because these textbooks are invariably structured around psychiatric diagnoses, they also tend to be **reductive** – in other words, they tend to treat biological influences as foundational, or as more important than others. By contrast, in this book we try to consider the links between 'bio', 'psycho' and 'social' in a more nuanced and conceptually sophisticated manner.

Finally, in these textbooks, the discussion of critics of psychiatry, and of the controversies associated with its diagnoses and assumptions, almost always seems to stop at the end of the 1960s. If one were to judge by such books, one might almost believe that all of the problems that these critics had raised were now solved. But this is not the case, and in the five decades since the 1960s there have been many more critiques of, and alternatives to, psychiatry. These critiques and alternatives have come from clinical psychologists and from those who use mental health services, as well as from psychiatrists themselves. In recognition of this, our book is also distinctive because it includes a chapter written entirely by mental health service users.

In writing this book we have therefore made a number of assumptions: for example, that psychiatric diagnosis does not necessarily provide the best way to approach mental health problems; that a more sophisticated psychological account of mental health problems will be useful; that mental health service users have valuable things to tell us about mental health difficulties and interventions. All authors have an **assumptive framework** – a worldview within which certain things are implicit and simply taken for granted. These assumptive frameworks are rarely made explicit, but we thought it would be helpful for you to have a sense of our starting points and assumptions so that you can take them into account as you read the book.

Importantly, we have not written this book as a polemic and we accept that you may agree or disagree with some of our judgements. Throughout the book we will be presenting evidence for and against different ways of conceptualizing mental health and illness, so that you can come to your own conclusions.

Of course, in attempting to write about mental health in a different way we had to think carefully about the language we used. There are many reasons for this, but perhaps the most important is that language contains concepts that structure our thinking. If we use concepts that are inconsistent or unhelpful, our thinking can become muddled. This meant that we needed to ensure that our approach was internally consistent, so it is to the issue of terminology that we turn next.

Terminology

One of the first challenges in learning about the psychology of mental health is the wide variety of terms and concepts used. Like the language used in relation to any other real-world phenomenon, none of these terms is neutral or value-free. All of them seem to imply something about the nature or the causes of the phenomena they describe, and all of them are more closely associated with certain disciplines and perspectives than with others. The term **mental illness**, for example, clearly suggests that our talk will be of matters related to health and sickness, that it will have a medical character but that it will also take a mentalistic or psychological focus. Another widely used term, **psychopathology**, makes exactly the same assumption because it adds the concept of disease – pathology – to the prefix 'psycho-', which is short for 'psychological'. In both cases, then, the terminology already assumes that our perspective upon these phenomena should be a fundamentally

---

BOX **1.1**
What is the DSM?

'The **DSM**' is The Diagnostic and Statistical Manual of the American Psychiatric Association. It contains the diagnostic criteria that American psychiatrists use in their practice. In Europe and the UK, psychiatrists most often favour the slightly different psychiatric diagnostic criteria set out in The International Classification of Diseases (**ICD**), produced by the World Health Organization. However, although they may use these criteria in their practice, for research purposes UK and European psychiatrists also tend to use the DSM.

Both the ICD and the DSM have been subject to frequent revisions. The ICD is currently on version 10, whilst the current DSM is known as DSM-IV-TR: version IV, text revision. As we went to press, both DSM-5 (the APA seem to have changed their numbering system) and ICD 11 were expected shortly.

At least in its current version, the DSM claims to be purely descriptive and a-theoretical, instead of depending upon concepts derived from theories. This means that it does not use earlier concepts such as **neurosis**: a collective term for forms of distress that involve exaggerations of everyday responses (e.g. excessive worrying) but do not involve distorted perceptions or unusual beliefs. Whereas the concept of neurosis was originally derived from psychoanalytic theory, the DSM purports to be no more than a set of descriptions of the disorders frequently observed by clinicians. These disorders are proposed by panels of experts, and are subject to a consultation process and approval by a central committee before they can be included in the manual.

Despite this, critics argue that the DSM is far from value-free and neutral. They suggest that in practice the DSM furthers the interests, not just of psychiatry, but also of the pharmaceutical and insurance industries (because, under America's insurance-based healthcare system, a diagnosis is needed in order to reclaim the cost of treatments such as medication).

Another concern frequently raised by critics is that the DSM has promoted the **medicalization** of everyday life: in other words, it encourages us to see everyday difficulties and stresses (for example, shyness) as 'symptoms' of 'illness' that then require 'treatment'. Certainly, the number of separate diagnoses within each version of the DSM has tended to increase with each revision, as the table shows. However, advocates of diagnosis argue that the system is simply becoming more accurate and refined over time, and that the changing numbers reflect this process of development.

TITLE	YEAR	DIAGNOSES
DSM	1952	106
DSM-II	1968	182
DSM-III	1980	265
DSM-III-R	1987	292
DSM-IV	1994	297
DSM-IV-TR	2000	297

Chapter 5 contains a lengthy discussion of psychiatric diagnosis and the issues that are frequently associated with it.

How we see or represent the world depends on how we choose to frame it, as well as upon what there is in the world for us to see

medical one, and that at its most basic level our concern is with people who are diseased or sick.

We think that this assumption is incorrect. In our view, when people are given diagnoses such as schizophrenia or depression it is neither accurate nor helpful to think of them as being medically ill or diseased. So in this book we will use the terms 'psychopathology' and 'mental illness' very infrequently, and even then only when they are already being used by the people whose work we are drawing upon. In their place, we will use the term **distress**. When we use this term, we use it to refer to just the same kinds of phenomena that textbooks of this kind usually call mental illness or psychopathology. We use distress to mean *all* of the different kinds of difficult or unusual experiences associated with the hundreds of psychiatric diagnoses currently employed. Distress is our term for the core subject matter of this book: the experiences associated with diagnostic categories such as schizophrenia and depression, and with the work of professions such as clinical psychology, psychiatry, social work and nursing.

However, to reduce repetitive language, we will occasionally draw on other phrases like *'mental health problem'*. This terminology is also open to challenge, because by locating these experiences in relation to health it also implies a link to illness. However, it is more ambiguous than 'mental illness', carries less conceptual baggage, and is easily understood because it is widely used.

Similarly, we will sometimes use the term **madness** to collectively describe experiences associated with the more

severe forms of distress. These include experiences such as hearing voices, which is an example of a **hallucination**: a general term for the perception of a stimulus that is not present. They also include advocating the unusual beliefs that clinicians call **delusions**: beliefs that can be shown to be either impossible or false, but which are sometimes proclaimed strongly by service users. These experiences are primarily associated with psychiatric diagnoses such as schizophrenia and bipolar disorder, and are sometimes collectively referred to as **psychosis**. There has been a recent debate in the UK about terms like psychosis and schizophrenia, and a 'Campaign against the Schizophrenia Label', which has received significant media attention. As with the other terms we favour in this book, we have used madness rather than psychosis because it mostly avoids the many connotations of illness or disease that accompany the alternatives.

You will probably be familiar with discussions about terminology from other areas of your studies. Because language supplies the concepts that structure our thinking and debating – sometimes very subtly, in ways we don't necessarily realize – it is vital to ensure that we are using appropriate terms. However, it's also important to realize that, in relation to distress, these discussions are often particularly contentious. Because distress touches the lives of so many people, and because the ways we understand it have very real implications for the ways that we respond to it, there are often very strong feelings about the terminology that is used.

For example, there is extensive disagreement about the term we should use to refer to people who experience distress. In recent years, the dominance of the medical perspective associated with psychiatry has meant that the term **patient** is very often used. Over the last 20 or 30 years, however, some of those who experience distress have organized themselves into activist groups and campaigned strongly for a change of terminology. They have argued that the term 'patient' implies a passive position where someone puts themselves in the hands of experts to be fixed. Some also object that the term inappropriately focuses almost exclusively on the medical and biological aspects of care (e.g. medication), rather than adopting a more holistic approach. As a result of these objections, some professionals now refer to those who use their services as **clients**. However, some groups have argued instead that they should be referred to as **consumers** (popular in the USA, Australia and New Zealand) or **service users** (popular in the UK), and many professionals have also taken up this language.

But these terms have also been challenged. Some suggest that they obscure the fact that many people are not always willing consumers of mental health services, unlike the consumers of other goods and services: some, for example, will be receiving compulsory treatment. Such critics have sometimes suggested that the term **recipient** is more accurate. And yet others have argued that, because they have had to cope not only with their distress, but also with psychiatric interventions which they have experienced as negative or unhelpful, the term **psychiatric system survivor** is most appropriate.

In short, then, there is no 'right' term to use and people in distress, like everyone else, have their own preferences and understandings. In this book we will usually use the term 'service user', since this is one of the terms most widely used in the UK. But we will also sometimes use other terms, where other people have used them or where the context demands it.

Stigma and discrimination

Language and terminology are important because of how they affect our thinking. However, they also matter in relation to service users and their experiences of distress because of the widespread discrimination to which such people are subject. The UK government regularly surveys public attitudes about 'mental illness': a survey (Office for National Statistics, 2010b) of 1,745 people revealed that

- 78% of people agree that 'people with mental illness have for too long been the subject of ridicule'
- 75% agree that 'people with mental health problems should have the same rights to a job as anyone else'
- 87% agree that 'we need to adopt a more tolerant attitude towards people with mental illness' (a fall from 92% in 1994)

At the same time, however, only 26% of people agreed that 'most women who were once patients in a mental hospital can be trusted as babysitters'. Only 34% agreed that 'less emphasis should be placed on protecting the public from people with mental illness', and only 33% agreed that 'mental hospitals are an outdated means of treating people with mental illness'.

This survey suggests that the public have ambivalent feelings about service users and distress. One way of understanding this ambivalence is to see negative attitudes as an example of **stigma**. This approach draws upon sociologist Erving Goffman's (1963) work *Stigma: Notes on the management of spoiled identity*, where he described the process of stigmatization as involving being viewed as socially deviant and linked with negative stereotypes. Since then, a number of researchers have drawn on this paradigm to suggest that experiencing distress or being given a psychiatric diagnosis can lead to one being stigmatized. Drawing on this insight, there has been a considerable amount of research into why mental distress is linked to negative attitudes.

Research suggests that the development of negative attitudes begins early in life. Rose, Thornicroft, Pinfold and Kassam (2007) asked 472 14-year-old school students 'What sorts of words or phrases might you use to describe someone who experiences mental health problems?' They reported that around 250 words were mentioned by the young people, including terms such as nuts, psycho, loony, weird, freak, spastic and demented. In their interview study of 1,737 adults, Crisp, Gelder, Rix, Meltzer and Rowlands (2000) reported that their respondents commonly perceived people who had been given a diagnosis of schizophrenia as unpredictable and dangerous, even though about half of them knew someone with a mental health problem. Unfortunately, research also shows that such prejudiced views are even reported amongst doctors (Mukherjee, Fialho, Wijetunge, Checkinski & Surgenor, 2002) and may be made worse by some nurse training (Sadow, Ryder & Webster, 2002).

Despite a huge amount of money spent on 'anti-stigma' campaigns the effects on public attitudes have been modest, leading some to suggest that attitudes about mental health may be different from other attitudes (Crisp et al., 2000). However, in a recent review, Read, Haslam, Sayce and Davies (2006) suggest that it may be the underlying assumptions of the anti-stigma paradigm which are the reason for the lack of change. These approaches are typically based on two assumptions, the first of which is that the public need to be taught to adopt a **biomedical model** of distress – to assume that distress is caused by diseases or illnesses of the brain or mind, and that these illnesses are what psychiatric diagnoses describe. The second assumption is that this will result in less discrimination, because people will be more tolerant if they think that an unusual behaviour is caused by a medical illness or disease; otherwise, they might hold the person morally responsible. Another problem noted by some critics of these campaigns is that stigma is seen as caused by problematic attitudes located inside individuals, rather than as a product of, or reaction to, discrimination at a societal level – in a similar manner to sexism and racism (Sayce, 1998).

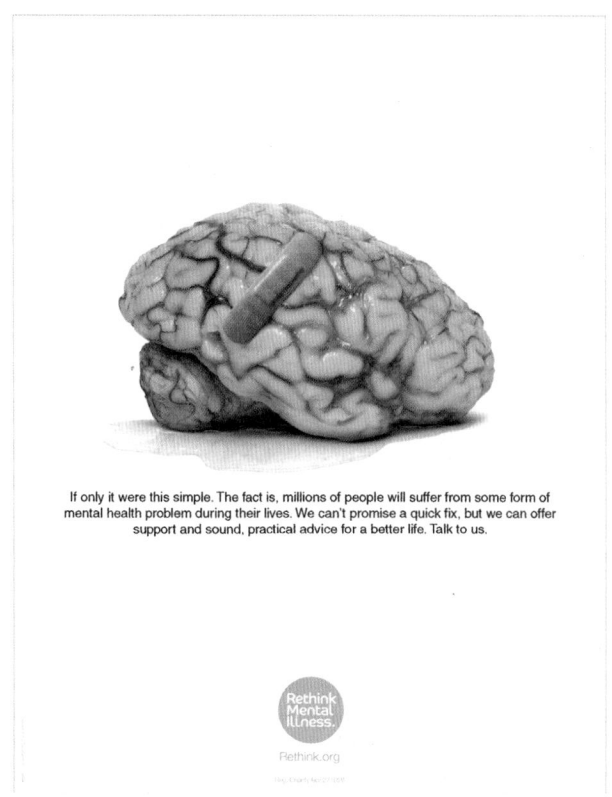

If only it were this simple. The fact is, millions of people will suffer from some form of mental health problem during their lives. We can't promise a quick fix, but we can offer support and sound, practical advice for a better life. Talk to us.

Rethink
Mental
Illness.

Rethink.org

This poster was part of an advertising campaign by a UK mental health charity. What does it make you think? Does it stigmatize people with mental health problems, or does it challenge their stigmatization? What does it suggest to you about the causes of distress?

A number of studies have reported that, whilst the public may use medical terminology, they place a 'greater emphasis on psychosocial than biogenetic explanations of schizophrenia' (Read et al., 2006, p. 311). Moreover, contrary to the assumptions of the anti-stigma paradigm, biomedical explanations are associated with more negative attitudes and behaviour than **psychosocial models**, in which mental health problems are seen as psychological in nature and caused by adverse life events and circumstances (Lam, Salkovskis & Warwick, 2005; Mehta & Farina, 1997; Read & Harré, 2001; Read et al., 2006). Why might this be? One possibility is that, if unusual experiences or behaviours are seen as biomedical in origin, they become more mystifying and unpredictable. Conversely, if they are seen as the result of someone's life experiences, they are perhaps more understandable. So public education programmes focusing on psychosocial explanations may well fare better than those that endorse biomedical approaches (see Figure 1.1).

Biomedical approach	Psychosocial approach
Sees the person's mental health problems as the main problem	Sees barriers in society as the main problem
Sees problems as a symptom of an underlying disease process and illness	Sees problems as an understandable response to adverse life events
Sees societal reactions as due to the stigma attached to having a mental health problem	Sees societal reactions as due to discrimination against a marginalised group (like racism, sexism etc)
Aim of public education is to remove perceived blame attached to the individual by 'blaming' the illness rather than the person	Rejects the relevance of notions of 'blame' and aims to promote diversity, reduce fear and increase empathy and understanding
Key public education slogan 'Mental illness is an illness like any other'	Key public education slogans: 'I'm crazy: so what?' 'It's normal to be different'

Figure 1.1 **Contrasting biomedical and psychosocial approaches to public education about mental health**

Discrimination

Although many people experience mental health problems, there is now substantial evidence that mental health service users experience significant discrimination across all areas of their lives (Sayce, 2000). For example, only 24% of people with long-term mental health problems were in work in England in 2003 – the lowest employment rate of any of the main groups of people with disabilities (Social Exclusion Unit, 2004). Almost half (47%) of Read and Baker's (1996) respondents said that they had been abused or harassed in public. Berzins, Petch and Atkinson (2003) reported that people with mental health problems suffered much higher rates of verbal abuse and physical harassment than the general public, with much of it committed by teenagers and neighbours.

Sadly, discrimination intrudes into even the most intimate relationships and can lead to many people with mental health problems feeling isolated (Mind, 2004) and being wary about telling other people about their own or another's distress (Mental Health Foundation, 2000). There has also been an increase in community opposition to nearby mental health facilities. Research suggests that residents' fears are fuelled by media reporting, and are associated – on occasion – with both vandalism and assaults (Repper, Sayce, Strong, Willmot and Haines, 1997).

Another domain within which mental health service users experience discrimination is the media. Headlines such as 'Schizophrenic Given Life for Murder' (*Daily Express*, 24 March 2009), and terms such as 'Psycho Cabbie' (*The Sun*, 4 June 2010), serve to associate mental health service users with violence and fear and help to spread negative attitudes. Indeed, many commentators see disproportionate media reporting as an important maintaining factor in more widespread discrimination. In one study of a range of print and broadcast media, stories about homicides and crimes accounted for 27% of all coverage of mental health (Care Services Improvement Partnership/Shift, 2006). Messages about the risks of violence posed by people with mental health problems were present in 15% of stories, most of which implied the risk was high.

News and entertainment media focus primarily on violence against others when addressing issues relating to mental illness, with these items receiving 'headline' treatment (Philo, 1994). These findings are robust (e.g. CSIP/Shift, 2006; Philo, 1996; Pinfold & Thornicroft, 2006) and influence the public's fear of unpredictability and violence (Philo, 1996). Levey and Howells noted (1995) that perceived dangerousness was not as important as the perceived difference and unpredictability of people with a diagnosis of schizophrenia. Moreover, they reported that reliance on fictional television was associated with higher ratings of unpredictability.

Rose (1998) compared UK TV news coverage in the summer and winter of 1986 with TV news and other programmes between May and July 1992. Although she found variety in TV genres like soap operas and comedies, the category of danger was very frequent. For example, a third of all camera shots in her collection of TV news relevant to mental health dealt either visually or verbally with danger, violence and crime. Moreover, on the news, nearly two thirds of all stories involving those with psychiatric diagnoses fell into the category of crime news, although crime news accounts for only 10% of news coverage. As well as increasing the general public's fear, negative media representations have an impact on people with mental health problems themselves. Half the respondents of a UK mental health charity's survey of mental health service users said that their mental health had been negatively affected and a third said others had reacted negatively towards them as a result of such reports (Mind, 2000).

The media bias against mental health service users is especially unhelpful because it largely ignores the available evidence. A UK study found that murders by mental health service users are infrequent and occur less than once a week (Large, Smith, Swinson, Shaw & Nielssen, 2008). Whilst this might sound alarming at first, it should be seen in the context of other statistics. First, only 10% of people convicted of murder in the UK are thought to have any mental health difficulties at the time of their crime (Department of Health, 2001), and 95% of all murders are committed by people who have never been given a psychiatric diagnosis (Institute of Psychiatry, 2006). Second, the number of people experiencing mental health difficulties at any one time is large – typically around one in six of the population, or – in the UK – roughly 7 million people. These figures show that the vast majority of murders are committed by people without mental health problems, and that the proportion of people with mental health problems who commit murder is extremely small. Other violent attacks by mental health service users (i.e. those not causing death) are similarly much less frequent than media reporting suggests, and when they do occur they are frequently also associated with the use of alcohol or other drugs (Fazel, Langstrom, Hjern, Grann & Lichtenstein, 2009).

In fact, contrary to public fears, people with mental health problems are far more likely to be victims of violence than perpetrators; for example, they are six times more likely than the general population to die by homicide (Hiroeh, Appleby, Mortensen & Dunn, 2001). A US study of people experiencing psychosis found that they were 14 times more likely to be the victims of violent crime than to be arrested for committing violence themselves (Walsh et al., 2003). They are also far more likely to be a danger to themselves than to other people; for example, one influential study found that 90% of UK suicides involve people with mental health problems (Barraclough, Bunch, Nelson & Sainsbury, 1974).

How might we change stigmatizing attitudes and discriminatory behaviour? As we have seen, promoting psychosocial rather than biomedical explanations may help. In addition, activists like Sayce (1998, 2000) have argued that lessons can be learned from broader disability campaigns. Here, campaigners argued that it was not a person's disability which was the problem (as might be expected from an individualistic biomedical approach), rather it was the way in which society unintentionally created barriers by organizing the environment in a way which was convenient only for people without a disability. In the same way, rather than focusing on individual experiences of stigma, we might see public attitudes to service users – fuelled by inaccurate media reporting – as socially-created barriers to their acceptance by others.

What is distress?

Throughout this book, then, we use 'distress' as a generic term to refer to all the phenomena and experiences that are sometimes called 'psychopathology' or 'mental illness'. But, as we have suggested, this is not just about a preference for a different way of describing these experiences: it also signals a different way of conceptualizing them. We will now describe in more detail how we conceptualize distress, and how – as a concept – it differs from concepts of mental illness or psychopathology.

When we talk about distress, we are talking about a highly variable and heterogeneous set of experiences. These experiences can include

- strong or overwhelming emotional states, of various kinds, that disrupt everyday life and prevent people from functioning
- habitual and repetitive patterns of acting – for example, in relation to personal hygiene, or to do with safety and security – that create anxiety if they are not carried out
- experiences of seeing and hearing things that other people do not see or hear, or of holding beliefs that are considered by others to be unusual and extreme.

In this book, we take these kinds of experiences as problems in their own right. This contrasts with the approach frequently taken in psychiatry, where service users' talk of these kinds of experiences can very quickly get re-interpreted as nothing more than symptoms of an illness. In psychiatric settings, doctors are frequently listening out for particular patterns of difficulty in order to match the person's experience with a pre-defined diagnostic category. However, this might mean that they miss some of the complexity and fluidity of people's actual experiences of distress: in attentively looking for patterns of symptoms, they may fail to notice the ways in which people's distress is linked to the circumstances of their situations. As a consequence, rich accounts of distress that engage with its meaning and detail in a person's life may be difficult to achieve from within a psychiatric framework.

From our perspective, however, experiences of distress are part and parcel of the other experiences of everyday life. They do not form a separate, unitary category of symptoms that can be understood separately from everything else. Experiences associated with distress – just like every other experience – are bound up with social and material conditions, personal biographies, life events and relationships. And, just like every other experience, they are influenced by our biological capacities, by the many, variable potentials produced by our nature as living, organic beings.

But if distress is not separate from other aspects of experience, and does not form a unitary category all to itself, how can we know where it starts and ends? How can we reliably and validly draw an objective line between distress – the province of services such as clinical psychology and psychiatry – and more everyday experiences of being unhappy, worried and so on?

Simply put, our answer is that we cannot draw such a line. We do not believe that it is possible to produce a set of criteria or definitions that transcend history, place and culture and that can be used objectively to discriminate between those who are clinically distressed and those who are not. In the DSM, the existence of a distinct line between normal and abnormal is taken for granted – even though it is recognized that only appropriately trained expert psychiatrists might be able to determine exactly where it lies. By contrast, we believe that there is no value-free distinction between behaviours and experiences that are considered normal and those that are considered abnormal. Neither is there any universal standard against which people's emotions, thoughts and actions can be judged, and by reference to which they can be categorized as deviant. On the contrary, the identification of distress *as* distress will always be entwined with prevailing cultural norms of emotionality, behaviour and morality.

However, this does not mean that cultural norms are the *sole* criteria against which distress might be identified. Sometimes a person's ways of acting or experiencing can make it difficult for them to live their lives as they would like, or can have a bad effect upon their physical health. When this happens, their behaviour is never somehow floating free of cultural norms: what we want to do in our lives, for example, is continuously influenced by the precepts, norms and values of our time and culture.

Nevertheless, there are patterns of activity and experience which would be unhelpful or damaging in most circumstances. Gradually starving yourself – perhaps because you have come to believe that only by doing so can you begin to meet all of the many expectations placed upon you – will damage your physical health, no matter where or when you live. Similarly, being so profoundly miserable that you are unable even to get out of bed is likely to prevent you from achieving your goals, whatever those goals are. In the same way, experiencing angry and abusive voices that no-one else can hear is likely to make you frightened, confused and distracted, and this will probably occur to some extent even in cultures where voice-hearing is not as thoroughly stigmatized as it is in the West. So, whilst these dysfunctional or damaging consequences are definitely not separate from wider cultural norms and values, they do not arise solely because of them: they are also a product of specific patterns of experience and activity.

To some extent, distress can also be identified with respect to the extent to which a person's actions and experiences are unusual and inexplicable. Again, cultural norms play an important role here, and in two ways. First, almost by definition, norms refer to the ways of acting and experiencing displayed by the majority. However, there are difficult issues involved in trying to agree the threshold at which an experience becomes seen as clinically significant (see Box 1.2 for a discussion). Second, norms are relevant because we are far more ready to ascribe distress to people when their ways of being in the world do not make sense to us. When what people say or how they act is not only unusual but also seems to lack any obvious explanation, we are more likely to conclude that they are experiencing distress of some kind. In other words, it is not just the frequency or rarity of someone's acts and experiences that counts – it is also the sense or the *meaning* that we are able to give to them.

Another issue is that there are significant numbers of people who receive treatment from psychiatric or clinical psychological services but who do not want these interventions. Some might be experiencing the transient states of extreme euphoria and intense energy that psychiatrists call mania; others might be hearing voices that are friendly and supportive, rather than angry or abusive; yet others might be very unhappy, worried or confused, but have nevertheless come to believe that the treatments are not working, or that they produce as many difficulties as they solve. Some such people might end up receiving services, not because they themselves are distressed, but because their behaviours and experiences are distressing to others around them. Others may end up receiving services because their behaviour leads them to fall foul of the law. Again, cultural norms are highly relevant here: but in cases like these those norms are either mediated by other people's experiences, or codified in legal or other requirements. These examples show how the identification of distress can be a compassionate move, perhaps by attempting to keep safe someone who might otherwise be a danger to themselves. But they also show how distress is always bound up with the wider structures of power that organize our lives, and by which interventions might be imposed against our will.

To summarize: distress is always conceptualized with respect to cultural norms, but these norms are not the sole criteria against which distress is understood. One consideration is that distress always has a subjective component, regardless of its location within culture. Another is that, intersecting with cultural norms, we also have

- Judgements about the extent to which a person's actions and experiences are harmful or dysfunctional
- Judgements about the extent to which they are unusual
- Judgements about the meaning of actions and experiences
- The influence of power relations

None of these judgements is simply objective, just as the operation of hierarchical power relations cannot simply be seen as 'objectively' correct. But whilst these judgements and influences do not escape the influence of cultural norms, they are not identical to them, either. Instead, they point to numerous ways in which the contexts, consequences and meanings of experience are part of its conceptualization as distress. They make it clear that distress is always socially and culturally positioned, that it will vary according to the specifics of time

---

BOX 1.2
The problem of thresholds

We have seen that one criterion for identifying experiences as mental health problems is how unusual they are. But what is the threshold beyond which an experience is considered so unusual that it is significant? This question is important, because research shows that some phenomena associated with distress are far more common than is usually supposed.

Of a random sample of 7, 076 Dutch people, Van Os, Hannsen, Bijl and Ravelli (2000) reported that, whilst 3.3% had 'true' delusions (i.e. meeting all diagnostic criteria) an additional 8.7% had delusions that were 'not clinically relevant' – that is, they were 'not bothered by it and not seeking help for it' (van Os et al., 2000, p. 13). Similar findings have been reported in relation to hearing voices (see Chapter 11).

Stein, Walker and Forde (1994) conducted a telephone survey in Canada to ask about experiences of social anxiety, finding that 61% of respondents reported being much or somewhat more anxious than others in at least one of the seven social situations surveyed. However, if the threshold at which a person's distress was considered clinically significant was moved, the prevalence of 'social anxiety syndrome' varied from 1.9% to 18.7%. Many diagnostic criteria are formulated without any empirical investigation of base rates in the general population. This may explain why there is a frequent disparity between numbers of people seen by mental health services and numbers of people in community surveys who meet diagnostic criteria.

Moffit et al. (2010) have suggested that many estimates of prevalence in community surveys undercount because they rely on retrospective accounts. Their prospective study, which followed participants between the ages of 18 and 32 and interviewed them four times during this period, found prevalence rates for DSM diagnoses that were twice those of other national surveys. They conclude by suggesting that 'researchers might begin to ask why so many people experience a DSM-defined disorder at least once during their life-times, and what this prevalence means for etiological theory, the construct validity of the DSM approach to defining disorder, service delivery policy, the economic burden of disease, and public perceptions of the stigma of mental disorder' (p. 907).

Because there are cultural norms about what might be regarded as grounds for distress, where the threshold for distress is set will have a considerable impact. One US study has suggested that 'about half of Americans will meet the criteria for a DSM-IV disorder sometime in their life' (Kessler et al., 2005, p. 593). If half of the population experiences something, is it unusual? To some extent, this depends on one's worldview. For example, Sigmund Freud, one of the founders of psychoanalysis, did not see it as his job to make people happy: instead he simply argued that 'you will see for yourself that much has been gained if we succeed in turning your hysterical misery into common unhappiness' (Freud & Breuer, 1895/2004, p. 306).

and place, and will be patterned according to broader socio-logical variables such as socio-economic status, gender and ethnicity. Conceptualized in this way, distress is quite different from mental illness or psychopathology, both of which imply objective disease states that can be identified in ways that are distinct from cultural norms.

Why not abnormal psychology?

Our claim that there are no objective criteria by which distress can be distinguished from other kinds of experience is a challenge to the idea that some kinds of experience – and perhaps even some kinds of person – are simply abnormal. But this is such a taken-for-granted idea that it even lends its name to the most commonly used title for textbooks like this one, which are typically described as books on abnormal psychology. This term is very widely used, perhaps because classifying some kinds of experience as abnormal makes it reasonable to describe them as expressions of psychopathology or mental illness. Since abnormal psychology is such a common term, we should explain why we do not use it in this book.

Whilst the notion that trained professionals can use objective criteria to distinguish between normality and abnormality is perhaps comforting, it is nevertheless mistaken. Speaking very generally, formal definitions of abnormality can be classed as medical, as statistical, or as social – but whichever kind of definition we use, we encounter contradictions and problems. Each kind of definition excludes some phenomena we might intuitively want to define as psychologically abnormal, includes some we would not want to define as abnormal, or smuggles elements of subjective opinion into what are ostensibly objective judgements.

For example, if we use a **medical definition of normality**, we will tend to class as normal those activities which contribute to health and wellbeing, and class as abnormal those that endanger life or wellbeing or which cause harm to bodily organs or tissues. But this means that many highly prevalent everyday activities – such as smoking, drinking alcohol, dieting, extreme sports, body-piercing and tattooing – would be classed as abnormal, because they all involve actual or potential damage to the body.

If we use a **statistical definition of normality**, we will class as abnormal those activities, behaviours and characteristics that are, numerically, relatively unusual in a given population. Statistical definitions of normality derived from psychology sometimes use psychometric instruments, normal distributions and similar procedures by which to distinguish those who are abnormal from those who are not. But without also drawing on cultural values and norms (for example, in deciding which experiences to include in psychometric scales) statistical definitions will always generate contradictions, because some highly valued attributes – being a member of the royal family, perhaps, or excelling at sport – are statistically highly abnormal.

If instead we use a **social definition of abnormality**, this will reflect the specific kinds of activities and experiences approved or disapproved of in that time and place, so will inevitably be subject to marked variation. This variation operates within as well as between cultures: groups and subcultures have their own norms of behaviour and conduct that sometimes differ significantly from those of the dominant or mainstream culture (Hebdige, 1979). Social definitions recognize the culturally normative dimension of distress that we described above, but when we try to formalize them it becomes apparent that we also have to invoke other (typically unspecified) criteria to decide *which* social norms, when, and where, to use as the basis of our decisions.

So concepts of normality and abnormality do not provide an objective basis for the identification of mental illness or psychopathology, and this in part explains why we have not relied upon these concepts in this book. But the term 'abnormal psychology' is nevertheless widely used, and seems acceptable to the majority of psychology lecturers and students. Despite this, there are other reasons why we choose not to describe this as a book about abnormal psychology.

Abnormal psychology is confusing and unclear

One reason we haven't used the term 'abnormal psychology' is that it is ambiguous: is it the psychology itself that is abnormal, or does the term refer to the psychology of abnormality? Common sense would suggest that it is the second of these options that most people have in mind; if so, this only leads to a second, thornier set of confusions.

As we have already discussed, there is no straightforward, objective way to distinguish abnormal behaviours and experiences from normal ones. Even more fundamentally, though, it is impossible to easily identify a body of psychological theory and practice that is both exclusive to abnormality and unconnected with other topics. Psychological explanations in abnormal psychology tend to draw upon just the same kinds of paradigms and theories as other psychological explanations – biological, cognitive, behavioural, social, developmental and so on. It does not seem necessary to assume that the psychological processes that occur in distress are fundamentally different or abnormal in comparison to those that occur in other, supposedly normal, experiences. There are many successful psychological models of distress that draw upon established psychological theories and concepts such as learning theory, attribution theory, schema and so on.

Abnormal psychology is not consistently psychological

A further way in which abnormal psychology is confusing is that it is not consistently psychological. Frequently, abnormal psychology entirely abandons psychology and turns instead to psychiatry. This is clearly demonstrated in the overall structure of most textbooks, which typically follow, more or less faithfully, the diagnostic categories associated with one of the major psychiatric diagnostic systems such as the DSM or ICD. But this necessarily means that the inconsistency also runs deeper: even where psychological explanations are offered, they are directed at problems already defined in psychiatric terms. So in abnormal psychology there is an unresolved tension between psychiatry and psychology, and frequent shifts from one to the other. Moreover, when this happens, abnormal psychology typically offers no rationale for this shift from a psychological mode of explanation and description to a medical, psychiatric one.

In this textbook, we try to avoid these confusions by presenting consistently psychological accounts of distress. This does not mean, of course, that we entirely ignore psychiatry: this would be impossible, given that so much of the evidence we have about distress is associated with it. Nor does it mean that we ignore any of the multiple facets of distress, such as its biological, cognitive or developmental aspects.

However, it does mean that we treat psychological explanations of distress as sufficient in their own right. Rather than subordinating them to psychiatry by applying them only to problems defined in the first instance as medical and psychiatric, we also use psychology to define the nature and character of people's distress.

Abnormal psychology is unhelpful

A third reason we haven't used the term 'abnormal psychology' is that it is likely to be particularly unhelpful for many of the people who will be expected to study it. As we note throughout this book, distress is very common and it is likely that most readers will know someone who has experienced it (see Box 1.3).

In this context, teaching that is framed from the outset as being about something abnormal will already import a range of assumptions that, for many readers, are likely to be difficult or unhelpful. It is hard to engage constructively with teaching that labels you, or the people you love and care for, as abnormal.

Even more seriously, this unhelpful aspect of abnormal psychology is not confined to its likely effects upon the learning and teaching of psychology. Although the majority of people who study psychology do not go on to have careers in the profession, they will nevertheless draw upon what they have learned at other points in their lives. This means that they will tend to possess a limited and restrictive set of conceptual frameworks when they themselves, or people in their lives, encounter mental health problems. These limitations, and the assumptions of abnormality which they reproduce, may act as barriers to people's ability to understand difficulties and respond to them appropriately.

Of course, *all* teaching and learning starts from a set of assumptions about what we imagine to be the nature of the topic and what students need to learn about it. We do not imagine that by avoiding the term 'abnormal psychology' we have somehow written a textbook that is free from any assumptions – far from it. We simply hope that the assumptions we started from will prove more helpful and appropriate for psychologists and many others who wish to engage with this topic.

Isn't this just anti-psychiatry?

Some readers might consider that our arguments so far are 'just **anti-psychiatry**'. By this, people mean the work of psychiatrists and others in the 1960s, like Ronald Laing in the UK and Thomas Szasz in the USA, both of whom were critical of the legitimacy of psychiatric claims. As we will see in Chapter 2, the so-called anti-psychiatrists were not a homogenous group, and there were important differences between the key figures. Moreover, both Laing and Szasz were unhappy with the term 'anti-psychiatry', and they were clearly not against all ideas and practices in this area, since they both continued to practise psychotherapy.

Many modern abnormal psychology and psychiatry textbooks give the impression that the challenges raised by the

---

BOX 1.3

I know someone who has a mental health problem

Many readers of this book will either know someone who has had a mental health problem, will have experienced a problem themselves, or may do so in the future. UK mental health campaigners suggest that about one in four people will, at some point in the course of their lives, experience clinical levels of distress. Elsewhere in this book, we ask whether such figures challenge common definitions of mental illness based upon notions of organic disease and dysfunction. For now, all we need to recognize is that such experiences are very common, so if you have experienced distress – or know someone who has – you are not alone.

In a survey of students attending an abnormal psychology class in the US, Patricia Connor-Greene (2001) found that almost every student reported knowing someone with a mental health problem, that quite often students knew several

such people, and that the people they knew were most often family members. She observed that taking part in such a class is not 'simply an abstract academic exercise; it is a potential source of knowledge and skills that could have a significant impact on students, families and friends' (Connor-Greene, 2001, p. 211).

We take this point seriously. Throughout the book we have sought to portray people in distress in a respectful manner, and to avoid an 'us and them' attitude. We have tried to investigate and present the evidence behind, for example, claims about particular mental health interventions, so that readers of the book can act as informed citizens when helping a family member to weigh up the pros and cons of different intervention options.

When reading about mental health, one can easily start to recognize oneself in the descriptions of certain kinds of problem. As we will see in later chapters, studies of the normal population suggest that many mental health problems are normally distributed, such that a lot of us experience them at a low level (i.e.

in a manner which does not get in the way of our lives or cause significant difficulties for us or those close to us). Thus, if you feel that you are a little obsessive because you like things to be neat and tidy, it does not mean you have a disease called obsessive compulsive disorder. This self-recognition problem is very common. If you asked the other students in the class if they have started to question whether they have a mental health problem, we think it is likely they will say that they have too!

If, however, you do have a problem that is long-lasting, and that is causing difficulties that get in the way of your life and causing you further distress, then you should consider seeking help. Most universities and colleges have mental health or counselling services, and these can be an appropriate place to start. For those who are not students, local voluntary services in your area can usually be identified by searching the internet. You could also try discussing your difficulties with your GP, who – if it is appropriate – will be able to refer you to more specialist services.

anti-psychiatry movement were addressed with a new edition of the DSM in the 1980s. However, this new manual did not solve the more fundamental conceptual problems noted by these critics – for example, that value judgements are necessarily involved in definitions of mental illness, and that there is no clearly evidenced biological basis for mental illness, and thus no physical tests for (say) schizophrenia in the way that there are for infections or viruses. Moreover, there has been a considerable body of empirical research over the last fifty years which has cast new light on some of the debates which began in the 1960s. Throughout the book we will draw on this research to demonstrate that there are continuing problems with the validity and reliability of diagnostic constructs. Likewise, we will draw on this research to show that a focus on the experience of forms of distress can yield results that are valuable to service users, researchers and clinicians.

It may help here to consider some of the debates in other areas of psychology, for example between different approaches to social psychology or between paradigms like learning theory and psychoanalysis. Here, too, there are debates about assumptive frameworks, key concepts, terminology and methodology. In these areas, too, we have had to accept that research is always, to some degree, a reflection of its time, affected by cultural norms and so on. Our contention is that this is also true in mental health, so throughout the book you will see debates analogous to those found in other areas of psychology.

In short, there are some similarities between aspects of our approach and the ideas of the anti-psychiatrists, but there are also significant differences. This book reflects the findings of the nearly fifty years of research and discussion that has taken place since the 1960s. The term 'anti-psychiatry' seems to exclude all of this more recent work, is simplistic, and carries far too much historical and conceptual baggage; for these reasons we would not use this label to characterize our approach.

From disorder to experience

Most mental health textbooks, then, focus on psychiatric disorders; Box 1.4 shows how disorder is typically defined within psychiatry, and discusses some problems associated with such definitions. By contrast, in this book we focus on experience. By this we mean that we will describe and try to explain experiences of distress without presuming that they are always caused by an underlying disorder of some kind. We will treat the difficulties themselves as something to be explained, rather than attributing them to an underlying disorder that in fact may not even exist.

In the last few years there has been a growing tendency for psychology to engage directly with the particularities of experience itself, rather than, for example, engaging with general biological or cognitive capacities. There have been three recent books on the psychology of experience, each one taking a slightly different focus. Ben Bradley (2005) emphasizes that experience is always relational and shaped by the simultaneous experiences of other people. He also discusses ways of thinking about the significance of time in relation to experience. Dave Middleton and Steve Brown (2005) show how our experience is made in part from our memories, exploring how they help give meaning to everything we see, hear and feel. Niamh Stephenson and Dimitris Papadopoulos (2007)

BOX **1.4**

DSM-IV definition of mental disorder

In DSM-IV each of the mental disorders is conceptualized as a clinically significant behavioural or psychological syndrome or pattern that occurs in an individual and that is associated with present distress (a painful symptom) or disability (impairment in or more areas of functioning). This syndrome or pattern must not be merely an expectable and culturally sanctioned response to a particular event, for example the death of a loved one. Whatever its original cause, it must currently be considered a manifestation of a behavioural, psychological or biological dysfunction in the individual. Neither deviant behaviour nor conflicts that are primarily between the individual and society are mental disorders unless the deviance or conflict is a symptom of dysfunction in the individual.

Reproduced in Stein et al. (2010, p. 1760)

This definition raises many issues that recur throughout this book: whether or not distress should be seen as a medical or biological problem, the relationships between individuals and their culture, the kinds of reactions we should expect people to show to unpleasant but common experiences such as bereavement, and so on. Notably, however, the definition also displays a continual concern with notions of **dysfunction**, and this raises some complex issues.

For example, Wakefield (1992) distinguishes between disorder and dysfunction. He argues that a disorder is a harmful dysfunction, and that what is considered harmful will be judged according to prevailing social norms. By contrast, a dysfunction – for example, of a cognitive mechanism designed to conduct a specific function – might be identified objectively, so is not subject to the same kinds of influences or biases. This suggestion is insightful: it avoids many of the difficulties associated with definitions of normality and abnormality whilst also recognizing that the notion of disorder is inescapably social in character.

However, as Kirk and Kutchins (1999) observe, we can only reliably identify a dysfunction if we can say with confidence what the *function* of a system or organ is meant to be. But in relation to human minds and brains, our knowledge of these functions is still remarkably limited. For example, we know that many neural systems frequently serve more than one function, that most basic abilities are enabled by multiple neural systems working in parallel, and that there are frequently many different neural pathways by which the same (or a similar) behavioural or cognitive goal can be reached. They argue further that many forms of distress are probably not dysfunctional in any simple sense: for example, that it may well be 'natural' and a sign that your neural systems are working as they should if you end up feeling deeply miserable because you have lost your job and have no immediate prospect of getting another.

focus mainly on the ways in which experience is shaped by the wider power relations of society, relations which regulate our experience and – at the same time – create contradictions that can put us somewhat at odds with their requirements.

These different perspectives on experience begin to show how it always spreads in two directions: 'outside' ourselves, into the social and material circumstances that give experience its character and content, and 'inside' ourselves, by way of the many thoughts, feelings and memories it consists of. In this book we will try to explore experience from both of these directions, in the hope that by doing so we can make even superficially baffling experiences more open to explanation. The alternative – attributing what we cannot readily understand to the effects of an underlying disorder – tends to produce unsatisfying, circular explanations: we know that Jenny has schizophrenia because she hears voices, and the reason she hears voices is because she has schizophrenia.

Whilst the kinds of experiences we will consider are quite varied, they are all of the kinds that mental health professionals might encounter in the course of their work. At the start of this chapter we presented Bess's story and suggested that her experiences are fairly typical of those that clinicians encounter. Here are some more examples:

Dave is a 45 year old man who is frustrated with his career. Although he has a well paid, highly respected job and a comfortable home, he is dissatisfied with other aspects of his life and his negative feelings have recently started to become overwhelming. At work, Dave feels that his talents are not being recognized, and that his manager is a bully who does not take his suggestions seriously. In recent months, this situation has begun to preoccupy Dave's thoughts. He has frequent trouble sleeping, and has started experiencing pains in his neck and back. His GP can find no physical cause for these pains, but since Dave recently began experiencing panic attacks he has referred him to a counsellor attached to the practice. Together with the counsellor, Dave has begun exploring how his responses to his manager are shaped by other experiences in his life.

Ellie is a 19 year old woman who got pregnant when she was just 15, although she has not seen her son's father since then. She has tried to provide her son with a stable home, but despairs that she is only surrounding him with the same kinds of instability and confusion that she experienced herself when she was growing up. For a long time now Ellie has felt very miserable, but she has come to believe that if only she had cosmetic surgery to make her body look 'younger', more attractive to men, she would feel much better. When her doctor would not refer her for cosmetic surgery of this kind, Ellie attempted suicide. Since then she has been taking anti-depressant medication and receiving cognitive-behavioural therapy.

Mark is a 25 year old unemployed man who lives with his mother and stepfather in a poor suburb. He never knew his own father, who left home when he was small. His mother remarried and had a daughter with her new partner, and Mark grew up feeling that he always took second place to his sister. Following a long and angry argument with his stepfather, Mark has been lonely and miserable and has started locking himself into his room. Alone at night, he has begun to hear angry male voices criticizing him. Mark is terrified by these experiences, but has not told anyone about them because he fears that people will laugh.

Like all of the other examples in this book, these are fictional – they are not descriptions of real people. Nevertheless, they are fictions closely informed both by clinical practice and by the research literature describing mental health difficulties. This means that we can use them to draw out important issues that are relevant to our understandings of distress – for example, how people are socially positioned. Dave is a middle-class professional, whereas Ellie and Mark are less wealthy and have fewer resources. Studies show that the incidence of psychiatric diagnoses varies with wider economic and social conditions and is patterned according to sociological variables such as class or socio-economic status, gender and ethnicity. Similarly, there is much evidence that women are more likely to be given some psychiatric diagnoses than men, and that overall they are more likely to experience distress. Nevertheless, as our examples illustrate, at the individual level these influences appear complex and uneven.

Ultimately, each of our examples is an attempt to reduce the messy complexity of a lived experience, in all its uncertainty and ambiguity, to a single narrative told from a specific point of view. Inevitably, doing this raises issues. For example, there are always other stories that could have been told: even though we have tried to illustrate something of the great diversity of distressing experiences, it is impossible to encapsulate the variety of experiences being lived out around us all the time. So we could have told many other stories; but we could also have told the stories we did tell in different ways. Mark's stepfather, for example, might have told a story that emphasized Mark's unreasonable behaviour, and described how he frequently becomes aggressive without any apparent justification.

Both psychiatry and psychology are imbued with interests – for example, those of commerce and professional status. Although the problems associated with these interests may be more acute in respect of psychiatry, psychology does not provide a neutral ground from which to approach distress

This suggests that there will often be tensions between what people say about distress according to how they have experienced it, how they have been exposed to it, and how they have been encouraged to understand it. Moreover, these tensions will often have moral, ethical or political dimensions to them. This is only to be expected: partly because distress often first becomes a matter for intervention when people flagrantly breach everyday moral codes and expectations, partly because distress is associated with inequality, disadvantage, discrimination and prejudice, and partly because the stigma associated with it can be used to discredit or denounce the actions and pronouncements of individuals. Stories about distress (like all stories, in fact) are never neutral: they are always told from a point of view, and that point of view always reflects a set of interests.

We have no definitive solution to these problems. We certainly cannot claim that the account we give in this book is somehow neutral, or that it fails to reflect our interests as academic and clinical psychologists. Instead, we have adopted two strategies to take account of these problems. First, we will continually emphasize the importance of *all* kinds of evidence when considering, weighing and assessing the claims made for different explanations of distress. And second, we have included in this book some of the views and perspectives of people who actually experience distress, so that our professional perspectives can be balanced by perspectives from those who have actually received mental health services.

All in the mind?

By rejecting psychiatric disease categories we might appear to be denying the reality of people's distress: if the categories aren't real, are we saying that the distress isn't real, either?

This is not the case. We have not based this book upon psychiatric diagnoses because of the extensive evidence regarding their lack of validity, poor reliability, dubious empirical grounding and much-discussed conceptual difficulties (we discuss this evidence in much more detail throughout the book, especially in Chapters 4 and 5).

In place of psychiatric diagnoses, we advocate consistently psychological explanations, but from a psychological perspective, people's distress is just as 'real' as it is from a psychiatric one. The pejorative term 'it's all in her mind' is sometimes used to imply that psychological distress should be something we can simply overcome by an effort of will. It is a moral judgement which ultimately implies that only those of weak character fall prey to psychological disorders. In this book we need to avoid such unjustified moralizing, whilst holding on to the idea that distress is fundamentally psychological. We can do so in a number of ways.

First, we should recall that nothing is simply 'all in the mind'. Mind, body and brain are intimately joined together, and anything that is 'in the mind' is simultaneously a state of the body–brain system. The denigration of psychological distress as being 'all in the mind', in other words, relies for its force upon the cultural commonplace of **mind–body dualism**. Mind–body dualism – also sometimes called **Cartesian dualism** – refers to a tendency, common in Western cultures and associated historically with the philosophy of René Descartes, to treat mind and body as distinct, separate substances with no necessary links between them.

Second, we should recall that pain, such as that from a broken leg, is just as much 'in the mind' as distress, but we

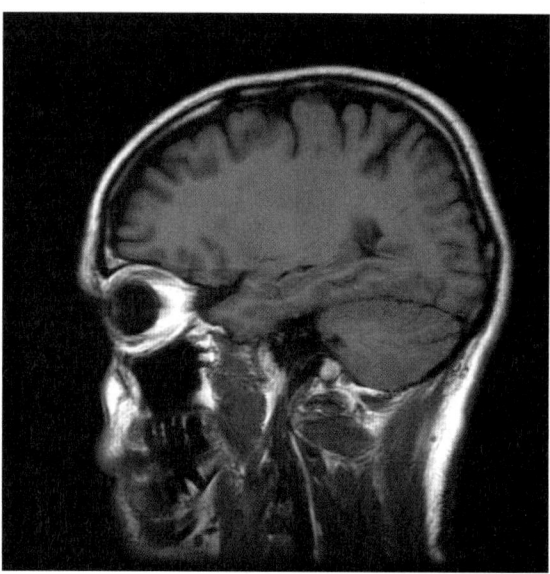

Anything that is 'in the mind' is also a state of the brain and body

don't understand it in these dismissive terms because there is a clear and visible explanation for its severity. Those who experience chronic back pain, by contrast, may also fall prey to such discrimination: having a visible cause for pain – or for distress – helps.

Third, the experiences of distress that are categorized by psychiatric diagnoses are, in any case, overwhelmingly psychological in character. There are no reliable biological markers for different diagnoses, no blood tests or scans that can be used to make diagnoses of depression or schizophrenia. Instead, there are reports – usually verbal – of various kinds of experience: unusual beliefs, profound unhappiness, extreme agitation, hearing voices and so on. These experiences may well also have aspects that are visible in the person's bearing and manner: people who are deeply unhappy, for example, often talk more slowly than other people, and sometimes more quietly. They may have difficulty thinking of words or concentrating on the flow of conversation, and may find it hard to motivate themselves. But the existence of these bodily elements does not necessarily mean that there is a physical disease called depression, although it does demonstrate, again, that psychological states are simultaneously states of the body and brain.

Fourth, we should always keep in mind that even when people's own actions seem to be unhelpful and self-defeating, this does not mean that they are simply responsible for their own distress. Putting this another way, just because how we respond to our distress can make a difference to the outcome, this doesn't mean that individuals should be held personally responsible for failing to respond in what, from an outsider's perspective, is the 'correct' manner. In actuality, most people's room to manoeuvre is far more limited than it might at first appear, and many simply do not have the resources to deal with their situation in ways that are markedly different. Moreover, just like everyone else, when people experiencing distress make choices, they always do so with limited knowledge of their consequences: we can know what we do, but cannot so readily know all of the *effects* of what we do.

Far from denying the reality of people's distress, then, psychological explanations begin with this reality and attempt to understand how it has been constituted. In our view, only the existence of a cultural prejudice against psychological explanations for distress prevents this from being more obvious.

Models of distress

In science, models are often used as an aid to thinking about and researching problems. Formal scientific models are derived from theories and bear a systematic relationship to them. There are also more 'informal' models that are most accurately located within a paradigm rather than a theory, and these are the kind of models typically used in relation to distress. We have already mentioned biopsychosocial, biomedical and psychosocial models of distress, but in the literature many more are described. Figure 1.2 shows some of the most commonly-cited models of distress, together with their most frequently used synonyms.

Whilst for convenience we have named these models as though they were separate and distinct entities, you need to be aware that in actual practice things are far more confusing. For example, it is possible to conceive of the diathesis-stress model as a variant of the biopsychosocial model, because it attempts to unite biology, in the form of an organic vulnerability or **diathesis**, with the psychological and social influences that cause stress.

However, it is equally possible to conceive of the diathesis-stress model as a variant of the medical or psychiatric model, because it posits that clinical distress only arises in people who are medically (biologically) vulnerable. Likewise, some family systems models are also psychoanalytic; and many psychological models are cognitive as well as behavioural. Similarly, many people would see the biological model as being the same as the medical or psychiatric one, whereas some would differentiate these.

Using models to understand distress can yield a number of advantages. Models simplify complex issues, making it easier to think about them and to generate ways of researching them empirically. They do this largely by selecting some aspects of distress as most relevant to enquiry, and others as less relevant: this assists with both theory and empirical research. Using a biological model of distress, for example, the primary focus of study will be what occurs inside the brain and body of someone experiencing distress; other influences will only be important to the extent that they make a difference to the body and brain.

Models also supply a mode of representation – an analogy or set of metaphors that is useful for communication and conceptualization. In the cognitive model, for example, the analogy is that the mind works like a computer, so we conceive of distress as caused by faulty information processing. In this way, models also organize events and phenomena into (possible) causal chains. If distress is cognitive and arises because of faulty information processing, the causal chains will implicate psychological mechanisms and strategies (attributions, perceptions etc.); if distress is biological, the causal chains will depend on biological phenomena such as features of the brain.

However, these benefits can also become limitations. Because models are analogies or metaphors for distress, rather than *actual* distress, they can easily be over-extended. Once we begin to think of distress in terms of (for example) a cognitive model, we might be tempted to keep on thinking of it this way even when we encounter aspects that might be better explained in other ways. For example, although some aspects of being extremely sad can be conceptualized cognitively (in terms of a set of negative cognitive biases), other aspects are probably better explained by reference to biological or social processes. This might seem to imply that a biopsychosocial model is what is needed, and whilst in a superficial sense this is obviously true, in practice most biopsychosocial accounts are inadequate (we discuss this issue in Chapter 4, especially in Box 4.5).

Another possible disadvantage of using models is that, in simplifying distress by focusing on what is most relevant from a given perspective, they might actually leave out what is most important, but we will never know this unless we start from the actual phenomena (the experience of being distressed, in all of its complexity and confusions) rather than from within the bounds of a model to which we have already made an intellectual or professional commitment.

A final disadvantage is that models of distress can be misleading with respect to causality because they might imply sets of relations that, in actuality, do not exist. For example, a biological model of distress that emphasizes the role of hormones might give the impression that these hormones only interact with each other, and lose sight of the fact that levels of hormones also fluctuate according to external influences such as social and relationship status.

There are also deeper conceptual issues with most commonly used models of distress because for the most part they accept boundaries that we might wish to question. For example, biological and social influences tend to be either kept apart or – when they are brought together – mediated by psychology. Whilst there is some sense in this, it then makes it very difficult to consider situations where biological and social influences might interact directly, without necessarily being psychologically mediated, such as in the development of an embryo in the womb, or in the very early days of a human infant's life.

Throughout this book we will sometimes have to make reference to models of distress, and you can use the table in this section to orient yourself toward them. However, whilst they can be useful, you should always bear in mind that they can also be misleading.

| Biomedical (biological) |
| Medical (psychiatric, illness) |
| Diathesis-stress (stress-diathesis, stress-vulnerability) |
| Behavioural |
| Cognitive |
| Humanistic (existential) |
| Psychodynamic (psychoanalytic) |
| Family systems |
| Psychosocial (sociocultural) |
| Biopsychosocial |

Figure 1.2 **Models of distress**

Overview of this book

This book is in two parts. The first part provides a foundation for the second by systematically setting out key concepts, debates and evidence. The aim of the first part is to supply a detailed account of distress that describes its character, identifies causal influences, and discusses responses to it. In the second part, we apply this account of distress to a subset of the most common kinds of mental health problems encountered by professionals in clinical psychology, psychiatry, social work and related disciplines.

Part 1

This part contains eight chapters which, read together, provide a consistently psychological account of distress. Although we frequently discuss psychiatric diagnoses in this part, we do not use them as explanations. Instead, we offer explanations that draw upon psychological theories and concepts, supplemented where appropriate with evidence and ideas from disciplines including neuroscience, anthropology, sociology, epidemiology and other relevant disciplines. In this way we provide an account of distress that avoids 'jumping ship' and uncritically importing wholesale a set of concepts and theories from psychiatry. Part 1 has eight chapters:

Introduction (this chapter)
History
Culture
Biology
Diagnosis and Formulation
Causal Influences
Service Users and Survivors
Interventions

History: To understand why we have the ideas we do today it is vital to look at how those ideas were developed, so in this chapter we provide a survey of the different ways that distress has been understood and treated over the centuries. Our history shows how there have always been competing strands of explanation and treatment for distress, some primarily implicating the body and its organs and some primarily implicating experiences, meanings, thoughts and feelings.

Culture: This chapter describes how distress differs between cultures. It discusses some of the great variability in the forms of distress, the variability in the ways that it gets linked to other aspects of experience, and the variability in the outcomes associated with it. As we have already suggested, distress is thoroughly bound up with culture, and this chapter illustrates the extent and consequences of this.

Biology: Our approach to biology treats it as an inescapable part of distress, but does not make the unfounded psychiatric assumption that it is always the ultimate cause of people's difficulties. In this chapter we explain why there are problems with biopsychosocial accounts of distress, and in their place offer an alternative view of the role of biology. We summarize evidence that supports our approach, drawing upon studies of attachment as well as upon recent work in psychology and neuroscience.

Diagnosis and Formulation: Textbooks of 'abnormal psychology' are usually organized around systems of psychiatric diagnosis, such as one of the versions of the DSM. This chapter presents some of the evidence that psychiatric diagnosis is not valid and reliable enough to provide a firm scientific basis for understanding distress. It then sketches an alternative, consistently psychological approach to classifying distress.

Causal Influences: In some instances, the causes of a person's distress might seem quite obvious; in others, they may seem mysterious or obscure. This chapter provides a detailed discussion of the notion of causality in relation to distress, showing how it is often more difficult to ascertain and understand than we imagine. We describe and evaluate the research methods used to establish causality in distress, and then review evidence showing that – regardless of the specific form that distress takes –it is associated time and again with a common set of causal influences.

Service Users and Survivors: Mental health service users sometimes describe themselves as *experts by experience.* This chapter draws upon some of that expertise and describes how the service user movement in the UK has mounted a series of challenges to the treatments offered by services. A discussion of the work of the 'Hearing Voices Network' shows how service users are continuing to challenge conventional services by organizing themselves to provide viable alternatives to conventional therapies.

Interventions: Here we describe the kinds of interventions for distress typically offered by Western mental health services. We describe psychiatric medication, psychotherapy, and community psychology interventions, using these to show how each offers different potential sources of help to people experiencing distress. A number of different mental health professionals are involved in offering interventions to people in distress – in the appendix to the book we describe some of the key professional groups and the kinds of settings within which they work.

Part 2

Part two of the book contains five chapters. In each one we discuss in detail one of the major kinds of distress that contemporary Western mental health services encounter.

We had to make some difficult choices about how we should present this material. On the one hand, we did not want to organize the material around psychiatric diagnoses. On the other hand, we knew that many mental health modules are structured in this way. This meant that we needed to present our material in a way that was useful to as many people as possible.

We have done this by structuring these chapters around broad forms of distress where there is some commonality in the underlying **phenomenology** of an experience. In psychology, phenomenology refers to exactly what an experience is like – what kinds of characteristics, features and subjective qualities it has. Reflecting some of its links with philosophy (phenomenology is also an important branch of philosophy), this usually means that efforts are made to include the bodily or **embodied** aspects of experience, as well as those usually described as mental or cognitive.

What does this look like in practice? Well, for example, it means that Chapter 9, 'Sadness and Worry', deliberately treats together aspects of experience that are usually treated separately in books organized according to the DSM classification. In other books, these experiences are likely to be addressed in two separate chapters, one focused upon 'Depression' and the other focused upon 'Anxiety Disorders'. Similarly, Chapter 11 on 'Madness' includes experiences that, in other textbooks, would be addressed separately in relation to psychiatric diagnoses such as schizophrenia and bipolar disorder.

Although the number of different kinds of distress we discuss in this way is fairly small, they will account for the vast majority of the referrals received by UK mental health services. The chapters are

Sadness and Worry
Sexuality and Gender
Madness
Distressed Bodies and Eating
Disordered Personalities

Each of these five chapters is structured in a similar way, and each one builds upon the concepts and evidence laid out in Part 1 of the book. Within each of these chapters there are sections on history and culture, a summary of the psychiatric diagnoses typically given to people experiencing this form of distress, a review of the evidence regarding causality, and a description of the kinds of treatments and interventions available for this kind of distress.

How to use this book

Sequence

Because most 'abnormal psychology' textbooks are structured around the diagnostic categories of the DSM, they often do not make a sequential, structured argument. This means that it is usually quite easy to dip into them, regardless of the order of the chapters, in order to read about specific diagnoses.

This book is a little different. In Part 1, especially, all of the chapters are linked so that together they provide a systematic argument that explains our approach to distress. The chapters in Part 2 are more like the chapters in other textbooks, in that it does not especially matter in which order you look at them. However, whilst these chapters can be read in isolation, you will get a lot more out of reading all of them if you first read the chapters in Part 1.

Questions

Each of the chapters has a set of questions associated with it. You can use these questions to check your own learning and make sure that you understand the material in the book in the way that we intend. There are guiding questions at the start of each chapter that will alert you to recurrent themes to keep in mind as you read. There are also summary or revision questions at the end, which you can use to check that your learning is proceeding adequately.

Boxes

All through the book we use boxes to introduce additional material alongside the main text. Some of the boxes simply contain material that, although linked to the main text, is easier to explain separately. Other boxes contain discussions of key theories, concepts or issues which will recur throughout the book.

Key terms and concepts

You have probably already noticed that whenever we use any specialist terms or language for the first time, the term is printed in **bold** and a definition or explanation appears very close by – mostly immediately afterwards, occasionally just beforehand.

Stories and experiences

Almost all of the chapters in this book start with a story about someone's experience. As we have already explained, these stories are all fictional but, at the same time, they are informed by clinical practice and by close readings of the mental health literature. You can read them as a very quick and accessible way of orienting yourself to the concerns and issues that each chapter raises.

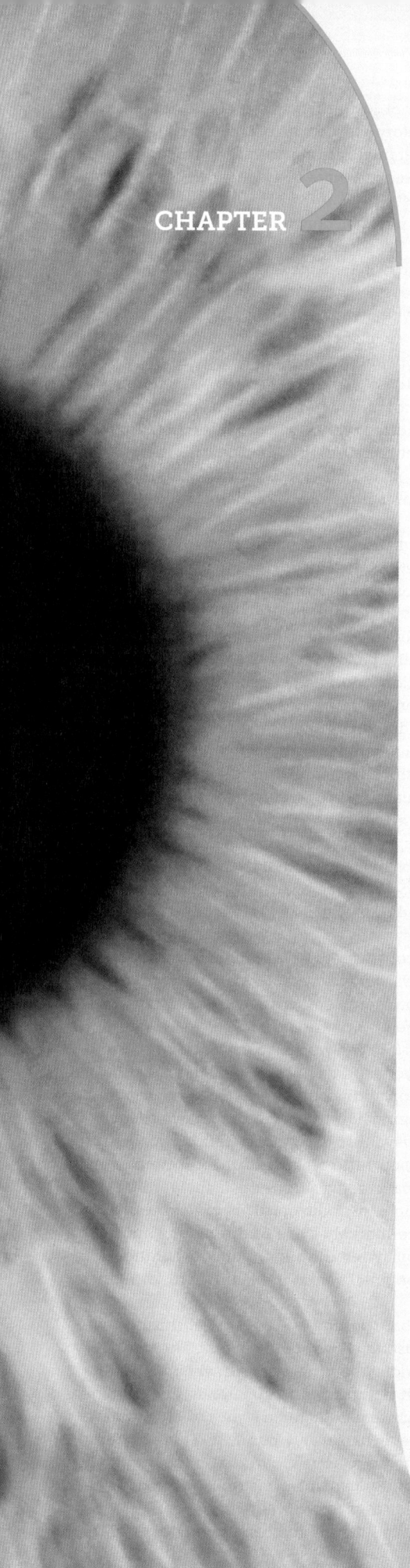

CHAPTER 2

HISTORY

Michael's story

Michael is a middle-aged man who is married with children. One day whilst at work he sees something strange which he struggles to understand – a ghostly figure in white approaching him. Later that day he hears a voice that tells him he is hearing the voice of God and that he should give up his life and follow God.

How might we understand this experience? As we will see in the next chapter, one context for understanding such experiences is a cultural one. For example, we might want to know what country the man lives in and what cultural norms exist – are religious visions and voices seen as unusual? Or are they seen as a normal and expected, even valued, experience within this culture? However, another context is a historical one because cultural norms vary over time. For example, in ancient Greece or in Europe until the late Middle Ages the man might be seen as a mystic or as someone called to a religious vocation by God. Alternatively, he might be seen as a heretic or as mistaking the voice of the devil for the voice of God.

If, on the other hand, these experiences took place in post-Enlightenment Europe, when ideas about distress began to change quite dramatically, moving from a religious-based worldview to a secular scientific one, we might wonder whether his experiences were caused by some kind of imbalance in his physical state, perhaps caused by a physical disease process. Alternatively, if this man lived in the late 19th or early 20th century, we might wonder whether these experiences signal some kind of inner conflict – perhaps they should be seen as a metaphorical sign of problems rooted in his early life experiences.

Finally, if these experiences occurred in the later part of the 20th century, we might wonder whether they were a response to sudden changes in the man's circumstances – for example, has he experienced recent negative life events? Are there conflicts in his family life or at work?

In this chapter, we examine how ideas of distress have been seen differently throughout history. Indeed, many of our modern ideas have deep historical roots.

By the end of this chapter you will:

1 Have an understanding of how distress came to be seen in the present era as an issue of health, within the domain of medicine
2 Understand how many modern debates (e.g. about the causes of distress) are rooted in historical debates about models of distress
3 Understand the social context of the development of our ideas about distress and treatments.

Introduction

In our ancient texts, there are examples of what might now be seen as instances of distress. For example, the Psalmist cries:

> All day long they carp at my words, their only thought is to harm me, they gather together, lie in wait and spy on my movements, as though determined to take my life.
>
> The New Jerusalem Bible (1985, Psalm 56:6)

Is this an example of what we would now call **paranoia** or a **persecutory delusion** (an unwarranted belief that others intend to harm us)? What we might now apprehend as madness was certainly mentioned in ancient stories and texts, and apparently unusual behaviour (descriptions of which today we might see as evidence of epilepsy) might be put down to the Hindu demon Grahi ('she who seizes') or an Indian dog-demon or, if one was Assyrian, the devil *migtu*. Ancient Egyptians delineated models of the self which was seen as split between Khat (the body), Ka (one's guardian spirit guide through life) and Ba (one's guide in the after life). Thus the health of the soul played an essential part in one's overall health. Such tripartite divisions were later seen in Plato, Islam and Freud. Medicine has a long history with evidence of some forms of Chinese, Egyptian and Indian medical systems dating back to 3000 BC and Hebrew systems back to 1000 BC.

Have humans always experienced forms of extreme distress or engaged in conduct that concerns and disturbs others? To some extent this question is unanswerable. Humans have existed for about 200,000 years but our evidence of how early humans saw the world is incomplete. Written forms of language only began to appear 5–6000 years ago (approximately 3000 BC), so we have no documentary evidence to explain our ancestors' lives earlier than this. Instead, we have to make inferences from other forms of evidence such as finds from archaeological digs, art, genetics (e.g. the distribution of certain DNA patterns across the world), linguistics (e.g. the relationship between different languages over time) and the remnants of oral traditions (e.g. cultural and religious stories passed down from generation to generation). Whilst these can tell us a lot about societies and cultures of the past we must also be careful not to exaggerate the status of our knowledge, which is necessarily limited. Even with written language we still need to interpret carefully, since meanings change over time and from context to context. As the British novelist L. P. Hartley put its it in *The Go-Between*, '[t]he past is another country: they do things differently there' (1953, p. 7).

In this chapter we aim to explain how we have come to view distress and disturbing conduct in the way that we now do. This is important, as it shapes the ways in which we address these issues. This is not just an abstract issue – without an understanding of history we can take our current ways of viewing distress for granted, failing to realize that there are other viewpoints. Moreover, there is a danger that we repeat the mistakes of the past.

As we noted in the previous chapter, definitions of distress are contested. One of the dangers in looking at the history of distress is to assume that 'it' remains unchanged but is simply labelled in different ways. However, this would be to underestimate the extent to which what is seen as a form of distress changes from place to place and from period to period. Bynum, Porter and Shepherd (1985) ask, 'Is there any such natural object of "madness" at all?' (p. 3) since the meanings of such terms 'change profoundly from epoch to epoch, in ways inexplicable unless viewed within wider contexts of shifting power relations, social pressures and ideological interests' (p. 4). Indeed, as Rose (1990) has observed, the very language and vocabulary we use makes new ways of seeing reality available to us.

We currently view distress as a matter of mental health – thus it is seen as something located in the mind (as opposed to the soul or the body or in relationships or the social context), and something that is to do with health and therefore in the province of doctors, hospitals and clinics (as opposed to the realm of the priest or the philosopher). As a result this leads to the kinds of interventions most associated with medicine, for example hospitals and medication. However, humans have viewed distress very differently over time in ways that were associated with very different kinds of interventions.

In the history sections of many textbooks on abnormal psychology or psychiatry, there is a narrative of a gradual progression from demonology to modern day enlightened views. We think this is an over-simplification. In Box 2.1 we discuss five problems encountered when approaching the history of a topic. We hope to avoid these problems in this chapter in a number of ways. Firstly, we hope to avoid a 'presentist' view of history by setting out the *historical context* within which ideas about distress have emerged, and by using, as much as possible, *the language and terms* used by people at the time. This is a difficult problem, as many of these terms (e.g. 'lunatic', 'madman') are now considered offensive. However, if we use modern terms (or even worse, go back through history to make *post hoc* psychiatric diagnoses of historical figures), we run the risk of simply imposing modern day conceptions of distress, thus obscuring how understandings have changed, often in important ways. For example, it can be instructive to look at terms in their historical context: for example, the 13th century word *lunatic* derives from the Latin word for the moon since, at that time, periodic episodes of madness were seen as caused by the monthly cycle of the moon. Similarly, the term **asylum** (usually referring to a public institution for those seen as mad) originates from the Latin word for refuge or sanctuary.

Secondly, rather than writing a 'ceremonial' history, we aim to present *contrasting views about distress*. The historian Andrew Scull (2011) notes how many treatments for distress were introduced with optimism and apparently good intentions only for them subsequently to be seen not only to have failed but to have been harsh and punitive. Thirdly, whilst many histories tend to emphasize a narrative of continuity – for example, associating particular historical periods with particular models of distress – we will describe some of the *discontinuities* and note how, although some models achieve

---

BOX **2.1**

Five problems encountered when doing history

Historians warn us of a number of problems to be aware of when we read historical accounts. The first of these is *presentism*. Presentist histories are those accounts written through the lens of the present, judging the past according to our current knowledge and values. A variant of this is so-called 'Whig' historical writing (noted in Richard Bentall's foreword) where the past is seen as ignorant or barbaric and we see present practice as enlightened, as if no further development or change will happen in the future. In such a view, history is seen as a straightforward account of progress with the practices of the present viewed as inherently better than those of the past. Instead, historians now prefer a *historicist* approach where an attempt is made to understand the past on its own terms.

A second problem occurs when historians write 'ceremonial' histories which serve to legitimize aspects of contemporary disciplines (and to ignore or downplay troublesome aspects or elements which do not fit with current ideas), rather than more critical histories, which put ideas in their political context. For example, the 19th century notion *Drapetomania* (see Box 2.3) could be seen as a way of justifying slave ownership.

A third problem occurs when the continuity of history is exaggerated (often with reference to 'masters' and 'pupils'), ignoring clear discontinuities. A fourth problem is when 'internal' factors (where one idea is seen to lead to another, or one theorist to lead on to another, in a progressive fashion) are over-emphasized. We also need to take account of 'external' factors, such as the cultural, political and economic contexts of ideas and practices. A related problem is where historians over-emphasize the notion of 'schools' of thought at a particular time – the so-called *Zeitgeist* approach. This is an over-simplification since there were often sharp disagreements within schools and, moreover, many theorists changed their ideas over time.

A final problem arises when historians adopt a 'great man' approach to history. The problem here is that important contributions by women, black people and other marginalized groups, such as those in distress, are neglected. In the 1970s and 1980s, feminist critics noted how much psychiatric theory was written by men about women and appeared to justify a hierarchical relationship between the sexes by reinforcing gender stereotypes. In 1972, American psychologist and psychotherapist Phyllis Chesler published *Women and Madness* (1972) in which she argued that double standards were applied to men and women in terms of mental health and that women were often punitively labelled as a function of gender, race, class, or sexual preference. In the 1980s this was followed by American feminist and literary critic Elaine Showalter's *The Female Malady*. She analysed depictions of hysteria and argued that cultural ideas about proper feminine behaviour had shaped the definition and treatment of women's mental health both in the past and the present. Similar arguments have been made by other groups who have been discriminated against throughout history, for example people from minority ethnic groups, the working class, gay and lesbian people, and so on.

---

some dominance at particular historical moments, there are *always other competing models* struggling for dominance. For example, throughout history it was far from obvious that medical explanations and treatments would become dominant – indeed, as we will see, this struggle for dominance was won by medical men only fairly recently (the middle of the 19th century). In this chapter we will attempt to understand how this dominance came about.

Fourthly, whilst some histories focus only on 'internal' factors – such as particular individuals and their theories – we will seek to describe *the broader social context* within which ideas and practices emerge. For example, we will discuss how the history of distress is also a history of *broader changes in institutions such as the Church, the academy, law and medicine* as well as a history of the emergence of – and struggles for dominance between – *new professional groups, such as psychiatrists*. A key influence, often neglected in histories, is the way in which *social policy* has shaped the way in which distress is viewed and treated, so we will describe the impact of policy changes over time (e.g. the building and subsequent closure of large public institutions or the laws regulating the treatment of those in distress). This does not mean that theories and models are not important – they form the assumptive framework within which interventions are constructed and the language with which they are justified. For example, the humoral model of distress (described further below) remained a dominant explanatory framework from ancient Greece to the 19th century and its echoes can still be seen in modern times when distress is explained in relation to purported chemical imbalances in the brain (Leo & Lacasse, 2008). We discuss debates about the biology of distress in Chapter 4. In most texts on the history of distress, two key explanatory models of are often referred to: a psychogenic model and a somatogenic model. In a **psychogenic model**, the causes of distress are generally seen to arise out of the mind. In a **somatogenic model** distress is seen as caused by the body. However, what is referred to much less is a **sociogenic model** where distress and disturbing conduct are seen as a result of a person's social location (e.g. suffering poverty and abuse), events in the world (e.g. particular negative life events) and their relationships with others. Sometimes the definition of a psychogenic model is broadened to include a person's response to events in the world. However, such accounts often give more prominence to explaining the variation in people's responses (usually due to a purported psychological mechanism) than to the environmental or social influences on that variation.

A fifth and final error that we hope to avoid is the production of a history that focuses only on medical men, philosophers and the efforts of social reformers, because, alongside the texts produced by the physicians of the day, a parallel documentary history exists, *written by the patients themselves*. These texts provide an insight into how distress was experienced at first hand. Moreover, they also document how those in distress experienced the treatments they received, treatments that often seem brutal to us now. One of the first historians to give an emphasis to the voices of those considered mad was the late Roy Porter in his *Social History of Madness* (1987). Another significant publication was Dale Petersen's *A Mad People's History of Madness* (1982). More recently, Gail Hornstein (2009) has provided an engaging account of her encounter with such narratives. She argues that, because 'the origins of madness remain elusive, and patients have always had their own distinct viewpoints' (pp. xvi–xvii), these first person narratives 'expose the limits of psychiatry's explanations and they offer competing theories and methods that might potentially work better' (p. xxii). She concludes that these narratives should be seen 'as protest literature, not as gibberish' (p. xvii).

This chapter is roughly chronological, beginning with ancient Greece and moving through the Middle Ages to the 17th, 18th and 19th centuries. We chart the way in which models of distress changed because of changes in the history of ideas (such as the development of science), the developments of new methods (such as the study of human anatomy) and social changes, for example the growth of both publicly-funded institutions and new disciplines such as psychiatry and psychology. We will see how there were struggles over how to best apprehend madness, with medicine largely winning this battle in the middle of the 19th century. The large numbers filling the asylums in the late 19th century drove a concern about chronicity, leading to worrying ideas that, in the 20th century, were used to justify the horrors perpetrated in Nazi Germany. With the 20th century came the birth of modern diagnosis, an array of psychological and pharmacological therapies and a new policy of **de-institutionalization** (i.e. the closing down of large mental hospitals and the development of new forms of treatment in the community). However, the 1960s brought a raft of challenges to psychiatry and, in the 1970s, 1980s and 1990s, the emergence of new ways of understanding distress as well as organized groups of mental health service users who campaigned for civil rights. We end the chapter by examining some recurring themes, such as the movement, over time, between the ideas that distress is primarily caused by either physical or mental processes.

A theme of this book is the need to understand more clearly the experiences of those in distress and to avoid making too many assumptions about those experiences. It is fitting, then, that we begin our journey through history by focusing on the experiences of those considered mad in their own words.

Guiding question

- *How did we arrive at our current ways of looking at and trying to help those in distress, or those whose behaviour others find disturbing?*

History from the patient's point of view: first person narratives as 'protest literature'?

John Perceval contended in 1838 that there was 'reasonableness in lunacy' and many of the works produced by those considered mad have attempted to document and explain their experiences. By definition, these authors were educated, literate and well-to-do, often publishing their accounts themselves, and most of them were men. However, one exception to this was Margery Kempe, born in 1373 to a prosperous burgess in King's Lynn. This illiterate woman dictated her account to a scribe. She first encountered distress following the birth of her first child and, for the rest of her life, moved between feeling that she was close to God and caught by the temptations of the Devil. She fought to escape the clutches of carnal desires through fasting and doing penance. She regularly saw visions and was consumed by bouts of weeping. Accused by others of being a 'false hypocrite' she sought the counsel of the mystic, Dame Julian of Norwich, and even undertook a pilgrimage to the Holy Land. The culmination of her religious quest was that she felt that God wanted to be joined with her in marriage. As Porter (2002) puts it, 'should we see Margery as turned by puerperal insanity, or think of her as a mystic? ... there is no master key to Margery's mind, and no one way of reading her life' (p. 177). But this dichotomy is not the only interpretation. The historian Gerda Lerner (1993) has highlighted Kempe's feelings about her marriage and the sexual relations it required, about which she wrote in such strongly negative terms as to suggest that 'her fourteen pregnancies were not voluntary' (p. 83). Kempe's pilgrimages, no doubt grounded in strong religious faith, also gave her a freedom from the demands of husband and family rarely available to a married woman of her class and time. In this example, we see in microcosm some of the debates about distress that run through this chapter. For example, is distress best understood in biological, psychological, religious, social or political terms?

Alongside a description of the experience of the manifestation of distress, another theme in these first person accounts is the injustice of the asylum system itself. In 1620 the *Petition of the Poor Distracted People in the House of Bedlam* (Campbell, 1996) was published – 'Bedlam' was a common term for the Bethlem hospital in London (and, to some degree, for madness and asylums in general) – which we will discuss later in the chapter. In 1774 Samuel Bruckshaw published *One More Proof of the Iniquitous Abuse of Private Madhouses* (Petersen, 1982). One of the best known first person accounts is that of John Perceval, son of the assassinated Prime Minister Spencer Perceval. Perceval spent 18 months in two expensive private asylums (Ticehurst and Brislington) and, in 1838, published *A Narrative of the Treatment Received by a Gentleman, during a State of Mental Derangement*. In it he wrote of how the medical staff did not talk or listen to him, saying he was treated 'as if I were a piece of furniture, an image of wood, incapable of desire or will as well as judgement' (Petersen, 1982, p. 94).

Patients, beginning with those in Bedlam in 1620, had petitioned parliament to report harsh, punitive and abusive treatment and their cases sometimes led to inquiries and changes in the law. They also had the support of advocates over the years, with the founding of organizations such as the Alleged Lunatics' Friend Society – 'the first organized manifestation of public apprehension about operation of the lunacy laws' (Hervey, 1986, p. 274) – the Friends of Insane Persons and the Society for the Protection of Alleged Lunatics (Coppock & Hopton, 2000), though their strategy was often one of challenging the accuracy of the diagnosis, hence the emphasis on 'alleged'.

However, one former American patient, Clifford Beers, became a powerful campaigner for reform. He had been a patient at a number of North American asylums between 1901 and 1903. Following his release he returned to working as a travelling salesman and dedicated his spare time to converting his notes into book form, eventually publishing *A Mind that Found Itself* in 1908. Given a diagnosis of **neurasthenia** (common symptoms of which included anxiety, depressed mood and a lack of energy), he felt he was the victim of a conspiracy and that the asylums were 'peopled by detectives, feigning insanity' (Beers, 1917, p. 64). Believing that his brother was an impostor, a fellow patient suggested that he test this by writing to his brother at his home address. When his brother duly arrived, Beers writes, 'the very instant I caught sight of my letter in the hands of my brother, all was changed ... Untruth became truth' (1917, p. 79). Despite this revelation he remained confined, keeping a record of the injustices he suffered. An activist of his day, he approached and gained the support of influential figures, including psychologist William James and subsequently, psychiatrists, policymakers and donors, until in 1909 he was able to set up his own organization the National Committee for Mental Hygiene – using the term suggested by the Swiss–American psychiatrist Adolf Meyer – which became the vanguard of the Mental Hygiene movement, a movement which led to the signing into law of the US National Mental Health Act in 1946.

In these first person accounts, then, we see a number of issues which will recur throughout the chapter: that madness may be understandable; that different models were suggested for understanding it (e.g. medical or religious); that those considered mad have often suffered harsh treatment in squalid conditions; and that, not only is recovery possible, but it has often been the activism of patients themselves which has brought about changes in mental health policy. In the rest of the chapter, we will look at how our views of mental distress have changed over a huge period, stretching from 1000 BC to the present day. It is important to note that this is not a global history. As we set out in the next chapter, culture has a huge influence on our understandings of distress. However, the account here focuses primarily on history from a European and North American viewpoint, as this is the context in which we live and work, and is also the context within which modern Western understandings of distress have developed. As a result, important developments in India, China or other parts of the world will not be covered here. To give an idea of the importance of such viewpoints, in Box 2.2 we outline the influence of the Islamic world on European knowledge.

BOX 2.2
Islamic approaches to distress in the Middle Ages

Modern histories of psychiatry and distress tend to promulgate a view that Europeans reverted to a form of demonology during the early Middle Ages and that a more institutionalized and elaborate system of demonology developed with the rise of Christianity resulting, for example, in the persecution of witches. This received view tends to see little of interest in this period until the Renaissance and the subsequent Age of Reason. However, this ignores the significant developments that took place in medicine, science and philosophy during this period in the Islamic world. During the time of the Islamic Golden Age (approximately 7th–13th century AD) and the Arabic Empire (approximately 10th–13th century AD), which stretched from Persia to Spain, a sophisticated system of medicine was developed. This drew not only on insights from Muslim traditions but also from Greek and Hebrew scholars whose work was translated into Arabic. Jim Al-Khalili (2010) argues that because the Islamic empire had a common language – 'from Cordoba to Samarkand' – and because they were intellectually curious and open to any work on merit, they were able to absorb and systematize knowledge from all over the world (e.g. ancient Greece, China, India). It has been argued that the Renaissance in Western Europe would

probably not have taken place if it had not been for the rediscovery of classical texts by Western European scholars, not only in Western European monastic libraries but also through knowledge assimilated from the Islamic world.

The Academy of Gundishapur, founded in Persia (now Iran) in the 3rd century AD translated Greek medical works and further developed Greek medicine until, during the 6th and 7th centuries AD, it was the most significant hospital in the Islamic world where students learnt to use a systematic approach to medicine. Gundishapur was also a centre of learning in philosophy, science and theology. Dols (1992) describes the development of institutions called maristans or bimaristans (Persian for 'place of the sick') in Cairo (Egypt), Aleppo (Syria) and Baghdad (Iraq) in the 7th and 8th centuries and in Granada (Spain) in the 14th century AD. Indeed, Porter (2002) suggests that these may well have served as a model for the asylums built later, in 15th century Spain at Valencia, Zaragoza, Seville, Valladolid, Toledo and Barcelona.

These institutions also cared for those in mental distress; the design of their buildings was influenced by Islamic ideas about the importance of architecture with pools, fountains and flower gardens designed to alleviate and heal distress (Fernando, 2007). At the maristans there was a systematic use of herbal treatments, including stimulants and sedatives, although there was also evidence of physical restraint and

beatings of patients (Fernando, 2007). There were even early manifestations of ideas which would not be more fully developed in Western Europe for several hundred years. For example, the Persian physician and philosopher al-Rāzi or Rhazes (865–925 AD) has been referred to as the first Islamic 'behaviour therapist' (Birashk, 2004, p. 382) because of his use of simple conditioned reflexes in treating mental distress.

Drawing on Persian influences, Islamic approaches to psychology were holistic rather than dualistic, seeing the self formed by a dynamic relation between the Qalb (or inner self), the Aql (or intellect), the Nafs Amara (or basic drives) and the body (Skinner, 2007). This tripartite division seems similar to earlier Egyptian and Platonic ideas. The Persian physician, philosopher and scientist Ibn Sina or Avicenna (980–1037 AD) believed 'that many disorders resulted from a lack of harmony between the brain and the body' (Birashk, 2004, p. 382) so that the purpose of remedies was to restore a homeostatic balance between these different elements. Traditionally, the more physical remedies were applied by herbal physicians (or Hakims) whilst spiritual remedies were addressed by spiritual guides (or Shaykhs). Specific kinds of music could be used either to balance forces in the Nafs Amara, or to weaken dissociation from the Qalb; this approach was common in Ottoman Turkish Asylums until just after the First World War (Skinner, 2007).

At intervals through the chapter we present seven timelines summarizing key events and placing them in a broad historical context. Figure 2.1 is the first timeline, covers a huge period, from 1000 BC to 1000 AD.

We begin our journey in the ancient world. The reader might be forgiven for asking what relevance this period has for us today but, as we will see, many of our modern notions of distress have their roots in this time.

The ancient Greeks: the emergence both of mythic and medical traditions of explanation

Roy Porter (1996) notes that '[p]re-Classical cultures certainly identified madness, but it is with the Greeks that madness first became an object of rational inquiry and literary depiction' (p. 278). In the Greek epic poems such as the *Iliad* (written somewhere between the 8th and 6th centuries BC) the heroes were puppet-like, subject to furious passions but lacking an inner self. Instead they were subject to the whims of external forces such as gods and demons. It was not until the 5th and 4th centuries BC that a more introspective mentality developed. At that time a number of Greek philosophers began to emerge and developed systematic approaches to reasoning gathering knowledge about the world: Socrates[1] (circa 470–399 BC), Plato (circa 428–348 BC) and Aristotle (circa 384–322 BC). They elevated reason and therefore wished to keep the irrational at bay. Thus Plato divided the soul (psyche) into three parts: the spirited (lover of victory); the appetitive (lover of gain); and the rational (lover of wisdom). For Plato, a healthy mind was achieved through the rational part of the mind (which he viewed as higher) being in control of the spirited and the appetitive (which he viewed as lower). However, it is important not to forget the social context in which these ideas developed. As Geoff Bunn notes:

> [T]he Greek philosopher Plato asserted the primacy of the brain because he thought that society should be ruled by intellectuals, or 'philosopher kings'. ... He associated each of the three souls with a different social class: reason, with the governors of the State; emotion, with the soldiers; desire, with the proletariat. The brain has always been a political as well as a biological object.
>
> Bunn (2011)

Both Porter (2002) and Scull (2011) identify two traditions in the classical Greek approach to making sense of madness: the cultural tradition represented in Homeric myth and Greek drama, and the tradition of Hippocratic medicine. The cultural tradition was represented most clearly in the theatre of the time, in which the heroes or heroines were 'crushed under ineluctable destiny, the rival demands of duty and desire, of individual, kin and state' (Porter, 2002, p. 14). This conflicted mind was often represented in Greek theatre by the chorus, whose voices spoke these contradictory thoughts out loud, or commented on the action.

---

1 Interestingly, Socrates apparently heard a voice a 'daemon' which no-one else could hear. In Plato's *Apology*, his Socrates recounts that he is 'subject to a divine or supernatural experience' which began in his childhood. It was 'a sort of voice which comes to me; and when it comes it always dissuades me from what I am proposing to do' (Leudar & Thomas, 2000, pp. 25–6).

The second tradition was medical, with the work of the physician Hippocrates (circa 460–370 BC) being of particular importance. Hippocrates argued that forms of insanity previously seen as supernatural in origin, such as the 'falling sickness' (what doctors would now call epilepsy), could be understood in the same manner as other illnesses. Mainstream Greek medicine held that illness was caused by imbalances in four categories of bodily fluids – the 'humours': blood, phlegm, yellow bile and black bile. An excess of yellow bile – or *choler* – could lead to mania, while an excess of black bile could lead to dejection – or *melancholia*. Aretaeus of Cappadocia (circa 150–200 AD) gave particularly detailed descriptions of melancholy in his *On the Causes and Signs of Diseases*:

> The patients are dull or stern, dejected or unreasonably torpid, without any manifest cause ... Unreasonable fear also seizes them ... But if the illness become more urgent, hatred, avoidance of the haunts of men, vain lamentations; they complain of life, and desire to die.
>
> Aretaeus (cited in Goodwin & Jamison, 2007, p. 65)

The Roman physician Galen of Pergamum (circa 129–200/216 AD) continued the humoral tradition into the Roman era. Scull (2011) contends that the humoral model, though often regarded as a purely somatogenic approach, was a holistic one in which the body and environment influenced each other: each person was naturally endowed with different proportions of the humours, whose balance could be disturbed by 'seasonal variation and developmental changes over the course of the life cycle' as well as by 'diet, exercise regimen, and sleeping patterns, and by emotional upsets and turmoil' (p. 11).

The Hippocratic system also saw a move from the Aristotelian notion that the heart was the centre of thought and emotion to one in which these were located in the brain. Hippocratic texts noted 'it is the brain too which is the seat of madness and delirium' (cited in Scull, 2011, p. 13).

Although Greek physicians were beginning to apprehend madness through rational means, cure was often still attached to a religious worldview. Thus, when ill, Greeks would visit the Asklepion, a temple of cure where the sick would receive religious medicine guided by priests. Moreover, the ancient Greek understanding of anatomy was limited, as there was a taboo against dissecting the human body which lasted until the time of the Roman physician Galen (Scull, 2011).

One way of summarizing the competing explanations of madness in ancient Greece is to note the establishment of a psychogenic model, best illustrated in the theatre of the time, in which heroes and heroines suffer madness as a result of tragic events and the clash of conflicting desires. However, on this view, distress was not seen as arising solely from within the mind but also as a result of events in a person's life and relationships, so there are also elements of a sociogenic model. Similarly, we can see the beginnings of a somatogenic model, in which distress is seen as caused by the body, illustrated in the notion of imbalances in the humours. However, Scull's (2011) argument that the humoral model was both somatogenic and sociogenic complicate such a neat division. At the same time, we see a tension between modes of explanation influenced by rationality and those influenced by religion, morality and the supernatural and, of course, this points to underlying tensions between

Figure 2.1 **Timeline 1000 BC–1000 AD**

Empires		Historical 'age'	Century	Key events
			1000 BC	
			900	
			800	
		Classical antiquity	700	Epic poem *The Iliad* written between 8th–6th centuries BC
			600	
			500	
			400	Socrates (circa 470–399 BC) Hippocrates (circa 460–370 BC) Plato (circa 428–348 BC) Aristotle (circa 384–322 BC)
			300	
			200	
	Roman Empire		100	
			100 AD	Galen of Pergamum (circa 129–200/216 AD)
			200	Aretaeus of Cappadocia (circa 150–200 AD) Academy of Gundishapur, founded in Persia
			300	313 AD: Emperor Constantine recognizes Christianity in the Roman Empire
			400	
			500	
Byzantine Empire		Early middle ages	600	Hospitals (maristans) founded in Cairo (Egypt), Aleppo (Syria) and Baghdad (Iraq)
			700	651 AD: Hotel Dieu hospital founded in Paris
			800	The Persian al-Rāzi (865–925 AD) utilizes treatments involving conditioned reflexes
	Arabic Empire		900	Avicenna (980–1037 AD)
			1000	

institutions. As we will see, these contrasting explanatory models and institutional tensions continue to emerge at different points throughout the history of madness. As we move from ancient Greece and the Roman Empire to Christianity in the Middle Ages, our focus will shift from the Mediterranean to Western Europe – Figure 2.2 outlines some key events in this period.

The rise of religious worldviews: Christianity and the Middle Ages

Following Emperor Constantine's recognition of Christianity in the Roman Empire in 313 AD, the pagan gods of the Asklepia were over time replaced by the God of Christianity. Many temples were destroyed to make way for Christian churches and monasteries, often incorporating places to care for the

sick. With the growing dominance of Christianity in Western Europe a religious worldview became a dominant mode in people's emotional experience and, unsurprisingly, religious explanations of madness became popular in the Middle Ages (roughly 5th–16th centuries AD). However, the Christian viewpoint allowed madness to be viewed in a range of ways. As Porter (1996) puts it:

> The contrasting models of mental alienation developed by the Greeks – madness as moral perversion, madness as disease – were assimilated within Christendom. But the Church added another conviction: religious madness as the expression of divine providence, regarded as a symptom of the warfare raged between God and Satan for the soul.
>
> Porter (1996, p. 282)

From this perspective, madness could be caused by Christianity's Satan (rather than the more diverse gods of

Figure 2.2 **Timeline 1000–1600**

Empires		Historical 'age'		Century	Key events
	Arabic Empire	High middle ages		1000	
				1100	1123: St Bartholomew's hospital in London founded.
				1200	Geel infirmary in Belgium established around the shrine of St Dymphna 1247: Founding of religious house of St Mary of Bethlehem in London 1288: Hospital of Santa Maria Nuova founded in Florence, Italy
Byzantine Empire		Late middle ages	European Rennaisance	1300	Islamic hospital (maristan) established in Granada in Spain 1373: Margery Kempe born 1377: Bethlem hospital caring for the insane by this time
				1400	Institutions for the insane built in Valencia, Zaragoza, Seville, Vallodolid, Palma de Mallorca, Toledo and Barcelona First peak of European 'witch craze' approximately 15th–16th century
				1500	1542: First Witchcraft Act becomes law in England (repealed in 1736) 1575: Houses of Correction established in England
				1600	

ancient Greece) or could be a sign of holiness, as seen in the lives of the saints. However, some forms of illness were seen as the result of God's vengeance or as the result of moral failings. Alongside such views, local animistic folklore beliefs were often tolerated and played a role in how madness was conceived.

A religious worldview was dominant, even for physicians. Thus the 17th century English doctor and Anglican clergyman Richard Napier reported that almost 300 of his patients suffered from some kind of religious anxiety or spiritual problem for which he recommended formal prayer, sometimes praying with his patients and writing short prayers for them to repeat (MacDonald, 1981). For example, an emotion dominant in Medieval times was *accidie* (a kind of spiritual laziness), for which there is no modern analogue (Harré & Finlay-Jones, 1986).

It was around this time that the European witch craze (approximately 15th–18th centuries) fuelled by the Catholic Church's Inquisitions (in which heretics were sought out, tortured and punished, often by execution) was at its height, having been building from the late 15th century – see Figure 2.3 for other developments in the seventeenth and eighteenth centuries. Estimates of the numbers killed range from 60,000 (Levack, 1987) to 300,000 (Ewen, 1929). However, there is debate about the extent to which the Inquisitors utilized notions of insanity. Sedgwick (1982), for example, argues that the witch craze had relatively little to do with madness and much more to do with the persecution of women (the majority of those accused of witchcraft were women) and others who were viewed with suspicion. The last execution for witchcraft in England was in 1682.

However, it would be a mistake to characterize this period as uniformly demonological. In Box 2.2 we saw that, during the Middle Ages, the Arab and wider Islamic world had developed a sophisticated holistic understanding of mental well-being, drawing on the insights of Hippocrates, Galen, Aretaeus and others and this extended even to Christian Northern Europe. Christian monks would combine this classical knowledge with herbal remedies based on experience, folklore and magic.

Increasingly detailed somatogenic models: from humours to nerves

By the beginning of the 17th century there was increasing scepticism about the supernatural and witches were seen as deluded rather than possessed. The Renaissance (roughly 14th–17th centuries) saw the assimilation in Europe of ideas from Greek and Islamic texts and, during the Enlightenment (roughly 17th–18th centuries), knowledge in a number of disciplines began to be gathered together and codified. Increasingly the Church's power was threatened by new discoveries in science.

The Scientific Revolution saw the gradual decline of humoral medicine (although it continued to exert some influence until the 19th century). Anatomists were beginning to develop much more detailed understandings of the body and started to conceptualize the body as a machine founded on the operation of two key systems: cardiovascular (i.e. the heart pumping blood through vessels around the body) and nervous (i.e. the brain and sense organs). Thus madness was seen as a result of failures in the sense organs and the nervous system. A number of candidate systems were proposed. The term 'neurologie' was coined by the 17th century Anglican Thomas Willis in his *Cerebri Anatome* (*Anatomy of the Brain*) of 1664 to indicate a physical lesion of the nervous system (Hunter & MacAlpine, 1963). In his own words, 'the true and genuine reasons for many of the actions and passions that take place in our body' were to be found in the 'anatomy of the nerves' (cited in Scull, 2011, pp. 32–3). Based on the results of his dissections of the human body, he contended that 'animal spirits' mediated between the body and mind.

The 'Age of Reason': the birth both of reason and unreason

In his *Discourse on Method* of 1637, the French philosopher René Descartes (1594–1650) had proposed a distinction between

Figure 2.3 **Timeline 1600–1800**

Historical 'age'	Decade	Key events
The Enlightenment	1600	The second peak of European 'witch craze' occurs in this century 1601–1602: Shakespeare writes *Twelfth Night* 1603–1606: Shakespeare writes *King Lear* 1605: First volume of *Don Quixote* published by Miguel de Cervantes 1656: Hôpital Général founded in Paris 1682: Last execution for witchcraft in England 1637: René Descartes publishes his *Discourse on Method* 1664: Thomas Willis publishes *Anatomy of the Brain* 1690: John Locke publishes his *Essay Concerning Human Understanding*
	1700	1758: William Battie publishes his *Treatise on Madness* 1774: Madhouses Act 1788: King George III confined and treated by Francis Willis 1792: Ticehurst House founded in Sussex 1793: Phlippe Pinel appointed physician of the infirmaries at the Salpêtrière and Bicêtre Hospitals 1796: William Tuke founds the York Retreat
	1800	Approximately 50 private madhouses established in England by this time

the mind and the body, as he declared 'I think, therefore I am'. In the previous chapter we referred to this distinction as an example of mind–body dualism, which could also be seen as a dualism between psychogenic and somatogenic models. Scull (2011) argues that Cartesian dualism had a profound influence on medical thought, in that it could justify medicine's jurisdiction over the mad: 'madness thus, was rooted in the body, the natural province of the physician' (p. 35). The Scottish psychiatrist W. A. F. Browne concluded that 'derangement is no longer considered a disease of the understanding, but of the centre of the nervous system ... the brain is at fault, and not the mind' (cited in Scull, 2011, p. 37). By way of contrast, as we saw in Box 2.2, Islamic medicine adopted a more **holistic** view (one which emphasized inter-relationships between different elements of the self) which attempted to avoid the problems caused by such dualistic approaches.

In Descartes' wake followed philosophers such as John Locke who, in 1690, argued, in his *Essay Concerning Human Understanding*, that all ideas were derived from the impressions of the senses, so were influenced by experience and education. For him,

> *mad Men* ... do not appear to me to have lost the Faculty of Reasoning: but having joined together some *Ideas* very wrongly, they mistake them for Truths; and they err, as Men do, that argue right from wrong Principles. For by the violence of their Imaginations, having taken their Fansies for Realities, they make right deduction from them.
>
> In Hunter and MacAlpine (1963, p. 237, emphasis in original)

Here, madness was no longer seen as the result of humoral imbalances but, rather, a result of a problem of thinking, of irrationality. For the French historian of thought Michel Foucault (1971), this moment of history was a defining moment in the history of madness – not only was it the birth of reason, but also its mirror image, unreason. For Foucault, unreason now became the defining feature of madness and he saw psychiatry as a monologue of reason about madness. We will discuss Foucault in more detail later in the chapter.

Ideas like those of Descartes and Locke laid the philosophical foundations for the development, much later, of cognitive

explanations of distress. Locke's view of delusions (or unusual beliefs) finds contemporary resonance in Maher's explanation that some delusional thinking may be triggered by anomalous perceptions or experiences (Maher, 1992). For example, a person with impaired hearing might start to become paranoid and suspicious because they misinterpret what is going on around them.

Although Locke's notions could justify optimistic views of the possibility of changing the thinking of those seen as mad, Scull (2011) observes that they could also be used to justify much fiercer treatment, in order to shock a person back into sanity by weakening irrational associations. Treatments could include whirling chairs, 'baths of surprise' (where people were unceremoniously dropped into vats of cold water by apparently solid floors designed to collapse), devices designed to make people think they were about to drown, and Joseph Mason Cox's swinging device. Benjamin Rush designed a 'tranquillizer' chair that '[e]ncased the madman's head in a padded box that excluded light and sound, and kept his arms and legs pinioned in place, while warm and cold water was applied to head and feet' (Scull, 2011, p. 35). In the late 18th century William Cullen, professor of the institutes of medicine in Edinburgh reported that, since fear diminished the 'irascible excitement of maniacs', he had concluded that:

> In most cases it has appeared to me necessary to employ a very constant impression of fear ... This awe and dread is therefore, by one means or other, to be acquired ... by their being the authors of all restraints that may occasionally be proper; but sometimes it may be necessary to acquire it even by stripes [whipping] and blows.
>
> In Hunter and MacAlpine (1963, p. 478)

It would be easy to argue that the Age of Reason was monolithic but it was not: the institution of the Church still had power in many countries and Descartes' work was placed on the Catholic Church's List of Prohibited books in 1663. As in other eras, there were other, competing, ways of seeing distress. Indeed, one aspect we have not discussed is that of the influence of literature and popular culture on how madness was understood and represented. Scull notes that:

> As we move from the medieval to the modern world, in plays, in broadsides, and in ballads, in the pages of *Don Quixote*, and in the pioneering novels and pulp fiction of 18th-century England ... a fascination with madness is everywhere. In the written word; on the stage; in political pamphlets; in songs on the street; in architecture and sculpture; in painting and in the new mass-produced engravings: images of Unreason surface.
>
> (2011, p. 21)

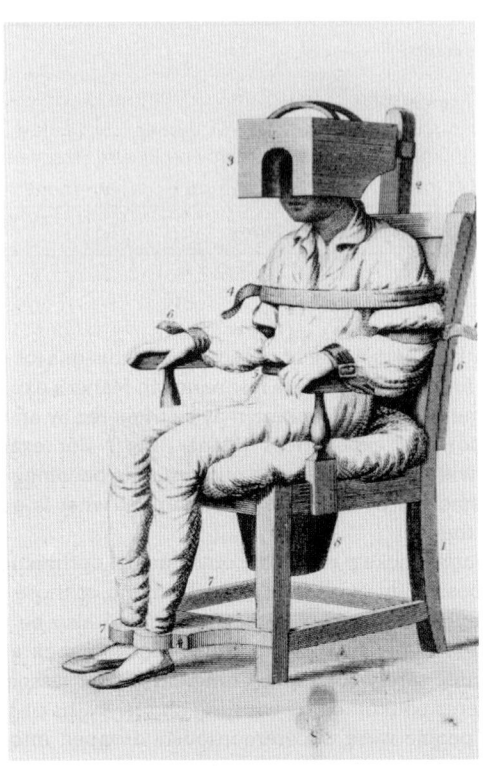

The tranquillizing chair of Benjamin Rush

For Scull, Cervantes' *Don Quixote* is a classic fictional representation of obsession and hallucination, as the hero tilts at windmills and perceives flocks of sheep as two onrushing armies. Porter writes of the image of the mad fool who could speak a poetic truth about the human condition: 'the Fool in *King Lear* and Feste in *Twelfth Night* outwitted logic in nonsense ditties ... gave voice to darker truths denied to sober speech' (Porter, 2002, p. 69). Shakespeare gave us other characters for whom madness was a theme: was Hamlet, for example, insane or play-acting (Scull, 2011)? Institutions for those seen as mad could also act as warnings. Porter (2002) notes how the image of 'Bedlam' (the Hospital of Bethlem in Moorfields, London) was conjured up in popular culture such as Hogarth's paintings and the engravings of the Rake's Progress (1735) where, after a time of high living, the central character, Tom Rakewell, ends up in Bedlam, mad and in debt, dishevelled and an object of curiosity for well-to-do visitors. However, Porter argues that Hogarth drew on these cultural representations to mock those viewing the artwork rather than to mock the Bethlem inmates, as it was common at the time for the public to visit Bethlem to view the inmates as a form of entertainment. We turn next to the development of institutions such as Bethlem.

The 'great confinement?' The madhouse, the asylum and the homogenization of those seen as insane

In most societies, until this time, it had been the family that was considered to be responsible for housing and feeding those afflicted with insanity, whilst the poor and destitute might resort to wandering the countryside and towns begging. Scull (2011) reports that the 'deranged beggar, like the leper, was a familiar part of the medieval landscape, wandering from place to place ... in search of alms' (p. 16) with the life of the poor and mad in the Hobbesian phrase 'nasty, brutish and short' (p. 17).

The quality of care both within and outside the family varied considerably according to one's wealth, social standing, location and kinship network. Some institutions were provided by the state: in England, 'houses of correction' were established in each county by a law of 1575. There were also institutions, often connected to religious centres, where the insane could go, both on pilgrimage and for healing. The Flemish village of Gheel surrounding the shrine of St Dymphna was seen as a place of healing (Porter, 2002). Other hospitals were established at the Hotel Dieu in Paris, the Santa Maria Nuova in Florence and St Bartholomew's in London whilst, in Spain, following the influence of Islamic medicine (see Box 2.2), seven hospitals had been established by the 15th century in Valencia, Zaragoza, Seville, Valladolid, Palma de Mallorca, Toledo and Barcelona (Scull, 2011). The religious house of St Mary of Bethlehem (Bethlem or 'Bedlam'), founded in 1247, was caring for the insane by 1377, although its provision was small-scale and it only had 20 inmates by 1598 (Scull, 2011).

By the middle of the 17th century, private for-profit madhouses (not to be confused with public institutions like asylums) were well-established in England and by 1800 there were around 50 licensed establishments and a veritable 'trade in lunacy' (Parry-Jones, 1972) developed in the commercial sector. Ticehurst House, in Sussex, was one such institution, founded in 1792, where the rich could 'live in separate houses in the grounds, install their own cooks, and ride to hounds' (Porter, 1996, p. 289). There was money to be made here and some mad-doctors such as Anthony Addington made considerable fortunes, but Scull (2011) notes that their profession lacked legitimacy: their competence and motives were questioned and they were figures of fun in the popular press. This questionable legitimacy was to be a continuing theme.

For the poor, it was a different matter and many institutions were brutal. The Bethlem received much censure, relying on 'physical restraint, blood-letting, purges and vomits' (Porter, 2002, p. 100). A Papal Indulgence was issued in 1446 as the 'miserable persons living there ... are so alienated in mind and possessed of unclean spirits that they must be restrained with chains and fetters' (cited in Scull, 2011, p. 19). Porter (1996) argues, however, that punishment was not an intention of these institutions (since official reports at the time revealed instances of humane practice alongside the more punitive), rather, the aim was to segregate the insane to preserve order and permit intensive treatment. Indeed, with new theories about the cause of madness developing, many of the owners of private madhouses began to publish case histories of their patients.

The link Porter makes between lunacy and the preservation of public order is significant. In his influential book *Histoire de la folie*, Michel Foucault – who originally trained as a clinical psychologist (Parker, 1995) – famously claimed that this period of history saw a 'great confinement' where lunatics, those considered 'idiots' and other outcasts from society (the poor, crippled, the aged, petty criminals, vagabonds, streetwalkers etc.) were confined in huge asylums. By the 1660s the Hôpital Général in Paris housed 6000 inmates. This segregation of sections of the population into a homogenous whole, Foucault argued, 'made possible the eventual formation of a single, overarching concept of deviancy' (Gordon, 1990, p. 8). Thus, for Foucault, the creation of these institutions meant that the originally heterogeneous population of inmates came to be seen as homogenous, all bearing the signs of insanity. This enabled the development of a new area of study and of treatment, and thus new professional groups.

Foucault was interested in how new ways of seeing and treating lunacy developed. He saw history as marked by sudden changes from one 'regime of truth' to another, often as the result of socio-political changes marked by new laws and institutions. Critics have argued that he neglected historical detail which did not fit his narrative sweep (Sedgwick, 1982) and some historians have suggested that Foucault's work overgeneralizes from the situation in France where, under the reign of Louis XIV, a vast bureaucracy of institutions grew in the service of his absolute monarchy. The situation in other countries was more varied (Still & Velody, 1992): Porter (2002) notes how in Russia, Poland, Scandinavia and the Balkans there were hardly any asylums until the second half of the 19th century. However, as we will see later with the rise of German psychiatry, having large captive populations facilitated the development of new kinds of observational studies.

Striking off the chains of the insane? The emergence of 'moral management'

Porter (1996) estimates that in England around 1800 about 5000 people – out of a total population of 10 million – were held in specialized lunatic asylums, with another 5000 in workhouses and jails. The dominant modes of treatment in these asylums were medication and mechanical restraint (in the form of manacles and chains), which often led to an increase in the violence they were supposed to quell. A common form of restraint – first used in Paris in the 1770s – was the **straitjacket**: a jacket of strong material with overly long sleeves which were then secured behind the wearer's back so they could not move their arms.

However, towards the end of the 18th century, new 'moral' (or psychological in modern parlance) methods had begun to develop. William Battie, physician to London's St Luke's asylum and owner of his own private madhouse, differentiated in his 1758 *Treatise on Madness* two types of madness: original and consequential. 'Original madness' referred to insanity that 'neither follows nor accompanies any accident' (Hunter & MacAlpine, 1963, p. 406): in other words, that has no obvious external cause. It was diagnosed especially in cases where madness was seen to run in a family and was thus thought to be hereditary (though see Chapter 4 for a discussion of the problematic assumptions underlying assertions of genetic hereditability of distress). 'Original madness' was seen as largely incurable, though the person might experience

long intervals of sanity. 'Consequential madness' was seen as 'consequential to other disorders or external causes' (Hunter & MacAlpine, 1963, p. 407): in other words, there was an obvious external cause or illness. For Battie this madness was 'as manageable as many other distempers', so the mad should not 'be abandoned, much less shut up in loathsome prisons as criminals or nuisance to the society' (Hunter & MacAlpine, 1963, p. 408). It could be relieved by the 'removal or correction of such disorders or causes', though recovery might be 'complicated with many other ill effects of those causes and disorders' (Hunter & MacAlpine, 1963, p. 407).

This was the approach adopted by the physician and clergyman Francis Willis in his treatment of King George III (popularized in the film *The Madness of King George*) who, in 1788, had been confined after proclaiming 'my lords, ladies and peacocks' at the opening of parliament (Sedgwick, 1982, p. 126).

A new form of treatment, 'moral management' began to be established, in which the doctor would, through sheer force of personality, subdue the sufferer and then use other psychological tactics to rescue the insane from their affliction by offering them the hope of cure. Here, then, was a move towards a more psychogenic model of madness. However, the emergence of moral management also constituted a challenge to medicine, as many of those espousing it were lay people, not medical men. For example, William Tuke, who founded the York Retreat, was a tea and coffee merchant, who became interested in the care of those considered mad after visiting York asylum, where a fellow Quaker had died. Appalled by the conditions, Tuke and his family raised funds and established the York Retreat in 1796, based on Quaker principles. The staff ate and lived with the patients and hoped that, through a rational and firm but kind approach they would strengthen the residual emotions of the insane and so enable a regeneration of the person through the development of self-control.

However, physicians too were adopting similar approaches. Thus, in Florence, Vincenzo Chiarugi argued that cure of the insane was possible through 'moral control' whilst in Paris in 1793 Philippe Pinel at the Salpêtrière and Bicêtre Hospitals (women's and men's hospitals respectively) did similar work 'inspired by the [French] Revolutionary ideals of liberty, equality and fraternity' (Porter, 2002, pp. 104–5). Pinel is perhaps best known for casting off the chains of the insane at these hospitals but this is the stuff of myth – apparently, a French historian challenged the accuracy of this story as early as 1880 (Gordon, 1990). However, Pinel was innovative in his approach: in one case he set up a mock trial to 'acquit' a patient, suffering from a delusion that he was to be executed (having misconstrued an overheard conversation during the revolutionary Reign of Terror of 1793–1794, when such executions were commonplace).

We described John Locke's ideas on insanity earlier: the pioneers of moral management could be seen as following the implications of his theory. Locke had contended that the mad were essentially rational but operating within a delusional fantasy world, so they sought to induce an educational discipline similar to that used with wayward children.

Andrew Scull argues that this was a significant episode in approaches to insanity, signalling a move from the external to the internal: from exterior restraints and physical coercion – which might force outward conformity but no more – to a regime designed to produce 'the essential *internalization of*

A painting of Philippe Pinel releasing lunatics from their chains at the Salpetrière Asylum in Paris in 1795, by Tony Robert-Fleury

moral standards' (Scull, 1993, p. 10, emphasis in original). Thomas Bakewell, a (non-medical) madhouse keeper, observed:

> Certainly authority and order must be maintained, but these are better maintained by kindness, condescension, and indulgent attention, than by any severities whatsoever. Lunatics ... should be treated as rational beings.
>
> Cited in Scull (2011, p. 45)

Gradually, throughout Europe and North America, the state began to take on responsibility for asylums and a new breed of doctor, the **alienist** (from the French aliéné – insane), emerged.

In the USA in the early 19th century a number of asylums along the lines of the York Retreat were established in Pennsylvania, Philadelphia, Boston, New York and Connecticut. In 1844 the Association of Medical Superintendents of American Institutions for the Insane, the forerunner of the American Psychiatric Association, was set up.

By the 1830s in England a new philosophy of non-restraint was established by two physicians: at the Middlesex asylum in Hanwell by John Conolly – see Figure 2.4 for other developments in the 19th century; and at the Lincoln asylum by Robert Gardiner Hill, where the years from 1829 saw a steady decrease in the amount of restraint until 1838, when there were no recorded cases of its use. In these institutions not even straitjackets were resorted to, security being achieved instead through the segregation of different categories of patient and 'surveillance by vigilant attendants and a regime of disciplined work and exercise designed to stimulate the mind, tire the body, and foster self control' (Porter, 1996, p. 295). Many asylums were located in the countryside and became self-sufficient on produce they grew themselves. In France, spa treatments were the order of the day. The increasing interest of physicians in the techniques of moral management was to prove one of the crucial factors in medicine securing the control of those considered insane, as we will see in the next section.

The medicalization of madness: the professionalization of asylum management

The 19th century saw the **professionalization** (i.e. the establishment of specific professional disciplines with their own training, rules and regulations) of those involved with the asylums. One of the most significant historians of this process is Andrew Scull, who published *Museums of Madness* in 1979 (he has subsequently offered a more nuanced analysis: Scull, 1993). Scull argues that the middle of the 19th century saw massive building programmes of institutions for those considered insane as a result of the advocacy of lunacy reformers such as Dorothea Dix in the USA. Dix argued that 'all experience shows that insanity reasonably treated is as curable as a cold or a fever' (Scull, 2011, p. 46). She advocated reforms for those in lunatic asylums (as well as those in almshouses and prison). Howard Becker (1963) coined the term 'moral entrepreneur' to refer to social reformers like Dix, and Scull argues that Dix was the 'moral entrepreneur most responsible for America's embrace of the asylum' (2011, p. 46). Similar campaigns in the UK and elsewhere led to successive inquiries and Acts of Parliament – in Table 2.1 we can see that there were successive waves of legislation, leading to successive waves of asylum building, helping to create the conditions for a new group of experts on madness. It was far from a foregone conclusion that medical men would secure control of these institutions; indeed, as we have seen, many advocates of moral treatment were laymen, whilst many abuses had been conducted in medically-run institutions like the Bethlem. Scull argues that medicine triumphed by adopting many of the tenets of moral treatment whilst still holding to a somatogenic model, contending that the cause of madness was to be found in the body and thus within their province. By the middle of the century 'the previously heterogeneous congeries of madhouse keepers had instead become a more and more organised group of specialists' (Scull, 2011, p. 50), with professional journals appearing in England, France and Germany. In England in 1841 medical superintendents (the so-called 'alienists') banded together to form the Association of Medical Officers of Asylums and Hospitals for the Insane, later to become the Royal Psycho-Medical Association and, in 1971, the Royal College of Psychiatrists. By 1853 it began publishing the *Asylum Journal*, which was renamed the *Journal of Mental Science* in 1858. On the first page of the first number in November 1853 was an editorial 'prospectus'. Recalling the tradition of Pinel and Conolly, the prospectus argued that, following the abandonment of mechanical restraint and the emergence of moral treatment a 'new school of special medicine' had been forming. This strategy would be seen again in psychiatry's response to the 'anti-psychiatry' movement in the 1960s (as we will see later in the chapter):

> Pinel vindicated the rights of science against the usurpations of superstition and brutality; and rescued the victims of cerebro-mental disease from the exorcist and the gaoler
>
> In Hunter and MacAlpine (1963, p. 1009)

It noted that 'the victory was not gained in one battle' but that now:

> The physician is now the responsible guardian of the lunatic, and must ever remain so, unless by some calamitous reverse the progress of the world in civilisation should be arrested and turned back in the direction of practical barbarism ... the public in all civilised countries have recognised the fact, that Insanity lies strictly within the domain of medical science.
>
> In Hunter and MacAlpine (1963, p. 1009)

Figure 2.4 **Timeline 1808–1897**

Year	Key events
1808	German physician Johan Christian Reil first uses the term 'psychiaterie' in his *On the Term of Medicine and its Branches, Especially with Regard to the Rectification of the Topic in Psychiatry*
1818	German physician Johann Heinroth publishes *Lehrbuch der Störungen des Seelenlebens* (*Textbook of the Disorders of the Soul*)
1831	Hanwell asylum opened in West London for the 'pauper insane'. It becomes well-known through its third superintendent physician John Conolly
1835	Physician Robert Gardiner Hill becomes resident medical officer at Lincoln lunatic asylum
1838	French law establishing asylums in each *department* (county) John Perceval publishes *A Narrative of the Treatment Received by a Gentleman, during a State of Mental Derangement* Esquirol publishes *Mental Maladies*
1841	Association of Medical Officers of Asylums and Hospitals for the Insane established in England
1843	Dorothea Dix publishes her *Memorial to the Legislature of Massachusetts* about the state of provision for 'lunatic paupers'
1844	Association of Medical Superintendents of American Institutions for the Insane established
1846	Alleged Lunatics' Friend Society publishes its first report in England
1851	In New Orleans physician Samuel Cartwright publishes his article on 'drapetomania'
1853	The *Asylum Journal* first published in England
1857	Bénédict Morel publishes his *Treatise on Physical and Moral Degeneration*
1865	Wilhelm Griesinger founds a University department of psychiatry in Berlin
1893	German physician Emil Kraepelin publishes the first edition of his *Compendium der Psychiatrie* (*Textbook of Psychiatry*)
1895	Freud and Breuer publish *Studies on Hysteria*
1897	Pavlov publishes *The Work of the Digestive Glands*

Medicine was winning a broader battle for recognition in society and 1858 saw Parliament pass the Medical Act, which legally recognized doctors and established the General Medical Council which set standards of qualification (to distinguish between qualified and unqualified doctors, popularly referred to as 'quacks') and powers of regulation. It should be remembered that, at this time, asylums contained people with a range of forms of distress, some of which would now be recognized unarguably as having an organic cause, such as those with **neurological** conditions (i.e. disorders of the nervous system); this issue will become important later when we examine the history of the schizophrenia concept. Increasingly, biologists and chemists were discovering the role of bacterial infection and viruses (penicillin, for example, was only discovered in 1943). Many of those in the asylums had a diagnosis of **General Paralysis of the Insane** which was subsequently found to be caused by **syphilis**, a sexually transmitted infection causing a range of physical and neurological symptoms which was only discovered in the early 20th century. Some critics have argued that, following the widespread use of the antibiotic penicillin after 1943, cases of GPI/syphilis no longer came to the asylums and no further miracle cures that treated underlying diseases were discovered. There was to be a revolution in pharmacology in the 1950s but, as noted in Chapter 8, these psychiatric medications managed symptoms rather than treating an underlying disease like an infection. However, in the early years of the 20th century, observers might have imagined that organic causes would eventually be discovered for all forms of mental distress found in the asylums. Suffice it to say that, for now, medical men were able to make the case for governance of those in the asylums. However, although medicine had taken over management of the insane, Scull (2011) suggests that their work continued to lack legitimacy in the eyes of many, and argues that they were as trapped in their asylums just as much as their charges.

Abuses and reforms of the asylums

One of the stocks in trade of the gothic novel was the confinement of the heroine in a madhouse presided over by unscrupulous characters (Scull, 2011), and, as we can see in Table 2.1, alongside a history of humane treatment there is a parallel history of neglect, abuse, inquiries and reforming legislation, a pattern which has continued to the present day.

In 1774 the Madhouses Act in England established that madhouses should operate under licences provided by magistrates who could carry out inspections at least once a year and check their record keeping – an important aspect of preventing abuses of confinement in private provision. Parliamentary investigations in 1807 led to an Act of Parliament of 1808 which allowed public money to be used to pay for County Asylums and, in the 1845 County Asylums Act, asylums were made compulsory for each county in England and Wales. In

Table 2.1 **Selected British mental health legislation 1774–1959**

Year	Act of parliament	Key provisions
1774	Madhouses Act	Established a Commission of the Royal College of Physicians to license and visit private madhouses in the London area.
1808	County Asylums Act	Allowed magistrates to build lunatic asylums with public money, where criminal and pauper lunatics could be kept instead of in workhouses and prisons, where they were disturbing other inmates.
1828	Madhouses and County Asylums Acts	Moved inspection of London private madhouses from the Royal College of Physicians to a 'Metropolitan Commission' and gave greater powers to magistrates for the erection of public lunatic asylums. Private asylums with a hundred patients or more were required to have a doctor living in the asylum.
1845	County Asylums and Lunacy Acts	Required every part of England and Wales to provide asylum accommodation for all its pauper lunatics. Converted the Metropolitan Commission into national Commissioners in Lunacy who would regulate almost all asylums, including their design and the way inmates were treated. All asylums with a hundred patients or more were required to have a doctor living in the asylum.
1858	Medical Act	Created the General Medical Council to regulate doctors and distinguish between qualified and unqualified doctors.
1890	Lunacy Act	A consolidation Act that incorporated civil liberties protections requiring most private patients to have a hearing before a magistrate (as public patients did) before they could be detained for any length of time. Fee-paying wards in public asylums were allowed, and the size and number of private asylums was effectively restricted to what it already was. This Act remained in force, with modifications, until 1959.
1913	Mental Deficiency Act	Required all local authorities to establish a Mental Deficiency Committee to identify 'mental defectives' in their area, providing suitable institutions (usually called colonies) for separating them. Four classes of people were counted as defective: idiots (the most severe), imbeciles, the feeble minded and moral defectives. Moral defectives could include people without intellectual impairment. National supervision (England and Wales) was provided by a Board of Control, developed from the previous Lunacy Commission. The Board of Control continued to supervise lunacy and mental defect until 1959.
1930	Mental Treatment Act	Introduced provision for the 'voluntary' (but still formal) admission to mental hospitals (previously lunatic asylums) of some 'persons of unsound mind' (previously lunatics).
1959	Mental Health Act (England and Wales)	Repealed the 1890 Lunacy Act, the 1913 Mental Deficiency Act and the 1930 Mental Treatment Act. Admission to hospital for mental disorders was to be informal (without paperwork enabling the hospital to detain), as it was for physical disorder, unless it was decided that the patient needed to be detained formally. Mental disorder covered mental illness, mental subnormality (later called handicap) and psychopathic disorder. However, it excluded admission for 'promiscuity' or 'other immoral conduct' alone. The Board of Control was abolished.

France, the statute of 1838 which enshrined the Napoleonic Code institutionalized some of Pinel's ideas. Each *département* (county) had to make provision for the mad, which included the building of asylums. To prevent unnecessary confinement, lunatics could only be admitted by doctors under certain rules, though, again, a lower threshold was required for the poor (Porter, 2002).

Porter (2002) notes that, in 1814, asylum reformers described, amongst others, the case of William Norris, an American marine detained in Bethlem who had been restrained in a metal contraption for ten years. A subsequent parliamentary inquiry led to further regulations and the sacking of staff at the Bethlem. Following a 300 page report by an Inquiry Commission, the 1845 Lunacy Act established a national Lunacy Commission.

The shaping of provision for those considered mad was thus not simply a case of 'internal' factors within the emerging discipline of psychiatry but 'external' factors such as the efforts of reformers and legislators. However, the expansion of the asylum system soon encountered a problem as more and more people were admitted yet fewer left, leading to new kinds of theories to explain this state of affairs.

Increasing populations and decreasing expectations: the emergence of notions of chronicity

Asylums became more established during the 19th century and the numbers of residents began to increase rapidly. Karl Marx, who would go on to write *Capital* and to co-author the *Communist Manifesto* with Friedrich Engels, was an assiduous reader of all kinds of official reports, which he used in his journalism. This is his account that appeared in the *New York Tribune* in 1858:

> The pressure upon these costly asylums on the part of the lunatic population may be illustrated by one case. When, in 1831, Hanwell (in Middlesex) was built for 500 patients, it was supposed to be large enough to meet all the wants of the county. But, two years later, it was full; after another two years, it had to be enlarged for 300 more; and at this time (Colney Hatch having been meanwhile constructed for the reception of 1,200 lunatic paupers belonging to the same county) Hanwell contains upward of 1000 patients.
>
> (Marx, 1858)

Porter (1996) notes that, in England, the total number of patients rose from about 5000 in 1800 to 100,000 in 1900, over twice the increase of the national population. In Italy, in 1881, 18,000 people were in asylums but, by 1916, there were twice as many. In the USA, things were no better, with a rise from about 5000 in 1850 to 150,000 by 1904. Some American asylums were huge, having up to 16,000 patients, and many European asylums had up to 5000 patients (Healy, 2002). In Germany the proportion of lunatics in asylums grew from one in 5300 in 1852 to one in 500 in 1911 (Scull, 2011).

Many hospitals were overcrowded and London's Colney Hatch, mentioned by Marx above, which accommodated 1,200 people at its opening in 1851 housed 2700 by the time it was renamed Friern Barnet in 1937 (Porter, 2002). As Scull notes, 'asylums seemed to serve as magnets, drawing forth an endless supply of mad folk from the surrounding community' (2011, p. 51).

However, it was not just the increase in numbers which was the problem, but the fact that the increasing rate of admission was not matched by a corresponding rate of discharge. The reasons for this were many, including varied and widening definitions of distress, more difficult cases being referred from the workhouses and jails, as well as the admission of those who we would now see as suffering from degenerative neurological conditions, little understood at the time. For example, at Lancaster Asylum, there were relatively few cures '[a]fter 1850 the figure never again reached 10 per cent, and the death rate was almost always higher than the cures' (Walton, 1985, p. 142). At Ticehurst, the median length of stay between 1845 and 1895 'fluctuated between twenty-two and thirty *years*' (Scull, 1993, p. 20, emphasis in original). Such a situation led to disillusionment: 'the asylum was changing character, from being the retreat for regeneration to a dustbin for derelicts' (Porter, 1996, p. 297).

Many institutions responded to this chronicity with increasingly custodial styles of management. Scull argues that this was because, embedded in the very notion of moral treatment, lay implicit contradictory tensions 'between repression and rehabilitation, between the imposition of moral discipline and the development of self-government and self-control' (Scull, 1993, p. 11). In the end, he argues, the tensions were often resolved in the direction of custodial control influenced by pessimism about the chances of recovery and the need to maintain segregation and order whilst meeting the demands brought about by the increasing tendency to admit people to asylums.

Commentators began to search for explanations for this chronicity; their preferred explanations reflected their respective worldviews. Some commentators drew on sociogenic explanations. Thus Marx (1858) saw the increase in lunacy as a direct effect of **capitalism** (an economic system based on the principles of the free market). Porter (2002) notes that others criticized the asylum system itself and the **institutionalization** (not a word used until the early 20th century) it produced. As early as 1816 John Reid, physician to the Finsbury Dispensary in London, had warned that asylums were 'nurseries of madness' and that:

> as soon as an unfortunate victim has been enclosed within the awful barriers of either the public, or the minor and more clandestine Bethlems, the destiny of his reason should, in a large proportion of cases, be irretrievably fixed.
>
> In Hunter and MacAlpine (1963, p. 724)

Moreover, he contended, '[m]any of the depots for the captivity of intellectual invalids may be regarded only as nurseries for and manufactories of madness' (Hunter & MacAlpine, 1963, p. 725).

However, others drew on somatogenic explanations, seeing the answer as lying in the body and in the perils of inheritance. Darwin's theory of evolution had been applied to human society, leading to the development of **Social Darwinism** (in which Darwin's notion of 'survival of the fittest' was interpreted as a moral injunction to prefer the strong over the weak) and other **degenerationist theories**. For example, in France, Morel produced his *Treatise on Physical and Moral Degeneration* in 1857, arguing that degeneration was cumulative over generations, each subsequent generation descending further into imbecility. In Italy, Lombroso viewed criminals and psychiatric patients as genetic throwbacks, shown by their physical features. By the late 19th century, theories of eugenics gained ground with some well-known followers such as the British psychologist Francis Galton, the novelist H. G. Wells and the playwright George Bernard Shaw. **Eugenics** was based on the idea that certain groups of people were genetically inferior and that if they were allowed to reproduce freely they would weaken the genetic composition of the general population. These theories would later be used to justify the horrors of Nazi psychiatry and forced sterilization in the US and Sweden, which we will discuss later in this chapter. In the USA another class of degenerationist theory was drawn on to justify slavery and, in Box 2.3, we can see how one New Orleans physician theorized that the desire of slaves to escape their captivity could be put down to a mental malady.

The large-scale institutionalization (almost industrialization) of madness which came with the 19th century is seen by Porter (2002) as a result of a number of cultural forces: the effect of a market economy in asylums; the growth of a paternalistic conception of the state which sought to help the unfortunate through the ministrations of experts; and the move from religion to a scientific secularism. The institution of the Church had lost power to the institutions of the academy and medicine. Where once the insane looked for cure to religious healers in monasteries, temples or shrines, now they looked to the secular hospitals and their staff. Not only that, but there had been a change in the way in which people were marginalized. Previously, being seen as sinful or lacking religious faith would be a reason to be marked out as Other. Now, however, it was irrationality and madness that truly marked one out, which may be signalled by the fact that the terms for inmates and their medical superintendents were *aliens* and *alienists*.

As well as causing problems, this growth of large institutions meant that, for those psychiatrists wishing to conduct research, there were captive populations. This would lead to the foundation of what Shorter (1997) terms the 'first **biological**

BOX **2.3**

Drapetomania: when the desire to escape from slavery is seen as a mental disorder

Drapetomania was a term coined in 1851 by the New Orleans physician Samuel A. Cartwright to denote a 'disorder' peculiar to negro slaves – the desire to run away from their owners:

> The cause, in the most of cases, that induces the negro to run away from service, is as much a disease of the mind as any other species of mental alienation, and much more curable, as a general rule.
>
> (Cartwright, 1851, p. 332)

Cartwright was a supporter of slavery in the deep South at a time, leading up to the American civil war, when the Southern States were becoming increasingly secessionist. He saw the slave as 'in the position that we learn from the Scriptures he was intended to occupy, that is, the position of submission' (1851, p. 332). His 'medical advice' was that slave-owners should inquire into any reasons for their slaves being 'sulky and dissatisfied' and address any problems:

> If treated kindly, well fed and clothed, with fuel enough to keep a small fire burning all night – separated into families, each family having its own house – not permitted to run about at night to visit their neighbors, to receive visits or use intoxicating liquors, and not overworked or exposed too much to the weather, they are very easily governed
>
> (Cartwright, 1851, p. 332)

However, if there was no apparent cause the slave-owner should whip 'the devil out of them' as a 'preventative measure' until they were in a submissive state.

In the same article, Cartwright also described another 'disorder' peculiar to slaves: *Dysaesthesia Aethiopica*, which he said was called 'rascality' by slave overseers:

> they are apt to do much mischief, which appears as if intentional, but is mostly owing to the stupidness of mind and insensibility of the nerves induced by the disease.
>
> (Cartwright, 1851, p. 333)

Included in the list of symptoms, Cartwright noted that they 'raise disturbances with their overseers and fellow-servants without cause or motive, and seem to be insensible to pain when subjected to punishment' (p. 333). He said that physicians in the Northern States had noticed these symptoms but that they 'ignorantly attribute the symptoms to the debasing influence of slavery on the mind'. Instead Cartwright saw this 'disease' as 'the natural offspring of negro liberty – the liberty to be idle, to wallow in filth, and to indulge in improper food and drinks' (1851, p. 333).

Cartwright's suggestion was never part of a formal diagnostic system (the American *Diagnostic and Statistical Manual of Mental Disorders* was not to appear for another hundred years), but Kutchins and Kirk (1999) note that his ideas were publicized throughout the English-speaking world. This is a salutary example of how diagnostic labels are shaped by the social and cultural values of a particular time and place.

---

psychiatry' (i.e. one viewing distress in biological terms) in which 'alienists attempted to enlist the neurosciences in caring for patients' (p. 69), and it is to this development that we turn as we enter the 20th century – see Figure 2.5 for historical developments occurring in the first half of the 20th century.

1900–1945: diagnosis, psychological therapy, eugenics and war

Classifying the mind: diagnostic classification and the rise of biological psychiatry

One of the most influential approaches to understanding distress has been the notion that there are different types or categories of disorder. In other words, there are types of problem which are distinguishable from one another. Thomas Sydenham, a physician working in the 17th century, had recommended that doctors follow the example of botanists and subdivide illnesses into different kinds. In 1733, the grandfather of modern classification, Linnaeus, in his *Genera Morborum*, described 325 distinct illnesses, including eleven specific forms of mental illness (Sedgwick, 1982).

The late 18th and early 19th centuries saw developments in classifying different forms of distress. In France, for example, Esquirol, one of Pinel's followers, published *Mental Maladies* in 1838, which attempted to resolve the tension between psycho- and somatogenic models by asserting that mental disorders were organic but with triggers in the person's life (an early version of the stress-diathesis model mentioned in Chapter 1). He and his students refined the understanding of epilepsy. In 1822, another Frenchman, Antoine Laurent Bayle, described *general paresis of the insane* which, once bacteriological study was possible, subsequently came to be seen as an effect of tertiary syphilis.

However, it was probably in Germany that most work on classification was conducted. It was here that the term 'psychiaterie' was coined by Johan Christian Reil at the turn of the 19th century (from the Greek words for soul and doctor). Here, as in other countries, there were debates about the causes of distress. Thus, in his 1818 text, Heinroth claimed that disorder came from the soul, not the body, while Griesinger, in 1845, asserted a somatogenic view that 'mental illnesses are brain diseases'. In 1865 Griesinger founded a University department of psychiatry in Berlin and, from this point onwards, a strong empirical research tradition developed in German psychiatry. Griesinger saw this tradition as a way of moving psychiatry from 'its closed-off status as a guild' instead enabling it 'to become an integral part of general medicine' (cited in Scull, 2011, p. 68). However, there was a problem: diagnosis in psychiatry was idiosyncratic, with multiple and contradictory classificatory schemes, most of which lacked any empirical foundation. Boyle (2002) describes early attempts as being:

> distinguished mainly by their vagueness and multiplicity; by the last decades of the nineteenth century it was obvious, even to the most uncritical observer, that the result was chaos.
>
> Boyle (2002, p. 92)

Figure 2.5 **Timeline 1907–1950**

Year	Key events
1907	First US state enacts compulsory sterilization laws
1908	Clifford Beers publishes *A Mind that Found Itself*
1909	National Committee for Mental Hygiene established in the USA
1910	Winston Churchill writes to the British Prime Minister recommending the detention and sterilization of 'the feeble-minded and insane classes'
1913	J. B. Watson publishes article on behaviourism
1914	First World War begins
1917	von Economo describes encephalitis lethargica
1918	First World War ends
1920	J. B. Watson conducts the 'little Albert' study
1935	Alcoholics Anonymous founded in the USA
1936	Moniz develops the prefrontal leucotomy
1938	Ugo Cerletti develops ECT
1939	Second World War begins Hitler initiates *Aktion T4* plan for the extermination of asylum inmates
1945	Second World War ends Film *Spellbound* released
1946	The Nuremberg 'doctor's trial' begins (ending in 1947) Cold War begins *Time Life* magazine publishes Charles Lord's harrowing photographs inside US asylums UK National Health service established
1948	Hendrik Verwoerd introduces apartheid in South Africa Albert Deutsch publishes *Shame of the States* in the USA
1949	Film *The Snake Pit* released World Health Organization publishes the *International Classification of Diseases* (ICD)
1950	National Association of Mental Health established in the USA Chlorpromazine synthesized in France

One of the most significant figures in German psychiatry was Emil Kraepelin. According to Richard Bentall, Kraepelin's 'big idea' was that '[m]ental illnesses fell into a small number of discoverable types, and these could be independently identified by direct observation of brain diseases, or by discovering the aetiologies of the illnesses' (2004, pp. 12–13). Thus different disease entities (which Kraepelin thought were related to different pathologies of the brain) could be identified with reference to different patterns of symptoms and the course and outcome of the disease. Kraepelin set out his conceptual approach in a number of editions of his *Textbook of Psychiatry*. He saw psychiatric diseases as classifiable by **symptoms** (subjective reports by the person) or **aetiology** (the study of causation). However, since aetiology at this time was

often unclear, his suggestion of a system based on symptoms was seen as a breakthrough. What was new about Kraepelin's approach was that he gathered detailed descriptive case studies and attempted to test his classificatory schemes on them. Bentall (2004) notes that Kraepelin had collected over a thousand such case studies by 1896. Here we see how the existence of large captive populations in the asylums together with a new professional discipline seeking to establish its legitimacy as a part of medicine formed the conditions for new classificatory and conceptual schemes.

Professor of psychiatry Arnold Pick described a case in 1891 that he diagnosed *dementia praecox* (i.e. a degenerative cognitive condition in younger people). By 1893, Kraepelin had included it in his *Textbook of Psychiatry*, differentiating *dementia praecox* from manic depression. He saw the former as a chronic degenerative condition in which emotions were atrophied, whereas the latter was characterized mainly by some form of abnormal mood but was not degenerative. Following this, the Swiss psychiatrist Eugen Bleuler coined the term *the schizophrenias* to signal a mismatch between perceptions and cognition. He felt the term dementia praecox was misleading, as not all patients had a deteriorating prognosis, and for some he thought the purported disease process had begun much earlier in life.

These days Kraepelin and Bleuler are held to be the originators of the modern conception of schizophrenia. However, Mary Boyle (2002) has argued that modern-day descriptions are very different from those of Kraepelin and Bleuler, the only common symptoms being delusions and hallucinations which are, of course, not unique to the diagnosis of schizophrenia but are associated with a number of other physical illnesses and psychiatric diagnoses. Moreover, Boyle points out the striking similarities between Kraepelin and Bleuler's descriptions of dementia praecox and schizophrenia and **post-encephalitic Parkinsonism**, a condition causing nerve damage similar to **Parkinson's disease** (a degenerative disorder of the nervous system) and thought to be the result of a viral infection. This was described by the Austrian neurologist and psychiatrist Constantin von Economo in 1917 though his term was Encephalitis lethargica. Von Economo differentiated between three forms of this condition: the **somnolent-opthalmoplegic form** (the symptoms of which included expressionless faces and sleepiness, often leading to coma and death); the **hyperkinetic form** (the symptoms of which included restlessness and involuntary movements); and the **amyostatic-akinetic form** (the symptoms of which included rigidity without a real paralysis and emotions which were mentally present but not facially expressed – he termed this form 'Parkinsonism'). Encephalitis is caused by a viral infection and there have been a number of reported epidemics over recent centuries, including a documented pandemic in Europe between 1916–1927. In Table 2.2 we can see some of the descriptions of von Economo's encephalitis lethargica, Bleuler's schizophrenia and Kraepelin's dementia – the similarities between them are marked. However, what is also surprising – given that Kraepelin and Bleuler are seen as the fathers of the modern schizophrenia concept – is the difference between their descriptions and modern-day descriptions of schizophrenia.

> It is remarkable that with the exception of delusions and hallucinations, not one of the phenomena described [in Table 2.2] ... appears in the index of a comprehensive academic text on 'schizophrenia' (Neale & Oltmanns, 1980). This striking discrepancy provides further support

for the conclusion that Kraepelin and Bleuler derived their concepts from a population which has little in common with today's 'schizophrenics'.

Boyle (2002, p. 70)

Indeed, Boyle argues that:

there are at least good circumstantial grounds for supposing that Kraepelin and Bleuler were for the most part dealing with the consequences of some forms of encephalitic infection and that a sizeable number of their patients would later have been diagnosed as cases of post-encephalitic Parkinsonism.

Boyle (2002, p. 74)

There is a further discussion of the history of the schizophrenia concept in Chapter 11.

However, just as the scientific status of somatogenic models was growing in Western Europe, another doctor was trying to establish scientific credentials in an altogether different direction, by developing what may be one of the most influential of all psychogenic models: psychoanalysis.

Table 2.2 **Some of the descriptions of dementia praecox (by Kraepelin), schizophrenia (by Bleuler) and encephalitis lethargica/post-encephalitic parkinsonism (by von Economo). Mary Boyle has argued that the similarities between the descriptions may indicate that many of Kraepelin's and Bleuler's patients were actually suffering from encephalitis lethargica/post-encephalitic Parkinsonism**

Encephalitis lethargica/post-encephalitic parkinsonism (von Economo)	Dementia praecox (Kraepelin)	Schizophrenia (Bleuler)
'In some cases the ataxia [lack of co-ordination] attains such a degree that the instability of gait, the deviation towards one side, the tendency to fall backwards on standing, the tremor, the giddiness and the nystagmus [involuntary eye movement] can only be ascribed to an involvement of the cerebellum in the inflammatory process'	'Constraint is also noticeable in the gait of patients. Often indeed it is quite impossible to succeed in experiments of walking. The patients simply let themselves fall down stiffly, as soon as one tries to place them on their feet'	
'In the now increasing somnolence [sleepiness – of the acute phase of the somnolent opthalmoplegic form of encephalitis lethargica] one often observes that the patients, left to themselves, fall asleep in the act of sitting or standing or even while walking...[somnolence] is repeatedly found in quite slight cases as the only well marked symptom'		'During acute thrusts [of schizophrenia], though rarely in the chronic conditions, we often encounter somnolence. Patients are asleep all night and most of the day. Indeed, they often fall asleep at their work. Frequently, this somnolence is the only sign of a new thrust of the malady'
'If...one lifts up the forearm of a patient [suffering from the amyostatic-akinetic form of encephalitis lethargica] the arm remains raised for quite a time after having been released, and is only gradually brought back in jerks and with tremors'	'[Ermes] found that a fall of the leg held horizontally only began after 205 seconds [in cases of dementia praecox], while in healthy persons it made its appearance on an average after 38 seconds, at latest after 80 seconds. There followed then [in dementia praecox] either a repeated jerky falling off with tremor or a gradual sinking'	
'A hypersecretion of the sebaceous glands [which produce an oily secretion on the skin and hair] (probably centrally caused) causes the peculiar shining on the faces of these patients'		'Hoche also mentions the markedly increased secretion of the sebaceous glands [in schizophrenic patients]'
'pupillary disturbances are very common. In patients [with the hyperkinetic form of encephalitis lethargica] one generally finds unequal and myopic [nearsighted] pupils with a diminished and sluggish reaction but sometimes also one-sided or double or complete absence of reaction or an absence of light reaction only. These pupillary disturbances often vary considerably [in the same patient]'	'[The] behaviour of the pupils is of great significance. They are frequently in the earlier stages [of dementia praecox] and in conditions of excitement conspicuously wide...here and there one observes a distinct difference in the pupils. The light reaction of the pupils often appears sluggish or slight'	'In the most varied [schizophrenic] conditions, [the pupils] are often found to be unequal without having lost their ability to react...this pupillary inequality is rarely persistent; it often varies within a few hours, becoming equal or reversed'
'Oedema [build-up of fluid causing swelling] of hands and feet...are...more frequent in the amyostatic than in the other forms of encephalitis lethargica'		'The tendency to edema [sic] is usually ascribed to poor circulation, but it may have other causes...in a physically strong female patient with a beginning mild schizophrenia, edemas were noted in the thigh area...At times more severe edemas may make movement painful'

Source: **Adapted from Boyle (2002).**

Treating the mind: the birth of the psychological therapies

Psychoanalysis

The grounds for the emergence of this new approach had been laid by practitioners of **hypnotism** (where the subject was put into a mental trance and a suggestible state). They had argued that there were hidden layers of the mind. In Paris at the Salpêtrière hospital, Charcot, building on the theories of Franz Anton Mesmer, had developed hypnotism as a method for distinguishing **hysteria** (a purported disorder, now discredited, said to occur largely in women, supposedly signified by a wide range of symptoms including anything from anxiety and fainting to insomnia and loss of appetite for food or sex). In 1885, Sigmund Freud (1856–1939) spent some months studying under Charcot. Freud had trained in medicine and physiology and went on to specialize in neurology. He worked with Josef Breuer, who described how he was treating his patient 'Anna O' who, he said, exhibited symptoms of hysteria. He induced hypnosis and interviewed her about what he felt were triggering events, at which point the symptoms disappeared. In 1895 Freud and Breuer published *Studies on Hysteria*. According to Porter (2002), Charcot had felt that sexual impulses lay at the root of much hysteria and Freud began to hypothesize that the origin of these symptoms was sexual abuse perpetrated by the father (the so-called pre-pubescent '**seduction theory**') and thus the symptoms represented **repressed memories**. He expounded this theory in a letter to his friend Wilhelm Fleiss in Berlin in May 1893 and in a public lecture on the aetiology of hysteria in Vienna in April 1896. However, by September 1897 he stated, in a letter to Fleiss, that he no longer believed in the seduction theory. Instead he had developed a theory of infantile sexuality – the **Oedipus complex** – in which the child is in love with the mother but jealous of the father. Freud thought he saw such **unconscious libidinal desires** (i.e. sexual desires outside conscious awareness) repressed in himself and contended that this was universal. For psychoanalysts this was a time when the foundations of the approach were laid: the unconscious and Oedipal sexuality. However, modern critics such as Jeffrey Masson – who trained as a psychoanalyst and gained access to Freud's unpublished papers before rejecting the approach in *Against Therapy* – argue that Freud was intellectually dishonest and that he changed his mind because he feared a loss of status and income because of vociferous rejection of his theory.

Over the rest of his life Freud continued to publish, often including detailed case descriptions of patients from his Viennese practice. In later work he outlined further key ideas: that there were unconscious mental states; that desires and memories could be repressed leading to neuroses; that infantile sexuality existed; and that there was a symbolic meaning to symptoms and dreams. He developed techniques which, he argued, enabled one to access these domains, for example **free association** (a technique involving the psychoanalyst encouraging patients to say whatever words came to mind in relation to a topic) and the interpretation of dreams, which he saw as a 'royal road to the unconscious'. In his therapy he also elaborated the theory of **transference** – that a patient may act towards the therapist in a manner reminiscent of how they had been treated by others – in other words, they transferred their feelings from others onto the therapist.

Freud also elaborated a model of the human psyche: the id (basic drives towards pleasure), the ego (the part of us which negotiates with others' needs) and the super-ego (the representation of moral constraints on action). In many ways, Freud built on ideas which were already in existence and he read widely, particularly about different cultures and times in history. It is therefore no surprise that his model of the psyche seems reminiscent of Plato's tripartite division of the soul, noted earlier. However, it was Freud who systematized these ideas and formulated them into both an explanatory model and a therapy. He saw himself as a scientist and in his hydraulic model of the unconscious (with its drives and pressures) we can see the influence of this. One might argue that in his hydraulic model of the psyche we see traces of the early humoral tradition based on the dynamic motion of fluids. Freud's ideas were incredibly shocking and influential at the time and continue to be so today. However, how his legacy is viewed depends on one's viewpoint. For Porter (2002), Freud's ideas were 'a Copernican revolution in psychiatry', whilst for Shorter (1997), committed to a somatogenic approach, this period is referred to only as 'the psychoanalytic hiatus'. Freud's was perhaps the fullest elaboration of a psychogenic model, and his ideas still have an impact today through his influence on the whole psychoanalytic movement. Thus modern theories of **attachment** – the idea that the nature of one's early relationships can influence one's mental health as an adult – can be directly traced back to psychoanalytic ideas through John Bowlby, David Winnicott and Melanie Klein.

A number of those influenced by Freud went on to change elements of the theory. The Swiss psychiatrist Carl Jung, for example, described a number of **psychological types** (e.g. introvert and extravert) but he increasingly argued that there was a collective unconscious – i.e. an unconscious shared with others. Following the persecution of the Jews by the Nazis, who called psychoanalysis 'the Jewish science' (Frosh, 2009), a substantial number of Jewish psychoanalysts, psychologists and psychiatrists emigrated, many going to the USA. Freud moved to London, where he died in 1939.

Psychoanalysis grew in the UK and the Tavistock Clinic, based in London, was founded in 1920 to practice psychoanalysis, drawing on insights gained from the talking treatments offered to soldiers from the First World War suffering from **shellshock** from the effects of war – what would now be seen as post-traumatic stress. Indeed, the identification of widespread shellshock (with 10,000 veterans receiving shellshock pensions) reinforced the emergence of the 'new psychology' (Miller & Rose, 1988), in which the causes of much distress were seen in psychogenic and sociogenic terms.

Interestingly, given its roots in the First World War, the Tavistock Clinic was also influential in the development of theories about groups (which were utilized during the Second World War) and on personality theory. However, psychoanalysis was not the only psychological therapy founded at this time – so too was one of its great rivals, behaviour therapy.

Behaviourism

In contrast to psychoanalysis, **behaviourism** was focused only on observable behaviours and there was scepticism about **introspection** (the reporting by a participant of their conscious thoughts). Although he did not identify himself as a behaviourist, the work of Russian mathematician and physiologist Ivan Pavlov in the late 19th and early 20th century on the

classical conditioning of reflexes (i.e. how associations could be learned by the pairing of an external stimulus such as a bell with an involuntary reflex such as a dog's salivation) was one of the earliest examples of the approach that was later termed behaviourism. The psychologist who most firmly established behaviourism was the American J. B. Watson, who outlined its central tenets in a key paper in 1913 (Watson, 1913) and in his 1924 book *Behaviorism*. Watson is famous for his 1920 Little Albert study in which he conditioned a fear response in an infant. The varied and contradictory accounts of this study provide a good illustration of some of the challenges in understanding historical episodes – see Box 2.4.

Watson had to leave his academic position at Johns Hopkins University because he was having an affair with his assistant and student Rosalie Rayner; he subsequently went to work for the J. Walter Thompson advertising agency. There were to be significant developments in the clinical application of behaviourism, but these would largely occur after the Second World War.

The emergence of behaviourism was significant in a number of ways. Firstly, whereas psychoanalysis posited internal

---

BOX **2.4**

Watson's Little Albert study and origin myths in psychology

J. B. Watson and Rosalie Rayner's study of conditioning of the nine month old baby Albert B. is one of the most quoted examples in both introductory psychology textbooks and behaviour therapy texts. However, Ben Harris (1979) and Franz Samelson (1980) have suggested that the way this study has been recounted since it was first published in 1920 can tell us a lot about psychologists' approach to the history of their discipline.

Harris (1979) provides a detailed account of the study, drawing on a number of primary sources and we'll use his account here. In the study Albert showed no fear response at an initial test either to a number of live animals (e.g. a rat, a rabbit, a dog and a monkey) or to various inanimate objects (e.g. cotton, human masks and a burning newspaper). However, he did show fear when a steel bar was hit with a hammer behind his back (Harris, 1979). Two months later, Watson and Rayner attempted to condition Albert to fear a white rat by presenting it to him and then hitting the steel bar with the hammer whenever he touched the animal – this occurred during seven pairings of the rat and the noise, conducted in two sessions a week apart. Five days later the generalization of the fear response was tested by presenting Albert with the rat, a set of familiar wooden blocks, a rabbit, a short-haired dog, a sealskin coat, a package of white cotton, the heads of Watson and two assistants (where Albert could touch their hair) and a bearded Santa Claus mask. There was a further reconditioning session five days later, when the noise was also presented for one trial each with the rabbit and dog as well as the rat. A final series of tests was conducted 31 days later to assess the permanence of the response. No attempt was made to decondition Albert, although Watson knew that Albert would be leaving the hospital a month before he himself left.

Harris (1979) reviewed a number of introductory textbooks and found a number of inaccuracies in the way they reported the Little Albert study. For example, the list of spurious stimuli to which Albert's fear was said to have generalized included: a fur pelt, a man's beard, a cat, a pup, a fur muff, a white furry glove, Albert's aunt who supposedly wore fur, either the fur coat or fur neckpiece of Albert's mother, and even a teddy bear. Harris (1979) notes that some accounts even included a happy ending by asserting that Watson removed the fear, sometimes describing this deconditioning in detail. Why did these inaccuracies occur? Harris (1979) argues that some of them were probably due to authors both relying on secondary sources rather than going back to the original accounts (with embellishments creeping in because of a 'Chinese whispers' effect) and wishing to present a neat and ethical story. Harris also puts some of the blame onto Watson himself, who gave contradictory accounts of the study at different times. However, Harris also notes how textbook authors, behaviour therapists and preparedness theorists appeared to have succumbed to the temptation to 'make experimental evidence consistent with textbook theories' (1979, p. 154) by altering or misinterpreting details of the little Albert study. He argues that authors' opinions about the validity of behaviourism led them to the read the study less critically than they should.

The way in which the Albert study has been used within psychology can be seen as an illustration of how disciplines develop certain origin myths on the basis of well-cited classic studies. These are not necessarily intentional attempts to defraud; rather, they arise 'as largely a byproduct of pedagogy: as a means to elucidate the *concepts* of a scientific specialty, to establish its *tradition*, and to attract students' (Samelson, 1974, p. 223).

In a companion study, Franz Samelson (1980) details further methodological flaws in the Little Albert study, inconsistencies in Watson's own accounts and the continued failure to replicate Watson's study. Drawing comparisons with psychologists' failure to recognize the apparent falsification of data by the British psychologist Cyril Burt on the heritability of intelligence, he asks two questions:

> Why did we not notice earlier (or say so in print if we had)? It seems, *now*, that anybody who read Watson's accounts carefully and critically could not fail to see some problems.
> Why did nobody helping to raise generations of undergraduates on Watson and little Albert replicate the study?
>
> Samelson (1980, p. 623)

There are a number of lessons to be drawn from these studies. Firstly, it shows the importance of going to primary sources – a good lesson for aspiring psychologists at a time when plagiarism has become a major concern. Secondly, it demonstrates that psychological knowledge is developed in a social context, and researchers and authors are not immune to temptations to interpret findings in ways that support their views. We can see in the little Albert affair evidence of some of the deadly temptations for historians temptations: presentism, the over-emphasis of continuity, and a tendency to write ceremonial histories which serve to justify current paradigms. A final lesson is the need, as Samelson (1980) has argued, to have 'a more critical understanding of our history and, more generally, for a more reflexive and self-critical attitude toward our activities' (p. 624).

psychic mechanisms which mediated between external events and distress, behaviourism did not. Thus it may be the first purely sociogenic model, in that distress could now be seen as the result of behavioural learning. Secondly, even though psychoanalysis articulated a psychogenic model of distress, many psychoanalysts were physicians. In contrast, behaviourism was developed by physiologists such as Pavlov and psychologists such as Watson. Behaviourism was thus the first approach which was based on the new discipline of psychology and psychologists did not, therefore, depend on insights gained from another discipline. Finally, whereas the hypotheses of psychoanalysis were hard to test empirically, behaviourism advanced the idea that its theories were testable.

Treating the body: new physical treatments

However, not all of the therapeutic developments in the treatment of distress were as benign as psychoanalysis and behaviourism, and the inter-war period saw the development of a number of troubling physical treatments. Many earlier approaches had been 'based in large part on an exterior, mechanical intervention upon a passive patient' (Sedgwick, 1982) and they had largely followed the humoral model of distress. Thus bleeding was seen as a cure-all right up to the 19th century. Alongside bleeding, the scalp might be washed with vinegar, and purgatives to cause vomiting could be used. However in the early 1930s Manfred Sakel, an Austrian psychiatrist, developed **insulin coma therapy** (whereby temporary comas were induced in patients through the administration of insulin). This became an extremely popular treatment and was widely used (Moncrieff, 2008). In 1936 the Portugese neurologist Antonio Egas Moniz developed the **prefrontal leucotomy** – a surgical technique for severing the connections to and from the prefrontal cortex. This was said to be of therapeutic value in treating depression and obsessions. In 1938 Ugo Cerletti introduced **electro-convulsive therapy** (ECT) in which an epileptic seizure was induced via the administration of electricity to the brain. We return to ECT in Chapter 8.

Finally, Henry Cotton, the medical director of Trenton State Hospital in New Jersey, developed a theory that madness was caused by infections, leading him to remove 'teeth, tonsils, stomachs, spleens, colons and uteri' (Scull, 2011, p. 78). Tragically, the 20th century had even worse treatment in store for some inmates of asylums as we will see as we switch our focus to Nazi Germany.

The participation of German psychiatry in the Nazi genocide

We saw earlier how social Darwinist and degenerationist theories became popular ways of explaining the increasing numbers and apparently increasing chronicity of distress of those in the asylums, and by the late 19th century, theories of eugenics had gained ground. Their proponents suggested a number of practices, including forced sterilization. From the perspective of today this seems obviously crude and racist and it can be hard to appreciate how popular a view this was. Yet, as we saw earlier, its proponents included some well-known figures, many of whom regarded themselves as liberal rather than right-wing. Another well-known advocate in the UK was Winston Churchill (later to become Prime Minister of Britain during the Second World War and again in the 1950s). Whilst Home Secretary in 1910–1911, Winston Churchill was an advocate of the confinement, segregation, and sterilization of the 'feeble minded' (Gilbert, 2009).

Despite such advocacy, proposals for legislation in the UK were derailed by opposition from religious groups (Scull, 2011). However, compulsory sterilization took hold in Germany, Sweden and the USA, where 40 of the 48 states had compulsory sterilization on their statute books by 1940 (Scull, 2011). In an almost unanimous ruling from the US Supreme Court, Oliver Wendell Holmes stated in the judgement:

> It is better for all the world if instead of waiting to execute degenerate offspring for crime, or to let them starve for their imbecility, society can prevent those who are manifestly unfit from continuing their kind. The principle that sustains compulsory vaccination is broad enough to cover cutting the Fallopian tubes. Three generations of idiots are enough.
>
> Scull (2011, p. 62)

A US state first enacted compulsory sterilization laws in 1907. In the US the Cold Spring Harbor Laboratory under Charles Davenport became a centre for eugenics research and in the first three-quarters of the 20th century approximately 60,000 sterilizations were conducted, a third of them in California (Stern, 2005). In Sweden, a eugenics law was introduced in 1934 and was only abolished in 1975. A media campaign in the late 1990s led to a government inquiry, which reported that over 62,000 sterilizations had been performed, about half of which were compulsory (Gamel, 2001).

The South African psychologist and theologian Hendrik Verwoerd used degenerationist theories to justify his policy of apartheid in South Africa, pursued after the Second World War when he was that country's Minister of Native Affairs and Prime Minister before the overthrow of Apartheid in 1994.

However, it was in Nazi Germany that eugenicists took their theory to its logical and horrifying conclusion – moving from mass sterilization to extermination. From 1934 to 1939, between 300,000–400,000 German patients had been sterilized (Scull, 2011), but in 1939 Adolf Hitler issued a decree mandating mass execution under the *Aktion T4* programme (named after the address of the headquarters at Tiergartenstrasse 4 in Berlin – Pilgrim, 2008). Under this programme, commissions 'marked mental patients for death often referred to as "disinfection" ' (Scull, 2011, p. 64). Other euphemisms included 'euthanasia'; patients were referred to as 'lives unworthy of living', following the title of psychiatrist Alfred Hoche's co-authored 1920 text *Allowing The Destruction of Life Unworthy of Living* (Pilgrim, 2008). Torrey and Yolken (2010) report that, in this programme, 70,273 were killed in gas chambers disguised as shower rooms, including 92% of patients transferred to the Hadamar asylum and 97% of those admitted to Obrawalde asylum in German Silesia. Many of those who took part argued that these killings, like euthanasia, helped to end suffering and so were a form of caring (Pilgrim, 2008).

The T4 programme ended in August 1941 following protests by members of the clergy but the killings continued in a more hidden fashion – in total about 200,000–275,000 patients were killed including about 100,000 who starved to death and an unknown number who were shot, or killed by lethal injection (Torrey & Yolken, 2010). The commander of the Treblinka death camp, Dr Irmfried Eberl, was actually a physician with psychiatric training (Strous, 2010). Many commentators note that it was on the patients in German asylums that the Nazis perfected the methods they later used as part of the 'final solution' to kill six million Jews. Franz Stangl, the head of the T4 programme became commander of the Sobibor death camp (Pilgrim, 2008). Haefner (2010) reports that, of the professors of psychiatry involved in these extermination programmes, two committed suicide after the war, one was sentenced to death and executed and another successfully hid for many years before being apprehended, subsequently committing suicide. Between 1946 and 1947, physicians who had participated in the death camps and other extermination programmes were prosecuted at the Nuremberg 'doctors' trial'. Pilgrim (2008) notes that, in the evidence examined, two psychiatrists (Karl Schneider and Ernst Rudin – famous for his research on schizophrenia) were singled out but escaped prosecution.

One of the most striking aspects of this episode of psychiatric genocide is how little it is discussed today – Strous comments that 'it has taken close to 60 years to confront this dark period in the history of psychiatry' (2010, p. 208). Indeed it is little discussed in textbooks on the history of psychology and psychiatry. Pilgrim notes that '[i]n some texts there is simply a complete silence about the history of eugenics in the profession, when genetic aspects are reviewed' (2008, p. 282) with the eugenic background of many key figures such as Ernst Rudin being ignored.

Strous (2010) raises key questions that resonate today:

> How was it that so many (senior and junior) psychiatrists, many with phenomenal international reputations, participated in and even initiated much of the genocide against mentally ill individuals? How was it that it has taken so long for psychiatry to confront this episode in our not-so-distant past?
>
> Strous (2010, p. 209)

The Nuremberg medical trials led to the establishment of a set of ethical principles called the **Nuremberg Code**, which required that research participants give full voluntary consent, the research should be of value to society, the results should not be attainable in any other way and studies should not result in death or serious injury. This code laid the foundation of the principles on which many institutional ethics committees in hospitals and universities are now based.

Unfortunately, even as this code was being agreed, Allied military investigation teams were going through the records of experimentation in the Nazi death camps selecting items deemed of military value whilst, in an irony of staggering proportions, one of the members of the medical tribunal, Dr Ewen Cameron, later went on to conduct some of the most unethical psychiatric experiments ever performed as part of an investigation into 'brainwashing' (Marks, 1979; McCoy, 2006).

1945–1970: the Cold War, the pharmacological revolution, de-institutionalization, the DSM, new psychotherapies and anti-psychiatry

No sooner had the 'hot war' in Europe and the Pacific ended, a 'Cold War' had begun. The **Cold War** (approximately 1946–1991) between the East (i.e. the Soviet Union and its allies) and West (i.e. the USA, NATO and its allies) began almost immediately. In this time of heightened military and diplomatic tension, psychiatry and psychology were pressed into service – see Figure 2.6 for an outline of historical events between 1951–70.

Psychiatry and the Cold War

Psychiatry and brainwashing

In the West there was concern during the war in Korea (1950–1953) at the apparent brainwashing of American prisoners of war (PoWs). The CIA funded a substantial series of research projects between 1950 and 1962 (McCoy, 2006). One recipient was Canadian psychologist Donald Hebb at McGill University, who studied **sensory deprivation** (a term describing an experimental condition where research participants had all sensory input reduced, for example by lying in a dark and soundproofed cubicle). After continuous isolation in this manner, participants began to experience hallucinations and a degraded ability to think clearly, and most students quit the study after 2 or 3 days. Under a psychological sciences research programme as part of the CIA's Project MKUltra, research funds of $7-$13 million were allocated annually for behavioural studies at major universities by channelling funds through a variety of legitimate and 'front' organizations, including The Society for the Investigation of Human Ecology at Cornell University. Ewen Cameron at McGill University's treatment facility the Allan Memorial Institute received such funding for research on unwitting and non-consenting psychiatric patients into a technique he termed 'depatterning'. This involved:

> First, drug-induced coma for up to eighty-six days; next, electroshock treatment three times daily for thirty days; and, finally, a football helmet clamped to the head for up to twenty-one days with a looped tape repeating, up to half a million times, messages like 'my mother hates me'. In contrast to Hebb's six-day maximum for voluntary isolation, Cameron confined one patient, known only as Mary C., in his 'box' for an unimaginable thirty-five days of total sensory deprivation
>
> (McCoy, 2006, p. 44)

Such accounts are shocking, so it is surprising to learn that Cameron had been a member of the Nuremberg medical tribunal (the 'doctors' trial') and went on to become not only the first Chairman of the World Psychiatric Association but also president of both the American and Canadian Psychiatric Associations. In the UK similar experiments using ECT combined with drug-induced comas were carried out by another eminent psychiatrist, William Sargant, the physician in charge of the Department of Psychological Medicine at St Thomas's Hospital in London (Streatfield, 2006).

Interrogation techniques based on the studies funded as part of these research programmes were used in Northern Ireland (Shallice, 1972; Watson, 1978), resulting in an investigation by the European Commission of Human Rights and the UK Attorney General promising never to use these techniques again (McCoy, 2006). Sadly, the ethical lessons do not appear to have been learnt and similar techniques have been used by the US in detention camps in Guantanamo, Afghanistan, Iraq and as part of the CIA's 'high value detainee' programme, in which a number of senior suspected Al-Qaeda members were interrogated in a series of secret CIA prison sites across the world including Poland and Romania (Marty, 2007).

The political abuse of psychiatry

In the Cold War psychiatry was used not only as a way of enhancing interrogation methods but, in the Soviet Union, as a way of confining **political dissidents** (i.e. those who questioned the prevailing political system), especially in the

Figure 2.6 **Timeline 1951–1970**

Year	Key events
1951	Carl Rogers publishes *Client-Centered Therapy*
1952	American Psychiatric Association publishes *Diagnostic and Statistical Manual of Mental Disorders* (DSM)
1953	B.F. Skinner publishes *Science and Human Behaviour*
1954	UK asylum population reaches its peak
1955	US asylum population reaches its peak
1956	Gregory Bateson and colleagues at Palo Alto describe the 'double-bind' theory of schizophrenia
1957	British psychiatrist William Sargant publishes *Battle for the Mind: A Physiology of Conversion and Brainwashing*
1959	Mental Health Act enacted in England and Wales
1961	R.D. Laing publishes *The Divided Self* Thomas Szasz publishes *The Myth of Mental Illness* Erving Goffman publishes *Asylums* Michel Foucault publishes *Histoire de la folie* Frantz Fanon publishes *The Wretched of the Earth* Enoch Powell gives 'water tower' speech at National association for Mental Health conference
1962	Ewen Cameron and colleagues publish 'The depatterning treatment of schizophrenia' in the journal *Comprehensive Psychiatry* Albert Ellis publishes *Reason and Emotion in Psychotherapy* Ken Kesey publishes *One Flew over the Cuckoo's Nest*
1963	The film *Shock Corridor* released
1965	Philadelphia Association founded
1966	Thomas Scheff publishes *Being Mentally Ill*
1967	David Cooper publishes *Psychiatry and Anti-Psychiatry*
1969	Stonewall riot in Greenwich Village, New York
1970	The Insane Liberation Front founded in Portland, Oregon The Socialist Patients Collective founded in Heidelberg in West Germany

1970s and 1980s. As Dr Georgi Morozov, director of the Serbsky Institute for Forensic Psychiatry in Moscow, observed, 'why bother with political trials when we have psychiatric clinics' (Wheen, 2010, p. 160). The diagnosis of 'sluggish schizophrenia' developed by Professor Andrei Snezhnevsky and the 'Moscow School of Psychiatry' was found to be particularly useful for this purpose (van Voren, 2010). One of the assumptions underlying its use was that, as Soviet Communism was a perfectly logical and satisfactory ideology, any questioning of this must indicate that the person was mentally ill. Symptoms could include 'reform delusions', 'struggle for the truth', and 'perseverance' (van Voren, 2010). Those confined ranged from Communists who simply wanted some reforms (such as Major General Pyotr Grigorenko) to anti-Communists. Detained dissidents included Valdimir Bukovsky and the biochemist Zhores Medvedev who wrote the book *A Question of Madness* about his ordeal (Wheen, 2010). At least 250 psychiatrists were involved in these activities; one commission, which investigated five prison psychiatric hospitals in Russia from 1994–1995, reported 2000 cases of detention on political grounds (van Voren, 2010). Because of the extent of this abuse, the Soviet Union was forced to withdraw from the World Psychiatric Association in 1983, returning conditionally six years later, the year the Berlin wall in Germany was toppled – the symbolic moment signalling the end of the Cold War. However, political abuse of psychiatry continues, particularly in China, which had carried out exchanges with the Serbsky Institute. In the 1980s the incidence of forensic psychiatric 'cases of a political nature' (the official term) was approximately 15%, dropping to a few per cent in the 1990s, although this still means hundreds, possibly even thousands, of detentions for political reasons (Munro, 2002). In China, the psychiatric literature equates political dissidence (e.g. mailing political literature or participating in political demonstrations) with violence and threat, popular diagnoses being paranoia, schizophrenia and personality disorder. More recently, psychiatric detention has been used as a way of dealing with the Falun Gong movement, a religious sect in China, seen by the authorities as a threat to the political system (Munro, 2002).

Whilst some commentators view such political abuses as unique exceptions from psychiatric practice and more to do with politics than psychiatry, Thomas Szasz (1994), the American psychiatrist who was a critic of psychiatry (discussed later in this chapter) argued that such instances occurred because of the place psychiatry occupies in contemporary society; he has stated that 'without psychiatric power there could be neither psychiatric abuse nor normal psychiatric practice, as we know it' (p. 136). Certainly the breadth of some diagnostic criteria, the subjectivity inherent in all judgment, and the legal powers that are granted to psychiatrists in many societies means that psychiatric power is often abused in totalitarian societies.

However, although the Cold War had an impact, a whole range of other developments have shaped our modern understandings of and treatments for distress.

For example, in the UK, immediately after the war, the newly elected Labour administration had established a freely accessible National Health Service (NHS) in the 1946 NHS Act. In the USA, the end of the Second World War had seen a huge number of veterans in distress, with 50,000 American soldiers in military hospitals as psychiatric casualties and nearly half a million GIs receiving pensions for psychiatric disability by 1947 (Scull, 2011). As we will see later, the Veterans Administration – the federal agency responsible for the care of veterans in distress – was to exert a powerful influence on the shaping of US clinical psychology. However, the post-war period saw calls for change to the asylum system alongside two revolutions occurring in the treatment of distress, one psychological (and delivered primarily by psychologists), the other pharmacological (and delivered by doctors) and by the middle of the 20th century the asylums had reached their zenith and were then to decline steadily over the rest of the century.

New psychological therapies

From behaviourism to behaviour therapy

Behaviourism had established a firm foothold before the Second World War but it is with the work of the psychologist B. F. Skinner that we see a thoroughgoing systematization of behaviourist principles, including the notion of **operant conditioning**: the shaping of voluntary responses by the use of reinforcement. His 1953 book *Science and Human Behaviour* showed the range of activity in which behaviourists had been engaged in the forty years since the publication of what has become known as Watson's behaviourist manifesto. The 1950s and 1960s saw increasing application of these ideas to clinical populations, and thus **behaviour therapy** was born. Beginning predominantly in the US, clinical psychologists often used these techniques in institutional settings like mental hospitals. Psychiatrist Joseph Wolpe developed the technique of **systematic desensitization** (by which a person with an unwarranted fear or **phobia** gradually learned to remain relaxed in the presence of an object they were previously frightened of). After initial scepticism, the psychologist Hans Eysenck, working in the UK, became a champion of behaviour therapy, while other psychologists such as Stanley Rachman developed techniques such as **response prevention**, in which a person with a compulsion to conduct a particular behaviour (e.g. continually checking that one has switched the oven off) learns to stay relaxed and to manage the fear that arises when one does not carry out the ritual. Psychologists based in institutions in the US and UK began to develop behavioural approaches such as the **token economy**, in which desired behaviour was rewarded with tokens which could be exchanged for activities or other rewards. Token economies became unpopular because they were too crude and institutionalized. Although behaviourism attracts criticism from some quarters for a tendency to reductionism and a neglect of the importance of the personal meaning of distress, Smail (1990) contends that it was the one therapeutic tradition which advanced a thoroughly environmental approach, in that problems were seen as occurring in the relationship between an individual and their environment – a sociogenic approach.

Client-centred therapy

However, just as behaviourism was beginning to flourish, another American psychologist was laying the foundations of a quite different approach. Influenced by the Viennese psychoanalyst Otto Rank's emphasis on the importance of the emotional experience in the 'here and now' and on a personality theory which stressed the centrality of a person's subjective reality, Rogers developed a whole new approach to psychotherapy, which became known as **client-centred therapy** (Rogers, 1951) In this approach the therapist adopted core values of genuineness in their responses, an empathy for their client and an unconditional positive regard, in order to facilitate a person's ability to heal themselves. Whereas psychoanalysis posited complex intra-psychic dynamics, client-centred therapy had less obvious theoretical baggage. In contrast to behaviourism's focus on the manipulation of behaviour, Rogers preferred a more facilitative non-directive approach and, indeed, Rogers and Skinner engaged each other in public debates about their respective approaches. As many of Roger's principles chimed with **humanist philosophy** (which asserted that those without religious faith could still act ethically and morally because of their faith in human values), his approach came to be seen as the vanguard of the tradition of **humanistic psychotherapy**.

Behaviourists saw the person in relation to their environment and history of reinforcement, whilst client-centred therapists focused on the individual, but in the 1950s and 1960s another therapeutic approach was developing, which focused on the individual in the context of their family relationships.

Family therapy

Following the Second World War, mental health researchers had begun to look in a sustained fashion at the impact of the family and the social environment on the aetiology of mental health problems. In 1949, in the USA, psychiatrists Theodore and Ruth Lidz published an article on the family environment of people with a diagnosis of schizophrenia (Lidz & Lidz, 1949). They argued that particular family patterns were a causative factor in the development of schizophrenia and talked of parents as 'schizophrenogenic', a term introduced by psychoanalyst Frieda Fromm-Reichmann. In 1956, in Palo Alto in the USA, Gregory Bateson, Donald Jackson, Jay Haley and John Weakland were influenced by **communication theory** (how information and meaning was conveyed) and **systems theory** (how the different elements in a system – such as members of a family or society – interacted with each other). Drawing on these ideas they developed their 'double-bind' theory of schizophrenia, arguing that contradictory and unresolvable messages between family members played a causative role (Bateson, Jackson, Haley & Weakland, 1956), a notion that R. D. Laing would later adapt, as we will see later in this chapter. Unfortunately these ideas have often generated more heat than light, in that a lack of maternal love was often asserted to be the cause of distress and mother-blaming terms such as 'schizophrenogenic mothers' or 'refrigerator mothers' were often used. However, the fierce response from more biologically-minded psychiatrists and from some relatives' groups has meant that some commentators have argued that it is now taboo to discuss any way in which family relationships might be a causal factor in the development of distress, particularly if it attracts a diagnosis of schizophrenia (Johnstone, 1993). Despite this, the field of family therapy has continued to grow since the 1950s and 1960s and is practised by a range of mental health professionals. In **family therapy**, distress is seen to arise from problems in relationships and communication between family members, so the therapist uses a range of strategies to help family members change the way they relate to one another. As we will see in Chapter 8, family therapy is now influenced by a range of ideas and the 'double-bind' theory is no longer in wide use. Family therapy could be seen as another example of a largely sociogenic model of distress, but we turn now to an example of a psychogenic explanatory model, one that draws very much on the ideas proposed by John Locke in the 17th century.

Cognitive behavioural therapy

The 1950s saw a fourth therapy tradition emerging with the work of another psychologist, Albert Ellis, who, disenchanted with psychoanalysis, and finding inspiration in adopting an approach to living based on **rationalist** principles (principles based on reason and logic) developed an approach termed **rational therapy** (later **Rational Emotive Behaviour Therapy**), publishing *Reason and Emotion in Psychotherapy* in 1962. A little later the American psychiatrist Aaron Beck, also disenchanted with psychoanalysis, began to focus on the importance of **cognition** (thinking) in the aetiology and maintenance of distress, particularly depression, publishing *Diagnosis and Management of Depression* in 1967 and broadening this approach to other forms of distress in his 1975 work *Cognitive Therapy and the Emotional Disorders*. In **cognitive therapy**, thoughts and beliefs were seen as influencing emotion, so a person's distress might be helped by changing their thoughts and beliefs. The work of Ellis, Beck and others chimed with growing concerns amongst research psychologists that a simplistically reductive behaviourist approach could not account for the influence of people's thoughts, beliefs and attitudes on their behaviour. Although Beck was a psychiatrist, many clinical psychologists began to practice **cognitive-behavioural therapy** (or CBT), a synthesis of both cognitive and behavioural therapies. Initially CBT therapists focused on common forms of distress such as sadness and worry (see Chapter 9) but in the 1980s and 1990s, especially in the UK, clinical psychologists used CBT approaches to understand madness (see Chapter 11). Although it has become fashionable to refer to a 'cognitive revolution', in which cognitive researchers and therapists were once again able to examine cognition after being oppressed by behaviourism, there is little evidence for this; cognitive research topics showed no decline during the time of behaviourism's prominence (Lovie, 1983). Rather this seems to be a case of psychology's preference for certain origin myths (Leahey, 1992 – see also Boxes 2.1 and 2.4).

The explosion of psychological therapies, especially psychoanalysis, had a massive influence on popular culture, particularly in Hollywood. In the film *The Snake Pit* (1949) a young psychiatrist used psychoanalysis to save a young female patient from the back ward of a State Hospital (Scull, 2011). Director Alfred Hitchcock made great use of psychoanalytic allusions in *Spellbound* (1945), in which the new head of a mental hospital (Gregory Peck) turns out to be an impostor and Ingrid Bergman uses her psychoanalytic expertise to unlock his amnesia. The film featured a bizarre dream sequence designed by the Surrealist artist Salvador Dalí. In 1963's *Shock Corridor* a journalist feigns insanity in order to discover the identity of a killer, which he succeeds in doing only to be subjected to ECT, never leaving the hospital again.

The birth of psychopharmacology

We noted earlier how, in the inter-war period, a number of physical treatments had been developed, including prefrontal leucotomy. This technique was adapted by the American surgeon Walter Freeman, who termed it a **lobotomy** (see Chapter 8). He was an enthusiastic proponent of psycho-surgery – according to Porter (2002), at one point he was performing a hundred transorbital lobotomies a week, often using an ordinary cocktail cabinet ice pick inserted through the eye socket. He performed about 3600 in all and *Time* magazine called him the man with the golden ice pick (Scull, 2011). In the USA over 18,000 such operations had been performed by 1951. It is hard to appreciate now how such irreversible and invasive procedures could be conducted on people without adequate supporting evidence. However, at that time the average family member would defer to medical authority. Moreover, the doctors were optimistic about these new treatments – an optimism that Scull (2011) has noted, has accompanied many new developments in psychiatry. However, as one British psychiatrist practising in the 1950s has observed:

> Tragically, the heart-warming optimism which greeted the much-vaunted 'physical methods', as these were called, proved to be illusory, and those who practised them, including myself, regard them in retrospect with more shame than pride.
>
> Rollin (2000, p. 12)

Psychiatrists had access to a range of medications, broadly falling into one of two types: sedatives such as barbiturates, paraldehyde and bromides and stimulants such as amphetamine (see Chapter 8 and Moncrieff, 2008). It was in this context that new medications began to be developed. In France, a new **anti-histamine** (used in treating allergies) called chlorpromazine was synthesized and, somewhat accidentally, it was discovered to have some sedative effects when tested on a group of psychiatric patients. This discovery transformed psychiatry and many commentators talk about this as the time of the **pharmacological revolution**: it was one of the harbingers of what Shorter (1997) terms the 'second biological psychiatry'.

Prescriptions of chlorpromazine increased massively – rising in France from a few hundred kilograms nationally in 1952 to over a million five years later. An interesting aspect of this is, as Joanna Moncrieff argues in Chapter 8, that whereas previously psychiatrists had seen drugs as compounds which could do a variety of things to alleviate symptoms, these drugs increasingly began to be marketed by pharmaceutical companies as addressing an underlying **biological disorder** (i.e. as acting on purported organic pathologies). They became known as **neuroleptics** (literally, taking hold of one's nerves) and **major tranquillizers**, although recently the term **antipsychotic** has become more popular, strengthening Moncrieff's argument.

An important effect of the discovery of drugs such as chlorpromazine was that pharmaceutical companies became a major influence on the shaping of diagnostic classifications (Healy, 2002; Moncrieff, 2008), partly because such drugs enabled more patients to be treated as out-patients rather than in-patients – what later became known as 'care in the community'. This reinforced the broader social changes taking place in relation to asylums, which is where we turn next.

The move from asylums to the community

In the 1950s the asylums of the US and UK reached breaking point. In the UK the number of people in the them rose, peaking in 1954 at around 148,100, falling by less than 12,000 by 1960 (Scull, 2011). In the US the peak occurred in 1955 at 558,900, falling to 535,500 by 1960 (Scull, 2011). A number of factors converged, leading to calls for a reform of the system for dealing with those in distress. An important factor was cost – the asylums cost huge amounts of money to run. In the US, for example, hospitals were paid for by local government – by each of the states –so there was a financial incentive to transfer care to the community which was funded by the federal (i.e. national) budget (Healy, 2002). In the UK, the asylums were placing an increasing strain on public funds, while the new drugs, such as chlorpromazine, meant treatment could be much cheaper.

Part of the impetus for change came from advocates of social reform, following successive exposés of the harsh and abusive treatment seen in many institutions. In the US in 1946, Charles Lord, who had worked as an attendant in a mental hospital (as he was a conscientious objector to military service), published photographs showing the state of these hospitals in *Time Life* magazine whilst, in 1948, Albert Deutsch published *Shame of the States*, describing one male ward at Byberry State Hospital in Philadelphia as 'like a scene out of Dante's Inferno' (cited in Scull, 2011, p. 96).

Moreover, in the UK, the law governing mental health care was rooted in in-patient treatment and was largely custodial in nature: there was much debate about how the law should be changed (Bean, 1980). A Royal Commission was set up and produced the Percy Report in 1957; this recommended that mental illness should be treated in much the same way as physical illness or disability and proposed the reform of hospitals, which were brought under the care of the Ministry of Health. The **Mental Health Act** was passed in 1959, specifically aimed at reducing the number of people subject to **compulsory treatment** – see Chapter 8. There was to be much more emphasis on voluntary and consensual (rather than compulsory) admissions to hospital, with shorter stays preferred over longer.

In Box 2.5 are some insights into life in a large psychiatric hospital in the UK in the 1950s and 1960s from the perspective of a nurse. The late 1950s saw the numbers in the asylums begin to decline. In the UK in 1961, the Conservative Minister for Health, Enoch Powell (later to become more notable for his right-wing and racist views on immigration), opened a conference of the National Association for Mental Health with a speech on how his forthcoming Hospital Plan would change psychiatric services. In this 'water tower' speech (the name deriving from the huge Victorian water towers which supplied the old asylums), he accelerated the process of **de-institutionalization** and **community care** (i.e. transferring care from hospitals to out-patient services). In his speech he argued that, on the then trend in the fall of in-patient admissions, only half of the current number of beds would be needed in 15 years time. He said of this statement of aims that it

Pilgrim State Hospital in Brentwood, Long Island in New York State was the largest psychiatric hospital in the world when it opened in 1931. By 1954 it had 13,875 patients and over 4000 employees. It was so large that it had not only its own railway station but its own services providing water, heat, electric light and sewage treatment, as well as its own fire department, police department, courts, farm, post office and cemetery

implied 'nothing less than the elimination of by far the greater part of this country's mental hospitals as they exist today'.

It is often claimed that it was the discovery of neuroleptics which led to the large-scale closure of the old asylums, but it was the result of a number of factors, of which drug treatment was only one. Healy (2002), for example, notes that in Japan asylum populations continued to increase during this period despite the use of chlorpromazine. He also points out that, in the UK, although the actual numbers of the asylum population peaked in the mid 1950s, the national population was itself increasing at this time and, when this increase is taken into account, the asylum population began to fall after 1915, forty years before the introduction of chlorpromazine.

Other factors drove the closure of the asylums, including the availability of welfare benefits, the development of community psychiatry, out-patient facilities and day hospitals, the institution of **therapeutic communities**, and social methods of **rehabilitation**, such as occupational therapy and industrial rehabilitation, as well as community re-settlement. Moreover, as we saw earlier, the 1950s and 1960s had also seen a range of new psychological therapies developing. The next significant development we'll examine, therefore, is the massive increase in the numbers of practitioners who could deliver these new treatments.

The post-asylum growth in the 'psy' disciplines

The post-war period saw a boom in the growth of what Nikolas Rose (1998) calls the 'psy' disciplines. The American Psychiatric Association, founded in 1844 by 13 asylum superintendents, had less than 5000 members in 1948 but over 12,000 in 1951 and 35,000 in 2003. Psychoanalysis was in the ascendancy, with the proportion of US psychiatrists who were psychoanalysts growing from a third at the end of the 1950s to form a majority of the profession in 1973 (Scull, 2011). However, this increasing interest in psychoanalysis was linked to a declining interest in working in large institutions, with the majority of psychiatrists working in private practice or out-patient clinics by 1947 whilst, by 1958, less than 16% worked in state hospitals (Scull, 2011). In the UK, the Royal Psycho-Medical Association (the national body representing psychiatrists) had over 600 members in 1921. It changed its name to the Royal College of Psychiatrists in 1971 and, by 2009, had over 15,000 members.

The move from asylum-based to community-based care influenced the development of a range of new professions, including **clinical psychology**. It is still a relatively young sub-discipline, emerging in the USA and UK during the Second World War, and it has grown significantly in the sixty years

BOX **2.5**

Life in a large psychiatric hospital in the 1950s and 1960s – a nurse's perspective

The following extracts are from the account of a charge nurse (male ward manager) written by Lewis (1995). He was employed in Lancaster County Asylum in Warrington, also known as Winwick Hospital, which, in its heyday, had up to 2000 patients and approximately 400 nursing staff.

> First impressions were the awesome size of the hospital and grounds, the huge size of wards and the mainly lack of privacy for patients. The smallest number of patients in a ward was about 30+ in the then refractory ward[1] of 3Up.[2]
>
> Lewis (1995, p. 98)

> The hospital had its own laboratory, mortuary, pharmacy, shoemakers/repairers, tailor's shop, engineers of all varieties, farm and market garden...Staff of various nursing grades and assistants supervised patient workers as did what were termed 'artisans' in the various workshops. Patients were paid and often tobacco, either thick twist or shag [types of tobacco], was a currency. There was too a staff-operated fire service headed by two full-time qualified firemen.
>
> Lewis (1995, p. 98)

> Wards: By present day standards these were enormous and in my early years consisted of a day room and dormitory. 1–5Up and Down had up to 60–70 patients but 6-7-8-9 were in the hundreds...dormitories with only a locker's width of space between each bed.
>
> Lewis (1995, p. 100)

> During the 1960s...iron railings which previously surrounded the hospital providing security were no longer thought necessary as most wards were now beginning to adopt the 'Open Ward' policy (p. 107) and so they became surplus to requirements. It was recognised also that the previously forbidding character of the hospital could be de-stigmatized somewhat by their removal. In 1965 the airing courts where previously patients took exercise were also being dismantled. (Airing courts were locked enclosures where patients exercised).
>
> Lewis (1995, pp. 106–7)

> As late as the 1960s patients also, on occasions when being admitted and showing aggressive tendencies could be brought in wearing a straitjacket and were consequently moved to a side room where s/he was released and protected from themselves by the horsehair padding approximately 6–8" deep, covering the walls and ceiling. On the floor was a mattress,

but no other facilities...or in some cases patients could be nursed in what were commonly called 'horse boxes', i.e. side rooms with split doors.

> Lewis (1995, p. 107)

> Bathing was a particularly institutionalized procedure. It consisted of whole blocks being designated for 'bath days'. Patients having removed their attire would stand in lines in the corridor outside the bathroom clutching their belongings under their armpits presenting a picture not unlike some of the newsreel film from internment camps. Systematically inspected for any bruising or unusual marks, then after being checked out by the 'crab' nurse! [nurse checking for sexually transmitted infections] were taken through to the baths (eight in number), there to be religiously scrubbed by staff under the auspices of the charge nurse. Bath water was drained after each patient and as wards commonly consisted of 60 or more patients, bathing continued over much of the morning.
>
> Lewis (1995, p. 107)

1   A refractory ward was where patients who were seen as not responding to treatment were placed (often for years).
2   The name of a ward – the hospital wards had names like 1Up and 1Down.

---

since then (Benjamin, 2005). Despite its youth, clinical psychology has grown rapidly. The membership of the American Psychological Association grew from 5391 in 1948 to 67,254 in 2010. Similarly, in 1945 the British Psychological Society's (BPS) Committee of Professional Psychologists – which included educational, clinical and other psychologists – had 77 members, while the figure for clinical psychologists alone is now over 10,000 (British Psychological Society, 2011; Hall, Lavender and Llewelyn, 2002) – this sharp growth can be seen in Figure 2.7.

The growth of clinical psychology has been hugely influenced by the socio-economic context in each country. Thus Hall (2007) notes that the founding of the UK's publicly-funded National Health Service in 1946 (in which most British clinical psychologists work) was a major influence on the development of the discipline. The adult mental health specialty has become a dominant force in the profession while, previously, most professional psychologists had worked primarily with children and families in child guidance clinics (Hall, 2007). In the US, the Veterans Administration and the United States Public Health Service provided a major boost to the training and employment of clinical psychologists both during and

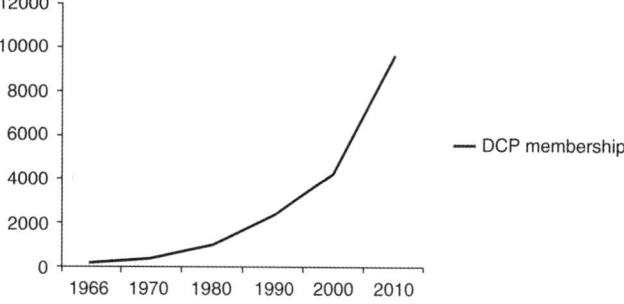

Figure 2.7 **The growth in the membership of the British Psychological Society's Division of Clinical Psychology (DCP) from its inception in 1966**

Source: **Hall et al. (2002) for 1945–2001 figures. British Psychological Society (2011) for 2010 figures.**

after the Second World War. Over time, clinical psychologists moved from conducting psychometric tests to aid psychiatric diagnosis to undertaking behaviour therapy and, subsequently, a much broader range of psychotherapy today, including cognitive behaviour therapy which is currently dominant in the discipline. British clinical psychologists largely remained dependent on psychiatry for referrals of patients for assessment and treatment, but with the publication of the Trethowan Report in 1977 it was able to accept referrals directly from General Practitioners, and so began to develop a more autonomous identity.

Of course, alongside the development of professional forms of help, there has been a steady growth over the last fifty years in the **self-help movement** (where people adopt coping strategies through their own reading or from learning from others with similar problems). Later in the chapter, and in Chapter 7, we will discuss the rise of self-organized groups of patients – the **service user/survivor movement**. However, it is worth noting here the tradition of self-help inaugurated by **Alcoholics Anonymous** (AA). AA was set up in the USA in 1935 by Bill Wilson and Dr Bob Smith who had both struggled to find ways of coping with their alcoholism. Influenced by others who had found support through religion and spirituality, they developed a self-help programme which was founded on showing empathy to their fellow alcoholics, encouraging them to see themselves as mentally ill rather than morally weak (the popular understanding at the time) and viewing themselves as in need of help from a higher power. By 1938 Wilson had codified the ideas of the movement into Twelve Steps – subsequent adaptations of the AA model to help people cope with other kinds of problem are, as a result called **Twelve Step programmes**, focusing on problems from narcotics to eating disorders. Although these organizations are founded on self-help, they often promote an illness model of distress and are therefore different from the activist groups described later and in Chapter 7, many of which are critical of biological psychiatry.

The process of de-institutionalization gathered pace in a number of countries over the next few decades. The total number of psychiatric beds in England and Wales has declined year on year: while in 1987–1988 it had stood at 67,122, in 2009–2010 the figure was 25,503 (Department of Health, 2010). Leff (2001) states that 'of the 130 psychiatric hospitals functioning in England and Wales in 1975, only 14 remain open, with fewer than 200 patients in each' (p. 381). In the USA the total number of psychiatric beds (in all types of organization) fell from 524,878 in 1970 to 211,199 in 2002, whilst the rate per 100,000 of the population dropped from 263.6 to 73.3 (Foley et al., 2006). Enoch Powell anticipated resistance to his plan to close the asylums but he underestimated how long the process would take.

The rate of decrease slowed in the 1990s, and in Figure 2.8 we can see how this policy has been followed in a number of European countries. In the UK many of the old asylums were sold to private residential developers – Friern Barnet hospital in London is now a residential development called Princess Park Manor, described on its website (www.princessparkmanor. net) as containing 'luxury apartments set within 30 acres of parkland'.

Advocates of de-institutionalization came from different ends of the political spectrum. In Italy, reform in the 1970s was led by the left-wing Italian psychiatrist Franco Basaglia (who we will discuss a little later), whilst in California it was supported by Reaganite Conservatives and, as we have seen, in the UK by the right-wing Enoch Powell (Scull, 2011). Since that time the political consensus has generally been in favour of de-institutionalization regardless of the political complexion of administrations (Scull, 2011).

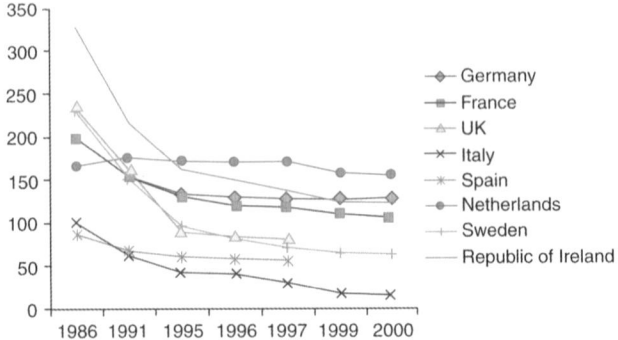

Figure 2.8 **The decline in psychiatric hospital beds in selected European countries**

Source: **Adapted from data provided in Knapp, McDaid, Mossialos and Thornicroft (2007). The figures are the number of beds per 100,000 of each country's population.**

Did community care 'fail'?

In the UK, as de-institutionalization progressed through the 1980s and 1990s, a number of media commentators began to argue that events such as homicides committed by people with psychiatric diagnoses showed that community care had failed (Rose, 1998) – a view which is not borne out by figures on homicide (see Chapter 8). This conclusion was endorsed by UK Health Secretary Frank Dobson in 1998 (Warden, 1998a). However, Thornicroft and Goldberg (1998) contend that such views are based on a number of myths and that community care was not adequately resourced. Indeed, the UK's National Director of Mental Health, psychiatrist Louis Appleby, noted that in the 1980s there had been 'a widespread belief that institutional care was expensive and that community care would be cheaper' (Appleby, 2007, p. 2). Laurance (2003a) suggests that one problem in the transition from institution-based to community-based services was that money was only freed up once the asylums had closed and been sold to developers, but this meant that there was not enough money to properly fund community mental health services. However, by the time they had been closed and sold off, lower property prices meant there was less money than envisaged and, moreover, the proceeds were often diverted elsewhere in the NHS. Thornicroft and Goldberg (1998) have argued that community care was 'only half-implemented: we should fully implement it before deciding whether it has failed or succeeded' (p. 1).

Before we leave the post-war period there are two significant topics to address, both of which touch on the legitimacy of psychiatry. As we saw earlier when we looked at the efforts of German psychiatrists at the end of the 19th and beginning of the 20th centuries, the systematization of diagnostic classifications has been seen as an important way for psychiatry to enhance its scientific legitimacy, and there were important developments related to this both in the US and internationally. However, within a decade of the publication of two significant diagnostic manuals, psychiatry was under attack from a range of critics, many from within its own ranks.

Attempts to systematize diagnosis

Modern **diagnostic categorizations** (definitions of different categories of distress with lists of indicative symptoms) did not emerge until the post-war period when international organizations began to be established; the World Health Organization took over the publication of the sixth edition of the *International Classification of Disease* (the **ICD**) in 1949. The American Psychiatric Association published the first edition of the *Diagnostic and Statistical Manual of Mental Disorders* (the **DSM**) in 1952. The diagnostic categories in the DSM were shaped by the psychoanalytic traditions which were dominant in American psychiatry at the time. As we saw in Chapter 1, these manuals are revised regularly – ICD-11 is to be presented to the World Health Assembly in 2015 whilst DSM-5 is reported to be due in 2013. Critics argue that psychiatric diagnostic categories change because of social and cultural changes over time. A particularly shocking example of how the social context can shape diagnostic formulations was seen earlier in Box 2.3, although that represents just one physician's opinion and, because there were no nationally or internationally agreed classificatory schemes, was not in wide use.

A more recent example of a change in diagnostic categories can be seen in the way in which psychiatry has viewed **homosexuality** (sexual attraction to one's own gender). In the first edition of the DSM the category of 'sexual deviation' was included, which was the diagnosis then used for homosexuality. By the second edition of the DSM in 1968 homosexuality was the first of 10 sexual deviations listed. The DSM drew on psychoanalytic notions, and, traditionally, psychoanalysis has viewed homosexuality as a mental disorder. Not only was homosexuality viewed as deviant but treatments were given to 'correct' sexual orientation. Many gay men at this time were subjected to sexual aversion therapy using electric shocks (Smith, Bartlett & King, 2004).

Following the Stonewall riots in New York in 1969, when lesbians, gay men, transvestites, transsexuals and others protested against police brutality, the gay liberation movement became increasingly militant about securing its members' civil rights. Following several protests at medical and psychiatric conferences in the 1960s and 1970s there was ongoing debate about viewing homosexuality as a mental disorder. This matched the concerns of some psychiatrists who wanted to rid the DSM of psychoanalytic notions considered to be unscientific (Kutchins & Kirk, 1999) and, in 1973, the Board of Trustees voted to remove homosexuality *per se* from the DSM, although a related category ('ego-dystonic homosexuality' or unhappiness with one's sexuality) was retained (Wilson, 1993). The removal of homosexuality as a disorder in its own right survived an attempt to overturn it in an American Psychiatric Association referendum in 1974 and, after further behind-the-scenes debate in the late 1980s, ego-dystonic homosexuality was quietly dropped with the publication of DSM-III-R in 1987.

Another example of a significant change in DSM diagnosis was the introduction in 1980 in DSM-III of **post-traumatic stress disorder** (in which a person suffers ongoing distress as a result of a traumatic event: for example, experiencing flashbacks of the event and avoiding situations which are reminiscent of it). It is widely accepted that this introduction was prompted by a wish to validate the experiences of US veterans of the Vietnam war.

Of course, the dispute over the classification of homosexuality was not the first time that psychiatry had received criticism. As we saw at the start of the chapter, patients and their friends and relatives have often been critical of the practices of

Many well-known people have experienced serious distress. Winston Churchill – British Prime Minister from 1940–1945 and 1951–1955 – suffered from bouts of depression which he referred to as his 'black dog' (Storr, 1989). In 2006 the British mental health charity Rethink Mental Illness unveiled this statue of Churchill in a straitjacket with the slogan 'judge me for the war effort, not because I had manic depression'. They argued that the statue was 'a celebration of the life of a man who triumphed over mental health problems' (Rethink Mental Illness, 2006)

psychiatry, though this was often focused on alleged misdiagnosis or abusive treatment. However, at the beginning of the 1960s a number of psychiatrists led the charge, challenging fundamental tenets of their discipline.

Anti-psychiatry: five books which challenged psychiatry

The years 1960 to 1961 saw five authors in four countries publish books which were to have a massive impact on attitudes to psychiatry in the subsequent decade.

In the UK, in 1960, the Scottish psychiatrist R. D. Laing published *The Divided Self* (Laing, 1960); an attempt, based on clinical case studies, to understand the lifeworld of people with a diagnosis of schizophrenia. Laing's work developed through the decade and was extremely influential. Over time he became more critical of psychiatry, arguing that it tended to individualize what were actually problems of living – problems rooted in relationships (e.g. in families) and in questions about the meaning of life. It was a largely sociogenic model, influenced by theories of family functioning (discussed earlier) which had begun circulating in the 1950s. However, Laing blended this with elements of Jean-Paul Sartre's **existentialist philosophy** (the idea that life is essentially meaningless and that we need to strive to create meaning in our own lives). Moreover, this was accompanied by a moral and political critique, asserting that psychiatry acted as an agent of social control. Over time, Laing increasingly argued that traditional psychiatry was ill-equipped to address these issues because of the power relationship between psychiatrist and patient and because he thought madness should be seen as a journey – at times a distressing journey – full of meaning, rather than an illness to be cured. Laing continued to publish works in the 1960s, co-founding the Philadelphia Association in 1965. One of the aims of the Association was to develop therapeutic communities as alternatives to traditional psychiatric in-patient care. The most famous was **Kingsley Hall** in the East End of London but it ran for only five years from 1965 to 1970. Laing's work became more mystical in focus and there were differences of emphasis between the various groups influenced by him. His work continues to be influential in that many contemporary psychological theories see psychotic experiences as having some meaning and as related in some ways to their life experiences and relationships. However, critics charge that Laing's work blamed families and relatives for what they saw as a biologically-caused illness.

In 1961, the Hungarian–American psychiatrist Thomas Szasz (pronounced Sahss) published *The Myth of Mental Illness: Foundations of a Theory of Personal Conduct*, in which he argued that physical medicine was scientific, being based on pathology for which there was physical evidence, whereas in psychiatry, judgements were more subjective and thus subject to social influence. Mental illness was simply a reified metaphor which was useful in warranting **coercive treatment**. He saw psychotherapy (he trained as a psychoanalyst) as justifiable so long as it was voluntary and consenting, and drew comparisons between psychiatric ideas and those of closed systems with their own unchallengeable assumptions, such as the Spanish Inquisition. Szasz's work continues to be influential in its focus on individual human rights, the need to limit the State's influence and the importance of consensual as opposed to compulsory treatment. Dying only in 2012, he outlived many of his contemporary critics.

Also in 1961 and also in the USA, the sociologist Erving Goffman published *Asylums: Essays on the Social Situation of Mental Patients and Other Inmates* (Goffman, 1961) based on participant observation he conducted at St Elizabeth's Hospital in Washington DC, a federal institution for over 7000 people. In *Asylums*, Goffman described these hospitals as 'total institutions' which totally governed the life of the patient. He traced the progress of the patient through the hospital, detailing significant aspects of this 'moral career'. He argued for the importance of context in shaping judgements of what was considered to be mentally ill conduct. Soon after *Asylums* was published, Ken Kesey's *One Flew Over the Cuckoo's Nest* appeared – a novel which became a stage play starring Kirk Douglas and, in 1975, a film starring Jack Nicholson which scooped five Oscars. Goffman's work was followed by the development of **labelling theory** – the notion that mental illness was actually the end result of a series of social processes whereby 'abnormal' behaviour was subtly reinforced (Scheff, 1966; Lemert, 1967). In the 1970s this work received some empirical support from the work of psychologist David Rosenhan (1973) who demonstrated that normal behaviours by people not in distress were seen as symptoms of mental illness

simply because a person was engaging with them whilst a patient of a psychiatric ward.

In France, in 1961, the French philosopher and historian Michel Foucault published his history of madness, *Folie et Déraison: Histoire de la Folie à l'Âge Classique (Madness and Unreason: A History of Madness in the Classical Age)*. A much truncated version was translated into English and published in 1965 as *Madness and Civilisation* (the full English translation was not published until 2009 when it appeared as the *History of Madness*, Foucault, 2009) and it began to influence thought in the UK, the USA and elsewhere. Foucault argued both that conceptions of madness were related to attempts to separate and confine groups of undesirables, and that the supposedly more humane moral treatments of the 18th century were no less repressive than earlier times – they simply replaced external repression with a more insidious control of people's minds. This had considerable influence as it challenged the traditional history of psychiatry as one of a progressive emergence from ignorance to enlightened values.

In Algeria, Northern Africa, 1961 also saw the publication of Frantz Fanon's *The Wretched of the Earth* (Fanon, 1963), a damning critique of the psychological effects of colonization and an exploration of the torture of Algerians by the French armed forces. Fanon was a black psychiatrist inspired by revolutionary struggles for independence, particularly in Algeria where he practised and where there were groups fighting the French colonial forces for independence, a fight that was eventually won in 1962. He pioneered a form of **socio-therapy**, connecting his patients' distress with their cultural backgrounds. Fanon's work influenced the work of black activists such as Malcolm X in the USA. Within the field of mental health, Fanon's work is relevant as it emphasizes not only the importance of culture in how we experience ourselves (see Chapter 3) but also how power exerts an effect on how we define our identities and how we are defined by others.

None of these authors defined themselves as anti-psychiatrists (Roberts & Itten, 2006) – the term anti-psychiatry was used by David Cooper, a South African psychiatrist, in his book *Psychiatry and Anti-Psychiatry* (Cooper, 1967). The term 'antipsychiatrie' was originally coined in 1908 by the German psychiatrist Bernhard Beyer (Szasz, 2009), though he intended it as a term of abuse to stigmatize criticism of psychiatry. The use of 'anti-psychiatry' to refer to critics of psychiatry in the 1960s implies that they were a homogenous group. However, as we noted in Chapter 1, there were often sharp differences among those labelled as anti-psychiatrists, particularly on political grounds: Szasz, as a libertarian on the right, considered the anti-psychiatrists 'self-declared socialists, Communists, or at least anti-Capitalists and collectivists' (Szasz, 1976b, p. 6). However, since the term is in common usage and is widely understood we will use it here.

There is a tendency in many textbooks to see challenges to psychiatry as very much a 1960s phenomenon, with only the work of Laing and Szasz being mentioned. Their ideas are often presented as outdated: overturned by developments in biological psychiatry. However, challenges to psychiatry have continued since that time both from within the 'psy' disciplines, but also from the service user/survivor movement. In the next section we will discuss these two traditions – Figure 2.9 outlines historical developments in the latter part of the 20th and the start of the 21st century.

Figure 2.9 **Timeline 1971–2007**

Year	Key events
1971	The Mental Patients' Liberation project founded in New York City The Mental Patient's Liberation Front founded in Boston, Massachusetts
1972	Mental Patients Union founded in London
1973	Franco Basaglia co-founds *Psichiatrica Democratica* American Psychiatric Association's Board of Trustees votes to remove homosexuality from the DSM
1975	Aaron Beck publishes *Cognitive Therapy and the Emotional Disorders* Film of *One Flew over the Cuckoo's Nest* released and wins five Oscars
1976	Anthony Clare publishes *Psychiatry in Dissent*
1977	The Trethowan Report is published by the UK Department of Health & Social Security – clinical psychology services are no longer dependent on psychiatrists for referrals of patients and can now receive them directly from General Practitioners UK Attorney General undertakes to never again use the interrogation techniques used in Northern Ireland
1978	Law 180 introduced in Italy following the campaign by *Psichiatrica Democratica* In the USA Judi Chamberlin publishes *On Our Own: Patient-Controlled Alternatives to the Mental Health System*
1979	Andrew Scull publishes *Museums of Madness*
1982	Peter Sedgwick publishes *Psychopolitics*
1983	Soviet Union forced to withdraw from the World Psychiatric Association because of psychiatric abuse against dissidents British Network for Alternatives to Psychiatry founded A new Mental Health Act enacted
1985	National Alliance of Mental Patients founded in the US Campaign against Psychiatric Oppression founded in the UK
1986	Martin Roth and Jerome Kroll publish *The Reality of Mental Illness* Survivors Speak Out founded in the UK First issue of *Asylum: A Magazine for Democratic Psychiatry* published in Sheffield
1987	*Stichting Weerklank (Foundation Resonance* – an organization for voice hearers) founded in the Netherlands Nottingham Advocacy Group established Roy Porter publishes *A Social History of Madness: Stories of the Insane*
1988	Hearing Voices Network established in the UK
1989	Dutch psychiatrist Marius Romme and science journalist Sandra Escher publish article on voice hearing in *Schizophrenia Bulletin*
1989	Lucy Johnstone publishes *Users and Abusers of Psychiatry: A Critical Look at Traditional Psychiatric Practice*
1990	President George H. W. Bush announces that the 1990s will be the 'decade of the brain' Richard Bentall publishes *Reconstructing Schizophrenia* Mary Boyle publishes *Schizophrenia: A Scientific Delusion?* First national hearing voices conference held in Manchester
1991	Cold War ends American psychiatrist Peter Breggin publishes *Toxic Psychiatry*
1994	End of apartheid in South Africa
2001	British critical psychiatrists Patrick Bracken and Philip Thomas publish article on *Postpsychiatry* in the *British Medical Journal*
2007	A new Mental Health Act in England and Wales

1970–present: new challenges to psychiatry from within and the rise of the service user/survivor movement

Challenges to psychiatry from within since the 1960s

In Italy, in 1973, the psychiatrist Franco Basaglia co-founded an organization called *Psichiatrica Democratica* (Democratic Psychiatry) which led to a restructuring of mental health services in Trieste. The asylum was closed down, with long-stay residents moving to group apartments and a network of 24-hour mental health centres was set up in the community. A nationwide campaign against asylums led to legislation in 1978 (law 180) and 1979 that effectively abolished new admissions to the asylums; instead, people with acute problems were to go to casualty services in general hospitals.

However, the challenge of the anti-psychiatrists was met by a response from within mainstream psychiatry. In the

UK, psychiatrist Anthony Clare responded in his *Psychiatry in Dissent* (Clare, 1976), adopting a pragmatic **biomedical** approach and arguing that accurate psychiatric diagnosis was possible and that many of the points made by the anti-psychiatrists were naïve and dangerous. Roth and Kroll's (1986) *The Reality of Mental Illness* (the title neatly mirroring Szasz's *Myth of Mental Illness*) adopted a similar approach, arguing that there was little evidence to support the claims of the anti-psychiatrists and that the future lay in further biological and genetic research. The active phase of anti-psychiatry had led to the consideration of alternatives to a somatic and biomedical model of distress (social, psychological, spiritual, political etc.). However, the resurgence of the biomedical model in the 1970s and 1980s marked a return, once again, to a somatic model of distress, symbolized by President George H. W. Bush's 1990 proclamation of the 'decade of the brain' to 'enhance public awareness of the benefits to be derived from brain research'. Indeed, this decade subsequently saw a rise of 70.1% in the number of prescriptions of psychiatric drugs (Rose, 2004).

Anti-psychiatry largely died as an active force in the 1970s due to the retirement of many of the key figures as well as the rise of community care, which was a challenge to the Therapeutic Community movement (Coppock & Hopton, 2000). The change in political climate was also a factor with the election of politicians, such as Margaret Thatcher in the UK in 1979 and Ronald Reagan in the USA in 1981, who had liberal economic but socially conservative policies.

However, in the 1980s and 1990s further challenges were made. For example, the American psychiatrist Peter Breggin published *Toxic Psychiatry* (Breggin, 1991), a damning and influential critique of physical interventions in psychiatry. In Holland, the Dutch social psychiatrist Marius Romme had been challenged by his patient Patsy Hage who **heard voices** (or 'auditory hallucinations') to accept that explanations other than biomedical ones were equally valid. Following a discussion on a Dutch TV show, Romme wrote with science journalist Sandra Escher about alternative ways of viewing the voice-hearing experience (Romme & Escher, 1989, 1993) and co-founded Foundation Resonance – an organization to provide information and a support network for self-help groups. There will be more discussion of this approach to voice-hearing in Chapter 7.

In the UK, much of this criticism came from clinical psychologists. Lucy Johnstone (1989, 2000) drew on case histories and empirical evidence to argue against simplistic biomedical approaches to emotional distress, which she suggested were often inhumane in practice. Richard Bentall (who wrote the foreword for this book and co-authored Chapter 11) and his colleagues (Bentall, 1990a; Bentall, Jackson & Pilgrim, 1988) argued that the empirical evidence for the concept of schizophrenia was weak because it was too broad a concept, and that more fruitful research would be conducted by focusing on symptoms. He also collaborated with the late American psychiatrist Loren Mosher and clinical psychologist John Read in editing a collection of critiques and alternative forms of intervention for those with a diagnosis of schizophrenia (Read, Mosher & Bentall, 2004). Mary Boyle (1990, 2002), whose work we examined earlier, argued that the assumptions underlying the DSM and schizophrenia in particular were deeply problematic and that there was a need for a new paradigm. By the end of the decade, clinical psychologists Craig Newnes, Guy Holmes and Cailzie Dunn (1999, 2001) had edited two collections which included contributions not just from psychologists and psychiatrists but from service users too.

These critics avoided the polemic and mystical obscurantism of some anti-psychiatric writings and by the end of the 1990s were joined by critical psychiatrists such as Patrick Bracken and Philip Thomas. Since, they argued, both traditional psychiatry and antipsychiatry had been 'united by the assumption that there could be a correct way to understand madness' (2001, p. 727), they suggested there was a need for what they termed **postpsychiatry**. This was not a new theory or therapy but, rather, a call to open up spaces 'in which other perspectives can assume a validity previously denied them' (2001, p. 727): in particular, the voices of service users. Other critical psychiatrists were represented by Joanna Moncrieff who critically examined the evidence base of psychiatric medication (2008) and by an edited collection by Duncan Double (2006).

We close the chapter by returning to the perspective of mental health service users and survivors, examining the more recent history of the modern service user/survivor movement. Some psychiatric commentators (e.g. Rissmiller & Rissmiller, 2006) suggest that the modern survivor movement has its origins in the anti-psychiatry movement of the 1960s, but survivor historians argue that this is not the case (Oaks, 2006; Survivors History Group, 2011). The British survivor activist, writer and poet Peter Campbell states that, in his opinion, 'anti-psychiatry and democratic psychiatry were very much professionally-led enterprises' (Survivors History Group, 2011, p. 13).

Challenges to psychiatry from without since the 1960s: the rise of the psychiatric survivor movement

As we saw right at the start of the chapter, the account of those in distress provides a different perspective from that of those ministering to them. Dain (1989) and Chamberlin (1990) have both provided histories of patients protesting against their treatment, as does Peter Campbell in Chapter 7. Judi Chamberlin was herself an ex-patient, Chamberlin (1990) gives an account of how, in 1868, Elizabeth Packard began writing a number of books and pamphlets about how her husband had forcibly committed her to the Jacksonville (Illinois) insane Asylum. Chamberlin's importance as a campaigner can be seen in the fact that, when she died in 2010, the *New York Times* carried an obituary.

The rise of the 'ex-patients movement' in the USA

The 1960s had seen changes in the forms of political struggles. The civil rights movement in the US had seen the development of Black Power, the movement expressing the desire of black Americans for self-determination rather than integration into white society. A similar change occurred within the women's movement: in a development known as second wave feminism, many feminists in the late 1960s and early 1970s argued that they did not just want to end formal inequalities but to challenge informal forms of inequality and gender stereotyping. These broader currents led to a more assertive civil rights focus amongst groups of psychiatric patients. As a result many patients organized their own groups and campaigns.

Chamberlin (1990) traces the roots of the ex-patients movement to the black, women's and gay liberation movements of the 1960s and 1970s. In particular she notes the importance of consciousness-raising activities and the wish, reminiscent of the separatist strategies of other movements such as Black Power, of many members of these groups to meet without mental health professionals. Chamberlin describes some of the first developments in this period:

> Among the earliest groups were the Insane Liberation Front in Portland, Oregon (founded in 1970), the Mental Patients' Liberation project in New York City, The Mental Patient's Liberation Front in Boston (both founded in 1971), and the Network Against Psychiatric Assault in San Francisco (founded in 1972).
>
> (1990, pp. 326–7)

A significant point was reached in 1978 with the publication of Judi Chamberlin's (1978) *On Our Own: Patient-Controlled Alternatives to the Mental Health System*.

Chamberlin (1990) describes how, in the early years of the movement, communication and organization were a challenge because of difficulties in obtaining funding. However, when survivors began meeting at the annual Conference on Human Rights and Psychiatric Oppression (first meeting in 1973), and communicating first person accounts, news, creative writing and political theorizing via *Madness Network News* (1972–86, based in San Francisco), the movement began to grow. The tenth conference, in Toronto, formulated a Statement of 30 Principles. McLean (1995) identifies some of the key values of the survivor movement in the US at that time.

The National Alliance of Mental Patients (now the National Association of Psychiatric Survivors) was set up in 1985 and 'strongly advocated for an end to compulsory psychiatric treatment, the development of user-run alternatives and the making of links with the wider disability movement' (www.mindfreedom.org/mfi-faq/intro-FAQs).

In 1986 a newsletter called *Dendron* was first published in Oregon. In 1990 newsletter readers protested at the American Psychiatric Association annual meeting in New York City and an alliance of 13 different groups was formed with the name Support Coalition International. In 2005 it changed its name to MindFreedom International.

Chamberlin (1990) reports on significant successes by the American ex-patients movement in relation to policy and the law, such as the securing, via lawsuits, of limited rights to refuse treatment, and an acknowledgement in the 1978 report of the President's Commission on Mental Health of the emergence of self-help groups across the USA. The linking of psychiatric ex-patients with the broader disability movement resulted in people with 'psychiatric disabilities' being included in the 1990 Americans with Disabilities Act which, in turn, influenced public policy in other countries, such as the UK's 1995 Disability Discrimination Act.

Chamberlin warned of the danger of a 'reformist "consumerism"' which fails to recognize the power imbalance in psychiatric treatment and which simply seeks small changes in the psychiatric system. In contrast, she argued for the 'liberation' of mental patients. However, she noted variation within the ex-patients movement:

> There are groups whose members promote the illness metaphor tag, National Depressive and Manic-Depressive Association; groups whose members promote self-help in conjunction with treatment for illness (e.g., Recovery, Inc.); groups whose members see themselves as consumers (e.g, the National Mental Health Consumers' Association); and groups whose members see themselves as liberationists (e.g. National Association of Psychiatric Survivors).
>
> (1990, p. 334)

However, Chamberlin recognized that one of the most important challenges was to reach the vast majority of psychiatric ex-patients who did not belong to an organized group.

The history of the service user movement in the UK

Several accounts have been given of the history of the British service user movement (e.g. Campbell, 1996; Crossley, 2005; Rogers & Pilgrim, 1991). Campbell begins his account in 1985 though he acknowledges there were earlier groups, such as the British Network for Alternatives to Psychiatry. However, a number of commentators point to the importance of the Mental Patients Union, so we will start our story there.

Unite and fight: patients get organized

Spandler (2006) describes how, in 1971, the short-lived Scottish Union of Mental Patients was formed by Tom Ritchie and Robin Farquason and other patients at Hartwood Hospital. In 1972, following the threatened closure of the Paddington Day Hospital, a therapeutic community in London, patients and staff formed a protest group to fight the proposals. From this protest, notes Spandler (2006), came the establishment of the **Mental Patients Union** (MPU), in which some members of the Scottish group were apparently involved. The process began in December 1972 with the publication of a pamphlet, *The Need for a Mental Patients Union: Some proposals*. The patients, staff and political activists involved drew inspiration from wider political debates, so the pamphlet argued that 'psychiatry is one of the most subtle methods of repression in advanced Capitalist society' (Roberts, 2008).[2] On its front cover it included picture of a fish caught on a hook (see over page) together with an adapted extract from the US psychiatrist and psychoanalyst Karl Menninger:

> An individual having unusual difficulties in coping with his environment struggles and kicks up the dust, as it were. I have used the figure of a fish caught on a hook: his gyrations must look peculiar to other fish that don't understand the circumstances; but his splashes are not his affliction, they are his effort to get rid of his affliction and as every fisherman knows these efforts may succeed.
>
> Spandler (2006, p. 55)

A subsequent meeting at Paddington Day Hospital in 1973 attracted 150 people, among them 100 patients and ex-patients and the meeting agreed that full membership of the union would be restricted to patients and ex-patients (Roberts, 2008). Spandler describes the activities of the MPU which included:

> Setting up its own headquarters and developing 'crash houses' for people to stay when in crisis to avoid hospitalization and psychiatric intervention. In addition, the MPU provided an advice and information service; advocated on behalf of patients in hospital; provided advice and representation at Mental Health Tribunals; and held

---

2 studymore.org.uk/mpu.htm

MPU meetings on psychiatric wards. They also produced regular newsletters and information regarding patients' legal rights and the side effects of psychiatric drugs and produced a comprehensive 'Declaration of Intent' and 'Drugs Charter'.

Spandler (2006, pp. 59–60)

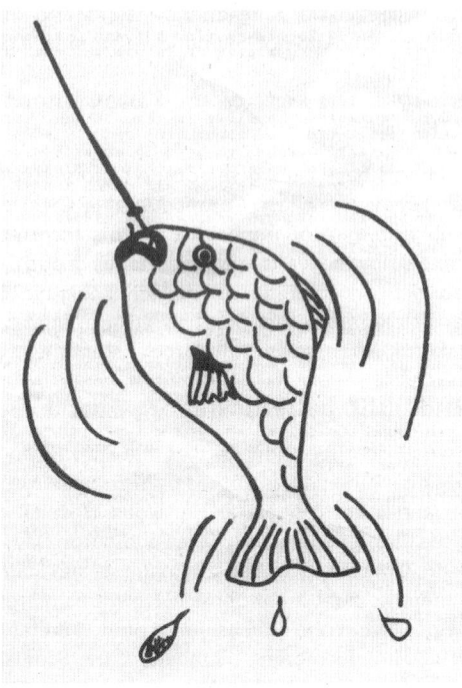

The picture of a fish on a hook drawn by Brian Douieb for the cover of the pamphlet 'The need for a mental patients' union: some proposals', written and distributed early in 1973

The MPU is regarded as the first overtly politicized group in the UK and it made links with other groups, including the SPK (see Box 2.6); a group of activists brought back an SPK pamphlet and translated it into English (Spandler, 2006).

The spider's web logo for the MPU alluded to how mental patients, like all human beings, were caught up in a web of psychiatry and social control

The MPU gave inspiration to groups such as Community Organization for Psychiatric Emergencies, founded in 1973, and led, in 1985, to the founding of the Campaign against Psychiatric Oppression: an explicitly anti-professional group which advocated avoiding contact with statutory services (Coppock & Hopton, 2000).

The mid-1980s saw a unique collaboration between a psychiatrist and patients. In Sheffield in 1986, the psychiatrist Alec Jenner, Lin Bigwood (a nurse), Phil Virden and a group of patients began to produce their own magazine, *Asylum: A Magazine for Democratic Psychiatry*. Early issues covered the *Psichiatrica Democratica* reforms in Trieste and it is still in existence at the time of writing (www.asylumonline.net).

Campbell (1996) describes how two conferences in 1985, an international conference of psychiatric survivors in Brighton in the summer and the national MIND conference in the autumn, brought service users to the fore. In 1986 both the Nottingham Advocacy Group and Survivors Speak Out were set up. Writing in 1996, Campbell notes with interest the considerable progress made:

> In ten years we have gone from a situation where less than a dozen independent user/survivor-led groups existed to a position (1995) where there are probably over 350 local, regional and national groups.

Campbell (1996, p. 219)

Campbell notes the influence of developments in the USA and elsewhere, particularly Holland, on the British service user movement (e.g. on the setting up of Patients' Councils). However, like Chamberlin, he debates what the aims of the service user should be: 'to improve mental health services, or to transform the position of mad persons in society?' (p. 222). He acknowledges that acceptance into the policy-making machinery has been surprisingly quick but strikes a note of caution in asking 'whether involvement in planning and consultative mechanisms really works' (p. 224) –Peter Campbell's views are examined at greater length in Chapter 7.

Crossley (2005) argues that the Mental Health Service User Movement needs to be understood as a social movement similar to other groups campaigning for rights or on other political issues such as the environment. However, like similar groups, the service user/survivor movement is not without threat. In the USA, for example, Rissmiller and Rissmiller (2006) end an article on the survivor movement by describing them as 'extremist' and 'having little scientific foundation' (p. 866). Similarly, the American psychiatrist Sally Satel, a fellow of the conservative think tank the American Enterprise Institute for Public Policy Research, has criticized the influence of what she sees as 'political correctness' in medicine (Satel, 2001). In one chapter she and her co-author assert that psychiatric survivor groups continually try to restrict the work of psychiatrists (Satel & Redding, 2005).

Many abnormal psychology textbooks neglect the influence of the service user and survivor movement, but it is important in influencing policy and practice; the issues raised by the movement are considered in more detail in Chapter 7.

The decades since the 1960s have seen further waves of legislation, mainly focused on the regulation of compulsory treatment but also addressing discrimination, as shown in Table 2.3.

BOX 2.6

'Madmen to arms!' – the Heidelberg socialist patients' collective

Helen Spandler (1992, 2006), Parker, Georgaca, Harper, McLaughlin and Stowell-Smith (1995) and Aust (2008) describe how, during the late 1960s, the West German psychiatrist Wolfgang Huber had begun politically-informed group-work sessions at a Day Hospital in the Psychiatric and Neurological University Hospital in Heidelberg. However, after Huber was sacked there were protests: patients (many of them students in group therapy with Huber) held a 'general assembly' to voice their opposition to Huber's dismissal. Subsequent protests included a hunger strike, patient teach-ins, occupations of offices and an occupation of the clinic by Huber and some of the patients. There was a continual struggle between the doctor and patients who wanted a new approach, including accommodation and other resources, and the University hospital hierarchy who resisted such a move. Out of these protests the *Sozialistisches Patientenkollektiv* (the **Socialist Patients' Collective:** SPK) was born in 1970.

The SPK 'argued that mental and physical illness was a revolt against an insane world of capitalism, alienation, pollution and repressive sexual morals' (Parker et al., 1995, p. 120). A SPK document entitled 'Patients' Info No. 1' stated 'the system has made us sick, let us give the death blow to the sick system!' (Aust, 2008, p. 110). The SPK aimed, in the titles of two of its pamphlets, *To make an army out of an illness* and to *Turn illness into a weapon*. The SPK developed methods of consciousness-raising: 'Individual Agitation, Group Agitation, Study Groups and Multifocus Expansion' (Spandler, 1992, p. 8). It saw mental illness as contradictory in nature in that it represented the results of a repressive society but, at the same time, carried the potential of a 'life affirming protest against capital' (Spandler, 1992, p. 10).

In contrast to anti-psychiatrists such as Laing, who seemed to think the response to symptoms was to voyage inside oneself, the SPK argued for the need to become aware of one's social conditions in a collective context.

Spandler (2006) suggests that the SPK's direct action tactics reflected the political philosophies of the Red Army Faction terrorist group (RAF; also known as the Baader Meinhof Group) – indeed, Huber's rallying cry was reportedly 'madmen to arms!' (Aust, 2008, p. 113). However, facing opposition from student groups, university administrators and the police, it disbanded in 1971. Subsequently, in the politically febrile atmosphere of early 1970s West Germany, a few former SPK members – about a dozen (out of approximately 300 members) – went on to become a large part of the so-called 'second generation' of the RAF after its founding members were arrested and imprisoned, and several ex-members of the SPK were later sent to prison on terrorism charges (Aust, 2008).

Table 2.3 **Selected UK mental health legislation 1983–2007.**

Year	Act of Parliament	Key provisions
1983	Mental Health Act (England and Wales)	Established a Mental Health Act Commission to oversee the treatment of patients subject to detention. Introduced controls over certain types of treatments used in hospitals, such as brain surgery, electro-convulsive therapy and mood-altering drugs. It required after-care provision for some ex-patients. Four categories of disorder were introduced: two referring to intellectual disability ('mental impairment' and 'severe mental impairment'); psychopathic disorder (a legal term referring to people whose conduct was 'abnormally aggressive' or 'seriously irresponsible' due to a disorder of some kind); and mental illness (which was undefined).
1984	Mental Health (Scotland) Act	Introduced principles similar to those of the 1983 English and Welsh Act into Scottish law.
1986	Mental Health (Northern Ireland) Order	Introduced principles similar to those of the 1983 English and Welsh Act into Northern Ireland.
1995	Mental Health (Patients in the Community) Act	Introduced new powers of supervision of some patients following discharge from hospital.
1995	Disability Discrimination Act	Made it illegal to discriminate against people on grounds of disability in relation to employment, receipt of services etc. A higher threshold was required for those considered to have mental health problems – these had to be 'clinically well-recognised'.
2003	Mental Health (Care and Treatment) (Scotland) Act	Introduced compulsory community treatment into Scotland. Similar to the 2007 English and Welsh Act, although there is a higher threshold in that evidence that a person's judgement is impaired by mental disorder is required.
2004	Mental Health (Amendment) (Northern Ireland) Order	Amended the 1986 Order, revising the criteria considered by Mental Health Review Tribunals.
2005	Disability Discrimination Act	Updated the 1995 Act and removed the higher threshold for disability due to mental health.
2007	Mental Health Act	Amended the 1983 Mental Health Act for England and Wales. Introduced Supervised Community Treatment (i.e. compulsory treatment in the community) and expanded the range of disciplines which could take on specific roles under the Act (see Chapter 8).

Chapter summary

Over the course of this chapter we have attempted to chart some of the changes in how we conceive of, and respond to, distress and behaviour that may worry or disturb others. Our aim was to set the topics covered in the rest of the book in a historical context. A key theme has been the way in which understandings of distress are contested. We think that a knowledge of the historical context within which debates emerged is helpful in understanding modern debates about, say, the effectiveness of medication or psychotherapy. Another key theme has been the ethical context of the interventions we develop to help those in distress. Although we no longer carry out thousands of leucotomies, modern interventions come with a number of ethical dilemmas: we explore these in further detail in Chapter 8, where we discuss a range of interventions for distress influenced by different causal models: somatogenic (medication); psychogenic (psychological therapies); and sociogenic (community psychology), as well as compulsory treatment and ECT.

Versions of the somatogenic model have dominated over the last two thousand years or so and in this chapter we have charted their rise and fall over time. In Chapter 4, where we examine the biological context of distress, we will see how modern debates about mind–body dualism are rooted in the debates we have discussed here. Moreover, we saw how new technologies such as human dissection led to new ways of seeing the body and the brain. In Chapter 4 we will see how that pattern has continued with the introduction of new machines which can scan the brain.

In Chapter 5 we discuss psychiatric diagnosis. The origins of debates about diagnosis can be seen in the different attempts to settle on classificatory schemes at the end of the 19th century and, again, in the middle of the 20th century. Moreover, those debates have also been influenced by challenges to the legitimacy of psychiatry from the anti-psychiatrists of the 1960s and other professionals from the 1970s to the present day.

We began and ended this chapter by discussing the perspective of those in distress on both their distress itself and the treatments they have received. In Chapter 7 we explore this in greater depth, including the development of self-help methods by the Hearing Voices movement which have clearly built on the work done by early service users and survivors such as the late Judi Chamberlin and others.

In Chapter 6 we discuss different causal models of distress. In the present chapter we have seen how psychogenic, somatogenic and sociogenic models have vied with each other for dominance over time. We have suggested that traces of earlier models (such as the humoral model of distress) can be seen in more modern times in the idea that the cause of depression is a 'chemical imbalance'. Moreover, we have seen how different professional disciplines, institutions and groups have privileged one or other of these models at various times. As we noted at the start of the chapter, our current way of seeing distress conceptualizes it as an issue of health. However, as we saw in Chapter 1, it seems that, despite this, ordinary people still draw on a variety of explanatory models. The causal models we discuss in Chapter 6 are also tied to different models of the mind (or soul, psyche or self) and in Table 2.4 we have summarized some of these different models. It is possible to see both continuities and discontinuities in how we have come to understand ourselves. In this chapter we have touched on how the way in which we understand distress is influenced not only by history but culture. However, as we noted at the beginning of the chapter, we have mainly focused on Europe and North America so, in the next chapter (Chapter 3), we examine the influence of culture in more detail.

Table 2.4 **Contrasting tripartite models of the self**

Egyptian	Platonic	Islamic	Freudian	Cognitive behavioural
Khat (the body)	appetitive (base desires)	the Qalb (inner self)	Id (basic drive towards pleasure)	Behaviour
Ka (one's guardian spirit guide through life)	spirited (desire for honour or victory)	the Nafs Amara (basic drives)	Ego (negotiates with others' needs)	Affect (i.e. emotion)
Ba (one's guide in the after life).	Rational (intellect)	the Aql (intellect)	Super-ego (moral constraints on action)	Cognition (i.e. thought)

End of chapter questions

1 What different ways of understanding distress have there been and why is it currently seen as an issue of health?
2 To what extent has the dominance of particular models been a result of struggles between different institutions and professional groups?
3 To what extent are modern debates about the relationship between biology and the social environment related to earlier debates between competing kinds of causal explanations such as somatogenesis, psychogenesis and sociogenesis?

Find out more

1 www.studymore.org.uk/mhhtim.htm
A very informative and detailed website about key historical events in the history of mental health.

2 Porter, R. (2002). *Madness: A Brief History*. Oxford: Oxford University Press.
A short introductory account by a social and medical historian.

3 Scull, A. (2011). *Madness: A Very Short Introduction*. Oxford: Oxford University Press.
Another short account, adopting a sociological approach to history.

4 Hornstein, G. A. (2009). *Agnes's Jacket: A Psychologist's Search for the Meanings of Madness*. UK edition. Ross-on-Wye: PCCS Books.
An engaging account of an American psychologist's encounter with first person accounts of madness, setting some of the themes in the context of contemporary debates, especially the service user/survivor movement.

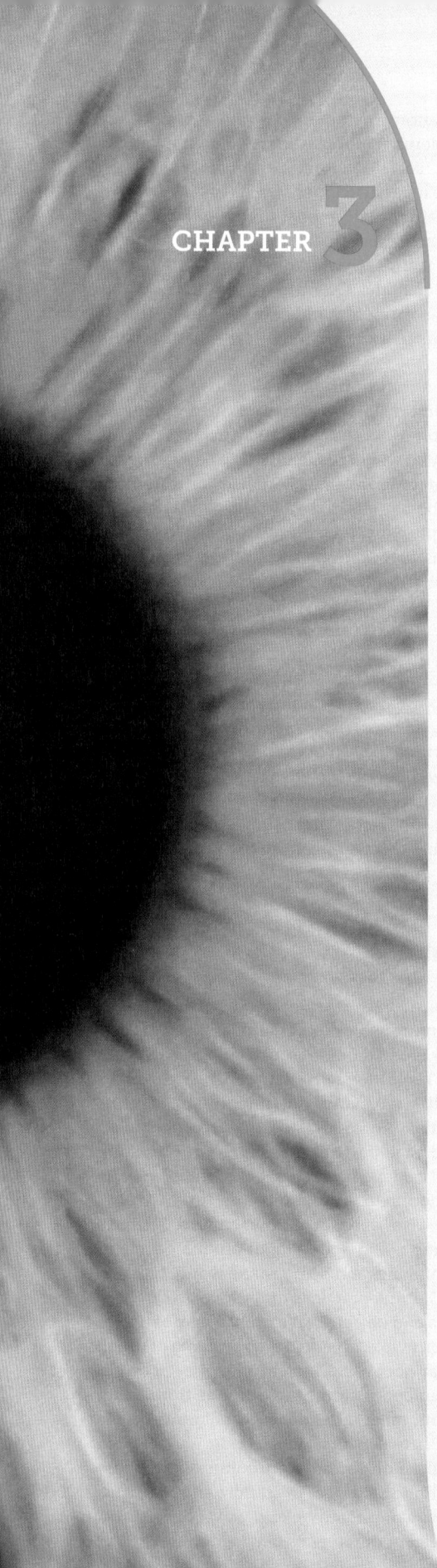

CHAPTER 3

CULTURE

Lala's story

Lala, a young woman living in a rural settlement in Peru, alienates her close relatives and the people of the community by behaving in a socially (and sexually) inappropriate manner before finally suffering a breakdown. She hears the voices of her ancestors, and believes that spirits surround her instructing her on how to achieve fulfilment in the after life. A local Shaman suspects she is *loca* (crazy) and believes her condition has emerged from the actions of supernatural forces. He prescribes a healing ritual, which calls for the active participation of most of her extended family, as he concludes Lala's *loca* results from the relatives' inappropriate behaviour. The Shaman recommends she returns home to her family, where she recovers rapidly, surrounded by family and friends.

Simon's story

Simon, a young white British man living in London, starts to behave strangely, retreating from family and friends and not showing up for work before finally claiming to be a descendant of Christ. He hears, and speaks to, divine voices and is preoccupied with his eventual crucifixion on the cross. Growing concern by family members leads to a consultation with a psychiatrist who requests that Simon be sectioned. Simon is admitted to hospital, where he is given psychiatric medication commonly used to treat schizophrenia. Simon does not have a history of 'mental illness', but a recent major bereavement sparks this a retreat from everyday life. He is put on a section, where he is required to take medication for up to a year. Although the persistent worry he experiences is reduced by the medication, he suffers side-effects, continues to hear voices and persists with his beliefs.

By the end of this chapter you should:

1 Have a working definition of culture
2 Understand the difference between emic and etic approaches to mental health and distress
3 Know the different prevalent rates for diagnosed mental disorders across cultures
4 Understand how various societies view mental health and distress and the differences between some of them

Introduction

Psychological approaches to mental health and distress aim to provide insight into the experiences, emotions, behaviour and states of mind that can contribute to the cause and/or maintenance of mental health problems. Psychologists and psychiatrists are scientifically trained to reach agreement about what problems look like, what to call them, how best to measure and eventually 'treat' them. However, let us pause for a moment to consider some of the issues relating to Lala and Simon; though we may be able to reach agreement on whether their behaviour is unusual or distressing to them and others, we may not be as confident about agreeing a standardized definition of the behaviour, or comparing the two sets of experiences. Do Lala and Simon both 'have schizophrenia' or a form of psychosis? When we look at culture and mental health, must we have a universal set of assumptions and questions about human experience? Is it the case that a Western orthodox understanding of mental health and distress is universally recognizable? Are the behaviours and states of mind described in Western medicine and psychology actually found throughout the world? Despite assurances by some traditional texts about the universal application of psychological and psychiatric models, several questions appear to remain.

Guiding questions

1 *To what extent do variations or similarities exist between cultures, in terms of the prevalence, incidence and course of traditionally defined mental 'disorders'?*
2 *Do different societies draw the same line between well-being and distress, sanity and madness?*

The first substantial question addressed in this chapter is '*To what extent do variations or similarities exist between cultures, in terms of the prevalence, incidence and course of traditionally defined mental "disorders"?*' We will address this by looking at a broad range of data, including the World Health Organization studies on 'schizophrenia'. It has been argued that if we were to find strong similarities in the prevalence, incidence and course of a disorder like 'schizophrenia', this would lend more weight to biological (or pathoplastic) models, which propose that while culture may shape the *content* of the symptoms of this disorder, the *form* of the symptoms remains the same. Incidence is a measure of the risk of disease, injury of death at any given time period (e.g. over the course of a year) and the occurrence of this within a population. Incidences are often expressed in terms of percentages. The biological model prioritizes a biological (neurological, brain structural and

physiological) explanation for the causes and maintenance of mental health problems. 'Pathoplastic' refers to the various influences (biological, social, cultural, psychological) on the *form* of a disease once it has developed.

According to the pathoplastic model, for example, people still have the illness 'schizophrenia', they may just attribute different meanings to it and it may manifest in different ways, according to cultural customs. Conversely, significant variations in the prevalence, incidence and course of 'disorders' in some societies invite us to ask whether we are measuring the same 'disorder' at all.

The second question is, 'Do different societies draw a line between well-being and distress, sanity and madness in the same way?' Perhaps some societies genuinely express distress and madness in ways that would not necessarily be recognized by Western medical definitions and diagnoses and perhaps there are emotions, bodily states, behaviours and states of mind that hold completely different meanings (Littlewood, 2002). If the variations between cultures are too great, does this make a universal model of mental health and distress problematic?

The vast literature on culture and mental health has developed largely within the disciplines of medical, cultural and social anthropology, and transcultural or cross-cultural psychiatry (Tseng, 2001) and psychology, but we will use this literature here to address issues specifically relevant to psychology. Before turning to each of the questions in turn, we must first address how different societies have made sense of issues relevant to the study of mental illness. It soon becomes clear that the different approaches can begin with quite different assumptions, leading to different questions and, ultimately, different answers.

What is culture?

Defining culture has never been easy and the debates between and within anthropology, psychiatry and psychology continue to rage. Too broad a definition of culture can often obscure some of the key differences between people within the same culture, and a too narrow definition can blind us to important similarities. According to social psychologists Kenrick, Neuberg and Cialdini (2010), a definition of culture can include the set of beliefs, habits, customs and discourse shared by people living in close proximity and time. Cultural anthropologists have also described how culture 'shap[es] experience, interpretation, and action [and] orients people in their way of feeling, thinking, and being in the world' (Jenkins & Barrett, 2004, p. 5). Cultural practices often involve symbols, language, rituals, dress and objects that signify a way of life for a society and a set of principles that make up systems of belief, moral codes and legal doctrine. This can also be cross-cut with differences in religious customs. An example from South Asia would be the noticeable differences in religious beliefs and rituals that exist between the Sikh, Hindu and Muslim religions. Thus, even though 'South Asian' cultures may share particular beliefs regarding selfhood, the family and marriage, for example, there would remain religious variations that would represent significant differences between these groups (Loewenthal, 2007).

The term 'culture' is often misused and is often put forward as a variable to be measured and compared. However, as

Arthur Kleinman, a leading US psychiatrist and medical anthropologist (2004, p.952) argues, culture is not a 'thing':

> [i]t is a process by which ordinary activities acquire emotional and moral meaning for participants. Cultural processes include the embodiment of meaning in habitus and physiological reactions, the understanding of what is at stake in particular situations, the development of interpersonal connections, religious practices, and the cultivation of collective and individual identity. Culture is inextricably caught up with economic, political, psychological, and biologic conditions. Treating culture as a fixed variable seriously impedes our ability to understand and respond.

Can we then say that a unanimous 'culture' is embraced by all who live in the same society or by those share the same geographical location? Not always; some societies contain a diversity of 'cultures' that may share certain moral or political beliefs, but diverge, say, on religious issues. British society, for example, contains a number of different cultural groups that can be further divided by religion and/or ethnicity. When studying culture and mental health, it could be argued that particular attention must also be given to the more specific domains of family, religion and spirituality, ethnicity, class, gender and sexuality within the overarching definition of culture, as these can have a dramatic impact on the organization of emotions, beliefs and norms of acceptable behaviour (Pilgrim & Rogers, 2002; Addlakha, 2008; Pilgrim, 2009). Furthermore, many 'sub-cultures' can exist within a society whose distinct set of behaviour and beliefs differentiate them from the larger cultural group as a whole, of which the sub-cultures are a part. Due consideration must also be given to issues of culture and migration, where it is possible for migrating groups to partly or fully retain their original beliefs and customs whilst living in a culture with a differing set of values on certain issues (Bhui, Bhugra, Goldberg, Sauer & Tylee, 2004).

Some parts of North American society are heavily influenced by Christian morals and ideals. How does this impact on what we define as culture?

It is clear, then, that defining culture is a complex affair. In textbooks, 'cultural differences' are often studied using geographical location as a way to distinguish differences between cultures. Furthermore, some cultural anthropologists have noted that the distinctions between 'industrialized' and 'developing' societies often operate under the implicit assumption that 'developing' nations refer to members of a society over 'there' and 'developed' nations refer to members of a society 'here', namely Europe and North America (Hopper, 2004). **Developing countries** are (broadly) countries of lower economic wealth, usually matched by less industrialization and technology. **Industrialization** is the shift from a broadly agricultural and rural society to an industrial and urban one, signalling technological and economic advances. However, there is no universal definition of this term. For the purposes of this chapter, we will stay largely within the bounds of 'geographical cultures', to avoid some of the more complex issues that warrant in-depth and prolonged discussion, which we do not have space for.

In addressing issues of culture in the context of mental health, we must ask questions relating to the particular customs and habits of a given culture and how they may play a role in the development of specific mental health problems; whether all cultures are equally mentally 'healthy'; whether specific behaviours and states of mind are found only in certain cultures and, lastly, whether being 'mad' or 'distressed' in one culture may lead to a better outcome. Furthermore, where migration has occurred, we need to ask how this experience impacts on an individual's mental health, especially when the 'host' culture has discriminated against the migrant or failed to accept their particular cultural beliefs (Fernando, 2003).

'Professional' cultures

'We have truth but they have customs' (Pascal, cited in Littlewood, 2002, p. 19).

It is worth noting that any discussion of culture and mental health must consider not only the wider cultural beliefs of a society, but the professional disciplines that are sanctioned by that society to measure and treat mental health and distress. This is because cultural beliefs regarding mental health are informed and shaped by professional experts who claim to know what causes mental distress and how best to manage or treat it. With the growth of psychiatry within the discipline of medicine in the early 19th and 20th century, distress and mental health became increasingly more medicalized in industrialized societies, with a whole set of human experiences (misery, anxiety, breakdowns) translated into terms such as 'illness' and 'disorder'. This has also begun to have far-reaching effects on countries undergoing economic development and rapid industrialization, where Western notions of mental health have grown in popularity, due to a number of factors, including the adoption of certain Western ideals (see Box 3.1).

The introduction of pharmaceutical companies into developing countries is another potential reason for an increasing interest in Western psychiatric views. In Europe and North America, mental health is still largely treated and measured as a *health and illness* issue, although the emphasis on biology and medication is much greater in North America than it is in Europe (Littlewood, 2002). Psychiatry has remained a subdiscipline of medicine and is largely in charge of the management of mental health issues in these societies. Unsurprisingly, the remaining dominant view (but not the only one) in mental health services is that mental distress is an 'illness' or 'disorder' to diagnose and primarily (but not exclusively, as psychological interventions are also recommended) treat with physical therapies (drugs). Thus, psychiatry has its own cultural practices and rituals that can shape the individual behaviour and attitude of each psychiatrist and client, such as standardized measurements, medication, institutionalization, consultations and codes of professional conduct. Clinical psychology also has its own culture, which at times is able to work alongside a psychiatric one, as it must operate in the context of a mental health team, while at other times may oppose psychiatry and create a new set of rituals and practices that can work independently (though, of course, clinical psychologists are still by and large employed by medical institutions).

What is often missing from references to culture and mental health in psychology texts is the recognition that the very idea of measuring people's distress using scales and defining mental distress according to an illness model has emerged from Western assumptions regarding mental health problems and the origins of the problem in the individual (in their genes, their history or personality). Rarely is there any discussion in these texts about how Western culture itself operates and defines what it means to be a person and part of society (Cole, 2005). Indeed, Kim Hopper, one of the cultural anthropologists working as part of the DSM-IV task force to include cultural features in the manual argues that it is rare for Western practitioners and researchers to acknowledge the assumptions regarding individualism and illness informing their work. **Individualism** as a philosophical tradition is concerned with the properties of the individual (deficits, illness, distress).

Furthermore, the DSM task force on culture reported feeling disappointed by the lack of more general discussion of cultural issues in the finalized DSM-IV (Kleinman, 1997). As Bentall notes (2003, p. 139) '*this* (DSM) *enterprise is, itself, culture bound*. It represents the efforts of [certain] members of one particular culture to make sense of human behavioural breakdowns'. Thus, psychiatry and clinical psychology have developed their own set of traditions, which have particular historical origins and politics. This professional culture, in turn, then impacts on the beliefs of a society regarding the nature of mental health and distress. In China, for example, though rates of clinical depression are still lower than in the West, rates have risen sharply over the last 25 years, due to the introduction of Western-influenced diagnostic and assessment tools (Kleinman, 1991). However, psychiatry and psychology are also affected by shifts in wider cultural beliefs regarding what is normal or abnormal. It would be highly unusual nowadays for a psychiatrist or psychologist to take seriously the 19th century diagnosis of drapetomania (an uncontrollable urge to escape slavery, often observed in African–American slaves). This is due to a shift in social attitudes regarding slavery, as opposed to a shift in scientific thinking. Ian Hacking, a philosopher of science, argues that professional cultures not only affect culture with the knowledge they produce, they in turn are affected by the cultural beliefs of the society they exist within. This can apply equally to sub-cultures – the removal of homosexuality from the DSM was strongly associated with political campaigns led by lesbian and gay activists.

The DSM-IV-TR has now been translated into 22 languages, including Chinese and Arabic, and continues to be regarded as an international template for the classification of mental disorders across the world. It is, therefore, unsurprising that wider societal beliefs about mental health and distress are in turn shaped by the language introduced by professional disciplines. Of course, Western psychiatry and psychology are not the only disciplines to shape local beliefs regarding mental health and distress. Traditional healers, for example, remain powerful figures in many non-industrialized societies; officially sanctioned traditional healing and medicine is legally recognized and is often the first place that many individuals turn to in times of distress (Jilek, 1993). Traditional healers have a well-established professional culture of their own (often dating back before the advent of modern psychiatry and psychology) including a set of culturally specific forms of assessment and treatment. Although traditional healers (who operate in a number of sub-Saharan African societies) may not adopt Western systems of diagnosis, for example, they do have an alternative version of diagnosis, known as *divination*. **Divination** is a process or ritual carried out by a healer to read signs of illness or possession. The healer may look at patterns in liquid or observe supernatural activity by achieving an altered state of consciousness. Unlike the individual consultations that take place in the average industrial nation, divinations may be performed publicly, especially if the patient's complaint is believed to be the result of collapsing social ties (Tseng, 2001). The healer then interviews the patient's family and relatives and, in doing so, builds a picture of his/her social field. Divination can be carried out by mixing specialist herbs or peering into medicated water to assess the ancestral roots that may have contributed to current social tensions (Laine, 2007). The healer may then see or hear the voices of dead spirits or witches who may have occupied the bodies of the relatives who are in conflict with the patient and are thus responsible for their illness. One treatment may be a public exorcism, where members of the community gather to witness the withdrawal of the evil spirit from the patient's body. This would be accompanied by dance and song, as a way to purify the patient and her/his wider community (Turner, 1974).

Studying culture in the context of mental health and distress

In addition to the contribution of professional cultures, how we make sense of the relationship between culture and mental health must depend on our understanding of people (psychology) and mental health more generally (Kazarian & Evans, 1998).

In non-Western societies, moral and community issues are more commonly addressed in the context of understanding

Despite a shift to industrialization in a number of non-Western societies, a sense of collective tradition still remains

When studying culture, it is always necessary to consider the interplay between the general cultural customs of a society towards unusual behaviour or distress, and the professional culture that has been developed to deal with them. The two may not resemble one another, but may variously be used by members of that culture. On a recent field trip to Zambia, one of the authors (Reavey) discovered there to be 42,000 registered faith healers and only four registered psychiatrists amongst a population of 11 million. There are a handful of clinics that offer cognitive behaviour therapy but this is extremely rare. Zambia is largely a rural country, where traditional medicine is still widely practised by faith healers to treat mental and physical illnesses. The origins of mental illness are believed to be medical, spiritual or religious, or a combination of these. Traditional medicine can involve the use of herbs, animal skins and tissue (fat, internal organs) to relieve symptoms, and

the healer will be paid for each visit. Faith healing can also include specific ceremonies where evil spirits or dead souls are exorcized by the faith healer, who is trained to go into altered states where she or he can communicate with the spirits. Furthermore, faith healers connected with Christianity can perform ceremonies where the patient is exorcized according to Christian doctrine, in the presence of the religious community. Both traditional healers and psychiatrists are responsible for treating mental health and distress and are officially recognized by Government bodies. In addition, the Zambian government has sought to increase the role played by medical practitioners (following Western principles of medical treatment) by developing a scheme that trains 'clinical officers' who are employed to perform a similar diagnostic and treatment role to psychiatrists, largely in outpatient clinics (there is only one psychiatric hospital in Zambia). The clinical officer is trained to use the DSM diagnostic system and to medicate patients. They are trained for only two years, following high school (this is roughly equivalent to UK A-levels).

The idea behind the use of clinical officers is that larger numbers of them can be trained to deal with mental health caseloads, by following the descriptive model of the DSM and prescribing established (Western) medications. The assumption is that following a well-established biomedical model will lead to more cost-effective and successful management of mental health problems, because they can be treated using standardized medical knowledge. The cultural picture for mental health and distress is, therefore, mixed. On the one hand, there is a strong belief in traditional medicine and the Christian faith, and on the other hand, there is a move towards establishing a psychiatric culture that resembles physical medicine involving short consultations (to monitor medication – case management) or, in extreme circumstances, short-stay hospital treatment. Other ethnographic reports suggest that most individuals living in sub-Saharan African societies rely on *both* traditional and Western psychiatric/psychological systems of support to tackle a variety of needs (Lefley, 1999).

the causes of mental distress, seeking an explanation in outside forces, rather than the individual's personality or possible biological dysfunction (Littlewood, 2002). In Western psychiatry and psychology, moral issues are usually replaced with concerns over symptoms of illhealth or 'states of mind' because the emphasis is on the search for a problem with the person's health, rather than their moral standing in the community. Furthermore, it has long been noted in anthropological writings that a positive belief in individualism is a key feature of Western societies, in which autonomy, independence, 'personality' and free-will are credited with greater significance than collectivity, religiosity, morality and dependency, which are more common to non-Western societies (Triandis, 1989,1995; Bharati, 1985). In non-Western societies, collective concerns may, in fact, overshadow individual needs.

Self and culture

Western societies have long been associated with the ideals of individualism and personal autonomy. **Individualism** is more often associated with liberalism and a form of 'I-consciousness' (Hofstede, 1984). **Liberalism** is the belief in the importance of equal rights in society.

According to theories and empirical studies in cross-cultural psychology, Western societies, personal life histories, internal beliefs, desires, commitments and thought are believed to provide the information we require to understand ourselves (Hofstede, 1980; Sadler, 2005). Another key assumption in Western culture is the existence of a 'unified self', based on the idea that we have stable and coherent personalities.

A national survey conducted in the US, for example, found that 97% of Americans believed strongly in 'being responsible for your own action's and 89% in 'being able to stand up for yourself'. They also believed that 'being in good health' and 'being able to express your feelings' was essential to good mental health (Cherlin, 1999, cited in Keyes & Ryff, 2003). Social psychological studies have also revealed how views on the self can actually moderate psychological well-being. For example, studies that have established a relationship between increased self-esteem, overall life satisfaction and psychological well-being have been unable to fully replicate these findings in collectivist societies (Ritter, Chaudry, Aigner, Zitterl & Stompe, 2010; Suh, Diener, Oishi & Triandis, 1998).

In **collectivist** (mainly non-industrial or developing) societies, selfhood may be more invested in community and family activities (though it is right to exercise caution here, as non-industrialized societies may adopt some individualistic values – see Box 3.2) rather than personal history and self-esteem alone. Collectivist societies are more often associated with traditionalism and a form of 'we-consciousness' (Hofstede, 1984). Selfhood is more widely dispersed, and grounded in shared activities and values. Having high self-esteem may not be valued, therefore, if as a result the individual stands out and appears to separate from the rest of the group. Such societies may also seek the attribution and resolution of certain experiences or problems, not in the individual's mind or body, but the community, and in particular, the family. This contrasts with much Western psychiatric or psychological intervention. Despite these differences in models of the person and the attribution of the cause of mental distress, psychiatry

BOX 3.2

Economic growth and the rise of eating disorders in Japan

The number of reported cases of **eating disorders** (anorexia and bulimia nervosa) has increased substantially in Europe and North America in the last fifty years. The term refers to a group of 'disorders' characterized by unusual eating habits, including restrictive or excessive food intake, which may have negative consequences for mental or physical health.

In fact, there was some discussion as to whether eating disorders should be included as culture-bound syndromes in the last version of the DSM, because almost no cases had been reported in developing or non-industrialized societies until fairly recently. The pursuit of thinness is reported by those diagnosed with these conditions, as the core feature is an intense fear of fat and poor self-image. The vast majority of cases are young females, a fact that has been attributed to a crisis in female identity, following conflicting demands for women's success in education and industry and their continued submissiveness and dependency in the domestic sphere. The increasing pursuit of individualism and personal success, along with the fragmentation of family ties, is also believed to be contributing to the growing number of eating disorders in these countries. Developing countries were thought to be immune because non-industrialized societies were more collective in outlook, had less access to food and supported strong family bonds (conditions opposite to those that foster eating problems). However, since the 1990s, cases of eating disorders have been reported in countries as diverse as Denmark and Nigeria. Why is this? One reason may be the growth of industrialism in previous non-industrialized societies and the adoption of consumer culture and individualism (although the simplistic view that non-industrialized societies merely mimic their industrial counterparts should be avoided). **Consumer culture** refers to societies in which the purchasing of material goods is driven by *desire* rather than need. One's social status and relationships are in part defined by how much one owns and has access to economic wealth. Greater wealth is desirable and affords greater social status. Ultimately, part of our identity is written into our success in acquiring wealth and goods.

A particularly interesting case is Japan, often considered to be the most economically developed society in Southern Asia. Since the Second World War, some of the conditions that have led to the increase of eating disorders in industrialized societies have arisen there, including individualism, conflicts between traditional and contemporary female roles and the growth of consumerism and the media in influencing and shaping public attitudes. Changes in the economic and industrial climate in Japan, as well as shifts in cultural attitudes, are believed to play a role in the sharp increase in eating disorders, according to leading experts (Nasser, Katzman & Gordon, 2001). Even though figures do not match US or European rates, anorexia has risen from virtually no reported cases in the mid-20th century to around 30 per 100,000. Another factor is the rapid growth of Western psychiatric diagnostic assessments and treatments, which may also explain why the number of cases identified by professionals has risen sharply. Despite this, it is unlikely that this alone would explain the sharp increase in eating disorders countrywide.

and psychology are still aiming for universalism. Attempts to compare individual symptoms across cultures are still pursued because the assumption is that, despite cultural differences in the content of symptoms and beliefs about the self, certain life events, genetic dispositions and stressors can still produce similar symptoms. According to this view, Lala and Simon could still initially be classified psychotic, regardless of the difference in the cultural ideas surrounding their behaviours and beliefs.

For example, if we were to treat 'schizophrenia' as a disease (that is, qualitatively distinct from the rest of human experience and one which runs its course regardless of human input or cultural content), our study of culture and mental health will probably involve some objectified and reliable measurement of schizophrenia. This standardized measurement can then be used to make comparisons across cultures, as in the study of medical conditions. Standardized definitions are also key to the development of certain (largely quantitative) methodologies. **Quantitative** research adopts standardized measurements of phenomena so that the relationships between elements can be measured and analysed mathematically. **Qualitative** research is interested in the meanings given by individuals to their beliefs, experiences and behaviours; the aim is not to standardize or mathematically measure meaning but to prioritize the individual's subjective meaning-making process.

In epidemiology, for example, it is necessary to establish an operational definition of a disease in order to measure its prevalence, course and outcome across different settings.

Epidemiology is the study of health and illness patterns in and across societies: it is a form of evidence-based medicine designed to identify risk factors for disease, usually based on large-scale quantitative methods.

Defining diseases, drawing causal chains for disease and the formulation of specific health strategies are important aspects of epidemiology and have been used in psychiatric research to establish prevalence, course and outcome across cultures. The assumption is that we are comparing like with like: only the cultural setting is considered to be variable, not the 'disorder' itself.

On the other hand, if we believe that cultures themselves define the terms of human experience, imposing different meanings on behaviours, thoughts, emotions and experiences and applying a universal name to them may not be possible. For example, the cultural psychologist Geertz claims that though all human cultures have some notion of what it is to be a human being (unlike, for example, an animal, rock or plant) the individualistic notion of self found in Western cultures is not universally recognized, as what it means to be an individual and a self is tightly bound by cultural convention and depends upon culturally specific language (Geertz, 1983; Cole, 2005). Emotions, behaviours and states of mind, therefore, may not be culturally equivalent, due to different language conventions (Leff, 1973). The Western understanding of depression, for example, does not translate readily into non-Western cultures, where there are different models of self (Pilgrim & Bentall, 1999). In the Western literature on depression, there has been a great deal of work linking particular self-constructs (the discrepancy between the ideal and actual self, for example) with depression (Hammen, 2005), but do these constructs resonate across all societies? A classic counter-example to a Western perspective on self can be found in Japan, in the syndrome *taijin kyofusho*, in which the individual is extremely fearful of her/his acceptability to others. If one considers the Japanese proverb *'the nail that stands out gets pounded down'* we can see that a DSM diagnosis of social phobia would miss the cultural subtleties and meanings that provide the context for that behaviour (Markus & Kitayama, 1991).

On a visit to an AIDS hospice in Lusaka, Zambia, one of the authors (Reavey) met patients described by the (extremely rare) local cognitive behaviour therapist as 'depressed'. Cognitive behaviour therapy (CBT) is a therapeutic practice aiming to change or modify and individual's thought processes and behaviour. When speaking to these people, Reavey found that asking questions about individual feelings and self-esteem (as one might do in the UK) had little resonance with these patients from rural communities, though, interestingly, the more educated urban dwellers were more able to address the question. Although anecdotal, this last example illustrates how differences between urban and rural communities can be crucial.

Emic versus etic distinctions

In practice, cultural studies of mental health and distress have been carried out by two different groups of researchers, who start out with different assumptions (Bentall, 2003). These can broadly be divided into the **emic** and **etic** perspectives. The former refers to an approach that prioritizes the meaning the person under observation attributes to their beliefs, experiences and behaviours, using their own cultural reference points. An etic approach gives greater priority to a universal definition of beliefs, experiences and behaviours, offered by a scientific observer. The main aim of is this approach is to be culturally neutral and objective and apply observations and measurements across cultures.

The etic or 'outside' perspective (as some anthropologists refer to it) follows in the tradition of behavioural psychology (Skinner, 1938), transcultural or cross-cultural psychiatry and anthropological approaches that link cultural practices to external or antecedent conditions, such as economic, social and ecological factors that may or may not be part of the vocabulary, beliefs or explanatory system of the inside group. This 'experience-distant' approach encourages the researcher to standardize categories and diagnoses, which can then be used to carry out cross-cultural comparisons. In methodological terms, this translates into the generation of hypotheses, used in large epidemiological or smaller experimental studies. Nevertheless, this perspective welcomes the exploration of cultural differences, in terms of the *content* of particular behaviours and symptoms. However, the assumption is that the *form* of the problem under investigation remains the same – depression is the same disorder, whether in India or North America.

The emic or insider perspective follows in the tradition of psychological studies of folk beliefs (Wundt, 1888) and in cultural and social anthropologists' pursuit of the 'native' participant's point of view (Malinowski, 1927; Sapir, 1924;

Mead, 1928; Sullivan, 1938) and, later, Kleinman & Kleinman, 1995). This 'experience-near' perspective privileges the participant's account of his/her experience, avoiding any unnecessary intervention or standardization of response by the researcher (Jenkins & Barrett, 2004). It often involves understanding mental health problems as extensions of normal human experiences, rather than as qualitatively distinct categories of disorder or illness, emphasizing the continuity between the ordinary and the unusual or 'extraordinary' (Sullivan, 1962). In methodological terms, this could take the form of an ethnographic or qualitative study, which would not involve testing a prior hypothesis, or a quantitative or experimental study of *specific* behaviours and experiences, rather than beginning with broader diagnostic categories. Emic knowledge is essential for a more empathic and complex reading of culture and psychological processes more generally.

There are differences between cross-cultural psychiatrists and psychologists, who adopt the invariant model of 'disorder' (typical of etic approaches), and anthropologists, who argue that important variations exist, resulting in a fundamentally different kind of experience (typical of emic approaches). According to the emic view, standardized measurement would be problematic. However, the emic and etic distinctions are not always strictly adhered to, as a number of psychiatrists and anthropologists have argued that careful emic knowledge is required *before* hypotheses can be developed, implying that neither approach should be used in isolation (Morris, Leung, Ames & Lickel, 1999; Cheng, 2002). In this chapter, we will draw on both emic and etic forms of knowledge, to address each of the substantive questions in turn.

Are the boundaries between mental health and normality similar or different across cultures?

In order to address the first question – 'To what extent do variations or similarities exist between cultures, in terms of the prevalence, incidence and course of traditionally defined mental "disorders"?' – we must first discuss what is meant by mental health and distress across a variety of cultural contexts.

Definitions of mental health problems rely largely upon definitions of normality, as the former are often identified via the impairment of a person's social or occupational status – in short, when there is some sort of disruption to normal social behaviours (Warner, 1996).

Definitions of normality, like definitions of health, vary widely across societies and depend upon a range of possible perceptions by members of that society or culture towards certain social behaviours (see Helman, 2000 & 2007, for an extensive discussion). Some distressing behaviours and thoughts involving a religious or spiritual dimension, for example, may be misinterpreted when standard Western categories of illness or disorder are adopted – see *Neurasthenia*, below. The use of a standard psychiatric category may miss important features of a particular cultural belief system that would be useful to explain, treat and, eventually, 'heal' the person (Loewenthal, 2007). In Japan, for example, 'fox possession' is a commonly recognized experience that can lead to distress and voice-hearing: the person believes they are possessed by a fox spirit who enters and speaks to them. Shamans, rather than psychiatrists, are commonly consulted and often perform religious rituals that enable the person to understand the nature of the possession by eventually establishing harmony with the fox spirit. This can even lead to the person becoming a Shaman themselves and carrying out religious rituals of the kind used to treat their own distress.

As well as unusual behaviours being read in different ways in different cultures, emotions can be constructed and experienced differently. In some African languages, for example, 'anger' and 'sadness' are not viewed separately and, in Japan, dependent emotions (honour, obedience, deference, selflessness) are viewed more positively than in the West (Leff, 1973). In Western psychology, emotion and cognition are often studied independently, indicating the assumption that thoughts and emotional states are distinct (consider the contrast between 'thought disorders' such as schizophrenia and 'affective disorders' such as depression). Despite there being significant similarities in conceptualizations of emotions across cultures, there are significant differences in the way in which emotion is seen to interact with mind and body processes (Leff, 1977).

Across different time periods and in different societies there have been countless recordings of 'odd,' 'abnormal' or 'unusual' behaviours: behaviours, emotions or states of mind that do not appear to fit with majority perceptions or actions (Littlewood & Lipsedge, 1982). Furthermore, it is clear that in every society what people consider 'normal' or 'abnormal' social behaviour can differ widely (Helman, 2000). In spite of this, there do appear to be behaviours and experiences that appear throughout the world, and that are considered to be problematic. These can include intense sadness (for no apparent reason), problems with eating, body dissatisfaction and culturally inappropriate beliefs, all of which are common everywhere (Nasser et al., 2001). Arthur Kleinman argues that the universal existence of human suffering underpins cultural displays of distress; the existence of abuse, poor communication, hostility, trauma and stress may lead to mental distress and/or poor mental health. Though most might agree that these behaviours, emotions and experiences are indeed universal and troubling (if they lead to social impairment), there is still a great deal of dispute about how to label them and whether the meanings assigned by different societies and cultures actually amount to the same thing (Littlewood & Lipsedge, 1997). If a local healer in Malaysia, for example, hears voices and interprets them as spirits who instruct her healing practices, should we use the same label for her behaviour as we would for a British-born man living in London who hears the voice of Christ? Although both individuals both share the *form* of behaviour or 'symptoms' (hearing voices), can they be regarded as equivalent, and should they necessarily be considered 'ill' or 'distressed'? In order to begin to address these kinds of questions we will be drawing on studies using both etic knowledge with a Western (often diagnostic) definition of mental disorder to measure 'abnormal' behaviours or experiences found across the world, and emic knowledge that has concentrated on the more local experience-near features. How we assess whether mental health and distress are universal may largely depend on the types of knowledge we draw on and the tools we use to measure them. Even then, definitions and eventual diagnosis used within the same 'culture' (Western culture) may differ across countries, due to differences in professional and clinical practices (see Box 3.1).

Prevalence rates across cultures

At the beginning of the 20th century, a number of investigations revealed different rates and forms of mental diseases in Western and non-Western societies. This is not surprising when we consider that the study of culture began with observations on the British temperament: in particular, the tendency towards repression and melancholia because of the climate (Jenkins & Barrett, 2004).

Since then, research has moved on to draw comparisons between 'developing' and 'developed' societies. One of the first to do this was Kraepelin (1904/74), in his study of the psychoses (including dementia praecox and manic depressive psychosis) in Java and Europe. Kraepelin compared the Javanese and European symptoms of these 'diseases', finding some similarities, yet also key differences. For example, he reported that there were fewer examples of delusions and hallucinations in the Javanese, which he attributed to an impoverished language system and greater reliance on sensual imagery for thought (Kraepelin, 1904/74). In fact, the view that European displays of madness and/or abnormality were less likely to occur in societies deemed 'primitive' or 'closer to nature', due to a lesser capacity for higher thought, was widely held, and was accompanied by anthropological studies that documented physical differences (e.g. skull size) between racial groups as a way of measuring intelligence and personality across cultures.

A study investigating the African mind, commissioned by the World Health Organization (WHO) in 1952, for example, went as far as to suggest that the underdeveloped frontal lobes of Africans could account for their poorly developed personality and primitive tendencies. It is clear that in the first half of the 20th century, cultural differences were observed through the lens of colonial and racist stereotypes, rather than by systematic scientific investigation.

Current practice in cross-cultural psychiatry and psychology is to count cases of mental disorder using objective and standardized measures, rather than relying on emic descriptions of distress and mental health found in qualitative anthropological studies. Prevalence rates can be measured with a range of instruments, including standard DSM or ICD diagnostic criteria or other recognized assessment tools such as the Present State Examination. The **Present State Examination** was designed in the 1960s to assess an individual's present mental state (questions refer to the past month only) in order to identify any mental disorder. The test includes a standard checklist of items, with some flexibility permitted in questioning.

It is important to note that different studies measure different populations for rates of mental health problems. Populations may consist of clinical samples (inpatient and outpatient services; GP or mental health services) or community samples. Accurate estimates are disrupted by differential access to services (leading to varying rates of formal diagnosis) and by different levels of acceptance of Western forms of diagnosis and assessment measures. This makes the determination of 'true' incidence difficult. However, a limited number of cross-cultural studies exist that reveal variations in mental health diagnoses across cultures.

The World Health Organization Collaborative Study on Psychological Problems in General Health Care (Ustun & Sartorius, 1995), for example, was an epidemiological cross-cultural study designed to examine the frequency, recognition and outcomes of psychological disorders in general health-care settings across cultures. Prevalence rates for a range of ICD-10 diagnoses varied significantly across different cultures (see Table 3.1). The authors of this study discussed some of the predictors of such variation, including health beliefs, help-seeking behaviour, diagnostic practices and patterns of response. A follow-up investigation (using a meta-analysis of the original results) of the cultural factors involved in the different prevalence rates produced several findings (Maercker, 2001). Current depression was less frequent in countries where values of self-mastery and personal strain were valued (e.g. Japan, China and Zimbabwe). In addition, generalized anxiety was negatively associated with countries that valued conservatism (e.g. Greece &Brazil: countries showing social control by the peer group and a preference for hierarchy). These findings also correspond to certain social theories that predicted higher rates of personal irritability in societies that value personal freedom (see Foucault, 1961).

Table 3.1 **Prevalence of mental disorders and presenting health complaints in the WHO general practitioner study**

Prevalence of most common ICD-10 diagnoses presenting complaints of patients attending health care facilities (per 1000)						
	Any ICD-10	**Current**	**Gen**	**Dep**			
	Mental disorder	**Depression**	**Anxiety**	**Alcohol**	**Psychological**	**Fatigue**	**Pain**
Rio de Janeiro	35.5	15.8	22.6	4.1	7.6	5.1	42.1
Paris	26.3	13.7	11.9	4.3	11	8.4	25.3
Gronigen (Holland)	23.9	15.9	6.4	3.4	12.8	5.7	28.2
Athens	19.2	6.4	14.9	1.0	2.2 '	5.1	21.9
Berlin	18.3	6.1	9.0	3.7	3.7	5.2	32.3
Ankara	16.4	11.6	0.9	1.0	2.6	5.6	40.5
Seattle	11.9	6.3	2.1	1.5	2.6	1.6	17.0
Verona	9.8	4.7	3.7	0.5	6.4	3.7	25.9
Ibadan	9.5	4.2	2.9	0.4	2.3	9.0	51.4
Nagasaki	9.4	2.6	5.0	3.7	1.3	9.5	21.3
Shanghai	7.3	4.0	1.9	1.1	0.2	13.3	26.2

Source: **Ustun and Sartorius (1995, tables on pp. 324, 326, 352).**

BOX **3.3**

Differences in psychiatric diagnosis in England and France

A study by Van Os and colleagues (1993) revealed significant differences between diagnostic and clinical practices in England and France, although both these countries are 'Western', industrialized or developed nations. Major differences were found between the way 92 English psychiatrists and 60 French psychiatrists conceptualized the cause, diagnosis and management of schizophrenia. In particular, each group of psychiatrists appeared to be influenced by their theoretical and philosophical traditions, which, in turn, directed their diagnostic and clinical work. In England, the tradition was that of Anglo-Saxon empiricism (the pursuit of truth through scientific experiments),while in France, it was continental rationalism (the pursuit of truth through thought and interpretation). This meant that in England, greater trust was placed in biological (neuro-biological and genetic) and behavioural theories, and, in France, in psychodynamic theories (that emphasize parenting) and familial dynamics. Incidence rates in the two countries were also different. France had higher rates of schizophrenia in individuals under 45 years of age and lower rates in those over 45. In France, there was a greater reluctance to diagnose schizophrenia after the age of 45 and a number of other problems ('pseudo psychopathy') were identified that English psychiatrists would not have recognized under the label schizophrenia. Cooper and his associates have also revealed differences between British and North American psychiatrists in the diagnosis of bipolar disorder and schizophrenia (Cooper, Kendell, Gurland, Sartorius & Farkas, 1969). These studies clearly point to key differences in incident rates, diagnosis and clinical practice in two Western cultures.

The World Health Organization studies of schizophrenia

In 1967 the WHO commissioned a series of studies investigating the incidence and course of schizophrenia, using broader local descriptions and Western (Schneiderian) criteria (see Chapter 2). **Schneiderian** refers to the work of Kurt Schneider, who described the symptoms of schizophrenia that differentiate the condition from other psychotic disorders as **first rank symptoms**, which mainly comprise a variety of hallucinations and delusions.

Since then, nearly thirty research sites in nineteen countries (Western and non-Western) have participated in such a study (Hopper, 2004). The WHO went to great lengths to include 'developing' and 'developed' countries in order to establish stable prevalence rates across the world. The three main studies – the International Pilot Study of Schizophrenia (IPSS, beginning in 1967), the Determinants of Outcome of Severe Mental Disorder (DOSMed, beginning in 1978) and the recently completed International Study of Schizophrenia (ISOS, beginning in 1982) – with follow-up periods ranging from two to five years (and in some sites, ten) have reported similar incidence rates across the world (between 0.7 and 1.3). DOSMed started with twelve sites but eventually reported from seven (Aarhus in Denmark, Chandigarh– rural and urban – in India, Dublin in Ireland, Honolulu in the US, Moscow in Russia, Nagasaki in Japan and Nottingham in the UK), in order to make cross-cultural comparisons of incidence rates and outcome. The ISOS study completed data collection in follow-up interviews of both the original ISOS study (24 years after the episode of inclusion) and the DOSMed cohort.

These studies report equally distributed numbers of individuals liable to schizophrenia (though we shall see that the course and outcome were significantly different across countries). Subsequently, the results have been used to gather further support for biomedical theories claiming that schizophrenia is a culturally invariant (in terms of prevalence and form) and genetically based disorder (Jablensky et al., 1992). If the prevalence rates of the WHO studies are correct, only the *content* of the 'symptoms' of schizophrenia can be considered variable, rather than the rate and quality of their *form*. However, there have been a number of criticisms of these studies, which point to definitional problems and poorly described inclusion and exclusion criteria (Kleinman, 1991). Firstly, Bentall has argued that it was inevitable that the initial IPSS study found consistent rates of schizophrenia across cultures, as only patients meeting the Western diagnostic criteria were included in the final cross-cultural comparisons (Bentall, 2003). Secondly, when examining the data from the second study (DOSMed), *there were statistically significant differences of* incidence across sites when a broader (as opposed to a Schneiderian) definition of schizophrenia was used (Jablensky et al., 1992). Thirdly, there are clear reported differences in the course and outcome of psychosis between developing and developed countries. Does this pose serious questions for a Western medical approach that claims to be able to measure and treat equivalent illnesses across cultures? If the course and outcome of psychosis varies markedly, are we talking about the same problem, or is the same 'disorder' better dealt with in some societies?

Cross-cultural differences in the course and outcome of schizophrenia

The findings of the WHO studies suggest significant differences between 'developed' and 'developing' countries in terms of the course and outcome of schizophrenia over time. In the initial ISOS study, 27% of patients from developing countries experienced a single psychotic episode, followed by complete recovery, compared to 7% of patients from developed countries. At the end of the follow-up period, this advantage extended to levels of disability, with 65% of patients in developing countries, compared with 56% of patients from developed countries, experiencing little or no long-term social impairment.

The DOSMed and ISOS studies later confirmed these initial observations, although the ISOS study suffered from the eventual inclusion of only India to represent the developing nations (note that Hong Kong was removed from this category following its substantial industrialized growth during the study's 15 year period). The later DOSMed was explicitly designed to investigate the link between culture and the course and outcome of schizophrenia (Jablensky et al., 1992), the final results making a strong case for the persistent and powerful effect of culture. After a two-year follow-up period, 37% of patients from developing countries experienced one

The rise of industrialization in certain cultures can be accompanied by an increase in certain forms of distress, such as eating problems and sadness and worry

psychotic episode, compared to only 16% in the developed world. Approximately 16% of patients in the developing countries experienced social impairment compared with approximately 42% of those in developed nations.

These results appear robust, even when attrition (drop-out rates), groupings (the distinction between developed and developing nations), diagnostic ambiguities (the removal of 'non-affective acute remitting psychosis') and gender and age and outcome measures are controlled for (Stevens, 1987; Hopper, 2004). Given that such findings appear stable and ultimately compelling, it is now time to turn to some of the reasons given for these persistent cross-cultural differences.

The task of measuring cultural differences is often complex and is commonly overshadowed by the requirements of a large-scale study to standardize measurement and operationalize terms. This is why a number of anthropologists have been openly critical of the WHO studies that have largely failed to provide emic knowledge of cultural practices, instead choosing to assign culture to a geographical location only (Kleinman, 1987; Hopper, 2004). Indeed, as the authors of the DOSMed study themselves lament, neither IPSS nor DOSMed was designed to 'penetrate in sufficient depth below the surface on which the impact of this unknown factor (culture) was established' (Jablensky et al., 1992, p. 89). Despite such shortcomings, several explanations, taken from three sub-studies of the DOSMed, have been assembled to explain the more favourable outcome among developing countries. Among these explanations are three key topic areas: (i) family relationships and expressed emotion, (ii) a lack of social stigma and employment opportunities and (iii) marriage and long-term relationships (see Hopper, 2004 for a fuller discussion of these factors).

Family relationships and expressed emotion

Expressed Emotion (EE) is the amount of emotion displayed in a family, and has long been found to have adverse effects on the course and outcome of individuals diagnosed with schizophrenia and bipolar disorder, especially in terms of relapse rates (Leff & Vaughn, 1985; Butzlaff & Hooley, 1998). High expressed emotion refers to the existence of hostility (the patient is blamed for the problem), emotional over-involvement (family members blame themselves and pity the individual with the problem) and critical comments (combining hostility and emotional over-involvement). High expressed emotion has been linked to a poorer prognosis for individuals with mental health problems and to the risk of developing certain mental health problems in the first place, and protective factors and a lower risk of relapse were found in families low in EE and high in emotional warmth (López et al., 2004).

The direction of this relationship (causal or maintaining), however, is still open to debate (Bentall, 2003). It is not clear, for example, whether EE *causes* the initial distress or whether living with a family member with high levels of distress *significantly contributes to* familial unrest and disruptive communication patterns (in other words, EE). The frequency and intensity of individual types of EE have been found in the WHO and other studies to vary across cultures, with the proportion of high EE among relatives of individuals with schizophrenia defined by the Western operational criteria, ranging from 8% in rural India (Wiget et al., 1987) to 67% in urban US (Vaughn, Snyder, Jones, Freeman & Falloon, 1984). Despite these claims,

some researchers have questioned the validity of Western definitions of EE. It has been pointed out that what counts as criticism, hostility and emotional over-involvement is culturally defined (Jenkins & Karno, 1992); further studies should adopt a combined emic and etic approach, using longitudinal designs (McGruder, 2004; Cheng, 2002).

Employment opportunities and social responses

The WHO and other later studies have largely shown that the family members of those with severe mental health problems in developing countries tend to be more supportive and proactive. Instead of being placed in psychiatric institutions or isolated community settings, those with problems tend to remain with their families, where employment is provided and a sense of purpose more likely (Warner, 1994). Here, the family is considered to be responsible for social and emotional welfare, and in some cultures, the entire social network may be involved in treatment and rehabilitation (Helman, 2000). Industrialized nations are not as well disposed to those who cannot contribute to the economic system and families tend to be less extended and more isolated (Warner, 1994). It has been argued that higher levels of social support, familial warmth and low stigma in some developing countries positively mediate the individual's emotional response towards their 'problem' and ultimately improve their outcome (Warner, 1996; López et al., 2004). This evidence from these powerful culturally mediating factors is compelling and makes it difficult to argue that mental health problems have a 'natural' course to follow.

Marriage and long-term relationships

In a subsequent analysis of marriage rates in the WHO studies, Hopper has recommended further investigations into the potential benefits of marriage or long-term partnerships in the study of psychosis (Hopper, 2004). For example, the long-term marital prospects of the participants in the developing countries are in stark contrast to those in the developed world. Jablensky & Cole (1997) have even argued that the data from the DOSMed point to how marriage may actually delay the onset of psychosis. In the ISOS study, 73% (74% of men and 71% of women) of the Indian cohort remained married at follow-up, compared to only 38% (28% of men and 48% of women) in the developed country cohort. Although the inevitable differences within cultures that result in various splits, due to class, gender, religious and caste distinctions, it is argued that the overall picture indicates the success of the social ethic Hindu Indian society (Shweder, 1990).

In support of the view that partnership may play a positive role in the course of schizophrenia in developing countries, other studies have also revealed the more universal buffering effects of long-term relationships and marriage. For example, married women with a diagnosis of schizophrenia in developed countries tend to fare better overall than men, as they tend to continue their relationships and participate in parenting (Jenkins, 1992). Rather than advocating marriage as a type of therapy (especially as domestic violence and abuse against women is far from uncommon in marriages, leading to significant mental distress), these results nevertheless point to the detrimental effects of isolation and seclusion in relation to the onset, course and outcome of schizophrenia and other mental health problems. Indeed, service users often report that stable long-term relationships are a positive force in buffering the effects of mental distress (Cherlin, 1999).

These lines of investigation remain speculative and require substantive and longitudinal evidence before conclusions regarding the exact nature of this positive relationship between developing countries and schizophrenia outcome can be understood. Furthermore, some authors, following a systematic review of the WHO data and further studies, have argued that the picture of better recovery rates in developing countries is not as straightforward as originally thought. For example, in a review of 23 studies in 11 low- and middle-income countries, Cohen, Patel, Thara & Gureje (2008) have argued that there is (a) greater variation of outcome and course across developing countries (e.g. good in India and poorer in Brazil and China), (b) levels of disability vary among developing countries (e.g. good in India and Indonesia but poorer in Nigeria and (c) social functioning and family relationships have so far not been examined in sufficient depth to determine whether developing countries as a whole provide better support for those diagnosed with schizophrenia (there being evidence of varying responses by families to 'mental illness' across developing countries). In sum, these authors conclude that further ethnographic and qualitative work is required to examine the quality of relationships and social support available across countries. They also argue that we should remain cautious about stating that those diagnosed with schizophrenia will always fare better in developing countries, before a more nuanced examination of the difference between countries is carried out.

Different cultural emphases, different problems?

In this section, we will discuss a range of different experiences and behaviours in order to assess whether some forms of mental health and distress are bound to specific cultures in particular ways. This focus will assist us with the second question raised at the beginning of the chapter, namely, 'Do different societies draw the same line between well-being and distress, sanity and madness?'

'Culture-bound syndromes' is the term for a unique set of behaviours and experiences recognized by members of a particular culture, and treated by them in a locally specific manner (Helman, 2000). They remain controversial, some arguing that such behaviours and experiences are merely different ways of expressing an underlying illness, and others that they cannot be inserted into existing Western diagnostic categories, given their symbolic and meaningful status in a society. These syndromes are characterized by behaviours that make sense and follow a given pattern in a population (Rubel, 1964). Of course, contemporary anthropologists have argued that all distress can be viewed as 'culture bound', as the expression of distress is always socially prescribed and never independent from human action (Littlewood, 2002).

The fourth edition of the DSM recognizes 'culture-bound syndromes', but only in a marginal sense, as they sit in the manual like an exotic enclave, dedicated to behaviours and beliefs that do not fit a traditional Western diagnosis. This is despite the existence of a DSM task force set up to advise and gather evidence on a variety of culture-bound syndromes

(including Western ones). However, we will not confine ourselves in this section, to a discussion of exotic beliefs from distant lands. Instead, we will look at a range of experiences, beliefs and behaviours that raise questions about the relationship between cultural emphasis and mental health more generally.

In the following sections, we will begin to see how certain behaviours can be viewed in a different light, according to their connection to particular cultural and religious beliefs on the nature of rationality and imagination, and of mind and body.

In order to illustrate this more fully, two main areas will be explored. First, we turn to different cultural constructions of dissociation and psychosis. **Dissociation** is the partial or complete disruption or disintegration of an individual's conscious or psychological functioning. It can be a response to trauma or drugs and can be adaptive in the short term, for example as a means to distance the individual from an unbearable experience. Over time, however, dissociation can dominate or even replace the individual's conscious perception of reality, especially at times of distress.

Dissociation Identity Disorder has often been associated with US culture and particular therapeutic practices there, and is characterized by the individual's display of a number of distinct identities or personalities (sometimes known as alters or alter egos), each with it own unique perspectives and ways of behaving. This diagnosis used to be called Multiple Personality Disorder.

We will examine the link between particular cultural beliefs on trauma and selfhood and the emergence of DID in the late 20th century. In addition, dissociation connected to particular religious and spiritual practices will be explored in order to assess the different ways in which these 'altered states of consciousness' are regarded in different religious and cultural communities (Clarke, 2010). Finally, we will examine how certain non-industrial societies have regarded psychotic states (e.g. hallucinations) as meaningful, and how resistance to psychiatric views of psychosis has also emerged in some European industrial societies (hallucinations are a sensory experience in which a person can hear or see something that others cannot).

We next explore the idea that different cultures have a variety of ways of expressing distress. Traditionally, examination of the various cultural 'idioms of distress' led some to claim that non-Western societies were more likely to express mental distress through the body – a process known as **somatization**: psychological stress or distress that leads to physical complaints.

The somatization thesis was often used to explain essential differences between Western and non-Western societies in the expression of distress, such as why South Asian patients presented with physical symptoms such as 'an aching heart' when depressed (see Lowenthal, 2007, for an excellent review of evidence relating to the somatization thesis).

The thesis has also been put forward as an explanation for why diagnoses of depression have traditionally been less common in the Eastern hemisphere, whilst diagnoses of 'neurasthenia' (nervous exhaustion) – that may resemble depression –have largely been higher (Kleinman, 2005). These two main areas illustrate how the lines between well-being, madness and distress can not only be drawn at different points but can lead to vastly different outcomes.

BOX **3.4**

Some 'culture-bound syndromes'

Koro (Malaysia, China, Africa). This is a belief in fatally retracting male genitals, or a belief in genital theft. It can cause widespread social concern or can remain the preoccupation of an isolated individual.

Wendigo psychosis (North America, Canada). The Wendigo (a malevolent spirit) is part of the traditional belief systems of various Algonquian-speaking tribes in the northern United States and Canada, most notably the Ojibwa/ Saulteaux, the Cree and the Innu/ Naskapi/Montagnais. Common to all these cultures is the conception of Wendigos as cannibalistic supernatural beings of great spiritual power. A person suffering from Wendigo psychosis craves human flesh, and believes that the evil Wendigo spirit possesses them.

Brain fag (West and South Africa). A condition mainly found in male students. It generally manifests as difficulty in concentrating on study and in somatic (physical) symptoms, including general fatigue and depression. It has similar symptoms to the Trinidadian illness *studiation madness*, whose main features include anxiety and depression.

Jinn (Middle East, North Africa). In Arabian and Muslim folklore, jinns are evil and grotesque demons with supernatural powers that they can give to people and then use to control them.

School refusal syndrome (UK). A behaviour identified in children who refuse to attend school.

Attention hyperactivity deficit disorder (mostly UK and US). This syndrome, involving hyperactive behaviour and a lack of concentration, has been found in increasing numbers, mostly in children, and is treated with prescribed medication (Ritalin).

DSM-IV-TR (2000)

Dissociation: spiritual enlightenment or illness?

Western professional practice is based on the assumption that what is rational can be clearly distinguished from what is *irrational*, and what is apparent (the real) from what is not (the imagined) (Littlewood, 2002). That is why states of dissociation and psychoses are often presented as prototypes of 'madness' in Western societies: they represent the opposite of the highly prized idea of a unified identity and self and adherence to the rational and the real (Hacking, 1996). Dissociation, according to Western diagnostic criteria, denotes a state of acute mental **decompensation**, in which certain thoughts, emotions, sensations, and memories are sectioned off, due to their often traumatic content; it represents the functional deterioration of a previously working structure or system in the human body and can occur as a result of trauma, fatigue, di/stress, disease or ageing.

Decompensation is a key feature of the Western bound disorder Dissociative Identity Disorder (DID: formerly known as multiple personality disorder) and is present in Post-traumatic Stress Disorder and other dissociative disorders listed in the DSM-IV. These disorders are considered to be signs of an underlying pathology, although significant questions have been raised about the cultural specificity of DID in particular, as this is rarely reported in Europe, in comparison with North America (Hacking, 1996; Littlewood, 2002). But is it always the case that individuals who experience dissociation are ill? To answer this question, we must move beyond Western scientific understandings of the real and the rational to discuss issues of religion, morality and spiritualism, as it is there that the boundaries between the real and the imagined not only shift but may crumble altogether.

Dissociation and multiple selves: Dissociative Identity Disorder in the US

Eric had suffered serious abuse as a child, and in psychotherapy began to reveal different personalities: 'quiet, middle aged Dwight, the hysterically blind and mute Jeffrey; Michael, an arrogant Jock, the coquettish Tian ...' To the therapist's astonishment, a total of 27 personalities were gradually revealed, Eric shifting personalities as many as nine times in a one-hour session. Some of the personalities would not talk to the therapist, whereas others would; some were aware of each other, and some were very reflective and insightful about Eric (based on Comer, 1999; cited in Loewenthal, 2007, p.105).

Although there is support for the idea that the self is made up of a 'community of internal voices' which resemble previous experiences and conversations (sometimes referred to as a 'dialogical self' – see Vygotsky, 1978; Thomas & Leuder, 2000; Osatuke et al., 2005), the idea that there is a unitary and consistent self is more familiar to Western professionals and lay people alike. The notion that several voices or personas can exist within one person is, therefore, often treated with suspicion in certain societies, and may only be openly addressed when some form of discrepancy or traumatic association between the various voices or personas exist. This explanation resembles the traditional Western approach to dissociation, in which an individual who experiences a series of traumatic events (commonly child sexual abuse in the case of DID) may avoid future pain by defending him or her self from painful memories by repressing them and splitting the self into a number of different **alters** (the distinct personalities displayed in DID).

A diagnosis of DID is more common in women than men (Hacking, 1996; Haaken, 1998). The alters can be regarded as fantasy-based characters or as different versions of the self. They develop in order to carry the burden of the painful memories and perform different roles, such as the protective adult alter who emerges in a situation that is stressful or volatile. One alter may be unaware of the behaviour or thoughts of another, which is why many 'multiples' (individuals diagnosed with DID) claim not to remember what some of their other alters have done. This is because they have split off aspects of their personality into separate components, and switches between alters may occur in different situations. DID can thus be understood as a strategy used by individuals with a history of trauma to cope with and defend against further pain. But how culturally specific is this coping strategy? Do all survivors of severe child sexual abuse behave in this way? The short answer to this is no. Socio-cognitive theorists (Spanos, 1994) have argued that DID has emerged out of certain cultural beliefs that legitimize the expression of difficult memories and experiences into separate components of the self. Psychotherapists can contribute to this process by providing further professional legitimation to this form of expression and by encouraging the client to see the different versions of themselves as distinct and separate personalities. According to this view, the disorder is a construction of therapist and client interactions, and not a naturally occurring phenomenon. Although such views regarding the construction of DID are controversial (Coons, Bowman & Milstein, 1988), it is interesting to note that DID is rarely diagnosed in Britain or Europe. Hacking, in a detailed exploration of this issue (1996), has suggested that hundreds of cases of multiple personality disorder emerged in the US within a relatively short period (beginning in the 1980s) and from a small number of therapists. This view was supported by Modestin (1992), who found that DID cases were reported by only 0.1% of the professional population. Spanos (1994) has also argued that if DID were a naturally occurring condition, there would not have been such a large increase in reports during the 1980s.

In short, DID may be considered less a 'condition' than a culturally specific social movement, supported by a small number of professionals and clients.

Despite the overwhelming focus on disruptive and highly culturally bound diagnoses in psychiatric and psychological literature, dissociation is not uncommon either in children (Bliss, 1980), or adults (Dorahy & Lewis, 2001) across all societies (Clarke, 2010). This includes dissociation related to coping with trauma, as well as dissociation related to religious or spiritual experience. The interesting thing to note is that the existence of dissociation *per se* does not lead to poor mental health, but, rather, the interpretation and purpose for which it is used. The question we must ask is whether in some societies and/ or religious communities, states of mind that are considered dissociative in one culture may be viewed very differently, even positively, in another.

Dissociation and religious experiences

My first experience of speaking in tongues was truly amazing. I had been a Christian attending a Baptist church for some time and had always wanted to connect with the holy spirit. The pastor in my church had always said that once you could speak in tongues, you had secured a special place in the kingdom of heaven. As the church orchestra began to play, I felt a presence taking over me, lifting me, running through my body. I felt light and I began to hear the voices of a thousand angels inside and outside my head. Everyone in the congregation was participating. Their eyes were closed, hands outstretched and then, some people began speaking in an unrecognizable language. I too began to join in, speaking in a language that I did not recognize. I felt euphoric, drunk almost, and overwhelmingly happy, as if my body was no longer my own, like I had been possessed by God himself. I was told by a friend that my trance lasted for about ten minutes, though it felt like it was hours before I came round again (description of glossolalia in a British Baptist church; personal correspondence).

In certain societies, what we might consider to be dissociative may in fact be connected to culturally or religiously specific states. Possession states share with DID the feeling that the core self is being substituted with another that contains new knowledge and motives. This can include possession by a spiritual entity or alteration of consciousness through a trance-like state (Loewenthal, 2007). Case studies from Singapore (Ng, 2000), Colombia (Pineros, Rosselli & Calderon, 1998), Senegal (Bullard, 2005) and other African societies (Helman, 2000) have shown possession and trance states to share certain features with dissociative states, such as amnesia, multiplicity and a loss of touch with reality. Possessions may also result from personally stressful and traumatic experiences such as isolation or abuse, although this is not always the case. Possession and trance states are often more connected to particular religious beliefs, such as the belief in reincarnation and spirits. But how useful is it to consider these experiences as a clear and stable form of mental disorder?

Witztum, Grisaru & Budowski (1996) describe states of *Zar* (spirit possession), common in parts of Africa, Asian and the Middle East. Despite being considered by some as a psychiatric or neurological disorder, *Zar* has been described as a culture-based syndrome that fulfils certain functions in a community, including the reinforcement of cosmological beliefs, the psychological manipulation of women, and when an exorcism is performed, the re-establishment of group ties (Al-Adawi, Martin, Al-Salmi & Ghassani, 2001, cited in Loewenthal, 2007). Like DID, it is women who appear to be more susceptible to spirit possession; possession is only accepted when the person thinks they are possessed and community members endorse this (Lewis, 1971). Although possession is considered to be abnormal and undesirable in certain circumstances (especially where the person is withdrawn or distressed), it is nevertheless endorsed by members of some societies and culturally normative (Helman, 2000). The solution or treatment can be a community-involved exorcism of the spirits, involving music and dance and a general acceptance of the person.

Glossolalia (speaking in tongues) is also a common feature of certain religious practices in parts of North America, India, Africa, the Caribbean and many Pentecostal churches across Europe and the US. It is an activity that usually takes place in church and is associated with higher spirituality and a closer connection to God. It involves a trance-like dissociative state in which the individual rolls or closes their eyes, tears at their clothes and may scream and fall over. Though considered dissociative in form, glossolalia is only considered to be abnormal when it is *uncontrollable* (Littlewood & Lipsedge, 1997). It is once again clear that different societies set different standards regarding what is acceptable, and many clinicians believe that religious practices should be taken into account when assessing the likelihood of there being underlying mental distress as the route cause of dissociation (Helman, 2007; Clarke, 2010). In the case of some religious communities, dissociation through glossolalia itself is not necessarily problematic; what matters is whether the person is able to control it or not. Even so, it is clear that cultural and religious metaphors run through these experiences and behaviours, including the example of Dissociative Identity Disorder in the US (many individuals who have been diagnosed with DID have claimed to have taken part in satanic rituals). Just as spirit possession and glossolalia cannot be understood without reference to the cultural and religious contexts in which they are embedded, neither can DID be comprehensible without reference to its emergence in particular therapeutic contexts and within particular (cultural) constructions of selfhood.

Are the boundaries between madness and sanity similar or different across cultures?

We are already well acquainted with the Western psychiatric (and variously) psychological view that psychotic behaviours – delusions and hallucinations – are clear signs of disorder and disease, or what we have euphemistically come to regard as *madness* (mainly contained as the symptoms of schizophrenia) (Bentall, 2003). However, this interpretation of hallucinations may not be universal, as some societies do not have such a clear public dividing line between imagination and reality or between spiritual and real consciousness (Al-Issa, 1995). Cultural anthropologist Erika Bourguignon, for example, found that hallucinations played a role in the ritual practices of 62% of the 488 societies she studied and were not necessarily considered to be a sign of illness.

Behaviour that is considered psychotic or mad according to Western psychiatric standards may be treated with respect and reverence and considered to be legitimate signs of authority and/or higher consciousness. Shamans and traditional healers (holy individuals who are believed to experience higher consciousness) may be initiated into their profession through a 'psychotic' experience (i.e. hearing voices), believing that this experience has led to a higher and more positive state of consciousness.

Communicating with spirits that are not visible to others could be considered a sign of a psychotic mental illness. However, many anthropologists would argue that there are noticeable differences between many shamans and healers and psychotic individuals (Krippner & Achterberg, 2000). American anthropologist Richard Noll, in comparing a DSM-III diagnosis of schizophrenia with shamanic behaviour, found the major difference to be the ability of the Shaman to voluntarily enter and leave his or her altered states of consciousness. The degree of organization and self-control required by shamans and healers would not necessarily be evident in an individual experiencing a full-blown psychotic episode, as diagnosed by a Western practitioner. Moreover, to equate the states of mind evidenced by shamans and healers with psychotic states or madness (as understood diagnostically) would be to deny the contribution they clearly make to their communities and cultures, on a practical and symbolic level. Often it is necessary to be aware of the symbolic content of unusual experiences and thoughts in order to pass reasonable judgment on them and to understand the constructive meanings underlying these kinds of experiences and behaviours (Littlewood, 1998). Despite such noticeable cultural differences in the values placed upon those who enter altered states of consciousness, it should be remembered that most people who hear voices or experience delusional states (people who would be diagnosed psychotic) in industrialized nations often do not come into contact with psychiatric or psychological services (Bentall, 2003). This indicates that the distinction between the imaginary and the real is more a prerequisite for Western psychiatric and psychological practice, rather than a simple reflection of what people in various countries experience or how they act upon such an experience (see Box 3.5). In other words, psychotic cases described in the Western literature are largely those who are known to psychiatric services, rather than a true reflection of those experiences in society (Clarke, 2010).

In all cultures, it appears that there are people who enter the realm of the imaginary (e.g. hearing voices) on a daily basis who may live independent lives, without any intervention by mental health services. Some societies clearly create valued roles for those who would otherwise go unnoticed (if they did not approach services) or be deemed sick or dysfunctional in Western societies. As in the experience of the shamans and healers, it appears that those individuals who believe they can control their experience, or are stronger than their voices, will probably not be distressed by them in Western countries and remain absent from professional psychiatric and psychological accounts (Romme & Escher, 1993).

The role of the Shaman varies across African and South American societies. Generally, the shamanic practitioner is considered to have access to the world of spirits and perform a number of healing rituals. Here a Zulu witchdoctor throws his bones on a straw mat, and by reading their layout receives messages from dead ancestors, which he relays to the Chief and rest of the tribe

Body, mind and society

A continuing theme in the mental health literature is the extent to which different societies (specifically, Western and non-Western) *express* mental health problems and distress in different ways. Many observers have pointed to the traditional Western emphasis, originating in Descarte's philosophical meditations, on mind–body distinctions (Cartesian dualism). Western models of mental illness typically locate causality either in the mind (e.g. cognitive models of depression) or in the brain (e.g. depression as a result of low levels of serotonin, dopamine or noradrenalin), as well as distinguishing both mind and body from the environment. Current treatments for mental illness address either the brain (psychiatric medication) or the mind (psychotherapy, counselling, CBT and all 'talking cures'), without much attempt to explain how either system operates in the context of the environment.

Eastern traditions have tended not to distinguish mind from body, but have instead emphasized the interdependency between mind, body and environment (Krause, 1998). Most Asian and Pacific cultures take a more holistic approach to mind, body and environment, with a more widespread

BOX **3.5**

Professional and lay interpretations of psychosis in European societies

In the early 1990s, the Dutch psychiatrist Marius Romme was challenged by one of his patients to accept an alternative view of the voice-hearing experience. After failing to accept his psychiatric interpretation of her voices (that hearing voices was a symptom of a mental illness), she described to him how in Ancient Greece, voice-hearing was part of normal experience. After Romme and his patient appeared on Dutch television, 450 voice-hearers called in, many of whom had never attended a mental health consultation. Around one third of callers reported being distressed by their voices. The main difference between those who had become patients was that they perceived the voice to be

stronger than they were, whereas the non-patients did not feel this way. As a result of this patient intervention, Romme and journalist Sandra Escher organized a national network for Dutch voice-hearers, where voice-hearers could meet, discuss their experiences and support each other, outside of psychiatric services. This organization, known as *Resonance*, takes the position that voice-hearing is part of normal human variation, rather than a sign of mental illness. The ethos of the group is self-advocacy, rather than professional intervention. Wherever possible, members are encouraged to avoid psychiatric services and accept their voices, by understanding why the voices may have emerged, and to create a dialogue with them. Many voice-hearers report troubled, stressful and traumatic events in their lives that lend meaning to the content of their voices. The purpose of these self-advocacy groups is to provide members with the space to explore their

lives and eventually to exercise more control over their experiences.

In the UK, the Hearing Voices Network (HVN) is a registered charity and has a number of local branches across the country, as well as a national helpline. A number of psychologists and psychiatrists in the UK are supportive of HVN, though it remains marginal in relation to statutory mental health services.

These self-advocacy groups provide individuals with the space to accept and respect their experiences. According to these networks, voice-hearing, when it is seen as part of normal human variation rather than an illness that requires a cure, can be integrated, understood, supported and respected.

Networks such as these demonstrate how lay views can create sub-cultures of their own. They also signal how it is possible for professionals to change their minds on certain issues, when presented with a viable alternative.

---

recognition that there is a symbolic correspondence between these elements, wherein natural substances and energies, as well as supernatural forces, are *indistinct* from mind–body processes (Marsella & White, 1982). Greater emphasis is also placed on the body in relation to the environment, which means that psychological processes (personality, feeling states), although considered to be important, may not be regarded as the *origin* of the problem. Although differences in cultural traditions still exist (see below for the diagnosis of neurasthenia), it is important to note that Western psychiatric and psychological professional cultures have been shown to shift non-Western perspectives on mind–body relationships towards a more Cartesian and hence Western medical view (see Krause, 1998).

Somatization

The term somatization refers to the existence of physical symptoms that have no identifiable organic cause. A popular proposal is that non-Western societies tend to view distressing experiences as physical symptoms – **somato-psychic**, in contrast to Western societies who take the view that psychological distress causes physical symptoms – **psycho-somatic** (Angel & Guarnaccia, 1989; Marsella & White, 1982). However, somatic complaints with no identifiable organic origin, are common in both Western and non-Western societies (Dubovsky, 1987), the difference being that the *expression* of distress through the body is accepted and even encouraged more readily by non-Western societies, due to a general belief in the lack of separation between mind and body.

In the mental health literature somatization is sometimes referred to as one of the 'idioms of distress', whereby mental distress is communicated through the body as physical complaints and/or symptoms. But what are the origins of

these observations, and are they correct? The proposal that non-Western societies are prone to somatizing mental health problems has a long history. Kraepelin, for example, argued that the Javanese people tended towards more sensorial expressions of illness, due to a deficit in higher thought functioning. Littlewood & Lipsedge (1997) argue in *Aliens & Alienists* (1982) that the history of the somatization proposal is based on a set of naïve and racist assumptions regarding the inability of non-Western people to recognize higher thoughts and feelings within themselves. In this section, we will consider the evidence regarding somatization and the extent to which it is *more common* in certain societies, or *more commonly acknowledged as a legitimate mode of expression*. A commonly held view in the psychiatric and psychological literature is that physical symptoms that have no organic origin are common across the world and reflect an individual's mental state (Kleinman & Kleinman, 1985). Stress, trauma, loss and physical and mental oppression can all lead to somatization, in any culture. The psychological mechanisms contributing to somatization are often viewed as dysfunctional responses in Western psychiatry and psychology, perhaps because of the emphasis on open expression of thought processes and the residing focus on the individual (as the source of the problem). Denial ('I don't have a problem'), suppression ('I can deal with it later') and repression ('I need to get that off my mind so I can concentrate on other things') (Dubovsky, 1997) are all believed to be the main mechanisms through which somatization develops.

We will discuss aches and pains and exhaustion and fatigue, as these complaints have been commonly discussed in literature with reference to their resemblance to Western models of depression and anxiety.

Common questions raised in psychiatry and psychology have been whether certain societies have a greater incidence of somatization or whether there are simply different ways of diagnosing and treating them. It is clear that in Eastern professional and lay cultures, somatization is accepted and considered to be a legitimate form of expression. But is it the case that somatization is less common in non-Western societies more generally?

A World Health Organization study (1997) collected data from 15 centres across Europe, Africa, Asia and North and South America (Gureje, Simon, Ustun & Goldberg, 1997). 25, 0000 primary care attendees were screened and interview data were collected from 5, 438 people. The interesting finding was that chronic pain was related to psychological distress across all of the centres, despite some variation. Furthermore, independent studies have not found higher rates of somatization in South Korean(see above) or Ghanaian samples (Ofori-Atta & Linden, 1995).

In the UK, Perkins & Moodley (1993), studied 60 acute admissions into psychiatric wards, finding that nearly 60% of those admitted did not think they had a psychiatric complaint and 40% believed they had a somatic complaint or that their problems were social in origin. In another British study, Bhui et al. (2004) compared symptoms in Punjabi (2006) and white English (173) participants attending a primary care clinic in London. Contrary to previous work, where South Asians have been commonly perceived to have a tendency to somatize distress, somatic complaints were equally prevalent in the Asian and white British sample. Furthermore, depression was higher among the Asian participants, which again fails to support the common view about Asian individuals and their tendency to express distress through somatization. Further studies have confirmed higher rates of depression in South and East Asian women in the UK, based on a household survey of 10,000 adults (Meltzer, Gill, Petticrew & Hinds, 1995 – report 1). This finding does not support the proposal that somatization in Asian populations, *replaces* or poses an *alternative* to psychological presentations of distress.

Culturally specific forms and diagnoses of somatization?

Although somatic complaints appear to be common in all societies, what is often missing from Western psychological accounts is the extent to which different cultures encourage somatization, and thus the extent to which it would be viewed as *dysfunctional* or *functional in* different cultural settings. One society, for example, may value a more indirect expression of unpleasant feelings, than another that places values on self-expression and emotional or individualistic accounts of adversity.

For example, consider the example below:

Over the past two years, Mrs Lin's physical symptoms have worsened and she has frequently sought help from physicians of both biomedicine and traditional Chinese medicine. When questioned by me, she admits to more symptoms – difficulty with sleep, appetite and energy, as well as joyfulness, anxiety and feelings that it would be better to be dead. She has an intense feeling of guilt about the stillbirth and also about not being able to be helpful in practical ways to her paraplegic brother. During the past six months she has developed feelings of hopelessness and helplessness, as well as self-abnegating thoughts. Mrs.

Lin regards her life as a failure. She has fleeting feelings that it would be better for all if she took her own life, but she has put these suicidal ideas to the side and made no plans to kill herself.

From Mrs Lin's perspective, her chief problem is her 'neurasthenia'. She remarks that if only she could be cured of this 'physical' problem and the constant headache, dizziness and fatigue it creates, she would feel more hopeful and would be better able to adapt to her family situation. For a North American psychiatrist, Mrs Lin meets the official diagnostic criteria for a major depressive disorder. The Chinese psychiatrists who interviewed her with me did not agree with this diagnosis. They did not deny that she was depressed, but they regarded the depression as a manifestation of neurasthenia, and Mrs Lin shared this viewpoint. Neurasthenia – a syndrome of exhaustion, weakness and diffuse bodily complaints believed to be caused by inadequate physical energy in the central nervous system – is an official diagnosis in China; but not in the American Psychiatric Association's latest nosology.

Case example from
Arthur Kleinman's research in China

Arthur Kleinman is the leading expert on somatization and mental distress in China. It is evident from his example that a diagnosis of neurasthenia is particular to Chinese (and East Asian) society and is used to *explain* the origins of low mood. This is contrary to a Western perspective, where a diagnosis of depression would actually be used to *explain* the physical symptoms. A diagnosis of neurasthenia is still commonly used in Chinese and East Asian societies, even though the diagnosis is not included in Western diagnostic manuals. Why is this? Is it because somatization is generally higher in Eastern societies? According to a study by Yen, Robins & Lin (2000), this idea is not supported, as *non-clinical* samples revealed no significant differences between the incidence of somatization in the Far East and the US. The difference appears to lie in the number of clients reporting somatic complaints to professionals and the manner in which the complaint was received.

Kleinman & Kleinman (1985) have argued that China is a more collectivist culture, where interdependency and social ties and bonds are valued over individualism. In many parts of Chinese society, individuals do not report feeling depressed or sad but express feelings of boredom, discomfort and symptoms of pain, dizziness and fatigue (Kleinman, 2004). Kleinman argues that interdependent individuals are more likely to express their distress in somatic complaints like exhaustion, so that social bonds and ties are maintained and the possibility of stigma is reduced. If an individual openly expresses distress ('I am unhappy about this relationship'), this is considered to be disruptive of social ties, especially when difficult social ties are likely to be the cause of the distress (Keyes & Ryff, 2003). In Japan, for example, Lock (1988) found that women with somatic complaints were more likely to receive interpersonal counselling, rather than a diagnosis of mental or physical illness. Furthermore, in a comparative study of the US and South Korea, Keyes & Ryff (2003) found an equal prevalence of somatic symptoms, the difference being that somatizers in South Korea did not also have symptoms of depression, as it was understood that this indirect expression of distress was socially supported and acknowledged. Conversely, somatizers in the US felt depressed and frustrated at the lack of support they received for their physical complaints and felt stigmatized and misunderstood by professionals.

In sum, this study and others have demonstrated that somatization in a collectivist culture such as South Korea and other East Asian societies is viewed as a constructive response to mental distress, whereas US participants, in a more individualistic culture, tend to report depression more often, due to feeling unsupported, undervalued and stigmatized. Studies on somatization raise questions for psychology and mental health, because the way in which certain cultures view the relationship between mind, body and environment affect how mental health and distress is experienced by the individual, how the practitioner diagnoses it and the types of treatment on offer. Sensitivity to different cultural traditions is necessary if the boundaries between mind and body, and consequently mental illness and health, are variable across cultures.

Migration

Migration refers to the movement of a group of people (sometimes large groups) from one place to another, sometimes over large distances. This can be either voluntary or involuntary, as in the slave trade or via human trafficking. The reasons for migration range from seeking better employment, educational opportunities or marriage to escape from war and/or oppressive regimes in the migrants' own country. Migration has contributed a rich texture to many developed societies, leading to an increase in the diversity of cultures, races and ethnicities in those societies (Bhugra & Becker, 2005). In the UK, the majority of permanent immigrants are members of ethnic minority groups and in the last British census (2001), those belonging to ethnic minorities had reached 4.6 million or 7.9% of the population. The largest ethnic minority population in Britain is Indian, then Pakistani, followed by mixed ethnic backgrounds, Black Caribbeans, Black Africans and Bangladeshis (cited in Bhugra & Becker, 2005). In this section, we will explore the relationship between trans-national migration (as opposed to urban–rural migration) and cultural identity with reference to mental health and distress.

Individuals who migrate tend to experience significant levels of stress and there are several hypotheses linking higher rates of diagnosed disorders such as schizophrenia in migrant groups. However, the reasons why some groups are more often diagnosed with particular difficulties are complex.

A number of reasons for these higher rates of diagnosis have been proposed, including racist and/or culturally insensitive professional practices in the UK, the stress of migration itself and difficulties with cultural bereavement and cultural identity.

Cultural identification; psychosis and African–Caribbean men

A number of studies conducted in the UK have shown higher rates of schizophrenia diagnoses in African–Caribbean groups (Bhugra, 2000). Several critics have put this down to the existence of racism in psychiatric practices (Fernando, 2003) and a propensity to misdiagnose African–Caribbean men (in particular) due to anti-social behaviour. Indeed, African–Caribbean men are significantly more likely to be compulsorily detained in psychiatric hospitals and to be given medication, than their white counterparts (Pilgrim & Rogers, 2010). In order to examine this issue, researchers at the Institute of Psychiatry invited a Jamaican psychiatrist, Fred Hickling, to reassess their diagnoses of schizophrenia (using detailed case notes) for African–Caribbean men to establish whether white psychiatrists were more likely to *over* diagnose this group. The study revealed broad agreement between the diagnoses made by Hickling and the British psychiatrists, suggesting that racism alone could not account for the elevated rates of schizophrenia diagnoses among African–Caribbeans in the UK. Furthermore, a community sample also found higher rates of psychosis among African–Caribbeans living in Nottingham (Harrison, Amin, Singh, Croudace and Jones, 1999). Given this evidence and the fact that there are lower incidence rates for psychoses in the Caribbean than in the British African–Caribbean community (ruling out a genetic vulnerability), several authors have explored the significance of migration in the development of psychosis, not only amongst first-, but second-generation African–Caribbeans in the UK and several European societies (Bentall, 2003).Furthermore, recent large scale meta-analyses of the data appears to support the role of migration as a significant risk factor for psychotic diagnoses (namely schizophrenia; see Cantor-Graae & Selten, 2005).

Ethnic density and parental absence

Several reasons emerge to explain these incidence rates in both first and second generation migrants. First, a recent study in London revealed that non-white people living in predominantly white neighbourhoods were more likely to be psychotic than non-white people living in predominantly non-white neighbourhoods. In one study, for example, equal rates of schizophrenia were found among Asians and whites and, interestingly, large numbers of Asians were living close by, leading to protective effects and greater levels of social support (Bhugra, 2004). Racial tension and isolation, therefore, may explain why higher rates of psychosis are found in some ethnic minority groups and not others (Boydell et al., 2001). Experiences of isolation, alienation and racial discrimination can lead to a number of negative emotional states, including poor self-worth and hypervigilance, all of which can affect psychological processes, such as attributions or self-representations (known to play a role in paranoia, psychosis and mania). **Hypervigilance** is a general sensory state referring to an individual's exaggerated sense of, and behaviours used to check for, perceived threat. This heightened awareness of threat usually results in fatigue.

Second, in an attempt to explain why the children of African–Caribbean immigrants were more vulnerable to psychosis, Dinesh Bhugra and colleagues found that out of 38 African–Caribbean hospital patients (diagnosed with schizophrenia), 12 (34%) had been separated from their mothers for a period of four years or more during childhood, and 19 (53%) had been separated from their fathers for a similar period (Bhugra et al., 1997). This suggests that migration may make it more difficult for some families to provide the sustained care and support that could protect their children from the adverse effects of significant life stressors (including racism), though more research is required to explore the relationship between parental absence, migration and childhood experiences. Third, challenges to cultural identity have been found to increase feelings of social isolation, experiences of discrimination, low self-esteem and alienation. **Acculturation** refers to a process of psychological transition when an individual moves from one culture to another. It also refers to the exchange or merging of cultural values, behaviours and feature that occurs when different cultural groups come into direct contact (e.g. by living in the same country). Although the groups remain distinct, each may alter over time as a result of its contact with the other.

Psychologist John Berry has described four outcomes of this process, which depend on whether the culture of origin or the host culture is identified with (see Table 3.2). The four outcomes are as follows:

1 *Integration* –the individual identifies with and adopts characteristics of both cultures
2 *Assimilation* – the individual rejects her culture of origin and embraces the host culture
3 *Separation* – the individual rejects the host culture and embraces his culture of origin
4 *Marginalization* – the individual does not commit to either culture.

If an individual is caught between two cultural identity groups, and rejected by both, a dissonance between the original and surrounding concept of self can then ensue, according to Berry. This is more likely to be experienced by the children of migrants, and can lead to marginalization, the most stressful of the four outcomes (Bentall, 2003; Bhugra, 2004). This, together with an increased risk of unemployment, a lack of social support (e.g. living in isolation from one's cultural

group), poverty and discrimination can result in a higher risk of long-term mental distress (Bhugra, 2004; Hwang & Wood, 2010). Furthermore, when an individual comes from a collectivist society it may be a significant challenge to their cultural identity to have to move to a society where individualism is held in high esteem, especially when he cannot make contact with members of his cultural group because of geographical isolation. When the stress of these experiences becomes overwhelming, distress can escalate and have a bad effect on self-esteem (Crisp & Turner, 2011).

Table 3.2 **The four types of acculturation**

		Identification with host culture	
		Yes	No
Identification with culture of origin	**Yes**	Integration	Separation
	No	Assimilation	Marginalization

Source: **Adapted from Berry & Kim (1988).**

The available evidence indicates that the children of immigrants are at particular risk of mental distress. However, more research is needed to establish the range of factors contributing to this: life events, racial and socio-economic discrimination, parental attachment and separation, employment and educational status, all deserve significantly greater attention if the relationship between migration, cultural identity and mental health and distress is to be understood.

Chapter summary

The relationship between culture and mental health and distress is ongoing and complex. In this chapter, we have discussed a number of issues that speak to this debate more generally, but in particular, we have discussed issues that speak more specifically to the role of culture in psychological approaches to mental health and distress. This is not a straightforward project, given the complexity of the definition and uses of culture in different research and practice traditions, in which particular views on measurement and methodological approaches differ.

Returning to the first major question raised in this section, 'To what extent do variations or similarities exist between cultures, in terms of the prevalence, incidence and course of traditionally defined mental "disorders"?', we can respond by discussing the differences in prevalence rates and the course of traditionally defined mental disorders between cultures, using the available evidence from large-scale studies.

However, it is also clear that increases in the use of Western diagnostic criteria and Western mental health professional cultures across the world may lead to more cases being identified. Furthermore, an increase in industrialization in previously non-industrialized societies may result in greater numbers of specific mental health problems, due to the growing appropriation of Western values (see the example of the growth of eating disorders in Japan). In exploring issues of dissociation, madness

and the relationship between body and mind in the second half of the section, we were able to address the second question 'Do different societies draw a line between well-being and distress, sanity and madness in the same way?' Once again, it is clear that different societies (and cultures) appear to have assigned a variety of meanings to states of mind and body. These are cut across with differences in religious practices and beliefs, as well as values associated with particular forms of expressions of mental states (see the example of dissociation and psychosis). Although somatic complaints (without any organic cause) are common throughout the world, for example, cultural labels and values are given to them, affecting the individual's own personal relationship to them and the treatment offered (for example, see diagnoses of depression and neurasthenia).

This brings us to another important point about the role of professional cultures in the measurement, diagnosis and treatment of mental health and distress across societies. A number of professional cultures may operate in a given society, but the one that may have the most impact, in terms of diagnosis and treatment, is often the one assigned the highest authority to speak on behalf of clients and patients. This can be due to government and industrial support (for example, from drug companies) for particular kinds of funding and clinical practice. And yet, in the case of the Hearing Voices Network in Holland and the UK, it is also clear that sub-cultures can develop as a means to resist the dominant point of view, leading to the creation of alternative reference points for users of the mental health system.

The last section, on migration, indicates that the study of culture is far from just a study of different geographical societies. A number of cultures contribute to European and North American societies, divided as they are by ethnicity and race and influenced by a number of religious practices. Issues of religion and spirituality are, therefore, clearly important in making sense of a particular cultural group, given the variety of religious and spiritual beliefs about the nature of mind and altered conscious states that exist.

In summary, culture is not a 'thing' that can easily be measured and *controlled* for. Culture is a way of life affecting us all. In psychology, we often forget that our beliefs about mental health and distress are shaped by wider cultural beliefs about the mind and body, what it means to be a person, a self and an individual (Ritter et al., 2010). We also tend to forget that the history of psychology as a discipline is such that the methodological traditions of psychology (as well as psychiatry as a continuous presence in some psychological research on mental health) affect how we look at the world and at people, how we measure them and ultimately understand them.

End of chapter questions

1 If different cultures have different standards for assessing psychological distress, what does that tell us about universal measurements?

2 Why do certain countries have better recovery rates for psychological distress (even for the so-called 'serious' psychotic states?), despite having less or no access to psychiatric treatments such as medication?

3 Does how we understand the mind and body affect the way we experience and professionally treat psychological distress?

4 Could a combination of quantitative and qualitative forms of assessment that do not rely on diagnostic categories produce a more accurate picture of rates and recovery from psychological distress?

Find out more

Helman, C. (2007). *Culture, Health and Illness* (5th edn). London: Hodder Arnold.

Jenkins, J. H. & Barrett, R. J. (Eds) (2004). *Schizophrenia, Culture and Subjectivity: The Edge of Experience*. Cambridge: Cambridge University Press.

Kazarian, S. S. & Evans, D. R. (Eds) (1998).*Cultural Clinical Psychology: Theory, Research and Practice*. Oxford: Oxford University Press.

Krause, I. B. (1998). *Therapy across Culture: Psychotherapy and Cultural Diversity*. London: Sage.

Littlewood, R. (2002). *Pathologies of the West: An Anthropology of Mental Illness in Europe and America*. New York: Cornell University Press.

Sadler, J. Z. (2005). *Values and Psychiatric Diagnoses*. Oxford: Oxford University Press.

Warner, R. (1994). *Recovery from Schizophrenia: Psychiatry and Political Economy*. London: Routledge.

Novels

Head, B. (1974). *A Question of Power*. Portsmouth NH: Heinemann International Literature & Textbooks.

In this autobiographical novel, Bessie Head describes slipping between psychotic hallucinations that torment, and wakefulness. Head explores these themes in the context of difficult social relationships and in the context of her being an exiled woman with a young son.

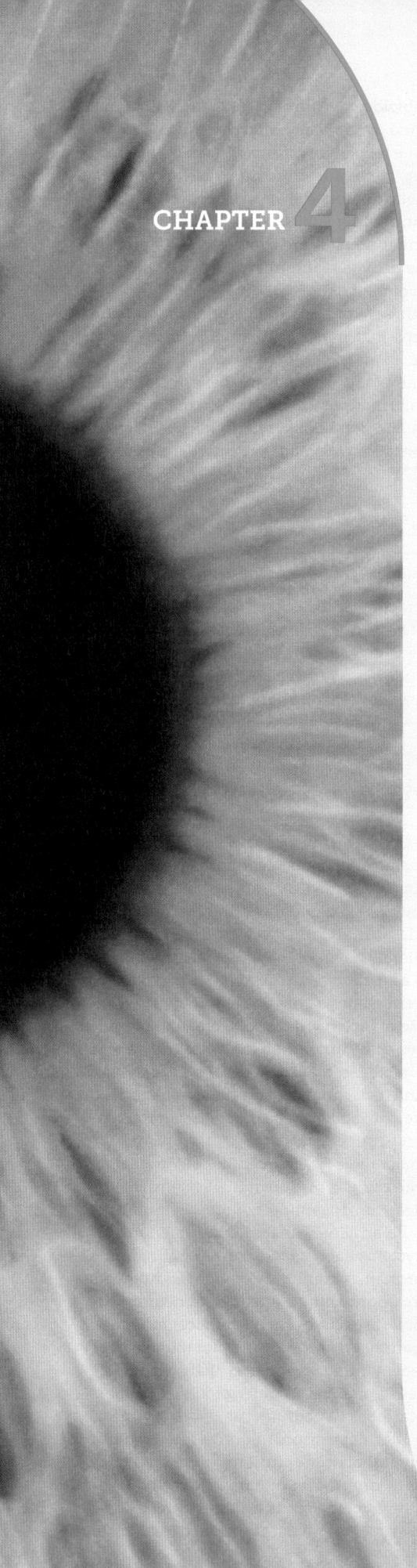

CHAPTER 4

BIOLOGY

Matthew's story

Matthew is a 22-year-old man who recently started hearing voices. He is a regular cannabis user, and his psychiatrist noted that cannabis may have caused his problems.

Matthew's mother is a black woman. His father, a white soldier, left home before Matthew was four. Matthew has only vague memories of his father, none of them pleasant: he remembers a lot of shouting, and once he saw his mother being hit. When he was growing up, Matthew's mother would never talk about his father; he quickly learned that it was best if he didn't, either.

At school, Matthew quickly became conscious of his mixed-race heritage and felt excluded by both white and black children. Although his teachers judged him to be quite bright, he never excelled at schoolwork and was often in trouble. As Matthew entered his teenage years he began to truant frequently. He began using cannabis when he was 15, and was soon smoking the drug most days. He also experimented with glue-sniffing and amphetamine.

Matthew left school at 16, and drifted into temporary, casual employment in various low-paid manual jobs – warehouse packing, stacking shelves in supermarkets, and so on. In between these jobs, he was unemployed and lived on benefits.

At the age of 20, during one of his more stable jobs, Matthew moved away from his mother's house and into a shared flat. Shortly afterwards, his mother traded the council house she had shared with Matthew for a small flat in another area. At first, Matthew continued to see her regularly, but became increasingly frustrated that she didn't seem to understand that his experience of growing up was very different from her own. They often argued, always about seemingly trivial or unimportant things, and his visits became less frequent.

As time passed, Matthew felt increasingly desperate to be in a relationship. About a month before his diagnosis, he had an embarrassing incident at a night-club. He was talking to an attractive woman and gave her his phone number. He went to the toilet, but when he came back she was talking and laughing with another man. Matthew was afraid she was laughing about him, so he left the club alone. Although he checked his phone obsessively in the days that followed, she didn't call.

After this incident, Matthew stopped going out. He stayed alone in his room, leaving only to get shopping and to claim benefits. After a while he began to hear voices whispering insults and abuse at him, especially at night. His sleep was disrupted, and he became afraid. His flatmates were concerned and called a GP. After a 20-minute conversation with Matthew the GP decided that a psychiatric assessment was appropriate. A member of the on-call team visited and gave Matthew a diagnosis of schizophrenia. He was taken into hospital and given antipsychotic medication.

After you have read this chapter you will be able to:

1 Describe some challenges to the idea that biology is the primary cause of distress
2 Explain why ignoring biology in relation to distress is inadequate
3 Describe Rose's 'lifelines' model of genes and environment
4 Describe Schore's account of brain development in infants
5 Explain the importance of plasticity and specificity in relation to distress.

Introduction

The vast majority of the research literature relating biology and distress falls into one of two broad camps. One camp – associated with psychiatry, abnormal psychology and biological psychology – positions biology as the primary cause of distress. The other– associated with social science and cognitive psychology –treats biology as largely irrelevant to distress. Students are typically faced with a difficult forced choice: they must agree with one camp or the other. Otherwise, they must attempt to accommodate the claims of both camps and find a balance between them.

In this chapter we suggest that this forced choice is inappropriate. Treating biology as the primary cause of distress ignores the many contradictions and gaps in the evidence base, and requires the naïve assumption that this evidence is somehow 'objective'. But ignoring biology is equally misguided because if we do so, we cannot explain how distress manifests itself in the bodies and brains of particular individuals, and the ways in which biological processes are both modified by, and productive of, everyday life experiences are obscured.

In this chapter we recognize that, for better and for worse, our experience is intimately, unavoidably, bound up with our bodies. In other words, our **embodiment** –the location and the character of our bodies within the world – contributes to all of the things we are ever able to see, hear, touch, taste and smell, all of the memories we form, and all the different moments we live through. Our bodies consist of many interlocking biological systems, so biology helps to make possible every experience we ever have. But this does not mean that we must assume that biology simply *causes* our experiences, which are always multi-layered (Connolly, 2002). We all have dreams, desires, wishes, hopes and beliefs, and we all experience pains and frustrations when these are challenged or blocked. All of these experiences *require* biology, but cannot simply be *reduced* to biology.

In the second half of this chapter we present an alternative way of thinking about the role of biology in distress. This alternative is drawn from the work of biologist and neuroscientist Steven Rose, and is based upon the notion of **lifelines**. A lifeline is the trajectory of a living creature as it grows, develops and ages, as it constantly modifies – and is modified by – the various environments it occupies. This focus on lifelines will let us move away from simple, static oppositions - for example, between 'nature' and 'nurture', biological processes and environmental forces. It will help us to recognize that at every level, including the biological, humans and their environments continuously and dynamically **interpenetrate** – that is, they quite literally come to include aspects of each other. From the lifeline perspective, genes and environments, for example, are not opposed. Genetic influence always occurs within environments, and is continuously subject to regulation by them. At the same time, environments are themselves continually being modified by the activities of humans, activities shaped, in part, by the actions of their genes.

At some points in this chapter we will be referring to brain structures and systems that may be unfamiliar to you. It is impractical, however, to define these as we have done for other ideas and terminology. Instead, we have included in this chapter various illustrations of the human brain and its components and systems. You should refer to these images if you want to know more about the brain structures and systems being discussed.

Guiding questions

Throughout this chapter, you should bear in mind these two questions:

1 *Why is the role of biology in distress so often seen as controversial?*
2 *How can we include biology, psychology and social influence* equally *in our thinking about distress?*

Biology: the primary cause of distress?

As we explained in Chapter 1, this is the way of thinking about biology that characterizes most 'abnormal psychology' textbooks. It underpins most medical and psychiatric thinking about distress, and lies at the core of the biomedical or 'diathesis-stress' model. It's also the way of thinking about distress that is frequently favoured by the media, and by commentators such as politicians. Currently, therefore, for many people in Western cultures, this is the dominant way of thinking about the role of biology in distress: one that considers the primary causes of distress to be biological influences such as genetic vulnerabilities, brain and other abnormalities, the effects of toxins and diets, drugs such as cannabis, and the influence and relative availability of hormones, neurotransmitters, peptides and other chemicals.

For example, schizophrenia is frequently said to be an illness caused by over-activity of dopamine systems in the midbrain; this is called the 'dopamine hypothesis'. Similarly, depression is said to be an illness that is due to abnormalities of **monoamine** systems such as that for serotonin, in the form of depleted neurotransmitter levels or reduced numbers of serotonin receptors (monoamines are a set of neurotransmitters that share some aspects of their chemical structure; the set includes dopamine, serotonin and norepinephrine). Alternatively, some recent thinking proposes that schizophrenia may be a neurodevelopmental disorder producing abnormalities in the temporal lobes (Woodruff et al., 1997); Strickland et al. (2002) propose that depression might be the result of irregularities in the **hypothalamic–pituitary–adrenal axis**, a term that summarizes a complex set of interactions and feedback loops between the hypothalamus and the pituitary and

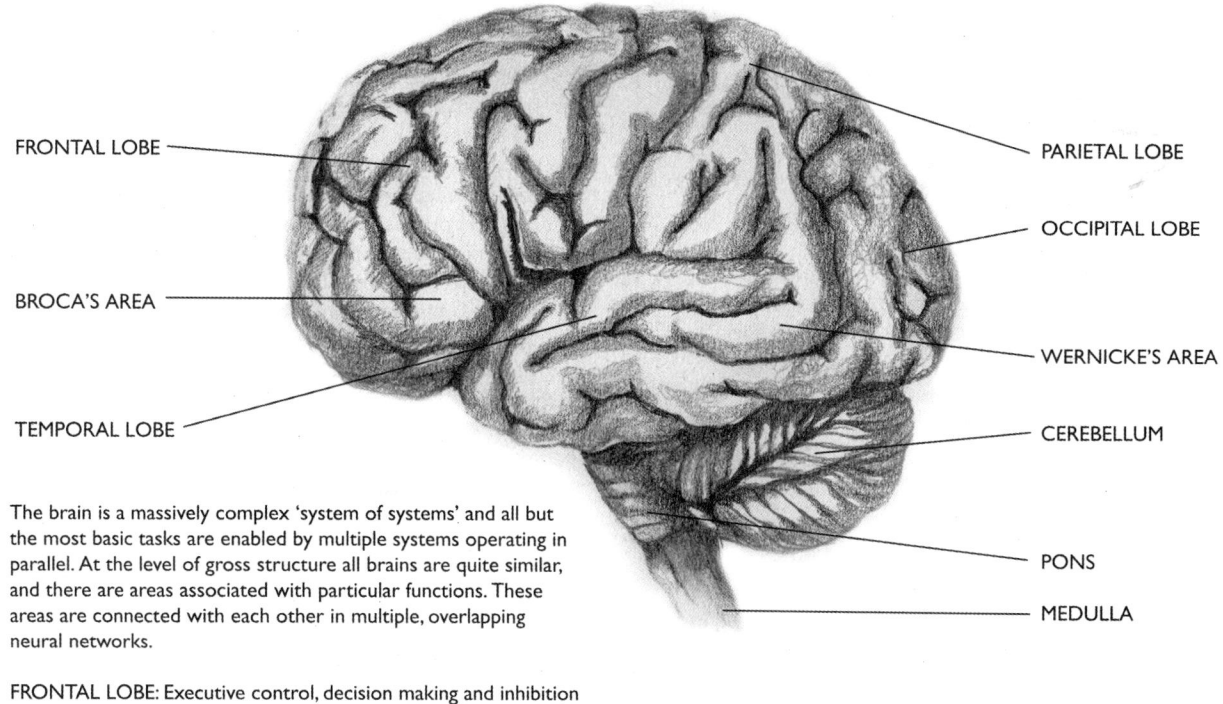

FRONTAL LOBE

BROCA'S AREA

TEMPORAL LOBE

PARIETAL LOBE

OCCIPITAL LOBE

WERNICKE'S AREA

CEREBELLUM

PONS

MEDULLA

The brain is a massively complex 'system of systems' and all but the most basic tasks are enabled by multiple systems operating in parallel. At the level of gross structure all brains are quite similar, and there are areas associated with particular functions. These areas are connected with each other in multiple, overlapping neural networks.

FRONTAL LOBE: Executive control, decision making and inhibition of impulses
PARIETAL LOBE: sensory input and integration
OCCIPITAL LOBE: vision
CEREBELLUM: motor feedback and control, some cognitive functions
MEDULLA and PONS: arousal, consciousness and the regulation of vital functions
TEMPORAL LOBE: auditory perception and memory processing
BROCA'S AREA: speech production
WERNICKE'S AREA: speech comprehension

An exterior view of the left hemisphere of the human brain, with some of the main anatomical features defined

adrenal glands; whilst Davidson and Henriques (2000) associate depression with uneven patterns of frontal hemispheric activity. This perspective is also associated with claims that scientists have found the 'gene for' various kinds of distress: both schizophrenia and depression are frequently described as illnesses with a strong genetic component. So although there are many disagreements about the precise character of these primary biological causes, in this way of thinking there is little doubt that these causes exist.

This way of thinking about biology in relation to distress is so influential that many people imagine that the primary biological causes of psychiatric distress are already accepted and understood. Those who are better informed may realize that things are not quite so straightforward, but many still assume that any disagreements or gaps in our knowledge primarily concern minor details. They imagine that cautionary statements about how little we actually know reflect no more than a good scientist's wariness of being overly-confident with respect to things that have not been definitively proved.

However, the truth is that clear and uncontroversial evidence for primary biological causes of distress (in the form of numerous well-designed, high-quality studies with large samples, replicated at different sites by independent researchers, and

with no significant pattern of contrary results) is extremely hard to find. For example, despite the evidence supporting it, there is also extensive evidence against the dopamine hypothesis of schizophrenia. First, excesses of dopamine are not found in *all* people given a diagnosis of schizophrenia, but they *are* also found in people given many other diagnoses (Bentall, 2003). So excessive dopamine is neither necessary nor sufficient as a cause of the experiences associated with a diagnosis of schizophrenia (see Box 4.1: Necessary and sufficient causes); nor – perhaps more importantly – is it exclusively associated with this diagnosis. Second, amongst people given a diagnosis of schizophrenia, dopamine levels are only excessive at the times when they are most distressed, not at other times (Bentall, 2003). Third, so-called antipsychotic medication, which works by reducing the levels of dopamine available in the brain, has a biological effect almost immediately after being ingested. However, it typically takes considerably longer for it to significantly influence people's experiences, and for about a third of patients it has little or no effect at all (Bentall, 2009; Thomas, 1997).

The same kinds of problems are associated with claims that depression is an illness caused by irregularities of monoamine systems such as that for serotonin, which can be treated using

BOX 4.1
Necessary and sufficient causes

Necessary causes are influences or events that always have to be present. If a biological defect was a necessary cause of clinical distress, then only those with this defect would ever become distressed and need clinical interventions, and no one without this defect would ever become clinically distressed.

Sufficient causes are influences or events that do not have to be present to cause distress, but which always result in distress occurring if they are present. If a specific trauma was a sufficient cause of clinical distress, then everyone who experienced this kind of trauma would become distressed. But not everyone who became clinically distressed would have to experience this particular kind of trauma: other traumas, and indeed other kinds of influence entirely, could be responsible instead.

selective serotonin reuptake inhibitors (SSRIs) such as Prozac. Despite these claims, evidence for the involvement of serotonin in depression is inconsistent and contradictory. Some studies have found reduced serotonin activity at relevant receptors (Drevets et al., 1999; Sargent et al., 2000). But some studies have found no significant differences between patients and controls (Meyer et al., 2004), and others have even found significantly increased serotonin activity in patients (Parsey et al., 2006; Reivich, Amsterdam, Brunswick & YannShiue, 2004). Reviewing this evidence, a leading American psychiatric textbook acknowledges that 'studies of serotonin function in depression suggest both hypofunction and hyperfunction' (Dubovsky, Davies & Dubovsky, 2001, p. 481). Similarly, a core text on psychopharmacology says that 'so far, there is no convincing evidence that monoamine deficiency accounts for depression; that is, there is no real monoamine deficit'(Stahl, 2000, p. 601).

Despite frequently asserting that distress is primarily caused by biological factors, psychiatry nevertheless distinguishes between **functional** and **organic diagnoses**. Functional diagnoses are those in which behaviour is judged to be dysfunctional but no consistent organic basis for the dysfunction has been shown, while organic diagnoses are those such as dementia, syphilis and Huntington's Chorea, where a biological cause of the dysfunction has been demonstrated. The vast majority of psychiatric diagnoses – including schizophrenia, depression, anxiety disorders, eating disorders, personality disorders and so on – are classed as functional. This is because more than a century of well-funded research, by thousands of researchers with access to an ever-improving set of technologies, has not demonstrated that any functional psychiatric diagnosis has a primary biological cause.

At this point, it is important to be very clear about the argument. Our claim is not that biology is irrelevant to distress, but that in most cases biology does not seem be the *primary cause* of distress. So it is not that there is no biological evidence at all in relation to these functional diagnoses: this immense, well-funded research effort has, unsurprisingly, produced masses of evidence, along with many claims about its significance. In recent years, for example, researchers have

linked schizophrenia to neurotransmitter systems including glutamate, serotonin, acetylcholine, gamma-butyric acid, prostaglandins and neuropeptides, as well as to dopamine. At the same time, they have also associated schizophrenia with physical features of the brain including enlarged ventricles, cerebral asymmetry, temporal lobe abnormalities, a thickened corpus callosum, a thinner corpus callosum, abnormalities of the basal ganglia and cerebellum, and reduced overall brain volume. Similarly lengthy lists of associations with brain features and processes can be compiled for many of the other common psychiatric diagnoses.

The problem, however, is that the overall pattern of this evidence is neither compelling nor clear. None of these biological features is present in every person given a particular diagnosis, and none of these features is confined exclusively to persons given that diagnosis. Indeed, some are observed in people with no psychiatric diagnosis whatsoever (although we rarely know how many, because population norms are for the most part not available). Whenever it seems as though a primary biological cause of distress might have been identified, alternative explanations are always available, contradictory evidence is always present, and methodological errors (inadequate control groups, improperly defined and small samples, flawed analyses) are relatively common. Very often, an initial proclamation of success is followed, sometime later, by a much less publicized failure to replicate initially promising findings. Moreover, the area of biology where these difficulties often seem to be most pronounced is also the area that might be thought to provide the clearest proof that the causes of distress are primarily biological: genetics.

Genetics and distress

Once biology is mentioned in relation to distress, many people think immediately of genetics. The media frequently present claims that 'the gene for' one disorder or another has been found, and it is widely assumed that many disorders have a strong genetic component. Schizophrenia, for example, is usually said to be strongly genetic, and most abnormal psychology textbooks assert that genetic influence accounts for around 50% of its incidence. However, there are good reasons to be sceptical of these claims and many researchers have taken issue with them (Boyle, 2002; Marshall, 1990; Rose, Lewontin & Kamin, 1984); in what follows we will draw primarily on the recent work of Jay Joseph (2003, 2006, 2010).

There are two strands to this research. **Behavioural genetic research** is the study of correlations between diagnostic categories and patterns of genetic relatedness. **Molecular genetic research** involves working with computerized analyses of DNA sequences. The two are linked, not least because molecular genetic methods have significant potential to generate false positives, so their deployment in the absence of good prior evidence from behavioural genetics might be questioned. Both historically and conceptually, then, behavioural genetics comes first.

Behavioural genetics

The most intuitively compelling claims in behavioural genetics come from twin studies. Most twin studies compare the prevalence of diagnoses such as schizophrenia in identical (monozygotic, or MZ) twins with the prevalence in same sex, non-identical (dizygotic, or DZ) twins. If both twins of a pair

The human brain viewed from the front, with the main features of the limbic system visible inside the cortex. Note that many links between this system and other brain regions are not shown: for example, links to the olfactory system and the frontal lobes.

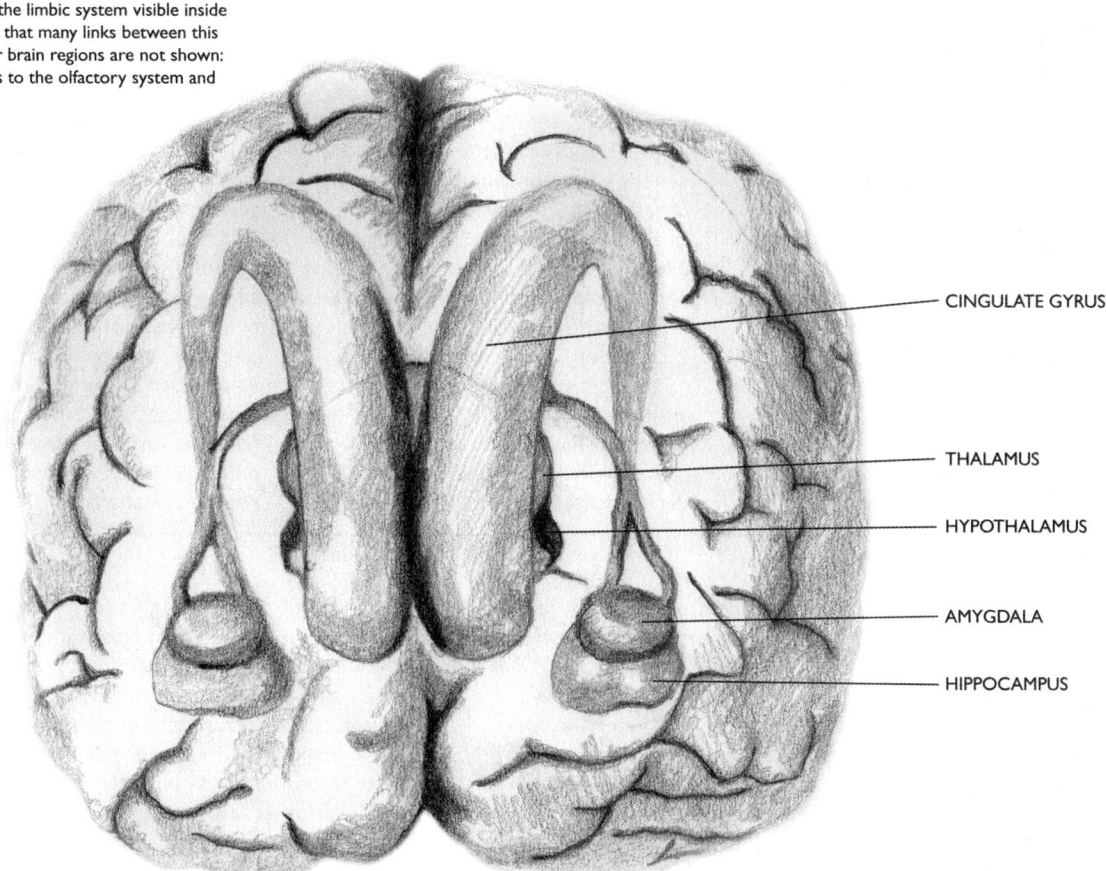

CINGULATE GYRUS

THALAMUS

HYPOTHALAMUS

AMYGDALA

HIPPOCAMPUS

The limbic system

have received a diagnosis of schizophrenia, the pair are said to be concordant. If schizophrenia were wholly genetic in origin, then the concordance rate for MZ twins, who are genetically identical, would be 100%. For DZ twins, who on average share half of their genes, the concordance rate would be 50%.

In a much-cited and authoritative review, Gottesman (1991) pooled the concordance rates from a number of studies and showed that, for schizophrenia, MZ concordance is 46% and DZ 17%. These figures already suggest that environmental influences are more important than genetic because, even for MZ twins, these influences account for more than half of the variance. But according to critics such as Joseph (2003), even figures such as this greatly overstate the contribution of genetics.

First, Joseph reminds us that there are two ways of calculating concordance rates: probandwise, and pairwise. In the probandwise method, if both twins were discovered independently in the sample, the pair is allowed to count twice (because twin A is concordant with twin B, AND twin B is concordant with twin A). In the pairwise method, by contrast, each pair only ever counts once.

In statistical terms both methods are legitimate, but statistics offers no criteria that determine which of the two methods we should apply in calculating concordance rates for schizophrenia. It should be obvious that probandwise concordance rates tend to be higher, though, and it is these that are used by Gottesman and other researchers in this field.

Joseph recalculated concordance rates in the studies analysed by Gottesman using the pairwise method, and produced concordance estimates of 40.4% for MZ twins and 7.4% for DZ twins.

Second, pooled analyses such as Gottesman's frequently fail to distinguish between older twin studies and more recent ones, even though more recent studies are methodologically sounder. This is an unusual position for scientists to adopt: it is usual to privilege newer research which utilizes the most recent technologies, and which has been designed in light of the known shortcomings of earlier studies.

With respect to twin studies, the most important technological advance is the determination of zygosity (whether the twins are MZ or DZ) by genetic testing, rather than – as in earlier studies – making a judgement on the basis of similar appearance (especially since these judgements were often made by researchers who were not blind to the research hypothesis – Marshall, 1990). In terms of design, the most important advance has been to use community samples of twins – rather than samples derived from institutional sources such as hospitals, which are more easily identified by researchers. Gottesman recognizes that these issues are important, and in his own writings he distinguishes between the pre-1963 studies and those carried out later which took account of them: nevertheless, he still calculates pooled concordance rates for *all* of the studies, not just the later ones. So Joseph calculated pairwise concordance rates for just the

---

BOX **4.2**
The heritability index

Genetic researchers make extensive use of statistics, and these figures frequently make it seem as though environmental influences upon distress account for little or nothing. The use of probandwise (rather than pairwise) comparisons in twin studies is one example of how numbers can be used to make environmental influence appear less important than it is. Another is the widespread use of the heritability or h² index. As Bentall (2009) observes, it is easy to misinterpret the h² index. When you are told that the heritability of

(for example) schizophrenia is 80%, it is easy to think that environmental influences contribute only 20% of its cause. But this is not what the h² index means.

The h² index is not an estimate of genetic causation, but an estimate of *variation* in genetic causation. It does not estimate how much genetic influence there is. Instead, on the basis of certain assumptions, it numerically estimates how much of the variability in causation is likely to be genetic in origin. So if environmental influences are relatively constant, then – however powerful they are – the *variation* in causation will mostly be down to genetic factors.

As Bentall says, this means that in a world where everyone smoked exactly 20 cigarettes every day, the h² index for lung cancer would be nearly 100%. Because one of the main environmental causes of lung cancer is constant, almost all of the observed variation would be down to genetics.

Of course, this would not mean that cigarette smoking does not cause lung cancer. And in the same way, a h² index of 80% does not mean that there is a disease called schizophrenia which is 80% caused by genetic influences. The misperception that there are strong genetic causes for (for example) schizophrenia is to some extent produced by misinterpretations of h².

---

nine twin studies of schizophrenia carried out since 1963, and obtained revised schizophrenia concordances of 22.4% for MZ twins and 4.6% for DZ.

So by using pairwise concordance and excluding dated, methodologically flawed research, the estimate for MZ concordance drops to 22.4% – strikingly lower than Gottesman's estimate of 46%. But Joseph then goes on to explore the detail of the twin method itself, showing how it makes a number of assumptions that, if invalid, would suggest that the differences between MZ and DZ twins can equally be accounted for by environmental influences. Key amongst these is the **equal environment assumption** or EEA. This is the assumption that environmental influence operates equally for both MZ and DZ twins – the assumption that MZ twin pairs are treated no more similarly than DZ twin pairs. If the EEA is flawed, then the twin method fails to separate genetic from environmental influences in the way that its advocates imagine.

Joseph questions the EEA. He observes that, compared to same-sex DZ twins, MZ twins are more likely to be mistaken for each other; more likely to be dressed and treated similarly by their parents; and more likely to spend time together, share friends, and be emotionally closer. Some twin studies have attempted to explore this issue. Shields (1954) calculated that there was a 'very close' emotional attachment in 47% of his MZ twin pairs, compared to only 15% of his DZ pairs. Kringlen (1967) gave a questionnaire to his twin pairs; Joseph's analysis of his results showed that 91% of his MZ twin pairs experienced 'identity confusion' in childhood, compared to just 10% of his DZ pairs. On a 'global evaluation' of twin closeness, 65% of Kringlen's MZ pairs were 'extremely close'; for the DZ pairs the corresponding figure was 19%.

Whilst these figures already suggest that the EEA is questionable, further evidence for its implausibility is provided by the findings from twin studies of people given a diagnosis of schizophrenia. The studies show that pooled concordance rates for same-sex DZ twins are 11.3%, whilst that of opposite-sex DZ twins is only 4.7%: with the same amount of shared genes, simply being the same sex more than doubles the concordance rate for schizophrenia diagnoses. Similarly, in most twin studies the concordance rates for DZ twins are

higher than for non-twin siblings (who also share an average of 50% of their genes), again suggesting that twins experience greater environmental similarity, which contributes to higher concordance for schizophrenia diagnoses.

So the method of comparing concordance rates in MZ and DZ twins is flawed. The EEA does not hold up, and this means that the method does not separate genes and environment. But there is another, apparently even more conclusive, twin study method that involves the comparison of MZ twins who have been reared apart. There are far fewer studies of this kind because twins are not often separated at birth; researchers then have to find these separated twins and count the incidence of diagnoses amongst them. This means that there are no systematic studies of schizophrenia using this method, although one review identified nine case studies, of which it is claimed that six pairs were concordant (S. Farber, 1981).

Joseph discusses the application of the twin method to studies of twins reared apart and shows that here, too, it is flawed. First, even twins separated at the very moment of birth have already shared a powerfully influential environment for the first nine months of their lives: their mother's womb. Second, to draw meaningful inferences from these very rare cases, we must assume that the environments of twins reared apart are no more similar than the environments of two randomly selected members of the population. But Joseph observes that MZ twins reared apart are always exactly the same age, always the same sex, and almost always the same ethnicity. They are also of strikingly similar appearance, so are likely to elicit similar responses from others. They are usually raised in the same socio-economic class and the same religion. To be included in research they must both be volunteers, and volunteers are known to share significant psychological characteristics. And finally, despite being separated, they are typically aware of each other's existence. Third, Joseph notes that the degree to which twins in studies of this kind actually were reared apart is frequently questionable. As he shows by returning to the original published research, few pairs were actually separated at birth. Very often the twin pairs in these studies shared important environments for lengthy periods of time after they were born. They frequently remained in contact even when separated, and sometimes the separation only happened for a few years, or consisted of living in neighbouring houses on the same street.

So despite their superficial success in separating genetic from environmental influence, twin studies mostly fail to do this. There are two other common behavioural genetic strategies: family and adoption studies. In family studies, the incidence of diagnosis is compared to the degree of genetic relatedness of different family members and patterns are sought. In adoption studies, the incidence of diagnosis in people who have been adopted is compared either with the incidence amongst their parents and birth families, or with the incidence in the adoptive families. However, both family and adoption studies are also typically flawed. Family studies are confounded by the truism that the degree of shared environment co-varies, at least in part, with the degree of shared genetic inheritance. Adoption studies suffer from a range of flaws similar to those associated with twin research, including the fact that adoption placement is rarely random and that adoption might itself be a risk factor for many disorders.

Molecular genetics

In recent decades new genetic research techniques have been devised, creating an approach known as molecular genetics. These techniques analyse gene sequences in biological tissue, using chemical processes and computerized analyses to first 'magnify' and then explore the available DNA (the part of the cell that contains genes). Joseph (2006) observes that, when these techniques were first established in the late 1980s, there was a wave of optimism amongst psychiatric geneticists that the genetic bases of distress would quickly be discovered. But twenty or so years later, this optimism has subsided. No breakthroughs have been made, and if anything the goal of identifying 'genes for' distress seems to have receded even further.

First, the human genome itself turns out to contain far fewer genes than anyone had anticipated: in the words of Craig Venter (leader of one of the research teams to produce the 'first draft' of the genome) 'We simply do not have enough genes for this idea of biological determinism to be right ... The wonderful diversity of the human species is not hard-wired in our genetic code. Our environments are critical' (McKie, 2001). Second, geneticists are discovering more about how environments impinge continuously on the processes of gene expression, finding that genes never simply act in isolation from environments. And third, as single genes 'for' disorders have not been discovered, 'it has become apparent that the genetic risk to psychiatric disorders is likely to be a multifaceted problem. Complexity is now a central theme in psychiatric genetics' (McInnis & Potash, 2004, p. 243).

Methodologically, molecular genetic research involves linkage studies, genome scans and association studies. **Linkage studies** try to identify genetic markers associated (linked) with specific diseases, using statistical analyses to estimate whether the linkage might have occurred by chance. A **genome scan** analyses the entire genome of an individual and compares its character to known markers for diseases and disease characteristics. Since 2005, **genome-wide association studies** (GWAS) have been the primary method used in psychiatric genetics. These studies compare the prevalence of putative genetic markers between groups of unrelated individuals given a diagnosis, and control groups of similar people without a diagnosis. Using computerized scanning techniques, the complete genome of individuals from each of the groups is then compared with previously identified markers of genetic variation called **single nucleotide polymorphisms** (SNPs). If some of the SNPs are more frequent in the group of people who have been given a diagnosis, these variations are said to be associated with it.

All of these methods involve both statistical analysis and a series of assumptions, one of which is that a mode of genetic transmission already exists. In the case of psychiatric diagnoses this is often said to have already been proved by behavioural genetics, but – as we have seen – this apparent proof is less conclusive than it might appear. If any of the assumptions underpinning association studies are violated, there is a substantially increased risk that they will produce false positives.

Moreover, there are a number of typical features of molecular genetic research and its methods which should lead us to adopt a position of scepticism with respect to many claims made on its behalf. First, because false positives are both relatively common and easy to generate (Beckwith & Alper, 2002), replications are always essential before findings can be accepted; this applies equally to the more recent GWAS method (Pearson & Manolio, 2008). Second, negative findings (disconfirmations) are of equal importance to positive findings, but these are harder to publish (Propping, 2005) and much less often publicized in the media (Conrad, 2002). Third, researchers frequently fail to correct the significance levels of their statistical analyse to take account of multiple searches, which are effectively multiple hypothesis testing (Joseph, 2006). Fourth, Joseph (2010) notes that the largely inconclusive findings of molecular genetic research in distress are frequently subject to rhetorical manipulation. For example, decades of failure to find genes consistently associated with psychiatric diagnoses get re-described as evidence for the 'complex genetic nature' of distress.

So there are features of molecular genetic research that artificially boost the likelihood that apparently significant genetic associations will be found, and there are also regular pronouncements that new genes for disorders have been discovered. To date, however, no genes have been consistently implicated and proven to have significant effects. Time and again, findings are not replicated in subsequent studies, and the overall picture seems to be that, at most, there are only very small effects from multiple genes. For example, recent studies of people given a diagnosis of schizophrenia have implicated genes called neuregulin 1, dysbindin (DTNBP1) and catechol-O-methyltransferase (COMT), but in each case the effects are very small, are mediated by environmental influences, and are not specific to people given this diagnosis. Moreover, there is no clear indication of specific impairments or defects associated with these genes: genetic inheritance may make a difference, but it doesn't seem to make that difference by producing observable biological impairments. In other words, any small effects associated with multiple genes seem to be non-specific, and largely dependent upon environmental circumstances for their variable influence. As Bentall (2009) observes, it is certain that if there were major genetic influences for psychiatric disorders they would have been discovered by now.

Biological causation in context

For most of the common illnesses in physical medicine there is good evidence about their causes; specific biological pathways have been identified and their workings detailed, and there is an evidence base about the most effective ways of treating them. But for the functional psychiatric diagnoses the picture is very different and there is no firm, evidence-based agreement about their biological causes or pathways. There are no precise linkages between particular kinds of distress and specific biological features or processes. There are no clear relationships between the basic findings of the cognitive, affective and social neurosciences and the characteristics of the diagnoses. There are no specific biological impairments reliably associated with any particular diagnosis. Instead, there is a great mass of inconsistent evidence, with no stable and definitive associations between any given biological feature and any diagnosis.

This, of course, is why there are no blood tests, brain scans or other objective medical diagnostic procedures that can be used to identify, confirm or rule out functional psychiatric diagnoses. Psychiatric diagnosis takes place on the basis of interview and observation, and involves self-reports of experience and expert assessments of mood and behaviour. It does not employ the biological tests common in physical medicine, because there simply are no biological features that have been shown to cause any disorder. On the basis of all of the evidence, we can conclude that bodies and brains play some part, somehow, in distress, but we cannot show that the causes of distress are primarily biological. Writing in the *American Journal of Psychiatry*, Kenneth Kendler, a lifelong advocate of biological causation, recently acknowledged that:

> We have hunted for big, simple, neuropathological explanations for psychiatric disorders and have not found them. We have hunted for big, simple, neurochemical explanations for psychiatric disorders and have not found them. We have hunted for big, simple genetic explanations for psychiatric disorders, and have not found them.

(Kendler, 2005, pp. 434–5)

Given this, what perhaps needs to be explained is not the biological basis of distress but the widespread belief that distress is primarily biological. We need to examine the wider context of this way of thinking, so as to understand how it became so deeply rooted and widespread. A number of important influences can be identified.

Culture

This way of thinking about biology reflects assumptions, deeply embedded in our culture, about the relationships between mind and body, and about what it is to be an individual (see Chapter 3). It also reflects a presumed hierarchy of scientific knowledge, where what are sometimes called 'hard' facts that are observable empirically (albeit only with the aid of powerful technologies such as fMRI scanners) are given precedence over so-called 'soft' knowledge, such as knowledge about the meaning of life events. From within this hierarchy, the meanings of Matthew's experience of anxiety, despair and humiliation in the nightclub, meanings that arise in the context of his long history of abandonment, alienation and social isolation, will seem to matter far less than the biological influence of his cannabis smoking.

In distress, evidence for the existence of such a hierarchy can be seen in a study by Calton, Cheetham, D'Silva and Glazebrook (2005) of papers presented at major international conferences on schizophrenia between 1988 and 2004. They examined 9284 abstracts by authors from 50 different countries, and categorized each one according to its primary orientation. They discovered that 75% of all the papers were predominantly biological in their orientation, whereas less than 5% took a predominantly psychosocial perspective. Out of almost 10,000 papers, less than 2% included any consideration of actual *experiences* of distress.

In contemporary Western societies, the media are vitally important carriers of culture. Newspapers, TV news and websites frequently report research which claims that the 'gene for' a particular condition has been discovered, or that its 'neural basis' has been shown in a brain scanner. But the media have a highly selective take on what is newsworthy, and they also apply particular strategies of presentation: in both senses they quite literally 'make' the news, as well as simply reporting it (Entman, 2007). Failure to replicate research finding the 'gene for' a condition is not often considered newsworthy, so is almost never reported. In the same way, the media don't tend to report imaging studies which challenge the idea that there are simple and direct links between brain regions and psychiatric diagnoses. These studies and their interpretations are complex, and don't fit the media template of simple, linear narratives with successful outcomes.

Research funding

A major influence upon what we know is the character and distribution of research funding. With respect to distress, significant amounts of research funding come from multinational pharmaceutical companies. For obvious reasons it is difficult to obtain precise figures, and of course not all pharmaceutical research is devoted to psychiatric drugs. Nevertheless, one assessment of drug company research spending for 2001 estimated it at £3.9 billion; another, for 2000, suggested that £10.4 billion was spent that year on research by the biggest five companies alone (Pfizer, Glaxo-Smith-Kline, Astra-Zeneca, Aventis and Novartis). By comparison, the UK Economic and Social Research Council, which distributes government funding for social research, had a total 2001 budget of just £72 million, of which only a tiny proportion was spent on research relevant to distress (Nightingale & Cromby, 2001). Similarly, Gagnon and Lexchin (2008) studied US pharmaceutical spending for 2004, and found that US companies alone invested $31.5 billion in research that year.

Moreover, the pharmaceutical companies spend significantly more on marketing and promoting their products, both to doctors and to the general public, than they do on research. In 2004, 13.4% of US pharmaceutical companies' income was spent on research, but 24.4% on promotion (Gagnon & Lexchin, 2008). In addition to advertising, this spending includes running public health campaigns to raise awareness of conditions for which they are able to offer treatment, and financing 'independent' pressure groups who then argue for new drug treatments for their illnesses (critics sometimes call these 'astroturf' campaigns, to distinguish them from the grassroots campaigns they mimic). The companies also promote their products through medical and psychiatric journals and conferences, and by using an array of marketing strategies (free lunches, funded visits to conferences in desirable locations, money to support meetings) that are designed to influence practitioners to prescribe their drugs rather than others (Ashmore & Carver, 2001). These marketing campaigns frequently emphasize biological causation, simply because doing so makes drug treatment seem like the obvious remedy.

Politics

There is a political aspect to the belief that biology is the primary cause of distress. This is because it might seem to shift some of the responsibility for distress away from social relations and material influences, locating it instead within individual, defective bodies and brains. This matters because epidemiological studies consistently show close relationships between social inequality and distress. For example, a review conducted by psychiatrists at the Maudsley Hospital showed that increased psychiatric morbidity (the tendency to be diagnosed with a range of common disorders) is consistently associated with markers of social inequality such as unemployment, low income and impoverished education, in countries including the UK, USA, Canada, Australia and the Netherlands (Melzer, Fryers & Jenkins, 2004). Similarly, there is a relationship between schizophrenia diagnoses and social inequality, with people born in poorer areas or to lower income families being much more likely to be given a diagnosis than people from wealthier backgrounds (Croudace, Bloom, Jones & Harrison, 2000; Eaton & Harrison, 2001).

However, not everyone exposed to social inequality experiences significant levels of distress; of those who do, not all get diagnosed with a disorder. From the perspective that biology is primary, this is usually taken as evidence that the minority of people exposed to inequality who *do* experience significant levels of distress already had some underlying biological vulnerability, which was then 'triggered' by social inequality and became a full-blown disorder. This, in turn, might seem to absolve politicians of any responsibility for people's distress.

There are many other possible explanations for this variation, explanations that recognize and work with the great complexity and contingency of human relations and social influence; we will return to this issue in much more detail in Chapter 6. For now, you should note that when biology is assumed to be the primary cause of distress, investigation of these complexities tends not to take place. This may help to explain why some political commentators promote biological causation.

Self-interest

Smail (2005) observes that it is often seen as inappropriate, even impolite, to suggest that self-interest might play a part in academic or scientific work. Yet it is a truism that we all have to survive and make a living in a harsh world that frequently demands compromises. So it is not unreasonable to suggest that we should try to be aware of the possible effects of self-interest and the compromises or biases it might produce. Indeed, this is why medical (and some other) journals now routinely ask authors to declare any sources of funding or support they have received for their work.

Moreover, despite such measures, there is good evidence that self-interest continues to bias findings. Ioannidis (2011) conducted a series of meta-analyses of brain-imaging studies reporting associations between various psychiatric diagnoses and brain volume abnormalities, in brain areas including the hippocampus, the putamen and the prefrontal cortex. By comparing effect sizes against the number of positive findings reported, he demonstrated that the number of significant findings being claimed was far more than the data were actually able to support. Ioaniddis concluded that there are strong biases in this literature, with selective outcome reporting and selective reporting of particular analyses as the most likely explanations. Similarly, Simmons, Nelson and Simonsohn (2011) show that researchers use strategic flexibility in their choices about which comparisons and hypothesis to test and which statistical analyses to publish, and that this serves to dramatically inflate the rate of positive findings.

Researchers who have dedicated their careers to a paradigm or theory have an obvious interest in sustaining their approach. So, when biological causes of distress are not found, there is an understandable tendency to declare that they are imminent and that there will soon be a 'breakthrough', rather than to concede that they may not exist. In this way, not only are current careers safeguarded: future research funding might also be secured. Recently, for example, there have been new hypotheses of schizophrenia based upon the role of glutamate (Gordon, 2010) or the patterns of neural oscillation and synchrony between different brain regions (Uhlhass & Singer, 2010).

Another, more subtle, influence upon researchers concerns their location within their given field. It is significantly easier to progress and be successful if your work is located within the mainstream of your discipline than it is if your work cuts across disciplines, and this bias operates independently of the quality of the work concerned (Brewer, 1999; Rhoten & Parker, 2004). This means that, on balance, work that promotes a narrowly biological perspective upon distress is more likely to be readily rewarded than work that attempts to integrate biological perspectives with theories and evidence from psychology or sociology.

Self-interest is not confined to individuals. Bentall (2009) explains how randomized controlled trials of the effects of psychiatric drugs can be subtly corrupted, and a series of recent studies have demonstrated that trials funded by drug companies are far more likely than others to find that drug interventions are successful (Bekelman, Li & Gross, 2003; Lexchin, Bero & Djulbegovic, 2003; Perlis et al., 2005). Academic journals have a well-known bias toward the selective publication of positive findings: it is far more difficult to publish an empirical paper that fails to prove its hypotheses than one that succeeds. Similarly, funding bodies have an interest in demonstrating that their money has been well spent, and universities have an interest in demonstrating that their staff's work is highly regarded, as do professional bodies such as the Royal College of Psychiatry and the British Psychological Society. Taken together, these interlocking interests are probably one of the fundamental reasons why scientific paradigms tend to be self-insulating and dismissive of challenges (Kuhn, 1970), although other factors undoubtedly contribute (Robertson, 2001).

Common sense

Finally, it is tempting to think of biology as the primary cause of distress because, sometimes, that does seem to be how biology operates. As we get older we all age and will eventually die and, clearly, our biology is the basis of this. Nevertheless, clear and uncontroversial examples of biology as the primary cause of distress remain elusive, although some do exist in related fields. For example, people born with an extra chromosome on their 21st pair (so that they have three chromosomes there, instead of the usual two) all have some degree of cognitive impairment and some of the distinctive facial features that we associate with Down's syndrome. This finding is long-established, has been replicated many times, and is uncontroversial: trisomy 21 *is* the biological cause of Down's syndrome.

Importantly, however, even in this uncontroversial instance, biological influence is far from being uniform. Whilst everyone born with the extra chromosome will experience some degree of cognitive impairment, the precise degree of impairment varies considerably. Some people with trisomy 21 have IQs almost in the normal range and can lead more or less independent lives. Others have IQs not much higher than 50, are largely unable to look after themselves, and will always be dependent upon social and personal care. There is extensive variation in the degrees of language and communication difficulties associated with the condition, with some people's abilities being greatly impaired and others barely affected. There is also extensive and related variation in the extent to which people are able to benefit from education and skills training in order to acquire useful skills and knowledge. Similarly, the extent to which people conform to the stereotypical visible appearance of a person with Down's syndrome is variable, as is their likelihood of having various medical problems (such as a susceptibility to heart disease and poor eyesight) that are known to be associated with the condition (Hall, 1984). So even this uncontroversial example of biological influence shows that outcomes vary widely, even where there is a known, primary biological influence.

As we saw in Chapter 2, the idea that distress is primarily a matter of biology is a fairly recent historical position. In the 1800s the medical profession made determined efforts to establish itself as the authority on distress, and today's common sense understanding arises in this historical context. Like other forms of common sense it continues to be challenged by other understandings, and does not always bear a necessary relation to the facts (Billig et al., 1988). Today's common sense understanding of distress is both historically and culturally specific and shaped by the influence of powerful professional, commercial and political interests. However, it must also be contextualized with regard to another influential strand of thinking which proceeds largely as though biology is simply irrelevant to distress.

Biology: mostly irrelevant to distress?

This is the way of thinking that characterizes much of the psychological and social scientific literature on disorder and distress. It underpins much work in sociology, social constructionism and social psychology, which tends to ignore or discount the ways in which distress is embodied within particular individuals. It is also implicit in many cognitive psychological accounts, which may acknowledge the biological, embodied aspects of distress but then quickly subordinate these to information processing explanations within which biology does not appear. In this way of thinking, it is as though biological influences simply have little or nothing to do with distress.

In cognitive psychology, distress arises from biases, deficits or defects in the processing of information and stimuli. For example, the profound unhappiness frequently associated with a diagnosis of depression is characterized as a 'cognitive triad' of negative beliefs about self, world and future; processing biases which lead to 'automatic' negative thinking and selective attending to stimuli; and the existence of schemas, organized collections of beliefs about self and world that endure across situations and profoundly organize activity

(Beck, 1967). Similarly, when people hear voices this might be explained in terms of an erroneous pattern of attribution, a failure to attribute the voice to their own thought processes and a bias towards explaining it as arising from a (frequently unseen) source elsewhere (Bentall, 2003). In these explanations, in order to understand distress we just need to understand the way that information gets processed. Biology only becomes relevant to the (very limited) extent that it is invoked within explanations of how this information processing occurs.

Alternatively, in social science and within some social and critical psychological accounts, distress is produced in **discourses** and narratives, is reified in categories and diagnoses, and is historically and culturally specific to particular places and times. These discourses and narratives are tied to institutions, such as prisons, clinics and asylums. The existence of these institutions already seems to 'prove' the validity of these ways of speaking and thinking, but they gain further legitimacy when people in other settings draw upon them to make sense of their experiences. Discourses and narratives, then, are not merely matters of language. On the one hand they reflect power divisions within society: not everyone has the authority to wield medical, psychiatric discourse, but those who do have this authority gain important degrees of power over others. On the other hand, discourses and narratives are only the verbal tip of shifting icebergs of social practices, such as medication, therapy, confinement, retreat, asylum or community care. Whilst none of these practices can be reduced to language, each is shot through with culturally and historically specific discourses that help to hold in place the various assumptions about the nature of the world that are made by their practitioners.

Frequently, in the way of thinking that treats biology as irrelevant to distress, the focus is not upon people's actual, lived experiences, but instead, upon the social processes and conditions within which distress appears, and upon the discourses, narratives and practices by which it is organized, made sensible and managed. Another way of saying this is that analysts try to understand the **conditions of possibility** for understanding an experience in a particular way, rather than grappling directly with the experience itself. These conditions of possibility are socioculturally and historically specific, and are often identified by analysing the discourses commonly used to construct and situate distress. The emphasis on these conditions of possibility can sometimes make it seem as though people might never have *experienced* distress if the categories and discourses that construct it as (for example) depression or schizophrenia had never been invented.

In many ways, social science and cognitive psychology are strikingly different enterprises. But with respect to distress they are frequently surprisingly similar, because both disciplines promote the notion that what is most important is what can be talked about, captured in language, and represented or reflected upon. The focus of one is mostly upon cognition, whilst the other often focuses upon language – but both downplay the importance of embodiment. For cognitive psychologists, distress can be traced back to deficits or malfunctions in information processing; for social scientists it can be traced back to socioculturally and historically specific ways of understanding experience. By strongly emphasizing these factors, both cognitive psychology and social science can give the impression that biology is largely irrelevant to distress.

It's important to recognize that in this way of thinking, the irrelevance of biology is rarely stated explicitly. In most writings on distress that adopt this perspective you will only notice the role accorded to biology by virtue of its absence, because of the way in which it is always pushed into the background. For example, cognitive psychologists do sometimes make reference to the biological aspects of distress, but at the same time typically fail to integrate them into their models and explanations. We see this in cognitive psychological accounts of paranoia premised upon the notion that emotions are an important part of this experience (e.g. Freeman, Garety, Kuipers, Fowler & Bebbington, 2002): in these accounts the ways in which emotions are embodied, and the significances of this for their influence upon our activity, are not adequately considered.

The relative absence of biology in this way of thinking, and the difficulty of integrating it, is sometimes discussed explicitly. Murphy (1995) argues that social scientists frequently sidestep the influence of biology by using 'rhetorical avoidance strategies' and by simply not conducting studies that would foreground biological influences. Newton (2002) describes various social science attempts to integrate the biological body, arguing that they often rely upon emotive appeals such as invoking 'scare stories' of ill health caused by lifestyle and social inequality. In his opinion we are still at the starting point of any serious integration of the two perspectives. Similarly, Bentall (2003) highlights the need to integrate social, cognitive and biological perspectives upon distress, whilst warning that we have barely begun to work at this complex but important enterprise.

It's equally important to recognize that the way of thinking which treats biology as irrelevant to distress is a *response* to the way of thinking that sees biology as its primary cause. We have already seen how this view of biology often dominates thinking about distress, and is bound up with various powerful interests. In this troublesome context, it is understandable that researchers examining social and psychological influences upon distress have sometimes responded by treating biology as simply too difficult or too dangerous to engage with. Indeed, whichever way we look at it, there is something of a gulf between – for example – accounts of distress rooted in an exploration of meaning as it is transacted in relationships, and accounts of distress rooted in an exploration of neurotransmitter levels in specific brain regions. Moving between these kinds of explanation raises deep conceptual problems which most researchers in both social and biological science have so far done very little to resolve (Bennett & Hacker, 2003; Cromby, 2007; Newton, 2007).

This way of thinking has nevertheless provided extensive evidence and valuable insights into how social and psychological factors are related to distress, evidence that has been vitally important in producing this book. Because it examines the social and relational influences that are often overlooked in other research, this way of thinking demonstrates that distress is not simply a matter of brain processes and biological activity; it is simultaneously the product of experience. By not rushing too quickly to assume that biological influences are the primary cause of distress, researchers have produced innovative and sophisticated social and psychological explanations. This has sometimes led to new interventions, such as the various cognitive psychological therapies offered to people given a diagnosis of depression. What is more, this

research situates notions of distress within the historical and cultural contexts that produced them. This reminds us that the boundaries between normal and abnormal, between everyday experience and distress, are fluid, variable, and contingent upon historical and cultural norms. It is a way of thinking more likely to engage with the *meanings* of distress, and for this reason is often associated with interventions that involve making material changes in people's lives and with helping them to talk about and understand their distress.

Nevertheless, as a way of approaching distress this way of thinking is incomplete. Distress, like *all* experiences, is embodied, and our embodiment is biologically supported. Many of the most difficult features of people's distress are associated with the way that it seems to have become a part of their embodiment. Being profoundly miserable, for example, is typically not solely a matter of having negative cognitive evaluations of self, world and future: it also includes feeling very unhappy, and other emotional and mood changes such as worrying more, tiredness, apathy, and changes in appetite, sleep, activity and energy levels.

A thorough understanding of distress must provide a framework that also makes it possible to consider its embodiment: we need a way of thinking about distress that neither wrongly assumes that biology is always causal, nor ignores it. To illustrate this, we will now consider the recent debate about cannabis use and schizophrenia. This debate clearly illustrates the importance of many of the influences we have discussed, showing how politics, the media, and the interests of researchers and other groups intersect to produce everyday understandings that are then all too easily taken as simply factual. The debate demonstrates both why we need to include biology, and why it is naïve to assume that it simply causes distress.

Cannabis and schizophrenia

In the UK, illegal drugs are classed in the categories of A, B or C, with class A drugs carrying the strictest legal penalties and class C the most lenient. In 2004, the UK government made a decision to downgrade cannabis from class B to class C. It is rare for people to be arrested for using or carrying class C drugs (although the police still have this option), so this was a significant change. For many years prior to 2004 campaigners had been asking for cannabis to be made legal, and there was significant public support for the change. The government's decision was initially welcomed by the police, many sectors of the media, the majority of the medical profession, and workers with people with drug problems.

Even before 2004, however, there had been some studies looking at the possible association between cannabis and schizophrenia. Perhaps the most well-known piece of research followed up conscripts to the Swedish army; it found that those who reported being cannabis users on joining the army were six times more likely than non-users to be given a diagnosis of schizophrenia during the 15 years that followed (Andreasson, Allebeck, Engstrom & Rydberg, 1987). This, and a handful of studies reporting similar findings, had already been considered by the Advisory Council on the Misuse of Drugs (ACMD), the scientific body that provides the UK government with evidence for its policies. Their expert assessment was that, on balance, the evidence of a causal association between

After caffeine, alcohol and tobacco, cannabis is the most widely used recreational drug in most Western cultures.

cannabis and schizophrenia was not sufficiently proven and that what risks there were did not justify keeping cannabis as class B.

In the period following reclassification, there was an upsurge of interest in the possibility that cannabis use causes schizophrenia. Psychiatrists at the Institute of Psychiatry in London, in particular, began to campaign in the media about possible dangers to mental health associated with the drug. Marjorie Wallace of the charity SANE (an organization for the families of people given a diagnosis of schizophrenia) also became a vociferous campaigner. A number of new studies were commissioned and reported, and the press and TV ran numerous 'scare stories' about cannabis and mental illness, with the frequent collaboration of psychiatrists. And instead of levying its usual charges for access, the website of the British Journal of Psychiatry began giving away academic papers on this topic 'in the public interest'.

By 2007 this campaign began to influence the government, which asked for a further review of the drug's legal status in view of its possible association with mental health problems. The ACMD carried out a detailed re-evaluation of the evidence. Early in 2008 they reported that their recommendation remained unchanged: there was still insufficient evidence of a causal link between cannabis use and schizophrenia. But in May 2008 the Home Secretary, Jacqui Smith, announced that she was overruling this advice: because of its links to mental health problems, she said, cannabis was to be re-classified as a class B drug.

It is unusual for government ministers to commission a report from experts and then go against their advice. Moreover, even though some within both the police and the medical profession welcomed the Home Secretary's decision, others adopted a more equivocal stance. For example, the Association of Chief Police Officers published a statement saying they agreed with the decision, but also saying they would not change the policy (introduced in 2004) of not arresting people for possession of small amounts of cannabis.

In all this, the idea of a causal link between cannabis use and schizophrenia was central. If this link could be shown to exist, it would be a clear example of biological influences causing distress. Statements by politicians and extensive media coverage of the issue will have given many people the impression that such a causal link had been conclusively demonstrated.

As we explain in Chapter 11, schizophrenia is a problematic concept and the diagnosis is applied to highly varied experiences with very different patterns of onset and outcome. There is also no evidence that the diagnosis is linked to a specifiable biological cause. Given this, the wide range of distressing experiences which might lead to the diagnosis are unlikely to be directly caused or uniformly influenced by cannabis. However, they might still have biological components, and the evidence suggests that there is something here that requires explanation. As you will see, though, the idea of simple biological causation remains questionable.

Cannabis and schizophrenia: an association

It cannot be doubted that there is evidence of an association between cannabis use and the diagnosis of schizophrenia. The 1987 Swedish study demonstrated this, as have numerous others in the UK, New Zealand and elsewhere. Arseneault, Cannon, Witton and Murray (2004) reviewed five studies conducted up to this time. They reported that rates of cannabis use in people given a schizophrenia diagnosis are twice those of the general population, and that between 20% and 40% of people given a schizophrenia diagnosis have used cannabis at some point during their lives. They concluded that, overall, cannabis use doubles the risk of being given a diagnosis of schizophrenia. Similarly, a review by Moore et al. (2007) concluded that cannabis use increases the risk of all psychotic-spectrum disorders, and that there is a dose-response relationship between the two: the more cannabis that is smoked, the greater the likelihood of a diagnosis. A small number of new empirical studies also added weight to this conclusion. For example, one study of 152 people in London who had been given a first-episode schizophrenia diagnosis found that 68% reported using cannabis and other drugs during their lifetime, and that cannabis use and gender (being male) predicted earlier diagnosis (Barnes, Mutsatsa, Hutton, Watt & Joyce, 2006).

One of the concerns that emerged in these studies is that the cannabis commonly available today may be more potent than that of some years ago; it is claimed that it contains roughly 12% of the active ingredient Tetrahydrocannabinol (THC), compared to 6% in the past. Another concern is that some people who had been given schizophrenia diagnoses might be self-medicating with cannabis, and that this might explain some or all of the association. Cannabis is well known for its tranquilizing properties, often associated with another of its active ingredients, Cannabidiol (CBD). The medications commonly given to people with a diagnosis of schizophrenia are tranquilizers and there is evidence that the effects of CBD may be comparable to this medication (Zuardi, Crippa, Hallak, Moriera & Guimaraes, 2006).

With this in mind, some studies looked in more detail at the separate effects of THC and CBD. At a 2007 conference in London, a team from the Institute of Psychiatry reported that THC reduced activity in the inferior frontal cortex: the frontal cortex is implicated in the inhibition of thoughts and behaviour, for example paranoid thoughts. Another study reported at the same conference by researchers from Yale University involved giving intravenous THC to healthy volunteers, and found that 50% subsequently experienced what were described as symptoms of psychosis. Similarly, a study of traces of THC and CBD in hair samples taken from 140 drug users found that those with only THC in their hair (rather than only CBD, or CBD and THC) had more of what were described as 'schizophrenia-like symptoms' (Morgan & Curran, 2008). This study, like a number of others, supported the idea that CBD actually has antipsychotic properties. So the effects of cannabis are not uniform: some of its chemicals might actually reduce the distressing experiences associated with a diagnosis of schizophrenia, and this might well account for some of the association between the two as people self-medicate. Nevertheless, the association still requires further investigation.

Association is not causation

As every statistics student knows, association – correlation – is not the same as causation. Just because two variables or phenomena co-vary does not mean that there is a causal relationship between them. Their co-variance may be random, or it may be caused by variation in some third variable or phenomena that influences them both. Self-medication with CBD is one example of a variable that might mediate the relationship between cannabis and schizophrenia diagnoses, but there are others.

Vulnerability to a diagnosis of schizophrenia is predicted by being a young male, being of minority ethnic status, living in an urban area, and being of low socio-economic status (Boydell et al., 2001; Harrison, Gunnell, Glazebrook, Page & Kwiecinski, 2001; Scully et al., 2002). In the UK, cannabis use, similarly, is predicted by being young, being male, being of dual ethnic heritage and living in an urban area (Home Office, 2006; UK Drug Policy Commission, 2010). Few studies have controlled for all of these variables, raising the possibility that variation in one or more of these may account for some of the observed association between cannabis use and schizophrenia diagnoses.

Epidemiological evidence

To conclusively demonstrate a causal link between cannabis use and the diagnosis of schizophrenia would require large-scale epidemiological work, like that conducted by Richard Doll in the 1950s which demonstrated the causal link between tobacco smoking and lung cancer. To date, no study of this kind has been conducted anywhere in the world. Such a study would require large samples and lengthy periods of time and would therefore be expensive and difficult to conduct. In this particular case, there is the further problem that the activity being studied is illegal in most parts of the world: this would make it even more difficult to recruit and maintain a suitably large, representative sample.

However, even though no relevant epidemiological studies have been conducted, there is related, population-level data which sheds light on the question of whether cannabis smoking causes the experiences associated with a diagnosis of schizophrenia. This data comes from two sources. First, as we saw in Chapter 3, there are variations in the prevalence of schizophrenia diagnoses in different countries. Second, for many countries, there is also evidence of the amount of cannabis smoked, in the form of records of the amount of the drug seized by the police each year. Police seizures never account for more than a small amount of the drug circulating, but it is reasonable to assume that they remain relatively stable as a proportion. This means that they provide a coarse indication of the amount of the drug being used: if seizures go up, we can suppose that more of the drug is being consumed, and vice versa.

In this way it is possible to compare the prevalence of cannabis smoking in different countries, and across time in the same country. Studies that have looked at this evidence have shown that rates vary markedly from one country to another, and that in many countries there are long-term trends of either increasing or decreasing usage. However, these differences in the amounts of cannabis consumed between countries, and the upwards and downwards trends of consumption within countries, seem to bear no consistent relationship to the prevalence of schizophrenia diagnoses. Similarly, even though cannabis in the UK today is said to contain more THC than in the past, rates of schizophrenia diagnosis have not gone up in line with this increase in the chemical supposedly responsible for causing it. In fact, a major element in the ACMD's recommendation not to reclassify cannabis as class B was research they commissioned which showed that, over the decade during which THC levels in the UK seem to have doubled, the prevalence of schizophrenia diagnoses actually fell slightly (Advisory Council on the Misuse of Drugs, 2008).

The clinical picture

Even though the epidemiological evidence doesn't demonstrate a causal link between cannabis use and schizophrenia, some clinicians still feel that the two are linked. But these clinical impressions might also be explained without invoking a causal biological link.

First, as we have seen, both the diagnosis of schizophrenia and cannabis use are predicted by being male, being young, having minority ethnic status and living in a city, and some clinicians might be mistaking this demographic association for a causal one.

However, clinicians might accept this and then argue that there are even closer associations between the two phenomena, because –at the intersection of this complex of variables – their experience is that it is those people whose cannabis use is most dysfunctional (i.e. sustained, prolonged and uncontrollable) who are most likely to be given a diagnosis of schizophrenia. Even this, however, is not necessarily evidence of a causal, biological link.

First, for people whose lives are already chaotic and troubled it is likely that heavy cannabis use is, on balance, not helpful. Although it might make their situation more bearable in the short term, the drug's biological effects upon memory and motivation, coupled with the hallucinatory effects that high doses can produce, might also exacerbate or compound the chaos and disorder of their lives (Henquet et al., 2010). Moreover, the financial cost of regular heavy use could further contribute to their difficulties. So there might well be a causal association that is not simply biological, but is instead mediated by the effects of cannabis use upon people's finances, social relations, and abilities to deal with other stresses and difficulties in their lives and relationships.

Second, with respect to diagnoses of schizophrenia, one of the most striking findings in recent years is a meta-analysis showing that 69% of women and 59% of men with such diagnoses report histories of childhood physical or sexual abuse (Read, van Os, Morrison & Ross, 2005). This is highly relevant because of the extensive evidence that physical and sexual abuse are strongly associated with dependency and dysfunctional patterns of use for all kinds of recreational drugs. For example, Cohen and Densen-Gerber (1982) found that 84% of a sample of 178 adults being treated for drug and alcohol problems had a history of child abuse or neglect. In Germany, Schafer, Schnack and Soyka (2000) interviewed 100 problem drug users and found that 70% of women and 56% of men reported histories of sexual abuse. Similarly, an American study with 46 Vietnam war veterans who had substance-dependency problems found that 77% had experienced some kind of severe childhood trauma (Triffleman, Marmar, Delucchi & Ronfeldt, 1995).

So rather than the association between dysfunctional cannabis use and the kinds of distress that lead to a diagnosis of schizophrenia being a causal biological one, it may also be that both are understandable responses to childhood abuse, trauma and neglect. Recreational drugs like cannabis can lighten mood, decrease pain, make isolation more enjoyable, and distract users from problems and difficulties in their lives: it is not surprising that their unrestrained use is more common amongst people who have been abused.

Conclusion

Recreational cannabis is not one drug, but contains many psychoactive chemicals (up to 60), and there is evidence that at least two of these (THC and CBD) have opposing effects: CBD tranquilizes, THC distorts perception. Cannabis is one of the most widely used recreational drugs, and the great majority of its users will not experience mental health problems. However, the idea of cannabis having a causal association with schizophrenia will make intuitive sense to those people who have tried cannabis once or twice and not enjoyed the experience. But the assumption that such unpleasant experiences are simply equivalent to the states of distress associated with a schizophrenia diagnosis (as in the Yale study mentioned above, where the effects of intravenous THC were described as 'symptoms of psychosis') remains unproven. The story of simple biological causation plays upon stereotypes of drugs, drug users and mental illness, binding them all together in a tabloid-friendly narrative that is politically influential and furthers the interests of psychiatry. But it conceals a far more intricate picture in which the associations between cannabis use and diagnoses of schizophrenia are extremely complex, and frequently mediated by non-causal factors that most studies fail to consider.

The debate about cannabis and schizophrenia illustrates how ideas about biology as the primary cause of distress have numerous sources, and can get recruited into the service of various interests. But it's important to recognize that these ideas also have very real consequences for people suffering distress. Matthew's psychiatrist focused on his use of cannabis when Matthew was given a diagnosis of schizophrenia. As a result, less attention was paid to the many other factors that may have predisposed Matthew to have distressing experiences: his troubled family background, poor education, relative poverty, minority ethnic status, lack of purpose in life, strained family relationships, and social isolation – his lifelong history of abandonment, neglect and marginalization. Due consideration of these factors would have produced a far more complex understanding of the relationship between Matthew's cannabis use and the experiences that led to his diagnosis. This understanding might have suggested that cannabis use was no more than one element of the explanation for Matthew's distress, that its influence was perhaps not simply biological, and that it might be understood more readily as a marker of other problems than a causal influence in its own right.

At the same time, the debate about cannabis and schizophrenia clearly illustrates why our accounts of distress cannot ignore biology. Cannabis is a psychoactive drug associated with diverse and multiple effects including euphoria, perceptual distortion, sedation, anxiety, and temporary motor, cognitive and memory impairment (Ashton, 1999). If cannabis did not have these embodied, biological impacts, if it did not produce alterations in mood, perception, appetite, motivation and other aspects of experience, it is unlikely that the notion of its being related to the diagnosis of schizophrenia would ever to have arisen. Indeed, if cannabis did not have (some of) these effects it is unlikely that it would ever have become established as a recreational drug in the first place! In everyday life, it is likely that the plausibility of the narrative that cannabis is a primary biological cause of schizophrenia depends on the embodied experiences of cannabis users and people who know them, just as much as it depends upon the research evidence. We simply cannot understand or appreciate the significances of cannabis (or any other recreational drug) without recognizing the ways that it impinges upon our embodiment – just as we cannot adequately understand distress itself without recognizing that it has profoundly embodied aspects.

So we need a way of thinking about biology in relation to distress that neither ignores it nor assumes that influence always flows in one direction, from biology to experience. We need a way of thinking that does not simply infer the character of experience from biological processes: there is evidence, for example, that moderate cannabis users have greater levels of life satisfaction and relationship quality than non-users (Shedler & Block, 1990). We need a way of thinking about biology in relation to distress that better matches the great mass of inconsistent evidence, and that does justice to the complexity and detail of the phenomena it claims to address. Crucially, we need an account that distinguishes adequately between *enabling* and *causing*: our biology enables distress, just as it enables every other experience we ever have. This does not have to mean that it is simply the primary cause.

Lifelines

Steven Rose (1997) offers a way of thinking about the role of biology based upon the notion of **lifelines**. A lifeline is the trajectory of an organism from birth to death. Lifelines are particular to individual creatures and reflect the specific features of their unique history and experiences. At the same time, the lifelines of members of a given species share many common features, since members of the same species tend to live for roughly the same amount of time, reproduce at the same point in their lifespan, have similar numbers of offspring, and so on.

Within the lifeline of an organism, biological influences are in continuous flow and exchange with influences from the environment. This happens at every stage of life, and to such an extent that no activity should be understood as *simply* biological. The biology of an organism is always, inextricably, bound up with both its present environment and with any previous environments that influenced its development and growth. To understand how thoroughly this is so, we need to start at the very basic level of single living cells.

Cells are bounded by semi-permeable membranes that allow a constant exchange of molecules with the environment immediately outside. Energy, for example, is generated by utilizing pre-existing molecules such as sugars and fats, or by photosynthetic processes requiring water and carbon dioxide. These molecules must constantly be allowed within the cell

---

BOX **4.3**

Enabling versus causing

Rom Harré (2002) proposes that when thinking about biology in relation to human experience it is often useful to distinguish clearly between enabling and causing. To enable something is to make it possible. As humans we are embodied creatures, so there is a clear sense in which the biological systems of our bodies are necessary to *enable* our experience – all of our experience. And because biology is always necessary to enable experience, it is easy then to assume that it is the *cause* of our experience. But this is often a faulty assumption.

For example, your experience of reading this paragraph is enabled by the biological systems that make vision possible: your eyes, the musculature that directs and focuses them, and the cortical receptors and neural assemblies that work upon the information coming from your retina. It is also enabled by the brain systems for memory and language that your brain uses to assemble these visual signals into words and phrases, in particular those systems associated with the left-hemisphere region called Wernicke's area. But this is not the same as saying that your experience of reading this paragraph is simply *caused* by these brain systems. It is also caused by the book itself, which generates the signals your brain registers and interprets. And the book's being in front of you and being able to generate these signals is caused, perhaps, by the support given to it by a table and the illumination given to it by a lamp or a window. It might also be caused by your prior decision to buy the book, or by your lecturer's requirement that you read it, and these decisions might themselves have been caused by further, more distal decisions, such as a decision to go to university, study psychology, or try to understand puzzling experiences.

So even for something as simple as your experience of reading this paragraph, causality is diffuse, multiple, and hard to pin down. In the face of this complexity, the simple story that the experience is caused by your biological systems is appealing. But as this example makes clear, this is an over-simplification: biology enables experience, it is not its sole cause.

---

membrane, whilst other waste substances must be expelled through it.

For single-celled creatures such as bacteria, the immediate environment is the world itself. This world is variable and potentially hostile, with unevenly distributed supplies of energy or food, and fluctuating temperature and pH levels. For single-celled creatures, survival depends partly on their ability to locate favourable conditions, for example by being sensitive to chemical concentration gradients and moving along them using flagella or cilia.

However, because movement is not always possible or effective, survival also depends on the ability to adapt to suboptimal conditions. For example, if bacteria that usually metabolize glucose are placed in a lactose-rich, glucose-poor environment they can begin to produce enzymes that allow them to feed off lactose in order to survive. They can do this because their DNA already contains the sequences necessary to produce these enzymes, although in normal circumstances these sequences are inactive. When the bacteria encounter a lactose-rich, glucose-poor external environment, this triggers signals that activate these usually dormant DNA sequences. So it is the interaction between the organism and the environment that determines which of its available DNA sequences, or genes, are active at any given time.

For the living cells of multi-cellular creatures such as humans, the situation is more complex. For these cells, the immediate environment is external to the cell but within the organism, so it tends to be less patchy, variable and unpredictable. So with no need to potentially activate previously unused DNA sequences, the cells of multi-cellular creatures lose this ability and become specialized as one type of cell rather than another – for example, as heart, lung or liver cells.

The cells of complex organisms thus benefit from a more stable immediate environment. But in order for this more stable environment to be maintained, *the organism as a whole* must respond to the external environment. Its numerous systems must strive to maintain a dynamic balance of near-optimal conditions for the many cells of its body, whilst its activities must be conducted in ways that facilitate their smooth operation. The various specialized cells must also continuously communicate with each other as, jointly, they create and maintain the inner environment of the organism. This means that the well-being, survival and reproduction of multi-cellular creatures can only be understood by also considering the actions and abilities of the organism, since the organism has abilities, properties and potentials that its individual cells do not.

Rose draws two far-reaching conclusions from these facts. First, that the boundary between organism and environment is never fixed: organisms constantly absorb parts of their environment, whilst at the same time excreting waste products or modifying their surroundings in ways that make survival and reproduction more likely. And second, that organisms are not 'the mere playthings of fate, sandwiched as it were between their genetic endowment and an environment over which they have no control' (1997, p.140). Instead, organisms constantly both modify and respond to their environments, and this occurs continuously whilst life persists.

These conclusions have a number of implications for the way we think about the role of biology, and in particular genetics, in distress. Genes influence development and growth by enabling cells to produce different kinds of molecules, as in the example of the bacteria which contain the DNA sequences that allow them to produce lactase enzymes. But the influence of these genes is already within one or more environments: it never simply occurs first, or in isolation. Within the cell, the environment of a gene includes the other genes that surround it, which themselves may regulate whether, when and how it becomes active. It also includes the wider environment of the cell itself, an environment constantly influenced by the immediate environment outside. And for multi-cellular creatures, this immediate environment is jointly created from the actions of many other cells communicating and working together, in interaction with the external environment.

This means that genes and environment are already thoroughly interpenetrated, at every single instant of development and growth. Throughout the unfolding of a lifeline, environments influence gene expression, which simultaneously influences the kinds of environments created or encountered. The fluid interdependency of genes and environment is such that those positions in the 'nature–nurture' debate which treat them as static entities are quite inadequate, especially with respect to our understanding of development. In fact, their interaction is so continuous and profound that even genes themselves are not simple fixed entities (see Box 4.4: What is a gene?). From the perspective of an organism's lifeline, its current state represents the sum total of the various dynamic interactions between all of the external environments it has encountered, the internal ones it has created, and all of the developmental transformations and modifications of the organism that have taken place. Both genes and environments are important in this, but their relationship is both fluid and complex.

For example, Rose observes, identical (MZ) twins have exactly the same genes. Yet even before birth they occupy very slightly different environments because the relative location of each embryo, with respect to both the placenta and the wider environment of the uterus, is a little different. As a direct consequence of these purely chance differences, each developing twin's access to nutrients, blood oxygen and so on will be slightly different, and with *every* instance of cell division these environmental factors will influence gene expression. Consequently, by the time that they are born, even 'identical' twins are not usually *so* identical that those who know them well cannot tell them apart. But both their resemblances and their differences arise from both genes and environment, operating *together* to produce both similarity and variation.

So Rose suggests that we replace the opposition of nature and nurture with a focus upon *temporally organized degrees of specificity and plasticity* in the unfolding of a lifeline. By this, he means that it is always both genes and environment *together* that bestow limits and potentials upon an organism. At any moment within a lifeline, their conjunction might create degrees of relative **plasticity**, where random or contingent influences can have a greater influence. At other moments, their joint influence will create greater **specificity**, meaning that outcomes are much less open to fluctuation and variation. So what counts is the degree of specificity or plasticity at any particular time: in other words, it is their **temporal organization** that it is important to understand. It is misguided to attempt to simply attribute plasticity or specificity either to genes or to environment: both are always operating synchronously.

Another implication of these facts is that analyses that attribute our actions to 'selfish genes', which supposedly drive our behaviour in their attempts to replicate, are misguided. These analyses presuppose that natural selection occurs only at the level of the gene, but, as we have seen, the survival and reproduction of multi-cellular creatures is dependent upon the activity and abilities of the *organism*. So it is a mistake to imagine that we can explain human activity by simple reference to the actions of genes that drive us for their own 'selfish' purposes. Human activity is conducted by humans, not genes, and it is the activity and capabilities of humans that determine whether or not their genes are transmitted to others. Whilst these activities and abilities are themselves open to genetic influences, they cannot be reduced to them because influences at the level of the organism are also always

---

BOX **4.4**

What is a gene?

In the popular imagination, genes are often seen as relatively fixed, discrete coding devices containing sets of instructions for their own replication. But at the level of cell biochemistry – where genes actually produce their effects – things are far more complicated than this.

Rose (2003) observes that the definition of a gene has changed significantly over time. An earlier idea of genes as abstract indivisible units that conferred particular properties was replaced in the 1930s with the notion that each gene codes for a particular enzyme. The subsequent discovery of the structure of DNA in 1953 showed how this coding could be managed, with each strand of the DNA double helix able to serve as a template. However, DNA sequences also code for proteins which are not enzymes (most enzymes are proteins, but many proteins do not function as

enzymes). Moreover, DNA does not itself create proteins, it does so only by means of its effects upon another molecule, RNA. A gene, then, could be defined as a region of a chromosome containing a DNA sequence which can be copied into RNA to provide a template for the synthesis of a protein. Seen this way, genes are relatively stable, discrete units that hold and pass on information. This is the notion of gene that has been made popular by writers such as Richard Dawkins.

Yet the reality is significantly more complex, varied and unstable. Cell nuclei contain long sequences of seemingly redundant DNA, so proteins are often coded for by elements of DNA dispersed widely across chromosomes. When cells reproduce, these DNA sequences come together in processes of splicing and editing that can create significant variation. Genes can actually be 'assembled' out of alternative DNA sequences, which means that the simple linear notion of 'one gene coding for one protein' is inaccurate.

Further adding to the complexity, it has also been discovered that these process of splicing and editing mean that the sequences of DNA that make up individual genes can 'jump' or move to other areas of the chromosome. Until the 1980s it was thought that this jumping was extremely rare, but research has increasingly shown it to be quite common. Like other aspects of gene activity, jumping occurs because genes are continuously interacting with the environments of their cells, which, in turn, are themselves continuously influenced by the environments beyond their walls.

So the picture of genes as fixed, discrete coding devices needs to be replaced with the modern understanding that genes themselves are somewhat fluid entities. As Rose observes, once we appreciate some of this complexity the simple idea of stable fixed genes 'for' individual properties will mostly fail to do justice to the complex reality of cellular reproduction that unfolds dynamically every time genes have some kind of effect.

significant. Moreover, for humans, this activity always occurs within social relations that mediate it, and that provide the resources and settings that make it possible. Human activity, then, is enabled by both genes and society, and conducted by active agents who are always influenced by biology and culture acting together. So our behaviour is not simply driven by 'selfish genes'. It reflects the operation of our biologically-enabled capacities for choice, reflection and deliberation, played out within social structures and relations, mediated by the resources of our culture, and more or less aligned with its taken-for-granted norms.

This more complex understanding also challenges many explanations for behaviour that draw on evolutionary psychology. However, this is not to say that evolution has nothing to say about the human condition, nor that we should reject Darwin's thinking. Currently, there are some who reject evolution and want to replace it with the theory of 'intelligent design'. There is no real evidence for the theory of intelligent design; it has very little scientific support, and most scientists see it as little more than an attempt to smuggle quasi-religious explanations into the curriculum. By contrast, although not every aspect of Darwin's theory is strongly supported by empirical evidence, there is extensive evidence for many of its claims. Similarly, whilst there are disagreements between scientists working with this theory, there is also a clear consensus that its key tenets are correct and that it provides valid and useful explanations for many phenomena in the life sciences. Nevertheless, as Rose points out, Darwin himself said that natural selection is only one of the mechanisms driving evolution, so it is paradoxical that some of those who claim to be following in his footsteps seem to want to discount all other influences. In a general sense, Darwinian evolution is relevant to our species, as it is to all others: but this does not mean that we can simplistically explain large areas of present-day human conduct with primary reference to the supposed activities of ancestors who lived in trees and caves.

To summarize: organisms and their environments are so thoroughly interwoven that the nature–nurture debate that oppose genes to environment is misguided. Instead, Rose argues that we should recognize how organisms and their environments are continually bound together or *interpenetrated* at every moment of the organism's life, including those moments when genes are being expressed. This means that rather than seeing genes and environment as opposing influences, we should recognize how they operate together to produce temporally organized degrees of plasticity and specificity. In order to demonstrate this, we have mostly talked about single-celled creatures, bacteria and enzymes, things that might seem to have little to do with distress. But discussing these examples has enabled us to begin clearing up some common misconceptions regarding the role of biology in human life; this sets the stage for the next part of our discussion.

BOX 4.5

What's wrong with the biopsychosocial model?

The biopsychosocial model attempts to understand distress by chaining together influences from each of three realms – the biological, the psychological and the social. Although problems with the model are widely acknowledged (Armstrong, 1987; Ogden, 1997) some argue that it is fundamentally correct and that only its implementation is troublesome (Marks, 2002; Spicer & Chamberlain, 1996). But in our view the problems run much deeper.

First, from the outset the biopsychosocial model was never clearly defined. It was proposed by Engel (1977), on the one hand as an alternative to psychodynamic theories, and on the other as a reaction against behaviourist notions of persons reacting blindly to their environments. But Engel never specified what the model should look like, nor did he link it to any theory. He just argued that such a model was valuable and then wrote about 'the' biopsychosocial model as though it had already been developed. However, nowhere in his writings does he undertake this development (Mclaren, 1998), and others who have claimed to be using 'the' biopsychosocial model have similarly failed to specify it. To the extent that the model has developed at all it has done so in relatively undisciplined ways; it means different things to different people, and there is still no clear agreement over its elements.

Second, research within the biopsychosocial model typically assumes that biology, psychology and the social are already separate and distinct, rather than understanding that they are already thoroughly entwined. Researchers then try to put the three influences together, instead of seeing that they are conjoined and exploring how their interpenetration is configured. Variables are typically considered side-by-side, as though they all have the same character; this ignores the real, qualitative differences between them. Social influence is probabilistic, not deterministic (Archer, 1995), involving active orientation toward norms rather than direct causal relations, and implicating 'distal' influences (Smail, 2005) that can't be manipulated experimentally. Consequently, when social and biological variables are treated identically, the resulting analysis can erroneously make social influence appear insubstantial and weak.

Third, there is actually little consideration of the *relationships between* biology, psychology and the social. Evidence is gathered using designs, methodologies and measures that already assume distinct separations between the three; and these assumptions then get reproduced within the evidence. By superficially appearing to join these three realms without actually doing so, the biopsychosocial model may do more to obscure the nature of the relationships between biology, psychology and society than to reveal them.

The biopsychosocial model thus tends to act as little more than a rhetorical gloss to justify the inclusion of variables from each realm, but actual attempts to explore the reciprocal relationships between these different influences are rare. Consequently, it tends to simply reproduce dominant trends, treating biology as more or less foundational but tacking on some discussion of social factors as contextual, or psychological factors as able to modify or ameliorate distress. This is why Read (2005) argued that what we typically have is actually a 'bio-bio-bio' model.

Body, brain and social relations

Damasio (1994) observes that not only is the brain embodied; the body is also 'embrained'. What he means by this is that it's a matter of convention rather than anatomy that we place the boundary of the brain somewhere near the base of the skull. In actuality, the nervous system is a seamless outgrowth of the brain that penetrates right through the entire body, all the way down to the tips of our toes. The brain is also awash with hormones, neurotransmitters and peptides, some released elsewhere in the body and others locally. In either case, these chemicals move so fluidly between 'body' and 'brain' that it makes little sense to think of them as entirely separate entities. What we have is a body–brain system (or more accurately, system of systems) which carries out all of the neural, hormonal and chemical activities that enable our experiences.

The body–brain system is open, dynamic and self-organizing. It is **open** because, as we have already seen, from the level of individual cells upwards it continuously responds to external, environmental influences. But neither these influences, nor the responses to them, are fixed and stable: both are **dynamic**. The body–brain system strives to maintain certain key variables (such as temperature, pH, the relative concentration of various salts) within strict limits. This striving is sometimes called homeostasis, but is more accurately described as **homeodynamics** since the equilibria it produces are always fluctuating around an optimal point, which itself fluctuates somewhat, according to environmental circumstances. Nevertheless, this shows us that the body–brain system is also **self-organizing**: although it responds dynamically to external influences, it tries to keep many of its responses within certain limits.

But what do these external influences consist of? Clearly, they include the things we eat and drink, since these get absorbed by our bodies. They also include temperature, sunlight, air and any other gas we might inhale. In unfortunate instances, they also include the effect of physical injury or trauma, or toxins in the environment. Recent work in the field of **epigenetics** – the study of how environmental influences can produce heritable changes in offspring – is beginning to show how some of these influences can interact with our biology (see Box 4.6). But because we humans are intrinsically social creatures, these external influences upon the body–brain system also include our social relations and cultural resources. At first, this might seem like a strange claim to make: society and culture are usually seen as relatively ephemeral, insubstantial things, and their influence as entirely separate from our biology. In fact, however, social and cultural influences are being built into our bodies right from the earliest moment of our lives. Perhaps the most obvious example of the interpenetration of the body and social influence is the vital role that language comes to play in our thinking and our actions.

The language you speak (or your main language, if you are fortunate enough to speak more than one) was probably acquired effortlessly by you during your infancy. As you learned it, your growing vocal system modified itself to gradually exclude all of the phonemes not included in your native tongue. Now, as an adult, you will find it difficult to produce the sounds of those excluded phonemes, so you will not be able to speak a foreign language like a native speaker. Social and

---

BOX 4.6
Epigenetics

In recent years there has been an explosion of interest in the area of biology known as epigenetics, with activity including presentations at international conferences, meetings, internet discussions, commercial funding interest, journal special issues and a textbook (Goldberg, Allis & Bernstein, 2007).

There are numerous definitions of epigenetics, and these have changed over time (Jablonka & Lamb, 2002). Historically, the term was used to describe microbiological events that could not be explained using genetic principles. Currently, it is used to refer to the study of the mechanisms whereby heritable changes in gene expression can occur, *without changes to the genes themselves*. Epigenetic research, then, takes very seriously the idea that organisms never develop independently of their environments. It tries to identify how environmental influences can produce biochemical changes that

modulate gene expression and which can be then be passed on to offspring. For example, processes during gene expression called methylation and histone modification are both open to environmental influence. Both have the capacity to 'silence' genes and prevent their expression, and both can produce heritable changes. Epigenetics is likely to be of growing significance in relation to health in the coming years, because it may help to explain some of the epidemiological variation in diseases such as cancer, and help account for many forms of intellectual impairment (Egger, Gangning, Aparicio & Jones, 2004).

So far there has been relatively little research into epigenetics and distress, although interest has accelerated rapidly in recent years, and there is some evidence of possible epigenetic effects. McClellan, Susser and King (2006) note that both the Dutch Hunger Winter and a famine in parts of China between 1959 and 1961 led to subsequent small increases in diagnoses of schizophrenia amongst offspring who were in the

early stages of foetal development whilst their mothers endured famine conditions. They speculate that folate deficiency might have influenced gene expression during foetal development, causing neural changes which render the offspring more vulnerable to diagnosis in later life, although they recognize that many other biological mechanisms could be implicated. Moreover, both of these famines were associated with significant social upheavals, raising the possibility that changes in economic status and disruptions to family life and relationships were also influential in producing the increase in diagnoses. Other published studies so far are similarly open to a multitude of explanations, and for the most part the research being conducted still depends upon unhelpful diagnostic categories. So, whilst for the moment we have little more than informed speculation, there is nevertheless the prospect that future epigenetic research might provide an important element of a framework that can integrate environmental and biological influences upon distress.

cultural influence, in the form of the sounds that constitute your language, has now become part of the habitual way that parts of your body work. But language does not only shape the way we use our lips, mouths and vocal cords. In the form of **inner speech**, the unspoken commentary that we experience accompanying the actions of ourselves and others, language also becomes part of the way that we think.

Vygotsky (1962) was one of the first psychologists to theorize and study this process. He argued that we internalize fragments of conversations, particularly those that are explicitly instructional, and then use them to guide our own activities. First of all, Vygotsky claimed, we take part in conversations with others. Next, we speak fragments of those conversations out loud to ourselves, using them to monitor and guide our actions. This **outer speech** is not 'egocentric', as Piaget claimed, but is instead a **transitional form** – it represents a stage in a transformation. Vygotsky says that outer speech is halfway between the shared conversations within social relations that it is derived from, and the mature, non-verbal inner speech that it will become.

Fivush (1991) illustrates this with the example of a little girl looking for her lost doll. When she asks her father for help, he prompts her to look in a series of places: 'Could it be in the kitchen? Have you looked there? Go and look there … It isn't there. Okay, have you looked under your bed? Go and look under your bed'; and so on. Fivush says that if this kind of conversation is repeated often enough, eventually the little girl will not need to actually ask her father to be able to imagine what he might say. Instead of asking him, she will 'replay' the conversation to herself, and use it to guide her search: first in the kitchen, then under the bed, and so on. At first she will do this by speaking her father's words aloud to herself, and when she does this she will copy his rhythms, his tone of voice, and the emotional quality of his speech. But after a while she will stop needing to speak his words aloud, and instead speak them silently to herself as inner speech. When this happens, the fragments of original conversation get shortened, truncated and stripped of **predicatives** (verbal terms or phrases that index or point to aspects of the current situation). They will become an integral part of her individual thought processes, which she will then be able to use to guide her own activities of thinking, reasoning, remembering and so on. This guiding activity is called **metacognition** – 'thinking about thinking' – and despite the fact that it occurs individually, in the intimate privacy of subjective experience, its origins are thoroughly social. Inner speech reflects not only the language of the culture where we first learned to speak, it also reflects the particular pattern of social relations within which we grew up.

Although as adults it is often difficult for us to see that inner speech is acquired in this way, some people are able to use the example of driving. Car driving is a skill typically acquired both later in life and outside the family home: for these reasons, the origins of its associated inner speech can often be more easily discerned. Many new drivers find that when driving in difficult conditions, or when they encounter an especially complicated situation, they find themselves speaking the words of their driving instructor when they encountered similar situations whilst learning. They may do this out loud – outer speech – or silently, as inner speech. Indeed, not only do they repeat their instructor's words, they are likely to repeat them in the instructor's (hopefully!) calm and reassuring tone of voice.

So even within the private, innermost recesses of thinking, there are social and relational influences helping us make sense of our activity. Moreover, these influences are not merely 'mental' or 'psychological', because they are enabled by systems in our bodies and brains that are specialized for this purpose. Gazzaniga et al. (1996) refer to the phenomenon of inner speech when they describe a collection of left-hemisphere brain systems they call '**the interpreter**' that functions to provide a continuous, running narrative upon our lives and activities. Gazzaniga has conducted research with **split-brain patients** – people who have had the fibres joining the two halves of their cortex (the corpus callosum) severed. This is done in very rare cases to limit the damage that would otherwise be caused by intractable epilepsy, and provides a chance to conduct some unusual studies. Gazzaniga's research with these people shows that inner speech is produced in the left hemisphere of the human brain, and that it generates culturally plausible and socially acceptable accounts of our activity, even on occasions when, because of experimental manipulations, the accounts can be demonstrably shown to be confabulations.

In the form of language, then, social influence becomes part of our own individual way of thinking, and there are brain regions dedicated to enabling this. So when it comes to talking and thinking, even when we are alone and our thoughts and sayings are wholly private, not shared with anyone else, social influence is nevertheless part of them. But this social influence is not merely 'psychological', because it has also become part of the normal operation of our bodies and brains. The physical movements that produce our primary language are now embedded within our bodies as habitual ways of using our lips, mouths and vocal cords. At the same time, the left-hemisphere systems associated with language and inner speech have taken up the vocabulary and semantic structure of this primary language, and use them to effortlessly generate personal narratives of experience. This is a clear example of what Rose calls the *interpenetration* of the organism and its environment, but here, the relevant environment is the social world of relationships and cultural resources, rather than the material environment of foodstuffs and objects.

Development

As the example of language shows, aspects of social relations and culture get built into the brain during the course of development and growth. We will now consider in more detail some of the pathways by which this might occur, and draw out some implications for our understandings of distress. We must start by recognizing that, unlike the young of most other species, newborn humans left to their own devices simply do not survive: right from the very first moments of life, we are dependent upon others for our well-being. Perhaps for this reason, humans come into the world biologically predisposed toward social relations. Within hours of birth, babies show a preference for faces (rather than random compositions of the elements that faces are made from). They 'recognize' the voices of their parents by responding preferentially to them, and are sensitive to markers of emotion such as tone of voice (Johnson, 1992). And, typically, parents respond to their babies with intense, mutual gazing, close mirroring of their expressions and movements, and large amounts of physical contact.

They use a tone of voice and ways of speaking ('**motherese**') specially adapted for their infant, and drastically rearrange their lives to accommodate its many needs.

Part of the reason that newborn humans are so thoroughly helpless is that their brains are still growing, and will continue to do so rapidly for some years after their birth. Many of the **glial cells** (which support the neuronal tissue) are not in place at birth, and important brain structures such as the orbito-frontal cortex, hypothalamus and hippocampus are only fully formed after the first three years of life. Both before and after birth, the sequence of brain development is largely under genetic control and so is relatively invariant. At predictable intervals, different regions of the brain undergo growth spurts, and this leads to the formation of new structures and the acquisition of new behaviours. For example, there is an explosion of growth in the human visual cortex at about eight weeks after birth (Yamada et al., 2000). Consequently, at about this time, babies get much better at tracking faces, and begin to spend longer periods of time gazing intently at their carers. Similarly, between three and nine months the amygdala and anterior cingulate grow particularly rapidly; these areas are important for emotion and feelings, and so the infant's repertoire of emotional responses extends and deepens greatly during this time. From the age of nine months or so and into the second year of life, connections are formed between the amygdala (and other parts of the subcortical limbic system) and the orbito-frontal cortex immediately above it. These connections enable the infant to monitor and inhibit emotional states; their acquisition adds yet further flexibility and sensitivity to its behavioural repertoire.

Growth spurts in the brain are characterized by two phases of activity. In the first phase, there is an abundant over-production of synaptic connections, so that many more connections are formed than will ever be needed. This over-production occurs at a staggering rate: during the first two years of life, the human brain forms approximately 30,000 new synaptic connections under each square centimetre of cortex *every second* (Rose, 1997). This proliferation of synapses, in turn, rests upon the prior over-production of cells in the womb, when the developing brain is forming precursor neuronal and glial cells at a rate of approximately one million every hour. Then, in the second phase, the neurones and synapses that are not being used are killed off, or pruned. The synapses that have not made functional connections with the dendrites of other neurones simply wither away and disappear, as do the neurones that have not connected themselves successfully to others. Both phases of activity are genetically programmed to occur, but – like all gene expression – both are open to external, environmental influences that condition precisely *how* they occur. And, just as with the example of language, these influences include social, cultural and relational forces.

For example, the growth spurt in the visual cortex at eight weeks enables the infant to get much better at identifying faces, tracking movements, and gazing at its carers. Carers typically respond to this new achievement by gazing back at the infant, and the intense mutual gazing that then ensues can be seen as an early channel of socio-emotional development. Feldman, Greenbaum and Yirimiya (1999) describe these early face-to-face interactions as 'highly arousing, affect laden, short interpersonal events'. They are typically characterized by the mutual co-ordination between infant and carer of gaze, facial expression, posture, tone of voice and movement, all of these effortlessly timed and co-ordinated. These interactions are important for socio-emotional development because their typical consequence is **affect synchrony** – the reciprocal, mutual regulation of emotional states in both infant and carer.

Vitally, the mutual responsiveness between infants and parents is not merely behavioural; it also has biological and biochemical aspects with direct consequences for brain development. For example, when parents cuddle their babies against their bodies, the heartbeat of both tends to synchronize. Infants respond to the dilated pupils of their parent's loving gaze by increasing their heart rate, and their brains respond by releasing more beta-endorphin in the orbito-frontal region. At the same time, dopamine is released in the brainstem and then migrates to the frontal regions. Beta-endorphin is one of the body's natural opiates and is associated with positive emotional states, whilst dopamine is subjectively stimulating and energizing. But in addition to their subjective effects, these interacting neurotransmitters accelerate the rate of uptake of glucose and insulin in brain tissue, so they increase the rate of neural development and the ease with which new synaptic connections can be formed. Conversely, an infant's biological systems also respond when its parents are unhappy, experience distress, or fail to meet its needs. The babies of emotionally unresponsive mothers tend to have lower levels of norepinephrine and dopamine (Jones, Field, Fox, Davalos & Malphus, 1997), and when babies are left to cry, their cortisol levels rise significantly (Gunnar & Donzella, 2002). Whilst moderate increases of cortisol can stimulate development, excessive levels have been shown to impede development in both the orbito-frontal region (Lyons, Yang, Mobley, Nickerson & Schatzburg, 2000) and the hippocampus (Caldji, Diorio & Meaney, 2000).

So the developing brain is dynamically self-organizing yet at the same time continuously open to social and environmental influences. Whilst the sequence of development is genetically controlled, its process is activity-dependent (Schore, 2001). Its outcome reflects not only the genes that prompted it but also the social and environmental conditions in which it took place. The baby's lifeline, begun in the womb, continues throughout infancy as the brain structures needed for adult life are formed. During this time the levels of neurotransmitters, hormones

Electrical impulses are transmitted along the axon to the terminal bulb. When they arrive they cause the vesicles to release neurotransmitting molecules into the synaptic cleft.

These molecules bind to receptor sites on the dendrite of the next neuron. When they do so, they influence the probability that this neuron will 'fire' its own electrical impulse.

A synapse

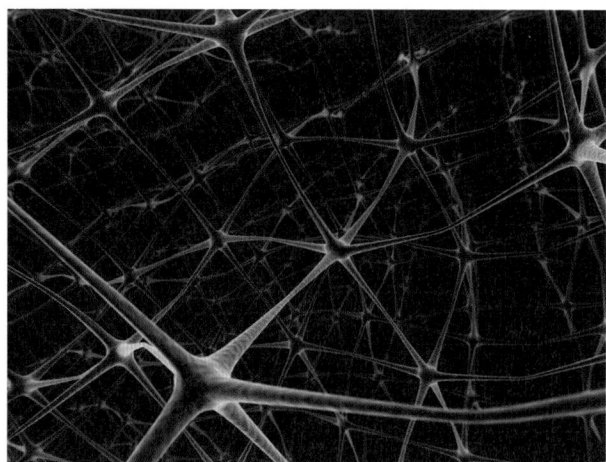

Neurons are connected together in patterns known as neural networks. Although the numbers of connections between them vary hugely, one neuron is frequently connected to many thousands of others.

and peptides in the baby's body and brain are continuously responsive to social influences, and also regulate some of the ways in which its brain and other biological systems develop. This means that whilst there are always degrees of plasticity within the lifeline, degrees of specificity can get built into our biological systems during these early years, because it is during this time that the basic brain structures that will endure throughout life are formed.

Temporal specificity and distress

Parenting need not be perfect – indeed, it is hard to know how we could ever decide what 'perfect' parenting might look like – but it does need to be **good enough parenting**, as Winnicott (1987) put it, in which parents and carers meet their child's basic needs for nutrition, warmth, and comfort. They have to be responsive to their child's emotional needs, too, offering comfort and reassurance that is fairly consistent across time, communicated sufficiently clearly, pitched at the right kind of level, and arrives relatively soon after it is first needed. Most parents do this without too much trouble, not perfectly, for sure, and certainly not all of the time, but, on balance, their care is usually good enough. Unfortunately, though, parenting is sometimes not good enough, and is sometimes accompanied by incidents of trauma and abuse.

Schore (2001) provides a necessarily speculative account that describes in some detail the possible effects upon the early development of the human brain of trauma, neglect and abuse. His work is framed by **attachment theory** (Bowlby, 1958), a psychoanalytic approach which proposes that a baby's relations with its parents or carers need to constitute an 'environment of adaptiveness' that is sufficient to enable it to develop adequate lifelong mechanisms for regulating emotion and coping with stress. The theory proposes that most babies have a primary **attachment relationship**, usually with their mothers, and that it is this relationship more than any other that sets the conditions for the development of systems of emotional control and stress regulation. Within this relationship, so long as care is 'good enough' the baby will learn to regulate its own emotions and control its own stress, both in

its relations with others and – by derivation from this – when it is alone. But sometimes, this 'good enough' kind of relationship does not occur. Sometimes parents and carers themselves are experiencing distress, and this might impair their ability to provide good enough care for their babies. Sometimes, too, more dramatic failures of care occur, including instances of severe neglect as well as of deliberate trauma or abuse.

In attachment theory, it is proposed that the relationships between carers and their infants provide the basis for emotional security – or its absence – in later life. Emotional security reflects the confidence, gained from early experience, that unpleasant emotional states will soon be alleviated and emotional needs will be met. Attachment relationships are usually categorized according to the patterns of activity that can be observed between carers and infants, using categories such as secure, insecure (often subdivided into avoidant and ambivalent) and disorganized. In a **secure attachment relationship**, carers respond to the emotional needs of infants appropriately, promptly and consistently, and as a consequence infants are better able to deal with potentially difficult situations such as being left alone for a short while. In an **insecure–avoidant attachment relationship**, carers show relatively little emotional response to their infant's distress, encouraging independence and self-reliance, and infants respond by becoming relatively autonomous when separated from their carers. They show relatively little distress when left briefly alone, but relatively little joy when their carers return. In an **insecure–ambivalent attachment relationship**, carers are somewhat inconsistent in their responses: sometimes they respond appropriately to their infant's needs, but at other times they fail to do so. Infants respond to this kind of care by coping relatively well with short periods of separation, but when the carer returns they display anger and reluctance, before eventually showing any degree of warmth.

The fourth category is disorganized attachment, and this is the primary focus of Schore's discussion. In a **disorganized attachment relationship**, rather than simply being the main source of comfort and security, carers themselves may become a source of fear and anxiety for their infants. In this kind of relationship, carers engage in fewer interactions overall with their infants, and tend to communicate with them less clearly. They use more aversive disciplinary techniques with their infants and, at the same time, display fewer positive reactions toward them. Their behaviour might be frightening or disorienting, veering from over-intrusiveness to extreme neglect. Rather than meeting their infant's emotional needs, such carers might appear to use their babies in an effort to meet their own. At the extremes, in such relationships, carers are overtly harmful to their infants, being extremely neglecting or deliberately abusive. Infants in a disorganized attachment relationship respond by showing contradictory patterns of activity and unusual stress reactions such as freezing and rocking. They sometimes cycle rapidly from one emotional state to another, so hysterical laughter can seamlessly become sobbing, and this in turn can transform quickly into a detached and 'blank' emotional state in which the child becomes silent and seemingly dazed and withdrawn. In extreme states, infants seem to 'dissociate' or disengage completely from their surrounding world. They become extremely still, their eyes are unfocused and staring, and they may adopt a curled, defensive bodily posture. In later life, disorganized attachment relationships may have adverse consequences for the person's ability to cope with stress, to regulate emotion, and to maintain supportive personal relationships.

Attachment theory proposes that infants and parents have the capacity to form strong emotional bonds that powerfully shape the infant's future sense of self

Schore (2001) states that, in a disorganized attachment relationship, infants are frequently in intense, enduring and extreme emotional states. The combination of over-stimulation as a consequence of abuse and under-stimulation as a consequence of neglect **dysregulates** (i.e. impairs the capacity for control and regulation) the activity of the infant's sympathetic and parasympathetic nervous systems. This produces extreme, rapid cycling between states of over- and under-arousal. These states are not simply psychological: like all psychological states they have simultaneous biological aspects, and are associated with corresponding changes in the infant's brain chemistry (van der Kolk & Fisler, 1994). Schore speculates that, as a result, disorganized attachment relationships can have profound lifelong consequences because they fundamentally alter the ways in which the infant's brain develops. Of particular concern is the development of the socio-emotionally dominant right hemisphere, and especially the growth of regulatory circuits between this hemisphere and the areas of brain beneath it that comprise the limbic system. Schore's argument is that the development and subsequent pruning of inhibitory and regulatory circuits, particularly within the orbito-frontal cortex of the right hemisphere, can be adversely influenced by a disorganized attachment relationship.

For example, extreme states of fear are characterized by excessive arousal of the sympathetic nervous system. Such states include the release of high levels of corticotrophin-re-leasing-factor (CRF), a hormone related to stressful experiences and the production of cortisol, and the release within the brain of noradrenaline. In these states, excitatory neurotransmitters such as noradrenaline and glutamate may be available at high levels within the developing brain, and corresponding high levels of metabolic activity will occur within the immature limbic system (Perry, Pollard, Blakely, Baker & Vigilante, 1995). These biological changes, driven by the infant's relation-ship with its carers, can have direct consequences for brain development. Excitatory neurotransmitters alter the rate of calcium metabolism in the infant's brain, and this is a critical 'neurotoxic' mechanism of cell death (J. Farber, 1981). As a result, excessive pruning of developing neural systems may occur. Consequently, infants within disorganized attachment relationships may fail to develop adequate neural connections, particularly within the right hemisphere, between the orbito-frontal cortex and the limbic system.

The orbito-frontal cortex is sometimes described as a **'convergence zone'** because it contains connections radiat-ing out to many other areas of the higher cortex, as well as downward to the subcortical limbic system: it is an important place where cortex and subcortex come together (Petrides & Milner, 1982). Consequently, Schore proposes that the exces-sive pruning of synapses and neurones in this area as a result of disorganized attachment relationships might have particularly important and lasting consequences. Impairment of the connections between the orbito-frontal cortex and the amygdala is especially important; the amygdala is a brain region closely associated with negative emotions, especially anxiety and fear (Le Doux, 1999). Trauma, abuse or neglect in the first years of life may permanently impair a person's ability to manage and dampen down their own fears and anxieties, so they may always be more prone to more severe, more unpredictable and more inconsistent extremes of anxiety and stress than others.

Neglect and abuse within disorganized attachment relation-ships may have other consequences, as well as leading to fail-ure to control and regulate stress and negative emotions. Both the amygdala and the orbito-frontal cortex have connections to the hypothalamus, a brain region implicated in regulating autonomic nervous system activity. Connections between the orbito-frontal cortex and the hypothalamus are laid down during the first two years of life, so trauma and abuse during this time may impact upon their development. Excessive prun-ing of these connections, especially in the right hemisphere, may result in an impaired ability to regulate arousal. This may produce a tendency toward **tonic immobility**: responses characterized by simultaneous sympathetic and parasympa-thetic nervous system activity (Berntson, Cacioppo & Quigley, 1991). These responses may produce the **dissociative states** sometimes experienced by survivors of abuse. In these states people seem to deal with inescapable trauma by cutting them-selves off, both from their own immediate experience and from the world around them. Abuse survivors who enter such states sometimes describe them as having helped to make the abuse tolerable, because it could almost seem as though it was happening to someone else.

The hypothalamus is also implicated in the production of rage and anger states (Beaumont, Kenealy & Rogers, 1996), and these too are usually subject to inhibitory control by connections with the orbito-frontal cortex. Just as early relational trauma might produce a tendency towards disso-ciation because the inability to inhibit immobility responses becomes impaired, so it might also be associated with uncontrollable outbursts of rage or anger. Schore suggests that relevant areas of the hypothalamus might fail to acquire dense synaptic connections with the orbito-frontal area, with the consequence that extremes of anger might both occur more often and be harder to anticipate, regulate or control.

Because the temporal sequence of brain development is largely under genetic control, the postnatal assembly of both limbic and autonomic nervous system circuits occurs according to a specific temporal pattern. Schore further speculates that this means that, within limits, it may be possible to specify the effects upon brain development of trauma and abuse occurring at different times during the infant's first few years. For example, during the last part of the first year of life and into the second year, the connections between the limbic area and the cortex above it are growing especially fast. As a result, neglect and abuse during this period of life might have particularly marked consequences for the development of the neural connections important for both empathy and emotional regulation. Each growth spurt in the developing brain might be seen as a 'sensitive period' during which adverse relational influences could have particular, enduring effects upon the infant.

Although there may be quite specific effects of this kind, disorganized attachments are not associated with any one particular psychiatric diagnosis. Schore (2001) argues that there is empirical evidence for the kind of orbito-frontal deficiencies and failures of affect regulation that are produced by disorganized attachments in people who are given diagnoses of schizophrenia, autism, manic depression, major depression,

obsessive–compulsive disorder, problem drinking and drug dependency. Disorganized attachment is associated with abuse, and in a review of the effects upon the brain of child abuse, Glaser (2000) links abuse to diagnoses of post-traumatic stress disorder, and suggests that there may also be links between abuse and a diagnosis of attention-deficit hyperactivity disorder (ADHD). Similarly, other studies of attachment have proposed links between the insecure–avoidant attachment category and diagnoses of schizophrenia (Dozier, Stevenson, Lee & Velligan, 1991).

Of course, attachment relationships – whatever their character – are never separate from the other social relations and material circumstances of people's lives (see Box 4.7). They are formed and played out in the actual, concrete circumstances of those lives, so they are always subject to a wide variety of other powerful influences. Trauma, abuse and neglect, and the kinds of harmful parenting seen in disorganized attachment relationships, do not arise out of nowhere. Whilst a small minority of people commit deliberate abuse, most parents and carers do the best they can with their children in what are sometimes difficult circumstances. This means that we must make a sharp distinction between recognizing that parents and carers have immediate responsibility for the well-being of their children, and falling into 'parent-blaming': the view that parents – particularly mothers – are wholly culpable for failures in the upbringing of their children. Recognizing

---

BOX 4.7
Contextualizing attachment

Schore's account has some limitations, many of which flow from its reliance upon attachment theory. Like all category systems, attachment categories conceal as well as reveal. Cramming the rich diversity of human relations into just four categories facilitates research and helps us think about the connections between early experience and distress in later life. At the same time, it obscures much of their richness and detail by prioritizing a relatively small handful of behaviours and treating these as having primary significance.

In practice, few attachment relationships fit neatly into just one of the categories (Kagan, 1998). One meta-analysis of disorganized attachment concluded that the behaviours associated with it occurred against an 'underlying' pattern categorized as avoidant (34%), ambivalent (46%) or secure (14%) (vanIjendoorn, Schuengel & Bakermans-Kranenburg, 1999). Moreover, not all infants form a primary attachment with their mothers: many become dependent upon two or more carers, and around 30% attach primarily

to fathers (Schaffer & Emerson, 1964). As a result, it is now common to assess attachment differentially to fathers and to mothers. Combined categories (e.g. insecure–disorganized) are common, suggesting that emotional security and carer's responsiveness are more nuanced and situationally variable than fixed attachment categories can easily allow.

There are also problems in assessing attachment relationships. Some are conceptual, to do with the extent to which researchers think they are assessing either the *actual* caregiver-infant relationship or its acquired internalized representation. Empirically, the 'Strange Situation Procedure' provides only a brief 'window' through which to examine the relationship, but many relevant behaviours occur relatively infrequently, and are subtle and fleeting (Green & Goldwyn, 2002). Other assessments suffer from problems of interpretation when they are qualitative, and problems of self-report, acquiescence and social desirability when they are questionnaire-based.

We must also beware of placing too much emphasis on the nature and quality of the relationship between an infant and a single carer, usually its mother, and so failing to recognize

the significance of other influences. Attachment theory can create the illusion of a single, primary relationship which is of overwhelming importance: if we fall prey to this, we easily forget that other influences are also highly significant. Childhood sexual and physical abuse is a significant risk factor for distress, and most abuse is committed by men, not women. Moreover, the prevalence of childhood physical abuse is patterned according to demographic and socio-economic variables, and is more prevalent in areas of relative deprivation and unemployment (Jack, 2004; NSPCC, 2006). Distress itself is more prevalent in conditions of social inequality, and parents and carers who are themselves experiencing distress might not always be able to shield their children from its effects. Sometimes, then, troubled attachment relationships might be best understood as markers of problems elsewhere.

Attachment theory is a useful way of thinking about some of the ways childhood experiences relate to distress in later life. However, difficulties in measurement and reliance upon a small number of relatively inflexible categories mean that studies often raise as many questions as they answer.

the importance of social and relational factors in creating a vulnerability to distress is not at all the same as claiming that parents or carers should be blamed for failures they may not have been able to prevent, and the consequences of which they had no way of knowing.

We must also emphasize that Schore's account is entirely hypothetical, in the sense that, whilst it rests upon an impressive array of good quality research, the studies he integrates are for the most part not direct tests of the hypothesis that disorganized attachment produces vulnerabilities to distress. His argument depends upon integrating a great many studies of more specific aspects of brain development and its links to social circumstances – for example, the research showing the effects of cortisol on hippocampal growth. However, we lack evidence that the various effects he integrates actually do come together in the way he suggests, and moreover – given the extent of measurement and intervention that would be needed – it is difficult to imagine how such evidence could ever be gathered.

Schore's account nevertheless provides one useful way of thinking about the way that biology and social relations might conjoin in the early years of life to produce degrees of specificity within the lifeline. This early specificity is produced by neither genes nor environment alone; it is the joint consequence of them both, acting together, as they always do. Schore's work allows us to conceptualize how enduring individual differences in temperament, differences which are all too easily assumed to be wholly biological, are, in fact, social at the same time. They are, as Rose says, environmental at the same time as they are genetic.

Temporal plasticity and distress

The preceding section described some of the ways in which our biology might be shaped at particular periods during development, to produce specific vulnerabilities and deficits that then endure throughout life. In this section we will present some of the evidence suggesting that, with respect to distress, our biology is constantly open to environmental influence: in other words, we will be concerned here with its **plasticity**. Steven Rose (1997, p. 132) describes plasticity as 'the capacity of a living system to adapt to experience and environmental contingencies, and to compensate for deficiencies'. Two features of this definition are particularly important. First, in using this definition Rose is specifically interested in development, and particularly the joint contribution of genes and environment. Second, Rose's focus on lifelines means that he is concerned with the capacity of the whole organism, not just the capacity of its brain, its nervous system, or any other component.

In neuroscience, much research into plasticity has been concerned with the developing motor and sensory systems, and has focused on the effects of specific trauma or lesions (because it is easiest to assess and quantify the effects of these kinds of changes to these brain systems; Beaumont et al., 1996). Moreover, much of the evidence for plasticity is very general and, unlike Schore's account, is rarely drawn coherently together in the context of a discussion of distress. In his account, Rose emphasizes the importance of **functional redundancy** during development: the fact that humans are such complex creatures that our biological systems may offer many possible pathways to what is, functionally, much the same outcome. In the presence of a certain gene that produces a particular protein, the function might be conducted one way: in the absence of this gene and protein, the same function might be achieved using another pathway. Nevertheless, we are not infinitely adaptable, and Rose uses the notion of the **norm of reaction** to describe this mixture of limits and flexibility. Within the kinds of environment for which a gene is typically prepared (and remember that the environment of a gene includes all of the other genes present) its phenotypic expression may vary widely, according to environmental factors. But outside of these limits, there are stark changes. Recall the example of trisomy 21 or Downs' syndrome, discussed earlier in this chapter: although there is extensive variation in the effects of having a third chromosome on the 21st pair, there are also limits; everyone with this genetic configuration experiences some of its effects.

In this section, we will follow Rose in emphasizing the whole organism – the whole person – whilst also, at times, talking about brains, genes, hormones and so on. We will also follow Rose's emphasis on development, taking it to include the ways in which our biological systems are plastic over the entire lifespan. In other words, we will, like Rose, emphasize some of the ways in which our biology is continuously open to environmental influences. These influences might be material, social, cultural or relational, and are often some mixture of all of these. In our account, then, plasticity does not simply refer to the neural or synaptic processes that might follow a lesion. It also refers to the various influences and processes – some neural and synaptic, others operating at a grosser level, others still operating primarily outside the individual – that demonstrate the continuous, dynamic responsiveness of our biological systems to the various influences upon them.

From this wider perspective, it should be clear that there is a sense in which large degrees of plasticity are already the norm for our species. Whilst we typically have difficulty adapting to gross neural insults, such as the loss of a section of brain tissue following a stroke, even in this unfortunate circumstance adaptation and recovery are often possible. Whilst recovery is not always good and much depends on the nature and extent of the initial lesion, a meta-analysis of 14 studies of stroke rehabilitation found that 65% of patients with motor-area strokes showed some degree of recovery (Hendricks, van Limbeek, Geurts & Zwarts, 2002). But neural plasticity is not simply an effect of injury: there is an important sense in which it occurs all the time, simply as an effect of experience. Kolb and Whishaw (1998) review evidence suggesting that experience is a major stimulant of brain plasticity that drives multiple brain changes including increased dendritic length, synapse formation and glial cell and metabolic activity. This should not be surprising, since every time we learn something new our brains must change in order to accommodate or encode this new information. So in a very general sense, our brains and neural systems are already equipped to provide significant degrees of plasticity, and experience is one of the primary forces driving the changes that occur.

There is also more specific evidence of plasticity with respect to distress. Taking a developmental perspective, despite the relatively gloomy picture painted by Schore there is extensive evidence that not everyone whose early childhood is difficult will experience clinical levels of distress in later life. Indeed, numerous studies of dysfunctional attachment or separation in early childhood seem to find little or no effect upon those children when they become adults (Kagan, 1984). Some of the most telling research of this kind does not depend upon the categories and assessment procedures of attachment theory, but instead explores the consequences of clearly defined early experiences of separation and loss. For example, a study of 38 American children orphaned during the Second World War and adopted into middle-class families found that only 20% had noticeable problems at follow-up some years later: the remainder were well adjusted and largely indistinguishable from other children (Rathburn, DiVirgilio & Waldfogel, 1958). More recently, large numbers of Romanian orphans were adopted into other countries after living their early years in well-documented, extremely harsh conditions of neglect and deprivation. One study looked at 219 of these children adopted into America, and found that their behaviours were more troublesome than non-adopted children. However, they were less troublesome than the behaviours of children receiving mental health services, and in fact most closely resembled the behaviours of children adopted from domestic sources (Groza, 1999).

Children described as having significant early attachment problems almost always experience unfavourable situations that endure throughout significant periods of childhood. Consequently, it is difficult to know whether adverse effects upon children are specifically due to attachment problems in the early years, or to the many years of suboptimal parenting that these children typically receive. One longitudinal study assessed 137 children who spent at least the first year of their lives living in a nursery characterized by minimal stimulation and multiple caregivers – risk factors said to be associated with attachment problems and later distress. When they were followed up at ages 12 and 14, these children's cognitive development and educational attainment was no different from that of the general population, although the incidence of psychiatric problems was between two and three times that in a comparison group (depending on which problems were being compared). However, further analysis revealed that in the great majority of cases the children with psychiatric problems had subsequently been physically abused, or had been placed with step-parents and carers who argued frequently and were not nurturing toward the children. Amongst those children who had been placed in benevolent homes after leaving the nursery, distress was no more prevalent than amongst a comparison group (Ernst, 1988).

Of course, this is not to say that there are no studies showing adverse effects upon children due to early experience. Kagan (1998) reviews the evidence and concludes that what matters most are typically not the very early years per se but the character of childhood as a whole. In his review, he finds that the two most widespread and enduring influences seem to be social class and perinatal, or intra-uterine, injury. Advocates of attachment theory might challenge Kagan's assessment, for example by pointing to studies showing relatively high rates of attachment problems amongst the Romanian orphans (e.g. O'Connor & Rutter, 2000). Similarly, disorganized attachment has only been recognized as a robust category in recent years, and it is claimed that its identification may provide new opportunities to reveal the associations between distress and early experience. However, even those excited by the potentials of disorganized attachment caution that the category is inherently heterogeneous and difficult to identify (Green &

Goldwyn, 2002). Clearly, then, these are complex issues, but it seems safe to conclude that there is some evidence for developmental plasticity with respect to distress.

There is also evidence of plasticity with respect to the course of distress as it occurs across the lifespan. Most obviously, although clinical distress is a risk factor for a subsequent diagnosis, substantial numbers of people who are given a diagnosis make a full recovery and are never diagnosed again. Others will have multiple episodes where their problems become so great that they require further clinical intervention, but will nevertheless eventually make a more or less full recovery. There is extensive variation here, not only between different degrees and kinds of distress but also between cultures (see Chapter 3). Nevertheless, even in the West, where outcomes are poorest, and for people given a diagnosis of schizophrenia where prognoses are often said to be the worst, recovery rates of around 50% are reported at five-year follow-up (Robinson, Woerner, McMeniman, Mendelowitz & Bilder, 2004).

If we focus upon the various biological systems and markers said to be associated with distress, we also see evidence for plasticity and variability. For example, Laruelle and Abi-Dargham (1999) used brain scanning techniques to look at dopamine activity in the brains of people given a diagnosis of schizophrenia, and found that their levels of dopamine were elevated only during the period when they were actively experiencing distress: after they had recovered, their levels of dopamine returned to normal. Some researchers claim that it is not so much high levels of dopamine that cause schizophrenia but increased numbers of dopamine receptors. This was challenged by a longitudinal study of four people given a diagnosis of schizophrenia which assessed the density of dopamine receptors in their brains at six and 24 months after diagnosis. Two of these four showed a significant reduction in distress between the two assessments; of these, one showed a large (25%) decrease in dopamine receptor density whilst the other showed a 13% increase. The levels of distress of the other two people showed very little change between the two assessments, but of these two, one had an overall decrease in receptor density of 56% whilst the other had an increase of 25% (Syvälahti, Räkköläinen, Aaltonen, Lehtinen & Hietala, 2000).

Similarly, enlargement of the cerebral ventricles is sometimes posited as a cause of schizophrenia. This claim is problematic, because enlarged ventricles are also observed in people with other diagnoses, and a further complication is that the size of the ventricles varies significantly over time in response to such influences as alcohol consumption, water retention, diet and pregnancy (Bentall, 2003). One study compared 24 people given a diagnosis of schizophrenia with 12 controls, using MRI scanning to assess ventricular volume. A baseline measure was taken at diagnosis, and another at follow-up around eight months later. It was found that although some of the patients had enlarged ventricles when they were first diagnosed, at follow-up their ventricular volume had reduced to within normal limits. Overall there were no significant differences in ventricular volume between patients and controls at eight-month follow-up, but greater change across time amongst the patient group (Puri et al., 2001).

To summarize: whilst the plasticity of human biological systems is not without limits, both with respect to distress and more generally there is extensive evidence that our organism's capacities are adaptable and modifiable, both in response to experience and in relation to trauma of various kinds. With respect to neural systems, plasticity seems to be greater in early life than later, although evidence from brain-imaging studies demonstrates that the relative size of some brain structures can continue to change as a result of adult experiences (e.g. Maguire et al., 2000). Anatomically it is largely confined to the fine-grained scale of neurones, dendrites and synapses, whilst physiologically it is enacted primarily by the reactivity to experience of various hormones and neurotransmitters. This suggests that distress is multiple, fluid and variable, not only in terms of experience but also at the level of the biological systems that enable it.

Chapter summary

Viewed from the perspective of the lifeline, the biological systems that enable our experience are continuously open to social and relational influence. Both the current state of these systems and their developmental history are always a product of genes and environment, biology and social influence, coiled tightly together in highly complex ways.

Experiences of distress, too, arise within specific lifelines. In the dominant way of thinking that treats biology as the primary cause of distress, genetic influences are particularly important. The lifeline perspective shows us how genes might play some part, but also shows that it is extremely easy to overstate genetic influences. Schore's work, for example, demonstrates that enduring differences in temperament – which appear early in development, so might appear to have a genetic origin – could be primarily relational in origin, even though they are associated with enduring biological differences. Similarly, epigenetic research shows how changes in environmental conditions can produce heritable differences in the characteristics of offspring. All this suggests that, in a climate where there is ideological and commercial pressure in favour of simplistic biological explanations, new claims to have found the 'gene for' a disorder should be treated with caution.

Conversely, the lifeline perspective also suggests that in future we need to pay more attention to the relationships between patterns of experience and biology. Rather than treat biology as irrelevant, we should investigate how aspects of our biological systems are already bound up with social and relational processes. Studies of distress in relation to social inequality, life events, attachment patterns, expressed emotion and trauma rarely make links between these variables and the biology of individuals who experience distress. Apart from the tendency to treat biology as irrelevant, there are methodological reasons for this. Nevertheless, it is to be hoped that future research into these social and relational influences will increasingly explore how their effects come to be biologically embedded.

Biology, then, always plays a part in our experience – but it is never separate, in principle or practice, from other influences. The focus on lifelines lets us include biology, rather than ignoring it, but at the same time prevents us from treating it as simply causal. And because the lifeline perspective understands biology as *already* in interaction with other influences, at every stage, the conceptual issue of understanding the *relationships between* biology, psychology and social influence becomes central, rather than being bracketed off. This is not to say that the lifeline perspective simplifies our understandings of distress: indeed, it often makes them more complicated. But distress, like every other human experience, is a complicated, heterogeneous phenomenon with multiple origins, so this complexity may be no bad thing.

End of chapter questions

1 What difficulties do Western cultural assumptions about the relationships between mind and body create for our attempts to understand the role of biology in distress?
2 Recent advances in genomics (gene science) and neuroscience mean that knowledge is accumulating at an ever-increasing rate. Will this new knowledge solve the conceptual problems associated with existing biological evidence?
3 Will it ever be possible to create a valid biopsychosocial model of distress?
4 Steven Rose's 'lifeline' model offers a sophisticated way of thinking about the relationships between genes and environments, but how can it be used to guide research?
5 Will it ever be possible to conduct experiments to prove or disprove Schore's theories about the way that the frontal lobes develop?
6 Can we include the effects of early childhood in analyses of distress without using troublesome categories such as those found within attachment theory?
7 How do the known problems of reliability and validity associated with psychiatric diagnostic categories impact upon our attempts to understand the associations between biology and distress?

Find out more

Films and plays

The science fiction film 'Gattaca' (1997) explores some of the ethical and personal issues that might arise in a society where our futures are defined entirely according to our genetic inheritance at birth. The film's title is a play on the designated letters for the four proteins that make DNA – G, T, C, A.

The musical 'Blood Brothers', first performed in 1983, is one of the longest running plays in London's West End, with many productions elsewhere in the UK and internationally. The plot follows identical twin brothers separated at birth who are raised in very different circumstances, but then meet and become friends.

Academic reading

Joseph, J. (2003). *The Gene Illusion: Genetic Research in Psychiatry and Psychology under the Microscope*. Ross on Wye: PCCS Books.
Joseph, J. (2006). *The Missing Gene: Psychiatry, Heredity and the Fruitless Search for Genes*. New York: Algora.
Rose, S. (1997). *Lifelines: Life beyond the Gene*. Oxford: Oxford University Press.
Rose, S., Lewontin, R. & Kamin, I. (1984). *Not in Our Genes*. Harmondsworth: Penguin.

CHAPTER 5

DIAGNOSIS AND FORMULATION

Lucy Johnstone

Sarah's story

Sarah is a single, white woman of 27. She says she was close to her mother, but her father died suddenly of a heart attack when Sarah was eight. This affected her mother very badly, and Sarah became her main emotional support. Since her father had been the main wage-earner, there was very little money, and Sarah lost her friends when she and her mother moved into rented accommodation nearer her mother's parents. A few years later, her mother re-married. Sarah reports that she was sexually abused by her stepfather over a period of five years, but did not feel able to tell anyone. She became quiet and withdrawn and did badly at school. Eventually she left home and trained as a nurse. She worked very hard and enjoyed this job, and met a partner whom she was planning to marry. This relationship broke down when Sarah was 25. Around the same time, she injured herself at work and had to take time off sick. After a few weeks she became very low in mood, and was prescribed medication. The injury required an operation, and Sarah felt that the care she received was poor. She particularly remembers lying in bed in pain for a long time before anyone would attend to her. While recuperating at home, she started to hear a critical male voice telling her, 'You are useless and dirty'. Over the next month, this voice became louder. It was joined by other voices telling her that she was responsible for the death of various former patients that she had nursed, and needed to be punished. Eventually, Sarah was referred for a mental health assessment and given a diagnosis of schizophrenia.

Learning outcomes

After you have read this chapter, you will be able to:

1 Identify some of the core assumptions underlying psychiatric diagnosis
2 Explain how psychiatric diagnosis differs from most medical diagnosis
3 Describe how issues of reliability and validity are relevant to psychiatric diagnosis
4 Explain what a formulation of distress is
5 Evaluate the relative strengths and weaknesses of formulation and psychiatric diagnosis.

Introduction

Working out why someone breaks down is very complex and challenging. As we have already seen, the lives of those who come into contact with psychiatric services almost inevitably consist of a confusing mixture of social deprivation, relationship conflicts and traumas. Their behaviour, beliefs and experiences can be highly unusual and disturbing, and sometimes frightening to themselves and others. How are we to understand this? The current dominant paradigm is to see them as suffering from mental illnesses, which are similar to physical illnesses but chiefly affect the mind. Those who support this paradigm hope that one day biological causes in the brain will be discovered. In the meantime, we need to have some way of grouping or categorizing these behaviours, beliefs and experiences if we want to develop effective interventions. The question of how to do this is fundamental to every aspect of theory and practice in mental health, including research and government treatment guidelines. The current categorization system, psychiatric diagnosis, is also deeply embedded in the criminal justice system, in medical insurance, in government treatment guidelines, and in pharmaceutical companies' development of new medications.

Because of the enormous implications of the question of how to define and categorize distress, diagnosis is one of the most controversial areas in psychiatry. On the one hand, the use of diagnostic terms such as schizophrenia goes largely unquestioned by many professionals, service users, lay people and the media. On the other, a substantial minority of researchers, clinicians and service users have long argued that psychiatric diagnosis is flawed in theory and damaging in practice.

This chapter outlines two different attempts to answer the question of how we should categorize distress. The first, psychiatric diagnosis, is modelled on medical classification and is largely carried out by psychiatrists by virtue of their medical training. It is based on the assumption that those who are clinically distressed are suffering from illnesses with primarily biological causes, such as changes in the brain's biochemistry. This gives rise to diagnostic labels such as schizophrenia, bipolar disorder, personality disorder and so on. Most research and practice is based on these terms, and we all have some familiarity with them, if only through the media. However, this language has increasingly come under challenge from service users and some professionals, as has the medical model itself.

The second approach is mainly used by clinical psychologists and is called **formulation.** A formulation is an individual summary of someone's difficulties, based on psychological theory. It can be seen as a kind of a story or narrative which attempts to link the service user's difficulties to the relationships and events in their lives, and the sense they have made of their experiences. Like diagnosis, formulation is used to decide on the most appropriate intervention, although in the case of formulation this is likely to be a psychological or social, not a medical one. Some clinicians see formulation as an alternative to the diagnostic approach, while others argue that it is best seen as an addition to diagnosis. There is an increasing interest in this approach, although it is less well-known than the diagnostic one.

In this chapter we will summarize the main debates about psychiatric diagnosis and formulation, including the views of service users who have been on the receiving end of psychiatric labelling. The first part of the chapter describes the history of psychiatric diagnosis and the assumptions it makes, and then sets out some of the problems associated with it. The second part of the chapter describes what psychological formulation is, explains how it is used by clinical psychologists, and provides an evaluation of its benefits and limitations.

Guiding questions

Throughout this chapter, you should bear in mind these two questions:

1 *How is psychiatric diagnosis similar to, and different from, diagnosis in general medicine?*
2 *How adequate is formulation as an alternative to psychiatric diagnosis?*

A brief history of psychiatric classification and diagnosis

Distress always seems to have been present in human history, although it has been understood in very different ways at different times (see Chapter 2). Psychiatric diagnosis as we know it today can be traced back to the work of the German psychiatrist Emil Kraepelin around the end of the 19th century (Bentall, 2003). Kraepelin believed that the severer forms of distress – those we call madness in this book – could be divided, like physical illnesses, into a small number of separate disorders based on their symptoms. The assumption was that one day these symptom patterns would be found to map onto underlying brain disease processes, and that each psychiatric disease would have its characteristic aetiology, presentation and outcome – again, like physical illnesses. He devoted his career to attempting to identify these patterns in distress, and concluded that there were three main types: dementia praecox, which roughly corresponds to present-day schizophrenia; manic depression, which is now referred to as bipolar disorder, and paranoia. Subsequently, the Swiss psychiatrist Eugen Bleuler coined the term schizophrenia, or 'split mind'.

Other psychiatrists elaborated on these ideas. Karl Jaspers clarified the distinction between symptoms that are understandable within the context of the person's life, such as anxiety after an upsetting event or depression after bereavement, and those that apparently arise from nowhere. The first group corresponds to what we would now call different forms of neurosis. The second group would now be called psychosis, and includes experiences that are unfamiliar to most of us, such as hearing critical and intrusive voices. Since these experiences do not make immediate sense, Jaspers believed that they had to be attributed to biological disease processes – a view that is shared by many modern-day psychiatrists. Kurt Schneider, another German psychiatrist, drew up an influential list of the 'first rank symptoms' which are said to be most characteristic of schizophrenia, a form of psychosis These include delusions (false beliefs) and hallucinations (false perceptions).

In summary, the mainstream assumption in psychiatry, dating back to Kraepelin, is that the severer forms of distress (which would today be diagnosed as schizophrenia, bipolar disorder, severe depression or paranoia) are best understood as disease processes. For this reason, enormous efforts have been devoted to trying to define and categorize them in the same way as diseases in the rest of medicine. Kraepelin's distinctions between psychosis and neurosis, and between the main types of psychosis, still form the basis of the much more elaborate diagnostic systems in use today.

However, as we saw in Chapter 2, different trends have always run alongside this tradition. For example, Carl Jung, the well-known psychiatrist who worked alongside Bleuler, believed that the unusual beliefs and behaviours of asylum inmates could be understood as symbolizing the conflicts in their lives. In other words, he favoured a psychological, not a medical, explanation of madness. As we show throughout this book, recent work in psychology and psychiatry has returned to the theme that much of what we call mental illness is, in fact, understandable within a full picture of a person's life events and relationships. For the moment, it is important to note that the act of giving someone a psychiatric diagnosis carries the message that their behaviour and beliefs are not understandable in this way and do not have any particular personal meaning. Instead, so-called psychotic symptoms such as unusual beliefs and experiences are seen as the outward manifestation of a biological disease process. This is similar to noting the confused speech of someone who is delirious in order to diagnose a fever: we would think it was odd if a doctor spent a long time discussing what the delirious person was actually saying. In a biomedical framework, it is not relevant or necessary to investigate the content of such speech, simply to note that it is present as a symptom. The strict biomedical approach to psychiatry treats psychotic experiences (unusual beliefs, hearing voices, etc.) in the same way.

The psychiatric classification of distress is outlined in the Diagnostic and Statistical Manual of Mental Disorders (American Psychiatric Association (APA), 2000), which is internationally the most widely-used system. It was first published in 1952 and is now in its fourth edition, with another (DSM-5) in preparation. This major revision is an enormously complex process, involving more than 500 leading clinicians, 13 work groups, 13 major conferences, and hundreds of peer-reviewed papers over the last decade (www.dsm5.org). An alternative and slightly different system is included as one chapter in ICD, the International Classification of Diseases (1993). This is published by the World Health Organization and is now in its tenth revision, with an eleventh due. The psychiatric section of this manual is mainly used in European settings, although DSM is usually preferred as a basis for research.

In the next section we will look in more detail at medical and psychiatric classification and diagnosis in order to understand why it is so controversial, and why many people have argued for alternatives.

Medical and psychiatric diagnosis

> Diagnosis is the Holy Grail of psychiatry, and the key to its legitimation.
>
> (Kovel, 1980)

> The critique of diagnosis is the critique of psychiatry.
>
> (Brown, 1990)

The purposes of diagnosis in medicine can be summarized as follows:

1 To indicate the correct treatment
2 To enable predictions to be made about outcome (prognosis)
3 To provide a basis for research. We cannot research a condition unless we have made some decision (provisional, at least) about how to define it and what name to give it
4 To indicate the probable aetiology, or cause, of the condition, based on the research findings
5 To enable professionals to communicate with each other in making their referrals, recommendations and treatment decisions
6 To provide information and, in some cases, relief for patients and their carers, who will naturally want to know what condition they are suffering from
7 To give patients and carers access to services, benefits, support groups and so on.

However, diagnosis has another even more important function when it is used in psychiatry: it supports the assumption that psychiatry is a legitimate branch of *medicine*. This view of psychiatry may seem too obvious to state. On the whole, we do not question the fact that people who break down are patients, suffering from illnesses. It follows from this that we expect them to be diagnosed and then treated by medication, administered by doctors and nurses in hospitals and clinics. Yet this language implies a particular way of understanding distress that is not inevitable, and indeed is widely disputed.

As it stands, though, psychiatry is assumed to be a branch of medicine, and as such it sits alongside the other natural sciences like biology, physics and chemistry. Classification systems are fundamental to the development of any science. All branches of science need to be based on a reliable and valid categorization of their basic units, whether these are atoms, chemicals or diseases. This in turn forms the basis of hypotheses that can be tested – for example, predicting how two chemical substances will react together. The gradual accumulation of such research findings enables us to develop the general laws that constitute a body of scientific knowledge.

It is important to note that without the starting point of a sound classification system, none of the rest is possible. For example, if you can't come up with a precise definition of an atom, and a reliable way of distinguishing one type of atom from another, you will not be able to make hypotheses about what happens when they interact, and there would be no foundation for the science of chemistry. The equivalent in medicine is being able to define and classify types of disease.

If you cannot come up with a clear description of the pattern of biological changes that we call 'cancer', you will not be able to work out whether someone is suffering from that disease as opposed to another, or indeed whether they are perfectly healthy. That in turn will mean that you have no solid basis on which to test your hypotheses about prognosis (outcome), aetiology (causation), treatments and so on. Whilst not all physical diseases can be diagnosed reliably or easily in our current state of knowledge, these general principles still hold.

We can see that the absence of a reliable and valid classification system would undermine the theory on which the day-to-day practice of psychiatry is based. Such a situation would raise very fundamental questions about whether psychiatry really is a legitimate branch of medical science. In other words, we might be in the paradoxical position of admitting that psychiatry is 'something very hard to justify or defend – a medical speciality that does not treat medical illnesses' (Breggin, 1993, p.7). This has far-reaching implications for psychiatry as it is currently practised, including the use of medical language (symptom, illness, patient, treatment, remission, prognosis, etc.), the typical settings (hospitals, wards, clinics), the medical training of key professionals (nurses and doctors) and the basic interventions used (medication, ECT). All of these taken-for-granted aspects of psychiatry would be challenged by a threat to its diagnostic system and hence to its current status as a branch of medical science. This is what is meant by the quotes at the start of this section.

Of course, in such a situation we would still be left with many very distressed and desperate people in urgent need of help. However, we might have to conclude that this help is not best delivered by psychiatry as it currently stands. For example, there might need to be a much more central role for psychological and social interventions, even in conditions such as psychosis, about which the strongest claims for biological causation have been made. In order to examine these arguments more closely, we need to do several things:

1 Clarify exactly what we mean by medical diagnosis
2 Understand how medical diagnosis differs from diagnosis in psychiatry
3 Identify problems with psychiatric diagnosis: reliability, validity, co-morbidity
4 Place psychiatric diagnosis in a cross-cultural context
5 Consider the extent to which psychiatric diagnosis is a social judgement
6 Discuss service user experiences of diagnosis.

What do we mean by medical diagnosis?

In medicine, diagnosis is a matching task. It is based on previous medical research that has identified patterns in the many different bodily complaints that people present with. Once researchers are reasonably confident that a meaningful pattern has been identified, it is given a label which we call a diagnosis – tuberculosis, multiple sclerosis, and so on.

The process of arriving at a medical diagnosis for a patient proceeds in several stages. Initially, someone goes along to their doctor with a complaint such as nausea, pain, loss of appetite or tiredness. There may also be more visible bodily features such as a rash, swelling or loss of weight. The doctor will try to identify whether the complaints fall into a known pattern of **symptoms** based on previous medical research. Symptoms are complaints that are largely subjective in nature

and that are typically associated with a wide range of conditions. For example, if someone presents with thirst and tiredness, diabetes might be suspected. However, because such complaints are often unobservable, and might have many possible causes, there may be a number of different possibilities at this stage and further investigations are needed.

The second stage is to narrow down the preliminary hypotheses by searching for characteristic **signs**. Signs in medical diagnosis are biological phenomena that can be observed and verified by other people, and that can be compared to an objective norm. Examples include blood cell counts and abnormalities that show up on X-rays. These features mean that, unlike symptoms, signs can be identified by carrying out tests: for example in the case of suspected diabetes, one sign would be the presence of sugar in the urine. It is assumed that there is some kind of biological mechanism associated with the sign and linking it with the symptoms – in the case of diabetes, poor re-absorption of glucose.

The possibilities are thus narrowed down until the doctor can be confident that the patient's signs and symptoms match one particular pattern. At this point, a diagnosis can be confirmed (Boyle, 1999). This is, of course, a simplification of a very complex process. Arriving at a diagnosis may take some time, and diagnoses themselves are only provisional labels, which may change as a result of ongoing medical research.

Before we look at the differences between medical and psychiatric diagnosis in more detail, it is important to note that a small minority of psychiatric diagnoses do fit reasonably well into this model. Some of these are listed under the heading 'Organic Mental Disorders' in DSM-IV (see Chapter 4 for an explanation of the distinction between organic and functional diagnoses). It is clear that the various sub-types of dementia, for example, are the result of changes in the brain which can be observed and verified with scans. The same is true of a minority of other conditions that are sometimes encountered on psychiatric wards, such as Huntington's Chorea, a genetically-transmitted neurological disease, and Korsakoff's Syndrome, which is the result of brain damage caused by heavy drinking. These are clearly genuine disease processes. However, it is unfortunate that they are seen as part of the remit of psychiatry, because the patients' main needs are for physical care and rehabilitation. These services could be delivered equally well without the additional stigma of a psychiatric label, and in fact should arguably fall under the remit of neurology.

There are also presentations which at first glance look like psychological distress, but turn out on investigation to have purely biological causes. For example, older adults sometimes react to chest or urinary tract infections by developing highly unusual ideas. The immediate and effective cure is a course of antibiotics. Similarly, we saw in Chapter 2 that many of the asylum inhabitants of the early 20th century were discovered to be in the end stages of syphilis. For obvious reasons, it is very important to identify the purely biological causes of a minority of psychiatric presentations and offer these patients the correct medical treatment. However, the vast majority of psychiatric problems do not fall into this category, which is why they are known as functional rather than organic disorders. This includes diagnoses such as schizophrenia and bipolar disorder, for which strong claims are made that biological causes will one day be found.

In summary, medical diagnosis is firmly based on research into the body and on a whole way of thinking about how the body works and how it can go wrong. As we saw earlier in this book, we can use the term 'biomedical model' as shorthand for all of this. The use of psychiatric diagnosis is based on these assumptions. To question psychiatric diagnosis is to question every other aspect of the theory and practice of the biomedical model of distress, since all of this is based on, and follows from, the use of this particular way of categorizing distress. We will now take a closer look at the differences between diagnosis in psychiatry and diagnosis in general medicine.

What are the differences between diagnosis in psychiatry and in general medicine?

Here is a list of some of the symptoms that make up the diagnosis that has been described as the 'prototypical psychiatric disease' (Boyle, 2002), or the 'heartland of psychiatry' (Goodwin and Geddes, 2007): schizophrenia. (The DSM-III-R (1987) version is used here because it gives the most detailed description of the criteria, although DSM-IV-TR (2000) is essentially the same.)

In the active phase:

Delusions
Prominent hallucinations
Incoherence or marked loosening of associations
Catatonic behaviour
Flat or grossly inappropriate affect

Bizarre delusions (i.e. involving a phenomenon that the person's culture would regard as totally implausible, such as thought broadcasting, being controlled by a dead person)
Prominent hallucinations of a voice with content having no apparent relation to depression or elation, or a voice keeping up a running commentary on the person's behaviour or thoughts, or two or more voices conversing with each other
Prodromal or residual symptoms: (i.e. preceding or following the active phase):

    Marked social isolation or withdrawal
    Marked impairment in role functioning as wage-earner, student or home-maker
    Markedly peculiar behaviour (e.g. collecting garbage, talking to self in public, hoarding food)
    Marked impairment in personal hygiene and grooming
    Blunted or inappropriate affect
    Digressive, vague, over elaborate or circumstantial speech
    Odd beliefs or magical thinking, influencing behaviour and inconsistent with cultural norms, e.g. superstitiousness, belief in clairvoyance or telepathy
    Unusual perceptual experiences, e.g. sensing the presence of a force or person not actually present
    Marked lack of initiative, interests or energy

(APA, 1987)

Like most of the other conditions listed in ICD and DSM, applying a diagnosis of schizophrenia differs in some important respects from diagnosis in general medicine.

Researchers have not found any signs to confirm the presence or absence of a hypothesized psychiatric disorder.

There are no objective indicators or signs that show if someone really is suffering from schizophrenia, bipolar disorder, personality disorder, and so on. It is often stated as a fact that functional psychiatric disorders are caused by 'biochemical imbalances', but there is no hard evidence to substantiate

these claims, and hence no way of testing for their presence (see Chapter 4).

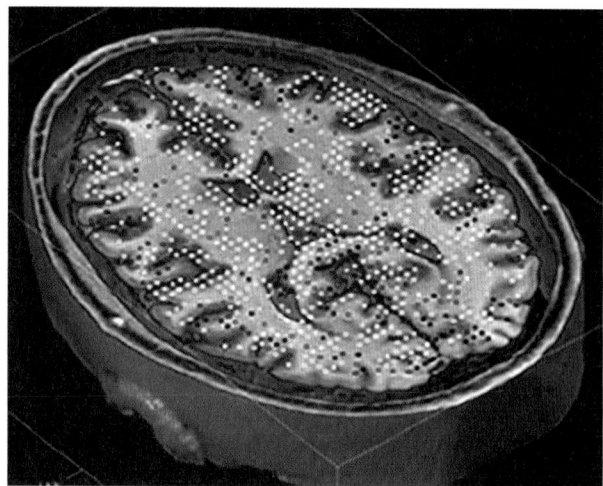

Despite having access to increasingly powerful technologies, researchers have been unable to reliably establish the existence of any signs associated with any functional psychiatric diagnosis

Because of the absence of signs to confirm or disconfirm the presence of a psychiatric disorder, DSM and ICD consist only of lists of subjective complaints ('symptoms').

The implications of a lack of research-based patterns of signs which can be linked with symptoms are profound. The committees of mental health professionals that draw up the DSM and ICD criteria have no way of checking whether any clusters of complaints are meaningful, rather than simply chance associations. In fact, without signs we are not only unable to distinguish reliably between different illnesses; we cannot clearly draw the line between health and illness at all. For example, hearing voices might have quite different causes in different cases, or it might overlap with normal experience. To use an analogy, psychiatrists are in an even worse position than a doctor who for some reason has no access to standard medical tests, and who guesses that a patient's tiredness and weight loss are due to diabetes, but has no definite way of distinguishing this from cancer or, perhaps, poor nutrition. In psychiatry, such tests do not even exist.

The 'symptoms' listed in ICD and DSM are not complaints about bodily functioning (pain, nausea, thirst, dizziness and so on). They are examples of beliefs, experiences and behaviours.

It is relatively simple, in principle, to work out how the body ought to be functioning and to draw up standards in order to compare the results of tests; for example, checking to see if someone's blood pressure or enzyme levels fall within an acceptable range. But there are no measurable and universally agreed standards for deciding on normal ways of feeling, thinking and behaving, because such judgements depend both on context (washing may be impossible if you are homeless) and culture (hearing voices may be acceptable in some societies or contexts – for example, spiritualist meetings.) There is no universal definition of exactly how meticulous you should be about your personal hygiene, or what is a reasonable level of initiative. In fact, a close look at the ICD and DSM symptoms of schizophrenia shows that every single one involves making a subjective judgement of some sort. How flat does your affect (your emotional expression) have to be, and who decides this? How much food are you allowed to store before it becomes 'hoarding', and when do your beliefs become delusions? At what point does your lack of hygiene become a medical symptom?

These points are even clearer in the case of the diagnoses of personality disorder (we discuss these diagnoses in detail in Chapter 13). Here are some examples of the criteria for diagnosing them (APA, 2000):

> *Conduct disorder*: Unable to sustain consistent work behaviour; fails to conform to social norms with respect to lawful behaviour; abandonment of several jobs without realistic plans for others; has never sustained a totally monogamous relationship for more than one year; travelling from place to place without a rearranged job or clear goal.
>
> *Borderline personality disorder*: A pattern of unstable and intense interpersonal relationships; markedly and persistently unstable self-image or sense of self; impulsivity in at least two areas that are potentially damaging, e.g. spending, eating disorders, reckless driving, inappropriate intense anger.

These examples raise the same questions as the criteria for schizophrenia. These are lists of thoughts, feelings and behaviours, not bodily symptoms. While we may recognize them as problematic and distressing, there are no objective standards to decide the cut-off with normality. Indeed, as we discussed in Chapter 1, whether or not we have ever been given a psychiatric diagnosis, all of us are likely to have had some of these experiences at some time in our lives.

Summary

We can all recognize individuals who fit the above descriptions, and they may indeed have serious problems and be in need of help. However, these 'symptoms' are not bodily experiences or measurable features like pain or blood sugar levels, as is the case in general medicine. They are examples of distressing and confusing thoughts, feelings and behaviours. In describing them as 'symptoms' of an 'illness', we have to make a subjective judgement about what are normal ways of thinking, feeling and behaving. This is completely different in principle from making a judgement about bodily functioning based on physical tests and objective norms. The process raises questions about the scientific status of psychiatric categories. It can be argued that the medical language of psychiatry (diagnosis, illness, disorder, symptom, etc.) conceals the fact that the process of psychiatric diagnosis is fundamentally unlike that in general medicine. As one critic has put it:

> Psychiatrists behave as if they were studying bodily functioning and as if they had described patterns there, when in fact they are studying behaviour and have assumed – but not proved – that certain types of pattern will be found there.

(Boyle, 2002, p.179)

In the absence of objective signs to confirm the presence of a biological disease process, psychiatry is left with a series of circular arguments. 'Why does this person hear voices?' 'Because they have schizophrenia'. 'How do you know they have schizophrenia?' 'Because they hear voices.' There is no exit from this circle via a sign, such as abnormalities detected by a blood test for dopamine levels, or a brain scan for structural abnormalities.

Problems with psychiatric diagnosis

There are various consequences of having a diagnostic system based on these intrinsically subjective criteria drawn up by committees, rather than on patterns of bodily symptoms and signs identified by researchers. As one might expect, reliability and validity are bound to be compromised. As one textbook on abnormal psychology puts it, 'Unfortunately, both reliability and validity have proven extraordinarily difficult to achieve' (Carson & Butcher, 1992, p. 25). This does not stop Carson and Butcher, and most other authors of similar textbooks, from using the terms uncritically as names and chapter headings. As we explained in Chapter 1, this is why in this book we avoid using these diagnostic terms as chapter headings and instead refer to broad categories of distress using ordinary language descriptions of experience. We will now discuss the consequences of basing psychiatric diagnosis on subjective norms in relation to a series of relevant headings.

Reliability

Reliability is a measure of the consistency of judgements that are made based on any given set of criteria. In psychiatry, this is usually tested by investigating the extent to which different clinicians will agree upon a diagnosis in any given case, using DSM as a basis for their decision. This is known as inter-rater reliability.

If, as has been argued, diagnostic criteria in psychiatry are ultimately based upon subjective judgements, one would expect reliability to be low. This is clearly the case in actual practice; any clinician will confirm that different psychiatrists have different diagnostic preferences, and service users commonly acquire a range of diagnoses during their contact with mental health services. Much effort has been expended in producing detailed and agreed criteria for every category of mental disorder in an attempt to increase reliability. DSM-III was a major revision requiring an enormous amount of work. Subsequent revisions have resulted in even more categories, so that Kraepelin's original three have been joined by about 400 others. Superficially, this would seem to help to make diagnosis more precise. However, the problem with this tactic is that the new criteria are still essentially based on subjective judgements. This means that while diagnoses may be based on more elaborate criteria, they are not necessarily any more reliable than before.

Studies into reliability produce very mixed results. Moreover, using clinicians who have been given extra training in applying DSM criteria, and who are presented with 'typical' examples of a particular condition, may not reflect real-life clinical practice. Even in these circumstances, clinicians only agree on a broad diagnostic category such as 'personality disorder' about 50% of the time (Kirk & Kutchins, 1994).

Co-morbidity

Another predictable problem is that many individuals will fit the criteria for more than one psychiatric disorder. This is known as **co-morbidity**. The National Co-morbidity Survey in the USA found that over 50% of people with one diagnosis also qualify for at least one other diagnosis, while 23% are assigned three or more diagnoses (Kessler et al., 2005) The opposite problem arises when two or more people with the same diagnosis have no symptoms in common. For example, one person given a diagnosis of schizophrenia may be withdrawn and hear voices, while another talks confusingly and believes that he is being persecuted by aliens. In the absence of a sign to decide the matter, there is no good reason for assuming that they are suffering from the same condition – and yet this frequently occurs.

One way of accommodating this 'fuzziness' of boundaries is the creation of what can be described as 'in between, just short of, and left over' categories (Mirowsky, 1990).The diagnosis of schizoaffective disorder lies somewhere in between schizophrenia and depression, whilst that of dysthymia applies to someone who is low in mood but just short of actual depression. Similarly, sub-categories with titles such as 'bipolar disorder not otherwise specified' and 'schizophrenia residual type' are used to sweep up any leftover cases. For some kinds of distress the 'not otherwise specified' category accounts for a very large percentage of people receiving a diagnosis – for example, over 70% of people given eating disorder diagnoses are in this category. While this offers more flexibility, it does not increase reliability. Instead, it suggests that diagnostic boundaries have been artificially imposed on the phenomena they are describing, rather than 'carving nature at the joints', or being a property of the phenomena themselves. In other words, it raises profound questions about their validity.

Validity

Reliability is a necessary attribute of a scientific classification system. If a category is not reliable, it cannot be valid, or in other words meaningful, making sense, and reflecting something in the real world. If one accepts that reliability has not been established for psychiatric diagnoses, then, by definition, they are not valid. However, we also need to be clear that even if reliability has been established, validity does not necessarily follow.

Setting aside the reliability problem for a moment, we can look briefly at the ways in which validity can be assessed. For the purposes of diagnosis, a valid construct should enable various types of prediction to be made. For example, it should be possible to decide which treatment will be most effective, and what the outcome of the illness is likely to be. This kind of predictive validity has been claimed for psychiatric diagnosis, although others have argued that it amounts to little more than guesswork, not backed up by evidence. For obvious reasons, the presence of biological signs that are reliably associated with particular diagnoses would also be relevant to the issue of validity, but as has been noted, these are not available. Although medication's efficacy is sometimes cited in relation to these issues, this is not accurate: as we explain in Chapter 8, psychiatric medication is not always beneficial, but even when it is, its effects are non-specific and so cannot meaningfully be said to be operating on disease-specific systems.

We can think about reliability and validity using some historical analogies. In Biblical times, people were quite convinced that madness was due to being taken over by evil spirits. We know that in the 17th century there was widespread agreement

When groups of Western people are asked to identify this character their reliability in doing so approaches 100%. But does this mean that he exists?

on how to identify witches. The criteria that were used seemed to be very reliable, at least in most people's minds; there were high levels of agreement about who was a witch, or who was possessed by spirits. However, since reliability does not necessarily mean validity, this does not mean that witches or evil spirits are valid scientific constructs, reflecting something that exists in the real world, even if people were thoroughly convinced that this was the reason for their unusual behaviour. Arguably, the same is true of diagnostic terms like schizophrenia and bipolar disorder. We can agree on the existence of people who behave in strange and disturbing ways, just as we do not doubt the existence of 17th-century women who were perceived as strange or threatening. However, the concepts used to explain this ('it must be schizophrenia/she must be a witch') do not necessarily relate meaningfully to reality, and do not necessarily function as explanations for what we observe.

Critiques of the validity of psychiatric diagnosis have been made since the beginnings of modern psychiatry in the 19th century. They were revived in a particularly strong form in the 1960s in popular books by R. D. Laing, Thomas Szasz and others (see Chapters 1 and 2). Laing argued that schizophrenia is not a valid category, since it does not explain anything, and the behaviours that it refers to can more plausibly be seen as a meaningful and understandable response to damaging family relationships (Laing, 1960; Laing & Esterson, 1964). Szasz also saw the concept of 'mental illness' as meaningless. He argued that the mind cannot be 'sick' in any sense except a metaphorical one – rather as we might describe the economy as 'sick' (Szasz, 1976a). Scheff, a sociologist, believed that mental illness is simply a kind of dustbin label which we use when we are unable to account for people's behaviour in any other way (Scheff, 1974). In other words, all these critics see mental illness as a social, moral or value judgement, not a legitimate medical concept. Although these critics are now widely dismissed as if the issues they raised were no longer relevant, the problems they identified have not gone away. For example, one of the public debates at the prestigious Maudsley Hospital in London in 2003 was on the topic 'Does schizophrenia exist?' The debate resulted, after a show of hands at the end, in a draw.

Cross-cultural perspectives

We can look at the same issues from a cross-cultural perspective. As we saw in Chapter 3, there are marked cultural differences in distress, and research and debate about diagnosis from cross-cultural perspective tends to fall into three main areas:

1 Patterns of diagnosis in minority ethnic groups in the Western world (e.g. Littlewood & Lipsedge, 1997). For example, it is well-established that African–Caribbean people living in the UK are up to twelve times more likely to be diagnosed with schizophrenia (Fernando, 2002).
2 Culture-bound syndromes, which often sound exotic to Westerners, such as the diagnosis of *dhat*, or intense anxiety about the discharge of semen, in India. These are listed in the appendix of DSM-IV.
3 Cross-cultural research looking at, for example, the incidence of schizophrenia diagnoses in the developing world (e.g. Warner, 2004).

The same problems with reliability and validity inevitably arise here as well, but the very obvious cultural context highlights something that may not be so immediately apparent from our earlier examples: that subjective judgements about diagnosis are ultimately tied to cultural norms. 'Normality' is defined within cultures, where it may seem too obvious to question, but it always plays a part in judgements about illness, health and distress (see Chapters 1 and 6). However, as we saw in Chapter 3, what counts as normal varies between cultures. For example, many Westerners might automatically assume that someone who regularly talks to his dead ancestors is 'mad', and such a person might be at risk of being given a diagnosis of schizophrenia. This involves a subjective judgement about what the person believes, how strongly the beliefs are held and so on, but such a judgement is also rooted in the cultural beliefs of a particular Western society. For most Westerners, hearing and talking to voices from dead people is seen as abnormal, although other cultures might see it differently.

One inevitable consequence is that those who are more culturally distant from the assumptions about normality on which DSM is based are more likely to be given a psychiatric label, because diagnosis reflects and reinforces the norms of the white, Western culture from which psychiatry has emerged. This may partially explain the higher rates of diagnosis of schizophrenia in African–Caribbeans living in the UK. For this reason, transcultural psychiatrists like Littlewood and Lipsedge (1997) have argued that psychiatric diagnosis needs to be carried out with special care with members of minority ethnic groups, so that culturally-specific ways of behaving are not misdiagnosed as 'mental illness'. They also argue that experiences such as paranoia can often, in minority ethnic groups, be seen as an understandable response to racism and disadvantage; if so, these experiences should not be treated as symptoms of a medical illness. They do not, however, question the validity of the diagnostic process itself, nor do they discuss the fact that the same principles apply within white culture – for example, the class and gender gap between psychiatrist and patient may partly account for the generally higher rates of psychiatric diagnosis in women and working class people.

A more radical critique comes from psychiatrist Suman Fernando (2002) who argues that since all psychiatric diagnosis is inherently laden with Western values and assumptions, it simply cannot be applied or understood in a non-Western culture. Western medicine, for example, assumes a split between mind and body that is completely absent in traditional African, Asian and Native American worldviews. Such cultures have no exact equivalent to our diagnostic practices, and may see what we would define as psychiatric disorders in religious, spiritual, philosophical or ethical terms instead. To seek to impose our models of medicine on their experiences is to fall into the assumption that our worldview is superior because it is more 'true'. Fernando describes this as a form of 'psychiatric imperialism' which is more subtle, but no less damaging, than more overt forms of colonialism.

If we accept this view, it could be said that all psychiatric conditions are 'culture-bound', as psychiatrists like Arthur Kleinman (1997) have argued. For example, eating disorders are a largely Western phenomenon, and the behaviours that we associate with them may seem quite as bizarre from the perspective of some cultures as *dhat* does to a European or American readership. The very existence of a DSM category of culture-bound disorders implicitly assumes that Western perspectives, unlike non-Western ones, are not influenced by culture. This is very much open to question.

Medical diagnosis should, if it lives up to its claims, be stable across cultures. If you have cancer or diabetes in the UK or the US, then given the right medical investigative tools, you will still be easily recognizable as having those same illnesses wherever you are in the world. You do not 'recover' as you get off a plane in a country where your experiences are held to be normal, as might be the case for someone who hears voices or believes they can talk to the spirits of their ancestors. This is yet another odd consequence of linking diagnostic judgements on cultural norms, and an indication that these norms are entangled with every psychiatric diagnosis.

Psychiatric diagnosis as a social judgement

So far, we have argued that psychiatric diagnoses inevitably have poor reliability and validity because they are based not on objective criteria but on essentially subjective judgements about people's thoughts, feelings and behaviour. This has far-reaching implications for psychiatry's status as a branch of medicine. It also raises the question of what kind of criteria we are using to make our diagnostic decisions. A close examination of the DSM and ICD criteria suggests that ultimately, these subjective judgements cannot be separated from social and cultural norms.

In other words, in labelling people with a disorder or illness, we are actually making a value judgement based on social/

cultural standards ('this is not the way we think people should behave in this society'), and not, as the diagnosis implies, medical or scientific ones. Interestingly, this is tacitly admitted within DSM, for example within the diagnostic criteria for schizophrenia which contain phrases such as 'bizarre beliefs ... that the person's culture would regard as totally implausible' and 'odd beliefs ... inconsistent with cultural norms'.

Other cultural prejudices will inevitably re-appear and be perpetuated through the diagnostic system. A particularly obvious example is the case of homosexuality, removed from DSM in 1974 when it became politically unacceptable to continue to describe it as a mental disorder (see Chapter 2). The controversy 'was not about research findings. It was a 20 year debate about beliefs and values' (Kirk & Kutchins, 1997, p. 56). It was part of the broader political campaign for civil rights for gay people.

With the passage of time and the liberalization of attitudes toward lesbian and gay people, we can now appreciate how this was a clear case of a social judgement disguised as a medical one. Similar issues arise in relation to the diagnosis of women. Feminists have long argued that the women who use psychiatric services can be understood as suffering from the pressures and contradictions inherent in women's social roles. For example, the enormous rise in eating disorders over the last 40 years, especially in women, can perhaps be partly attributed to pressures placed on their appearance and weight. Women are also more frequently given diagnoses of depression than men. It has been argued that this may reflect the fact that they are more likely to experience poverty and sexual abuse, along with inequality in jobs, pay, and so on, while carrying the major burden of childcare (see Chapter 9). This debate surfaced in a particularly controversial form in the 1980s in relation to the proposed diagnosis of 'Masochistic Personality Disorder' (see Box 5.1). Feminists argued that this diagnosis simply pathologized women whose behaviour might be entirely understandable in relation to their circumstances – perhaps domestic violence. In such a case, the effect might be to leave women in an even more powerless position than before, by diagnosing a social or relationship problem

as an individual failing. American psychologist Paula Caplan made her point by proposing a diagnosis of 'Delusional Dominating Disorder', which was said to apply to men who have an 'inability to identify and express a range of feelings; a tendency to feel inordinately threatened by women who fail to disguise their intelligence' and so on. The controversy was unresolved, and the diagnosis was re-named Self-defeating Personality Disorder and placed in the appendix in DSM-III-R. The full story is told in Kirk and Kutchins (1994).

Summary

Once again, it is important to be clear about the argument. No one would deny that most of the people who present to mental health services have serious problems. The issue is whether diagnosing these problems as 'symptoms' of an 'illness' is a legitimate process. Equally, there is nothing intrinsically wrong with using subjectivity – or what is sometimes called 'clinical judgement' – to tell us about a person's difficulties: as we explained in Chapter 1, there is no way of identifying distress that does not implicate cultural norms, whatever other information is used. However, the problem arises when subjectivity is presented as objectivity, or to put it another way, when social and cultural judgements are presented as if they were medical ones about bodily problems. This raises questions about the whole practice of psychiatry and its status as a branch of medicine. It also suggests that psychiatric diagnosis may leave service users in a worse situation than before. Their problems may not only be misunderstood, but framed in a way that is very unlikely to lead to the help they need. It is therefore very important to listen to service users' accounts of their experience of psychiatric diagnosis.

Consequences of diagnosis for service users

Whether or not the process of psychiatric diagnosis is valid and reliable, it has been extensively documented that it has a powerful impact on service users and their relatives (e.g. Pitt,

---

BOX **5.1**

Masochistic personality disorder

Here are the diagnostic criteria for Masochistic Personality Disorder, later re-named Self-defeating Personality Disorder.

A pervasive pattern of self-defeating behaviour, beginning by early adulthood and present in a variety of contexts. The person may often avoid or undermine pleasurable experiences, be drawn to situations or relationships in which he or she will suffer, and prevent others from helping him, as indicated by at least five of the following:

1   chooses people and situations that lead to disappointment, failure or mistreatment even when better options are clearly available

2   rejects or renders ineffective the attempts of others to help him or her

3   following positive personal events (e.g. a new achievement), responds with depression, guilt or a behaviour that produces pain (e.g. an accident)

4   incites angry or rejecting responses from others and then feels hurt, defeated, or humiliated (e.g. makes fun of spouse in public, provoking an angry retort, then feels devastated)

5   rejects opportunities for pleasure, or is reluctant to acknowledge enjoying himself or herself (despite having adequate social skills and the capacity for pleasure)

6   fails to accomplish tasks crucial to his or her personal objectives despite demonstrated ability to do so, for example,

helps fellow students write papers, but is unable to write his or her own

7   is uninterested in or rejects people who consistently treat him well; for example, is unattracted to caring sexual partners

8   engages in excessive self-sacrifice that is unsolicited by the intended recipients of the sacrifice.

Would you say that this diagnosis is more likely to be applied to a woman or a man? Why do you think this?

Feminist author Phyllis Chesler wrote, in her 1972 book *Women and Madness*, 'What we consider "madness"...is either the acting out of the devalued female role or the total or partial rejection of one's sex-role stereotype'. Does the diagnosis of Masochistic Personality Disorder support this statement?

Kilbride, Welford, Nothard & Morrison, 2009). On the positive side, this may include:

Comfort and reassurance

People experiencing distress – and those who care for them – naturally want to know 'what is wrong'. Since mental illness is commonly described as something you 'can't help', like other diseases, there may be a sense of release from guilt and blame, both for the individual so diagnosed and for his/her relatives.

Access to services

Both in the UK and the USA, a diagnostic label is required in order to qualify for many services and to access available welfare benefits, although in the UK most psychiatric care is provided by the state, not private hospitals.

A sense of community

There are self-help and support groups, books and websites for every psychiatric category, offering information, understanding and a sense that you are not alone with your problems.

It is worth noting that many of these benefits can also be achieved in other ways: for example, access to services could be enabled by expert professional judgements without using diagnostic classifications, and groups like the Hearing Voices Network already provide a sense of community, support and trust without relying upon diagnoses: instead, people are united by their common experiences. Nevertheless, for the moment psychiatric diagnosis is frequently helpful for these kinds of reasons, even though it is also typically accompanied by a series of negatives.

Stigma

Stigma is an internal feeling of shame, inadequacy and differentness as a consequence of societal discrimination (see Chapter 1). It has been argued that a DSM diagnosis can 'exacerbate clients' symptoms and inhibit the healing process in therapy' by feeding into people's negative beliefs about themselves (Honos-Webb & Leitner, 2001, p. 37) Stereotyped public perceptions of the 'mentally ill' as weak, irresponsible and potentially violent may be taken on as a central part of the client's identity, and the implication that they are abnormal and crazy, and 'permanently stuck with this disorder', can induce a sense of alienation and despair that is profoundly anti-therapeutic. Psychiatric labels are notoriously *sticky*; in other words, it is much more difficult to transcend this aspect of your identity even when you have recovered than if you have been given, say, a diagnosis of pneumonia or heart disease.

Some diagnoses are more stigmatizing than others. This is particularly true of personality disorder diagnoses, which tend to carry implications of badness as well as madness by association with criminal behaviour or psychopathy (now referred to as Anti-Social Personality Disorder). In addition, the diagnosing of something wrong with your personality – with who you are, not just how you feel or behave – carries particularly profound implications of permanence and lack of hope (Castillo, 2000).

Discrimination and social exclusion

Access to services comes at a price. As a result of spending time in a psychiatric hospital, people can face very real discrimination, which may feed into their sense of shame and inadequacy. This includes social isolation, difficulty in getting employment, housing and insurance, obstacles to gaining custody of or access to one's children after divorce, being threatened and physically attacked, harassed and intimidated at work, and so on (Sayce, 2000, and see Chapters 1 and 11). Stigma and discrimination combine to create social exclusion. In other words, service users encounter barriers to all kinds of social participation, including employment, education and use of public services.

The sick role

The sick role is the term that has been coined for the social position that one enters after being diagnosed as 'ill'. There are common cultural understandings about what it means to be sick or ill; for example, that you are not responsible for your condition, and need to rely on expert help to get better (Parsons, 1951). This may be largely true for asthma or multiple sclerosis. However, if psychiatric breakdown is the result of crises and conflicts in people's lives and relationships, it may not be helpful for them to be encouraged to hand over responsibility for their recovery to the professionals, and wait for the pills to cure them. The perceived passivity of psychiatric patients is a common source of irritation for clinical teams, but staff rarely appreciate that the act of diagnosis has invited them into this position. The resulting sense of frustration on both sides is very untherapeutic.

Loss of personal meaning

Loss of personal meaning is perhaps the most serious consequence of psychiatric diagnosis. If hearing voices, or being low in mood, or intensely anxious, or fearing that you are being poisoned by your relatives, are diagnosed as the 'symptoms' of an 'illness', there is a danger that professionals will see no more reason to enquire into them than they would into the meaning of a rash, or a fever. Factors such as past abuse, neglect and trauma may not be seen as relevant, except as part of the psychiatric history. In other words, the content of the experience may be ignored, so the opportunity for linking it to the person's current difficulties may be missed. As a result, people may end up being tried on numerous different medications and re-admitted over a period of years, without resolving

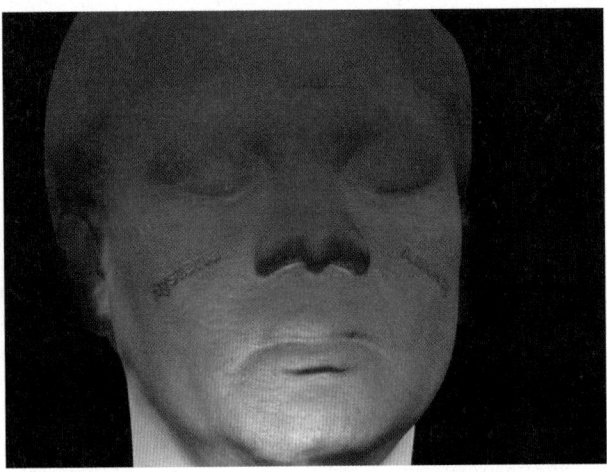

When distress gets treated as a medical illness, the personal meanings of people's experiences are downplayed

the difficulties that brought them into contact with services in the first place. This is known in the UK as the 'revolving door' phenomenon, when service users continue the pattern of admission, discharge and re-admission over many years. It can be argued that this common pattern is in part initiated and maintained by the act of diagnosis.

Responses to the problems of psychiatric diagnosis

The present system

A common response to critiques of psychiatric diagnosis is the contention that 'you have to categorize people's difficulties somehow'. This leads to attempts to reduce some of the disadvantages of diagnosis; for example, the Royal College of Psychiatrists anti-stigma campaign 'Changing minds: Every family in the land' (Cowan & Hart, 1998). The key themes of such campaigns are usually that psychiatric breakdown is 'an illness like any other', and there should be no shame in experiencing it. This argument reflects the assumption that problems seen as biologically caused will not be stigmatized (see Chapter 1).

There are two main problems with this kind of response. The first is that it does not seem to be very effective in reducing public prejudice (Read, Haslam, Sayce & Davies, 2006; also see the discussions in Chapters 1 and 11). The second problem is that it assumes the validity of psychiatric labels in the first place. Critics would argue that these conditions are not illnesses like any other, or indeed illnesses at all, and that we need to replace diagnosis with something entirely different. This might well reduce discrimination and stigma anyway, by rendering distress more understandable.

As a variation on this theme, it is sometimes suggested that we should come up with new versions of particularly stigmatizing labels, such as 'dopamine dysregulation disorder' or 'salience syndrome' instead of schizophrenia. There is a current trend to replace the diagnosis of schizophrenia with the less precise and perhaps less alarming general term 'psychosis'. However, such a broad category implies even greater problems of reliability and validity, without fully avoiding biomedical assumptions and all the problems therein.

Another suggestion is that DSM and ICD should be based on a dimensional approach rather than, as at present, a categorical one. The latter assumes that there is a definite cut-off between those who are and are not 'ill', and that different illnesses can be clearly distinguished from each other. It is the failure to fit any type of distress into a categorical system that has led some to propose a dimensional approach instead.

In fact, DSM states that 'there is no assumption that each category of mental disorder is a completely discrete entity with absolute boundaries dividing it from other mental disorders or from no mental disorder. There is also no assumption that all individuals described as having the same mental disorder are alike in all important ways' (APA, 2000, p. xxxi). However, while physical diseases do not always fall into discrete categories, serious problems are implied by a having a diagnostic system in which a *majority* of people cannot be fitted into any single category.

In a dimensional approach, it would be assumed that everyone varies along a number of different dimensions, such as anxiety, emotional stability and aggression, with no clear cut-off point. The definition of abnormality would then depend more on statistical frequency – that is, how common it is to be rated beyond a certain point on a scale. This approach has the advantage of common sense: as we have noted, we all experience some degree of the 'symptoms' listed in DSM at some time in our lives. It does not, however, address the problem of whether it is valid to think of distress in the same way as bodily problems. Abandoning this premise would imply a complete change of paradigm along with the introduction of dimensional scales, with non-medical language and very different assumptions about the whole nature of distress. Nor does it necessarily solve the issues about subjective social judgements. Who would choose the dimensions and on what basis? DSM-5 is currently considering a kind of compromise whereby categorical diagnosis would be supplemented by dimensional assessments (see Box 5.2).

Another common response is to claim that the diagnoses in DSM and ICD were never meant to be understood in the sense used in general medicine. Instead, they are said to be intended as purely descriptive terms, not based on any particular theory or implying any particular aetiology. In other words, they are a shorthand and convenient way of referring to particular patterns of symptoms, perhaps the best one we have at present. The abstract of DSM-IV thus claims that it is a 'descriptive approach that attempt(s) to be neutral with respect to theories of etiology' (APA, 1994). If DSM is simply a collection of summaries that may be useful in practice, then reliability and validity would not be expected, and arguably are not essential for day-to-day practical purposes.

These are surprising admissions, and inconsistent with the efforts devoted to improving the reliability of DSM categories – a task which is doomed to failure if indeed there are no clear demarcations between the categories, which is exactly what the reliability studies have found. Moreover, this position does not explain why DSM and ICD continue to use the language of medicine (diagnosis, sign, symptom, illness, patient, and so on), which is based on the biomedical model of distress as a result of bodily dysfunction. Nor does it explain why the task of applying such terms falls to doctors. If these are not diagnoses in the sense used by medicine, then it is not clear what they are. To use them is therefore very confusing, since it conveys the clear message to service users, carers and other professionals that medical illnesses are being identified.

In an attempt to include some of the factors that a diagnosis inevitably leaves out, DSM diagnoses from edition IV onwards have been intended to be supplemented by information from five different 'axes'. Two of these axes refer to non-medical information: axis 4 codes psychosocial problems such as loss of employment, poverty or social isolation, while axis 5 allows the clinician to record how well the person is functioning in various aspects of their life such as work, leisure and relationships. It is obviously useful to have a way of giving a more complete picture of the person's medical, social and relationship context, and in this respect, the axes can be seen as performing some of the functions of a psychological formulation. However, psychiatric referrals frequently make only scant reference to these axes and the information associated with them usually gets subordinated to diagnoses, which many psychiatrists assume to be more informative. So whether this goes far enough is open to debate, and of course these add-ons do not solve the problems of reliability, validity, and so on. Nor do they reduce the other consequences of diagnosis, such as stigma and discrimination.

BOX **5.2**

DSM-5

The fifth version of the Diagnostic and Statistical Manual (DSM) of the American Psychiatric Association, or DSM-5 is currently being finalized and some important revisions are being suggested.

Categorical classification may be supplemented by 'cross-cutting dimensional assessments'

The dimensional criteria will consist of difficulties that tend to cut across diagnoses. For example, low mood, insomnia and so on may be present alongside the core criteria for a great many diagnoses. The DSM workgroups are discussing ways in which these additional problems can be assessed, alongside a decision about the main diagnosis. In addition, it is proposed that the severity of such difficulties can be rated, because unlike in categorical systems, a symptom does not have to be either present or absent. For example, someone with a categorical diagnosis of schizophrenia might also be rated as suffering from moderate insomnia and severe anxiety.

There may be a new diagnosis of 'Psychosis Risk Syndrome'

This diagnosis might be given to those who do not currently meet existing diagnostic criteria for schizophrenia or bipolar disorder, but who are judged to be at high risk of doing so in the near future. Whilst this new diagnosis might have some advantages in terms of allowing vulnerable people earlier access to services, it is also troubling because it might allow psychiatrists to interpret the boundary between health and distress even more flexibly than they do at present.

A number of other new diagnoses have been proposed

One of the other new diagnoses being proposed is 'Internet Addiction'. Whilst we might accept that some people over-use the internet, it is important to consider all the implications of introducing diagnoses that cover such broad areas of everyday life.

Clarifying boundaries

All the work groups helping to produce DSM-5 have been asked to work towards the general principles of clarifying the boundaries between mental disorders, and those between specific mental disorders and normal psychological functioning. It remains to be seen how successfully this will be accomplished, not least because some of the proposed new diagnoses seem very likely to blur these boundaries even further.

Developing alternative approaches

One way of side-stepping the problems of psychiatric diagnosis as a basis for research and intervention is to adopt a 'complaint-based' approach. In this, a specific difficulty such as hearing voices (hallucinations) or having very unusual beliefs (delusions) can be investigated, without the assumption that it belongs to a broader diagnostic category such as schizophrenia. Working on this basis, researchers have found various life events or characteristic ways of thinking that are associated with such experiences. For example, there is evidence that people who experience clinical paranoia are particularly likely to jump to conclusions (Bentall, 2003), while hearing voices is often associated with bereavement or trauma. Psychologist Richard Bentall has argued that if all of the so-called 'symptoms' can be accounted for in this way, there will be no illness of schizophrenia or bipolar disorder left to explain: we will have as complete an account as we need for the purposes of intervention, prognosis and so on (see Chapter 11).

Service user-led organizations such as the Hearing Voices Network (HVN) have taken this argument further. They believe that hearing voices is a normal variation of human experience, and does not necessarily imply any kind of pathology. Using the description 'hearing voices' as a starting point, rather than diagnostic terms or medical language like 'symptom', their research has found that many people cope well with their voices without ever coming to the attention of psychiatric services. In cases where voices cause distress, self-help strategies can bring relief. The HVN has grown into an international movement which offers alternatives to biomedical psychiatry (see Chapter 7).

Psychiatrists such as Suman Fernando believe that from a cross-cultural perspective, incorporating non-Western assumptions would mean that psychiatry 'would need to give up its outdated model of the individualized person (and)

rewrite its diagnostic systems in line with a holistic understanding that addresses the connectedness between people, the environment and the cosmos'. However, if such changes were to occur, it might be difficult to recognize the result as 'psychiatry' anyway (Fernando, 2003). In fact, although all societies seem to recognize some sort of madness, Fernando does not believe that a universal language about what we call mental illness is possible, since each model would only be valid within its own culture. He does, however, have a number of suggestions for the practice of multicultural psychiatry in the West, which incorporates many of the features for which service users of all ethnic backgrounds are campaigning. This includes 'diagnosis ... being superseded in importance by an understanding of the individual in the context of family and society ... Psychiatrists would move away from seeing "symptoms" such as hallucinations as "disorders"... towards seeing them as experiences with meaning and significance' (Fernando, 2003, p. 213).

Is psychiatric diagnosis fit for purpose?

At the start of this chapter, we summarized the purposes of medical diagnosis as follows: indicating treatment; predicting outcome; providing a basis for research; suggesting aetiology, or cause; enabling professionals to communicate with each other; giving information and relief to patients and carers; giving access to benefits and other resources. Diagnosis in general medicine is (mostly) able to fulfil these functions by matching patterns of bodily signs and symptoms to clusters that have been identified by researchers. This is not possible in the vast majority of cases in psychiatry.

As we have discussed, the contrast with general medicine is not always clear-cut. Many diagnoses of physical illness do not meet all these criteria. The diagnostic concepts may still be at an early stage of development, or we may know little about aetiology in a given case. Sometimes the boundary between mental and physical conditions is still disputed, as in Chronic Fatigue Syndrome. Further research may clarify these questions. However, if psychiatric diagnosis does not meet acceptable standards of reliability and validity, this kind of incompleteness will not just apply to some diagnoses, but to all aspects of all functional diagnoses.

If this is the case, then everything will be a best guess. Treatment will be a case of 'We haven't tried this medication, so maybe we should give it a go'. Outcome predictions will be along the lines of 'We can't say anything very precise, but some people do recover, although others don't'. An honest discussion about aetiology will acknowledge that 'We think that biochemical abnormalities are involved, but hard evidence is lacking'. Service users and relatives may feel initial relief on being told 'We know what is wrong – it is bipolar disorder'. However, if such categories are not valid, this statement is itself open to question, and may not lead to the hoped-for effective treatment, and so on.

Equally worryingly, research that is based on non-valid categories will be fundamentally flawed. If there are no satisfactory criteria for distinguishing schizophrenia from other diagnoses, or from normality, the results of research are bound to be inconsistent and contradictory. This may help to explain why, over 100 years since syphilis was identified as the causal factor in a large number of asylum inhabitants, there have been no other comparable breakthroughs in the field of mental health, despite the enormous advances in investigative techniques and in other branches of medicine during that time.

One might ask why, if this is the case, psychiatric diagnosis survives. The answer is complex. Service users and carers may gain a sense of relief from guilt and blame (see Box 5.3). The medical training and status of psychiatrists and psychiatric nurses is justified by the diagnostic approach. The pharmaceutical industry makes enormous amounts of money from selling medical solutions to psychiatric problems; indeed it contributes to the development of DSM (Kirk & Kutchins, 1997) and has actively supported the emergence of new diagnoses such as 'Social Phobia', for which medication can be prescribed (Johnstone, 2000). In the US, having a psychiatric diagnosis gives access to medical insurance and government health schemes such as Medicaid. Finally, it has been argued that there are wider social and political reasons why psychiatric diagnosis survives. We have already noted that diagnosis is embedded in other aspects of society, including criminal law, insurance and government policy. Additionally, vulnerable and disturbed people are not always welcome as relatives, friends or neighbours; it may suit all of us to see them as suffering from a medical problem which is someone else's role to treat. The alternative solutions – providing housing and employment, tackling poverty, re-building communities – are far more challenging and expensive (Johnstone, 2000).

It should now be clear why the issue of psychiatric diagnosis is so controversial, and why some professionals see formulation as a more promising way forward.

BOX 5.3
Service user views

I am labelled for the rest of my life...I think schizophrenia will always make me a second class citizen...I haven't got a future.... I'll never be able to erase the ink that's been put on me. (Honos-Webb & Leitner, 2001)

Interview with Kjell Magne Bondevik, former Prime Minister of Norway, about the four week's sick leave for depression during his time in office:

How did the diagnosis make you feel? What effect did it have on you? 'I had never heard of "depressive reaction" before...One of the effects it had on me is that I chose to be open about my condition...I did think that maybe this could be a contribution to fighting the stigma around mental health problems...And the fact is that in the end being open did not harm me. The reactions were overwhelmingly positive'. (Mitchell, 2010)

I already knew something was wrong with me. Now I knew I was mad...The diagnosis becomes a burden...you are an outcast in society...It took me years to feel OK about myself again. (Lindow, 1992)

A British consultant psychiatrist talking about his experience of depression:

When I was told that I was depressed it gave me a framework of understanding and a first grip on what was happening, not just for me but for my wife and children who had been equally frightened by my behaviour...What's more, diagnosis implied that this was an illness and therefore not my fault – important for someone whose depression has always been riddled with guilt. Illness meant treatment and the possibility of cure. (Shooter, 2010)

An American clinical psychologist and campaigner talks about being diagnosed with schizophrenia:

I was apprised most definitely that I was a person with schizophrenia, that this was a deteriorating brain disease, and that I would probably spend the rest of my life under the care of state hospitals...Now I had hit rock bottom...It was hard to muster much hope about what the future held for me...But in the mental health field, I have found considerable understanding from many co-workers. In retrospect, I see that despite my schizophrenia, I have been able to have a fulfilling career as a psychologist/advocate. Yes, the diagnosis has had quite an impact on my life, but the biggest impact has probably been giving me a purpose and a passion to try to improve the lives of others. (Frese, 2010)

The killing of hope...it almost feels like, well, your hands are tied, your cards laid and your fate set. (Horn, Johnstone & Brooke, 2007)

How do you account for these very different reactions? Do they constitute evidence for continuing, refining, or abandoning the practice of psychiatric diagnosis? To what extent would the damaging aspects have been avoided, and the helpful aspects preserved, if these people had been offered the chance to develop a formulation of their difficulties instead?

Formulation

As we have seen, views on psychiatric diagnosis are divided. Many professionals, including most psychiatrists, wish to retain it and believe that its shortcomings can be overcome in time. While acknowledging its limitations, they see it as the best available option at present. Others, including some psychiatrists, believe that it is misconceived in principle and unhelpful in practice. These professionals argue that diagnosis is based on an invalid model of distress and will therefore always be problematic. They do not deny that service users are often in urgent need of help and support, but they believe that this distress is often best understood in very different, non-medical terms – for example, as a psychological response to trauma, which is associated with many kinds of mental health problems (see Chapters 9–13). From this perspective, the answer is not to improve diagnosis but to replace it with a different understanding of distress, even – or perhaps especially – in the case of psychosis.

As we have seen, service user views on psychiatric diagnosis are split. Although some find it helpful, there is widespread dissatisfaction with an overly narrow approach which pays insufficient attention to other factors. Those who are active in the service user/survivor movement have called for more recognition of the reasons behind people's breakdowns. As Jacqui Dillon, UK chair of the Hearing Voices Network puts it, 'Instead of asking "What is wrong with you?" we should be asking "What has happened to you?" ' (Dillon, 2011, p. 155). This implies a formulation-based approach, which has some features in common with the alternative approaches to diagnosis discussed above.

What is a formulation?

All formulations:

1 Summarize the service user's core problems
2 Show how the service user's difficulties may relate to one another, by drawing on psychological theories and principles
3 Suggest, on the basis of psychological theory, why the client has developed these difficulties, at this time and in these situations
4 Give rise to a plan of intervention which is based on the psychological processes and principles already identified
5 Are open to revision and re-formulation.

A formulation can be defined as 'a hypothesis about a person's difficulties, which draws from psychological theory' (Johnstone & Dallos, 2006, p. 4). In other words, it is an individual summary, developed collaboratively with the service user, which looks at all aspects of a person's life in order to try and explain how and why their problems arose, and what interventions, if any, will be useful. If we see service users, as they often see themselves, as wrestling with a messy, complex mixture of traumatic life events, relationship conflicts and adverse social circumstances, then the main question we need to ask is not 'What kind of illness is this?' but 'What kind of problem is this?' A formulation can help us to work out the possible answer. In other words, 'Formulations can best be understood as hypotheses to be tested' (Butler, 1998, p. 2).

All formulations are based on the assumption that, even in the case of the more severe forms of distress, 'at some level it all makes sense' (Butler, 1998, p. 2). No matter how unusual or alarming someone's experiences and behaviour, it is assumed that they can be made understandable in the context of that person's life events and the sense they have made of them. In other words, unlike diagnosis, formulations give a central role to personal meaning. A formulation will include important life events such as bereavement, trauma and so on, but this is only the first step. Not everyone reacts to these events in the same way. The death of a parent might mean anything from 'Now I can be free from my mother's demands' to 'Now my father will never apologize for the way he hurt me', or 'Everyone important to me will inevitably leave me'. These are the personal meanings that need to be explored and clarified, and which will help to explain later difficulties with self-confidence, relationships, trust, and so on.

It usually takes time for both the professional and the service user to understand these processes, so there are likely to be several sessions before a provisional formulation can be developed. As new information and insights emerge, the formulation will need to be updated. Unlike a diagnosis, it is a work in progress, and always open to revision. Again, unlike a diagnosis, a formulation is drawn up jointly with the service user and respects their view of its accuracy and usefulness.

Formulations can take various forms, according to the therapeutic approach they draw upon. A cognitive–behavioural formulation, for example, might consist of a diagram showing the links between thoughts such as 'I'm worthless', feelings such as hopelessness, and behaviours such as avoiding people. A systemic formulation would have a strong focus on family relationships, whereas a psychodynamic formulation might include unconscious fears and wishes (see Chapter 8 for descriptions of different therapeutic approaches). For the purposes of this chapter we have shown you an integrated formulation, since the majority of therapists describe themselves as working in this way. In other words, they draw on a number of different therapeutic models in their formulations and interventions. Whichever therapeutic model is used, we can immediately see how different it will look from the diagnosis of schizophrenia that Sarah was given. Box 5.4 sets out a possible formulation of Sarah's difficulties: you should read it now.

While formulations are a central part of most therapies, they do not have to be used or developed solely within that context. There is a growing literature on using formulation within teams, in which a group of professionals come together to share their ideas about a service user and plan a care package based on the resulting formulation. This may be particularly useful in the case of service users with more complex and challenging difficulties who are not currently able to make use of individual therapy. In such cases, the outcome may be to help the team understand disturbed behaviour and develop a clearer and more consistent approach to it, and the interventions might include giving staff support with their feelings, trying new approaches, or putting the service user in touch with voluntary agencies (there is an example of this in Chapter 13).

Other purposes of formulation include: providing an overall map of the service user's difficulties, identifying missing information, predicting future difficulties, increasing the service user's sense of trust and enhancing collaboration with the service user. Good practice suggests that formulations should be constructed collaboratively with the service user whenever

BOX **5.4**
A formulation for Sarah

Re-read Sarah's story on p. 101.

You were close to both your parents, and your father's death was a huge blow. Because of your mother's distress and money worries, you felt you had to support her so that at least you had one parent to look after you. This was particularly difficult when you had lost contact with your own friends and former way of life. As a result your own grieving was put on hold. In addition, you did not fully understand the reasons for your father's death. As an eight year old, you wondered if you were in some way responsible, since he died while shopping for a bicycle for your birthday.

You have strong feelings of guilt and shame about the sexual abuse that you were subjected to. These feelings, plus your desire to protect your mother's happiness, prevented you from confiding in her. Instead, you withdrew into yourself. The only solution was to leave home as soon as you were old enough. Your mother and stepfather still live together, and you still feel very confused and frightened about whether or not to reveal this family secret. At an emotional level, your stepfather seems to have the same power over you as he did when you were a young girl. You find visits home extremely stressful for this reason.

Nursing allowed you to build up some self-confidence and, as someone used to caring for others, you found that you were very good at it. Looking back, it seems as if this may have been another situation in which you put others' needs before your own, and perhaps it was inevitable that at some point, your own needs and feelings would catch up with you. There were several triggers for this. When your partner left you, it brought back unresolved feelings of grief and rejection about your father's death. The injury prevented you from continuing the job that was a major source of satisfaction and self-worth. Without hard work as a distraction, issues from the past started coming to the surface. A key event was the time you spent waiting for pain relief in hospital. You felt abandoned and angry, and this incident seemed to encapsulate the feelings of pain, anger and loneliness associated with the abuse you suffered. Despite all the care you have given to others, there seemed to be no-one to care for you when you needed it. Alone in your flat, some of these conflicts emerged in the form of the voices you hear. The voices can perhaps be understood as expressing unresolved guilt, shame, anger and grief about the abuse and about your father's death.

You are someone with many strengths. You have survived some very traumatic and difficult times, and are highly valued in your profession. You have good friends and have been coping very well until the recent crisis. All this will help you to overcome your current difficulties.

possible and expressed in ordinary language, rather than professional jargon, held tentatively and revised as necessary, include the service user's strengths as well as their difficulties, and be based on an awareness of social and cultural factors. This contrasts with the process of psychiatric diagnosis, which is an expert judgement, not open to negotiation with the service user, and held to be a 'truth' that is independent of social or cultural factors and judgements (although, as we have argued, this is not actually the case).

We have said that a formulation is based on personal meaning: the sense that the service user has made of their experiences. It also assumes that the service user has agency – the ability to make changes in their life – as opposed to depending on an expert professional to prescribe a solution (the sick role). This may partly explain why formulations can be challenging for service users to hear. On the one hand, a formulation does not carry the risk of stigma and discrimination, but on the other, it does not bring the immediate relief that may be experienced after diagnosis. In fact, as some research suggests, the initial reaction may be one of sadness or distress, as the person faces up to painful events and feelings. In the words of Ron Coleman, a former psychiatric patient who is now a campaigner, letting go of your diagnosis 'means taking back responsibility for yourself, it means that you can no longer blame your illness for your actions ... but more important, it means that you stop being a victim of your experience and start being the owner of your experience' (Coleman, 1999, pp. 160–1).

Formulation and diagnosis: additions or alternatives?

Professionals take different views about whether formulation should be regarded as an addition to, or an alternative to, psychiatric diagnosis. As we have seen, formulation has some potential to function as an alternative to diagnosis. Currently, however, the majority of psychiatrists and psychologists occupy a midway position. Whilst many see formulation as a useful addition to diagnosis, particularly in the broad category of neurosis (depression, anxiety, eating disorders and so on), most do not yet see it as a replacement for diagnosis. Many psychiatrists and psychologists argue for the use of diagnosis in order to indicate the broad nature of someone's difficulties, coupled with a formulation to fill in the details as they apply to a particular individual (Eells, 1997; Weerasekera, 1996). Others see these two ways of conceptualizing someone's difficulties as incompatible, at both a theoretical and a practical level. Arguably, it does not make sense to tell someone that their problems have primarily biological causes, and are at the same time a result of their life experiences and the sense they have made of them. In practice, this may lead to situations such as someone being given medication to remove their symptoms of depression while at the same time having counselling to express and release their feelings. Clearly this is confusing for the service user, and may undermine the attempt to do psychological work with them. However, as we have already noted, the centrality of diagnosis to the whole practice of psychiatry means that replacing it with formulation would mean a very radical change in approach and a challenge to many professional and business interests.

Limitations of formulation

It might be objected that a formulation is, as we have argued in the case of diagnosis, intrinsically subjective, open to bias and so on. This is true, but is not necessarily an argument against it. Most proponents of formulation argue that it does not claim, or need, to meet scientific standards of reliability and validity, since they see mental health professionals as dealing with human distress, rather than medical illnesses. We would not expect these situations to fall into neat clusters, although we may be able to draw upon our knowledge about typical reactions to certain events (for example, there is a great deal of information about common responses to bereavement, trauma and abuse, and about common causal factors in distress; see Chapter 6). However, their impact will obviously vary from person to person, and it is the job of a formulation to work out exactly how they apply in each individual case.

The case for formulation as a credible alternative to diagnosis would be strengthened by the development of broad-level categories of distress in addition to individual narratives. For example, it might be possible to rename the diagnosis of schizophrenia, in many cases, as 'dissociative response to severe trauma'. Other psychiatric diagnoses could perhaps be replaced by 'attachment difficulties' or 'unresolved bereavement', and so on. In fact, some of the existing DSM/ICD diagnoses are actually a type of broad-level formulation implying psychosocial rather than medical causes – 'bereavement reaction' for example, and PTSD. A formulation-based approach would not assess such categories solely in terms of reliability or validity (although if conducted thoroughly, a formulation is likely to be more valid, at least in terms of ecological and face validity), because it would not be trying to create a parallel version of medical diagnosis. Rather, the aim would be to develop a series of loose categories that are based on psychological evidence about the effects of trauma, abuse, bereavement and so on, and that might give some pointers to the most effective forms of intervention in such cases. These categories might also be able to perform some of the other functions that psychiatric diagnosis claims, and perhaps fails, to fulfil, such as indicating aetiology, predicting outcome, providing a basis for research, and so on.

It should be noted that formulation is not without its own limitations and challenges. Whilst there are published resources that clinicians can draw upon to help them include social influences (e.g. Hagan & Smail, 1997 a,b) there is nothing to prevent a formulation from ignoring social and cultural factors and focusing purely on deficits, exactly as diagnoses do. Equally, there can be no guarantee that they will be constructed collaboratively. Perhaps the best that can be said is that formulations can, at least in principle, and if sensitively developed and used, sidestep these traps, whereas they are arguably an unavoidable consequence of diagnosis.

We should also note that though formulations can and should include cultural factors, the concept of formulation is itself a Western psychological construct, rooted in Western assumptions. As a result, there are certain service user meanings that would probably not be accepted by most psychologists; for example, he or she might well take the position that the belief that your ancestors are guiding you should be understood symbolically, not literally. As we have seen, distress may be understood in very different ways in other cultures, and it is not clear that psychological formulation as currently conceived can always accommodate this more successfully than psychiatric diagnosis. To a large extent, whether or not formulations include cultural factors depend on the theories they draw upon.

Finally, there is the paradox that although formulation has been recognized as a central skill of clinical psychologists for many years, there is very little research evidence to support its use. Is formulation more acceptable to service users? Does it improve therapy outcomes? Does a formulation-based approach cut costs, and reduce admission and the use of medication? Although there is good evidence for the kind of psychological theories that would support a formulation-based approach (for example, links between trauma and experiences such as hearing voices and having unusual beliefs; see Chapter 11), there has been very little investigation into the effectiveness of formulation itself. Nor is it clear how formulation could be evaluated. If it constitutes a central part of most therapies, including CBT, it will be almost impossible to separate the effects of formulation from the effects of the therapy itself. Moreover, while it makes sense to ask whether a diagnosis is accurate, in the sense that the patient's complaints match a particular set of signs and symptoms, the same question does not apply so readily to formulation. What is the 'accurate' version of the personal meaning behind someone's distress, and who should judge this? Formulations may be more appropriately judged by their usefulness than their 'correctness', although this in turn raises questions of 'useful in what way?' and 'useful to whom?'.

Chapter summary

The table below summarizes the key differences between formulation and diagnosis.

Diagnosis	Formulation
Obscures social contexts	Can include social contexts
Individualizes	Includes relationships
Not culturally sensitive	Can be culturally sensitive
Expert-driven	Collaborative
Stigmatizing	Non-stigmatizing
Medical consequences	No medical consequences
Social consequences	No social consequences
Removes agency ('sick role')	Promotes agency
Removes personal meaning	Based on personal meaning

It can be seen that despite the tendency to use diagnosis and formulation alongside each other, they start from different, indeed opposing, assumptions. In fact, critics of diagnosis argue that formulation can be an answer, or antidote, to the well-documented theoretical and practical drawbacks of psychiatric diagnosis (Johnstone & Dallos, 2013). Formulation is an under-researched approach with its own limitations and pitfalls. However, many psychologists believe that it does in principle offer a way of reintroducing personal meaning, personal agency, personal relationships and social and cultural contexts into mental health work.

Lacking research support, and without the backing of powerful professional and business interest groups, formulation is likely to remain a minority approach for the time being. Nevertheless, the growing number of publications on the topic in recent years – including British Psychological Society Guidelines on good practice for its use (Johnstone, Whomsley, Cole & Oliver, 2011) – suggests that this may change in the future.

End of chapter questions

1 Psychiatric diagnosis contains an inescapable element of subjective judgement: does that mean that it is unscientific?

2 Will it ever be possible to create a culture-free system of psychiatric diagnosis?

3 To what extent can the stigmatizing effects of diagnoses such as schizophrenia be alleviated by changes in terminology – for example, by calling it psychosis?

4 To what extent are the changes being proposed for DSM-5 likely to address the problems identified by critics of psychiatric diagnosis?

5 Is the DSM just one example of a wider phenomenon of 'medicalizing' everyday life?

6 What are the differences between a psychological formulation and a factual account of a person's life and experiences?

7 Why might some clinical psychologists be unwilling to entirely dispense with diagnosis and just use formulations instead?

8 Re-read the formulation for Sarah in this chapter. One of the main purposes of a formulation is to indicate possible interventions. What interventions might follow from this formulation? What interventions might follow from the diagnosis? What differences do you notice?

Find out more

Films and books

The classic novel *Catch-22* by Joseph Heller describes in a humorous and satirical way some of the paradoxes associated with classification systems that try to objectively determine aspects of experience such as sanity and madness. *Catch-22* describes how anyone who would be willing to fly a military aircraft in battle must be mad, so could be excused from doing so on the grounds of insanity. At the same time, to show concern for your own safety in a war is good evidence of rational thought and sanity, which means that anyone taking advantage of this catch must by definition be entirely sane. *Catch-22* was made into a film in 1970.

Academic texts

Boyle, M. (2007). The problem with diagnosis. *The Psychologist*, 20(5), 290–2.

Johnstone, L. & Dallos, R. (2013). *Formulation in Psychology and Psychotherapy: Making Sense of People's Problems*. Second revised edition. London, New York: Routledge.

Johnstone, L., Whomsley, S., Cole, S. & Oliver, N. (2011). *Good Practice Guidelines for the Use of Psychological Formulation*. Leicester: British Psychological Society.

Kutchins, H. & Kirk, S. (1997). *Making Us Crazy: DSM – The Psychiatric Bible and the Creation of Mental Disorders*. New York: Free Press.

Scheff, T. J. (1974). The labeling theory of mental illness. *American Sociological Review*, 39, 444–52.

Szasz, T. (1976a). Schizophrenia: The sacred symbol of psychiatry. *British Journal of Psychiatry*, 129, 308–16.

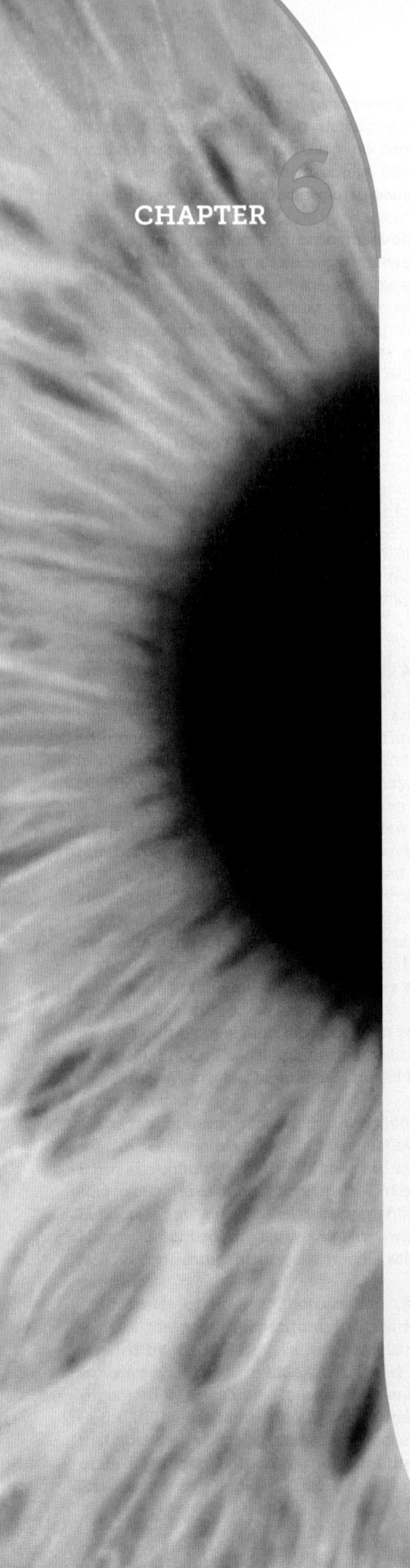

CHAPTER 6

CAUSAL INFLUENCES

With Lucy Johnstone

Don's story

Don is a university student with a dilemma. His best friend, Sally, is also a student. Recently, Sally has confided that she has started having some difficulties in her life.

Some years ago, in the wake of her parents' divorce, Sally became very unhappy and was treated with anti-depressant medication for a period of six months. Since she came to university, Sally has been fine, experiencing only the same kind of routine ups and downs as other students. But now, with final examinations rapidly approaching and the pressure of a large dissertation to complete, Sally has found herself becoming worried and unhappy. Instead of working, she often finds herself just staring into space, unable to stop worrying about what she will do after university, and wondering what will happen to the friendships she has made. She feels miserable much of the time, doesn't feel like eating, and finds it hard to concentrate on her work. She often feels like all she wants to do is sleep. These difficulties have worried Sally so much that she has been to see her doctor, who has recommended that Sally begins another course of anti-depressant medication.

Sally is unsure about this. Although when she took it before the medication improved her mood, it didn't help her to concentrate. In fact, it mostly made concentration more difficult: because Sally wasn't worrying so much about the consequences of not working, she often found it even harder than before to motivate herself.

Sally has turned to Don for advice. Don wants to help her, but he doesn't know what to say. Although he's not an expert, he can clearly see that Sally isn't as happy and contented as she was. But what advice should he give? It all seems to depend on what's causing her problems. If her unhappiness is simply an illness, a matter of brain chemistry, then surely she should just take the medication, even if this means that her work suffers. But if her unhappiness is caused by other things – and from what he knows about Sally, Don suspects that, at least in part, it is – then maybe medication is not the best idea, and perhaps he should recommend that Sally uses the university counselling service.

Don has tried asking friends for their opinions (without identifying Sally, of course). But their views seem to be polarized according to the subject they are studying. His medical student friends say Sally has a brain chemical imbalance and needs to take the medication; his social scientist friends say that Sally should try to reduce the conflicts between the different roles she occupies; and his psychologist friends say Sally is unhappy because of the way she thinks about her situation, and suggest she should try to change her ways of seeing the world. After listening to all of them, Don is just as confused as before.

After you have read this chapter, you will be able to:

1 Explain why causal influences upon distress are difficult to identify and research
2 Evaluate the strengths and weaknesses of the various research methods typically used to identify causal influences upon distress
3 Describe the kinds of causal influence upon distress that researchers have explored
4 Describe how these influences get translated into practice by mental health professionals.

Introduction

As Don's story shows, thinking about causal influences upon distress is something that people do in everyday life, as well as in clinical and scientific settings. In this chapter we will describe some important issues that need to be considered in order to understand causal influences upon distress. First, we will discuss the part played by everyday social influences in the identification of distress, and in generating evidence for its causes. This includes an acknowledgement that in the case of distress, as we have seen elsewhere in this book, the role of cultural assumptions is particularly prominent. We will go on to list some of the difficulties that arise when trying to identify and assess causal influences upon distress. Next, we will describe the different kinds of research methodology that are typically used to investigate the causes of distress, and assess their strengths and weaknesses. After this, we will briefly summarize each of the major categories of causal influence upon distress that research has explored. This summary will be followed by a discussion of the ways in which these influences come together in the lives of individuals to supply the resources and possibilities through which personal agency and meaning appear for them. Then, in the final section of the chapter, we will describe some of the ways that clinicians think about and model these causal influences.

Guiding questions

Throughout this chapter, you should bear these two questions in mind:

1 *How can we understand the ways that different causal influences upon distress interact with each other?*
2 *To what extent does research into the causes of distress clarify how clinicians should proceed?*

Causal influence, social process

In everyday life we often find ourselves saying things like, 'This happened because he thinks that' or 'The reason she said that was because she's this kind of person'. Psychologists who have studied the antecedents, frequency and effects of these kinds of statements call them **causal attributions**: everyday, common-sense explanations of behaviour and its consequences (Hewstone, 1989). They have shown that causal attributions are

quite frequent in everyday social interaction, and that they can fulfil various functions. Sometimes they seem to work more as assertions of identity or morality than as accurate explanations; for example, descriptions of why something happened can be used to blame one person and excuse another. Rather than simply providing a dispassionate account of 'what actually happened', causal attributions frequently cast a positive light on those who make them, or establish the relevance of one or more social norms. At the same time, this means that they often have the effect of questioning the actions or motives of others by, for example, casting them as thoughtless, impolite or morally deficient. So everyday causal attributions are as much about what is legitimate as they are about what is accurate: they are about morality, ethics, values and norms, as well as about the truth of facts, events and situations.

Usually, when we make a causal attribution, we do so in good faith. When we claim to know the reasons why something occurred, we typically tell the truth as we see it. But this does not necessarily mean that we are correct, and classic social psychology experiments show that we are frequently *not* correct (Jones & Harris, 1967). We are wrong so often that social psychologists have coined a term for one of the most frequent mistakes: the **fundamental attribution error**. This refers to a common tendency to over-emphasize internal or dispositional factors (such as personality or motivation) in accounting for the activity of others. Simultaneously, the fundamental attribution error means that we tend to underestimate the significance of contextual, situational or environmental factors when we explain why other people acted as they did.

The fundamental attribution error is made so frequently that some have claimed it is the 'bedrock' of social psychology (Ross, 1977). Psychologists have also described the error in terms of a **correspondence bias** (a tendency to make assumptions about a person's dispositions from behaviours that can be explained entirely by the situations in which they occur (Gilbert & Malone, 1995), and more recently it has been reformulated in discursive social psychology as a pattern of speech in everyday social interaction (Potter, 1996). So the fundamental attribution error continues to be important in explaining how humans understand each other, and how they account for their own and other people's activities. It might become relevant to Sally's problems if one of her friends were to explain her current difficulties by suggesting that she had 'always been a worrier'. Sally herself might well deny this, arguing that she had coped well until recently and this is why she is confused and upset to suddenly find herself struggling. It is also inevitable that, during these discussions, Sally and her friend would make social comparisons or draw upon social norms and culturally-sanctioned values and expectations.

There are two reasons why these social psychological phenomena are relevant here. First, it is often overlooked that the processes by which people first come to the attention of mental health services in everyday life are social and interactional. People do not typically get referred to services just because they hold unusual beliefs, for example. Indeed, evidence suggests that relatively large proportions of the population hold beliefs that many would class as delusional, but the vast majority of these people are not receiving any kind of treatment and have never been in contact with mental health services (e.g. van Os, Hannssen, Bijl & Ravelli, 2000).

Similarly, being deeply sad or intensely worried does not, of itself, usually result in people receiving interventions.

Typically, what actually happens is that others – family, friends, neighbours or colleagues – notice that someone is behaving in unusual ways, saying things that do not make sense, or seems to be inexplicably overcome with emotion and finding it hard to function. These people may then encourage the person concerned to seek treatment, or sometimes – where the person appears to be a danger to themselves, or others – they might themselves notify relevant services.

But even where other people are not immediately involved and individuals are reflecting privately upon their own experiences, their reflections rely upon the norms, values and expectations of their own culture and situation. Individual decision-making is a kind of conversation with oneself: it uses similar cultural tools, relies upon the same cultural norms, and is broadly aligned with prevailing principles, values and ethics (Billig, 1987; Vygotsky, 1962). Before deciding to speak to the doctor about her difficulties, Sally would no doubt have compared her recent experiences with those of others around her, and with what she imagines to be 'normal' for people in her kind of situation. Alternatively, if Sally had been reluctant to seek help but was behaving in ways that upset or worried others (crying loudly in her room, wandering the streets at night), they might have sought professional help on her behalf.

This means that everyday judgements about the nature, level and causes of people's distress have an inescapable social and cultural dimension. Decisions to seek help are made against a backdrop of socially sanctioned values, norms and expectations for conduct, by reference to which we judge whether or not help is appropriate. However, in emphasizing this we are not saying that all ways of behaving should be seen as equally acceptable. Nor are we denying that some people's feelings, thoughts and actions are strikingly different from those of others; so different, sometimes, as to make them distressing, alarming, or occasionally even dangerous. We are simply recognizing that, even in circumstances where behaviour is obviously very far from everyday social norms, those norms and expectations are still part of the process whereby these people get identified.

This leads to the second reason why these social psychological phenomena are relevant here. Clinicians make judgements about the nature of people's distress, and hence about the kind of intervention that will be offered, on the basis of many bodies of knowledge. Their starting point will be what they know about the person: their difficulties, their context and their history. They will interpret what they know in conjunction with theories of the nature and causes of distress, and with regard to their own clinical experience. Similarly, when it comes to devising an intervention, clinicians will draw upon their professional training (e.g. as social worker, occupational therapist, psychologist or psychiatrist). Their decision about an intervention will also be informed by the evidence base for its efficacy, and local knowledge of the resources currently available.

Clinicians must consider so much knowledge of this kind that it is easy for us to imagine that this knowledge is the *sole* basis of their decisions. Consequently, we may forget that their reasoning, too, is continuously informed by norms, morals, values and expectations. Professional training, research evidence and clinical experience mediate and modify the judgements that clinicians make, but their fundamentally normative aspect persists and social norms are still relevant. This is why clinical decisions in psychiatry and medicine are informed by medical ethics, and why the work of clinical psychologists is regulated by the ethical codes of professional bodies: in the UK this includes the codes of the British Psychological Society and the Health Professions Council.

Moreover, it is not only clinicians who rely upon normative values and expectations when they make judgements: so do the researchers who generate the evidence on which clinicians rely. Work within the discipline of Science and Technology Studies (e.g. Latour & Woolgar, 1986) clearly shows that science is in no sense separate from society, and that its processes and findings are thoroughly permeated with social influence. Importantly, this does not mean that we should simply dismiss science and its findings as biased or irrelevant: we need systematic, sensitive and thorough empirical investigations in order to improve our understandings of distress. However, it does mean that we should not naively imagine that science can somehow just leave social influences and cultural norms behind. As biologist Gunnar Myrdal said in 1944:

> Cultural influences have set up the assumptions about the mind, the body and the universe with which we begin; pose the questions we ask; influence the facts we seek; determine the interpretation we give these facts; and direct our reaction to these interpretations and conclusions.
>
> Myrdal, in Gould (1981 p. 23)

If what Myrdal says is true for the so-called 'hard' sciences like biology, it must apply with even more force to our understandings of distress. As an element of human experience, distress is always bound up with the cultural influences and social relations that shape both its content and meaning.

Causality

Perhaps the most fundamental reason why science is important here is that causality – of anything, not just distress – is frequently much more difficult to establish than it appears. Many causal chains have the potential to extend back almost infinitely: she did this because of that, which was because of that, which was because of … and so on, until we reach the 'ultimate' conditions of possibility 'because she was born', or 'because there is a universe for her to be part of' (see Box 4.3). As philosopher David Lewis puts it: 'Any particular event that we might wish to explain stands at the end of a long and complicated causal history. We might imagine a world where causal histories are short and simple; but in the world as we know it, the only question is whether they are infinite or merely enormous' (Lewis, 1987, p. 214).

For practical purposes, then, we often restrict our exploration of causality to those factors most relevant to our present purposes. This principle is likely to serve us well in relation to distress, where it makes sense to focus primarily on those causal influences that are at least partially amenable to modification: aspects of ourselves, our societies and our relationships that we might be able to change to some degree. In this way, we hope that some meaningful intervention can follow from the identification of causality.

At the same time, one reason why a sophisticated understanding of science as a social process is necessary when we think about causality in distress is that – like other aspects of human experience – causality in distress is *multiple, complex and over-determined*. Causality is *multiple* in the sense that both research and clinical experience demonstrate that there are many possible causes of distress, and that in most instances more than one contributes. Causality is therefore *complex*: it is usually not just a matter of multiple influences, but of how these influences interact with each other. The potential for influences to cause distress depends upon their many consequences for other aspects of the person's life, as well as upon precisely how they impinge upon experience in a given moment. This in turn means that causality is frequently **over-determined**. On the one hand, it will usually be possible to 'explain' a person's distress in more than one way, and for each explanation to be largely in accord with the known facts. On the other hand, it will often seem that at least some of these explanations are mutually exclusive: if one is true, one or more of the others must be false. So we need a relatively sophisticated understanding, because the kind of causation involved is rarely as straightforward as that which occurs between, for example, the molecules of two different compounds interacting in a test-tube.

We can begin to develop this more sophisticated understanding by recalling the distinction that was first presented in Chapter 4 between **necessary causes** – those that always have to be present for a phenomenon to occur – and **sufficient causes**: those that do not always have to be present, but always cause a phenomenon to occur when they are (see Box 4.1). This distinction begins to untangle some of the complexity of causation in distress, because in most cases the causal influences are neither sufficient nor necessary. But this means that we also need to move away from the naive idea that causes simply determine outcomes, and instead adopt the more sophisticated understanding that causes influence probabilities. From this perspective, causality can be defined quite simply as *an increase in the probability of x following the occurrence of y*. For example, if distress is more likely following trauma, then – providing other influences are controlled for or taken account of – we can assume that trauma is a cause of distress. Whilst this notion of causality could still be conceived mechanistically, it does seem to leave significant room for human agency and interpretation. Although it is rarely stated explicitly, this 'probabilistic' theory of causality was formalized in the 1970s by philosopher Patrick Suppes and in practice is widely used in the human and social sciences (Cartwright, 2007).

Mirowsky and Ross (1989, pp. 57–61) offer three criteria for identifying probabilistic causal influences of this kind:

> *Association*: there is a correlation between the supposed influence and some kind or level of distress. This correlation appears in multiple studies and across numerous populations, and appears to be robust.
>
> *Nonspuriousness*: the observed correlation between influence and distress is a real association between them. It is not the side-effect of some other influence, or an artefact of research methods.
>
> *Causal order*: to be causal, the influence must come before the distress. In practice, causal order is often difficult to establish, not least because many effects might also be causes. Misery, poor sleeping and an inability to concentrate might cause someone to perform badly at work and lose their job; but being made unemployed can cause misery, sleeplessness and difficulty concentrating and making decisions. Causal order must nevertheless be established if influences are to be accurately identified.

To understand causal influences upon distress, we need to move far beyond the notion that causes operate singly and in a mechanical fashion. In our lived experience, there are always multiple influences interacting to shape how we think and feel, to regulate what we do, to give our experience its particular character and meaning. At any given moment of our lives there are many, many influences upon us, each of which can arise, be triggered or play themselves out in an almost unlimited number of ways. The world we occupy is an open-ended one, in which the unexpected can always occur: a world where many things are more likely than others, but relatively few things are entirely inevitable.

Contingency

The open-ended character of the world has to mean that causal influences upon distress operate **contingently**: in other words, they interact with each other, and with objects and events, in ways that it is frequently impossible to predict in advance. There are very many possible influences upon distress, each of which has the potential to trigger other influences, in different ways. And each of these further influences is also open to still other influences, including those not directly related to distress, with which they nevertheless interact.

However, contingency is not the same thing as *randomness*: just because the causes of distress operate contingently, this does not mean that they don't conform to any patterns at all. It simply means that, at the level of individual cases, these patterns are frequently difficult to discern. But how does psychology typically deal with contingency? An example will help to make this clearer.

Psychologists conducting memory experiments sometimes test recall using lists of nonsense syllables like SOT, NIM or PLE. This is because, if they used lists of real words, they could not control for familiarity, for the almost infinitely different prior associations each word might have for each of their participants. Familiarity, and the availability and nature of word meaning, strongly influence recall: but the character of their influence is wholly diffuse, unpredictable and contingent. In order to establish rigorous experimental control, then, it makes sense to use nonsense syllables.

Experimental psychology contains many procedures of this kind, where elements of everyday life get 'translated' into purified or sanitized versions. These procedures are attempts to ensure that a uniform set of expectations and experiences can be delivered to participants. In this way, variables of interest can be isolated and sound inferences made about the extent to

In mathematics, the 'butterfly effect' is an example of contingency. It describes how very small changes in one system can produce large, unpredictable changes in another – so a butterfly flapping its wings in one place might eventually cause a tornado somewhere else

which effects can be attributed to their operation. On the basis of these inferences, putative causal models can be generated.

The need for these kinds of procedures is taught very early in most psychology courses. Consequently, they can quickly sink into the background, becoming part of what is simply taken for granted about the conduct of psychological research. So it is useful to pause for a moment in order to reflect upon what they signify, because when we impose these kinds of conditions upon participants we are effectively making an important admission.

Effectively, we are acknowledging that the real world is so messy and unpredictable that it is actually *impossible* for psychologists to properly capture its multiple, diverse and complex lines of influence using discrete variables. We are acknowledging that, even within the highly constrained and artificial confines of the experimental cubicle, everyday influence and causation are subject to more unpredictable variation than our measures could ever capture. We are also acknowledging that, if we did try to do this, it would be noticed by our participants who would then, inevitably, make some changes to what they do, with the result that the phenomena we set out to investigate became, at least in part, something different. So by using nonsense syllables or other artificial stimuli, we effectively acknowledge that we must sacrifice some of the richness, diversity and fluidity of everyday life in order to generate consistent findings.

From the perspective of experimental psychology, and within other research traditions that prize the derivation of causal laws, such sacrifices are both sensible and necessary. Without them, it would be extremely difficult to generate meaningful findings that can be generalized, and that might in future be replicated. But the continuing need for them highlights an important but inconvenient truth.

This inconvenient truth can be stated reasonably simply: the influences upon what we do are usually multiple and often unknowable; neither we nor anyone else can necessarily identify them easily; and they may change, more or less subtly, from moment to moment. And this holds, not just for particular individuals, but for all of us, all of the time. Whilst this does not mean that causal associations cannot ever be established, it does mean that they cannot easily be reduced to deterministic causal laws.

Some psychologists and social scientists have tried to explain why individual human activity is not subject to deterministic causal laws. Rom Harré (2002) argues that human activity is not 'caused' so much as guided. As thinking creatures who have agency and choice, we sensitively and creatively interpret the norms relevant to our situation. Our choices are not caused by these social and cultural norms, but they are guided and shaped by them. From a slightly different perspective, John Shotter (1993) argues that many of our everyday interactions are characterized by what he calls 'joint action'. What he means by this is that, as I respond to you and you respond to me, our interactions can become so open-ended that outcomes can emerge that were unintended in advance by *either* of us. From Shotter's perspective, most of our social relations and interactions are intrinsically uncertain and open-ended in this way.

Similarly, social theorist Margaret Archer (1995) argues that all social causation is necessarily probabilistic rather than deterministic. The social world is immensely dynamic and complex, and any event or situation is the outcome of multiple, intersecting lines of influence, coming together in ways that those who enacted them were frequently unable to foresee.

Even in very simple social situations – like this game with wooden blocks – it is very difficult to predict exactly how people's actions will come together to shape outcomes

For example, whilst most people who walk into a bank simply deposit or withdraw money, every now and again one of them will pull out a gun and commit a robbery. So although broad patterns of social causation can be discerned, there will always be some variation in how people respond to and deal with the various social influences that impinge upon them.

Psychologist Ben Bradley (2005) provides an extended discussion of contingency, complexity and chance. First, he observes that the meaning of what we do is *always* contingent upon the actions of others, but that these actions are usually out of our control and frequently cannot be predicted. For example, walking down the street we knock a cyclist off his bike; he gets up unhurt, we apologize, he grumbles and cycles away. Alternatively, walking down the street we knock a cyclist off his bike; he falls into the path of a passing car and is killed. In the first case we are involved in a trivial incident that will quickly be forgotten; in the second we may face a charge of manslaughter. This example shows that, as Bradley (2005, p. 70) puts it, 'the meaning of what we do depends on the patterns of coincident events which our actions help to make'.

Moreover, what might appear to be a coincidence at the individual level may well be nothing of the sort when viewed from another perspective. A classic example of this is Durkheim's explanation for the distribution of (individual) suicide rates in terms of **anomie**. Anomie describes how there can be mismatches between small-group norms and those of wider society, and how there can be an absence of a distinct social ethic to unite people: in both senses, then, it refers to phenomena operating at the level of societies rather than individuals. Durkheim's thesis is an old one now, but recent evidence (e.g. Lewis & Sloggett, 1998) suggests that it is still relevant today. Bradley also observes that even where events seem to be random, they might nevertheless occur more commonly than we suppose. As he puts it: 'An event that is so rare that it is one in a million will be plentiful in a population of three hundred million' (p. 78).

Contingency is relevant to accounts of distress because it helps us to understand why one person rather than another ends up experiencing clinical levels of distress. This can be illustrated using a very trivial example. Whilst preparing a meal earlier, I picked a freshly washed fork from the washing-up rack and re-used it during cooking. I picked that fork simply because the washing-up rack is nearer to the cooker than the drawer where the rest of the forks are stored. After I've used it, it will get washed again, and go back in the rack once more. Once there, it might be picked another time for re-use from the washing-up rack. The more times this happens, the more that fork will endure wear and tear from washing, heat and so on, so the more likely it is that that particular fork – rather than any of the others in the drawer – will eventually break. For reasons that are entirely contingent on other, largely unrelated factors – the initial choice of one fork rather than another (itself a consequence of a prior, random choice to use that fork to eat with); the layout of my kitchen; the various meals I cook and eat each day; how often I wash up and put the dishes away – one fork might end up receiving considerably more wear and tear than any of the others.

Of course, people are not forks, and the processes by which they become distressed are far more complex than those involved in cooking and dishwashing. But similar principles of contingency apply: more so, in fact, precisely because the relevant process and situations are both more complex and more numerous. Sometimes, random events precipitate chains of meaning, activity and behaviour that have unforeseen, unintended consequences: but sometimes, numerous relatively uncommon events can coincide within one person's life.

You should also note that this principle of contingency begins to explain why not everyone exposed to 'the same' social circumstances will end up experiencing clinical levels of distress. First, because causality is probabilistic rather than deterministic, we should not expect social circumstances to impact uniformly anyway. Second, just like the different forks in the same kitchen, people in superficially similar social circumstances nevertheless get exposed to a wide range of different stressful influences. And third, these various influence will sometimes operate **synergistically**: one cause and its effects sometimes magnify the influence of another cause and its effects. Box 6.1 provides an example that illustrates this principle; you should read it now.

BOX **6.1**
Synergistic causation

At first glance it might appear that contingency always dilutes the impact of different causal influences. However, it is more accurate to recognize that contingency means that causal influences are always mediated by other factors. Whilst this sometimes means they get weakened, it can also mean the opposite: sometimes, causal influences interact synergistically so that the effects of one get magnified by the effects of another.

For example, both sexual abuse and social inequality are separate causal influences upon distress, but together their effects may be synergistic (Cromby & Harper, 2009). To understand why, we must think about how experiences of sexual abuse might actually be lived by people on lower incomes and with fewer resources. Compared to wealthier people, people on lower incomes tend to live in smaller houses, with more cramped living conditions and more shared space. They are less likely to have second homes, country cottages, prolonged holidays, or other means by which to easily and regularly gain respite from an abusive home. These material facts mean that, on average, sexually abused people from poorer backgrounds will more often find themselves in closer proximity with their abuser, with fewer opportunities for respite. Consequently, contact with the abuser is likely to be more frequent, sustained or intense: characteristics which are known to make the negative effects of sexual abuse worse. So social inequality, itself a causal influence upon distress, can magnify the effects of sexual abuse: another, separate causal influence.

It's also important to realize that some people's experiences have simply been consistently and overwhelmingly traumatic. Priest (2006) describes a client, Alison, who is constantly engulfed with an overwhelming feeling of dread that something awful might occur; Alison's fears disable her, harming her relationships and limiting her choices. Priest explains:

> Alison begs to be told why every time her life, uncharacteristically, seems to be going well, a feeling of dread creeps up on her and soon she is cloaked, enshrouded in desolation. Yet this same woman talks about how, at the age of four, her father used to hide in a cupboard in her bedroom, terrorizing her. At other times, she witnessed his alcohol-fuelled violence towards her mother. When her parents finally split up when she was seven, there followed a series of moves between refuges and relatives. At nine her new stepfather tried to rape her. The father of her first child, whom she bore at 15, ended up in prison for murder. Her next boyfriend poured a glass of bleach over her whilst she was in the bath. Another boyfriend locked her in a shed along with a pair of rats and a baby kitten. Through repeated experiences of awful things happening in her life, she has acquired an acute sense of dread that something awful is about to happen, because it so often has. (Priest, 2006, p. 26)

Alison's story clearly illustrates why it is vital to recall that, in everyday life, ALL causality operates on the basis of contingency.

To summarize: if we are to understand causal influences upon distress we need a relatively sophisticated understanding of causation. This involves recognizing the distinction between necessary and sufficient causes, and understanding the relevance of association, non-spuriousness and causal order. We have to appreciate that causation is multiple, complex and over-determined, and recognize how influences come together contingently.

Difficulties

This more sophisticated way of thinking about causal influences in distress is also necessary because some of the most important causal influences are particularly difficult to research empirically. We can understand these difficulties in a number of ways:

- Many important influences are difficult to explore prospectively: for example, the impact of parenting and child-rearing practices only becomes apparent many years later. This is one of the reasons why, although studies of attachment are relevant to understandings of distress, their findings are often considered controversial.
- Important influences like parenting and education occur over long periods of time, happen in many different places, and usually involve a variable range of significant others (for example teachers, grandparents, family friends). No observational study could possibly encompass *all* of the facets of all of these influences, and no observational study could encompass *any* of them without potentially transforming what was observed.
- Many important influences are not amenable to experimental manipulation: for example, distress is patterned according to socio-economic status, gender and ethnicity, but none of these variables can be manipulated in experiments. Whilst they can be used to stratify samples and form groups, our understanding of their impact is always dependent upon prior interpretation, contextualization and categorization.
- Many important influences are sensitive, shaming and difficult to speak about: for example, abuse, trauma, and some adverse life events and their effects. As a result, people with these kinds of experience may seem to be under-represented in some samples simply because they choose not to disclose them to clinicians and researchers (Read, van Os, Morrison & Ross, 2005).
- Many important influences upon distress are difficult for the person themselves to identify, so might not always be spontaneously mentioned. Over and above the ways that shame and embarrassment may prevent people from telling all that they know about their own experiences, there is the issue that – just like the rest of us – people experiencing distress are unable to ever fully articulate the influences upon their lives. Clinical experience shows that distress is always somewhat **ineffable**, or incapable of being fully expressed in words (Smail, 2005). So even where the important influences helping to produce a person's distress are not especially shameful, their significance might nevertheless not be recognized, so might simply not be noticed.
- Many important influences are mediated by their *meaning* in people's lives. Meaning is notoriously difficult to quantify and is always bound up with the minutiae of people's specific experiences.

Amongst other things, these difficulties have implications for how we take account of the views of mental health service users. In this book we have attempted to incorporate these views, in order to give people's own experiences and understandings the importance they deserve. But as these difficulties suggest, taking seriously what service users say does not mean that clinicians should discount or ignore other sources of knowledge and evidence. The views of service users are absolutely vital if we are ever to create properly *human* interventions when faced with the distress of others. At the same time, as clinicians go about their work they must remember that people themselves may not always be able to say just why they feel and act as they do. There is a subtle but important difference between, on the one hand, listening sensitively to an account and taking it seriously, and on the other hand, treating it as a complete explanation for the person's distress. This difference means that is always clinically necessary to interpret what people say, as well as to listen empathically to what they are saying.

Researching causality

Given the nature and the extent of these difficulties, it should be clear that conducting research into causal influences upon distress is far from straightforward. Before we consider some of the evidence, then, we must briefly reflect upon how it is produced. Whilst this research is conducted using a wide range of methods and designs, amongst the more common are experimental methods, surveys, epidemiological studies, case studies and qualitative methods. Table 6.1 summarizes the strengths and weaknesses of each of these approaches, and we explain these in more detail below.

Experimental methods

Research evidence is often said to be organized into a hierarchy, within which the best evidence is frequently said to come from controlled experiments. Although in practice experiments can be extremely complex, the principles underpinning them are relatively simple and will already be familiar to many readers:

- A relevant population is defined
- A random sample of this population is compiled
- People in the sample are randomly allocated to either an experimental or a control group
- People in the experimental group are subject to some kind of intervention, people in the control group are not
- Appropriate measures are taken from both groups, both before and after the intervention
- If the before–after difference for the experimental group is significantly greater than for the control group, the intervention is said to have been influential.

There is no question that experiments are a powerful means of demonstrating causality. However, as even this very simplified description shows, applying them to the study of causal influences upon distress is difficult. One obvious issue is that experiments are designed to measure the impact of something that can be manipulated, such as an intervention: but most often when we are studying causal influences upon distress we are not actually intervening or manipulating anything. Rather than doing something to our research participants, we

Table 6.1 **Research methods for studying causality in distress**

Method	Strengths	Weaknesses
Experiments	Definitive test of causal order Clearly defined variables	Unable to manipulate core variables Low external validity Artificial samples Difficult to measure meaning
Surveys	Large, ecologically valid samples Address (reports of) actual experience Some grasp of causal order	Reliance on self-report Sampling frame biases
Epidemiology	Clinically comprehensive samples Addresses (medical records of) actual experience	Uses unreliable and invalid diagnostic categories Endorses biomedical approach
Case studies	Generative of new hypotheses Detailed exploration Identify rare sequences Some grasp of meaning	Impossible to generalize
Qualitative studies	Some grasp of causal order Detailed analyses of small samples Analyses of social and personal meanings of distress Generative of new hypotheses	Unable to test hypotheses Frequently difficult to generalize Often difficult to relate to quantitative findings

are observing, recording, measuring and classifying things that have already happened to them. We are using these observations and measurements to look for both associations (for example, between levels of trauma and levels of distress) and differences (for example, between people with different experiences and different kinds of distress). But the traumas and experiences have already occurred: neither they nor their effects can be manipulated experimentally.

There are other well-known problems surrounding the use of experiments to establish causality with respect to distress. First, their power to conclusively demonstrate causal influence comes at a cost: narrowness of scope (Cartwright, 2007). Experiments have high **internal validity** (they enable experimenters to be confident that the experimental variables were related to any observed changes) but low **external validity** (it is difficult to generalize to the real world from the artificial circumstances they require). They demand rigorous selection and very high levels of control of all the relevant variables in order to be valid: but these levels of selection and control inevitably limit their wider relevance. Second, crucial elements of personal meaning and subtle nuances of agency and choice are difficult to operationalize as variables and manipulate within experimental designs. This can sometimes mean that investigators use relatively crude indicators that fail to capture significant variation and may obscure important effects. Third, many experiments are conducted using **convenience samples** – participants who happened to be readily available, and whom we imagine are suitable. The most commonly sampled group is university psychology students, but people in other institutions (hospitals, schools, prisons) are also widely used. Underpinning the use of such samples is an assumption that all people are much more alike than they are different, but with respect to the causes of distress this assumption is questionable.

In their discussion of the value and limitations of using experiments to explore causal influences upon distress, Mirowsky and Ross (1989) observe that ethical and practical constraints mean that is usually impossible to reproduce experimentally the kinds of influences and effects known to be important with respect to distress. It would, for example, be both ethically unacceptable and practically difficult to induce enduring and profound unhappiness in experimental participants. So instead, experiments often use weak or limited manipulations: for example, different small monetary rewards might be given to explore the association between wealth and happiness. The superficial plausibility of this procedure may blind us to two obvious facts. First, all of the rewards will actually be *tiny* compared to both the levels of income and the income differentials (the substantial relative differences in income between rich and poor) that exist in everyday life. Second, all of the rewards will be fleeting and temporary, compared to the longer durations involved in everyday work and employment.

Alternately, analogue experiments are sometimes used: for example, researchers might try to experimentally test the hypothesis that overwhelmingly difficult or impossible circumstances produce distress. They could do so by giving one group an anagram that can be solved, and another a sequence of letters that looks like an anagram but does not make any word: they could then measure levels of frustration and unhappiness in both groups. But as Mirowsky and Ross (1989, p. 69) say: 'In what way is the unsolvable anagram like a life of poverty, being laid off, or having cancer? Can it really represent them? How much is the experimentally induced frustration and annoyance like the demoralisation, powerlessness, depression, anxiety and malaise felt by the poor, the unemployed and the sick?'

Finally, Mirowsky and Ross (1989) observe that researchers also conduct what they term 'fake' experiments: studies that look like experiments into the causal influences of distress, but are not. One of the most common fakes is the substitute experiment and the most widely-used substitution is to replace humans with animals. When making the substitution, the researcher assumes that all of the important processes and contents relevant to the phenomenon of interest operate, in equal measure, in the substitution. But is this assumption justified? For example, is the learned helplessness of a dog subjected to inescapable electric shocks (Seligman, 1975) really just the same, in all of its details, processes, contents and meanings, as the profound misery of a human unable to change a difficult situation?

Survey methods

Survey methods rely upon interviewing large numbers of people: face to face, by telephone or online. When used to identify causal influences upon distress, surveys typically ask about the occurrence of a predefined range of experiences associated with distress (such as changes in appetite, weight and sleep patterns, difficulty concentrating, hearing voices, feelings of persecution, and so on). Very often clinical interview schedules are used; the interviewer will first be trained in using them, and may already have clinical experience.

If large random samples and reliable and valid clinical instruments are used, surveys can give a reasonably good picture of the mental health of a population. By looking for patterns of association and difference in the level and nature of people's experiences of distress, and associating these with demographic and other information (e.g. about life events or traumatic experiences), researchers can use survey data to draw inferences about the causes of distress.

Compared to experiments, surveys have the advantage of working with people's reports of their actual experience. They explore real variation in stable characteristics such as age, gender and ethnicity, and investigate whether differences in these characteristics are consistently associated with differences in the experiences of distress that people report.

Most surveys are cross-sectional: they look at people's reports of their experiences at a single point in time. This means that they are less effective at identifying causal sequences, although Mirowsky and Ross (1989) show that there are nevertheless ways in which causality can be explored using survey data. For example, some characteristics (e.g. year of birth) are stable and precede data-gathering, so can be treated causally. Similarly, there are established sequences in everyday life that can be used to establish causality: levels of income, for example, are caused by (rather than causal of) different kinds of employment, and people have to first get married before they can get divorced. Surveys can also be used longitudinally: people can be asked about both their income and their experiences of distress at one point in time, and then again ten years later. If levels of distress at time 2 are associated with levels of income at time 1, any causal association between them must flow from the earlier income level to the later distress.

But survey methods, too, have their problems. One is that they entirely depend upon the preconceptions of the researcher: issues and experiences not probed during the survey will simply never appear in the research, no matter how important they might actually be in people's lives. This limitation means that the ability of surveys to work with the meanings of relationships and life events is also quite restricted. Another problem is that surveys rely on self-report data: this means that they can only ever include what participants are both willing and able to tell researchers. Finally, there is the issue of how participants are identified: what *sampling frame* is used. Although surveys do not usually restrict themselves to institutional populations (e.g. university students or hospital patients) they always require some systematic basis for selecting participants. Common sampling frames include

the electoral register, or the telephone book. Other methods involve knocking on every tenth door in areas selected for their demographic characteristics and asking for an interview, or stopping people out shopping in town centres. However, all of these methods are quasi-random rather than random, and all have slightly different potential to reach the entire population. To some degree, each of these sampling frames will tend to exclude those people with the most chaotic and disordered lifestyles: people who don't register for elections, have telephone landlines, open the door to strangers with clipboards or make themselves available to interviewers in town centres. But with respect to the causes of distress, these might be the very people whose experiences are the most relevant.

Epidemiological studies

Epidemiology is the branch of medicine that involves the study of how frequently different diseases occur in different populations. Variations in the prevalence of diseases are linked to other variables: demographic characteristics, occupation and employment histories, lifestyle choices, and so on. As with surveys, researchers collect this information about relatively large samples and then look for associations and differences: this then allows inferences about causality to be made.

With respect to the causes of distress, epidemiology currently provides the bulk of the available evidence. However, it should immediately be clear that this evidence is somewhat problematic. Because it is medically led, epidemiological research works with the idea that distress has a medical basis and takes the form of organic diseases associated with psychiatric diagnostic categories. This introduces difficult-to-quantify distortions into the evidence, since these categories are not sufficiently reliable and valid and do not relate to demonstrable organic diseases (see Chapters 4 and 5).

A strength of epidemiological research is that its medical character means it can more readily access and include in-patient, clinic and hospital populations, as well as community samples. Epidemiologists frequently use clinical information gathered by doctors and other professionals, rather than information supplied directly by those experiencing distress. This means that the direct consent of these people is not always needed, so it might sometimes be more effective than survey research at gathering information about people with the most extreme levels of distress.

Epidemiological research is nevertheless subject to all of the difficulties associated with the biomedical model of distress. It frequently presents researchers who do not wish to adopt this model with a dilemma (Rogers & Pilgrim, 2003). On the one hand it often provides the most comprehensive picture of associations between demographic and lifestyle characteristics and distress. On the other, its use can seem to imply some endorsement of the biomedical model, because reproducing the results of research produced using diagnostic categories can have the effect of making those categories seem more 'real', more useful, than they are.

Case studies

Case study research has a long and respected history in medicine and many other scientific disciplines: large parts of astronomy, for example, are about single cases such as particular planets. However, case studies have fallen out of favour in recent years as experimental methods and randomized controlled trials (RCTs) have increasingly been promoted. Whilst it is impossible to generalize from case studies, they are nevertheless useful for generating new hypotheses, exploring complex phenomena, identifying rare occurrences, and beginning to identify some of the meanings associated with complex quantitative findings. With respect to distress, famous case studies include Freud's therapeutic work with Dora and 'The Wolfman', both of which contributed to the development of psychoanalytic theory and therapy.

Qualitative research

Qualitative research includes many different types of method. These methods differ greatly with respect to the kinds of data they use, and in both the kinds of assumptions they make about the nature of the world (ontology) and the kinds of things we can know about it (epistemology). In general, however, qualitative research deals with language, images, and other non-numerical data: qualities, not quantities. It is primarily concerned with what people say, rather than how often they say it, and it tends to work directly with this information rather than using rating scales or questionnaires to turn it into numerical indices.

Qualitative research is not designed to test hypotheses, so does not usually feature in discussions of the relative influence of different causal influences upon distress. By its nature, most qualitative research has little to say about such things, although Dehue (2002) suggests that ethnography can be used effectively in this way. Ethnography is a qualitative method, first used in anthropology, that combines diaries, observations and reports from participant observers (people who take part in a situation but also record their activities) with evidence from other sources: documents, codes of practice, memos, regulations, instructions and guidance given in meetings and training sessions, and so on. Clearly, a strength of ethnography is that it does not just rely upon self-report, and Dehue argues that it can produce complex and sophisticated accounts of how causal influences play themselves out.

Nevertheless, for the most part, qualitative research is useful for exploring the *texture* of causality, and charting how the *meaning* of different causal influences impacts upon people's experience. Because it engages with more of the minutiae of experience, qualitative research can uncover some of the many different ways in which contingent causal influences upon distress operate. Indeed, only qualitative research can engage directly with the contributions of personal agency and personal meaning to both shaping and ameliorating distress. Qualitative research can also assist with the generation of new hypotheses and the investigation of complex cases, and in recent years it has increasingly been used to study experiences of distress (Harper, 2008).

Summary

All of the methods used to research causal influences upon distress have both weaknesses and strengths: all introduce more or less subtle biases into the patterns of findings they produce. Experimental research is often held up as the most powerful, but with respect to questions of causality in distress it is often quite limited. Survey research is probably the least overtly biased; however, the majority of evidence has been gathered using epidemiological research methods that rely upon psychiatric diagnostic categories. Qualitative research is not designed to demonstrate causality, but may nonetheless have an important complementary role because of its ability to explore meaning and subjectivity.

Recognized causal influences

When the many sources of evidence about causal influences upon distress are reviewed, certain influences can be seen to recur time and again. Whatever research method is used, and whatever psychiatric diagnoses may be invoked, researchers very often identify broadly similar clusters of influence upon people's experiences. These clusters can be categorized as relational, biological and social, and each can be broken down into various sub-categories (see Table 6.2). However, it is important to note that the literature does make reference to other possible causes of distress than those we have listed. Age, for example, is often thought to interact with these other influences and to modify their impacts in various ways (see the discussion of lifelines in Chapter 4). Moreover, we could have said much more about each of the categories of influence we do identify (and in fact we will do so at many points throughout the book: for example, in each of the chapters in the second part. So this account is not intended to be comprehensive: merely to give you an adequate grounding on which to begin thinking about the primary causal influences that researchers have studied.

Table 6.2 **Causal influences upon distress**

Relational	Biological	Social
Families	Neurotransmitters	Inequalities
Early experience	Brain structure	Gender
Trauma and abuse	Genetics	Ethnicity

Relational influences

When people think about the causes of distress, one of their first guesses is likely to be about relationship factors. Did the person have an unhappy childhood? Have they got friends? Have they been involved in an argument or conflict of some kind? While it might seem intuitively obvious that people's relationships, especially in early family life, are influential in the development of later distress, this is actually one of the most controversial ideas in psychiatry, especially in relation to the more severe forms of distress.

There is obviously considerable interaction and overlap between different types of relationship influences. For the sake of clarity we will consider this large area under three subheadings: family relationships, early experience, and trauma and abuse.

Family relationships

The causal role of family relationships is widely accepted in some forms of distress, such as the experiences associated with diagnoses of depression, eating disorders and borderline personality disorder. However, it is controversial when applied to the diagnosis of schizophrenia. The issue surfaced in a particularly heated form in the 1960s, when it was associated with unorthodox psychiatrists such as R. D. Laing in Britain and Thomas Szasz in the USA (see Chapter 2). The quote below is typical of the response that is still generated by this debate:

> Theories of family pathogenesis have in the past been widespread and are still held by some professionals. This has resulted in relatives being blamed and stigmatised for the patient's illness.
>
> Tarrier (1991, p. 483)

In other words, any implication that family relationships might have a causal role in the development of experiences associated with diagnoses of schizophrenia runs the risk, then and now, of being characterized as blaming the parents, ignoring the service user's suffering, and denying the reality of their distress.

For this reason, it is important to be very clear about the terms of the debate. In line with our earlier discussion about the nature of causality, we need to bear a number of general principles in mind when presenting arguments for the causal role of family and other relationships in distress, particularly in the severer forms of breakdown. Such factors, if they exist, will be neither necessary nor sufficient; in other words, not everyone from a disturbed family background will experience distress in later life, and nor will the presence of such experiences inevitably lead to long-term difficulties. If family relationships are a factor, they are highly likely not to be the only factor; causes will be multiple, complex and over-determined. This might, in principle, allow a role for biological influences such as inherited temperament. In any individual case, we are likely to find that the various factors have acted together synergistically to magnify the final effects. For example, stressful family relationships may lead to a lack of confidence, which may make it harder to find or keep employment, which may in turn mean that the person spends more time at home where relationships are stressful, and so on.

In such a controversial area, we need to be as sure as we can that the association between family relationships and distress is, to a degree, a causal one, not simply a correlation. We can help to avoid implications of blame if we remember that parents are at least partly the product of their own families of origin, and so on in an infinite regression. Moreover, families are themselves shaped by powerful social pressures which may place limits on their ability to care for their children, and – as Smail (2005) observes – are primarily conduits for external influence, rather than the origins of all that occurs. As Wilkinson & Pickett (2009, p. 209) put it: 'When parents suffer more adversity, family life suffers'. Indeed, they suggest that the 'poor parenting' that is said to characterize some deprived families can perhaps be understood not as inadequacy, but as an adaptive response to adverse environments. Some parents may believe that children need to be treated harshly in order to be tough enough to survive the environment they are born into.

Family therapists would start from the position that all parents are doing their best given the circumstances they find themselves in. Moreover, loose categories like schizophrenia will include all sorts of individual causal pathways, which may or may not implicate family tensions in any particular case.

With these many caveats, a properly scientific account cannot afford to ignore the possibility that family relationships may sometimes contribute to the more severe forms of distress, as well as to others. And in fact there is a large body of evidence from various theoretical orientations (including psychoanalytic, systemic, humanistic and cognitive–behavioural) which suggests that relationships, especially but not only childhood ones, do have a causal role in the emergence of all forms of distress (Harrop & Trower, 2003). In relation to the experiences associated with a diagnosis of schizophrenia, a pattern has been identified of extreme difficulty in separating and helping young adults to achieve independence; blurred boundaries in relationships; identity confusion; confused and contradictory communications; emotional and physical/sexual intrusiveness; difficulty in dealing with anger and sexuality; and social isolation (see Johnstonea, 1999, for a summary). Some of the key studies are longitudinal and prospective, and provide good evidence for a causal link (Doane, West, Goldstein, Rodnick & Jones, 1981; Goldstein, 1985).

While much of this literature dates back several decades, it has been supported by more recent findings that suggest that even where there is a family history of schizophrenia diagnoses (which is often said to indicate some genetic or temperamental component), the quality of family relationships is the key influence upon whether offspring do eventually break down (Tienari et al., 1994).

It should be noted, however, that the argument that family relationships can be causal influences upon the more severe forms of mental distress is still disputed by some. In part, this may be because thinking about causal influences frequently fails to adequately recognize their complexity. Additionally, many accounts that implicate families tend to treat them as relatively isolated systems, rather than understanding that they are also subject to much wider external powers and influences. Consequently, the currently popular version of family intervention in psychosis, which is based on the concept of High Expressed Emotion (EE: a measure of hostility, criticism and over-involvement on the part of the relatives of those given a diagnosis of psychosis) distances itself from suggesting that High EE is a causal influence. Instead, this approach treats family influence merely as a factor that may influence recovery once a psychotic breakdown has occurred.

Early experience

Additional evidence for the importance of family dynamics as a factor in later distress comes from research on attachment. Attachment theory describes how the quality of our early bonds with caregivers acts as a template for later relationships, and a context in which we learn how to empathize, regulate our emotions, and so on (see Chapter 4). The theory proposes that we are all influenced by our early attachments, but there is growing evidence of their particular relevance in either protecting us from, or creating vulnerability to, distress in later life. Early experiences of being loved, cared for and wanted seem to help people survive the impact of stress in later life. Conversely, experiences of feeling unwanted, insecure and marginalized seem to make people more likely to experience clinical distress, and less able to cope with difficult events. And as we have already seen (Chapter 4), there is growing evidence of the effects of both good and poor attachments on the development of the brain.

There is thus an emerging consensus that disturbed attachment relationships are a risk factor for a range of psychiatric diagnoses, including psychosis and personality disorders (Liotti & Gumley, 2008). People given a diagnosis of borderline personality disorder, in particular, are often seen as having a failure of early attachments, leading to a lifelong difficulty in regulating emotions and forming stable relationships (Bateman & Fonagy, 2006). The pathway to psychosis is less clear, although it has been suggested that infant attachment disorganization may decrease the ability to deal with the overwhelming feelings arising from traumatic life events (Liotti & Gumley, 2008; Moskowitz, Schafer & Dorahy, 2008).

Trauma and abuse

This area overlaps with the two previous ones. We now have strong evidence that physical, emotional and sexual abuse in childhood can be causal influences upon distress later in life, as can violence, rape and domestic abuse in adulthood. This includes the effects of domestic violence on both adults (mainly women) and children. Domestic abuse is witnessed by an estimated 750,000 children in the UK every year (Department of Health, 2006).

However, abuse is neither a necessary, nor a sufficient, cause of breakdown: by no means has everyone with psychiatric difficulties been abused, and the majority of people who are abused do not experience clinical levels of distress. Nor does trauma and abuse necessarily occur within the family; bullying at school, bereavement, severe physical illness and disability, battlefield combat, torture, or being caught up in a natural disaster like an earthquake, can all be extremely traumatic. As discussed earlier, such influences may be synergistic. Someone with a secure attachment is likely to be more able to cope with subsequent experiences of trauma or abuse, whereas someone lacking this basic early security will be more vulnerable to the effects of trauma, especially if it occurs at the hands of the primary caregivers and is part of the same pattern of neglect.

Awareness of the prevalence of abuse in the lives of people with psychiatric problems has fluctuated over the years. Although the link was acknowledged by both Freud and Jung, as Judith Herman reminds us in her book 'Trauma and recovery', 'The knowledge of horrible events periodically intrudes into public awareness but is rarely retained for long. Denial, repression, and dissociation operate on a social as well as an individual level' (Herman, 1997, p. 2).

Currently, the part that trauma plays in the development of more long-lasting and serious distress is still controversial. John Read and others (Read et al., 2005; Larkin & Morrison, 2006) have summarized a range of evidence which demonstrates that although there is a general relationship between child abuse and adult pathology of all types, this has typically been ignored or downplayed in relation to diagnoses of psychosis (see Chapter 11). Evidence that this is a causal link comes from the fact that there is a dose-dependent relationship between the number and severity of types of trauma, and the likelihood of a later diagnosis. In fact, childhood abuse appears to increase the risk of being given a diagnosis of psychosis by up to nine-fold, and experiencing the most severe types of abuse raises the risk 48-fold, a relationship that holds in prospective studies (Janssen et al., 2004). The link also holds after controlling for factors such as substance abuse, ethnicity, gender and education (Bebbington et al., 2004).

This perspective is gaining acceptance in countries including New Zealand and the UK; for example a briefing paper from the Department of Health in the UK states that 'Violence and abuse is a core mental health issue affecting 70% or more of women service users and a significant number of men ... The effects of child sexual abuse can be a significant contributory factor to all diagnoses and presentations from depression, anxiety, eating and obsessive compulsive disorders and peri-natal mental ill health through to bipolar disorder, psychosis/schizophrenia, dual diagnosis and personality disorder ... Department of Health policy is that adult mental health services should acknowledge and address the links between violence and abuse and mental ill health' (Department of Health, 2008, p. 1).

Biological influences

As we have seen (Chapter 4), biology plays a part in all human experiences, both 'normal' and 'abnormal': regardless of any causal influence it might exert, it certainly helps to *enable* every experience we ever have (see Box 4.3). However, we must beware of simplistic cause-and-effect explanations that see distress as the straightforward consequence of faulty genes, biochemical imbalances, brain defects and so on. The distinction between mind and body, nature and nurture, is to a large extent an artificial one. Our bodies allow us to have certain types of experience – to see, to hear, to move, to form relationships with others – and these in turn feed back into the development of our physical selves, starting very early in life when a baby's brain forms new synaptic connections in response to its relationship with a caregiver. This means that, even when we seem to be seeing biological causes of distress, we might actually be seeing the longer term consequences of earlier social and relationship influences whose effects are now encoded in biological processes. There is nevertheless much discussion of the role of possible biological causes of distress, which we will summarize under three headings: neurotransmitters, brain structure and genetics.

Neurotransmitters

In books on psychiatry and abnormal psychology it is commonly stated as a fact that when people are given such diagnoses as schizophrenia or bipolar disorder, their problems are caused by 'biochemical imbalances'. The biochemicals in question are neurotransmitters, chemicals in the brain that carry messages between cells by travelling across the gap, or synapse, between them. It is believed that mood is regulated by neurotransmitters (among their many other functions), although this theory is itself speculative. In fact, we know relatively little about the extraordinarily complex ways in which the brain and its 200-plus neurotransmitters work. There are a number of practical difficulties which currently limit our knowledge and hence our ability to draw conclusions. These include the following:

There is currently no way of directly studying or measuring neurotransmitter levels in the live human brain.

It is possible to take indirect measurements, via metabolites in the blood or urine, but these have failed to find consistent evidence of altered neurotransmitter levels in people given a psychiatric diagnosis.

The brain's trillions of synapses contain different kinds of neurotransmitter receptors (more than a dozen for serotonin, for example), and many neurotransmitters seem to serve more than one function. Consequently we are a long way from being able to make precise and definite statements about how any of these transmitters work.

Evidence suggests that the phrase 'biochemical imbalance' is misleading: neurotransmitters are in a constant state of flux and change as the body seeks to regulate its functions (Rose, 1997): they do not get stuck in a state of 'imbalance'.

It is important to emphasize, once again, that in drawing attention to these problems we are not denying the role of biology or biochemistry in distress. Neurotransmitters are involved in everything we think, feel or do. Statements such as 'neurotransmitters are *thought to be* involved with major depression', often found in pharmaceutical company leaflets, are self-evidently true, but they tell us very little about causation, because neurotransmitters are undoubtedly involved in every other kind of human activity as well.

In fact, much of the evidence about neurotransmitters and distress has worked backwards from studies of medication (see Chapter 8). Drugs described as anti-depressants were found to act significantly on the serotonin system, giving rise to the hypothesis that serotonin system defects cause the experiences that lead to a diagnosis of depression. Similarly, drugs described as antipsychotics act significantly on the dopamine system, and this gave rise to the dopamine hypothesis of schizophrenia. But just because (for example) artificially increasing the amount of serotonin is helpful for some people who have been given a diagnosis of depression, their sadness was not necessarily caused by an initial lack of serotonin. This would be rather like claiming that, because aspirin can alleviate headaches, headaches are caused by a lack of aspirin. These kinds of claims are simplistic and questionable: both headaches and clinical sadness can have many causes, and both are undoubtedly enabled by multiple brain systems operating in parallel.

There are numerous discussions of the role of neurotransmitters elsewhere in this book:

- in Chapter 4, 'Biology'
- in the 'psychiatric medication' section of Chapter 8, 'Interventions'
- in relation to the various experiences of distress in Chapters 9–13.

You should refer to the information in these chapters if you want to know more about how neurotransmitters have been related to specific kinds of distressing experience, or if you want to better understand the effects of medication. But with respect to causal influences our conclusion is that – whilst no-one can yet know for certain, either way – the evidence suggests that it is most useful to think of neurotransmitter systems primarily *as enabling* experiences of distress rather than as *causing* them in some simple way.

Brain structure

Investigations into abnormalities of brain structure in distress have produced mixed results, and the overall picture is inconsistent and contradictory. For example, studies of people given a diagnosis of schizophrenia have variously found enlarged ventricles, temporal lobe abnormalities, cerebral asymmetries, a thicker corpus callosum, a thinner corpus callosum, abnormalities of basal ganglia and the cerebellum, and reduced brain volume. Whilst there is a considerable body of evidence of this kind, there is little consensus between studies as to which neurological features (if any) are characteristic of schizophrenia, and there is certainly no abnormality which is universal. Nor is there any abnormality which is found only in people with one diagnosis, such as schizophrenia, and not in people with any other diagnosis. Moreover, control groups in these studies are not always adequate, sample sizes are frequently small, and results are rarely replicated. Sometimes it is claimed that this confusing picture arises because different patterns of abnormality cause different kinds of schizophrenia. Whilst this might seem reasonable (since different brain regions and systems enable different aspects of psychological functioning), in fact it multiplies the difficulties, because neither are there consistent patterns of evidence linking specific brain abnormalities to specific impairments of mental health.

The conceptual issues that apply here are similar to those in the discussion of neurotransmitters. Changes in brain structure, if they were to be reliably established, could just as easily be the result as the cause of distress: we know, for example, that experiences such as early trauma and neglect can impact on both the structure and functioning of the brain (see Chapters 4 and 11). We also know that even mundane, everyday activities such as taxi driving are associated with statistically significant changes in the size of brain structures (Maguire et al., 2000). Similarly, some structural changes may simply reflect ongoing processes and may not be permanent: for example, ventricular size is known to vary according to dehydration, diet, medication status and pregnancy. It is also very likely that some brain changes (which are often only identified at autopsy) are the consequence of factors such as long-term use of medication. Post-mortem evidence that the brains of people given diagnoses of schizophrenia sometimes contain more dopamine receptors has been used to support the idea that schizophrenia is caused by dopamine system irregularities. However, a known effect of the medication that inhibits the action of dopamine in the brain is to cause the brain to produce more dopamine receptors.

Genetics

As we explained in Chapter 4, in recent years the search for single genes for schizophrenia and other diagnoses has been replaced by a recognition that the situation is bound to be far more complex. Researchers now talk about a great number of genes, each of which is hypothesized to contribute a small potential risk. However, as with brain biochemistry, our knowledge of genetics is still limited. Although scientists have recently completed the enormous task of decoding the human genome – making a list of the sequences of DNA that make us the living creatures we are – some experts have suggested that we are at least a century away from actually understanding what all of this means and how it works. We have copied out a massive book whose language is still largely incomprehensible to us. We do know that the processes involved are extremely complex: gene activity *always* takes place within an environment which influences its course, each gene may make several proteins, and each protein may perform more than one job. Conversely, a whole number of genes may interact to produce a single physical characteristic.

Moreover, many geneticists now acknowledge that there is a much greater role for the environment than had originally been suspected, simply because it was found that we possess far fewer genes than originally assumed. So far scientists have only been able to identify specific genes for a very small number of physical illnesses, such as cystic fibrosis and Huntington's chorea, but these relatively simple forms of transmission, in which it does make sense to talk about a gene for a certain condition, are atypical. Despite regular optimistic announcements in the media, no gene or set of genes has been definitively identified for any functional psychiatric diagnosis. Announcements about 'breakthroughs', which regularly appear in the press, refer not to the discovery of genes themselves, but to markers, indicators that certain genes may (or may not) be found nearby. Identifying a marker is a long way from finding the possible defective gene that may be associated with it – it took ten years to move from marker to gene in the case of Huntington's chorea. Commonly, research that finds initial indications of a gene or marker is based upon small sample sizes or inadequate control groups, and is not subsequently replicated.

In practice it is extremely difficult to untangle the relative contributions of nature and nurture, and even studies that superficially appear to do so – such as behavioural genetic studies using the twin method – in practice fail to separate these influences. Many studies also have methodological problems, and the general picture is that the more rigorous the study, the smaller the genetic contribution that emerges. This conclusion is reinforced by more recent studies of molecular genetics, which have failed to find significant, replicable genetic effects in association with functional psychiatric diagnoses, even for diagnoses such as schizophrenia for which strong claims of genetic causation have been made. It is also consistent with the clinical observation that most people with a diagnosis of schizophrenia have no relatives with the same diagnosis.

As if all this wasn't complicated enough, the growing field of epigenetics is showing that social and psychological experience – in other words, nurture – can change the way that genes are expressed even during someone's lifetime, and even more remarkably, that such changes can be passed on to one's offspring (see Box 4.6). For example, stress from being separated from one's mother can affect gene expression, and thus the nurture of one generation might influence the nature of the next one. Epigenetic processes have already been identified in people with a range of psychiatric diagnoses.

However, before we start talking about epigenetic aspects of schizophrenia and other diagnoses, we must remember a key point that was raised in Chapter 5. In psychiatric diagnoses the 'symptoms' are not bodily ones such as rashes, tumours or stomach pains, but *beliefs, experiences and behaviour*. Patients are said to be confused in their thinking, or withdrawn, or afraid of voices in their heads, or whatever. It is clear what is, or could be, inherited in diseases such as cystic fibrosis. It is not at all obvious how the beliefs and behaviours which are said to be the 'symptoms' of mental illness could be determined by or passed on in the genes, even in principle. Beliefs, behaviours and feelings arise in response to particular situations, past and present, and can only be understood in those contexts. The link from genes to behaviour is almost infinitely long and complex, and includes all the developmental, environmental, social and cultural influences that a human being is exposed to, not to mention their own capacity to make sense of all these and their capacity for choice in deciding how to react.

Of course, none of this is to deny the significance of genetics. As with neurotransmitters, it is only common sense to accept that we are a mixture of both what we have inherited and the environmental influences on us. However, there remains an important paradox that undermines claims that there are *specific* genetic causal influences upon (for example) schizophrenia. The paradox arises because, on average, these diagnoses are associated with impaired relationships, which

means that **reproductive fitness** – the ability to pass on genes to the next generation – is also impaired. This in turn means that the incidence of schizophrenia should be falling gradually, year on year, as the relevant genes become less prevalent in the population. But instead, the incidence of schizophrenia diagnoses remains relatively stable. Fluctuations in the incidence of this and other diagnoses seem to be largely in response to social and economic shifts, and do not follow the continuous downward trend that specific genetic influence would predict.

Because we are still such a long way from being able to be clear about how genetic and environmental influences combine to produce distress, it is impossible to come to a final resolution of this paradox. However, one distinct possibility is that any genetic influences associated with distress are actually non-pathological. Rather than being intrinsically disease-related, these genes may also be associated with outcomes and behaviours that are adaptive.

For example, it may be that sensitivity and reactivity to the emotions of others has a genetic component. Being able to understand and respond to other people's feelings is adaptive, and may be associated with many positive outcomes: forming and maintaining good relationships, being an effective employee or manager, functioning well in groups, and so on. However, exactly the same capacity may be less adaptive when people find themselves in extremely toxic, highly emotionally-demanding, stressful, traumatic or abusive situations. In such circumstances, what is a generally adaptive genetic trait might be unhelpful, since it will mean that the effects of stress, trauma and abuse are felt more keenly. This fits with the results of the Tienari et al. (1994) study discussed earlier, where psychosis, even in those with a family history of difficulties, emerged only in the context of unfavourable family dynamics. This led the researchers to suggest that the inherited factor might be something akin to a general sensitivity to the environment.

Social influences

Psychiatry has on the whole been reluctant to acknowledge the role of social factors in the development of distress, although the tradition known as social psychiatry does focus on social and cultural contexts, drawing on related fields such as sociology and social psychology. It has debated the role of **social drift** (sometimes called social selection) versus **social causation** as explanations for the higher prevalence of distress in more deprived sections of the community. Social drift suggests that people with psychiatric problems tend to move down the social scale as their ability to cope with more highly skilled jobs diminishes, and lower salaries or unemployment force them to move to cheaper neighbourhoods. Conversely, social causation argues that the greater stresses of such lifestyles and environments contribute to the development of mental health problems in the first place.

Critics have argued that social drift is a less challenging position for psychiatry, because it allows for a primary role for biological causal factors. Common sense, and our discussions about the complexity of causal mechanisms, suggests that both social causation and social drift could apply. In any case, there is strong evidence for the relevance of both specific and general social factors in the development of distress, including extensive research clearly demonstrating the influence of social causation.

Social inequalities

There is a well-established general relationship between lower socio-economic status and higher rates of distress (Melzer, Fryers & Jenkins, 2004). In fact 'for nearly every kind of "mental illness", disease or disability ... poorer people are afflicted more than richer people, more often, more seriously, and for longer' (Gomm, 1996, p. 112). For example, having a parent with low socio-economic status more than triples the risk of being given a diagnosis of severe depression, even after controlling for family histories that might be thought to indicate genetic predisposition (Ritsher, Warner, Johnson & Dohrenwend, 2001). Similarly, the probability of being given a diagnosis of schizophrenia as an adult rises dramatically with increasing levels of deprivation at birth (Harrison, Gunnell, Glazebrook et al., 2001; Werner, Malaspina & Rabinowitz, 2001).

A series of classic studies by Brown and Harris (Brown, 1996) tried to unpick some of these links in relation to working class women in London. The researchers found that the women were more vulnerable to a diagnosis of depression if they had three or more children aged under 14 living at home, had lost their mother before the age of 11, and had no confiding relationship. Stressful events in the present triggered the onset of unhappiness, and these events tended to be class-related; for example, eviction from one's home or one's husband being sent to prison (Brown, Ni Bhrolchain & Harris, 1975).

Working class families are more likely to be poor, and a later study in the Brown and Harris series found that poverty doubled the risk of single mothers becoming distressed, probably by its direct and indirect influence on almost every other area of their lives (Brown & Moran, 1997). Population studies show that poor mental health is strongly associated with low income and material deprivation (Fryers, Melzer, Jenkins & Brugha, 2005). For example, people on incomes lower than the average wage are twice as likely to develop mental health problems (Social Exclusion Unit, 2004).

Given the general relationship between poverty and poor mental health, it is not surprising that unemployment shows the same relationship. Unemployed people are significantly more likely to be given diagnoses of depression, psychosis and other mental health problems (Warner, 2004). Once you have been given a diagnosis, your chances of getting another job are significantly reduced – in the UK, only 20% of people with mental health problems are in employment and only about a third of employers are willing to take them on (see Chapter 1).

The homeless, who are nearly always unemployed, have higher rates of mental health problems of all types than the general population. This includes a substantial proportion of people given diagnoses associated with the more severe difficulties, such as psychosis and personality disorder. There are also very high rates of drug and alcohol abuse. Rough sleepers (people forced to sleep wherever they can, sometimes outdoors) do worst, with 30–40% reporting difficulties including self-harm and experiences associated with diagnoses of depression and psychosis (MIND, 2009).

The picture we have painted so far is one in which restricted incomes, resources and opportunities mean that causes of distress arise more frequently and more intensely and, when this happens, disadvantaged people have fewer options for managing or absorbing the effects. They may lack material advantages: having more money, owning your own home in a better, more settled neighbourhood, having access to a car, being able to afford to go away on holiday. Many of the other relevant resources are less tangible, and are sometimes described as 'social capital': knowing who to ask for help, knowing how to approach institutions and authorities in order to resolve problems, having the confidence to persist in the face of bureaucratic obstacles, and so on.

Thus far, we have considered social factors that apply to specific individuals or groups. Two epidemiological summaries add weight to the role of general levels of social inequality across whole societies, and the impact this may have on the overall prevalence of distress. While both implicitly assume a biomedical model, taken together they make a very strong case for the causal role of social inequality in a whole range of ills.

Richard Wilkinson is an epidemiologist whose latest book summarizes thirty years of research into social inequalities (Wilkinson & Pickett, 2009). He presents an overwhelming set of data in support of the hypothesis that, above a certain level of material wealth, more equal societies do best on almost every measure. The bigger the gap between the richest and the poorest members of a society, the worse it performs on numerous measures – mental and physical health, violence, crime, obesity, education, community life, and so on. The crucial factor here turns out not to be absolute material deprivation, harmful although that can be, but relative inequality within societies, which ultimately affects the security and social cohesion of the whole community. Moreover, equality brings benefits across the board: for example, the richest members of the USA have a lower life expectancy than the poorest inhabitants of, say, Greece, which is a much more equal society. Everyone benefits from living in a country which is friendlier, happier and more

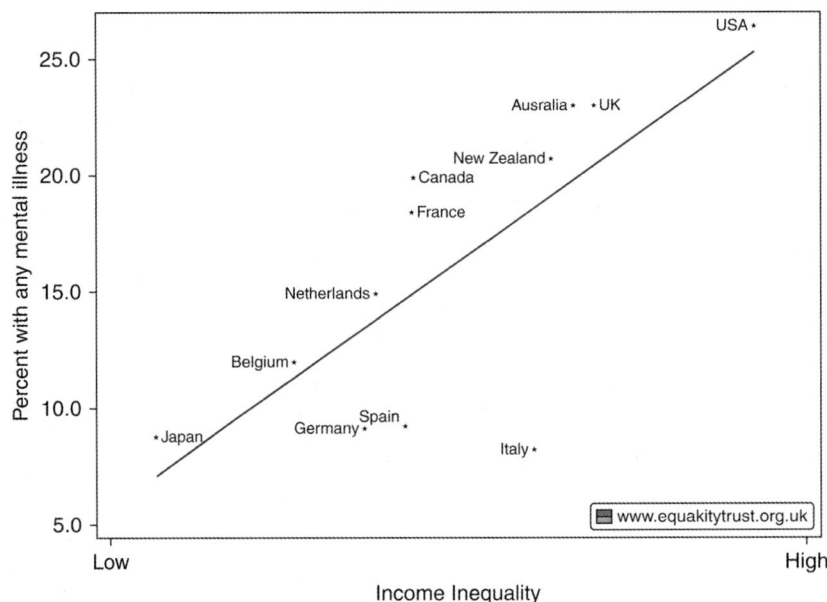

As this graph shows, there is a relationship between levels of income inequality and the prevalence of clinical distress

cohesive, with less violence and drug abuse and fewer people marginalized and excluded. Wilkinson's work is given added impetus by a recent World Health Organization report (WHO, 2009), which found that as countries get richer, rates of mental illness increase, and that this needs to be understood and treated less in terms of individual pathology and more as a response to the complex consequences of inequality.

The implications are very important. Despite the unquestioning use of biomedical concepts such as 'mental illness', these bodies of work give strong support to the role of social causation in distress. In fact, Wilkinson and Pickett (2009, p. 181) estimate that 'across whole populations, rates of mental illness are five times higher in the most unequal compared to the least unequal societies'. Currently, the UK and the USA both feature in the top four most unequal societies of the 23 that they surveyed. They suggest that 'if Britain became as equal as the four most equal societies (Japan, Norway, Sweden and Finland), mental illness might be more than halved', while if the USA did the same, 'mental illness ... might ... be cut by almost two-thirds' (2009, p. 261). However, the trend for both countries in the last 30 years has been in the opposite direction.

These epidemiological studies provide the background to our knowledge about specific social causal factors. They also demonstrate that, as mental health professionals and as a society, we need to look beyond interventions at an individual, family or service level, valuable though those may be in their own right. We also need to promote social justice in society as a whole.

Gender

Distress varies with gender, which influences the likelihood that men and women might suffer distress, the kinds of distress they are likely to experience, and the ways that psychiatric services respond to these needs. Men, for example, are more likely to be given diagnoses of alcohol or substance dependency, and of anti-social personality disorder. Women, by contrast, are more likely to receive diagnoses of eating disorders, anxiety, depression and borderline personality disorder, and to self-harm. A significant proportion of women are given a diagnosis of post-natal depression (Department of Health, 2002). Research into diagnoses such as schizophrenia and bipolar disorder does not always show such clear gender differences, although some studies suggest that men are more vulnerable than women to a diagnosis of schizophrenia (Scully et al., 2002).

Overall, however, it is women who are disproportionately represented in psychiatric statistics (Busfield, 1996), and there is now a substantial body of work which links this to the circumstances of women's lives (Department of Health, 2002). This includes the fact that gender is strongly associated with social inequality, due to the on-average differences in wealth and opportunity between men and women that exist in most societies: women earn less, hold lower status jobs, and are more often unemployed than men. Women who are lone parents and older women are especially likely to live in poverty. In addition, they are more likely than men to be the victims of domestic violence (between 18% and 30% of all women in the UK), sexual abuse (up to 30% of all girls) and all forms of sexual violence, including rape (Department of Health 2002). These factors are compounded if women come from a black/minority ethnic background, with the risk of racism supplying additional barriers to employment and social inclusion.

Psychological pressures associated with female gender roles include the expectation that women should care for others, including children, the sick and elderly, while taking on the major part of domestic responsibilities, even if they have paid employment. Historically, a number of writers have argued that women's distress can be seen as a response to the pressures of expected gender roles (Chesler, 1972). More recently, this analysis has been applied to diagnoses such as borderline personality disorder, and some clinicians see the criteria for this diagnosis – anger, distrust, difficulty in forming relationships – as an understandable consequence of the sexual abuse that frequently forms part of these women's histories (Proctor, 2007).

In fact, traditional gender roles do not seem to be especially beneficial for either sex: for example, the expectation that men be strong, independent providers who can shrug off emotional and physical pain is associated with fewer and later visits to their GP: this can lead to delayed diagnosis of what are sometimes serious problems that could have been treated more effectively if recognized earlier. Similarly, there is evidence that consistent suppression of emotional reactions has deleterious effects on the immune system and may be associated with a wide range of health problems (Herbert & Cohen, 1993). With respect to distress, male gender roles are often said to be closer to the norm for effective functioning in our society (Chesler, 1972): this may be a further reason why men receive fewer psychiatric diagnoses than women. Another may be that male gender stereotypes influence men's responses to distressing situations – resulting in more drink and drug use, street violence and disorder, rather than an increased likelihood of being given a psychiatric diagnosis.

Ethnicity

Belonging to an ethnic minority group increases the likelihood of experiencing some kinds of clinical distress. Black and ethnic minority people are over-represented in psychiatric services, more likely to receive diagnoses such as schizophrenia, and more likely to be judged by professionals as dangerous (Ferns, 2005). Men from black and mixed white/black groups are three or more times likely, and women from these groups two or more times, than the general population to be admitted to psychiatric hospital (MIND, 2009). African–Caribbeans in the UK seem to do particularly badly; they are up to six times more likely to be given a diagnosis of schizophrenia (Meltzer, Gill, Petticrew & Hinds, 1995a,d). The picture is more mixed for Asians in the UK.

In part, these increased rates of diagnosis are due to the association between minority ethnic status and poverty. Ethnic minority groups, asylum-seekers and refugees are more likely to be unemployed and therefore poor. As a result, ethnic minority people are more at risk of homelessness – and the homeless are, by definition, poor. However, large-scale studies controlling for this association have demonstrated that ethnicity represents an independent causal influence. One of the largest UK studies used census data to explore how the likelihood of being given a diagnosis of schizophrenia in London varies according to ethnicity. This study showed that black and Asian people were 50% more likely than white people to be given a schizophrenia diagnosis (King, Coker, Leavey, Hoare & Johnson-Sabine, 1994). Ongoing experiences of subtle, minor – perhaps unintentional – prejudice and discrimination, as well as experiences of overt racial abuse and violence, may impact upon people from ethnic minorities and make them more likely to experience distress. The explanation that prejudice and discrimination are causal of distress in this way is further supported by rarely-considered evidence that (white) Irish people living in England are significantly more likely to be given a diagnosis of schizophrenia than English white people (Bracken & O'Sullivan, 2001). This research also raises the interesting possibility that many of the studies which have shown that ethnic minority people are over-represented in mental health services have nevertheless under-estimated this difference, because they have typically counted Irish people in with other 'white' people.

It is also well-established that once ethnic minority people receive a diagnosis, they are likely to be treated differently. Black people in the UK are more likely to be compulsorily detained or sent to locked wards, are more often given physical treatments such as medication and ECT and in higher doses, and less often referred for counselling and therapy (Ferns, 2005). It is not surprising that ethnic minority groups often experience services as 'inhumane, unhelpful and inappropriate' and say that their values and worldviews are not understood or even acknowledged by services (Sainsbury Centre for Mental Health, 2002, p. 9).

Conclusion

In concluding this summary of established causal influences, we cannot emphasize strongly enough that **none** of them is either a necessary or sufficient cause of distress: none appears in every case, and none of them invariably results in clinical distress. Their contributions to causality must therefore be multiple, complex and over-determined, operating on the basis of increased probability rather than invariant determination. Moreover, there are many, many ways in which these influences interact – both with each other, and with other influences. Their influence is always *contingent*, always mediated by other influences. It will never be possible, for example, to predict that someone will experience distress – or what kind and level of distress they might experience – simply on the basis of knowing their socio-economic status, gender, ethnicity and family history.

Our conclusion therefore has to be that there is no simple answer to the question of what causes distress, and there is certainly no general answer which applies to all individuals This means that causality in distress is likely to remain a controversial issue (see Box 6.2).

However, this does not mean that we cannot try to make sense of people's distress, as long as we remember that whatever can be said at a general level will always need adapting to specific individuals and their lives. Another way of putting this is to emphasize, again, that distress is a form of experience, so it consists of feelings, beliefs, expectations, habits, behavioural responses and activities. It is in the lives of individuals that social forces, material influences and biological capacities come together to produce every kind of experience, including those associated with psychiatric diagnoses. This means that

---

BOX 6.2
Controversies about causality

Although there is extensive evidence for each of the causal influences we have identified, there are also many controversies surrounding that evidence.

For example, the links between social inequality and distress are no longer disputed, but explanations remain contentious. Not all of the evidence indicates the direction of causation, and Melzer et al. (2004) argue that the association 'is no doubt complex and not all one way'. The causal factors in individual cases are even less clear, and the exact mechanisms by which social inequality exerts harmful influence are still being identified. However, Wilkinson and Pickett's epidemiological work, coupled with other recent enquiries, make an extremely strong case that social inequality does dramatically influence distress.

Psychiatry largely accepts the role of social causation in relation to diagnoses of depression, but sees it as more contentious in the case of diagnoses such as schizophrenia. Even so, there is good evidence that being born in

a deprived area to parents classed as unskilled or unemployed increases your later likelihood of being given a diagnosis of schizophrenia (compared to a random selection of controls from the birth register) more than eight times (Harrison, Gunnell, Glazebrook et al., 2001).

Controversies also accompany other causal influences. Gender differences are sometimes attributed to women supposedly being 'weaker' or more prey to strong hormonal influences. Similarly, it is sometimes argued that black people get diagnosed with schizophrenia more often because they are genetically vulnerable. Relational explanations are likewise criticized as 'family blaming', or challenged because they might stigmatize abused people.

Explanations that posit biological influences are similarly controversial. One issue is that diathesis-stress explanations are flawed because evidence for the diathesis part of the explanation is lacking or flawed. Another is that explanations predicated upon the diathesis-stress model typically invoke relatively simple, mechanistic notions of causality. Consequently, the question of why bereavement, job loss, or abuse in childhood leads to breakdown in

one person and not another meets the response 'because they were vulnerable' – but this vulnerability is, in turn, evidenced by the fact that those people broke down. This circular reasoning has the effect of reducing environmental causes to 'triggers', depriving them of their personal meaning and significance. As Boyle (2002, p. 13) says:

> The vulnerability-stress hypothesis...has proved to be an extraordinarily useful and effective mechanism for managing the potential threat to biological models...Its usefulness lies in its seeming reasonableness (who could deny that biological and psychological and social factors interact?) and its inclusiveness (it encompasses both the biological and the social – surely better than focusing on only one?) while at the same time it firmly maintains the primacy of biology...by making it look as if the 'stress' of the model consists of ordinary stresses which most of us would cope with, but which overwhelm only 'vulnerable' people. We are thus excused from examining too closely either the events themselves or their meaning to the 'vulnerable' person.

we must now consider the role of personal agency and meaning in shaping the form and content of responses to challenging psychosocial events.

Personal agency and meaning

Throughout this book we reject the assumption, common in both psychiatry and psychology, that human beings can be studied as if they were objects, as in the natural sciences, reacting mechanistically to the environment and to each other according to predictable causal laws. This position is implied by quotes such as:

> If you think of the brain as a computer, in the schizophrenic the wiring is 99% correct but there is a fault ... Like the computer, most of the time it works OK but if you stress it too much it crashes.
>
> Murray (1994, p. 6)

Instead, we endorse two other assumptions. The first is that human beings are agents: they are capable of making choices and taking actions for themselves, as opposed to simply being acted on. The second, equally important, assumption is that human beings are meaning-creators with the capacity to reflect upon and learn from our experiences. These meanings will shape our response to those events.

At first sight these two assumptions may seem to contradict some of the other messages of this chapter. We have emphasized the huge and often damaging impact of social inequalities, trauma and deprivation in relationships, and acknowledged that our bodies mediate and limit our responses and reactions. In this context, it might seem odd that we are now emphasizing personal agency and meaning. However, this apparent contradiction arises largely because of the (Western) cultural presupposition that we should understand 'individuals' as separate from their society and culture. As we have already discussed (Chapter 3), it is common in the West – perhaps especially amongst psychologists – to imagine that humans go through life as fundamentally distinct and isolated creatures, and that social influences impinge upon them only to provide the context or backdrop to their many individual actions and experiences. By contrast, once we stop imagining that individuals are simply separate from their society and culture, we can begin to appreciate how social forces and cultural resources come together with bodily capacities *to make personal agency and meaning possible*.

In other words, personal agency and meaning are already in large part *produced by* society and culture. Social and cultural influences do not just provide backgrounds and set limits and constraints upon agency and meaning, they actually supply many of their raw materials and conditions of possibility. Personal agency and meaning *depend upon* social and cultural influences and resources just as profoundly as they depend upon our having a brain and body with which to apprehend the world and act upon it. With respect to distress, this means that the choices people can make and the meanings they can create are not simply determined by their social position: there is always some room to decide what to do and how to understand the world. At the same time, personal agency and meaning are not wholly individual and idiosyncratic and there is no 'absolute' freedom. Both the choices actually available to people, and the various meanings they are able to make and sustain, always depend heavily on their social and material

circumstances. Where people live and work, the relationships they have, the opportunities they encounter, the limitations to which they are subject, the kinds of explanations for behaviour and events that are deemed acceptable amongst their peers – all of these influences interact to shape what people are able to do, what they *imagine* they are able to do, and how they are able to make sense of their own lives.

This picture was painted by a mental health service user. What meanings do you see in it? What meanings do you imagine it has for the person who painted it?

If we did not believe in people's capacity to change, then there would be little point in training for professions in psychology, psychiatry or psychotherapy. At the same time, there are various reasons why we must always be careful not to overstate the influence of personal agency in distress:

- None of us is ever fully aware of all of the possible consequences of our choices; when people are experiencing distress, this already limited awareness is sometimes even further compromised
- Previous life experience provides many of the frameworks of choice and meaning that people use; because this experience can never be 'un-lived' or wished away, changing these frameworks can be slow and difficult
- People's actual ability to make meaningful life choices and select between meanings in their lives is *always* mediated – and often severely limited – by the powers and resources (both material and cultural) that are currently available to them
- Over-stating personal agency can actually make people's distress worse if it leads them to fail in efforts to change circumstances that are actually *impossible* for them transform
- Over-emphasizing personal agency can also lead to a blaming stance ('You ought to be able to pull yourself together and get over this; other people manage to cope') which fails to take into account the many personal, social and cultural barriers that a person may be facing.

Belief in the importance of personal agency and meaning is a core tenet of psychological approaches from CBT to psychoanalysis. It is also consistent with many of the other research findings we have discussed. Wilkinson & Pickett (2009) suggest that the impact of poverty is at least partially due to the personal meaning it has for the individual, in terms of feeling devalued. There are numerous other clues that tell us that at least some differences in people's reactions to events are accounted for by their personal meanings. Attachment theory suggests that those who are able to make a coherent narrative out of difficult early relationships are better able to transcend their damaging effects. Unemployment seems to have a particularly destructive impact on men because of social and personal expectations that a man's role is to have a job (Warner, 2004). The Brown and Harris studies also suggest that the emotional toxicity of events is related to the sense of humiliation and entrapment that accompanies them (Brown, 1996).

Ultimately, there are deep conceptual and philosophical questions here. These questions revolve around issues of free will and determinism, the sharp divide between individuals and their society that is frequently presupposed in Western cultures, and the disciplinary divides separating psychology, psychiatry and neuroscience from sociology, cultural studies and economics. Sociologists and other social scientists discuss these questions in terms of the relationship between agency and structure, and they have been raised in relation to neuroscience by philosophers of science (Bennett & Hacker, 2003). They are of continual relevance to understandings of distress, even though they are not always sufficiently emphasized.

Putting this into clinical practice

The many possible interacting causal factors in distress must be translated into practice by clinicians who daily work directly with service users. However, not only is there a confusing array of different psychotherapeutic models (everything from psychoanalysis to narrative therapy to neurolinguistic programming), there are also combinations such as CAT (Cognitive Analytic Therapy, which integrates elements of personal construct theory, systemic theory, and object relations theory: see also Chapter 8, 'Interventions'). This great variety means that it is only possible to speak in quite general terms about how clinicians understand these causal influences in their practice.

Incorporating relationship influences

All of the 'talking therapies' have a great deal in common, and all of them very much depend on the relationship between client and therapist. This is made explicit in relation to the person-centred approach founded by Carl Rogers (1961), which highlighted the central importance to this relationship of the so-called 'core conditions'. These are:

- Accurate empathy. This is the ability to put yourself in the client's shoes and gain a sense of their experience as it feels to them.
- Warmth, or unconditional positive regard. The therapist accepts and respects, or 'prizes', the person for who they are, rather than on the basis of how they behave.
- Genuineness, or congruence. The therapist is true to him or herself, and within the limits of the session, acts and speaks consistently with his/her feelings.

Together, these core conditions provide the foundation for the development of a trusting relationship with the therapist (the **therapeutic alliance**, as it is sometimes called). Research has established that the quality of the therapeutic relationship is the essential and most powerful vehicle and predictor of change in all therapies (Margison et al., 2000). It may account for the equally well-established finding that 'despite different philosophical emphases and applications, models of psychotherapy tend to achieve broadly similar outcomes' (Paley & Lawton, 2001, p. 13).

Broadly speaking, some therapies see the therapeutic relationship as one with the potential to heal past scars and nurture new ways of being: in these approaches, the relationship itself is seen as the most powerful vehicle for change. Other therapies are more focused on the particular problems that the person brings to therapy, and the potential solutions that might be applied. In both kinds of approach, however, it is accepted that a good relationship between therapist and client is vital if therapy is to succeed. In principle, at least, most therapies allow for the inclusion of personal meaning and agency into distress via a respectful and trusting relationship, something that is often lacking in standard psychiatric treatment.

Frequently, people are expected to accept medical treatment for their psychiatric illness alongside the psychological, therapeutic work. Depending on their views about the role of biological influences, this may be seen by some as unhelpful and even contradictory. Moreover, the effects of medication on people's ability to feel emotions might mean that it is harder to release and work through painful feelings, which is often a necessary part of coming to terms with traumatic events (Kendall, Burbeck & Bateman, 2010).

Incorporating biological influences

As we have seen, the biomedical model of distress, or variants of it, is currently dominant in Western mental health care. This model allows the limited inclusion of social and relationship factors alongside the usual medications for the hypothesized underlying illness. At present in Britain, only psychiatrists and other medically-trained professionals are able to prescribe psychiatric medication, but this has changed in some US states and may do so in the UK. Moreover, both time and resource pressures and the very limited training that most professionals have in any kind of therapy means may also make it more likely that services will promote versions of this model. For these kinds of reasons, clinical psychologists are nearly always required to work within and alongside psychiatric models and practices.

Consequently, psychologists do not need to strive to incorporate biological influences into clinical practice, because they are frequently already dominant. What we perhaps need instead is a better way of integrating them, one which – for example – includes recent evidence about the effects of trauma on the developing brain, but which does not arbitrarily prioritize biological over psychosocial factors (Read, 2005b). As we explain at the end of this chapter, there is still considerable work to be done in order to develop and promote this more sophisticated, fully-integrated kind of perspective.

Incorporating social influences

We have seen that it is no longer denied by professionals or by policymakers that social influences contribute to distress.

The key question is whether, and how, this is actually incorporated into clinical practice. The lack of a coherent, integrated model of distress is a significant hindrance to this task. In its absence, recognition of social and cultural contributions to distress is piecemeal, and frequently operates alongside, not as a replacement for, the dominant biomedical model. In the UK, this means that whilst nearly all psychiatric services offer help with arranging benefits, supported housing, access to voluntary services and self-help groups and so on as part of the intervention, this does not usually imply that distress is seen as a direct result of or response to social factors. It is much more likely that such influence will be seen within a diathesis-stress or biomedical model as 'triggers' of the 'mental illness' that has brought the person into contact with services.

Within clinical psychology, the social causes of distress are most obviously emphasized within the subgroup of practitioners who describe themselves as community psychologists. As we explain in Chapter 8, community psychology is a general approach rather than a specific therapy or intervention. It aims to develop an understanding of people within their social worlds and to use this to reduce distress through social action. Rather than working primarily with individuals or families, community psychologists frequently work in consultation with organizations and communities, supporting people to gain more control and influence over their lives through social action at a local level. Practitioners associated with community psychology have begun to outline some principles of a social model of distress, including an end to 'them and us' thinking about those who experience distress; a holistic understanding of distress that sees people within their social, rather than medical contexts; a commitment to taking seriously people's own accounts of their distress and its meaning to them; an awareness of power relationships, inequality and internalized oppression; and a partnership approach to research, rather than the traditional expert-led evidence-based paradigm (Tew, 2005).

In relation to culture and ethnicity, the picture is rather similar. There have been some attempts to develop transcultural models of mental health, but these mainly consist of introducing adaptations to existing models to make them more 'culturally sensitive'. This might include using translators, trying to match client and therapist ethnicity, add-on specialist services for particular groups of service users, and so on. However, even with such adjustments, Western notions of distress remain dominant. It is not obvious how a less Westernized model could be put into clinical practice, or even whether this could be delivered at all within existing services, despite widespread staff training in cultural awareness.

It is probably fair to say that clinical psychologists as a whole do not see it as a main part of their role to work with social influences in distress. At a purely practical level, this is understandable: there are other professionals and voluntary workers who have greater knowledge of the resources that might be helpful, and can put service users in touch with them. At another level, however, the danger of not giving social factors sufficient weight is that interventions become implicitly individualized and blaming. Smail (2005) has described this as a process (not conscious or deliberate on the part of the therapist) of mystifying people about the origins of their distress. There is a risk that psychological interventions will be framed in purely psychotherapeutic terms – building self-esteem, or coming to terms with feelings about abuse. While these may

be useful as far as they go, the more urgent need may be for better housing or meaningful employment. Both psychiatry and psychology – psychiatrists and psychologists – have some way to go before the strong evidence for the causal role of social factors is adequately integrated into practice.

Towards integration

Partly because causal factors are complex, and precise causal mechanisms are still largely unknown, models of intervention in distress remain conceptually unclear and confused. A simplistic version of the biomedical model usually fills the gap. Combined, but not integrated, with equally simplistic versions of social or psychological factors, this can lead to contradictory and unsuccessful attempts at intervention.

The lack of an agreed, integrated model of distress also has major implications for mental health practice. In most multidisciplinary mental health teams in the UK, for example, a number of models tend to be held in parallel. A survey of 100 different professionals found that these could be categorized along six different dimensions, including medical, social, psychotherapeutic and cognitive–behavioural (Colombo, Bendelow, Fulford & Williams, 2003). When given a description of a fictional patient, psychiatrists and psychiatric nurses were more likely to understand it in biomedical terms (e.g. 'he has a genetic vulnerability to schizophrenia'), whereas social workers tended to come from a psychotherapeutic perspective ('he has unresolved emotional difficulties stemming from his childhood'). Patient and carer groups were divided in their views, but reported finding it hard to challenge the dominant medical perspective if they disagreed. Typically, there is no meaningful attempt to integrate or even acknowledge the existence of these very different, and sometimes contradictory, views about distress. Instead, the hierarchy of power relations within services means that the default position often becomes a biomedical one, whose shortcomings remain largely unchallenged.

Both staff and service users can become trapped in the conflict between models that are fundamentally incompatible. For example, the biomedical model is based on the assumption that 'you have an illness which is not your fault, and it is our job to treat it', while the psychotherapeutic model assumes that 'your problems are an understandable response to your life circumstances, and you need to play a part in overcoming them'. This is clearly a mixed message about personal responsibility. In practice, it can be played out as a rapid change from 'rescuing' to blaming patients when they don't seem to be helping themselves enough, although this passivity is itself partly a result of labelling them as having an 'illness'.

However, the problem is more serious than having a multiplicity of conflicting and unintegrated models. The various vested interests in the dominant biomedical model mean that those who challenge this orthodoxy can encounter strong resistance. A number of professionals have testified to the hostility that such views arouse, sometimes with damaging results for their careers. Similarly, an enduring theme in service user/survivor literature is the struggle to have their own views heard. 'Being treated in a medicalized way, as if they had physical illnesses, formed the basis of negative evaluations and complaints on the part of most users in every aspect of their management. This ranged from a dislike of the aloof and cool attitude of psychiatrists during interviews ... to the rejection of physical treatments as a response to personal distress. In summary, the professional discourse and the lay discourse about personal distress are incompatible' (Rogers, Pilgrim & Lacey, 1993, p. 176). Both in theory and in practice, then, the need is urgent for a coherent, integrated model of distress that is workable within our own cultural context.

Chapter summary

We have seen that the question of what causes distress is extraordinarily complex., The framework that UK clinical psychologists use in their practice to summarize and integrate the hypotheses about the causes of distress in relation to an individual service user is the formulation. Best-practice formulations are an integration of biological, psychological and social factors. Most crucially of all, they are based on the *personal meaning* to the service user of the events and experiences in their lives (Johnstone, Whomsley, Cole & Oliver, 2011). By clarifying how experiences and meanings are linked, formulations aim to promote the service user's greater agency, or ability to take control of their life (see Chapter 5 for an example of a formulation, and a comparison between formulation and diagnosis).

But although formulation can provide a basis for understanding distress at an individual level, the task of developing a thoroughly integrated, general account remains incomplete. The only conclusion we can come to is that causes are multiple, complex, over-determined and contingent, and that the various influences can act synergistically to produce outcomes which are never entirely predictable from our knowledge of the background factors. This gives us hope: there is no such thing as an inevitably bad outcome, even to the most damaging life experiences. It also points to the crucial importance of personal agency and personal meaning in shaping reactions to life circumstances, and of course it is these inescapable aspects of being human that mean that there is the possibility of recovery for anyone, whatever they have suffered.

However, it also makes simple answers to the question of what causes distress impossible. Indeed, the one thing we can say with certainty is that simple 'single cause' answers do not exist, and we should be highly suspicious of anyone, from whatever theoretical stance, who claims otherwise. This does not mean that there is no possibility of understanding people's distress, or of working with them to make its causes clear, but it does mean that there is still much work to be done before a comprehensive understanding is achieved.

End of chapter questions

1 Which social psychological processes are relevant to the identification of causal influences in distress, and how?

2 What does it mean to say that causality in distress is complex, multiple and over-determined, and how would you apply this understanding of causality to the diagnosis of schizophrenia?

3 Evaluate the research methods typically used to explore causal influences upon distress: what are the strengths and weaknesses of each?

4 What kinds of causal influence have been identified in relation to experiences of distress? Answer this question with respect to any one psychiatric diagnosis.

5 Why is the possible causal influence of family and relationship factors in relation to diagnoses such as schizophrenia still seen as controversial?

6 Why must we be wary of over-stating the importance of personal agency in relation to understandings of the causes of distress?

7 In what ways would an integrated model of causal influences upon distress be helpful to psychologists in clinical practice?

Find out more

Films and books

The film 'Sliding Doors' (1998) has nothing to say about distress, but illustrates perfectly the way that contingency operates in daily life. The film shows what difference it makes to the central character's life whether she misses, or catches, a specific train.

The novel 'The Dice Man' (Luke Reinhardt, 1971) is a clever parody of the idea that we can live entirely according to contingency. The central character gives responsibility for all of his important decisions to a set of dice, letting the dice throws determine the course of his life.

Accessible academic reading about causality is quite rare! One account can be found in:

Read, J. & Sanders, P. (2010). *A Straight-Talking Introduction to the Causes of Mental Health Problems*. Ross-on-Wye: PCCSBooks.

Another readable account (although it is biased in favour of survey methodologies) appears in:

Mirowsky, J. & Ross, C. A. (1989). *Social Causes of Psychological Distress*. New York: Aldine de Gruyter.

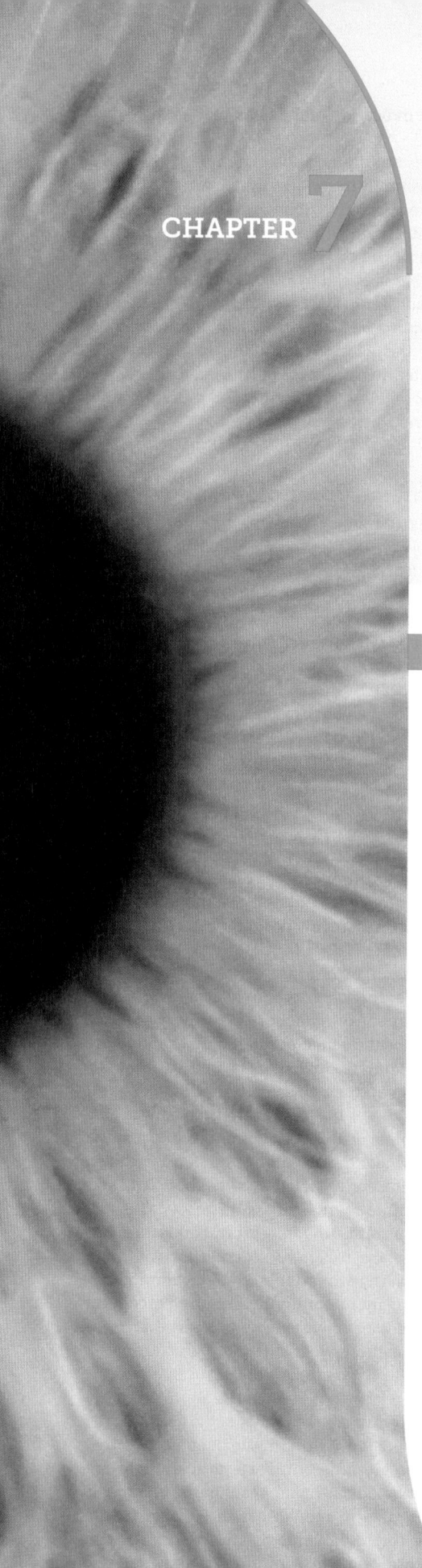

CHAPTER 7

SERVICE USERS AND SURVIVORS

In many textbooks, the words of those who experience mental distress are often heard only indirectly, as case examples described by researchers and textbook authors. Rarely do we get the chance to hear the voices of those who have experienced distress in their own words. To attempt to address this issue, this chapter is authored by three people with first-hand experience: of distress, of mainstream mental health services, and of collaborative self-help alternatives. As a result, there is no fictional case story in this chapter, as the whole chapter is informed by the authors' experiences and insights.

Learning outcomes

By the end of this chapter you should know:

1 What the service user/survivor movement is
2 What its key concerns are
3 How this movement has developed alternative forms of support like the Hearing Voices Network
4 What it is like to hear voices and what helps people to cope with distressing voices.

Guiding question

● What is the service user/survivor movement and why is it important?

SERVICE USERS/SURVIVORS AND MENTAL HEALTH SERVICES

Peter Campbell

Introduction

Collective action by mental health service users has been an important feature of the mental health scene over the last 25 years. As we saw in Chapter 2, throughout history the mad (see Box 7.1 for a discussion about the language used to describe mental distress) have regularly protested their case – both that they are not actually mad and that society mistreats them as mad people (Porter, 1987). But such protests have usually been individual and ineffective in gaining major changes to mental health services. There are certainly a few examples of collective action in pursuit of positive change: the Alleged Lunatics' Friend Society (1845–1863), often cited as the first service user-led advocacy group, is one (Hervey, 1986). Yet it is not until the 1970s that we see the first signs of coherent independent action by service users, and not until the late 1980s and, particularly, the 1990s, that significant numbers of service users and their organizations are drawn into collaborative attempts to change mental health services for the better. In this chapter, as the authors are all based in the UK, the examples we will give will tend to be UK-based, but there are similar developments around the world that we will refer to (and some prominent international organizations are listed at the end of the chapter in the further reading and resources section).

BOX 7.1
Language and concepts

Mental health is a controversial field in which language and concepts are often contested rather than agreed. Service user activists regardless of the strength of their opposition to the medical model often support demedicalized language and concepts:

Distress or *mental distress* rather than *mental illness*
The term 'the mentally ill' is not used
Neither are diagnostic labels like *schizophrenic, anorexic, manic depressive*
Instead more plain English descriptions are used:
Eating distress (anorexia/bulimia)
Hearing voices (auditory hallucinations)
Health anxiety (hypochondria)

Self-definition is seen as a positive good that people must struggle for, having ended up with a psychiatric diagnosis which stigmatizes and mystifies. As part of this, new collective terms are used:

Consumer (common in the 1980s but seen by many activists as giving the misleading impression that they are freely choosing consumers of services when, for instance, compulsory treatment is not a choice).
Recipient (a counter to 'consumer' that emphasizes the often passive or involuntary nature of the relationship).
Service user (a neutral term now commonly used).
Survivor (this term carries an explicit criticism of services although what is being survived may differ as in *psychiatric survivor* or *mental health system survivor*.
Service user and *survivor* are often now used alongside each other in literature written by activists.

Nowadays, involving service users collectively in the development of mental health services has become a necessity, dictated by government, and one which service providers cannot avoid, whatever their underlying feelings. Service users have a voice in every mental health sector: service development and monitoring, training, research and anti-discrimination work. In some areas service users are running their own mental health services. It is now impossible to enter into any significant discussion in the mental health field in the UK and other parts of Europe without ensuring the presence of service users in the debate. While it is possible, as we shall see, to question how credible the user voice actually is or to suspect that users wield influence rather than power, they are now a presence in aspects of mental health services in which their presence would have been inconceivable a quarter of a century ago; this is an indication of the change in climate that has occurred.

This chapter outlines the dimensions of action by the service user/survivor movement in the last thirty years. It recognizes that in some areas positive change has been achieved but is realistic in pointing out where there have been failures and identifying some of the obstacles to effective action. An underlying question that is raised by the material discussed is the extent to which a substantially powerless group like mental health service users can ever achieve radical as opposed to tokenistic change. Is the widespread failure to achieve the former due to the limitations of service users and their organizations or to the impossibility of changing the mental health system from outside the corridors of power?

The service user/survivor movement – a diverse movement

Some commentators (Crossley, 2006; Rogers & Pilgrim, 1991) have characterized action by mental health service users as a 'new social movement'. Whether service user activists themselves think there is a 'service user/survivor movement' and, if so, that they are part of it, is a slightly different matter. The *On Our Own Terms* research project that looked at action in England in 2000–2001 used a very broad definition of a movement to try to establish what activists felt: 'the term "movement" implies that these individuals, groups and organizations share some common goals and are moving in a similar direction.' (Wallcraft, Read & Sweeney, 2003, p. 20). Employing these criteria, they found that, while most of those surveyed felt there was such a movement, a minority felt there was not, or that they were not a part of it or did not want to be a part of it. When we talk about service user action as a movement it is very clear that we are not necessarily describing activity that is close-knit, coheres together well or is guided by a set of clear, commonly agreed aims and objectives.

On the contrary, the service user/survivor movement is notable both for the variety of its actions and the variety of views that inspire them. Action includes traditional campaigning work, demonstrations and lobbying as well as ongoing collaboration through representation on committees and working groups. Involvement in research and training is also important. Although a great deal of action is directed to changing mental health services, groups and individuals are also involved in work to challenge society's perceptions of, and responses to, people with a mental illness diagnosis. Creative and artistic work is also a feature in many groups and a number (e.g. *Survivors' Poetry*) are exclusively dedicated to them. Campaigning and educating around themes of discrimination and stigma is becoming more common, and any perception that the focus of service user activists is now or has ever been exclusively on mental health services is seriously mistaken.

While recognizing the diversity of service user action, it is important to be aware that not all activists want the same outcomes. This does not usually mean that activists will actually be directly opposing and working against each other, but that their priorities are different. For example, there are differing views on how radical or far-reaching a change is either possible or desirable in mental health services. Some activists are working for improvements in services. Others seek major change (Rose, 2001a,b). A number of activists view services as incapable of meaningful reform and focus more on the creation of alternatives (e.g. Stastny & Lehmann, 2007). A significant section of the movement has also moved beyond commenting on the experience of using mental health services to involve themselves in debates about the nature of mental illness/distress itself – a more challenging and controversial field. While some activists seem relatively happy with the dominance of the medical world-view in services, others see this as a key issue rendering them powerless and incompetent and seek to develop a social model of madness and distress to challenge the medical hegemony.

It can indeed be argued that the movement would benefit from a clearer definition of its aims and objectives and its underlying beliefs. But that does not mean it does not have any. One of the difficulties currently facing the movement in the UK is that it appears relatively weak organizationally at a national level and this may hinder the sense of an overall direction. There has also been a long-standing reluctance amongst activists to tell other service users what they should be doing or believing in. In the 1980s, when action was reaching a new level, network groups like *Survivors Speak Out* adhered to a belief in self-advocacy, which emphasizes encouraging people to speak and act on their own behalf, rather than persuading them to adopt a common line on issues. Service users who had long experience of having other, more powerful, people telling them what their lives were about, did not want to repeat the process with their fellows. This laudable sentiment was important in shaping how action developed and in encouraging diversity rather than coherence. It may also have led to some of the difficulties the movement faces twenty years later.

The service user/survivor movement – underlying beliefs

Nevertheless, despite the very real diversity of action and views, there are underlying shared beliefs and experiences that bind activists together and justify a view of action as part of a movement. At the most basic level, activists share the experience of being on the receiving end of the mental health system. This includes, but is by no means confined to, personal experience of using mental health services. While use of services is a key area of concern, it is important to recognize that the lives of service users are lived within society as well as within services and that this is increasingly the case. So while the experience of diagnosis, acute ward care or compulsion may be shared and problematic, service users will also be brought together by being caught up in the welfare benefit system, experiencing poverty and being the target of discrimination by employers and harassment by the public. As the movement has developed and grown larger it has become apparent that, in fact, significant areas of experience are not necessarily shared. The life and experience of someone with a diagnosis of a psychotic mental illness who hears voices and is regularly admitted to an acute ward under a section of the Mental Health Act is markedly different from that of someone with depression who simply takes anti-depressants from her GP and sees a counsellor regularly. Yet there are common elements. They both experience mental distress. They have both ended up in a powerless and devalued social grouping. If they are activists, it is likely that they are both, directly or indirectly, protesting against their predicament.

But activists do not just criticize negative aspects of the mental health system. They also put forward a more positive vision of people with a mental illness diagnosis. In the first place, they are bound together by their desire to see a more sensitive and sophisticated approach to mental distress and madness, one which gives recognition and space to the aspects of these experiences that can be positive. They are fighting for a more nuanced perception of what madness really is. Furthermore, the actions they are involved in are all challenging to some degree the assumption that they are an irredeemably incompetent group whose members have a significant lack of insight into their own needs, replacing it with the proposition that they are essentially competent and contributing like everyone else, although they may sometimes be temporarily incompetent to make certain decisions as a result of their distress. This proposition and the demonstration of its truth are revolutionary in their implications. Against a deep-rooted negative judgement of their worth in society (The SANE (Schizophrenia A National Emergency) advertising from the early 1990s – 'You don't have to be mentally ill to suffer from mental illness'– played perfectly to such negative stereotyping), service user activists are asserting their ability to make a positive contribution and demanding the opportunity to do so. They may not always have the same priorities but they share a belief in the capacity rather than the incapacity of those diagnosed mentally ill.

This shared assertion of their capacity carries over into a powerful belief in self-help and self-organization. Scepticism about the expertise of mental health professionals which may arise from their personal experience within services, has become coupled with an emphasis on the individual's own expertise and on the value of people offering mutual support, comfort and understanding beyond that which professionals can offer. At the same time, most activists place a high value on self-organization, in which action groups are controlled by, or completely made up of, people who have used services. Although as the movement grows larger it is becoming increasingly difficult to keep track of the true character of groups, it is certainly the case that independent, service user-led action groups remain a key element within it.

Over the years, the service user movement has sometimes been criticized for being essentially a negative voice with nothing positive to offer. Although such criticism is much less likely nowadays, there are a number of aspects of mental health services that activists have opposed widely and consistently since the 1970s. Most obvious of these is the place of compulsory treatment (see Chapter 8) – a unique feature of mental health services. It is worth noting at this point that only a minority of services users end up being detained under mental health legislation, though the number of people so detained rose by 20% between 1996 and 2006 just as the number of voluntary admissions was going down (Keown, Meyer & Scott, 2008). Service user activists have been almost united in the last quarter of a century in opposing any extension of compulsory powers to the 1983 Mental Health Act. They have also argued powerfully that the implications of having services backed up by compulsion are not fully appreciated by many mental health professionals. They point particularly to the negative effect of compulsion on therapeutic relationships, and stress the psychological damage that forced treatment and seclusion (or what some survivors would describe as psychiatric assault and solitary confinement respectively) can do to a recipient. They argue that while compulsory powers continue to exist, no patient can really be informal/voluntary. Although their voice has only had limited influence so far (the amended Mental Health Act 2007, which regulates compulsory psychiatric treatment in England and Wales, did extend compulsory powers), it seems clear that opposition to compulsion will remain at the bedrock of service user activism for the foreseeable future.

Many service users object to being given psychiatric treatment compulsorily. In the period leading up to the new Mental Health Act (2007) a number of demonstrations were organized. This photograph was taken in London in 2002 at a rally organized by a group of service users/survivors called *No Force*. Those attending the rally marched from the headquarters of the Department of Health, past the Houses of Parliament to the old site of Bethlem Hospital (now the Imperial War Museum)

It is often stated that the service user/survivor movement is opposed to the 'medical model', and it is certainly true that scepticism about the medical approach to mental distress/madness is common among activists. Nevertheless, it is less clear that all activists are saying the same thing when they oppose the medical model. Some, perhaps a minority, seem to be offering a far-reaching criticism of the model, possibly involving disagreement over the concept of mental illness or a deconstruction of the process of diagnosis. Others seem less concerned with such a fundamental assault and are more interested in services where there is greater choice and flexibility but where the medical approach still plays an integral role. As in other areas of service user action, there is often a noticeable difference between the more and less radical sections of the movement.

Opposition to discrimination is another shared position, and here the situation is more straightforward. Discrimination against service users and the associated stigma are universally opposed. Discrimination has come to be seen as a central element in the lives of service users and as an issue that must be addressed if their increased presence in the community is to make any real sense in terms of equal citizenship. It is notable that in the last decade service user activists have been quite likely to identify discrimination as bringing them greater problems than their own mental health difficulties. In the 1980s, it would have been less common for service users to talk of mental health services themselves in such a way. There has been an appreciable shift in what activists see as the critical issues. While more radical activists may go further in pinpointing mental health services themselves as a key generator of discriminatory attitudes and practices, challenging discrimination has become an important shared objective for the entire service user/survivor movement. Indeed, those who use mental health services can be seen as surviving a wide range of forms of discrimination (see Box 7.2).

Discrimination has a bearing on employment. As we saw in the introductory chapter, people with a diagnosis of a long-term mental illness have high rates of unemployment compared with the general population and with many other groups of disabled people. This is not entirely due to discrimination, but it is clear that many employers are reluctant to employ people with a history of mental distress. In recent years British and other governments have woken up to the importance both of employment and of barriers to employment in their drive to promote social inclusion. Unfortunately this has led to a heavy emphasis on getting people back into paid work while overlooking the unpaid contribution that many service users make in the charitable sector.

Redefining experience

Characterizing service user action as mainly concerned with the improvement of mental health services is one possible response to the action of the last thirty years. There is some justification for seeing things this way, as this is probably the aspect that government and service providers in general are most interested in. However, taking this position risks underplaying the wider significance of the service user/survivor movement in its attempts to redefine the role and status of people with a mental illness diagnosis. At the most basic and practical level, service user action has given small but significant numbers of service users the opportunity to move out of dependent and stigmatized roles and take active, often paid, roles in mental health services and elsewhere. Having a mental illness diagnosis and a history of service use has on occasion become an advantage rather than a disadvantage. Although such changes may only have affected a minority, there has been a wider knock-on effect and, for the first time, service users have won access to an audience that is not automatically going to dismiss what they say and do. A revaluing of personal experiences has become a genuine possibility.

One indication of the wider challenge to conventional thinking is in the area of language, where new terminology is being championed. In particular the 'illness' component of people's problems is questioned by the replacement of the term 'mental illness', 'mental distress', or just 'distress', and a

BOX 7.2
The survivor predicament

People with a mental illness diagnosis can be said to be 'surviving' an obstacle course including the following obstacles:

Their distress. Disagreeing with the way their problems are conceptualized or the type of response on offer does not usually mean people are saying they do not have problems.

Not being listened to. This refers not so much to a total lack of therapeutic interaction (as on many acute wards in hospital) but to the quality of hearing that is going on (not really being listened to). It is complicated by the belief of many professionals that people with a mental illness diagnosis do not have insight/do not know what is in their best interests.

Compulsion. People with a mental disorder can be detained and treated against their will, even if they have decision-making capacity.

Abuse of power. For example, people who self-harm may be stitched up without anaesthetic in Accident and Emergency departments. People detained by the police for assessment under the Mental Health Act can be held in solitary confinement in police cells.

Poverty. A high proportion of people with severe and enduring problems are unemployed and dependent on welfare benefits. The problems they face may be as much due to poverty as to ongoing mental distress.

Harassment. People with a mental illness diagnosis face a range of discriminations. These include physical and verbal harassment by other members of the public or neighbours.

greater sensitivity is demanded around the use of diagnostic terms like bipolar disorder or schizophrenia. At the same time, people with a mental illness diagnosis are looking for different ways to describe themselves – as service users, mental health system or psychiatric survivors, mad instead of mentally ill or mental patients. This is an ongoing process that does not seem likely to result in people deciding a definition for themselves which has universal or even wide acceptance, but is more to do with exercising the right to self-definition and demanding respect for the definition so chosen. It might be argued that some of the choices made are superficial and do not imply a fundamental challenge to the negative status of those diagnosed mentally ill. However, they are examples of a more complicated process of redefinition that lies behind and goes beyond the mere shaping of better mental health services.

The challenge posed by the service user/survivor movement is one based fundamentally on personal experience: an experience that is, moreover, potentially seriously compromised in the view of the general public. Although many service user activists have other expertise, what they bring to the table is their personal experience of living with mental distress and using mental health services. It is this personal experience and their reflections on it that they are demanding be valued on a par with professional expertise. This would be revolutionary enough in itself. But their personal experience is also one that

society, including most mental health professionals, routinely denigrates as flawed by mental illness/madness. There is a large gulf here and it is not surprising if the credibility of the service user movement and the effectiveness of its contribution has frequently been called into question. Listening to and valuing the talk of mad people still goes significantly against the grain.

Origins and influences

Although in recent years it has become clear that the movement in the UK can trace its origins at least as far back as the early 1970s, it was in the 1980s that service user action reached an important new level. In the mid-1980s there were half a dozen independent service user action groups. By 1990 there were at least 50, and major voluntary organizations like Mind were establishing their own service user networks. There were a number of reasons for such growth in activity.

One undoubted factor was the UK Conservative government's new enthusiasm for the National Health Service 'consumer' as part of its plan to introduce market economics into the provision of health services. It became important that the views of service 'consumers' should be elicited in detail in order that services should become as efficient and as cost effective as possible. This new approach opened the doors to mental health service users, who were frequently invited into meetings with managers and other stakeholders to give their views on services. Although their agendas and those of Margaret Thatcher's governments may in fact have been significantly different, service users' path to influence was smoothed by Thatcherite economics.

Since the 1960s there had been a growing concern about civil rights in Western industrialized societies. A succession of oppressed/disadvantaged groups had begun to campaign for positive change in social attitudes and practices: black and minority ethnic groups, women, lesbians and gay men, and disabled people. By the 1980s, some of these groups had achieved substantive change. With such examples before them, it was extremely likely that, in due course, the mad/people with a mental illness diagnosis would also start to take action to challenge their diminished status within services and within society. Mad people may have been mad but they were not stupid! They could see the gains other oppressed groups had already made. They could appreciate the constructive possibilities of collective action.

Many of those who became involved in service user/survivor action in the 1980s had been involved with mental health services for considerable periods of time. Nevertheless, they still felt themselves part of the community in a way that, as we saw in Chapter 2, preceding groups of mental health service users probably did not. Although many of them had received care and treatment in isolated asylums, these had not become their homes. They had returned to the community and lived there between periods of crisis, so could feel for themselves the disparity between being told they were the same as everyone else and actually being routinely discriminated against by their fellow citizens. It is possible that the growth of action in the 1980s had something to do with the existence of a critical mass of service users who were both able to take action (rather than being on the back wards of asylums) and who had too little left to lose by doing so. The climate was right. The desire was there.

A number of commentators (often from outside the service user/survivor movement) have emphasized the links between anti-psychiatry and the growth of service user action (Crossley, 2006). There is currently some dispute about the importance of this link. It is certainly true that anti-psychiatry, although at its strongest in the 1960s and early 1970s, still provided in the early 1980s much of the language and many of the concepts through which criticism of psychiatry was conveyed. It is also true that mental health workers who knew or supported R. D. Laing, seen as a leading member of the anti-psychiatry movement, played an important role in groups like the British Network for Alternatives to Psychiatry (BNAP), in which numerous important service user activists gained their first taste of action. On the other hand, it seems likely that many service user activists at that point had never read, let alone absorbed, the writings of leading critics of psychiatry like Laing, Szasz or Cooper. Although no proper study has been made of the links between anti-psychiatry and service user action in the 1980s, it is notable that numerous service users who were active at this stage play down the influence of anti-psychiatry on them and emphasize instead what they learned from fellow service user activists in the UK and other countries, particularly the USA and the Netherlands. In both these countries, and in Scandinavia, significant action by service users had started earlier and gone further both in terms of organizational development and gains made. In the Netherlands there was already a properly funded Clients' Union and a national Patients' Council Organization. In the USA action groups were quite widespread, although their influence varied from state to state. Judi Chamberlin, a well-known activist, was to have particular influence in the UK through her visits and her book, *On Our Own: Patient-Controlled Alternatives to the Mental Health System* (Chamberlin, 1978).

In truth, the service user/survivor movement at this early stage was being influenced from different directions. Some groups, certainly some individuals, were more radical than others. While, in the broadest sense, anti-psychiatry influenced the direction of some actions, other actions were affected by different influences. It is not clear that anti-psychiatry believed in, or was even much concerned about, 'loonies taking over the asylum'. Yet involvement in consultations about service development has become a key activity of service user action groups. The provision of independent and collective advocacy services has also become a key issue for the service user/survivor movement. Again, the inspiration for this did not come from anti-psychiatry, which appeared to have little to say about advocacy, but from the advocacy and patients' council system established in the Netherlands. It seems fair to say that while anti-psychiatry has always held a special fascination for those who try to make sense of the development of mental health services in the UK, it is only one of a number of influences on service user action in the 1980s. Much action was actually carried out under the banner of self-advocacy, a concept that did not even originate in the mental health field but in the field of learning disability.

When the nature of service user action at this time is closely examined, it can be seen that the contribution of allies was often extremely important. Allies are those (including mental health professionals) who may not describe themselves as service users but who support the aims of the movement. *Survivors Speak Out*, a significant networking group founded in 1986, was greatly helped by allies in its early years. Many local groups also received assistance from allies, whether members of the group itself or supporters from outside the group. The issue of service user-only groups was important at this time. Many activists felt that they needed a space without allies where they could develop their critique and self-confidence away from the danger of allies (usually mental health workers) 'taking over'. At the same time, many mental health workers were angry and uncomprehending when activists opposed their presence in groups. In recent years, the heat has gone out of this debate to some extent: it appears that the message that wanting your own space does not imply a rejection of a collaborative approach has been generally accepted.

Range of actions undertaken by the mental health service user/survivor movement

In Box 7.3 we see examples of the range of groups and organizations which make up the contemporary service user/survivor movement. It is important at the outset to remember that action is not just taken by independent service user action groups, although they are integral to the movement. Individuals also take action on their own, outside groups. Furthermore, a significant number of activists are involved in action within large voluntary organizations that are not themselves service user-led organizations. Charities like *Mind*, *Rethink* and *Together*, for example, all have service user involvement mechanisms within them. Finally, it is useful to be aware that action, in its broadest sense, is now frequently taken by service users who are paid for their time and may even earn a good living by doing so, for example as researchers, freelance trainers, or service user development workers.

It is also important to recognize that, while the service user survivor movement is about taking action for positive change, mutual support and self-help is a prominent activity. Indeed, the *On Our Own Terms* research revealed that self-help support is the commonest type of activity taken by groups which remain, ostensibly, action groups (Wallcraft et al., 2003).

Actions: consultation and monitoring

Obtaining information about the experience of using/consuming mental health services is one of the main, if not the main, activities in which government and service providers want service user activists to become involved. The provision of such 'consumer evidence' has become a key task of local action groups and a portion of the funding they receive may often be attached to providing such information. Most groups spend some time on this type of work and it is often their main activity.

The mechanisms used in the consultative process are varied and a combination may be used within the same consultation. Questionnaires are often used, sometimes devised in collaboration with service users and distributed by them. Consultative meetings take place which may involve service providers going to meetings of the local service user action group but almost certainly mean the local group sending representatives to committees, working groups and meetings set up by service providers. Service user representatives may or may not receive specific support to enable them to canvass their constituency.

BOX 7.3

Some important elements in the service user/survivor movement

International level

World Network of Users and Survivors of Psychiatry (WNUSP)

European Network of Users and Survivors of Psychiatry (ENUSP)

Neither well resourced but still operating as networks. Produced, with MindFreedom International, The Declaration of Dresden against Coerced Psychiatric Treatment (2007)

National level

United Kingdom Advocacy Network (UKAN). Based in Sheffield

National Survivor and User Network (NSUN). Based in London

Voxx (Voices of Experience) The Scotland-wide Network

Service User-led groups focussing on particular aspects

Hearing Voices Network (HVN)

National Self Harm Network (NSHN)

Bipolar UK (previously MDF):Organization for those with a diagnosis of bipolar disorder

Local

Action often appears stronger at local than national level. Groups are mainly small (with a core membership of less than 30) and many, although usually funded and often employing a paid worker, do not have a certain financial future. Estimates of the number of local groups in UK vary from 600 to over 1000.

Networks associated with national charities

Mindlink: probably the largest network group in the UK, advises Mind on its policies, campaigns and so on

Perceptions – linked to Rethink

Individuals

It is difficult to know how many service users are taking action outside groups, but the number in paid employment as researchers, trainers and consultants has grown substantially over the last ten years.

In addition to providing input into work around the development of new services, local service users may be involved in monitoring existing services, sometimes using *User Focused Monitoring* (UFM), a system designed to facilitate service user involvement in the monitoring process (Rose, 1998a). Representatives from local groups may also take part in the selection process for new staff.

Actions: training and education

Service user activists have placed a high priority on involvement in the training and education of mental health professionals. Survivors Speak Out had an (unpaid) training officer on their first co-ordinating group in the mid-1980s. Now all the mental health professions are required to involve service users (and carers) in their training and education programmes.

The degree of service user involvement in training and education can vary considerably. Quite often it is restricted to individuals, either members of local action groups or freelance trainers, devising and running specific sessions on training programmes. But, increasingly, it can also mean that service users are involved in curriculum development and the evaluation of trainees. In some places, special groups have been set up to facilitate the input of service users in the training field, for example SAGE (Salomons Advisory Group of Experts) for the Clinical Psychology programme at Canterbury Christ Church University (Cooke & Hayward, 2010).

Actions: research

Since the mid-1990s there has been a move towards greater involvement of service users in the research field. This has focused not only on maximizing service user involvement in professionally-led research but also on the development of service user led research, where service user researchers devise, carry out and control the entire research process. Good examples of user-led research are *Strategies for Living* (Mental Health Foundation, 2001) and the *SURE* (Service User Research Enterprise) at the Institute of Psychiatry; see also Sweeney, Beresford, Faulkner, Nettle & Rose (2009) and Wallcraft, Schrank and Amering (2009).

Actions: alternative understandings

It is an important feature of the service user/survivor movement that it has not restricted itself to the provision of evidence about what it is like to use mental health services. Instead, a significant number of activists and their organizations have extended their critique beyond the quality of services to the true nature of madness/mental illness itself. In many ways, this is a much more controversial and challenging activity, as it usually calls into question professional expertise and understandings and promotes the validity of insights from people who, by the very nature of their problems, are traditionally supposed to lack insight.

Two organizations that have challenged professional understandings and suggested alternative forms of practices are the Hearing Voices Network (adopting a radical new approach to major psychiatric symptoms – auditory and visual hallucinations) and the National Self Harm Network. Both these groups have made some progress in gaining a sympathetic audience for analyses based on direct experience. There are now approximately 180 local Hearing Voices Network groups in England; a later section of this chapter will discuss the Network in more detail. *Self-harm (Perspectives from personal experience)*, originally published by Survivors Speak Out, became a best-seller in its field (Pembroke, 1995a) and the National Self Harm Network (adopting adopted a harm reduction approach: see Chapter 13, Box 13.7) was set up to support survivors and to campaign, for example to change the way people who self-harmed were treated by hospital staff (Cresswell, 2005; Pembroke, 1995b).

Actions: service provision

Providing services run by service users themselves has not been a high priority for the service user/survivor movement until now. Nevertheless, some groups have been involved in service provision but on a relatively small scale, and local groups may provide support groups or drop-in services of some kind. Occasionally they may run a centre providing a number of services, as *Having a Voice*, a group in North Manchester, has done.

Since the 1970s, service users have called for alternative crisis services, including crisis houses, and have often wanted these to be run by service users themselves. In reality, only a small number of crisis houses have been established over the years and more often than not they have been run by mental health professionals. At the time of writing, Kaya House, run by Barnet Voice as a weekend crisis resource, was the only service user-led crisis resource in existence in the UK, but this, too, has now closed, due to problems in securing continuing funding.

Actions: anti-discrimination and media work

As outlined earlier, discrimination has become increasingly important to service user activists. Activists have been involved for many years in attempting to influence the media (one of the major sources of discriminatory messages about service users – see Chapter 1). This work has moved from protesting about media coverage, through developing better contacts with the media, to creating material for the media. One very successful project was run by *Mental Health Media* (not a service user-led organization), which provided local service users with the skills both to carry out anti-discrimination work and to train other service users.

Actions: arts and creativity

Artistic work of various kinds plays an important part in the service user/survivor movement. Many groups undertake artistic activities of some kind, a few devoting all their energies to such work. The messages of the movement have been conveyed in art, music, drama and poetry and prose writing. *Survivors Poetry* has been a particularly successful example of an arts-oriented group. It was set up by four survivor-poets in 1991 and provides poetry workshops and performances by and for survivors. It also has become involved in publishing poetry books and its magazine *Poetry Express* (now only available online: www.poetryexpress.org/) has a very wide circulation.

What has the survivor movement achieved in the UK?

There are real barriers to any clear-cut delineation of the achievements of the service user/survivor movement. One of these is connected to the diversity of actions and views contained within the movement. There is no substantial agreement about what the movement wants to achieve or, indeed, what it is possible for it to achieve. For some people the fact that service users are widely involved and that there are now hundreds of groups, while in the early 1980s there were four or five, is achievement enough in itself. For others, the number of groups is irrelevant if concrete changes in the mental health system are not detectable. For them, involvement without change is meaningless.

Another difficulty is that, over the years, a great deal of the most impressive action has taken place at a local rather than a national level. This has meant that positive change has often

been small scale. As a result it has not always been easy to detect and has often not been properly documented. The fact that a significant portion of the movement's wider demands do not seem to have been achieved, or have only been partially achieved, should not be taken to mean that local action groups have been unsuccessful. Sometimes the opposite is the case, and it is not until you talk to local activists than you can appreciate the positive changes that are happening. The very fact that many local groups have been operating for substantial periods suggests that local activists continue to believe that action at a local level is worthwhile.

Nevertheless, there are good grounds for being circumspect about the extent to which service user activists have been able to change mental health services, and it is important to draw a distinction between the fact that service users are involved (which they conspicuously are) and the possibility that their involvement is having a major effect (which is more difficult to substantiate). Involvement and involvement that changes things are two quite different matters. Thirty years on we need to be clear headed about the impact of service user action and refuse to be satisfied by the fact that service users are now there or thereabouts in the corridors of power. We need to be cautious about drawing too much comfort from the declaration that attitudes have changed (which they undoubtedly have) without seeing clear evidence that they have altered enough to transform service provision and mental health practice.

Achievements: involvement in care and treatment

One of the underlying objectives of the service user/survivor movement has been to maximize the autonomy of service users, to win them greater control and influence over their own lives, and to empower them. In the context of mental health services, such empowerment has usually been closely connected to giving individual service users more influence over their care and treatment. The last thirty years has seen a great deal of activity towards this objective, some of it originating from the service user/survivor movement, some of it from government. There is no doubt that there are now greater opportunities for service users to be involved in planning their care and treatment, through the *Care Programme Approach* (a care-planning process), crisis planning, advance statements (statements about how someone would like to be treated if unwell: see Chapter 8), the latter being an issue that service user organizations had particularly championed. At the same time, the amount of information available to service users has increased, even if the choices available to them remain largely unaltered. We are living in an era of 'user-centred' services and it might be supposed that collaboration between service user activists and service providers has helped to give greater autonomy to service users.

While there is some justification for such a claim, it is important to be realistic about the actual degree of autonomy achieved. Leaving aside the reality that a significant number of service users are actually being forced to receive care and treatment against their will, the available evidence suggests that service users' influence over their own treatment remains quite limited. A Healthcare Commission report (2007) found that half of the service users surveyed had no say in the choice of medication prescribed and that one third of service users in the community had no information about the side-effects of their medication. It also discovered that 50% did not receive a copy of their care plan. Meanwhile a report on patient involvement in acute ward situations showed that, although it was possible to increase involvement through specifically targeted initiatives, improvements were occurring within a 40% to 60% involvement threshold rather than anything higher (Healthcare Commission, 2008). It seems that half of the users of NHS services feel they are not involved enough in their own care and treatment. Despite the positive work of recent years, mental health service users are in a similar position.

When we talk about service user-centred services, we need to be aware just what the levels of individual involvement in care and treatment actually are. In the light of these it might be hard to argue that the service user/survivor movement has done a great deal for the autonomy of service users within services.

Achievements: independent advocacy

The development of independent mental health advocacy has been one of the most significant changes in services over the last 30 years. In the early 1980s, independent advocacy barely existed. In the 2007 amended Mental Health Act there is a right to independent advocacy for all detained patients. This is a remarkable change for which a substantial part of the credit must go to service user activists and their organizations. The demand for advocacy has been a fundamental part of the demands of the service user/survivor movement since the mid-1980s and service user action groups have often taken the initiative in pursuit of proper advocacy services when other agencies – both statutory and voluntary – have been much less enthusiastic. There are strong grounds for saying that service user activists took the lead in the development of independent advocacy in the United Kingdom. The *United Kingdom Advocacy Network* (UKAN), a service user-led organization established in 1991, played an absolutely crucial role not only in promoting advocacy and supporting advocacy groups but also in producing key documents, a code of good practice for advocacy and training manuals (UKAN, 1994, 2001, 2004). Advocacy is a mechanism that can help empower service users in their journey through services, and is a vital element in good service provision.

That we have come as far as we have with mental health advocacy is largely due to the efforts of the service user/survivor movement. It is perhaps the best example of successful collective action by service users.

But even in relation to advocacy, the story is one of less than total success. The service user movement's enthusiasm has been for service user-led advocacy. That is, advocacy, perhaps provided by service users themselves, but certainly provided by organizations that are service user-controlled. And it is precisely this element that has been marginalized as we have moved towards acceptance by the British government of the value of advocacy and the establishment of a right to advocacy in the amended Mental Health Act. While the service user/survivor movement can rightly be proud of its contribution to the development of advocacy in this country, it must also feel rueful that it appears that the more important advocacy has become, the less acceptable it has become for service users to have meaningful control over it. As advocacy continues down the road towards professionalism, it is not clear what role

service users will have in its provision. Perhaps, when push comes to shove, service users still remain regarded as a little deficient as credible operators.

Achievements: the Mental Health Act and compulsory treatment

Although traditional campaigning has not been a particularly strong feature of service user action in the last 30 years, the movement has always campaigned around the use of compulsion and changes to the Mental Health Act. This is hardly surprising. Although only a minority of service users have ever been compulsorily detained, compulsion is a uniquely problematic feature of mental health services and it seen by many service users as having an impact even on informal patients. Indeed, it is quite common for service users to claim there is really no such person as an informal patient, as everyone knows that legal powers exist to prevent an informal in-patient leaving an acute ward in a hospital if the appropriate professional thinks fit, until they can be assessed under the Mental Health Act. It is also clear that some of the practices that tend to accompany compulsory detention and treatment – solitary confinement in police cells or seclusion rooms, restraint, forced injection of drugs – are both traumatic and controversial. Furthermore, for many activists, the fact that mental health legislation permits compulsory treatment of individuals even if they are no threat to themselves or others and retain the capacity to make treatment decisions is fundamentally discriminatory, and draws an unacceptable line between people with a mental illness diagnosis and all other groups in society. There is more discussion of these issues in Chapter 8.

For these important reasons, most service user activists and their organizations have campaigned against compulsion and resolutely opposed any extension of compulsory powers in the English and Welsh Mental Health Act (the law is slightly different in Scotland: see Chapter 8). In particular, they worked against the introduction of community treatment orders since they were first discussed in the mid-1980s, seeing such orders as a significant and unnecessary extension of compulsion into community settings. It can certainly be argued that their opposition delayed the move towards community treatment orders, particularly in the late 1980s, but such a move proved unstoppable and both the introduction of aftercare under supervision in 1996 and, more significantly, of supervised community treatment in the amended Mental Health Act (2007), can only be seen as defeats. Not only has compulsion been extended beyond the hospital, but it is still possible to be detained in police cells – which some survivors describe as solitary confinement – and the relevance of capacity to decisions about detention and treatment has not been conceded.

Faced with such a comprehensive rejection of their position (the right to advocacy notwithstanding), some activists would argue that, while they have lost the battle, they have at least won greater recognition for the negative effects of compulsion. There may be some truth in this view. Certainly, mental health professionals, including psychiatrists, seem to have adopted a more cautious approach to the acquisition of new powers during the long discussions leading up to the amended Mental Health Act (2007). Some of this reluctance may have come from listening to the protests of service user activists. On the other hand, there is danger in placing a high value on more enlightened attitudes unless practice itself is changing. In this respect, the fact that compulsory admission has risen by 20% between 1996 and 2006 at a time when voluntary admissions are declining does little to suggest that the efforts of a service user/survivor movement opposed to compulsion has yet had much success.

The slowness of change

As has already been suggested, it may be difficult to gain an accurate impression of the impact of the service user/survivor movement because change has been small scale and at a local rather than a national level. Although service user activists can claim to have influenced the major changes that have occurred in services since the 1980s, it is probably true to say that the fact service users call for a particular change is not usually by itself enough to secure such a change. It is only when there is strong support from other stakeholders that change takes place.

The mental health service system is resistant to change and, even when change does occur, it is slow. Although it has been obvious since at least the 1980s that service users want greater opportunities for talking and listening to be built into services (Rogers, Pilgrim & Lacey, 1993), it is only now, in the second decade of the 20th century, that this demand is receiving a serious response from government. At the same time, it is clear that in the 1980s, local service user action groups were very concerned about the non-therapeutic character of acute ward care (GPMH/Consortium, 1988). But it was not until more prestigious, non-survivor organizations took on research into acute care problems ten years later that changes began to be made (Sainsbury Centre for Mental Health, 1998). These examples illustrate the very real limits on the capacity of service users to stimulate speedy change in services, and are a reminder that the service user/survivor movement can be more accurately be seen as having influence rather than power.

The service user/survivor movement: problems and challenges

Although the service user/survivor movement has been more successful at securing small scale, local change rather than large-scale, national change, its actual existence is itself an important change. As already mentioned, service users are active in areas of mental health services that they would never have dreamed possible in the early 1980s. A notable absence has been transformed into a real presence, and the movement has won an important degree of respect. In recent years, many commentators and mental health professionals have begun to talk of service users and service user activists in particular as 'experts by experience', an expression which confers a degree of respectability on the evidence they are providing and the activities they are undertaking. This is an indication of progress, but should not be exaggerated.

Although service user evidence and argument is now clearly part of the process, it may still rank lowest on the scale of validity. For example the Cochrane Collaboration place 'service user opinion' at the bottom of their hierarchy of evidence (Department of Health, 1999). A number of factors still limit the credibility of the service user contribution.

Problems and challenges: representation

One of these problems, one that has dogged the service user/survivor movement throughout its history, is the issue of representativeness. Service users and service user organizations have been regularly accused of not representing their constituency: the wider group of service users. As a result, the significance of the evidence they produce or the views and arguments they put forward can be called into question. These misgivings can mean that some mental health professionals describe some service users as 'professional users', a term that implies that the person is not representative of the broader constituency of service users. Although this term is often left relatively undefined, it clearly relates to the proposition that service user activists are not 'real' service users, are different from ordinary service users and not in touch with their views and opinions. By becoming articulate and competent, by establishing their own organizations and developing their own analysis and critique of mental health services, they can be seen to have separated themselves from ordinary service users and become unable to represent them. In many ways, it is a trap from which the service user activists cannot escape. By becoming more effective they have become less credible.

Alongside doubts about representativeness, the assignation 'professional user' also reveals a certain degree of dismay and trepidation that service users are becoming organized in their own groups, becoming 'professional'. While it is acceptable for mental health professionals to have their own organizations and lobby for their own causes, fear and apprehension build up when service users do likewise. It is almost as if they have broken the rules of the game, a game that should be run by professionals for professionals. While evidence from atomized, individual service users (consumer evidence) is welcome as raw material that professionals and professional groupings can mould in their own way, when service users develop their own analysis and lobby collectively for change, the establishment becomes deeply unsettled. The term 'professional user' is, in part, based on genuine concerns about representativeness but is also an easy derogatory term designed to keep service user activists in their place.

Even so, the charge of not being representative cannot just be shrugged aside. There is no doubt that certain groups of service users are not well represented among activists and that activists find it difficult to reach certain groups of service users to elicit their views and opinions. Until recently, people from black and ethnic minorities have not been adequately involved in the movement. Older people and young people are also largely uninvolved and their voices are not being heard. The core of the service user movement is white adults who have had considerable use of specialist mental health services but have been able to avoid major dependence on them. People who simply use primary care services play much less of a part.

The issue of representativeness needs to be explicitly addressed and this may not be happening at present. For example, it is not always made clear by mental health professionals when representativeness is essential and when it is not. Good ideas, proposals and initiatives should not be ruled out simply because a majority of service users do not support them: they still deserve a sensitive hearing. At the same time, it would help service users if there were more consistency. Service user activists have complained over the years that representativeness seems to become an issue only when activists come up with suggestions and demands with which service providers do not agree. Finally, if representativeness is so important, service user organizations should be given the means to become more representative and to make better contact with hard-to-reach groups. There is no real evidence that service user activists are unaware of these issues, indeed the opposite is the case. Concerns about representation are shared by activist and service providers alike. What is needed is effective collaboration to improve the situation.

Problems and challenges: the process of involvement

The mechanics of involving service users remain problematic even after 30 years. Although a good deal has been written over the years about how to involve service users (not just mental health service users), it appears that the same mistakes are regularly made (Newbiggin, 2005). By and large, there is insufficient appreciation of the difficulty of involving service users successfully and sufficient resources of time, energy and money are very often not being devoted to it. Moreover, it is still the case that service users involved in committees are put off by the use of jargon, the amount of paperwork involved and an overall lack of support to enable them to be effective representatives of their group. Although it is likely that the failures of the involvement process gain more publicity than the successes, a strong impression remains that many organizations are not good at involving service users.

Token involvement has been a common complaint of service user activists, and this continues. This is partly because of the problems outlined above, but it is also due to a perception that service users are not being involved at the levels where decisions are actually made. Many service users have talked about being on committees or working groups on which they feel the decisions are being made elsewhere, either before or after the meetings they are attending. This is a vital issue and goes to the heart of the 'service user involvement' industry that has grown up in mental health services. While it is no doubt better to be involved than to be excluded from the process of changing mental health services, it is by no means clear, even at this advanced stage, whether service providers see the involvement of service users as a means of changing services according to their wishes: there is a fear that consultation processes may act as a democratic smoke screen, sanctioning changes that have been decided. Certainly for radical activists, manipulation of this kind is seen as a more than likely feature of the involvement process.

A question that arises in relation to service user involvement is the degree to which activists are able to set their own agendas. They are usually very much the junior partners in collaboration. It is they who are being invited to become involved, not those handing out the invitations. This might mean that they end up pursuing the goals and agendas of service providers rather than doing what they want to do. Of course, there is often significant overlap between the two agendas, and activists are quite happy to follow the lead of service providers. On the other hand, service user action groups may feel constrained to pursue certain types of action and activity because this is what they are being funded to do. It may be useful to think of a spectrum of service user action ranging from that which is freely and spontaneously chosen, through

to involvement that is really desired, to involvement, which, to some extent, feels as if it has been forced on activists. In all this it is important to be aware of the relative powerlessness of service user activists in deciding the nature and content of the involvement process.

Service user action originally took place on the fringes of or outside mental health services. In the early 1980s, groups tended more towards a position of separatism rather than collaboration with services; in other words, following other civil rights campaigns, they wished to include only service users and chose not to engage with mental health services for much of the time, as they were considered resistant to reform. As a result, they tended to offer their critiques from a position outside services. This has changed very substantially over the years. Now, almost all service user groups and most activists are actively involved in services and bringing forward their views and ideas from within rather than outside. Collaboration, even partnership, is now the name of the game. This situation seems to be accepted, even welcomed, by many activists, despite some of the evident practical difficulties in the involvement process. Nevertheless, for some, the dangers of co-option are very real and they would claim that the movement has identified itself too strongly with mental health services.

As a result, they would argue, activists have lost their independence and their more radical demands have been lost. For them, provider-led involvement of service users has gone too far and the service user/survivor movement has become too much like a rubber-stamping machine, approving ideas that have actually been decided elsewhere.

Beyond services: discrimination and social exclusion

This chapter has so far focused on the work of service user activists in relation to mental health services, because this is where activists have taken most of their action. But service users are not just service users: they are citizens, too. Their relationship to the wider society beyond services is extremely important, particularly as more and more service users are spending greater amounts of time living in the community. And in the community, the reality of life for service users is that it is still likely to contain widespread discrimination and social exclusion (Thornicroft, 2006).

While awareness of discrimination on the grounds of a mental illness diagnosis has certainly increased in recent years, service user action to combat it has been fairly modest. There have been no strong service user-led campaigns, apart from Mental Health Media's *Open Up* initiative, which aims to give local service users the skills to conduct anti-discrimination work at a local level. This is due less to a lack of desire to undertake such campaigns as to an absence of resources and expertise. There have been a number of discrimination campaigns, the most recent being the *Time for a Change* campaign in England, well-funded and jointly led by four non-service user-led organizations: Mind, Rethink, Mental Health Media and the Institute of Psychiatry. Whilst service users were involved in the campaign, the extent to which they had an opportunity to create the messages, as well as publicize them, is unclear.

There are real difficulties in setting up a campaign against discrimination on the grounds of a mental illness diagnosis.

Mental health remains a contested field. Many service users object to anti-discriminatory messages that convey support for a medical model approach to their predicament (e.g. that 'mental illness is an illness like any other'), as many find this reductive and too reliant on medication as an intervention. Similarly, many service users dislike talking about those who experience distress as 'tragic and brave'; this kind of language has alienated disabled people in the past because it is patronizing and tends to focus only on one aspect of a person's identity: their distress. There is also an issue around difference. A significant number of activists might oppose messages that downplay the differences between people with a mental illness diagnosis and the majority of the population, instead, over-playing the similarities. This can be linked with an approach where people claim to 'see the person, not the illness'. For this group, differences are real, albeit not necessarily the same differences that the majority of society would identify. Difference should be given a proper value and celebrated: it should not be denied. A final difficulty relates to the origins of discrimination, which many activists see as lying, to a significant extent, within mental health services themselves.

The danger is that in any wide-scale campaign, the more radical voice of service users would be lost in blander messages that do not respect the realities of living in society with mental distress. On the one hand, the oppressive nature of mental health services may be toned down. On the other, approaches which celebrate madness, like those adopted by the group *Mad Pride* (see Box 7.4), may be marginalized. The Time to Change initiative (www.time-to-change.org.uk) is the largest scale mental health anti-discrimination project yet contemplated in England. It is vital that it truly reflects the views and lifestyles of service user and service user activists and honestly confronts the realities of their lives.

Where are we now? Where are we going?

After 25 years of activity, service user action seems to have achieved a degree of permanence. It is unlikely that British

The Mad Pride logo

and other governments will cease seeking the involvement of service users in the foreseeable future. Their commitment to 'user-centred' services seems long-term and will not make sense without a considerable degree of service user involvement at the collective level. But service user involvement and the service user/survivor movement are not the same thing, however closely interlinked they may appear. It is by no means clear that government is particularly concerned how user involvement is delivered – whether by independent service user-led organizations or by voluntary organizations for service users. Although there are a large number of local service user action groups in existence, perhaps more than 600 in England now, many are small and relatively unfunded and in competition in certain fields with voluntary organizations. There is nothing to suggest that the number of independent groups might not fall away in the future and that they become less important conduits of service user views and opinions than voluntary groups.

Service user-led groups live within certain constraints. They are not usually well-funded, key members are vulnerable to a recurrence of their mental distress and they often lack the financial and management skills needed to run their organizations effectively. For these and other reasons, service user action groups may appear less credible than voluntary organizations and may lose out in the battle for funding and influence. At a national level, mental health charities like Mind, Rethink and Together already dominate the field. With the continuing absence of a strong service user-controlled national networking organization, it is more than possible that voluntary organizations will increasingly be seen as the voice of service users.

The challenge of just keeping going is a very real one for service user action groups. The challenge of being effective is even greater. A movement that began with a focus on mental health services must now look at the whole span of service users' lives within services and within society. Community care without equal opportunity and equal citizenship is no longer sufficient. But to achieve equal citizenship, it seems likely that service user activists will have to enter into broader alliances with groups who are experiencing similar problems of social exclusion. In particular, service users may need to work for common goals with the disability movement, something that has only begun to occur in a meaningful way in the last two or three years. The movement now needs to broaden its horizons and move beyond collaboration within the mental health services alone.

This chapter has argued for the need for realism when assessing the service user/survivor movement. On the one hand, it is no longer possible to complain, as did the 1985 House of Commons Select Committee Report on Community Care, about the difficulty 'of hearing the authentic voice of the ultimate consumers of community care'. Service users are talking, teaching, researching, every day in every corner of England. On the other hand, many of the changes service users have worked for over 30 years have not happened. On the one hand, it is vitally important that the movement has entered the debate about the true nature of madness/mental illness. On the other, even as 'experts by experience', service user activists are deprived of credibility or can be accused of not being representative.

We are living in an era of sound bites, where those with the power are prone to refer to heart-warming concepts

BOX **7.4**
Mad Pride and direct action by survivors

In 1999, a group of survivors based in London and the south-east of the UK set up an organization called *Mad Pride*. Drawing inspiration from other civil rights and liberation struggles, the idea was to reclaim madness in the same way that gay and lesbian people reclaimed the word 'gay' and black people reclaimed the term 'black' (Barnett, 2008). Such a strategy attempts to turn a term of abuse into a positive identity. Mad Pride's ethos was a blend of a punk rock and anarchist ethos of 'do-it-yourself' direct action – its logo is based on the traditional anarchist symbol – aiming to make their point in a humorous manner. The roots of Mad Pride began in 1997, a year when celebrations were planned by a London NHS Trust to mark the 750th anniversary of Bethlem Hospital. A group of survivors formed *Reclaim Bedlam*, arguing that this event should be a commemoration, not a celebration, because of the abusive way in which patients had been treated over the previous 750 years (Shaughnessy, 2000). By 1999 this group had formed Mad Pride and engaged in a number of events on

their own and in collaboration with other groups. Direct actions included picketing conferences of the Royal College of Psychiatrists and the headquarters of the Association of British Pharmaceutical Industry with a giant syringe and fancy dress straitjackets. They also produced a book, *Mad Pride: A Celebration of Mad Culture* (Curtis, Dellar, Leslie & Watson, 2000) and music, organizing a free music festival in London in 2000 (attended by 4000 people) and a fundraising CD, *Nutters with Attitude*. Sadly, with the suicide of Pete Shaughnessy (one of the group's founders) in 2002, the group became a little less active in the UK, although there are occasional music gigs and there was a demonstration against government cuts to welfare benefits in London in 2010. However, the Mad Pride ethos continues to be influential both in the UK and internationally.

In the UK, for example, there have been a series of bed pushes, in which groups of survivors in pyjamas and colourful costumes push a bed from one location to another to raise awareness. For Valentine's Day in 2005, the artist Aidan Shingler created a design incorporating a Valentine's heart with a syringe in it (alluding to the way service users are given neuroleptic injections in

their buttocks). A demonstration (called 'Kiss it!') in London marched to the site of the old Bethlem Hospital holding placards designed by Aidan Shingler with messages like 'kiss goodbye to institutional violence', 'stop the pricks!', 'compassion not compulsion' and 'psychiatrists: restrain yourselves!'. In 2008 a South London group called Creative Routes organized the *Bonkersfest* festival with music, poetry, art and comedy (Barnett, 2008).

In the USA, MindFreedom International (www.mindfreedom.org/campaign/madpride) has promoted the Mad Pride ethos and there have been events around the world: in Australia, Canada, Ghana, Ireland and the USA. Using humour as a way of engaging the public, MindFreedom has also instigated 'Normality screenings' where people dress up in colourful costumes and ask the public if they want to be screened for 'normality'. Janet Foner, on the MindFreedom website, defines normality as 'a serious and persistent "chronic mental illness" afflicting much of the general population' and she describes ten warning signs to be vigilant for (www.mindfreedom.org/campaign/madpride/other-info/normality-screening/10-warning-signs-of-normality).

like empowerment and partnership to reassure people that we are all on the same side and the right sort of progress is being made. In fact, despite the changes of the last 30 years, mental health service users are still a disadvantaged group in society and not notably in control or empowered in relation to services. The partnerships are still unequal, the empowerment frequently illusory. Although it is very clear that service user action is now a permanent feature of the mental health scene, but whether we talk in terms of user-centred consumerism or liberation, it is evident that there is still a very long way to go.

THE HEARING VOICES NETWORK

Eleanor Longden and Jacqui Dillon

As Peter Campbell has noted above, one of the key contributions of service user/survivor activism in the UK in the last 20 years has been the development of new ways of understanding mental distress and new ways of helping people to cope with it. The Hearing Voices Network has been at the forefront of attempts to change the way in which voice-hearing (auditory

hallucinations) is understood. In this section of the chapter we describe the work of the Network. Voice hearing is also discussed in Chapter 11.

What is voice-hearing?

Hearing voices refers to the hearing of human speech that does not originate from an objective source. These voices can be heard internally (inside the head) or externally (through the ears), or even from other parts of the body such as the stomach. There may be one voice or several, and they can talk to the person, about them, or a combination of both. Voices may be male or female and of various ages. As well as speaking they may laugh, scream, sing, whisper or shout. Traditionally, psychiatrists have referred to the experience as **auditory hallucinations**, but we prefer the phrase 'hearing voices' as a more neutral description that uses ordinary language to describe a subjective experience.

The phenomenon of voice-hearing has been documented throughout human history (Leudar & Thomas, 2000), and reported voice-hearers include such notable figures as Socrates, Joan of Arc, Charles Dickens, Carl Jung, Mahatma Gandhi, Virginia Woolf and Anthony Hopkins. There are many circumstances in which people may hear voices. These include the periods between wakefulness and sleep, and in association with bereavement, spiritual/religious experiences, sensory deprivation, physical illnesses like Parkinson's Disease (a disease of the nervous system), hypnosis, and the use of psychotropic drugs like cocaine (Watkins, 2008). Furthermore, research suggests around 13% of the general population (i.e. not including psychiatric patients) have heard voices at some point in their lives (Beavan, Read & Cartwright, 2011). Despite this, voice-hearing is often seen as a major symptom of mental illness, particularly schizophrenia. However, many individuals experience their voices as related to aspects of their life history:

> I had been extensively bullied at school ... the typical themes for the voices are that I am stupid, ugly and worthless. The bullying seemed to be carried on by the voices, although I didn't connect the two things at first.
> I thought I was bad because the voices called me all sorts of names. Later, I realised that the voices were related to [my] abuse, because they have the characteristics of those who abused me.
>
> Quoted in Romme (2009a, p. 46)

> The relationship with my voices has always been related to suppressed emotions ... I believe my voices are emotions that I denied myself. They talk about abuse, self-doubt, insecurity and inadequacy.
>
> Quoted in Escher (2009, p. 56)

> My therapist made it clear that there was a similarity between my voice and my [abusive] stepfather. As soon as she told me that I got a flashback and saw my stepfather. I also understand that they are not really similar but that the voice resembles him and tells me the same things.
>
> Quoted in Romme (2009b, p. 68)

The hearing voices network

Since its launch in 1991, the Hearing Voices Network (HVN), a registered charity, has earned a reputation as a creative and influential grassroots movement that promotes positive explanations for voice-hearing and supports individuals in finding frameworks for developing their own ways of coping. Although it recognizes that voice-hearing can be tormenting and debilitating for some people, the HVN disputes that the experience is a meaningless 'symptom' of mental illness. Instead it suggests that voice-hearing is a socially significant and psychologically interpretable event, which is closely related to (usually painful and unresolved) experiences in a person's life. Correspondingly, the Network believes that understanding and accepting the emotional meaning of one's voices is an important part of recovery, claiming that such exploration provides a way for the person to learn to cope not only with their voices, but also with the social and psychological problems that underlie the voice-hearing experience (Baker, 2009; Dillon & Longden, 2011; James, 2001).

'The freedom to hear voices': the work of Romme and Escher

The emphasis the HVN places on accepting voices, making sense of them, and acknowledging the subjective reality of the voice-hearer originates in the pioneering work of the Dutch psychiatrist Marius Romme and his co-researcher Sandra Escher (e.g. Romme & Escher, 1989, 1993, 2000). Their innovative approach was developed through collaboration and partnership with voice-hearers themselves, and is based on the premise that (a) voice-hearing is a normal human experience that is common in the general population, (b) has a personal, understandable meaning in relation to life history, and (c) is frequently provoked and maintained in response to overwhelming events (Corstens, Escher & Romme, 2008). This stance is consistent with the growing body of research showing how many voice-hearers – and indeed, many service users diagnosed with schizophrenia – have experienced adverse life events, particularly, though not exclusively, childhood abuse (e.g. Hammersley, Read, Woodall & Dillon, 2008; Johnstone, 2007; Longden, Madill & Waterman, 2012; Read, van Os, Morrison & Ross, 2005).

Part of Romme and Escher's rationale for developing their approach was the negative, reductive way in which voice-hearing is often treated in Western mental health services (Hornstein, 2009). Because psychiatry has traditionally seen voices as a meaningless symptom of illness, people are rarely asked about the content, impact or emotional relevance of their voices, and psychological therapy is generally not considered as a treatment of choice (Johnstone, 2011). As a result, mental health services often have little to offer voice-hearers who seek help beyond medication, or for whom the voices do not cease after medication has been prescribed. However, while some people have found medication beneficial, a significant number do not, and many are understandably concerned about the long-term use of antipsychotics (Holmes, Hudson & May, 2008) – see Chapter 8. Furthermore, some individuals experience their voices as symbolic and meaningful, and therefore wish to improve their relationship with their voices rather than get rid of them entirely (Romme, 2009a).

In contrast, Romme and Escher's perspective suggests that 'rejecting the meaning of the voices is the same as rejecting the person'(Corstens et al., 2008, p. 320). This new way of understanding voice-hearing did not come from academic theory or clinical research, but was the suggestion of one of Romme's own patients. Patsy Hage had been tormented by menacing voices since adolescence and, when she came to Romme's attention, was on the verge of suicide. Although she had been given a diagnosis of schizophrenia, Patsy was adamant about the reality of her voices, and was keen to find an explanation for them beyond being 'mentally ill'. One notable inspiration was a controversial book by the psychologist Julian Jaynes, *The Origin of Consciousness in the Breakdown of the Bicameral Mind* (1976), which argues that until a few thousand years ago, humans did not possess reflective consciousness and heard voices (which they attributed to gods) that guided social cooperation and decision-making. Jaynes called this 'the bicameral mind', claiming that voice-hearers in modern times relapse to this ancient mental structure under the influence of extreme stress. Patsy was absorbed by this theory and was sufficiently inspired by it to one day respond to Romme's dismissal of her voices with a memorable challenge: 'You believe in a God we never see or hear, so why shouldn't you believe in the voices I really do hear?' (quoted in James, 2001, p. 31). To a conventional psychiatrist, trained to understand 'auditory hallucinations' as a by-product of mental illness, this was a startling proposition and it took Romme many months to gradually come to accept that Patsy really did hear voices and that they made sense to her. Essentially this required abandoning what his medical training had taught him and following the lead of one of his own patients, simply because what she said 'made more sense than any other theory he had heard' (Coleman & Ellis, 2008, p. 6). Indeed, according to Coleman (2004, p. 13):

> Romme ... in his own words is a traditional psychiatrist ... [but] when he listened to Patsy Hage and explored what she was saying, it was then in my opinion he stopped being a traditional psychiatrist. When he asserted in public for the first time that hearing voices was a normal experience and that voice hearing was not to be feared, he stopped being a traditional psychiatrist. When he continued his work despite being ridiculed and criticized by his peers, he stopped being a traditional psychiatrist and in my opinion became a truly great psychiatrist.

Having accepted the reality of Patsy's voices, Romme began to consider whether voice-hearing could actually be considered a normal human variation. Furthermore, both Romme and Escher felt that in order to help people who were unable to manage their voices, they must find people who were able to cope successfully.

Consequently, Romme and Patsy appeared on Dutch television to discuss voice-hearing, inviting anyone who shared the experience to contact them. The response was surprising: over 450 people phoned in, 150 of whom had never had any contact with psychiatry and led happy, high-functioning lives. In many cases they actually valued their voices. This was an astonishing finding for Romme, who had only ever considered voice-hearing to be indicative of a mental illness, usually schizophrenia. These results led to an important realization: that perhaps the real problem was not hearing voices itself, but rather the person's inability to cope with either their voices, or with the painful, unresolved life events that evoked the voices' presence. It also inspired an important query: could the methods used by those living happily with their voices be successfully employed by those who were not?

Thus began an exploration of the voice-hearing experience that continues to the present day. It was also the beginning of another paradigm shift, in which stigmatizing labels began to be challenged and discarded; the concept of the *schizophrenic* and *auditory hallucinations* receded, to be replaced by the newly defined *voice-hearer* and *hearing voices* (James, 2001). Paul Baker, a British mental health worker who witnessed Romme and Escher publicly deliver their findings for the first time, later recorded: 'Fundamental to this approach ... has been its emphasis on partnership between voice hearers themselves and professionals ... this was a refreshing change from most of the approaches I had come across before which rarely, if ever, gave such importance to the views of those who had actually experienced the mental health difficulties under consideration' (Baker, 1989, p. 11). Romme (2000) has since argued that voice-hearing is a normal sign of human difference and diversity, in which the 'liberation' of voice-hearers is comparable to the civil rights movements of the 1960s. In this respect, Romme (2000) suggests that psychiatry must change its attitudes toward voice-hearing just as it changed its punitive, persecutory

attitudes towards homosexuality. Warwick (quoted in James, 2001, p. 41) makes this political point explicitly:

> How much longer is psychiatry going ... [to continue] labelling first one thing, then another, as mental sickness? Look at the record of psychiatric blundering that has quietly been crossed off with no apologies, let alone any compensation for the many victims. Masturbation, homosexuality, having a child out of wedlock ... these are but a few of the many natural ways of human nature, that in Britain at least, no longer qualify for diabolical forms of treatment psychiatrists inflict upon those they are empowered to label mentally sick.

HVN affirms this viewpoint, and in the past ten years its approach has become increasingly popular, powerful and influential, dispersing across the world in the form of research, training, media coverage, national networks, conferences, publications and self-help groups (see Box 13.5). These activities inspired and led to what is now collectively referred to as 'the Hearing Voices Movement', a philosophical and social trend in which groups of voice-hearers, organized outside the psychiatric system, develop ways to support one other, empower themselves, reclaim ownership of their experiences, and disseminate hopeful messages about recovery (May & Longden, 2010). There are now hearing voices networks in 21 countries across the world, including Australia, Denmark, Germany, Japan, the Netherlands, New Zealand and, most recently, the USA. The work of these national networks is coordinated and supported via *Intervoice: The International Network for Training, Education and Research into Hearing Voices*.

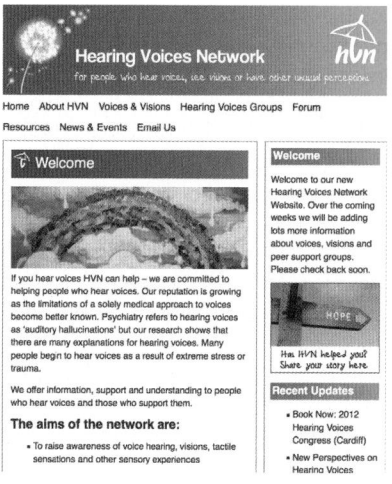

The website of the English National Hearing Voices Network

An information and support network

The main ambition of the HVN is to promote positive, non-stigmatizing explanations for voice-hearing and provide individuals with a framework for developing their own ways of coping – see Box 7.5 for the Network's objectives. Specifically, the Network aims to:

5 Raise awareness of voice-hearing, visions, tactile sensations and other unusual sensory experiences.

6 Give men, women and children who have these experiences an opportunity to talk freely about this together.

7 Support anyone with these experiences seeking to understand, learn and grow from them in their own way.

What are hearing voices groups?

Establishing peer support networks is an important objective for the HVN. As part of this goal, it has invested considerable energy and resources into setting up and supporting hearing voices groups (Downs, 2005a). These can be seen as a communal space in which individuals assemble to support one another, share their feelings, develop coping and self-management strategies, and ultimately reduce their sense of stigma, shame, isolation and distress (Dillon, 2006; Romme, 2009c; May & Longden, 2010). Different groups operate in different ways, and vary according to the emphasis they place on emotional support, promoting citizenship and social inclusion for their members, and/or education and campaigning initiatives to challenge stigma and disseminate positive, respectful information about voice-hearing (Downs, 2005a). In addition to voice-hearers themselves, groups may also welcome relatives, friends and mental health workers to their meetings.

Within groups many helpful and healing processes occur. Principally, their emphasis on collective support and empathy means they play an important role in providing 'a safe-haven where people feel accepted and comfortable' (Downs, 2005a, p. 5). Similarly, Morland (2003, p. 12) suggests that: 'By giving people a safe place to go, they may start to share their experiences and give and receive support which is of benefit to them'. Because voice-hearing often creates feelings of shame, confusion and alienation, finding a forum in which experiences can be openly and freely discussed may prove extremely beneficial. In turn, the knowledge and insights generated within the group can be a valuable complement to individual, psychotherapeutic work that is done outside the group with a mental health professional.

BOX 7.5

Objectives of the Hearing Voices Network

The Network uses the following to achieve its aims:

Diverse membership

Membership is comprised of people who hear voices, their friends, relatives and allies, mental health workers, academics, researchers and members of the public.

Newsletter

Members of the Network receive the quarterly *Voices* newsletter free of charge, which provides information on HVN activities, useful publications and personal accounts, stories, coping strategies and creative pieces from voice-hearers.

Information

The HVN publishes reports on its annual national conferences as well as a range of books and pamphlets on various aspects of the voice-hearing experience, including personal accounts, coping strategies, and the use of medication. Such outreach work has helped promote tolerance, awareness and positive explanations for voice-hearing, as well as spread the ethos of the Hearing Voices Movement to a wider audience.

Self-help groups

There are now over 180 Hearing Voices self-help groups established in England (Scotland and Wales have their own Networks, as does Ireland). Although most groups run in the community, they also operate in a variety of other venues including acute and secure settings (both hospitals and prisons), and a number of specialist groups have been developed for women, BME communities and for children and young people.

Training

The HVN provides national and international training sessions in both statutory and voluntary sector organizations on voice-hearing awareness, supporting voice-hearers, self-help group facilitation skills, working and living with paranoia, working with childhood sexual abuse and other allied subjects. Training is usually delivered by voice-hearers themselves ('experienced-based experts') in partnership with 'experts by profession', such as psychologists, nurses and psychiatrists.

Conferences and seminars

Over the last 20 years the Network has held conferences and seminars for voice-hearers, relatives and workers, as well as providing trainers and speakers for events throughout the UK and overseas.

Helpline

The Network provides a confidential helpline, run by voice-hearers, which offers support and advice to anyone troubled by voices, visions or other unusual experiences.

Research

The Network has increased the understanding and further development of more psychological approaches to voice-hearing by facilitating and supporting ongoing social and scientific research.

Media

The Network has regularly liaised with both the national and international media over the past decade, resulting in numerous positive broadcasts and publications about its work and the voice-hearing experience.

Promoting an innovative approach

The HVN has advanced its work through productive partnerships with professionals, relatives and community groups, therefore supporting many people to end safely their reliance on statutory mental health services. Additionally, its approach has now become more commonplace and accepted within mainstream mental health services. For example, the Healthcare Commission (2008) recognizes the provision of hearing voices groups as a sign of good practice. Similarly, recent literature has begun to advocate the importance of exploring and privileging the relationships voice-hearers have with their voices, and how these dynamics can be used to generate feelings of autonomy and control (e.g. Chin, Hayward & Drinnan, 2009; Corstens, May & Longden, 2011; Longden, Corstens, Escher & Romme, 2012; Trower, Birchwood & Meaden, 2010).

There have now been a number of studies investigating the positive impact of attending Hearing Voices groups (e.g. Escher, 1993; Meddings, Walley, Collins, Tullett & McGowan, 2006; Newton, Larkin, Melhuish & Wykes, 2007; Romme 2009c; Wykes, Parr & Landau, 1999). The results are very consistent, and can be summarized as follows:

1 *New knowledge*: Groups can generate important insights into individual experiences (e.g. linking negative feelings to a negative voice, questioning a voice's perceived power and purpose) as well as providing helpful frameworks for understanding voice-hearing more generally (e.g. as a response to life events).

2 *Solidarity and positive group identity*: Group members can provide opportunities to respect and validate one another's stories. This can help individuals to accept the voice-hearing experience and cultivate a healthy, positive identity as someone who hears voices.

3 *Social gains*: Group attendance confers valuable social benefits, such as building independence, developing self-confidence, self-esteem and self-awareness, overcoming social anxiety, improving communication skills and increasing the capacity and opportunity to socialize.

4 *Normalization*: It can be affirming and reassuring for individuals to recognize their own situation in the experiences of other members.

5 *Overcoming fear of the voices*: Talking about negative voices may reduce isolation, fear and avoidance, and ultimately increase the person's sense of control. Furthermore, it generally feels less threatening to discuss one's experiences with other voice-hearers.

6 *Hope and inspiration*: Hearing how other members have transformed their relationships with their voices can motivate people to learn positive new coping strategies. These could include short-term distraction techniques (e.g. listening to music), in addition to more long-term aims (e.g. exploring the symbolic meaning and significance of the voices). Box 7.6 gives some examples of different ways to cope with voices.

7 *Mutual support*: Psychiatric service users are often passive recipients of care. A group dynamic of reciprocal support and encouragement allows individuals to provide care for others, which in turn can develop a stronger sense of autonomy and self-determination amongst individual members.

These processes are eloquently summarized by one young woman with personal experience of group participation (quoted in Romme, 2009c, p. 82), who states that: 'The group became a natural part of my life, something I would not want to be without ... Creating a "fellowship" around voice-hearing gives the experience the recognition, the weight of reality, the value, that it truly has to every voice hearer.'

In this respect, an important element of the HVN's philosophy is inclusion. For example, while traditional mental health services often arrange self-help initiatives according to a person's diagnosis (e.g. schizophrenia), the HVN advocates creating groups on the basis of shared experience (voice-hearing) irrespective of psychiatric status (Downs, 2005a; May & Longden, 2010). Similarly, while groups in psychiatric services may expect service users to conform to a medical, illness-based explanation for voice-hearing, the HVN encourages members to seek solutions within their own preferred framework, without any prejudice or fear. The Network mostly promotes psychological understandings of voice-hearing. However, it does not put forward any particular explanatory model as more legitimate than another. Rather, it provides a space where all perspectives are respected and all experience is seen as valid. Explanatory frames of reference for voices might therefore include cognitive, trauma-focused, spiritual, political, philosophical, parapsychological models, and so on. In this respect, primacy is given to the subjective reality of the voice-hearer, who is credited with unique wisdom, insight and expertise about his or her own experiences. Within this equation, recovery and empowerment are the main objectives and self-help the guiding force (Dillon & Longden, 2011). According to Reeves (1997) this kind of self-help cannot be prescribed; it requires courage to set out on a journey of self-discovery, personal input being the most powerful tool for change. Coleman (2004) similarly uses a travel metaphor to describe the process of reclaiming one's life from distressing voice-hearing experiences. According to his perspective, while changing from 'victim to victor' can be difficult and distressing, a good map – something that self-help groups can provide – makes the journey much easier.

Mental health workers can assist in organizing self-help initiatives through the provision of resources, infrastructure and other practical help. However they cannot, by definition, supply or be responsible for peer support. The philosophy, form and function of a Hearing Voices group should therefore be defined by its members. For example, problems may arise if a professional emphasizes a particular explanatory framework for voice-hearing that is contrary to the preference of group members. Similarly, a worker may try to prioritize clinical agendas, whereas the members may be more concerned with attaining social or occupational goals. To prevent the ethos of HVN becoming corrupted or colonized by well-meaning yet misguided workers, the Network has developed a Charter that addresses issues of empowerment and ownership (Dillon & Longden, 2011). This ensures that groups operate within the HVN's user-led philosophy by retaining a focus on *self-help* rather than *treatment* (Johnstone, 2011). The importance of this distinction is its emphasis on the personal choice, control and autonomy of group members, who are encouraged to actively take responsibility for their own healing rather than being passive recipients of medical interventions.

BOX 7.6

Possible strategies for coping with distressing voices (see also Downs, 2005b; May & Longden, 2010; Smith, Coleman & Good, 2003; Coleman & Smith, 2006; Corstens, Longden & May, 2012)

Short-term techniques

To use when acutely distressed by voices

- Distraction (e.g. watch TV, do crossword puzzles, go shopping, tidy the house, browse the internet).
- Talk to a supportive family member, friend, or mental health worker.
- Take some exercise.
- Focus on a positive emotion (e.g. watch comedy films, read inspirational quotes, look at photos of loved ones).
- Self-soothe to reduce anxiety (e.g. meditation, yoga, massage, deep breathing exercises, prayer, guided relaxation CDs, calming music, a warm candle-lit bath, aromatherapy oils).
- Talk, read aloud, sing or hum (as this can interrupt a process linked to voice-hearing termed **subvocalization**, whereby one's vocal chords make minute movements accompanying inner speech).
- Visualize a mental barrier between yourself and the voices.
- Find a 'safe place' where you can go and wait for it to pass. This could be your bed, a comfortable armchair, or another quiet peaceful spot.

Long-term strategies

Ways to make sense of the voice-hearing experience

- Use a 'Voice Diary' to get to know your voices (e.g. how many are there? Are they male or female? How old are they? What do they say? What situations or emotions trigger them and how do they respond?). Share the diary with someone you trust and begin looking for patterns.
- 'Time share' with the voices: schedule a time for them (e.g. between 7.30 and 8.00 p.m.), and refuse to listen until then.
- Only listen to the positive and/or least negative voices ('selective attention'), or try to use the positive voices as allies against the negative ones.
- Talk to the voices: ask them questions, challenge them, and/or set boundaries. Remain calm and respectful, yet assertive. Use a mobile phone to talk to them in public without drawing negative attention. Or use 'voice dialoguing' techniques to let someone you trust speak directly to the voices.
- Join a self-help group, or set one up.
- Educate yourself about the voice-hearing experience. Read books, do research online, and speak with other voice-hearers.
- Explore what the voices say in order to regain power and control (e.g. do their threats and predictions ever come true? Is it possible to disobey their commands with no obvious repercussions? Is the power they claim to have consistent with the power they actually have?).

- Accept that the voices themselves are not the problem, they are the result of a deeper, underlying problem. Your task is to find out more. Use the voices as clues to emotional conflicts that can be understood and channelled in new ways.

Self-care strategies

To increase general well-being

- Create a 'Comfort Box' filled with reassuring items (e.g. photos, letters, birthday cards).
- Make a list of your strengths, talents, or positive things other people have said about you. Regularly remind yourself of your hopes, dreams and aspirations for the future.
- Get help with practical issues like finances, housing and medication.
- Find and repeat a positive mantra.
- Go back to basics: get plenty of sleep, a good diet and enough exercise.
- Organize regular treats for yourself.
- Build up a support network.
- Set positive, achievable goals.
- Regularly engage in enjoyable, meaningful activities.
- Express yourself using music, dance, painting, or drawing.
- Ask solution-focussed questions. This is different from problem-solving, because it emphasizes strengths rather than conflicts and difficulties (e.g. 'What has helped me stay hopeful?'; 'How do I cope?'; 'What have I done to stop things getting worse?'; 'When this happened to me in the past, how did I handle it?').

Chapter summary

While orthodox psychiatry sees the elimination and suppression of voices as a primary aim, the Hearing Voices Movement offers an alternative paradigm which views voice-hearing as meaningful, interpretable and originating within the context of one's personal history. Within this optimistic and emancipatory framework, (a) self-help and peer support initiatives are used to generate a safe, creative space in which individuals can reclaim control over both their voices and their lives, and (b) voice-hearing is constructed as an acceptable human experience that can be lived with —even celebrated – rather than an abnormal, pathological 'symptom' that can only be endured (Dillon & Longden, 2011; Johnstone, 2011; May & Longden, 2010). Finally, primacy is increasingly being given to the expertise of experience, with academic, clinical and professional knowledge bases collaborating with voice-hearers themselves in ever more equitable ways.

End of chapter questions

1 What is the service user/survivor movement and what has it achieved?
2 Why was there a need for such a movement?
3 How is it related to other campaigns for civil rights?
4 What are the aims of the Hearing Voices Movement?

5 How does the approach of the Hearing Voices Movement differ from that of traditional psychiatry?

Find out more

1 Beresford, P. (2010). *A Straight-talking Introduction to Being a Mental Health Service User*. Ross-on-Wye: PCCS Books.

2 Romme, M., Escher, S., Dillon, J., Corstens, D. & Morris, M. (Eds) (2009). *Living with Voices: 50 Stories of Recovery*. Ross-on-Wye: PCCS Books.

3 UK-based organizations
- Bipolar UK (previously MDF): www.mdf.org.uk/
- National Hearing Voices Network: www.hearing-voices.org/
- National Self Harm Network: www.nshn.co.uk/
- National Survivor and User Network: www.nsun.org.uk/
- Survivors History Group: www.studymore.org.uk/mpu.htm
- United Kingdom Advocacy Network: www.u-kan.co.uk/
- Voxx (Voices of Experience): www.voxscotland.org.uk/

4 International organizations
- European Network of Users and Survivors of Psychiatry: www.enusp.org/
- Hearing Voices Network USA: www.hearingvoicesusa.org/
- Intervoice: www.intervoiceonline.org/
- MindFreedom International: www.mindfreedom.org/
- World Network of Users and Survivors of Psychiatry: www.wnusp.net/

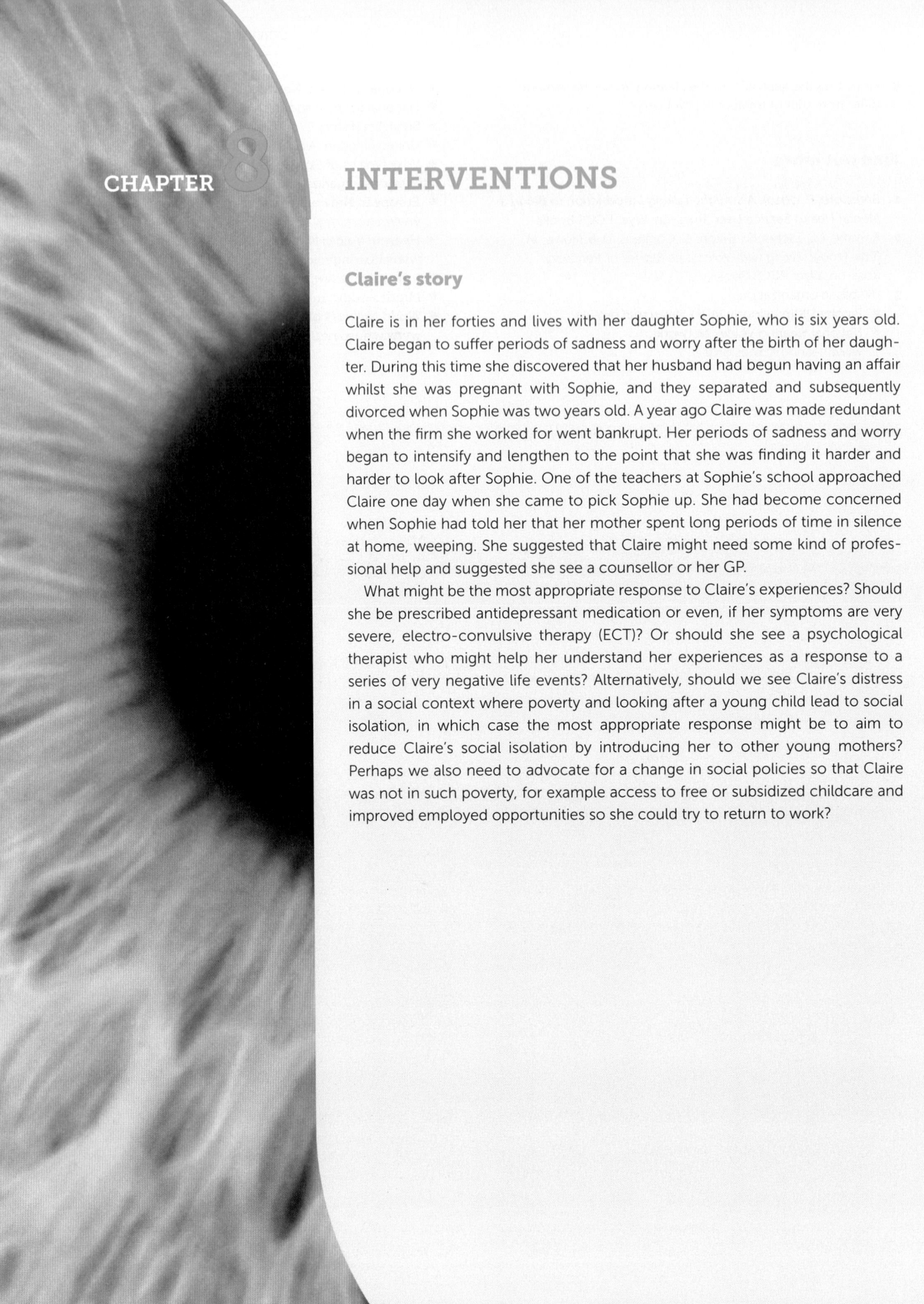

CHAPTER 8

INTERVENTIONS

Claire's story

Claire is in her forties and lives with her daughter Sophie, who is six years old. Claire began to suffer periods of sadness and worry after the birth of her daughter. During this time she discovered that her husband had begun having an affair whilst she was pregnant with Sophie, and they separated and subsequently divorced when Sophie was two years old. A year ago Claire was made redundant when the firm she worked for went bankrupt. Her periods of sadness and worry began to intensify and lengthen to the point that she was finding it harder and harder to look after Sophie. One of the teachers at Sophie's school approached Claire one day when she came to pick Sophie up. She had become concerned when Sophie had told her that her mother spent long periods of time in silence at home, weeping. She suggested that Claire might need some kind of professional help and suggested she see a counsellor or her GP.

What might be the most appropriate response to Claire's experiences? Should she be prescribed antidepressant medication or even, if her symptoms are very severe, electro-convulsive therapy (ECT)? Or should she see a psychological therapist who might help her understand her experiences as a response to a series of very negative life events? Alternatively, should we see Claire's distress in a social context where poverty and looking after a young child lead to social isolation, in which case the most appropriate response might be to aim to reduce Claire's social isolation by introducing her to other young mothers? Perhaps we also need to advocate for a change in social policies so that Claire was not in such poverty, for example access to free or subsidized childcare and improved employed opportunities so she could try to return to work?

By the end of this chapter you should:

1 Be able to describe what medication, psychotherapy and community psychology interventions are.
2 Understand the theories of change on which they are based.
3 Be aware of some of the debates concerning these interventions.
4 Understand how the efficacy of interventions is investigated.
5 Be aware of the limitations of efficacy studies.

Introduction

In this chapter we introduce and review three broad approaches to interventions to address distress: psychiatric medication, psychological therapies and community psychology. We will generally use the term 'intervention' rather than 'treatment' as the latter tends to imply a medical approach; indeed, when this term is used in the psychiatric literature, it is often understood as referring only to medical treatments like ECT, medication or admission into hospital. Since there is so much debate about the utility of these three forms of intervention, readers who are on psychiatric medication or receiving psychotherapy and who have not encountered criticisms of these therapies may decide to discontinue them. We would suggest readers consult Box 8.1 prior to making any decisions.

The first section concerns psychiatric medication, which is by far the most common intervention mental health service users receive. Rogers and Pilgrim (1993), in their survey of 516 UK psychiatric service users (who had experienced at least one hospital admission), reported that 98.6% had received psychiatric drugs of one type or another. Interestingly, Anderson, Brownlie and Given (2009) reported a correlation between medication and poverty: 31% of the poorest quarter of the population (household income less than £12,000) had used medication, compared with only 17% of the richest quarter (household income of £38,000 or more).

The UK Healthcare Commission (2007a) noted that 92% of their service user sample had taken medication. Groups campaigning for service users have often criticized mental health services for placing too much emphasis on medication, for prescribing over recommended limits and for prescribing similar drugs simultaneously. It seems there is some evidence for this: the Healthcare Commission reports the results of an audit by the Royal College of Psychiatrists' Prescribing Observatory for Mental Health (POMH-UK), which revealed that 36% of people were prescribed more than 100% of the maximum recommended daily dose of antipsychotic medication. The Commission also noted that 91% of people were taking two or more medications. The National Institute for Health and Clinical Excellence (NICE) publishes regular guidance for the NHS, and current NICE guidelines recommend only one antipsychotic medication be used at any one time. However, the Commission reported that the POMH-UK audit had found that 43% of people were on more than one antipsychotic medication (Healthcare Commission, 2007).

BOX **8.1**
Should I decide to stop my treatment?

Critiques of mental health interventions are, by their nature, general criticisms. It is a truism that interventions benefit some people some of the time and, if you are receiving an intervention, the authors in this chapter are not in a position to know whether or not you, personally, are benefitting from it.

If you are taking psychiatric medication, and you decide that you want to stop or reduce it, we recommend that you seek advice from reputable sources. The general advice is to reduce medication gradually, since this helps minimize withdrawal symptoms, and not to stop it suddenly altogether. Benzo.org.uk have advice on reducing benzodiazepines, some of which applies more generally. Other online resources include:

- The 'coming off' website: www.comingoff.com
- The Icarus Project guide: http://theicarusproject.net/alternative-treatments/harm-reduction-guide-to-coming-off-psychiatric-drugs
- Mental health charity Mind's website: www.mind.org.uk/campaigns_and_issues/report_and_resources/809_coming_off_medication
- This is also a useful text: Read, J. (2005). *Coping with Coming Off*. London: Mind.

We would advise you to read around the topic, talk things over with supportive friends and family and any health professionals involved in your care. For example, General Practitioners and mental health professionals can also provide advice and support.

We will also examine compulsory psychiatric treatment, which is governed in by the 2007 amendment to the 1983 Mental Health Act. Following admission to hospital, service users generally receive medication but may also receive ECT, which is also covered in this chapter. Although controversial, this is still very widely used, particularly, as we will see, with elderly people: Rogers and Pilgrim (1993) reported that 48% of their sample had received ECT at some point.

Talking therapies have become increasingly popular over the last few decades and we will also examine these. Rogers and Pilgrim reported that 60% of their sample had received some form of talking therapy. This form of intervention 'received the biggest vote of confidence out of all the therapies evaluated, with almost three quarters of the sample reporting that they had been useful' (1993, p. 623). Anderson, Brownlie and Given (2009) noted that whilst 40% of their representative general population sample had discussed their emotional lives with a health professional at some point, the vast majority reported that this was with a GP, and only 16% of people had ever had contact with a 'talk-based' professional. Again, there was a relation between inequality and talking therapies, although less marked than with medication: half of those in the lowest income quartile had used formal sources of emotional support, compared with 38% of those in the highest quartile.

Given these links between interventions and inequality, we will finally discuss community psychology, whose practitioners hope to design interventions focused on addressing inequality and its effects

Guiding questions

1 *What considerations might go into judging which is the most appropriate intervention to help with a person's distress?*
2 *How can we judge the efficacy of an intervention?*

PSYCHIATRIC MEDICATION

Joanna Moncrieff

There is no doubt in my mind about this medication. It gave me my life back.

> A comment on citalopram, an SSRI type antidepressant (Scottish Association of Mental Health, 2004).

I wasted a year of my life on this drug. I was a zombie.

> A comment on venlafaxine, another antidepressant
> · (Scottish Association of Mental Health, 2004).

Although I felt very well, I felt as if I had absolutely nothing to talk about. I kept wondering about whatever [it] was that had been so interesting during most of my life that I had suddenly lost ... But I was very much in contact with reality and for that I was thankful.

> A comment on taking haloperidol, an antipsychotic
> (Moncrieff, Cohen & Mason, 2009)

[i]t did help me, but my personality has been so stifled that sometimes I think the richness of my pre-injection days – even with brief outbursts of madness– is preferable to the numbed cabbage I have now become ... in losing my periods of madness I have had to pay with my soul.

> A comment on taking a depot antipsychotic injection
> (Wescott, 1979)

People's responses to taking psychiatric drugs vary enormously. Some people feel that drugs can help reduce their distress, and help them to function normally again. Some feel drug treatment has even 'saved their lives'. Others find that psychiatric drugs induce unpleasant and sometimes unbearable feelings such as grogginess, dopiness, emotional flattening and agitation. Others, like the authors of the last two comments cited above, feel that psychiatric drugs provide some relief from intrusive thoughts and emotional turmoil, but at considerable cost.

The use of drugs is the central form of treatment in modern day psychiatry. Most people who are referred to psychiatrists are prescribed one form of drug or another and many psychiatric patients take several drugs simultaneously for long periods of time. Many more people are prescribed psychiatric drugs by their General Practitioners. Psychiatric services revolve around the rituals of drug administration and devising and supervising drug regimes forms a large part of the work of many mental health professionals. Drugs occupy this pivotal role in mental healthcare because they are viewed as 'chemical cures' (Moncrieff, 2008). By this I do not mean they are believed to reverse or eliminate psychiatric disorders entirely. They are regarded as cures because they are claimed to act on the underlying biological defect that is claimed to give rise to particular psychiatric symptoms. It is the idea that they act in a specific way, on the basis of a disease, that gives modern psychiatric drugs the status of medical treatments. It marks them out from earlier drugs used in psychiatry, which were regarded as forms of chemical restraint.

In this section I will discuss mainstream views about how psychiatric drugs work and when to use them, and I will look at the evidence that supports these views, and discuss its weaknesses. I will also present an alternative way to think about psychiatric drugs by seeing them as psychoactive substances like alcohol and heroin. I will explain how this alternative view helps us to understand the full range of effects that psychiatric drugs produce, and how by doing so it enables us to make better judgements about when drugs may be helpful, and when they are likely to do more harm than good.

Models of psychiatric drug action

In order to provide a clear way to think about the nature of psychiatric drugs I have outlined two alternative ways of understanding how they might affect people. I have called these different 'models' of drug action the disease-centred model and the drug-centred model. Their contrasting features are summarized in Table 8.1.

The **disease-centred model** is the standard view that psychiatric drugs work by correcting a defective or diseased brain. According to this model, drug treatment makes your brain more normal by helping to reverse the underlying biological abnormality that leads to experiences of distress. The disease-centred model is based on the way most drugs work in physical medicine. Insulin, for example, compensates for the underlying deficiency of insulin in diabetes and anti-asthma drugs help to reverse the lung problems that cause wheezing. Even pain killers, although they do not target the underlying disease, work by acting on the biological pathways that give rise to pain.

Like most medical drugs, psychiatric drugs are named and classified according to the diseases they are thought to reverse or treat. Thus drugs that are thought to help correct the disease process that leads to depression are called 'antidepressants'. Drugs that are thought to rectify the abnormality that gives rise to the symptoms of schizophrenia or psychosis are known as 'antipsychotics' and drugs that are believed to correct an underlying mood control defect are referred to as 'mood stabilizers'.

The alternative way of thinking about psychiatric drugs is what I have called the **'drug-centred' model**. According to this view, psychiatric drugs, like all psychoactive drugs, modify the functioning of the nervous system and by doing so produce altered mental states.

Table 8.1 **Alternative models of drug action**

Disease-centred model	Drug-centred model
Drugs help correct an abnormal brain state	Drugs create an abnormal brain state
Therapeutic effects of drugs derived from their effects on an underlying disease process	Therapeutic effects derive from the impact of the drug-induced state on behavioural and emotional problems
Paradigm: insulin for diabetes	Paradigm: alcohol for social anxiety

The drug-centred model suggests that drugs can sometimes be helpful because the features of the altered drug-induced state superimpose themselves onto the manifestations of distress. One example of this is when a socially anxious person drinks alcohol in order to reduce their anxiety. Alcohol is not thought to be helpful because it corrects a deficiency of alcohol within the brain, nor because it corrects another chemical imbalance. It is thought to help because one of the characteristic features of alcohol intoxication is that it reduces social inhibitions, which may be helpful (if used in moderation) for someone who finds social situations anxiety-provoking.

However, by stressing that drugs are chemicals that alter the normal functioning of the body and the brain, the drug-centred model allows us to see both the positive and the negative effects of drug treatment. Drugs do not simply target psychiatric symptoms. They affect all areas of mental and emotional functioning and they have physical effects too. In addition, since drugs are extraneous chemicals, the body tries to counteract their effects, with both predictable and unpredictable consequences.

Psychoactive drugs

Psychoactive drugs are chemical substances that, by acting on the central nervous system, produce changes in perception, mood, consciousness and behaviour. The most familiar psychoactive substances are recreational drugs like alcohol, heroin, cannabis and LSD. When we think of recreational drugs, we refer to the altered mental states they produce as 'intoxication'. Psychiatric drugs also produce states of intoxication. The features of these states vary according to what sort of drug is taken. Just as the effects of cannabis differ from those of alcohol or heroin, so the effects produced by 'antipsychotics' are different from those produced by drugs like Valium, which differ again from the effects of Prozac, for example. The characteristic features of the intoxicated or drug-induced state depend on the chemical structure and nature of each drug. Recreational drugs, by definition, produce effects that many people find pleasurable or enjoyable. Not all altered states are pleasurable, however, and there are many other psychoactive substances that produce effects that most people find unpleasant.

Psychoactive drugs act by altering the functioning of brain chemicals, called neurotransmitters, that are involved in the transmission of nervous impulses. As we saw in Chapter 4, these chemicals include substances like dopamine, noradrenalin, serotonin, acetylcholine, endorphins and many more. They are involved in helping the electrical impulse that travels along the nerves to cross the gaps between nerve cells that are known as 'synapses' (Figure 8.1).

When the electrical impulse arrives at the terminal of one neuron, it causes release of a neurotransmitter from the vesicles in which it is stored. The transmitter travels across the synapse and attaches to receptors on the surface of the next neuron. The bonding between the neurotransmitter and the receptor activates (or sometimes inhibits) the nervous impulse in the second nerve cell. Many psychoactive drugs act on neurotransmitter receptors, either blocking or enhancing the receptors' ability to transmit impulses. Opiate drugs like heroin and morphine, for example, stimulate receptors that are

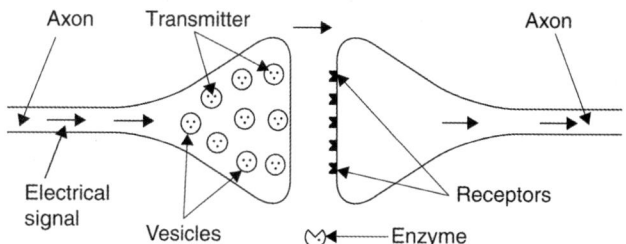

Figure 8.1 **Transmission of nervous impulses**

Source: **Moncrieff (2009). Used with the kind permission of the publishers.**

usually activated by the body's natural pain-killing chemicals, the endorphins. The neuroleptic or antipsychotic drugs block dopamine receptors and stop the chemical dopamine from transmitting its messages in a normal fashion. Drugs can also affect neurotransmitters by directly stimulating their release, acting on the processes by which they are made, or acting on the mechanisms by which they are inactivated or removed from the synapse. One of the ways in which neurotransmitters are inactivated is by their re-absorption or re-uptake into the nerve cells. Stimulants like amphetamine and Ritalin directly stimulate the release of noradrenalin and dopamine into the synapse and reduce their re-uptake from the synapse. Antidepressants are claimed to act by inhibiting the re-uptake and deactivation of the neurotransmitters serotonin and noradrenalin.

Although there is variation in individuals' response to all drugs, psychoactive drugs produce their characteristic range of effects in anyone who takes them, whether or not they have a psychological problem. Most psychoactive drugs also have physical effects, and often the physical and mental effects are linked. Alcohol and benzodiazepines, for example, produce a state of both physical and mental relaxation, and stimulant drugs like amphetamines and cocaine stimulate both mental and physical processes. Some drugs used in general medicine for their physical effects on bodily systems also have psychoactive effects, like steroids, for example, and antihistamines.

An important feature of all psychoactive substances is that, by altering mental processes, they impair the user's ability to evaluate their own functioning. When people are under the influence of a psychoactive substance, they may not be able to judge their actions and behaviours very well. Peter Breggin, a well-known critic of psychiatric drug treatment, has called this effect **'spell-binding'** (Breggin, 2006). We are familiar with this effect in relation to alcohol. When people are intoxicated, they are often over-confident about what they can do, and do not realize that their reactions are slowed and their abilities reduced, which is why there are legal restrictions on drinking and driving. What it means in relation to psychiatric drugs is that while people are taking a drug, they may not be able to give a fully objective account of how it has affected them. It may only be after they have stopped taking the drug that people realize the full extent of the drug's impact upon their functioning.

Any drug taken over a long period, including psychoactive drugs, stimulates the body to try and counteract its effects. This can mean that the effects of the drug get weaker with continual use. The body is said to become 'tolerant' to the presence of the drug. Moreover, when the drug is stopped, **withdrawal symptoms** occur, because the drug is no longer present to oppose the adaptations the body has made to its presence. For example, in long-term opiate users, the body reduces the number and sensitivity of its opiate receptors to counteract the effects of the drugs. Users therefore have to keep increasing their dose to get the same high that they achieved when they first started using. When they stop using, or miss a fix, they develop withdrawal symptoms, which are caused by the under-functioning of their endogenous opiate system, making sensations more painful, and stimuli more intense.

However, the body's adaptations do not always perfectly balance the effects of the drug, leading to unexpected effects. Antipsychotic or neuroleptic drugs reduce the effects of dopamine by blocking the special receptors on brain cells that communicate dopamine's effects. To counteract this effect the body makes more dopamine receptors and increases their sensitivity to dopamine (Samaha, Seeman, Stewart, Rajabi & Kapur, 2007). The condition known as **tardive dyskinesia,** a recognized side-effect of antipsychotic drugs, which consists of abnormal repetitive twitching-type movements, usually affecting the face, may be due to over-compensation of the dopamine system and other neurotransmitter disturbances.

Evidence on psychiatric drugs

Randomized controlled trials

Psychiatric drugs, like other medical treatments, are tested to see if they are effective in placebo-controlled randomized trials (Box 8.2).

In these trials, people are randomly allocated to be given either the real drug or an inert tablet called a placebo. The improvement in symptoms in both groups is then measured using various rating scales, consisting of items thought to be relevant to the condition concerned. If the drug is found to be superior to placebo to a statistically significant degree, it is declared to be efficacious.

The **randomized controlled trial** involves randomly allocating study participants and including a control group who receive a placebo (i.e. a chemically inert tablet like a 'sugar pill'). It was devised to control for a number of factors that could influence the outcome of treatment studies, for example, by giving the erroneous impression that treatment was useful when it was not. A **control group** (or comparison group) is necessary because distress can fluctuate naturally, so it is necessary to compare people who receive treatment with those who do not. A control is similar to the experimental group receiving the intervention in every way except that they do not receive the intervention. Ideally, to reduce any effects of expectation, they should receive something that is similar to the intervention minus its active ingredient. For example, depression is known to be self-limiting, in that many people will improve without any treatment over a period of time: this is known as **spontaneous remission** (Goldberg & Huxley, 1992). So if you gave a tablet to a group of people who were depressed and then observed that they improved, you could not say that the improvement was due to treatment, because they might have improved anyway. Only if people who take

---

BOX **8.2**

Randomized controlled trials

Start by defining people who might receive the treatment to be tested (for example people with depression for a trial of a treatment for depression) – *the population*

Select a *sample* for the study (often younger and older people are excluded, as well as people with other conditions, like physical illness)

Randomly divide the sample into groups

Give groups the *different treatments* to be studied (e.g. in a placebo-controlled trial, one group is given the drug and the other the placebo)

Measure and compare the *outcomes* of the different groups

From Moncrieff (2009a).
Used with the kind permission of the publishers.

the tablet improve more than another similar group who do not take the tablet can you say that the tablet *might* have been helpful. A comparison group is also needed because people may improve because of 'non-specific' aspects of treatment or care. For example, the process of articulating one's problems aloud, the experience of being listened to by a caring professional, and the general advice and support that people receive when they seek treatment for a mental health problem, may all help them to improve; these 'non-specific' factors will be discussed further in the section on psychological therapies. **Random allocation** was introduced to ensure that there were no systematic differences between people allocated to different treatment groups. Placebo tablets are used to control for the effects of the '**placebo effect**'. This is the notion that people improve because they expect that treatment will be helpful. They believe in the benefits of treatment and this belief leads to an improvement in their mental state. The placebo effect is especially useful where there is a subjective component, such as pain (Benson & McCallie, 1979). With forms of distress such as depression, where hopelessness is one of the characteristics, it is logical that the placebo effect will also be strong. Ideally, the study participant should not be able to work out whether they are receiving an active or inert medication. However, participants can often work this out by comparing any effects they experience with the list of **side-effects** (or unwanted effects of the drug) given out as part of the study. One solution to this is to use an **active placebo**– in other words, a drug that produces some side-effects (so a participant feels they are on an active medication). When active placebos are used comparison group outcome scores are generally higher, reducing the difference between the experimental drug and the placebo (Moncrieff, Wessely & Hardy, 1998).

Since expectations can have a powerful effect on a study, it is important that the participants are not informed about (i.e. are 'blind' to) whether they are in the intervention or comparison group– this is known as a 'single blind' trial. However, the expectations of health professionals can also exert an effect, so they also must be unaware of whether their patient is in the normal or comparison group. A 'double-blind' trial is one where neither the participant nor professional knows which condition they are in. However, it has been found that the researcher's knowledge of the participant's status can influence the outcome, so the highest level of blinding is 'triple-blinding', where even the researcher does not know who is in which group. Few studies are of a triple-blind nature.

Because double-blind randomized controlled trials are carefully designed to minimize the influence of things like selection and the effects of expectation, they are often referred to as the 'gold standard' of treatment research. Large trials are regarded as providing especially reliable evidence on the benefits or otherwise of interventions. Meta-analyses are also regarded as providing high quality evidence. A meta-analysis is a combination of the results of a number of different trials of the same treatment. But in fact meta-analyses are only as good or as poor as the trials that they combine, a fact that is sometimes overlooked. By combining studies, meta-analysis is a powerful instrument that can yield results that look strongly positive. But a meta-analysis of poorly conducted trials, as well as adding together their results, also summates their deficiencies or biases.

Randomized controlled trials are designed to indicate whether the drug being tested improves the outcome for the participant more than the 'control' treatment. In a trial comparing a drug with a placebo, the groups are compared on a measure of outcome, such as the score on a depression rating scale. Statistical tests are applied to see if there is a genuine difference between the scores of the two groups. If the difference is big enough, and the study has enough participants, the probability that the difference just occurred by chance will be low. When the probability, or the p value as it is also known, is less than 5%, or 0.05, then we say by convention, that the result is statistically significant. This means that we accept that there is a real difference between the outcomes of the two groups. However, although conventionally the result is accepted as real, 5% of the time it will still occur by chance. If, for example, we do 100 tests, or use 100 different measures of outcome (as many studies do), then even if there is no real difference between the groups, on average five of our results will be 'statistically significant'.

Problems with randomized controlled trials

It is important to realize that, although randomized controlled trials are designed to reduce various sources of bias, there remain considerable problems with conducting valid trials of interventions for distress (Table 8.2).

Firstly, people who participate in randomized controlled trials may not be the same sort of people who seek help from psychological, medical and psychiatric services. Some trials recruit subjects through advertisements, which mean that people may enter trials who would not ordinarily present to clinical services. In addition, in order to test whether an intervention is efficacious for a particular form of distress, studies often focus on people with only one diagnosis. Such people are not at all representative of the people seen in mental health services, who typically have complex problems and multiple diagnoses. The results of trials may therefore not be **generalizable** to the people seen in normal clinical practice.

Secondly, although most drug trials are meant to be double blind, the side-effects of drugs often '**unblind**' trials by enabling participants and researchers to guess who is taking the drug and who is on the placebo. We know that most people who take part in trials of psychiatric medication can guess the identity of the tablets they take better than would be predicted by chance (Fisher & Greenberg, 1993). Positive expectations about the benefits of drug treatment will therefore not be adequately controlled and may lead to 'amplified' placebo effects in people who are allocated to take the 'real' (i.e. experimental) drug as opposed to the placebo (Thomson, 1982).

Thirdly, most trials are conducted with people who are already taking drug treatment of some sort, so the group who are allocated to placebo must be withdrawn from their prior treatment at the start of the trial. This may lead to withdrawal symptoms, which may be mistaken for a worsening of the underlying problems. This is particularly problematic if people

Table 8.2 **Problems with randomized controlled trials in mental health**

- Selection of participants
- Unblinding
- Medication withdrawal
- Dropouts
- Analysis and presentation
- Publication bias
- Influence of drug-induced effects

have been taking treatment for a long time before entering the trial.

Most studies only collect follow up data from people who stay in the trial, but we know that many participants drop out, or fail to complete the study, for a variety of reasons: this is known as **attrition**. If the reasons for drop-out differ between people taking the drug and people taking the placebo, the remaining groups may no longer be comparable and outcomes will reflect these differences as well as any drug-placebo differences. In order to counteract this problem, data for drop-outs is often included in the analysis, but the outcomes are usually only *estimated*, by using the last observation made before drop-out (the last observation carried forward method).

The way that data is analysed and presented can influence the way a trial is interpreted. Most trials use a number of outcome measures, but many selectively report the positive measures and omit the negative ones. Linked to this problem is the fact that many trials that are essentially negative are never published, or published later than others (Melander, Ahlqvist-Rastad, Meijer & Beermann, 2003). This '**publication bias**' means that the published literature is likely to overstate the benefits of drugs.

Finally, randomized placebo-controlled trials only establish that a drug is different from a placebo. They do not establish how or why it is different, nor do they distinguish between disease-centred effects and drug-centred effects (see below).

Evidence for disease-centred effects

The disease-centred model suggests that the difference between a drug and a placebo is attributable to the impact of the drug on the underlying brain abnormality that is thought to produce the 'symptoms' of mental disorder. However, this explanation assumes that any psychoactive effects psychiatric drugs produce are trivial and do not affect the outcome of the study. But we know that psychiatric drugs have profound psychoactive effects, which are bound to impact on psychiatric symptoms. For example, antidepressants have been shown to be slightly superior to placebo in randomized controlled trials. However, they all produce drug-induced effects that may affect the results. Many have sedative effects, for example, which will improve rating scale items that relate to poor sleep, anxiety and agitation, which are included in all depression rating scales (Moncrieff & Cohen, 2006). Some may blunt or dampen down emotions, which will reduce the expression of depressed feelings (Price, Cole & Goodwin, 2009). It is therefore only possible to tell whether a particular drug acts on a disease process if the impact of the psychoactive (and physical) effects the drug has been taken into account.

To establish that a drug acts in a disease-centred way, a number of things need to be demonstrated. Preferably, as in many areas of medicine, you would show how a drug interacted with a demonstrable disease process. However, no specific pathology has been demonstrated for any form of distress currently found in psychiatric diagnostic manuals. It has been suggested that schizophrenia and psychosis are caused by an increased amount of dopamine in the brain and that depression is caused by a lack of serotonin or noradrenalin (see Chapters 4, 9 and 11). However, these are only theories and there is no consistent independent evidence that there are specific abnormalities of dopamine in psychosis or schizophrenia (Moncrieff, 2009), or of serotonin or noradrenalin in depression (Moncrieff, 2008). Why, then, does the idea that distress is caused by a chemical imbalance seem to have become so dominant? Lacasse and Leo (2005) argue that this is a consequence of a 'disconnect' between drug company advertisements and the research literature.

In the absence of a demonstrable disease mechanism to justify a disease-centred model, it should at least be possible to show that drugs that are claimed to act in a disease-centred way are superior to other drugs. However, there is little evidence for this. Drugs that have been shown to be superior to placebo or equivalent to antidepressants in depression trials include benzodiazepines, opiates, many antipsychotics and stimulants (Moncrieff & Kirsch, 2005). In addition, antidepressants themselves come from many different chemical classes and can have few pharmacological properties in common. Thus it appears that almost any drug that has noticeable psychoactive effects has an impact on depression.

Studies that compared antipsychotics with sedative drugs also fail to confirm the superiority of antipsychotics. Although two studies showed that an early antipsychotic, chlorpromazine, was better than barbiturates (Casey, Lasky, Klett & Hollister, 1960; Casey et al., 1960), comparisons with benzodiazepines do not find antipsychotics to be superior overall (Wolkowitz & Pickar, 1991). A randomized study from the 1960s, which compared chlorpromazine to opium, also found that the two drugs were equally good at producing improvement (Abse, Dahlstrom & Tolley, 1960). However, even if antipsychotics were found to be superior to other sedatives, this does not necessarily confirm that they have a disease-centred action. The drug-induced effects they produce, particularly the restriction of cognitive processes and emotional responses, may make them superior to other sedatives which lack these properties in terms of reducing psychotic symptoms.

Characteristics of different psychiatric drugs

Because research has been based on the assumption that psychiatric drugs act on disease mechanisms, the psychoactive effects they induce and their long-term effects on physical and mental functioning have received scant attention. In the following section, I describe what is currently known about the effects of the main types of psychiatric drugs under the headings by which they are currently classified. Table 8.3 outlines this classification.

As I have already mentioned, some members of some classes actually resemble drugs from other classes, and a drug-centred approach would suggest that the current classification is wholly unsatisfactory, since it fails to categorize drugs according to the nature of the effects they induce. However, it is difficult to classify drugs satisfactorily in a drug-centred manner, because of a lack of information about the range of effects they induce.

Antipsychotics

Chlorpromazine, the first drug to become known as an 'antipsychotic', was first used in patients in asylums in France in the early 1950s (Delay & Deniker, 1952). However, it was originally developed as an anti-histamine (i.e. as an allergy treatment) and its use in psychiatry was serendipitous (Healy, 2002). Its use rapidly spread to other parts of Europe and North America. To begin with, these drugs were viewed as acting in a drug-

Table 8.3 **Current psychiatric drug classification**

Overall class	Subclasses	Examples (brand names)
Antipsychotics (also known as neuroleptics, major tranquilizers)	Old (also known as 'typical')	e.g. chlorpromazine (Largactil), haloperidol, trifluoperazine (Stelazine) and depot* injections like zuclopenthixol (Clopixol) and flupenthixol (Depixol)
	New (also known as 'atypical')	Clozapine, olanzapine (Zyprexa), risperidone (Risperdol), quetiapine (Seroquel)
Antidepressants	SSRIs (Selective Serotonin Re-uptake Inhibitors)	Fluoxetine (Prozac), paroxetine (Seroxat), sertraline (Lustral), citalopram (Cipramil)
	Tricyclic antidepressants	Amitriptyline, imipramine, clomipramine, nortryptyline, lofepramine
	MAOI (Monoamine oxidase inhibitors)	Phenelzine (Nardil), moclobemide (Manerix)
	Others	Venlafaxine (Efexor), mirtazapine (Zispin)
'Mood stabilizers'	Lithium	
	Anticonvulsants	Valproic acid (Depakote), carbamazepine, lamotrigine
	Antipsychotics	Olanzapine
Anxiolytics	Benzodiazepines (also used as general sedatives)	Diazepam (Valium), nitrazepam, chlordiazepoxide (Librium), lorazepam
	Buspirone	
	SSRIs	
Stimulants		Methyl phenidate (Ritalin, Concerta), amphetamine (Dexedrine), amoxetine (Strattera)

Notes: *A depot injection involves a regular injection of a compound into the body, which gradually releases a medication into the body over a period of time (days and weeks).

centred fashion. Pierre Deniker, one of the first psychiatrists to use these drugs, described how they produced a neurological 'disease' that replaced and suppressed the symptoms of schizophrenia (Deniker, 1960). Before they became known as antipsychotics, they were named after the particular effects they induced. Deniker and colleagues named them 'neuroleptics' after their ability to 'seize hold' (lepsis in Greek) of the nervous system. In Britain they were referred to as 'major tranquillizers' for many years.

The conventional disease-centred view suggests that antipsychotics work by correcting an underlying abnormality of dopamine function, or dopamine and serotonin function. From a drug-centred perspective, antipsychotics work by inducing abnormal states, whose characteristics depend on the nature of the drug. The older antipsychotics all reduce dopamine activity by blocking dopamine D_2 receptors and by this means they produce a state that is similar to the neurological condition known as Parkinson's disease. **Parkinson's disease** is caused by reduced activity of dopamine in a part of the brain called the basal ganglia, which controls movement and also influences thought, emotion and motivation. People who have used older antipsychotic medications, either as patients or as volunteers, report that they cause sedation, cognitive impairment or slowing, emotional blunting and decreased motivation or initiative, accompanied by feelings of physical restriction (Moncrieff et al., 2009; Belmaker & Wald, 1977; Healy & Farquhar, 1998). These effects can reduce the impact

of psychotic symptoms, which is extremely useful for some people who are locked into a psychotic and troubling internal world. In such cases, the ability of the drugs to dampen down these experiences can allow people to engage with external reality once more, and resume their lives. However, the drugs do not just target symptoms, and their general 'deactivating' effects are often disliked by users (Breggin, 1997). Over 50% experience significant adverse effects (Barbui et al., 2005), and some people decide that these negative effects outweigh the benefits of medication (Rogers et al., 1998).

The new **atypical antipsychotics** are a mixed bag of drugs (they were described as atypical because they were thought to cause fewer side-effects than the older 'typical' or more conventional drugs). Some appear to act in a similar fashion to the older drugs, and have prominent dopamine-blocking properties. Some, like olanzapine and clozapine, appear to act slightly differently. They are less likely to induce Parkinson's symptoms, but they cause a marked increase in appetite and many people who take them gain extraordinary amounts of weight. However, the altered state they produce is also characterized by mental impairment and emotional indifference (Moncrieff et al., 2009).

There are numerous randomized controlled trials that show that antipsychotic drugs reduce psychotic symptoms more than placebo in an acute episode. This is not surprising given the drug-induced effects they produce, although the difference in rates of 'response' to drug and placebo was only 17% in a recent meta-analysis (Leucht, Arbter, Engel, Kissling & Davis, 2008). However, we do not know whether antipsychotics improve the ultimate outcome of a psychotic episode, since we know that most people will recover in any case, at least initially.

As well as acute treatment, it is usually recommended that people who have psychotic episodes should take antipsychotic drugs on a continuing basis in order to prevent a relapse (National Institute for Health and Clinical Excellence, 2002). Trials of continuation treatment show that people who stop antipsychotics have higher relapse rates than those who continue. However, these trials are flawed because they ignore the withdrawal effects of antipsychotics, and there is also evidence that stopping antipsychotics may, in itself, precipitate or bring forward a relapse (Moncrieff, 2006; Viguera, Baldessarini, Hegarty, Van Kammen & Tohen, 1997). In addition, long-term treatment causes the body to produce more dopamine receptors, which may counteract any beneficial effects and may produce the drug-induced condition known as tardive dyskinesia. Tepper and Haas's (1979) review of 44 previous epidemiological studies reported a **prevalence** rate (i.e. how many cases there were at a particular time) of 24–56% of tardive dyskinesia amongst 'chronic neuroleptic users'. Woerner et al. (1991) reported that prevalence varied from 13.3% of those using neuroleptics in a voluntary hospital to 36.1% of patients in a State hospital. Those prescribed atypical neuroleptics appear to be at a lower risk: Tenback, van Harten, Slooffand van Os (2010) reported an **incidence** rate (i.e. how many new cases in a fixed time period) of 0.74% over two years, while Schwartz, Saba, Hardoby, Virk and Masand (2002) reported an incidence of 3% for outpatients receiving risperidone and 5% for those prescribed olanzapine over 1–2 years. As well as involuntary movements, tardive dyskinesia is associated with general intellectual decline (Waddington, O'Callaghan, Larkin & Kinsella, 1993). Therefore, despite the standard recommendations, the balance between the benefit and harm of long-term antipsychotic treatment is not straightforward.

As well as causing Parkinson's disease-like symptoms and tardive dyskinesia, antipsychotics can impair cardiac conduction, cause hormonal imbalances such as increased prolactin secretion, which leads to reduced libido, male breast growth and lactation, and some studies suggest they produce mild shrinkage of brain tissue (Moncrieff & Leo, 2010). They are all associated with weight gain, but the new antipsychotics, and particularly olanzapine and clozapine, can cause extraordinary weight gain, along with diabetes and abnormal lipids. Some studies suggest they increase the risk of premature death (Joukamaa et al., 2006), but a recent study contradicted this finding (Tiihonen et al., 2009).

Antidepressants

Drugs that are now referred to as 'antidepressants' were also first introduced in the 1950s. The first drugs of this sort were initially regarded as useful because they were similar to stimulant drugs like amphetamine (Crane, 1956). Gradually the idea arose that, unlike stimulants, they could work in a specific way to reverse the underlying biological basis of depression and help return someone to normal. At that stage, the idea that they were drugs with psychoactive effects was forgotten.

The mainstream view is that antidepressants work by correcting an underlying deficiency of noradrenalin or serotonin, which has been said to play a part in producing

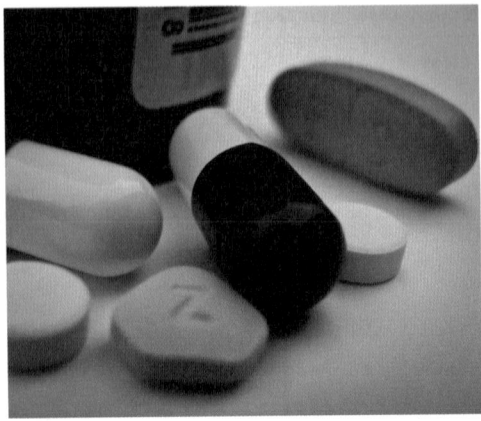

Psychiatric medication remains the form of intervention most people receive in mental health services

symptoms of depression. According to a drug-centred model, antidepressants come from a variety of chemical classes and have a range of quite different psychoactive effects. The earliest drugs that came to be called 'antidepressants', drugs classed as **monoamine oxidase inhibitors** (MAOIs), had similar effects to stimulants. In contrast, the **tricyclic antidepressants**, such as amitriptyline, are chemically similar to early antipsychotics, and share many of their effects. They are extremely sedating, impair mental functioning and some have been shown to block dopamine in animal studies (Moncrieff, 2008). **Selective serotonin re-uptake inhibitors** (SSRIs) have milder psychoactive effects in volunteer studies (Dumont, de Visser, Cohen & van Gerven, 2005). Commonly reported effects include drowsiness, feelings of cognitive impairment, agitation (and other so-called 'activating' effects like anxiety), emotional blunting and emotional instability (Goldsmith & Moncrieff, 2010). There has been heated debate about whether they can induce suicidal behaviour. Several, but not all, large-scale analyses suggest SSRIs are associated with increased suicidal thoughts and acts, especially in children (Gunnell, Saperia & Ashby, 2005; Whittington et al., 2004), which may be linked to their emotional effects (Teicher, Glod & Cole, 1990).

Current guidelines recommend antidepressant treatment for people with a diagnosis of moderate to severe depression (National Institute for Health and Clinical Excellence, 2004a). These recommendations are based on placebo-controlled studies that indicate that antidepressants are a little better than a placebo at improving the symptoms of depression, but not much. A recent meta-analysis, which included unpublished studies to reduce publication bias, found that the difference between the drugs and placebo was only 1.7 points on the 54 point Hamilton Rating Scale for Depression (Kirsch, Moore, Scoboria & Nicholls, 2002), which is unlikely to represent a clinically relevant effect. Continuation treatment is recommended for people who experience severe and recurrent episodes, based on studies that show increased rates of relapse in people who are converted from antidepressant treatment to placebo. As with antipsychotic trials, however, the impact of withdrawal effects on these studies has not been considered.

There is no doubt that many people feel they have been helped by taking antidepressants. In placebo-controlled trials however, many people are helped by placebo. Others have not found antidepressants useful, and some people feel they have been harmed by them. From a drug-centred perspective, it is difficult to see how the psychoactive effects induced by anti-depressants can be useful in people experiencing feelings of depression. Indeed, it seems difficult to justify the prescription of mind-altering drugs to people who are feeling depressed, except maybe for the careful use of sedatives to improve sleep, or calm agitation or anxiety. Being in a drugged state may effectively distance someone from their current emotions, but it is unlikely to help them recover in the long term. Indeed, it may act as barrier to dealing with the interpersonal problems that so often contribute to depression.

The adverse effects of antidepressants depend on their class. The tricyclic antidepressants have largely been replaced by newer drugs because they were heavily sedating, and carried the same cardiac conduction risks as antipsychotics, which made them highly dangerous in overdose. SSRIs such as fluoxetine (Prozac) and paroxetine cause drowsiness too, but coupled with unpleasant activating effects, emotional effects and possibly increased suicidal ideation. They do not have the dangerous cardiac effects of tricyclics, although venlafaxine, a commonly prescribed serotonin and noradrenalin re-uptake blocker, is associated with potentially dangerous cardiovascular effects (Howell, Wilson & Waring, 2007).

Drugs used for people with a diagnosis of manic depression

'Mood stabilizers' is a term that has been introduced into psychiatry by the pharmaceutical industry and has no agreed meaning (Harris, Chandran, Chakraborty & Healy, 2003). It refers to drugs that are used for the treatment of people with a diagnosis of what was called manic depression, but is increasingly referred to as 'bipolar disorder' (which is covered in Chapter 11). For many years, lithium was the only drug that was regarded as a specific treatment, but various other drugs, notably some used in epilepsy such as carbamazepine and sodium valproate have now been branded as 'mood stabilizers.' Some new antipsychotics, such as olanzapine, are also being promoted for this indication.

The standard view is that drugs for manic depression reverse an underlying instability of mood. From a drug-centred perspective, all drugs that are referred to as mood stabilizers have sedative effects that are likely to impact on symptoms of mania, in particular. Lithium is a particularly toxic drug, whose dangerous effects include suppression of the nervous system, which occurs at doses just above those used for treatment. Volunteer studies show that lithium impairs mental abilities, is unpleasant to take, reduces creativity and does not reduce normal mood variability (Judd, Hubbard, Janowsky, Huey & Attewell, 1977; Squire, Judd, Janowsky & Huey, 1980).

The main use of these drugs is the long-term treatment of people with a diagnosis of bipolar disorder. Some of the trials of lithium and other 'mood stabilizers' show that relapse rates are lower in people taking drug treatment compared with those taking placebo (Geddes, Burgess, Hawton, Jamison & Goodwin, 2004), although some do not show any effect (Bowden et al., 2000). However, again, these trials are confounded by withdrawal or discontinuation effects. There is strong evidence that stopping lithium, especially abruptly, increases the chance of having a relapse over and above the natural history of the distress (Baldessarini, Tondo & Viguera, 1999). In other words, people who have taken lithium for a period of time and then stop taking it are more likely to relapse than if they had never taken it in the first place. A recent placebo controlled withdrawal study of olanzapine also showed evidence of a discontinuation effect, with almost all of the excess relapses in the placebo group occurring shortly after randomization, which coincides with withdrawal of previous treatment (Tohen et al., 2006). Placebo controlled trials of lithium and other drugs for manic depression do not, therefore, give a fair comparison. They may merely reflect the problems induced by coming off these drugs.

Again, many people with a diagnosis of bipolar disorder feel they have been helped by drugs. Others manage their distress without long-term drug treatment. From a drug-centred perspective, drugs with sedative properties are likely to reduce the symptoms of acute mania, and they may reduce manic relapses, although the evidence for the latter remains inconclusive. However, even if it were clearly shown that drug treatment reduced relapse rates, the balance between benefit and harm of long-term treatment would need careful consideration. As well as sedative effects and mental dulling, all drugs currently used as 'mood stabilizers' cause weight gain and various hormonal and metabolic disturbances. Lithium frequently causes hypothyroidism, can impair renal function, and carries a constant threat of dangerous toxicity.

Stimulants

Stimulant drugs, which include amphetamine and Ritalin, are still referred to by the altered state of artificially enhanced arousal that they produce. They increase heart rate, reduce sleep and, if given at high doses, people become more active. However, at lower doses, they produce a state of calmness and heightened and highly focused attention, without increasing activity (Breggin, 2001). They are used for the treatment of children and increasingly also adults diagnosed as having hyperactivity or attention deficit disorder (ADHD). It used to be said that stimulants exerted a 'paradoxical effect' in people with a diagnosis of ADHD that was different from the effects they produced in other people, especially recreational users. However, it is now recognized that these different effects are simply a consequence of dose, and that even at therapeutic doses, stimulants clearly show signs of increasing arousal. Some authors suggest that stimulants have a disease-centred effect in people with a diagnosis of ADHD, by acting on some unconfirmed abnormalities of the dopamine system (Spencer et al., 2005). Others, however, maintain that, consistent with a drug-centred model, the well-recognized psychoactive effects of low dose stimulants account for the effects that are seen in people with a diagnosis of ADHD (Breggin, 2001).

Randomized placebo-controlled trials show that stimulants can improve attention and concentration in the short term, and may reduce hyperactivity. However, a meta-analysis of these trials suggested that they were generally of poor quality, and there was evidence of publication bias (Schachter, Pham, King, Langford & Moher, 2001). In other words, there are likely to be further unpublished negative studies. There has only been one large long-term study conducted in children, the Multimodal Treatment study of children with ADHD (known as the MTA study). There was no placebo group in this study, but a group who received intensive 'medication management' was compared with other groups, including one that received a behaviour therapy programme. At 14 months the 'medication management' group performed better than the behaviour therapy group on some outcome measures, although not those rated by the blinded independent rater (The MTA

Cooperative Group, 1999). However, three-year results showed no differences between those who were allocated to, or took, medication versus others (Jensen et al., 2007).

The adverse effects of stimulants include emotional and cognitive effects. Animals given stimulants become overly focused on trivial, repetitive and meaningless tasks. Likewise, adults and children taking these drugs can develop obsessive–compulsive behaviours such as repeated checking, and also show reduced initiative and can become overly placid, depressed and 'zombie-like' (Breggin, 2001). Stimulants have also been shown to reduce growth. In the MTA study, children who took stimulants were 4 cm shorter than other children in the trial (Swanson et al., 2007). They also increase the activity of the heart, which can on rare occasions lead to sudden death (Nissen, 2006).

Benzodiazepines

Benzodiazepines include well-known drugs like diazepam (Valium), chlordiazepoxide (Librium) and lorezepam (Ativan). Their effects are similar to those of alcohol, and the state of intoxication they produce is characterized by feelings of calmness and relaxation, sedation and social disinhibition. They also produce muscular relaxation and induce sleep. They work by enhancing the action of gamma aminobutyric acid, known as GABA, which is the brain's main inhibitory neurotransmitter. They were extensively prescribed from the 1960s onwards to people who were labelled with anxiety and neurosis, especially women, often for long periods of time. In the 1980s it was recognized that when people take benzodiazepines for more than a few weeks, they become physically dependent and experience debilitating withdrawal symptoms if they stop taking them. Subsequently benzodiazepine use declined. Benzodiazepines continue to be prescribed for the treatment of insomnia and anxiety, but only short-term treatment is now recommended. They are also frequently prescribed to in-patients in psychiatric hospitals for purposes of sedation. They can cause dangerous respiratory suppression in overdose, but they are usually safer than other sedative drugs like alcohol and barbiturates, and they do not have the adverse cardiac effects associated with antipsychotic drugs.

Conclusions

The disease-centred view of drug action suggests that psychiatric drugs work by reversing an underlying brain abnormality. The model relies on the psychiatrist, as the expert in the nature of the presumed underlying disease, to judge what drug is suitable for each individual. This view is consistent with theories about the biochemical nature of psychiatric disorders, but there is little evidence that directly supports the idea that mental disorders are caused by biochemical abnormalities, or that psychiatric drugs have specific effects on underlying disease processes.

In contrast, the drug-centred model suggests that psychiatric drugs work, or appear to work, by inducing psychoactive effects that alter the normal state of consciousness, thought and emotions in anyone who takes them. Drugs may be useful because, by suppressing mental activity in differing ways, they can dampen down mental distress and reduce accompanying behavioural disturbance. This view of psychiatric drugs suggests the need for a more collaborative approach between professionals and service users. Since it is the mind-altering

properties of psychiatric drugs that determine whether or not they may be useful, it is ultimately up to the service user to judge whether these effects might help their particular circumstances, or whether they might do more harm than good.

Whichever model one prefers, it is important for those considering taking psychiatric medication to knowhow effective a drug is for a particular form of distress, the likely main effects and side-effects of the drug and, lastly, by what criteria they will judge its utility (e.g. impact on distress, everyday functioning, quality of life, sex life).

COMPULSORY PSYCHIATRIC TREATMENT

> It felt horrible because I was locked away for so many days and I couldn't go out and be free.
>
> It felt like a prison.
>
> I felt like I had done something wrong, that I was a criminal.
>
> So I felt, you know, being in hospital was one way of keeping me safe.
>
> It was very scary so you did need that containing place [hospital] if you are going to be challenged to that extent. It was terrifying.
>
> I need people around me so I don't go and stab myself or do anything really stupid.
>
> Comments by a number of mental health service users who have had experience of compulsory treatment (from Gilburt, Rose & Slade, 2008)

In Chapter 2 we saw how, over the last two hundred years or so, a series of laws have been passed to govern mental healthcare. One of the most controversial areas of mental health law is that, in certain circumstances, treatments can be given to people without their consent. The most frequent interventions given compulsorily are medication and ECT. A form of intervention which was used much more regularly in the past than now (Bentall, 2010) is **psychosurgery** (also known as **neurosurgery** for mental disorder). This is a 'a surgical operation with the aim of destroying brain tissue for the treatment of mental disorder' (Care Quality Commission, 2010, p. 93). Psychosurgery reached its peak in the 1940s and 1950s, the predominant operation being **leucotomy** (also known as frontal lobotomy – see Chapter 2), in which the connections to and from the prefrontal cortex were cut. In the 12 years between 1942 and 1954, there were 10,365 leucotomy procedures performed in England and Wales (Tooth & Newton, 1961). The use of psychosurgery is now very carefully regulated by law and it is now so rarely used that there was only one request for it in England and Wales in 2009–2010 (Care Quality Commission, 2010). As a result, it will not be discussed further here.

Why give treatment compulsorily?

This approach is based on the assumption that sometimes, when a person is in an extreme state of distress, their judgement might be so impaired that they could harm themselves or others: for example, they might attack another person because they wrongly believe that person wants to kill them. Most industrialized countries have laws enabling people to be given compulsory psychiatric treatment, though there are some variations between countries (e.g. within Europe) in when it can be used. In the US the terms **involuntary commitment** or civil commitment are used to refer to compulsory admission to hospital, while in Canada the term is **mandatory treatment**. There can even be differences within the same country.

Despite these variations, there are some common themes and ethical dilemmas. In this section we will focus on compulsory treatment in England and Wales because the authors are most familiar with it, it addresses both compulsory treatment in hospital and in the community (as in other countries such as Australia, Canada and the USA) and because it has raised some new issues for clinical psychology since, in England and Wales, the law has recently allowed psychologists to become involved in the administration of compulsory treatment.

In some jurisdictions (e.g. Scotland), specific evidence of impaired judgement must be presented before the person can be compulsorily treated. Elsewhere (e.g. in England and Wales) this is not required and a person can be treated under the Mental Health Act (MHA) so long as they have a sufficiently serious 'disorder or disability of mind' for which there is a treatment available. Treatment would usually involve admission to a psychiatric hospital and forcible administration of medication (e.g. via an injection) or electro-convulsive therapy (ECT) – see the later section in this chapter.

Is it ever ethical to treat someone compulsorily?

People can be given general health treatments against their will in certain very restricted circumstances: for example, if they have a dangerously infectious disease which could kill others. However, apart from these relatively rare situations, there is little compulsory treatment in general healthcare. Thus, for example, a terminally ill person could refuse treatment which might slow the progress of the disease affecting them. However, within the mental health field, compulsory treatment is used regularly and is understandably controversial. Proponents argue that if a person's judgement is impaired because of their distress, they might do something (e.g. harm themselves or others) that they would not have done were they not distressed. However, critics argue against its use. Janice Hartley and Tamasin Knight (two British psychologists who have received psychiatric treatment) and British clinical psychologist Rufus May (who was treated compulsorily as a teenager: see his account in Romme, Escher, Dillon, Corstens & Morris, 2009) have argued that compulsory treatments are unethical because they are inhumane and breach human rights such as autonomy (May, Hartley & Knight, 2003). See Chapter 7 for examples.

What is the Mental Health Act?

Most countries have laws regarding compulsory treatment but there are differences both in the criteria for its use and in the rates with which it is used (Salize & Dressing, 2004). In most countries, compulsory mental health treatment is reserved for cases where, as a result of their distress, a person is considered to pose a serious risk to themselves or others. In Scotland, compulsory treatment is governed by the Mental Health (Care and Treatment) (Scotland) Act 2003 whereas in Northern Ireland, compulsory treatment is governed by the Mental Health Northern Ireland Order (1986), which was amended by a further order in 2004.

The law governing compulsory psychiatric treatment in England and Wales is the 1983 Mental Health Act, which was amended in 2007 after much debate and criticism from many service user groups (see Chapter 7). In England and Wales, if a person is considered at risk, agreement must be reached between two doctors (usually a psychiatrist and GP) and an **Approved Mental Health Professional** (usually a social worker but sometimes a community mental health nurse or other professional). The person responsible for organizing the person's care is termed the **Responsible Clinician** (RC). Previously only a psychiatrist could take this role, but now other mental health professionals, such as clinical psychologists, can do so, provided they fulfil the specialist requirements. The involvement of clinical psychologists in treating people compulsorily has been the subject of much debate (e.g. Cooke, Kinderman & Harper, 2002; Diamond, 2002; Harper, 2005, 2006; Holmes, 2002; Pilgrim, 2005; Taylor, Gillmer & Robertson, 2003). Proponents argue that having a psychologist RC might make sense if a service user was receiving essentially psychological interventions; it could be a way of designing care around a psychological formulation. Critics argue that the role itself means that psychologists would be drawn into a specifically social control function and that it would disrupt trust between psychologist and client (Holmes, 2002). However, currently very few clinical psychologists appear to have taken up the role: Gillmer and Taylor (2011) noted they were the only two non-medical RCs in England and that there was only one in Wales.

The Act has a number of sections outlining the rules for the use of compulsory treatment in different sets of circumstances; this is the origin of the slang term '**sectioned**', meaning to be compulsorily admitted for psychiatric treatment. Section 2 of the Act concerns admission to hospital for assessment (for which the maximum stay allowed is 28 days). Section 3 governs admission for treatment (which can be for up to six months, although it can then be renewed).

One of the most controversial aspects of the 2007 amendment to the Mental Health Act was that it introduced the practice of **Supervised Community Treatment**: in other words, a person no longer has to stay in hospital to be given treatment compulsorily. Instead, provided they agreed to follow their **Community Treatment Order** or CTO (e.g. to take medication, attend day centres or allow visits by mental health professionals), they can now be treated at home. This idea was first raised whilst the Mental Health Act was being revised in the 2000s, when some commentators warned that there was nothing to prevent these orders being used more often than intended: a prediction that seems to have been borne out. In 2009–2010 (the first full year for which figures are available) 4103 CTOs were used: considerably more than the government's original estimate of 400–600 per year (Lawton Smith, 2010). The use of CTOs fell slightly in 2010–2011 when 3834 were used (NHS Information Centre, 2011). In the US this procedure is termed **outpatient commitment** or **assisted outpatient treatment**. In Canada, new mental health legislation, which came into effect in 2000, introduced community treatment orders into the Canadian mental health system.

What is meant by risk of harm to self or others?

The most serious risks of harm are **self-harm** (discussed in Chapter 13), suicide and homicide. **Suicide** is much more common than homicide: for example, the UK saw 4421 suicides in 2006, of whom 3350 were men and 1071 women (9% were aged under 25, 41% aged 25–44, 34% aged 45–64 and 16% 65 and over – National Confidential Inquiry into Suicide and Homicide by People With Mental Illness [NCISH] 2009). Only about a quarter of these people had been in contact with mental health services in the 12 preceding months. Even if a person is admitted into hospital this does not remove the risk; in 2005, 161 psychiatric in-patients killed themselves (NCISH, 2009). **Homicide** is much less common: there were 773 deaths initially recorded as homicide in England and Wales in 2007–2008 and 73% of the victims were male (Povey, Coleman, Kaiza & Roe, 2009). Among female victims, 73% knew the main suspect, compared to only 48% of male victims (Povey et al., 2009). The proportion of homicides committed by those in distress is approximately 10% in the UK, and this has been falling as a proportion of overall homicides over the last fifty years (Povey et al., 2009) – even though the overall homicide rate has been increasing – see Figure 8.2. To put the numbers of homicides and suicides into some kind of context, 2538 people died in road traffic accidents in 2008 (Office for National Statistics, 2010a).

It is a surprise to many people that only about 10% of homicides are committed by those in distress. Some researchers argue that negative and stereotyped media reporting about mental health has exaggerated the risks posed to others by people in distress (Care Services Improvement Partnership/ Shift, 2006; D. Rose, 1998b). A diagnosis of major mental illness appears to be far less predictive of violence than being 'young, male, single, lower class, and substance abusing or substance dependent' (Hiday, 1995, p. 123). Indeed, people with psychiatric diagnoses are six times more likely to die by homicide than the general population and they are also at a raised risk of dying as a result of suicide and accident (Hiroeh, Appleby, Mortensen & Dunn, 2001).

Based on their meta-analysis, Large, Smith and Nielssen (2009) conclude that homicide rates by people with a diagnosis of schizophrenia are correlated with the rates of all homicides. Dorling (2005) argues that overall murder rates are related to social conditions: for example, as women's social power has

increased in recent years, so the murder rate of women in the UK has fallen. In contrast, there are more men killing other men: he concludes that this is because the 'lives of men born since 1964 have polarised, and the polarisation, inequality, curtailed opportunities and hopelessness have bred fear, violence and murder' (p. 39).

Who is most likely to receive compulsory treatment?

Young men, particularly those from a minority ethnic group background, are the most likely to be subject to compulsory treatment (Audini & Lelliott, 2002; Care Quality Commission, 2010; Mental Health Act Commission, 2009). For example, compared with the national average, the following ethnic groups are more likely to be detained under the MHA when admitted to a psychiatric ward: Black Caribbean, Black African, Other Black and White/Black Caribbean Mixed groups, White Irish, Other White and Other Mixed groups (Care Quality Commission, 2011). Moreover, some black and dual heritage (e.g. white/black) groups are more likely to be referred to mental health services from the criminal justice system, such as by the police (Care Quality Commission, 2011).

That young men from black minority ethnic groups experience an increased use of compulsory treatment and are over-represented in secure psychiatric facilities is a well-established finding. Explanations for this have included that it reflects a genetic vulnerability amongst black men for psychosis, that it reflects institutional racism and that it reflects the effects on young black men of living in a racist society. There is no evidence for the genetic explanation; for example, Hickling and Rodgers-Johnson (1995) reported lower incidence rates for diagnoses of schizophrenia in Jamaica compared with African–Caribbean people in the UK and Holland. Dein, Williams and Dein (2007) suggest that the over-representation reflects higher rates of distress amongst the African–Caribbean population and a late presentation to services. Boydell et al., (2001) reported a higher prevalence of schizophrenia diagnoses among black people living in majority white areas in the UK compared with black people living in residential areas where the majority of people were black. This study has been replicated (Das-Munshi, Becares, Dewey, Stansfield & Prince, 2010), though the nature of any causal relationship remains unclear (Lester, 2010). However, it is suggestive that being in a majority white area can lead to distress (see also Read, 2004a). There is also evidence that cultural misunderstanding (Littlewood & Lipsedge, 1997) and institutional racism (Fernando, 1991) play a part. Boast and Chesterman (1995) found that, at each stage of black men's contact with the mental health and criminal justice systems, there was an incremental increase in discrimination. They suggested that the formation of stereotypes was significant, as these modified the social judgments of professionals (e.g. about diagnosis and risk).

Lastly, a greater proportion of those living in London and the North West of England receive compulsory treatment (Department of Health/National Statistics, 2010). Bindman, Tighe, Thornicroft and Leese (2002) note that socially deprived areas with poorer mental health services tend to have higher rates of compulsory treatment.

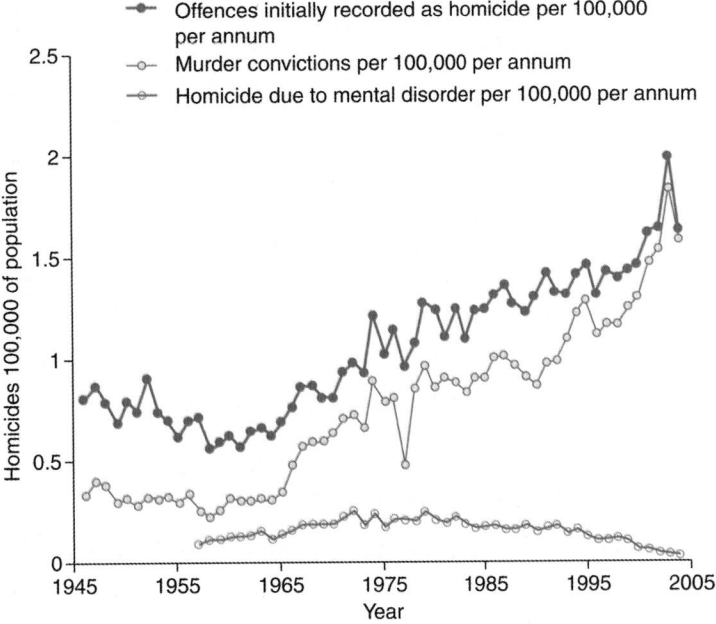

Figure 8.2 **Overall homicides in England and Wales compared with those due to mental disorder**

Source: **Large et al. (2008).**

The rise in the use of compulsory treatment in England and Wales

A 2010 census of mental health in-patients reported that 49% had been admitted under the Mental Health Act (Care Quality Commission, 2011). This is quite a high figure, although the Mental Health Act Commission suggests that part of the reason for this is the lack of adequate services in the community that might prevent an admission; they also note that other countries have proportionately more psychiatric beds (Mental Health Act Commission, 2009).

There has been an upward trend in the use of compulsory treatment since the 1980s, with the overall number of detentions in hospital as a result of the MHA reaching 49,417 in 2009–2010 (Department of Health/National Statistics, 2010). This number is double the number of detentions in the 1980s, as can be seen in Figure 8.3.

Figure 8.3 includes three lines: the top one represents the number of people admitted to hospital under section 2 of the MHA for assessment. We can see that it has seen the largest increase, from just over 10,000 in 1984 to 26,122 in 2007–2008 (Mental Health Act Commission, 2009). The second line down includes people who came into hospital voluntarily and consensually (i.e. 'informal admissions'), but who were then prevented from leaving because of concerns about risk of harm and were then detained for compulsory treatment. This also has seen a substantial increase, though not as great as section 2 admissions. The third line (near the bottom of the graph) represents those people who were admitted for treatment straight away under section 3 (i.e. without an admission first for assessment). There appears to have been little change here. It is unclear why these numbers have increased, though some commentators note that the big increases in the 1990s reflect negative media coverage of mental health as a result of homicides committed by people in distress, notably the killing of Jonathan Zito by Christopher Clunis in 1992 (leading to a well-publicized inquiry) and the killing of Lin and Megan Russell by Michael Stone in 1996, leading to a trial, an appeal, a re-trial and an inquiry (Laurance, 2003a).

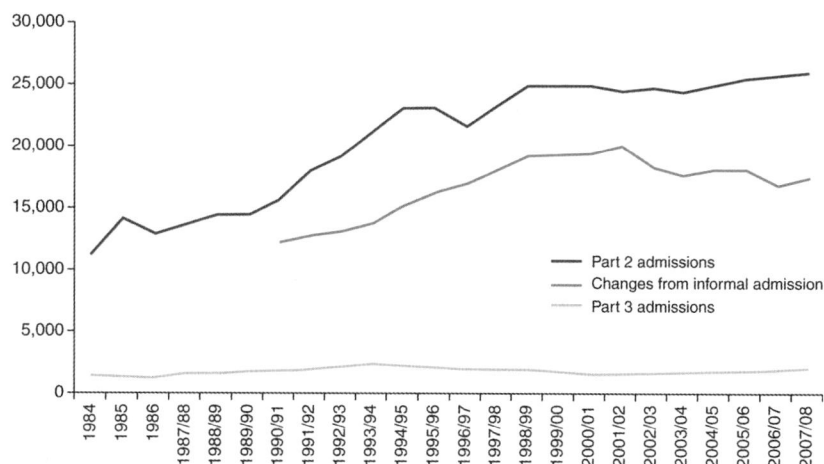

Figure 8.3 Admissions to hospital under the Mental Health Act in England and Wales between 1984 and 2008

Source: **Mental Health Act Commission (2009).**

ELECTRO-CONVULSIVE THERAPY

After every treatment he would say how do you feel and I'd say God I feel awful, just awful. What I finally realized was that as long as I said I felt bad I kept getting them because he thought I needed more treatment. So the next time I said I feel much better now ... He said oh maybe we'd be able to stop these soon. After the next one I said I felt great. And then he stopped them. That was what all the other patients around the hospital taught each other – that if you wanted to stop getting these things, don't say how bad you feel, say how good you feel. Then they will think they're working and leave you alone.

Woman aged 32

But I did the ECT treatments and let me tell you; it pulled me out of my suicidal stage. Things began to look brighter in my life. Unfortunately I am now having a relapse. I am starting again my ECT treatments Monday. Yes is it scary, yes it is expensive, yes some people do not benefit, but I have completely benefited by it. The only problem is now is that I need more of it to go on. The only problem that I had during my sessions and even now is the memory loss that I have. I cannot remember things back to two years ago.

Woman, age unknown
Service users who have received ECT
(from Rose, Fleischmann & Wykes, 2004, p. 289)

What is ECT?

Electro-convulsive therapy or ECT (also known as electro-shock therapy) involves placing electrodes on a person's head and then passing an electrical current across the brain to stimulate convulsions, of the kind that can be seen during an epileptic seizure. It is unclear how it achieves its effects: as NICE notes, '[a]lthough ECT has been used since the 1930s, there is still no generally accepted theory that explains its mechanism of action' (National Institute for Health and Clinical Excellence, 2003, p. 9). Muscle relaxants and an anaesthetic are administered so that the person's body is immobile (otherwise the person would move as they convulsed) – this is known as 'modified ECT' ('unmodified ECT' is administered without drugs). Many people are surprised that ECT is still a common treatment, as it is very controversial. Readers may recall its portrayal in the film *One Flew over the Cuckoo's Nest* when McMurphy (the character played by Jack Nicholson) receives the treatment and he appears to have lost his personality, seeming like a zombie. ECT is also discussed in Chapter 11.

What are the origins of ECT?

ECT originated with the Italian neurologist Ugo Cerletti. Following reports that those with epilepsy appeared to experience fewer psychotic symptoms, he experimented with inducing epileptic reactions in animals. In an abattoir, seeing pigs prepared for slaughter, he noted how they were initially stunned and then convulsed following the administration of an electric current through their temples and he decided this would be appropriate for humans. The 'discovery' of

ECT was serendipitous rather than theory-based. Indeed, there is considerable debate about its mechanism of action (Johnstone, 2003; Read, 2004b).

How often is it used?

The most recent survey of the use of ECT in England was in 2002 (Department of Health, 2003). This revealed that, between January and March 2002, 2272 people received the treatment, which would suggest that, if ECT administrations are constant over the course of a year, approximately 9000 people received ECT in 2002. Of the 2272 receiving ECT in the first quarter of the year, 1608 were women and 664 were men. Forty seven per cent of women and 45% of the men were aged 65 and over. The majority of people received 6–8 administrations. Of the 2272 total, 616 were detained under the Mental Health Act: only 28% of these had consented to the procedure. Seventy six people were treated under 'emergency' powers (i.e. when ECT is reported to have been given as a 'life-saving' measure; for example, because the person is so depressed they have stopped eating). Three hundred and seventy people were given the treatment without their consent (this is allowed once a second doctor has agreed). Of those in hospital voluntarily, 98% consented to the treatment. However, Rose, Wykes, Bindman and Fleischmann (2005) report that a third of patients who had signed a consent form did not feel they had freely consented. ECT administration has been falling gradually over the last 20 years (see Figure 8.4).

When is it used?

ECT used to be prescribed for a variety of forms of distress, including diagnoses of schizophrenia. However, nowadays, its use tends to be more restricted. The National Institute for Health and Clinical Excellence (2009a) recommends that ECT is considered only in relation to depression and, even then, only 'for acute treatment of severe depression that is life-threatening and when a rapid response is required, or

when other treatments have failed' (p. 41). It is not to be used routinely for people with a diagnosis of moderate depression unless 'their depression has not responded to multiple drug treatments and psychological treatment' (p. 42). The 2002 Department of Health survey reported that, of those given a diagnosis, 81% of those receiving ECT had a diagnosis of 'mood disorder' whilst 7% had diagnoses of schizophrenia, or schizotypal or delusional disorders.

What are its side-effects?

A number of side-effects have been associated with ECT. For example, a range of memory problems have been reported, including retrograde amnesia, anterograde amnesia and service users' own accounts of memory loss (Read, 2004b). Initially, reports of memory problems were the source of much debate. However, there does now appear to be a consensus from a range of studies that a range of cognitive problems can follow ECT administration (McElhiney, Moody, Steif et al., 1995; Neylan et al., 2001; National Institute For Health and Clinical Excellence, 2003; Robertson & Pryor, 2006). However, there are other potential side-effects. Read (2004b) and Johnstone (2003) note reports of brain damage visible at autopsy. There also appears to be a slight but significant elevated risk of death following ECT, both during the course of treatment but also continuing some time afterwards (Johnstone, 2003; Read, 2004b; Read & Bentall, 2010a), though the causal mechanism is unclear. ECT recipients have mixed views about ECT, although the majority appear to report adverse effects and negative experiences of ECT (Johnstone, 1999b; Rose et al., 2003, 2004).

Is ECT effective?

The effectiveness of ECT is heavily contested. The two NICE (2003, 2009a) reviews concluded that it was effective in certain circumstances, such as in cases where people have a diagnosis of severe depression. However, Read and Bentall (2010a) note that many studies inadequately control for methodological problems. For example, few studies explain how blindness to the experimental conditions was achieved. Moreover, as we have noted elsewhere in this chapter, a placebo-controlled study is the most rigorous. In the case of ECT, a placebo form of ECT – so-called **'sham ECT'** – is administered. This involves the participant going through a procedure identical to that of ECT, including receiving anaesthetic and muscle relaxants and even having the electrodes placed on the head, but with no electric current passing through the brain. Read and Bentall (2010a) note that when only these placebo-controlled studies are examined, ECT appears to have only a slight benefit during the course of treatment, but that this falls away as soon as treatment stops. They report that there is no evidence that ECT saves lives or reduces suicide (indeed, they note evidence that it may increase suicide risk). Johnstone (2003) argues that ECT researchers themselves have stated that intensive nursing support might be efficacious when a person is so depressed they have stopped eating. Given the elevated risk of death and the risks associated with having a general anaesthetic, Read and Bentall (2010a) conclude that 'the very short-term benefit gained by a small minority cannot justify the risks to which all ECT recipients are exposed' (p. 344).

Administrations

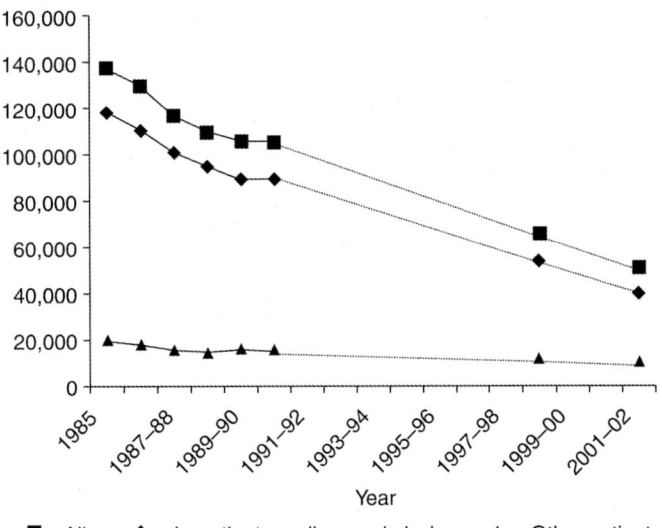

Figure 8.4 **Number of ECT procedures administered in England between January–March in the years 1985 to 1989–90, 1998–99, 2001–02**

Source: **Department of Health (2003).**

PSYCHOLOGICAL THERAPIES

Paul Kelly and Paul Moloney

Counselling provided space to talk and be listened to, a chance to discover myself and my potential. A place to be heard and understood, a chance for personal growth, development and change.

Psychotherapy provided understanding, validation and acceptance of experience from my perspective. Opportunity to talk over the stresses in social and family life and traumatic experiences in psychiatric system.

It was disturbing and unsettling, confusing, like brain washing.

Brought up a lot of issues we didn't have time to deal with. Finished when therapist changed jobs, finished very badly.

Service users' comments on psychological therapies from Rogers and Pilgrim (1993).

This section focuses on another class of interventions for distress: psychological therapies. It will begin with an overview of what psychotherapy is, including a brief description of some of the main schools, leading on to a discussion of the evidence for whether psychological therapy is an effective way of treating psychological distress, a question that is closely connected with the issue of power as it arises within the therapeutic relationship, and beyond. The section will conclude with a discussion of some of the possible implications of this critique for the clinical practice of psychotherapy.

What is psychotherapy?

The word 'psychotherapy' originates in the Greek words 'psyche' (breath, spirit, or soul) and therapeai (to cure). In modern usage, the term refers to a broad range of 'talking treatments' carried out by professionals with the aim of alleviating distress or facilitating psychological change (McLeod, 1994; Pilgrim, 1997). Most forms of psychotherapy involve verbal communication between the therapist and the client but can also include other forms of communication such as art, drama or music. These treatments can be provided by any of a wide range of professional groups as part of their role – including psychologists, social workers and educators– as well as by practitioners who describe themselves solely as psychotherapists. Practitioners of psychotherapy can be working in public health and social care services, such as the NHS, or in private practice, and they may draw upon a variety of different theoretical approaches in their work.

Historically, most cultures have developed ways of addressing personal problems through social rituals such as religious practices like shamanism (Fancher, 1996). These rituals often have an element of personal inquiry, and in the ancient Hellenic world, for example, many thinkers saw philosophical discussion as a way of helping people deal with their problems in living (Howard, 2000). However, the notion of paid professionals specifically trained in the theory and practice of healing distress through conversation distinguishes psychotherapy from other forms of human helping relationships and makes it a fairly recent social invention, originating in 19th-century Europe (Cushman, 1995; Fancher, 1996). Since this time the field has greatly expanded, to the extent that talking treatment is considered – at least in Western cultures – as a viable way to find greater personal authenticity on the one hand and to overcome clinically significant misery, on the other (Erwin, 1997; McLeod, 2003). Most writers on psychotherapy tend to see its increasing availability as a sign of medical or humanistic progress (see Beck, 1991, for instance). However, the growth of psychotherapy may just as easily have been a response to the isolation and loneliness that went with 20th-century urbanization (Gellner, 1993; Stivers, 2004).

Estimates suggest that there are over four hundred different forms of psychotherapy in existence today (McLeod, 2004; Morrall, 2008), and it is obviously not within the scope of this section to describe all of them. In order to simplify this task, therefore, we have focused most of our discussion on the three broad families of individual therapies which are often cited in textbooks as the best known and most widely practised, and which offer competing paradigms of the theory and application of talking treatment (Dryden, 2007; McLeod, 2003): psychoanalysis, cognitive behavioural therapy, and the humanistic and existential therapies.

Psychoanalysis

As we saw in Chapter 2, it is generally agreed that psychotherapy as a formal profession in Western cultures has its origins in the work of an Austrian doctor, Sigmund Freud, who in the late 19th century developed psychoanalysis (Cushman, 1995). This school is largely based on Freud's notion that conscious thoughts, feelings and behaviours are determined by unconscious mental dynamics. Freud believed that psychological distress or psychopathology arises when unconscious thoughts, feelings or impulses are blocked from conscious awareness because they may be disturbing to the person. Psychoanalysts believe that our conscious minds censor out the most disturbing thoughts and feelings, and they are therefore interested in the client's dreams and fantasies as a way of observing these unconscious thought processes. Therapists in this tradition often make use of methods such as **free association** – in which the client is encouraged to say whatever comes into their mind– in order to help them to express their hidden thoughts, feelings and motivations. Another commonly used method is to examine how the client relates to the therapist. It is assumed that these reactions can provide a window into the emotional attitudes that the client has acquired toward key people in their lives, such as their parents, for instance: reactions that may still be distorting their relationships with others. This expression of the 'echo' of past relationships in current relationships is termed the **'transference'**. As the client reflects upon this transference of feelings as reported by the practitioner, the way is cleared for them to become less stuck in the past and to live a more purposeful life, open to the here and now (Bateman & Holmes, 1995; Jacobs, 2006).

A number of variants of Freud's ideas have been developed over the past century and these have been given the generic term 'psychodynamic' psychotherapies. They can be distinguished from psychoanalysis by their differing emphases on the nature and importance of the unconscious, their focus upon the extent to which the therapist makes use of their own intuitions about the client, and in the relative brevity of the process of treatment, but all have their roots in Freud's original theories (Corrigall, 2003; Jacobs, 2006; Lomas, 1999).

Cognitive–behavioural therapy

Cognitive–behavioural therapy (CBT) was developed as a model of therapy from the integration of behaviour therapy and cognitive therapy. **Behaviour therapy** emerged from its parent discipline of behaviourism in the early 20th century. **Behaviourism** is associated with the work of theorists such as Ivan Pavlov, a Russian physiologist (Gray, 1979) and B.F. Skinner, an American psychologist (Skinner, 1974) who endeavoured to develop a scientific approach to the study of human behaviour. The emphasis of behaviour therapy is on the measurement and treatment of observable problem behaviours – such as compulsive hand-washing or extreme and 'irrational' fears (often described as phobias) – through processes like **graded exposure**, in which a person employs cognitive–behavioural coping strategies as they expose themselves to feared objects or situations, working through a hierarchical system in which they move from the least to the most feared level. However, behaviour therapy was criticized for ignoring subjective human experiences such as beliefs, memories and feelings, which were increasingly thought to play a role in the genesis of distress. Cognitive therapy emerged during the 1960s and is especially linked with the work of an American psychiatrist, Aaron Beck (Beck, 1991). **Cognitive therapy** is based upon the idea that psychological distress is sustained by maladaptive beliefs that have been acquired at an early stage in life – for example, 'I am a bad person'. The aim of cognitive therapy is to assist the client to develop more helpful or realistic beliefs about themselves, others and the world around them (Weishaar, 1996). CBT developed during the 1970s as an integration of the ideas and practices of cognitive therapy and behaviour therapy. CBT therapists therefore use a combination of behavioural techniques, such as the testing out of fixed problematic beliefs in a range of different circumstances, while drawing upon cognitive therapy methods. These may include the use of educational literature, aimed at helping the client to manage their symptoms more effectively and methods such as **'Socratic dialogue'**: a systematic attempt to help the client to question and challenge their unhelpful beliefs about themselves (e.g. 'I must achieve perfection in anything I attempt' or 'I am unlovable and worthless') and their world. CBT is considered to be one of the more structured and goal-directed forms of therapy (P. Gilbert, 2009).

The humanistic and existential therapies

These therapies owe their existence to humanistic and existential philosophies, which emphasize that the quest for meaning is central to our lives (Cooper, 2003; van Deurzen, 1998; Binswanger, 1946). Perhaps the best-known example of humanistic therapy is the **Person-Centred Approach**, associated mainly with the work of an American psychologist, Carl Rogers, in the 1950s. It emerged as part of what became known as the **Third Force in Psychotherapy**, itself a reaction against the dominance of psychoanalysis and behaviour therapy in the mental health field at that time. Rogers believed that more attention should be paid to an individual's personal meaning system in contrast to the focus within behaviourism on the objective measurement of observable behaviours. His work also emphasized positive aspects of psychological development in contrast to the focus on psychopathology within psychoanalysis. Rogers believed that psychological distress arises when our natural tendencies towards individuality and emotional honesty are thwarted by the oppressive conventions of society or, worse still, by the abusive conduct of others. Rogers recommended that the therapist should endeavour to provide the client with a safe and accepting relationship as a kind of antidote to these experiences. Based upon the three core principles of unconditional positive regard, empathy and genuineness, this relationship would enable the client to slowly give voice to unacknowledged feelings and desires, and to rekindle their inbuilt self confidence and openness to others (Raskin, 1996).

In summary, these three approaches can be viewed as relying respectively upon the use of insight, learning or love as the main vehicle for inducing positive change (Smail, 1987), while in terms of the therapist's role, three distinct types of character can be distinguished: the calm parent of the psychoanalyst, the pragmatic instructor of the CBT therapist, and the thoughtfully honest friend, as personified in the humanistic counsellor (Howard, 1998).

Despite the many fundamental theoretical and practical differences between schools of psychotherapy, they nevertheless share some common aspects. For example, most of them attempt to identify and ameliorate the hitherto concealed factors that are presumed to underlie the client's manifest feelings or actions. This is true even of behavioural treatments, which, by helping the client to understand what is reinforcing problematic behaviours, seek to reveal to the client things about themselves of which they were not previously aware (Mair, 1992). Moreover, most schools now recognize that in therapy, the formation of a trusting, collaborative relationship between both parties is essential, although some approaches give more weight to the importance of this relationship than others (Beck, 1991; Cheshire & Pilgrim, 2004; Jacobs, 1999; Rogers, 1980; Winter, 2008). This relationship has been seen as one of the key 'non-specific' factors in psychotherapy. In recent years there has been a movement toward the integration of different therapeutic approaches. Surveys suggest that up to half of all practicing therapists describe themselves as 'integrative practitioners', who will draw upon theoretical perspectives and techniques from different kinds of therapy so as to fit each client's personal style, preferences and problems (Dryden, 2007; McLeod, 2003). The field has also seen a growing emphasis upon credentialized training and registration under the aegis of professional bodies (such as the British Psychological Society or the United Kingdom Council for Psychotherapy) as a guarantor of therapist competence, ethical commitment and expertise. This emphasis upon technical skill also reflects the extent to which therapists in public health services are increasingly governed by national treatment guidelines from the National Institute for Health and Clinical Excellence (NICE), which recommend predetermined or so-called 'manualized' treatment programmes, particularly in relation to the use of CBT. This trend was seen most clearly in the UK's *Improving Access to Psychological Therapies* programme, an attempt to use standardized psychological techniques to cure and prevent mental illness on an industrial scale (Marzillier & Hall, 2009; Newham IAPT, 2007).

Does psychotherapy work?

Given the diversity of theories and practices within the field of psychotherapy, it is perhaps not surprising that research into whether psychotherapy is an effective treatment for personal distress is a complex and contested field.

The demand for psychological therapies has grown in recent years

Since the 1950s, many thousands of research studies have been carried out examining whether clients' problems are reduced following treatment with psychotherapy. The broad consensus appears to be that this is the case (Lambert & Ogles, 2004). However, to demonstrate that these improvements are the result of psychotherapy rather than some other common factor (e.g. the simple passage of time, or patient expectations), investigators in this field increasingly rely on the evidence from randomized controlled trials (RCTs). As we saw in the previous section (Box 8.2), the purpose of these experiments is to control all possible factors that may influence the outcome so that any improvement in psychological functioning can be confidently attributed to the treatment alone (Cooper, 2008). On the basis of meta-analyses of RCTs, many forms of psychotherapy do seem to lead to significant improvements in the mental health of up to a quarter of recipients (e.g. Smith, Glass & Miller, 1980; Lipsey & Wilson, 1993). Furthermore, when psychotherapy is compared to medication for the treatment of forms of distress such as depression or panic, the evidence appears to show that it is at least as effective in the short term and perhaps more helpful when considered over a period of a year or more post-treatment (Chilvers et al., 2001; Gould, Otto & Pollack, 1995). However, this finding must be tempered by the fact that, as we saw in the previous section, there are increasing doubts about the effectiveness of many widely used psychoactive drugs, including the so-called antidepressants and antipsychotics (Breggin, 1993; Moncrieff, 2008).

In addition to the question of whether psychotherapy is helpful, researchers have turned their attention to whether certain forms of psychotherapy are more potent than others, when applied to specific kinds of psychological problem (Chambless & Ollendick, 2001). In a review of this evidence, Roth and Fonagy (2005) produced a comprehensive guide to specific therapies that appear to be most effective for a range of different clinical presentations. This type of evidence is increasingly used by organizations such as NICE in its clinical treatment guidelines for clinicians and patients, the intention being to assist both parties in choosing the most helpful treatments for specific diagnoses, such as depression or anxiety (e.g. NICE, 2004a, 2004b).

On the basis of this evidence, can we conclude that talking treatments are a well-established and effective way of helping the distressed person? Unfortunately, the answer to this question is more complex than it may appear. A more critical examination of the research evidence points to a number of serious problems with the findings upon which these claims of effectiveness are based. For instance, there appear to be some fundamental methodological flaws in many, if not most, of the studies that are included in the meta-analyses of psychotherapy outcome (Bolsover, 2004; Epstein, 1996; Mair, 1992; McLeod, 1994). Many of these reflect the factors noted earlier in Table 8.2. These include the use of inadequate control groups (Holmes, 2002); a reliance on non-clinical treatment groups such as university students (Epstein, 2006); systematic participant attrition from treatment (Eisner, 2000); the use of flawed outcome measures (Tolman, 1994) that rely exclusively upon self report and are subject to participant and researcher bias (Epstein, 1996; Frank & Frank, 1991). In a detailed analysis of these flaws, Epstein (2006) concludes that 'against rigorous standards of clinical science, psychotherapy has rarely, if ever, gone through a definitive test of its effectiveness. At best, its outcomes are indeterminate; psychotherapy is most likely ineffective' (Epstein, 2006. p. 14). There are further problems. For example, if a therapy is compared only with treatment as usual (often simply being prescribed medication) rather than with a competing psychotherapy, this will exaggerate the efficacy of the intervention. Similarly, an attempt to control for therapist factors means that many RCTs utilize the same set of therapists who provide all the therapies to be compared (e.g. supportive counselling versus CBT). However, often the therapists in the study are more experienced in – and have a preference for – one of the therapies. This appears to influence study outcomes in that, generally, outcomes are better for the therapy the therapist is more experienced in and has a preference for: Luborsky et al. (1999) term this the 'therapist allegiance' effect. Moreover, proponents of the non-preferred therapy may argue that the version of their therapy in the RCT is not an accurate one. Sometimes a comparison intervention like 'supportive counselling' or 'befriending' is originated and manualized by adherents of the experimental intervention. In one recent review, Lynch, Laws and McKenna (2010) argue that the closer the methodological design of a CBT RCT to that of a double-blind trial, the less effective CBT appears to be.

Finally, there is a lack of research into whether the apparent gains made in psychotherapy are maintained in the long term, and the research that does exist gives little reassurance (Härkänen, Knekt, Virtala & Lindfors, 2005). For example, in one such study, Lipsitz, Mannuzza, Klein, Ross and Fyer (1999) found that among clients followed up ten to sixteen years after treatment for a specific phobia, approximately three quarters had re-experienced a clinically significant return of their problems, and felt that their lives were impaired as a result.

This overall picture becomes even less encouraging in the light of the doubts that have been voiced about the validity of meta-analytic studies, which, as we saw in the previous section, are only as dependable as the quality of the data upon which they are based and cannot be taken at face value (Charlton, 2000). Indeed, there has been a longstanding debate about the relevance of RCT methods *themselves* to the assessment of talking therapies (Guy, Thomas, Stephenson

& Loewenthal, 2011). Some writers have objected that it is impossible to provide an adequate placebo treatment for any therapy under investigation, because a truly convincing placebo would amount to a new form of psychotherapy (Mair, 1992). Thus, whilst the gold standard in pharmaceutical research is the double-blind (or even triple blind) RCT, RCTs of any psychotherapy are often not single-blind. Some commentators have questioned the 'drug metaphor' assumed by most psychotherapy RCTs: that an RCT can help determine the 'active ingredient' in a therapy like a pharmaceutical RCT (Stiles & Stiles, 1989). Others have argued that the interactions between clients, therapists and, particularly, the techniques that are used are simply too dynamic and various to pass through the crude sieve of the RCT approach, a method that is better suited to the study of inert and easily dispensed physical treatments such as tablets (Marzillier, 2004; Smail, 1978), although even here, as we saw in the previous section, the psychological processes of the placebo effect are very pronounced (see also Goldacre, 2009). All these difficulties are summarized in Table 8.4.

Table 8.4 **Additional problems with RCTs in psychotherapy efficacy studies**

- Impossibility of blinding clients, therapists or researchers to condition
- Challenge of randomization
- Impact of therapist's preference for a particular therapeutic orientation
- Therapy fidelity
- Comparison with another therapy or only treatment as usual?
- Length of follow-up

As a result of these methodological debates, the situation is now quite confusing for service users and mental health professionals alike, both proponents and critics of CBT arguing that the evidence supports their position. For example, Lynch, Laws and McKenna (2010) note that:

> CBT for schizophrenia thus finds itself in the unusual position of being recommended in the revised NICE guideline (NICE, 2009b), despite having failed in all of the treatment studies that used both control interventions and blind evaluations (p. 14)

Some solutions have been proposed: for example, Luborsky et al. (1999) suggest that researchers should select therapists who have an allegiance to that therapy; others suggest more of a focus on common factors (Shapiro & Paley, 2002) or a transtheoretical approach (Prochaska & Norcross, 2010). At the time of writing, these debates have not been resolved and indeed may never be so, because they hinge upon irreconcilable views of psychological functioning and of the extent to which that can be measured by standardized and experimental means (see, for instance, Kline, 1988).

Proponents of RCTs argue that equivalence may be a methodological artefact, in that the successful elements of comparison therapies like the 'supportive counselling' treatment (which has often been the comparison intervention in RCTs of CBT for diagnoses of psychosis) are successful because they are similar to the active ingredients of CBT (Tarrier, Haddock, Barrowclough & Wykes, 2002). Critics, however, argue that a better research strategy would be to embrace a broader range of research designs than RCTs and to focus on the common

factors between therapies rather than the often small differences between 'brand name' therapies (Paley & Shapiro, 2002; Shapiro & Paley, 2002). There is much that we do not fully understand, even about CBT, which is probably the most studied form of psychotherapy. For example, the development of **third wave behavioural therapies** like **Dialectical Behaviour Therapy** (DBT), which emphasizes developing one's mindfulness (see Chapter 13) and **Acceptance and Commitment Therapy**, which emphasizes the need to adopt an accepting stance towards oneself (Hayes, Follette & Linehan, 2004), has raised questions about what the active ingredients of CBT are. For example, one review of studies of these ingredients in CBT for people with diagnoses of anxiety or depression– termed **component studies** – by researchers influenced by the third wave therapies concluded that:

> almost without exception, component studies found no difference in effectiveness between the cognitive and behavioural elements of CBT. Nor did cognitive interventions provide 'added value' to behavioral interventions. Taken together, these studies provide a substantial body of research showing that cognitive interventions are not a necessary component of the therapy
>
> Longmore and Worrell (2007, p. 184)

They conclude that there is a need, instead, to focus future research on 'behavioral change, constructivism and attentional control' (Longmore & Worrell, 2007, p. 184).

In addition to the problems with the outcome evidence for the effectiveness of psychotherapy, there is also evidence that non-qualified amateurs can be as effective in delivering therapy as qualified professionals (Dawes, 1994; Stivers, 1999). In one sense, this finding is not surprising, given that, when it comes to rating the effectiveness of talking treatment, a number of researchers have shown that a range of so-called non-specific factors consistently emerge as being two to three times more potent than the therapist's ability to deploy therapeutic techniques, which themselves may account for as little as 10% of the variance in treatment outcome (Howard, 2005). Non-specific factors include the availability of support in the client's life outside the consulting room and the quality of the therapeutic relationship itself (Bohart, 2000; Bergin & Garfield, 1994; Mahrer, 1998). The importance of the client's environment is further supported by the consistent finding that the closer any clinical study comes to a public health service setting in which service users are likely to be struggling with a wide range of social adversities, the less successful psychological treatments have been shown to be (Bostock, 1998; Epstein, 1996). Some researchers (e.g. Seligman, 1995) draw a distinction between studies of **efficacy** (an attempt to clarify how powerful an intervention is through the kind of RCTs based in research settings with highly selected participants) and studies of **effectiveness** (where interventions are evaluated in actual service settings with 'real' clients who have complex sets of problems). Unsurprisingly, the vast majority of studies are of efficacy rather than effectiveness (Cahill, Barkham & Stiles, 2010).

In summary then, it could be argued that after nearly 60 years of strenuous efforts, the field of psychotherapy research is still riven with debate and uncertainty, as it has failed to conclusively demonstrate that one therapeutic approach is more effective than any other, or that trained practitioners are more helpful than their untrained counterparts.

Our currency, your problem: the question of power in psychotherapy

It is clear that many mental health service users value the opportunity to receive talking therapy, which can represent a chance to feel that they have been listened to and that their problems have been acknowledged and perhaps understood (Rogers & Pilgrim, 1993; Rogers, Pilgrim & Lacey, 1993). At its best, psychotherapy can therefore be seen as a kind of bridge, which allows the troubled and the alienated to have their experiences recognized and validated, so that they can begin to feel that they are less isolated from the rest of society (Fancher, 1995; Feltham, 1999). What is less clear is whether this enthusiasm reflects the curative properties of therapy *per se*, or the way in which any encounter with a sympathetic and thoughtful individual will be preferred to, for example, medication (Davies, 1997; Rogers, Pilgrim & Lacey, 1992).

Talking treatments could be seen as representing a set of healing rituals that are common to all human societies (Frank & Frank, 1991). Such rituals are all about influence. It may be that clients are increasingly well informed consumers of treatment, which will mean that their encounters with health professionals are not as one-sided as they used to be (Iliffe, 2008); indeed the US-based *Consumer Reports* conducted an influential study of psychotherapy in the 1990s (Seligman, 1995). With the rise of consumerism there has been more debate about choice in psychological therapy. However, even when psychotherapy is viewed within a consumer context there is still a power relationship between therapist and client, which means that the therapist will usually have the most say over the nature and parameters of the treatment. Conversely, it is the client who will be required to disclose their personal insecurities and who will – from this disadvantageous position – be entering a space that is largely defined and controlled by the professional (Pilgrim, 1997).

There are obvious risks in this situation, and the radical humanist scholar Jeffrey Masson has garnered numerous and well documented accounts of the financial, emotional or sexual exploitation of clients by some of the leading figures in 20th-century therapy and counselling (Masson, 1988). For Masson, abusive conduct comes ready-made with the therapist role, which confuses friendship with professional service and requires the practitioner to show their superior psychological acumen: a recipe for condescension and moralism (and see Pilgrim, 1997). Furthermore, most of the accounts of abuse that Masson describes involve men exploiting women. It is hard to deny that this speaks both to the oppression of women in the wider world, and the failure of practitioners to have developed approaches to therapist education and supervision that take a full account of this situation (Bates, 2004; Dineen, 1999).

Proponents of talking treatment have countered that most forms of helping relationship entail some kind of power difference and that informal helpers will not necessarily be more benign. Indeed, many people seek out therapists because they cannot find a sufficiently compassionate or impartial friend or family member to whom they can turn for consolation or advice (Pilgrim, 1997; Smail, 1996). Moreover, there are hopes that the potential for exploitation can be reduced if therapists are required to register with a professional body that oversees the standards of training and practice, though there is little empirical evidence in support of this argument and many commentators remain sceptical (Pilgrim, 2009; Postle, 2007).

Leaving aside the question of direct exploitation, clients can only make an informed choice about their treatment when there is some transparency about the aims, methods, limitations and possible harmful effects of treatments *and* of the kind of relationship therapists are offering (Davies, 1997; House, 2003). The recommendations for the training of counsellors, therapists and psychologists and the ethical codes that are intended to govern their work certainly endorse this kind of openness (e.g. British Association for Counselling & Psychotherapy, 2007; British Psychological Society, 2002, 2006). However, these directives gloss over the problem that a professional consensus about these matters may be impossible to achieve, because authoritative accounts of what psychotherapy *is* or of what it *does* that meet with common agreement, or that are not tied up with the interests of one professional grouping or another, are hard to achieve (House & Bohart, 2008; Erwin, 1997).

This theme is nowhere more evident than when we consider the way in which power operates in particular schools of psychotherapy. For instance, CBT practitioners are taught to view themselves as scientifically trained Socratic teachers. However, unlike the historical Socrates, who seems to have radically questioned *everything*, including the basis of his own knowledge (Howard, 2000), CBT, like many approaches in mental health, is based on certain core and unquestioned assumptions about the causes and treatments of psychological distress. Despite this apparent certainty, there are many criticisms of the scientific validity of the standard cognitive explanations of the relationships between thinking, feeling and behaviour, many of which – as we saw in relation to medication research – were developed post hoc (Bracken & Thomas, 1999; Fancher, 1996). Furthermore, critics have argued that because CBT practitioners have traditionally questioned the emphasis placed on the therapeutic relationship by other traditions, there is a danger that guidance could slide into coercion, just as an overenthusiastic teacher might unwittingly cross the boundary that divides encouragement from indoctrination (Guilfoyle, 2008; Kendall, 2004).

By contrast, humanistic therapists place their relationship with their client at centre stage, and for many the results can be both nurturing and encouraging (Scott Gordon, 2000). For others, however, the optimistic Rogerian focus upon personal growth – the belief that we can overcome or reconcile ourselves to personal adversity as long as we are honest about our feelings and experience the therapist's positive regard enough – can mean that the tragic realities that confront us all are not faced (Clarke, 1999; Howard, 1998). By the same token, the ardent projection of warmth and empathy run the risk of making the therapist seem unreal and unworthy of trust, while also blinding them to the many subtle ways in which they might be shaping the conversation (Howard, 1998; Proctor, 2002), for example through the (not necessarily intentional) use of reinforcement (Truax, 1966). The assumptions of many therapeutic traditions owe a lot to the historical context within which they were born. The assumptions of person-centred therapy are based on the kind of uncritical Western individualistic humanism that was popular in the 1950s and 1960s but that has come under more criticism in the decades since.

Finally, psychodynamic therapists vary widely in how much they use their 'real' relationship with their clients to address issues of power and to acknowledge the limits of their own authority. Critics argue that a disregard for these questions could lead to the client experiencing a denial of their feelings about the present and therefore of what they are actually bringing to the therapy session (Lomas, 1999; 2003; Simpson, 2004). On the other hand, the psychodynamic therapist's efforts to try to be emotionally neutral and to probe beneath the surface of what the client is saying could make the therapeutic encounter seem rigid, cold and undermining (France, 1988; Sands, 2000).

A more general problem lies in the important social and cultural differences that can sometimes divide paid therapists and their clients. On the whole, practitioners tend to be middle class, relatively well resourced and white. In contrast to this, especially in public health services such as the British NHS, clients are more likely to be working class, poor, socially isolated and from a minority ethnic background (Davies, 1997; Pilgrim & Rogers, 2005; Williams, 1999). Over the years, sociological research has generally shown that individuals from less privileged backgrounds are less inclined to value intense self-reflection as the best means of dealing with their difficulties or of achieving their personal goals (Kearny, 1996; Richards, 1995). Instead, the experience of persistent social and material disadvantage – of powerlessness – is more likely to teach that being able to talk about a problem is not the same as being able to solve it. Indeed Smail (1993) has argued that one might need adequate economic and other resources before this kind of therapeutic help is found useful. This sobering picture is confirmed by the large body of social health survey and clinical evidence that demonstrates that social deprivation and the widespread abuse of power underpin much of the emotional pain and confusion that prompts people to seek the help of a psychotherapist (Davies, 1997; Proctor, 2008; Rogers & Pilgrim, 2003).

In the previous section we discussed the potential for harm from medication. However, any intervention has the potential for harm, a fact that is not as well-recognized by the general public, who tend to prefer talking treatments to medication (Rogers & Pilgrim, 1993). Some practitioners have recognized the potential harmfulness of the psychotherapies. Some of the potential dangers flow from the assumption common to many psychotherapies that the client can improve their lot through an inward re-sculpting of their thoughts and feelings.

There is thus the potential for a client to feel they are themselves to blame for their difficulties because they are unable to muster the necessary reserves of insight or will-power that seem to be essential for achieving positive change (Davies, 1997; Willoughby, 2001; Ryan, 1971). From a broader societal perspective, this exclusive psychotherapeutic focus upon the individual's inner landscape can deflect attention from the need to alter the external world that gave rise to their problems in the first place (Smail, 2005).

Implications for clinical practice

Many psychotherapists have recognized that psychological distress owes much to the world in which people live. For instance, the idea that psychological disturbance might be a form of 'social neurosis' was explored by the American psychoanalysts Alfred Adler, Karen Horney and Otto Fenichel during the first half of the 20th century (see Totton, 2000, for a fuller discussion). In the 1960s, as we discussed in Chapter 2, the British psychiatrist R. D. Laing suggested that madness might be a valid response to an insane world (Kotowicz, 1997; Laing, 1967). The early 1980s marked the publication of an influential volume on critical psychiatry, edited by the British psychologist David Ingleby. Amongst other things, this book sought to show how psychoanalytic ideas could be adapted so as to provide a method and a language for exploring the social production of individual distress (Ingleby, 1981).

Feminist approaches

The last quarter of the 20th century saw the development of feminist approaches to therapy that have sought to mould their assumptions and methods to the experience of women as a disempowered and often oppressed group (Chodorow, 1978; Eichenbaum & Orbach, 1983; Irigaray, 1993). While these approaches critiqued what they viewed as the **patriarchal** nature (i.e. the dominance of men) of the main schools of psychotherapy, they do not seem to have been as potent a force for social change as their advocates might have hoped. In part, this may be because much of the theoretical work was not as accessible as it might have been (Jardine, 1989; Kitzinger & Perkins, 1993). Moreover, in common with many other schools of therapy, feminist theorists have not addressed the longstanding issue of the exclusion of men, the elderly and psychotic patients from psychological therapy (Rogers & Pilgrim, 2003). Individuals from these groups are more likely to be deemed unsuitable for talking treatment, and often find themselves facing the more unpleasant or coercive kinds of psychiatric interventions (Hollingshead & Redlich, 1958; Rogers & Pilgrim, 2003) though see Brown (2009).

Given the growing awareness of the link between personal distress and social context, it was perhaps inevitable that some practitioners might try to bring parts of the outside world into the consulting room itself, to be worked upon and perhaps repaired within that setting. The schools that most strongly advocate this position are the so-called narrative and systemic therapies.

Narrative approaches

The narrative therapies (e.g. White & Epston, 1990) are founded upon postmodernist ideas, and therefore seek to question received notions of therapist expertise and of individualistic conceptions of the client's problems lying within their own heads. Here, distress is conceptualized as the result of a mismatch between our life narratives and our actual lives. Thus, for example, if a person has a story about themselves: that they are 'a schizophrenic', with its associated vocabulary of deficit (Gergen, 1990), it becomes harder to see themselves in any other way. Moreover, these stories are so powerful that when things happen that don't fit with this dominant narrative (say, for example, we are successful at something) they tend to get forgotten. Within narrative therapy, the therapist becomes a fellow traveller, working alongside the client and perhaps their family or other members of their community, to explore times when a person has done something that does not fit with the dominant problem story and to build an alternative narrative or **counter-narrative**. This can shift the focus toward the client's strengths and locates their distress in the unhelpful narratives that have been constructed (Besley, 2002; Payne, 2006). In this way, some narrative therapists seem to have helped some clients to secure more control over their circumstances (White, 2007). However, critics argue that there is a danger that changing a narrative may not substitute either for the way in which emotional pain is felt in the body or for the need to change the client's position in the real world (Held, 1995).

Systemic approaches

Systemic therapy is most often practised in public health settings, and particularly in child and adolescent therapy services, perhaps because the approach lends itself to multi-agency working (Newnes & Radcliffe, 2005). It draws upon ideas from **systems theory**, which aimed at understanding the relationship between different elements in a system, such as subsystems like grandparents, parents and children. In common with proponents of other therapies, early family therapists had originally trained as psychoanalysts but then rejected a focus on what they saw as a decontextualized individual, on the unconscious and on the past. Instead they focused on the dynamics of relationships between family members in the present. Different traditions of family therapy emphasized different aspects, for example interactional sequences, hierarchical relationships between different subsystems or behavioural patterns. However, a common element was the focus on the system or social group in which the distressed individual lived. This group is typically a family, which may be helped to come to terms with the problems of the client, or to see that the things that they themselves do and say might be the main catalysts for the client's malaise (Dallos & Dallos, 1997). In terms of research and publication this is a vibrant field, and recent years have seen the development of feminist and multi-cultural versions of systemic treatment (McGoldrick, 1998). However, as with other forms of therapy, critics have questioned the extent to which apparent changes can be sustained beyond the boundaries of the consulting room, given the many external pressures that such families often face (Dineen, 1999; Epstein, 1996).

Feminist, narrative and systemic family therapies still depend upon the application of quite specific techniques. In contrast, there have been attempts to define talking treatment as a highly personalized craft, which is close to other forms of art such as painting or poetry. Drawing upon humanistic and psychoanalytic ideas, these practitioners see their work as an inherently ethical endeavour that is in many ways unique for each client, and bound up with ideas about how we should live and how we should treat one another (Gordon, 2009; Lomas, 1999; Scott Gordon 2000).

Despite the wide diversity of alternative approaches that have been described in this necessarily selective review, it is still possible to identify shared themes. All the therapies tend to have the goals of helping the individual to develop a clearer, less self-blaming view of the likely roots of their problems, and encouraging them to access the kinds of solidarity and material resources that might improve their self-confidence and well-being (Miller & McLelland, 2006; Smail, 1996).

What, then, can we conclude about the value of talking therapy? As we have seen, the question of whether psychotherapy of any tradition is the best solution to distress is to some extent a question of ethics and politics as well as of method. Arguably, it is above all a question of scientific and clinical evidence, which is still incomplete. Interestingly, one proponent of RCTs and of cognitive–behavioural therapy accepts that the role of talking treatment is modest and that social justice and a redistribution of wealth is necessary:

> Much of mental distress no doubt has its roots in, or is at least exacerbated by, social deprivation and inequality and their psychological consequences. A good dose of social justice and redistribution of wealth would do the world's health a lot of good. In the meantime, any psychological treatment can only be a sticking plaster over the wound of such inequality
>
> Tarrier (2002, p. 292)

As with psychiatric medication, it is apparent that many people report that therapy is helpful. However, it is clear that many issues remain to be resolved in relation to its effectiveness. These include fundamental questions about what 'help' actually means and what the limitations and risks of such help might prove to be. In view of the current state of evidence, perhaps therapists should demonstrate humility in relation to claims about what they can offer, which might be limited to simple, but at times important elements, such as comfort, exploration and clarification of the origins of personal problems, and encouragement to find the external resources needed to deal with them – where of course such resources exist in the first place. Talking therapy might sometimes even help some people to join with others and to find common cause in beginning to tackle some of the shared environmental roots of their distress: an approach that would take it into the margins of community psychology, which focuses upon issues of inequality (Bostock, Noble & Winter, 1999; Diamond, 2008). It is to this approach to intervention that we turn next.

COMMUNITY PSYCHOLOGY

Rachel Cox, Guy Holmes, Paul Moloney, Penny Priest and Mike Ridley-Dash

So what is different about this [community psychology] course and mental health related therapy groups? The balance of power is central to the outcome. From the moment of first contact and referral from a GP, the balance shifts from client to health professional. As clients we wait for an appointment, we come to your workplace, we wait until you are ready. We hope you don't cancel or are late. We know nothing about you, but you already know something personal about us. We retell our story again and again until it is watered down to a couple of sentences on a page and lost. We hear your reassurances about confidentiality and your apologies when records go missing. We are assessed, discussed, judged and allocated. Some of us are told we don't fit the criteria for the help on offer. Our choices diminish as our part in the process becomes less relevant. We drown when no one is looking, not wanting to bother anyone. We are discharged.

The *Psychology in the Real World* courses demand that we are and remain proactive from the beginning. We choose. We apply and turn up to the venue, which is new to all of us, both facilitators and participants. We are all nervous. Some of us have met before. We are remembered. We are not defined by our problems, diagnoses or hang ups. We have coffee breaks together ... To those expecting these courses to be therapy groups there may be disappointment; to those not wanting this, relief.

Elisabeth X, cited in Holmes (2010, p. 85)

Sense of community can also be associated with negative aspects of social life. The nature of exclusion of 'others' can lead to harmful social consequences. Local social cohesiveness can be at the expense of minority groups and newly arrived immigrant groups.

Pretty, Bishop, Fisher and Sonn (2007, p. 19)

Definitions and origins of community psychology

Orford (2008) defines community psychology in the following way:

> The central idea of community psychology is that *people's functioning, including their health, can only be understood by appreciating the social contexts within which they are placed.* It is 'community' psychology because it emphasises a level of analysis and intervention beyond the individual and his or her immediate interpersonal settings. (p. xii, emphasis in original)

There is a debate amongst community psychologists about how best to define the field. In the UK it has come to encompass many of the ideas in Table 8.5.

In many ways, community psychology sits on the margins of mainstream psychology. It is not covered as a major approach in many psychology or mental health textbooks. Few psychologists are employed directly as community psychologists: rather, psychologists from a range of sub-disciplines such as clinical or educational psychology practise community psychology. However, it is a growing field with a range of textbooks (e.g. Kagan, Burton, Duckett, Lawthom & Siddiquee, 2011; Nelson & Prilleltensky, 2010; Orford, 2008) and journals (e.g. the *American Journal of Community Psychology*, *The Community Psychologist* and the *Journal of Community & Applied Social Psychology*).

The cultural influences and historical precursors of community psychology in different parts of the world also make for different and sometimes distinct approaches. In Europe, Marie Jahoda is often cited as one of the earliest and most influential people in shaping community psychology, particularly through her work on unemployment and its relationship to mental health (see, for example, Jahoda, 1979). American psychiatrist Richard Warner's historical analysis picked up on this and revealed that recovery rates from mental health problems and unemployment figures were inversely correlated. According to Warner (2003), pessimism and neglect is often spawned by poor economic conditions, and this can lead to declining standards of care, poor outcomes for people accessing mental health services and decreased quality of life. Warner has shown that interventions focused on people's social and economic conditions can be effective and can have a greater impact than those focused on insight (e.g. supported employment increases the likelihood of employment from 20% to 60% for people given diagnoses like schizophrenia). In the UK, the British Psychological Society now has a Community Psychology section (http://cps.bps.org.uk/) and there is a European Community Psychology Association (www.ecpa-online.eu/).

In North America, community psychology grew out of clinical psychology and developed as a separate discipline. Its emergence is often credited to the 1965 Swampscott Conference in Boston, where psychologists were encouraged to be active participants in solving the general problems of society and thus become 'social change agents' and 'political activists' (Rickel, 1987). Within the US, community psychology is represented by Division 27 of the American Psychological Association: the Society for Community Research and Action (www.apa.org/about/division/div27.aspx). The Australian Psychological Society also has a College of Community Psychologists (www.groups.psychology.org.au/ccom/).

In Latin America, community psychology is closely linked with liberation psychology, which is seen as originating from the work of the Jesuit priest and social psychologist Ignacio Martín-Baró (Martín-Baró, 1996). Burton and Kagan (2011) believe that liberation has its origins in the interaction of two types of agents or activists: external catalytic agents (e.g. intellectuals, political activists, committed professionals) and the oppressed groups themselves. There is an active process of dialogue between these two sets of people in which there is a gradual decoding of the world, as people grasp the mechanisms of oppression and dehumanization. They compare this to the mental health survivor movement in the UK (see Chapter 7), in which people's confidence, self-esteem, sense of personal power and psychological well-being can improve both through developing an understanding of the sources of marginalization and organizing with others to do something about it. They suggest that professionals can learn from the experiences, analyses, training programmes and writings of people who have received services. It is not possible to provide a comprehensive review of the history of community psychology here, but the interested reader is referred to Burton, Boyle, Harris and Kagan (2007) for a review of British community psychology and Reich, Riemer, Prilleltensky and Montero (2007) for a worldwide review.

Given its focus on promoting social change, it is perhaps not surprising that there are many areas of debate within

Table 8.5 **Key themes in definitions of community psychology**

- Placing people in their social contexts, focusing analysis and interventions on the social causes of distress and correcting the individualistic bias in psychology
- Sharing ideas and valuing diversity of knowledge
- Learning from and working collaboratively alongside others (rather than doing things to them)
- Analysing the impacts of power and disempowerment
- Questioning whose interests are served by various theories, policies and practices
- Focusing help on people in society who have been marginalized and oppressed
- Creating and nurturing self-supporting systems or communities
- Resisting oppression, silencing and social injustice
- Promoting social change
- Engaging in participatory and action research

community psychology (see Box 8.3). For example, how much community work professional psychologists engage in both inside and outside work and whether clinical psychologists are the most apt or skilled people to be involved in community work are important questions to consider (Holmes & Newnes, 2004; Smail, 1994, 2001). Most community activism happens without any help (or interference) from professional psychologists. Makkawi (2009) has warned that psychologists can have a deleterious effect on community activism in that community psychology interventions can undermine the development of grassroots groups and campaigns. For example, community psychology programmes to assess and treat post-traumatic stress not only run the risk of individualizing and medicalizing such distress (Summerfield, 1999) but divert energy, attention and resources away from self-sustaining, mentally healing and politically engaged groups. Even when they are not so damaging, attempts at community psychology can be naive and misguided (see Holmes, 2005, for a description of the author's comical attempts to intervene in a school environment).

Whilst community psychologists have critiqued mental health systems' focus on the individual in terms of understanding and alleviating distress, they have not always been quick to critique the damaging effects that communities and community groups can have, both on members of those groups and on others. Group dynamics such as scapegoating and splitting can increase people's propensity to hurt members of both in-groups and out-groups, and local social cohesiveness can be at the expense of people perceived as outsiders like minority groups and newly arrived immigrant groups (Pretty et al., 2007).

There is debate about whether it is possible for professionals working for the state (e.g. in the NHS) to fully practise in accordance with the principles of community psychology. Critics contend that state employees run the risk of unintentionally being agents of social control because they are regulated by government policy and because the NHS is essentially a provider of medical services (Parker, 2007). *Music and Change*, founded by clinical psychologist Charlie Alcock, is a UK programme inspired by community psychology principles that has flourished by being outside the bureaucratic obstacles of public sector organizations (Zlotowitz, Alcock & Barker, 2010). The programme is run as a charity (MAC-UK) and aims to address the social and mental health needs of young people living on a socially deprived estate in North London. It engages young people in innovative ways, such as 'street therapy' in which workers engage young people in informal ways, aiming to build trust and rapport, and uses a mobile recording studio and electronic gaming facilities that appear of greater interest to people than traditional mental health interventions. Rather than be the sole expert providers, *Music and Change* workers support and train young, interested, local people to be peer facilitators.

However, non-public sector organizations also have downsides. They often need to devote large amounts of energy and time to securing and maintaining funding, which is often of a fixed-term nature and from a range of funding bodies, each of which might have its own aims. Bostock and Diamond (2005) defend NHS community psychology, as they believe it can helpfully serve to shape psychological practice, underpinning a range of interventions with its values (such as focusing on social causes of distress, devolving power and utilizing people's strengths), and increasing the amount of community-based group work, campaigning, advocacy and action research in which psychologists might become involved. For example, Bostock et al. (1999) and Harris (2005) have shown how clinical psychologists can put their expertise in research methodology into the hands of marginalized communities with high levels of social deprivation in order to assist them to gather data that they can use to campaign for better housing and social conditions in their locality.

Theoretical frameworks informing community psychology

Mental health services have traditionally viewed their clients' difficulties as located within intra-psychic processes brought about through biochemical imbalances (Boyle, 2002), faulty thought processes (Brewin, 1996) or inner conflicts (e.g. Freud, 1917/1974). In contrast, community psychologists view distress as largely resulting from social inequality, so interventions are not solely aimed at the level of the individual or even the family but at various community levels (from the neighbourhood up to national and international levels). Gradually, mental health policymakers have begun to acknowledge the need for interventions at multiple levels (e.g. Social Exclusion Unit, 2004).

As we saw in Chapter 6, Wilkinson's epidemiological research (e.g. Wilkinson, 1996, 2005) provides evidence of the destructive

---

BOX **8.3**

Key debates within community psychology

- Contested definitions of what 'the community' is (Baldwin, 1987).
- What is the 'psychological' element in community psychology: is there a danger of psychologizing community development (Smail, 2001)?
- If community development is already conducted by other groups, why do we need community psychology (Holmes & Newnes, 2004; Smail, 1994)?
- How can professionals use their power and expertise to serve the community without becoming too dominant or colonizing a community's own resources (Makkawi, 2009)?
- How might community psychologists avoid imposing Westernized and medicalized notions of mental health (Makkawi, 2009)?
- How might community psychologists aim for the transformation of social relations rather than simply an amelioration of problems (Kagan, Burton, Duckett et al., 2011)?
- How can the twin perils of cynical pessimism and unrealistically naïve utopianism best be avoided?
- How might community-level change best be evaluated?
- Are community psychology programmes sustainable over the longer term?
- How can community psychology programmes aim for longer-term change when their funding may be short-term?
- What is the boundary between community psychology and political action as citizens (Holmes & Newnes, 2004; Smail, 2001)?

effects of poverty and inequality and it is this that community psychology seeks to address. Wilkinson's research reveals that amongst developed countries it is not the richest societies that have the best physical and mental health, but those that have the smallest income differences between rich and poor. In this context a number of commentators have suggested that some communities may have inadequate **social capital**, the social glue that binds a community together. Social capital refers to both the number of social networks (community organizations like churches and youth groups) there are in a community and how strong the links between them are. Wilkinson's view, that the lack of social capital experienced by the poor and other marginalized groups is instrumental in causing health problems, has been taken up by community psychologists (see also Friedli, 2009; Pickett & Wilkinson, 2010; Wilkinson & Pickett, 2009). In the UK, although ministers under different government administrations have referred to Wilkinson's work, there has been little movement towards reducing income inequality, revealing the lack of power that community psychology and evidence in general have in bringing about social change.

Community psychology has sometimes been associated with **empowerment**. Empowerment refers to ways in which groups with less power – for example, those with little access to economic resources – attain greater power. However, critics have noted that the term has become increasingly individualized and seen as an internal psychological construct related to an individual's self-confidence, with psychological interventions described by people providing one-to-one therapy as 'empowering clients' without them actually gaining more power in society (Burton & Kagan, 1996; Smail, 1995).

Community psychology can be applied at different levels. Bronfenbrenner's (1979) **ecological model of systems** conceptualizes systems as having four levels:

micro – involving the individual and their immediate/proximal systems, such as home, school and work.
meso – where links exist between an individual's proximal systems, such as between home and school.

exo – involving more distal systems that influence proximal systems, such as local councils and school governing bodies, which impact on the micro and meso systems.
macro – involving large-scale systems characterized by social structures and ideologies, such as the policies of governments and multinational companies, aspects of capitalism such as maximizing profits and off-loading costs, unemployment rates, the role of gender and religion in society.

Addressing the needs of individuals by intervening at different levels reflects some key points of difference between clinical and community psychology interventions. These are summarized in Table 8.6.

Community psychology and effectiveness

We saw earlier how methodological problems meant that many RCTs of medication were flawed and we also saw how, because of the specific problems affecting RCTs of psychotherapy, many psychotherapists have argued they are an inappropriate way of assessing the utility of psychotherapy. Indeed, there have been some criticisms of NICE, the key UK body which evaluates the efficacy of interventions (see Box 8.4 and Guy et al., 2011).

The Midlands Psychology Group (2010) note that, although the guidelines are supposed only to guide professional decision-making, they are now used to set standards, an example of **function creep** (where an original goal is revised to include additional goals). Some critics are concerned about the influence of the pharmaceutical industry on guideline development. Thus Healy et al. (2007) argue that 'the pharmaceutical industry has captured the guideline process and is using it as a mechanism to gain and control markets' (p. 138).

Some community psychology researchers have raised similar questions about the evaluation of community psychology interventions. Much community psychology evaluation

Table 8.6 **Differences between the traditional focus of clinical psychology and community psychology**

Clinical psychology	Community psychology
More likely to work with individuals	More likely to work with groups and communities
Work confined to clinical populations	Work likely to involve the diverse groups in a local community
More likely to take place in a consulting room in a clinic	More likely to take place in a community setting
Focus on symptomatic change in the individual through individually-focused therapies	Focus on community-level change through collective action
Work influenced by psychiatric diagnosis	Work influenced by mapping needs at community level and identifying sources of oppression
Work influenced by 'top-down' treatment guidelines (e.g. NICE)	Work influenced by 'bottom-up' feedback from community collaborators
Evidence base privileges RCTs	Evidence base privileges diverse research methods, especially those that emphasize community action and participation
More likely to be short-term or time-limited	More likely to be long-term and build and grow over time
Reactive and ameliorative in aim	Preventative and transformational in aim (e.g. advocacy, campaigning and acting to bring social change)

BOX 8.4
The problem of being NICE

What is NICE?[1]

The National Institute for Health and Clinical Excellence (NICE) describes itself as 'an independent organization responsible for providing national guidance on promoting good health and preventing and treating ill health'

It produces guidance in three areas of health:

- public health– guidance on the promotion of good health and the prevention of ill health for those working in the NHS, local authorities and the wider public and voluntary sector.
- health technologies – guidance on the use of new and existing medicines, treatments and procedures within the NHS.
- clinical practice – guidance on the appropriate treatment and care of people with specific diseases and conditions within the NHS.

NICE's guidance is developed 'using the expertise of the NHS and the wider healthcare community including NHS staff, healthcare professionals, patients and carers, industry and the academic world'.

Criticisms of NICE

A number of criticisms have been made of the guideline development process. For example, Barker and Buchanan-Barker (2003) argued that the membership of the Schizophrenia Guideline Development Group was dominated by mental health professionals. Indeed, the two service user representatives on the group developing guidelines on self-harm resigned because they felt the group was unwilling to question aspects of assessment and treatment (Midlands Psychology Group, 2010; Pembroke, undated). Winter (2010) argues that the recommendations of the NICE guidelines on depression reflected the allegiances of the members of the Guideline Development Group in that of those members 'who were psychologists or psychological therapists, the majority were cognitive behavioural in their therapeutic orientation' (p. 6).

The Critical Psychiatry Network submitted a comprehensive critique of the notion of ADHD to NICE's stakeholder consultation on this diagnosis. In the table listing consultation responses, the network's submission is noted, but the developer's response is:

Thank you very much for your comprehensive and detailed critique of the concept, diagnosis, classification and treatment of ADHD and related categories. Unfortunately, we are unable to dismiss the diagnosis as we would be left without a guideline to undertake. (NICE, 2006, p. 34)

Interestingly, the introductions to many guidelines note debate about the reliability and validity of diagnostic categories (e.g. the introduction to the guideline on borderline personality disorder), but this clearly does not stop the development of the guideline. There are four different versions of each guideline: Learmonth (2006) notes the differences between versions:

The Quick Reference Guide and shortened Guidelines are essentially synopses of the full Guidelines, but with all caveats and ambiguities removed. The effect of this is to make them read as hugely more 'authoritative' statements of fact, whereas the full Guidelines allow for far more questioning of both process and outcome. (p. 2)

---

1   Further information on NICE can be found at: http://www.nice.org.uk/aboutnice/howwe work/how_we_work.jsp, retrieved 30 October 2012

---

involves action research (Lewin, 1946), for which publication in peer-reviewed journals may not be a priority, as the research is focused on programme evaluation (e.g. to secure continued funding, as many community projects have only short-term funding). Many evaluations are thus published in the so-called 'grey literature' (e.g. reports for charities) rather than peer-reviewed publications which often privilege theory-driven experimental results.

A significant problem is that community psychologists are focused on community-level rather than individual-level change, so the usual outcome measures traditionally completed by participants in RCTs may be inappropriate. Kagan et al. (2005) describe this problem in their evaluation of a community participatory arts project:

> Perhaps most importantly was a clash of ideologies between artists, evidence based ideas in formal health services and researchers. At times we felt as researchers that we [were] translators of the evidence-based requirement of the health services to the artists, when we were, ourselves, highly critical of many of the positive assumptions of this approach. (p. 16)

NICE has published a briefing examining the evidence base for public health interventions in promoting positive mental health (Taylor et al., 2007), though it excluded community psychology interventions. Because community psychologists are interested in community-level change, evidence of their effectiveness is evaluated by criteria such as the reduction and prevention of the social causes of distress, combating inequality and injustice and promoting acceptance of diversity, and the promotion of social and environmental change in order to prevent rather than simply react to people's difficulties. There is evidence that working with people in groups and at a neighbourhood and community level can have more transformative potential than simply working with individuals. For example, solidarity with others can lead to a more positive sense of identity for oppressed individuals (Drury & Reicher, 2009; Nelson, Prilleltensky & MacGillivary, 2001) and create possibilities for mental health service users to challenge discrimination (see Chapter 7). Peer support amongst service users has increasingly become a focus of research (Davidson et al., 1999; Pistrang, Barker & Humphreys, 2008). In their review of research on social relationships and health, Berkman, Glass, Brissette and Seeman (2000) found that bolstering social networks provides social support and helpful identification with others, increased access to resources and material goods, and opportunities to bring about social change through co-ordinated action. There is even evidence that accessing green spaces can ameliorate health differentials between the poor and the well-off (Hartig, 2008). The British Psychological Society (2008) has published a discussion paper on socially inclusive practice that highlights several projects: lessening discrimination in the workplace and reducing workplace stress; challenging prejudice about mental health in schools; and *Evolving Minds*, a community mental health project. There are many more examples of the effectiveness of such work from across the world (e.g. Holmes, 2010; Nelson et al., 2001; Nelson & Prilleltensky, 2010; Orford, 2008; Reich, Riemer, Prilleltensky & Montero, 2007; Watkins & Shulman, 2008).

Community psychology interventions

Community psychology interventions vary both in scale and scope. For example, Watkins and Shulman (2008) include a description of the *Green Belt Movement* in Kenya, which has grown from a small, tree-planting project to a point where it now involves over 100,000 people, mostly women meeting together in small groups, 'decoding the social lies' that they feel are promulgated in their society, analysing the causes of local and national environmental degradation and campaigning to protect their environment. However, community psychology interventions also occur at a much smaller scale and, in this section, we describe three projects (*Space to Write, Psychology in the Real World* and *WELD* and *MELD* groups) of which, as employees of the UK NHS, we have first-hand experience. We then go on to describe The White City project, which occurred outside the confines of the NHS.

Space to Write

Space to Write was a 12-week writing group co-facilitated by a trainee and a qualified clinical psychologist. The group provided an alternative means for local people to access psychologists (rather than through a waiting list for individual therapy) and highlighted the value of supportive relationships, solidarity and collaboration for mental well-being. The group facilitators had a background in research aimed at contextualizing and de-individualizing mental health problems (e.g. Priest, 2007; Ridley-Dash & Bostock, 2007) and attempted to utilize this approach in the group. Providing a 'space to write' was one way of helping people who had previously attended psychiatric day services to reclaim opportunities for solidarity that had been taken away from them through the closure of that service. The modest aims were initially to provide a safe space in which group members could feel comfortable and be able to express themselves creatively through writing, to provide a social meeting space in which group members could enjoy conversation and each other's company, and to assist group members to express their aspirations and have their personal aims met through being part of a supportive group.

Previously entrenched in providing one-to-one interventions to people referred to a CMHT, the facilitators experienced *Space to Write* as one way of following the encouragement of Bostock and Diamond (2005), who emphasized the need for psychologists to broaden their 'focus from individual and reactive interventions; providing opportunities to voice the links between social circumstances and psychological well-being; [being mindful of] our limitations as psychological therapists and advocates for social change; and working collaboratively with others' (p. 25). The group was evaluated via participant observation, structured interviews with group members, written material from group members and personal accounts

written in the final session. Positive aspects of particular importance to group members included:

1. The relaxed and fun approach to meetings, which took the pressure off participants. This lack of stress led to a greater sense of spontaneous creativity.
2. The involvement of group facilitators in writing exercises, which both created a sense of solidarity within the group and encouraged group members to write.
3. The writing exercises, which did not focus on group members' difficulties but helped to foster their strengths.
4. The ability of group members to make their own drinks at break times, rather than having them prepared by staff, helped to give them a sense of ownership over the space and increased the sense of conviviality within the group.
5. The medium of writing enabled group members to explore ideas in more depth than they might have done otherwise.

Some of the benefits of *Space to Write*, such as creating a 'space to think' where people could provide each other with mutual support and solidarity, continued after the group ended. A *Newsgroup* was set up, in which participants negotiated a space to meet and write in the community team premises in return for keeping other people informed about news and events in the team. Rather than pressing for progressive change, this group was mostly concerned with finding space within a system they often experienced as oppressive in which people could connect with others and feel safe in a friendly environment that they themselves created. Such an intervention can be seen as **ameliorative** (i.e. enabling people to cope better without fundamental changes in their relationship to society) rather than **transformative** (i.e. transforming their social circumstances), in that it did not seek to challenge or change the practices of the team or wider community. It could also be interpreted as obfuscating the impact of oppressive societal influences on service users (Albee & Fryer, 2003). However, given the limited power of service users (and psychologists) to transform services, niches such as *Space to Write* and the *Newsgroup* can be important in terms of providing group members with time and space to interact, opening up dialogues that differ from those that normally occur in individual consultations and forming a bedrock of solidarity from which activism might later grow.

Psychology in the Real World

Psychology in the Real World is an umbrella term under which a number of groups, courses and ventures have been set up by Guy Holmes and others in Shropshire over the past decade. Rather than bringing people together because they have a shared problem or diagnosis, *Psychology in the Real World* ventures bring people together who have a shared interest. For example, *Understanding Ourselves and Others* brings together people who are interested in exploring a variety of theories about people's behaviour; *The Black Dog* enables people to critique ideas about depression; *Toxic Mental Environments* brings people together who want to analyse the social causes of distress and try and bring about social change; *Thinking about Medication* and *Out of the Box* attracts people who want to discuss a wide range of issues about medication and support each other in coming off psychiatric drugs; *Walk and Talk* enables participants to access the benefits of being in the countryside; *This is Madness* brings people together who want to critique and bring about change in mental health services.

When people take action collectively to stand up to injustice it can be incredibly empowering. Here, mental health service users, survivors, friends, relatives and professional allies take part in the 2005 'Kiss it!' rally in London against compulsory treatment (see Chapter 7). The placards were designed by artist Aidan Shingler.

It is not possible to describe all the philosophies and aims of these groups here (see Holmes, 2010, for comprehensive descriptions and evaluations of the groups and how to set up such groups), but many *Psychology in the Real World* philosophies overlap with community psychology philosophies and practices elucidated in this chapter.

The groups have been characterized by the following:

- They occur in non-mental health settings, such as arts and education centres, libraries, along river paths and at local pubs.
- People are not referred to the groups by health professionals; the groups are open to all and are advertised in ordinary local community facilities as well as within mental health services. Staff from helping professions also often attend.
- They are often designed and co-facilitated by people who have previously attended other *Psychology in the Real World* ventures, many of whom have long histories of psychiatric treatment, and are based on ideas that grow out of these groups.
- They are not 'skills for ills' groups (i.e. groups to learn coping strategies for particular forms of distress) but respect the fact that, as one participant put it, 'there are as many recoveries as there are people', each person's reactions to their life experiences are unique and complex, and there are a myriad causes of distress, all of which may benefit from collective critique.
- Participants explore theories and research relating to the causes of distress but look beyond immediate factors to 'the causes of causes', for example aspects of 21st century consumer capitalism that damage us all.
- Research findings are discussed and critiqued. Thus the validity of drug company research might be questioned. There might be an exploration of the lessons to be learned from the Milgram obedience study (Milgram, 1963). However, unlike NICE, the evidence of group members' lived experiences and reflections on those experiences are given just as much weight.

- The healing effects of groups (for which there is a considerable evidence base, see MacGowan, 2008) is brought to the fore, as is the 'wisdom of crowds' (Surowiecki, 2004).
- Both during and on ending the groups participants are encouraged and assisted to move from critique to action to bring about social change.

The groups have been evaluated in numerous ways (see Holmes & Gahan, 2007; Holmes, 2010) and have been shown to have impacts on various aspects of people's lives and the communities they inhabit. There have been gains that enable participants to exert more power over the conditions of their life in a way akin to Hagan and Smail's (1997a,b) work on power-mapping (where there is an attempt to include a consideration of a person's experience of power in psychological assessment and formulation). By being members of a non-stigmatizing and valued group, and later taking on roles such as campaigner, activist, group facilitator, conference presenter, researcher and published writer, participants have described personal benefits as well as brought about some change at levels beyond the micro-level.

The groups have enabled there to be some challenge to stigma associated with mental health services. One member of *Thinking about Medication*, having reduced her dose of antipsychotic medication, commented: 'I used to think of myself as a schizophrenic but this group has really opened my eyes … I now think of myself as a woman'. Participants with no history of mental health service involvement have commented on attaining greater understanding and less fear of people with 'psychotic' diagnoses or histories of admissions to the psychiatric hospital. As one participant put it, 'It was so good to realise that in spite of or because of all our faults and failings we are all mortal and members of the human race and it's OK not to be scared of those who live and express themselves differently'. Examples of social action include lobbying of drug companies to manufacture drugs in doses that would better assist tapered withdrawal; feeding back difficult experiences of taking and trying to come off medication to mental health professionals; meeting local politicians as part of a campaign to protect from development the area where *Walk and Talk* takes place and to ensure greater access for the local community. A loose nexus of people who have met on these courses support each other and have set up their own groups, projects and campaigns that run without any professional involvement. Group members, many with considerable histories of psychiatric service involvement, have described the groups at conferences and training events and have gone to other parts of Britain and inspired and assisted other groups to set themselves up. For example, *The Living with Medication Group* in Leicester was set up through assistance and liaison with the *Thinking about Medication Group*. In turn, the Leicester group have helped another medication group in Nottingham to start. In addition, several *Walk and Talk* groups have sprung up around the country, and *Walk and Talk* has been part of a wider movement locally and nationally towards combining the benefits of walking, accessing green areas and meeting with other people in your local community.

These kinds of networking activities have enabled members to change the way they view themselves and other people in society and engage in critical analysis of the causes of distress, as well as laying some foundations for collective action on a larger stage. However, it would be misleading to imply that everyone coming to a *Psychology in the Real World* venture has gone on to become an activist. Some just come to one venture but report the types of benefit people get from other interventions (e.g. greater self-understanding; help to leave abusive partners). Some make friends. Others at least spend time in a non-toxic environment. And whilst community-wide impacts are modest, especially compared to more revolutionary changes that have arisen from community interventions in other parts of the world, the groups have provided an alternative to one-to-one psychotherapy, with evaluations indicating that such ventures can meet needs (such as the alleviation of loneliness and a sense of powerlessness) on which individual psychotherapy may not have an effect.

Women, men, empowerment and learning disability: the WELD and MELD groups

Compared to the general population, people with learning disabilities (the British terminology for intellectual disability or mental retardation) are multiply disadvantaged. They are more likely to be poor, unemployed and socially isolated, to have chronic health problems and to have a shorter life span than the mainstream population. People with learning disabilities also tend to be excluded from mainstream health and education services (Department of Health, 2007) and from roles and activities that many of us take for granted like the opportunity to have a sexual relationship or to become a parent. Learning disability services have often viewed their service users as passive vessels to be filled with whatever activities are deemed appropriate, resulting in people who have 'never said no to anything in their lives' (Stenfert-Kroese & Holmes, 2001). A lot of the distress experienced by people with learning disabilities reflects the disordered environments in which they have to live, and while psychologists have taken some account of this pervasive reality, their work has often been confined to the immediate context in which individuals and their problems are located (Rapley, 2004). The few disciplines that go beyond this include community and feminist psychology, both of which highlight how personal malaise and well-being arise from the interplay of social, economic and material power (Bostock, 1998; Kitzinger & Perkins, 1993; Orford, 2008).

On this basis, the WELD and MELD groups were established to help people with learning disability negotiate a clearer and less self-blaming view of the causes of their problems, to find solidarity and friendship with others, and to begin to develop skills that might enable them to exert more positive influence upon their world. The groups were established as men-only and women-only groups, in acknowledgment of the fundamental differences between the experiences of women and men with learning disabilities, differences that are often ignored (Clements, Clare & Ezelle, 1995). The acronyms WELD and MELD were collaboratively devised to reflect these themes and stand for 'Women/Men Empowerment Learning Disability'. The letter E also designates a range of possible alternate words, including 'enjoyment', 'energy', 'escaping' and so on, symbolizing the open-ended nature of both of these forums.

From the outset, the approach was one of working alongside service users. Staff tried to be mindful of the power imbalance between themselves and participants and how easy it would be for them, with the best of intentions in the name of client empowerment (Illich, 1977), to set the terms of the discussions in advance. Instead, the staff sought to offer a framework within which people could build their skills and confidence and then begin to set their own goals and to work in ways that suited them.

Both of these groups started with a small nucleus or steering group of several individuals with a learning disability, at whose disposal the staff placed their own practical skills in organizing meetings and facilitating discussions. The aim was to gradually pass these skills over to the participants who, it was hoped, would be able to learn through practice in a supportive environment. These skills included things like chairing meetings, organizing the meeting rooms, acting as a contact point for new members, taking part in presentations, public speaking, political action and acting as consultants. For many attenders the opportunity to acquire capacities of this kind and to set their own agenda was an alien experience, frightening and alluring in equal measure. Nevertheless, an important feature of both the WELD and MELD is that participants are not told what to do or what the ultimate aim of any meeting should be, beyond the idea of getting together and talking about things that might interest them.

Patriarchy has appeared central to the experiences of group members. Some of the men talked about the way in which their male identity had felt compromised by their inability to acquire the badges of respectable masculinity, such as a job, a girlfriend, the ability to drive and to perform manual or DIY skills. Some of the men also described how they felt vulnerable to harassment and attack because of others' perceptions of their relationship with masculinity. Women in the WELD talked about having to face frequent emotional or sexual exploitation, being subjected to violence (including domestic abuse), of being defined through their bodies and positioned as needing a male partner in order to be classed as 'fully feminine'. Unfortunately, none of these experiences is unusual for women within this client group (see Brown, Stein & Turk, 1995). Childless women within the group also described how they had felt dissuaded by others from becoming a mother. In contrast, women who had been able to become parents described how they had become the focus of intense and even hostile scrutiny from health and social care professionals, describing professionals as having a fundamental disbelief in their ability to be 'good enough parents'. For many this played a key role in the eventual removal of their children. The emerging literature on learning disability and gender (e.g. Clements et al., 1995; Department of Health, 2007; McCarthy, 1999) confirms that such experiences are common.

Most participants needed several years to consolidate the necessary trust, mutuality and organizational skills to feel confident about themselves and about what they were doing. This underlines the way in which self-confidence is not something that a person simply develops within themselves: rather, it is developed through engaging with others in a supportive context. It thus comes from the 'outside' rather than the 'inside', through our engagement with the world (Smail, 2005). Often these kinds of opportunities are not available to people with learning disabilities because of societal barriers like prejudice and discrimination, so they may need a longer period than others to acquire such confidence. The paid workers in WELD/MELD often felt it was best to let people learn from being given the freedom to fail and to learn from their own mistakes rather than intervening when the workers believed that they knew best (one commented that they had 'learned the value of sitting on their hands and keeping their mouth shut').

Sometimes there has been a need for staff to use their power as professionals to help each group promote itself in order to gain the necessary recognition and resources, for example by writing about the group and acting as a contact and information point for anyone who might be interested in joining the groups. However, this worked against the need for participants to be 'the face' of the group; in community psychology ventures like these, finding the right balance between differing roles can be difficult.

Through joining these groups, some people have made new friends, gained in self-assurance and have been able to exert a modest influence upon local Adult Learning Disability services and other aspects of their world. The groups have been involved in some local campaigns, for example to improve local road-crossing facilities to enable people to attend the groups safely and independently. However, this should not distract us from the necessarily limited nature of these developments, given the minute amount of power available to people with learning disabilities, or from the fact that very few of them are involved in activities of this kind. As far as the rights and entitlements of people with learning disabilities are concerned, what is needed is fundamental change within many aspects of society.

Social action therapy: The White City project

Working in the NHS imposes constraints on people trying to do community psychology, as it is an organization dominated by treating individual illness rather than addressing the social and material conditions that lead to physical illness and distress. The projects described above often struggled to move from amelioration of distress to social transformation. More transformative projects are easier to set up outside the confines of the clinic, where there is freedom from Health Service policies and bureaucracy. The White City project (Holland, 1991, 1992a, 1992b), is a good example of a community psychology venture that was able to do this.

Sue Holland is a clinical psychologist who, in the 1980s, developed a mental health project for women in White City, a council housing estate in an area of West London. Unlike many psychologists working with people suffering social deprivation, Sue also lived on the same estate. The team was very small: Holland, a part-time social worker and a part-time administrator (Holland, 1992a). Her approach was informed by feminism; sociological theory about racism, sexism, homophobia and classism; psychotherapy; and theories of social change. It followed a four-stage model. Women could exit or continue at the conclusion of each stage, depending on their preferences.

Most of the women seen by the project were receiving psychiatric medication. Holland termed this point at which the women entered the project as 'patients on pills' (see Figure 8.5). She argued that, within the traditional approach to treatment, these clients were not seen fully as people but rather as 'symptom-bearing machines' (1991, p. 59). In this first stage of

Individual level **Focus on symptoms: 'patients on pills'**
Women sometimes feel so bad about themselves that they can't face their everyday life. We go to the doctor complaining of 'nerves' and get given pills to calm us down (tranquillizers) or cheer us up (antidepressants). We then see ourselves as having a 'medical' problem. Sometimes the doctor will send us to see a psychiatrist who continues the regime of, usually stronger, mood changing drugs. We now see ourselves as a 'psychiatric case', passively expecting to be cured.
Personal level **Focus on meaning of experiences: 'person to person psychotherapy'**
White City Mental Health Project offers women an alternative to pills. Talking to a woman therapist helps us to explore the meanings of our depression and so reveals our buried feelings, such as anger and guilt. We can then take charge of all our painful 'ghosts from the past'.
Social level **Focus on shared meanings: 'talking in groups'**
Now, freed from our personal ghosts, we can get together in groups and discover that we share a common history (HER-STORY) of abuse, misuse and exploitation of ourselves as infants, as girls, as women, as working class women, as black women ... Now we can see, and say together, what we really want!
Political level **Focus on fighting injustices of race, gender and class: 'taking action'**
Having changed ourselves from patient to person, from a state of depression to self and self-other awareness, we can now use our collective voice to demand changes outside in our community ... in our schools, our health centres, our community centres, our housing, transport, and in anything else that affects our lives.

Figure 8.5 **Sue Holland's social action psychotherapy**

Source: **Adapted from Holland (1991, 1992a, b).**

intervention, following an assessment, the women would be offered ten weekly sessions of psychodynamic psychotherapy. This gave opportunities for the women to explore their subjective experience of the world and begin to make interpretative links between the past, the present and their hopes for the future. The aim was to help the women tell their own story and to understand the meaning of their 'symptoms' (e.g. as understandable reactions to their life experiences). Some women who had experienced very difficult early life experiences (such as child sexual abuse) might be seen for longer and Holland also allowed her ex-clients to contact her again in the future, for example for an 'emergency' session after a stressful life event.

After the individual therapy sessions were concluded, participants were given an opportunity to join a group with other women. Since the women all lived on the same housing estate, they had a lot of experiences in common. Here the focus was on enabling them to connect their subjective experience with the experiences of other women, where common themes might emerge: for example, similar reactions to oppression such as racism. Groups were also set up for women with a shared identity e.g. an African–Caribbean women's history group.

Once the women had moved from individual psychotherapy to group work they began to see that the roots of their difficulties often lay outside themselves, in the inequalities they saw all around them. It was at this point that the project became more transformative. The project's participants got together to set up a self-help counselling and advocacy group called *Women's Action for Mental Health*. Freire's (1970) notion of **conscientization** is applicable here, meaning that one needs to develop a critical awareness of society in order to understand the roots of one's own oppression. A key aspect might be to explore personal, social and economic contradictions (e.g. why are so many people in industrialized countries unhappy, despite apparent material wealth?). The solidarity developed through joint work enabled the White City women to campaign for local issues like better housing conditions, but it also enabled them to challenge the wider 'social systems and structures that ... limit people's needs and choices' (Holland, 1992a, p. 72).

Holmes (2010) has adapted Holland's model as a way of conceptualizing all types of group work. His model shows the different ways people are conceptualized when they engage in different types of group work, and how community psychology ventures such as The White City project and *Psychology in the Real World* can help people to move on from learning how to cope with individual problems (Quadrant 1) to exploring the roots of their problems (Quadrant 2), coming to see the causes of those problems as rooted in the way our society is structured (Quadrant 3) and subsequently taking action to transform local communities and aspects of national and international policy that are the 'causes of causes' of distress (Quadrant 4).

Conclusion

Whilst individual treatments have some advantages over community psychology interventions (e.g. they enable people to more

easily disclose abusive experiences that induce shame), and are championed by many both within and outside Health Services, there does appear to be a renewed interest in the social and community context of both distress and help. For example, Paul Gilbert, author of the popular self-help text *Overcoming Depression*, has written of 'the benefits of fostering a psychology of mutual support and building social capital' (Gilbert, 2009, p. 402). Whilst it is individuals that experience distress, community psychology offers scope for theories and interventions that go beyond the individual, including the reduction of oppression, inequality and other causes of distress in our society. However, one of the key challenges for community psychology is the extent to which interventions are genuinely socially transformative. As we have seen, there are debates within community psychology about how to judge whether an intervention is transformative. On the one hand, critics might contend that some interventions, including the examples in this chapter, are rather parochial and predominantly ameliorative, perhaps because they are small-scale or conducted within public sector services. On the other hand, those participating in these kinds of projects report a wide variety of benefits, many of which were gained through involvement in a communal activity rather than something solely aimed at individual change.

Kagan et al. (2011) propose that in the future community psychologists should approach their work by considering both the extent and the scope of change they are aiming for. Thus the extent of change could range from no change (e.g. preserving the status quo), through some quantifiable change or improvement in people's lives but with no fundamental change in social relations, to a situation in which there is a qualitative change in social relations. The scope of change could range from a local or short-term focus, through a medium-range or medium-term focus (e.g. in a city or region), to a long-range and long-term focus (e.g. at national or international level). The extent to which an intervention thus colludes with current power structures and is ameliorative or transformative depends on where it is located between these two axes. Local interventions can be transformative if they are longer-term and lead to a qualitative change in social relations. And from little acorns, mighty oaks do grow.

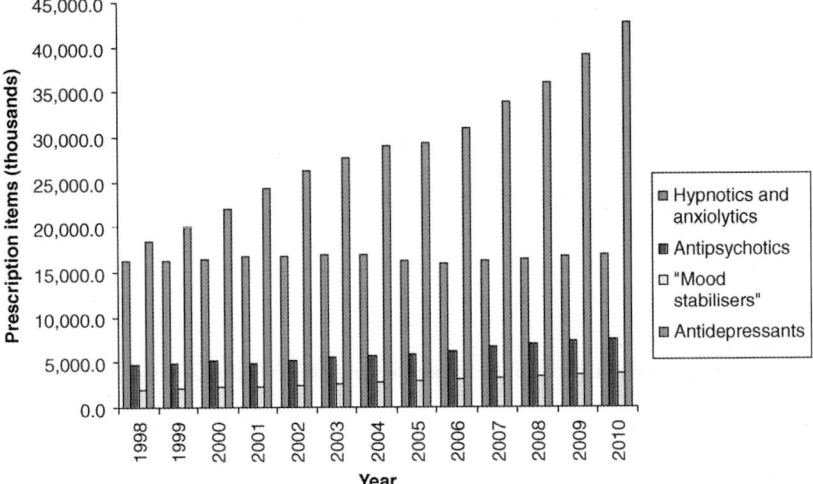

Figure 8.6 **Trends in prescriptions of major classes of psychiatric drugs 1998–2010**

Source: **Ilyas & Moncrieff (2012).**

Chapter summary and conclusions

In this chapter we have discussed three broad approaches to intervention: medication, psychotherapy and community psychology. We have also examined the use of compulsory treatment and ECT. The debates about the efficacy and effectiveness of interventions might leave some readers feeling bewildered – does this lead to the nihilistic conclusion that no interventions 'work'? In fact, the conclusion is very much the opposite: many interventions, including placebos, appear to have good outcomes. Instead, the difficulty comes in trying to understand *how* they 'work', in trying to compare one kind of intervention with another and in choosing the most appropriate intervention for an individual.

In much of the research and professional literature, the choice of therapeutic intervention is related to diagnosis. For example, we are told that a drug is specifically antipsychotic or that a psychotherapy is effective 'for' a particular diagnosis. However, as Joanna Moncrieff has shown, current psychiatric drugs are not this specific and, as Paul Kelly and Paul Moloney have demonstrated, the shared 'non-specific' factors of psychological therapies are as important as, if not more important than, the differences between 'brand name' therapies. Moreover, as we have argued elsewhere in the book (e.g. Chapter 5), diagnostic categories themselves often lack reliability and validity, so do not provide an effective basis for choosing a therapeutic approach on their own. With the current state of knowledge, clinicians often lack the evidence to predict in advance whether a particular intervention will be effective for a particular person. The fact that a particular approach is effective for a particular *group* (i.e. a sample of research participants) does not necessarily mean it will work with the particular *individual* client a therapist is seeing.

Some commentators have suggested that researchers should use more clinically meaningful analyses so that professionals (and their clients) have a better idea of the chance that an intervention will be effective for a particular individual. The **number needed to treat** (NNT) criterion is one example. Within psychotherapy, this statistic illustrates how many clients a therapist would need to conduct an intervention with before, on average, one client gained more benefit than if they had been in the control group. For example, Kuipers et al. (2002) report the NNT for their trial of CBT for psychosis (see Chapter 11 for further discussion of similar CBT interventions). It was '6 at the end of treatment and 3 at the end of follow-up' (p. 534). In other words, when the therapists were seeing clients for therapy, they needed to see six clients in the experimental condition for one person to gain a benefit they would not have obtained from receiving the control condition. One of the reasons such numbers are higher than might be expected is not that the experimental interventions do not lead to any improvement, rather that, as people also improve in the control group, improvement in the experimental group accordingly needs to be higher so that there is a statistical difference between the groups. Unfortunately, this statistic is still rarely cited in studies – indeed Kuipers et al. (2002) note that they had not reported it in their original outcome study. Shearer-Underhill and Marker (2010) analysed 100 randomly selected papers published in the APA's *Journal of Consulting and Clinical Psychology* between 2000 and 2008, finding that only four reported this statistic.

Given the partial state of our knowledge it could be argued that clinicians should be more transparent with those who use their services, acknowledging that choosing the most appropriate intervention is essentially a process of trial and error; they could invite their clients to collaborate in judging whether a chosen intervention is effective in their case. One could also argue that it is important for accessible and comprehensible information on the state of the evidence and the pros and cons of a range of interventions to be made available to service users, so that they can have an informed discussion with their clinician about the most appropriate intervention for them.

A number of key themes have been addressed in this chapter. Firstly we reviewed some of the difficulties faced by researchers assessing competing claims about efficacy and effectiveness. To some degree this relates to a debate about the most appropriate means of assessing the outcome of interventions, for example, whether this should be evaluated by changes in symptom rating scales for individuals or by change at a community level. In addition, whose views of outcome are given priority? Rose, Thornicroft and Slade (2006) ask 'who decides what is evidence, or more precisely, whose versions of evidence are given priority?' (p. 110). Perkins (2001) and Rose et al. (2006) note that the views of clinicians and researchers are often given precedence in the literature over the views of the recipients of interventions. For example, Perkins (2001) argues that clinicians may focus only on symptomatic change, while service users may be more interested in increasing their quality of life (see also Harper, Gannon & Robinson, 2013).

It seems that there is a need for more rigorous assessments of medication and ECT (e.g. triple-blind trials with 'active' placebo controls). For example, there is also a need to fully consider the influence of the placebo effect (see, for example, the issues raised by Goldacre, 2009 and Kirsch, 2009). However, given the difficulty of providing proper 'blinding' or active placebo controls in trials for the psychotherapies, there is a need for a paradigm shift in the evaluation of these interventions. The 'drug metaphor' on which psychotherapy RCTs are based has led researchers to focus on modest differences between brand name therapies rather than the more powerful factors they share. RCTs have, perhaps, hindered rather than helped research progress. One intriguing suggestion is that efficacy may have less to do with brand name therapies and more to do with whether therapists seek feedback from clients and adapt their practice accordingly (Miller, Hubble & Duncan, 2008).

Secondly, we explored the ethical dimensions of interventions. One of the key maxims in medical ethics is 'first, do no harm': a recognition that any intervention (psychosocial as well as physical) can do harm as well as good. How do health professionals manage this dilemma? Is it ever ethical to give someone treatment against their will? These kinds of questions remind us that interventions in mental health are not simply technical matters but, rather, go to the heart of values like autonomy, consent, the avoidance of harm and the promotion of well-being.

Finally, we discussed the social context of interventions. Why are poorer people more likely to receive medication as a treatment? Why are men from minority ethnic backgrounds more likely to be treated compulsorily? Tackling poverty and racism requires changes not just in mental health services, but also in society as a whole. Moreover, the individualism prevalent in much of the mental health literature can blind us to the epidemiological evidence about the social causes of distress (Mirowsky & Ross, 2003; Pilgrim & Rogers, 2002) and lead to an emphasis on reactive individual-level interventions rather than preventative community-level ones. How might psychologists develop such interventions more fully and evaluate them appropriately? Moreover, might a community and psychosocial epidemiological perspective on mental health lead to recommendations for public policy, as called for by community psychologists like Prilleltensky and Nelson (2002)?

As we saw in Chapter 2, historically, the popularity of classes of treatments has often had less to do with efficacy and more to do with the cultural norms and values of the time, especially the dominance of particular models of distress (e.g. psychogenic, somatogenic or sociogenic). Nikolas Rose (2004), for example, has argued that, whilst over the 20th century a range of developments (e.g. the rise of psychological therapies) had led us to think of ourselves as 'psychological selves', an increasing interest during the late 20th and early 21st centuries in technological developments in the life sciences (e.g. molecular genetics), means that we are increasingly conceiving of ourselves as 'neurochemical selves'. In Figure 8.6 we can see the huge increase in prescription of antidepressants and to some extent antipsychotics over recent years, an increase seen in a number of other countries too. Hundreds of millions of pounds are spent on this medication every year. Although some of this rise can be accounted for by the rising costs of drugs, it is also clear that rates of diagnosis and prescriptions are rising. The danger here is that this encourages us to ignore the social context of distress and its ethical and political dimension, seeking instead a 'technical fix'. Do psychologists involved in public debates about these issues have a responsibility to consider the ethical and political issues here as well as the technical ones?

End of chapter questions

1 What might be the implications for mental health services of adopting a 'drug-centred' model of drug action?
2 Since the placebo effect is generally far more powerful than any experimental intervention, could a new class of interventions be developed that harnesses it for more effective use on its own (as opposed to it only being seen as something to be controlled for)?
3 Since it is hard to 'blind' participants in traditional psychotherapeutic research trials, how might study methodologies need to be changed in order to better assess the efficacy and effectiveness of psychotherapies?
4 What might a mental health service based on community-level interventions look like?

Find out more

1 Moncrieff, J. (2009). *A Straight-Talking Guide to Psychiatric Drugs*. Ross-on-Wye: PCCS Books.
An accessible introduction to psychiatric medication.

2 Read, J. (2009). *Psychiatric Drugs: Key Issues and Service User Perspectives*. London: MIND/Palgrave Macmillan.
An interesting introduction to the perspective of mental health service users on medication.

3 www.compsy.org.uk/
A website based in Manchester in the UK by community psychologists Mark Burton and Carolyn Kagan. It lists upcoming events, reports from previous conferences, academic papers, links and other resources.

4 www.musicandchange.com
An innovative project designed by a clinical psychologist on community psychology principles.

5 http://psychologyintherealworld.co.uk
A resource for those interested in learning more about these groups featured in this chapter.

6 Pilgrim, D. (2009). *A Straight Talking Introduction to Psychological Treatments for Mental Health Problems*. Ross-on-Wye: PCCS Books.
An accessible introduction to psychotherapies including a focus on ethical issues and research.

7 Perry, P. & Graat, J. (2010). *Couch Fiction: A Graphic Tale of Psychotherapy*. London: Palgrave Macmillan.
A graphic novel about a psychotherapist and client – a nice introduction to psychotherapy.

8 Bentall, R. P. (2010). *Doctoring the Mind: Why Psychiatric Treatments Fail*. London: Penguin.
A well-researched account of interventions for distress, describing their history and the current state of knowledge.

9 Prochaska, J. O. & Norcross, J. C. (2010). *Systems of Psychotherapy: A Transtheoretical Analysis* (7th edn). Belmont, CA: Brooks/Cole, Cengage Learning.
An interesting attempt to identify commonalities and differences in the range of therapy approaches, outlining a broad integrative framework.

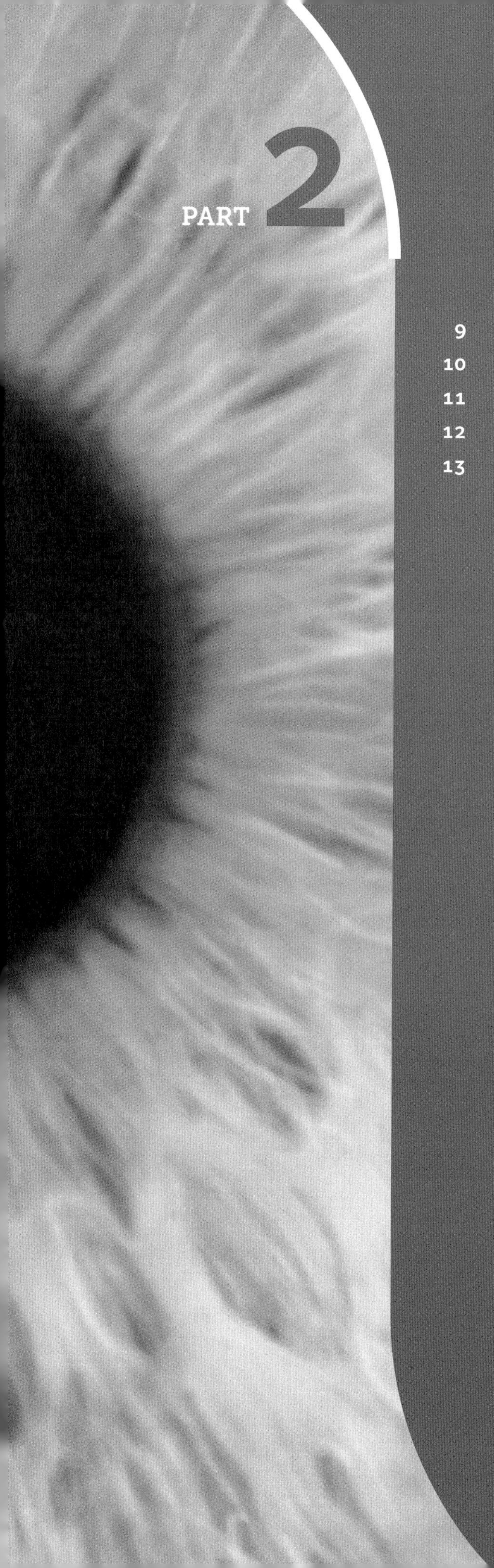

PART 2

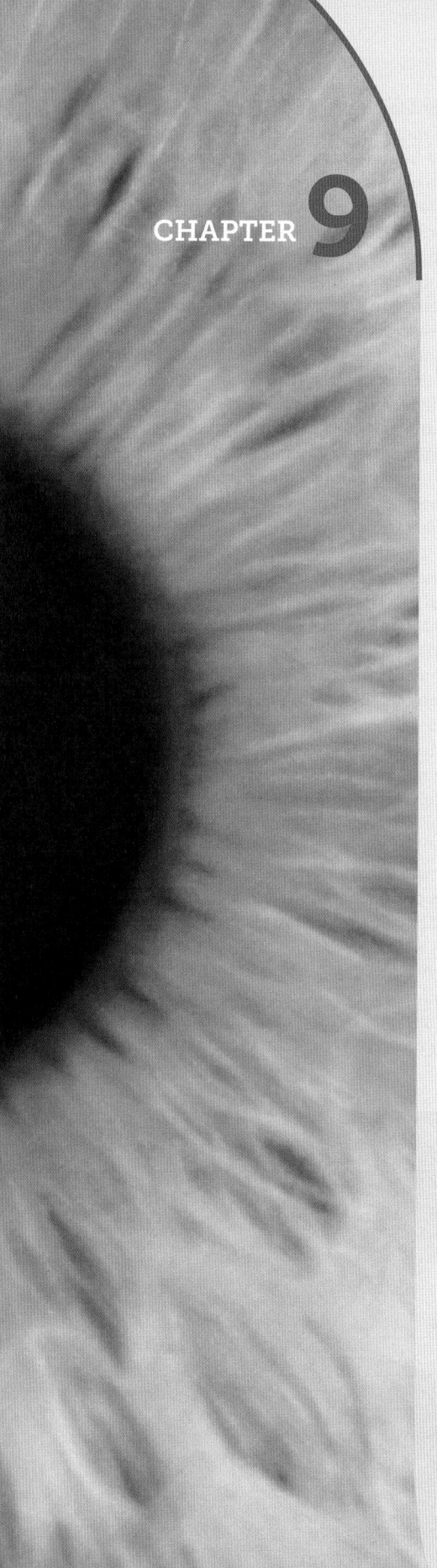

CHAPTER 9

SADNESS AND WORRY

Jane's story

Jane's parents were both teachers. She and her younger brother grew up in a large, comfortable house in a small city. Jane's father was a quiet man who died suddenly of a stroke when Jane was 18. By contrast, her mother was an outspoken woman who set exceedingly high standards for her children.

As she grew up, Jane increasingly felt that she was letting her parents down: it sometimes seemed that her brother was the favourite, and that she was failing to match the levels of capability and energy expected of her. By the age of 15 or 16, Jane began to recognize that her parents' marriage was not the perfect union her mother had always led her to imagine; however, it was impossible to discuss this understanding with either of her parents.

When Jane first went to university she developed intense preoccupations with her weight and appearance, but these concerns subsided when she met her current partner, Dave. At the end of their studies, Jane and Dave married, and both moved straight into demanding, well-paid jobs. After a few years, Jane gave birth to a daughter.

Jane first came into contact with mental health services when her daughter was five years old, after referring herself to her GP. She told her doctor that she regularly experienced inexplicable bouts of crying and lengthy periods of intense misery when she felt so overwhelmed with despair that she could barely talk. Jane confided that her husband increasingly seemed distant and arrogant towards her, and that she felt unsupported by him. She sometimes felt that only her daughter, Emily, gave her anything to live for; at the same time, because of her failure to control her own moods, she constantly felt that she was letting Emily down.

Sam's story

Sam is the oldest of three children. He remembers how, when he was small and his parents were always arguing, he would tell stories and invent games to distract his brother and sister from the shouting downstairs. When he was 12, his parents separated. For years afterward his mother was often absorbed in her own misery, leaving Sam to attend to his siblings.

When he was 18, Sam's mum started a new relationship: shortly afterwards, Sam started seeing Bridie, a girl he knew from school. When Sam was 19, Bridie got pregnant and they moved into a flat together. They had a son; then, two years later, a daughter. But the relationship did not last: as the years passed Bridie became increasingly distant, and Sam eventually discovered that she had been having a series of affairs. Their separation was bitter, with much arguing over money. Bridie moved out and left the children with him; now she sees them only a few times each year.

This story continues on the next page

Not long after, Sam met a new partner. Dawn is more considerate and patient than Bridie, and she too has children from a previous relationship. Everything was fine until Dawn and Sam moved in together and the two sets of children began arguing and competing. This causes tension between Sam and Dawn, and Sam often lies awake at night wondering how to help everyone to get along.

Sam's work involves driving. Recently, he has started experiencing panic attacks: sometimes as he gets into his van, sometimes as he parks at a customer's address, sometimes at seemingly random intervals. Increasingly, he finds it difficult to breathe in public places, and feels out of breath and dizzy when he imagines people looking at him. His sleep is disturbed: he often either fails to fall asleep or, alternatively, wakes early and is unable to sleep again. He frequently feels miserable, but tries to keep this away from his family for fear of making things worse.

Sam's most recent panic attack occurred whilst he was driving his van and found himself stuck in a traffic jam that was going to make him late home. This made him fear that he might not be safe to drive, so he contacted his GP and asked for help.

Learning outcomes

After you have read this chapter you will be able to:

1 Describe how experiences of sadness and worry have varied across time and between cultures
2 Identify the psychiatric diagnoses commonly given to people experiencing clinical sadness and worry
3 Describe the primary causal influences upon sadness and worry
4 Explain which interventions are commonly given to people experiencing clinical sadness and worry.

Introduction

This chapter is about the experiences of people like Jane and Sam. The most striking aspect of Jane's problems is that she is sad and unhappy; the most striking thing about Sam's problems is that he is preoccupied and worried. However, you should notice that Jane's distress consists of worry as well as sadness, and that Sam is miserable as well as worried. Jane is very concerned that she is failing her daughter; in the past, she had been intensely worried about her appearance. Sam feels miserable about his life and relationships, but tries to hide his misery and spends lots of time worrying how to solve his problems.

Sadness and worry are common experiences in everyone's life, so most readers will be able to imagine something of how it feels to be either Jane or Sam. But although we all get miserable or worried sometimes, those who end up receiving clinical treatment typically have difficulties that are greater or more pervasive than most of us typically experience, and that may endure for longer. However, as David Smail (1993) observes, it

is also the difficulty of identifying an immediate explanation for their levels of sadness and worry that differentiates the experiences of people like Jane and Sam from those of other people. Someone who has recently lost a loved one because of bereavement might be just as profoundly miserable as Jane; someone who was fortunate enough to survive a horrific accident might be just as anxious as Sam. By contrast, for people like Sam and Jane, although sadness and worry seem to have run out of control, there is, at first glance, little reason for them to be as worried or miserable as they are. It is only once we look in more detail at the totality of their lives and experiences that we can begin to gain some sense of the reasons for their difficulties. Smail observes that it is as much this difficulty in accounting easily for their sadness and worry as any particular feature of their experience, which marks them out as people who might end up receiving mental health services.

Clearly, moderate degrees of sadness and worry have adaptive value: worry makes us alert to threats and may induce reasonable caution in the presence of danger; sadness encourages withdrawal and disengagement, and may assist in the management of changes in social status. Consequently, there are good reasons why our species has biological systems that enable these kinds of experiences. However, this does not mean that sadness and worry are discrete biological responses that can sensibly be separated out from all of the other aspects of our experience. So, in this chapter, sadness and worry are not code words for 'depression' and 'anxiety disorder'. Rather, they are everyday language terms describing particular kinds of distressing experiences, experiences which – when they become persistent or dominant – may be associated with clinical interventions.

To some degree or other, experiences of sadness and worry characterize the lives of people who have been given most – perhaps all – kinds of psychiatric diagnosis. In this chapter we will focus on people whose *predominant* experiences are of sadness, worry or both. However, it is vital to realize that we are doing this solely to simplify and organize the material. Whilst you are reading, you should not forget that significant degrees of sadness and worry are experienced by the great majority of

Sadness and worry are very common experiences

people who receive mental health services. There are nevertheless many people, like Jane and Sam, whose distress seems to consist primarily of some mixture of unhappiness, misery, sadness, anxiety, worry or fear: this chapter is about experiences like those.

In order to put these kinds of experiences into a properly psychological context we'll first look at how they have appeared and varied over time, and how they differ across cultures. We'll then describe some of the forms that they commonly take in contemporary Western culture, and the psychiatric diagnoses people experiencing them are most likely to receive. We'll outline some of the social, psychological and biological influences thought to be influential in producing these experiences, then discuss the kinds of treatment and intervention people are usually offered.

Guiding questions

Throughout this chapter, you should bear in mind these two questions:

1   *What difference does it make to our understanding once we recognize that sadness and worry often occur at the same time?*
2   *How do social, psychological and biological influences come together to produce experiences of sadness and worry?*

History and culture

History

Experiences of sadness and worry have been described for as long as humans have made records of their activities: unsurprisingly, it appears that we have always had things to worry or to be miserable about! Both the Bible and the Koran make reference to experiences of misery and anxiety, as did the ancient Greeks. Writing in the 1st century AD, Solanus of Ephesus described a condition called **melancholy**, which was thought to be caused by an excess of black bile and was characterized by 'mental anguish and distress, dejection, silence, animosity toward members of the household, sometimes a desire to live and at other times a longing for death, suspicion on the part of the patient that a plot is being hatched against him, weeping without reason, meaningless muttering, and, again, occasional joviality' (Melechi, 2003).

In more recent history, too, distress characterized by sadness and worry has been widely recognized. In the Middle Ages, it was recorded that monks sometimes fell prey to **accidie**, a mixture of misery, boredom and disgust characterized by a loss of faith in God and a failure to perform required duties (Harré & Finlay-Jones, 1986). Shakespeare's play 'Macbeth', written in the early 1600s, is about the murder of a king and its consequences. Lady Macbeth, one of the central characters, is an accomplice to her murderous husband. In the weeks after Macbeth kills the king she is agitated, restless and unable to sleep: racked by profound anxiety and guilt, Lady Macbeth engages in compulsive rituals of hand-washing. In 1623, not long after the time that Macbeth was first performed, Richard Burton's influential book 'Anatomy of Melancholy' was published. Burton's text described melancholy as an experience that 'goes and comes upon every small occasion of sorrow, need, sickness, trouble, fear, grief, passion, or perturbation of the mind, any manner of care, discontent, or thought, which causes anguish, dullness, heaviness and vexation of spirit, any ways opposite to pleasure, mirth, joy, delight'. Five editions of the book were published during Burton's lifetime, and it influenced other writers including Samuel Johnson, Charles Lamb and John Keats.

Another illustration of how experiences of sadness and worry were recognized historically is that until the early 1800s there were two statues at the gates to London's famous Bethlem Hospital. One, sometimes called 'Melancholy Madness', showed a manacled figure contorted and shrunk in the depths of misery; the other, 'Raving Madness', was of a figure frozen in extreme terror. So there was profound sadness at one side of the entrance and extreme worry at the other, and all those who entered the asylum necessarily passed between them. The two figures were described by the poet Christopher Smart, who was confined to Bethlem in the 1760s. He said of them: 'That on the left is melancholy or sullen madness, the other downright distraction'.

Forms of sadness and worry, then, may have been capacities of our species for as long as we've been able to reflect upon ourselves – but this does not mean that they have remained constant and unchanging. Solanus observed that melancholia was much more common in men than women, and occurred primarily in middle age; today, diagnoses of both depression and anxiety disorders are given to more women than men, and some studies find that diagnoses of depression are given least in mid-life (Ross & Mirowsky, 2008). A contemporary of Solanus, Rufus, noted that melancholia was also common in old age, and that the most extreme cases were amongst women; today, diagnoses of depression and anxiety disorders are less common in later life, and the group most at risk of suicide are young and adolescent men (Form, 2000).

Accompanying this demographic variability, there is also historical evidence of variation in the prevalence of sadness and worry. Although some studies have suggested that levels of sadness and worry remain fairly stable over time (Murphy et al., 2004) others have shown marked fluctuations in their prevalence in accord with changing social and material conditions. One study conducted in the USA found a strong birth-cohort effect for anxiety: two meta-analyses showed a 20% increase in symptoms of anxiety between students in 1952 and those in 1993. The increase was attributed primarily to decreases in social connectedness and increases in environmental dangers such as crime (Twenge, 2000). Similarly, Lewis (1993) compared psychiatric morbidity (profound, persistent unhappiness, anxiety and panic attacks) in two UK community samples of approximately 6000 people. In 1977, 22% of the sample reported such feelings: by 1986 this had risen to 31%. Another UK study by Klerman (1988) found that diagnoses of depression, drug and alcohol dependency have all increased markedly since 1945, particularly amongst the generation born in the years following World War II. Some other European countries also demonstrate increases over this time frame; for example, Hagnell, Lanke, Rorsman and Ojesjo (1982) found marked increases in diagnoses of depression in community samples from Sweden between 1947 and 1972.

History also provides evidence for variation in the meaning of experiences of sadness and worry, and how they are configured with respect to other elements of people's lives.

Harré and Finlay-Jones's (1986) analysis of accidie amongst mediaeval monks shows how this condition was thoroughly bound up with religious duty and the obligation to serve. Accidie included the experience of disgust at the self for failure to perform duties, and simultaneous marked disenchantment with God and the Church. Far from being optional elements, these religious dimensions were seen to be core, defining features of the experience. Similarly, whilst Richard Burton's 'Anatomy of Melancholy' describes experiences that are in some ways quite similar to contemporary psychiatric notions of depression, there are also significant differences, one of which is that these experiences appear far more variable than those described by contemporary psychiatry: Burton characterizes them as 'irregular, obscure, various, so infinite, Proteus himself is not so diverse' (in Greek mythology Proteus was the 'God of the Sea', capable of almost infinitely changing his shape). Another difference is that, in Burton's time, melancholy was often associated with great feats and outstanding achievements. Unlike contemporary depression, which is often associated with apathy, lack of motivation and difficulties in concentrating and working, melancholy was associated with insight, clarity, analytic precision and expressive power. A third difference between melancholy and depression is that some, including Burton himself, characterized it as 'flatuous melancholoy'. The theory of the four humours, which underpinned Burton's account, supposed that melancholy was caused by an excess of black bile, which in turn would produce flatulence. Consequently, along with other illnesses thought to be caused in this way (such as asthma: Gabbay, 1982) excessive flatulence was frequently observed amongst those who were diagnosed as melancholic.

Culture

Cross-cultural analyses also demonstrate significant variation in the ways in which sadness and worry are experienced and understood. With respect to experiences of sadness, it is often said that there is an important dimension of cultural diversity in the extent to which people in different cultures emphasize its physical and somatic aspects, versus the extent to which they **psychologize** or, in other words, emphasize its emotional and cognitive aspects. In the West, people experiencing profound sadness tend to emphasize low mood, irritability, difficulty in concentrating, and so on. Kirmayer (2001) argues that this Western tendency is deep-seated and associated with various problems. It may lead scholars to mistakenly lump all 'Eastern' cultures together in one group and all 'Western' in another, rather than engaging in thorough, sensitive explorations of cultural difference. It also obscures the extent to which, even in Western cultures, people who experience sadness and worry complain of physical aspects such as excessive tiredness and aches and pains.

One of the most influential studies of cultural differences in sadness was conducted by Kleinman (1986). With his colleagues, Kleinman looked closely at 100 people at the Hunan Medical College in China who had been given a diagnosis of **neurasthenia**. Neurasthenia was said to have been the product of 'nervous exhaustion', and its symptoms included such complaints as headache, backache, muscular weakness, fatigue, noises in the ears, irritability and lack of concentration, hopelessness, morbid fears and phobias, dizziness, insomnia, poor appetite, indigestion and sweating. Today,

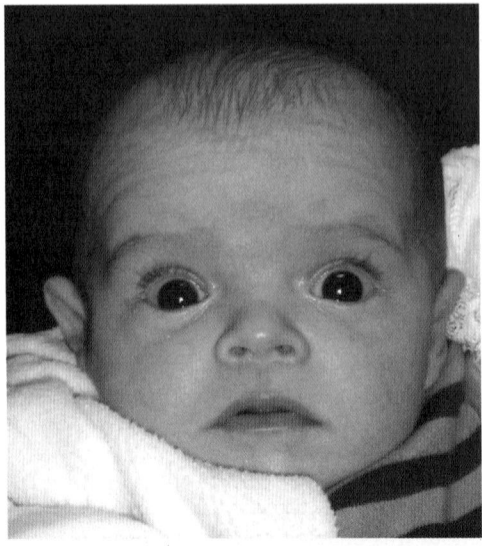

The capacity to experience the world in the ways that we in the West call 'sad' and 'worried' seem to be given to us by our biology, but the forms these experiences take are thoroughly shaped by culture

this diagnosis is not widely used in the West, although it was popular from about 1880 to 1930. Rather than simply disappearing, it is sometime said to have been re-conceptualized so that Western patients who formerly received this diagnosis are today given a diagnosis of chronic fatigue syndrome (CFS, or myalgic encephalopathy – ME: Wessely, 1990). As the description of its symptoms demonstrates, although neurasthenia contains elements of both sadness and worry, its symptoms were primarily physical rather than psychological.

In China the everyday term for neurasthenia is *shenjing shuairuo* – literally, 'neurological weakness' – and Kleinman observes that the prevalence rates for Chinese diagnoses of neurasthenia closely mirror those for diagnoses of depression in the West. By contrast, Kleinman found that diagnoses of depression were very rarely given in China. Of the 100 people who took part in his research in China, all of whom had been diagnosed with neurasthenia, Kleinman concluded that 87 met the Western criteria for major depressive disorder. Using Western criteria (from DSM-III), his team found that anxiety disorders were also widespread amongst these 100 people, and that there were also a smaller number of culture-bound syndromes. Another 44 of the 100 were found to be suffering from previously undiagnosed chronic pain.

Although Kleinman's study has been the most influential, there have been others that have similarly demonstrated a difference in the degree to which, compared to people from other cultures, Western people emphasize the emotional and cognitive aspects of sadness and worry. Kleinman proposed that we could understand this difference by distinguishing between a disease, which is biological and constant, and an illness, which is culturally specific. He recommended that clinicians should always work with the illness, not the disease, since it is the illness that determines the form the symptoms appear to take and that shapes the expectations and understandings of patients. At the same time, as an anthropologist, Kleinman was sensitive to the danger that this distinction might allow forms of cultural imperialism to proliferate. He recognized that it makes no more sense to posit an underlying disease called 'depression' which manifests in some cultures as 'neurasthenia' than it does to suppose the opposite.

Kleinman's work fostered debates regarding the extent to which the differences he found are differences in presentation rather than experience. People in the West who experience profound sadness also find that their sadness has somatic components, and there is evidence that Chinese people confide in their friends (but not necessarily their doctors) that their neurasthenia includes experiences of sadness and worry. Related to this is the fact that it is sometimes claimed in the West that CFS is a form of 'masked' depression, characterized by a mixture of anxiety and unhappiness (Hyland, 2002; Sharpe, Hawton, Clements & Cowen, 1997). Explanations for these cultural differences include the extent to which psychological 'illness' is seen as legitimate in each culture, culturally specific codes of etiquette which prohibit the expression of some experiences but permit others, differences between languages in the extent to which they supply psychological categories and descriptions, and culture-specific norms for non-verbal communication. Another important factor might be the wider, culture-specific conceptual frame within which experience is understood, which for Westerners is dualistic and separates mind from body (Jenkins, Kleinman & Good, 1991).

Some studies of sadness have failed to find the kinds of marked differences between cultures that were expected. Krause and Liang (1992) studied symptoms of depression amongst older adults from Japan, Taiwan and the USA and found no marked differences in their cross-cultural manifestations. By contrast, other studies have found marked differences even within subcultures and minorities. Manson, Shore and Bloom (1985) studied sadness amongst the Hopi peoples of North America, and found that it takes five distinct forms: worry-sickness, unhappiness, heartbreak, drunken-like craziness (with or without consumption of alcohol) and disappointment-pouting. Although, for Western psychiatrists, people experiencing any one of these conditions might be said to be experiencing major depression, amongst the Hopi they are seen as five distinct conditions, each with its own causes and each requiring its own forms of intervention. Similarly, research has found that African–Americans experience a more equally balanced mix of emotional and somatic symptoms than do white Americans (Chang, 1985), and that African–Americans given a diagnosis of depression experience more anger, and are more likely to attempt suicide, than white Americans (Myers, 1993).

Cultural variation in experiences of sadness is bound up with differences in idiom and metaphor. For example, in Afghanistan, extreme sadness is said to be characterized as a form of weakness and to be associated with the feeling of the heart being squeezed by a hand (Weiss & Kleinman, 1988), whereas in Japan it is characterized as 'darkness and rain'. There are also different cultural norms for body posture, which can then appear clinically as forms of non-verbal communication. In some African cultures, for example, a downcast gaze is a form of politeness to those in authority, but in the West tends to be read as a sign of misery. Wider cultural norms are also relevant, since by definition it is only against these norms that 'abnormality' becomes sensible. In Buddhism, suffering is highly valued, which may mean that people from Buddhist cultures emphasize their misery more than people from others (Obeyesekere, 1985). Such cultural norms also influence the specific emotions that are bound up with sadness: for example, in the Western Judaeo-Christian tradition the emphasis upon guilt means that it is more frequently found as a component of sadness there than it is in other cultures (Kaiser, Katz & Shaw, 1998).

Experiences of worry, too, vary across cultures. Like experiences of sadness, this variation can be seen with respect to the objects and events with which it is associated; its demography and character; and its associations with other aspects of experience. Beginning with objects and events, amongst Western populations generalized anxiety about work is common, and is frequently associated with concerns about poor memory, impaired concentration and loss of interest. By contrast, in Nigeria there are relatively high levels of generalized anxiety concerning procreation, sterility, impotence and the various tasks involved in maintaining a large family (Al-Issa & Oudji, 1998). Similarly, agoraphobia is a Western fear of going outdoors, and in Japan there is a superficially similar fear called *taijinkyo fusho* or TKS, which, like agoraphobia, is characterized by a desire to stay at home. But agoraphobia is associated with panic attacks and fear of fainting, whereas TKS is associated with shame and fears of harming others. And whereas in agoraphobia people are anxious about embarrassing themselves, in TKS they are worried about offending or embarrassing others. Consequently, unlike agoraphobia, TKS often includes anxiety about emitting offensive odours, breaking wind, or having physical deformities (Takahashi, 1989).

In addition, there are more clearly delineated culture-specific experiences of worry. Amongst the Inuit, 'kayak-angst' describes an acute panic state that can occur whilst seal-hunting. Hunters sitting immobile in their boats waiting for seals to surface may become dazed and experience vertigo and spatial disorientation, so that they find it hard to orient themselves to the horizon. Kayak-angst often afflicts groups of hunters simultaneously, rendering them helpless and stricken with dread until they are rescued by others (Pfeiffer, 1982). Amongst Islamic peoples, *waswas* or 'whispered promptings of the devil' is an obsessive–compulsive reaction that can occur whilst washing before prayer. Those affected believe themselves insufficiently clean, so find it hard to stop washing; they may also repeat the introductory invocations and raising of the arms at the start of prayer more often than is usual. However, waswas is not seen as an illness but as the temptation of the devil, and it commands respect amongst others for the piety and devotion it signals (Pfeiffer, 1982).

In the West, many studies show that women are more commonly given anxiety disorder diagnoses than men, but this difference is not always replicated in other cultures. Whereas Western diagnoses of agoraphobia are more commonly given to women than men, Japanese TKS is distributed evenly between men and women (Al-Issa & Oudji, 1998). Other studies show both differences and similarities between cultures. A study comparing test anxiety in Mexican and American schoolchildren found much higher levels of anxiety amongst the Mexican children. However, girls from both cultures scored higher than boys, as did children from both cultures whose SES was lower (Diaz-Guerrero, 1976). Similarly, the large scale 'Epidemiological Catchment Area' (ECA) study in the USA (Robins & Regier, 1991) found that women were more anxious than men in all of the ethnic groups identified in the study. Yet the same study also suggested other variation: obsessive–compulsive behaviours were most common amongst white Americans and least common amongst Hispanics, with African–Americans somewhere between. By contrast, generalized anxiety was most common amongst low SES people of all cultures, but Hispanic people had the lowest levels overall.

As with cross-cultural studies of sadness, people from different cultures use local, idiomatic expressions to describe their experiences of worry, and these may only imperfectly map onto their actual experiences. In some African countries, 'brain fag' is a kind of anxiety associated with academic performance and is said to include pains in the neck, burning sensations as though the scalp were being rubbed with chilli, burning feelings in the centre of the head and the sensation that the scalp is rippling (Collignon & Gueye, 1995). In the Caribbean, *ataque de nervios* is characterized by short intense bursts of shouting, crying, trembling, heat rising from the chest into the head, and aggression (Barron, 1994). Yet amongst Hispanic people in the USA and in Costa Rica, *nervios* is marked by headaches, insomnia, misery, lack of appetite, fear and anger (Low, 1981). In the West, anxiety is also associated with fear, trembling, and lack of appetite, but Western accounts also emphasize blushing, tightness in the stomach, and experiences of nausea and dizziness.

To summarize: experiences of both sadness and worry show clear evidence of historical and cross-cultural variation. This variation encompasses the character of the experiences, how they are configured with other elements of people's lives and activities, their prevalence and their demographic distribution. This variation should not be greatly surprising, because it is well established that cultures vary greatly, between each other and over time. Sadness and worry, as forms of experience, are constituted in part from the raw materials of the cultures where they appear. Moreover, it is with reference to the changing norms of particular cultures that experiences of sadness and worry are assessed, and against which they might be judged as excessive. It is therefore only to be expected that their character, meaning and distribution will show both historical and cross-cultural variation.

Contemporary Western forms of sadness and worry

Tolstoy's great novel, *Anna Karenina*, opens with the line: 'Happy families are all alike; every unhappy family is unhappy in its own way'. Whilst this might seem a little unfairly dismissive of happy families, it does usefully highlight how everyone's experience of sadness and worry is different. Distress is always marked by contingency and particularity, so excessive abstraction will always tend to conceal significant elements of its meaning. Nevertheless, it is useful for our purposes to describe, in very general terms, some of the more common patterns of experience of sadness and worry that have been identified within contemporary Western cultures.

To place these patterns in their proper context we need to recall that, compared to many cultures of the world, Western cultures have a particularly individualized notion of the person, that people within Western cultures tend to downplay somatic symptoms and emphasize emotional or affective difficulties, and that Western people commonly understand their experiences within a dualistic framework that takes for granted the separation of mind and body. We also need to recall that contemporary Western psychiatric conceptions of depression and anxiety disorder are relatively recent. Moncrieff (2008, p. 120) shows that 'it was not until the 1950s that something resembling the modern conception of depression began to emerge'. Although sadness seems to be a longstanding human capacity, before the 1950s its psychiatric categorization as 'involutional melancholia' was seen as relatively rare, and mostly confined to old age and to people admitted to psychiatric hospitals. Similarly, Tyrer and Baldwin (2006) describe how the contemporary diagnosis of generalized anxiety disorder was only constructed in the early 1980s as a kind of 'residual' category left over from the breaking down of the earlier diagnosis of 'anxiety neurosis'.

In Western cultures today, for those who are predominantly sad, their misery is typically greater, more enduring, more resistant to explanation or intervention than everyday misery. Clinically, sadness is often characterized by a low or negative mood, loss of interest and enjoyment in usual activities, and excessive tiredness. However, there is significant variation in the ways that people experience sadness: some people don't mention negative mood, but talk of bodily symptoms such as fatigue and muscle and joint aches. For others, 'low mood' does not seem to capture the nature and extent of their misery and they talk instead of having no mood, no feeling, of being unpleasantly numbed and devoid of any emotions whatsoever. Other common features of sadness include difficulties in concentrating and making decisions, negative views of the self and noticeable pessimism. These emotional and psychological states usually also have accompanying physiological dimensions, although again there is some variation in how these appear. While some people sleep more, eat more and become markedly apathetic, others do the opposite: they eat less, sleep less and become more agitated.

In their lifetime, some people will experience just one bout of profound sadness, whereas others will recurrently drift into and out of deep unhappiness. Jane's current period of sadness was preceded, whilst she was at university, by a period of deep insecurity, manifested as eating problems and concerns about her appearance. Sometimes, sadness is punctuated by periods of rapid activity and positive mood, and is often also characterized by anxiety and irritability. Episodes of profound sadness are frequently triggered by dramatic, life-changing events such as bereavement, unemployment, the birth of a child or the end of a significantly valued relationship. Sometimes, however, their origins are more mysterious, more reflective of the totality of the person's life and relationships than of any single incident.

Experiences of worry are sometimes more enduring and consistent than experiences of profound sadness. Clinically, these may appear as frequent feelings and thoughts of impending doom or threat, sensations of dizziness or faintness, intense restlessness and agitation, exaggerated startle responses, difficulties in concentration, irritability and insomnia. Sometimes, intense worry includes brief experiences of **de-personalization** or **de-realization**, in which either the self, the surrounding world, or both, are experienced as fundamentally strange or unreal and the person feels profoundly detached from things that are happening. These experiences frequently also have physiological dimensions, which can include heart palpitations, hyperventilation and heightened muscular tension, dryness in the mouth, tight chest and difficulty in breathing, a frequent need to urinate, hot flushes, sweating, tremors, and numbness and tingling around the mouth and in the fingers and toes.

For many people their experiences of worry are very general: they can arise in almost any situation, and can get attached to an extremely wide range of objects, events, places and people. Smaller numbers of people have intense worries that are far less general and seem to be tied to very particular objects, places or situations. These **phobias** can be triggered by creatures such as spiders or moths, activities such as flying or travelling in cars, or events such as dental appointments (see Box 9.1).

Some worried people may not experience themselves as particularly anxious, but nevertheless feel compelled to repeatedly conduct certain activities, often in particular, ritualized ways. These activities might include obsessive tooth-brushing, domestic cleaning, or checking of door locks and organizing of personal possessions. If for some reason these rituals are not carried out, these people very easily get overwhelmed with intense worry. A significant minority of people have intense, disabling worry that can be linked to a particularly traumatic event or set of experiences, such as a horrendous accident, or participation in a war. When worry is tied to such events it is sometimes accompanied by **flashbacks**: moments in which vivid memories of trauma get re-lived involuntarily, and which are accompanied by severe emotional impacts. As in Sam's story at the start of the chapter, these states of worry may take the form of **panic attacks**: relatively brief but intense periods of overwhelming anxiety alongside pronounced physiological effects such as breathlessness and dizziness. Panic attacks are extremely unpleasant and associated with numerous kinds of difficulties in everyday life.

BOX **9.1**

Some phobias

Reflecting the massive diversity and contingency of our experiences, it seems that people can develop powerful fear reactions to almost anything. Some phobias are quite common: fear of dentists, hospitals, doctors, flying, spiders or other insects. Some studies find evidence for biological predispositions toward fear responses for evolutionarily old stimuli, such as snakes and spiders, as compared to modern stimuli such as guns and syringes (Ohman & Minecka, 2001), although there are many problems with such claims (McNally, 1995). In any case, as this (partial!) list shows, there are phobias for an incredible variety of objects, activities and events. In each case, phobia means 'fear of'.

Achluophobia – darkness.
Acrophobia – heights.
Agliophobia – pain.
Arachnophobia – spiders.
Astraphobia – thunder and lightning.
Ataxophobia – disorder or untidiness.
Bacteriophobia – bacteria.
Barophobia – gravity.
Bathmophobia – stairs or steep slopes.
Batrachophobia – amphibians.

Belonephobia – pins and needles.
Bibliophobia – books.
Botanophobia – plants.
Catoptrophobia – mirrors.
Chionophobia – snow.
Chromophobia – colours.
Chronomentrophobia – clocks.
Claustrophobia – confined spaces.
Coulrophobia – clowns.
Dendrophobia – trees.
Dentophobia – dentists.
Domatophobia – houses.
Dystychiphobia – accidents.
Ecophobia – the home.
Elurophobia – cats.
Entomophobia – insects.
Ephebiphobia – teenagers.
Equinophobia – horses.
Gamophobia – marriage.
Genuphobia – knees.
Glossophobia – speaking in public.
Gynophobia – women.
Heliophobia – the sun.
Haemophobia – blood.
Herpetophobia – reptiles.
Hydrophobia – water.
Iatrophobia – doctors.
Insectophobia – insects.
Koinoniphobia – rooms.
Leukophobia – the colour white.
Lilapsophobia – tornadoes and
              hurricanes.

Lockiophobia – childbirth.
Mageirocophobia – cooking.
Megalophobia – large things.
Melanophobia – the colour black.
Microphobia – small things.
Mysophobia – dirt and germs.
Necrophobia – death or dead things.
Noctiphobia – the night.
Nosocomephobia – hospitals.
Obesophobia – gaining weight.
Octophobia – the figure 8.
Ombrophobia – rain.
Ophidiophobia – snakes.
Ornithophobia – birds.
Pathophobia – disease.
Pedophobia – children.
Pteridophobia – ferns.
Pteromerhanophobia – flying.
Pyrophobia – fire.
Scolionophobia – school.
Selenophobia – the moon.
Somniphobia – sleep.
Tachophobia – speed.
Technophobia – technology.
Tonitrophobia – thunder.
Trypanophobia – injections.
Venustraphobia – beautiful women.
Verminophobia – germs.
Wiccaphobia – witches and
              witchcraft.
Xenophobia – strangers or foreigners.
Zoophobia – animals.

It is important to note that experiences of sadness and worry very commonly appear together. It is understandable that people who are sad and miserable, whose outlook is bleak and whose ability to function socially is impaired, might also worry: about themselves, their relationships, their job, their future, and their ability to cope with the problems they are experiencing. Similarly, extensive worry is simply inconsistent with happiness, and worry might itself make sufferers miserable. Consistent or profound worry will inevitably impact upon people's lives in various ways: restricting their choices and giving them a more fraught, strained character, negatively influencing their working lives, and impairing their relationships with other people.

Psychiatric diagnoses

Many people who receive treatment for sadness or worry will be treated by their doctor with medication or a referral to counselling or therapy (in the UK currently, the referral is likely to be to an IAPT service), and many of these will receive no formal diagnosis. Those who are referred for treatment for experiences of sadness or worry by specialist mental health services typically receive one or more of the following psychiatric diagnoses:

Unipolar depression
Bipolar depression
Post-natal depression
Psychotic depression
Seasonal affective disorder
Generalized anxiety disorder
Panic disorder
Obsessive–compulsive disorder
Post-traumatic stress disorder (PTSD)
Avoidant personality disorder
Obsessive–compulsive personality disorder

As with many other psychiatric diagnoses, there is good evidence that people who are given these diagnoses are not very distinct from each other, and that the diagnoses do not represent discrete, unitary diseases. Andrews, Anderson, Slade and Sunderland (2008) observe that if these diagnoses represented distinct diseases, the rates of co-occurrence between them would be at chance levels, but both epidemiological evidence and clinical experience shows that rates of co-occurrence are considerably higher. A review by Brady and Kendall (1992) found that between 16% and 62% of children in samples identified as either anxious or depressed showed features of both forms of distress. Dunner (1998) studied a large sample of psychiatric patients and found that 55.6% of those referred for panic disorder also had a history of major depression, whilst 21.6% of patients referred for major depression had experienced at least one panic attack. Similarly, a World Health Organization study of patients in general practice found that experiences of depression and anxiety very commonly appear together (Sartorious, Ustun, Lecrubier & Wittchen, 1996). Indeed, the diagnostic criteria for major depression also make reference to experiences of agitation, restlessness and anxiety, and clinically, sadness and worry appear together so frequently that some psychiatrists (e.g. Tyrer, 2001) have called for a mixed diagnosis of **cothymia**. It now seems widely accepted amongst psychiatrists specializing in this field that

people given a diagnosis of generalized anxiety disorder cannot be differentiated reliably from those given a diagnosis of depression (Stein & Rauch, 2008), and there is also increasing scepticism about the utility of diagnoses of post-traumatic stress disorder (McNally, 2009).

Not only is it difficult to separate experiences of sadness and worry from each other, it is also difficult to separate them from the experiences that characterize other psychiatric diagnoses. Labbatte, Young and Arana (1999) studied a sample of 49 patients given a diagnosis of schizophrenia, finding that 43% had experienced panic attacks and 33% had at some time met the criteria for panic disorder. Although fears and phobias are extremely common and there are no fixed patterns, longitudinal research shows that they can sometimes predict the later experience of more extreme forms of distress (Tien & Eaton, 1992). Similarly, numerous studies and reviews suggest that around 25% of patients given a diagnosis of schizophrenia also meet the diagnostic criteria for major depression (Hwang & Bermanzohn, 2001; Kilzieh, Wood, Erdmann, Raskind & Tapp, 2003). Psychiatrists consider bipolar disorder or manic depression to be a form of psychosis (see Chapter 11), and cluster analyses of the symptoms of people given this diagnosis show that they overlap significantly with the symptoms of those given a diagnosis of schizophrenia (Bentall, 2003). Moreover, the 'negative' symptoms that form part of a diagnosis of schizophrenia look very like the core symptoms of major depression; conversely, the diagnostic criteria for major depression allow for the occasional presence of hallucinations and delusions.

Unsurprisingly, then, the authors of the literature reviewed in this chapter frequently acknowledge the difficulty of drawing meaningful conclusions due to their reliance on diagnostic categories. The diagnosis of generalized anxiety disorder is sometimes mentioned as especially troubling, since its validity has long been questioned (Breslau & Davis, 1985; Stein & Rauch, 2008) and some studies show that it overlaps with diagnoses associated with depression by up to 70% (Carter, Wittchen, Pfister & Kessler, 2001). Diagnoses of depression are similarly problematic, with the UK National Institute for Clinical Excellence saying that the diagnosis of depression 'is too broad and heterogeneous a category, and has limited validity as a basis for effective treatment plans' (National Institute for Health and Clinical Excellence, 2007a). In future, it may be that single symptom research will be better able to unpick the patterns of influence and prevalence that accompany experiences of sadness and worry. Nevertheless, most of the studies reviewed in this chapter have been conducted using these and other related psychiatric diagnostic categories: caution is therefore needed when interpreting these findings.

Prevalence and distribution

Even at levels requiring clinical intervention, experiences of sadness and worry are extremely common. Almost everyone knows at least one person who has taken 'antidepressant' medication, had a 'breakdown', suffered panic attacks, or had a strong phobic reaction to something. The diagnosis of depression is sometimes described as the common cold of psychiatry (Rosenhan & Seligman, 1989); similarly, taken together, the various anxiety disorder diagnoses comprise the largest single category of psychiatric diagnoses.

Using a clinical interview schedule, Jenkins, Lewis, Bebbington et al. (1997) conducted a survey of community mental health in the UK. They found that 16% of a random sample of over 10,000 people scored above the cut-off point for one or more disorders. Of these 16%, nearly half were allocated to a so-called 'residual' category of 'mixed anxiety/depression'. The study found significant differences in psychiatric morbidity between women and men, and significant variation associated with social class, unemployment, age and marital status. With respect to gender, Jenkins et al. (1997) found that women consistently reported more symptoms of all kinds than men. They categorized all of the diagnoses in their study that were associated primarily with sadness and worry into a general category of neurotic disorder: over 19% of women in their sample fell into this category, but only just over 12% of men. Using the same general category, they also found a social class gradient, with disorders far less likely amongst the most affluent and increasingly likely amongst those in manual occupations. People categorized as either unemployed or economically inactive had 'strikingly higher' rates of neurotic disorder (with the exception of older people in retirement). Ethnicity emerged as a factor, with black people more likely to fall into the neurotic disorder category, but further analysis found that this association was explained by a combination of social class, age and family type.

These findings are broadly similar to those of many other studies carried out in the UK, the USA and elsewhere in recent years. The consistent picture emerging from these studies is that experiences of sadness and worry are stratified according to social inequality, gender and age, and that other variables such as immigrant status, ethnicity, family background and marital status are also influential. However, as we consider the various subcategories of diagnosis associated with sadness and worry, this general picture inevitably becomes somewhat less distinct. There are three numerical reasons for this: the population of people affected is smaller, the number of studies that have been conducted is smaller, and the sample sizes in these studies are often smaller. As the range of distressing experiences associated with each diagnosis is reduced (because the diagnosis is more specific), the degrees of contingency within the various interacting influences upon the person's experience become proportionately more marked (see the section on 'contingency' in Chapter 6): consequently, smaller samples and fewer studies make generalization less reliable.

Causal influences

When we begin to think about causal influences in relation to sadness and worry it quickly becomes clear that there is no single pathway or route by which people become distressed. Because these are lived experiences, rather than organic diseases or brain dysfunctions, we should not imagine that they are unitary or homogenous. They will always be shaped by the great multiplicity and contingency of the human world, even though similar kinds of influences, pathways and processes might frequently be involved. Often, for example, specific fears – phobias – can be traced back to dramatic life events, occasions or relationships, but occasionally those who have them seem unable to explain what may have caused them. One of us knows a psychologist colleague who

has an intense phobia for garden peas, but claims to have no idea why! Similarly, people given a diagnosis of seasonal affective disorder sometimes struggle to explain why their mood varies according to the time of year. By contrast, people given a diagnosis of PTSD can trace their problems back to a specific incident or time in their lives: indeed, the diagnostic criteria for PTSD are unique in that they explicitly recognize the impact upon the individual of particular external circumstances.

The causal influences associated with clinical experiences of sadness and worry have been conceptualized and studied within epidemiology, psychology and psychiatry. Each discipline has separately hypothesized possible individual characteristics and mediating pathways or processes linking causal influences to individual experiences. Quite often, these accounts have treated sadness and worry independently. Their separate conceptualization is sometimes helpful because it provides partial recognition of the specificity of individual experiences of distress and reveals something of the diversity of its causes. At the same time, separating sadness and worry in this way can make it more difficult to understand the extent to which they very often co-occur.

There is another difficulty that arises when interpreting the evidence for causal processes in sadness and worry, which flows from the way that the evidence is fragmented across disciplines. Consequently, each discipline emphasizes the aspects most central to its own interests: for example, psychology typically highlights cognitive processes, whilst psychiatry often gives primary importance to biological influences. This separation has allowed each discipline to simplify the phenomena it studies, facilitating the identification of processes and influences. At the same time, it can make it difficult to understand how different causal processes operating at social, biological and psychological levels are already bound up with each other. Consequently, we can very easily end up with a list of sometimes incompatible causes, but able to say relatively little about how these causes interact.

These difficulties are further compounded because, in practice, they intersect. Each therefore magnifies the effect of the other, whilst also to some extent obscuring the overall picture and making it even harder to think clearly about causality (see Box 9.2). You should bear these issues in mind as you read the rest of this section.

Social inequality

Sadness and worry are all but ubiquitous in experiences of distress, and the association of social inequality with distress has been demonstrated repeatedly in studies from many countries. Consequently, there is some debate about the reasons for the associations between social inequality, sadness and worry, but no question that strong associations exist. For example, a large study of patients in general practice in Belgium and Luxembourg included 13,699 people who consulted their doctors (Annsseau et al., 2008). Of these, 13.4% were found to meet the diagnostic criteria for generalized anxiety disorder, 11% met the criteria for major depression and, altogether, 17.8% met the criteria for one or both diagnoses. Across this large sample there were strong associations with social inequality, measured using level of education and type of employment. 12.8% of patients with a degree met the criteria for diagnosis, compared to 22.1% of those without;

BOX **9.2**

Complexities of psychological causation

Anne's story

Anne is a university student. In her early childhood, her father regularly took her to the dentist. She never enjoyed going (who does?!) but had no particular problems. By the time she entered her teenage years, her parents had separated. Anne was living with her mother, who – Anne knew – had a profound phobia about dental treatment. When Anne's mother first took her to the dentist when she was 14, Anne had a panic attack. Now, eight years later, she is unable to receive dental treatment without first taking medication, and dreads the thought of ever visiting the surgery.

Anne's story illustrates some of the difficulties that accompany attempts to provide neat explanations for even relatively simple forms of distress. Simple phobias are most often explained using classical conditioning, but Anne experienced no aversive stimulus, no painful incident, that transformed her experience. Whilst her panic attack could itself be seen as an aversive stimulus that partially accounts for her continuing phobia, classical conditioning cannot explain why this panic attack occurred.

A social learning theorist might say that, having first learned from her father that dental surgeries are relatively unthreatening, Anne later learned the opposite from her mother. But why should this later learning suddenly take precedence over years of earlier learning? Rather than answering this question, suggesting that her mother's modelling was more salient just pushes it elsewhere, because then we must explain this difference in salience.

A Freudian explanation of Anne's problems might engage with their oral location, and with the links within Freudian theory between oral tendencies and dependency, particularly between mothers and daughters. Other psychoanalysts might invoke notions of identification, or emotional containment: maybe Anne's father was able to contain her fears in a way that her mother was not, precisely because Anne *knew* that her mother was herself terrified.

Whilst this explanation seems more plausible, it must assume that Anne's deep fears already existed long before they suddenly became a phobia; but Anne had already attended the dentists for many years without difficulties. We might posit 'primal' fears to explain this: but then we would have to both account for where *they* came from, and also explain why their course of development was so distinctive in Anne's case.

In short, even with a very simple example of this kind, we can see that simple, mechanistic 'cause and effect' psychological explanations are often insufficient. However, this does not mean that Anne's distress is wholly incapable of explanation. But it does show that any viable explanation could only be generated in a process of sensitive and thorough discussion with Anne that engaged fully with the *meanings* of her difficulties.

Finally, just to add further complexity, it is quite possible that Anne's phobia could be removed in a relatively quick process of progressive desensitization. Just because conditioning theory does not provide a satisfactory explanation does not necessarily mean that it cannot provide a solution.

---

similarly, there was a marked gradient related to employment status with 27.7% of unemployed people meeting the criteria for one or both diagnoses, compared to just 15.5% of people in management roles. Annsseau et al. (2008) found that sadness and worry were equally associated with social inequality, but some other studies have found more of an association between inequality and sadness (Kessler, 2002), and an Australian survey (Hunt, Issakidis & Andrews, 2002) showed that people given a diagnosis of generalized anxiety disorder were significantly likely to be unemployed or poorly educated.

Two kinds of explanation are typically offered for the associations between social inequality, sadness and worry. One is that inequality is difficult, distressing and inevitably causes sadness and worry, which for some individuals reaches clinical levels. The other is that because clinical levels of sadness and worry impair relationships, obstruct employment, and generally impede life chances, they cause downward social mobility. Both of these kinds of explanation seem plausible, and it is possible that, to some degree, both may occur. Clinicians do sometimes see some evidence for downward social mobility amongst their patients, as a result of their distress. Nevertheless there are many large-scale studies suggesting that clinical sadness and worry are caused by social inequality. Fan and Eaton (2001) followed up a sample of 1824 people born in America between 1960 and 1965, and found that median household income at age seven was a strong predictor of 'general emotional distress' and depression in adult life. In their community study, Annsseau et al. (2008)

reported that social inequality seemed to be causal of sadness and worry because there was a **dose-response relationship** (i.e. a tendency to co-vary) between level of education and distress. A dramatic study in Australia by Page, Morrell and Taylor (2002) showed that conservative governments, which have historically tended to be associated with greater levels of social inequality, were also associated with higher suicide levels.

Although few studies have set out to directly compare both of these hypotheses (that social inequality causes clinical sadness or worry, or that sadness and worry produce social inequality) one study has done so. Ritsher, Warner, Johnson and Dohrenwend (2001) carried out a large scale, longitudinal study of families with and without histories of major depression. Three generations were assessed, spanning the period between 1977 and 1994, and in total 756 people were included in the research. By making various inter-generational comparisons, their study found strong evidence for the hypothesis that inequality causes depression and no significant evidence for the hypothesis that depression causes inequality. In their sample, people born to parents who were poorly educated were twice as likely to be given a diagnosis of depression in adult life as controls, and their risk was more than tripled if their parents worked in manual or unskilled occupations. In a separate analysis of families without any history of major depression (and thus with no obvious genetic predisposition), people born to poorly educated, unskilled parents were five times more likely than controls to be given a diagnosis of depression as adults.

Gender

Women are far more likely than men to receive clinical interventions for sadness or worry. In the community study by Jenkins et al. (1997), 19% of women were classed as having a neurotic disorder, compared to 12% of men; similarly, Annsseau et al. (2008) found that 20.8% of women in their sample met the diagnostic criteria, compared to 13.3% of men. This difference is fairly typical of many others which have looked at gender differences in the prevalence of diagnoses associated with sadness and worry, and which commonly show that women are roughly twice as likely to receive such diagnoses as men.

One explanation for women's higher rates of sadness and worry is domestic violence. Although men are occasionally the victims, this kind of violence is far more commonly meted out by men against women. A World Health Organization multi-country study of women's health and domestic violence in ten countries (Garcia-Moreno, Jansen, Ellsberg, Heise & Watts, 2005) found rates of severe physical violence against women ranging from 4% in Japan to 49% in Peru. Rates of sexual violence and emotional abuse were also variable but frequently strikingly high. In all of the countries surveyed, women who had ever experienced physical or sexual violence were significantly more likely to report higher levels of crying, inability to enjoy life, and tiredness, and significantly more likely to have contemplated or attempted suicide.

Differences in economic status may also help to explain the different rates of sadness and worry in women and men. Despite increasing levels of gender equality in the West in recent years, on balance women are still at a relative disadvantage. They tend to earn less money than men, and are more likely to occupy lower-paid, lower status and more precarious jobs. In the UK, figures for 2009 showed that mean pay for women was 16.4% less than that for men (Office for National Statistics, 2009). However, despite increasingly being in employment, in most families women are still the primary carers of children (Himmelweit, 1998), and they typically undertake more than their fair share of other household or domestic responsibilities.

There is also evidence that, in heterosexual relationships, women typically do more nurturing, caring and apologizing than men, and consequently may be less likely to have their own emotional needs met (Perrons, 2000). **Emotion work** is a sociological concept that refers to the ways people are sometimes expected to manage, cultivate, refine and display their emotions in line with employers or other expectations (Hochschild, 1979). Studies of emotion work show that women often express dissatisfaction with what they perceive to be their male partners' reluctance or inability to share 'emotional intimacy' in the relationship. Many women feel that, as a consequence of this, they have to make more effort to sustain these heterosexual relationships than their male partners (Duncombe & Marsden, 1993). Moreover, the gendered division of emotion work does not only operate in the home. For example, Pierce (1997) studied law firms in the USA and found that not only did men typically earn more money, but also that there were striking differences in the emotional repertoires expected of men and women. Men were expected to adopt an aggressive 'winner takes all' stance characterized by intimidation, attempts to humiliate others and strategic, opportunistic flattery. By contrast, women were expected to be intuitive and anticipatory to the emotional needs of others, especially men, and to bolster the emotional status of others through deferential treatment and status affirmation.

Arguably, women also experience more pressure to conform to conventional standards of appearance and behaviour, and the social pressures this involves may produce some sadness and worry. Cash, Ancis and Strachan (1997) studied women's satisfaction with their own bodies in relation to a range of variables, including conformity to traditional beliefs about women's role in society, and the extent to which women adopted traditional gender attitudes during everyday male–female social interactions. They found that whilst proclaimed beliefs about women's role were unrelated to body satisfaction, traditional attitudes within everyday social interaction were significantly associated with stronger and dysfunctional investments in stereotypically feminine standards of appearance. An experimental study by Fredrickson, Roberts, Noll, Quinn and Twenge (1998) found that increased objectification (produced by asking participants to try on a swimsuit) led to raised levels of body shame, followed by restrained eating, but that when gender was introduced as a variable, this effect only occurred amongst women.

Sometimes biological factors are invoked to explain the gender imbalance in diagnoses of sadness and worry, with women seen as more prey to hormonal disturbances and mood swings. Whilst this view may have some intuitive appeal in relation to women given diagnoses of post-natal depression, it is a truism that the birth of a baby always involves profound, enduring and sometimes unsettling changes in parent's lives, whatever effect it also has on the mother's hormones. In recent years, numerous scholars have pointed out the lack of evidence for direct hormonal effects of this kind, and provided alternate explanations that engage closely with the social and material circumstances of women's lives (Lafrance, 2009; Mauthner, 1995; Stoppard & McMullen, 2003). In Jane's story at the beginning of this chapter, we see how she feels ignored and unsupported by her husband but is expected to devote significant amounts of energy to childcare whilst also managing a highly demanding job.

Clinically, it is frequently more useful to see the diagnosis of post-natal depression and other manifestations of this gender imbalance in the context of the broad gender role expectations associated with both men and women. Compared to men, women are expected more often to be carers and nurturers, to be emotionally responsible for others, and to take a passive, supportive role. Hankin and Abramson (1999) observe that girls are more likely than boys to be confronted with emotional responsibility for life events within the family. When circumstances become difficult, it is easy to see how someone who has regularly adopted a caring role might tend to respond by becoming worried or sad. By contrast, men in our culture are more often expected to be providers and protectors, and to be dominant, active, directive and controlling. When circumstances become difficult, then, men are less likely to become overtly worried or sad, but far more likely than women to be given diagnoses of substance- or alcohol-dependency disorders. When adverse life events and circumstances arise, the broad pattern of gender expectations associated with both women and men may help to make them differentially vulnerable to different kinds of distress.

Family and childhood influences

Numerous studies have documented associations between adverse childhood circumstances and sadness and worry in later life; of these, many place particular importance upon the characteristics of families. For example, Oakley-Browne, Joyce, Wells, Bushnell and Hornblow (1995) recruited 65 women who had recently been given a diagnosis of major depressive disorder, and a community sample of 81 women who had never been given diagnoses. Amongst other comparisons, the women's childhood experiences of care and neglect were assessed using a questionnaire. The analysis showed that childhood experiences of low maternal care made it four times more likely that the women would be given a diagnosis of major depression as adults.

Many studies of these influences have explicitly considered experiences of sadness and worry together. Phillips, Hammen, Brennan, Najman and Bor (2005) investigated 816 adolescents who had been born to Australian mothers from 1981 to 1984, and who had been assessed at numerous points over the intervening years. They found that adolescents who had been given diagnoses of anxiety disorders were significantly more likely than either controls or those who had been given diagnoses of depression to have been exposed to stressors such as maternal anxiety, divorce and relationship changes, and had experienced a greater number of total adversities. Moffit et al. (2007) followed up a cohort of 1037 children born in New Zealand in 1972 and 1973, 96% of whom were still in the study 32 years later. Their study explored risk factors for diagnoses of generalized anxiety disorder and major depression, including proportions of family members given diagnoses, socio-economic status in childhood and maltreatment before age 11, together with a range of assessments of psychological variables taken at various ages. They found that some risk factors were shared and that those who had scored highest on many of them were most likely to meet criteria for both diagnoses, but also that there were some significant differences between the antecedent risk factors for each diagnosis.

Similarly, Biedel and Turner (1997) used interviews to assess levels of anxiety disorder in children whose parents had been given diagnoses of anxiety disorders, depressive disorders or both, and compared these with controls. They found that children born to parents from all three groups were all equally more likely than controls to meet the diagnostic criteria for an anxiety disorder. They also found that distressed children born to parents who were given diagnoses of depressive disorders met the criteria for a broader range of disorders than did those born to parents who had been given other diagnoses. However, some studies find that the diagnoses associated with both sadness and worry are predicted more or less equally. Sachs-Ericsson, Verona, Joiner and Preacher (2006) studied 5614 people aged from 15–54, who had provided information as part of a USA National Comorbidity Study. They used participant memories of having been called names as children by their parents as an index for the character of relations in the childhood home. Their analysis found that those who had been called names had 1.6 times as many symptoms of anxiety and depression as those who had not been abused in this way, and were twice as likely to have been given either a mood or anxiety disorder diagnosis at some point in their lives. However, such measures cannot capture all adverse family influences: in Jane's story, for example, it is clear that the exceedingly high and gender-specific expectations of her mother were a factor in her later distress, even though nothing so overt as name-calling ever took place.

Overall, whilst there is some confusion about the extent to which particular kinds of childhood and family experiences may be associated with specific forms of sadness and worry in later life, there is nevertheless good evidence that these influences exert significant causal force.

Life events

In everyday life, sadness and worry are unremarkable components of our reactions to a wide variety of distressing events, and these associations are so powerful that they sometimes enter into diagnostic criteria. For example, the criteria for major depression in DSM-IV exclude people who meet the other criteria but who have been recently bereaved; conversely, diagnoses of PTSD are entirely dependent upon the prior occurrence of unusually stressful events. Moreover, there is good evidence linking clinical sadness and worry to the prior occurrence of adverse life events, and it is widely accepted in psychiatry that people given diagnoses of major depression may have experienced an 'excess of life events' in the period before they came into contact with services (Burton, 2006).

A number of studies have taken advantage of large-scale natural disasters such as earthquakes to chart their association with sadness and worry. Coincidentally, Nolen-Hoeksema and Morrow (1991) had administered a battery of measures of distress to a cohort of students in California, just two weeks before a large earthquake in 1991. They administered the same measures again at both seven days and ten weeks after the earthquake, and found that those students who had already been reporting symptoms of stress and depression were significantly likely to have further deteriorated. Similarly, Mcleish and Del Ben (2008) measured symptoms in a population of 156 psychiatric outpatients before and after Hurricane Katrina devastated the American city of New Orleans in 2005, and found increases in the symptoms associated both with diagnoses of depression and diagnoses of post-traumatic stress disorder.

Other studies have demonstrated associations between life events, sadness and worry using individual self-reports and correlating these with symptom assessments. Kendler, Hettema, Butera, Gardner and Prescott (2003) conducted blind ratings of the levels of humiliation, entrapment, loss and danger associated with the life events reported by 7322 adult twins. They found that experiences of loss or humiliation made people more likely to meet the diagnostic criteria for major depression and for generalized anxiety disorder. People whose experiences were characterized by loss and danger were more likely to meet the diagnostic criteria for generalized anxiety disorder, whilst people who experienced combinations of humiliation and loss were especially likely to meet the diagnostic criteria for depression. Blazer, Hughes and George (1987) assessed the occurrence of life events in a community sample of 2902 adults, and found that men who reported four or more adverse life events in the recent past were more than eight times more likely than others to meet the diagnostic criteria for generalized anxiety disorder. Similarly, Finlay-Jones and Brown (1981) assessed 164 women attending a UK general practitioner who had recently experienced severely threatening life events. They found that severe loss was significantly more likely amongst those women meeting the criteria for depressive disorders, whilst severe danger was more likely in women meeting the criteria for anxiety disorders.

Childhood abuse

As with many other forms of distress, childhood experiences of sexual or physical abuse are common amongst people with clinical levels of sadness and worry. A meta-analysis of the effects of childhood sexual abuse by Paolucci, Genuis and Violato (2001) considered 37 studies involving 25,367 people and found significant associations with diagnoses of PTSD and depression, as well as with suicide. Similarly, a wide-ranging review of published studies by Putnam (2003) showed that a range of psychiatric diagnoses are associated with childhood sexual abuse but that diagnoses of depression are the most common psychiatric outcome. However, Schaaf and McCanne (1995) examined 475 college students, some of whom had experienced sexual abuse, physical abuse or both, and found strong associations between these experiences and symptoms consistent with a diagnosis of PTSD. A review by Polusny and Follette (1995) found higher levels of general psychological distress in people who had experienced childhood sexual abuse, associated with greater tendencies towards dysfunctional, re-victimizing or abusive adult relationships, binge-eating, somatization and suicidal behaviours.

Other studies looking at the effects of both physical and sexual abuse have uncovered associations with sadness and worry. Mancini, Van Ameringen and MacMillan (1995) took histories from 205 women admitted consecutively to anxiety disorder clinics in Canada. They found that childhood sexual abuse was reported by 23.4% and childhood physical abuse by 44.9% of the women. Young, Abelson, Curtis and Nesse (1997) assessed 650 patients referred to a specialist outpatient clinic, and found that 35% of people who met the diagnostic criteria for either major depression or panic disorder had experienced sexual, physical or emotional abuse as children. Similarly, Koverola et al. (2005) collected information from 203 women attending USA children's clinics. They found associations between a measure of maternal victimization, which includes abuse of various kinds, and symptoms of depression. They also found numerous other consequences, some of which impacted upon children.

Psychological processes

Psychological processes never occur in isolation from other aspects of experience: cognitions, beliefs, attributions and so on only arise and become influential in the ongoing stream of experience, where they are continuously bound up with the powerful material and social influences that shape our lives (Bradley, 2005; Smail, 2005). Psychological explanations for sadness and worry often strongly emphasize cognitive processes, and in doing so they can minimize or obscure the significance of the external influences that continuously shape our activity and experience. In reality, individuals and their worlds are always intimately related, in each and every moment. Failing to recognize this sufficiently can easily lead to something akin to victim-blaming, where we imagine that people persist with their unhelpful patterns of thought simply because they lack the good sense or the willpower to change them. But it is nevertheless useful to consider psychological processes because, once circumstances lead people to adopt unhelpful beliefs and habits of thinking, these processes can then become a part of their problems, helping to 'lock them into place', and further contributing to their distress. There is also some evidence that psychological processes can predispose people to have more extreme or frequent distressing responses to life events, and so play some part in precipitating people's difficulties, and that they can also impede people's attempts at recovery.

Sadness

With respect to sadness, the two most influential recent approaches are the cognitive models developed by Beck (1967) and Abrahamson, Seligman and Teasdale (1978). Beck hypothesized that vulnerability to clinical experiences of sadness and worry is produced by consistent patterns of automatic thoughts, characterized by negative views of self, world and future. This **negative triad** of views is said to be caused by an underlying **negative schema**: a collection of interrelated beliefs about the self, negative in character and acquired in childhood, usually as a result of adverse life experiences. Because of this negative self-schema, individuals have a set of cognitive biases toward pessimistic, negative or critical interpretations of events and experiences. These biases include **arbitrary inference** (drawing conclusions in the absence of appropriate evidence); **selective abstraction** (taking details out of context and magnifying them); and **over-generalization** (assuming that, for example, all future events will go badly because one event has). As a consequence of these and other biases, said Beck, when faced with adversity, some individuals more readily develop the kinds of reactions that are associated with a diagnosis of depression. However, it is important to remember that describing these information-processing strategies as 'biases' can tend to obscure their origins in past experience, where – for whatever reason – they may have been adaptive; similarly, focusing too much on cognitions and schema can sometimes obscure the extent to which current social and material circumstances contribute to sadness.

The other influential cognitive theory of sadness gives a central role to attributions. Abrahamson et al. (1978) proposed that vulnerability to extreme sadness arises when individuals persistently make attributions – causal explanations – that are unhelpful. They identify three features of a person's attributional style that may cause problems. First, when people make attributions that are *internal rather than*

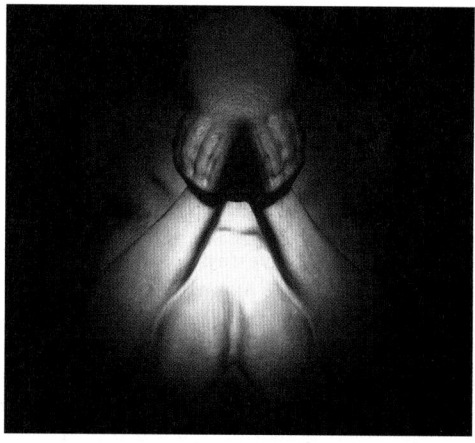

Psychological processes never occur in isolation from other aspects of experience. This is a sculpture by Jaume Plensa

external: always blaming themselves rather than situations when things go wrong. Second, when their attributions are *stable rather than unstable*: when they focus on things that are unlikely to change, rather than things that are temporary or variable. And third, when people make attributions that are *global rather than specific*: when they refer to all or most aspects of their lives, rather than a specific situation or task. For example, if you fail a psychology test an internal, stable, global attribution might be 'I am just too stupid to pass tests'. This attribution is internal because it blames a personal attribute (lack of intelligence), stable because such attributes don't change very much, and global because it is applied to all tests. By contrast, an external, unstable and specific attribution might be 'I had a bad day, and besides I hate psychology'. This is external because it blames the 'bad day', unstable because each day has the possibility of being different, and specific because it recognizes that psychology tests can be especially annoying. Because this theory has its origins in Seligman's (1975) theory of learned helplessness, it also provides a way of beginning to think about how unhelpful attributional styles might be learned as a result of negative prior experiences; in other words, how cognitive processes are shaped in social relations. However, this theory does not consider the ways in which attributions are always made in social situations and bound up with present circumstances (Chapter 6; Hewstone, 1989).

There are also other, less influential, psychological theories of clinical sadness. Psychoanalytic theories (e.g. Freud, 1917) identify the cause of extreme sadness as the real or symbolic loss of a loved object (in psychoanalysis, 'objects' includes people!). They understand clinical sadness as a regressive phase that may include elements of anger towards the lost person, perhaps coupled with guilt, either at one's own anger, or in relation to any positive experiences that occur. Behavioural theories propose that vulnerability to clinical sadness is the outcome of being exposed to reinforcement schedules that fail to positively reinforce, or alternatively even negatively reinforce, constructive behaviours that promote useful activity (Lewinsohn, Youngren & Grosscup, 1979). Consequently, people become inactive, withdrawn and lack motivation, and may be drawn into a 'behavioural vacuum' in which sadness gets established as a chronic condition.

There is research evidence in support of each of these psychological theories. For example, Beck's theory is supported by studies using **dichotic listening** (where two different audio stimuli are presented simultaneously, one in each ear) which have demonstrated that people given a diagnosis of depression have an attentional bias that makes it harder for them to ignore negative information (Ingram, Bernet & McLoughlin, 1994). Similarly, a number of studies have shown that attributional style may predict sadness: students with more global and stable attributional styles and lowself-esteem were sadder than others in the five days following a difficult exam (Metalsky, Joiner, Hardin & Abrahamson, 1993). Behavioural theories are supported by studies showing that behavioural interventions that provide graded positive reinforcement and reinforce alternate coping strategies can have beneficial effects (Jacobson, Martell & Dimidjian, 2001). Likewise, there is extensive evidence (some of it reviewed in the 'childhood influences' section above) that childhood and parenting patterns may be associated with later vulnerabilities; much

of this evidence can be read as offering some support to both psychoanalytic and behavioural accounts.

A more recent cognitive account of sadness is given by Bentall (2003). His integrative model incorporates both attributions and cognitive biases, and links them to various aspects of the self that research has shown to be associated with clinical sadness: lowself-esteem, overly demanding self-standards, discrepancies between ideal self and actual self. As we explain in Box 9.3, psychological accounts of sadness frequently downplay its bodily or embodied aspects. Unusually for a psychological model, however, Bentall's model also explicitly includes possible biological processes, suggesting that clinical sadness could be in part precipitated by the disruptions to circadian rhythms and sleep patterns described by Healy (1987: see the section on 'biological processes' below).

Worry

With respect to experiences of worry, different psychological processes have been hypothesized as involved in different kinds of difficulty. Panic attacks are often thought to involve **catastrophic misinterpretation** in which ordinary bodily sensations are mistaken for serious problems: for example, thinking that chest pain caused by indigestion is actually a heart attack. These misinterpretations or attribution errors are themselves productive of anxiety, and the anxiety they produce – breathlessness, stomach-clenching – might then also get misinterpreted in similarly catastrophic ways. Consequently, people who make these attribution errors can quickly spiral uncontrollably into extreme states of breathless panic in which they are genuinely terrified that something physically awful is happening to them. Like other attribution errors, the origins of tendencies to misattribute in this way can frequently be traced back to prior negative experiences. From start to finish, these states can last for up to thirty minutes, and once the attack has ended its highly unpleasant character can leave people extremely wary of a recurrence, but this wariness itself may feed forward into future situations to make subsequent catastrophic misinterpretations even more likely. This kind of 'fear of fear' can also sometimes lead people to develop a pattern of repeated, recurrent panic attacks that is very distressing and disabling. People may also develop 'safety behaviours', habits intended to avoid panic attacks or manage them if they occur. People who experience repeated panic attacks have been shown to be more preoccupied with their bodily states than controls (Ehlers & Breuer, 1992), and are also more vulnerable to cognitive expectancy effects: simply being told that something will be negative or difficult can make them likely to experience a panic attack, even in the absence of actual threats (Sanderson, Rapee & Barlow, 1989).

Panic attacks are also sometimes explained psychologically in terms of classical conditioning, where sufferers come to pair internal cues, such as dizziness or raised heart rate, with aversive consequences. However, this kind of explanation is most commonly applied to phobias, which are often said to be produced by these kinds of processes: within this paradigm is it is well established that once a stimulus has been paired with a particularly aversive outcome, encountering the stimulus in future might generate a severe anxiety response. For example, after being in a car crash people sometimes feel extremely anxious next time they get into a car, or, in some cases, when

BOX **9.3**
Sadness as embodied experience

There are relatively few psychological accounts of sadness that don't either invoke psychiatric diagnoses or disembody sadness (by emphasizing information-processing strategies with no necessary connection to human bodies).

An account by Cromby (2004) used the notion of transactional scripts (Wiener & Marcus, 1994): broad categories that characterize typical patterns of talking and relating. The 'Helpless–Helpful' script characterizes environments where people are rewarded for positioning themselves as incapable or describing themselves as inferior. The 'Powerless–Powerful' script characterizes environments where people are rewarded for placating others and ingratiating themselves. Finally, the 'Worthy–Worthless' script characterizes environments where people are rewarded for apologizing and deploying self-deprecating discourses.

Weiner and Marcus ask us to imagine three people growing up in different homes where one of these scripts predominated. If asked to complete the Beck Depression Inventory, all three might agree with the statement that 'I can't make decisions at all any more' (Beck, 1967). However, for each, *the meaning of their agreement would differ.*

The person who grew up with the Helpless script would mean something like 'I don't know how to manage responsibility'; for the Powerless script, 'I am not permitted to make meaningful decisions'; and for the Worthless script something like 'I am not good enough to make decisions' (Weiner & Marcus, 1994, p. 223).

Cromby (2004) used this idea of transactional scripts alongside work from neuroscience. First, he argued that the verbal aspects of these scripts could become embodied in individuals through a neural system called the 'left brain interpreter' (Gazzaniga, 1988).

However, sadness involves much more than just ways of talking. It also involves ways of feeling, experiencing and holding the body. We see this clearly in people who are profoundly sad. Their tone of voice, gestures, postures and expressions are all thoroughly imbued with misery. These *embodied* aspects of sadness are also completely bound up with our ways of talking and relating, and we might begin to understand them with reference to Damasio's 'somatic marker' hypothesis.

Damasio (1994) describes a neural system that facilitates decision-making in social settings by temporarily re-enacting brain and body states from the past. He calls these body states somatic markers, and we experience them as *feelings* that subtly guide our decision-making by making us favour some options over others. Somatic markers are acquired in social relations, so their character reflects experiences of – for example – different transactional scripts. Persons who grew up with one script rather than another would acquire a different set of somatic markers.

This could make sense of the fact that the diagnosis of depression contains paradoxical bodily patterns (both agitation and apathy, both over- and under-eating, both insomnia and hypersomnia). The 'Hopeless' script might generate somatic markers associated with apathy and hypersomnia, whereas the 'Worthless' script might generate markers associated with agitation and insomnia. Similarly, all three scripts could generate somatic markers that make all available options feel unavailable, perhaps explaining why people given a diagnosis of depression often find decisions difficult.

---

they just cross a road, or see cars travelling at speed. Similarly, the extreme fear some people experience when they think about going to the dentist is often associated with personal or family histories of unpleasant experiences at the dental surgery. Histories of traumatic experiences that may be associated with processes of classical conditioning have been found in relation to people with fears about dentists, accidents and dogs (De Jongh, Muris, Ter Horst & Duyx, 1995; King, Clowes-Hollins & Ollendick, 1997; Kuch, Cox & Evans, 1996; Locker, Liddell, Dempster & Shapiro, 1999).

Frequently, people's worries are more general, tied neither to specific life events or experiences, nor to specific objects or circumstances. Psychological explanations for these more generalized forms of worry sometimes implicate information-processing biases that might predispose people to preferentially allocate attention to threatening stimuli or threatening information. Whereas most people are biased to avoid such stimuli because they are inherently unpleasant, it is suggested that people who are prone to excessive worry have the opposite bias and tend to process threatening stimuli more often and more deeply. This bias toward unpleasant or threatening stimuli may also be associated with beliefs that worrying about threats is somehow protective or useful. Versions of the **Stroop test** (which allows psychologists to assess experimentally the amount of information-processing associated with different kinds of stimuli by comparing the reaction times associated with them in alternate conditions), have shown that people prone to anxiety do tend to devote more cognitive effort to threat-related stimuli (Mogg, Bradley, Williams & Matthews, 1993). As with other psychological accounts, we have to link these suggestions to understandings of the wider context, for example by considering what kinds of parenting styles or early life events might have produced a tendency to focus excessively on the possibility of threat. In Sam's case, for example, it seems that his excessive worrying was learned very early in his life and is associated with his desire to care for others (see Box 9.4).

In the wake of sudden and traumatic experiences, some people have a range of distressing reactions including flashbacks to the moment of the trauma, and momentary but deeply unsettling feelings that either they or their surroundings are not real. People experiencing these reactions are frequently given a diagnosis of PTSD, and there are numerous competing psychological theories of how they occur. Behavioural or conditioning accounts draw upon principles of classical conditioning to suggest that the traumatic event gets associated with contingent features of the situation where it occurred. As a result, conditioned responses are built up between these seemingly random environmental features and the shock of the trauma, so that when these superficially harmless environmental features are encountered again they have the power to re-evoke the trauma. However, whilst

BOX **9.4**
Why worry?

Smail (1984, 1987, 2005) argues that what can superficially appear as 'irrational' cognitive biases or information-processing errors are better conceptualized as understandable responses to environments and events. Notice how, in Sam's story, he had great responsibility to care for others: as a child, he told stories to his siblings to distract them from the sound of their parents arguing. Now, he and his wife are having relationship difficulties and Sam is desperately trying to resolve their problems. But his efforts have so far failed, causing broken sleep, dizzy spells and panic attacks.

We can imagine that a well-meaning friend might advise Sam to just stop worrying. Such advice clearly has Sam's best interests at heart, but misses the vital point that for Sam *worrying probably isn't a simple matter of choice*. Sam has spent much of his life learning that, in various ways, he is responsible for the emotions of others. Worrying about others is what Sam does, and – manifest as loving concern and attentiveness – is no doubt part of what makes him an attractive person. But now, his own situation has become so difficult that this worrying is damaging his health and making it difficult for him to work. Yet this doesn't mean that he can simply stop it, because this way of being and relating is an integral part of who he is. Just as, once we've learned, we can't forget how to ride a bicycle, so we can't simply 'unlearn' our basic, acquired ways of relating to other people (Priest, 2006).

This understanding is supported by evidence showing that people who worry excessively often believe that their worrying is necessary, indeed vital, if negative outcomes are to be avoided (Davey, Tallis & Capuzzo, 1996). Studies suggest that people like Sam have stable, powerful beliefs that worrying is helpful and must be undertaken if problems are to be avoided (Borkovec, Hazlett-Stevens & Diaz, 1999). People who worry excessively claim that their beliefs help motivate action, solve problems, avoid difficulties, prepare appropriate plans to deal with them, and give reassurance by making them feel that they are doing all they can. Worrying about certain aspects of problems, or about minor difficulties, may also serve to distract people from thinking about bigger, more difficult or distressing issues in their lives, and there is some evidence that worrying helps to block difficult emotional states (Borkovec, Lyonfields, Wiser & Deihl, 1993). There is also evidence that people who worry more than others are more likely to be perfectionistic, intolerant of uncertainty, and to take responsibility for others (Ladouceur, Talbot & Dugas, 1997; Pratt, Tallis & Eysenck, 1997; Startup & Davey, 2003). This evidence further suggests that, for someone like Sam, worrying isn't optional.

To make sense of worry, then, just as with other forms of distress, it will usually help to both place it firmly within the context of people's previous life experiences, and relate it to their present situation.

---

these accounts are superficially appealing they fail to explain the range of experiences associated with traumatic reactions and, like other behavioural accounts, they also largely exclude *meaning*. This means that conditioning accounts often struggle to explain why one particular feature of an event or situation, rather than another, becomes the focus of a conditioned response.

In behaviourist psychology, notions of stimulus generalization are sometimes used to help account for this, and stimulus generalization is central to another psychological account of these experiences which emphasizes emotional processing (Foa, Steketee & Rothbaum, 1989). Here it is proposed that due to the profound shock of a trauma, many disparate and abstract contextual features associated with it will subsequently evoke fear responses.

Psychological responses to trauma have also been explained using the **theory of shattered assumptions** (Janoff-Bulman, 1992). This theory proposes that the shock of trauma can be so great that it thoroughly challenges and changes pre-existing core beliefs about the basically benevolent character of the world. Consequently, people who experience trauma are then left struggling to understand their relation to the world, to such an extent that they may sometimes experience both themselves and the world as somewhat unreal. This theory goes some way toward explaining the experiences of dissociation, re-realization and de-personalization that sometimes accompany or follow traumatic events. However (and perhaps unsurprisingly), evidence suggests that the people who are most prone to severe traumatic reactions are not those who previously felt the most secure, but those who *already* viewed the world as a threatening and unsafe place.

Perhaps the most comprehensive psychological theory of responses to trauma has been proposed by Joseph, Williams and Yule (1995). Their psychosocial model includes consideration of the characteristics of the traumatic event, the person's coping strategies and their (sometimes unintended) effects, pre-existing dispositional or personality factors, and the level of relational and social support the person receives. Unusually for a psychological theory, Joseph's model also includes some consideration of the biological mechanisms that may enable trauma, by incorporating Brewin's account of two complementary neurally-based memory systems – verbally accessible memory and situationally accessible memory – that together may enable the various features of trauma (a more comprehensive account of Brewin's theory appears in the next section, on biological processes).

Biological processes

Just like psychological processes, biological processes are thoroughly bound up with other aspects of people's lives, and the evidence frequently suggests that our biology *enables* sadness and worry rather than simply causing them (see Box 4.3: Enabling versus causing). In the absence of clear evidence of brain injury, trauma or other organic insult or problem (e.g. impairments of hormonal systems) it seems unwise to conclude that the causes of sadness and worry are simply biological. Although they are always enabled biologically (like all experiences), their causes frequently lie elsewhere. Differences in the biological systems of people experiencing clinical sadness and worry, then, frequently reflect or mediate these external circumstances rather than being causal in their own right.

Sadness

Current biological explanations for clinical sadness often implicate monoamines (a set of neurotransmitters with some aspects of their chemical structure in common; the set includes dopamine, serotonin and norepinephrine). Rather than starting with a hypothesis about the neural basis of extreme sadness, these explanations have worked backwards from the discovery that drugs that impact upon these neurotransmitter systems can also influence people's mood. Consequently, much of the evidence for these explanations is provided by studies showing that certain drugs alter the availability of these neurotransmitters. Ingestion of a drug called physostigmine, which inhibits the availability of norepinephrine, causes brief but intense low mood (Janowsky, El-Yousef, Davis & Serkerke, 1972). Selective-serotonin reuptake inhibitors (SSRIs), such as Prozac, prevent serotonin from being reabsorbed from the synapses in the brain and so cause levels of brain serotonin to gradually increase. Similarly, so-called tricyclic antidepressants (TCAs) and monoamine oxidase inhibitors (MAOIs) increase the availability of serotonin, norepinephrine and dopamine. All three of these classes of drugs are associated with increases in positive mood and reductions in patterns of negative thinking.

A widespread problem with accounts of sadness that invoke neurotransmitters is that they depend upon notions of a monoamine imbalance. Moncrieff (2008) describes how, since the 1950s, drug companies have worked to promote the idea that an 'imbalance' of serotonin is responsible for the experiences that lead to a diagnosis of depression. However, although many psychiatrists and lay people presume that this hypothesis has been proved beyond doubt, eminent psychopharmacologists observe that in fact there is simply no good evidence for it. As LaCasse and Leo (2005, p. 1212) say: 'Contemporary neuroscience research has failed to confirm any serotonergic lesion in any mental disorder, and has in fact provided significant counterevidence to the explanation of a simple neurotransmitter deficiency'. They note that not only does neuroscience provide no evidence for an 'imbalance' of monoamines such as serotonin or norepinephrine, it does not even supply any evidence to say what an ideal *balance* of these neurotransmitters might be.

A further weakness of these accounts is that they typically fail to specify why some individuals rather than others might have these deficiencies or imbalances in their neurotransmitter levels. The body-brain is a massively open 'system of systems', and levels of neurotransmitters are known to fluctuate according to external influences (see Chapter 4). However, studies of the influence of serotonin and norepinephrine have rarely tried to identify the ways in which external (social and material) influences might be related to the availability of these neurotransmitters. This is in part because it would be unethical to conduct controlled studies of this kind upon humans, although it is sometimes seen as permissible to do so with animals.

Raleigh, McGuire, Brammer and Yuwiler (1984) conducted a series of studies with vervet monkeys, who spontaneously form social hierarchies with a leader or 'boss monkey' at the top and others arranged below. The researchers took advantage of this to conduct experiments measuring levels of blood serotonin whilst manipulating the monkeys' social hierarchy. They found that the boss monkey had the highest serotonin level, and that as they moved down the social hierarchy the serotonin levels of the other monkeys became progressively lower. They then isolated the boss monkey and observed what happened. After isolation, the boss monkey's serotonin levels plummeted. Amongst the monkeys remaining in the colony, a new boss monkey soon emerged, and this monkey was found to have the highest serotonin levels. Importantly, however, the new boss monkey's serotonin levels were not higher *before* it became boss monkey: they were only raised *after* it became the boss monkey. In other words, the change in serotonin levels was caused by the change in social status, not the other way around. However, apart from the difficulty of making generalizations to humans from other species, this study can be questioned for relying upon blood serotonin levels, because these bear an uncertain relationship to levels of serotonin in the brain. The study nevertheless suggests that, if serotonin is implicated in clinical sadness, it is primarily as a means of mediating social and material influence.

A similar kind of explanation was put forward by Dinan (1994), who proposed that serotonin deficiencies in humans might be caused by excessive levels of cortisol, produced as a consequence of living in stressful environments or being frequently subjected to adverse life events. Continuous activation of stress responses may increase cortisol, which may in turn reduce serotonin by disrupting the hypothalamic–pituitary–adrenal axis. If this could be shown to be the case, then a very specific biological pathway by which social and material influence impacts directly upon body-brain systems to enable experiences of sadness would have been identified. However, a large-scale community study assessing levels of salivary cortisol amongst patients in general practice who were receiving antidepressant treatment failed to find any evidence at all for increased cortisol levels. In contradiction to the monoamine hypothesis, the research also found that serotonin levels amongst women in the study given a diagnosis of depression were elevated, not lowered (Strickland et al., 2002).

An alternative biological account of sadness proposes a role for differential patterns of hemispheric activation. Brain-imaging studies of people given a diagnosis of depression show that, on average, their right frontal lobes are more active than their left. By contrast, controls without a diagnosis tend to show the opposite, with more activation in the left frontal lobes than the right. The right side of the brain is sometimes thought to be more important for processing emotion than the left, which is often more closely involved in processing language (Davidson & Henriques, 2000). The frontal lobes are especially active in planning and reasoning and play an important role in behavioural inhibition. However, the precise ways in which such a pattern of activation might be associated with the moods, thoughts and actions that lead to a diagnosis of depression remain unknown. Moreover, just as with neurotransmitters, evidence from brain-imaging studies makes it abundantly clear that brain activation states are always influenced by the contexts experienced by the person whose brain it is (Davidson, Jackson & Kalin, 2000).

Healy (1987) sets out a biological explanation for experiences of clinical sadness that implicates **Circadian rhythms**: the biorhythms or 'body clocks' that govern sleeping, wakefulness and levels of energy and activity. These rhythms are associated with a variety of biological and psychological effects including variation in body temperature and cognitive performance and differences in appetite. Circadian rhythms are usually 'set' by environmental cues known as 'zeitgebers' (literally 'time givers') that help them to produce a pattern of activity that might be appropriate for the latitude and time of year (Roenneberg et al., 2007). This usually happens automatically and gradually, so that we tend to be blind to the important role played by these environmental signals and to imagine that our bodies follow a simple 'natural' pattern of activity. However, the unpleasant experience of jet lag – where we are abruptly thrown out of synchronization with the daily rhythms of our environment – shows quite dramatically how much we are actually dependent upon these environmental zeitgebers.

Healey notes that when life circumstances become difficult, people often experience disruptions to their everyday routines. Over a period of time, persistent disruptions to daily routines may cause our Circadian rhythms to become de-synchronized with our environments. When this happens we experience difficulty in sleeping and waking, changes in appetite, and a range of subtle cognitive impairments. These effects then make it even more difficult for us to cope with whatever difficulties we are trying to resolve, so may precipitate further stress and consequent disruption to daily routines. Subtle cognitive impairments, appetite changes and disruption of sleeping and waking are very often prominent features of clinical experiences of sadness. Healey therefore suggests that clinical sadness might be the consequence of chronic circadian dysrhythmia, which may be produced by difficult life events and circumstances.

Worry

Biological explanations for clinical experiences of worry have some interesting parallels with those for sadness. Within the brain, serotonin and norepinephrine are sometimes implicated, as is **gamma-aminobutyric acid** or **GABA**, an inhibitory neurotransmitter that dampens down the rate of neural firing. As with sadness, researchers identified a possible role for these neurotransmitters in experiences of worry by working backwards from the observed effects of drugs that seemed to have a beneficial effect. There are also suggestions that particular brain structures are involved in the generation of clinical worry. Studies using classical conditioning have shown that fear and anxiety responses are enabled by systems that include the amygdala. The amygdala is an important part of a relatively distinct subcortical circuit of structures with projections to the visual and frontal cortices, often known as the limbic system (Le Doux, 1999; Panksepp, 1998).

In very general terms, then, it could be proposed that experiences of worry may be associated with high levels of activity in the limbic system. One of the functions of this system seems to be that it constantly scans the environment for threats, so increased activity here might reasonably be thought to be associated with a greater propensity to perceive imminent threats. The limbic system is linked, via the hypothalamus, to the sympathetic nervous system, and through this linkage has the ability to quickly initiate states of physiological arousal when possible threats are encountered. Levels of activity within the limbic system are known to be capable of being influenced by both serotonin and norepinephrine. Greater availability of serotonin is associated with reduced limbic system activity, whilst increased limbic activation is associated with increased levels of norepinephrine. Conversely, higher levels of GABA are associated with reduced activity and with lower levels of worry.

It is sometimes suggested that the limbic system can enter into a continuously hyperactive state called **limbic kindling**. Although this phenomenon is historically more closely associated with epileptic seizures, it is sometimes also linked to diagnoses such as PTSD. However, in these circumstances it remains unclear to what extent this hyperactivation simply enables the ongoingpsychological trauma the person is experiencing, and to what extent the kindling is spontaneous or internally driven, as opposed to being continuously activated by external influences.

In addition to these general mechanisms, more specific biological explanations are sometimes proposed to enable particular experiences of worry. With respect to panic attacks, it has been suggested that a biological over-sensitivity to atmospheric carbon dioxide may lead to **suffocation alarm**, causing increased breathing and hyperventilation (Klein, 1993). Alternatively, a specific role has been proposed for the neurotransmitter norepinephrine, with suggestions that elevated levels of this neurotransmitter may trigger panic attacks. However, another biological explanation points to the similarity between panic attacks and conditioned fear responses, and suggests that combinations of influence and early life events may predispose some people to develop especially active 'fear networks' centred upon the amygdala and its projections to the hypothalamus and brain stem (Gorman, Kent, Sullivan & Coplan, 2000).

For some people, worry is managed by adopting rituals and routines, such as overly frequent checking of tasks or needless repetition of activities such as hand or body washing. Because people with brain damage sometimes subsequently adopt such repetitive or ritualistic ways of behaving, it has been proposed that there is a specific neural substrate to these experiences of worry. Based upon the pattern of injuries observed and also upon what is known about neuroanatomy, it has been suggested that impairments in the frontal lobes and basal ganglia might prevent persons from inhibiting their own behaviour patterns, resulting in repeated checking (Jenike, 1986). However, the great majority of people who develop these rituals have no history or evidence of brain injury or trauma, so this explanation cannot account for more than a few experiences of this kind.

Specific brain mechanisms are also thought to enable the flashbacks and intrusive thoughts that sometimes follow traumatic events. Brewin (2001) discusses the evidence that extremely high levels of emotion improve memory for central details but impair memory for peripheral details. He proposes a **dual representation theory** in which one memory system stores consciously processed verbal or narrative aspects of a traumatic event, whilst a separate system stores images, sounds and feeling states or bodily reactions: in essence, all of the sensory, non-verbal aspects. Flashbacks, then, consist of information held in this sensory register. There is good neuroscientific evidence to support the existence of these separate memory systems, and the theory accounts for the fact that flashbacks involve much more than simply 'seeing' the event over again. During a flashback, vivid images of a traumatic event are accompanied by powerful physical reactions: people may almost feel as though they have been punched in the stomach at the same time as they 'see' the trauma again, and it is in large part this embodied dimension that makes flashbacks so profoundly unpleasant. Brewin's theory suggests that flashbacks arise when sensory memories co-exist with incomplete narratives, a proposal which has similarities with recent suggestions regarding the workings of repression (Ellis & Cromby, 2009). However, it is important to realize that Brewin describes a general process of interaction between memory systems common to our species: consequently, his account requires an understanding of neural systems as open and dynamic if the variations in people's responses to trauma are to be understood.

Lifelines, plasticity and specificity

Experiences of sadness and worry frequently exhibit significant variation within individual lifelines, so it seems that degrees of both plasticity and specificity are usually present. You should recall that both plasticity and specificity are produced jointly by social and material circumstances acting upon elements of our biology, including upon our genes (Chapter 4). As in the research into causal processes, though, it is difficult to provide a definite account of plasticity and specificity in sadness and worry. This is because in some areas relevant research has not been done; and because the research is fragmented across psychiatric diagnostic categories, or framed by assumptions that make its interpretation difficult.

Specificity

Numerous studies have found evidence for genetic influence upon people who experience clinical levels of sadness and worry. Estimates of heritability in samples of people who have been given the various anxiety disorder diagnoses range from 30–45% (Smoller, Gardner-Schuster & Misiaszek, 2008); estimates of heritability amongst people who have been given diagnoses of depression vary from 22% (McGue & Christensen, 2003) through 48% to 75% (McGuffin, Katz, Watkins & Rutherford, 1996). The great majority of these studies and meta-analyses depend upon behavioural genetic approaches and are subject to the various confounds and problems of overestimation common to this kind of research (see Chapter 4, and Box 4.2: The heritability index). The research may show a similar pattern to that identified by Joseph (2003) in relation to diagnoses of schizophrenia, with more recent, better-designed and conducted research typically producing lower heritability estimates.

There is also evidence for heritability from studies of molecular genetics, which suggest moderate genetic effects. These studies identify a wide range of candidate gene mechanisms: one recent review identifies more than 15 possible genes that may increase the risk of being given a diagnosis of either major or bipolar depression (Kato, 2007); another review identified 13 possible genes associated with one or more of the anxiety disorder diagnoses (Smoller et al., 2008). This work suggests that any genetic influences upon sadness and worry are not reducible to the effects of single genes, but may arise as a consequence of particular gene combinations.

On balance, this evidence seems to suggest that there is some variable genetic influence in relation to clinical experiences of sadness and worry, and that genetic influence is moderate, largely non-specific, not associated with single genes, and consistently dependent upon environmental interactions. Interpretation of these studies is frequently difficult, however, because of the assumption buried within many of them that specificity is produced by genes acting alone. As we have seen, however, even biological changes that occur very early in life are also produced by the effects of environments. Environmental influences continuously modify whether, how and when genes are expressed, so that studies that attempt to isolate genetic influence tend to be simplistic. Schore's (2001) account of the ways in which early attachment failures may be associated with the development of brain systems to produce later vulnerabilities to anxiety incorporates genetic components. However, he also compiles evidence to suggest that early experiences characterized by inconsistent extremes of emotion from primary caregivers may impact upon the developing brain to produce excessive pruning of downward, inhibitory projections from the frontal areas to the amygdala and limbic system, especially in the right hemisphere. Lacking rich networks of these inhibitory connections, such people may be permanently more vulnerable to extremes of worry and sadness than others and this may be an important form of early specificity (see Chapter 4).

Pynoos, Steinberg and Piacentini (1999) review some of the literature linking early childhood trauma to later vulnerabilities to distress, focusing particularly on experiences of worry. They provide a schematic account of how early vulnerabilities may be produced that clearly demonstrates something of the great complexity and contingency involved. Traumatic events vary in their content, complexity, objective and subjective features; their immediate impact is mediated by any coping strategies, but may be prolonged if they involve some permanent loss (e.g. of a parent due to bereavement). However, the impact of events will also be mediated by 'proximal secondary stresses' such as possible changes in family living circumstances, changes in family or community resources or changes in social support. A further set of mediating influences are associated with 'proximal trauma reminders': wholly contingent aspects of people's environments and situations that may inadvertently re-evoke aspects of the traumatic event. The highly variable effects of the great complexity associated with the initial trauma are subsequently subject to further mediation from 'child-intrinsic' factors (such as temperament, disability, acquired developmental competencies or pre-existing difficulties) and 'ecological' factors such as physical illnesses or disabilities of parents and carers, parents' and carers' own experiential history of loss and trauma, and numerous influences related to schools, peers and the wider social environment. Finally, all of this variation is yet further moderated by age-specific effects, since children's abilities to monitor and regulate their own emotions and to engage in play and other activities that may assist in coping become progressively greater as they mature.

Pynoos et al. argue that this massive complexity means that much more research is needed before distinct patterns of influence between early experience and later distress can be discerned, but that there are nevertheless already some studies which begin to make these connections. For example, they cite Bouwer and Stein's (1997) finding that a significant proportion of adults who experienced repeated panic attacks had a history of traumatic suffocation experiences. Pynoos et al. briefly review evidence suggesting that any specific impact of early trauma with respect to worry might occur through alterations to tonic autonomic and **catecholaminic** activity (catecholamines are a subset of the monoamine neurotransmitters), alterations to the functioning of the hypothalamic–pituitary–adrenal (HPA) axis, reduced cortisol responses and changes in left hippocampal volume. A similar review focusing on sadness also identified the possibility of changes to the HPA axis, in conjunction with the **locus coeruleus-norepinephrine (LC-NE) system** (Meyer, Chrousos & Gold, 2001). The LC-NE system begins in the pons and radiates upward, and has close connections with the HPA axis and the sympathetic nervous system.

Plasticity

So whichever brain and body mechanisms are involved, there is plentiful evidence that early trauma can be associated with later experiences of sadness and worry: as we saw in the section on 'causal processes', above, experiences of bereavement, abuse, parental neglect and difficult life events are all common amongst people receiving treatment. It is nevertheless vital to emphasize that not everyone who experiences early trauma goes on to experience clinical sadness or worry. In other words, despite the strong evidence for some degree of early specificity, there are also degrees of plasticity and the long-term effects of trauma can often be minimized. Nevertheless, those who experience such events will never be able to 'unlive' them: they will always be people whose lives have been transformed, in some way or other, by the events they have experienced. Moreover, there are many people like Jane and Sam, whose lives have not been marked by any particular or dramatic instances of trauma but who nevertheless experience periods of disabling sadness and worry during their lives.

The evidence suggests that as we move out of the early years, plasticity and specificity continue to be present. Eaton, Kessler and Wittchen (1994) review numerous surveys of the prevalence of clinical experiences of panic, and find lifetime prevalence rates – across countries, and in different studies – ranging from one person per thousand to 35 per thousand, with similarly wide variation for phobias (five per thousand to 142 per thousand) and for general experiences of worry (25 per thousand to 107 per thousand). With respect to lifespan variation, Eaton et al. find a relatively flat incidence of experiences of phobia, but a mid-life peak for both men and women for experiences of panic (with the incidence being much greater amongst women). With respect to broader, non-specific experiences of worry, however, Lieb, Becker and Altamura (2005) find that prevalence rises steadily with age so that worry is most pronounced amongst older adults, particularly women. With respect to sadness, numerous studies provide evidence to suggest that ageing is a protective factor and that the incidence of new clinical referrals declines with increasing age (Form, 2000; Henderson et al., 1998), although others still caution that profound sadness is 'perhaps the most frequent cause of emotional suffering in later life' (Blazer, 2009, p. 118).

Evidence from within individual lifelines also demonstrates plasticity. Having once been distressed enough to received treatment makes people more likely to experience severe distress in the future. Although 54% of people receiving treatment for clinical sadness have recovered within six months and 88% have recovered within five years (Keller, Lavori, Mueller & Endicott, 1992), some studies show that 85% of people will experience at least one further episode of clinical sadness within 15 years of their first (Mueller et al., 1999). However, these studies are typically based upon people receiving treatment from specialist clinics, who are already those

with the most severe problems, and the likelihood of distress recurring is probably lower for people whose problems are less severe. A study of American female twins, designed primarily to explore genetic effects, found that although having experienced a previous episode of clinical sadness is a risk factor for subsequent episodes, recurrence is more strongly predicted by stressful life events (Kendler, McGonagle, Swartz, Blazer & Nelson, 1993). Similarly, a study with a random sample of 1710 adolescent students in America conducted over a one-year period found that over 80% of those who experienced an episode of clinical sadness did not relapse (Lewinsohn, Hops, Roberts, Seeley & Andrews, 1993).

With respect to worry, a five year follow-up study of 210 UK patients seen by psychiatric outpatient clinics found that 60% had a favourable outcome (Seivewright, Tyrer & Johnson, 1998). A US study conducting 12-year follow-ups of nearly 500 people given one or more of the diagnoses associated with worry (generalized anxiety disorder, social phobia and agoraphobia) produced a less favourable picture, presumably because the multiple diagnoses were illustrative of a greater extent and variety of difficulties, but still demonstrated recovery in nearly half of those given diagnoses (Bruce et al., 2005). However, another study in the US which tracked 167 people given a diagnosis of generalized anxiety disorder for five years found that only 38% recovered (Yonkers, Dyck, Warshaw & Keller, 2000). In this research, poorer outcomes were associated with lower quality of life (indexed by variables such as low SES, health problems and marital status), poor quality family relationships, and with pre-existing complex difficulties (indexed by the presence of other psychiatric diagnoses).

Interventions

Ideally, interventions for sadness and worry will be supported by a good evidence base for their efficacy. In the UK, the efficacy of treatments for forms of sadness and worry is currently assessed by NICE, the National Institute for Clinical Excellence. The evidence base used by NICE in determining its recommendations largely consists of studies based upon psychiatric categories. Consequently, NICE itself frequently makes recommendations based upon these categories, whilst sometimes also acknowledging the many limitations they impose. Even though research into treatments for sadness and worry often considers them largely separately, in practice there is considerable overlap between the approaches that may prove beneficial for both.

Pharmaceutical interventions

In the Western world today, probably the most common pharmaceutical treatment for both sadness and worry is with SSRIs. Although these drugs were originally marketed as 'antidepressants' and prescribed primarily for people given a diagnosis of depression, SSRIs are now also commonly prescribed for people given diagnoses of panic disorder and generalized anxiety disorder. The best known of these drugs go under the brand names Prozac and Seroxat, although there are now many drugs of this kind available. All of them work in a similar fashion, by slowing down reabsorption of the neurotransmitter serotonin. Serotonin is released into the synaptic cleft when a neuron discharges, but is usually quickly reabsorbed. SSRIs block the mechanism whereby serotonin is reabsorbed, meaning that levels in the brain rise gradually. Raised levels of serotonin can be associated with feelings of contentment and satisfaction, and these feelings might help to counter the misery and numbness of clinical sadness and the tension and agitation of clinical worry (although they are unlikely to help everybody – see Box 9.5). SSRIs were originally marketed as being largely free of the undesirable effects often associated with other drugs used to treat sadness and worry. It is true that they are less dangerous in overdose than other drugs and that they do not interact so dangerously with other substances; nevertheless, their undesirable effects still include nausea, insomnia, weight changes, decreased libido, digestive disturbances and headaches. There is also evidence, some of which seems to have been initially suppressed by the manufacturers, that both Prozac and Seroxat can be associated with agitation and, perhaps related to this, it also appears that they may carry a small but significant increased risk of suicide.

Tricyclic antidepressants – TCAs – are also widely used. Despite their name, which implies some specificity to sadness, TCAs are also prescribed for people given diagnoses of panic disorder, PTSD and generalized anxiety disorder, as well as for people given diagnoses of depression. Like SSRIs, TCAs inhibit the reabsorption of serotonin; however, they also have the same effect for norepinephrine and, to a lesser extent, dopamine. Like serotonin, increases in both norepinephrine and dopamine can be associated with positive feelings. These feelings may help to counteract misery and so can be helpful for people experiencing sadness and worry. However, TCAs also raise the levels of other neurotransmitters, particularly acetylcholine, so have many other effects too. These can include such unpleasant effects as blurred vision, constipation, increased appetite, weight gain and impaired sexual functioning.

The third class of drugs sometimes used to treat both sadness and worry are the monoamine oxidase inhibitors or **MAOIs**. Monoamine oxidase acts as an enzyme in the brain that assists in the breakdown of the neurotransmitters serotonin, norepinephrine and dopamine (an enzyme is a chemical that makes the reaction of two more other chemicals proceed more efficiently). By lowering the levels of monoamine oxidase, MAOIs raise the levels of serotonin, norepinephrine and dopamine present at the synapses. Accordingly, like SSRIs and TCAs, MAOIs can produce positive feelings that may be beneficial for people experiencing clinical sadness or clinical worry. However, MAOIs have numerous significant harmful effects as well as their desired ones. They also raise brain levels of **tyramine** (a naturally-occurring monoamine), and high levels of tyramine cause sudden increases in blood pressure, which can lead to strokes. Because tyramine is also released in the brain when we consume many common foodstuffs (including cheese, wine, chocolate and pickles) the use of

---

BOX 9.5
Do antidepressants work?

It is widely assumed that so-called antidepressants are highly effective remedies for clinical sadness, but is this true?

Kirsch, Moore, Scoboria and Nicholls (2002) studied the efficacy of numerous antidepressants, including compounds submitted for approval by the American Food and Drug Authority (FDA). Their study, which was unusual in that it included data from unpublished studies, showed that 18% of patients showed more improvement on active drug treatment than on placebo. Whilst an 18% gap might be seen as slightly disappointing, it does represent a significant difference between controls and people receiving treatment.

However, this 18% difference was produced by an average increase of only 1.7 points on the Hamilton Rating Scale for Depression (a widely used instrument). In clinical terms this is far too small to allow conclusions to be drawn; one commentator upon the study described it as 'vanishingly small' (Brown, 2002). The study's authors concluded that 'the pharmacological effects of antidepressants are clinically negligible' (Kirsch et al., 2002, p. 1).

Kirsch et al.'s study included modern SSRI drugs that work on the serotonin system. However, numerous large-scale trials of earlier drugs that work on other neurotransmitter systems similarly failed to indicate clear advantages of drug treatments.

A large, well funded and designed study by the UK Medical Research Council compared the relative efficacy of imipramine, phenelzine, ECT and placebo (MRC, 1965). Whilst the study seemed to show that ECT had some positive effects, the differences between the antidepressant drugs and the placebo were negligible.

In America, a similarly well funded study compared imipramine, chlorpromazine and placebo (Raskin, Schulterbrandt, Reatig, Chase & McKeon, 1970) in 714 people. Despite excluding 159 black people from the analysis on the grounds that their response to imipramine was 'poorer', the authors were only able to conclude that 'although imipramine did have beneficial effects, these effects were generally small'.

There are also methodological problems associated with many studies, including the failure to use active placebos, frequent unblinding of research participants (so that researchers are able to guess whether they were in placebo or treatment groups), and failures to distinguish between the effects of withdrawal from antidepressants and the resurgence of clinical distress.

It is sometimes argued that inconclusive results can be explained by features of the populations studied, because the drugs are most effective for severe distress but most studies include people with mild and moderate distress. However, there is little or no evidence that these drugs are more effective for people with severe problems; what evidence there is mostly suggests they work best for people with moderate problems. Moncrieff (2008) argues this is not surprising, since these are people who are quite motivated to seek help, but not so overwhelmed by distress that nothing would seem to help.

This evidence does NOT mean that people taking antidepressant drugs should suddenly discontinue them, especially if they seem to be beneficial. However, it does raise doubts about the strong claims of drug companies, and challenges the belief that clinical sadness is simply caused by neurotransmitter imbalances.

MAOIs is always subject to strict dietary restrictions. For these reasons, MAOIs are not usually offered unless other pharmaceutical treatments fail. They are most commonly prescribed for people given diagnoses of depression, bipolar disorder/ manic depression and panic disorder.

Some drugs, called **benzodiazepines**, increase the levels of gamma-amino butyric acid or GABA. The best known of these drugs is diazepam (brand name 'Valium') but there are numerous other drugs with similar effects, including many that break down more quickly. They are very fast acting, and work by raising levels of GABA in the brain. Because GABA is an inhibitory neurotransmitter which slows down levels of neural activity and firing, increased levels have a calming effect. This effect may be beneficial for people who are severely worried, and benzodiazepines are often prescribed for people given diagnoses of generalized anxiety or panic disorder. However, benzodiazepines quickly create marked physical dependency and are associated with an unpleasant withdrawal syndrome. For this reason, it is less common these days for people to be given them for long-term treatment: previously, before the withdrawal syndrome was widely recognized, Valium was so frequently and widely used that it went by the nickname 'mother's little helper'! However, there is still concern about the substantial numbers of people who do receive long-term prescriptions for benzodiazepines, and in recent years some evidence that people have become dependent after buying benzodiazepines for themselves from internet pharmacists.

Even the newest of these classes of drugs, the SSRIs, have been in use for some time now. After 20 years, drugs are considered to be 'off licence': this means that other manufacturers are free to make cheaper, generic versions. So if you were to be prescribed an SSRI in the UK today, for example, you would probably receive cheap, generic fluoxetine – the name of the active chemical compound involved – rather than the more expensive, branded 'Prozac'. Exactly the same thing happens with other medications such as over-the-counter painkillers, where for example you can choose between the branded and expensive 'Nurofen' or the generic and cheap ibuprofen: whichever one you buy, however, the psychoactive ingredient is exactly the same. Like other businesses, pharmaceutical companies are profit-driven and need to generate continuous income for their shareholders. They can therefore face difficulties when popular drugs go off licence because their profits can be hit hard.

One effect of this is that companies continually strive to replace older, off-licence drugs with new compounds, and this has been happening with drugs to treat sadness and worry. The pharmaceutical companies are now producing a newer class of compounds that are being generically marketed as **atypical antidepressants**. These newer drugs include such brands as Wellbutrin, Cymbalta and Effexor. Like TCAs and MAOIs, these new compounds increase levels of norepinephrine and dopamine, as well as raising serotonin. Their possible benefits are therefore similar to those of TCAs and MAOIs, but their undesirable effects seem to be less dangerous and unpleasant. These effects nevertheless still include such responses as sexual dysfunction, raised cholesterol and raised blood pressure, and – in the case of Wellbutrin – a slight risk of heart palpitations and seizures. Like the older 'antidepressants' the possible beneficial effects of these new 'atypicals' are not specific to sadness, so they are also being prescribed for people experiencing clinical worry.

Physical interventions

ECT

Electro-convulsive therapy or ECT involves passing electrical currents through the brain. It is still used with people experiencing profound clinical sadness, although less frequently than it was during the last century. It is sometimes described by psychiatrists as a 'treatment of last resort', for example when it is considered that a person is at immediate risk of committing suicide and has not responded to other treatments.

ECT was first used clinically in the 1930s, as a way of inducing seizures. At that time, some people believed that epilepsy and schizophrenia were mutually exclusive, which might mean that schizophrenia could be cured by inducing a controlled episode of epilepsy. Seizures were induced by malarial fever and by injecting drugs such as insulin or metrazol, but all of these methods were unreliable and dangerous. An Italian psychiatrist visiting a slaughterhouse noticed that pigs killed by applying electrical currents to their heads experienced what looked like an epileptic seizure before they died, and this led to the method being used with humans (Read, 2004b). Psychiatrists subsequently found that ECT might also have some beneficial effect for people experiencing profound sadness.

In ECT, the person is first given both a muscle relaxing drug and an anaesthetic. Then, whilst the person is unconscious, a current of between 70 and 130 volts is applied to the brain using electrodes placed at the temples. This induces an immediate seizure, although the person remains largely still throughout because they have been immobilized by the muscle relaxant. Typically, one course of treatment will involve this procedure being repeated up to three times in a week, usually for a period of up to four weeks.

ECT induces **retrograde amnesia** (i.e. it impairs recall of the past), particularly for recent events, and also has effects on the ability to form new memories in the period immediately following treatment. In some cases it also seems to cause longer-term, possibly permanent, memory impairment. Its other effects include confusion, nausea, muscle aches, headaches and – less often – heart irregularities and blood pressure changes.

ECT is controversial for a number of reasons. First, there is a lack of good-quality research into its benefits, and concern that its effects have been over-stated. A large-scale study by Kendell (1981) concluded that its benefits were only modest and restricted to the short term (less than four weeks.) But there is a lack of good-quality evidence and, even today, most studies of ECT fail to include adequate – or often even any – control group (Read, 2004b).

Second, psychiatrists freely admit that they have no idea why ECT might produce benefits. They speculate that it releases neurotransmitters which then have beneficial effects, but there is no evidence for this. Nor is there any reason to suppose that any transmitters that are released are likely to be those that are of specific benefit. What is certain, though, is that ECT impairs memory and induces a temporary period of flattened emotion and cognitive confusion. It is possible that, for some people in the depths of profound sadness, the retrograde amnesia and emotional blunting that ECT causes might serve to temporarily isolate them from the burden of their experience, whilst the associated cognitive impairment may prevent them from worrying about their difficulties by making all thought very difficult. For profoundly distressed, deeply miserable people, it is conceivable that blocking out memories of the recent past and temporarily preventing them from feeling deep emotions might bring some short-term relief. However, in every case this would need to be weighed against the fact that ECT is a form of brain trauma which may cause permanent or irreversible damage (Breggin, 1997).

Third, there is good evidence of a marked risk of death following ECT. Read (2004b) reviews the literature on this, showing that whilst the American Psychiatric Association describe the risk as being in the region of one per 10,000 patients, many studies have produced death rates far higher than this. The highest death rate in any of these studies is one per 100 patients, but rates of one per 200 patients are common.

Fourth, ECT remains controversial because both the treatment and its effects are widely seen as frightening. Many people still suspect that, at least in the past, ECT was used primarily to control and stupefy troublesome or difficult patients, rather than for any genuine therapeutic reason.

Psychosurgery

Psychosurgery is sometimes still used with people experiencing sadness and worry. People given a diagnosis of depression who do not respond to other forms of treatment may be given surgery to sever connections to the prefrontal cortex. The many connections to the prefrontal cortex collate information about the body and feelings; severing some of these connections is therefore likely to flatten emotions and have an effect on mood (Malhi & Bartlett, 2000). Surgical treatments are also sometimes used to treat people with obsessive behaviours, and with people given diagnoses of depression, manic depression or bipolar disorder. An operation called a **sterotactic subcaudate tractotomy** is often used (Poynton, Bridges & Bartlett, 1988): this involves using micro-surgical techniques to sever connections between areas including the basal ganglia, the caudate nucleus and the amygdala. Psychosurgical treatments are irreversible, frequently have many effects other than those that are desired, and always carry the surgical risks associated with any form of brain surgery. For these reasons there is considerable concern about their ethical status, and they should only be used after all other possible treatment options can be shown to have comprehensively failed (Marino & Cosgrove, 1997).

Psychological interventions

Psychological interventions for sadness and worry are usually categorized according to the kind of therapy upon which they are based. However, as with interventions for other forms of distress, you should always remember that other 'non-specific factors' – such as the quality of the relationship between therapist and client – are always important determinants of outcomes.

Cognitive and cognitive–behavioural

The most common kind of psychological treatment for clinical sadness and worry is individual psychotherapy. In the UK, currently this will mostly be cognitive–behavioural therapy or CBT. NICE guidelines recommend CBT as the preferred psychological treatment with the best evidence of long-term efficacy for people given diagnoses of generalized anxiety disorder and panic disorder (National Institute for Health and Clinical Excellence, 2007b). NICE recommends that adults judged to be experiencing mild depression are treated with computerized CBT, and those judged to be experiencing moderate or severe depression are treated with medication, preferably SSRIs, and either CBT or interpersonal therapy (National Institute for Health and Clinical Excellence, 2009b). In a separate guideline dealing with children and adolescents, NICE do not recommend that medication is used but instead favour a range of psychological therapies, most often CBT but also guided self-help, interpersonal therapy and family therapy (National Institute for Health and Clinical Excellence, 2005). A general discussion of individual therapies such as CBT appears in Chapter 8; here, we describe its application specifically to sadness and worry by identifying some of the elements of CBT typically used to tackle specific kinds of difficulty, and reviewing some of the research evidence for its efficacy.

CBT to tackle clinical sadness is usually informed by the psychological theories put forward by Beck (1967) and by Abrahamson et al. (1978); see the section on 'psychological processes', above. In practice, this means that therapy aims first to identify unhelpful patterns of thinking and information-processing: negative beliefs, negative automatic thoughts, and internal, global and stable pessimistic attributions. So as to both provide information about these cognitive processes, and also to help clients generate insight into them, procedures such as diaries and 'thought-recording forms' are frequently used. By discussing the information from these monitoring exercises with clients, therapists can help them to identify situations, people and places with which they are most likely to experience difficulties, and to identify the particular unhelpful beliefs, thoughts or attributions that accompanied these difficulties. Having done so, therapists aim to help clients to challenge and change these ways of thinking, by helping them to realize for themselves that their beliefs are not always correct, their automatic thoughts are sometimes mistaken or irrelevant, and their pessimistic attributions sometimes overly self-critical or doom-laden. NICE reviewed 16 trials comparing the efficacy of CBT for clinical sadness to medication such as SSRIs, finding that short-term effects (within one month) are broadly comparable, but that at one-year follow up, people treated with CBT were less likely to relapse than people treated with medication (National Institute for Health and Clinical Excellence, 2009a). NICE also cites four studies showing that CBT has a large effect compared to waiting-list control groups, and reviews a series of studies showing that its effects are roughly comparable to those of other psychological therapies.

People who have experienced one bout of clinical sadness are more likely than the general population to experience another (Mueller et al., 1999), and also more likely to be given other related diagnoses, including those associated with worry and psychosis (Burton, 2006; Keller et al., 1992). This will often be because the social and material circumstances that caused the original problem have either not changed, or have recurred in the same or a similar form. However, sometimes it may be because recovered people – understandably enough – are prone to thinking that new experiences of low mood are the beginning of another episode of clinical sadness, and consequently can more easily fall back into the kinds of negative thinking patterns that therapy aims to transform. In recent years, **mindfulness-based cognitive therapy – MBCT** – has been developed to address this problem. In MBCT, monitoring and other techniques are used to encourage clients to develop different relationships with their negative feelings: to treat them as passing events rather than the beginning of a trend, to minimize rather than maximize their significance and import, to recognize that their feelings are not necessarily an accurate representation of their actual situation, and so on. A study by Ma and Teasdale (2004) showed that MBCT can reduced the likelihood of a further incidence of clinical sadness by between 42% and 62% (depending on the severity of the client's problems).

Self-monitoring procedures are also employed with clients receiving CBT for clinical worry, but here they are used to identify and then challenge patterns of catastrophic thinking and fixed, irrational beliefs and behaviours. Clients are also frequently given relaxation training, using breathing techniques and progressive muscle relaxation to teach them how to manage and reduce physical tension in their bodies. Once they have gained some proficiency at using these techniques, clients may be encouraged to rehearse using them in situations where they typically find that their worrying causes problems. These initial attempts to overcome difficulties can often generate further information about the ways in which worrying functions for the client, leading to the identification of further strategies to either minimize the worrying or reduce its impact. Ladoceur, Dugas and Freeston (2000) found that, compared to a waiting-list control group, people given a diagnosis of generalized anxiety disorder who received CBT had both clinically and statistically significant reductions in erroneous beliefs, problem orientation and cognitive avoidance, and that 77% of the CBT group no longer met the criteria for a diagnosis.

Clients who receive CBT for panic attacks are similarly asked to undergo self-monitoring to identify possible exaggerated threat perceptions and tendencies to make catastrophic interpretations of bodily feedback. They will also commonly be taught breathing techniques and receive educational input about physiological responses relevant to panic attacks. Once they have learned the breathing techniques and begun to accept that many of the bodily sensations that terrify them are actually harmless, they may be asked to undergo graded exposure to some of these sensations: for example, by ingesting a dose of caffeine. Then, in the safety of the clinic and with a supportive therapist nearby, they can practice using their breathing and reassuring themselves with new information, and so gradually learn to control their panic. A meta-analysis by Oei, Llamas and Devilly (1999) assessed 35 studies of the use of cognitive therapy with people experiencing panic attacks, finding that the majority showed clinically significant improvements (symptom reductions of more than two standard deviations toward the norm of the non-diagnosed population) in the short term, although longer-term benefits were less clear.

Although CBT is recommended by the relevant NICE guidelines, those guidelines also acknowledge that the evidence base for its efficacy is still developing. In particular, there is a shortage of good, long-term follow-up studies, and some of those that have been conducted raise serious questions as to whether CBT is actually superior to any other form of psychological intervention (see Box 9.6).

Behavioural

When clients have very specific worries or phobias, behavioural techniques have traditionally been used, although in recent years cognitive techniques have also been introduced. The two primary behavioural techniques are **systematic desensitization** (progressive introduction of more frightening versions of the feared stimuli whilst the client is in a relaxed state) and **flooding** (introduction of the feared stimuli in its full form whilst the client is in a relaxed state). If we take a quite common phobia as our example – arachnophobia, or fear of spiders – therapy using systematic desensitization might begin by exploring the client's experiences of and beliefs about spiders, so requiring the client to engage in discussion about them. Once the client is able to do this relatively comfortably, the next stage might be to introduce a small picture of a spider into the room; this might be followed by a larger picture, then a video, and perhaps an immersive 'virtual reality' representation. As these steps proceed, clients are helped to relax, encouraged to breathe deeply and remain calm, and to talk about their fears so that any deeply irrational elements can be challenged. The 'ideal' final stage of this process would be to enable the client to handle a live spider without panicking. By contrast, flooding aims for the same end point but omits the slow build-up: the client is simply encouraged to relax and breathe deeply, and once a stable, calm state is reached the live spider is introduced. The client is then helped to stay calm whilst encountering the spider; by this means the phobic reaction can be extinguished all but instantaneously. A recent variation of this technique combining cognitive prompts with similar behavioural strategies for claustrophobia showed impressive and lasting improvements following single one-hour sessions of treatment (Ost, Alm, Brandberg & Breitholtz, 2001).

For some people who experience clinical sadness, social isolation is a significant contributory factor to their problems (Segrin, 2000). It has been suggested that people experiencing sadness have difficulty relating to others, and sometimes present themselves in ways that others struggle to accept (Lewinsohn & Hobermann, 1982). Social skills deficits are not unique to sadness, and it is unlikely that they are always causal, although some longitudinal studies suggest this: Segrin and Flora (2000) assessed 118 students at the start of their college careers and again at the end, finding that those with the worst social skills were more prone to sadness and loneliness later, and that they were more likely to suffer as a consequence of adverse life events. Consequently, social skills training may sometimes be offered to people experiencing sadness. This training may include help and advice to practise relating to other people in a wide variety of situations including everyday conversation, meeting new partners and job interviews. Training methods may include information, modelling, skills of listening and of assertiveness, role-play and rehearsal and 'homework' assignments in which people are asked to practise what they have learned in a specific and bounded setting.

BOX 9.6

How effective are psychological therapies for sadness and worry?

All the therapies reviewed here are supported by evidence of their effectiveness. But what does 'effectiveness' actually mean? Westen and Morrison (2001) discuss this issue at length, showing that many outcome studies of psychotherapy for people experiencing sadness and worry may be overly optimistic.

First, they describe the many different definitions of 'effectiveness', showing that differences in definition influence reported outcomes. Then they identify other issues, including that

- many studies base their calculations only upon people who complete therapy, simply ignoring those who dropped out
- many studies assess treatment shortly after it ends; very few follow people one year later or more
- many studies only assess transient states rather than enduring difficulties
- the efficacy of many therapies has simply not been tested

Next, they present a series of meta-analyses of high-quality, randomized controlled trials of therapies for people given diagnoses of depression, generalized anxiety or panic disorders. Summarizing their findings, they say

> The average empirically-supported therapy for the disorders we examined leads to substantial initial improvement in pathological states for roughly half of the patients who pass a series of rigorous inclusion and exclusion criteria. ... The limited data available suggest, however, that the majority of patients do not show sustained improvements over 1 to 2 years, particularly for generalised affect states (depression and GAD).
>
> Westen and Morrison (2001, p. 884)

Their meta-analyses identify two key issues. First, participants in studies are carefully selected and not always representative of those typically encountered in clinical practice. From one perspective, this is valid: it reduces error variation, making it more likely that subtle effects will be detected. Consequently, many studies only include participants who meet the criteria for just one diagnosis, rather than also having difficulties such

as substance or alcohol dependencies. However, this excludes large proportions of the patients who actually get referred for therapy, and selectively excludes those people with the most complex, severe and enduring problems.

Second, there is very little evidence about the extent to which the benefits of therapy are sustained for longer than six months. For people given a diagnosis of depression, the limited data showed that, for those who completed therapy, no more than 38% showed sustained improvement after two years. If this figure is recalculated to include those who dropped out, only 27% still show improvement after two years.

Nevertheless, Westen and Morrison argue that their analysis does *not* show that psychological therapy for sadness and worry doesn't work. First, outcomes were markedly better for people receiving therapy for panic attacks than they were for people receiving therapy for enduring sadness and/or worry. Second, many interventions may be better at dealing with transient states than enduring problems. And third, we perhaps need to recognize that brief psychological interventions can only succeed for people with the least complex and enduring forms of distress.

Chapter summary

In this chapter we have seen how sadness and worry often appear together in people's experiences of distress. We have sketched out some of the ways they are bound up with the cultural influences of their time and place, including the Western psychiatric diagnoses with which we frequently associate these experiences. We have also explored the literature on the many causes of sadness and worry, and considered some of the clinical interventions frequently offered to address them. In conclusion, we should emphasise again that *most* experiences of distress include significant elements of sadness and worry. We have devoted a separate chapter to these experiences because, in the West today, some people's experience of distress seems to consist largely of sadness, worry or both. Nevertheless, it is important to remember that sadness and worry are frequently also associated with *all* of the other kinds of distressing experience discussed in this book.

End of chapter questions

1   How should we understand cultural and historical variation in experiences of sadness and worry: does it make sense to distinguish between culturally specific 'illnesses' and biologically universal 'diseases'?

2   What are the benefits and costs of (a) treating sadness and worry as separate experiences of distress, and (b) treating them as aspects of the same kind of distress?

3   How might we identify the most significant causal influences upon experiences of sadness and worry?

4   What is the evidence for the effectiveness of psychological interventions for sadness and worry?

5   How good is the evidence that some interventions for sadness and worry are better than others?

6   How adequate is the 'serotonin hypothesis' as an explanation for the experiences that lead to a diagnosis of depression?

7   Why does gender difference seem to be so important in relation to experiences of sadness and worry?

8   In what ways do psychological accounts of sadness and worry tend to disembody these experiences?

9   In what ways do medical and psychiatric accounts of sadness and worry tend to individualize these experiences?

10   What are the consequences of analysing experiences of sadness and worry separately from the experiences associated with a diagnosis of schizophrenia?

Find out more

Films and books

'Amélie' (2001) tells the story of a socially anxious woman who nevertheless tries to bring happiness into the lives of everyone else she meets, whilst struggling with her own loneliness and need to be loved.

'About a Boy' (2002) has as one of its central characters Marcus, a 12-year-old boy caring for his mother, who is overcome by sadness. In a light-hearted way, the film shows how his mother's sadness impacts upon Marcus, causing him to behave in ways that would otherwise be inexplicable.

'Synecdoche, New York' (2008) tells the story of a theatre director who is struggling with the profound sadness and worry induced by a range of challenges that accompany his attempt to stage an innovative new play.

Classic novels about sadness and worry include Charlotte Perkins-Gilman's 'The Yellow Wallpaper' (1892) and Sylvia Plath's 'The Bell Jar' (1963). A recent memoir by Augusten Burroughs, 'Running with Scissors' (2002) describes the author's sadness and worry during his teenage years, difficulties associated with his sexuality and with his mother's own distress. Burrough's story was filmed in 2006 as a comedy.

The novel 'Waterline' (2011) by Ross Raisin is a moving and detailed account of a man's descent into misery following the death of his wife. Raisin's novel is rich in detail and clearly shows how people in distress, even when they appear to be acting irrationally, are actually following chains of reasoning. The novel also demonstrates how contingency plays a significant part in the ways that causal influences generate distress.

Academic reading

Healy, D. (1997). *The Antidepressant Era*. Harvard, MA: Harvard University Press.

Smail, D. J. (1984). *Illusion and Reality: the Meaning of Anxiety*. London: Dent.

Smail, D. J. (1993). *The Origins of Unhappiness*. London: Constable.

Smail, D. J. (2005). *Power, Interest and Psychology: Elements of a Social Materialist Understanding of Distress*. Ross-on-Wye: PCCS Books.

CHAPTER 10

SEXUALITY AND GENDER:
Diversity, deviance and disorder?

Alice's story

Alice is a 28-year-old black woman who has been in a committed and also monogamous heterosexual relationship for just over six years. She is emotionally satisfied with the relationship and she and her partner Andrew are able to enjoy a variety of sexual practices, including oral sex and masturbation that lead to them both achieving orgasm. Alice enjoys these aspects of her sex life very much but has difficulties with penile vaginal intercourse. Often when Andrew and Alice attempt this type of intercourse, Alice experiences a tightening of her vaginal muscles, such that the penis cannot always enter. Both Alice and Andrew feel very distressed by this, especially as Alice's 'reaction' appears involuntary. Andrew has never been openly critical of Alice but has often felt frustrated by their inability to have penis-in-vagina intercourse very often. Alice has sensed this in Andrew and feels anxious about having sex and ashamed of her inability to give Andrew what he feels or says he needs.

Both Alice and Andrew would like to share the experience of intercourse, and feel that something is missing in their relationship. They would like professional help to be able to achieve this type of sexual intercourse and be able to reach what they expect to be deeper levels of intimacy.

Sajid's story

Sajid is a 45-year-old South Asian gay man who has been in a committed and also monogamous relationship for ten years and has always been very content with the emotional and sexual side of his relationship – until recently. Sajid has been open with his family about being gay, and although some extended family members have been unhappy about his identity, on the whole his close family has been supportive. Sajid and his partner Simon have always talked openly about what they each wanted from sex and intimacy and had never experienced problems in fulfilling each other's sexual needs until recently, when Sajid became withdrawn and started experiencing difficulties in getting an erection. Sajid claims his difficulties are down to being tired and stressed at work, but Simon believes Sajid is unhappy with their physical relationship, which he thinks started when Sajid's sister had a baby. This difference of opinion about the cause of the problem has resulted in arguments and has created tension in the relationship. Rather than continuing to engage in any form of sexual intimacy, Sajid has withdrawn completely and Simon has begun to wonder if their relationship has a future.

Monogamous refers to a relationship that is exclusive, involving only two sexual or intimate partners.

Learning outcomes

By the end of this chapter you should:

1 Know what is included in the section 'Sexual and Gender Identity Disorders' in the DSM-IV-TR and the use of the terms sexual dysfunction, sexual disorder and gender identity disorder

2 Understand why there is so much debate about these categories

3 Understand the identified causal processes associated with sexual problems generally and specific diagnoses of sexual dysfunction

4 Examine some of the social contexts that define particular sexual behaviours and gender identities

5 Know what kinds of interventions are available and whether they are considered to be effective

Introduction

This first part of this chapter is about the experiences of people like Alice and Sajid. Both have what have traditionally been defined broadly as problems with having sex or what might justify a sexual dysfunction diagnosis. Yet both Alice and Sajid are also part of a relationship, and part of a wider community and culture. **Sexual dysfunction** is a diagnostic term referring to a difficulty an individual or couple may experience with any aspect of the human sexual response cycle (HSRC), including desire, arousal and orgasm. For Alice, Andrew's growing frustration with her has led to her sexual withdrawal. For Sajid, his difficulties in being open about his relationship have resulted in withdrawal and tension between him and his partner. It is clear, then, that sexual problems cannot be separated from the relationship in which they occur. Sexuality and relationships often have to be viewed together, as a dynamic and complex set of issues that are both individual and interpersonal.

We live in a sex-saturated culture where a fulfilling sex life is considered key to our happiness and mental well-being (Attwood, 2005; Tiefer, Hall and Tavris, 2002). Sexual pleasure is now seen as something we are entitled to as part of a healthy lifestyle, rather than merely fulfilling our reproductive duties, that is, having sex purely to produce children (Hawkes, 1996). Yet we are also instructed to 'work' hard at our relationships, to ensure we are satisfying our partner(s) and are constantly being reminded to maintain high levels of sexual desire, perfect bodies and attractiveness. But do these standards fit with the reality of many people's lives? As we shall see, a number of problems related to our sexuality can occur over the course of a lifetime that may affect our ability to have sex or to be intimate with another person. High rates of sexual problems in community surveys suggest that generally, there are significant barriers to achieving a fulfilling sexual life, as well as feeling good about being sexual and experiencing pleasure. And the impact of such problems is clear, with people being four to five times more likely to report unhappiness and dissatisfaction as a result of a sexual problem (Laumann, Paik & Rosen, 1999; Laumann et al., 2005).

Guiding questions

1 *Which social, psychological and biological factors come together to explain the difficulties individuals may have with sex and sexuality?*

2 *Should problems with having sex or 'unusual' sexual behaviours or gender variances be viewed as mental disorders?*

What's 'normal', sex-wise?

Given the high rates of sexual problems in the general population, clear-cut distinctions between 'normal' and 'abnormal' sexuality are difficult to find. In this chapter, we consider the issues associated with sexuality and mental health to be complex and burdened with a variety of historical, cultural, legal and political concerns (Rubin, 1984). The causes of sexual difficulties are also numerous, including interpersonal (between a couple), psychological (trauma, worry, sadness), chemical (via prescribed medication, alcohol or recreational drugs) and social factors (via family and religion) or a combination of them all.

In mental health circles, what is considered sexually 'disordered' or 'problematic' has changed over time, and is often culturally bound. Although homosexuality was removed from the DSM in 1973 because there was no evidence to suggest it was a rare or abnormal sexual practice, what continues to generate difficulties for lesbian, gay, bisexual and trans individuals is the discrimination they can experience from wider society, leading some to seek professional help (Rubin, 1984; Davies & Neal, 1996). **Homosexual** refers to an individual who is sexually attracted to a member of the same gender. What is not normal as such, and what causes distress, may not be an individual's sexual identity or sexual practices as such, but the negative responses potentially encountered by others, including family, friends or wider society. In this chapter, we discuss lesbian, gay, bisexual and transgender issues in relation to mental health, but we do not wish to imply that these practices are in any way problematic, as they are part of the natural variation of human sexuality. Rather, our discussion will cover evidence suggesting how discriminatory practices against minority groups can contribute to their distress (sadness, worry, substance abuse) in general.

Similar questions over the removal from the DSM of what many deem to be ordinary variations in human sexual desire and behaviour are now being raised in relation to the group of behaviours known as the 'paraphilias' in the DSM. These behaviours include exhibitionism right through to child sex offending, yet all are listed under the same diagnostic category. As Silverstein (2009) notes, however, given the increasing use of the internet and young people's greater exposure to 'alternative sexual practices', what we see as perverse or disordered will gradually narrow and be redefined as activities that form part of a wide range of sexual preferences and tastes that will ultimately be accepted as normal variations of human sexual desire.

Many have argued that even if certain behaviours are deemed 'unusual', as long as they are consensual, they cannot in themselves be seen to be 'disordered'. At best, those behaviours involving non-consent (such as aggressive and/

BOX **10.1**

Some definitional pointers (taken from the Oxford English Dictionary)

In this chapter, we will be using a variety of different terms in relation to sexuality and sexual problems, so perhaps it is best to make clear what some of these terms mean.

Sex: sexual activity. * Interestingly, the Oxford dictionary includes specifically 'sexual intercourse' in the definition, which makes the assumption that 'real' sex involves penetration.

Sexuality: (1) capacity for sexual feelings. (2) a person's sexual identity.

Sexual desire: (1) a strong sexual feeling of wanting to have something or wishing for something to happen. (2) strong sexual feeling or appetite.

alternative[3] sexual practices that exist in society, we highlight the debates that are currently taking place in the academic and clinical fields as to whether such behaviours constitute an identifiable and discrete mental disorder. In this respect, the chapter covers some of the material that other textbooks do, but in a way that is far more searching and critical.

Within this chapter, we explore (1) problems with having sex, (2) the kinds of sexual attraction that have been classified as disordered or paraphiliac and (3) issues relating to the diagnostic category Gender Identity Disorder. We will discuss how each of these issues relating to sexuality and gender is potentially defined according to diagnostic criteria, and present critical commentaries on those diagnostic practices. The main thrust of the chapter will be on problems with having sex, where we will look more closely at possible risk factors and interventions. For (2) and (3), we will mostly concentrate our efforts on a broader discussion of the controversies surrounding these topics, as well as covering some of the literature on causation and intervention.

or abusive sex) should be deemed criminal rather than pathological. Chess Denman further makes a distinction between behaviours that are transgressive (unusual) or coercive (involving non-consent) (Denman, 2004).

Topics covered in this chapter

As we must limit our discussions to areas of sexuality (and, later on, gender identity) relevant to mental distress, we concentrate on a limited number of issues covered in the mental health literature generally and ones that come to the attention of mental health professionals. In doing so, we wish to make clear that the sources of the distress associated with some sexual problems are not clear cut, uni-causal (have one cause only) or necessarily individual. Problems relating to gender identity and sexuality are listed under the categorial heading **Sexual and Gender Identity Disorders** in the DSM-IV-TR, which includes (a) **Sexual dysfunctions:** difficulties in having sexual relations with another person, (b) **Paraphilias:** sexual attraction to unusual objects or sexual activities that are deemed unusual in nature and (c) **Gender Identity Disorder:** the current diagnostic category for a person who views their current biological sex as contrary to their perceived gender identity (usually opposite to the one they were assigned at birth).[1] This can result in the person holding a strong desire to become a member of their preferred gender identity. In this chapter, although we cover a number of the issues related to these diagnostic categories, we do not describe them in any straightforward diagnostic way. Instead, our discussion covers a number of debates relating to the validity of traditional diagnostic practices, as we wish to make clear the controversies surrounding the application of the label of 'mental disorder' to sexual problems and gender variance.[2] Similarly, whilst we describe some of the more

Historical considerations

Throughout history, sexuality has been subject to a variety of moral and religious sanctions and prohibitions. Since classical antiquity, religious and spiritual leaders, medical practitioners and therapists alike have linked sexuality to psychological well-being, intellect and rationality as well as illness and disease (Weeks, 2003). It is no surprise, then, that sexuality and gender have been scrutinized in medical circles since the Enlightenment period, with a view to identifying 'pathological' or 'abnormal' sexual and gender-inappropriate conduct, which may pose a threat to general psychological well-being and pose a threat to moral society. Women in the mid to late 19th century were labelled with a host of sexual deviancies if they contravened even slightly the moral codes for appropriate feminine behaviour. Diagnosis relating to excessive emotion was closely linked to women's physiology, especially dysfunction in their menstrual cycle and reproductive capacities; indeed the term 'hysteria', frequently diagnosed at that time, originates from the term 'womb' (Chesler, 2005; Ussher, 1989). These ideas linking sex, gender and mental distress are clearly outmoded and unfashionable, although we must not think that cultural assumptions regarding socially acceptable gender roles do not continue to influence diagnostic practices (see Horwitz, 2002).

Establishing sexual and gender 'pathology' in general has remained complex, due to the often difficult separation between moral cultural values and scientific classification (Sadler, 2005). This has never been more apparent than in the case of homosexuality, which was only removed from the DSM in 1973, due to a change in opinion amongst members of the American Psychiatric Association (APA), and subsequent to the intervention of gay rights activists. Although ego-dystonic homosexuality (homosexual desire that is out of keeping with self-image) remained a category of disorder until 1987, the APA and World Health Organization now agree that homosexuality

---

1   Diagnostic titles are reviewed and may be revised for the forthcoming DSM-5.
2   **Gender variance** refers to holding gender traits that are contrary to one's biological sex (according to culturally prescribed norms of gendered behaviour.

---

3   We acknowledge that what have been traditionally defined as alternative sexual practices – bondage, sadomasochism and attraction to unusual objects – are not uncommon in general population studies.

should be considered a normal variant of human sexuality. Yet it is worth mentioning that a diagnostic category, 'Sexual Disorders Not otherwise Specified' (listed in DSM-IV-TR, 2000), contains the description 'Persistent and marked distress about sexual orientation' (APS, 2000, p. 582), which, commentators have argued, retains a way of pathologizing homosexuality by reframing it as a 'means by which distress occurs' (Lev, 2006). Many have argued that allowing such a form of distress to be used in diagnostic terms entirely obscures the oppression and discrimination that causes such distress, as opposed to some internal dysfunction possessed by the individual.

Unfortunately, sexual discrimination cannot yet be confined to the history books and continues to operate in every society to some degree (in lay as well as clinical quarters), depending upon specific religious and cultural practices (Herdt, 1997). Each society has its own views on sexuality (which can often be contradictory), and although there is overlap between countries, there are specific religious, ethnic and cultural practices that inevitably influence personal and professional views on the matter.

Culture, sexuality and the body

Different cultures have more or less rigid ideas about what is normal when it comes to sexuality and relationships (Jankowiak, 2008). In Western societies, the development of this state of affairs is incredibly complex (for an excellent overview, see Weeks, 2003). In the 18th and 19th centuries, sexuality moved from the domain of religious orthodoxy to a more secular concern with psychological morality, with marriage at the pinnacle. Monogamous heterosexual relationships continue to define what is appropriate and acceptable, despite same-sex relationships being recognized as legitimate sexual identities in some societies.[4]

However, what is defined as 'normal' does not always match actual behaviours, as many sexologists and anthropologists have discovered a much greater variation than traditional representations of sexual behaviour would allow – in desires, fantasies and practices in their empirical work (Weeks, Holland & Waites, 2003). A **Sexologist** is a scientist who studies human sexual behaviour. Their methods include naturalistic observations, experimental work with individuals in a laboratory and large-scale survey work with interviews. In other words, what people report doing, or what we observe people doing is not always representative of what they actually do or what they fantasize doing.

In Western European societies, messages about sex are freely available in the media and form part of how we understand ourselves as individuals. But it is important not to forget that certain states in North America continue to prohibit or do not officially recognize same-sex marriages (Weeks, 2011).

Despite some degree of freedom in certain areas of the Western world, sex is still viewed as a private act; a part of ourselves that should not be revealed outside of our close relationships: a hidden part. Despite such privacy, sexual identity is still a significant way in which to position and see ourselves and a way to feel (de)valued. It can also be visibly written into the way we look, how we dress and groom our bodies, and is,

of course, based in part on the gender category (or categories) we fit into (Fausto-Sterling, 2000; Smith-Pickard & Swynnerton, 2005). Whether we are gay, straight or bisexual, our sexuality has become an identity that matters (Weeks, 2003). This is precisely why any shame or discrimination we might face as a result of our sexuality (which lesbian, gay, bisexual and trans people undoubtedly do) may make us feel out of place and devalued, and contribute to poor self-esteem and self-belief.

Within all this, the body plays a significant role. Our sexuality is often highly stylized through our bodies, and what is deemed to be sexually attractive and desirable. The reasons for removing hair from our face, legs, chests, underarms or genitalia is a recognition that some bodies are more attractive (hairless, slender, symmetrical bodies) to the same or other sex than others in current Western thinking (Bordo, 1997). As well as a variety of home- and salon-based techniques to beautify our bodies, cosmetic surgery has become a further way in which a significant minority are choosing to 'correct' body dissatisfaction (Heyes & Jones, 2009).

In recent years, the voluntary uptake of cosmetic surgery has added to existing pressures on individuals to adhere to standards of the 'body beautiful', with more women, in particular, electing to have surgery to alter their genitalia (labiaplasty; vaginal tightening) or increase or reduce breast size (Braun, 2005). The 'designer vagina' is now a well-known term, referring to women who surgically alter the outer and inner parts of their genitalia to achieve ultimate genital 'beauty'. The literatures on this topic present different ideas about the success of cosmetic surgery to enhance self-esteem and sexual pleasure, with some writers arguing that surgery can lead to greater sexual satisfaction and others, taking a more cultural viewpoint, stating that surgery not only fits with the increasing medicalizing of sexual behaviour but in fact reinforces traditional and stereotypical gendered behaviours, in which women still conform rather than challenge the unrealistic expectations placed upon their bodies (Tiefer, 2004). This has the effect of restricting ideas of beauty – and hence sexuality – to a restrictive script, making it clear that individual change, rather than social change, is required to achieve sexual pleasures. Furthermore, studies have suggested that cosmetic surgery can lead to greater sexual dissatisfaction, and it is certainly not without its risks (Braun, 2005).

Sex and gender

It is impossible to talk about sex and sexuality without also talking about gender to a great extent, as it is impossible to understand psychology without also understanding the social. 'Sex' is often still used interchangeably with 'gender', although more writers, academics and professionals, recognize a distinction; sex pertaining to sexual acts and gender relating more usually to identity.

Where gender and 'sex' are still used interchangeably, most often it is when working from a perspective that recognizes two biological sexes, male and female, that are fixed and easily identified. Gender, then, is talked about as something more social. A number of problems arise with this. The body is maintained as central to that identity, and regarded as existing in only one of two fixed realities. This ignores current knowledge about biological variation (Johnson, 2004), as evidenced by people who are identified as 'intersex' at birth. (**Intersex** is the term for

---

4   **Heterosexual** refers to an individual who is sexually attracted to a member of the opposite sex/gender.

BOX 10.2
Classifying sexuality

Although we use a variety of terms to describe various categories of sexuality in everyday life, these terms have not always been used and can be considered problematic. The term 'heterosexual', for example, was not introduced until 1892 in a translation of neuropsychiatrist Krafft-Ebing's *Psychopathia Sexualis* (1886); the term implied that individuals were attracted *either* to the opposite *or* the same gender. Krafft-Ebing described over a thousand case studies of various sexual 'perversions', including **sadomasochism** (the process of administering or receiving acts of pain or humiliation for the purpose [usually] of sexual arousal and pleasure), transsexualism and homosexual behaviour, and in doing so

made the difference between what was considered to be 'normal' and 'abnormal' more distinctive. After some time, however, and after discussing sexuality with a number of gay male patients, Krafft-Ebing reached the conclusion that homosexuality should not be considered a mental disorder or a perversion, but an orientation, just like heterosexuality.

The categorization of sexuality into homosexuality or heterosexuality has been widely criticized by a number of authors, who have argued that our sexualities are not as clear cut as such categories suggest. What we fantasize about, or who we are attracted to, may not be reflected in the behaviours we actually engage in or report. Also, it is worth mentioning that the gender of the person we are attracted to may not be a fixed or defining feature of our sexuality. Prior to the introduction

of the terms heterosexual or homosexual, there was greater emphasis on the actual sexual practices individuals engaged in. Furthermore, bisexual communities often challenge the gender-defining features of sexuality.

Alfred Kinsey, a famous North American sexologist (scientist of sexual behaviour and attitudes) argued that many individuals do not fit neatly into an established category and instead used a dimensional scale (0–6; 0 being exclusively heterosexual and 6 exclusively homosexual) to measure an individual's sexual preferences. Many have followed Kinsey's lead, arguing for a more dimensional (as opposed to categorical) and contextual version of how sexuality works.

Richard von Krafft-Ebing – A pioneer for classifying sexual perversions: 1840–1902.

---

people with gender characteristics that may be indistinguishable as typically *either* male *or* female or typically *both* male *and* female[5] [Blackless et al., 2000; Fausto-Sterling, 2000].) Using 'sex' and 'gender' interchangeably is further confused where sexual identities in contemporary Western societies are largely determined not only by the sex/gender of the individual, but by the sex/gender of their partner/s (for example, homosexual, heterosexual and bisexual – see Box 10.2). This chapter makes a distinction by defining sex as 'sexual activities' and gender as 'sexed identities', to highlight that a change in gender does not necessarily imply a change in sexual partner.

The ways sexuality is linked to gender are complex and go far beyond identifying gender as determined by genitalia or sexual orientation (Chau & Herring, 2004). Western cultures have only two acknowledged genders: male and female. Anyone claiming to be neither, a mixture of both, a blending of genders or 'indefinable' is often deemed 'odd', 'confused' or even 'disordered'. Recently, a greater diversity of stories have become visible through the use of the internet, where people can experience more freedom in their communications, representation and play, as well as through research methodologies and critical thinking that can explore gender issues with more nuance by exploring how individuals might play with, move beyond and actively disrupt gender categories in their personal, public and sexual lives (Whittle, 1998; Farr, 2010; Ferreday & Lock, 2007). This is also in no small part due to the increase in those working in the area of lesbian, gay, bisexual, transgender, queer and questioning (LGBTQQ) perspectives in psychology (Clarke & Peel, 2007) that have criticized traditional psychological research on gender and sexuality for (either implicitly or explicitly) assuming heterosexuality is 'normal' and minority sexualities 'problematic' (Johnson, 2007).

Discrimination regarding sexual and gender identity, and its relationship to mental distress

Although to some extent sexuality has become more liberalized in certain societies, due to changes in law and cultural values (Baumeister, 2001; Jankowiak, 2008), there are still certain groups who are more likely to experience abuse and discrimination. In many countries of the world, individuals are killed for illicit sexual acts, including same-sex sexual practices, infidelity and open displays of affection. Furthermore, it is still the case that female children and adult women are often more subject than men to abusive and violent acts involving sex[6], which can have profound and long lasting effects on sexuality (one's ability to have sex, or experience sex that is pleasurable) and psychological wellbeing (Finkelhor & Browne, 1986; Jehu, 1989; Warner, 2000; Briere & Elliot, 2003; Baker, 2004). These include sexual abuse in childhood as well as culturally sanctioned acts such as genital mutilation.

It is also still the case that certain men and women experience higher levels of discrimination and violence as a result of being lesbian, gay, bisexual or transgendered. **Transgender** refers to individuals who diverge from culturally prescribed gender roles. This includes individuals who have undertaken gender-corrective surgery to transfer from the gender they were assigned at birth to the gender that fits their personal identity. **Cisgender** refers to individuals whose gender assigned at birth matches their socially ascribed gender role or identity. Such discrimination can lead to higher rates of distress among these groups. A recent UK national survey by King et al. (2003) at the Royal Free Hospital in London found

---

5 The term 'intersex' replaces the formerly used 'hermaphrodite'. Between one and two newborn children per 1000 are identified for 'corrective genital surgery', an issue which introduces other concerns and, sometimes, related debates (Blackless et al., 2000).

6 We are in no way suggesting that boys and adult men do not experience child sexual abuse or adult rape. We are making a more general point about certain groups having being identified as more subject to these experiences than others.

significantly higher rates of distress (e.g. diagnoses of depression, anxiety and substance abuse) among lesbian, gay and bisexual (LGB) participants, signalling the need for mental health professionals to be alert to the discrimination experienced by these groups when assessing their difficulties and planning treatment. Other studies have also indicated higher rates of mental distress among LGB groups, especially bisexual individuals (Jorm, Angermeyer & Katschnig, 2000; King et al., 2003; Chakraborty and McManus, 2011), making it difficult to ignore the role of discrimination in the development and maintenance of distress in these groups.

Furthermore, if an individual is distressed by their sexual orientation, rather than aiming to 'correct' their orientation (which was a common practice in the early and middle 20th century) the aim has become one of encouraging clients to accept their orientation. **Conversion therapy** or 'reorientation/reassignment therapy' describes a therapeutic technique designed to reorient an individual from a homosexual or bisexual to a heterosexual orientation.

Conversion therapy is still practised in some parts of the United States and elsewhere. **Gay affirmative therapies**, on the other hand, are designed to encourage and provide support to individuals, offering respect by positively reinforcing their sexuality identity, rather than trying to alter it (Davies & Neal, 1996). Indeed such therapies are now recognized in the clinical literature, and training programmes for clinical psychologists and psychotherapists are available. Gay affirmative therapy is a form of psychotherapy that encourages gay or bisexual clients to learn to accept and celebrate their sexual orientation rather than change it to a heterosexual orientation.

It is clear that sexuality can have a profound impact on mental health through sexually abusive and violent acts, as well as through discrimination and prejudice (potentially resulting in verbal and physical violence) towards a person's sexual and gender identity. Gender and sexual orientation, therefore, should be considered important factors in assessing overall vulnerability to abuse and discrimination and their potential impact on psychological well-being. However, rather than viewing minority gender and sexual identities as problems in themselves, affirming and supporting the individual's identity is advocated (Davies et al., 1996).

Defining 'problems'

It is perhaps obvious that what we consider to be a problem with gender and sexuality is far from straightforward. As the section on history and culture indicates, definitions of sexually problematic or troublesome sexual behaviour have varied across time and setting. What has not changed is the overriding focus on the individual as the source of the problem, and in the latest version of the DSM, no background information on partners and their behaviour is required.

Many conventional psychiatric or psychology text books on mental health cover 'gender and sexual disorders' in terms of the major related DSM categories, but, in contrast, we would argue that these issues should not be explored as an internal problem relating only to the individual. Not only are sexual problems relatively common, they are tightly bound to circumstance and *relationships*, as well as socio-cultural, political and economic factors. Therefore, although we may speak of individuals experiencing difficulty in having sex, we do NOT automatically assume such difficulties constitute an internal or individual 'dysfunction'. Whilst some individuals have medical conditions leading to such problems or long-standing difficulties with intimacy (arising from childhood relationships) the causes of which can be located in their individual circumstances or history, we do not think that examining the individual as the source of the problem is the only pathway to understanding. Following the work of sex therapists Kaschak and Tiefer (2001) in their influential text *A New View of Women's Sexual Problems*, we define sexual problems as 'discontent or dissatisfaction with any emotional, physical or relational aspect of sexual experience' (Tiefer, 2001). In their view, this approach does not place undue emphasis on the medical aspects of sexual functioning but broadens the agenda to include all of the following: socio-cultural, political and economic factors, partner and relationship factors, psychological factors and medical factors. In addition, there are two further themes that underline the labelling of sexual problems, that is (a) whether they cause distress and (b) whether they are legal. Both are riddled with controversy and debate. The definition of and controversies surrounding gender variance and related diagnoses will be discussed later in the chapter.

Causing distress

First, a sexual response or behaviour may be considered problematic and suitable for professional treatment if it is long term, frequent and causes significant distress and/or disruption to occupational, social or interpersonal functioning (e.g. relationship difficulties). For example, an individual's preference for lots of sex can become disruptive if that person has to make excuses at work or forgo other important relationships to satisfy their desire for sex. This in itself can lead to distress and may even put the individual at risk (in terms of violence and/or in relation to sexually transmitted infections), if their demand for sex leads to an increase in stranger contact. However, whether a behaviour or identity is distressing is entirely culturally defined. For example, what counts as sexual compulsion may be related to how much sex we think people should be having, based on our own experience.

Non-consensual or illegal behaviour

Second, sexual preference and/or behaviour involving individuals who do not offer consent or who cannot legally provide consent is included in the DSM and ICD. There are numerous examples of how definitions of (and requirements for) consent are defined in law that warrant careful scrutiny of the social context (for an excellent overview, see Weeks, 2011, 32–4); however, there is general agreement that behaviours involving non-consensual sexual activity can be a significant source of distress for non-consenting individuals. However, whether such behaviour should be considered psychologically disordered – as in the DSM – or simply criminal, is a matter of considerable debate, which is what we will focus on when covering issues of consent. However, we wish to make clear that to dispute the labelling of behaviours that involve non-consensual acts as mental disorders does not in any way imply that we do not consider such acts as they are currently defined to be utterly unacceptable and criminal. Any suggestion that our perspective might support acts of abuse or sexual acts involving children would be completely wrong and misguided.

Problems with having sex

The problems people experience having sex have been commonly described in the literature as a disruption in **sexual functioning**: the ability for the person to be able to experience desire, to be aroused, to physically engage in a sexual act and experience orgasm.

Traditionally, any problems with the ability to function sexually are identified in the medical, psychiatric and psychological literature as disruptions in a normal human sexual response cycle (HSRC), as defined by sexologists William Masters and Virginia Johnson (1966) and developed by Helen Singer Kaplan. The **Human Sexual Response Cycle (HSRC)** is a model of sexual stimulation and activity developed by sexologists William Masters and Virginia Johnson. Based on scientific observation they argued there are four stages of sexual response: excitement, plateau, orgasm and resolution.

Sexual problems in the psychiatric and clinical literature are therefore referred to as sexual dysfunctions. Masters and Johnson conceptualized sexual problems/dysfunctions as anxiety-induced inhibitions related to gaps in sexual knowledge and learned attitudes and behaviour. They believed that with appropriate guidance and instruction, sexual problems could be directly addressed and resolved in a relatively short period of time.

In their clinical observational studies of 10,000 men and women, individuals and couples were invited to have sex in front of researchers, who would then measure a range of physiological responses, from arousal through to orgasm. From these observations, Masters and Johnson concluded that there were four stages to the HSRC: (1) Excitement phase (initial arousal) (2) Plateau phase (at full arousal, but not yet at orgasm) (3) Orgasm and (4) Resolution phase (after orgasm). Disruption to any of these four universal phases (although there is no specific difficulty associated with the fourth phase as such) results in a label of sexual dysfunction (Masters & Johnson, 1970). Masters and Johnson's work has been extremely influential in the field of medicine and sexology and forms the basis of the DSM diagnostic categories for sexual dysfunction. Despite this, significant criticisms remain of their work, especially relating to the physiological bias inherent in their depiction of sexual desire and the linear progression of the stages (Tiefer, 1997).

The main point here is that problems with having sex have been reported to have a significant negative impact on an individual's quality of life, through their effect on the individual's self-esteem and intimate relationships. It is perhaps self-evident, given the importance placed upon sex in many societies, that such difficulties can lead to a drop in self-confidence, self-image and mood (Fugl-Meyer, Branholm & Fugl-Meyer, 1991).

General prevalence rates and issues concerning problems with having sex

There have been very few large-scale surveys that have attempted to measure how many individuals have problems with having sex (or sexual 'dysfunctions' as they are commonly referred to in the literature). We discuss a number of these studies here, to locate our observations of sexual behaviour and sexual problems more generally. Before we do, it must be said that some of the key researchers in the field have questioned whether 'sexual dysfunction' is an appropriate term to use, especially to describe women's sexual difficulties, given there are situational factors that more accurately explain why a significant number of women experience low sexual desire and pain during sex: situational factors such as power inequalities, general emotional well-being and the quality of the emotional relationship with a partner are among some of the relational and social factors identified (Rosen & Laumann, 2003; Bancroft, Loftus & Long, 2003). **Low sexual desire or hypoactive sexual desire** refers to the absence of sexual thoughts, fantasies or desire for sex and is considered to be a sexual dysfunction in the DSM.

Contrary to the ICD or DSM classifications, physical descriptors (pain, erectile dysfunction) of 'sexual dysfunctions' were thought to be poor predictors of sexual difficulty in a US community study of nearly 1000 black and white women aged between 20 and 65 years (Bancroft et al., 2003).

Another difficulty in measuring prevalence rates for sexual problems is, of course, that not everyone may consider what they do to be a problem, even if it meets the criteria for a sexual dysfunction. A study by Fugl-Meyer and Fugl-Meyer (1999), for example, found that 69% of men with erectile problems were distressed, in comparison to only 45% of women who were unable to reach orgasm. Despite this, attempts have been made to generate prevalence rates, and recent figures suggest sexual dysfunction to be fairly prevalent in community samples (Simons & Carey, 2001, see Box 1.4). A recent global study across 29 different countries, involving over 27,000 men and women aged 40–80, also found that age significantly increased the likelihood of these types of difficulties, especially for men (Laumann et al., 2005). Furthermore, sexual problems of this nature were more common (almost twice as common) in East and South Asia than in other regions of the world. According to the US National Health and Social Life Survey carried out with 1749 women and 1410 men between the ages of 18 and 59, sexual dysfunction is more prevalent in women (43%) than men (31%) (Laumann et al., 1999) and is associated with various demographic characteristics, including age and educational attainment. It is also more common among women and men with poorer physical and emotional health (Laumann et al., 2005). Moreover, sexual dysfunction is highly associated with negative experiences of sexual relationships and overall well-being. These findings suggest that sexual functioning is tied to a variety of physical, psychological and social factors, including interpersonal difficulties, gender, class and overall psychological well-being. We will discuss each of these factors in turn, and cover some difficulties in more depth. Before we do so, let us recall the two personal stories of Alice and Sajid that we introduced at the beginning of the chapter.

Alice and Sajid's stories at the beginning of the chapter illustrate the complexities of thinking through why some people experience difficulties with sexual functioning. Although both Alice and Sajid's difficulties are located in specific sexual functions, the origins of those difficulties may not be immediately obvious. That is why when we are looking for the origins of problems with having sex we have to consider a wide range of factors, rather than assuming there is a straightforward link between physiological functioning and sexual expression.

Psychiatric diagnoses

Individuals are diagnosed with a sexual dysfunction if they fulfil the following three criteria: they experiences significant

BOX 10.3
Sexual 'dysfunction' and diagnosis

There are nine sexual dysfunction categories listed in the DSM. A diagnosis is made on the basis that what the individual is experiencing leads to a significant disruption in sexual functioning and is distressing and/or disruptive to them. The dysfunctions listed relate to the Masters and Johnson sexual response cycle and include dysfunctions relating to desire, arousal, orgasm and, less so, resolution. Pain is a further inclusion criterion.

1 *Erectile dysfunction*: persistent and recurrent inability to gain or maintain erection until penetration has been completed.
2 *Vaginismus*: persistent and recurrent involuntary spasms of the outer third of the vagina, preventing intercourse (with an object or penis).
3 *Dyspareunia*: genital pain experienced during or after penetration by both women and men.
4 *Sexual aversion disorder*: aversion to and avoidance of sexual contact with a sexual partner.
5 *Premature ejaculation*: persistent and recurrent onset of orgasm with minimal sexual stimulation before or shortly after penetration in men. Women can ejaculate prematurely but this is not listed as a problem.
6 *Female sexual arousal disorder*: persistent and recurrent difficulty with genital swelling and lubrication for sexual activity.
7 *Female orgasmic disorder*: inability to reach orgasm despite adequate sexual stimulation.
8 *Male orgasmic disorder*: inability to reach orgasm despite adequate sexual stimulation.
9 *Hypoactive sexual desire disorder*: persistent and recurrent absence of desire for sexual activity or sexual fantasies.

---

levels of distress, the difficulty is persistent and their problem has not arisen as a result of a diagnosis for another Axis I disorder. There are nine different 'sexual dysfunctions' listed in the DSM (see Box 10.3). Both Alice and Sajid would be eligible for a diagnosis as their difficulties cause them significant levels of distress, they have experienced difficulty for a long period of time and they are free of other mental health diagnoses. However, it is worth noting that community studies have revealed that around a third (32%) of those reporting sexual problems have more than one difficulty with sexual functioning, a quarter have more than two, around 8% have three and 1% have difficulties in all four areas of sexual function outlined by Masters and Johnson (Johnson, Phelps & Cottler, 2004). Diagnosis is therefore highly controversial once again and hotly contested in the sexological literature by leading researchers (Bancroft et al., 2003; Laumann et al., 2005). Furthermore, diagnostic categories have been further criticized because they do not tend to map onto people's actual experience of their sexual difficulties, especially those of heterosexual, lesbian and bisexual women and gay and bisexual men, due to assumptions regarding what is 'normal' (see below; Cove & Boyle, 2002; Kaschak & Tiefer, 2001; Nicholls, 2005; Sadler, 2005)

Diagnostic issues for Alice

To illustrate this: it is very possible that Alice would be diagnosed with a disorder named **vaginismus**, which is a diagnosis made on the basis of a reported involuntary vaginal spasm that occurs when penetration is attempted. Alice has reported this herself and would potentially qualify for this diagnosis. What else would we need to know before making an assessment of Alice's needs? What are the potential drawbacks of labelling Alice with a 'disorder' that potentially strips away some of the important contextual details of her problem? After all, Alice is able to experience sexual desire and satisfaction, so should the context of her problem be investigated further?

What are some of the problems that have been empirically identified in relation to the practice of diagnosis for women's sexual difficulties? Interestingly, the definition and measurement of vaginal spasm has not been standardized, so self-reports are used (Reissing, Binik, Khalife, Cohen & Amsel,

2004). However, when a range of physiological measures have been used to differentiate women with a diagnosis of vaginismus from women who experience pain during intercourse (**dyspareunia**), differences could not be found on those physiological measures. Indeed, Alice could be diagnosed with both vaginismus and dyspareunia, making such distinctions irrelevant in her case. The major difference seemed to be the lack of willingness to endure pain from the vaginismus group, as compared with the dyspareunia group, who will proceed to intercourse despite experiencing pain. What this tells us is that discrete diagnostic categories for problems in sexual functioning are not meaningful when we consider that the individual's appraisal of the situation is more central to the behaviour than some identifiable and discrete set of symptoms for each disorder (see De Kruiff, 2000, cited in Reissing et al., 2004; Balon, 2007).

Studies suggest that the presence of pain is insufficient to explain levels of sexual satisfaction and orgasm in women; it is the actual appraisal of the pain that predicts the repercussion of painful intercourse (Farmer & Meston, 2007). Furthermore, the interpersonal dynamics of sexual encounters predict levels of sexual satisfaction far better than the presence of pain (dysfunction) alone. This provides support for the idea that the more comfortable women are in sexual situations, the more likely they are to report satisfactions and be able to orgasm, despite some difficulties with certain sexual functioning (i.e. being penetrated). When sexual dysfunction is diagnosed, however, the focus of concern is often treatment in the presence or absence of a symptom (e.g. pain during penetration or vaginal spasm). What empirical studies point to is the need to investigate further the impact of partner dynamics, the type of stimuli given by partner, and levels of sexual arousal and lubrication, in order to understand the situational factors. **Sexual arousal** describes sexual excitement at the thought or anticipation of sexual activity.

It is even more difficult to discuss Alice's problem as a clear indicator of a 'disorder' when pain during intercourse occurs in 15–20% of young women between the ages of 18 and 29 (Laumann et al., 1999; Farmer & Meston, 2007), making her experience far from uncommon or 'atypical'.

BOX **10.4**
Gender and sexual abuse

Sexual abuse is not an uncommon experience. Although men do report experiences of child sexual abuse and adult rape, women and girls in particular are subjected to sexual abuse in large numbers (up to 33% of girls are sexually abused as children and 20–25% of women are raped as adults). **Child sexual abuse** refers to sexual contact (this can include exposing oneself, as well as verbal and physical contact) with a child. **Sexual abuse** is the coercion of another adult person (using either verbal suggestion or physical force) by another to engage in sexual activity.

Sexual abuse and violence in childhood and adulthood can have profound effects on a person, contributing to long-term distress associated with not only sexuality, but also a wide range of mental health problems (see Chapter 6 for an in-depth discussion). Many victims of sexual abuse do not come forward, and even when they do, the conviction rate in the UK for both child sexual abuse and adult rape is shockingly low (7% for child sexual abuse and 8% for adult rape). A number of academics and activists believe that the shame associated with sexual abuse and a victim-blaming culture contributes significantly to the long-term distress experienced by victims and survivors (Reavey & Warner, 2003; Gavey, 2005; Warner, 2009).

There is extensive literature on the long-term effects of trauma, including child sexual abuse as well as adult rape, on psychological well-being. The relationship between experiences such as child sexual abuse and later psychological well-being are complex and should not be treated as straightforwardly causal. A variety of factors contribute to whether an individual goes on to develop specific issues with sexuality in adulthood, such as the level of support they receive after the abuse has stopped, whether they are believed, whether the abuser has been punished and the quality of relationship they have now, and have had with other family members. Sexual trauma can also be accompanied by physical and emotional abuse, as well as neglect, and it is the specific configuration of these for each individual that informs our understanding of their potential difficulties. In other words, when we look at issues of abuse and trauma we also need to look closely at the relationships and/or familial dynamics that surround the actual experience of trauma, as those relationships will contribute to the formation of self-identity and the long-term effects of the abuse. For example, if and when a child informs her mother that she has been abused by her step-father, the quality of the relationship between the mother and daughter, as well as if the mother believes the daughter and supports her will impact strongly on the daughter's ability to work through what has happened. Therefore, it is not only the abuse but also the surrounding relational context that impacts on the individual's mental well-being.

A variety of issues have been addressed in this literature, including the impact of trauma on mental health and quality of life generally (Finkelhor & Browne, 1985; Warner, 2000) as well as the link between abuse and a variety of mental distress, including sexual problems, eating problems, relationship issues, hearing voices and chronic fear responses. Sexually abusive experiences can lead to specific and difficult emotional experiences related to sexuality, including difficulties with trust, fear of intimacy and sex (Maltz & Holman, 1987, poor body image, feelings of interpersonal powerlessness and low sexual self-worth. Moreover, a range of specific problems related to sexual functioning have been identified by a number of authors, including pain during intercourse for men and women (Jehu, 1989), vaginal spasms in women, and low sexual desire and sexual avoidance in both men and women with a history of either rape or child sexual abuse (Heiman, 2002). A further issue to be considered is the evidence pointing to higher rates of sexual revictimization among community and clinical samples of women with a history of child sexual abuse (Coid et al., 2001). Experiences of sexual trauma in childhood, therefore, can have an even greater negative impact and be heightened by repeated sexual trauma in adulthood. John Read, a clinical psychologist working in New Zealand, has referred to this as the 'dose response': the longer and the more repeated the attacks that a person experiences, the greater the severity of mental health problems, including psychotic experiences (Read, 2005).

Diagnostic issues for Sajid

Sajid fulfils the criteria for **Male Erectile Dysfunction (MED)**: the inability to develop or maintain an erection during sexual activity. Around 52% of men between the ages of 40 and 70 years of age are diagnosed with erectile problems, so Sajid's problems cannot be regarded as rare or atypical. Erectile difficulties can be the result of medical conditions (e.g. diabetes, high blood pressure) as well as life style (e.g. smoking, alcohol consumption) and medication. It would be important to rule out any physical complaints before arriving at the conclusion that Sajid's problems are psychological, or the result of a specific disturbance in sexual functioning.

Causes, maintenance and risk

The causes of sexual problems are many. Some authors, for example, have argued that disorders such as dyspareunia should be reclassified as pain 'disorders', rather than sexual dysfunctions (Binik, 2005). Others have argued that a completely new view of women's sexual problems should be adopted to account for the linking of sexual problems to gender roles and relationship difficulties (Tiefer, 2006). In this section, we explore a range of factors identified as linked to individuals and couples experiencing problems with having sex. Over the past 25–30 years there has been a shift in thinking about sexual problems as mostly psychological to a consideration of the combination of the biological, psychological, social and cultural aspects of a person's difficulties (Wincze, Bach & Barlow, 2008).

Culture

In the Global Study of Sexual Attitudes and Behaviours (Nicolsi, Laumann, Moreira, Palik & Gingell, 2004)—an international survey study of sexual problems across 29 countries, involving 13,882 participants— clear cultural differences were found in levels of sexual problems lasting for two months or more. Sexual problems, including a lack of interest in sex for women and inability to have an orgasm and erectile difficulties for men, almost doubled in Middle East, East Asian and South Asian countries. In Middle Eastern countries, average rates for women who were not interested in sex were as high as 43.1%. This indicates how cultural practices can contribute to an individual's sexual difficulties, including rigid gender role expectations which lead to a lack of foreplay (which will decrease women's enjoyment and cause lubrication difficulties) and a bias towards male pleasure via penetration.

Age

Rates of sexual problems increase significantly with age, according to the GSSAB (Laumann et al., 2005). In the Massachusetts Male Ageing Study, 34.8% of men between the ages of 40 and 70 were recorded as having a sexual problem. For men, in particular, a range of physical problems associated with ageing can affect sexual functioning (Diokno, Brown & Herzog, 1990). These include vascular disease, cardiovascular problems, hypertension, neurological problems (stroke, brain damage) diabetes and a diagnosis of depression (Kubin, Wagner & Fugl-Meyer, 2003). For women, satisfaction with their sexual relationships was most closely associated with relationship adjustment and did not relate to age (Hawton, Gath & Day, 1994), although the US National Health and Social Life Survey (1999) revealed lubrication difficulties increased in post-menopausal women, though these did not greatly affect satisfaction.

Gender

The rates of problems with having sex are different for women and men (43% and 31% respectively). Furthermore, women's quality of life may be more negatively affected by the difficulties they experience with sex. We must be cautious, however, in interpreting these findings, as these difficulties have been argued to be the product of many different risk factors that are bound to the context of women's lives, rather than any fixed internal properties of women, or any 'medical' malfunction (Kaschak & Tiefer, 2001). In this text, *A New View of Women's Sexual Problems*, Kaschak and Tiefer have argued that women's sexual difficulties are intimately tied to a wide range of contextual factors. These include (i) the impact of cultural expectations (women are more likely to play a submissive role in sexual encounters, leading to lower sexual satisfaction – Boyle, 1993), (ii) much higher rates of sexual violence (inside and outside intimate relationships), (iii) inexperienced male partners who, through a lack of motivation or knowledge, cannot adequately stimulate and fulfil their partner (Kaplan, 1974), (iv) higher rates of reported child sexual abuse, (v) higher rates of unhappiness, especially amongst married women, and (vi) the emphasis on penetration as 'real sex', which in a high percentage of women does not lead to orgasm (Hite, 1976; Bancroft, 1989; Boyle, 1993; Nicolson & Burr, 2003). Interestingly, health problems did not lead to an increase in sexual problems for women as they do for men. The only positive association between health-related problems was an increase in pain during sexual intercourse for women with a urinary tract infection (Laumann et al., 1999). Many feminist authors have demonstrated theoretically as well as empirically the unequal relations that exist between women and men

---

BOX **10.5**

Prevalence rates for diagnosed sexual dysfunction in a community sample*

Male Orgasmic Disorder – 0–3%
Erectile Disorder – 0–5%
Male Hypoactive Sexual Desire Disorder – 0–3%
Premature Ejaculation – 4–5%
Female Orgasmic Disorder – 7–10%

From Simons & Carey (2001)

*Rates increase significantly with age.

---

more generally. The language we use to describe women and men's sexuality, for example, is full of assumptions about how men and women should behave (Weatherall, 2002). In short, standards for men and women differ: women can be criticized for exercising authority and assertiveness over their sexual relations, because they are deemed too 'masculine', just as men can be negatively evaluated if they exhibit more passive sexual tendencies, because they are deemed too 'feminine'. Even though some may argue we live in a more equal society overall, we must remember that the question of sexual inequality is still fiercely debated (Fausto-Sterling, 2000; Denman, 2004; Attwood, 2005). And issues of inequality can, of course, lead to relationship problems, sexual difficulties and complications, as well as sexual abuse between adults as well as children (Ussher & Baker, 1993).

Relationships and childhood

Becoming sexual with someone and feeling comfortable expressing sexuality with that person or persons can be as much to do with issues of intimacy and trust as well as any issue relating to sexual functioning per se (Tiefer, 2004). Sex is often an intimate act and heavily relational. If we look beyond masturbation, sex takes place with another person or persons and thus involves some type of relationship (although we are not prescribing which relationship). Sexual relationships can be influenced by the important relationships we have had in the past, such as parental bonds, as well as by relationships in the present.

We have already mentioned that child sexual abuse and experiences of sexual trauma more often than not take place in the context of a relationship in which emotional investments are involved (Warner, 2009). That is why some researchers have examined attachment issues for individuals who experience difficulties with sexual functioning more generally. Feeling disempowered by your mother as a child, for example, can lead to difficulties in forming relationships with adult women and has been shown to contribute to the development of erectile difficulties and premature ejaculation in clinical and non-clinical samples (Kinzle, Mangweth, Traweger & Biebel, 1996). Indeed, in one study, family background, as measured by the Biographic Inventory of Diagnosis of Behavioural Disturbance (BIV), was a better predictor of later problems with having sex than was sexual abuse. Growing up in an 'unhappy

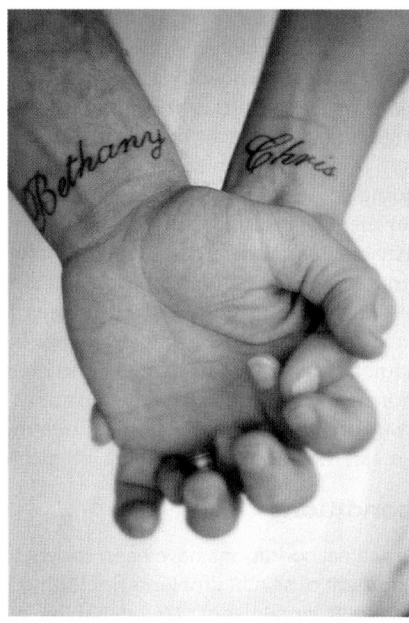

As sex often takes place between people, the role of relationships is important for understanding sexuality

family', therefore, may be as powerful a predictor of later sexual problems than experiences of abuse alone. This was particularly the case for men as opposed to women, although this may be because instances of abuse against male children were reported to be single incidents and less violent than those reported by women.

Life events

What happens to us in our lives plays a vital role in our ability to feel sexually fulfilled. Unemployment, interpersonal conflict and relationship difficulties, as well as infertility, have all been identified as contributory factors to the development and/or maintenance of sexual problems.

Whether we are happy or unhappy in our relationship(s), if we are bored or under-stimulated or if we are faced with a tragedy or trauma in our lives, all these make a great difference to our sexuality. Our childhood, including developmental factors, also impacts greatly on our ability to engage in sex positively (Bancroft, 2003). How open our parents are about sex, whether we were encouraged to feel positive about our bodies, and society's moral codes on sex and sexuality, all contribute to our sense of well-being across time (Levine, 2005). We have already discussed how abusive relationships and traumatic events may impact negatively on sexuality but there are other factors on a list of general life events that must also be considered as contributing to problems. A number of studies, for example, have pointed to the impact of stress and resulting emotional problems on sexuality, including one's willingness to engage in sex, as well as the presence of sexual desire more generally (Laumann et al., 2005). Other issues have been highlighted, such as the link between erectile dysfunction and low sexual desire in men without long-term employment (Johnson, Phelps & Cottler, 2004), due to decreases in self-esteem and feelings of powerlessness (Rosen, 2007). Interpersonal factors also play a very significant role. Relationship difficulties and

disputes, for example, can lead to a significant fall in sexual desire (Brezsnyak & Whisman, 2004). If we think back to Alice and Sajid, it is clear that though interpersonal conflict may not have been the initial cause of the problem (although we cannot know this on the basis of the limited information supplied, and should always pursue this line of enquiry), the result has been a significant increase in tension and disruption to the relationship, leading to feelings of isolation, sexual withdrawal, frustration and emotional distancing. Finally, the inability to conceive has been known to lead to problems with having sex in men but not women, due to an increased pressure to perform and the forced timing of sex, i.e. around ovulation (Monga, Alexandrescu, Katz, Stein & Ganiats, 2002).

Thoughts and feelings

Our mood and the way we think about sex (e.g. as a chore or something exciting) can have a profound effect on our ability to feel sexual (Kaplan, 1974). Being angry with someone, for example, can greatly dampen any sexual desire we might have for that person and may hinder our ability to have sex with them. Being sad can also hamper our ability to feel pleasure or to be motivated to engage intimately with another person. Much of the literature covering the role of emotion in relation to sexual problems has focused on diagnostic categories such as 'depression' and 'anxiety' to measure whether there is any relationship between those conditions and sexual problems. The relationship with sexual problems is well documented in the literature, particularly for individuals already diagnosed with 'mood disorders' (e.g. depression). And yet it is difficult to know precisely the direction of causality. A person's low mood may have resulted in sexual difficulties, or the sexual difficulty itself may have led to a lower mood. A prescribed medication for low mood (e.g. antidepressant medication) could also be a factor.

The relationship between anxiety and sexual difficulty is also less than clear. For example, a study measuring the impact of mild threat on sexual arousal during the viewing of erotica found that the physiological component of anxiety (e.g. sympathetic nervous system functioning), when activated, had a neutral and/or even facilitative effect on sexual arousal in men and women with and without sexual problems (Palace, 1995). A study by Nobre and Pinto-Gouveia (2006) looked at men and women with and without diagnosed sexual dysfunctions, measuring the relationship between emotions ('anxiety'-type emotions and 'depressive'-type emotions) and automatic thoughts that may occur during sexual activity. Emotions were assessed by the Emotional Reactions (ER) subscale, where participants described emotional reactions (worry, sadness, disillusion, fear, guilt, shame, anger, hurt, pleasure, satisfaction) to a list of automatic thoughts (AT subscale) that may occur during sexual activity. Results showed that both men and women with sexual dysfunction had significantly less positive emotional reactions to automatic thoughts during sexual activity. However, negative emotions associated with anxiety were weaker in comparison to emotions relating to sadness, disillusionment and lack of pleasure (depressive-type emotions). In sum, negative emotions per se do not appear to account for sexual difficulties, but specific emotions relating to sadness, disillusionment and a lack of pleasure more generally, may do.

Chemical substances

As well as the range of psychological, social and cultural factors examined so far, it is important to be mindful of chemical influences on sexuality. This can include prescribed medications, including psychiatric medications, as well as legal and illegal substances, such as alcohol, marijuana and cocaine.

Substance use

There is some evidence to suggest that substance abuse plays a role in the development of difficulties with sexual functioning (Schiavi, Stimmel, Mandeli & White, 1995). Although this has been observed in clinical samples (who may be heavier substance users), it is necessary to investigate whether there is also a trend in the general population, in order to form a more representative picture of the role of substance use in the development of sexual problems. As part of the Epidemiological Catchment Area Study (a large community study investigating prevalence rates for mental health problems across the US), 3004 individuals from a variety of ethnic and cultural groups in the district of St. Louis took part in a study measuring the relationship between substance use and 'sexual dysfunction'. It was found that low sexual desire was significantly associated with marijuana and alcohol use; pain during sex was linked to illicit drug use (excluding marijuana), and those using illicit drugs in the population at large experienced inhibited sexual excitement. It can be seen that substance use is positively related to risk for sexual problems, though it is unclear which specific mechanisms are involved.

Prescribed psychiatric medications

Problems with having sex among individuals who take or are given (via depot injection – an injection that is delivered deep into the buttock or leg muscles) psychiatric medication has been widely acknowledged in the psychiatric profession, especially among individuals prescribed traditional (as opposed to atypical) antipsychotic medications and the SSRI antidepressants (Aizenberg, Zemishlany, Dorfman-Etong & Weizman, 1995; Clayton et al., 2002; Baggaley, 2008).

The side-effects of such medications can be a loss of sexual desire, erectile difficulties and lubrication problems. Indeed, problems having sex has been identified as one of the major causes of service users abandoning medication use and seeking alternative forms of help. This is related to the general reduction in quality of life reported by service users. Given that medication is the first line of treatment offered to those in primary health care settings (e.g. General Practitioners) for common mental health problems like 'depression', it is unsurprising that sexual difficulties are far from rare and continue to complicate further the lives of those experiencing other forms of mental distress.

Biological factors

The preceding sections outlined the impact of chemical substances on sexual activity, but a number of biological factors have also been identified in relation to individuals who experience sexual problems. These include the role of sex hormones, vascular disease and neurological impairment. Animal and human data are often combined to improve our understanding of the exact biological mechanisms that contribute to the development of sexual problems.

Furthermore, with the rise of medications such as Viagra™ and Cialis™ for men's sexual problems, a new era of debate has begun to tackle the issue of possible organic causes for sexual problems. **Viagra** is the commercial name for the drug sildenafil, used to treat erectile dysfunction in men and low sexual desire in women. **Cialis** is the commercial name for the drug Tadalafil, used to treat male erectile dysfunction.

The search is now on for an equivalent medication for women, leading some sexologists to lament that sexuality has become over medicalized to suit the profit-making demands of the pharmaceutical companies (Bancroft, 2003). We have already examined the impact of ageing, as well as the contributory role of certain medications and substances. Both ageing and substance/medication use involve biology but there are further biological factors that require examination, including the impact of medical conditions and hormones. Of course, we must always remember that biological treatments do not necessarily mean there is an identifiable biological cause.

Medical conditions

A variety of medical conditions have been shown to play a role in the development of sexual problems, including HIV (Wilson et al., 2010; Cove & Petrak, 2004; Meyer-Bahlburg et al., 1993), Alzheimer's (Zeiss, Davies, Wood & Tinklenberg, 1990), diabetes (El-Rufaie, Bener, Abuzeid & Ali, 1997), irritable bowel and bowel disease (Fass, Fullerton, Naliboff, Hirsh & Mayer, 1998), neurological disorders and heart disease (Stahl, 2001). Many of these conditions increase with age but many are associated with life style and socio-economic status (SES). For example, poorer health and being at higher risk for almost every disease is associated with lower SES (Ilsey & Baker, 1991). But, more specifically, a range of medical conditions have been associated with problems in having sex.

It is now well established that blood flow to the penis can be adversely affected by heart disease or blocked arteries (Stahl, 2001). Cardiovascular disease or CVD (a disease of the heart or blood vessels) has also been shown to lead to endothelial (the cells that line all blood vessels) dysfunction in both men and women. The effects of endothelial dysfunction can lead, for men, to problems getting and maintaining an erection and, for women, problems with arousal and orgasm (Bailey & Hoffman, 2008). Lower urinary tract symptoms can also lead to ejaculation pain and loss and erectile difficulties in men (Rosen, Altwein, Boyle, Kirby & Lukacs, 2003). Finally, diseases such as diabetes and multiple sclerosis are understood to be implicated in damages to the central nervous system leading to problems with arousal and lubrication. However, caution must be applied to interpreting a straightforwardly causal relationship between medical conditions and sexual problems. Other psychological and social factors may impact on the individual's response to their medical condition, as well as the response of their partner. For example, anxiety associated with changes to one's sexual responses may lead to avoidance and withdrawal. The quality of the overall relationship may also be put to the test when there is a change in an individual's ability to have or enjoy sex to the extent they had previously. A study with diabetic women and a group of controls found that although there were higher levels of lubrication difficulty in the group with diabetes, the most significant predictors for sexual problems in both groups was marital conflict and low mood (Enzlin et al., 2002).

Hormones

Certain hormones play a significant role in levels of desire, arousal and a general ability to have sex (e.g. getting and maintaining an erection) (Regan, 1999). Three main hormones (there are more) have been associated with sexuality and the development of physical gender characteristics and sexual activity: testosterone (an androgen), oestrogen and prolactin. All three are present in both men and women, although women produce more oestrogen (especially around ovulation) and men much greater levels of testosterone. **Testosterone** is found in both sexes but is often described as a male sex hormone; it is secreted by the testes and involved in the production of male sex characteristics such as enlargement of the testes and the growth of facial hair. **Oestrogen** is a sex hormone found in both sexes but is more commonly described as a female sex hormone. It is secreted by the ovaries and is responsible for the regulation of the reproductive cycle in women and the generation of typical female sexual characteristics. **Prolactin** is a hormone involved in the regulation of lactation.

Some human and animal studies suggest that testosterone is associated with higher levels and frequency of sexual arousal, behaviour and orgasm, although many other studies have failed to replicate these findings (Baumeister, Catanese & Vohs, 2001). There has been considerable debate in this area with no clear conclusions. For example, although higher levels of testosterone are found in men more generally, within-gender variation has yet to be fully explored. Furthermore, testosterone levels are poorly correlated with sexual interest and drive when they are within the average range. Sex drive is much more likely to be affected by external stimuli (sights, sound and touch) than by variations in sex hormones, except in extreme cases.

Given the complexity of hormones and their role in sexual desires, arousal and activity, what role, if any, do they play in sexual difficulties?

Oestrogens are important in maintaining the condition of the vaginal lining and its elasticity, and in producing naturally-occurring vaginal lubrication. Low levels of oestrogen can, therefore, negatively affect the body's ability to do this. In women, drops in oestrogen (and to a lesser extent testosterone) generally occur around menopause, with around a quarter of women reporting a reduction in sexual desire and a lack of vaginal lubrication, which is why some women choose to take a hormone replacement. However, it is important to note that naturally-occurring lubrication can always be replaced by external (manufactured or natural) lubrication (of which there are many brands on the market). For example, external lubricants can be used for vaginal and anal sex, as well as by trans women having vaginal sex.

In men, oestrogens have no known consistent function. An unusually high level, however, may reduce sexual appetite, cause erectile difficulties, produce some breast enlargement, and result in the loss of body hair, with potential negative effects on self-esteem and body image. **Body image** refers to an individual's perception of their body shape and size and the sexual attractiveness of their own body.

Certain medications can alter levels of oestrogen (e.g. certain cancer medications), as can some surgical procedures such as hysterectomy and ovariectomy.

Large deficiencies of testosterone may cause a drop in sexual desire, and excessive testosterone may heighten sexual interest in both sexes (Regan, 1999). In men, too little testosterone may cause difficulty obtaining or maintaining erections. Given that testosterone levels decrease with age in men,

it is not surprising that the rates for problems with having and maintaining an erection increase. Finally, high levels of prolactin have been linked to erectile problems. Interestingly, antipsychotic medication raises levels of prolactin, which could be why large numbers of men taking this medication have difficulties developing and maintaining an erection (Gutierrez, Glen & Stimmel, 1999).

Lifelines, plasticity and specificity

Experiences of sexual problems, like other forms of distress, demonstrate a large degree of variation across an individual's life span, making clear the existence of both plasticity and specificity. As we have outlined in the chapter on causal processes, this makes the task of assigning clear causal markers difficult, a challenge that also applies to an account of plasticity and specificity. The difficulty is a lack of research in this area, as well as the continual problem of co-morbidity, making it difficult for sexual problems to be examined empirically as entirely distinct from other forms of identified (and diagnosed) problems. And yet, as we have already discussed, sexual problems can occur as a result of multiple factors that can change and transform themselves across the life span, including medical complaints, age-specific problems and the impact of early negative experiences.

Very few studies have found evidence for a genetic influence upon people who experience sexual difficulties. The few studies that have been conducted have adopted behavioural-genetic approaches and often rely upon survey techniques, which are subject to the problems of over-estimation found more generally in this type of research. The very few genetic studies that do exist, however, have found moderate estimates of heritability for orgasmic responses among female twin samples, using questionnaire measures (Dunn et al., 2005; Dawood et al., 2005). And yet, orgasm responses increased significantly when orgasm was calculated via masturbation, as opposed to penetration alone, and it must be noted that these were not adoption studies. To date, much of the research is speculative, and authors of a recent review (Burri, Cherkas & Spector, 2009) suggest that whilst there are avenues of possibility for genetic research on sexual problems, we should exercise caution in looking to genetic causes alone, given the speculative nature of much of the research and the small sample sizes to date. Furthermore, they argue that sexual problems are likely to have multiple causes, as opposed to some inherited tendency for internal dysfunction. This of course ties into the extent to which early experiences play a role in the development of sexual problems, which can have a lasting effect on physiological and psychological functioning. Given that child sexual abuse is not uncommon in the life histories of women, it is vital that these factors are taken into account (Leonard & Follette, 2002).

The literature on the link between early childhood experiences and adult sexual difficulties is vast. Many such studies point to the existence of sexual abuse in the histories of women and men with current sexual difficulties, though the relationship between child sexual abuse experiences and male sexual difficulties is less clear (Sarwer, Crawford & Durlak, 1997).

In a recent US community sample of over 3000 women, childhood emotional, physical and sexual abuse was associated with sexual dysfunction relating to pain and overall satisfaction, but not overall sexual activity (Lutfey et al., 2008). Other studies have demonstrated similar findings relating to sexual difficulties, although it is necessary to make clear that not everyone with a history of sexual abuse experiences difficulty in having sex. One of the avenues for making a more refined judgment of the role of early sexual experiences has been discussed in a recent review of the link between how people cope with sexual abuse, the more general beliefs they have about sex and their internal sexual schemas. For example, Rellini and Meston (2011) found that sexual function and satisfaction in a group of women who had experienced childhood sexual abuse was partially mediated by negative affect preceding sexual stimuli. Furthermore, if women had sexual schemas (thoughts about themselves) that were more conservative or embarrassed and less open or direct about sex, this partially explained their negative reaction towards sexual stimuli. In other words, a history of childhood sexual abuse itself could not account for low sexual satisfaction necessarily; it had to be accompanied by particular sexual schemas and negative emotions. This is an important point about how we read early childhood experiences, as a history of sexual abuse alone cannot provide a complete account of later sexual/emotional difficulties. For example, we must bear in mind that it is normal for other forms of emotional abuse to co-occur with sexual abuse. In a study by Kessler, Davis and Kendler (1997), approximately 85% of individuals reported other forms of early adverse experiences alongside sexual abuse, such as emotional and physical abuse as well as neglect. Moreover, individuals who have had early negative sexual experiences are more likely to encounter further abuses in adolescence and adulthood (Classen, Palesh & Aggarwarl, 2005), making it likely that an engagement across the life span involving multiple factors is necessary to fully understand the consequences of negative early experiences and their potential impact on sexuality and mental health more generally.

Gender is a further consideration in the argument for a more specific and lifespan perspective on sexuality. Although gender differences appear to play a role in the development of sexual difficulties, as we have seen, they do not necessarily point to any genetic contribution, but may say more about the cultural contexts where sexuality is lived out. In relation to early childhood sexual experiences, it appears that a history of child sexual abuse has different effects (in general) for men and women. For example, Sarwer, Crawford and Durlak (1997) found that men with histories of child sexual abuse did not necessarily experience sexual difficulties in the long term, in comparison to women (Rind et al., 1998). However, they caution against a reading of the data that would support biological differences between men and women and point to the specific circumstances and socio-cultural conditions under which abuse takes places for men and women. For example, women are more likely to experience multiple episodes of abuse, potentially leading to long-term sexual problems. Furthermore, an underreporting by men, as a result of shame for not being adequately masculine, may result in more general psychological difficulties, rather than specific difficulties with sexuality. In line with Paris's (1997) suggestion that men may be more prone to externalizing their problems, as opposed to internalizing them, men's emotional difficulties as a result of adverse early experiences may manifest themselves in ways other than sexual problems. However, there is evidence to suggest that men are just as likely to experience difficulty in being intimate with another person as a result of negative early experiences with sex (Lisak, 1994). In conclusion, gender may mediate the effects of negative early sexual experience on adult sexuality, but this does not mean that these early experiences do not impact on general mental health. We must, though, exercise caution in assuming that all experiences of child sexual abuse will lead to long-term difficulties.

As with all experiences, it is important to be aware of the various ways in which individuals cope with adverse experiences and how such coping strategies impact on sexuality and mental health more generally. Such coping strategies can include withdrawal, avoidance, denial and dissociation, which in the short term may be beneficial (e.g. they lower heart rate) but in the long term, perhaps less so. Some researchers have begun to look at how the reactions and coping strategies adopted by individuals who have experienced early sexual abuse can impact on their long-term mental health. For example, children experiencing abuse or neglect may learn to dissociate from their present circumstances (i.e. they may psychologically disengage their mind from the immediate event and take their mind elsewhere): a strategy that has initial beneficial effects, such as decreasing physiological arousal and imagining a better place. In the long term, however, such coping strategies may become habitual, automatic and hence uncontrollable to some extent, so that the person has difficulties in reading their own emotions and that of others. This may have a biological correlate, as researchers in neurobiology have found that dissociation, depending on the age of the child, as well as the frequency and severity of abusive episodes, can lead to alterations in brain structure – especially maturation of the hippocampus and limbic system, affecting memory and threat perception – and changes in neuroendocrine functioning (Vander Kolk, 2003). Furthermore, chronic stress responses as a result of abuse can lead to a variety of long-term alterations in biological functioning, including cortisol-hypersecretion and excessive glucocorticoid levels (known to be involved in regulating stress responses and mood) (Weber & Reynolds, 2004).

However, it must be noted that these physiological responses are both mediated by a whole host of psychological and social factors. Van der Kolk (2003) argues that physiological arousal and emotional response, for example, will be moderated by the quality of parental-child attachments, as well as the response of the parent (if they are aware of the abuse) to the child's experience. The parent's response (and the child's internalization of this) will thus impact on the child's ways of coping in the present situation, as well as providing a model for interpreting the world (including their social relationships) in the future. In other words, social relationships, especially the levels of attachment experienced by the child, will mediate the long-term impact of adverse experiences. In the absence of adequate parental guidance, children may rely on their own strategies of coping, which may be disorganized and chaotic, resulting in long-term biological, psychological and social disruption that may persist across the lifespan as they continue to encounter new intimate and social relationships more generally. This has important implications for sexuality and the development of relationships, as in both physiological and psychological terms. If an individual is set up to anticipate threat or to experience a stress response even in the absence of danger, such anticipation may impact on their ability to engage in sexual activity and intimate relationships, or relax if they do.

The problem with diagnosis

According to the DSM, a diagnosis of 'sexual dysfunction' should only be administered when other organic causes are ruled out, or if the individual has already received another major mental health diagnosis. For example, if an individual has been diagnosed with 'depression' and they have sexual problems, they cannot also be diagnosed with a sexual dysfunction. It is assumed that the sexual problem is a by-product or 'symptom' of the depression, rather than a 'disorder' in its own right. Furthermore, we have already noted that medical treatments for depression can lead to sexual problems, so the sexual problem is seen to be a by-product of the major mental health problem. Here, the limitations of diagnostic practices become clear. A person may have sexual problems and be miserable because of unresolved long-term anxieties: about their relationships, their feelings of self-worth or their place in the social world. Such underlying feelings can have effects on several areas of life, leading to difficulties with being able to trust people, or being intimate and hence able to share sexual experiences with another person. These emotional issues arguably become lost if carved up into different diagnostic categories, and if a search for a treatment to tackle symptoms of a discrete disorder becomes the focus. Many have criticized this approach in relation to the 'sexual dysfunctions', calling for their removal from the DSM (e.g. Karasic & Drescher, 2007). Furthermore, many have argued that dysfunctions are often still defined according to heterosexual 'norms' and the ultimate goal of engaging in penetration. For example, even though there is a premature orgasm category for men, there is no equivalent for women (as penetration can still go ahead even if women do orgasm, or in situations where this is not the goal of the sexual encounter).

Summary

There is no single explanation for why people experience difficulties having sex. Sexual problems appear to be relatively common in the general population and not everyone experiences distress as a result of them. Nevertheless, when an individual becomes distressed by being unable to have or enjoy sex, a variety of psychological, cultural, social (interpersonal and at a wide societal level) and biological factors must be considered. Here we have discussed a range of factors, including culture, age, life events, trauma and abuse, medication and other biological risk factors. Whatever the cause might be, it is important to remind ourselves that although one person may start out with 'the sexual problem', we cannot assume that the origins of the problem lie in that individual only. The present context may have contributed to the problem, and the solution might be to treat the individual whilst also exploring their relationship dynamics and social circumstances more generally. Even though a problem may begin with one individual, the origin of the problem may be far from individual and may have begun in early relationships, bad sexual experiences and/or abuse, or sex-negative cultural norms. In other words, *the personal is often interpersonal* and cultural.

If we think back to Alice, we might be tempted to think that her difficulty in having penetrative sex fits neatly into a diagnostic category (vaginismus), and that the best way forward would be to treat her individually, with a view to finding out why she had developed this problem in the first place. However, a more comprehensive investigation would look to the historical, interpersonal and social-cultural factors that provide a clue to all aspects of her life. Both Alice and Andrew would therefore need to be included in the examination, not just Alice. The quality of Alice and Andrew's communication

skills, whether the frustration and distress resulting from the couple's inability to have penetrative sex is leading to further unhappiness, withdrawal and overall fear of intimacy in the couple and their understanding of femininity and masculinity within the wider culture they are part of, would all be under investigation. This would be just as applicable to Sajid. Even though stress (life events) may have precipitated Sajid's problems in developing an erection, the tension and dispute between Simon and Sajid as a result of this leads to further emotional conflict and withdrawal. As well as asking questions about Sajid, involving his age and life style (e.g. work commitments), we may also ask why the problem developed at that particular time. If the problem started when his sister gave birth to her first child, we may wish to explore with Sajid whether any unresolved issues to do with family remain.

In sum, there are many questions we would need to ask before arriving at an explanation for an individual's sexual difficulties; we might even question whether a causal explanation is achievable or even desirable (many therapists argue it is how a client views the situation in the *here and now* that is important, not any definitive idea about the cause of the problem). Even if we have a good idea why a problem originally occurred, we may have to also deal with how it is being maintained or made worse by looking at how other people respond.

Interventions for people who have problems having sex

Over the past 90 years, significant changes to the treatment for individuals experiencing problems with having sex have occurred. At the beginning of the 20th century, psychoanalytic perspectives concentrated on revealing the underlying conflicts connected with sexual repression, which did seem to address a general European unease with sexuality (Weeks, 1985). However, as cultural values shifted more towards liberalism (although this is not entirely straightforward, see Hawkes, 1996), especially during the 1960s and 1970s in Europe and the United States, views of sexual difficulties shifted once more to a concern with educating people about their bodies and providing direct and practical/behavioural solutions to their sexual problems (Leiblum & Rose, 2000). The work of Masters and Johnson in their influential text *Human Sexual Inadequacy* (1966, 1970) encouraged therapists to identify practical solutions to specific sexual difficulties based on direct observation of physiological responses. This is why the practice of '**sex therapy**' in Europe and the US has become an independent branch of therapy, specifically designed to directly address sexual and relationship issues, using a variety of psychological, medical, social and behavioural approaches (Annon, 1974; Leiblum & Rose, 2000; SARP-ED, 2006; SARP-vaginismus, 2006; Kleinplatz, 1998, 2003, 2004). **Sex therapists** are therapists who predominantly treat people's difficulties with having sex. In the UK, the main advisory body for sexual and relationship therapists is the College of Sexual and Relationship Therapists (COSRT) (formerly known as the British Association for Sexual and Relationship Therapy [BASRT]). **College of Sexual and Relationship Therapists [COSRT]** is a UK charity for sexual and relationship therapy.

The focus of such organizations was at one time the preservation of 'marriage', and indeed many therapists referred to themselves as marriage counsellors. In recent years, however, BASRT/COSRT changed its policies and practices to include much broader views on sexuality that include minority sexual groups and those in non-monogamous relationships. This is largely due to a growing number of LGBT activists, working as therapists, who have argued strongly that many of the ideas underpinning sex therapy have been based on traditional heterosexual views of relationships and sexuality, which are not only biased against gay men, lesbians, bisexuals and transgendered individuals, but also sustain unequal gender relations (Davies & Neal, 1996).

Although attitudes towards sex have become more liberal in Western Europe and some areas of the US, some have argued that this has not led to a more psychological view of sexuality, but a more medicalized one (Tiefer, 2001; 2006; Braun, 2005; Croissant, 2006). For example, over the past ten years the medical model of sexual problems has become the main way in which to treat sexual problems (Winton, 2001), following the success of drug treatments like Viagra for specific difficulties such as erectile dysfunction. **Impotence**, or **male erectile dysfunction** refers to the inability to develop or maintain an erection.

BOX 10.7
Women's experiences of sexual problems

In the very few studies of women's experiences of sexual problems, a number of significant issues arise. For example, in an in-depth qualitative study of British women, Bellamy (2008) found that although the women (largely heterosexual) in his study were often blamed for any sexual difficulty in their relationships, the women cited their partner's sexual incompetence and unrealistic demands as the main cause of their own inability to orgasm or their experiences of pain during intercourse. Furthermore, women's 'inability' to reach orgasm in the context of penetrative sex (a very common occurrence amongst heterosexual women – see Hite, 1976) was not distressing to them *but* caused significant anxiety for their partner (see also Nicolson & Burr, 2003). Bellamy's findings concur with the *New View of Women's Sexual Problems* outlined in Kaschak and Tiefer's work, stressing the importance of relational factors and wider socio-cultural expectations for men and women's sexual desire and behaviour generally, in making sense of sexual problems. A further test of the validity of the *new view* was further demonstrated by Nicholls (2008). In a questionnaire study comprising 49 women's own accounts of sexual difficulty, only 15% of women's sexual difficulties were reported in psychological or medical terms; 65% were relational and 20% contextual/external, with only 8% individual/ psychological (8%) or medical (7%) factors described. This data further supports the idea that to understand sexual problems, a more relational model of women's sexual difficulties is required, highlighting once again the limitations of a medical/diagnostic model that concentrates on individual factors only.

The 21st century has witnessed many new drug and hormone treatments, with increasing numbers of treatments purchased via the internet (e.g. sexual performance enhancing drugs such as Viagra), without any clinical intervention or research investigating the long-term effects of these drugs. This has, of course, led to significant concerns over individuals exposing themselves to health risks, especially older individuals with underlying health problems. Furthermore, individuals wishing to transfer or modify their gender have also turned to hormone-altering drugs, without any clinical intervention whatsoever (Johnson, 2007).

The basic structure of sex therapy[7]

Sex therapy involves a number of stages designed to identify specific sexual problems, usually ones that correspond to a sexual dysfunction listed in the DSM.

A sex therapist can operate from a range of perspectives, including psychiatric, systemic, psychodynamic, cognitive–behaviour, existential and humanistic. It is self-evident that

---

7 We are indebted to Dr. Meg Barker, a committee member of COSRT, for providing valuable information on the practice of sex therapy, as well as information relating to COSRT.

the therapist's prior expertise will affect the range of treatments they offer.

An important aspect of this type of therapy is the significance attached to relationship dynamics. Clients will often be seen as a couple, the aim being to increase sexual and communication skills between partners. In the main, sex therapy operates through a number of interlinking elements.

1 *Assessment* – In order to identify a specific sexual or relationship difficulty, the client must first of all be assessed. An assessment usually occurs in the first or second session when the client's life history, including their medical history, is taken. A medical examination can also accompany the verbal assessment, but according to COSRT guidelines, this is not compulsory.

2 *Relational dynamics* – Sexual problems often arise as a result of poor communication or deeper relational conflict. One partner may be more controlling, or there may be significant cultural differences leading to sexual tension; one partner may have lost interest in the other: a common problem. Whatever the conflict, the therapist works closely with the couple to identify better ways for them to communicate and work together as equals.

3 *Organic causes* – One of the advantages of carrying out a medical examination before beginning therapy is that organic causes may be identified. Not always –if the problem is 'psycho-somatic'– but sometimes, underlying health problems such as diabetes or high blood pressure contribute to an individual's ability to have sex, so a course of drug treatment may be beneficial. Furthermore, psychiatric medication can sometimes contribute to the onset of sexual dysfunction (Miller, 1997; Knegtering, Blijd & Boks, 1999).

4 *Communication and sexual skills* – A problem may arise when an individual or a couple is unaware of some of the basics of human anatomy. Informing clients about what the body can and cannot do, as well presenting them with a full sexual menu, is vital for increasing confidence and enabling better communication. If a woman is experiencing difficulties with penetrative sex because her partner is neglecting to provide her with pleasure prior to penetration, then some obvious difficulties regarding vaginal dilation and lubrication and, most importantly, enjoyment may occur. This ties in with improving communication more generally; the couple will be encouraged to be more open about their desires and to communicate what they find pleasurable as well as what they do not. If there are communication problems, any underlying tensions are less likely to be resolved, making sex more unlikely and/or problematic.

5 *Behavioural techniques* – A wide range of behavioural techniques are now used to increase sexual pleasure. These include relaxation techniques, as well as some of the traditional behavioural interventions, such as systematic desensitization. In the case of the latter technique, a person who is fearful of some aspect of a sexual encounter can be gradually introduced to it at a pace that will not induce anxiety. A man who encounters premature ejaculation may benefit from gradually learning to respond to sexual cues more slowly. Another technique used as homework is often referred to as *sensate focus*, in which couples are encouraged to engage in massage and caressing, but without direct genital contact. This technique is used by therapists to increase eroticism within sexual encounters

and to take away the pressure of aiming for orgasm, as well as to increase each partner's knowledge of their partner's experiences of arousal and pleasure. **Sensate focus** is a therapeutic technique developed by sexologists Masters and Johnson in couples therapy. Partners are instructed to sensually touch each other without touching the genitals, progressing to full sexual activity. The aim is to gradually reduce anxiety about sex.

6 *Tackling beliefs* – Because sex is such a private affair, many people gain knowledge of sex through the media and culture. The media can transmit scientific information well, but it can also reinforce myths and prejudices, such as 'women should not initiate sex' or that 'men should always be ready for sex'. If a client holds beliefs that are unhelpful or harmful to themselves or others, the therapist will explore these beliefs and encourage more helpful and informed ones.

Interventions

In this section, we explore a variety of psychological interventions used for both couples and individuals, concentrating mainly on techniques used in sex therapy. The most common approach within sex therapy is cognitive–behaviour therapy, where an individual or a couple's way of thinking or behaving is linked to the problem and worked with closely. Given that many see therapists as a couple, some therapists also refer to their approach as cognitive-interpersonal, to make clear the dynamic and relational nature of sexual difficulties. As well as interventions facilitated by a qualified therapist, there are also a number of self-help texts available to individuals experiencing difficulties, a form of therapy often referred to as **biblio-therapy**.

A number of cognitive–behavioural techniques are used by therapists to increase desire and arousal, reduce anxiety and increase sexual skills. These include 1. systematic desensitization 2. start/stop squeeze techniques 3. reinforcement and 4. sensate focus. These techniques are often combined with relaxation techniques and communication skills training. They can also be used in combination with approaches that encourage clients to explore the way they think about sex, their partner or being in a relationship more generally (which can include gender roles or the power dynamics of the relationship). If a sexual or relationship issue is being explored as part of **couples therapy**, then the feelings between the couple are explicitly explored. Couples therapy can also be referred to as a systems approach.

1 *Systematic desensitization* – This is a commonly used behavioural technique for problems experienced by women who are unable to engage in vaginal penetration, as well as men experiencing premature ejaculation. The idea is to gradually reduce an individual's anxiety over time by exposing them to the situation whilst they are relaxed and in control. In the case of women who experience difficulty with penetration, a vaginal dilator or other object, such as candles or fingers, are inserted gradually into the vagina while the woman relaxes. She may begin by inserting smaller objects and then increase the size steadily until she has the equivalent of a fully erect penis. Initially the woman would do this alone until she is ready to involve her partner. This treatment is reported to be effective in 63–100% of cases (Kleinplatz, 1998).

2 *Start/stop squeeze techniques* – These are the standard techniques used to tackle premature ejaculation. To begin with, the man is stimulated manually or orally (by himself or his partner) until he is close to orgasm. He then stops or instructs his partner to stop until the pre-orgasm feeling disappears. This is then repeated daily for up to half an hour. The process is then repeated during genital contact, using slow, then faster, movements. The squeeze technique involves the partner firmly squeezing the head or base of the penis just prior to ejaculation. This helps to reduce the erection and prevent ejaculation, although it may take a few sessions to achieve this. After a number of sessions, the couple can attempt this during sexual intercourse, where the man lies on his back and his partner withdraws every few minutes to squeeze. After a while, the couple can repeat this and gradually increase the rate of thrusting.

3 *Reinforcement and direct masturbation* – This can also be referred to as directed masturbation training (Heiman, 2002). A person experiencing difficulties with becoming aroused or someone with low levels of desire may find it useful to combine erotic thoughts and fantasies with masturbation. Once orgasm has been achieved using masturbation (by themselves and/or with a partner), a client may then move on to other forms of sex with a partner, using the same combination of erotic thoughts and fantasies with the sexual act.

4 *Sensate focus* – Masters and Johnson developed a series of exercises to deal with issues relating to performance anxiety and to increase knowledge of the individual's own and their partner's erotic preferences and zones of pleasure, without the pressure of genital contact and orgasm. The goal of sensate focus is to heighten sexual sensation (arousal and pleasure through massage and touch) rather than sexual performance (physiological responses such as orgasm, erection or lubrication) (Wincze & Carey, 2001). The couple will be instructed to suspend all genital contact in order to concentrate on non-genital touching and/or massage, with the aim of focusing on the pleasure of touch, rather than any sexual end-state such as orgasm. Over time, the couple should become highly aware of the non-genital areas on the body that can give and receive pleasure. The couple will also be encouraged to communicate what they enjoyed about the experience. Over time, often weeks but sometimes months, the couple may be able to move onto a gradual touching of the genitals and then to other forms of sex, including oral, vaginal or anal sex.

Developing communication and sexual skills

Although in popular culture sex is meant to 'just happen' between people, what we like and don't like is actually quite difficult to communicate, especially if we do not wish to upset, offend or even provoke anger in a partner. In other words, if a person is unhappy with the quality of the sex they experience, they may blame themselves for the problem or decide to say nothing, through fear that the relationship will come under threat (Litvinoff, 1992). It may also lead to individuals faking pleasure, which has been well documented in relation to women and orgasm (Potts, 2000, 2002). However, increasing explicit communication about what an individual likes and dislikes has been successful in treating sexual problems (Rose, Leiblum & Spector, 1994). Furthermore, using diaries and homework assignments to document sexual techniques, or using video and film material to directly demonstrate sexual techniques, can be used as additional ways to increase the person's knowledge of sex, which may help to develop sexual skills as well as communication between partners (Kaplan, 1974; Crowe & Ridley, 2000). It is vital, however, to consider the cultural basis of sex when exploring issues relating to skills and communication. Before entering therapy, and while therapy is taking place, the couple and indeed the therapist are bound by how the partners see each other, what expectations there are on men and women to have sex in a particular way (especially given that penetrative sex is still seen to be the only 'real sex' in many cultures), and the roles that exist within a relationship (Jankowiak, 2008). For example, although a heterosexual couple may present with a sexual or relationship problem on the basis that the woman has 'lost interest' in sex, we may discover further into the therapy that she is in fact resistant to sex, not because she has lost interest in it, but because she is angry that her partner maintains a traditional masculine role (where he believes it is his right to have sex) within the relationship and refuses to help her deal with child-care issues and housework. His lack of support and his demands, are issues requiring communication and resolve, not the problem with sex per se (Kleinplatz, 2001, 2003). Moreover, this 'problem' is not an unusual one based on the specific dynamic of this relationship only, but part of how relationships are organized more widely and endorsed by cultural conventions (i.e. where women are often more responsible for child care).

Medical treatments

Prior to 1983, difficulties in developing and maintaining an erection were regarded as psychological. This view was famously overturned at a urology conference, when one of the well respected urologists, Dr. Brindley, dropped his trousers to reveal a drug induced erection (using another drug called phentolamine, which is a general smooth-muscle relaxant that increases blood flow). The problem with phentolamine was that it does not specifically operate on the penis, but causes all the muscles in the man's body to relax. What was needed was a drug that would act directly on the smooth muscles in the penis: that drug was released onto the market in the late 1990s, with the commercial name of *Viagra*.

The use of medication for men having difficulties in developing and maintaining an erection has increased dramatically since 1998, when Viagra (clinical name, sildenafil) was introduced into clinical settings. Viagra is taken as a pill, rather than as an injection, making it more user-friendly. Furthermore, it can only induce an erection when the man is already sexually aroused (as it relies on the brain sending messages to the penis indicating arousal and thus claims to be able to incorporate the psychological dimension of arousal). Within a relatively short space of time, the drug has become available online: the consumer receives no medical check-up and may not be experiencing any identifiable sexual problem. A drug originally designed to treat erectile dysfunction or 'impotence', it is now also used as a recreational drug, to increase sexual intensity, performance and stamina (Grace, Potts, Gavey & Vares, 2006; Tiefer, 2006).

The majority of Viagra users are men; some women have been known to experiment with the drug to increase blood flow to the vagina and thus enhance sexual pleasure, though there is no systematic evidence that this works (Potts, 2005). One major criticism of the widespread use of Viagra is that it leads to an over-emphasis on biological functioning in accounting for sexual problems and sexuality more generally (Marshall, 2002). As we have seen, sexual problems are often relationship problems, and fixing an erection may fulfil only one of the partners, and even then, only temporarily. Moreover, despite the zeal with which Viagra is prescribed (currently around 25 million worldwide are using the drug), clinical reports indicate success rates of only 16 to 44% (Bach, Wincze & Barlow, 2001).

Annie Potts, a social psychologist, has carried out in-depth qualitative work examining the experiences of men and women who have had Viagra introduced into their sexual lives. Although some participants were positive about the effects of the drug, many more raised concerns over the quality of the sex they experienced when the drug was used. Although men taking the drug could successfully maintain an erection, their female partners reported that other sexual contact besides penetration had virtually disappeared, and the ultimate goal had become penile vaginal penetration, which for them was unsatisfactory (Potts, 2002; Vares & Braun, 2002).

It is worth noting again that many psychiatric medications can cause sexual problems, including erectile difficulty and lack of arousal. Some practitioners have prescribed Viagra or Cialis to counteract the effects of existing psychiatric medication, making the picture more complex still. Some authors have argued that medications for sexual problems induced by psychiatric medication are treating an **iatrogenic problem**: a problem created by the treatment itself. Greater care should be taken when assessing the benefits and limitations of medications that lead to sexual problems, as well as the dose levels.

Summary of treatments and interventions

This section has covered a number of treatments available for people who encounter problems with sex. The person is always assessed first in order to establish whether there is a medical or psychological basis for treatment (or both) and then treated either as an individual or, more often, with their partner. A variety of behavioural techniques are available that both partners can try, as well as a range of interpersonal activities to increase sexual skills and communication between partners. In recent years, a number of medical treatments have been developed for use with men who have erectile problems or for both men and women who have hormonal imbalances.

Confusing social 'deviance' with mental disorder?

Robin is a 43-year-old heterosexual man who has been married for over 20 years. He has three children, two girls and one boy, aged between six and fourteen. In every area of life, he is a well functioning and socially skilled individual who has a large group of friends and an active social life. Despite his outward appearances of 'respectability', Robin frequently engages in sexually masochistic practices with others (some familiar, others less so) at a specialist club. For example, he gains sexual arousal from being beaten with a stick and bound with chains. Although there is an element of

humiliation involved, Robin finds this exciting and sexually gratifying. After a number of months, Robin begins to find his sexual fantasies leaning more towards masochism, rather than to 'regular' sex with his wife. He would like his wife to share with him in his activities but fears she will reject him if he discloses this desire to her. His thoughts and behaviours are also leading to a significant level of distress because Robin and his wife are supposedly monogamous. He seeks advice from a counsellor, because of the distress his thoughts and behaviour cause him.

One of the questions we will consider in this section is whether Robin's behaviour is in itself problematic, or becomes problematic because of its social consequences: the potential reaction of his wife and the perceptions of society more generally. Robin's behaviour could be diagnosed as a paraphilia (in particular, sexual masochism), because not only is the behaviour deemed unusual, but significantly, it is causing distress.

Generally, issues relating to attraction or arousal from 'unusual' stimuli are treated in texts on mental health and abnormal psychology as clear examples of mental disorder, but we will be tackling these issues rather differently. Instead of providing a standard discussion of the causes of behaviours deemed sexually problematic, we will make clear the current controversies surrounding the labelling of them as mental disorders. In other words, rather than attempting to resolve those controversies once and for all, we are inviting further thought and discussion relating to their status as mental disorders. At the same time, we will also examine issues relating to attraction or arousal from non-consenting others, though from a standpoint that emphasizes harm and questions their status as mental disorders.

Variation in sexual arousal

The list of attractions to so-called 'fetish' and 'unusual' objects seems endless. On reading popular as well as psychiatric/psychological literature, we learn that it is possible to be sexually attracted to a broad range of objects and activities, from shoes, to eating sushi from a (usually) naked woman's body – Nyotaimori. In the main, men have been shown to engage in more varied sexual acts than women. Some researchers have linked this to greater evidence of hypersexuality among men, leading to greater sexual exploration and thrill-seeking (Kafka, 1997). However, we must exercise caution in reaching the conclusion that women are inherently less sexual or less adventurous, given the historical restrictions placed on women's sexuality more generally.

It is also necessary to point out that the majority of individuals who engage in such behaviour are NOT distressed by their activities and do not necessarily experience general mental health problems. Examining the social histories of people who regularly participate in Bondage-Domination-Sadism-Masochism (BDSM), we find that such behaviours are carried out in the community, often without any intervention by mental health professionals (Langdridge and Barker, 2007). One has to ask 'why do such behaviours continue to be deemed evidence of mental disorder?' This is a question with no straightforward answer.

In recent years, the DSM has made some concession by shifting its definition of 'unusual' sexual behaviours from 'sexual

What is clinically described as 'sexual disorders' can often reflect criminal and legal definitions

deviations' to the supposedly more neutral term of 'paraphilias' (meaning 'to one side of love') coined by the sexologist John Money[8] (paraphilia means powerful and persistent sexual interest other than in copulatory or precopulatory behaviour with consenting adult human partners – given this definition, oral sex and mutual masturbation could be included!).

Yet the question remains as to whether or not such activities simply form the basis of broad and varied expressions of human sexuality (despite moral and social prohibitions), or whether they meet the criteria for an actual mental disorder. A recent survey of 1915 men in Germany published in the Journal of Sexual Medicine found paraphilia-type sexual arousal in over 60% of men, with only a very small (1.7%) proportion of men finding these arousal patterns distressing (Ahlers et al., 2011). Although many academics and practitioners in the field of psychiatry have argued that the paraphilias constitute a distinct mental disorder (one that is distinct from other forms of distress), there are others who have questioned the empirical and scientific basis of this judgment.

Problems with diagnosis

In 2007, a book including a range of perspectives on gender and sexuality diagnoses was published (Karasic & Drescher, 2007). Its authors included sex therapists, psychiatrists, social workers and psychotherapists, offering an academic perspective on some of the continuing problems with diagnostic practice relating to sexual behaviours. One of the main issues raised in the volume was whether the judgments informing diagnoses of sexual disorders were based on social or political perspectives, as opposed to scientific classifications of individual internal dysfunction (see also Marshall, 1997). A major complaint was that sexual and gender diagnoses are value-laden and based on a **deviance model (criminal act)**, as opposed to empirical evidence of a discrete psychological disorder.

_____
8   Like many sexologists, John Money's contribution to the understanding of sex and gender is noted, though his work has also attracted considerable controversy, as some authors have argued he promotes the idea that people who are attracted to unusual objects or practices are by definition 'disordered'.

Impairment or social judgment?

The DSM clearly states that neither deviant behaviour (e.g. political, religious, or sexual) nor conflicts that are primarily between the individual and society are mental disorders, unless the deviance or conflict is a 'symptom of a dysfunction in the individual' (2000, p. xxxi). Two eminent writers in this field, the sexologist and physician Charles Moser and sex therapist Peggy Kleinplatz (2005) have argued strongly for the removal of the paraphilias from the forthcoming DSM-5 on the basis that their inclusion was based on flawed logic, inconsistent definitions of 'dysfunction' and a general lack of empirical evidence that would lend support to the idea that paraphiliac behaviour was a clear-cut sign of 'internal dysfunction' (a requirement for inclusion in the DSM). The first argument they discuss relates to the DSM's statement that people diagnosed with paraphilias show an impairment in 'normal' sexual relating (e.g. to another adult). Yet Moser and Kleinplatz (2005) argue that there is no empirical evidence for this statement: individuals diagnosed with paraphilias tend to have a broad range of sexual interests, including 'normative sexual interests' and behaviours (Earls, Martin & Lalumière, 2007; Langevin, Lang & Curnoe, 1998). Furthermore, 'unusual' sexual interests are commonly found in the general population and are rarely a sole substitute for sex involving another consenting adult (Ahlers et al., 2011; Renaud & Byers, 1999). Community studies with men, for example, have revealed that unusual sexual desires are more common than expected and not linked to clinical cases alone (Ahlers et al., 2011). In a study of sexual attraction to children, using self-report and a physiological measurement of arousal (a penile plethysmograph measures blood flow in the penis), a quarter of men in one community sample reported arousal or were measured as being aroused on the physiological measure when showed sexually provocative pictures of children (Hall, Hirschmann & Oliver, 1995). It is important to remember that a diagnosis of paedophilia can be made on the basis of fantasy alone, and does not depend upon the person acting out his/her fantasies. In this sense, a third of the men included in the study cited above could be labelled 'mentally disordered', even though they represent a significant minority of men who have never acted on their fantasies. However, researchers involved in revising diagnostic criteria for the forthcoming DSM-5 argue that studies already exist, using fMRI technology, which have demonstrated differences between paedophiles and non-paedophilic men, and predict that this technology will be used in the future to diagnose individuals with paraphilias (see Blanchard, 2010).

Engaging in paraphiliac behaviour can lead to a diagnosis, even though many individuals engage in the behaviour without distress or negative repercussions. Furthermore, Karasic and Drescher (2007) argue that the 'removal' of the sexual behaviour becomes the focus of concern (as a result of the diagnosis), which obscures the often non-sexual difficulties (emotional, behaviours, interpersonal) faced by the individual.

Specific paraphiliac characteristics?

Some researchers have argued that individuals diagnosed with a paraphilia from a clinical population have been found to have certain sexual and psychological characteristics, such as hypersexual desire (Kafka & Hennen, 2003) and distinct personality profiles, such as low agreeableness, high neuroticism and low conscientiousness (Fagan et al., 1991). Furthermore, poor social

BOX **10.8**

List of Paraphilias included in the DSM-IV-TR (2000)

There are three groups of paraphilias:

i. Sexual arousal that is directed at an inanimate object rather than a person:

Fetishism

Recurrent sexual arousal from inanimate objects

Transvestic fetishism –Sexual arousal from cross-dressing. Cross-dressing is the term for an individual who adopts the dress code of the opposite sex. In the context of transvestism this activity often leads to sexual arousal.

ii. Sexual arousal resulting from experiencing or inflicting pain and suffering

Sexual Masochism

Sexual arousal from experiencing humiliation

Sexual Sadism

Sexual arousal from inflicting harm or humiliation (psychological and/or physical)

iii. Sexual desires and arousal directed at non-consenting individuals. These behaviours are criminalized by many societies.

Exhibitionism

Sexual arousal resulting from exposing the genitals to strangers

Voyeurism

Sexual arousal resulting from observing someone naked without their consent

Frotteurism

Sexual arousal resulting from a thought or the actual act of rubbing oneself against a non-consenting other

Paedophilia

Sexual attraction towards children—usually prepubescents. In this category there are two subtypes: paedophilia exclusive, where the person is exclusively attracted to children and paedophilia non-exclusive, where the person is attracted to children and adults. Only 7% of clinical cases are exclusive.

---

skills have been put forward as an explanation for why some individuals choose to engage sexually with objects or children, although this has been discredited by those arguing that many socially unskilled individuals do not have paraphiliac interests; neither do individuals diagnosed with paraphilia necessarily lack any social skill whatsoever (LeVay & Valente, 2002). Others have argued there are no distinctive characteristics of those diagnosed with paraphilias, if one looks to community samples for a more even distribution (Brown et al., 1996; Laws & O'Donohue, 2008).

It has been argued by Moser and Kleinplatz (2005), for example, that those with paraphiliac interests do not constitute a discernible group in terms of aetiology or personality characteristics. Many receive not one but many diagnoses and their behaviour changes dramatically over time, making it difficult to locate their sexual behaviour in any distinct or stable personality type (Laws & O'Donohue, 2008). As sex therapists working with this group of clients, they argue that the only thing this group of individuals have in common is their shared sexual interest, which makes them indistinguishable from individuals with 'normal' sexual interests in a number of important respects.

The presence of a specific behaviour does not qualify an individual for a diagnosis, they argue. Other 'characteristics' must be present, such as shared personality characteristics or other shared cognitive deficits. Yet the literature cannot easily distinguish those with paraphilias from those with other forms of distress. That is, there is no distinct class of paraphiliacs. Karasic and Drescher (2007) argue that paraphiliac sexual behaviours are associated with mental disorder because they are often socially unacceptable or illegal. If diagnosed, the specific sexual behaviour can become the focus of concern due to social and legal restrictions, with the aim being to correct or cure the morally questionable conduct (Laws & O'Donohue, 1997). According to Moser and Kleinplatz (2005), focusing on the removal of the specific sexual behaviour, as therapy does when a diagnosis of paraphilia is made, only serves to obscure the underlying emotional causes that could be intimately tied to the individual's life history and be the reason for the development of particular sexual behaviours.

Distress

Distress relating to the sexual practice itself is rarely a problem for individuals diagnosed with paraphilias. According to Drescher (2010), such individuals only come to the attention of professionals when their behaviour has been deemed socially unacceptable. Even though the DSM states that the distress associated with the sexual behaviour should be long-term and present at the time to qualify for a diagnosis, this practice is not upheld and the 'unusual' nature of the sexual behaviour is instead enough to qualify for a diagnosis. Furthermore, Moser and Kleinplatz (2005) have argued that if the distress could be alleviated via support and the reduction of stigma, would these individuals then still qualify for a diagnosis? They think not.

Discrimination

The discrimination (either direct or imagined) experienced as a result of paraphiliac behaviours is often the main reason for distress, as opposed to the sexual practice itself. This raises the question as to whether such individuals should then be diagnosed with a mental disorder if they are dealing with the effects of discrimination rather than managing the distress associated with their sexual behaviour. Many have argued that a minority status and external prejudice should not be the source of a mental disorder diagnosis. For example, what if the 'impairment in social, occupational or other important areas of functioning' (one of the diagnostic criteria: APA, 2000, p. 566) was not the result of the sexual behaviour/interest per se but arose as a consequence of other people finding out about it? If a person's employer found out about their sexual preferences, this could lead to a whole host of negative and stressful events, which could cause distress. The individual could be sacked and the reason could be included on their employment record. They may experience difficulty in finding a job, and be socially excluded and isolated, which could lead to isolation and intense misery. Participating in a social support group may remedy these feelings, rather than a treatment targeted at their sexual interest or the emotional consequences of their social isolation.

BOX 10.9
Treatment for child sex offenders

Treatments for 'child sex offenders' (commonly referred to as 'paedophiles', though this not a term we wish to use[1]) has always courted controversy, inciting passionate reactions from members of the public and professionals alike. **Paedophile** is a psychiatric diagnosis (a paraphilia) used to describe adults who have a sexual preference for pre-pubescent children (aged 13 years or below). If the person diagnosed is 16, their preference must be for an individual five years their junior.

The popular media often portrays this group of individuals as incurable 'monsters', deserving of scorn and violent retribution for the horrific crimes they commit (Bell, 1993). It is not unusual to hear calls for the castration of individuals who offend against children, and even the reintroduction of the death penalty (Kitzinger, 2002). However, many have argued that such passionate reactions are often responsible for offenders' reluctance to speak openly and honestly about the reasons why they offend, which in turn can lead to greater shame and re-offending. It is important to note that around a third of all sex offenders are adolescents who require early intervention and help, to prevent them from engaging in offending behaviour in the long term.

In 1991[2] the British government introduced a Sex Offenders Treatment Programme (SOTP) in prisons, which now treats over 600 inmates a year. It is based on a cognitive–behavioural approach that encourages individuals to explore the thoughts and feelings that motivate them to offend. Although the programme can include adult rapists, the majority of treatment records relate to child sex offenders.

The programme involves the teaching of self-management skills in the context of group therapy and is based on a relapse-prevention programme once used for alcoholics. The programme is delivered in group situations, as attending a group is considered beneficial in establishing a supportive context in which to explore thoughts and feelings that non-offenders would find difficult and/or abhorrent. In an evaluation of the programme, it was found that being part of a group increased self-esteem and decreased feelings of inadequacy. Given that feelings of inadequacy and a lack of appropriate adult relationships are risk factors for individuals who offend against children, the group context has led to significant improvements in these areas and is well justified (Beech, Fisher & Beckett, 1999; Fisher, Beech & Browne, 1999).

The main aim of the programme is to develop the offender's awareness of their behaviours, thoughts and feelings in relation to their offence, and of the situations that increase the likelihood of offending.

The SOTP includes a number of core areas for therapeutic intervention, listed below. These interventions are specifically designed to prevent relapse by encouraging offenders to a) recognize that what they have done is wrong, b) take responsibility for their acts, c) increase empathy with their victims and d) acknowledge the consequences of their acts on their own lives.

Denial and Minimization Sex offenders typically deny both the full extent of their sexually deviant behaviour and the risk they pose of re-offending in the future (Nichols & Molinder, 1984). Breaking down denial is seen as an important prerequisite for change, as offenders need to admit to their deviant behaviour in order for them to take responsibility for their offences. Without a clear understanding of what the offending behaviour involves, the offender cannot develop the skills necessary to prevent re-offending.

Damage to Victims Sex offenders frequently demonstrate very little remorse for their behaviour and do not appear to recognize the damage they do to their victims. They frequently blame the victims for the offence and misinterpret the victims' behaviour as provocative. It is argued that improving empathy by educating offenders about the harmful effect of abuse will strengthen their motivation not to offend (Salter, 1988).

Justifications and Distorted Thinking About Offending Sex offenders typically develop a belief system that 'gives them permission' to carry out their offence(s), and justify their actions in order to minimize their own feelings of guilt and responsibility. Over time these beliefs become deeply entrenched. Only through treatment can offenders be made aware of their distorted patterns of thinking and be taught to recognize and challenge them.

Deviant Sexual Fantasies Finkelhor (1984) has suggested that the first precondition of offence behaviour is motivation. This frequently takes the form of thoughts or fantasies about deviant activity, by which the individual becomes sexually aroused. Treatment is aimed at teaching the offender to modify or control deviant arousal and to develop arousal to appropriate, non-deviant fantasies as an alternative. Whilst the presence of deviant sexual preference is known to underpin the behaviour of some sex offenders, its range and intensity varies considerably between different types of sex offenders (Barbaree & Marshall, 1989); sex offenders who re-offend are more likely to be those who show deviant arousal (Harris, Rice, Quinsey & Chaplin, 1996).

Relapse Prevention Based on the work of Marlatt and Gordon (1985) in the field of addictions, the treatment aim is to get offenders to recognize situations, feelings, moods and types of thought which put them at risk of re-offending. An ability to describe strategies to prevent relapse, along with an awareness of risk situations and warning signs, has been shown to be correlated with a reduction in recidivism (Marques, Day, Nelson et al., 1991; Ryan & Myoshi, 1990; Ryan & Lane, 1997).

Lifestyle and Personality Problems in being correctly assertive, low self-esteem and the failure to develop a capacity for intimacy in adult relationships appear to be common characteristics of sex offenders (Abel, Becker and Mittelman, 1987; Marshall, 1989, 1993; Marshall, Hudson & Hodkinson, 1993; Pithers, Kashima, Cumming, Beal & Buell, 1988). They may suffer from depression, anxiety and social isolation and lack the confidence and skills needed in adult, social and intimate situations. Pithers et al. report that general social skill deficits were the precursors of sex offences in 59% of child abusers and 50% of rapists studied. Comprehensive cognitive–behavioural

---

1 'Paedophile' originates from the Greek 'child (paed) love/friendship (phile)'.
2 This programme was revised in 1994: the revisions included a 100% increase in treatment hours.

BOX 10.9

Continued

programmes address these deficits with a view to improving the offenders' general level of functioning in society.

Sex Education A number of offenders are likely to have poor knowledge about sex and to require sex education. Understanding of the emotional aspects of sexual activity is also held to be beneficial in helping offenders to function more appropriately in relationships and to improve their ability to understand the viewpoint of their partner (Beech, Fisher & Beckett, 1999, p. 13).

Do these programmes work?

In order to assess the efficacy of the SOTP, an evaluation study was conducted and published in 2003 by Friendship, Mann and Beech in order to measure pro-offending attitudes and re-offending rates in sex offenders. The individuals were first of all categorized as low or high deviancy (measured according to the number of victims; abused boys or both boys and girls; committed abuse outside as well as inside the family) as well as low and high denial (e.g. individuals could be classified as low denial/high deviance; high denial/low deviance; high denial/ high deviance and so on). The vast majority of men who attended the SOTP in prison reported significant therapeutic benefit. On release into the community, 76% of men reported the treatment as 'very helpful', with a further 20% stating that the treatment had 'helped quite a lot'. However, the programme was also found to reduce reconviction rates to a significant extent, especially where prisoners were given the revised longer treatment hours (160 hours as opposed to the original 80), rendering the treatment successful in reducing pro-offending attitudes, increasing empathy towards the victim and reducing reconviction rates. Having said this, only 14% of men in the high deviancy group produced a treatment effect and were still socially incompetent at the end of treatment, presenting with low self-esteem and a high emotional connection with children. This is of great concern, given that individuals who do not establish positive adult attachments on release are more likely to re-offend in the community. The recommendation at present is for high deviancy individuals to repeat the SOTP programme.

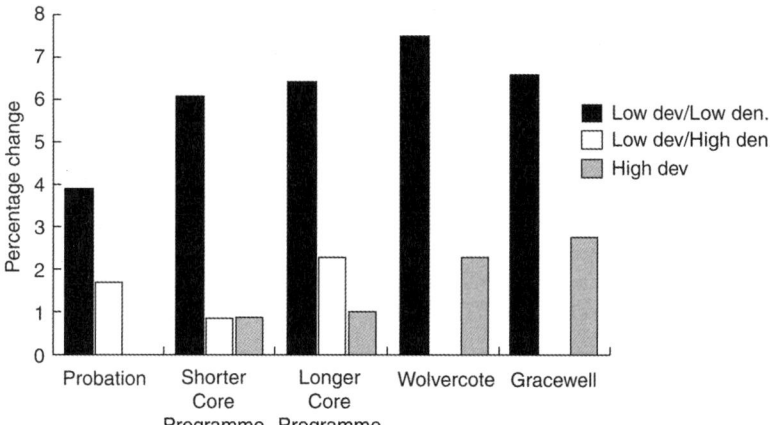

Figure 10.1 **Percentage showing overall change in a comparison of community and resident treatment programmes. The results reveal that resident programmes are more successful in both low and high deviancy groups of men**

Source: **Beech, Fisher and Beckett (1999).**

A further argument justifying the inclusion of the paraphilias relates to there being 'an impairment in the capacity for reciprocal, affectionate sexual activity' (APA, 2000, p. 567). Yet according to Moser and Kleinplatz (2005) individuals diagnosed with paraphilias are no more likely than others to find it difficult developing and maintaining relationships than 'normal' adults, though this view is questioned by those working on refining the diagnostic criteria for the forthcoming DSM-5 (Kafka, 2010).

Summary

Although people may find what some people do disturbing and morally questionable, many questions surrounding the labelling of certain sexual identities, choices and desires as 'pathological' remain and continue to be hotly debated in the mental health field. Moreover, consensual and non-distressing behaviours such as sadomasochism or cross-dressing are practised widely and do not necessitate any professional intervention, according to some, given that the adults are practising in a risk-aware manner (Langdridge & Barker, 2005, 2007). In contrast, behaviours where consent is absent (e.g. sex between an adult and a child) attract a very different kind of debate about whether they should be treated as mental health issues, or as plainly criminal.

Despite the controversy surrounding these issues, many therapists remain committed to working with individuals who experience distress as a result of feeling stigmatized or with those who engage in illegal activities, such as sexual offences. There are a range of behavioural therapies (aversion therapy, orgasmic reorientation and covert conditioning; see Box 10.9 on sex offending), drug treatments, such as antidepressants and cognitive therapies to treat individuals diagnosed with paraphilias (Laws & Marshall, 1991). The key point raised in these debates is the importance of maintaining a clear separation between consensual behaviours and those that do not involve consent. The two should always be viewed and treated as distinct: non-consent should be treated as a criminal matter.

When individuals are attracted to 'unusual' objects or non-consenting sexual activities, they are currently eligible for a diagnosis of mental disorder, if the activity causes sufficient distress or if it is illegal. This position is controversial, however, with a number of service users and mental health professionals arguing for the removal of these categories from the diagnostic manuals. But the question remains: should those who commit offences against non-consenting individuals be treated by the criminal justice system, not by mental health services? The debates surrounding this issue continue to rage and are not currently resolvable.

GENDER, VARIANCE AND DISTRESS

Allan Tyler

Susan's story

Susan is 32 years old and was raised in North London by Jewish parents. Susan was identified as male at birth and raised as a boy, called Frank. As Frank, she displayed behaviours that her parents considered inappropriate for a boy. Frank told her parents she was a girl trapped in a boy's body and when she grew up she would be a woman, which caused them a great deal of concern. As a teenager, she experienced regular bullying and even death threats from schoolmates about her feminine behaviours. Frank struggled to identify with other boys physically and was self-conscious about any form of undress. Frank was deeply unhappy with the masculine features of her body and would experiment with changing her appearance with make-up, clothing and by 'tucking' her penis, which she described as 'disgusting'. When she left school, Frank began spending more and more time as Susan, which her family learned to accept. Her close friends were all very supportive and noticed her confidence grow. Susan now lives as a woman. She no longer experiences the bullying that she experienced as a boy, but sometimes struggles to know how to deal with the reactions of strangers when she is recognized as transgendered. Susan has always been frustrated by the amount of medical bureaucracy that she has had to go through to receive the treatments to alter her physical appearance to match her identity. Susan's appearance has become more feminine since she has been taking hormones and she has had extensive electrolysis for hair removal from her face. She hopes to have a number of surgeries, to have breast implants, soften the line of her jaw and reduce the size of her Adam's apple as well as major abdominal surgery to create a vagina.

Zen's story

Zen is 26 years old. Zen was identified as female and raised as a girl. Zen uses the female pronouns (she, her), and identifies herself as a 'boi', a term she uses to position herself as masculine, but neither male nor female. She dresses in gender-neutral attire and obtained a doctorate, which she says was in part so her title would also be gender-neutral. Zen is often mistaken in public for a man, which she does not correct; however, it does cause her difficulty when she uses public toilets. Zen's girlfriend, Twila, identifies as a lesbian and plays up her role as 'the wife'. Zen is considering taking testosterone and having 'top surgery' to remove her breasts and reconstruct her chest as masculine, but she has not been approved for surgery by her doctor because she does not meet the criteria for Gender Identity Disorder in the DSM. Zen has recently investigated

having the surgery conducted privately but cannot afford the cost in England, so is looking at options in Thailand. However, Zen's girlfriend is concerned about the legitimacy and safety of the services advertised and wants her to take things more slowly. Zen and Twila have talked about what the changes to Zen's body will mean, and how the changes will affect the way Twila is attracted to Zen sexually.

This section highlights the problems with defining sex and gender–defining them as one and the same thing that can only stay the same. It looks at how the DSM defines gender variance as a disorder (e.g. Gender Identity Disorder), and the tensions that exist between diagnostic definitions and the variety of some people's lived experience. Finally, it looks at some example of stresses that people may face in dealing with transgenderism. The section will focus on particular transgender experiences, specifically those that intersect with the attention of professionals in the fields of psychology and psychiatry. The inclusion of transgender experience in this chapter is not intended to pathologize or categorize it, but to look critically at pathologies and categories. In writing about particular, sometimes negative, experiences, we recognize the limits we face in discussing diverse populations with a broad range of experiences and accept that there are huge challenges in finding examples and language that are adequately representative whilst also being accessible.

Definitions

Cisgender is the term used to describe people who continue to identify with the gender that they were assigned at birth through their bodies and their behaviours. The term avoids the use of the word 'normal' and hence the social construction of transgender as 'abnormal' (Green, 2006; Schilt & Westbrook, 2009). **Social construction** recognizes that the way people talk about something constructs and reinforces social rules for knowledge and understanding (Howitt, 2010).

Transgender is a term that is commonly used in a variety of ways. It may be used as an umbrella term for all individuals who 'transgress' norms of gender or specifically to those individuals identifying, appearing or acting as *neither* exclusively male *nor* female. Transgender discards the *requirement* that the individual make a 'complete' transition from one gender to the 'opposite' one according to prescribed, socially conventional criteria, as illustrated in Zen's story above. Whilst the term transgender is increasingly used in place of 'transsexual' (for example, Susan might describe herself as a transgender woman), it also makes room for individuals who challenge their assigned gender, whether or not they conform to medical criteria (Weeks, 2011). **Transsexual** is the term with which most people will be familiar, which refers to individuals who alter their bodies to reflect a different gender from that which was assigned to them at birth. Likewise, transgender includes individuals *during* a time of transition, when their social, legal and biological status is identifiably in a state of flux (Playdon, 2004), examples of which are discussed later in this section. Transgender also reinforces the distinction between 'gender' and 'sexuality' (as discussed on pp. 222–23). For example, whether a person identifies as male or female does not necessarily relate to whether they are sexually attracted to men or women (Johnson, 2004). Differentiating between transsexual and transgender highlights a shift of recognition about what is considered acceptable or required behaviour for women or men. Since homosexuality is a real possibility for many cisgender men and women, it is a problem if it is not recognized as a possibility for transgender people as well (Johnson, 2004).

When transgender is used as an umbrella term, distinctions are usually drawn between different types. For example, people who use costume for theatrical performance or social 'events' might refer to themselves as drag queens (men dressed as women) or drag kings (women dressed as men) (Halbarstam, 1998; Volcano & Halbarstam, 1999) but baulk at being referred to as a transvestite. Transvestite can literally be defined as 'cross-dresser', meaning a person who wears clothes that transgress the prescribed norms for their named gender (Weeks, 2011), but a distinction is made between drag and transvestism. Drag has social norms in the theatre (for example, in British pantomime) and has been a part of gay social scenes even at times and in places where homosexuality was illegal or considered a mental illness (Cole, 2000); whereas, **transvestite**[9] more usually describes a person who cross-dresses, whether for emotional or psychic reasons or as sexual fetish (Weeks, 2011), and is usually only used in relation to (heterosexual) men.[10] Whilst originally attributed to male homosexuality, 'there is no necessary relationship between the two' (Weeks, 2011, p. 217). It is interesting to note that in the DSM-IV-TR, transvestic fetishism is only diagnosed in heterosexual males, implying that such behaviour is only deemed unacceptable or 'pathological' when identified in particular sexual groups, but not in minority groups such as gay men, women and bisexuals (Lev, 2006). It can be argued that this is but one example of a particular sexual behaviour labelled dysfunctional or pathological when it goes against certain social norms of behaviour – in this case, heterosexual men dressing in women's clothing – and being sexually aroused would contravene dominant codes of masculine behaviour. Psychology professionals have reflected on how or why gendered rules of dress cause distress for the individual, the importance of those rules and whether clothing is significant to the individual's identity or behaviour. One obvious problem with attributing wearing gender-specific clothing to mental disorder is that fashions and social norms change and cultural and historical boundaries between appropriate dress for men and that for women shift (an obvious example is the acceptability of trousers for women), highlighting a problem for institutionally defined standards of dress (Wilson, 2003). Therefore, an obvious criticism of the DSM-IV is that using or wearing a particular type of clothing is not in and of itself a psychiatric disorder and that experiences or expressions of distress remain the locus of attention.

Significantly, cross-dressing behaviours – even in childhood play – remain as (problematic?) diagnostic criteria elsewhere in the DSM-IV-TR in the diagnosis of Gender Identity Disorder (GID) in Children (see Box 10.11).

Gender, bodies and science

The first attempts at gender-reassignment surgeries in the early 20th century preceded the introduction of the word

'transsexual' by Harry Benjamin in 1954 (Weeks, 2011) and to that extent, transsexuality has always been a medicalized phenomenon (Bornstein, 1994; also Butler, 2004, and King, 1996). The phenomenon positions people along a continuum of 'completion'– where surgery is seen as the normalizing stage for the transsexual body – as well as between two binary categories of male and female (Chau & Herring, 2004; Playdon, 2004). Both Susan and Zen will experience extended periods of time when they will experience a place that is neither fully male nor female, whether it is their aim to cross it to a surgically normalized body (as in Susan's case) or to live within it, pushing at legal and medical boundaries and their restrictions (like Zen). (**Trans** is used as an umbrella term to include all transvestite, transgender and transsexual identities.)

Anne Fausto-Sterling (2000) highlights a number of very different diagnostic criteria that have been used and discarded throughout history to determine gender: psychological, anatomic, physiological, and/or biological (Fausto-Sterling, 2000). With advances in embryology, endocrinology, surgery, psychology and biochemistry, the distinctions which are currently held as medical 'truth' about gender may well be regarded in the future as mere attempts at guesswork and postulating (Fausto-Sterling, 2000), with some already arguing for recognition of multiple biological genders (Blackless et al., 2000) and sexualities (Johnson, 2004).

Recent research tentatively offers some evidence of differences in brain anatomy between cisgender males and Male-to-Female Transsexuals (MTF) who have not yet been treated with hormones; MRI data for the MTF show a significantly larger volume of regional grey matter in the right putamen compared to cisgender men, although the pattern of regional grey matter variation seen in MTF data is more similar to that of cisgender men than to cisgender women (Luders, Sánchez, Gaser, Toga & Narr, 2009). Possible links between genetics and trans-identification are both supported (Hare et al., 2009) and challenged (Ujike et al., 2009). One might also criticize research that shows links between hormone patterns and sex-differentiation in the brains of laboratory animals for dogmatically extrapolating animal models to human gender identity (Gooren, 1990). At best, there is currently no conclusive agreement across the scientific community. There is, however, sociological and anthropological evidence that transgenderism exists across numerous geographically and historically diverse cultures (Oetomo, 2000; James, 1998).

> # BOX **10.10**
> ## DSM-IV-TR
>
> ### Transvestic Fetishism
>
> A. Over a period of at least six months, in a heterosexual male, recurrent, intense sexually arousing fantasies, sexual urges, or behaviours involving cross-dressing.
> B. The fantasies, sexual urges, or behaviours cause clinically significant distress or impairment in social, occupational, or other important areas of functioning.
>
> Specify if:
>
> *With Gender Dysphoria*: if the person has persistent discomfort with gender role or identity

---

9 The term transvestite was first used by Magnus Hirschfield in 1910 (Weeks, 2011).

10 The DSM IV-TR specifically refers to heterosexual men only.

BOX 10.11
DSM-IV-TR

Gender identity disorder

A. A strong and persistent cross-gender identification (not merely a desire for any perceived cultural advantages of being the other sex).

In children, the disturbance is manifested by four (or more) of the following:

1 Repeatedly stated desire to be, or insistence that he or she is, the other sex

2 In boys, preference for cross-dressing or simulating female attire; in girls, insistence on wearing only stereotypical masculine clothing

3 Strong and persistent preferences for cross-sex roles in make-believe play or persistent fantasies of being the other sex

4 Intense desire to participate in the stereotypical games and pastimes of the other sex

5 Strong preference for playmates of the other sex

In adolescents and adults, the disturbance is manifested by symptoms such as a stated desire to be the other sex, frequent passing as the other sex, desire to live or be treated as the other sex, or the conviction that he or she has the typical feelings and reactions of the other sex.

B. Persistent discomfort with his or her sex or sense of inappropriateness in the gender role of that sex.

In children, the disturbance is manifested by any of the following:
In boys, assertion that his penis or testes are disgusting or will disappear, or assertion that it would be better not to have a penis, or aversion toward rough-and-tumble play and rejection of male stereotypical toys, games and activities;
In girls, rejection of urinating in a sitting position, assertion that she has or will grow a penis, or assertion that she does

not want to grow breasts or menstruate, or marked aversion toward normative feminine clothing.

In adolescents and adults, the disturbance is manifested by symptoms such as preoccupation with getting rid of primary and secondary sex characteristics (e.g. request for hormones, surgery or other procedures to physically alter sexual characteristics to simulate the other sex) or the belief that he or she was born the wrong sex.

C. The disturbance is not concurrent with a physical intersex condition.

D. The disturbance causes clinically significant distress or impairment in social, occupational or other important areas of functioning.

Code based on current age

Specify if (for sexually mature individuals):

Sexually attracted to males
Sexually attracted to females
Sexually attracted to both
Sexually attracted to neither

Gender and the DSM

The DSM-IV-TR contains a category of sexual disorder labelled Gender Identity Disorder (GID) (see Box 10.11), while some critics propose to replace Gender Identity Disorder with diagnostic criteria and language that would emphasize instead the lack of congruence between the individual's experienced gender and assigned gender at birth. The literature that refers to gender identity as 'disordered' claims a variety of triggers, including childhood abuse, problematic paternal relationships and hormonal *abnormalities*, although no conclusive evidence has been found to support these claims. These 'triggers' were the same as some of the 'causes' that previous versions of the DSM listed to cite homosexuality as a mental disorder nearly 40 years ago. Similarly, a number of therapists, researchers and gender activists have stated that what we refer to as 'gender dysphoria' is but one part of a whole variety of gender-variant experiences, which are part of the diversity of human sexuality and gender. GID is a diagnosis given to both adults and children. In the West, the only form of recognized treatment is a series of gender-reassignment surgeries supported by hormone and psychological therapies, with psychological therapies adopted to alter transgender identities having very limited success.

Prescribing gender

The psychiatric category that aims to describe transgender experiences has attracted controversy in recent decades for many reasons and is often the site of tensions within the transgender and professional communities. Where many

people feel empowered by a formal recognition of their experience, others assert that constructing the phenomena around gender dysphoria as a 'mental disorder' reinforces stigma against individuals and arguably constructs the issue as a lack of mental health, rather than a physical issue that can be corrected through surgery. Perhaps more radically, the identification of a single phenomenon denies that a biological gender is subject to several separate, if interrelated, physical features – such as the genitals and the hormones – (Fausto-Sterling, 2000) or something which is more flexible (Garfinkel, 1967; Kessler & McKenna, 2000; Butler, 1993). People who deny the possibility of a 'real' mismatch between the physical and psychic self for transgender people claim that gender is fixed and that surgery is merely cosmetic.

A person may choose or feel compelled to have medical treatment so that their physical appearance matches their gendered self. A person must live for a minimum of one year (as authorized by the clinician) in their transgender identity before they will be considered for surgery. This is referred to as the 'real-life experience' (RLE) (Bockting, 2008). Although significant gains in medical and surgical treatments for gender-variant individuals have been made in recent years, many still question the relevance of including a strict criterion that allows only those who meet the diagnostic criteria to receive treatment. The surgeries performed are major and, with the exception of breast augmentation (implants), irreversible. The RLE gives the person time to explore and address a number of related issues (Bockting, 2008). One difficulty with the GID diagnosis is the limited inclusion of those wishing to transform gender (i.e. those wishing to pass as identifiably male or female, and preferably heterosexual). Only those diagnosed with GID are granted access to pharmaceutical (e.g. hormone treatment) and surgical treatments (e.g. breast implants [MTF], mastectomy and chest surgery Female-to-Male [FTM]), vocal pitch surgery, and sex reassignment surgeries to remove internal reproductive organs (FTM) and/or reshape existing genital structures to create a penis and scrotum or vagina with clitoris and labia (MTF & FTM).

Some people seeking medical treatment (as in Zen's story) do not fit simply into the Gender Identity Disorder category (Lev, 2004), yet still seek medical and surgical treatments in varying degrees (Lev, 2004). Many have described how this has led to individuals fitting their story to meet the GID diagnostic criteria (see Johnson, 2007) and, through controlling the way they make themselves look (Speer & Green, 2007), act to incite approval from psychiatrists who are positioned to make the final decisions about whether or not to endorse medical or surgical treatments.

The individual seeking medical intervention is assessed for psychological competence to maintain lifelong adherence to self-administered pharmaceutical treatment (for example, testosterone injections for FTM transmen) and the possibility of complications from surgery (such as unwanted scarring), factors which extend beyond the social obstacles that many transgendered and gender-variant people face (Johnston, 2007). Often the success of surgery is dependent upon a range of factors including prior mental stability, successful adaptation to the new gender role prior to surgery, an adequate understanding of the potential limitations of the surgery (Lawrence, 2003) and a recognition of personal expectations for social, family and romantic relationships (Winterkjaer & Dalchow, 2004).

The psychiatrist's role must also be to assess clients for comorbid signs of an enduring mental illness which, to the frustration of many trans-identified clients, positions the clinician as the gatekeeper of safe, medical treatment. Transgender individuals sometimes express a desire to see the removal of gender identity from the DSM, but fear this would result in a denial of access to treatment. Some, for example, make the compromise of being labelled as mentally disordered as a means of accessing safe, medical gender-reassignment surgeries and legal prescriptions for hormones where provision is made through private insurance (as in the United States) or through national health care (as in the United Kingdom).[11]

Debates about diagnosis

The reality for many individuals is that to be considered 'legitimate', the transsexual person must meet a number of criteria in order to be recommended for medical treatment (Lindemann, 1997; Califia, 1997). They must share their identity with their family and friends, as well as change their name, socially and legally, to one that 'fits' with their gender identity. Psychology professionals must be mindful of the stresses that an individual might face in complying with standard requirements. For example, for Susan to carry a passport and driver's licence on which her name is Susan but her gender is still legally identified as male makes it difficult for her to 'pass' as

a woman. (**Passing** is the ability to conceal one's transgender identity and 'pass' without being recognized as transgender.) This act of concealing may also be a source of stress for individuals, where authenticity does not exclude acknowledging one's past reality.

Whilst medication, surgery, passing and an invisible reintegration into society are often the indicators of success for an individual like Susan, these options are not possible or available to everyone. Criteria on which candidates have previously been rejected as candidates for surgical therapy include age, homosexuality, fetishism, sadomasochism, having a face or body that won't pass (that is, to be 'somatically inappropriate'), 'refusal to aspire to be a feminine woman or a masculine man' or just 'uppitiness' (Califia, 1997, pp. 224–5). The criteria, therefore, can mean that one cannot just be a woman or a man; one must be a *particular type* of woman or man. In Zen's case, this presents real problems for her.

The DSM-IV's criteria for GID has recommended diagnosing long-standing cross-gender identification through culturally – material and historically – marked indicators such as boys playing with dolls or girls playing rough games. The individual is (often) expected to consistently 'perform' in a manner befitting their biologically opposed gender, through manner, dress and sexual partner-attraction. Some feminist critics have pointed out that transgender or gender-variant persons perform such hyper-masculine or hyper-feminine roles that they reinforce traditional – and often outdated – stereotypes (Lorber, 2007), such as through clothing choices that are emphatically gendered. Psychology professionals should be mindful that many individuals are learning how to construct a gendered self, sometimes with little or no experience and often in secret. The rules for gender attribution, otherwise taken for granted in daily life, are painstakingly studied by the transgendered person striving to 'pass', requiring constant effort 'to produce an effect of naturalness by deliberate action' (Connell, 2002, p. 67). Others have taken the view that the transgender individual, especially one who does not pass as male or female, 'challenges, threatens and undoes the belief in gender certainty for all of us' (Johnson, 2007, p. 457). Some authors have argued that the DSM should remove all reference to behaviours related to social non-conformity in GID (see Box 10.11), as this contradicts the DSM's mission to exclude behaviours that in themselves are not symptoms of mental disorder, but merely socially non-conforming.

Possibilities

Under the direction of the DSM, the sign of a 'successful' transsexual is one who 'passes' invisibly as heterosexual, a notion which not only denies diversity but ignores the reality of the social group and the physical body *in transition*. In addition, the diagnostic criteria deny the possibility of a mentally healthy, socially well-adjusted and accepted *transgender* individual, in favour of the pre-operative *transsexual* who must display a significant level of distress or impairment of personal, social and occupational functioning. The person who seeks gender transformation has historically been seen as an unfortunate victim, not as an empowered person making empowered choices. Some writers argue that transsexuals are fully participating in the shaping of their own lives and bodies, and in doing so, change the medical practices that are working to shape them (Prosser, 1998, p. 8). With a surgically completed and officially

---

11 In stark contrast, gender-reassignment surgery is a state-sanctioned provision in Iran, where homosexuality is illegal.

approved gender identity unavailable to those who fail the stringent, yet subjective, criteria of their nominated health care professionals, some will make the choice to live on the margins of society as cross-dressers or within the gay community. For male-to-females, there is the (extreme) option of castration, which is more culturally acceptable within India's *hijra* identity than in western society (Wartmann, 2005). In any case, some may turn to drug addiction or alcoholism as a means of escape (Wartmann, 2005) and a small number will seek to take their own lives (Clements-Nolle, Marx & Katz, 2006).

Even without significant distress, and even after treatment, a person can still be labelled as mentally disordered, according to current DSM criteria. As Kelly Winters argues, 'The ambiguity concerning the mental illness of individuals whose gender dysphoria was successfully treated with hormones or surgeries contradicts the efficacy of those treatments' (Winters, 2007, p. 83; Winters, 2008). In her view, rather than emphasizing the 'non-conformity' aspects of those with gender variance, as the DSM does, the diagnostic criteria should only include reference to the distresses associated with gender dysphoria. Following this, Winters and others advocate replacing GID with a new diagnosis defined as chronic distress, rather than any reference to social non-conformity that includes only those who are distressed as a result of their physical sex characteristics and NOT (a) those who have successfully undertaken treatment, (b) those who are distressed as a result of social prejudice and intolerance or (c) gender non-conformists who do not experience distress.

Interventions

The treatments for gender variance or gender dysphoria continue to be controversial, with some arguing that fewer restrictions should be placed upon individuals wishing to undergo treatment. Others have argued that gender variance is a sign of mental disorder, believing that medical treatment actually worsens the core 'symptoms', to the extent that medical and surgical procedures serve to reinforce a disordered cross-gender identification (Federoff, 2000). According to this

view, changing one's gender, is not going to 'make better' the belief that one is the opposite gender.

Despite these reservations, sex reassignment surgery in recent years (with greater knowledge and better surgical techniques) has been found to be successful in the majority of cases (Green & Fleming, 1990) although the validity of using only observational evidence or studies without control groups is disputed by some authors (Murad et al., 2010). In a review of controlled studies from 1970 to 1989 with a one-year follow-up, 97% of FTM surgeries and 87% of MTF surgeries were satisfactory (out of 130 FTM and 220 MTF surgeries). Furthermore, sexual satisfaction and general psychological well-being were found to significantly increase after MTF surgeries (Lief & Hubschman, 1993; Smith, van Goozen, Kuiper & Cohen-Kettenis, 2005). However, it can be argued that the commitment to medical and legal procedures acts to reinforce binary gender roles (Lindemann, 1997). For example, some lesbian women express concern about the current emphasis on transgender and acknowledge that there are tensions as well as opportunities in group membership and individual identities (Sinfield, 2004). FTM invisibility is a problem that highlights the material, symbolic nature of gendered subjectivity. Contemporary western society has little recognition of FTM equivalent of transvestism, partly because when women adopt a masculine costume it is simply seen as unisex and thereby neutral in gender (Garber, 1997; Wilson, 2003).

Section summary

The debates within and around gender variance and reassignment are multiple and complex. The language that we use to describe gender does not necessarily represent the complexity of individual experiences. Advances in biology and medicine enable new discoveries about gender but challenge both public and professional beliefs. Professional standards and criteria intended to benefit individuals in distress have the potential to realize new opportunities for openness between the client and the professional, between psychology and medicine, and between the body and the mind.

Chapter summary

Our sexuality, sexual relationships and gender identity can be seen as key to our psychological well-being and happiness more generally. Who and what we are attracted to sexually also forms an important part of our self-identity because it enables us to assess whether we appear to fit in or whether we are seen as 'different' from the norm – even though it is clear that a norm of sexual behaviour is hard to find. Even though we are taught that sex is natural (especially sex between a man and a woman – often termed 'heteronormative'), significant variations in sexual tastes, orientations and practices exist and many struggle to know how to communicate what they find pleasurable, or actually know what they desire. (**Heteronormativity** is the view that men and women should adhere to a biologically prescribed set of gender-specific behaviours (e.g. women as exclusive care-givers). Within this, heterosexuality is viewed as the only natural and normal form of sexual orientation.)

Why people have problems with sex is complex, involving a variety of possible causes and risk factors. These can be cultural, psychological or biological, or induced via medication. Many therapists believe that the individual should be seen with their partner, as part of a relationship, so that the entire set of relational dynamics, not just the individual's sexual problem, can be assessed.

As well as problems with sex per se, there are individuals aroused by objects or non-consenting individuals, who are diagnosed with a mental disorder (a paraphilia) if their activity causes distress (either for them or another person) or disrupts their social or work activities. This includes individuals who experience great distress as a result of being born 'the wrong sex', as in the case of gender-variant or transgender individuals. What unites these groups is the unusual or criminal aspect of their activities.

A growing number of mental health professionals and lay people argue that social taboos should not be included in a manual for mental disorders. If distress or disruption is caused, they argue, it is often not as a result of the sexual practice itself, but through the discrimination and stigma faced by such individuals. In the case of those who engage in sexual activity with non-consenting individuals, such as children, they argue that those individuals should be dealt with by the legal system, as their behaviour is criminal, rather than any sure sign of mental disorder. Given the significant rates of child sexual abuse across the world, it is clear that behaviour such as this is not unusual and not committed by distressed individuals or those who have lost touch with reality.

Issues relating to sexual 'disorders' in mental health circles continue to be fiercely debated. They are highly complex, especially when they involve criminal acts, as the boundaries between criminality and abnormality become blurred. Although the status of sexual problems in the next version of the DSM continues to be hotly contested and debated, it seems that they are likely to be included, for now at least.

The debates within and around gender variance and reassignment should be regarded as separate from discussions of sexuality more generally. We have included these topics in the same chapter here because they have traditionally been combined in a single category in the DSM, even though that may change in the forthcoming DSM. The transgender communities have been at the forefront of challenging traditional medical models of gender variance and many continue to dispute its inclusion as a mental disorder. Professional standards and criteria intended to benefit individuals in distress may lead to new opportunities for openness between the client and the professional, between psychology and medicine, and between the body and the mind. However, it seems likely that tensions between professionals and transgender individuals and others (professionals and lay people) in support of a non-pathologizing model of gender variance will continue for some time to come.

End of chapter questions

Sexual problems

1 If problems with sex or experiencing orgasm during sex are common, should they be viewed as mental disorders?
2 Should we always view sexual problems in the context of the relationship in which they occur?
3 Are problems with sex linked to levels of distress more generally?
4 Why do women experience higher numbers of sexual problems than men?

Sexual disorders

5 Are paraphilia-type fantasies uncommon?
6 Does unusual sexual attraction always lead to distress?
7 Are sexual disorders a matter of social/moral/legal, as opposed to scientific judgement?

Gender identity and transgender

8 Should transgender individuals be viewed as disordered?
9 Is gender variance in itself distressing?
10 What are the practical benefits of receiving a diagnosis relating to transgender?

Find out more

Ames, J. (ed.) (2005). *Sexual Metamorphosis: An Anthology of Transsexual Memoirs*. New York: Vintage.

Bancroft, J. (ed.) (2003). *Sexual Development in Childhood*. Bloomington IN: Indiana University Press.

Bancroft, J., Loftus, J. & Long, J. S. (2003). Distress about sex: A national survey of women in heterosexual relationships. *Archives of Sexual Behavior*, 32(3), 193–208.

Califia, P. (2003). *Sex Changes: Transgender Politics* (2nd edn). Berkeley CA: Cleis Press.

Crowe, M. & Ridley, J. (2000). *Therapy with Couples: A Behavioural-Systems Approach to Couple Relationship and Sexual Problems*. Oxford: Blackwell.

Kaschak, E. & Tiefer, L. (2001). *A New View of Women's Sexual Problems*. New York: Haworth.

Kleinplatz, P. J. (ed.) (2001). *New Directions in Sex Therapy: Innovations and Alternatives*. Philadelphia PA: Brunner-Routledge.

Laumann, E.O., Nicolosi, D. B., Glasser, D. B., Paik, A., Gingell, C., Moreira, E. et al. (2005). Sexual problems among women and men aged 40–80y: Prevalence and correlates identified in the global study of sexual attitudes and behaviours. *International Journal of Impotence Research*, 17, 39–57.

Laumann, E. O., Paik, A. & Rosen, R. C. (1999). Sexual dysfunction in the United States Prevalence and predictors. *JAMA*, 281, 537–44.

Stryker, S. & Whittle, S. (2006). *The Transgender Studies Reader*. New York: Routledge.

Novels or popular texts

Ames, J. (ed.) 2005. *Sexual Metamorphosis: An Anthology of Transsexual Memoirs*. New York: Vintage.

Armstrong, L. (1978). *Kiss Daddy Goodnight*. New York: Pocket books. An autobiographical account of child sexual abuse.

Bornstein, K. (2006). *Hello Cruel World: 101 Alternatives to Suicide for Teens, Freaks and Other Outlaws*. New York: Seven Stories Press.

Brown, C. (1992). *The Playboy* (a graphic novel). London: Drawn and Quarterly.

Easton, D. & Liszt, C. (1997). *The Ethical Slut*. Eugene OR: Greenery Press. A book about having open multiple lovers and friends, in the polyamory sense.

Fraser, S. (1989) *My Father's House: A Memoir of Incest and of Healing*. London: Virago. An autobiographical novel about a father sexually abusing his daughter.

Hall, R. (1982). *The Well of Loneliness*. London: Virago. A lesbian novel written in 1928.

Malone, C., Farthing, L. & Worrell, M. (1996). *The Memory Bird: Survivors of Sexual Abuse*. London: Virago. A collection of autobiographical essays about experiences of child sexual abuse.

Schreiber, F. (1977). *Sybil*. London: Warner books. An account of child sexual abuse and Dissociative Identity Disorder.

Spring, J. (1987). *Cry Hard and Swim: The Story of an Incest Survivor*. London: Virago. An autobiographical account of child sexual abuse.

Walker, A. (1983).*The Color Purple*. London: Women's Press. An autobiographical account of child sexual abuse in the context of a family.

Winterson, J. (1991). *Oranges Are Not the Only Fruit*. London: Vintage. On experiences of coming out as a lesbian.

Films

Boys Don't Cry (1999). Director: Kimberly Peirce. Transgender, sexual relationships, discrimination and sexual violence.

Bus Stop (1956). Director: Joshua Logan. Kidnapping and trying to enforce a 'normal' married life on someone.

Just Like a Woman (1992). Director: Christopher Monger. Transvestism, heterosexuality.

Kinsey (2004). Director: Bill Condon. A biographical account of the famous sexologist.

Ma Vie en Rose (1997). Director: Alain Berliner. Gender variance, gender dysphoria in childhood.

Mysterious Skin (2004). Director: Gregg Araki. Child sexual abuse, working as a male teenage prostitute and obsession with alien abduction.

Secretary (2002). Director: Steven Shainberg. Sado-masochism, bondage, sexual relationships.

TransAmerica (2005). Director: Duncan Tucker. Gender dysphoria and transsexual subjectivity, with specific references to clinical care, relationships with family.

The Adventures of Priscilla: Queen of the Desert (1994). Director: Stephan Elliot. Drag, gender dysphoria, transsexual identification, transphobia, queer families.

The Color Purple (1985). Director: Steven Spielberg. African American woman's experience of incest and survival.

The Woodcutter (2005). Director: Nicole Kassell. Convicted sex offender; starting new sexual adult sexual relationship, stereotypes of 'paedophiles'.

Twin Peaks – Fire Walk with Me (1992). Director: David Lynch. Child sexual abuse through incest; murder, sexual promiscuity.

CHAPTER **11**

MADNESS

John Read and Richard Bentall

Susan's story

Susan is in her late thirties and has been given a diagnosis of schizophrenia. She first became involved with mental health services in her late twenties when she started hearing distressing voices following the birth of her first child. Susan was sexually abused by an uncle who lived in the same house and who babysat her while her parents went out. The abuse started at a very young age and her uncle warned her that she would be sent away if she ever told anyone. He would blame her for the abuse, saying he only abused her because she wanted him to. As soon as she could, Susan left home and married her first boyfriend. Her husband, Nick, was gentle and kind and didn't abuse her. After a few years Susan became pregnant and gave birth to a baby boy. However, very soon after the birth, she began hearing a voice calling her names. Soon after this, more voices appeared. Some seemed neutral towards her and one seemed to say positive things, but the others were all very negative and distressing. Some of the voices told her to kill herself. She was very disturbed by this but when the voices told her to kill her son she decided to seek help. She saw a psychiatrist and was admitted to hospital. However, she was very worried that her son would be taken away. She was put on antipsychotic medication. She still seemed to hear voices, however, and she found the medication slowed down her thinking. When she told the doctor and nursing staff about this, they increased the dose and kept her in hospital. As a result she decided to tell them that things were better and later sought out a psychotherapist. Talking to the therapist over many sessions, she realized that the voices began after the birth of her son and that seeing him had brought back memories of the abuse; she had managed to distract herself from the memories over the years. She also began to realize that the negative voices sounded like her abusive uncle. She joined a local hearing voices group and learned some useful coping strategies, like asking the positive and neutral voices to argue back against the negative voices which they did. She also refused to talk to the voices during the day but would make an 'appointment' to talk to them in the evening. She slowly came off the medication with the support of her husband, friends and family and has been living with her voices for several years now. The family are doing well.

Leroy's story

Leroy is in his late twenties and has been involved with mental health services since his teens. He comes from a tough neighbourhood and used to be bullied on the street and at school. As a result he tended to stay at home in his room and didn't have many friends. He spent a lot of time reading science fiction, playing computer games and browsing on the internet. His relationship with

This story continues on the next page

his parents wasn't very good, however. They were very critical of him and there always seemed to be arguments at home. Leroy was quite bright, though, and was successful enough academically to go to university. He moved quite some distance away from home but he didn't seem to settle at university. He found it hard to make friends and spent increasing amounts of time alone in his student flat. He was doing an engineering degree and found the course quite stressful. One night, trying to complete an assignment, he stayed awake until the early hours and, as time went on, his sleeping pattern started to change so that he overslept during the day and began to miss lectures. At night he would spend hours on the internet. He began to feel that he was being watched so he avoided going out: he would rush to the nearby shop on campus and then return to his flat without talking to anyone. He started to feel that lots of apparently mundane things had a special significance to him. When people talked to him he thought they were indirectly criticizing him; he began to think that lots of people around him were talking about him behind his back and trying to catch him out and humiliate him. He started to develop quite a complicated belief system involving fellow students, thinking that they were working for British intelligence services. He spent long hours on the internet researching this. When he thought that TV presenters were sending him coded messages he became even more afraid. One night he was so scared that he started shouting at people in his corridor, telling them that he knew they were spying on him and reporting on his activities. The students became worried and told his personal tutor. However, when his tutor knocked on the door Leroy felt so paranoid that he barricaded himself in his apartment and his GP and the police had to be called. The door was forced open and he was taken to hospital under the Mental Health Act (see Chapter 8). He was transferred to a hospital in his home town and stayed there for several weeks, receiving antipsychotic medication. He found this whole experience very traumatic. When he came out of hospital he moved back in with his parents but found the argumentative atmosphere quite difficult. However, his community psychiatric nurse (CPN) helped him to get an apartment of his own. The CPN introduced him to a group of other young black men who were also mental health service users. They played five-a-side football regularly and he started to make friends in the group. Recently he's begun seeing a clinical psychologist who has helped him to understand some of the reasons why he began having unusual experiences. He's recently begun a creative writing class at the local college and has hopes of starting an online web magazine of science fiction short stories.

Learning outcomes

By the end of this chapter you should:

1 Have some knowledge of traditional biomedical approaches to understanding madness through psychiatric classifications like 'schizophrenia' and 'psychosis'

2 Have an appreciation of some of the problems with this approach

3 Have an understanding of an alternative approach focused on specific problematic experiences or 'complaints'

4 Have some knowledge of the social factors and psychological processes involved in the development of these psychotic experiences, and be able to evaluate the evidence for and against them

5 Have an understanding of the main approaches to helping people who have these experiences and be able to evaluate the evidence for and against them

Introduction: attempting to define madness

The term 'mad' has been with us since the 13th century but, in common with the other forms of distress discussed elsewhere in this book, madness is referred to within mainstream psychiatric classifications by a variety of technical rather than more everyday terms. **Psychosis** generally refers to psychiatric diagnoses in which there is an assumed loss of contact with reality, usually characterized by hearing or seeing things others cannot hear or see (**hallucinations**) or holding beliefs that others consider strange and unusual (**delusions**). The diagnosis most often used to label such experiences, **schizophrenia**, is considered the most severe of all, but people with primary diagnoses of **bipolar disorder** (which involves extreme fluctuations of mood) or major depression (see Chapter 9) may also be considered to be on the psychosis spectrum if they are experiencing hallucinations and delusions. Hence, this chapter, while focusing primarily on the complaints and experiences considered to be symptoms of schizophrenia, also covers mania, which is usually associated with the diagnosis of bipolar disorder.

It is interesting that, with this form of distress more than others, a mental health service user's identity is seen by others as bound up with their diagnosis. Thus, for instance, people may be referred to as a 'psychotic' or a 'schizophrenic', losing any sense of their individuality. The notion of madness evokes a mixture of fascination and fear in many of us. Most of us are frightened by the madness of others and many of us may have had moments when we fear we are going (or have gone) mad ourselves.

Chapter 2 of this book identified several themes running through the history of attempts to understand extreme human distress. The current chapter will throw more light on three of the questions raised there: Is madness understandable? Are treatments (today) sometimes abusive? and Is recovery possible? We will provide research evidence to support our conclusions that the answer to all three questions seems to be yes.

We begin, however, with consideration of two of the other themes identified in Chapter 2. The first is that, as a result of the considerable debate about terms, concepts and models in mental health, key ideas about madness are heavily contested. While this may seem obvious, there are still many experts, as we shall see, who claim that they know what schizophrenia or psychosis is, many seeming to take for granted that it is a brain disease with a strong genetic component. By contrast, Scottish psychologist Jim Geekie argues that madness is an 'essentially contested construct', meaning that, like concepts such as beauty and truth, there will probably never be universal agreement on how to define it, let alone what causes it (Geekie & Read, 2009). Box 11.1 offers brief excerpts taken from websites during 2011, illustrating just how contested madness remains today and that the conventional view that schizophrenia is an illness similar to those encountered in relation to our physical health is just one of many. Apart from the improbability of reaching agreement *within* any one culture, we have already seen, in Chapter 3, that the complexity and diversity that emerges when we consider the huge variations in definitions and explanations *between* different cultures may render agreement impossible.

The second theme, an extension of the first, is that the different views of madness held at different times do not, as most psychology textbooks and histories of psychiatry imply, represent a gradual progression from demonology to modern-day enlightened views but, rather, are determined by broader social changes. As in the past, there are powerful social and economic forces in play today. One example, rarely if ever mentioned by psychology textbooks, is the pervasive role – in professional training, research funding, drug licensing bodies and so on – of the pharmaceutical industry (Healy, Thase, Cannon et al., 2003; Moncrieff, 2007; Mosher, Gosden & Beder, 2013). Critics argue that the pharmaceutical industry promotes a medical model of human distress because, within this approach, the most common form of intervention is medication, so the promotion of a medical model approach would lead to increased sales of their products. For example, a recent internet survey found that that more than half the top schizophrenia websites are funded by drug companies and that these websites espouse a significantly more biological approach, to both causation and treatment, than websites that do not receive funding from the pharmaceutical industry (Read, 2008).

Guiding question

- *How might we best understand those experiences of distress which are seen as characteristic of madness?*

History and culture

In Chapter 2 there was a discussion of how the common-sense notion of madness, based on predominantly Western ideas, has changed overtime. It noted that there had been competing constructions of, and explanations for, the kinds of experiences now seen as associated with madness. For example, we saw that when Socrates appeared to have heard a voice it was thought of as a divine gift (something that still holds true today in modern spiritualist churches). Leudar and Thomas (2000) detail the history of the experience of hearing voices, examining Socrates' daemon, Achilles' voices in Homer's Iliad and Schreber's 'souls' as described in his memoirs. However, it is often difficult to understand these kinds of experiences

The website of Intervoice, an international web-based organization of the Hearing Voices Movement

in their original context because our current ways of thinking about madness have been so shaped by concepts developed over the last 100 years or so. As a result, in this section we will focus less on the history of the experience of madness per se, but rather on the history of its definition within psychiatric classifications.

History: the invention of schizophrenia

The development of the concept of schizophrenia was introduced in Chapter 2 but we will give a more detailed account here because of its importance. The history of scientific endeavours in relation to madness is sometimes presented as if there was a significant breakthrough, about 100 years ago, involving the discovery of a new illness, which came to be called schizophrenia. In arguing here that this was more an invention than a discovery, we are not, of course, arguing that the experiences that came to be called 'schizophrenia' (such as hearing voices or believing that everyone is out to get you) don't exist. We are arguing that applying a medical-sounding word to these experiences and a vast array of other thoughts, feelings and behaviours is not the same as discovering an illness. By using the term 'invention', rather than 'discovery', we are trying to highlight the fact that the whole notion of an illness called schizophrenia was more a construction, located in the minds of the inventors, than something that actually existed out in the real world waiting to be discovered.

Emil Kraepelin and Eugen Bleuler, still regarded by many today as the grandfathers of modern psychiatry, were jointly responsible for the invention of the schizophrenia concept. Throughout the 19th century, progress in physical medicine had been impressive and the motivation to seek similar successes in relation to madness was very strong. In 1822 Bayle found the physiological cause for one form of madness, identifying a type of brain damage in dementia paralytica or paresis, which was later identified as syphilis. This fuelled hope that other mental illnesses with physiological causes might be discovered. However, in the words of Bleuler himself: 'After Paresis was excluded ... for 70 years theoretical psychiatry stood entirely helpless before the chaos of the most frequent mental diseases' (Bleuler, 1911/1951, 1924, p. 372).

BOX 11.1

A range of views on 'what is schizophrenia', taken from Internet sources

National Institute of Mental Health (US Government)

www.nimh.nih.gov/health/topics/schizophrenia

Schizophrenia is a chronic, severe, and disabling brain disorder.

www.schizophrenia.com

Schizophrenia is a chronic, severe, and disabling brain disorder.

National Association of Mental Illness (NAMI): an influential US organization funded largely by drug companies

www.nami.org

Schizophrenia is a serious and challenging medical illness.

JANSSEN, a division of Ortho-McNeil-Janssen Pharmaceuticals, Inc.

http://www.choicesinrecovery.com/

Schizophrenia is a severe mental illness. ... Years of research have shown that schizophrenia is a biologically based brain disease.

The Royal College of Psychiatrists (UK)

http://www.rcpsych.ac.uk/mentalhealthinfoforall/problems/schizophrenia/schizophreniakeyfacts.aspx

What is schizophrenia? It is a mental disorder which affects thinking, feeling and behaviour.

What causes schizophrenia? It seems to be a combination of different factors. These include genes, subtle brain damage at birth or viral infections during pregnancy and childhood abuse.

MIND: The UK's leading mental health charity

http://www.mind.org.uk/help/diagnoses_and_conditions/schizophrenia

Many people prefer to look at schizophrenia 'holistically', and argue that these symptoms are logical or natural reactions to adverse life events. In other words, an extreme form of distress. They emphasize the need to think about individual experience, and the importance of understanding what the experiences mean to the individual. Hearing voices, for instance, holds a different significance within different cultures and spiritual belief systems.

Intervoice: an international organization run by people who hear voices

www.intervoiceonline.org

We say: Accept that the voices are real and belong to you. Accept that the voices may have meaning (metaphoric or literal) based on your life experiences. Whilst it is the case that some people define hearing voices as a symptom of medical illness, other voice hearers are able to live with their voices and consider them as a positive (or at least manageable) part of their lives.

Campaign to abolish the schizophrenia label

http://www.asylumonline.net/resources/campaign-for-the-abolition-of-schizophrenia-label/

The idea that schizophrenia can viewed as a specific, genetically determined, biologically driven, brain disease has been based on bad science and social control since its inception ... The concept of schizophrenia is unscientific and has outlived any usefulness it may once have claimed. The label schizophrenia is extremely damaging to those to whom it is applied.

A problem confronted by researchers at this stage was the lack of consensus about how to describe these forms of distress. Indeed, it has been said that, at the end of the 19th century and the beginning of the 20th, no self-respecting psychiatrist could manage without their own personal system of psychiatric classification (Kendell, 1975). The researcher of this period whose influence was to prove most enduring, Emil Kraepelin, set out to solve this problem, and developed an approach to classifying disorders that evolved over successive editions of his *Textbook of Psychiatry for Physicians and Students*. Kraepelin believed that mental health problems could, in principle, be classified in three ways: by identifying clusters of symptoms that occurred together and which had a common outcome; in terms of their pathological anatomy; and, finally, in terms of their aetiology (for example, whether a consequence of a hereditary disposition or trauma). The assumption here was that, as in general medicine, the kinds of experiences which a patient reported (e.g. hearing a voice) were seen as a symptom of an underlying disease which could only be inferred from these observable signs. Because of the absence of data on either pathological anatomy or aetiology, Kraepelin had to rely on observations of his patient's symptoms. This did not trouble him, because he assumed that all three methods of classification would yield the same result (Kraepelin, 1907). Hence, by identifying patients

with common symptoms, Kraepelin assumed that he would find patients whose problems were the result of common neurobiological and aetiological processes.

Kraepelin assiduously collected data on his patients' symptoms, lamenting in 1896 that he had collected data on only a thousand cases, which was scarcely sufficient for his purposes (Bentall, 2004). Nonetheless, by this time he had reached the conclusion that the severe psychiatric disorders – those we now term the psychoses – fell into three main categories: dementia praecox (literally, senility of the young), manic depression and paranoia.

The first of these was conceived as an irreversible disorder characterized mainly by cognitive dysfunction (Kraepelin's observations of the attentional, memory and reasoning difficulties of his patients seem strikingly modern), hallucinations and delusions. Manic depression encompassed what we now know as unipolar depression and bipolar disorder, and was thought to have a much better outcome, with most patients recovering from their difficulties. The term 'paranoia' was reserved for conditions in which delusions were experienced in clear consciousness and without the presence of hallucinations or negative symptoms.

It was a Swiss psychiatrist, Eugen Bleuler, who, objecting to the term 'dementia praecox' (he thought the condition was not a dementia and not always praecox), replaced it with the term 'schizophrenia'. It is interesting to note that Bleuler's famous 1911 monograph on the topic was entitled *Dementia Praecox or the Group of Schizophrenias* (Bleuler, 1911/1951), showing his awareness of the diversity of problems that Kraepelin had lumped together. In this book, Bleuler praised Kraepelin for his clinical concepts and Freud for enlarging the theoretical concepts available to psychopathologists. Hence, although he eventually fell out with Freud (whom he saw as far too dogmatic), Bleuler's conception of schizophrenia was influenced by psychoanalytic ideas, and emphasized subtle emotional abnormalities rather than cognitive dysfunction. For Bleuler, hallucinations and delusions were secondary symptoms that were the product of the patient's efforts to adjust to these more fundamental symptoms of emotional ambivalence, inappropriate affect, loosening of associations and autism (by which he meant a retreat into a preferred world of fantasy; a concept different from the modern diagnosis of autism).

The final important step from Kraepelin to the modern concept of schizophrenia was taken by another German psychiatrist, Kurt Schneider (1959), who came to prominence after the end of the Second World War. Schneider proposed a list of 11 'first-rank symptoms' by which schizophrenia might be identified, all of which were types of hallucinations or delusions. Although Schneider's intention was purely pragmatic – he was simply attempting to identify symptoms that were diagnostically useful and certainly did not intend them to be regarded as central to its definition – his efforts influenced a subsequent generation of American psychiatrists, who began to identify a subgroup of people who were given a diagnosis of 'Schneider-positive schizophrenia'. This eventually led to the current DSM conception of schizophrenia, which emphasizes **positive symptoms** (the presence of abnormal experiences) like hallucinations and delusions over **negative symptoms** (the absence of normal experiences) like apathy, anhedonia (an inability to experience pleasure) and flat affect (where one's emotions seem flattened).

Note that, according to Kraepelin's own account, to establish the existence of a medical illness scientifically it was necessary to demonstrate at least three things: (1) that there exists a group of people with a certain set of symptoms in common which seem to occur together more often than would be expected by chance, and which tend not to be found in people with other illnesses; (2) that there is some kind of physical pathology causing the symptom group, which tends not to be found in people with other illnesses; and (3) that people with the illness share a broadly common outcome if untreated. Interestingly, both Kraepelin and Bleuler acknowledged in their writings that these criteria had probably not been met when they were writing.

Symptoms

All Kraepelin could do, in the absence of any anatomical findings (see below), was make lists of behaviours that appeared to go together and apply a label, such as 'dementia praecox'. By 1913 he had listed a total of 36 groups of psychic symptoms and 19 types of bodily symptoms. One person could have symptoms entirely different from a second, and totally in contrast to a third. Kraepelin asserted, nevertheless:

> We are justified in regarding the majority at least of the clinical pictures which are brought together here as the expression of a single morbid process, though outwardly

they often diverge very far from one another. (Kraepelin, 1913/1919, p. 3)

Bleuler simply acknowledged:

> We do not as yet know with certainty the primary symptoms of the schizophrenic cerebral disease. (1911, p. 349)

Box 11.2 provides just a few examples of the long list of different behaviours, thoughts and feelings assumed, by Kraepelin and Bleuler, to be symptoms of their new illness. Some of them appear to have more to do with breaking the social conventions of a particular time and place than with being symptoms of a biological illness.

Causes

Bleuler admitted:

> The pathology of schizophrenia gives us no indication as to where we should look for the causes of the disease. Direct investigation for specific cause or factors has also left us stranded.

> (1911, p. 337)

Similarly, Kraepelin acknowledged that causes 'are at the present time still wrapped in impenetrable darkness' (1913, p. 224). The key words are 'at the present time'. The same words have been used repeatedly ever since, and are still used today, by researchers in search of a biological cause of schizophrenia.

Outcomes

In 1913 Kraepelin wrote:

> The undoubted inadequacy of my former classification has led me once more to undertake the attempt to make a more natural grouping. ... Recovered cases were not taken into account because of the uncertainty which still exists, but only such cases as had led to profound dementia. (pp. 89, 90)

Kraepelin apparently genuinely thought that he had discovered an incurable, degenerative illness. But some people in his grouping got better. One way to deal with this was to assume they had not really suffered from the illness in the first place. Making this manoeuvre left Kraepelin with a group of people who really did not get better, which he used as evidence that the illness existed. The logic involved might be described as circular. The famous American psychiatrist Harry Stack Sullivan (Sullivan, 1927) soon complained:

> The Kraepelinian diagnosis by outcome has been a great handicap, leading to much retrospective distortion of data, instead of careful observation and induction. (p. 760)

Bleuler had already abandoned the idea that everyone with the disease ended up with dementia. He acknowledged that 'It is impossible to describe all the variations which the course of schizophrenia may take' (p. 328), adding that 'We have not discovered any correlation between the initial disease symptoms and the severity of the outcome of the illness' (p. 261).

Clinical psychology and schizophrenia

The Kraepelinian concept of schizophrenia continues to be influential today, particularly in North America, largely as a consequence of the widespread use of the DSM diagnostic

BOX **11.2**

Symptoms of an illness or broken social norms?

They laugh on serious occasions, are rude and impertinent towards their superiors, challenge them to duels, lose their deportment and personal dignity; they go about in untidy and dirty clothes, unwashed, unkempt, go with alighted cigar into church. (Kraepelin, 1913, p. 34)

The patients sit about idle, trouble themselves about nothing, do not go to their work. (p. 37)

Patients are in love with a ward-mate with complete disregard of sex, ugliness, or even repulsiveness. (Bleuler, 1911, p. 52)

It hardly makes any difference to the patient whether he is addressing a person in authority or someone more humbly-placed whether a man or a woman. (p. 49)

A hebephrenic [an early subtype], whose very speech was confusion, held the cigar-holder to the mouth of another patient suffering from muscular atrophy....He did this with a patience and indefatigability of which no normal person would ever be capable. (p. 48)

Even decades later ... nuances of sexual pleasure, embarrassment, pain or jealously, may emerge in all their vividness which we never find in the healthy. (p. 46)

Many schizophrenics display lively affect at least in certain directions. Among them are the active writers, the world improvers, the health fanatics, the founders of new religions. (p. 41)

Perversions like homosexuality and similar anomalies are often indicated in the whole behaviour and in the dress of the patient. (Bleuler, 1924, p. 188)

system. Most historical accounts of psychosis have emphasized only the role of the psychiatric profession in our evolving understanding of psychosis, but it is worth spending a few moments considering how clinical psychologists have thought about this problem.

The profession of clinical psychology was formally established in the United States and Britain after the end of the Second World War, largely because of a perceived shortage of physicians willing to work with severe mental illness. In the United States, it was agreed at the outset that the profession would require a doctoral-level qualification (Benjamin, 2005), whereas, in the UK, training evolved more gradually from the 13-month course (focusing mainly on psychometric assessment) initially established (Derksen, 2001). In both countries, however, the new cadre of mental health professionals quickly became interested in developing new psychological therapies based on scientific principles discovered in the psychological laboratory. In the UK, this ambition became manifest in the methods of behaviour therapy (for example, systematic desensitization) inspired by Pavlovian conditioning theory, and focused on people with anxiety problems. In the USA, however, many newly qualified clinical psychologists went to work in the large state hospitals, and attempted to help severely institutionalized patients with diagnoses of psychosis.

The conditions that the psychologists found in the hospitals could fairly be described as appalling, with vast numbers of patients crammed into huge wards, supervised by poorly qualified and often abusive staff, sometimes abandoned for decades with almost no therapeutic input of any kind. Faced with this mountain of need, one approach adopted by psychologists involved simple operant conditioning techniques (very similar to those employed by animal trainers) to reward behaviours, usually self-care behaviours, that might facilitate discharge from hospital. Using detailed single case studies, it was sometimes possible to demonstrate very dramatic effects. There was no focus on the nature of people's experiences of distress. Rather, staff were often encouraged to ignore them in the hope that this process of extinction (removal of rewards) would allow them to go away (Ayllon & Michael, 1959). The ultimate form of this type of therapy was the **token economy** system, in which whole wards were subjected to systematic programmes

of reward-manipulation (Ayllon & Azrin, 1968). Although this kind of treatment was ultimately seen as dehumanizing and simplistic, careful research showed that it was very successful, particularly in terms of facilitating the discharge of people who had become highly institutionalized, so that they could live in the community (Dickerson, Tenhula & Green-Paden, 2005).

The heyday of behaviour modification for psychosis was over by the early 1980s. The gradual promotion of care in the community meant that techniques such as the token economy were no longer relevant. In the words of one prominent American psychologist, schizophrenia became behaviour modification's 'forgotten child' (Bellack, 1986). In the face of this development, clinical psychology's attitude towards psychosis has developed in two contrasting ways.

Mainly in the United States, psychologists have embraced the Kraepelinian model and the DSM system, but sought to modify some of its assumptions. Perhaps the most important manifestation of this approach was the stress-vulnerability (also known as the diathesis-stress) model of psychosis, developed mainly by researchers at the UCLA Schizophrenia Research Centre. This model sees information-processing deficits as an important (perhaps genetically determined) vulnerability factor that only results in psychotic episodes during periods of stress (Nuechterlein & Dawson, 1984). Most recently, researchers working in this framework have observed that cognitive deficits correlate poorly, if at all, with positive symptoms, but strongly predict social functioning, leading to the argument that it is cognitive dysfunction rather than hallucinations and delusions that marks the core of schizophrenia (Green, 1998).

In the UK and continental Europe, the kinds of problematic experiences associated with psychosis were ignored for many years, but from the beginning of the 1980s, began to be viewed within a quite different framework. Starting with a series of case studies, clinical psychologists began to experiment with cognitive–behavioural techniques inspired by the work of Aaron Beck (1976), the American psychiatrist famous for developing cognitive therapy for depression. This work eventually culminated in a series of fairly large-scale randomized controlled trials which showed detectable, although by no means dramatic, effects on voice-hearing and the holding of beliefs seen as delusional – so-called positive symptoms

(Tarrier & Wykes, 2004). From the point of view of the present discussion, this work led to an interest in the psychological processes involved in these kinds of experiences, an emphasis on emotional more than information-processing factors, and also an acknowledgement that environmental factors, specifically social adversity, play a major causal role in these kinds of experiences (Bentall & Fernyhough, 2008; Garety, Kuipers, Fowler, Freeman & Bebbington, 2001). Alongside the move to research particular experiences, the term 'psychosis' seems to be increasingly used instead of schizophrenia or associated diagnoses, though some commentators have warned that this move may not lead to the fundamental reconceptualization for which some of its proponents hope (see Box 11.3).

Chapter 3 outlined some of the debates concerning the relationship between culture and distress, in both how distress is defined and how it is treated. For example, Al-Issa (1995) has noted that how hallucinations are viewed varies from culture to culture. Something that might be considered a hallucination in one culture might, in another, be considered normal, such as in societies where there is less of a clear dividing line between the supernatural and the material world. Indeed, in some cultures, such as Maori in New Zealand, voice-hearing is regarded as either a natural, everyday experience or as a gift (Taitimu, 2007). Al-Issa suggested that these cultural differences also influenced how these experiences were treated. In Chapter 3 some of these issues were discussed, with a

particular focus on the diagnosis of schizophrenia. For example, it was noted that countries considered to be part of the developing world have better recovery rates than in the developed world for people with a diagnosis of schizophrenia. Since these debates have already been discussed we will not repeat them here. However, we will focus on one aspect of culture: how madness is understood by the public. This is an important issue, as it influences how people experience distress, and how others respond to it. It may also influence policy-makers' decisions about the best way of allocating funds for research and treatment.

Cultural influences on how madness is seen: stigma and prejudice

In Chapter 1 the stigma, prejudice and discrimination which mental health service users face was discussed. A diagnosis of schizophrenia attracts considerable stigma. Research findings that people given this diagnosis are subject to negative attitudes are remarkably consistent over place and time, with dangerousness and unpredictability at the core of the stereotype (Angermeyer & Matschinger, 2003; Read, 2007; Read, Haslam, Sayce & Davies, 2006); children appear to learn this prejudice early in life (Jorm & Wright, 2008).

The perception of dangerousness associated with certain diagnoses was discussed in the section on compulsory treatment in Chapter 8. The perceived association between distress

---

BOX **11.3**

Is the notion of psychosis more useful than that of schizophrenia?

In this chapter, we have chosen to focus on psychotic experiences rather than diagnostic terms like 'schizophrenia' and 'bipolar disorder'. In much recent mental health research, there has been an increasing use of the term 'psychosis' in place of these diagnoses. This is seen by some as a potentially paradigm-changing move: providing an alternative to problematic categorical diagnoses, enabling researchers to examine commonalities between the experiences of those with different diagnoses. However, some commentators have argued that the increasing popularity of the term, while bringing some positive benefits, also runs the risk of being less radical than some of its proponents hope.

Mary Boyle (2006), for example, has identified a number of problems in the literature using the term. She notes that the term is used ambiguously, variously as: identical to schizophrenia; a generic term including schizophrenia but also including other diagnoses (e.g. bipolar disorder); and finally, as a precursor to

schizophrenia. Boyle raises three key questions about this concept. Firstly, she asks whether the term psychosis is really a radical alternative if it is used interchangeably with 'schizophrenia'. She also notes that medical language and assumptions still permeate the literature even when continuum models are investigated.

Secondly, Boyle suggests that, even in research focusing on the impact of the environment and life experience, psychosis is presented as a stable category with an implied biological cause (as we saw in the 'stress-vulnerability or biopsychosocial model' section). Moreover, in this literature, links with environmental factors are sometimes presented, by biologically oriented researchers, as provisional and described in very indirect ways, implying that causal links are more debatable than biological ones. She suggests that some of the recent work on trauma, whilst acknowledging the effects of environmental causal influences, then focuses much more on intrapsychic processes than on social processes.

The third problem Boyle identifies is that much of the psychosis literature draws on a discourse of deficit. Thus a number of studies compare people with

psychotic experiences with the general population, interpreting any differences as due to purported information-processing deficits. She argues that such a focus on deficit can obscure the role of the environment and can imply that the cause of distress is biological in origin.

Boyle supports researchers who focus on particular problematic experiences like voice-hearing rather than global categories like schizophrenia and psychosis (as we have attempted to in this chapter). She supports the emphasis on continuum models and the use of general psychological theory and argues for a clearer delineation between psychotic experiences and negative life events (e.g. abuse but also more mundane problems like serious communication and relationship problems and in families, racism, extreme social isolation, etc).

However, there is continuing debate about this within the field. Some researchers argue that the notion of psychosis provides a way of challenging the category of schizophrenia. They also contend that a focus on psychological processes, rather than obscuring the link between trauma and psychotic experience, can provide a way of demonstrating the link.

and dangerousness continues, despite evidence that any actual danger is grossly exaggerated (Mullen, 1997). Contrary to the popular notion of the violent schizophrenic, people with this diagnosis are about ten times more likely to be the victim of a violent crime than to commit one (Brekke, Prindle, Bae & Long, 2001). Many users of psychiatric services suffer serious assaults as adults. One study found that in the year prior to hospitalization, 63% had suffered violence from partners and 46% of those living at home had been assaulted by family members (Cascardi, Mueser, Degiralomo & Murrin, 1996). Sexual assaults as adults are experienced by the majority of female service users and about a quarter of male service users (L. Goodman, Salyers, Mueser et al., 2001; Read, van Os, Morrison & Ross, 2005). In a study of women attending a US psychiatric emergency service, adult physical assaults outside of a relationship were reported by 29%, whilst 37% reported adult sexual assaults or rapes and 42% stated that they had experienced one or more physical assaults within an adult relationship. Rates of physical assault were particularly high for the women given a diagnosis of psychosis (Briere, Woo, McRae et al., 1997). Assaults also occur in mental health settings themselves (Tummey & Tummey, 2008).

Nevertheless, the stereotypes, negative attitudes and fears persist and are reflected in discrimination in many domains, including the workplace and housing, and can also lead to rejection by family and friends (Sayce, 2003; Wahl, 1999). They can also lead, via anticipated and actual discrimination and **internalized stigma** (where the stigmatizing attitudes of others are adopted – internalized – by service users themselves), to decreased life-satisfaction and self-esteem, and to increased alcohol use, depression and suicidality (Read, 2007; Sayce, 2003).

Although there is good reason for mental health professionals to hold the media partly responsible for perpetuating prejudice (Angermeyer & Schulze, 2001), the fundamental cause may be closer to home. Health professionals have worse attitudes than the public towards those who are distressed (Jorm, Korten, Jacomb et al., 1999). One survey of mental health service users and their families found that 'The overwhelming belief was that they experience more stigma and discrimination from mental health professionals than from any other sector of society' (Walter, 1998).

One of the themes of this book has been how views about distress are contested and one of the key areas of contention, as we have seen in other chapters, concerns the explanations given for the causes of distress.

Public opinion about the causes of distress

It is interesting to note that surveys in 22 out of 23 countries find that, when asked about the causes of schizophrenia, the public (including people given a diagnosis of schizophrenia themselves, and their family members), while expressing many different opinions, consistently place much greater emphasis on social causes than on biological/medical factors (Read et al., 2006; Read, Magliano & Beavan, 2013). The exception is the USA, where the public seems to have recently moved towards a more biological perspective, perhaps as a result of strident advertising campaigns from the drug companies (see below).

For example, a survey of Australians found that respondents believed the most likely cause of schizophrenia was 'Problems from childhood such as being badly treated or abused, losing one or both parents when young or coming from a broken home'; this was rated as a likely cause by 91%. 'Day-to-day-problems such as stress, family arguments, difficulties at work

or financial difficulties' was endorsed by 90%, 'The recent death of a close friend or relative' by 88% and 'Traumatic events' by 87%. 'Inherited or genetic' causes were endorsed by 70% (Jorm, Christensen & Griffiths, 2005). When Londoners were asked about schizophrenia, 'Overall subjects seemed to prefer environmental explanations referring to social stressors and family conflicts – e.g. "being mercilessly persecuted by family and friends and having come from backgrounds that promote stress" ' (Furnham & Rees, 1988, p. 218). Another London study found that the most endorsed causal model of schizophrenia was 'Unusual or traumatic experiences or the failure to negotiate some critical stage of emotional development', followed by 'Social, economic, and family pressures' (Furnham & Bower, 1992, p. 204). 'It seems that lay people have not been converted to the medical view and prefer psychosocial explanations' (p. 207). 'Subjects agreed that schizophrenic behaviour had some meaning and was neither random nor simply a symptom of an illness' (p. 206).

These findings, in countries as diverse as the USA, China, Ethiopia, India, Japan, Russia, Mongolia, Germany, Greece and Turkey is remarkable, especially given the millions of pounds spent over the past two decades to convince the public they are wrong. The goal of all this expenditure has been to increase what has become called 'mental health literacy' (Jorm, 2000), a term for the extent to which we, the public, agree with biologically-oriented psychiatrists and the drug industry that mental health problems are brain diseases with strong genetic bases. When people given a diagnosis of schizophrenia express the same views as the majority of the public they are often told they have no insight, which sometimes comes to be seen as another symptom of their illness (Lysaker, Yanos & Roe, 2009).

The relationship of causal beliefs to attitudes

Many destigmatization campaigns have adopted the 'mental illness is an illness like any other' approach, designed to educate the public to believe that human distress, confusion and despair are symptoms of biologically-based mental illnesses. The idea is that if we think of people as ill, we won't hold them responsible for their negative behaviours and will, therefore, be more accepting of them. For example, a Canadian study, emanating from the World Psychiatric Association schizophrenia campaign, funded by the drug company Eli Lilly, portrays the belief that schizophrenia is a 'debilitating disease' as 'knowledgeable' and 'sophisticated'. (Thompson et al., 2002).

Numerous studies show, however, that rather than biological and genetic causal beliefs being related to positive attitudes, the opposite is the case. A review of twelve studies showed that all but one found either that bio-genetic beliefs about the causes of mental health problems are related to negative attitudes or that psychosocial causal beliefs are related to positive attitudes (Read et al., 2006). For example, two New Zealand studies found that young adults with bio-genetic causal beliefs experience people with mental health problems as more dangerous and unpredictable, and are less likely to interact with them, than those with psychosocial causal beliefs (Read & Harré, 2001; Read & Law, 1999). In a US experiment, participants in a learning task increased electric shocks faster if they understood their partner's mental health problems in disease terms than if they believed they were a result of childhood events (Mehta & Farina, 1997).

Another New Zealand study compared the effects of two versions of a video on two groups of undergraduate mathematics students. Viewing a video of a person describing hallucinations and delusions followed by a bio-genetic explanation significantly increased perceptions of dangerousness and unpredictability, but a video of the identical behaviours explained as reactions to adverse life events led to a small (though statistically non-significant) improvement in attitudes (Walker & Read, 2002). Unsurprisingly, a **normalizing approach** (in which experiences are explained as within the range of normal responses) is more effective than a **pathologizing** one (in which experiences are seen as symptoms of an illness) in reducing stigma about psychosis (French et al., 2011).

Studies of 5025 Germans have found that belief in either 'brain disease' or 'heredity' increased fear, but if psychosocial stressors were seen as the cause, reactions were more favourable (Angermeyer & Matschinger, 2003). Further analysis of the same data confirmed that bio-genetic causal beliefs (particularly brain disease) were particularly predictive of perceived dangerousness and a desire for **social distance** (Dietrich, Matschinger & Angermeyer, 2006).

The same research team analysed interviews with 745 Russians and 950 Mongolians plus their original sample, which had consisted of West and East Germans (Dietrich et al., 2004). They found that the belief that schizophrenia is a brain disease was associated with a greater desire for social distance in three of the four samples, and the belief that heredity is a cause was associated with a greater desire for distance in all four samples.

The relationship between bio-genetic causal beliefs and negative attitudes also exists among professionals and mental health service users. Mental health staff with a biological perspective assess the people they are trying to help as more disturbed (Langer & Abelson, 1974), and are less inclined to involve service users in planning services (Kent & Read, 1998). A US study presented a biological explanation to some service users and a psychosocial explanation to others, and found that those given the biological explanation made fewer efforts to change themselves or their situation and consumed more alcohol to try to cope with their problems (Fisher & Farina, 1979). A UK study found that service users who accepted their diagnosis felt they had less control over their condition and that depression in psychotic service users is 'linked to patients' perception of controllability of their illness and absorption of cultural stereotypes of mental illness' (Birchwood, Mason, MacMillan & Healy, 1993, p. 387).

One recent review found that 90% of all studies in this field show that bio-genetic causal beliefs are related to negative attitudes or that psychosocial causal beliefs are related to positive attitudes, or both (Read, Haslam & Magliano, 2013). Another recent review, by one of the most prolific researchers in the field, German psychiatrist Professor Matthias Angermeyer, and his colleagues, confirmed that bio-genetic causal beliefs 'were related to stronger rejection in most studies examining schizophrenia' and concluded that 'Biogenetic causal models are an inappropriate means of reducing rejection of people with mental illness' (Angermeyer, Hozinger, Carta & Achomerus, 2012, p. 367).

Contemporary Western forms of distress

Prevalence

In Chapter 3 we saw that the claim that schizophrenia rates were the same around the world, and that this indicated that schizophrenia was biological in origin, was problematic because of a number of methodological flaws, including how the diagnostic criteria were defined and assessed. Saha, Chant, Welham and McGrath (2005) reviewed the prevalence estimates for the diagnosis of schizophrenia from 188 studies drawn from 46 countries. They reported an estimated median **point prevalence** (i.e. the number of people meeting diagnostic criteria at a particular point in time) of 4.6 per 1000 people and a **lifetime prevalence** (i.e. how many people would meet the criteria over the course of their lifetime) as 4 per 1000. However, they noted that there was considerable variability with estimates varying 3.4-fold for point prevalence, despite the fact that their methodology ignored 20% of the variation of the distribution in the tails of the graphs and they acknowledged that rates would have been 'much higher' (4.23) if they had not done this.

Weissman et al. (1996) reviewed population-based epidemiological studies using similar methods from 10 countries (the USA, Canada, Puerto Rico, France, West Germany, Italy, Lebanon, Taiwan, Korea and New Zealand) and reported that lifetime prevalence estimates for the diagnosis of bipolar disorder varied from 0.3/100 in Taiwan to 1.5/100 in New Zealand.

However, these estimates need to be treated with considerable caution, not only because of methodological problems with the studies in relation to issues of measurement but because they are based on diagnostic concepts that are themselves problematic. As we will go on to argue in more detail in the next section, the diagnosis of schizophrenia, for example, lacks validity and reliability, thus rendering prevalence estimates deeply flawed. And later in the chapter we will suggest that an alternative approach to the use of these categories is to focus on particular kinds of experience, such as hearing voices or having unusual beliefs. It is possible to examine prevalence in a different way, then, by investigating how common these experiences are.

A number of studies have examined the prevalence of voice-hearing in the general population. Tien (1991) reported the results of a large (18,000 participants) US population survey of psychiatric symptoms. An estimated 11–13% had experienced hallucinations at some time in their lives (twice as many women as men). Voices occurred throughout the lifespan but appeared to be more commonly experienced by older people. Van Os et al. (2000) collected data using a structured diagnostic interview schedule from 7000 Dutch people randomly selected from the general population. They specifically excluded abnormal experiences considered to be caused by drug-taking or physical illness. They reported that 1.7% of their sample met the criteria for 'true' hallucinations, but a further 6.2% met all the diagnostic criteria for delusions except the criterion of accompanying distress.

Similar studies have been conducted into the holding of unusual beliefs (or delusions). Van Os et al. (2000) reported that 3.3% of their sample had 'true' delusions whilst 8.7% had delusions that were not associated with distress and did not require intervention. Poulton et al. (2000) interviewed a whole birth-cohort of children in Dunedin in New Zealand at the age of 11, using a structured diagnostic interview schedule, and followed them up at the age of 26. This 15-year longitudinal study found that 20.1% of the 26-year-olds held beliefs which met the diagnostic criteria for delusions, with 12.6% judged as being paranoid.

Similarly, a Swiss study found that about 5% of the population experience hypomanic episodes, with 10% experiencing less severe subdiagnostic hypomanic symptoms (Angst, 1998). A Swedish study found that 82% of recently bereaved elderly persons experienced hallucinations and/or illusions such as feeling the presence of their deceased spouse. Thirty percent reported hearing the voice of their loved one within the first month of their death, and 6% were still hearing them 12 months later (Grimby, 1993). A recent review of 17 studies of the prevalence of hearing voices in the general population found that the median (midpoint) was 13.2% (Beavan, Read & Cartwright, 2011).

Thus, when particular experiences are examined, we can see that they are much more common than the traditional prevalence estimates for the diagnoses of schizophrenia and bipolar disorder imply. In the next section, we examine some of the reasons why diagnoses like these are flawed and outline an alternative approach based on experiences.

The DSM

Chapter 5 discussed some of the issues involved in classifying different kinds of distress, focusing in particular on the American Psychiatric Association's Diagnostic and Statistical Manual, or DSM. The lists of behaviours, feelings and thoughts considered to be indicative of each of the many mental health problems in the DSM-IV-TR (APA, 2000) represent a huge amount of work on the part of psychiatrists. Their goal is to bring some order to the hundreds of ways that humans experience emotional distress and become disturbed or disturbing. Their belief is that categorizing unusual or abnormal human behaviour will help us understand its causes and will lead to the development of more effective treatments.

In this chapter we are continuing to focus on the kind of psychotic experiences associated with the experience of madness. The two main diagnostic categories which these experiences normally attract are bipolar disorder and schizophrenia. We will look at both of them in this chapter, particularly schizophrenia.

In DSM-IV a person may be give a diagnosis of bipolar I disorder or bipolar II disorder. The criteria for a bipolar I disorder include experiencing major depression (see Chapter 9) and one or more manic or mixed episodes. In a **manic episode**, a person has an abnormal and persistently elevated, expansive or irritable mood lasting at least a week. These moods would have at least three of the following features: grandiosity; decreased need for sleep; more talkative than usual; racing thoughts; distractibility; agitation; and engaging in behaviour without apparent cognisance of its consequences (e.g. excessive spending or promiscuity). In a **mixed episode** the person's moods fluctuate between depression and mania. A person might have psychotic experiences when in a depressed, manic or mixed episode; for example, in a manic episode a person might have very grandiose beliefs about themselves. The criteria for a bipolar II disorder are broadly similar except that a person's mood is considered **hypomanic** (a milder form of mania where a person is affected, but not as seriously as in a manic episode). The criteria exclude anyone having psychotic experiences (for which a bipolar I diagnosis would be considered). The ICD-10 definition is broadly similar, though the DSM-IV criteria mean that only a single manic or mixed episode is required, whereas the ICD-10 criteria require both depression and mania or two mixed episodes.

To receive a diagnosis of schizophrenia using DSM-IV-TR you need two of five Characteristic Symptoms for at least a month. These are: (1) hallucinations, (2) delusions, (3) disorganized speech (an expression of thought disorder), (4) grossly disorganized or catatonic behaviour (a kind of stupor marked by an extreme rigidity or laxness of limbs), and (5) negative symptoms (American Psychiatric Association, 1994, p. 285). Negative symptoms might include blunted affect (lack or decline of emotional response), alogia (lack or decline in speech) or avolition (lack or decline in motivation).

To receive the diagnosis of schizophrenia there must have been a marked decline in one or more major areas of functioning such as work, interpersonal relations or self-care, and there must have been continuous signs of these problems for at least six months. If the signs have been present for more than one month but less than six, the diagnosis of schizophreniform disorder is used. Psychotic symptoms lasting less than a month may be diagnosed as brief psychotic disorder, and some other conditions may be classed as psychotic disorder not otherwise specified.

The first problem with the diagnostic construct of schizophrenia is that there are 15 ways (1+2 v. 3+4; 1+2 v. 3+5, etc.) in which two people can meet the DSM criteria for schizophrenia without having any of the characteristic symptoms in common. This can be illustrated with a brief example of two mental health service users: Jim and Debra. Jim hears voices and is considered by psychiatrists to have very disordered thoughts but no other symptoms. Psychiatrists consider Debra to have delusional beliefs and a range of negative symptoms, but no other symptoms. Both Jim and Debra could meet the criteria for a diagnosis of schizophrenia even though Jim has none of Debra's symptoms and vice versa. The term for this sort of construct is 'disjunctive'. This problem was highlighted more than 40 years ago by British psychologist Don Bannister in his famous paper 'The logical requirements of research into schizophrenia' in which he argued that 'Disjunctive categories are logically too primitive for scientific use' and he concluded that: 'Schizophrenia as a concept, is a semantic Titanic, doomed before it sails, a concept so diffuse as to be unusable in a scientific context' (Bannister, 1971, p. 181).

To make matters worse, according to the DSM, you only need one symptom if the voices you hear keep up a running commentary on your behaviour, or if they talk to each other, or if the delusions are bizarre. When 50 senior American psychiatrists were asked to differentiate bizarre and non-bizarre delusions, the researchers concluded: 'The symptom of bizarre delusions does not have adequate reliability' (Mojtabi & Nicholson, 1995, p. 1807). So you can be given a diagnosis of schizophrenia on the basis of just one symptom, for which psychiatrists struggle to agree a definition.

For DSM-5, the American Psychiatric Association has proposed 'elimination of requirement that only one characteristic symptom be present because no unique diagnostic specificity for these characteristic symptoms in comparison to others has been identified' (American Psychiatric Association, 2010). The American Psychiatric Association also proposes that at least one of the two required symptoms be hallucinations, delusions or disorganized speech. This would reduce the number of ways that two people can receive the same diagnosis without having any symptoms in common from 15 to 12. Nevertheless, the construct would remain disjunctive and, therefore, scientifically meaningless.

Problems with the traditional psychiatric account

To ask whether schizophrenia exists is not to question whether people sometimes have experiences that are unusual or difficult to understand, and sometimes suffer extreme emotional pain and confusion as a consequence. The issue we wish to address here is: does the diagnostic category of schizophrenia meet accepted requirements for establishing a scientific concept? This issue was discussed, to some extent, in Chapter 5. As in that chapter, to address this question we must ask whether there is agreement about when to use the concept (reliability) and whether it is useful in terms of understanding or explaining anything (validity) (Bentall, 2003; Boyle, 1999, 2002; Read, 2004a, 2004c)?

Reliability

As we saw in Chapter 5, a central test of whether a construct is scientifically reliable is whether a reasonable level of agreement can be reached about whether the thing in front of a group of observers is, or is not, the construct in question. In our case we are interested in whether psychologists, psychiatrists or other experts can agree on whether one person meets the diagnostic criteria for schizophrenia and another does not. As early as the late 1930s it had been concluded that: 'It is clear that the Kraepelinian system is inadequate on precisely these grounds' (Boisen, 1938, p. 235). It was accurately predicted, nevertheless, that:

> There always will be many who will use the existing system of classification irrespective of whether or not it has any meaning, and even those who decry the orthodox classification will invoke it as an atheist when off guard invokes God.

Jellinek (1939, p. 161)

Early psychologists, some working in hospitals before the formal establishment of the clinical specialty, tried to develop tests with the aim of improving diagnostic procedures. Before the midpoint of the century, however, some had concluded that 'The psychiatric taxonomy which psychologists have been constrained to adopt is so inadequate, even for psychiatry, that no patching can fix it up' (Roe, 1949, p. 38). In the same year it was discovered that clinicians agreed with each other's diagnoses in only between a third and a half of cases (Ash, 1949). One of the largest reliability studies ever undertaken, using the **test-retest** approach (where people are diagnosed and then re-diagnosed after the passage of some period of time), found that consistency for schizophrenia was only 37% (Hunt, Wittson & Hunt, 1953).

These sorts of findings led to a concerted effort to improve diagnostic procedures, and thereby reliability (Read, 2004c). But by 1962 one leading group of researchers (Ward, Beck, Mendelson, Mock & Erbaugh, 1962) found that agreement between pairs of clinicians for schizophrenia was still only .53 or – using the correct statistic (kappa), which allows for agreement by chance – .42 (Read, 2004c).

Later, it was observed that massive differences existed in the way that the schizophrenia concept was employed in different countries. When 134 US and 194 British psychiatrists were given case descriptions, 69% of the former gave a diagnosis of schizophrenia, but only 2% of the latter (Copeland, Cooper, Kendell & Gourlay, 1971). In 1973, following the observation that the schizophrenia concept was also being employed very broadly in the USSR (now Russia), the World Health Organization concluded that Kraepelin's attempt to create a concept of dementia praecox had been unsuccessful (World Health Organization, 1973).

Widespread public concern about this problem was prompted by a famous study in which normal people, admitted to psychiatric hospitals after saying they heard the words 'empty' and 'thud' when no one was around, were given a diagnosis of schizophrenia. Many of the people being treated in the hospital, but none of the staff, recognized that these **pseudo-patients** (people playing the role of a psychiatric patient) were not distressed and were engaged in normal activities whilst on the ward (though, these too, were interpreted by staff as psychiatric symptoms). A follow-up study, in which hospital staff were told that they would be sent pseudo-patients for assessment, resulted in staff reporting that 21% of their patients were pseudo-patients, even though the researcher had deliberately sent none (Rosenhan, 1973).

In 1992, a group of researchers identified 16 different systems for classifying schizophrenia. Out of 248 people, the number given a diagnosis of schizophrenia in terms of these systems ranged from 1 to 203 (Herron, Schultz & Welt, 1992). In 1996 US psychiatrist Howard James stated that schizophrenia is 'an unscientific and unprovable nosological construct, which has outlived its usefulness in the lexicon of modern psychiatry' (p. 148). A more recent study of African–American people found no significant relationship between diagnoses of schizophrenia by clinicians and *either* of two diagnostic processes used by researchers, with agreement rates of just 11% and 13% (Whaley, 2001).

Validity

In Chapter 5 we noted that to establish a construct's validity it is necessary to investigate whether the construct is related to observations to which the theory underpinning the construct says it should be related. In the case of the illness theory of schizophrenia, these observations include: (a) a set of symptoms that occur together more often than would be expected by chance and which tend not to occur in people given a diagnosis of other mental health problems; (b) some degree of predictability in terms of outcome; c) a consistent biological cause, and (d) responsiveness to treatments. Next we will examine evidence touching on the first two of these four issues: symptoms (a) and outcome (b), and return later to causes and treatments.

a) Symptoms

Statistical analyses of the association between different symptoms have usually employed factor analysis. Factor analysis attempts to reduce a matrix of correlations between variables (in this case, ratings of symptoms) to the minimum number of dimensions (Blashfield, 1984). According to Kraepelin's original conception of schizophrenia, we would expect a single factor of symptoms to emerge from this exercise (indicating that a person having one symptom of the disorder would be likely to have most of the others).

Modern investigations began with the work of Peter Liddle (1987), who attempted to test a suggestion by Tim Crow (1980) that there was not one syndrome of schizophrenia, but two. Crow (and subsequently Andreasen & Olsen, 1982) hypothesized that positive symptoms such as delusions and hallucinations were caused by a dysregulation (i.e. an impairment) of the dopamine system, whereas negative symptoms such as flat affect and social withdrawal were caused by cerebral atrophy. Liddle, however, found three clusters of psychotic symptoms: positive symptoms; negative symptoms; and symptoms of cognitive disorganization, a schema that is not consistent with either the Kraepelinian model or Crow's two-factor model. Similar results, or an even greater number of factors, have been reported by subsequent researchers (e.g. Murphy, Shevlin, Adamson & Houston, 2011).

A general problem with these studies, as Maric et al. (2004) have pointed out, is that they tend to be based on clinical samples that are affected by a statistical phenomenon known as **Berkson's bias**, which is that, since people with multiple symptoms are probably more likely to seek help than those with only a few symptoms, the observed correlation between symptoms is likely to be inflated in clinical samples when compared with samples drawn at random from the community. Maric et al. (2004) used epidemiological data collected in the Netherlands to show that this bias accounted for the apparently high number of people observed with both positive and negative symptoms. In their general population sample, the two types of symptoms occurred together much less often.

As we would expect, symptoms leading to a schizophrenia diagnosis are found in other diagnostic groups in the same way that people given a diagnosis of, say, tuberculosis and lung cancer will share some symptoms. Hallucinations and delusions are therefore often reported by service users with other diagnoses such as bipolar disorder (Goodwin & Jamison, 1990) and major depression (Lattuada, Serretti, Cusin, Gasperini & Smerald, 1999). With the schizophrenia diagnosis, however, the situation goes well beyond what we find in medicine, with most people given a diagnosis of schizophrenia actually meeting the criteria for one or several additional diagnoses, suggesting that the diagnostic criteria are not doing their job of properly distinguishing between different kinds of problem. This issue is often referred to as co-morbidity (Crow, 2010). For example, in the analysis of data from a large, US epidemiological study, it was found that individuals with a DSM-III diagnosis of schizophrenia had a risk 14 times greater than chance of also meeting the diagnostic criteria for depression and a 46 times greater than chance of also meeting the diagnostic criteria for mania. Surprisingly, the authors of the study concluded that 'The most likely explanation for co-occurrence is that having one disorder puts the affected person at risk of developing other disorders' (Robins, Locke & Reiger, 1991). An alternative, and more parsimonious, interpretation is that there are significant problems with the categorical nature of the classificatory system itself. In other words, this system does not, in the words of the 18th-century scientific taxonomist Carl Linnaeus, 'cleave nature at its joints'. As we have seen in the other chapters focused on different forms of distress, this problem is regularly encountered, and a number of studies have now reported high levels of co-morbidity between schizophrenia and obsessive–compulsive disorder, panic disorder, personality disorders, substance abuse, PTSD, anxiety disorders (Craig & Hwang, 2000) and dissociative disorders (Ellason & Ross, 1995).

b) Outcomes

Kraepelin believed that a diagnosis of schizophrenia always resulted in a poor outcome for the person; hence his assumption that it was a type of dementia. However, an examination of the evidence of long-term outcome studies reveals that,

in contrast to this assumption, there is massive variation in outcomes, and many people given a diagnosis of schizophrenia subsequently recover.

Estimates of long-term recovery rates range from 13% (Stephens, Richard & McHugh, 1997) to 72% (Thara & Eaton, 1996), with most falling between 30% and 55% (Ciompi, 1980, 1984; Harding, Brooks, Ashikaga et al., 1987; Harrison et al., 2001). By the turn of the century there was increasing evidence of rates in excess of 50% (Kruger, 2000).

A clear demonstration of outcome variability was provided by Manfred Bleuler (1978), the son of Eugen Bleuler. From a 20-year study of hospitalized people with a diagnosis of schizophrenia at the Burgholzi Clinic (where his father had worked), he found the following stable outcomes: severe – 15%; moderate – 17%; mild – 38%; recovery – 30 %. Swiss psychiatrist Luc Ciompi (1980) found similar variability in a 37-year study: severe – 20%; intermediate – 26%; minor – 22%; recovery – 30%.

In Vermont, Harding and colleagues (1987) studied 'the sickest group in the hospital'. The people making up their sample had been hospitalized for ten years at the outset of the study. In the 12 months preceding the follow-up assessment, an average of 32 years later, 82% had not been in hospital, 40% were employed (despite two thirds being 55 or older) and 68% had few or no symptoms. In 2001 a World Health Organization review of outcomes in 18 countries reported an average recovery rate, after 15 or 25 years, of 48% (Harrison et al., 2001).

Ciompi concludes:

> There is no such thing as a specific course for schizophrenia. Doubtless, the potential for improvement of schizophrenia has for a long time been grossly under-estimated. What is called 'the course of schizophrenia' more closely resembles a life process open to a great variety of influences of all kinds than an illness with a given course.
>
> (1980, p. 420)

Importantly, it has been repeatedly demonstrated that outcomes in poorer countries (e.g. Nigeria and India) are far superior to those in wealthy industrialized societies (Bresnahan, Menezes, Varma & Susser, 2003; Harrison et al., 2001; Warner, 2004, 2008); this was discussed in Chapter 3.

Kraepelin's idea of a consistently negative outcome, which influenced psychiatry for a century, has been challenged by some significant forces within psychiatry. In their 2001 review of data from the WHO *International Study of Schizophrenia* (ISoS), Harrison et al. (2001, p. 513) conclude:

> Because expectations can be so powerful a factor in recovery, patients, families and clinicians need to hear this ... The ISoS joins others in relieving patients, carers and clinicians of the chronicity paradigm, which dominated thinking throughout much of the 20th century.

If the assumptions of the Kraepelinian paradigm are problematic, how might we go about developing an alternative way of viewing the kinds of distressing experiences that have often been associated with the notion of schizophrenia? In the next section, we will outline an alternative approach.

An alternative approach to researching psychotic experiences

Researching reliable constructs

There have been many attempts to break the construct of schizophrenia into smaller, more reliable, categories.

Traditionally, this has been attempted by trying to define various subtypes of schizophrenia. For example, DSM-IV, (APA, 1994) suggests the following subtypes: paranoid, disorganized, catatonic, undifferentiated and residual. However, these categories are often theoretically- rather than empirically-based. Another and, in our view, a better approach is to see which kinds of problematic experience or complaint (or 'symptom' within a medical framework) actually occur together, using statistical techniques such as factor analysis and cluster analysis. As discussed in Chapter 5, when we follow this approach, it is useful to think in terms of dimensions along which experiences might vary, rather than discrete diagnostic categories (McGorry, Bell, Dudgeon & Jackson, 1998; Read, 2004c). Normal human behaviours, thoughts and feelings vary significantly over time and between differing social contexts. So do those considered abnormal.

As we have already seen, efforts along these lines have suggested that psychotic experiences can be described in three or more underlying dimensions (Liddle, 1987). A recent attempt to build a model of psychosis on this basis has been proposed by van Os & Kapur (2009), who suggest that all those with diagnoses of severe mental illness, whatever their categorical diagnosis, can be mapped onto five dimensions: Liddle's positive, negative and cognitive disorganization factors plus factors of mania and depression.

In addition to this search for reliable groupings of behaviours and experiences, as we have seen in other chapters, there has also been an increasing focus on specific behaviours and experiences, free from any diagnostic assumptions. Once we focus on definable and measurable constructs like hallucinations, delusions and mania rather than larger-scale heterogeneous categories like 'schizophrenia', significant progress is made in our ability to understand and to help. Constructs like hallucinations and delusions can themselves be broken down into clinically valuable and highly reliable dimensional variables such as duration, intensity, frequency, conviction, disruption and distress (Kingdon & Turkington, 2005; Morrison, 2004). As

with any area of research, however, there are debates about the most appropriate definition of these concepts. Definitions of delusions, for example, have been subject to considerable debate (see Box 11.4).

The DSM-IV devotes just three of its 886 pages to its only dimensional measure. *The Global Assessment of Functioning Scale* (GAF) records the clinician's judgement of overall level of functioning. Its inclusion is an advance, an acknowledgement that mental health is a matter of degree. Dimensional measures of mental health are more reliable than diagnoses. When clinicians were asked to assess 258 people in terms of *degree* of psychopathology, inter-rater reliability was high and the researchers concluded that 'independent judges may not agree regarding what a person has, but they show remarkable agreement in deciding how severe it is' (Rosenthal et al., 1975, p. 42). The DSM-IV's GAF (and its two trial dimensions measuring relational and social/occupational functioning – (pp. 758–60) also have high levels of inter-rater reliability (Hilsenroth et al., 2000).

A review of studies comparing dimensional and categorical representations of behaviours considered indicative of schizophrenia concluded that the dimensional approach appeared to be more useful in terms of yielding information on a person's needs and outcome (van Os & Verdoux, 2003). Largely due to the lobbying efforts of Dutch psychiatrist Professor Jim van Os, the first draft of the DSM-5 includes a system for rating the severity of specific types of psychotic experiences such as hallucinations and delusions (American Psychiatric Association, 2010). If included in the final version, due out in 2013, this would be a significant step towards a more helpful, and scientific, approach to assessment.

The dimensional approach, covering a range of severities and frequencies, is also helpful in showing how many of the general population have psychotic experiences (Johns & van Os, 2001). Earlier in this chapter we described how van Os et al. (2000) had reported much higher rates of hallucinations and delusions than might traditionally have been expected. The Hearing Voices Network, discussed in Chapter 7, is making it

---

BOX **11.4**

Debates about delusions

We have argued in this chapter for the need to focus on particular kinds of experience like auditory hallucinations or delusions. These constructs appear to be reliably measurable but, even here, there are definitional debates about what constitutes a delusion (Boyle, 2002). For example the DSM definition of a delusion views it as a false belief and yet Maher (1992) argues that this diagnosis is often made without an independent empirical investigation of a person's belief claims. The DSM suggests that a delusional belief is one held despite incontrovertible evidence to the contrary. This implies that all beliefs have a truth value that is empirically verifiable but many are not – for example, how might

one disprove a belief in time travel or the devil? Moreover, it also implies that all normal beliefs are evidentially-based but what about moral, political or religious beliefs – are such beliefs based simply on evidence? The DSM definition asserts that a delusional belief is not ordinarily accepted by other members of a person's culture or sub-culture but it offers no guidance on what the appropriate cultural comparison group for a person might be and how one might go about gathering evidence on this, particularly when surveys suggest that there are high rates of belief in Western societies in ghosts, clairvoyance, UFOs and so on (Harper, 2011). Heise (1988) has argued that delusions are beliefs considered to be lacking social value or currency. He suggests that the diagnosis of delusion is a social act where the diagnoser's view

of reality is privileged over that of the holder of a belief. For example, one of the authors (JR) once had a client who had the 'delusion' that he was being watched 24 hours a day, wherever he went. It turned out that this was true; his mother, out of genuine concern for his deteriorating mental health, had arranged for friends and relatives to follow the client when he went out and to peak in through the windows when he was home. But she had not told him about this. Debates like these mean that the term 'delusion' is contested as critics argue that it is a pathologising term. Alternatives include 'unshared beliefs', 'having an alternative sense of reality' and, as one mental health survivor Dr Tamasin Knight has suggested 'beliefs that might not be easily confirmable' (Hornstein, 2009, p. 136).

easier for the millions of people that these figures represent to talk more openly about their experiences without fear of being deemed crazy. Awareness of such high numbers in the general population should help to normalize what are often seen as very rare and very strange experiences. In Chapter 1 it was noted that these experiences seem to be a part of normal human experience and it is curious how they have come to be seen as 'abnormal'. However, perhaps we need to question what we mean by the word 'normal' (Kingdon, 2009).

Despite the evidence detailed here, many psychologists and psychiatrists continue to use the categorical, rather than the dimensional, approach. Perhaps part of the attraction is that categorizing creates the impression that we then know what it is we are looking at, and even what has caused the behaviours we have just labelled (as in 'the hallucinations are caused by the schizophrenia'). For some psychiatrists, it may also bolster their belief that the complexities of human distress are indeed just like medical illnesses, which can be categorized via the same diagnostic process used by their colleagues in other branches of medicine.

Causal processes

In Chapter 4 it was argued that a consistent flaw in much mental health research has been the failure to conceptualize the way in which biology and the social world interact. That chapter also discussed how biochemistry and genetics were given primacy in discussions of causal processes. We see this, for example, when researchers talk of 'the biological basis of behaviour' and in many textbooks, these 'biological bases' often appear first in any discussion of causal factors. In contrast, Chapter 4 argued that these elements enable rather than cause, that the social and biological are mutually influential and that causal processes are often probabilistic rather than deterministic. As a result, the approach adopted within this book has been to identify the evidence for a variety of causal factors in the development of distress without necessarily giving any one factor a predetermined primacy. Indeed, discussions of causal processes in earlier chapters often present the social factors first. However, we think that dominant conceptualizations of schizophrenia are so associated with simplistic and reductive accounts which make unwarranted claims about biochemistry and genetics that we need to address these issues first before moving onto the evidence considering social and psychological factors, even though, as we will see, these appear to be much more important in the development of psychotic experiences than is often supposed.

As with other chapters, much of the material we will draw on is based on studies where the diagnosis of schizophrenia has been used rather than an approach focused on particular experiences. Therefore, as with earlier chapters, we will endeavour to recover what we can that is useful from these studies and, where possible, draw on evidence linked to particular kinds of problematic experience. There is a need for researchers to focus more on these experiences in future rather than global and heterogeneous categories like 'schizophrenia'.

The stress-vulnerability or bio-psychosocial model

The third piece of evidence needed to establish the validity of the construct of schizophrenia is about causation. We begin with a discussion of the **stress-vulnerability model**. This assumes that we inherit varying degrees of genetic susceptibility to mental illnesses. The greater this inherited vulnerability, the smaller the amount of stressors required to trigger the illness. This is an example of an approach that claims to provide a **bio-psychosocial model** of the causation of distress. This model is presented in most psychology textbooks as if it were a balanced integration of biological and psychosocial perspectives. However, in Chapter 4 we described problems with this model, namely that it lacked definition and that, by treating the 'bio', 'psycho' and 'social' as discrete factors, rather than as interpenetrating elements, it failed to establish a clear explanation of the development of forms of distress.

In 1977 Zubin and Spring published their landmark paper 'Vulnerability: A new view of schizophrenia'. Their stress-vulnerability model offered the possibility of a genuine integration of psychosocial and biological research. Unfortunately, rather than embrace this opportunity, biological enthusiasts distorted the model by decreeing that the purported heightened vulnerability to stress must be biological in origin (usually genetic, but with some attention to perinatal factors). Psychosocial factors were thereby relegated to mere triggers, or exacerbators, of a genetic predisposition without which schizophrenia could supposedly not develop. However, Zubin and Spring had included in their proposal a discussion of 'acquired vulnerability' which could be 'due to the influence of trauma, specific diseases, perinatal complications, family experiences, adolescent peer interactions, and other life events that either enhance or inhibit the development of subsequent disorder' (Zubin & Spring, 1977, p. 109). Surprisingly, much more attention has been focused on hypothesized biological vulnerability rather than acquired vulnerability.

A genetic predisposition to schizophrenia?

It is often assumed that there is a strong genetic predisposition to schizophrenia. We have already discussed the first problem with this assertion, that there is really no such thing as schizophrenia because of the poor reliability of the construct. Nevertheless it is important to evaluate the evidence that has been put forward to support the argument that there is a genetic predisposition to the experiences and behaviours that tend to lead to receiving this diagnosis. The evidence for this comes in two forms: studies of families and, more recently, studies of genes.

Family studies

A common assumption is that if something runs in families then it is genetically inherited. As we discussed in Chapter 4, this is a dubious assumption. Any mental health problem or psychological characteristic can be passed down to the next generation by non-genetic processes. If political values tend to run in families, do we assume that they are genetically determined? We all learn much of our behaviour, including how to deal with stress, from our parents. For example, it can be depressing to grow up with depressed parents. Alternatively, or in addition, family members tend to share certain environmental factors, such as poverty, that increase the chances of mental health problems, including having psychotic experiences.

As we established in Chapter 4, studies of twins tell us little or nothing about causation. Researchers have found that if one identical (monozygotic – MZ) twin is given a diagnosis of schizophrenia there is a certain percentage chance that the other will too, and that this chance is higher than the concordance rate for non-identical (dizygotic – DZ) twins. The researchers assume that the environments of MZ and DZ twins are about the same. A leading analyst of genetic research into schizophrenia, Jay Joseph, points out:

> However, this 'equal environment assumption' has little basis in the evidence. MZ twins' more similar social and physical environments contribute to MZ-DZ concordance rate differences. Because it is widely understood that MZ twins are treated more similarly, encounter more similar environments, and experience a greater level of identity confusion than DZs, there is no reason to accept that MZ-DZ comparisons measure anything more than the *environmental* differences distinguishing the two types of twins.
>
> Joseph (2004, p. 69)

A better research design would involve studying people who had been born to a parent given a diagnosis of schizophrenia but then, at a later stage, adopted. Several studies claim to have found a higher than expected rate of schizophrenia among these samples than among other adoptees. However, most of these studies actually only found statistically significant differences by greatly expanding the definition of schizophrenia to include non-psychotic schizophrenia-spectrum disorders. Furthermore, many reviewers, including Joseph, have pointed out serious methodological flaws in these studies. For example, often they include children who were not adopted early (thereby contaminating the research with environmental factors). Moreover, they also suffered from the **selective placement bias**, whereby the best potential adoptive parents are in a position to choose from a range of potential adoptees and may well be put off adopting children with a biological family history of mental health difficulties, since potential adopters are usually informed of any difficulties in the adoptee's family background. Finally, many of the studies analysed their data wrongly and some even made up some of their data (Joseph, 2004, 2006; Rose, Lewontin & Kamin, 1984).

Amazingly, only one adoption study has taken an interest in the quality of the families into which the participants had been adopted. In this study it was reported that children whose biological parents had been given a diagnosis of schizophrenia were at a higher risk than those whose biological parents did not experience distress. However, despite this apparent support for a biological account, the authors also reported that 'all adoptees who had been diagnosed either as schizophrenic or paranoid had been reared in seriously disturbed adoptive families' (Tienari et al., 1987, p. 482).This study therefore found strong evidence of an interaction between genetic and environmental factors.

The search for a schizophrenic gene

In the last two decades, family approaches to studying the roles of genes in psychosis have given way to molecular approaches, using increasingly sophisticated technologies to identify associations between psychiatric diagnoses and particular locations on the human genome or, in some instances, specific alleles of genes. The earliest studies of this kind were published to enormous fanfare, as if some kind of fundamental breakthrough had occurred. (Indeed, the role of the media (Leo & Lacasse, 2008) and the internet (Read, 2008) in promoting unsubstantiated biological theories as if they were fact has recently been

subject to increased scrutiny.) A fundamental problem that has emerged from prodigious efforts using this approach has been the difficulty in replicating findings (Crow, 2008). For example, in 2008 an *American Journal of Psychiatry* paper (Sanders et al., 2008), described by the journal's editor as 'The most comprehensive genetic association study of genes previously reported to contribute to the susceptibility to schizophrenia' (i.e. a review of all previous studies) found 'nothing outside of what would be expected by chance' (Hamilton, 2008, p. 421). The genes targeted in this study had been chosen because they had been reported as associated with schizophrenia in a number of previous studies.

Current thinking in the molecular genetics of psychosis has converged on a number of important conclusions. First, it is clear that there are no genes of major effect for psychosis (that is, no particular genes which, on their own, confer a high risk of psychosis). At this stage in the research, we can take this as a fact rather than as a type-2 (false negative) error: if any genes of major effect did exist they surely would have been discovered by now.

This leads to the second conclusion now favoured by many genetic researchers, which is that psychosis must by highly polygenic. Taking an unusual (and debatable) approach to estimating how many genes might be involved, one study recently arrived at an estimate of more than a thousand, each conferring a tiny increased risk (International Schizophrenia Consortium, 2009). This is a remarkable estimate given that, currently, the human genome is thought to contain only about 26,000 genes.

Finally, most genetic researchers now believe that few, if any, genes confer a specific risk of a schizophrenia diagnosis. Indeed, in the International Schizophrenia Consortium Study, many of the genes identified were thought to confer a risk of also receiving a diagnosis of bipolar disorder. Indeed, some molecular geneticists have argued that this kind of evidence is sufficient to reject the Kraepelinian view of schizophrenia (Craddock & Owens, 2005).

As was discussed in Chapter 4, a further complication is that it has been increasingly recognized that genetic factors cannot be understood without considering the environmental context. Different genes are switched on and off in different tissues in the body and, at least in the case of central nervous system genes, this process is influenced by environmental factors, particularly various kinds of stress. Indeed, some researchers have argued that it is only by understanding these epigenetic mechanisms that progress in understanding the role of genes in psychosis will be achieved (Read, Bentall & Fosse, 2009).

Schizophrenia is a brain disease?

Most brain research into psychosis or schizophrenia seeks, and often finds, differences between people with or without the diagnosis in question, and then concludes that the differences confirm the researcher's belief that people with the diagnosis are suffering from an illness with a purely or primarily biological aetiology. However, there are three significant problems with the assumptions underlying this approach. Firstly, this approach assumes that the schizophrenia diagnostic construct has good reliability. However, if one set of researchers is using a different definition of schizophrenia from another set, any differences discovered are going to be very difficult to interpret. Secondly, if the brains of people with a diagnosis of schizophrenia are different from 'normal' brains, does that mean we have found the cause of the behaviours, thoughts and feelings that led to the diagnosis? When we are grieving the loss of someone we loved, our brains act differently from usual. Is our sadness caused by the brain's slower functioning or by our loss? The idea that brain differences necessarily imply a biologically-based illness or disease is, on careful thought, untenable. What use would a brain be if it did not respond to the environment? We shall see later, for instance, that childhood trauma can cause enduring changes in the structure and functioning of the human brain. The third problematic assumption is the fact that one of the things that can change the brains of people with a diagnosis of schizophrenia is something they really do have in common: the treatment they receive, primarily medication, as we saw in Chapter 8.

Biochemistry

As discussed in Chapter 4, one of the most widely held biological theories of schizophrenia suggests that psychotic experiences are the product of some kind of over-activity in basal ganglia circuits that employ the neurotransmitter dopamine. The theory was originally based on indirect evidence from the effects of antipsychotic drugs on the brain (Ross & Read, 2004). It was noted in Chapter 8 that these drugs were discovered adventitiously and, when they were first used in the 1950s, very little was known about their effects on the brain. It was discovered later that antipsychotics had the common property of blocking dopamine D2 receptors, and that the extent to which they did this correlated with their potency (Seeman et al., 1976). Researchers in search of a biological cause argued that, if drugs that appear to ameliorate symptoms of schizophrenia also block the dopamine system, the cause of schizophrenia was likely to be over-activity of the dopamine system. Critics have argued that this is like saying that headaches are caused by a lack of aspirin in the body (Jackson, 1986). However there is some empirical support for the proposition that increasing the amount of dopamine in the brains of people without psychotic experiences can sometimes lead to psychotic (typically paranoid) states (Angrist & Gershon, 1970), for example in people with a diagnosis of Parkinsonism taking drugs such as l-dopa (that increase dopamine transition) and also from drug abusers or volunteers taking dopamine **agonists** (drugs that activate dopamine receptors).

These observations from the effects of drugs are no more than suggestive, however. Firm evidence for the dopamine theory would require direct observation of abnormalities in the brains of people having psychotic experiences. This kind of evidence has proven remarkably difficult to obtain. An early approach was to measure the amount of homovanilic acid which is a **metabolite** of dopamine (i.e. a substance produced by the metabolism of dopamine) in the cerebral-spinal fluid, hoping that this would indicate that too much dopamine was being secreted at the neurone. When this approach failed, researchers turned their attention to investigating, either at post-mortem or in living brains, the number of dopamine receptors. However, despite some positive reports, it was soon discovered that the drugs used to treat people with a diagnosis of schizophrenia not only caused a blockade of the dopamine system but also initiated an attempt to compensate for the blockade. A 1982 review of post-mortem studies found that increased dopamine levels were found only in those who had been receiving antipsychotic medication shortly before death; the dopamine levels of those who had been drug-free were normal. It was concluded that 'these findings do not support the presence of elevated DA [dopamine] turnover in the brains of schizophrenics' (Haracz, 1982, p. 440).

Developments in imaging techniques have enabled researchers to study biochemistry in greater detail than before. For example, in **positron emission tomography** (PET), positron-emitting radioisotopes – short-lived radioactive substances – are introduced into the body in order to produce three-dimensional coloured images of their concentration in body tissue. **Single photon emission computed tomography** (SPECT) produces a computerized cross-section of physical structures in the body based on their differential absorption of gamma-rays. Some recent studies have attempted to examine differences in the density of different types of dopamine receptors (DA_1, DA_2, etc.). The advantage of these techniques is that they can be used to study living people who have not yet been prescribed antipsychotic dugs. At the beginning of the 21st century, a number of reviews of the research on the dopamine theory were published. One acknowledged that 'few studies have provided convincing evidence of altered dopaminergic activity' (Copolov & Crook, 2000, p. 110), reporting that 11 of the 13 studies using the new neuroimaging techniques had found no significant differences in dopamine receptor density. Another concluded that 'findings on dopamine and other neurotransmitters, as well as enzymes involved in the synthesis and degradation of neurotransmitters, have been inconsistent' (Dean, 2000, p. 561). A third argued that 'In spite of decades of extensive research, the causes and exact sites of the presumed dopamine-mediated hyperactivity remain elusive' (Gainetdinov, Mohn & Caron, 2001, p. 527). Another concluded: 'While postmortem and imaging studies have identified numerous alterations in brain structure and function in schizophrenia, the fundamental nature of the pathological process associated with this illness remains poorly understood' (Laruelle, 2000, p. 372). The author of this last review undertook a novel neuroimaging study using PET, finding that people who had only recently experienced distress, but not those who had been distressed for some time, showed a greater increase in dopamine secretion compared to controls (Laruelle & Abi-Dargham, 1999). This led him to argue that the dopamine system functions abnormally only during the onset of severe psychotic experiences, implying that it plays a proximal rather than aetiological role in these experiences. In Chapter 4 it was noted that this is suggestive of plasticity and variability in brain systems.

An important missing element in most versions of the dopamine theory is an account of what the dopamine system actually does. Recent research has provided strong evidence that it is important in rewarding learning (Montague, Dayan, Sejnowski, 1996), but there is also emerging evidence that it plays a role in the anticipation and avoidance of threat (Moutoussis, Williams, Dayan & Bentall, 2008). Interestingly, there is evidence from animal studies that the dopamine system can be sensitized by repeated exposure to extremely threatening experiences (Selten & Cantor-Graae, 2005), which may help to explain why unpleasant early life experiences appear to increase the risk of psychotic experiences (see below).

Neuroanatomy

The anatomy of the brain has also been examined by researchers hoping to establish a physical disease process underlying psychosis, and these studies have been facilitated by the development of modern imaging techniques such as **computerized axial tomography** (CAT), in which a computer images a slice of body tissue using x-rays and **magnetic resonance imaging** (MRI), in which images are produced through the use of magnetic fields and radio waves. However, despite the undoubted sophistication of these techniques, much of this research suffers from the sort of methodological and conceptual difficulties that have beset biochemical studies.

For example, one of the widest reported neuroanatomical findings is enlargement of the fluid-filled cavities – ventricles – in the brain, which is claimed to be a consequence of reduction in brain tissue. Some of the problems with claims of this nature were discussed in Chapter 4. This phenomenon was in fact reported in the earliest modern brain imaging study of this time, using what would now seem a primitive CAT scanner, conducted by Johnstone, Frith, Crow, Husband and Kreel (1976). A meta-analytic review of the literature from 58 relevant brain imaging studies reported that cerebral volume in people with a diagnosis of schizophrenia was 2% less than in controls, and that the ventricles were 26% larger (Wright et al., 2000). Another more recent meta-analysis of 66 studies of people with a diagnosis of first-episode schizophrenia found evidence of a reduction in whole brain volume and in the volume of the hippocampus, but increased ventricular volume (Steen, Mull, McClure, Hamer & Lieberman, 2006).

The problem is how to interpret findings of this sort. As noted in Chapter 4, similar observations have been made in relation to people with many other mental health problems, such as depression and alcoholism (Copolov & Crook, 2000), raising questions about specificity. Another difficulty is the confounding effects of antipsychotic drugs. Recent studies with both animals and humans have confirmed that antipsychotic drugs can cause neurodegeneration (Weinmann & Aderhold, 2010; Weinmann, Read & Aderhold, 2009) and a reduction of grey-matter volume (Lieberman et al., 2005; Vita & de Peri, 2007). Indeed, a recent longitudinal MRI study of 211 people with a diagnosis of first-episode schizophrenia, followed up for an average of more than seven years, found that reduction in brain volume was significantly predicted by duration and dosage of antipsychotic drugs, even after controlling for substance abuse and illness severity and duration (Ho, Andreassen, Ziebell, Pierson & Magnotta, 2011).

A third complication is that, even if we can be sure that a reduction in brain volume is somehow associated with distress (rather than confounding factors), this tells us nothing about the causes of the differences seen on the CAT or MRI scans.

For example, some research has reported that, in identical twins who are discordant for schizophrenia (that is, one of the twins has the diagnosis and the other does not), the affected twin has larger ventricles than the non-affected twin (Reveley, 1985). However, as the twins are genetically indistinguishable, this actually supports an environmental causal explanation. In this context, it is particularly interesting to note that some structural brain changes that have been observed in those having psychotic experiences, for example reduced hippocampal volume, have also been reported in studies of people who have been subjected to trauma such as sexual abuse (Nemeroff et al., 2006).

Uniform prevalence?

As discussed earlier, another argument used to support the notion that schizophrenia is a medical illness is that it exists in the same proportion everywhere in the world. This claim has been used to argue that cultural or environmental factors are irrelevant and the cause must therefore be of the kind associated with medical illnesses. In fact, however, many medical illnesses show huge variations between populations and locations. As a 1987 review of prevalence studies points out: 'If schizophrenia has no such differences it would be a unique disease and that fact alone would be one of its most significant aspects' (Torrey, 1987, p. 599).

This review, of over 70 studies, found that the highest rate – 17 per 1000 in part of Sweden – was 55 times greater than the lowest rate: 0.3 per 1,000 amongst Amish people in the USA. There was actually a complete absence of schizophrenia diagnoses among 3000 Kwaio adults in Melanasia. Even after removing some of the lower rates the reviewer still concluded that 'a ten-fold range of prevalence for schizophrenia is supported by this data' (Torrey, 1987, p. 605).

Psychosocial causes

We have already discussed how the distorted version of the stress-vulnerability model (with sensitivity to stress wrongly assumed to be always genetically inherited) relegates psychosocial factors to mere triggers or exacerbators of distress. However, we shall see next that a long list of life events and circumstances are important causal influences on the development of psychotic experiences. Indeed, some of these have been shown to be highly predictive, even after controlling for family history of mental illness. This does not mean that genetics plays no part. As has been argued in this chapter and elsewhere in this volume, it is impossible to separate genes and environment and therefore meaningless to try to calculate which is more important. Although we are clear that there is no specific genetic predisposition to schizophrenia or psychosis it is possible – we would suggest probable – that we do inherit different levels of sensitivity to stress.

We would also like to point out that it is very rare for one life event or circumstance, by itself, to lead to the development of psychotic experiences. What increases our chances of going mad is a combination of events over time, an accumulation of the effects of multiple stressors (Read & Sanders, 2010). We shall present these stressors, or adverse life events and circumstances, in three sections: sociodemographics, childhood events and events in adulthood. Then we will summarize the theories that try to explain *how* these events lead to psychotic experiences. Once again, many of these studies research the diagnostic category of schizophrenia using clinical diagnoses or research measures. If we were being strictly scientific we would not report the findings of such studies, because of the problems of reliability and validity. However, this has been the approach taken by the majority of researchers for decades, so to ignore all those studies would be problematic. Fortunately, an increasing number of researchers are taking the more scientific route of investigating specific experiences and complaints, like hallucinations, delusions, or mania, often adopting the dimensional approach discussed earlier. Where findings of this nature are available we will draw on them, as we believe they enable a clearer delineation of causal processes.

Poverty

Poverty is perhaps the most powerful predictor of psychosis out of all the risk factors, social, psychological or biological (Read, 2010; Read, Johnstone & Taitimu, 2013). This is not because being poor, by itself, drives people crazy. It is because poverty is related to many of the more direct causes of madness, such as childhood neglect and abuse, and because poverty often involves reduced access to resources that help us through difficult times, such as psychotherapy or just having a nice holiday to get away from it all for a while.

An early US study famously reported that people from the poorest social classes (V: unskilled, manual) were three times more likely than people from the wealthiest two classes (I & II: business, professional and managerial) to be treated for mental health problems in general (Hollingshead & Redlich, 1958). Contrary to the notion that milder forms of distress, but not schizophrenia, are socially caused, the diagnosis having the strongest relationship with class in this study was schizophrenia. The poorest people were eight times more likely to be given a diagnosis of schizophrenia than the wealthiest.

By 1976 a review had concluded:

> There have been more than 50 studies of the relationship between social class and rates of schizophrenia. Almost without exception, these studies have shown that schizophrenia occurs most frequently at the lowest social class levels of urban society. The evidence comes from research in Canada, Denmark, Finland, Great Britain, Norway, Sweden, Taiwan, and the United States – an unusually large number of countries and cultures for establishing the generality of any relationship in social science.
>
> Kohn (1976, p. 177)

A Tennessee study of 10,000 first admissions to hospital again confirmed that the diagnosis most strongly related to socio-economic status was schizophrenia (Rushing & Ortega, 1979). The relationship between being given a diagnosis of schizophrenia and poverty was described as 'one of the most consistent findings in the field of psychiatric epidemiology' (Eaton, 1980. p. 149).

A more recent British study found that children growing up in economic deprivation were four times more likely to develop 'non-schizophrenic psychotic illness' but eight times more likely to grow up to be given a diagnosis of schizophrenia than non-deprived children (Harrison, Gunnell, Glazebrook, Page & Kwiecinski, 2001). Even among children with no family history of psychosis, the deprived children were seven times more likely to later be given a diagnosis of schizophrenia, demonstrating that a genetic predisposition is not necessary. A well-documented relationship between urban living and psychotic experiences also remains after controlling for the presence of psychiatric diagnoses in family histories (Lewis, David & Andreasson, 1992; Mortensen et al., 1999).

It must also be noted that, as we saw in Chapter 6, there is convincing evidence that *relative* poverty is an even stronger predictor than poverty per se. In their book, 'The Spirit Level', epidemiologists Richard Wilkinson and Kate Pickett report multiple studies demonstrating a far stronger relationship between relative poverty and a range of social, health and mental health outcomes (including 'severe mental illness') than between poverty per se and the same outcomes (Wilkinson & Pickett, 2009) – the graph in Chapter 6 (Image on p. 254) provides a very clear illustration of this. There is good

evidence to support the relative poverty hypothesis in relation to madness. A study of 17 electoral wards in South London found that high inequality (measured by degree of distribution of a composite deprivation score) was associated with the incidence of schizophrenia diagnoses (after adjusting for age, sex, absolute deprivation and ethnicity), but only in the group of the most deprived wards (Boydell, van Os, McKenzie & Murray, 2004). A similar South African study, comparing seven municipalities, found no significant relationship between a poverty measure (percentage of residents above or below the national poverty line) and being treated for a first episode of psychosis. However, the study did find a significant relationship with inequality, measured by the mean annual income of the top 10% wage earners divided by the mean annual income of the bottom 10% (Burns & Esterhuizen, 2008). The relationship remained significant after controlling for gender, age, ethnicity, urbanicity and employment status.

Chapter 6 included a discussion of social drift and social selection theories. These have attempted to explain the relationship between poverty and madness with the notion that madness causes poverty, rather than the other way round. The idea behind these theories is that people who have psychotic experiences cannot function well, and cannot earn a living, so they inevitably move to economically deprived areas, where housing is cheap. However, most longitudinal studies find that the poverty precedes the psychosis (Read & Dillon, 2013; Read, 2010). The famous New Haven study, like some studies before it (e.g. Lapouse, Monk & Terris, 1956) and some after (e.g. Lee, 1976; Wheaton, 1978), tested the social drift theory and found it wanting. They investigated whether 'class V patients had drifted to the slums in the course of their lives' and whether schizophrenics were downwardly socially mobile, but no evidence of such social drift was found. The study also rejected the weaker social selection theory because 91% of the people with a diagnosis of schizophrenia were in the same social class as their parents, rather than a lower class as predicted (Hollingshead & Redlich, 1958). More recently, several large epidemiological studies have shown that poverty (Samele et al., 2001) and exposure to an urban environment (Mortensen et al., 1999) during childhood, rather than adulthood, is associated with an increased risk of attracting a diagnosis of psychosis.

There is another reason, besides direct social causation, why so many poor people are given a diagnosis of schizophrenia. By 1977 there were nine studies showing that more severe diagnoses are given to poorer people than wealthier people with the same presentation (Abramowitz & Dokecki, 1977). A tenth study found that psychiatrists assigning severe diagnoses on the basis of class genuinely believed they were basing diagnoses on patient behaviour rather than occupation and education. Thus there was 'intellectual denial of social status effects and a subconscious utilization of status information' (Lebedun & Collins, 1976, p. 206). This important line of research has not been adequately pursued since, although some recent studies have reported mixed results (e.g. Swaggerty-Valdes, 2009). British clinical psychologist Lucy Johnstone has concluded:

> A number of studies have found that severer diagnoses are given to working- than to middle-class patients, regardless of symptoms; that the former are seen as having a poorer prognosis; and that professionals are less interested in treating them.
>
> Johnstone (2000, p. 238)

Ethnicity

Ethnicity is another powerful predictor of receiving a diagnosis of schizophrenia. This has been demonstrated in Australia, Belgium, Denmark, Germany, Greenland, the Netherlands, New Zealand, Israel, Sweden, the UK and the USA (Read, Johnstone & Taitimu, 2013). In the UK, for example, the incidence rates for schizophrenia are 3.6 times higher among all ethnic minority groups combined than among whites, and Afro-Caribbeans have been found to be nine or 12 times more likely to be given a diagnosis of schizophrenia than white people (Fearon et al., 2006; Read & Dillon, 2013). Studies focusing on specific psychotic or psychotic-like experiences rather than diagnoses also find higher rates, but not as high as studies using diagnoses (raising the issue, again, of whether the diagnostic process might be biased; see below). For example, a recent British study found that such experiences were twice as common among Black Caribbeans and 4.6 times as common among Black Africans, compared to White British (Morgan et al., 2009).

The factors that link ethnicity to a diagnosis of schizophrenia have been shown to be poverty, unemployment, discrimination and social isolation (particularly from people of the same ethnicity). For example, a Dutch study recorded experiences of discrimination in 4067 people (Janssen et al., 2003), and then used the experience- or complaint-focused methodology we have advocated rather than relying on diagnosis. Those who had reported discrimination in two or more domains (skin colour/ethnicity, gender, age etc.) were three times more likely to be experiencing psychotic hallucinations than those who had reported no discrimination, and five times more likely to be experiencing psychotic delusions. Findings that admission rates for ethnic minorities are lower in neighbourhoods where there is a high concentration of the ethnic group (Boydell et al., 2001) 'suggests that social causation, in the form of reduced exposure to direct prejudice and increased social support, is a likely cause of the effect' (Halpern & Nazroo, 2000, p. 34). This has been further explored, and confirmed, using qualitative methodology (in-depth interviews) (Whitley, Prince, McKenzie & Stewart, 2006).

Despite the strength of the evidence linking minority status to psychosis-risk, it seems likely that biases in the diagnostic process also contribute to the higher rates of diagnoses of psychosis recorded from ethnic minorities. One study of 656 people in a US psychiatric hospital, for example, found that even when a semi-structured instrument and DSM criteria were used, Whites were more likely than African–Americans to receive a diagnosis of bipolar disorder and less likely to be given a diagnosis of schizophrenia (Neighbors, Trierweiler, Ford & Muroff, 2003). Another study in the UK found that male Afro-Caribbean inpatients were 95 times more likely than white male patients to be given a diagnosis of **cannabis psychosis** (McGovern & Cope, 1987). This diagnosis is given when a psychotic episode is regarded as having been primarily caused or triggered by cannabis use (the apparent association between cannabis and the diagnosis of schizophrenia was discussed in Chapter 4). A subsequent survey of British psychiatrists found that 57% thought cannabis psychosis was more common among Afro-Caribbeans. Of these, 95% believed Afro-Caribbeans smoke more cannabis than other ethnic groups and 21% thought they were more susceptible to a psychotic reaction to the drug (Littlewood, 1989).

Evidence of bias in relation to the process of reaching a diagnosis of schizophrenia has been found in studies comparing diagnoses made with and without knowledge of the subject's ethnicity (Goodman, Siegel, Craig & Lin, 1983), studies showing that when structured diagnostic protocols are used fewer people from ethnic minorities are diagnosed than is the case in real-life clinical settings (Whaley, 2001), studies showing that black people are more likely to be given a diagnosis of schizophrenia than their white counterparts with the same symptoms (Strakowski et al., 1995; Strakowski, Shelton & Kolbrener, 1993), and studies showing that ethnic minorities are given a diagnosis of schizophrenia on the basis of fewer symptoms than the number required for white people (Teggin, Elk, Ben-Arie & Gillis, 1985). The bias can occur both at the level of what constitutes a symptom (e.g. hallucinations being more readily perceived by psychiatrists in African–Americans than in other people) as well as at the level of deciding that a given symptom is indicative of schizophrenia (Trierweiler et al., 2000).

Adverse events in childhood and adolescence

One of the striking aspects of psychotic experiences is that they seem to begin most frequently in adolescence. Harrop and Trower (2001, 2003) have examined this issue in detail, and note that many of the characteristics of these experiences (e.g. conflicted family relationships) mirror the features of normal adolescence. They suggest that psychotic experiences may occur as the result of a difficulty in moving through adolescence, developing a coherent sense of self and important peer relationships outside the family. There are a number of reasons why teenagers may experience such a 'blocked adolescence' and we examine some of them in this section.

Loss of parents

One study found that the loss of one's mother during childhood is significantly higher (55%) in people given a diagnosis of schizophrenia than for other diagnoses (23%) (Friedman et al., 2002). A study of people with a diagnosis of first-episode psychosis found, after controlling for parental history of 'mental illness', that they were 2.4 times more likely than a control group to have been separated from one or both parents, 3.1 times more likely to have had a parent die and 12.3 times more likely to have had their mother die, before the age of 16 (Morgan et al., 2007).

Problematic parenting

Chapter 6 included a discussion of whether parenting plays a role in the causation of mental health problems. As that chapter established, this has been seen as rather controversial for many years. Some have even argued that this issue should be ignored because it was **family-blaming**; in other words, some felt that such an assertion held families morally responsible for the development of distress. Pressure groups, like NAMI (National Association for Mental Illness) in the USA, which appear to speak for families but which receive significant funding from drug companies, have campaigned effectively on this point. (One of us – JR – once had a research paper showing that the public rejects bio-genetic causes rejected by a prominent psychiatric journal, partly on the basis of a reviewer who wrote that 'these findings will be totally unacceptable to NAMI'). Accusations that research studies are family-blaming are based on two false assumptions. Firstly, it is not the case that finding a relationship between certain family patterns or parenting styles and subsequent psychosis (or anything else) implies that parents intentionally set out to cause problems in their children. Almost all parents do the very best they can for their children. It's just that some people are, inevitably, better parents than others. Secondly, there is a difference between a scientific finding and moral condemnation. As we recently explained, in the *American Journal of Psychiatry*:

> While it can be tempting to ignore childhood adversity, out of fear of being accused of family-blaming, many childhood adversities occur outside the family and those that occur within families tend to be intergenerational and are therefore areas in which many families need assistance.
>
> Read & Bentall (2010b, p. 717)

Nevertheless, as discussed in Chapter 6, for decades most researchers have restricted themselves to the issue of discovering whether parenting affected **relapse rates** (i.e. whether a person experiences an increase in symptoms or is rehospitalized) rather than the onset of distress, thereby avoiding being accused of family-blaming. Many studies of Expressed Emotion (EE), a measure of parental criticism, hostility and over-involvement, did indeed find that it increased relapse rates for people given a diagnosis of schizophrenia (e.g. Vaughn & Leff, 1976). However, one group of researchers ignored the taboo on researching EE *before* a diagnosis of schizophrenia. The parents of 64 troubled adolescents, none of whom had any psychotic experiences, were assessed for EE. Fifteen years later none of the adolescents (now adults) whose parents had both been rated Low EE, but 36% of those whose parents had both been high EE, were given a diagnosis of schizophrenia (Goldstein, 1987). It has since been confirmed that the parents of children with schizophrenia-spectrum diagnoses 'were more likely to direct harsh criticism toward the child than were parents of depressed children or parents of normal controls' (Hamilton, Asarnow & Tompson, 1999, p. 463). Numerous studies by attachment researchers (see below) have found low rates of parental care combined with high rates of control in the childhoods of people later given a diagnosis of schizophrenia (Read & Gumley, 2008).

The idea that family patterns of interaction may be related to specific experiences or complaints has quite a long history. In the 1960s, Lyman Wynne and Margaret Singer, two US researchers, reported that **communication deviance** (CD; a form of vague communication associated with unfocused attention) in parents was associated with the development of **thought disorder** (where a person's thoughts are inferred to be incoherent and confused on the basis of incoherent and confused speech) in children (Singer & Wynne, 1965). Goldstein and his colleagues later found that when the parents had scored high on communication deviance, 10% of their adolescents met the criteria for schizophrenia diagnoses 15 years later, compared to none of those whose parents had been low on CD, and that those given a diagnosis of schizophrenia were particularly likely to experience thought disorder (Doane, West, Goldstein, Rodnick & Jones, 1981). This finding was replicated in Tienari's Finnish adoption study (see above), in which it was found that children considered to be genetically predisposed to develop psychotic experiences went on to become thought disordered only if their adoptive parents showed communication deviance (Wahlberg et al., 1997).

Child abuse and neglect

The issue of whether child abuse can help cause psychosis has been equally controversial (Read & Bentall, 2012). However,

after decades of silence on the issue, the last 15 years have seen a rather spectacular burst of research activity (Larkin & Read, 2008; Read et al., 2009; Read, Fink, Rudegeair, Feliti & Whitfield, 2008; Read et al., 2005). A recent review found, from an analysis of 59 studies, that an average of 55% of male, and 65% of female, psychiatric inpatients had been either sexually or physically abused as children (Read et al., 2008). These reviews report numerous studies, using clinical diagnoses or research measures, showing that childhood emotional, physical and sexual abuse, and childhood neglect, are related to the development of psychotic experiences.

Ten out of eleven recent large-scale general population studies have found, even after controlling for other factors (again including family history of diagnoses of psychosis) that child maltreatment is significantly related to having psychotic experiences. The maltreatment variables studied were: neglect, sexual, physical, emotional and psychological abuse, bullying and witnessing violence in the home. For example, a prospective Netherlands study controlled for both family mental health care and history of hallucinations or delusions in first-degree relatives and found that people who had been physically, sexually, emotionally or psychologically abused as children were nine times more likely than non-abused people to have serious psychotic experiences (Janssen et al., 2004).

Nine of the 11 studies tested for, and found, a dose-response relationship (i.e. that the greater the severity of the abuse, the greater the chance of having psychotic experiences). For example, a recent prospective study, of 6437 British children, found that those who had been exposed, at age eight or ten, to either overt bullying or relational bullying (rejection by peers) were twice as likely to have psychotic experiences at age 12; while those who were victims of both types of bullying were 4.7 times more likely to do so (Schreier, Wolke, Thomas et al., 2009). The dose-response relationship between severity of abuse and distress is also found in smaller studies specifically targeting people with psychotic experiences or people who had experienced abuse (Kilcommons, Morrison, Knight & Lobban, 2008).

Even *within* samples with diagnoses of psychosis or schizophrenia, child abuse is related to longer duration before people present for help (sometimes referred to as 'untreated psychosis'), poorer premorbid functioning, substance abuse, other diagnoses (especially depression and PTSD), unemployment, poor engagement with services, low medication compliance, low satisfaction with diagnosis and treatment, and, most importantly, suicidality (Lecomte et al., 2008; Read et al., 2008).

The relationship between adverse events in childhood and these sorts of negative outcomes is confirmed by seven studies of people having psychotic experiences for the first time (Conus et al., 2010). One of these studies (Fisher et al., 2009) found a relationship between these experiences and abuse in women but not in men (which might be explained by gender-specific responses to trauma, and the greater likelihood of abused males entering the criminal justice system or killing themselves). The largest first-episode study to date found that child physical or sexual abuse was significantly related to numerous outcomes, including substance abuse (see below) and suicide attempts, and, crucially, that the trauma preceded the psychotic experiences in 98% of the cases (Conus et al., 2010).

The first meta-analysis of studies relating childhood adversity to psychosis (in which the current authors were involved) focused on sexual abuse, physical abuse, emotional/psychological abuse, neglect, parental death, and bullying (Varese et al., 2012). Significant associations between adversity and psychosis emerged across all research designs, with an overall odds ratio of 2.8 (p < .001). For example, clinical case-control studies indicated that patients with psychosis were 2.7 times more likely to have been exposed to childhood adversity than controls. We concluded that 'these findings indicate that childhood adversity is strongly associated with increased risk for psychosis' (p. 661). Furthermore the 'estimated population attributable risk' was 33%, meaning that if all six types of adversity could be magically eliminated, so would one third of all cases of psychosis.

In keeping with our belief that more is learned once we abandon current diagnostic categories, it seems that the relationship between child abuse and specific psychotic complaints crosses diagnostic boundaries. For example, in a sample of adults with a diagnosis of bipolar disorder, those who had been sexually abused as children were twice as likely to experience some form of auditory hallucinations and six times more likely to hear voices commenting (Hammersley et al., 2003). A study of people with a first-episode diagnosis of bipolar disorder found that the 25% who had been physically or sexually abused in childhood or adolescence had poorer premorbid functioning and poorer engagement with treatment (Conus et al., 2010).

Numerous studies have demonstrated a relationship between abuse and the actual content of hallucinations and delusions (see Box 11.5). Over 100 years ago, psychoanalyst Karl Abraham (1907/1955, p. 17) noted that a woman who was sexually abused as a child and then again by her husband 'saw the devil, bearing her husband's features and carrying a spear, with which he thrust at her' (1907, p. 17). More recently a study of severely maltreated children found that the content of the hallucinations or illusions were strongly reminiscent of episodes of traumatic victimization (Famularo, Kinscherff & Fenton, 1992). The same has been found to be true for many adolescents (Heins, Gray & Tennant, 1990) and adults (Dillon, 2010; Romme & Escher, 2006; Romme, Escher, Dillon, Corstens & Morris, 2009) who suffered childhood sexual abuse. High rates of sexual delusions have been found in incest survivors with diagnoses of psychosis (Beck & van der Kolk, 1987). Indeed, two studies have found that the content of just over half of the psychotic experiences in adults with a diagnosis of schizophrenia who were abused as children are obviously related to the abuse (Bowe, 2002; Read, Agar, Argyle & Aderhold, 2003). A third found that 12.5% had hallucinations with similar themes and content to their traumas, and 45% had hallucinations in which the themes were the same, but not the content (Hardy et al., 2005). A recent Australian study found that among young people at 'ultra high risk' for the development of psychotic experiences, the presence of attenuated (mild) psychotic experiences with sexual content was significantly related to a history of sexual molestation or rape, and that this relationship remained significant when other traumatic experiences, a diagnosis of Posttraumatic Stress Disorder (PTSD; see Chapter 9), age and sex were adjusted for (Thompson et al., 2010).

The final important finding to report from this fast-growing body of literature is that abuse disclosures by people with a variety of psychiatric diagnoses, including schizophrenia, seem to be reliable (Read et al., 2008; Read et al., 2005). One study found 93% test-retest reliability for reports of sexual coercion by inpatients (Chandra, Deepthivarma, Carey, Carey & Shalinianant, 2003). Evidence to corroborate the reports of mental health service users that they experienced sexual abuse in childhood has been found in 74% (Herman & Schatzow, 1987) and 82% (Read et al., 2003) of cases. One study specifically demonstrated that 'The problem of incorrect allegations of sexual assaults was no different for schizophrenics than the general population' (Darves-Bornoz, Lemperiere, Degiovanni & Gaillard, 1995, p. 82). The most recent, and comprehensive, study (Fisher et al., 2011) found that disclosures of childhood sexual or physical abuse, or neglect by adults, meeting the diagnostic criteria for a psychotic disorder had high levels of concurrent validity (correlated with responses to the **Parental Bonding Instrument** – a retrospective measure of one's childhood relationships with one's parents), good convergent validity (with clinical case-notes), and were reasonably stable over time (test-retest reliability). Moreover, their reports of childhood abuse were not related to the severity of psychotic symptoms. This last finding is particularly important because some mental health professionals still think that one should not believe a person who has psychotic experiences when they report abuse or neglect, and that there is, therefore, little point asking them about it (Read, Hammersley & Rudegeair, 2007).

Substance abuse

Being given a diagnosis of schizophrenia has been linked to the use of a range of legal and illegal substances including cannabis, cocaine, amphetamines, hallucinogens and alcohol (Murray, Grech, Phillips & Johnson, 2003). As discussed extensively in Chapter 4, however, it remains an open question whether any of these substances are causal factors, as often supposed, or whether they are used to self-medicate (either for complaints considered indicative of schizophrenia or for the emotional reaction to adverse life events, or both). Any relationships between receiving a diagnosis of schizophrenia and substance abuse may be explained by causal factors common to both, such as poverty and child abuse (Shevlin, Murphy, Houston & Adamson, 2009). The topic is mentioned here, under 'adverse events in childhood', because recent research suggests that, if anything has any predictive value, it is heavy cannabis use early in adolescence (Caspi et al., 2002). Consistent with this hypothesis, a recent large general population study (Houston, Murphy, Adamson, Stringer & Shevlin, 2008) found that neither childhood sexual abuse nor cannabis use independently predicted the development of psychotic experiences, but that there was a significant interaction effect if the first use of cannabis was before the age of 16. In other words, if people had both been sexually abused and used cannabis before the age of 16, they were more likely to have psychotic experiences later in life. However, in a study of undergraduate students, current usage was a better predictor of the development of psychotic experiences than age of first use (Richardson, Gallagher & Garavan, 2011), perhaps because many university students smoke cannabis for the first time when they get to university.

Adverse events in adulthood

Physical assault and rape

A very high proportion of mental health service users, especially those with a diagnosis of psychosis, have been assaulted and raped as adults. The studies involved, however,

BOX 11.5

The content of hallucinations and delusions is often related to childhood trauma

Heins et al. (1990):

> A man who had been raped several times by an uncle at the age of seven heard voices telling him he was 'sleazy' and should kill himself.

> A woman who had been sexually assaulted by her father from a very young age and raped as a teenager had the delusion that 'people were watching her as they thought she was a sexual pervert and auditory hallucinations accusing her of doing 'dirty sexy things'.

> A woman whose father had raped her monthly from the age of eight and who was raped several times by a cousin at the age of eleven heard voices calling her a 'slut' and a 'whore'.

Read and Argyle (1999):

> A woman who had been sexually abused by her father from age five heard male voices outside her head and screaming children's voices inside her head.

> In another example, involving command hallucinations to commit suicide, the patient identified the voice as the perpetrator of the child abuse.

> A man who had been sexually abused from the age of four believed his body was asymmetrical and that women only wanted sex with him because of the thrill of being with a freak.

Read et al. (2003):

> One person, sexually abused between the age of 8–9 years, heard auditory hallucinations in the form of the voice of the abuser.

> Another's medical records read 'Sexual abuse: Abused from an early age.... Raped several times

> by strangers and violent partners'. This person believed 'was being tortured by people getting into body, for example "the Devil" and "the Beast"' and 'had bleeding secondary to inserting a bathroom hose into self, stating wanting to wash self as "people are trying to put aliens into my body"'.

> Another, whose records reported childhood sexual and physical abuse and multiple rapes, believed that 'has never been a child but is an old man who had his penis gouged out and had silicone injected into chest and hips'.

> Another, whose chart documents childhood sexual abuse also documents 'olfactory hallucinations (smells sperm)'.

> Another, who suffered 'ongoing sexual abuse by relative who is a violent person' hears 'the voice of the relative telling to jump from the bridge and kill self. Has already tried to commit suicide several times'.

often do not determine which came first – the assaults or the psychosis. However, an important recent study of over 2,000 Danish women found that the 103 who attended the Aarhus Centre for Rape Victims were ten times more likely to be given a diagnosis of a psychotic disorder (e.g. schizophrenia) in the subsequent five years, after controlling for whether or not they had previously been given a diagnosis of psychosis (Elklit & Shevlin, 2010).

A New Zealand study of 200 people using a community mental health centre shows the benefits of (i) examining the interrelationships and cumulative effects of different adverse events over the life span and (ii) studying specific experiences or complaints. Childhood physical abuse and childhood sexual abuse were strongly correlated (confirming previous findings that abused children are often exposed to multiple types of abuse). Childhood sexual abuse and adulthood sexual assault were also strongly correlated (suggesting that if a person has been abused as a child, others are more likely to abuse them later in life). Hallucinations were experienced by 18% of the group in which no abuse was reported, 47% of the group reporting abuse (physical or sexual) as a child, 42% of the group reporting abuse (physical or sexual) as an adult and 86% of the group who had been abused both in childhood and adulthood. However, in this particular sample, only adult sexual assault was significantly related to the occurrence of delusions or thought disorder (Read et al., 2003). How many of the adult assaults occurred before the first episode of psychosis was not determined.

War

When elevated rates of psychotic experiences were identified in Vietnam veterans it was automatically assumed that any diagnoses of schizophrenia were misdiagnoses and that these

experiences were therefore somehow non-psychotic (Van Putten & Emory, 1973). Recent research, however, has noted marked similarities between the complaints experienced by people given a diagnosis of PTSD and those leading to a diagnosis of schizophrenia (Larkin & Morrison, 2006; Moskowitz, Schafer & Dorahy, 2008; Muenzenmaier, Castille & Shelley, 2005).

When research scales such as the Minnesota Multiphasic Personality Inventory (MMPI) are used (thereby reducing the influence of clinician biases based on diagnostic preferences or beliefs about the relationship between trauma and psychotic experiences) the highest elevations following combat exposure are on the subscales purporting to assess responses characteristic of schizophrenia and depression (Elhai, Frueh, Gold, Hamner & Gold, 2003). One medication study identified 55 male war veterans with 'psychotic combat-related PTSD' (Pivac, Kozaric-Kovacic & Muck-Seler, 2004). A case study reported delusions of parasites under the skin and around orifices following multiple rapes in the Bosnian war (Oruc & Bell, 1995). A study of MMPI profiles of childhood sexual abuse survivors and combat veterans found that both had elevated scores on the schizophrenia subscales, and that childhood sexual abuse survivors and combat veterans are much more similar than different in their clinical presentation (Elhai, Frueh, Gold, Gold & Hamner, 2000).

In a group of prisoners of war, those who had experienced the most severe traumas were found to be markedly more likely to be given a diagnosis of schizophrenia (Beebe, 1975). One in five Somali refugees in London (most of whom had fled because of war and risk to their lives) reported having psychotic experiences (Bhui et al., 2003).

In the 1990s it was discovered that approximately two thirds of Israel's psychiatric inpatients aged 65 or over were holocaust survivors, and that the majority of these had been given a diagnosis of schizophrenia (Laub, 2005; Read & Masson, 2013).

Explanatory models explaining how adversity leads to psychosis

Chapter 6 included a discussion of the causal role of a variety of traumas in the development of a range of forms of distress. But why might people experience different kinds of distress? Now that the relationship between psychotic experiences and complaints and a range of adverse life events has been established, many researchers have focused on understanding the processes by which events in childhood can lead to hallucinations or delusions later, sometimes many years later. The cognitive model offers important explanatory accounts and it also underlies a range of interventions, which are discussed below. We shall also briefly describe contributions focused on psychodynamic theory, attachment and dissociation. We begin, however, with an attempt to produce a genuine integration of biological, psychological and social factors.

The traumagenic neurodevelopmental model

As noted earlier (and in Chapter 4), brain researchers studying schizophrenia often operate as if the brain existed in a social vacuum, ignoring the fact that a primary function of the brain is to react to the environment. In Chapter 4 there was discussion of how the development of the structure and biochemistry of the brain in childhood was influenced by its environment and some interesting research on the effects of attachment and childhood abuse and neglect were reviewed. Chapter 6 also identified trauma as playing a significant causal role in the development of distress. The **traumagenic neurodevelopmental model** of psychosis (Read, Perry, Moskowitz & Connolly, 2001) is based on similar research demonstrating that the findings from brain research – which are traditionally cited as evidence that schizophrenia is a brain disease – are also found in studies of the brains of abused children (see Box 11.6). Thus the heightened sensitivity to stress evidenced by dysregulation of the brain's stress regulation mechanisms is not necessarily inherited: it can be caused by childhood trauma. The authors also reviewed research linking child abuse and neglect to the cognitive and emotional difficulties in childhood that are typically interpreted as early signs of mental health problems rather than the result of adverse events in childhood. Even reviewers sceptical about whether a causal relationship has been demonstrated acknowledge:

> There are studies that have found HPA dysregulation in abused girls and in women who were physically or sexually abused in childhood. Heightened sensitivity to stress has long been considered a central feature of schizophrenia, and recent research has found patients with a first episode of psychosis to have enlarged pituitary glands compared with normal controls, independent of antipsychotic treatment.
>
> Morgan and Fisher (2007, p. 8)

An explicit test of the traumagenic neurodevelopmental model found that within a sample of people given a diagnosis of schizophrenia, those abused as children (especially those emotionally abused) experienced greater dysregulation of the hypothalamic–pituitary–adrenal axis (HPA – see Chapter 4), measured by cortisol levels, than their non-abused counterparts (Braehler et al., 2005). Further support for the model comes from studies showing that problems in childhood attachment can alter the structures, neurochemistry and connectivity of the brain. Like childhood physical and sexual abuse, severe child neglect affects the ability of the HPA to regulate the body and brain's stress response (Corbin, 2007; Strathearn, 2007).

This genuinely integrated approach is not only applicable to psychosis. A recent study found a relationship between adverse childhood experiences and 18 different outcomes, which parallels the cumulative exposure of the developing brain to the stress response with resulting impairment in multiple brain structures and functions (Anda et al., 2006, p. 174).

Psychodynamic theory

Although Freud had initially thought that people who experience psychosis could not be treated with psychoanalysis because they could not form a transference, there is some evidence that psychodynamic therapy can be effective for psychosis (Alanen, de Chavez, Silver & Martindale, 2009; Summers & Rosenbaum, 2013). Freud's successors have contributed greatly to understanding psychosis (Koehler, Silver & Karon, 2013). Among the most famous of these have been Carl Jung (1939, 2009), Harry Stack Sullivan (1974), Bertram Karon (Karon, 2007; Karon & VandenBos, 1994) and Frieda Fromm-Reichman (1954), whose treatment of Joanne Greenberg was immortalized in the best-selling book *I Never Promised you a Rose Garden* (Greenberg, 1964) and, more recently, in a film (Mackler, 2008).

Since neither of us are psychoanalysts we will let three people who are, and who have devoted their lives to working with people given a diagnosis of schizophrenia, summarize the psychodynamic perspective:

> It is only in the uniqueness of the history of each individual, and in the meanings that each person assigns to that history and to their symptoms, that any true cause can be discovered. Although people given a diagnosis of schizophrenia are very different from each other, their symptoms

---

BOX 11.6

The traumagenic neurodevelopmental model

Brain differences do not necessarily imply a brain disease that has nothing to do with life events.

Brain abnormalities found both in adults given a diagnosis of schizophrenia and severely abused children:

- over-activity of the hypothalamic–pituitary–adrenal (HPA) axis
- dopamine, norepinephrine and serotonin abnormalities
- hippocampal damage
- cerebral atrophy
- ventricular enlargement
- reversed cerebral asymmetry.

Read et al. (2001)

very often represent manifestations of, or defenses against, chronic terror. Any human being can develop such symptoms under enough stress, and every patient's life, as subjectively experienced, would drive anyone psychotic. (Conscious and unconscious meanings determine severity of stress). Probably something, large or small, happens early in life which changes existing fantasies, which then change how later experiences are met, which again change the fantasy structures, and so forth. When experience, as given meaning by conscious and unconscious fantasies, is literally unbearable, when one seems on the brink of annihilation, blatant psychosis results.

Silver et al. (2004, p. 209)

Perhaps one example of how psychodynamic defence mechanisms can help psychologists, and their clients, understand psychotic experiences is the idea that when you hear the voice of the person who has traumatized you in childhood one way to defend yourself against the terror of remembering is, without being aware of the process, to repress the memory of the events while simultaneously projecting the voice out onto the external world so that it seems to have nothing to do with your own life.

Attachment theory

We have already summarized the research on child abuse and neglect and on problematic parenting. In Chapters 4 and 6, attachment theory was drawn on to develop an explanation of how these kinds of experiences might lead to the development of distress. Unsurprisingly, many children who grow up to develop psychotic experiences do not appear to have been securely attached to caregivers. A recent review reports that almost all studies using the Parental Bonding Instrument in relation to people given a diagnosis of psychosis or schizophrenia find high rates of the 'affectionless control' pattern, in which parents are experienced as having exhibited low care and high overprotection. This has been found in Australia, Austria, Canada, England, Italy, Norway and the USA. The review also reported numerous studies showing high rates of insecure and disorganized attachment during childhood in people who later received a diagnosis of psychosis and schizophrenia (Read & Gumley, 2008).

Attachment theory can help us integrate psychodynamic theory (from which it derives) with cognitive perspectives. One's attachment style is a cognitive template, or internal working model, of relationships. An attachment perspective is also relevant to the traumagenic neurodevelopmental model's focus on dysregulation of the stress response, because an integral component of secure attachment is our ability to regulate our emotions when faced with interpersonal stressors such as rejection. Recent reviewers have argued that 'Attachment theory has the potential to provide a useful theoretical framework for conceptualising the influence of social cognition, interpersonal and affective factors on the development and course of psychosis, thus integrating and enhancing current psychological models' (Berry, Barrowclough & Wearden, 2008, p. 472). However, as with any model, there are some criticisms, which were discussed in Chapter 4, Box 4.7: Contextualizing attachment.

Dissociation

Dissociation is a partial or complete disruption of the normal integration of a person's conscious or psychological functioning, and is a common response to trauma, as it allows people to distance themselves from experiences that are too much for them to cope with by 'spacing out' or 'switching off' (Dell & O'Neil, 2009).

The relationships between psychosis, trauma and dissociation are the focus of increasing research attention (Longden, Corstens, Escher & Romme, 2012; Moskowitz, Read, Rudegeair, Farrely & Williams, 2009). High levels of dissociative experiences or complaints have been found in people with a diagnosis of psychosis, and vice versa (Elhai et al., 2003; Ross & Keyes, 2009; Schafer, Ross & Read, 2008). The developmental integration of the various separate affective states of the human infant requires a safe and consistent social environment in which a primary caregiver attends to the child's needs and minimizes trauma. Ongoing social stressors can inhibit the integrative process, in part by impairing the capacity of the hippocampus to provide the contextual component of memory, resulting in the creation and persistence of separate affective and cognitive states: in other words, of dissociation. The absence of an integrating frontal 'executive' function and the impoverishment of the capacity for contextualization leaves the emerging adult vulnerable to the intrusions of these persistent isolated intra-psychic states into each other (Moskowitz et al., 2009; Read et al., 2008).

In addition to the characteristic complaints of dissociation, including memory lapses, identity confusion and affective instability, psychotic experiences are also logical consequences of this uninhibited internal dialogue. For example, decontextualized voices – signals, as it were, from one compartmentalized state to another – are easily misunderstood as originating externally. Likewise, decontextualized feelings of fear are easily ascribed to people and events occurring in the present social environment, generating paranoia. Abrupt shifts between states, especially at times of stress, can easily generate disorganization of thought (Liotti & Gumley, 2008; Payne, Nadel, Britton & Jacobs, 2004).

Cognitive research

Cognitive researchers, mostly in the UK, have been the most prolific in seeking to understand the psychological mechanisms involved in psychotic experiences or complaints. Although a wide range of complaints have been studied, hallucinations and delusions have received the most attention.

Hallucinations

Researchers have converged on a consensus account of the mechanisms involved in hallucinations, which assumes that they occur when internal, self-generated mental contents are attributed to a source that is alien or external to the self (Bentall, 1990b). In the case of auditory-verbal hallucinations, or voice-hearing, it is inner speech (the internal dialogue which forms an important role in everyday thinking) that is misattributed. The primary evidence that this is the case comes from studies that have recorded the physiological concomitants of inner speech in people who hallucinate. As a result of studies using **electromyography** – a way of recording the tiny electrical impulses in muscle tissue – we have known for more than half a century that voice-hearing is accompanied by covert activations of the speech musculature (Gould, 1948; Inouye & Shimizu, 1970; McGuigan, 1966); these kind of covert activations, known as **subvocalizations**, occur during normal verbal thought, and are thought to be neuromuscular echoes of the phase of childhood when children learn to speak to themselves, first out loud and then silently (Berk, 1994). Recent studies using PET and **functional MRI** (fMRI: a specialized type of MRI which measures blood-flow related to neural activity) have confirmed that voice-hearing is accompanied by activations of the frontal brain regions involved in speech generation, and in the more posterior regions involved in speech perception (Jones & Fernyhough, 2007).

Psychological studies using signal detection (Barkus, Stirling, Hopkins, McKie & Lewis, 2007; Bentall & Slade, 1985; Rankin & O'Carrol, 1995) and other methods (Bentall, Baker & Havers, 1991; Brebion, Amador, David, Malaspina & Shariff, 2000; Johns et al., 2001; Morrison & Haddock, 1997) have confirmed that people from non-clinical samples who have a high predisposition towards hallucination, and also people who hear voices, show impairments in their performance of **source monitoring** (the skill of distinguishing between self-generated thoughts and perceptions) compared to appropriate controls. A series of electrophysiological studies, (Ford & Mathalon, 2004) showed that, whereas normal inner speech is associated with signals from the frontal cortex which suppress activity in the auditory cortex, these signals are absent in people who hear voices. Hence it seems likely that the poor source monitoring of people who hear voices is a consequence of the failure of this mechanism which, in non-voice hearers, prevents self-generated speech from being mistaken for the speech of other people.

There are two possible psychological mechanisms that might link trauma to this impairment. First, poor source monitoring might be a vulnerability factor which only causes voice-hearing when a person experiences uncontrollable, trauma-related thoughts and memories. This hypothesis is plausible because the uncontrollable intrusive thoughts of PTSD victims are, in many ways, phenomenologically similar to voices, and because experimental studies show that spontaneous thoughts of this kind are particularly difficult to source monitor (Johnson, Hashtroudi & Lindsay, 1993). An alternative possibility is that trauma somehow directly interferes with the source monitoring mechanism.

Paranoid delusions

Paranoid beliefs (beliefs characterized by a feeling of threat and where the person thinks others are actively conspiring to harm them) tend to arise against a background of chronic victimization and powerlessness (Janssen et al., 2003; Mirowsky & Ross, 1983). There is also evidence that both people with a diagnosis of psychosis (Dozier & Lee, 1995) and ordinary people with sub-clinical paranoia (Pickering, Simpson & Bentall, 2008) tend to have severe attachment difficulties. These observations may help to explain why early separation from parents (Morgan et al., 2007) and being unwanted at birth (Myhrman, Rantakallio, Isohanni & Jones, 1996) increase the risk of later having psychotic experiences, and also why immigrant groups (who are vulnerable to victimization in the host country) are especially likely to have these experiences, typically with a paranoid theme (Harrison, Owens, Holton, Neilson & Boot, 1988; Selten et al., 2001).

The core of paranoia is the excessive estimation of personal threat (Bentall et al., 2009). As the striatal dopamine system plays a role in anticipating aversive events, it seems likely that, at the neurochemical level, dopaminergic abnormalities (long implicated in psychosis: Laruelle & Abi-Dargham,

1999) underlie this excessive threat anticipation (Moutoussis, Williams, Dayan & Bentall, 2007). This abnormality, in turn, seems to be associated with problems of emotion and reasoning which are quite distinct from the source monitoring difficulties of those who hear voices.

Three separate mechanisms have been proposed in the psychological literature, with some evidence to support each. First, it has been suggested that delusions in general are associated with a tendency to jump to conclusions, that is, a tendency to make decisions on the basis of very little information. Although the precise nature of this deficit is currently a matter of controversy, the balance of evidence suggests that it is more evident in those with a diagnosis of delusion than in those with other kinds of complaints (Dudley & Over, 2003; Garety et al., 2005; Garety, Hemsley & Wessely, 1991; Moritz & Woodward, 2005).

Second, it has been argued that those with paranoid beliefs may have a difficulty in **theory of mind** (ToM) – the ability to understand other's mental states. Frith (1994) argued that a sudden loss of ToM skills would be likely to lead to persecutory beliefs if the person assumed that others were concealing their true intentions. Consistent with this idea, empirical studies have clearly demonstrated that ToM skills are impaired during acute episodes of psychotic experiences, but the evidence for a specific association with paranoia is inconsistent (Brune, 2005; Corcoran, Cahill & Frith, 1997; Corcoran et al., 2008; Drury, Robinson & Birchwood, 1998).

Third, it has been argued that paranoia arises as a consequence of severe problems of self-esteem and an **external locus of control** (where one believes that causal agency for events is located outside, rather than inside, oneself), especially if the individual attempts to fight against feelings of low self-worth by attributing the causes of misfortunes to malevolent others (Bentall, Kinderman & Kaney, 1994). Arguably, these kinds of cognitive bias are especially likely to develop against a background of attachment insecurity and victimization. Consistent with this account, those with paranoid beliefs show highly unstable self-esteem (Thewissen, Bentall, Lecomte, van Os & Myin-Germeys, 2008; Thewissen et al., 2007) as well as marked discrepancies between implicit and explicit self-esteem (McKay, Langdon & Coltheart, 2007; Moritz, Werner & von Collani, 2006). However, an **externalizing attributional bias** (the specific tendency to attribute negative events to the actions of others) only seems to be present during acute episodes of paranoia (Janssen et al., 2006) when the individual also feels they are uniquely special in some way: in other words experiencing **grandiose beliefs** (Jolley et al., 2006), and when they believe that persecution is completely undeserved (Janssen et al., 2006).

Lifelines, plasticity and specificity

In common with the forms of distress discussed in the other chapters in this book, no conclusive explanatory account of madness is yet available, largely because researchers have used invalid and unreliable constructs like schizophrenia. However, as researchers have focused on particular kinds of experience, it is possible to outline some potentially fruitful avenues for further investigation of their causal pathways. Following the lifelines approach advocated by Steven Rose (2001), described in Chapter 4, we can see that any explanatory account needs to see genetics and biochemistry in a complex interplay with the social environment. One promising avenue may be how both the effects of childhood abuse and the strategies (e.g. dissociation) that children use to cope with it become physically embodied, enabling the development of experiences like hearing voices. Another promising avenue may be how poor attachment experiences become physically embodied and also feed back into the development of fear, anxiety and poor trust in others, leading to the development of paranoid and other unusual beliefs. As we are still at an early stage in the development of this more nuanced and less reductive approach to researching distress, such accounts are necessarily provisional.

Recent years has seen more attention paid to the process of recovery by researchers. Service users have also increasingly spoken about the factors that helped them to recover. British clinical psychologist Dr Rufus May (pictured here addressing a crowd at the 2002 No Force rally in London about compulsory treatment: see Chapter 7) has spoken about his own recovery from the psychotic experience he had as a teenager, which had resulted in admissions to hospital. He recovered by drawing on support networks outside of mental health services. In the UK his story has been featured in national newspapers (Stuart, 2006), a BBC Radio 4 programme and a Channel 4 TV drama documentary. You can read his story in Romme et al. (2009), and at www.rufusmay.com)

The perspective of experience-based experts

When experts debate the causes of psychosis, we rarely include the voices of those who actually have these experiences (Geekie & Read, 2009; Read, 2012; Romme et al., 2009). As we saw in Chapter 7, they have much to contribute (Bullimore, 2010; Dillon, 2010; Lampshire, 2009; Longden, 2010). For example, Wilma Boevink, from the Netherlands, suggests another mechanism by which childhood trauma can lead to psychosis:

> I don't think that abuse itself is a strong cause for psychosis. It hurts, but it is too simple. I think that the threat and the betrayal that come with it feed psychosis. The betrayal of the family that says you must have asked for it, instead of standing up for you. That excuses the offender and accuses the victim. And forces the child to say that the air is green, while she sees clearly that it is not green but blue. That is a distortion of reality that is very hard to deal with when you're a child. You are forced to betray yourself. That is what causes the twilight zone. What makes you vulnerable for psychosis.
>
> Boevink (2006, p. 19)

Interventions

Earlier in this chapter, in the section on culture, we saw that the public prefer psychosocial causal explanations to understand distress. They also prefer psychosocial treatment approaches for people in distress (see Chapter 8). This holds true even for people given a diagnosis of schizophrenia, for which psychosocial interventions are preferred over medication (Read et al., 2006). This has been demonstrated in Australia, Austria, Canada, China, England, Germany, Hong Kong, India, Italy, Japan, Russia, Slovakia, South Africa, Switzerland and Turkey (Read & Dillon, 2013). For example, when Austrians are asked what they would do if a relative began having psychotic experiences, the most common response is 'talk to them' (Jorm, Angermeyer & Katschnig, 2000). When asked about treatments for people with a diagnosis of schizophrenia, the most preferred treatment in Germany is psychotherapy for 65% of respondents, compared to psychiatric drugs – 15% – and ECT – 1% (Riedel-Heller, Matschinger & Angermeyer, 2005). For Australians, the reasons for rejecting antipsychotic drugs include: 'have more risks than benefits', 'lack efficacy because they do not deal with the roots of the problem', and 'are prescribed for the wrong reasons (e.g. to avoid talking about problems, to make people believe things are better than they are, as a strait jacket)' (Jorm et al., 2000, p. 404). One review (Angermeyer & Dietrich, 2006) reported that eight out of nine studies had found that 'The particular liking of psychotherapy is more developed for schizophrenia than for depression'. However, as discussed in Chapter 8, medication is still the most common treatment for all forms of distress. Before discussing present-day treatments in more detail, we will look briefly at the history of physical interventions.

From rotating chairs to lobotomies

Chapters 2 and 8 discussed some of the history of treatments in psychiatry, but here we will focus specifically on the history of treatments for those seen as mad. There is a long history of less-than-helpful treatments based on the idea that there is something wrong with the brains, bodies or genes of people deemed to be mad. In the 18th and 19th centuries these included blood-letting, purgatives (laxatives), forced vomiting, rotating chairs (to settle the 'disordered motions' of the nerves in the USA, but in Britain, to unclog the blood), inoculation of scabies, and force-feeding chimney soot or woodlice (Read, 2004d).

The early part of the 20th century saw the addition of 'calming boxes' (cages), suspension from the ceiling, and ice-cold body packs. Drugs were used by Kraepelin to cause fever and Bleuler to cause vomiting, but both acknowledged the goal was to subdue rather than cure (Read, 2004e). Another approach, fortunately largely limited to New Jersey, was to surgically remove body parts and organs assumed to be causing madness, including teeth, tonsils, testicles, ovaries, gall bladders and colons. Many died (Bentall, 2009, p. 35). In the 1930s, primarily in Scandinavia, Germany and the USA, genetic theories had led to eugenics programmes in which tens of thousands of people given a diagnosis of schizophrenia, and other people considered mentally ill or defective, were sterilized. Twenty years earlier Bleuler had written:

> Lomer and von Rohe have again recommended castration, which, of course, is of no benefit to the patients themselves. However, it is to be hoped that sterilization will soon be employed on a larger scale ... for eugenic reasons.
>
> Bleuler (1911/1951, p. 473)

In Germany, the same genetic theories led to the murder of approximately a quarter of a million mental patients, at least half of whom were given a diagnosis of schizophrenia. The deaths were described as 'mercy killings' and justified by diagnoses such as 'life devoid of value' (Read & Masson, 2013). With tragic irony, this annihilation of the majority of the people in one country with a supposedly genetically-based illness provided further evidence against the theory that had been used to justify the murders. While the prevalence, of course, had been drastically reduced, the incidence (new cases) was unaffected (Fuller Torrey, 2010).

During the 1940s and 1950s well over 100,000 people given a diagnosis of schizophrenia and other mental health problems (an estimated 50,000 in the UK alone) were given lobotomies, which consists of cutting the connections to and from the prefrontal cortex. Despite the severe adverse effects involved, including reduced intellectual functioning and deadened emotions, its inventor, Portuguese neurosurgeon Egas Monitz, was awarded the Nobel Prize (Bentall, 2009).

Shock therapy

Ugo Cerletti administered the first electric shock designed to cause a seizure, in Italy, in 1938. Electroconvulsive therapy (ECT) was by no means the first attempt to shock people back into sanity. Previous attempts included being forced to stand next to cannon fire, dropping people through trap doors into ice-cold baths, and causing convulsions by overdosing with insulin.

Although nowadays used most often for depression, ECT was devised to treat schizophrenia and is still recommended for that diagnosis in most countries. The idea that people given a diagnosis of schizophrenia could be cured by inducing grand-mal epileptic seizures developed from the belief that schizophrenia and epilepsy did not co-occur in the same person. People with a diagnosis of schizophrenia had blood taken from them to be given to others with epilepsy and psychiatrists sought ways to cause epilepsy in people given a diagnosis of schizophrenia. Having observed pigs being stunned in a slaughterhouse, Cerletti discovered that electric shocks to the head caused seizures (Read, 2004b,d).

Sixty years later, as was discussed in Chapter 8, there is no robust evidence that ECT has any benefits for people given a diagnosis of either depression or schizophrenia, beyond the treatment period (typically about eight electric shocks over a three-week period). Comparisons with sham or simulated ECT, in which people are given the general anaesthetic but not the electric shock, find that a minority of those given ECT do have slightly faster improvement in mood during treatment, but any differences between the two groups disappear once the treatment ends (Gregory, Shawcross & Gill, 1985; Read & Bentall, 2010). Indeed, the two most recent studies on people given a diagnosis of schizophrenia found no difference, even during treatment (Sarita, Janakiramiaiah, Gangadhar, Subbakrishna & Rao, 1998; Ukpong, Makanjuola & Morakinyo, 2002). There is also no evidence to support the oft-made claim that ECT saves lives by preventing suicide (Read & Bentall, 2010).

Unsurprisingly, administering about 150 volts to the brain, in which the nerve cells are designed to deal with tiny fractions of one volt, causes brain damage. The most common damage comes in the form of retrograde amnesia, the inability to remember past events, and anterograde amnesia, the inability to retain new information. For some people these memory problems are temporary. However, one review identified four studies of memory loss at least six months

post-ECT (n = 597), with a frequency range of 51% to 79%, and a weighted average of 70.2% (Rose, Wykes, Leese, Bindman & Fleischmann, 2003). Four studies (n = 703) found a range for 'persistent or permanent memory loss' of 29% to 55%, with a weighted average of 38%.

Despite repeated claims, for 50 years, that ECT is safe, the first large-scale prospective study of cognitive outcomes following ECT did not occur until 2007. It found that autobiographical memory was significantly (p < .0001) worse than pre-ECT levels both shortly after ECT and six months later. The degree of impairment was significantly related to the number of shocks. Women and older people (both of whom are given ECT more frequently) were particularly impaired. Even using a conservative definition of two standard deviations worse than pre-ECT scores, 38 (12.4%) met the criterion for marked and persistent retrograde amnesia (Sackeim et al., 2007).

In the 1940s it had been argued that ECT worked precisely because it *does* cause brain damage and memory deficits. Walter Freeman, who imported ECT from Europe to the USA, wrote, in a paper entitled 'Brain damaging therapeutics':

> The greater the damage, the more likely the remission of psychotic symptoms. Maybe it will be shown that a mentally ill patient can think more clearly and more constructively with less brain in actual operation.
>
> Freeman (1941, p. 83)

ECT also involves a slight but significant risk of death, the most common causes of which being heart attacks and strokes (Read & Bentall, 2010).

Despite the lack of evidence of efficacy in relation to psychosis, official statements on the issue vary. The American Psychiatric Association's Task Force Report states that 'ECT remains an important treatment modality, particularly for patients with schizophrenia who do not respond to pharmacological treatment' and notes that, in the USA, schizophrenia and related conditions (schizophreniform and schizoaffective disorders) constitute the second most common diagnostic indication for ECT (APA, 2001). In the UK, as we saw in Chapter 8, the NICE guidelines recommend that ECT 'is used only to achieve rapid and short-term improvement of severe symptoms after an adequate trial of other treatment options has proven ineffective and/or when the condition is considered to be potentially life-threatening, in individuals with: severe depressive illness, catatonia, a prolonged or severe manic episode' (NICE, 2003). The UK's Royal College of Psychiatrists states that 'ECT is unlikely to help those with mild to moderate depression or most other psychiatric conditions. It has no role in the general treatment of schizophrenia' (RCP, 2010).

In 2011, a 154-page research report commissioned by the Food and Drug Administration in the USA (to help it decide whether to classify ECT as a 'high risk' procedure) concluded 'Little evidence exists supporting the long-term effectiveness of ECT'. The panel voted ten to eight that ECT should be classified as high risk for people with depression, and (making the odd assumption that electric shocks to the brain are differentially dangerous for people with different diagnoses) by 13 to 4 for schizophrenia (Wilson, 2011).

Antipsychotic drugs

a) First generation, 'conventional' antipsychotics

The discovery of chlorpromazine in the 1950s has already been discussed in Chapters 2 and 8. As it was seen to induce a 'euphoric quietude' it was tried on people in French psychiatric hospitals. Within a year of its first use, two million Americans were receiving it (Johnstone, 2000) and, by 1970, about 250 million people worldwide had taken antipsychotics (Jeste & Wyatt, 1979).

One of the claims made in support of their effectiveness was that they made community care possible. As discussed in Chapter 2, there is little evidence supporting this assertion and much against it (Warner, 2004). In most countries, the decline in hospital usage had begun well before 1954, when chlorpromazine was introduced, and can be explained by other, usually economic, factors. Scull (1984) argues that in England and Wales the number of inpatients had peaked around 1930.

Other evidence for the efficacy of the conventional antipsychotics (used before the introduction of the atypical antipsychotics in the early 1990s) came from studies comparing the relapse rates of people on the drugs with the relapse rates of people whose drugs were replaced with placebos. A review of 29 such studies, totalling 3519 people, found a difference in relapse rates in every study (Davis, Schaffer, Killian, Kinard & Chan, 1980). However, when the numbers from the 29 studies are combined, we see that relapse occurred in 55% of the people whose drugs were replaced with placebos and in 19% of those remaining on the drugs. To make a crude comparison, we can subtract the 45% benefiting from placebo from the 81% benefiting from the drugs. Based on this calculation, the drugs only appeared to benefit 36% of the people who took them.

However, in a recent review the proportion improving with placebo was around 19%, while 29% improved with haloperidol (Leucht et al., 2009), suggesting that only 10% of participants benefited from taking it.

One of the studies (Vaughn & Leff, 1976) found that the drugs did make a difference for those living with hostility and criticism and who were unable to get out of the house very much: 53% on drugs relapsed compared to 92% on placebos. For those living in more supportive home environments the drugs made little difference: 12% on drugs and 15% on placebos relapsed.

As noted in Chapter 8, these conventional or first-generation antipsychotics have a range of serious adverse effects. These include dry mouth, tachycardia (rapid heart beat), weight gain, constipation, urinary retention, delirium, akathisia (feelings of extreme agitation and restlessness), tremor, rigidity, dystonia (a neurological movement disorder causing muscle contractions) and oculogyric crisis (involuntary movement of the eyeballs). Another adverse effect, as noted in Chapter 8, is tardive dyskinesia, which involves uncontrollable movements of the tongue, lips, face, hands and feet. The average prevalence among people on conventional antipsychotic drugs is 30% (Llorca, Chereau, Bayle & Lancon, 2002). Among people over 45 years old, 26% develop tardive dyskinesia after just one year on the drugs and 60% after three years (Jeste, Caligiuri, Paulsen & Heaton, 1995).

The pharmaceutical industry has acknowledged that tardive dyskinesia is irreversible in 75% of cases. A 1992 estimate, based on everyone who had ever received the drugs to that date, was 86 million cases, 57 million of which were irreversible (Ross & Read, 2004). By 1983 tardive dyskinesia had, justifiably, been described as 'one of the worst medically-induced disasters in history' (Breggin, 1983, p. 109).

b) Second-generation atypical antipsychotics

As we saw in Chapter 8, in the 1990s the new atypical, or second generation antipsychotics (SGAs) – risperidone, olanzapine, sertindole and quetiapine – were introduced. It was claimed that the new drugs were more effective. It was also claimed that they produced lower rates of tardive dyskinesia and this was used as a major marketing tool (Mosher et al., 2013). However, in its final letter of approval to Janssen, the FDA made explicit its conclusions about the relative merits of risperidone (an atypical) and haloperidol (a conventional). Robert Temple, director of the FDA's Office of Drug Evaluation, told Janssen:

> We would consider any advertisement or promotion labeling for RISPERDAL false, misleading, or lacking fair balance under section 502 (a) and 502 (n) of the ACT if there is presentation of data that conveys the impression that risperidone is superior to haloperidol or any other marketed antipsychotic drug product with regard to safety or effectiveness.
>
> Whitaker (2002, p. 277)

A 2000 review of 52 studies, involving 12,649 people, concluded that 'there is no clear evidence that atypical antipsychotics are more effective or are better tolerated than conventional antipsychotics' (Geddes, Freemantle, Harrison & Bebbington, 2000).

Indeed, the new atypicals have an additional range of adverse effects, including: glucose intolerance and diabetes (especially in men); obesity, which, besides the social stigma involved, can lead to hypertension, cardiovascular disease, hyperlipidaemia (an excess of lipids in the blood) and, again, diabetes; sexual dysfunction (in about 50%); lactation in women and breast swelling in men; decreased motivation and ability to experience pleasure; and a form of depression called neuroleptic dysphoria. It can be difficult to separate the impact of drugs from the impact of lifestyle (for example, many people with a diagnosis of schizophrenia smoke cigarettes and do not exercise), but recent reviews also indicate that antipsychotic drugs reduce life expectancy (Weinmann & Aderhold, 2010; Weinmann et al., 2009). They can also reduce the volume of the brain, via neurodegeneration (Ho et al., 2011) thereby – paradoxically – causing some of the abnormalities cited as evidence that schizophrenia is a brain disease (Moncrieff & Leo, 2010).

A recent review of 38 clinical trials of SGAs (Leucht et al., 2009) found that 24% and 41% of participants improved significantly when taking placebo and SGAs respectively. This suggests that only 17% of people taking the drugs benefitted from them. In 2010 a review of research on risperidone, a widely-prescribed atypical antipsychotic, was published by the Cochrane Collaboration, whose evaluations of medical treatments are regarded as the most rigorous and independent. It found only ten drug-placebo comparisons that met their inclusion criteria, all but one conducted by drug companies (Rattehalli, Jayaram & Smith, 2010). It concluded:

> Risperidone appears to have a marginal benefit in terms of clinical improvement compared with placebo in the first few weeks of treatment but data are limited, poorly reported and probably biased in favour of risperidone. The margin of improvement chosen by the researchers as their outcome may not be clinically meaningful ... Data became considerably more homogeneous (and positive) when the one study independent of industry funding was removed ... It is, however, associated with movement adverse effects, increased prolactin level, and the outcome of marginal improvement is difficult to interpret as being

clinically relevant. We know that increased prolactin can cause sexual side effects which has not been reported in the included trials. There is also the worry that these studies are, at the very least, moderately prone to bias favouring risperidone. (p. 2)

Global effects suggests that there is no clear difference between risperidone and placebo. ... Risperidone causes many adverse effects and, even in the included studies where these effects are particularly poorly reported, these effects are important and common. Data in this review does not support or refute the sustained use of this drug ... People with schizophrenia or their advocates may want to lobby regulatory authorities to insist on better studies being available before wide release of a compound with the subsequent beguiling advertising. (p. 18)

Unsurprisingly, perhaps, many people stop taking these drugs. In one study, of about 1400 American people, 74% stopped within 18 months mainly because they found them to be ineffective or because of the side-effects, or both (Lieberman et al., 2005).

It is striking that in media reports concerning people with a diagnosis of a mental health problem, especially where violence is involved, mention is often made that a person had stopped taking their medication, but the reasons why someone might do this are seldom examined.

Although large numbers of people prescribed these drugs stop taking them, few psychiatrists have stopped prescribing them. The vast majority of people given a diagnosis of schizophrenia are immediately given antipsychotics. Their usage continues to increase. For example, in the UK, prescriptions of antipsychotics rose from 2.3 million in 1987 to 7.2 million in 2006. There appears to be a puzzling difference between the research evidence and the claims made by the pharmaceutical industry in their successful efforts to persuade governments all over the world to fund these drugs, despite their being about ten times as expensive as conventional antipsychotic drugs. Of particular concern is the increasing use of antipsychotics for elderly people who have never had psychotic experiences (Mosher et al., 2013; Ross & Read, 2004) and troubled teenagers who are deemed to be at risk of having psychotic experiences and receiving a diagnosis of schizophrenia in the future (Bentall & Morrison, 2002). In the USA, antipsychotic prescribing to those under the age of 18 recently quadrupled in six years (Cooper et al., 2006). Studies conducted to date have produced no evidence that antipsychotics are effective in preventing psychosis in people judged to be at high risk of developing this condition (Marshall & Rathbone, 2011). For example, one study found no benefit of risperidone (a popular SGA) over placebo when both groups were also given psychological therapy (Yung et al., 2011). It is feared that the new diagnoses of 'Psychosis Risk Syndrome' or 'Attenuated Psychotic Symptoms' Syndrome proposed for inclusion in the DSM-5, which have very broad and inclusive criteria, will further increase the use of these drugs with young people, whose brains are particularly susceptible to the adverse effects because they are still developing (Morrison, Byrne & Bentall, 2010; Ross, 2010).

Psychosocial treatments

Contrary to the belief that the sorts of psychological treatment approaches used for problems like depression and anxiety are inappropriate or ineffective for psychosis, there is no reason to assume that psychotic experiences are so severe or so biological that these approaches are not just as useful with these problems. As noted in Chapter 8, many mental health service users often express a preference for psychological and psychosocial interventions over medication (Byrne, Davies & Morrison, 2010). A number of books have described and summarized the research evaluating the effectiveness of a range of psychosocial treatments for psychosis, including family therapy and group therapy (Alanen et al., 2009; Bentall, 2009; Garfield & Mackler, 2008; Gleeson, Killackey & Krstev, 2008; Johannessen, Martindale & Cullberg, 2007; Pilling et al., 2002; Read & Dillon, 2013).

A meta-analysis of 37 studies calculated that 66% of people improve as a result of individual psychotherapy, compared to 35% who improve without treatment. The result was the same with or without medication. Of the three types of psychotherapy assessed, cognitive–behavioural (68%) and psychodynamic (67%) had equally high rates of improvement, with supportive therapy (62%) not far behind (Gottdiener, 2004).

For some time after the introduction of the antipsychotics in the 1950s psychoanalysts led the struggle to keep psychological approaches alive. In 1956 the Italian psychiatrist and psychoanalyst Gaetano Benedetti founded what was to become the interdisciplinary International Society for Psychological and Social Approaches to Psychosis (www.isps.org), which today has branches in 15 countries, publishes a book series (12 at last count) and a research journal: *Psychosis: Psychological, Social and Integrative Approaches*, promotes the full range of psychosocial approaches, and describes how various models can be integrated (Garrett & Turkington, 2011). We focus here, however, on what has become known as the Soteria approach and on the approach that has been most researched: cognitive therapy.

The Soteria model

In 1998 Loren Mosher (1933–2004), an American psychiatrist, resigned from his profession because of what he saw as its narrowly biological focus and its financial dependence on and acquiescence to the pharmaceutical industry (Mosher, 1998). Before his resignation, however, he had been Director of the Center for Studies of Schizophrenia at the National Institute of Mental Health, and had founded and edited what remains one of the leading research journals in the field, *Schizophrenia Bulletin*. Inspired in part by the work of another highly influential dissident psychiatrist, Ronnie Laing (Laing & Esterson, 1970), at Kingsley Hall in London, Mosher established Soteria House in California in 1971. In his own words:

At its core was the notion that psychosis should be dealt with face to face without the usual external impediments of theory, artificial institutions, professionally acquired belief systems and practices and without chemical alteration of consciousness by antipsychotic drugs. It focused on finding shared meaning and understanding of the subjective experience of 'schizophrenia' (actually 'personal or developmental crisis' was the operant term), including the experience of others involved in the interactional process. In doing so the approach eschewed the medical (or any other) theoretical model. Its facility was a home in the community, rather than a hospital. It utilized non-professional staff specially selected and trained to relate to and understand madness without preconceptions, labels, categories, judgements or the need 'to do' anything to change, control, suppress or invalidate the experience of psychosis. Antipsychotics were not ordinarily used for at least the initial 6 weeks.

Mosher (2004, pp. 350–1)

Dr Loren Mosher, the American psychiatrist who established Soteria House in California in 1971

In fact, at the six-week follow-up, 76% of Soteria residents had not received antipsychotic medications, compared to 2% of the people treated in hospital with whom Mosher compared his approach. (It is important to note that although highly critical of diagnostic labels such as schizophrenia, Mosher ensured that all people in both groups had received such a diagnosis. This meant that in the eyes of the system he was trying to change the two groups were comparable, and also that if he was able to demonstrate that the new approach was more effective that result could not be dismissed with arguments that they were less disturbed than the hospital group in the first.) There were comparable reductions in symptoms between the two treatment groups. In fact, at the two-year follow-up, the Soteria group had better outcomes than those in the treatment-as-usual group at the hospital, not only on symptom measures, but also on quality of life measures such as social functioning and being employed. Those who had received no medication at any stage were the most improved (Mosher, 2004; Mosher, Hendrix & Fort, 2005).

Unfortunately, such projects and studies, comparing unmedicated and medicated people, have been rare (Calton, Ferriter, Huband & Spandler, 2008), largely because of the assumption that it is irresponsible not to prescribe medication to everyone given a diagnosis of schizophrenia. By 2009, one reviewer examining similar projects could find only five such studies (one more in the USA, and the others in Switzerland, Finland and Sweden). The extent to which the projects resembled Mosher's Soteria project varied. However all the later studies found that people who were unmedicated had better outcomes than those who were medicated (Bola, Lehtinen, Cullberg & Ciompi, 2009; Romme et al., 2009). As well as being at least as effective as hospital-based and medication-based

treatment, the alternative approach has none of the adverse effects of the drugs, mentioned earlier. Of equal importance is the fact that those who receive care tend to prefer the alternative approach (Agar-Jacomb & Read, 2009)

Cognitive therapy

The most extensively researched individual psychological therapy for patients with psychosis is cognitive-behaviour therapy (CBT), which was introduced in Chapter 8. This approach had two roots. The first was behaviour modification (based on Skinnerian conditioning theory), which enjoyed some success as a technique for rehabilitating people who had become severely institutionalized in hospital (Dickerson et al., 2005), but which was eventually abandoned as simplistic, arguably dehumanizing, and impractical in community settings. For example, on 'token economy' wards, patients were reinforced for looking after themselves by being given plastic tokens which could later be exchanged for treats of various kinds. The second root was cognitive therapy, a brief therapy for people experiencing depression developed by the American Psychiatrist Aaron Beck (1976), in which patients would be gently encouraged to examine and abandon their pessimistic assumptions about the world. Today, CBT encompasses a broad collection of therapeutic strategies designed to help people with a wide range of problems, with a number of important common features, which include: (i) an emphasis on treating specific problems as defined by the client; (ii) an emphasis on the importance of a tailored formulation (a model of the client's difficulties and how they have arisen: see Chapter 5) that is shared between the therapist and the client; (iii) a focus on examining and questioning the client's way of interpreting experiences; (iv) a structured plan for therapy which will include the client undertaking homework assignments; and lastly (v) the expectation that therapy will be completed in a timely fashion (six months of weekly sessions are common in the treatment of depression). It should be noted that, although CBT is often thought to be a fairly prescriptive approach to therapy, CBT therapists are generally aware of the importance of a warm and collaborative therapeutic alliance with the client.

CBT for psychosis began with single case studies in which attempts were made to help people cope with their voice-hearing (Slade & Bentall, 1988) or to overcome their fears considered delusional (Chadwick & Lowe, 1995). These experiments led eventually to a number of reasonably large and moderately successful randomized controlled trials with people who had failed to benefit from antipsychotic drugs (e.g. Sensky et al., 2000), people with a diagnosis of first episode of psychosis (Tarrier et al., 2004), people thought to be at risk of relapse (Gumley et al., 2003) and even people who were thought to be at risk of a first episode of psychosis (Morrison et al., 2004).

As noted in Chapter 8, specific strategies are designed to exploit the client's ability to reason almost scientifically about what has happened in his or her life (hence the term **collaborative empiricism** is sometimes used to describe the approach). Clients are therefore encouraged to weigh up and evaluate the evidence for their distressing beliefs, to propose alternative accounts of their experiences, and to try simple behavioural experiments to test out their expectations. For example, a client who is terrified that others can hear his or her abusive voices might be encouraged to ask other people whether this is the case, to carry around a tape recorder to see whether the voices are physically audible, or to keep a record of how others react when the voices become particularly loud.

CBT is currently recommended for the treatment of psychosis by the UK's National Institute for Clinical Excellence, which advises the National Health Service about which treatments to invest in for specific conditions. Some of the debates about the effectiveness of the psychotherapies, including CBT, were discussed in Chapter 8. CBT is still the focus of controversy, with some critics claiming that it does not beat placebo treatments, by which the critics seem to mean less structured forms of psychotherapy (Lynch, Laws & McKenna, 2010). Several meta-analyses have reported that CBT is effective in reducing the severity of problematic psychotic experiences, but not the risk of relapse (Pilling et al., 2002; Wykes, Steel, Everitt & Tarrier, 2008); however, it should be recalled that this kind of treatment remains at an early stage of development – just over 30 trials carried out over about a decade at the time of writing, as opposed to, in the case of antipsychotics, many thousands of drug trials conducted over more than half a century (Bentall, 2009).

One of the difficulties has been gaining approval for studies of psychological therapies in the absence of antipsychotic drugs, because of the false assumption that everyone must be on these drugs (Bola et al., 2009). A small but very important CBT study recently circumvented these objections by studying people who had been prescribed the drugs but refused to take them or had come off them. A response rate analysis found that 35% and 50% of participants achieved at least a 50% reduction in psychosis symptoms scores by end of therapy and at 15-month follow-up respectively (Morrison et al., 2012).

As with other fields of psychotherapy research, the choice of methods and outcome measures employed in the trials has become an important point of contention (Morrison, 2009). Based on comparisons with drugs, the most commonly measured outcome is symptom-severity, but that might not be what is most important to the client, for whom quality of life might be more important (Morrison, 2009).

Early intervention

In many parts of the world, including Scandinavia, the USA, the UK, Australia, New Zealand, Germany and Canada, there has been a concerted effort to develop early intervention, or first-episode, services for people with troubling psychotic experiences. These services are based on the belief that these problems are indeed treatable, that the chances of recovery are higher than previously thought, and that the earlier people receive help, the greater the chance of a speedy recovery (Johannessen, 2004; Yung, Killackey, Nelson & McGorry, 2010).

For example, an evaluation of the Early Psychosis Prevention and Intervention Centre (EPPIC) in Melbourne found that eight years after treatment, EPPIC patients had fewer psychotic experiences and were more likely to be in paid employment than a matched control group of people who had received generic mental health services. The study also recorded the costs involved and concluded that 'Specialized early psychosis programs can deliver a higher recovery rate at one-third the cost of standard public mental health services' (Mihalopoulos, Harris, Henry, Harrigan & McGorry, 2009, p. 909).

The balance between medical and psychological treatments may vary from one service to another but the majority of the young people involved will be given antipsychotic medication and thereby exposed to the risk of the kind of adverse effects identified above. Indeed, the risks may be greater for adolescents because their brains are still developing and because some of the side-effects, such as sexual dysfunction and severe weight gain, affect the ability of young people to engage effectively in the developmental tasks of adolescence and early adulthood, such as dating, finding a career and establishing a secure identity (Bentall & Morrison, 2002).

A recent extension of the early intervention approach has been to try and identify people at an earlier stage, before they become overwhelmed by psychotic experiences. Within this approach, psychotic experiences are seen as signs of a **prodrome**: the stage immediately before the point where somebody might become overwhelmed and then attract a diagnosis of psychosis. This approach was pioneered in Melbourne, where researchers attempted to identify people with sub-clinical prodromal signs (usually attenuated symptoms and reduced social functioning), which, it was thought, might indicate an impending breakdown. In an initial study, about 40% of the sample went on to have such a breakdown (Yung et al., 1998), a result that has been replicated in some (Cannon et al., 2008) but not all (Yung et al., 2006) subsequent studies. Clearly, these findings have important practical and ethical implications.

Some researchers have attempted to see whether antipsychotics can prevent the onset of a breakdown in high-risk samples. So far the findings have been equivocal (McGlashan et al., 2006), but, in any case, it is difficult to see how this approach can be justified given the risk of antipsychotic side-effects and the fact that 60% of all those receiving medication would not have had a breakdown (Bentall & Morrison, 2002). Psychological therapies are not without ethical hazards, as we saw in Chapter 8, and there is also the risk of stigmatization as a result of being a client of such a service – but at least there is no physical risk to the client. A pilot study of CBT for people with the kind of problematic experiences seen as symptoms of a prodrome reported a reduced risk of developing more serious problems in the short term (Morrison et al., 2004), but much more work is required to determine whether this approach really is effective.

Initiatives by experience-based experts

As Peter Campbell noted in Chapter 7, since the 1960s organizations of patients – or, as they prefer to be called, service users or consumers, psychiatric survivors or experience-based experts – have developed a range of strategies to resist what many see as a coercive and pessimistic medical model of psychiatry. As well as protesting against diagnostic labelling, the overuse of drugs and any use of shock therapy, they often provide alternative services (Campbell, 2006; Chamberlin, 2004).

A wonderful example, with obvious relevance for the subject of this chapter, is the Hearing Voices Network (www.intervoiceonline.org), also discussed in Chapter 7. The network has active groups in Australia, Austria, Denmark, England, Finland, Germany, Ireland, Italy, Japan, the Netherlands, New Zealand, Norway, Palestine, Scotland, Spain, Sweden, Switzerland, the USA and Wales. Inspired in large part by the work of Dutch psychiatrist Marius Romme, the groups provide support to other voice-hearers and training for professionals on how to support voice-hearers without labelling, patronizing or pathologizing them, stressing the meaningfulness of people's experiences in the context of their life histories (Beavan, 2011; Beavan & Read, 2010; Romme et al., 2009; Romme & Escher, 2012).

Professor Marius Romme and Dr Sandra Escher have pioneered an innovative approach to understanding the voice-hearing experience and helping people cope with distressing voices

The recovery approach

Consistent with the gradual acknowledgement that people who have psychotic experiences have much to contribute to our understanding of how to assist them (Romme et al., 2009) many countries have adopted various branches of what has become known as the **recovery movement**. Like early intervention services, this rejects the idea that people with psychotic experiences are suffering from an irreversible or chronic condition. Richard Warner, a US psychiatrist and a renowned expert on recovery from psychosis (Warner, 2004), defines the movement like this:

> The recovery model refers to subjective experiences of optimism, empowerment and interpersonal support, and to a focus on collaborative treatment approaches, finding productive roles for user/consumers, peer support and reducing stigma. The model is influencing service development around the world. ... Remission of symptoms has been precisely defined, but the definition of 'recovery' is a more diffuse concept that includes such factors as being productive and functioning independently. Recent research and a large, earlier body of data suggest that optimism about outcome from schizophrenia is justified. A substantial proportion of people with the illness will recover completely and many more will regain good social functioning ... A growing body of research supports the concept that empowerment is an important component of the recovery process. Key tenets of the recovery model – optimism about recovery from schizophrenia, the importance of access to employment and the value of empowerment of user/ consumers in the recovery process – are supported by the scientific research.
>
> Warner (2009, p. 374)

Asking about adverse life events

A prerequisite for any treatment plan is a formulation (ideally agreed between the helper and the person seeking help) of the causes of the problem(s) for which the person or family is asking to be helped. The formulation approach was introduced in Chapter 5 as an alternative to the categorical diagnostic system embodied in the DSM and ICD classification manuals. A prerequisite for a formulation is a full understanding of the

person's life history and current social circumstances. Many researchers recommend that all service users, including those with a diagnosis of psychosis, are routinely asked about traumatic events (e.g. Conus et al., 2010; Read et al., 2007). Research, however, tells us that mental health professionals very often avoid asking about child abuse and neglect, or about rape and assault in adulthood (Read et al., 2007). Moreover, some studies have found that people given a diagnosis like schizophrenia are particularly unlikely to be asked about these issues and are less likely to be offered trauma-focused therapy (Agar & Read, 2002; Read & Fraser, 1998a, 1998b).

A one-day training programme about when and how to ask about abuse, and how to respond, was developed and evaluated in Auckland, New Zealand (Cavanagh, Read & New, 2004; Young, Read, Barker-Collo & Harrison, 2001) and, in 2007, presented in the professional journal of the Royal College of Psychiatrists in the UK (Read et al., 2007). In 2008 the England Department of Health published a briefing paper on *Implementing National Policy on Violence and Abuse* (NHS Confederation, 2008). Consistent with the policy on which the Auckland training programme was based, the document states (p. 1):

> Department of Health policy is that adult mental health services should acknowledge and address the links between violence and abuse and mental health by ensuring staff, once satisfactorily trained, raise issues of violence and abuse routinely and consistently in assessments (both at first contact and at assessment reviews).

It should be noted (p. 2) that the Department of Health understands that:

> The effects of child sexual abuse can be a significant contributory factor to all diagnoses and presentations from depression, anxiety, eating and obsessive compulsive disorders and perinatal mental health through to bipolar disorder, psychosis and schizophrenia, dual diagnosis and personality disorder diagnoses.

We leave the last words on this topic to a group of service users (mostly with diagnoses associated with psychosis) who, during the planning of the Auckland training programme, were asked what they thought about asking all mental health service users about child abuse.

> There were so many doctors and registrars and nurses and social workers in your life asking you about the same thing, mental, mental, mental, but not asking you why.

> I think there was an assumption that I had a mental illness and you know because I wasn't saying anything about the abuse I'd suffered no one knew.

> I just wish they would have said, 'What happened to you? What happened?' But they didn't.
>
> Lothian and Read (2002)

Prevention

Prevention of mental health problems is given little or no space in most psychology textbooks. Given how much research psychologists and others have conducted into the causes. This seems unfortunate.

> Successful primary prevention in psychiatry is often not psychiatric in nature. Successful interventions include providing a healthy start to life through adequate prenatal

care and home-based services for high-risk parents, the provision of preschool for socially deprived children, and developing employment for parents of poor families.

Warner (2005)

One of the saddest things about biological psychiatry's over-emphasis on genes and biochemistry is that, because of the accompanying assumption that psychotic experiences are not caused by adverse events, it has led to the belief that nothing can be done to prevent them (Boyle, 2004). In this approach, the model of prevention is more properly termed **secondary prevention**: identifying symptoms before a person meets the criteria for a psychiatric diagnosis. Thus mental health professionals attempt to identify at-risk teenagers and refer them to mental health services to be treated (often, but not always, with drugs). **Primary prevention**, on the other hand, involves targeting the causes of a problem. Now that it has been established that psychosis is largely caused by the same factors that increase risk for many other mental health problems, it is clear that primary prevention of psychotic experiences is entirely possible (Clements & Davies, 2013). As Warner (2009) has indicated, such programmes will not necessarily be focused on specific forms of distress, because they are primarily caused by the same sorts of social adversities. For example, in an all-too-rare study using a psychosis-related outcome measure for a primary prevention approach, an environmental enrichment programme at age three to five was found to reduce scores on a measure of schizotypal personality in adulthood (Raine, Mellingen, Liu, Venables & Mednick, 2003). It also reduced anti-social behaviour.

A 2004 paper, entitled 'Preventing "schizophrenia": Creating the conditions for saner society', put it this way:

> Many mental health professionals see more human pain in a week than most of us see in a lifetime. Paradoxically, these societally-ordained witnesses seem paralysed into silence about the source of the pain flowing over them. To ask a human being to sit day after day with often frightened and sometimes frightening survivors of the worst that life can throw at people, *and* to find the energy, and hope, to simultaneously try to plug the source, seems unfair. On the other hand, an exclusive focus on the distressed individual may be stopping us focusing on what we mean by mental health, healthy families, healthy communities and just societies. If we focus more of our debate here, we might learn more about how to enhance their development.

Davies and Burdett (2004, p. 279)

The famous American psychologist, George Albee, adds:

> Psychologists must join with persons who reject racism, sexism, colonialism, and exploitation and must find ways to redistribute social power and to increase social justice. Primary prevention research inevitably will make clear the relationship between social pathology and psychopathology and then will work to change social and political structures in the interests of social justice. It is as simple and as difficult as that!

Albee (1996, p. 1131)

There are some debates about prevention, however. For example, Boyle (2004) has noted that the prerequisite of any prevention programme is clarity about what it is that is to be prevented and a clear explanatory causal model with a delineation of interventions that can address causal factors. As we have seen in this chapter, although much progress has been made in this direction, particularly in attempting to understand the causal processes implicated in specific experiences (rather than global and heterogeneous diagnostic categories), much remains to be understood. Moreover, there is an assumption that the prevention of such experiences is always a preferred aim. Whilst this may be true of many mental health service users it may not be true of all: some may wish to learn to live with their psychotic experiences rather than eradicate them. A good illustration of this debate is the following conversation between one of the authors (RB) and the Dutch psychiatrist Marius Romme (discussed earlier in relation to his work on voice-hearing):

> As we walked through the pristine white corridors of the brand-new conference centre one morning, Romme and I discussed our different approaches and, in the middle of this conversation, he said something that I will never forget:
> I really like your work on hallucinations, Richard. But the trouble is, you want to *cure* hallucinators, whereas I want to *liberate* them. I think they are like homosexuals in the 1950s – in need of liberation, not cure.

Bentall (2003, p. 511, emphasis
in original)

Chapter summary

In this chapter we have discussed debates about how best to define madness and located this form of distress in its historical and cultural context, in particular how it has been addressed by clinical psychologists and how professional understandings have influenced public attitudes. We have discussed how madness is conceptualized by the DSM, including some of the problems with psychiatric conceptualizations, particularly issues with the reliability and validity of diagnostic categories. We have also outlined an alternative approach which is consistently psychological, focusing on particular experiences like hearing voices. We have described a range of causal factors and explanatory models from different theoretical traditions. Finally, we have reviewed the evidence for a number of different interventions.

The way in which madness has been understood has often reflected dominant intellectual fashions. Throughout the 20th century it has been understood primarily within a simplistically reductive biomedical model. However, recent years have seen researchers examine particular psychotic experiences, finding that they can be understood using concepts and principles from mainstream psychology. As a result, a number of more complex causal models have been developed, as have a range of interventions, psychosocial as well as biomedical. Hopefully, these developments will pave the way for an increase of the quality of care received by those who experience the forms of distress associated with madness.

End of chapter questions

1 Given that many psychotic experiences are more common than traditionally thought, should they be understood as variations of human experience rather than symptoms of an illness?

2 Is it possible to research the early life experience of people who have psychotic experiences without this being seen as 'blaming families'?

3 Is a focus on particular experiences or complaints the best alternative to the use of global diagnostic categories like schizophrenia?

4 Given the evidence in support of psychosocial interventions, why is medication by far the most common treatment for people with a diagnosis of schizophrenia?

Find out more

Readers should also consult the further reading and resources section in Chapter 7 where publications and organizations associated with the Hearing Voices Movement are listed.

1 Bentall, R. (2003). *Madness Explained: Psychosis and Human Nature*. London: Penguin.
A detailed account of the issues discussed in this chapter.

2 Bentall, R. (2009). *Doctoring the Mind: Why Psychiatric Treatments Fail*. London: Penguin.
An accessible discussion of the recent history of psychiatry and its dominance, illustrated with personal and clinical stories.

3 Boyle, M. (2002). *Schizophrenia: A Scientific Delusion?* (2nd edn). London: Routledge.

A critical examination of the notion of schizophrenia, including a discussion of its history, its implicit assumptions and alternative ways of understanding psychotic experiences.

4 British Psychological Society (2000). *Recent Advances in Understanding Mental Illness and Psychotic Experiences: A Report by the British Psychological Society*. Leicester: Author. Available from: www.schizophrenia.com/research/Rep03.pdf
This report was an attempt to develop a consensus view of psychotic experiences by British clinical psychologists from a range of traditions. It is a little dated now (a second edition is underway), but still provides a concise examination of relevant research, drawing also on the insights of users of mental health survivors.

5 British Psychological Society (2010). *Understanding Bipolar Disorder: Why Some People Experience Mood States and What Can Help*. Leicester: Author. Available from:http://psychminded.co.uk/news/news2010/October10/Understanding-bipolar-disorder.pdf
Another, more up-to-date, consensus report by British clinical psychologists, this time focusing on a specific diagnostic category: bipolar disorder.

6 Geekie, J., Randal, P., Lampshire, D. & Read, J. (Eds) (2012). *Experiencing Psychosis: Personal and Professional Perspectives*. London: Routledge.
Pairs of chapters discussing aspects of psychosis from the viewpoint of an 'experience-based expert' and researchers.

7 Read, J. & Dillon, J. (2013). *Models of Madness: Psychological, Social and Biological Approaches to Psychosis* (2nd edn). London: Routledge.
An edited volume critically examining the illness model of schizophrenia, an elaboration of social and psychological models of understanding madness and a review of a range of alternative forms of intervention including Mosher's Soteria House, mentioned in this chapter.

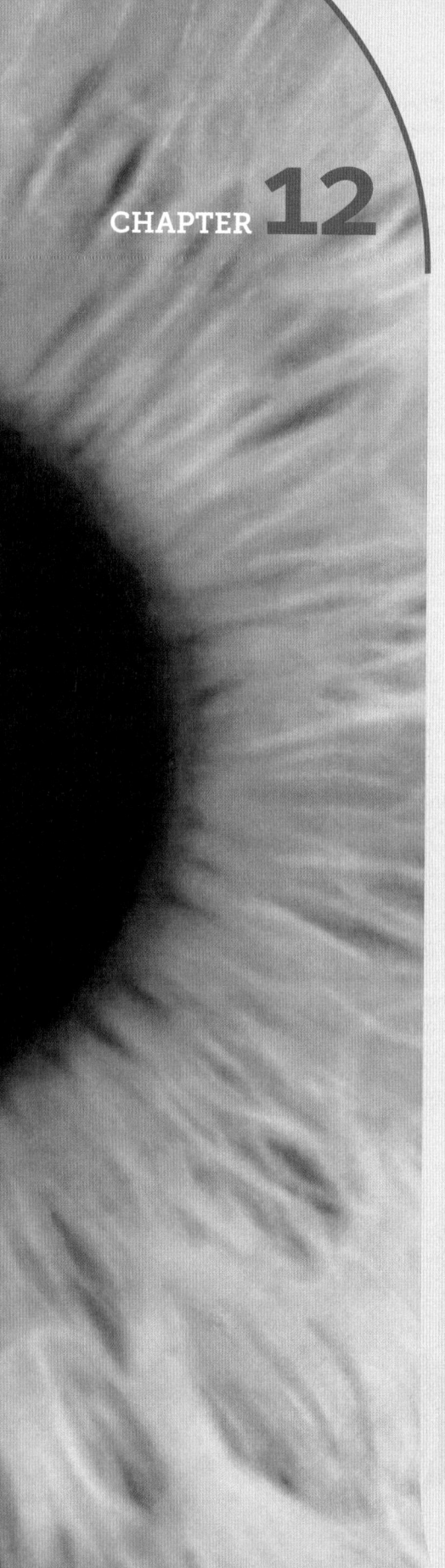

CHAPTER 12

DISTRESSING BODIES AND EATING

Carmel's story

Carmel is a 13-year-old girl from a suburban district in the south of the UK. She is mixed race; her mother is white South African born and her father is African–Caribbean British born. Carmel is highly academically able and usually finds school a pleasure, as she has many friends. Of late, however, Carmel has been showing signs of withdrawal: turning up for school late and disappearing rapidly after the home time bell has rung. Her appearance has altered considerably and she has a lost a considerable amount of weight. Her movements are more sluggish and her eyes more sunken and tired-looking. Her fingernails are split and her hair is thinning. When one of her friends called for her after school one day, they found Carmel irritable and distracted. After some persuasion, Carmel allowed her friend to come into the house and into her bedroom. There her friend found a horde of high-calorie snacks; doughnuts, chocolate and crisps, hidden in her clothes chest. She asked Carmel what was going on and why they hadn't seen as much of her. Carmel responded by talking to her friend about what had been happening at home. Her parents had been arguing a lot and spending less and less time at home together. As a result Carmel felt very lonely and a little rejected. When she asked her father to help her with her homework, he just looked at her blankly and said he had better things to do. Her mother was more helpful but had started acting strangely and using her mobile phone more often. Her mother had also joined a gym and lost a lot of weight, as well as wearing more makeup. Carmel looked at herself alongside her mother and felt that perhaps she could do more to improve the way she looked, as her body had started changing and becoming more 'plump' in certain places. After several failed attempts at restricting her eating completely, she began fasting during the day and secretly bingeing at night in her room. After bingeing, Carmel would feel terrible; guilty, ashamed and out of control. She would immediately vomit and hide any remnants of her activities. Even though she did feel bad, she also felt that she had got into a routine and didn't really know how to stop. No-one at home had really noticed and she simply became better at making excuses for skipping meals. She told her friend that she felt as if things had spiralled out of her control and she wanted help, but didn't know how to ask for it and who to ask.

By the end of this chapter you should:

1 Know how eating problems and weight-related concerns have been defined in the mental health literature.
2 Understand why weight and body image concerns are at the centre of eating-related problems.
3 Understand what kinds of risk factors are associated with these problematic experiences
4 Know what are considered to be symptoms of eating disorders.
5 Know what kinds of interventions are available and whether they are effective.

Introduction

It is not uncommon to be unhappy with our appearance and sometimes feel as if we would be able to sort out other problems in our lives if we could simply 'look better'. As many of the magazine advertisements tell us, we should 'look better and feel better', especially when attached to advertisements for weight loss. Eating patterns and weight concerns are highly related in the type of problems reported to clinical psychologists and psychiatrists. And yet concerns over weight and eating problems are by no means uncommon in many Western industrialized societies, and a growing number of non-Western countries (Nasser, Katzman & Gordon, 2001).

Like Carmel, many of us have used eating as a way to cope with distressing events and experiences in our lives and have often found ourselves spiralling out of control so that getting back to healthy eating is difficult. In the long term, however, eating problems, involving food restriction, bingeing (eating too much in one go) and purging (vomiting or using laxatives) can lead to persistent distress and contribute significantly to feelings of sadness and worry that may well have been there all along. (**Purging** refers to behaviours that serve the purpose of controlling weight, including the removal of food from the body, such as vomiting, the use of laxatives, enemas, diuretics, and over-exercising.)

Perhaps no other issue relevant to mental health and distress has been subject to greater public speculation, fascination and scrutiny as problems related to weight management and eating habits. Every time we pick up a popular magazine there are circles drawn around the body parts of celebrities to signal they are too thin or, more likely, overweight, and numerous articles feature their eating habits and lifestyles. Many of us seem obsessed, or at least fascinated, by hip and waist measurements, weight charts, Body Mass Index ratings and whether or not we fit into conventional model of attractiveness. (**Body Mass Index** is the measure of body fat currently used in the UK. It is defined as the individual's body weight divided by the square of his or her height. This figure is then categorized as low weight, average weight, overweight or obese.)

Western societies and a growing number of rapidly developing industrial societies appear obsessed with dieting, exercise regimes and achieving the ideal body weight. Many studies have revealed how our body weight and eating habits are perceived to be integral to our moral standing, attractiveness, intelligence and overall sense of personal control. If we fail to control our eating and hence our weight, we are more likely to be labelled lazy, unhealthy, irresponsible and selfish (Malson, 2009). 'Fat', therefore, is a constant enemy and a visible sign that we have failed to reach the cultural ideal: the slim, attractive and, hence, morally upright citizen.

But do these standards fit with the reality of many people's lives? Why do women and girls appear to be particularly struck with the 'thin ideal', more so than boys and men? Even though a small percentage of girls and women, and an even smaller percentage of boys and men, are seen by mental health professionals for the treatment of their eating behaviours and body weight issues, there is a much larger proportion of the non-clinical population who are restricting their food intake, using laxatives and vomiting to prevent weight gain. Community samples once again reveal that concerns over weight fuel the use of dieting, exercise and purging techniques to promote weight loss in about 25–30% of young girls and women (McVey, Tweed & Blackmore, 2004).

Furthermore, adolescent longitudinal studies reveal that dieting and unhealthy weight-control behaviours predict outcomes relating to binge-eating, restricted eating and starvation, as well as obesity, five years later (Neumark-Sztainer et al., 2006). (**Obesity** is a medical term describing excess body weight, to the extent that health and life expectancy is threatened. **Weight-control behaviours** are those that support the maintenance of ideal weight. This can include dieting behaviours such as calorie control, food restriction and purging.)

Although it is entirely appropriate to ground our discussions of distressed eating in relation to wider eating patterns in the general population, it is perhaps wise not to lose site of the fact that between 10 and 15% of individuals diagnosed with anorexia (characterized by extreme food restriction and starvation) die from their condition, and that extreme distressed eating has the highest death rate of all mental health problems. Furthermore, weight and body image concerns and dissatisfaction, along with eating problems, are likely to be also closely related to other forms of distress, such as feeling out of control, anxiety, low self-worth and unhappiness (Polivy & Herman, 2002; Cole-Detke & Kobak, 1996; Dozier, Stovall, Chase & Albus, 1999). (**Body image** is the individual's perception of their body shape and size and the sexual attractiveness of their own body.)

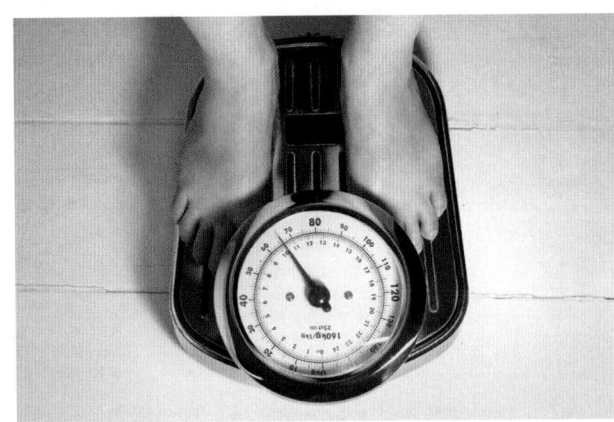

How much is too much? The widespread use of measurements such as the Body Mass Index (BMI) means we are now able to judge our weight against standardized categories (e.g. under and over weight, as well as obese) although these measurements have been widely criticized

Thus, we have come a long way from talking about 'slimmer's' disease' and have begun to address eating issues more thoroughly as the complex and multifaceted phenomenon they are.

Guiding question

- *Is distress over weight and body image at the centre of eating problems?*

Topics covered in this chapter

In order to put these experiences relating to eating problems into a properly psychological context, we will first look at how they have appeared and varied over time, and how or whether they differ across cultures. We will also examine the psychiatric diagnoses associated with these problems, which are grouped under the heading 'eating disorders' in diagnostic manuals. (**Eating disorders** refer to a group of 'disorders' characterized by unusual eating habits including restrictive or excessive food intake, which may have negative consequences for mental or physical health). In the section on risk factors, we tackle restricted eating, starvation, bingeing and purging together, as there appear to be few distinct causes to distinguish the 'eating disorders' listed in the diagnostic manuals (see below) (Jacobi, Hayward, de Zwaan, Kraemer & Agras, 2004). Perhaps more than any other mental health problem covered in this book, culture will also be discussed not only as a comparative background but as a causal process, given the vast literature on both. We will then outline some of the social, psychological and biological factors thought to be influential in producing these experiences, and discuss the kinds of treatment and intervention on offer.

Finally, even though a growing number of mental health professionals and health care providers argue for the inclusion of obesity in the DSM and ICD, to date there is no agreement on whether obesity represents a problem related to mental health, or simply to health. Moreover, given the increasingly large numbers of individuals labelled obese, especially in the West, the inclusion of obesity in a diagnostic manual of mental disorders would result in vast numbers of individuals being labelled mentally ill or disordered.

For the most part we will focus on individuals who engage in eating behaviours designed to reduce their weight, as the mental health literature has concentrated its efforts on these particular problems.

Problems relating to eating and weight loss are listed in the DSM under the categorical heading 'eating disorders', and include (a) anorexia nervosa(b) bulimia nervosa(c) binge eating disorder and (d) eating disorders not otherwise specified. (**Anorexia nervosa** is characterized by a refusal to maintain healthy body weight (as defined by the Body Mass Index) and a persistent and excessive fear of weight gain. **Bulimia nervosa** is the restriction of food intake, sometimes for long periods, followed by purging behaviours such as the use of laxatives and vomiting.)

Binge Eating Disorder is the consumption of large quantities of food (up to 4000 calories) within a very short time (e.g. 2–3 hours). Purging and dieting do not necessarily accompany bingeing episodes. **Eating Disorders Not Otherwise Specified (EDNOS)** refers to behaviours that resemble anorexia and bulimia nervosa to some extent but do not fully meet the criteria for the main eating disorder diagnoses.

In this chapter, we will cover a number of the issues related to these diagnostic categories, but our discussion of risk factors and interventions for these problems will not be separated according to diagnostic categories. It is worth noting that some individuals diagnosed with one eating disorder may qualify for another, at some point in their life (Fairburn and Wilson, 1993). As ever, diagnostic categories are much more fluid and interlinked than is often implied in the clinical literature (Grilo, 2006). In this chapter we will identify some of the overlaps between different experiences relating to problem eating, such as food restriction, bingeing and purging.

What's normal? Contemporary Western forms of eating problems and weight concerns

In Western and Westernized cultures, eating patterns involving dieting are not uncommon, and aspiring to be thin is hardly 'abnormal'. Conversely, overeating and rates of obesity have soared over the past 20 years, with approximately 20% of the UK population categorized as 'clinically obese' (Department of Health, 2006).

The cultural ideal for women, for example, is thin or slender, which has come to be equated with sexual attractiveness and femininity (Bordo, 1993). Given that a significant number of young people and women more generally are dissatisfied with their bodies and, more specifically, their weight, it is unsurprising that clear-cut distinctions between 'normal' and 'abnormal' weight concerns and eating patterns are difficult to establish. Unless an individual makes it clear that they suffer distress because of eating or dieting, or their weight drops below the recommended level as measured by the Body Mass Index, they can continue to eat very little or binge without any clinical intervention. Even then, some young girls and women who are starving themselves and achieving a dangerously low weight may not admit to having a problem and may feel content. Pro-anorexia websites, for example, reveal a certain pride in an anorexic identity (or 'ana' identity), and a refusal to talk about starvation and extreme thinness as anything but beautiful and mentally 'healthy' (Giles, 2006; Riley, Rodham & Gavin, 2009). In fact, individuals diagnosed with anorexia are recognized in the literature as extremely resistant to treatment, due to a reluctance to relate their behaviour to an 'illness'. Instead, some young women describe their body weight and starvation in positive terms and as a sign of achievement.

In this chapter, we consider eating patterns related to weight concerns as complex and multi-factorial. The causes and risk factors for such difficulties are once again numerous, and can be psychological (trauma, worry, sadness), cultural (based on ideals relating to body size and beauty) social and interpersonal (embedded in family relationships and identity) or a combination. As far as biological factors are concerned, genetic inheritance has been suggested as a possible risk factor. However, most of the biological research has concentrated on the biological changes that occur *after the onset* of an eating problem.

In short, biological factors can help explain why problematic eating patterns are *maintained*, but not, in the main, how they are *caused*.

History and culture

Historical considerations

Historical examples of self-induced starvation or problem eating are easy to find, though the reasons for them are diverse. Self-induced starvation in the context of religious beliefs and practices, for example, was motivated by spiritual concerns with purity and the attainment of a higher consciousness (Bell, 1987). Examples of religious observants starving themselves and wandering the deserts in Palestine and Egypt during the 4th and 5th centuries can be found in documents relating to practices of religious devotion.

Female saints, in particular, would engage in self-starvation in order to gain greater access to God (St. Catherine of Siena, who lived in the 14th century, is a noteworthy saint who refused to eat, right up until her death, aged 32). Interestingly, starvation and low weight was also linked in medieval times to demonic possession amongst women in particular. Catherine of Siena made sure she ate something each day in order to avoid being labelled a witch, as one of the measures of witchcraft would be any fluctuations in weight, established using the government's official scales. It is clear that though there are differences in how starvation was understood and experienced, the relationship between gender, purity and starvation remained strong. This goes back as far as 400 BC, when Hippocrates wrote a script entitled 'On the disease of young women' where he describes a 'condition' very similar to anorexia (Silverstein & Perlick, 1995). In the document, Hippocrates (460–370 BC) speculates that drastic weight loss can be due to abnormal menstrual cycles, and recommended marriage and pregnancy as the best treatment. Ironically, bingeing and purging among adult men during the classical period of ancient Greece and Rome was not uncommon, and was often associated with celebrations and banquets and not due to weight concerns. Furthermore, there was no suggestion that this behaviour was abnormal.

By the 19th century, self-starvation became seen as an illness affecting predominantly young girls and resembled (to some extent) contemporary definitions of 'eating disorders', in the sense that emphasis was placed upon the 'psychosomatic' origins of self-starvation and emaciation. Marce (1860), for example, described a form of hypochondria, resulting in 'inappetency' among pubescent girls after an episode of accelerated physical growth. He reported that death was the result of such starvation in some cases, and advocated the use of force-feeding to combat the effects of the condition. Charles Lasegue in 1873 and William Gull in 1874 both published works on wasting diseases, in which they discuss severe and unexplained weight loss that was not attributable to any known physical disease. Gull coined the term anorexia nervosa (meaning nervous loss of appetite), distinguishing it from other forms of hysteria. However, the difference between 19th-century descriptions and more contemporary ones is that 'fat phobia' was never mentioned in the former. In fact, some have argued that it was only after World War Two that fat concerns began to emerge in patients (Shorter, 1997).

Refusing to eat has also been used throughout history to signal political resistance. Ghandi used this strategy in the 1930s in India in protest against British rule, as did IRA prisoners during the conflicts in Northern Ireland in the early 1980s. A refusal to eat can be a powerful way to demonstrate defiance and can lead to significant action. It is important to note that some individuals who are diagnosed with an eating disorder describe their own experience of self-starvation and/

BOX **12.1**

Problem eating and self-starvation diagnoses

Three major eating disorders are listed in the DSM.

Anorexia Nervosa

There are two types of anorexia nervosa: (i) restrictive type (restricted eating only) and (ii) purging type (involving bingeing followed by vomiting or use of laxatives).

1 A refusal to maintain appropriate body weight for age and size. Body weight is less than 85% of that expected.
2 An intense fear of gaining weight despite being underweight.
3 An undue emphasis on weight in self-evaluation. Denial that weight is seriously under that which is expected.

4 Amenorrhea: the cessation of at least 3 menstrual cycles if menstrual cycles have already occurred.

Bulimia Nervosa

1 Recurrent episodes of binge eating (a typical binge can be between 2000 and 3000 calories).
2 An undue emphasis on weight in self-evaluation.
3 Recurrent compensatory behaviours, including vomiting, excessive exercise or laxative use after eating.
4 Compensatory behaviours must last on average for three months and occur at least twice a week.

Binge Eating Disorder

1 Recurrent binge eating.
2 Significant levels of distress accompany binge eating

3 Bing eating occurs at least twice a day for a period of six months

Eating Disorder Not Otherwise Specified (EDNOS)

1 The criteria for Anorexia Nervosa are met, except that the individual has regular menstrual cycles.
2 The criteria for Anorexia Nervosa are met except that, despite substantial weight loss, current weight is in the normal range.
3 The criteria for Bulimia Nervosa are met, except that binges occur less than twice weekly or for less than three months.
4 An individual of normal body weight who regularly engages in inappropriate compensatory behaviour after eating small amounts of food.
5 An individual who repeatedly chews and spits out, but does not swallow, large amounts of food.

or purging as a protest and a way to regain control over their lives (Malson, 1998; Hepworth, 1999).

In summary, self-starvation and problem eating have been recorded throughout history, although the reasons for them have varied according to context (religious versus secular, for example). It was not until the 19th century that problem eating was officially treated as a psychological condition and entered the psychiatric realm. Eating disorders did not receive a separate category in the DSM until 1983, when they were removed from the 'disorders of childhood and adolescence' section.

Culture

Until relatively recently, eating disorders were thought to be 'culture-bound syndromes', existing in so called Western or industrialized societies where 'thinness' is considered an important ideal for the attainment of female beauty, and dieting, amongst females in particular is actively encouraged (Miller & Pumariega, 2001). We will review the evidence relating to the direct impact of socio-cultural ideals on eating problems later in the chapter. For now, we will concentrate on the question of whether eating problems are universal or culturally specific (although it is advisable to be aware that many cross-cultural studies narrowly use DSM criteria to measure the prevalence of eating disorders *diagnoses*; Hsu, 1996). Prevalence refers specifically in epidemiology to the total number of cases of a disease or disorder in a population at any given time. The figure provides an estimate of how common a disease or disorder is and allows for comparisons over time.

Diagnosed eating disorders have been rising since the early 1990s, a fact attributed to exposure to thinner female body shapes and the equation of success and self-control with a well controlled and thin physique, especially in the West (Malson, 1998). Changes in attitudes towards eating and body image have been linked to a number of significant changes in the latter part of the 20th century in Western societies, mostly affecting women. These include a rise in consumerism, the prizing of individualism over more collective concerns, increasing conflict between generations and the disruption of traditional gender roles, leading to identity confusion over female roles in particular (Gordon, 2000). **Gender roles** are the set of prescribed norms (relating to emotions, behaviour, thinking) considered to be socially and culturally appropriate for individuals of a particular sex (male/female).

Consumerism is a socially and economically driven desire to purchase goods and services in ever greater amounts. The emphasis is on the consumptions of goods that can be used to secure higher social standing and a more valued identity.

As fashion models in these countries appear to be getting progressively thinner and articles on weight loss are on the increase, public concerns over weight have also been rising.

Despite the recognized links between Western/industrialized cultures and diagnosed eating disorders, weight concerns and eating problems have also been found in highly developed non-Western societies in increasing numbers since the early 1990s, although the numbers are in the main smaller than in Western/industrialized societies. Since weight concerns and body image form a major component of the diagnosis of eating disorder, some cross-cultural researchers have concentrated on the prevalence of diagnosable eating disorders (mainly anorexia and bulimia), as well as body image perception and dieting behaviours. However, as we shall see, weight concerns

Dolls play an important role in shaping young girls' perception of body image. The appearance and often unrealistic body shape of the doll continue to be sources of inspiration for young girls

are not the only factors influencing the development of eating problems or self-starvation in non-Western societies.

The universal rise of eating problems?

A number of writers in recent years have suggested that eating problems should no longer be seen as unique to Western societies (Nasser, 1997; Keel & Klump, 2003). The reasons for this view are diverse, but many have pointed to the growing influence of Western cultural norms on rapidly developing nations. These include east and south east Asian countries such as Japan, China, South Korea and Hong Kong; South Asian countries such as India; sub-Saharan African countries such as Ghana, Zambia and Nigeria as well as Mexico, Chile, Brazil and Argentina in Latin America. When reviewing this evidence, however, we must be mindful of the quality of some of the research studies, as a significant proportion of the empirical evidence emerges from case studies, rather than formal epidemiological studies (Gordon, 2001). Another consideration is the increased use of Western-based diagnostic manuals and psychiatric treatment in the latter decades of the 20th century, which may account for the greater number of observed cases. Prior to this, local healers and medical non-specialists in some non-Western countries would have been responsible for dealing with problems, without the use of any formal diagnostic terminology. Another difficulty with studies that rely on diagnostic criteria to measure incidence (usually only anorexia and bulimia) is the much greater spectrum of problem eating and weight concerns that are distressing but not diagnostically coherent, in other words, they do not strictly meet the criteria for anorexia and bulimia but have many similar features.

It is interesting for example that EDNOS (Eating Disorders Not Otherwise Specified) is not used as a measure in the majority of prevalence studies, when many have argued it to be the most commonly found eating disorder (Machado, Machado, Gonçalves & Hoek, 2006).

A number of studies in south east Asia have identified an increase in diagnosed eating disorders and weight-related concerns in clinical and community samples. Japan has seen the biggest rise, which many have attributed to accelerated industrial growth since the Second World War, leading to changes in family structure, the rise of consumerism and extreme tensions between traditional and contemporary gender roles (Gordon, 2001). There is also a large media presence in Japan that celebrates thinness, especially amongst Japanese schoolgirls. A similar picture is emerging in other south east Asian societies where wealth is increasing, including Hong Kong, Singapore, South Korea and Taiwan (Lee, 2001). And due to the increasing influence of Western advertising in lower-income Asian countries, such as Malaysia, Indonesia and the Philippines (Waterson, 2000), eating disorders are reported to be on the increase. Traditionally these cultures have prized 'plumpness' as a sign of health and fertility, especially in women. And yet, as in Western countries, it is women who make up the eating disorders population in south east and south Asia. More patients are being seen in clinical settings, and prevalence studies reveal similar incidence rates to Western societies as well as high rates of dieting and weight concerns among school children and college-age women in southern and east Asia (Huon, Mingvi, Oliver & Xiao, 2002). This is despite an overall lower than average BMI (Body Mass Index) in southern and south east Asian societies than in Western societies (Lee, 2001). In sub-Saharan Africa, data are more limited, but isolated cases of eating disorders have been reported in countries such as Ghana (Bennett, Sharpe, Freeman & Carson, 2004), Nigeria (Oyewumi & Kazarian, 1992) and in black South Africans (Szabo, Berk & Allwood, 1995). In South Africa, in particular, the political situation has been linked to a rise in eating disorders in the black population, due not only to 'Westernization' but also to urbanization and the subsequent revision of gender roles (from disempowerment to empowerment for women, through increased access to education and employment) and, to some extent, the adoption of Western ideals of body size and beauty, via access to Western media (Szabo & Le Grange, 2001).

Despite many key similarities, there are also some notable differences in the meaning attributed to loss of appetite across cultures. Some authors, such as Sing Lee, the director of the Hong Kong eating disorders centre, have argued that an ability to eat (resembling anorexia) is not exclusively linked to weight concerns, a finding similar to that of Keel and Klump (2003) in their ample meta-analysis of Western and non-Western societies. In a study by Lee and colleagues over a 12-year period with over 70 Chinese patients, all the participants resembled those diagnosed with anorexia according to Western definitions, yet only 41% experienced 'fat phobia'. Furthermore, in a study of female secondary school students in Ghana, individuals identified for self-starvation reported doing so, not because they were afraid of being fat, but because starvation was a method of self-control aimed at 'perfectionist moral and academic standards' (Bennett et al., 2004).

Lee, along with other prominent clinicians, has called for a broadening of understanding of the meanings underlying eating problems and self-starvation across different cultural contexts as well as in the eating disorders literature more generally. Lee has argued that, rather than a desire to be thin, what individuals share is a desire to exert control over lives that are often beset by family conflict, abuse and oppression (Lee, 2001). Similarly, the literature emerging from South Africa, which has seen rapid political reorganization and urban regeneration, suggests a more complex picture of why women and girls experience problem eating, related to gender identity and the negative impact of changing expectations of black women in particular (Szabo & Le Grange,

2001). Urban regeneration is the rebuilding and often the transformation of cities and countries according to social and economic need.

Within cultural differences?

For many years, eating problems (notably anorexia) were considered the provinces of white, affluent and highly educated girls and women (Andersen & Hay, 1985; Malson, 1998; Bordo, 2009a). This has changed somewhat over time, with a growing proportion now coming from lower social classes (McClelland & Crisp, 2001). However, with the emergence of studies on bingeing and purging (not just starvation and food restriction) in the community as well as clinical samples, a more nuanced picture has begun to emerge. Given the existence of a growing number of multi-cultural societies, it is important to be aware that cultural differences are not simply observable in different geographical locales, but can be evident within the same country, due to ethnic sub-cultural differences. A number of important findings have established significant cultural differences in how black, white, Asian and Latin American women view their bodies, and in rates of eating problems. Part of those differences has been attributed to different values in relation to body size and weight. In a US sample, African–American women held the most positive beliefs about their body size, followed by Asian women, whilst white and Latin American women held the most negative views relating to body image (Altabe, 1998; Fernández-Aranda, 1999).

These findings on body image do appear to translate into different rates of eating problems, with greater numbers of white women meeting the criteria for an eating disorder diagnosis, especially those relating to weight concern (e.g. anorexia and bulimia nervosa) (Striegel-Moore, 1997. In a study comparing black and white women who met the criteria for binge eating disorder, significant differences were also found in (a) concerns over weight, with black women holding more positive views of their weight; (b) a previous history of bulimia, with white women being eight times more likely to have a history; (c) seeking treatment for bingeing, with black women less likely to pursue treatment; and (d) a current diagnosis for another DSM Axis I 'disorder', with white women being more likely to be diagnosed with depression, social phobia and substance abuse and dependency (Mitchell, Hatsukami, Eckert & Pyle, 1985).

In sum, higher rates of distress for binge eating disorders have been found amongst white women in comparison to black women (Pike, Dohm, Striegel-Moore, Wilfley & Fairburn, 2001). Finally, we must also consider that sexual orientation may play a part in the development of eating problems. A study by Siever with gay men, lesbians and heterosexual women revealed that heterosexual women and gay men were more likely to express body dissatisfaction. The author argues this is due to a shared emphasis on being thin, which is seen as the key to pleasing men (Siever, 1994).

Psychiatric diagnoses

People referred for treatment related to eating problems and starvation typically receive one of the following psychiatric diagnoses (see Box 12.1, above):

Anorexia Nervosa
Bulimia Nervosa

Binge Eating Disorder
Eating Disorder Not Otherwise Specified (EDNOS)

As with other psychiatric diagnoses, there is good evidence that these diagnoses are not completely distinct from each other. As Fairburn, Cooper & Shafran (2003) and Fairburn, Cooper, Shafran, Wilson & Terence (2008) point out, both anorexia and bulimia share core features: an over-evaluation of eating, shape and weight. Furthermore, both restrict their food, use compensatory strategies to reduce weight (vomiting , etc.), are consumed by thoughts and concerns about weight and engage in constant body-checking. Moreover, longitudinal data suggest that the transitions from anorexia (restricting type) to bulimia and/or EDNOS is so common that anorexia should be regarded as only a temporary stage in the long-term course of an eating disorder (see Eddy et al., 2002). This makes sense when we consider that anorexia (restricting type) usually begins in adolescence and bulimia develops in early adulthood.

If we think back to Carmel's story, we can see that although Carmel shows signs of self-starvation (so could be diagnosed with anorexia), she is also showing signs of bulimia. This is not unusual. In fact, around half of those diagnosed with anorexia subsequently go on to be diagnosed with bulimia (Collier & Treasure, 2004). Whilst there is some evidence that the rarer forms of eating problems, such as anorexia (restricting type), are modest predictors of treatment outcomes (Hay & Fairburn, 1998), the majority of individuals who experience eating problems do not fit current diagnostic criteria and fall into a category called Eating Disorders Not Otherwise Specified (EDNOS). Despite this, the majority of researchers do not use the ENDOS category to measure rates of eating problems, preferring to stay within diagnostic boundaries and measure the least common eating problems, such as anorexia and bulimia. An accurate picture of prevalence in the community is therefore difficult to establish.

EDNOS resembles anorexia and bulimia in its features and certainly its severity but does not have any specific criteria, other than those excluding it from other diagnostic categories (Fairburn and Bohn, 2005; Zimmerman, Francione-Witt, Chelminski, Young & Tortolani, 2008). A review of US psychiatric outpatients by Zimmerman and colleagues, found the most common form of eating problem to be EDNOS, rather than the two major disorders (anorexia and bulimia) described in the DSM. When EDNOS was combined with binge eating, 92% of the sample of 2500 met the criteria for EDNOS. However, it is interesting to note that EDNOS does not have any distinct features as such, but is defined according to what it fails to do (i.e. meet exact criteria for the other major disorders). The review concluded that although the vast majority of patients fail to meet the criteria for the two major eating disorders *they do appear to have a combination of problems* that require clinical treatment.

Thus, even amongst the diagnostic categories, a high degree of symptom-combining occurs in individuals with eating problems. This result has been replicated across a number of studies, especially those with longitudinal designs (Fairburn & Harrison, 2003; Herzog et al., 1999). As a result, some authors have argued that separating the eating disorders into discrete diagnostic categories does not make sense, given that individuals in different diagnostic groups share so many features, including risk factors/cause, extreme dietary restraint, binge eating, over-evaluation of control over eating, body-checking and avoidance and self-induced vomiting and/or compensatory behaviours (Fairburn and Bohn, 2005; Milos, Spindler, Schnyder & Fairburn, 2005). An emphasis on the similarities between eating problems thus has solid empirical backing, and is often referred to as a 'transdiagnostic' approach (Fairburn, 2008) since it acknowledges the blurred boundaries between diagnostic categories. A **transdiagnostic approach** acknowledges that many overlapping dimensions exist across disorders (e.g. eating disorders), implying that we should think about disorders in terms of their overlapping or behavioural/psychological dimensions, instead of retaining the idea of distinct categories of illness/disorder.

As well as encountering difficulties in distinguishing between separate eating disorders, it is well recognized that very few people experience eating problems without some other form of distress. Research estimates that between 82% and 93% of individuals diagnosed with eating disorders are also diagnosed with another Axis I disorder (Braun, Sunday & Alalmi, 1994). The most common co-diagnosed difficulties are depression, substance abuse, personality disorder (69%) and anxiety (especially obsessive compulsive disorder – Altman & Shankman, 2009).

Sadness and worry are very commonly experienced by individuals with eating problems, either before or during an eating disorder diagnosis. In a study of women diagnosed with an eating disorder (anorexia – AN; or bulimia – BN) or with major depression (MD), anxiety disorders were common in all three clinical groups (AN, 60%; BN, 57%; MD, 48%). In 90% of AN women, 94% of BN women and 71 % of women diagnosed with major depression, anxiety disorders occurred *before* any eating related problem, although panic disorder tended to develop afterwards (Bulik, Sullivan, Fear & Joyce, 2007). Diagnosed major depression among individuals diagnosed with an eating disorder has also been found in high numbers (Braun et al., 1994). Eating disorders are also over-represented in samples relating to substance abuse and self-harm, when compared with other psychiatric patients (Grilo, Levy, Becker, Edell & McGlashan, 1995; Paul, Schroeter, Dahme & Nutzinger, 2002), and nearly 70% also meet the diagnostic criteria for an Axis II personality disorder (Braun et al., 1994).

Given the difficulties associated with applying discrete diagnostic categories to people's eating problems and weight concerns, and the degree of overlap between a variety of diagnostic categories, it is extremely difficult to see eating problems as isolated or discrete forms of disorder or distress.

Prevalence and distribution

As with other forms of distress discussed in this book, studies of the prevalence and distribution of experiences of weight concern and problem eating have mostly been conducted using psychiatric diagnostic categories. As ever, caution is needed when interpreting these findings, especially since 90% of people with eating problems at clinical level do not refer themselves for treatment and therefore do not appear in clinical statistics (Fairburn, Welch, Norman, O'Connor & Doll, 1996).

Even at levels requiring clinical intervention, eating problems and weight concerns are extremely common, especially if obesity were to be included in the mix.

The rise in media attention relating specifically to weight concerns has led to the increased visibility of eating problems, body image and weight concerns, especially in Western

Table 12.1 **Rates of DSM-IV eating disorders in 2500 psychiatric outpatients**

Eating Disorder	Current, n (%)	Remission, n (%)	Past, n (%)
Anorexia nervosa	0 (0.0)	12 (0.5)	25 (1.0)
Bulimia nervosa	18 (0.7)	23 (0.9)	29 (1.2)
Binge-eating disorder	63 (2.5)	18 (0.7)	15 (0.6)
Eating disorder NOS	84 (3.4)	6 (0.2)	61 (2.4)

Source: **Zimmerman et al. (2008).**

Table 12.2 **Prevalence rates for diagnosed eating disorders in a US community sample (2028 girls and women aged between 12 and 23)**

Anorexia nervosa – 0.39%
Bulimia nervosa – 0.30%
Eating disorders not otherwise specified – 2.37%
Overall community rate for eating disorder – 3.06%

Source: **From Machado et al. (2006).**

cultures and increasingly in other non-Western industrialized countries (Nasser et al., 2001). The group most likely to be affected by eating problems relating to dietary restriction, weight loss and compensatory behaviours such as vomiting, excessive exercise and laxative use, is girls and women. Females are in fact around ten times more likely to develop a diagnosable eating disorder (Striegel-Moore, 1997), which has been attributed to greater perceived social rewards for women of lower weight and thinner body shape (see below for a more detailed discussion). Women are also more likely to experience a range of body image problems, are more likely to binge eat and use extreme weight-control measures (vomiting, laxatives etc.) than men (Grilo, 2006).

Using a clinical interview schedule, Favaro, Ferrara and Santonastaso (2003) conducted a community survey of eating disorder prevalence in Italy with over 1300 18–25 year old women. They found that (AN) and (BN) were diagnosed in 2.0% and 4.6% of participants respectively across their (limited) lifespan. The prevalence of atypical ED (EDNOS) was 4.7% and that of binge eating disorder (BED) was 0.6%. Other prevalence studies have revealed lower levels of the main disorders, anorexia and bulimia nervosa. For example, in a review of eating disorders across Europe, 0.3% of young women met the criteria for anorexia (Hoek & van Hoeken, 2003) and 1% for bulimia (Hoek & van Hoeken, 2003). Binge eating disorder (BED) is estimated to occur in 1–3% and EDNOS itself is thought to occur in around 2.7% in a population of young women (Machado et al., 2006). However, if 'sub threshold' populations are included in prevalence rates, there is a significant increase in all eating problems (Grilo, 2006), with a further 1.5–2% diagnosed with anorexia and 2% bulimia in community samples, if only one of the official diagnostic criteria is removed (Wittchen, Nelson & Lachner, 1998). Furthermore, persistent binge eating was reported by 4% of young people in a survey of 4746 adolescents (Ackard, Neumark-Sztainer, Story & Perry, 2003).

Risks and maintaining factors

As with all forms of mental distress, eating problems, self-starvation and weight concerns appear to have a variety of identifiable risk factors. Interestingly, although a great deal of emphasis is placed on the separation of eating problems into distinct diagnostic categories, in traditional psychology textbooks the relevant sections on causes and risk factors tend to merge the categories, with the effect of suggesting no clear aetiology for those distinct categories (see Bennett, 2003 and Davey, 2008 for examples of this). Of course this once again raises questions regarding diagnoses, but also leads to

questions over what is known about the causes of *specific* eating problems. To date, the literature is better able to point us in the direction of identifiable risk factors rather than any definite causes. This means we may have a fair picture of which factors are involved but little information on how they operate to produce difficulties. In this section, we will focus on a variety of risk factors including socio-cultural processes, gender, age, family relationships, sexual abuse and biological factors. (**Socio-cultural** refers to the relationships between the organization of society as a whole (e.g. institutions, work, family, education) and the production of cultural values, identities, beliefs and rituals.)

Socio-cultural factors: body image and weight concerns

Perhaps no other factor has received as much attention as that relating to socio-cultural influences on the development of eating problems. This applies to the two major diagnostic categories anorexia and bulimia (Stice, 1994), but less so to binge eating disorder. The Western idealization of the 'thin' or 'slim' body, which appeared in the 1980s, has led to increases in eating problems and weight concerns in Western populations and beyond (Striegel-Moore, Silberstein & Rodin, 1986; Hsu, 1989; Malson, 1998). Some have argued that it is by no means coincidental that the recent preoccupation with the 'thin ideal' and a decrease in women's body size portrayed in the mass media has led to a rise in eating problems (Wiseman, Gray, Mossiman & Ahrens, 1992), especially given that the core feature of the current diagnostic criteria for the main two eating disorders is 'fear of fat' and 'body dissatisfaction'. (The **mass media** is a broad range of technologies used to communicate information, news and entertainment to the population (within and across countries). Technologies include television, the internet, newspapers, film and radio.)

However, it is also important to note that not all eating problems, especially self-starvation, are driven by a fear of fat. Many others have pointed to other motivations, such as political defiance, religious dedication and the exercising of control over one's life, in Western and non-Western contexts (Lee, 2001). As Katzman and Lee (1997) have argued, the portrayal of distressed eating as some sort of 'appearance disorder' can be denigrating to those who express only a desire for greater control over their lives (rather than a desire to be thin) in situations where they are powerless, such as in zones of political conflict (Szabo & Le Grange, 2001). These alternative meanings must still be read within their socio-cultural context. Nevertheless, the majority of socio-cultural work has concentrated on the link between intense body image dissatisfaction, weight concerns and the development of problematic eating.

Feminist scholars (Bordo, 1993, 2009b; Malson, 1998, 2009) have been at the forefront of developing theories relating to the link between these kinds of difficulties, namely gender development and the socio-cultural contexts that give rise to mild as well as extreme concerns over weight, which can develop into distressed forms of eating. **Feminism** is a collection of movements whose primary aim is to promote equal rights for women. A **feminist** is a person who adheres to the principles of feminism.

We must always remind ourselves that extreme eating problems and weight concerns are experienced most often by girls and women. It is essential, therefore, that these are viewed as gendered phenomena, within a wider socio-cultural context in which thinness and dieting behaviours are encouraged (Polivy & Herman, 2002. Concerns about weight are pervasive in Western cultures, and a growing number of non-Western industrialized societies (McVey, Tweed & Blackmore, 2004). However, we need to concentrate on specific aspects of these socio-cultural influences to establish particular risk factors for certain individuals and not others. These are (i) the impact of the media, (ii) living in a consumerist culture, and (iii) body dissatisfaction and increases in dieting behaviour.

The impact of the media

There are a number of robust studies that have directly measured the impact of exposure to media images: specifically, the development of weight concerns, weight-restricting behaviours and eating problems in relation to magazine reading and television watching. Not only are measures of body dissatisfaction higher through exposure to media images of underweight women, individuals also directly learn how to diet, binge and purge via the media (Fairburn & Harrison, 2003). These socio-cultural influences, it has been argued, also operate via processes of social comparison and the avoidance of social disapproval (Wertheim, Paxton, Schutz & Muir, 1997), rather than a straightforward desire to be thin. Furthermore, young women exposed more frequently to magazines portraying idealized female body types are more likely to experience body dissatisfaction and to endorse dieting (Tiggemann & Slater, 2004).

Dieting alone can increase an individual's risk for eating problems, especially bingeing, but also for severe food restriction (see below). To find out if exposure to media messages is sufficient to predict body dissatisfaction and problem eating, Groesz, Levine and Murnen (2002) reviewed the impact of the media across 25 separate studies, leading them to conclude that exposure to media portrayals of slender ideals led to body dissatisfaction in a significant number of participants. Stice, Schupak-Neuberg, Shaw and Stein (1994), in an empirical study of over 200 young girls, found a direct link between media exposure to the thin ideal and 'eating disorder symptomatology'. They also found that women were likely to model their eating on the extreme eating and exercise regimes of women in the media. A further finding was that media exposure increased gender-role endorsement, which in turn was related to ideal-body internalization. Television watching has also been studied in order to determine the effect it has on body image and eating patterns. For example, body dissatisfaction and social comparisons (between the woman's body shape and the models) were significantly correlated with the amount of time young women spent watching certain television channels, such as music channels (e.g. MTV), in which idealized body shapes were featured. Celebrity worship is another contributory factor in relation to television viewing and its impact on body image. Maltby, Giles, Barber and McCutcheon (2005) found that

adolescent girls who had formed a 'para' social relationship[1] with a celebrity and who believed their celebrity had a good body shape (equivalent to an 'ideal' female shape) experienced a poorer body image themselves. Interestingly, although this relationship was found in 14–16-year-old girls (and not the boys), the effect had all but disappeared in the 17–20-year-old group and the adult group, for both men and women. The indication is there is a greater vulnerability to celebrity worship and poor body image in younger girls (who are more likely to develop eating problems).

Clearly, these studies indicate that exposure to the media, via magazine or television, may lead young girls and women to question their body size, and in some cases result in body dissatisfaction and eating problems. However, a cautionary note should be added when interpreting these studies. Despite being dissatisfied with their bodies, only a minor proportion of young girls and women go onto develop severe problems with restricted eating, starvation or problematic eating.

A qualitative study of 67 adolescent young women revealed how socio-cultural messages, presented via the media, were deemed to be important in relation to how the girls felt about their bodies and through exerting pressure to be thin. However, the girls described how the desire to be thin did not necessarily result in body dissatisfaction, as many other emotional factors were involved, including self-esteem and self-belief (Tiggemann, Gardiner & Slater, 2000). Though the evidence for a powerful media effect is clear, other factors should be taken into account to establish why only some young girls and women go on to develop serious and long-term problems with how they perceive their bodies and the way they eat.

Body image distortion and body dissatisfaction

There is little doubt that the pervasiveness of body dissatisfaction in Western societies (and a growing number of non-Western societies) is the result of the idealization of slender bodies and the constant invitation for women to self scrutinize, to bring themselves in line with this ideal. Certain groups, such as professional and non-professional models, ballet dancers and gymnastic champions, who prize a slender physique highly, have higher rates of body dissatisfaction coupled with diagnosed eating disorders (Ravaldi et al., 2003). But does body dissatisfaction lead to body image distortion in everyone diagnosed with anorexia? **Body Image Distortion (BID)** involves a person holding an inaccurate and exaggerated view of their body weight and size. For individuals diagnosed with anorexia nervosa this manifests as the underweight individual perceiving themselves to be grossly overweight. In clinical terms, BID is characterized as a cognitive distortion that is persistent and rigid.

A 'disturbance in perception of body shape' or 'body image distortion' is among the diagnostic criteria for the two major eating disorders listed in the DSM (anorexia and bulimia nervosa) and a number of researchers have suggested there is a close link between body image distortion and eating problems (Horne, Van Vactor & Emerson, 1991). But at present the empirical research does not fully support the hypothesis that

---

1 A 'para' social relationship refers to a relationship that is one-sided. The relationship is usually fantasy based but nevertheless very significant to the individual, who usually has an extensive knowledge of the other person's life. The most common form of parasocial relationship is between a celebrity and his/her fan, though sports fans could be included as an audience group.

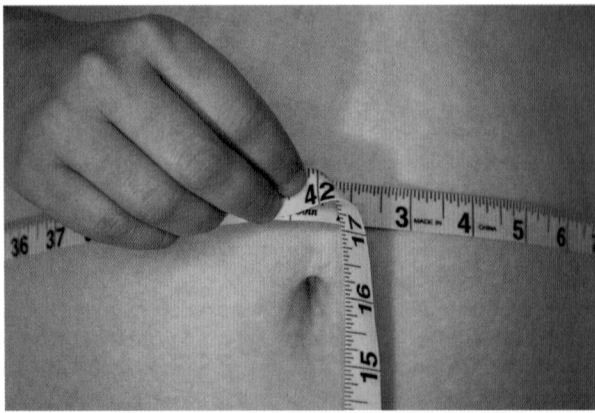

A number of societies have shown an increasing obsession with measuring and standardizing body shape

body image disturbance is present in *all* individuals diagnosed with an eating disorder, which calls into question the idea that it is a core feature of *all* major eating difficulties. For example, in a study of 214 patients diagnosed with eating disorders (anorexia, anorexia and bulimia and bulimia only), many, but not all, held a current body image distortion, suggesting there was no clear-cut overall perceptual distortion between the diagnostic groups. In a meta-analysis of 66 studies, from 1974 to 1993, Cash and Deagle (1997) found that body image dissatisfaction (measured in terms of attitudes) distinguished groups of individuals diagnosed with eating disorders from control groups, but body image distortion (where individuals over-estimate their body size) did not. Similarly, a preliminary study of 44 patients in therapy for bulimia and anorexia (Fernández-Aranda, 1999) found that most patients did not tend to have any impairment or distortion in their perception of body size.

Gender identity

We have already established that body dissatisfaction and problem eating is much more common in girls and women. The link between adherence to traditional gender roles and problem eating has received empirical support (Hsu, 1989; Murnen & Smolak, 1997). However, apart from greater engagement with media influence, it is not clear what other effects gender has on the development and maintenance of such difficulties. One explanation links the issue of power to weight concerns and eating problems. Women are perceived to gain greater power through their appearance and sexual displays and are culturally supported in adhering to normal standards of beauty (Fallon, Katzman & Wooley, 1994). However, they are perhaps less supported in displaying power in other ways, such as through employment, status and politics, which are still more associated with male power. A number of authors have therefore argued that women face contradictions in the way they are supposed to conduct and assert themselves as individuals. Gender is a multifaceted and complex matter for all individuals to negotiate and in the following section we will look further into the literature on gender to reveal a number of factors relevant to problem eating, weight concerns and issues relating to control. These include (a) control and confusion: female development and maturation; (b) the conflicting roles and expectations that young girls and women face in a

changing society; and (c) the complex relationship between mothers and daughters.

Control and confusion: female development and maturation

Eating problems and weight concerns largely develop in adolescence, often around puberty. Adolescence is a difficult time for many, especially those whose life experiences have not been positive, or those who have experienced childhood abuse.

Higher than normal rates of childhood sexual abuse are found in individuals diagnosed with anorexia or bulimia. Such abuse can have an adverse effect on how young girls view themselves and their bodies (Walsh & Burns, 2000). Child sexual abuse is sexual contact with a child; it can include exposing oneself, as well as verbal and physical contact.

According to Bemis (1978), self-starvation enables the developing girl to retain a child-like, pre-adolescent, pre-pubescent body, which can enable the suppression of mature sexual characteristics, thus helping the individual to avoid thinking about sex, or about sexual abuse.

The question for us here, though, is why some girls experience difficulties specifically related to the development of adult female characteristics and why this can lead to serious weight concerns and eating problems. Young women may feel they can gain control by controlling their weight and presenting a more culturally acceptable persona (Polivy & Herman, 2002). Thus, although body dissatisfaction may be one reason why girls strive to achieve the perfect body, the underlying reason may be to gain a sense of control and to give purpose to a life that is chaotic or uncertain. Although entirely plausible, this explanation does not address the issue of why girls choose weight or appearance over other strategies and why so many young women believe that appearance is important to their sense of self and a sense of achievement. The answer is, of course, that the ways in which we cope with uncertainty and loss of control are manifested via the culturally acceptable – and gender-acceptable – ways of dealing with difficulties. For girls and young women, this may involve turning their distress back on themselves and finding solutions that are culturally acceptable, and appropriately feminine (Ussher, 1989).

Control through dieting

One of the risk factors for eating problems is dieting (Collier & Treasure, 2004). A number of factors have been linked to girls starting diets as a way to refuse the maturing female body (itself a risk factor for eating problems), which coincide with the onset of adolescent teasing, social comparison (comparisons between themselves and their peers, or characters in the media) and living with a mother with eating problems (Cooper, Whelan, Woolgar, Morrell & Murray, 2004). In a community study of 938 11–12-year-old girls in the US, Killen, Hayward, Wilson et al. (1994) found that girls with signs of eating problems (those linked to bingeing and purging) and weight concerns were usually heavier and more sexually mature, which was linked to greater body dissatisfaction and a sense of inadequacy. In particular, as the visible signs of maturity appear, young girls begin to engage in behaviours (restricted eating, purging) that resist the onset of maturation in order to avoid attention and criticism from others. In some girls, this is specifically linked to sexual maturation. For example, in a group of women diagnosed with anorexia, one of the reasons given by women for initial food refusal was the delay or cessation of signs of sexual maturation (Malson, 1998). There are several reasons why particular individuals feel this way, including child sexual abuse, family dysfunction and general low self-esteem (Waller, Hamilton, Rose, Sumra & Baldwin, 1993). Family dysfunction involves regular misconduct, conflict and poor communication amongst family members. It can also include emotional, sexual or physical abuse.

A further reason is the explicit rejection of femininity, which girls link to the maturing female body. For example, in an interview study with women diagnosed (professionally or self-diagnosed) with anorexia, starving oneself was related to a refusal to be associated with some of the negative aspects of femininity, such as 'highly emotional, sexual, vulnerable and out of control' (Malson & Ussher, 1996). Through starvation, the feminine body could more easily be disrupted, because signs of femininity such as menstruation and the development of breasts and hips are absent. To stop one's body from menstruating and thus developing feminine signs, the women felt they were able to reject the more negative and unruly aspects of femininity.

Conflicting roles and expectations that young girls and women face in a changing society

To varying extents, normative or socially ascribed gender roles are difficult to avoid. They form part of the way we see ourselves and the way we respond to events and interpersonal relations, and gender roles form the expectations that others have of us (Bem, 1993). Whether we choose to look at gender in terms of fixed personality traits (traditionally selflessness and expressiveness for women; assertiveness and independence for men) or as social constructs (in the form of language, images etc.) in which we are compelled – but not forced – to invest (Burr, 2000), gender is a powerful influence on our sense of who we are and how we should express ourselves (see also Chapter 10 for a fuller discussion).

Traditionally, gender roles included masculine and feminine traits relating to emotion, cognitions and behaviours. For example, assertiveness – a sense of mastery and control and autonomy – has traditionally been linked more to masculinity, while passivity, dependency and selflessness have traditionally been seen as 'feminine' traits (Bem, 1993). Others have argued that eating disorder patients directly reveal high levels of 'negative feminine' traits. These include passivity and dependency and a need for excessive praise and approval from others, notably men, due to poor self-esteem (Boskind-Lodahl, 1976). **Self-esteem** is a psychological term for an individual's overall appraisal of their self-worth. It can operate in a specific domain (I am worthless because I am fat) or be more global in presentation (I am simply worthless). It can relate to how someone thinks (cognition) and how they feel (emotion).

However, gender roles are rapidly changing in modern societies, as women enter the workforce in greater numbers and have become educated to the same or similar levels as men. This is the case not just in the West but in countries undergoing rapid industrial growth, leading to shifts in gender roles cross-culturally (Lake, Staiger & Glowinski, 2000; Nasser et al., 2001).

Despite recent changes in gender roles, however, contradictions and ambiguities relating to women's (and men's) roles remain. Girls and women are now expected to be assertive, educated and career-minded and simultaneously (hetero)

sexually attractive (which means slim), sufficiently feminine, and yet still mindful of and fully accommodating to male desires (Gill, 2006). Ironically, greater 'freedom' for women has led to greater role confusion and distress for some. Some theorists have argued that 'eating disorder' patients are affected by a strong sense of failure to manage these contradictions and ambiguities (Steiner-Adair, 1986).

In other words, for these individuals, there is a discrepancy between their ideal self (masculine and assertive) and their actual self (feminine and passive). The discrepancy theory proposed by Steiner-Adair (1986) argues that eating disorders develop from the self-perception of a lack of traditionally masculine characteristics, rather than from an abundance of negative feminine characteristics (Lancelot & Kaslow, 1994). According to this theory, contemporary demands on women to be more masculine are incompatible with their early and current feminine socialization experience (Turner, 1992).

An alternative perspective suggests that though there may appear to be more gender equality in some societies, the very fact that women's bodies are steeped in unrealistic expectations and must accord with male desires is also *reflective* of gender inequalities, which can cause distress (Bordo, 1992). **Gender inequalities** are the differences between access to rights that arise from one's membership of a gender category (male/female).

Indeed, empirical studies have shown that women and girls spend considerably more time than men on grooming their appearance and generally worrying about their bodies, which some argue is directly linked to socio-cultural pressures (Lancelot & Kaslow, 1994; Wertheim, Paxton, Schutz & Muir, 1997).

A review by Lancelot and Kaslow (1994) found some support for Boskind-Lodahl's theory linking negative feminine gender traits specifically to eating disorders, but it was difficult to ascertain whether they were linked only to eating disorders or to more general levels of distress, such as low self-esteem and a diagnosis of depression or anxiety. They did find that women who invest in the idea that they have to be 'everything' – both masculine and feminine – in order to succeed in today's society (which supports Steiner-Adair's discrepancy theory) were more likely to report eating problems (Timko, Striegel-Moore, Silberstein & Rodin, 1987). However, the specific link between problem eating and being a type of 'superwoman' needs further exploration, as it has also been implicated in the development of women's 'depression' and other forms of distress (see Nolen-Hoeksema [1990] on dual role theory and depression).

The complex relationship between mothers and daughters and gender transmission

One of the key ways in which gender messages are transmitted to girls is through the mother–daughter relationship. What we see our mothers do can significantly shape how we develop, or indeed reject, certain gender characteristics. Furthermore, mothers are still primarily responsible for feeding us, so it is unsurprising that researchers have tended to focus on this relationship over and above other family relationships.

Many feminist authors have argued, of course, that that the relationship between mothers and daughters should always be understood against a wider socio-cultural background. Gender roles are prescribed by wider social structures such as education, medicine and the law, which inform family members how they should behave and understand their emotions and needs (Bordo, 1993). In this way, simplistic 'mother-blaming' perspectives can, and should, be avoided, to reveal a more culturally contextual and complex picture (Ruskay Rabinor, 1994).

We will explore family relationships (including the role of fathers) in more depth later in the chapter, but for now, we are interested in how gender messages and meanings are transmitted via the specific relationship between mothers and daughters, as this area has received the most attention. Indeed, a consistent finding is that the mothers of individuals diagnosed with eating disorders are more likely themselves to be problem eaters and have other forms of distress (Hodes, Timimi & Robinson, 1997). Daughters then 'model' the behaviour of their mothers who transmit subtle messages regarding weight and appearance concerns.

An alternative explanation focuses on issues of autonomy and control in the mother–daughter relationship, rather than imitating behaviours per se. For example, in their questionnaire study of 30 mothers and their daughters aged between 16 and 19, Ogden and Steward (2000) found that the daughters were more likely to report eating restraints and body dissatisfaction if the mother reported lower belief in her own and her daughter's autonomy and if both mother and daughter thought that projection (the possibility that the mother's ideas could be passed onto the daughter) was something they considered to be important. They did not find any direct relationship between the mothers' and daughters' weight concerns.

Feminist psychoanalytic authors have also identified a number of factors leading to loss of control and subsequent eating problems. Feminist psychoanalytic authors Luise Eichenbaum and Susie Orbach (1983) describe in detail how daughters who develop 'anorexia' do so as a result of feeling ambivalence and shame in expressing their needs. Such feelings can be unconsciously encouraged by the mother, wishing to show her daughter how to abandon her own needs in order to care for others and thus become 'suitably feminine'.

Others have focused more explicitly on how the maternal body evokes a fear of fat in young girls who have an unstable relationship with their mothers. Susan Bordo (1993) has argued that eating problems and weight concerns are a form of dis-identification from the maternal body (perceived as round, plump and 'larger') as a way to achieve separation from the mother and gain a greater sense of autonomy. However, rather than destroying the mother–daughter bond through problem eating and starvation, some feminist therapists have argued that daughters in fact want to transform their relationship with their mother and to make it more empathic and reciprocal (Ruskay Rabinor, 1996).

Family and childhood influences

As we noted earlier in the chapter, eating problems, together with other forms of psychological distress, appear to some extent to run in families (Ogden, 2009). A systematic review of the eating disorders literature reveals that the majority of these studies suggest higher rates of eating disorders, affective disorders and some anxiety disorders (OCD, depression, panic disorder, generalized anxiety disorder) in family members of anorexic and bulimic patients (Jacobi et al., 2004). Furthermore, individuals diagnosed with eating disorders have consistently higher levels of adverse childhood experiences with their carers/parents, including early separation

anxiety or childhood abuse (Friedberg & Lyddon, 1996; Troisi, Massaroni & Cuzzolaro, 2005; Ward, Ramsay, Turnbull, Benedettini & Treasure, 2000). And, insecure attachment styles have been found to be higher in women diagnosed with eating disorders (Troisi et al., 2005). In a study that compared individuals diagnosed with a wide range of eating disorders with controls, Ward et al. (2000) also found that insecure styles of attachment consisting of both compulsive care-seeking and compulsive self-reliance characterized the eating problem group. Furthermore, expressed emotions in families can lead to poorer social adjustment and dropping out of treatment (Szmukler, Eisler, Russell & Dare, 1985).

However, there are disagreements amongst leading researchers about the precise role that families play in eating problems. Some have proposed caution when assigning a causal role to the family, as there appears to be no consistent structure, dysfunction or behavioural pattern across all families (Eisler, Lock & Le Grange, 2009).

Systems theory

Approaches that concentrate on family dynamics and attitudes are often referred to as *family systems theory*. In Minuchin's structural family systems theory of eating disorders (Minuchin, Rosman & Baker, 1978), the whole family system, not the individual with the eating problem, is the focus of concern. And the family is thought to be involved in the *development* and *maintenance* of the problem. In other words, the 'problem' is dispersed across the family system, rather than within the individual only. Furthermore, the establishment of appropriate boundaries between family members is considered vital for the development of healthy relationships; failure to achieve this can lead to significant problems. According to Minuchin, families who have a member with an eating problem share at least one of a number of important characteristics relating to boundary violation, namely (a) *enmeshment* (b) *overprotection* (c) *rigidity* and (d) *lack of conflict resolution*. *Enmeshment* refers to an over-involvement and intrusion by parents into their children's lives. Furthermore, parents are often over-critical and dismissive of their children's emotional needs. *Overprotection* is related to perceived high levels of parental control and over-investment in parenting per se by the child. *Rigidity* refers to difficulty in challenging familial rules and the status quo. This is especially pertinent to the development of eating problems, as such difficulties usually begin in adolescence when changes to family relationships are highlighted. For example, an adolescent's need for greater autonomy and independence is likely to disrupt the familial status quo. Finally, *lack of conflict resolution* characterizes a family that is unable to openly acknowledge conflict and avoids any such open conflict, thus failing to resolve it.

There is some empirical support for Minuchin's approach, although the familial dynamics described have also been found in families with other forms of distress, making the stated factors indirectly as opposed to directly causal (Polivy & Herman, 2002; Lacey & Price, 2004). For example, one study found not only adversity in childhood and family background, but also depression, to be higher in a group diagnosed with bulimia, but not anorexia (Webster & Palmer, 2000). Furthermore, a study of 74 family triads (the parents and their child) found that parents who had children diagnosed with anorexia were more likely to deliver a double message to their daughters: one in which they were outwardly affectionate and nurturing whilst neglectful of their daughter's emotional needs and feelings (Humphrey, 1989). In the same study the daughters diagnosed with bulimia were more likely to have families who were similar to those described by Minuchin, as they were characterized by greater enmeshment and rigidity.

Life events

There is some evidence that individuals diagnosed with eating disorders experience a greater number of stressful life events than community controls (Troop & Treasure, 1997). In clinical and community studies, the available evidence does appear to support the presence of precipitating life events leading up to the onset of a clinically recognizable eating problem (Raffi, Rondini, Grandi & Fava, 2000). For example, in a study comparing over 100 ED patients with two community cohorts, using the life events and difficulties schedule developed by social psychiatrists George Brown and Tyrril Harris (1978), 67% of those diagnosed with anorexia and 76% of those diagnosed with bulimia were found to have experienced a major life difficulty, including difficulties with family and friends (Schmidt, Tiller, Blanchard, Andrews & Treasure, 2000).

In a study comparing adolescents with an ED diagnosis (bulimia and anorexia) with a control group of adolescents across an 18-month period, significantly higher levels of stressful life events were reported in individuals with an ED diagnosis, especially those with a diagnosis of bulimia (Strober, 1997). Welch, Doll and Fairburn (1997) also found elevated rates of stressful life events in the bulimia group, in a study comparing bulimia patients and non-eating disordered controls, one year prior to the development of the eating problem. In particular, they found negative life events relating to family and other social relationships, as well as threats to physical safety, to be especially common in the bulimia group. One possible mediating factor is how individuals with an ED diagnosis cope with adverse or stressful life experiences, with some of the evidence pointing towards a greater tendency for individuals diagnosed with anorexia to use avoidance strategies when trying to cope and those diagnosed with bulimia adopting a more ruminative coping strategy, meaning they continuously and repetitively turn things over in their mind (Troop & Treasure, 1997). In general, those diagnosed with eating disorders were found to experience greater levels of helplessness in comparison to controls.

The difficulty with the studies listed above is they are all retrospective rather than prospective. **Retrospective** describes the process of looking back at events that have already taken place. **Prospective** refers to an event in the future that is likely to happen. Prospective studies are studies where participants are interviewed, observed or measured *before* an event occurs, and are better because they do not rely on people's memories of events. In a rare prospective study, Sohlberg, Norring and Rosmark (1992) measuring the relationship between stressful life events and outcome one, two and three years after individuals were diagnosed, suggests that although life events were significant prior to the onset of the problem, they did not predict the outcome after three years.

In sum, life events do appear to play a role in the development of eating problems but further information is needed in order to establish exactly how they lead to *eating-specific difficulties*, given that they are also involved in the development of a variety of mental health problems (Bentall, 2003).

Childhood abuse

A number of authors have noted the link between a history of childhood abuse and the development of eating problems. A particular focus in the literature has been on the role of child sexual abuse (CSA), considered to be a recognized risk factor (Polivy & Herman, 2002). For example, some authors have explored the idea that purging food can be symbolic of ridding the body of unwanted substances (e.g. semen) so that the person can feel cleansed and more in control. Others have argued that restricted eating is linked to a desire to delay the onset of sexual maturation and thus protect the feminine body from any further abuses which increases feelings of control (Walsh & Burns, 2000). Thus, the visible signs of sexuality and sexual availability (which could invite male attention and thus abuse) are actively stopped, in order to protect the person from further harm.

A number of large empirical studies have been carried out to test the hypothesized link between eating problems(EP) and childhood sexual abuse. However, the results appear uncertain (Pope & Hudson, 1992). For example, Smolak and Murnen (2002) completed a meta-analysis of 53 studies to determine whether there was a positive relationship between EP and CSA. Although a significant relationship between EP and CSA did emerge, it was unclear which aspects of the eating problem (body image or binge eating) were linked to CSA. Another meta-analytic study found an association between EP and CSA only in individuals who binged and purged (those diagnosed with bulimia), but not in those who only restricted their eating (those diagnosed with anorexia) (Wonderlich, Brewerton, Jocic, Dansky & Abbott, 1997). Once again CSA was more likely to be significant in the group diagnosed with bulimia who had a number of other mental health problems, not eating problems alone. Thus, some have argued that eating problems are a way to cope with generally higher levels of distress that can develop as a result of CSA (Rorty, Yager & Rossotto, 1994). Paul, Schroeter, Dahme & Nutzinger (2002) confirmed this in their study measuring rates of self-harming behaviour and eating problems which resulted from experiences including childhood sexual trauma. Early sexual trauma was linked to eating problems, especially in those who also self-harmed.

Favaro et al. (2003), in a community study of 934 women 18–25 years old, found that being a victim of childhood abuse was a significant factor in the development of eating problems. However, they concluded that CSA could not be treated as a causal factor, because the data was correlational, which could only imply a relationship between the two factors. In sum, individuals with eating problems can have a number of mental health problems resulting from CSA that are not eating-specific (e.g. self-harm, dissociation, low mood and anxiety).

Thoughts and feelings

Cognitions

How people think about themselves has an obvious impact on their mental well-being. This is true of eating problems as much as any other form of mental distress. The central cognitive (and diagnostic) feature of the major eating disorders is *an over-evaluation of body shape, eating and weight* (Fairburn, 1981). Self-evaluation is largely determined by the individual's ability to achieve perfection in body shape, eating and weight, and failure to do so leads to low self-esteem and the maintenance of problematic eating. However, many have argued that the preoccupation with body shape, eating and weight are masking other enduring negative self-beliefs. Certain eating behaviours (starvation and binge eating) develop in response to underlying emotional distress and self-awareness (Heatherton & Baumeister, 1991), the argument being that the eating problem provides an opportunity to dissociate from, or avoid thinking about, difficult emotions and/ or traumatic experiences (Geller, Cockell, Hewitt, Goldner & Flett, 2000). Furthermore, core negative self-beliefs are believed by many to be predisposing factors in the development of eating problems (Cooper, Todd & Wells, 2005).

Cognitive studies have revealed a number of maintaining factors associated with diagnoses of anorexia and bulimia. These include perfectionism/cognitive rigidity, experiential and emotional avoidance, pro-anorectic beliefs and the response of close others to the condition, as well as thoughts relating to the importance of control (Cooper et al., 2005; Schmidt & Treasure, 2006).

In the main, cognitive research has concentrated on emotional and cognitive factors that *maintain* rather than *cause* eating problems. However, some have linked the development of certain cognitive styles to *personality factors* that are believed to be *dispositional* and *trait*-like (and hence causative), rather than state-bound (lasting only as long as the eating problem) (Schmidt & Treasure, 2006). Personality characteristics identified for individuals diagnosed with anorexia and bulimia (and which are said to be predictive) are (i) perfectionism (ii) low self-esteem (iii) dependency and non-assertiveness. **Perfectionism** is the firmly held belief that perfection can be achieved. In clinical terms, this means the belief that anything less than perfection is a sign of failure, and can be a threat to self-belief and esteem.

However, many of these 'characteristics' are also commonly identified for individuals with other psychiatric diagnoses, including anxiety and depression (Shafran & Marshall, 2001). Again, it is difficult to work out why an eating problem develops in place of or alongside expressions of sadness and/or worry. Many have argued that weight-related self-schemata must be operating in addition to more general characteristics, in order for eating problems to develop (Vitousek & Hollon, 1990).

Some cognitive processes, such as perfectionism, thoughts about control and positive beliefs about the person's eating problems, have been linked to issues of weight and body shape, although a number of authors have argued that these are not the only factors involved in the development and maintenance of positive thoughts about the problems (Lee, 2001; Schmidt & Treasure, 2006).

Intrapersonal and interpersonal factors

Schmidt and Treasure (2006) reviewed the evidence relating to intrapersonal and interpersonal factors affecting the thought processes of those diagnosed with anorexia, from a culture-free perspective. **Intrapersonal** refers to thoughts, emotions and communication taking place within the individual. **Interpersonal** refers to thoughts, emotions and communication taking place between individuals. They argued that anorexia is not necessarily linked to cultured and gendered thoughts about weight and body image and should be seen more as a defence against any social threat. Unlike other work, which emphasizes individual cognitive processes only (intrapersonal), they argue that because self-starvation often works to reduce social threat (and thus initially has an adaptive function), we have to take into account threats coming from the person's individual personality characteristics (perfectionist/obsessive compulsive) as well as difficulties arising from family interactions (interpersonal factors). Interestingly, the treatment evidence indicates greater success for psychological therapies that are strongly family or interpersonally focused, rather than therapies involving individuals only (McIntosh et al., 2005).

Cognition and bingeing

Cooper et al. (2005) have developed a cognitive maintenance model relating to binge eating (mainly but not exclusively related to diagnoses of bulimia). They measured maintaining factors before, during and after bingeing, as well as asking patients to describe their dietary and compensatory behaviours (vomiting, exercise, laxatives etc.). They found that the triggers for bingeing were interpersonal stress and physical sensations (such as feeling full or hungry), as well as low mood, anger and speculated 'personality disorder' (Fassino, Leombruni, Pierò, Abbate-Daga & Giacomo Rovera, 2003). Thus the emotional triggers were not necessarily related to weight or eating. For the 12 women patients interviewed, bingeing provided a means of comfort and avoidance of emotions and thoughts related to the initial trigger. They also identified four types of thoughts that completed the bingeing cycle: (i) thoughts reflecting cognitive and emotional avoidance (positive beliefs about eating); (ii) negative beliefs about weight and shape; (iii) permissive thoughts (negative self statements and all-or-nothing (dichotomous) thinking; and iv) thoughts of no control.

Finally, a further line of investigation into cognitive factors has been the study of meta-cognitive beliefs, in order to understand how individuals interpret their own beliefs and thought processes.

Meta-cognitions, for example, can reveal how certain beliefs are viewed as positive or anxiety-provoking (e.g. worry is dangerous for me). Studies on meta-cognitions are rare, but one carried out with a group of anorexia patients, and control dieters and non-dieters found higher levels of meta-cognition in the anorexia group, including the views that worry was dangerous and uncontrollable, a belief that it was important to control one's thoughts and an elevated awareness of their thoughts and thinking processes (Cooper, Grocutt, Deepak & Bailey, 2007). These results, although preliminary, suggest that as well as having to cope with an eating problem, individuals may be using unhelpful coping strategies (in the form of meta-cognitions) that maintain anxiety and/or obsessionality.

Emotions

It might seem obvious that emotions have a part to play in eating problems, but it is only relatively recently that researchers have begun to empirically examine their role (Fox, 2009).

Many have suggested that individuals who develop eating difficulties do so as a result of being unable to recognize emotions in others (Kucharska-Pietura, Vasilis, Masiak & Treasure, 2004), express their own emotions, or as a way to divorce themselves from stressful emotions (Copper et al., 2005; Legenbauer, Vocks & Rüddel, 2008). Waller, Kennerley and Ohanian (2007) have also described how restricted eating and bingeing/vomiting are all used as a means to avoid or suppress emotions. Restriction can be used to delay emotion and binge/purging can be used after an emotion has been activated, to reduce its effect.

But which emotions play a role in eating problems? A number of key emotions have very recently been identified, including disgust, anger and shame. Many believe that these emotions arise from the individual's family background and developmental history, and become more fixed over time. However, a recent edition of the journal *Clinical Psychology and Psychotherapy* (2009) included a number of papers that identified a range of core emotions in the development and maintenance of eating problems (which they grouped into the diagnostic categories anorexia and bulimia). Fox and Power (2009), for example, argue that self-disgust is a motivating emotion in eating disorders, as well as high levels of anger that cannot be appropriately channelled. Because anger is then believed to be threatening, it is directed away from the self (towards which it is initially directed) onto the body (Fox & Harrison, 2008), leading to extreme body dissatisfaction. These emotions have also been found in individuals diagnosed with depression, which often accompanies eating disorders. Davey and Chapman (2009) offer an alternative to Power and Fox's analysis when they suggest that anxiety, rather than disgust, mediates behaviours relating to eating disorders. They argue, using data from a community sample, that disgust alone does not represent an independent risk factor. Shame (characterological [or self shame] and body shame have also been implicated in the development of eating disorders, in terms of shame related to past relationships as well as shame pertaining to the eating problem itself (Swan & Andrews, 2003; Goss & Allan, 2009). Shame itself can prevent women from disclosing their difficulty, in everyday life and in therapy. Finally, there is some research which suggests that individuals diagnosed with an eating disorder experience difficulty in recognizing their own and others' emotional states, which some have argued to be a result of an emotionally impoverished early environment (Fox, 2009; Harrison, Sullivan, Tchanturia & Treasure, 2009).

In the literature, difficulty with recognizing emotional states is sometimes referred to as alexithymia. **Alexithymia** is a condition in which people have difficulty reading and interpreting emotions.

A study of 70 women diagnosed with an eating disorder and 70 matched controls revealed higher levels of alexithymia in the eating disorder group, as well as difficulty with imagining other people's emotional experiences (Bydlowski et al., 2005). However, after controlling for depression, the difference in alexithymia scores between individuals diagnosed with an eating disorder and the controls was not significant, which supports wider research suggesting alexithymia is not specific to eating problems, but is a feature of a number of mental health problems (but only when distress is present, and often not when the person is in recovery). For example, alexithymia scores for individuals diagnosed with an eating disorder appear to return to normal when the person has recovered, which suggests that these emotional difficulties are *state* rather than *trait*-like in character (Beales & Dolton, 2000).

Biological factors

In this section, we will review the evidence relating to three different areas of biological functioning (a) genetic factors, (b) neurotransmitter functioning, (c) endogenous opioids, and (d) neuroendocrine functioning.

One of the difficulties involves establishing whether biological factors are the result of changes in eating behaviour and weight loss, or an underlying cause of such changes.

Genetic factors

The search for the identification of genetic factors has expanded in the eating disorders field in recent years (Keel & Klump, 2003). Indeed, it does appear to be the case that diagnoses of anorexia and bulimia run in families, and the growing consensus is that genetic factors may play a role (Collier & Treasure, 2005). However, there still appears to be disagreement about whether individuals with anorexia and bulimia have a shared genetic vulnerability, or whether there are key differences in the genetic pathways.

In a study of 1831 relatives of 504 probands (individuals diagnosed with anorexia or bulimia), the authors found a significant increase in diagnoses of anorexia and bulimia in first-degree relatives, as well as evidence of milder forms of eating problems (Strober, Freeman, Lampert, Diamond & Kaye, 2000). Klump, Miller, Keel, McGue and Iacono (2001) found, in a community study, a concordance rate of over 50% for MZ twins and none for DZ twins, suggesting a shared genetic risk for anorexia and bulimia.

As well as relying on cross-transmission eating disorders diagnoses only, research examining personality traits associated with anorexia (perfectionism, rigidity, obsessiveness) have found higher rates of eating problems in family members. This has led some to argue that more research into the different and broader genetic pathways for anorexia and bulimia is needed, given that temperamental and personality traits can differ between the two diagnostic groups (Collier & Treasure, 2004; Keel & Klump, 2003).

While these studies are informative in terms of highlighting a familial transmission of eating problems, they do not allow us to separate environment from biology in any clearly defined way. Many behaviours that run in families may be learnt as opposed to inherited, which is why adoption studies would shed greater light on the matter. To date, there is one adoption study on anorexia or bulimia (Klump, Suisman, Burt, McGue & Iacono, 2009), which examined 123 adopted and 56 biological sibling pairs. The results propose significant genetic influences on eating problems, body dissatisfaction and weight preoccupation, lending support to previous familial transmission studies. Researchers have also tried to establish specific gene loci on specific chromosomes. Some genetic linkage studies have proposed chromosome 1 is linked to anorexia but not bulimia (Grice et al., 2002). And chromosome 10 has been associated with bulimia purging type (Bulik et al., 2003). However, replication of such studies is difficult and the results are yet to be firmly established (Grilo, 2006).

Neurotransmitter functioning in the hypothalamic region

The hypothalamus is involved in the regulation of appetite and has thus been identified as a potential site for the development of eating disorders. Animal studies reveal that lesions in the lateral hypothalamus lead to loss of appetite and starvation, which are features of an anorexia diagnosis. The argument is that higher levels of serotonin, which result from hypothalamic lesions, lead to mood improvement as well as feelings of being full.

However, individuals diagnosed with anorexia do not report appetite loss and often think about and crave food greatly, so the association between the lateral hypothalamic region and eating disorders is weak. Furthermore, more recent imaging studies have found lower levels of serotonin in individuals diagnosed with anorexia during periods of both starvation and in recovery (Kaye et al., 2005). Although some authors have identified serotonin as a factor in eating disorders, its exact function remains unclear, and empirical evidence is weak.

Endogenous opioids

Endogenous opioids (naturally occurring opiates) are a compound released in the body in order to reduce pain (Dean, Bilsky, Luby & Koval, 2009). A consequence of this release, however, can be a lifting of mood and feelings of euphoria. Endogenous opioids are released during an initial period of dieting and reinforce a state of starvation-dependence (Marrazzi et al., 1997). This may especially be the case for those who hold addictive personality characteristics. Davis and Claridge (1998), for example, have found that patients diagnosed with both bulimia and anorexia score highly on addictive personality traits, making them more susceptible to the effects of euphoria caused by increased endogenous opioids. However, some researchers have found lower levels of endogenous opioids amongst individuals with a diagnosis of bulimia, especially given that lower levels are associated with craving, although this finding has not been consistently replicated.

Given that opioid systems are activated by food deprivation, one study set out to examine how blocking opioids might lead to an improvement in 'symptoms'. One study by Luby and Koval (2009) did find that opiate blockade using naltrexone (an opioid antagonist) was shown to be effective in some but not all individuals with diagnoses of anorexia and bulimia. Interestingly, naltrexone is a drug commonly used to treat substance-dependence, and there appears to be some crossover between individuals diagnosed with bulimia and substance abuse and dependency.

Neuroendocrine functioning

Because hormonal (neuroendocrine) functioning is associated with appetite and feeding, there have been some investigations into its role in the development of diagnosed eating disorders. Leptin is a hormone communicating information on the body's fat stores/energy reserves to the brain, which maintains normal levels of neuroendocrine function. Decreased serum levels of leptin have been found in some individuals with an anorexia or bulimia diagnosis (Blüher & Mantzoros, 2004).

However, according to this theory, it is the loss of weight and lower body fat (through starvation and diet) that causes decreases in leptin, suggesting that pre-existing levels of leptin are not responsible. Again, this suggests that the eating behaviours themselves are responsible for maintaining biological changes, rather than any dispositional biological impairment.

Lifelines, plasticity and specificity

Experiences of eating problems, like other forms of distress, demonstrate a large degree of variation across an individual's lifespan, making clear the existence of both plasticity and specificity in the development and maintenance of these problems. We have already noted throughout the chapter how a number of researchers and clinicians have begun using a transdiagnostic approach, simply because individuals tend to migrate from one diagnostic category to another over their lifetime. This makes a straightforward causal explanation for discrete diagnostic categories problematic. Another factor to consider is the cultural specificity of some forms of problem eating. For example, a meta-analytic study by Keel and Klump (2003) has suggested that the diagnostic category bulimia nervosa is non-existent in areas of the world not exposed to Western media, suggesting a cultural, rather than a biological, cause. However, they argue that rates for anorexia are relatively consistent worldwide, even in locations that have not been subject to Western influences. The authors suggest that anorexia may well have a genetic component, given the similarity in worldwide prevalence rates, whereas bulimia is likely to be a culturally created eating problem. We must nevertheless be wary of reaching a conclusion that self-induced starvation is motivated by Western ideals of beauty. Even in countries that have not had significant exposure to Western ideals, religious beliefs may be present, suggesting a social/cultural explanation, as opposed to a genetic cause for self-induced starvation (Lee, 2001). We must also remember at all times that, in the vast majority of cases, eating problems manifest in girls and women, which has not been accounted for in any genetic explanation (Levine & Smolak, 2006).

Given such a large level of migration between diagnostic categories, some researchers investigating the potential genetic inheritance of eating disorder diagnoses have adopted a behavioural checklist that is relevant across the diagnostic categories. In this way, body dissatisfaction, bingeing, weight concerns and psychological traits believed to be relevant to eating disorder diagnoses in general (such as perfectionism, rigidity, obsessive thoughts) can be assessed to establish whether there is a link between these general psychological traits in families.

As already noted, there is still much debate about the heritability of eating problems. Although over 30 twin studies have now been conducted, many have been subject to methodological and statistical criticisms, and there are doubts about the validity of the Equal Environments Assumption (see Chapter 4 for further information). Twin studies, as we have noted, cannot provide a definite answer to whether shared behaviours have been developed because of a shared environment, or inherent genetic characteristics. The only adoption study on eating problems has been conducted recently by Klump et al. (2009, see above); it provides potential evidence for substantial genetic effects on a range of behaviours related to problematic eating and eating disorder symptoms. The authors argue that this is the first adoption study to provide significant support for the existence of genetic risk factors for eating disordered behaviours, as opposed to shared environmental risk factors.

Further molecular genetic work may be needed to establish specific genes relevant to eating disorders. The authors also note that the identification of genetic risk factors does not rule out the importance of cultural and other environmental factors in the development and maintenance of eating problems. For example, *non-shared* environmental factors (experiences that siblings do not share, such as child sexual abuse, critical peer commentary, engagement in weight-concern sports) were not investigated, in the recent adoption study by Klump and colleagues. And yet they have been argued to be crucial in understanding the onset and course of eating- and body-related issues (Klump, Wonderlich, Lehoux, Lilenfeld & Bulik, 2002). The authors only measured environmental factors shared between siblings at the time of the study, neglecting to investigate pre-puberty factors, such as early childhood. Other twin studies, for example, have shown less evidence for genetic influences and more for shared environments when investigating psychological traits such as perfectionism and rigidity, which are relevant to eating problems (Kamakura, Ando, Ono & Maekawa, 2003).

Moreover, replication of this initial adoption study is required, to establish whether the results – which only suggest a genetic component of eating problems – are uniformly consistent; greater and more representative (and cross-cultural) samples, and measures of past and present, shared and non-shared sibling environments are also necessary. And, of course, eating problems generally co-exist with other forms of mental distress, presented in terms of diagnoses of depression, anxiety and substance abuse, making it difficult to arrive at a straightforward link between eating problems and genetic inheritance (Levine and Smolak, 2007).

Because eating problems largely begin in childhood, it is important to think about not only a set of potential risk factors for the onset of the problem, but to also think specifically about the family circumstances that surround the individual, both in terms of ongoing family conflict and whether or not treatment is being supported by family members. We have already discussed how family conflict, parent–child relationships and child sexual abuse can contribute to eating-related and body- and weight-related problems, but we must also be mindful of how the immediate familial conflict can affect the course of the problem; in other words, what keeps the problem *going* can be as important as what started it in the first place. As we shall we see later on in the chapter, treatment options are largely family-based, because of the age of the diagnosed individual, so it is important to assess the impact of familial support in relation to the course of the difficulty and long-term recovery. It is also important to bear in mind that the younger the individual is when their eating problems is identified, the more likely they are to recover, if given early social support (Pike, 1998; Stice, 2002).

In a number of studies, high levels of parental criticism, including maternal critical comments, and low self-directedness in the individual are related to poorer treatment outcomes, as well as substantial changes in the eating problem itself. For example, in a study measuring the impact of parental behaviours, when there were high levels of parental criticism and low self-directedness, individuals originally diagnosed with anorexia restrictive type began engaging in bingeing and purging type behaviours, enabling them to maintain the self-control necessary for food restriction (Strober, Freeman & Morrell, 1997; Tozzi et al., 2005).

A further issue worthy of consideration is habituation, which may involve physiological as well as psychological components. When we refer to **habituation**, we mean how we become used to responding to distress in a particular way – a way that becomes familiar and even reassuring to us. For example, studies indicate that dieting behaviours may reduce serotonin levels (and, some have argued, lead to a lowering of mood), such that binge eating may be used as a way to restore serotonin levels (and make the individual feel better). In other words, bingeing may make us feel better and become a way of re-establishing positive mood, in the short term at least. Once this process has begun, however, the biological processes involved may further maintain this cycle of dieting followed by bingeing. Walter Kaye and colleagues, for example (1998), have shown how food restriction can lead to neuropeptide abnormalities. Disruption to normal peptide functioning (as a result of food restriction) can thus lead to a number of psychological and physiological events, such as menstruation stopping (amenorrhea), rigid thinking and mood disturbances (Kaye et al., 1998). However, it appears that when an individual is in recovery and normal weight is restored, neuropeptide and neuroendocrine abnormalities are no longer present. Again, it is important to be mindful of the how physiological changes may lead to the persistence of psychologically distressing thoughts and behaviours. We must also be aware that whilst these physiological processes contribute to the maintenance of eating problems, they are not the cause of them, since they often disappear once the individual has recovered.

Finally, another relevant issue is the extent to which other forms of mental distress are present before the start of an eating problem, or whether they develop as that problem proceeds. In other words, we must take into account co-morbidity. The answer to this question is far from straightforward. A number of studies have suggested that a diagnosis of depression, anxiety or poor psychosocial functioning in general can predict increases in binge eating in non-diagnosed *and* diagnosed (eating disorders) girls and women (Keel, Klump, Miller, McGue & Iacono, 2005; Spoor et al., 2006; Gilbert & Meyer, 2005). Interestingly, the degree of depression in individuals diagnosed with anorexia does not appear to predict the onset of binge eating, suggesting that depression itself cannot explain the cause of particular types of eating problems (e.g. bingeing), though we can be clear they often exist alongside eating problems and can predict continuing problems with eating and body dissatisfaction. In a 10-year follow-up study of individuals with diagnosed eating disorders, Schork, Eckert and Halmi (1994) found that the greater number of diagnosed difficulties (e.g. diagnoses of depression, anxiety, substance abuse), the more likely the individual was to experience a sustained problem with eating. Therefore we need to turn our attention to the specific set of difficulties an individual may experience at any given time to make sense of why certain behaviours, thoughts and feelings appear when they do, and persist or disappear after a period of time.

Summary

There is no single explanation for why individuals develop eating problems and severe weight concerns: we can only identify particular risk factors.

Eating problems appear to be relatively common in the general population and not everyone experiences distress as a result of them. A variety of psychological, cultural, social (familial and at a wider socio-cultural level) and biological factors must be considered in terms of both the *development* and the *maintenance* of eating problems. We must also not forget that it is primarily girls and women who develop the major eating problems and weight concerns, which must, therefore, involve a detailed examination of gender factors.

Here we have discussed a range of risk factors, including socio-cultural factors, body image, gender, life events, trauma and abuse along with other biological risk factors that may lead to eating problems. These risk factors appear pertinent to all eating problems in various ways. Although the diagnostic categories appear to describe a number of different types of behaviours, many researchers and clinicians have argued that the underlying risk factors are so similar, and the core fear of weight gain the same, that differentiating the categories is extremely problematic (Fairburn, 2008). Furthermore, given that eating problems usually develop during adolescence, it is important to consider familial dynamics that may underpin the individual's distress.

If we turn our attention back to Carmel, we might be tempted to think the best way forward would be to treat her eating problem as the sole problem, rather than looking at her family situation. However, a more comprehensive investigation would examine both personal and interpersonal factors that would provide clues to all aspects of her life – her mother and father's relationship and/or her mother's and father's emotional relationship with her. Her mother's dieting and weight loss, for example, and her father's emotional distance may be factors that have significantly contributed to Carmel's distress and isolation and her choice of strategy to deal with them (e.g. dieting and withdrawal).

In sum, there are many questions we would need to ask before arriving at a causal explanation for an individual's eating problems. Even if we have a good idea why a problem originally occurred, we also must deal with the ways in which it is being maintained or made worse by looking at how other people respond and react to it.

Interventions

An individual diagnosed with an eating disorder can be treated as an inpatient in a general psychiatric hospital or specialist treatment centre, or as an outpatient. However, the vast majority of individuals with serious eating problems never reach treatment because they either deny they have a problem or they see their restricted eating or bingeing as a way of successfully dealing with other problems in their life. As a result, over 90% of individuals in this latter category are not in clinical treatment (Fairburn et al., 1996) and may frequently use the internet or other resource to deal with their difficulties. These forms of self-help or guided self-care can be extremely useful and are judged to work for some (Ghaderi & Scott, 2003). One four-year follow-up study, for example, found no difference between guided self-care (with significantly reduced therapist contact) and standard cognitive–behaviour therapy (Schmidt, Treasure & Garthe, 2003).

Treatments for diagnosed eating disorders involve a complex assessment of the difficulties a person is facing, as well as knowing when it is best to tackle them. If a person is starving and close to death, it may not be the time to attempt

in-depth psychotherapy. A safer course may be to tackle weight gain and the effects of starvation before embarking on more in-depth discussions surrounding the causes and maintenance of the problem. Furthermore, although eating behaviours (separated out into clear eating disorder diagnostic categories) were once thought to be the target for treatment (reducing restricted eating or reducing bingeing), it is now recognized by some leading practitioners that the most important aspect of treatment is what people *across* diagnostic categories share – that is, an intense fear of weight gain and body image concerns, driven by cultural incentives (Fairburn, Cooper, Shafran & Wilson, 2008). The argument, which has empirical support, is that many individuals transfer from one diagnostic category to another over time and during relapse, with the biggest cause of relapse being *body image disturbance*, regardless of whether someone is diagnosed with anorexia or bulimia (Keel, Dorer, Franko et al., 2005). The final point to consider is that as with other forms of mental distress, individuals experiencing them have a variety of complex and overlapping difficulties to contend with. Dealing with an eating problem as if it were the only problem may obscure other important issues, such as intense sadness, worry and long-term developmental difficulties. As we have seen from previous sections, the co-occurrence of several problems, including substance abuse, diagnosed depression and anxiety and personality disorder is common in individuals diagnosed with an eating disorder.

The following sections include a discussion of the major treatments for eating problems, including (a) promotion of weight gain; (b) cognitive–behaviour therapy; (c) family therapy; and (d) drug treatment. In each section, the extent to which each therapy is effective will be reviewed.[2]

In doing so, it is necessary to consider both short- and long-term treatment success and the factors relevant to relapse, in order to establish clearly whether the positive effects of treatment actually last (Herzog, Dorer, Keel et al., 1999).

Weight gain

It is estimated that around 6% of individuals diagnosed with anorexia die as a result of starvation. Many practitioners argue, therefore, that it is essential to promote weight gain before beginning any other form of psychological treatment. There is some evidence to suggest that patients whose weight is higher when they leave inpatient services fare better than those with relatively little weight gain (Castro, Gila, Rodriguez & Toro, 2004).

According to the National Institute of Clinical Excellence (NICE) guidelines for the treatment of eating disorders, individuals are encouraged as inpatients to gain on average between 0.5 and 1 Kg each week: as an outpatient this decreases to an average of 0.5 Kg. Weight gain continues until the individual has reached a BMI of at least 18 (regarded as normal weight). Various techniques are used to achieve weight gain. If an individual is dangerously ill and at risk of death, force-feeding through a nasogastric tube (through the nose to stomach) may still be used to instigate initial weight gain, but only in extreme circumstances. In **nasogastric feeding**, a plastic tube is inserted through the nose, past the throat and into the stomach. It is a medical technique used to administer

---

2 With the added proviso that treatment studies have been criticized for measuring 'symptom reduction' only.

food or medication when a person cannot eat, or refuses to do so. It is controversially used to force-feed individuals with a diagnosis of anorexia who are of a very low body weight and dangerously close to death.

By law, psychiatrists *are* permitted to use force-feeding to prevent death and to ensure weight gain, as patients are not perceived to be mentally competent to make therapeutic choices and/or to refuse treatments (Treasure, 2001). Given that most patients are children requiring their parent's consent to treat them, it is not uncommon for the child's point of view to be discounted in favour of the parent. However, some have argued that individuals who starve themselves are intelligent and aware of the dangers, and should be given the right to make an informed decision, even if it results in their death (Russon & Alison, 1998). Despite exercising caution with regard to force-feeding practices, one study involving nearly 400 female inpatients found that nasogastric feeding led to higher weight gains and did not affect treatment satisfaction in comparison with patients who were fed using reward systems (Zuercher, Cumella, Woods et al., 2003). In severe cases where death is likely, it has been argued that force-feeding is valid, to increase body weight and thus avoid death, though this view continues to cause intense controversy.

An alternative to force-feeding is the operant approach. Based on a behaviourist principle, the idea is to offer rewards to individuals who gain weight. Measuring food intake is obviously insufficient, as food can be brought up and calories used up in excessive exercise. Rewards might include visits from family or friends, although some argue that denying patients (especially very young patients) such rights to visitation under any circumstances is counterproductive and punishing. The promotion of weight gain is complex and the setting under which weight gain is promoted even more so. For example, a study by Gower et al. (2000; cited in Grilo, 2006) discovered that patients who were hospitalized fared worse than those who were treated as outpatients. However, it is difficult to ascertain whether those who were hospitalized had more severe problems in the first place than those who were not. Randomized control trials of inpatient and outpatient settings are needed to determine further the effect of different treatment settings on weight gain (Grilo, 2006).

Cognitive–behaviour therapy

Cognitive–behaviour therapy for eating disorders was developed by Christopher Fairburn and colleagues at the University of Oxford in the early 1980s, and is largely concerned with factors that *maintain* eating problems (Fairburn, 2008). The therapy focuses on both restoring a healthy diet and tackling the over-evaluation of body shape and weight, commonly found in clients referred for eating-related problems. Although cognitive–behaviour therapy was initially developed to manage problems associated with bulimia nervosa (Fairburn, 1981), a revised version of this model has been argued to be effective for all eating disorders, since they have the same core features (preoccupation with and fear of weight gain and dissatisfaction with body shape) (Fairburn et al., 2003). This 'transdiagnostic' model thus advocates the use of cognitive–behaviour therapy to address all eating problems, with more sessions (40 as opposed to 20) proposed for those diagnosed with anorexia, simply to promote initial weight gain before therapy begins.

The primary aim of cognitive–behaviour therapy is to tackle the underlying (dysfunctional) core beliefs relating to eating, body shape and weight. Whereas others may judge their self-worth with respect to success at home, work and other areas of life, the individual with an eating problem judges their self-worth almost exclusively in relation to their ability to control eating and weight. This dysfunctional *core* belief, it is argued, serves to maintain problems with eating and should be the main focus of treatment (rather than the specific eating problem itself). All other associated behaviours, such as food restriction, vomiting, excessive exercise and laxative use, are argued to be *part* of the problem but must be treated as secondary to the main dysfunctional core belief system: *body dissatisfaction and an intense fear of weight gain and fat.*

If restricted eating is not adhered to and the dietary regime is broken, the individual sees this as evidence that they have lost control. Such perceived loss of control is reported to be a major reason for binge eating (Fairburn et al., 2003). Other triggers for binge eating include intense mood changes which are temporarily relieved through binge eating for some individuals (across *all* diagnostic categories).

There are four major stages in Fairburn and colleagues' enhanced cognitive–behaviour therapy (see Fairburn et al., 2008 for a detailed discussion of each of the stages).

Stage 1: Engaging the patient

This is the longest and most intense part of treatment (eight sessions over four weeks). It involves devising a formulation of the problem (and diagnosis – see Chapter 6 for further discussion of these terms) with the individual in order to assess the severity or disruptive nature of the difficulty. A formulation involves generating a hypothesis about how the problem is kept going (maintained) and devising practical ways for the client and therapist to overcome it. This is the most difficult phase, because individuals with eating problems are often reluctant to admit they experience difficulties as a result of their eating behaviour or weight restriction. It is also the most important stage because success at this stage can predict longer-term success. The individual will also be informed that they will be weighed once a week for the duration of treatment and must keep a record of their eating patterns and the feelings associated with them. Alongside this, the therapist will provide information on healthy eating and dieting and the establishment of a regular meal plan and alternative eating pattern. Family members and friends may be called upon at this stage to help with the establishment of regular eating (if agreed by the client).

Stage 2: A review and revision (if necessary) of the original formulation

This is a shorter phase (two sessions) and involves the therapist and client reviewing the original formulation, including a review of any progress and a measure of change (using standardized psychological assessment measures), including general psychological well-being as well as a measure of bingeing and purging and eating patterns. If the client is unduly negative about their progress, the therapist may wish to assess levels of depression. If present, antidepressant medication can be used. Stage 2 also involves planning for stage 3.

Stage 3: Addressing the major maintaining factors

At this stage (eight weekly sessions), the focus of treatment is the cognitions and behaviours that keep the problem going

Dieting cultures: many women in Western countries report being on a diet that restricts food intake. But when does dieting become dangerous?

(maintaining factors). These include the over-evaluation of weight and body shape, restricted eating, body-checking and dieting and bingeing. The over-evaluation of weight and body shape is the most complex in relation to self-evaluation and requires several sessions to decipher its significance, and then to provide alternative means of self-evaluation. To begin with, the client will be required to make a daily assessment of the importance that weight and body shape play in terms of their self-evaluation. This can be represented in a pie chart. Generally, clients start off with a disproportionate section of the chart allocated to body/weight concerns. They will also be asked to write down the number of times they make checks on their body (body-checking) and to write down their interpretation of why they are body-checking and how they feel after they have checked (feeling fat, disgusted etc.).

The primary task for the therapist is to gently challenge the client's appraisal, to find out *when* and *where* the client is most likely to feel dissatisfied with their body and, with the client, to find other aspects of their life that they can value more. This is not a straightforward process: it must be handled with extreme sensitivity and must be carried out jointly with the client. Towards the end of this stage, the client may then be ready to explore why they over-evaluate themselves in relation to their body shape and weight (e.g. to assert control, to overcome shame or humiliation). The client may then be ready to make adjustments to their dietary regime (restricted eating, bingeing and/or purging), which has helped maintain the over-evaluation of body shape and weight. Tackling beliefs associated with certain eating patterns (e.g. eating certain foods will cause weight gain) is the main target of treatment at this stage and eventually leads to the client's implicit rules about dieting being gradually reduced and the cycle broken.

Stage 4: Looking to the future: how to maintain positive change and prevent relapse

In the final stage of treatment (three fortnightly sessions) the aim is to ensure the changes that have occurred so far in treatment are maintained and the risk of relapse reduced. Depending on which problems still remain, the client and therapist make up a plan for dealing with these problems. Furthermore, when setbacks do occur (as inevitably they will), the client is shown that they should treat these as temporary and solvable, rather than devastating and permanent. The

most important part of this stage is to teach clients to think about setbacks in non-catastrophic ways. Developing a plan of action to deal with setbacks or slip-ups enables the client to see themselves as an *active* participant, rather than a *passive* recipient of an illness. This will enable a more proactive engagement with any future difficulties and will hopefully develop the problem-solving skills of the client. However, clients must be reassured that they can seek help if it is needed.

In addition to the treatment procedures outlined above, Fairburn and colleagues also recommend addressing four further maintaining factors for individuals with eating problems (Fairburn et al., 2003). These will vary depending on the individual (and there are sub-groups who experience these difficulties with greater intensity). The four maintaining factors are:

- Clinical perfectionism: levels of perfectionism that are severe and enduring. When goals are not met, distress usually occurs, so it should be the aim of therapy to reduce expectations and to show the client that not obtaining such high levels of attainment will not result in disaster.
- Core low-self-esteem: in addition to low self-esteem in regard to body shape and weight, there are some individuals who experience low self-esteem on a more general level. The eating problem alone will not tackle this core low self-esteem, so steps must be taken to address this in treatment.
- Difficulty in coping with intense mood changes (mood intolerance): some individuals experience difficulty in coping with emotions such as anger, frustration or disgust. Some may turn to substances to deal with this difficulty because they believe they are incapable of dealing with changes in mood (which makes the mood change appear greater). As a result, the goal of treatment is to enable clients to recognize that they can deal with mood change and to identify problem-solving strategies that will help them do this.
- Interpersonal problems: relationship difficulties (family, friends or partners) can lead to low self-esteem and can help to maintain eating problems. One of the reasons for this relates to feeling in control. If relationships are difficult and the individual feels out of control, exerting control over eating may lead to a greater feeling of self-mastery in general and a better therapeutic outcome in the long term.

How effective is cognitive–behaviour therapy (CBT)?

No other form of therapeutic treatment for eating problems has been more systematically studied than CBT, which has been heralded as the treatment of choice in the NICE (National Institute for Health and Clinical Excellence) guidelines, after systematic review of its efficacy and evidence base (Wilson & Shafran, 2005). However, most of the research conducted on CBT efficacy has been with adults with diagnoses of bulimia (Fairburn et al., 2008). CBT does appear to be more effective than either family therapy or interpersonal therapy in treating bulimia, within a shorter period of time. **Interpersonal therapy** focuses on the interpersonal context in which a person lives, such as their intimate relationships and family, and concentrates on building a set of interpersonal skills with the client to enable the establishment of stronger and more fulfilling relationships and greater sense of personal well-being. In the Cochrane Collaborative meta-analysis of randomized

BOX 12.2

A conversation about the over-evaluation of weight and shape between a therapist and client in cognitive–behaviour therapy

THERAPIST: We've decided that today we are going to focus primarily on the shape side of things. I'd like to go back to why we are doing this. If we look back at the diagram that shows the things that are driving your eating problem (referring to the patient's formulation) you can see that at the top are your concerns about your shape and weight. Clearly we need to focus on them since they seem important in keeping your eating problems going and they really worry you.

PATIENT: Yes, my shape is the main thing I worry about. I really bothers me – the fact that I can't get it off my mind – and it is so awful. I hate it.

THERAPIST: Well, to start with, we need to talk about the way we all evaluate or judge ourselves, something most of us don't even think about. All of us have a system, or way, of judging ourselves, and if we are meeting our personal standards in this respect, we feel reasonably good about ourselves, whereas if we are not, we feel bad. So if we take a typical person, there will be various things that he or she will judge him or herself by. For example, relationships with others are often important – and children, if one has some – and one's relationship with friends. Other things that are likely to be important are pastimes – say, sport or singing, music, cooking, or whatever. And one's appearance, too, may be important, Now, if things are going well in these various areas of life, one feels fine, but if they are not, one feels bad – indeed, feeling bad is the best clue to an area's importance. If one feels really bad when an aspect of life

is not doing well, this strongly suggests that this aspect is very important to one's self-evaluation. Does that make sense?

PATIENT: Yes, I think so. The way I look, for example, makes me feel really bad. I won't go out some days.

THERAPIST: Exactly. So this indicates that your appearance is very important in how you see, or judge, yourself. Now a good way of representing all this is to draw a pie chart with the various slices representing the various aspects of your life that are important to you, and the bigger the slice, the more important that aspect is. Let me show you (*sketches out a 'balanced' pie chart*). Now what I would like us to do together is to try to draw your pie chart. What we first need to do is list the things that are important in the way you judge, or evaluate, yourself. What might they be?

Source: Fairburn et al. (2008, pp. 600–1).

controlled studies of CBT and waiting-list patients, eight separate studies showed a significant remission (defined as four weeks or more) in 40% of CBT patients, compared with 5% of the waiting-list group (Wilson, Grilo & Vitousek, 2007).

Furthermore, CBT has been shown to significantly reduce bingeing in 76% of clients and purging in 69% of clients after only three weeks (Wilson, Loeb Walsh, 1999). However, these short-term benefits are not necessarily maintained. If we compare interpersonal therapy (which takes a great deal longer: 12–18 months) and CBT, they both perform equally well in the long term (at one-year follow-up – see Agras et al., 2000a). At best, however, CBT reduces bingeing and purging in about 40–60% of cases, so more research is needed to ensure greater numbers of clients or patients make long-term recoveries (see Agras et al., 2000a; Wilson, Grilo & Vitousek, 2007; Schmidt, Treasure & Garthe, 2003).

In a rare study with adolescents diagnosed with bulimia *or* EDNOS, a comparison was carried out between family therapy and cognitive–behaviour therapy guided self-care (a form of CBT that is self-directed with little therapist intervention; Thiels, Schmidt, Treasure and Garthe (1998) argue that guided self-care is as effective as CBT). Although the guided self-care group had a greater reduction in bingeing and over-evaluation of body shape and weight at six months follow-up, the differences between the family therapy and CBT self-care group had disappeared at 12 months (Schmidt et al., 2007). Whilst CBT may again reveal positive results more quickly, the advantages over other forms of therapy do not appear to last. The picture for clients diagnosed with anorexia is even more uncertain. In the very few studies that do exist, one year of CBT was found to be more effective than nutritional counselling in post-hospitalized patients. Overall treatment failure and drop-out rates combined were also much lower in the CBT group (22% compared with 52%) (Pike, Walsh, Vitousek, Wilson & Bauer,

2003). Two years later, however, a randomized control trial was conducted, published in the same journal; it compared two specialized forms of therapy (CBT and interpersonal therapy) with a non-specific case-management group (which involved an experienced therapist delivering a non-directive form of psychotherapy). The results reveal that interpersonal psychotherapy was the least successful mode of treatment, followed by CBT and the case-management group (McIntosh et al., 2005). In this study, at least, other factors appear to influence the success of treatment. The authors speculate that the professional experience of the therapist and the success (or otherwise) of the therapeutic alliance are likely to determine success, rather than the specific treatment approach. Perhaps most important was the emphasis, in the case-management group, on issues that the client chose to pursue, which may have lead to a greater sense of control and autonomy in therapy, leading to an increase in perceived therapeutic empathy more generally.

Family therapy

Despite ongoing debates about the exact role of the family in the development and maintenance of eating problems, most researchers and clinicians agree on the benefits of involving the family in the treatment of younger individuals (Lock, Le Grange, Agras & Dare, 2005; Eisler, Simic, Russell & Dare, 2007). There are many different forms of family therapy; what they share in common is a focus on family dynamics: improving how family members communicate with one another and adjusting boundaries within the family, if they are not well established (such as if a parent is over-involved with or over-protective of their child). Another focus is to explore issues of autonomy and control within the family and to assess whether the child or young person could be granted more autonomy and control over their life (Lock,

Le Grange, Agras & Dare, 2001). The treatment can involve parental re-feeding (if the patient is currently underweight) with the guidance of a therapist and structured family therapy sessions. In addition to a structural family therapy approach outlined by Minuchin et al. (1978: see above), there are many other different types of family therapy used to treat problems related to eating, body shape and weight. One of the better known approaches used in the UK for young people and their families is the **Maudsley method**, developed by Gerald Russell and colleagues at the Maudsley Hospital in London. The aim of the Maudsley method is to involve parents in the initial phase of treatment, aimed mainly at the restoration of weight and the regulation of dieting behaviour. This treatment is commonly used to treat young people with a diagnosis of anorexia. This first phase of treatment involving the parents in promoting weight gain also emphasizes the need for parents to separate the problem eating behaviour from their child. This provides space for the family to openly discuss their frustrations and concerns about what may have caused the problem and for the therapist to reassure the parents that they are not to blame. A non-blaming position by the therapist is important, in order to engage the family in therapy and to encourage a more positive line of communication between the individual with the eating difficulty and other family members (Lock, Agras, Bryson & Kraemer, 2005). By the time weight is restored and eating patterns stabilized, the family is then ready to address more fully, issues relating to independence and autonomy, family boundaries and the roles of each of the family members. At this stage families can be taught how to communicate more effectively with one another, and to jointly solve problems when they arise.

Some feminist authors have criticized general family therapy for not appearing to address one of the major features of eating problems: socio-cultural norms relating to appearance, body shape and weight and their relationship to gender norms (Fallon, Katzman & Wooley, 1994). In feminist family therapy, there is greater acknowledgement of the relationship between culture, gender and eating-related problems. **Feminist family therapy** uses feminist theory to explore the relationship between wider cultural messages about gender (as well as a variety of socio-political and socio-economic factors such as race, class and disability, that can impact on family life) in the generation and maintenance of family difficulties and psychological distress. The approach advocates the establishment of egalitarian relationships within the family and a non victim-blaming position.

Feminist family therapy concentrates not only on the family system but also on the gender-specific changes that occur during adolescence, such as concerns about being properly 'feminine' and being 'thin'. The family is educated about the pressures that all women face in adhering to a particular and culturally defined standard of beauty, as well as how girls are more likely to find it difficult to express autonomy, due to the societal emphasis on caring and nurturing. Finally, the feminist family approach attempts to uncover and analyse power structures and hierarchies within the family. It also explores the possibility of any underlying sexual abuse that may have contributed to the development of the problem (sexual abuse has often been associated with eating problems and many other forms of distress, especially in girls and women, with whom it more frequently occurs; Baker, 2004).

How effective is family therapy?

The Maudsley method has been found to be more effective in treating younger individuals diagnosed with anorexia than individual forms of therapeutic support (such as CBT), after a one-year follow-up; although it must be noted that these were non-chronic outpatients (Russell, Szmukler, Dare & Eisler, 1987; Eisler, Dare, Russell, Le grange & Dodge, 1997). Whether or not family therapy is effective depends on a number of factors, including a) whether the individual with the eating problem considers the family to be the problem and experiences high levels of 'maternal' criticism and b) whether the individual with the eating problem is old enough to want to be autonomous and see a therapist one-to-one (Russell et al., 1987).

In a study of diagnosed anorexia, comparing 'conjoint' versus 'separated' family therapy (CFT: all family members are involved; SFT: family members are seen individually) over a one-year period, the latter was more successful for individuals perceiving high levels of criticism from their mothers. However, both forms of therapy had a positive effect on mood, eating-related symptoms after a one-year follow-up (Eisler et al., 2000). SFT proved more effective for improving symptoms, while overall psychological improvements in the areas of sexuality and mood were seen in the CFT group. In a five-year follow-up study comparing the CFT and SFT groups once more, few differences were found between the two therapeutic approaches, except in the case of individuals who had reported high levels of maternal criticism, who did not experience an increase in positive effects when offered CFT (see also Lock et al., 2010). In a further randomized controlled trial with 84 older individuals diagnosed with anorexia, family therapy (and a psychoanalytically informed psychotherapy) was found to be more effective than cognitive analytic therapy and a non-specific low contact therapy (Dare, Russell, Treasure & Dodge, 2001).

In sum, there are very few studies measuring the effectiveness of family therapy in comparison with other treatment forms, but initial results appear to be in favour of a family therapy approach, especially for younger individuals and those who do not experience specific difficulties with maternal criticism.

How effective are drug treatments?

Most studies measuring the effectiveness of medication have examined antidepressants for eating disorder diagnoses (Agras et al., 1992; Bellini & Merlt, 2004), although there is a growing number of studies examining the role of antipsychotics (see below). It is unsurprising that antidepressants have received the most attention, as people with eating problems are also likely to feel very unhappy. The co-occurrence of eating disorder diagnoses and clinical depression is well known. The evidence for drug treatments in comparison with placebo are quite mixed, however. A placebo is a false medical intervention. Patients given a placebo can sometimes experience a perceived or actual improvement in their medical condition. Placebo conditions are often included in randomized controlled trials to assess the effects of psychological suggestion in medical intervention. Randomized controlled trials are a form of scientific study in which a form of treatment is tested. Before treatment begins, the patient identified with a specific illness or condition is placed in one of a number of treatment trials. The treatment trials are then systematically compared to measure how effective each treatment has been in tackling the specified

BOX **12.3**

Creative resistance: a poem on anorexia by a member of an online anti-anorexia service user website

Anorexia

There I was a while ago lost with no hope and happiness nowhere to be seen.
You came along and offered to me a ticket that would make everything better.
You lied to me and made me feel like everything was going to be fine.
Instead you tortured me and took me away from my loving family and friends.
You convinced me that all I needed was you and for that to happen I had to follow your impossible rules.
You crushed my dreams and made me feel like being happy was illegal.
You made me feel that I was never good enough and that I didn't deserve to live.
You tricked me into thinking your voice was my own and your expectations were my thoughts.
You ripped me open and turned my heart into a black cold rock and you sucked out all that was in me and made me skin and bone.
You took away all my energy and made me work like I was your slave with no time to rest.
You made me work so hard with everything. House work, cooking, cleaning, the list just goes on and on never coming to an end.
You dug a deep hole for me with no way to get out.
You locked me in a tiny cage and threw away the key.
Now I am here fighting for you to be out of my life forever.
Just leave me alone; don't you know that you are not wanted?
I am not some sort of puppet that you can control for your own entertainment.
I am a human being, not a character in a horror movie that you can just watch and laugh at.
You put me through so much pain and misery; how could you do this to me? Don't you have any feelings at all?
I am sorry to disappoint you but I choose not to take your road to death and fall into more of your traps.
You can no longer control me! I am putting my foot down.
How dare you take every little thing that was left in me and call me all those nasty names.
How dare you just sit there and laugh at me and the people who try to help me as we go through so much heartache and distress.
You are a monster, a life destroyer; I don't even think you deserve a name.
I am going to get better whether you like it or not and I don't care how long it takes, this nightmare will come to an end!
Until the day you are finally out of my life forever I will not stop fighting.
Food is my worst nightmare, mirrors are the reflection of disgust, everyone hates me, I am alone forever,
I don't deserve to live; all this bullshit you tried to tell me and for a minute you had me convinced but I no longer want to be on your leash. Now watch me untie this tangled knot that you have tied together so hard.
I am no longer going to listen to you. I am opening the door for you to get out of my life; take it, you are no longer welcome here anymore.
I don't want an apology or your sympathy. You don't deserve my forgiveness. You don't even deserve to exist.
My hate is all I have to offer you.

By Marie (aged 14 years) – Insider

www.narrativeapproaches.com

This is an example of poetry written by one of the online members of the Anti-Anorexia league, a group of individuals who are actively trying to resist their eating problems and develop a strategy to overcome and rebel against cultural norms related to body shape and weight. The group is supported by a group of narrative therapists who specialize in eating difficulties. The online archive include personal stories as well as art and poetry, all aimed at addressing ways to overcome severe eating difficulties.

illness/complaint, preferably over a period of time. Some studies reveal an increase in weight and general well-being and a reduction of negative core beliefs surrounding body shape and weight using antidepressant medication, though slight (Claudino et al., 2006). However, these results have not been replicated in larger-scale RCT studies. A further meta-analysis of 29 studies reporting significant differences in placebo and drug treatment groups found the effect size of the difference to be very modest in clinical terms, for diagnosed bulimia, using a number of different antidepressant medications (Bacaltchuk & Hay, 2002). A **meta-analysis** is a quantitative measurement and comparison of the results of a number of empirical studies that are broadly testing similar hypotheses. Furthermore, the drug-taking group was more likely to drop out of treatment. The other problem was that remission (stopping bingeing and purging) was only observed at one week. Longer-term data is obviously needed. In a double-blind RCT study of 93 outpatients after weight recovery, no significant difference was found between placebo and the group receiving fluoxetine (an antidepressant) at one-year follow-up (Walsh et al., 2006). A further problem with using medication is that although certain medications may reduce binge eating for some, the core beliefs maintaining the eating problem do not generally improve. As Grilo (2006, pp. 102–3) notes, 'a core behavioural symptom of BN is not alleviated and, in fact, may be strengthened (i.e. helping the BN to become a "stronger dieter") by these medications ... [and] the heightened unhealthy dietary restraint will eventually fail and lead to repeated bingeing'.

Antipsychotics

Antipsychotics have supposedly been manufactured to treat diagnosed psychotic disorders, such as schizophrenia, although they are also used in the treatment of dementia, bipolar disorder, Posttraumatic stress disorder and psychotic depression (see Chapter 8 for a full discussion of drug treatments).

The second-generation antipsychotics (e.g. clozapine, olanzapine) are notorious for causing weight gain. Some recent studies have attempted to assess whether antipsychotics should be used to promote weight gain in individuals with eating problems and whether such weight gain may lead to an improvement in the thoughts and feelings associated with eating problems. Although some very modest improvements have occurred in weight gain (as expected), it is very difficult to know how these drugs are working (given that they were designed for a completely different set of problems). Some have argued that it is their general mood-stabilizing properties that serve as a temporary anxiety reducing agent (Attia & Schroeder, 2005). However, given the severe side-effects that these drugs can produce and that in some patients a serious amount of weight gain occurs, it seems unlikely that in the long term these drugs will prove effective, especially for individuals whose main concern is body shape and weight gain (Grilo & Mitchell, 2009). Finally, in a meta-analysis review of controlled studies relating to both antidepressants and antipsychotics, Attia and Schroeder (2005) found very little evidence for the effectiveness of either antidepressant or second-generation antipsychotics.

Chapter summary

Many of us have expressed our emotions and dealt with problems by eating too much or too little. Eating problems generally are not uncommon, especially when we bring binge eating and general overeating into the equation. But when weight and eating become our obsession, we may find it difficult to break the cycle. Eating problems are no longer specific to people living in developed countries who are more individualistic in their thinking and emotional expression (Ioannou & Fox, 2009). They are now found throughout the world and to some extent this can be accounted for by the rise of Western ideals and media messages that are now freely transmitted to a growing number of non-Western countries. The risk factors associated with eating difficulties and weight concerns are multifaceted and complex and cover a range of socio-cultural, psychological, familial and biological features. However, it must be remembered that eating problems often occur alongside other mental health diagnoses, such as depression and especially anxiety, and substance abuse and personality disorder (Bulik et al., 2007). This makes the identification of a single set of causal processes specific to eating problems, difficult to establish. Despite this, we have been able to review some of the available risk factors, including socio-cultural factors such as the influence of the media, body dissatisfaction and body image distortion; gender identity issues and gender-role conflicts (Hamilton & Waller, 1993).

We have also made clear the relationship between family conflict and eating problems and relationship problems more generally. A whole range of life events and traumatic episodes have also been covered to establish the role of negative events in the person's life, as well as more individualistic explanations that focus on thought patterns and feelings, especially around weight-related concerns and self-esteem. Finally, we have considered the extent to which biological factors play a role in the development and maintenance of eating problems, resulting in an overall conclusion that they do appear to play a part, at least in the maintenance of eating difficulties. We have covered the variety of ways in which eating problems have been treated by mental health professionals, as well as through self-guided help manuals, though it is important to recall that over 90% of individuals with eating problems will never ask for treatment. The major interventions covered in this chapter were (a) weight gain (b) cognitive–behaviour therapy (c) family therapy and (d) drug treatment. These treatments have been shown to be successful (to varying degrees) for some individuals, although less so for individuals with severe or chronic weight loss. However, we must always exercise caution when it comes to applying a singular treatment model for all individuals, as many have a combination of difficulties that need specific and complex treatment interventions.

End of chapter questions

1 Weight concerns are common: what do they tell us about the values in our society?
2 Why do girls and women seem to experience greater distress relating to body image?
3 Why is self-worth linked to body image concerns for individuals with problem eating?
4 Are diagnosed eating disorders discrete categories?
5 Are family therapies more effective for younger people?
6 Why does cognitive–behaviour therapy appear to work for those who binge and purge?

Find out more

Fairburn, C. (2008). *Cognitive Behaviour Therapy and Eating Disorders*. New York: Guilford Press.

Fairburn, C. G., Cooper, Z., Shafran, R., Wilson, R. & Terence, G. (2008). Eating disorders: A transdiagnostic protocol. In D. H. Barlow (ed.), *Clinical Handbook of Psychological Disorders: A Step-By-Step Treatment Manual* (4th edn). New York: Guilford Press.

Grilo, C. M. & Mitchell, J. E. (2009). *The Treatment of Eating Disorders: A Clinical Handbook*. New York: Guildford Press.

Keel, P. K. & Klump, K. L. (2003). Are eating disorders culture bound syndromes? Implications for conceptualising the etiology. *Psychological Bulletin*, 129, 747–69.

Lock, J., Le Grange, D., Agras, W. S. & Dare, C. (2001). *Treatment Manual for Anorexia Nervosa: A Family-Based Approach*. New York: Guilford Press.

Malson, H. & Burns, M. (eds) (2009). *Critical Feminist Approaches to Eating Dis/Orders*. London: Routledge.

Nasser, M., Katzman, M. A. & Gordon, R. A. (2001). *Eating Disorders and Cultures in Transition*. London: Brunner Routledge.

Zimmerman, M., Francione-Witt, C., Chelminski, I., Young, D. & Tortolani, C. (2008). Problems applying the DSM-IV eating disorders diagnostic criteria in a general psychiatric outpatient practice. *Journal of Clinical Psychiatry*, 69, 381–4.

Films

Girl Interrupted (1999). Directed by James Mangold.
Sharing the Secret (2000). Directed by Robert Greenwald.
The Karen Carpenter Story (1989). Directed by Joseph Sargent.
The Best Little Girl in the World (1981). Directed by Sam O'Steen.
When Friendship Kills (1996). Directed by James A. Contner.
The David Cassidy Story (2000). Directed by Jack Bender.
The Father I Knew (1999). Directed by Michael Landon.
Kate's Secret (1986). Directed by Arthur Allan Seidelman.
For the Love of Nancy (1994). Directed by Paul Schneider.

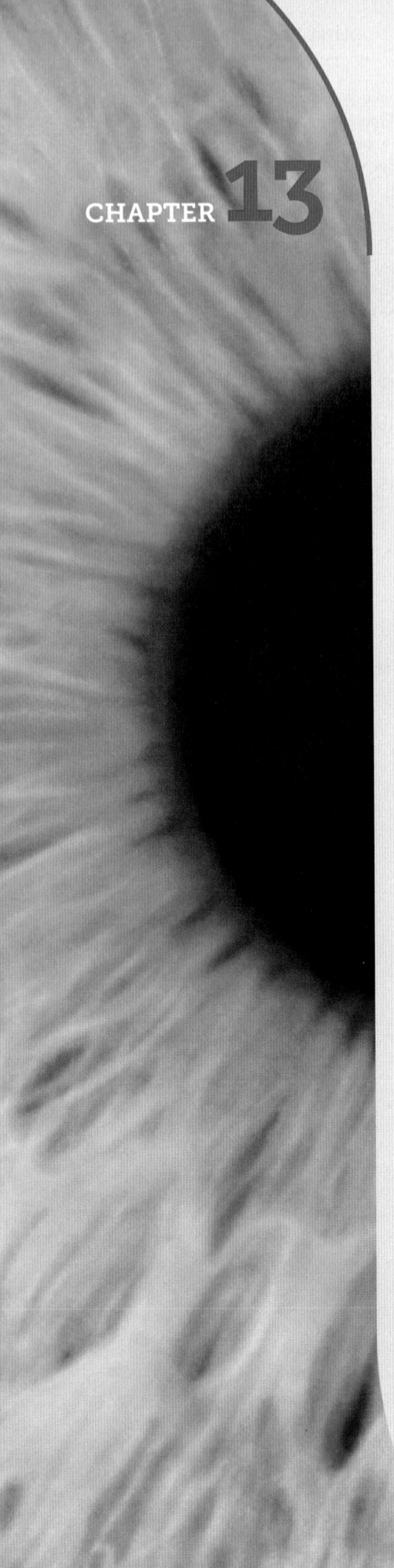

CHAPTER **13**

DISORDERED PERSONALITIES?

Salima's story

Salima is in her early twenties and has recently been diagnosed with Borderline Personality Disorder. Her childhood was difficult: her father was violent towards her mother and occasionally towards her and her sister, usually when he was drunk. Her mother lacked self-confidence and would criticize Salima. Salima was sexually abused by her father for several years but was afraid to tell anyone. During the abuse, Salima would try to mentally escape it, sometimes leaving her body in her mind. She began to regularly feel waves of feelings that made her feel disgusting and worthless. One day she found that if she cut herself the pain would be intense enough to distract her from the other feelings. She also began to hear strange sounds. One day this sound became the clear sound of a man's voice: it called her a 'bitch' and a 'slag' and other horrible names. She was very frightened and began to fall behind at school. This gave her mother and father more reasons to criticize her. Subsequently she was taken into the care of the local authority. Her father had denied the abuse and her mother sided with her father. Unfortunately, she was sexually abused when she was staying with one foster family. By now Salima was finding it very difficult to trust others. As more care placements broke down and her self-harming continued she was referred to mental health services whilst still a teenager. She was given a number of different diagnoses over time and a number of different kinds of psychiatric medication. Salima regularly found herself at the Accident and Emergency department because of a deep wound or because of an overdose she had attempted. Her psychiatrist told her recently that he thought that borderline personality disorder (or 'emotionally unstable' personality disorder) was the most appropriate diagnosis to make.

Carl's story

Carl is in his early thirties. He also had a difficult upbringing. His father spent long periods of time in prison for petty crime and, during these periods, his mother began to work as a prostitute and subsequently became a heroin user. Carl's parents often criticized him and beat him. He didn't really enjoy school and he started to truant more (so he cannot read or write very well). He and his friends formed a gang that got into trouble with the police. From a young age, Carl had problems with his temper and felt quite low and empty inside. He spent time in the care of the local authority because of the physical abuse and his mother's heroin usage. He served prison sentences for petty criminal and, later, violent offences. Carl doesn't really trust others: his philosophy is that the powerful win so you need to make sure you are more powerful than others. If he perceives others have wronged him in some way (e.g. by 'disrespecting' him) he can become extremely violent and finds it hard to set limits on what

This story continues on the next page

is a reasonable response. He first saw a psychiatrist when he was in care in his teens and was regularly getting into fights with other children. The psychiatrist then gave him a diagnosis of conduct disorder. In prison he was prescribed antipsychotic medication to calm him down and other medication to help him sleep. Because of his history the courts recently requested a psychiatric report when he was prosecuted and this records that he has been given a diagnosis of antisocial (or dissocial) personality disorder.

Learning outcomes

By the end of this chapter you should:

1 Know what is meant by the term 'personality disorder'
2 Understand why there is so much debate about this category
3 Understand what kinds of causal processes are associated with the problematic experiences seen as symptoms of personality disorder
4 Know what kind of interventions are available and whether they are effective

Introduction

This chapter is concerned with a category of problems known as personality disorders. We will see that this broad category includes a wide range of very different problems and behaviours, as we saw in the stories of Salima and Carl: from difficulties in relating to others and managing often powerful emotions, to difficulties in feeling empathy for others. Although many people with this diagnosis pose no risk to themselves or others, some may harm themselves (e.g. by cutting themselves) or others (e.g. through violence). Because of this, those with this diagnosis are often stigmatized by the public and even by mental health professionals (we discussed stigma in Chapter 1). At times, some commentators have argued, people have been given this diagnosis as a 'diagnosis of last resort' or a 'diagnosis of exclusion': in other words, it is a diagnosis reached after other diagnoses, through a process of elimination (although some have used this term to refer to how people with this diagnosis are often excluded from accessing services). Sometimes, because of the difficulties that some people with a diagnosis of personality disorder have in relating to others, strong emotional reactions are invoked in others, including mental health professionals. We have seen in other chapters that critics argue that many psychiatric diagnostic criteria reflect certain cultural values. Sarbin and Mancuso's (1980) book title posed the question: *Schizophrenia: Medical Diagnosis or Moral Verdict?* Similar arguments have been made about personality disorders (e.g. Blackburn, 1988; Pilgrim, 2001; Weinstock & Nair, 1984).

This category of problems are termed the *personality* disorders because they are seen as extreme manifestations of normal personality traits that are relatively stable over long time periods. But does it make sense to say that personalities are 'disordered'? Indeed, what do we mean when we refer to 'personality' as an explanation for distress or disturbing conduct? We will see that this diagnosis is one of the most

hotly contested, with critics arguing that it is invalid, unreliable, value-laden and a mechanism for social control. In addition some service users argue that the diagnosis is invalidating and stigmatizing. In line with our approach, we will attempt to move beyond the debate about diagnostic categories and examine particular kinds of experience and behaviour that may be experienced as problematic. We will describe some of the causal processes associated with these specific kinds of problem, arguing that, in many respects, these experiences can be seen as a legacy of emotional neglect and physical and sexual abuse in childhood. We will also review a number of interventions associated with these forms of distress.

Later in the chapter we will discuss the different sub-categories of personality disorder found in psychiatric diagnostic manuals. However, when we focus on causal processes and interventions we will focus on two sub-categories in particular: antisocial personality disorder (APD) and borderline personality disorder (BPD): see Table 13.2 for core themes in the definitions of these categories. This is because these are the categories which have received most interest from clinicians and researchers; they are currently, for example, the only personality disorders with a guideline from the National Institute for Health and Clinical Excellence (see Kendall et al., 2009 for a summary of their recommendations). Moreover, as Widiger and Mullins-Sweatt (2009) put it, 'there have been no adequate empirical studies on the treatment of (for instance) the avoidant, schizoid, paranoid, histrionic, narcissistic, obsessive–compulsive or dependent personality disorders' (p. 213).

Guiding question

- *Is the notion of personality disorder a helpful way of making sense of people's difficulties in relating to others?*

History and culture

History

Across history there have been many accounts of people who have had difficulty in controlling their passions or who have been seen as breaking societal rules about behaviour according to the mores of the time. For example, at the beginning of the 17th century English clergyman John Downame published *Spiritual Physick to Cure the Diseases of the Soul, Arising from Superfluitie of Choller, Prescribed out of God's Word* – the second edition had the snappier title of *A Treatise on Anger!* In the book, Downame describes different kinds of anger, including 'unjust anger' which 'hath not always a true cause, but sometime fained & imaginary' (Hunter & Macalpine, 1963, p. 55). A modern day psychiatrist might see such behaviour as indicative of paranoid personality disorder.

In order to understand the history of personality disorder it is first necessary to understand the history of the notion of personality itself. Although the term 'personality' has been in the English language since the 14th century, it only came to acquire its modern meaning of 'unique and distinctive character' in the late 18th century. Indeed, many commentators argue that the modern Western conception of a bounded, individual self with a unique character differentiating it from others developed after the European Enlightenment in the 17th and 18th centuries (Rose, 1989; Stainton Rogers, Stenner, Gleeson & Stainton Rogers, 1995). As the historian John Lyons puts it,'[u]nder the sails of philosophy, religion, politics, and the arts the self was invented shortly after the middle of the eighteenth century' (1978, p. 16). Because we are socialized into the concepts of a self and of personality from an early age it can be difficult to realize not only that it is a relatively recent concept but also that it is a very Euro-American one. The anthropologist Clifford Geertz (1984) has noted that the concept of a self-contained individual is quite unusual in other cultures across the world. In contrast, many other cultures place much more value on collective rather than on individual identity and there is a more distributed notion of the self – the self is seen as always in relation to others – than is often found in Europe or North America.

Personality disorder is a relatively recent addition to psychiatric classification. Kraepelin identified the 'morbid personality' in 1904. However, Théodule-Armand Ribot had published *Les Maladies de la Personalité* in 1885. Indeed, although the term 'personality' had been in use since medieval times, it was only with William James in the USA and Ribot in France that the notion of personality began to be drawn on, particularly in relation to so-called multiple personalities. Personality disorders were included in the first edition of the American Psychiatric Association's diagnostic manual. However, as Lane (2009) points out, much of the material on personality disorders in DSM-I was adapted from descriptions in memos by US military medical personnel in the second world war. As Lane notes, what was considered appropriate conduct in the military (with its focus on hierarchy and discipline) is very different from the range of behaviour seen in civilian life. He argues that such a transposition of diagnoses from the military to a civilian manual made 'the temporary frustration of the US War Department a basis for establishing lasting pathologies in the population at large' (Lane, 2009, p. 59).

A brief history of personality theory and its problems

In the 1950s and 1960s, two key approaches to the study of personality were dominant. Firstly, there were theorists such as Hans Eysenck and Raymond Cattell who argued that the key factor in determining people's personalities were traits or dispositions like 'extraversion' which could be measured, for example, through personality questionnaires. This was often contrasted with the idea that people simply experienced different states without necessarily exhibiting the consistency over time and across situations that the notion of trait implied. Secondly, there were theorists influenced by the Freudian psychoanalytic notion that personality was formed by early experience. Later psychoanalytic theorists such as Alfred Adler, Heinz Kohut and Karen Horney developed these ideas and psychoanalytic theories of personality had an influence on the first edition of the American Psychiatric Association's DSM. One version of psychoanalytic theory was that people could be differentiated into different psychological types which varied according to the relative dominance in a person of introversion and extraversion, sensation and intuition and thinking and feeling. Isabel Briggs-Myers and her mother, Katharine C. Briggs, drew on Jungian notions of personality types developing a psychometric instrument: The Myers-Briggs Type Indicator (Myers & Myers, 1995).

In 1968 the psychologist Walter Mischel criticized these approaches (Mischel, 1968). He argued that there was too much dependence on questionnaire studies rather than observation of what people did in everyday situations. He noted that correlations between personality factors and actual behaviour were weak and that, when one looked at people's behaviour across situations, there was less consistency than would be predicted from traditional personality theories. This 'situationist' critique, as it came to be known, then led to theorists arguing for an interactionist view of persons and situations.

The *Interpersonal circumplex* was developed by American psychologist Timothy Leary. Before he became a part of the 1960s counterculture and famous for his advocacy of LSD, Leary had conducted research using the Minnesota Multiphasic Personality Inventory (MMPI) scale. Leary (1957) was interested in the contribution of personality to relationships. He suggested that interpersonal relationship styles were best theorized along two axes: hate–love (changed to hostile–friendly in some contemporary versions) and dominance–submission. He argued that different aspects of personality could be seen within the four quadrants (see Figure 13.1).

The *Leary Interpersonal Behavior Test* was developed in order to locate people in the circumplex. Leary completed a number of psychological tests himself (including, in a comical episode, some he had himself designed) whilst he was serving a 20-year prison sentence for possession of marijuana. Vale (2008) describes how Leary planned to escape prison (which he subsequently did) and realized that he needed to ensure he was placed somewhere with less security. As a result he deliberately completed the tests in such a way that he would be profiled as a conforming person who would not try to escape and who liked gardening and forestry! The circumplex model was popularized again in the 1980s by Kiesler (1983) and Wiggins (1982), and continues to influence some contemporary interpersonal theorists (e.g. Birtchnell, 2002).

The **Five-Factor Model** was originally developed by two US Air Force psychologists, Ernest Tupes and Raymond Cristal in the 1960s, using items from Raymond Cattell's 16 PF personality scale. The model was popularized in the 1990s by Digman (1990), Goldberg (1993) and Costa and McCrae (1992). Cattell rejected these developments and, until his death in 1998, continued to argue that 16 factors fitted the data better. The five factors are: extraversion, agreeableness, conscientiousness, neuroticism and openness to experience. Assessment is most commonly conducted using the *Neuroticism-Extroversion-Openness Inventory* (Costa & McCrae, 1992).

However, the methodological problems identified by Mischel in 1968 still dog the field to some extent. For example, many studies are based on factor analysis. In personality research, this statistical method shows whether items from a test are correlated with each other and whether some items are more strongly correlated together than others, producing factors (i.e. clusters of highly correlated items). The problem with using factor analysis to differentiate clusters of questionnaire items is that the results are highly dependent on what the scale items are. Moreover, their selection is likely to be influenced by the researcher's implicit theory of personality. Stainton Rogers et al. (1995) note that when participants complete a personality inventory like the *Eysenck Personality Questionnaire* they will encounter items like 'do you like to

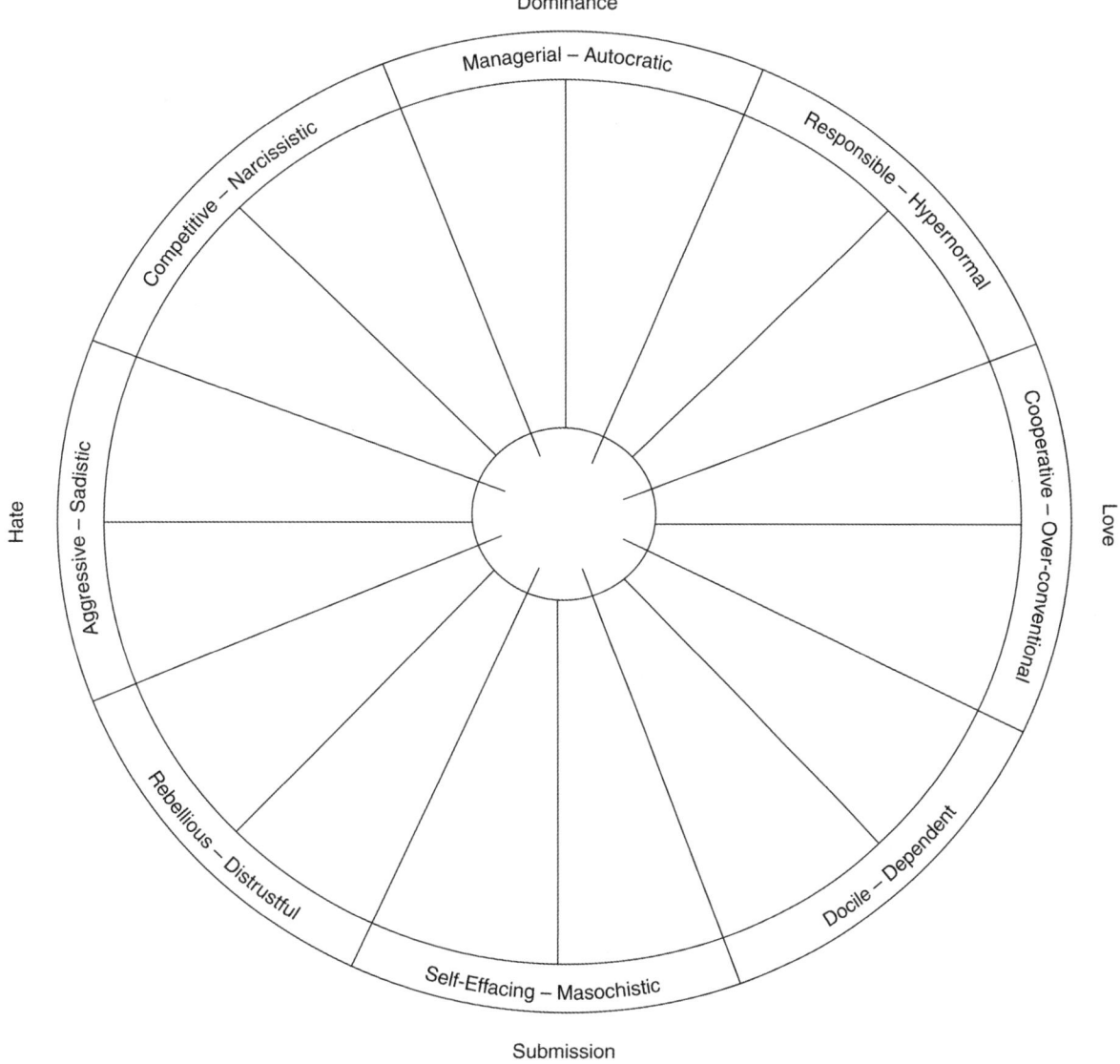

Figure 13.1 **Timothy Leary's interpersonal circumplex (adapted from Timothy Leary's estate: www.timothylearyarchives.org/)**

go to parties?' and 'are you impulsive?'. Answering repeated questions with similar meanings makes it clear to participants that the questionnaire is designed to look at extraversion and introversion. As these are ways of being that we are familiar with in culture, it is straightforward to represent ourselves in this way by responding consistently to the items. However, rather than such scales finding a thing called 'personality', Stainton Rogers et al. (1995) argue that all that they do is test the extent to which the scale-designer and participants 'share a common understanding of "what people are like" ' (pp. 50–1).

The notion that personality arises from an interaction between the person and the situation is, however, problematic. Stainton Rogers et al. (1995) identify three problems. Firstly, it is, as we argued earlier in this volume, impossible and nonsensical to separate the person and the environment: it is impossible for a person not to be in some kind of context (even if that context is an experiment). Secondly, two situations which

appear observably similar may, in fact, have very different meanings for the participants. Stainton Rogers et al. (1995) give the example of two lovers meeting versus a meeting between two ex-lovers who decide to continue a friendship: the two situations might appear similar to an observer but they have very different meanings for the two people concerned. Lastly, they argue that it is hard to capture the temporal context: the way that, in life, different circumstances open up and close down different possibilities for action as we move through time. They point out, for example, that to be 'rebellious' means we are in a particular relationship with our circumstances: in other words, our circumstances have presented us with something (e.g. conventional standards of some kind) against which we rebel.

In a recent article (Mischel, 2009) noted that his critique had been misrepresented in textbooks over the years and that, provided researchers focused on the meaning a situation had for a person, it was possible to observe 'stable, distinctive, and highly meaningful patterns of variability' in people's actions, thoughts, and feelings across different situations (2009, p. 285). He termed these behavioural signatures 'if ... then ... situation-behaviour relationships'.

Although over time it appears that interactionist and integrationist approaches have become more popular in the literature (Webster, 2009), recent years have seen a resurgence of trait theories in the form of the Interpersonal circumplex and, especially, the 'big five' personality factors.

Stainton Rogers et al. (1995) also emphasize the moral nature of personality descriptions. How we describe a person's personality is not a value-free matter. If we think of an earlier term for personality, 'character', we can see this clearly. The notions of morality and character are bound up with each other. When we describe others, our descriptions are imbued with evaluative comments: whether we like or dislike the person, whether we think they are a good person and so on.

Culture and personality

Unlike many of the other forms of distress discussed elsewhere in this book, personality disorder is not something that has an analogue in ordinary everyday language other than, perhaps, in descriptions of others' negative character traits. The category covers a wide range of problematic and distressing experiences and behaviours that have been conceptualized by Western psychiatry as problems relating to a person's personality. The notion of personality has been used as a way of explaining why some of these experiences and behaviours can endure over time. The notion of personality itself is also, as we have seen, peculiarly linked to Western notions of the individual. In more collectivist societies, for example, there is a very different conception of what it is to be a person. Moreover there is debate about whether the traits measured by personality tests are distributed universally across cultures (see Box 13.1).

A headline in the American satirical newspaper *The Onion* reads 'New Study Reveals Most Children Unrepentant Sociopaths' (7 December 2009: www.theonion.com/articles/new-study-reveals-most-children-unrepentant-sociop,2870/). The piece states that the fictional study found that 'an estimated 98 percent of children under the age of 10 are remorseless sociopaths with little regard for anything other than their own egocentric interests and pleasures'. This humorous story emphasizes that expected norms of behaviour are inextricably linked with cultural values. In Western industrialized cultures we do not have the same expectations of children as we do of adults, so we accept the rather self-focused actions of children and do not see them as selfish or as psychopaths.

One of the major criticisms of the personality disorders is that, although diagnostic manuals aim to study universal disorders, they imply, perhaps more so than other diagnostic categories, particular cultural values and normative assumptions. In other words, they reflect particular ideas about what a normal personality for a man and woman should be (here, we are using the term 'culture' to cover not only nationality, skin colour, ethnicity, for example, but also the values that different societies have in relation to gender and so on). But is this right?

It can be easy to take it for granted that one's own cultural values are normal and those of other cultures abnormal. Indeed, Gaines (1995) warns that other cultures can be exoticized by describing a number of Western beliefs and practices which might seem bizarre to those from other cultures, including Catholic nuns' vows as a form of 'spirit marriage' and beliefs in persecution by the CIA, FBI and so on.

In a recent German study, Leising, Rogers and Ostner (2009) attempted to delineate the value judgments implicit in the DSM-IV personality disorder criteria, since the DSM 'states how a person should not be, but never states how a person *should be* or *why*' (Leising et al., 2009, p. 230, emphasis in original). As a result, for each of the 79 criteria they created an opposite

---

BOX **13.1**

Are personality trait descriptions culturally universal?

Is what is considered a personality disorder in one culture the same in other cultures? We will consider the issue of cultural bias in Box 13.5 but, to some extent, the answer to this question depends on whether personality traits are culturally universal. For example, is the concept of extraversion equally meaningful in all cultures?

An indication of how cultural values might influence how dimensions of personality are evaluated in different cultures can be seen in Costa, Terracciano and McCrae's (2001) analysis of a compilation of over 23,031 *Revised NEO Personality Inventory* data from

26 cultures: this is one of the groups of researchers proposing the Five-Factor Model of personality. They reported that there were some gender differences, though the causes were unclear. The differences were broadly consistent with gender stereotypes, with women scoring higher on neuroticism, agreeableness, warmth, and openness to feelings, whereas men scored higher on assertiveness and openness to ideas. Interestingly, the size of the gender difference varied across cultures. Most significantly, though, the researchers reported that the gender differences were small when compared with individual variation within the genders.

Costa et al. (2001) assumed that the Five-Factor Model was universally applicable, but a recent study casts some

doubt on this assumption. De Raad et al. (2010) adopted a psycholexical approach, in which personality traits are researched via the ordinary language terms we use to describe others. Different personality taxonomies and scales and people's ratings on them are then factor-analysed to investigate whether there are clusters of related items. De Raad et al. used 14 trait taxonomies from 12 different languages (predominantly European plus Filipino and Korean), and concluded that a three-factor solution best fitted the data. Those factors were: extraversion, agreeableness and conscientiousness. Emotional stability (also termed neuroticism) was less meaningful across cultures. This is interesting, since it is a key item in categories such as borderline personality disorder.

statement. They then asked 28 student raters to sort these statements into stacks of similar statements. Cluster analysis was then used to differentiate the statements into 10 clusters (see Table 13.1).

Table 13.1 **Clusters of values implied in the DSM-IV personality disorder criteria**

Be self-reliant and independent
- Be able to tolerate real and imagined separation
- Take care of yourself

Be self-confident, but in a realistic manner
- Be well grounded
- Have a stable, positive and realistic self-image
- Be self-confident and autonomous

Get along with others
- Be confident and relaxed in social situations
- Be flexible and adaptable
- Consider yourself equal to others
- Be accountable and act responsibly

Tolerate uncertainty and imperfection
- Have courage and trust in yourself
- Focus on what really matters

Look for the good in people

Be conventional
- Be sexually modest
- Express yourself clearly
- Adhere to cultural norms
- Have ordinary experiences and realistic fantasies
- Be only mildly, if ever, depressed

Have self-control
- Be able to control your impulses and emotions
- Display anger only when appropriate, and with moderate intensity

Connect with others emotionally and treat them fairly
- Display consistent and authentic emotions
- Display appropriate emotional involvement
- Treat others fairly, with empathy and respect

Enjoy social relationships and activities

Be trusting
- Be suspicious only with good reason
- Have trust in other people
- Be trusting in social situations
- Assess your relationships with others realistically

Source: **Leising et al. (2009).**

Laid out in this way, the statements describing the implicit 'undisordered personality' (Leising et al., 2009) capture the Manual developers' normative assumptions; they look rather like a modern guide to etiquette in the exhortations to be 'sexually modest', to 'look for the good in people', 'be trusting' and so on. Looking through the statements, it is possible to detect a tone of moral evaluation. Indeed, the criteria for some categories, like antisocial personality disorder, appear to be concerned with social deviance, like committing crimes and breaking other social rules. As a result, critics have argued that the category of personality disorder is less to do with mental health or personality and more to do with the transgression of moral codes of behaviour. Moreover, they argue, the definitions of personality disorder are so broad that many aspects of conduct could be inappropriately labelled as personality disordered, particularly given the increasing medicalization of everyday life (see, for example Chapters 1, 2 and, especially, 3).

Contemporary Western forms of distress

There have always been people who seem to exhibit strong characteristics and who, because of circumstance, have been led into difficulties by those characteristics. This is the stuff of many novels and films, for example. As we have argued elsewhere in the book, rather than focus on somewhat heterogeneous diagnostic categories, we need to look at particular problematic experiences. For example, some people experience significant difficulties in relating to others, finding it hard to trust them, or going through a recurring pattern of getting close to people but then being overwhelmed by fear and pushing them away. To some extent, these kinds of feelings can be experienced by anyone, but they are often exacerbated if a person has had a bad experience in a relationship, particularly if their trust in another person has been compromised. Similarly, all of us from time to time might find it hard to contain our feelings: we may get angry at something someone has said or laugh out loud whilst reading a funny story in a quiet train carriage. However, some people may find it so hard to cope with their emotions that they cannot resist reacting impulsively if they get a sudden rush of emotion, or they may have to engage in acts of self-harm in order to 'let the feelings out'. Others may experience different kinds of difficulties in relating to others in that they seem quite hardened and do not seem to think or feel about the feelings of others. They may engage in risky behaviours, seeing themselves as mavericks, breaking social conventions. Sometimes this is combined with aggressive behaviour towards others. This kind of behaviour has been praised in the West, at least in certain domains of life – for example in some sports, during wartime and in business and finance – and it is also found in the criminal world (Taylor, 1984). Indeed, later in the chapter we will see how it may even be adaptive in these circles.

Some of the other problematic experiences seen as symptoms of personality disorder overlap with other categories of disorder, such as **obsessive–compulsive personality disorder** (where a person is purportedly preoccupied with perfectionism and orderliness) and **paranoid personality disorder** (where a person is seen as hostile and suspicious), so they do not have separate analogies in everyday life.

Prevalence

As we will see later in the chapter, many commentators have criticized the categories of personality disorder for poor reliability and validity. However, as Rogers and Pilgrim (2003) point out, since epidemiological research is based on psychiatric categories, we have to try to distil what we can about the underlying experiences and processes. Hopefully, future epidemiological research will focus on specific kinds and dimensions of experience (or symptom) rather than heterogeneous categories.

A large-scale British survey in 2000 reported that about one in 25 adults were assessed as having a personality disorder of some kind: approximately 44 per 1000 (Singleton, Bumpstead, O'Brien, Lee & Meltzer, 2001). The prevalence was slightly higher among men than women (54 per 1000 men and 34 per 1000 women) and the most prevalent type of personality disorder was obsessive compulsive personality disorder, with a prevalence of 19 per 1000 adults. Prevalence rates are generally higher in clinical populations: Zimmerman, Rothschild and Chelminski (2005) interviewed 859 psychiatric outpatients in the US and reported a prevalence rate of any disorder of 31.4% which rose to 45.5% if **Personality Disorder Not Otherwise Specified** (in which a person meets many criteria for personality disorder but does not fit into a particular sub-category) was included.

Huang et al. (2009) compared prevalence estimates based on the International Personality Disorder Examination used in the World Health Organization World Mental Health surveys of 21,162 people. The Western European results were based on samples from five countries (Belgium, France, Germany, Italy and Spain) and was only based on 'husbands and wives in the same family' (Huang et al., 2009, p. 46). Rates of 'any PD' (i.e. personality disorder) varied from 2.4% in Western Europe to 2.7% in Nigeria, 6.8% in South Africa, 7.6% in the USA and 7.9% in Colombia, with an average of 6.1%.

However, as we have noted, prevalence figures like these need to be interpreted with caution (which are discussed below), as personality disorder is a contested category: a fact that obviously has implications for assessment.

Psychiatric diagnosis

The history of diagnosing personality disorder

Bourne (2011) has described how modern notions of personality disorder developed from the idea that conduct seen as immoral was a result of some kind of pathological deficiency and disease. Theorists cited both moral and social environmentalist explanations, the former pointing to a decrease in self-restraint as a result of the decline in religious faith, and the latter to poor social conditions. Given that immoral individuals often appeared to have an intact reasoning ability, therapeutic efforts focused on increasing a person's self-control.

Personality disorders exist as a category in the two main diagnostic manuals, the DSM and the ICD. However, there are some differences both in how they are conceptualized and in the terminology and content of the various sub-categories. They have been a category in the DSM since its first edition in 1952, but over the course of the five editions there have been a number of changes both in how personality disorder is conceived as a major category and in the composition of its various sub-categories. We noted earlier Lane's (2009) observation that many definitions were adapted from those used by the US military. However, he points out that, whereas the military definitions conceptualized problems as ones of 'reaction', the DSM instead conceptualizes them as pertaining to 'personality'. He reports that what had been conceptualized in the first edition as 'traits' were transformed, in the second edition, into 'deeply ingrained maladaptive patterns of behavior' which were 'life-long' and 'determined primarily by malfunctioning of the brain' (American Psychiatric Association, 1968, pp. 41–2, code 301). As a result, characteristics that might have been seen as habits have, instead, come to be viewed as chronic and caused primarily by biological factors, leading to a more pessimistic prognosis.

A major change occurred with DSM-III, published in 1980, in which personality disorder was presented not as a discrete diagnostic category along with all the others but, rather, as lying on a second axis. This meant that it was seen as a disorder that could be experienced by a person with another diagnosis. In contrast, ICD-10 maintains personality disorder as a diagnostic category similar to other categories rather than as a separate axis like the DSM.

DSM-IV defines personality disorder as 'an enduring pattern of inner experience and behaviour that deviates markedly from the expectations of the individual's culture' (American Psychiatric Association, 2000, p. 689). This pattern is seen as manifested in two or more areas: cognition, emotional response, interpersonal functioning and impulse control. The pattern is seen as affecting a range of domains of a person's life, leads to distress or impairment in functioning, and is stable and long-term (i.e. extending back into childhood).

ICD-10's definition is very similar to that of DSM-IV: personality disorder is seen as present if 'the individual's characteristic and enduring patterns of inner experience and behaviour deviate markedly as a whole from the culturally expected and accepted range (or "norm")' (World Health Organization, 1992, p. 149), although here, such deviation only needs to be seen in one or more areas. The areas concerned are virtually identical to those of DSM-IV.

The current 11 DSM-IV and nine ICD-10 sub-categories can be seen in Table 13.2. There is quite a lot of overlap between the two systems, but there are some differences which First (2009) regards as lacking any conceptual basis. The DSM suggests that the sub-categories can be grouped into three clusters (see Table 13.3) and we include them here as, increasingly, studies refer only to the clusters rather than the sub-categories which compose them.

Only three of the DSM sub-categories have remained relatively unchanged over time: paranoid, schizoid and antisocial personality disorders were present in the first edition (see Table 13.2 for the core themes in these categories). Hysterical personality disorder was introduced in DSM-II but was renamed as 'histrionic' in DSM-III. Four sub-categories were introduced in DSM-III: schizotypal, narcissistic, avoidant and dependent. However, a number of disorders have been removed: 'passive–aggressive' (removed in DSM-IV); 'cyclothymic' (removed in DSM-III); 'inadequate' (removed in DSM-III); 'dyssocial' (removed in DSM-II; not to be confused with dissocial which is the ICD-10 term for antisocial personality disorder).

Problems with prevalence

As we noted earlier, prevalence rates for personality disorders should be interpreted with caution, as they are based on contested categories: a fact that has implications for assessment measures. The best prevalence data comes from studies of the general population, with samples as large as possible so as to both counteract any methodological deficiencies and be sensitive enough to detect rare conditions. As a result, we will be examining four recent prevalence studies: in Table 13.4 we can see some of their methodological details.

Table 13.5 shows that there are substantial differences in prevalence rates across the studies. Thus the most prevalent category varies from avoidant (Torgersen, Kringlen & Cramer, 2001) to antisocial (Samuels et al., 2002), obsessive–compulsive (Grant et al., 2004) or personality disorder not otherwise specified (Coid, Yang, Tyrer, Roberts & Ullrich, 2006). The overall rates themselves vary and, in the case of the Samuels et al. (2002) and Grant et al. (2004) studies, even vary within the same country. Thus Grant et al. (2004) state that '[o]verall 14.79% of adult Americans ... or 30.8 million, had at least one personality disorder' (p. 948). In Samuels et al.'s study the overall rate was 9% (although, interestingly, they note that the overall rate of ICD-10 personality disorder was only 5.1%). And for Coid et al.'s (2006) UK study the rate was half that, at 4.4%.

Table 13.2 **DSM-IV and ICD-10 personality disorder sub-categories**

DSM-IV	ICD-10	Key common themes
Paranoid	Paranoid	Pattern of suspiciousness and mistrust of others whose motives are seen as hostile
Schizoid	Schizoid	Withdrawal and detachment from others with a limited range of emotional expression
Schizotypal	This is placed under the schizophrenia, schizotypal and delusional disorder categories	Cognitive and perceptual distortions, eccentric behaviour and discomfort around others
Antisocial	Dissocial	Disregard for, and violation of, social obligations and others' rights
Borderline	Emotionally unstable: Impulsive type Borderline type	Unstable emotions and difficulties in close relationships leading to impulsive behaviour
Histrionic	Histrionic	Excessive emotionality and seeking of others' attention
Narcissistic	Not included	A need for admiration coupled with grandiosity and a lack of empathy for others
Avoidant	Anxious (avoidant)	Hypersensitivity to negative evaluation and rejection by others and feelings of insecurity and inadequacy leading to social avoidance
Dependent	Dependent	A strong desire to be taken care of by others and fear of abandonment leading to submissive, passively compliant and 'clinging behaviour'
Obsessive–compulsive	Anankastic	Preoccupation with a sense of control, perfectionism and a need for orderliness and a lack of flexibility in thinking
Personality disorder not otherwise specified	Personality disorder unspecified	The person meets the general criteria for personality disorder but is not classifiable in one of the current categories

Table 13.3 **DSM-IV clusters of personality disorder sub-categories**

Cluster A 'odd-eccentric'	Cluster B 'dramatic-emotional'	Cluster C 'anxious-fearful'
Paranoid	Antisocial	Avoidant
Schizoid	Borderline	Dependent
Schizotypal	Histrionic	Obsessive–compulsive
	Narcissistic	

How might we make sense of this variability? It is difficult to know whether these varied results are due to differences between countries (or between regions in the US) or to methodological differences between the studies. One difference between them was that they each used different assessments. Zimmerman et al. (2005) note that personality disorder prevalence rates are higher when structured interview methods are used rather than the unstructured interviews usually seen in everyday clinical practice. However, all the studies reported here used structured interview schedules, albeit different ones – although Torgersen et al. and Coid et al. (2006) used different iterations of the SCID. Clark and Harrison (2001) note, however, that the inter-rater reliability of these structured interviews varies considerably from study to study; this can

be seen in Table 13.4 (see also Table 13.6) in the ranges of the small number of studies they cite. The schedule used by Grant et al. (2004) had not been used in previous personality disorder research and no figures on convergent validity are available (i.e. the extent to which scores on it correlate with other personality disorder assessments). As a result we do not know if it is more likely to over-diagnose personality disorder than other assessments.

As we saw in Chapter 5, problems of reliability in diagnosis can lead to inconsistent and contradictory results. And as we will see later, problems of poor reliability and intercorrelations within personality disorders and between them and Axis I disorders mean that we need to treat prevalence figures with caution.

Given the high prevalence figures for personality disorder, some researchers have wondered whether associated behaviour might actually be functional in certain ecological niches, as we will see later in the chapter.

A number of problems with the notion of personality disorder have been reported by commentators. To a large extent these problems mirror those inherent in the notion of personality itself, as we saw earlier. Criticism of the personality disorder category is widespread amongst mental health professionals. In one survey of 146 psychologists and psychiatrists from 42 countries about their views of the DSM 'the personality disorders led the list of diagnostic categories with which respondents were dissatisfied' (Maser, Kaelber & Weise, 1991, p. 275): 56% of the professionals considered the category

Table 13.4 **Studies of the prevalence of personality disorder**

Study	Torgersen et al. (2001)	Samuels et al. (2002)	Grant et al. (2004)	Coid et al. (2006)
Location	Oslo, Norway	Baltimore, USA	USA	England, Scotland & Wales
Sample	2053 people from National Register	742 people re-interviewed from a 1997 study of prevalence (aged 34–94)	43,093 people participating in the National Epidemiologic Survey on Alcohol and Related Conditions	626 people participating in the British National Survey of Psychiatric Morbidity
Method	Structured Interview for DSM-III-R Personality	International Personality Disorder Examination	Alcohol Use Disorder and Associated Disabilities Interview Schedule-DSM-IV Version	Structured Clinical Interview for DSM-IV Axis II disorders
Mean inter-rater reliabilities of the assessment (from Clark & Harrison, 2001)	0.71 over five studies (range: 0.57–0.86)	0.71 over three studies (range 0.46–0.99)	–	0.89 from one study
Diagnostic system	DSM-III-R*	DSM-IV	DSM-IV (only assessed 7 of 10 disorders)	DSM-IV

Note: ***Only the disorders present in DSM-IV will be reported.**

Table 13.5 **The prevalence of DSM-IV personality disorders in Norway, USA and the UK**

Prevalence (%)	Torgersen et al. (2001)	Samuels et al. (2002)	Grant et al. (2004)	Coid et al. (2006)
Paranoid	2.4%	0.7%	4.41%	0.7%
Schizoid	1.7%	0.9%	3.13%	0.8%
Schizotypal	0.6%	0.6%		0.06%
Antisocial	0.7%	4.1%	3.63%	0.6%
Borderline	0.7%	0.5%		0.7%
Histrionic	2.0%	0.2%	1.84%	0%
Narcissistic	0.8%	0.03%		0%
Avoidant	5%	1.8%	2.36%	0.8%
Dependent	1.5%	0.1%	0.49%	0.1%
Obsessive–compulsive	2%	0.9%	7.88%	1.9%
Personality disorder not otherwise specified	–			5.7%
Any	13.4%*	9%	14.79%	4.4%

Note: ***Includes personality disorders not in DSM-IV.**

problematic. However, some of the most challenging criticism has come from people who have received this diagnosis.

Service users' views and experiences

As we noted in Chapter 7, 'service users' views have increasingly been sought by clinicians and researchers. Indeed Flanagan, Davidson and Strauss (2007) called for service users to be included in the workgroups drawing up the DSM and for the diagnostic criteria to include subjective experience, 'since people's experiences of a disorder may indicate major underlying processes and may differ from the characteristics

of the disorder objectively perceived by outside observers' (p. 391). Indeed, a small qualitative interview study by Miller reported that those with a diagnosis of borderline personality disorder gave highly consistent descriptions of their difficulties but these 'differed markedly from clinical descriptions' (p. 1215). For example,'[r]ather than having an impaired sense of self they seemed to have a sense of themselves as impaired' (p. 1216).

Compared with other forms of distress, the general public encounter people with a diagnosis of personality disorder relatively rarely. A survey of the Scottish public, for example, reported that only 3% knew of anyone with the diagnosis, compared with 7% for schizophrenia and 48% for depression (Braunholtz, Davidson & King, 2004). This may be related to the greater prevalence of depression but it may also be influenced by the stigma attracted by personality disorder and, of course, levels of stigma may well be influenced by how prevalent a mental health problem is. As with diagnoses of psychosis, when personality disorder is mentioned in the media it is often in association with violent crime: many service users dislike these diagnoses because they fear the negative reactions of others. In contrast to other mental health problems, personality disorder has historically attracted considerable stigma within mental health services, as we will see in more detail when we look at interventions.

In a qualitative study, Nehls (1999) interviewed 30 women with a diagnosis of borderline personality disorder. She identified three themes common in their experience. Firstly they described the negative effects of living with this diagnostic label. Secondly, they felt their personal experience was invalidated when professionals said their self-destructive behaviour was manipulative. Finally, they asserted that mental health services intentionally set limits on their access to care.

In one British study (Haigh, 2002), the researcher conducted focus groups with service users with a personality disorder diagnosis and consulted with professionals and mental health charities. The report noted that many service users felt labelled both by society and mental health professionals and noted that 'there was a strong feeling that many professionals did not understand the diagnosis, often equated it with untreatability and sometimes hid it from service users' (Haigh, 2002, p. 1). Not all of those with this diagnosis view it negatively, however. A service user writing in a magazine produced by the UK Virtual Institute of Severe Personality Disorder states:

> At the time I felt some sense of security in the fact that the experts had all agreed I had a personality disorder. The labelling process meant I had been ordered or normalized in some way.
>
> Anonymous (1999, p. 3)

Given that the notion of personality has become central to people's sense of self-identity it is, perhaps, not surprising that being told one's personality is disordered in some way is experienced as invalidating, as if one has failed at being a person in some fundamental way. In another study, 50 people in the UK with a personality disorder diagnosis were interviewed (Castillo, 2003). One of the author's participants stated that personality disorder was 'a label they put on people when they can't treat or figure out what's wrong with you' (Castillo, 2003, p. 69).

Commentators have noted that psychiatric diagnostic frameworks are deficit-based (Gergen, 1990). If identity is, as feminist writer Jill Johnston has put it, 'what you can say you are according to what they say you can be' (Johnston, 1974, p. 68), how might service users feel about themselves when applying the diagnostic criteria for personality disorder to themselves? As another of Castillo's interviewees commented:

> It is no wonder that those of us with a Personality Disorder diagnosis feel like second-, or more like third-class citizens (life's rejects). You only have to look at the definitions given in ICD 10 and DSM IV and read comments such as 'limited capacity to express feelings – disregard for social obligations – callous unconcern for others – deviant social behaviour– inconsiderate of others – incompetence

– threatening or untrustworthy'. The list is endless, but one thing that these comments have in common is that they are not helpful in any way.

> Castillo (2003, p. 128)

In a magazine article written by a black woman with a personality disorder diagnosis, the author makes a similar point:

> So if my personality is disordered, does that mean I'm: a) Less of a person, with no identity and a disordered character and personal qualities or b) Too much of a person with too strong an identity and a character and personal qualities that are too distinctive to fit into society's norms? I'm not sure which is worse. Either way I end up feeling like someone who clearly does not belong, whose personality is not what society finds acceptable and so bars me from fitting into the jigsaw of the world around me.
>
> Kalikhat (2004, p. 26)

A network has formed between mental health professionals critical of the diagnosis borderline personality disorder and women with this diagnosis, called Women at the Margins. Articles based on presentations given at a conference organized by Women at the Margins appeared in a special issue of the UK publication *Asylum: The Magazine for Democratic Psychiatry* (see below).

Disordered personalities or problems in relationships?

One of the major problems with the diagnostic criteria for personality disorder is whether the difficulties identified are best conceptualized as problems within an individual's personality or as problems between two or more people. For example, both Salima's and Carl's difficulties involve how they relate to other people. Family therapists have argued that many mental health problems are best conceptualized as problems *between* rather than *within* people (Burnham, 1986; Tomm, 1990). They

Special issue of *Asylum* magazine on women and borderline personality disorder. The illustration on the cover is by Maddy Smith

have proposed that traditional explanations in mental health are based on individualistic causal explanations in which A leads to B in a linear sequence. In contrast, systemic family therapists propose that, within a system like a family, circular causal models have more explanatory power. Circular causal explanations include the fact that when something happens it may cause something else, but it also simultaneously causes feedback. An example might help here: see Figure 13.2.

Imagine a heterosexual couple, Marion and Geoff, who are encountering difficulties. Geoff is depressed and tends to isolate himself at home a lot and withdraw. An individualistic approach to this might state that Geoff's withdrawal is characteristic of depressed people. However, imagine that we ask Geoff why he withdraws so much. He says that Marion approaches him a lot, trying to talk with him and asking him to help with some household tasks. He says he feels like she is nagging him and withdraws further. We could again adopt an individualistic approach. We could understand Marion as a nagging partner. Imagine that we were to talk to Marion and she explains that she gets worried when Geoff isolates himself. She fears this only increases his feelings of sadness and hopelessness. As a result, she tries to engage him in conversation to cheer him up and, as she has heard that physical activity can help reduce these feelings, she suggests helping with some household tasks. When Geoff withdraws further, this increases her concern and she steps up her efforts to engage him. Hearing from both Marion and Geoff, we can see that their actions are not just caused by their individual feelings and personalities but by their reactions to each other's actions. Figure 13.3 illustrates this circular explanation.

The American Psychiatric Association's research agenda document includes relationship problems in its chapter 'personality disorders and relational disorders' (First et al., 2002). It acknowledges that the DSM is based on an individualistic model and that to include relationship problems in the next edition 'would require a conceptual shift in the DSM's exclusive focus on the diagnosis of individual patients. In contrast, relational disorders always involve two or more individuals' (First et al., 2002, p. 157).

However, many of the diagnostic criteria reflect relational concerns:

- psychological dependence on other people (dependent personality disorder)

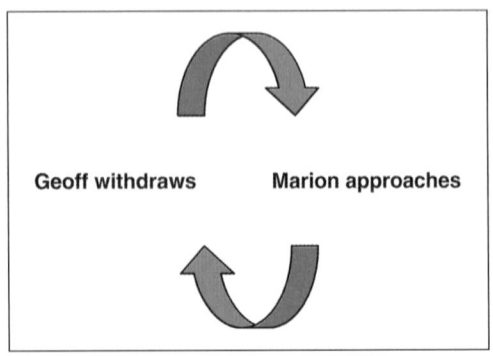

Figure 13.3 **Illustration of circular causality in Marion and Geoff's difficulties**

- a disregard for the safety of the self or others (antisocial personality disorder)
- unstable relationships (borderline personality disorder)
- going to great lengths in order to secure concern and support from others (histrionic personality disorder)

The preference of diagnostic manuals like the DSM for individualistic rather than relational descriptions may reflect a Western cultural preference (see later discussion) but next we address another problem: reliability.

The reliability of personality disorder diagnoses

In Chapter 5 we discussed some of the problems with the reliability of psychiatric diagnoses, particularly inter-rater reliability: in other words, whether two interviewers will give a person the same diagnosis. In many studies of reliability, agreement between raters is measured by the kappa (κ) statistic, producing a value of 0 if there is no agreement and 1 if there is perfect agreement. However, as Kirk and Kutchins (1992) note, this is a much-contested area with a lack of consensus even about what constitutes a good measure of agreement, some commentators asserting a value of 0.4 and below is fair and others arguing it is poor. They have attempted to make explicit the interpretative standards implied in a seminal paper by Spitzer and Fleiss (1974), in which average kappa values of 0.4 and below are seen as 'poor', values over about 0.7 are seen as 'only satisfactory', with the category between them labelled as 'no better than fair'.

There are many sources of variability in reliability studies, including how many raters are involved, across how many sites, how much training they are given, whether they conduct joint or separate interviews, how long a gap there is between interviews and even the subtly different wordings of diagnostic schedules (Zimmerman, 1994). Different assessment measures are also associated with different authors and research groups and this can have implications for research. Thus if a research group who know each other well and share assumptions about the phenomena they are examining achieve high reliability ratings, it is not that surprising. But this does not tell us much about how these criteria might be interpreted in everyday clinical practice, where the clinician does not have the author or research team present. It is worth noting that everyday clinical practice is also different from research trials, as the latter focus

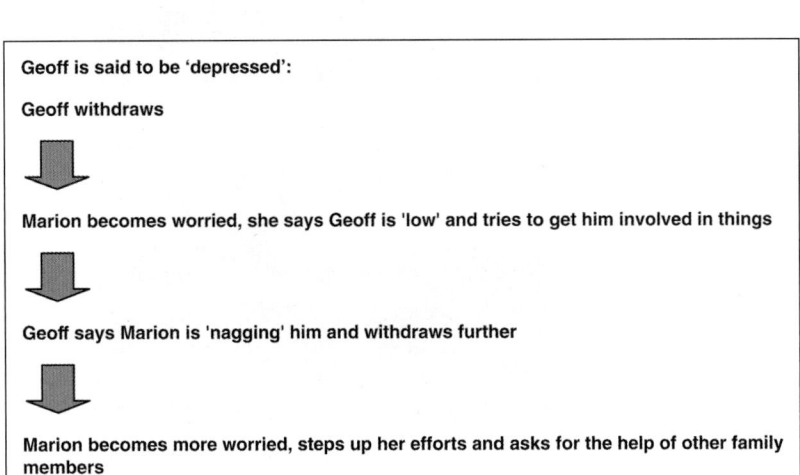

Figure 13.2 **A repetitive sequence in Marion and Geoff's relationship**

on highly selected samples, often with a high rate of attrition (i.e. the researchers end up with fewer participants than they started with). Mellsop, Varghese, Joshua and Hicks (1982) found lower levels of agreement between three psychiatrists independently using unstructured interviews in an ordinary clinical setting than the DSM-III field trials. However, Garb notes that 'there is evidence that a significant number of clinicians do not adhere to criteria when making diagnoses' (Garb, 2001, p. 2041) and Westen suggests that, when making axis I diagnoses, clinicians appear to ask questions derived from the DSM criteria, but they make axis II diagnoses 'by listening to patients describe interpersonal interactions and observing their behavior with the interviewer' (Westen, 1997, p. 895).

Low inter-rater reliability has been one of the most longstanding problems with the diagnosis of personality disorder. In a review of studies of pre-DSM-III-R reliabilities for personality disorder diagnoses, Grove (1987) cited inter-rater reliabilities ranging from 0.06–0.77 and described considerable variation in the methodological design and quality of studies. It was hoped that the conceptualization of personality disorders as lying on another axis (axis II) from other mental health problems would resolve this problem, but reliability has continued to be problematic. Perry (1992) reviewed the results of studies examining the reliability and diagnostic concordance of structured interview and self-report questionnaire methods in the diagnosis of personality disorder, reporting that agreement between these different

methods was low, which was 'not scientifically acceptable' (1992, p. 1645).

Table 13.6 shows the inter-rater and test-retest reliabilities for personality disorder diagnoses as measured using a variety of structured clinical interviews. The ranges are generally large.

Has DSM-IV led to any change? Nathan and Langenbucher (1999) report that the DSM-IV field trials had made 'no real progress in addressing the substantial reliability problems of personality disorders ...' (1999, p. 82). Coolidge and Segal (1998) note that 'poor diagnostic reliability has always been the bane of personality disorder assessment, and although agreement rates are as high as ever they are still modest at best' (pp. 594–6). Zanarini et al. (2000) conducted a reliability study using DSM-IV criteria. Although data were missing for several categories (as not all raters saw all interview tapes) inter-rater reliabilities remained variable, ranging from 0.58 for paranoid personality disorder to 1.00 for antisocial personality disorder, whilst test-retest reliabilities ranged from 0.39 (paranoid personality disorder) to 1.00 (narcissistic personality disorder).

Farmer (2000) also notes problems of overlap between the criteria in the different sub-categories of personality disorder, suggesting that 'at least a subset of DSM PDs represent variants of the same underlying construct(s), and as such cannot be differentiated at the symptom level' (2000, p. 834). This may account for some of the problems with co-morbidity (see below).

Table 13.6 **The reliability of personality disorder diagnoses***

Sub-category	Inter-rater reliability (κ) ranges of diagnostic interview schedules**	Test-retest reliability (κ) Ranges of diagnostic interview schedules***
Cluster A		
Paranoid	0.52–0.71	0.46–0.59
Schizoid	0.71	–
Schizotypal	0.55–0.86	0.61
Cluster B		
Antisocial	0.70–1.00	0.71–0.84
Borderline	0.75–0.96	0.40–0.85
Histrionic	0.71–0.87	0.43–0.74
Narcissistic	0.77–0.87	0.43–0.78
Cluster C		
Avoidant	0.45–1.00	0.67–0.71
Dependent	0.52–0.92	0.42–0.77
Obsessive–compulsive	0.36–0.92	0.24–0.56

Notes: **A figure was not available for every schedule in every sub-category. DSM-III diagnoses were used throughout, apart from the SCID-II test–retest reliability figures.

**The Diagnostic Interview for Personality Disorders (DIPD), Personality Disorder Examination (PDE), Personality Disorder Interview (PDI) and the Structured Interview for the DSM Personality Disorders (SIDP).

***The DIPD, the SIDP and the Structured Clinical Interview for DSM Personality Disorders (SCID-II).

Source: **Zanarini et al. (2000).**

It is usually the case that the broader the category, the more agreement between assessors. For example, there is more agreement between raters on whether a person does or does not have a personality disorder in general than on what type of personality disorder they have. As a result, researchers are increasingly presenting their results in the form of the three DSM-IV clusters rather than the different sub-categories. Many prevalence studies report results for the three DSM-IV clusters of personality disorders. But how reliable are the clusters? Tyrer et al. (2007) adapted a version of the clusters for the ICD-10. They reported test-retest reliabilities using two different assessments: 0.53 for cluster A, 0.78 for cluster B and 0.40 for cluster C. It seems that the presentation of findings in clusters only may mask the differences in reliability and validity of the sub-categories and assume more homogeneity between the sub-categories than is warranted.

Diagnostic instability over time

The DSM states that patterns indicating personality disorder need to be 'stable and of long duration' with an onset which 'can be traced back at least to adolescence or early adulthood' (American Psychiatric Association, 2000, p. 689). This, of course, assumes that the elements measured by personality assessments do not change over time. First et al. (2002) note that this stability is '[f]undamental to the validity of a personality disorder' (2002, p. 137). We have already discussed Lane's (2009) observation that when the DSM compilers constructed the criteria, they focused on chronicity. However, Farmer (2000) comments that 'long-term stability studies generally suggest modest to poor stability' (p. 835).

Two recent studies have investigated temporal stability in some detail. Baca-Garcia et al.'s (2007) sample consisted of 10,025 patients at a hospital in Spain who had been assessed using ICD-10 on at least ten occasions across a range of settings (emergency room, inpatient and outpatient) from 2000 to 2004. They noted that the 'temporal consistency of mental disorders was poor, ranging from 29% for specific personality disorders to 70% for schizophrenia' (p. 210). The stability between the first and last evaluation across all settings achieved a kappa of 0.3 which is considered very low.

Sanislow et al. (2009) conducted a study on 733 participants in the Collaborative Longitudinal Personality Disorders study, focusing on four sub-categories: schizotypal, borderline, avoidant and obsessive–compulsive. Data (including blind ratings) were collected at multiple points over ten years. Sanislow and colleagues noted that, initially, the different sub-types were differentiated. However, over time, the overall severity of problems and the differentiation between the sub-categories decreased and the correlations between them increased. Interestingly, the average initial ratings of the severity of participants' problems were defined as at 'sub-clinical' level anyway.

It therefore appears that personality disorder diagnoses may not be stable over time. Like Salima, some people receiving this diagnosis report having received a number of other diagnoses before, and poor temporal stability is an indication of this. Another reason may be the high level of co-morbidity found with personality disorder, and it is to this that we turn next.

Co-morbidity

In addition to her personality disorder diagnosis, Salima also heard voices. Traditionally, hearing voices (or auditory hallucinations) has been seen as related to psychosis, especially schizophrenia. Thus Salima might be given two simultaneous diagnoses. This is not the only way to view these experiences, of course. Salima tends to dissociate as a coping strategy and one could argue that voice-hearing is related to dissociation, as there are strong links between trauma, dissociation and psychosis (e.g. Moskowitz, Schafer & Dorahy, 2008). Some of these links were also discussed in Chapters 7 and 11.

Researchers have reported a high level of co-morbidity of the personality disorder category and other diagnostic categories. This is a problem, because if the majority of people with a diagnosis of personality disorder also have other mental health problems, this may indicate that the categorical system does not adequately capture people's experiences.

Zanarini et al. (1998) assessed 504 US inpatients with a diagnosis of personality disorder to see how many met the criteria for borderline personality disorder and then, how many of these could also be given an Axis I diagnosis. The interviewers were blind to clinical diagnosis and used a semi-structured research interview schedule. Of the 379 patients who met the criteria for borderline personality disorder, 125 also met DSM-III-R criteria for at least one non-borderline Axis II disorder. However, 96.3% met criteria for a mood disorder, 88.4% for an anxiety disorder, 55.9% for PTSD and 53% for eating disorder. Substance-use disorders were significantly more common among male borderline patients, while eating disorders were significantly more common among female borderline patients.

In Coid et al.'s (2006) UK study, 32% of participants identified as having a cluster A disorder were also identified as having a cluster B disorder, 48% of people with a cluster A disorder had a cluster C disorder whilst 27% of those with a cluster C disorder also had a cluster B disorder. Miller (1994) notes that the average person with a diagnosis of borderline personality disorder meets the criteria for two other personality disorders.

A number of explanations have been put forward to explain these very high levels of co-morbidity. Blais and Norman (1997) asked a US nationally drawn sample of mental health professionals to rate 280 patients known to them, using a symptom checklist containing all the DSM-IV personality disorder criteria. They reported the **discriminant validity** (i.e. the extent to which a measure differentiates between two or more constructs) to be weak and suggested that, as a result, levels of co-morbidity would remain high. In other words, the sets of criteria for the sub-types of personality disorder did not adequately discriminate, so the same symptom could attract more than one diagnosis.

This may partly explain the problems of correlation within the personality disorder sub-categories and with Axis I diagnoses, but there may be a more fundamental problem: the Axis I and II system itself. Livesley (2001), for example, suggests that this distinction lacks a clear rationale. Coolidge and Segal (1998) argue that, because of this division,

> [c]linicians were now more than subtly forced to evaluate each of their patients for a personality disorder. It was estimated that 40% to 50% of all patients with an Axis I diagnosis might also have an Axis II personality disorder.
>
> Coolidge and Segal (1998, p. 591)

Lynam and Widiger (2001) suggest that the levels of co-morbidity follow the pattern that might be expected from a dimensional perspective, utilizing the Five-Factor Model. However, as Widiger and Mullins-Sweatt (2009) note, the fact that 'persons meeting the diagnostic criteria for the same personality disorder may not even share many of the same traits' (p. 213) renders research into aetiology and intervention deeply problematic.

However, another possible explanation is that the experiences captured by lists of personality disorder symptoms represent sub-clinical levels of problems more commonly associated with other diagnostic categories. For example, symptoms of obsessive–compulsive personality disorder are remarkably similar to those of obsessive–compulsive disorder. Claridge (1997) has argued that the personality dimension of schizotypy may be linked to the development of later psychotic symptoms, so might the symptoms of schizotypal personality disorder be a sub-clinical representation of problems which, if they worsen, become seen as symptoms of psychosis? If a dimensional system of classification of problems were to be accepted, perhaps many of the current categories of personality disorder would become redundant.

Personality disorder not otherwise specified

This category is listed at the end of the DSM personality disorder category. It is intended to provide a personality disorder diagnosis for a person who meets the general criteria for personality disorder but does not fully meet the criteria of the other categories, or meets the criteria for a category removed in later editions of the DSM. In the ICD, 'unspecified personality disorder' may be given as a diagnosis if a person meets the criteria for several sub-categories. However, despite there being ten different sub-categories of personality disorder, this (or personality disorder unspecified for those using ICD-10) is one of the most commonly used. For example, this diagnosis was the third most frequent personality disorder amongst 1516 patients at Norwegian Therapeutic Day Hospitals (Wilberg, Hummelen, Pedersen & Karterud, 2008). It accounted for 17% of the total sample and 22% of those given another personality disorder diagnosis. In a Dutch study, Verheul, Bartak and Widiger (2007) interviewed 1760 patients referred for psychotherapy using the Structured Interview for DSM-IV Personality Disorders (SIDP-IV). They reported that the prevalence of personality disorder not otherwise specified was 21.6% if only one personality disorder could be given, or 70.8% if co-occurrence with 'formal' personality disorder was allowed. In contrast, in the general population the rate is lower: Coid et al.'s (2006) normal population study reported a prevalence of 5.7% (weighted).

First et al. (2002) note that there have been numerous changes in the coverage of personality disorder, with a number of new categories appearing and older ones disappearing. Given this, one reason for the high levels of co-morbidity reported is that clinicians may still want to use older sub-categories.

Personality disorder: whither or wither?

So the DSM personality disorders vary in their reliability and over time and appear to be highly co-morbid both with personality disorder sub-categories and with other DSM Axis I disorders. They have been criticized for adopting Euro-American-centric normative cultural values and, despite having many sub-categories, the non-specified category is one of the most frequently used in practice. It is, perhaps, no surprise that the British psychiatrist, Peter Tyrer (an editor of the *British Journal of Psychiatry*), stated in *Personality Disorders: Diagnosis, Management and Course*:

> The current categorical diagnoses of personality disorder ... [a]lthough these are now well known to most clinicians, mainly because of the well-oiled publicity that always accompanies a new edition of the Diagnostic and Statistical Manual of Mental Disorders (DSM) they, in the current language of medical science, have little evidence base.
>
> Tyrer (2000, p. 22)

However, despite these problems, the category of personality disorders has stayed with us. As the authors of a popular abnormal psychology textbook put it:

> Despite problems with the diagnosis of personality disorders, we should not dismiss the utility of trying to make such diagnoses. These disorders are prevalent, and they cause severe impairment in people's lives. Some of the problems with diagnosis stem from the fact that the personality disorders have been the subject of serious research for a much shorter time than have most of the other diagnoses considered in this book. As research continues, the diagnostic categories will most likely be refined, perhaps with a dimensional system, and many of these problems may be solved.
>
> Davison, Neale and Kring (2004, p. 411)

What is interesting here is that it is assumed that personality disorders constitute a meaningful category (for example, it is assumed they are prevalent) and that the problems with them are essentially ones of refining the diagnosis: these are common responses to criticism of diagnoses (e.g. Boyle, 2002). They have not been the focus of much research, although much of the research that has been conducted has been deeply critical of the category, even from those who find it useful, as the quote from Tyrer, above, shows. It is clear that, for commentators such as these, the dimensional system offers some hope. In the next section we will discuss some of the key issues in the debate about categorical and dimensional systems.

Categorical versus continuum models

As we saw in Chapter 5, the diagnostic classification systems have been criticized because they are based on a categorical system of diagnosis (where problems are seen as either absent or present) rather than a dimensional one (where problems are seen to lie on a continuum). We have argued that psychiatric categories are imperfect representations of people's experiences of distress. Community surveys suggest that the distressing experiences that people report do not fall into neat categories. Rather, they follow very broad patterns with overlaps (Mirowsky & Ross, 2003). This patterning seems more consistent with a dimensional approach and formulation-based models.

The personality disorder category has been a focus of much of this debate and this is, in part, why it was conceptualized on a different axis with DSM-III. However, this has not stemmed the debate. In a review, Trull and Durrett (2005) conclude that a dimensional approach has many advantages. However, despite this, the DSM developers have continued to conceptualize personality disorders as discrete categories, although in DSM-IV reference was made to the debate about whether a dimensional system would be better. However, the DSM compilers have proposed a mixed categorical and dimensional model for DSM-5 (see Box 13.2).

What might a wholly dimensional approach consist of? There are two broad approaches to what the dimensions

BOX 13.2
Towards DSM-5 and ICD-11

Currently both the DSM and ICD schemes are being revised. DSM-5 is likely to be published in 2013 and some proposed revisions have been made public, though these may well change over time. ICD-11 is not due to appear until 2015, and no proposed revisions to the personality disorder category have yet been published.

Following a number of years of sustained criticism of the categorical approach to classification, the DSM compilers have decided to adapt the current system. Current proposals at the time of writing suggest that they will not totally abandon a categorical approach, as some advocates for dimensional approaches have argued. Instead, they are proposing a hybrid dimensional-categorical model. The proposed new definition will view the essential features as impairments in identity and sense of self (e.g. self-directedness) and in the capacity for effective interpersonal functioning (i.e. empathy and intimacy). To diagnose a personality disorder, the impairments must meet all of the following criteria:

- A rating of mild impairment or greater in self- and interpersonal functioning on the Levels of Personality Functioning (from 'no impairment' to 'extreme impairment').
- Either:
  - a 'good match' or 'very good match' to one of five personality disorder types (antisocial/psychopathic; avoidant; borderline; obsessive–compulsive; schizotypal)
  - or a rating of 'quite a bit like the trait' or 'extremely like the trait' on one or more of the six personality trait domains (negative emotionality; detachment; antagonism; disinhibition; compulsivity; and schizotypy).
- Features are relatively stable over time and consistent across situations.
- They are not better understood as a norm within an individual's dominant culture.
- They are not solely due to the effects of a drug or a general medical condition.

In other words, the current personality disorder categories are to be cut by half. The introduction of personality trait domains is an attempt to draw on dimensional approaches. However, the six trait domains are different from the factors in the Five-Factor Model (extraversion; agreeableness; conscientiousness; neuroticism and openness to experience). They are assessed by looking for particular trait facets: the trait of 'suspiciousness', for example, falls under the negative emotionality trait domain.

The DSM-5 website (www.dsm5.org) indicates how current personality disorder categories could be conceptualized in the proposed system. As an example, we could look at antisocial personality disorder. This obviously matches the antisocial/psychopathic type. Associated traits might include those from the antagonism domain (e.g. callousness, aggression, manipulativeness) and from the disinhibition domain (e.g. irresponsibility and impulsiveness).

---

might be: dimensions of personality, or dimensions of particular types of problematic experience. We turn to personality-related dimensions first. Widiger and Mullins-Sweatt (2009) have recently proposed a dimensional approach to personality disorder, basing it on the Five-Factor Model of personality. Since each of the five factors has six facets, this means there are 30 different elements from which to construct such a profile. Widiger and Mullins-Sweatt provide different profiles of the DSM-IV personality disorders using the Five-Factor Model. McCrae and Sutin (2007) note that these approaches show promise but they also point out that such profiles have so far been based on the ratings of clinicians and researchers rather than on the results of an empirical study of problematic behaviours in the population. Morey, Gunderson, Quigley and Lyons (2000) asked 144 patients diagnosed with personality disorder (via a structured interview) to complete an inventory to assess the Five-Factor Model. They reported that the five-factor profiles they identified seemed quite similar across the disorders, suggesting that a dimensional approach might not address problems of co-morbidity and discriminant validity.

However, as Block (1995) notes, a focus on five globally defined factors risks losing important information from the items underlying those factors. Indeed Paunonen and Ashton (2001) demonstrated that the underlying facets were better predictors of 40 behaviours (ranging from religiosity and whether they donated blood to alcohol consumption and committing traffic violations). This is analogous to the argument that broad diagnostic categories such as 'personality disorder' may be less useful than delineating the specific underlying problematic experiences such as impulsivity.

As we have discussed earlier, the Five-Factor Model is not the only dimensional model of personality; there are others, including the circumplex model. It is worth noting that some personality dimensions specifically focus on certain kinds of distress. Thus, some researchers have suggested that psychosis-related problems might best be viewed as a personality trait. Thus Eysenck and Eysenck (1976) proposed a personality dimension of psychoticism whilst Claridge (1997) proposed a dimension of schizotypy.

First et al. (2002) identify a number of candidate dimensional models of personality and, whilst noting some overlap between them, they were concerned at the continued proliferation of models, arguing this might continue 'until an authoritative or governing body imposes or compels a uniform classification of general personality functioning' but, they reported, 'no comparable authority or control is present in the classification and assessment of general personality functioning' (First et al., 2002, p. 131).

In addition to dimensional theories of personality, the second type of dimensional approach might be to focus on different forms of problematic experiences, rather than personality traits, enabling us to locate people on dimensions representing emotional dysregulation, self-harming behaviour and so on. A dimensional assessment might indicate commonalities in a person's problems that cross the boundaries between categorical diagnoses, which is important given the problems of co-morbidity, noted earlier. For example, the kind of experiences that might be seen as indicative of obsessive–compulsive and avoidant personality disorder could be viewed as part of a continuum of mood-related distress. Similarly, experiences indicative of paranoid, schizoid or schizotypal personality disorder could be seen as existing along a dimension of psychosis-related experience. Such a dimension might be focused on a particular kind of experience, like hearing voices (see Chapter 11).

A significant hurdle for a dimensional approach is its clinical utility and this has often been the reason cited for not abandoning categorical systems. For example, First et al . (2002) comment:

> It would be difficult to replace the existing diagnostic categories with a dimensional model of personality (e.g., to have the model accepted by practicing clinicians) if the model was inconsistent with or failed to provide useful clinical information with respect to these fundamental validators [such as temporal stability, heritability, neurochemical correlates and childhood development] of a personality disorder diagnosis. (p. 137)

Of course, this statement assumes that the current categories provide reliable information in relation to these validators, an assumption questioned by other researchers, as we have noted.

One of the concerns in relation to utility is how complicated a dimensional system might be to use. For example, Allen Frances, who chaired the DSM-IV taskforce has argued that 'the multiple, complicated, confusing, and cumbersome systems suggested for DSM-5 would be far too unfamiliar and time consuming to ever be used by clinicians' (Frances, 2010). However, as we saw in Chapter 5, a categorical system is not necessarily any more clinically useful than a dimensional system. The categorical system is said to be useful because a diagnosis conveys important information. However, as we have seen, a categorical diagnosis on its own does not always convey such information if it is unreliable, or if two people can be given the same diagnosis when they have different sets of experiences ('symptoms'). Moreover, when it comes to treatment, as we will see in the last section of the chapter, the most robust indicators are changes in particular problematic experiences, not global ratings of the severity of personality disorder. As Manning (2000) puts it, 'superimposing a diagnosis on a person's symptoms and situation does not add, but rather removes, information' (p. 624). Saying a person has a diagnosis of personality disorder may not convey a lot of clinically useful information, as one will still need to ask for more detail about the particular forms of distress the person experiences.

For mental health professionals who use formulations rather than diagnoses, a dimensional approach may be much more useful than a categorical approach. A challenge for dimensional approaches, however, is whether the dimensions should be personality traits or a focus on kinds of experience. If personality traits begin to take up a more dominant role certain issues will be crucial: whether the elements of personality facet profiles identified are strongly correlated with each other, that they are robust and reliable over time and across situations, that it is possible to meaningfully discriminate between profiles and that they explain enough of the variance in problematic personality and relationship-related experiences. As Alwin et al. (2006) note:

> Whatever the advantages of dimensional representation, both categories and dimensions are essentially abstractions that provide no more than a global guide to dysfunction. While traits provide summary descriptions of behaviour, they do not explain behaviour because the causes of the trait-relevant behaviour remain to be identified. (p. 8)

Causal influences

As we discussed in Chapter 6, distress results from the complex interplay of a range of different influences. In this section we will describe some of the key influences identified by researchers.

First et al. (2002) report that DSM-III included four childhood antecedents of personality disorders, of which only one – that those with a diagnosis of antisocial personality disorder engaged in behaviour considered to be conduct disordered as children – has remained. They note 'it is unclear why there would be so much empirical support for one personality disorder with almost no data on the childhood antecedents for most of the other personality disorders' (p. 140). In this section, we will not be identifying the causes of personality disorder per se. Throughout the chapter we have identified a number of criticisms of the concept of personality disorder which render aetiological research on such categories problematic. However, as much of the research literature is framed as addressing the causes of particular disorders, we will have to distil what we can about causal processes from them. Where possible we will focus on causal processes linked to particular experiences (or symptoms), since this seems the most useful direction for future research. Indeed, it may be that on those occasions when researchers find a causal process linked with a diagnostic category, it is because that process strongly influences a particular kind of experience considered characteristic of or distinctive about the category. For example, the link between antisocial personality disorder and conduct disorder is not surprising, since the criteria required for each diagnosis are very similar; this might simply imply that their difficulties started earlier rather than that one disorder 'caused' another.

Culture and personality disorder

A recent systematic review noted that, within both inpatient and secure health settings, proportionately fewer black people than white people appeared to receive diagnoses of personality disorder (McGilloway, Hall, Lee & Bhui, 2010). However, in Singleton, Meltzer, Gatward, Coid and Deasy's (1998) survey (see Box 13.3) more black prisoners appeared to meet the criteria for personality disorder:

> Being born in the UK was also significantly associated with having evidence of personality disorder. Once country of birth had been taken into account, people who classed themselves in the Black or 'other' ethnic groups were more likely to be assessed as having personality disorder than those in the White group.
>
> Singleton et al. (1998, p. 27)

Similarly, Grant et al. (2004) reported that Native Americans were 1.6 times more likely to be diagnosed with avoidant personality disorder than white people. Black people, Native Americans, and Hispanic people were all more likely to meet the criteria for paranoid personality disorder than white people.

Does this indicate a difference of prevalence rates in the UK health and penal systems and between different ethnic groups? Possibly, but it also may reflect methodological differences. For example, Grant et al.'s prevalence rates in general are higher than other studies and use a novel assessment, so it is possible their study over-estimated prevalence rates, though whether that would cast doubt on the prevalence within different cultural

BOX 13.3

Is personality disorder common amongst prisoners?

In July 1997 the UK prison population was 61,944, of which approximately a third were on remand (i.e. awaiting trial), with the remainder sentenced. Singleton et al. (1998) interviewed 3142 male and female prisoners from 131 prisons, both sentenced and remanded. All received interviews administered by a trained lay person (rather than a clinician) and a self-completion SCID-II screening instrument (Structured Clinical Interview for DSM-IV). In addition, a fifth were routinely selected for clinical follow-up interviews with a psychiatrist or psychologist who administered the Structured Clinical Interview for DSM-IV (SCID-II). Findings reported for the whole sample are based on multiplying the results for this smaller sub-sample by five. Singleton et al. (1998) reported that of those who had a clinical interview, 64% of sentenced male prisoners met the criteria for a personality disorder

(78% of male remand prisoners). The highest prevalence of personality disorder sub-categories were: antisocial (49% of sentenced men, 63% of men on remand and 31% of female prisoners), paranoid (20% of sentenced men, 29% of men on remand and 16% of female prisoners) and borderline (20% of female prisoners).

These figures need to be interpreted with caution. For instance, since the criteria for antisocial personality disorder include rule-breaking, it is not surprising that a person with a history of criminal offending will meet them. Similarly, the participants were prisoners who were confined and denied liberty, and there is some evidence that this can have negative psychological effects on prisoners (Haney, 2006).

Singleton et al. (1998) reported that the two risk factors most strongly associated with a personality disorder diagnosis were economic activity status prior to coming to prison (i.e. those who were living off crime showed more evidence) and the number of stressful life events the prisoners had experienced:

the odds of meeting the diagnostic criteria for personality disorder rose to 9.50 for those who reported 11 or more events compared with those who had experienced none. The most commonly reported stressful events for all groups were:

- running away from home
- serious money problems
- separation or the breakdown of a steady relationship
- the death of a close relative or friend.

About half the women and about a quarter of the men interviewed reported having suffered from violence at home, while about a third of the women reported having suffered sexual abuse, compared with just under a tenth of the men.

A quarter of the female sentenced prisoners had been taken into local authority care as a child, as had a third of the men on remand. Two-fifths of the prisoners had left school before they were 16 and a tenth had left before they were 13. Perhaps as a result, from a quarter to a third of prisoners had not been working prior to coming to prison.

---

groups is unclear. Singleton et al.'s results were not based on actual diagnoses the prisoners had been given by health professionals whilst in prison, but were hypothesized on the basis of research interviews. We do not know, for instance, how their survey findings compare with the number of people who have actually been given a personality disorder diagnosis by health staff. McGilloway et al. (2010) suggest that the differential rates may be due to racial bias in diagnostic labelling. Cultural bias has been reported in the research literature It is possible that this might be more likely to affect everyday NHS practice when compared with interviews conducted by researchers.

Cultural bias in the diagnosis of personality disorders?

Mikton and Grounds (2007) asked 220 forensic psychiatrists in the UK to provide diagnoses for different case-vignettes. They noted that, using a vignette describing possible DSM-IV antisocial personality disorder, 'Caucasians' were 2.8 times more likely to be given a diagnosis of personality disorder than 'African–Caribbeans'. Interestingly, they reported that there was no apparent cultural bias in the diagnosis of borderline personality disorder, but diagnosis of antisocial personality disorder also varied according to the ethnicity of the clinicians.

Stowell-Smith and McKeown (1999a) were intrigued that more white than black people were given a diagnosis of psychopathy in the British forensic psychiatry system. They thought it was particularly noteworthy since black people are over-represented in the diagnosis of schizophrenia. They therefore conducted a discourse-analytic examination

of psychiatric reports on white and black patients in an English maximum security hospital. They noted that, in the reports on white patients, there was a particular focus on their inner worlds and the fantasies that were seen as driving their violent behaviour. In contrast, in the reports on the black patients, this narrative style was less prominent. Their inner subjective world was seen as less evident or influential; instead, there was a flat description of behaviour. In a sense, then, the question raised was whether fewer black people received a diagnosis of psychopathy because, in some ways, they were seen as having less of an inner world and less of a moral sense. A further study (Stowell-Smith & McKeown, 1999b), which used Q methodology to understand how mental health was viewed for black and white men by mental health professionals, service users and others, provided further support for this hypothesis. A recent study of the first 100 referrals to a London personality disorder service suggests this pattern may be continuing: whilst a third of the local resident population were Bangladeshi, only 9% of those referred to the service were (Garrett, Lee, Blackburn, Priestly & Bhui, 2011).

White Europeans – colloquially termed White Anglo-Saxon Protestants (or WASP) – have been one of the most dominant cultural groups in Western Europe and North America for the last few centuries and Gaines (1992) has argued that the DSM manual as a whole implies a particular kind of person: 'the ideal self is a gender- (male), ethnic- (German Protestant) and age-specific (adult)' (1992, p. 3). Thakker and Ward (1998) argue that the DSM's 'underlying thesis of universality based on Western-delineated mental disorders' (1998, p. 501) is problematic.

Alarcón, Foulks and Vakkur (1998) detail a number of ways in which culture can influence the diagnosis of personality disorder; for example, by not taking into account the base rate of behaviours in a wide range of cultures. However, Alarcón (1996) states that the DSM compilers ignored half of the recommendations made in relation to personality disorder by the NIMH-sponsored Culture and Diagnosis Group. Comments on paranoid and schizoid personality disorder were largely accepted, whereas 'those for narcissistic, histrionic, and avoidant were almost totally ignored' (1996, p. 260).

Cultural differences in the diagnosis of personality disorder are significant when comparing different countries. Paris (1998) notes that 'Axis II diagnoses have a different prevalence in different societies' (p. 289). An example of the differences between two cultures can be seen in Cooke, Michie, Hart and Clark's (2005) comparison of diagnoses of psychopathy in North America (Canada and the USA) with those in the UK, using data from offenders and some forensic psychiatric patients. Comparing scores on Hare's (1991) *Psychopathy Checklist–Revised* (PCL-R) they reported that the factor structure was similar in both data sets. However, they found that the diagnosis in North America required a higher score. They also reported that symptoms related to emotions were more reliable across cultures whereas those relating to interpersonal style (e.g. arrogant and deceptive or impulsive and irresponsible behavioural styles) did not discriminate equally well. Thus, even in two very similar cultures (with regard to language and history) there can be important differences. However, in recent studies, some researchers have argued that personality disorders may be particularly prevalent in particular cultural contexts like the business world or the military.

Psychopaths in suits? The search for the 'successful psychopath'

Given that we find many people who meet the criteria for psychiatric diagnoses in the general (i.e. non-clinical) population, researchers have long wondered whether the same is true of antisocial personality disorder and psychopathy. These questions have been voiced more loudly in the wake of recent financial crises and evidence of fraud and malpractice in the world of banking and finance. There is a popular image that, to be successful in business, one needs to be uncaring. As Mr Burns says in the cartoon series The Simpsons, 'I'll keep it short and sweet. Family, religion, friendship. These are the three demons you must slay if you wish to succeed in business' (Season 8, Episode 21, 'The old man and the Lisa').

Unfortunately clinical researchers tend to do their research with clinical or prison populations, so they are unlikely to meet those who might be considered to be 'successful psychopaths'. However, a number of studies have shed light on this question.

Lynam, Whiteside and Jones (1999) gave *Levenson's* (Levenson, Kiehl & Fotzpatrick, 1995) *Self-Report Psychopathy Scale* (LSRP) to 1958 US undergraduates. The scale includes items like 'for me what's right is whatever I can get away with' and 'success is based on survival of the fittest; I am not concerned about the losers'. They found that 96% of the items were endorsed by more than 10% of the sample. Indeed, the mean endorsement rate across all items was 24%, so it would seem that these tendencies are well represented amongst college students at least.

Are there domains where people exhibiting these tendencies might find success? What kinds of ecological niches would be most conducive? Two that have been suggested are the military and the business world.

In his book *On Killing* (Grossman, 1995), Lt. Col. David Grossman, a former Army Ranger, West Point Psychology Professor and Professor of Military Science, argues that it is intensive training that encourages soldiers to overcome an inhibition against killing. However, in their study of soldiers from the Second World War, Swank and Marchand (1946) stated that 2% could be classified as 'aggressive psychopaths'.

There has been rather more research into business people. Babiak and Hare (2007), for instance, discuss a number of case studies of successful business people who appear to meet many of the criteria for **psychopathy**. Mullins-Sweatt, Glover, Derefinko, Miller and Widiger (2010) surveyed lawyers and two groups of psychologists (those interested in applying psychology in the legal realm and clinical psychology academic staff). Participants were asked if they had ever known anyone they would characterize as a successful psychopath. Participants supplied a number of examples, including a police detective, a university dean, a mayor and successful academics. Interestingly, whilst half of the lawyers chose a client, the modal choice for both psychologist groups was a current or former colleague! They concluded that 'the successful psychopath is distinguished from the unsuccessful (or prototypic) psychopath via differences in conscientiousness' (pp. 556–7). In other words, those who might be considered to have psychopathic tendencies and to be successful tended also to be conscientious.

Babiak, Neumann and Hare (2010) used data gathered from 203 people participating in US corporate management development programmes. The authors completed PCL-R ratings based on face-to-face meetings, observations of work interactions and other evidence. For some participants, they had the results of 360-degree assessments, in which the perceptions of the person's peer-workers and others were recorded. They also had access to performance appraisals conducted by the employing companies. Eight (3.9%) of the sample had PCL-R scores of 30 or higher, which is the common research threshold for psychopathy, higher than in other community samples. They were of quite high status: vice-presidents, directors, managers and supervisors in companies. Babiak et al. reported that psychopathy was positively associated with in-house ratings of charisma/presentation style (e.g. creative and strategic thinking with good communication skills) but negatively associated with ratings of responsibility/performance (e.g. being perceived as a team player). They suggested that the fact that some companies perceived 'psychopathic executives' as having leadership potential despite some poor ratings from colleagues was evidence 'of the ability of these individuals to manipulate decision makers' (p. 190).

Board and Fritzon (2005) wanted to investigate whether business managers exhibited psychopathy. They defined **Psychopathic Personality Disorder** (PPD) as represented by emotional detachment (superficial charm, egocentricity and remorseless use of others) and antisocial behaviour. They compared three samples: 39 male business managers (recruited via informal and business networks); 768 male patients from a maximum security psychiatric hospital with a legal classification (under the 1983 Mental Health Act) of mental illness ('MI patients'); and 317 male patients from the same hospital with a legal classification of PPD. All participants completed the MMPI scales for DSM-III Personality Disorders, which produce scores for the eleven different sub-categories.

On only the histrionic items did the business managers score significantly higher than the two clinical samples (although scores on the compulsive and narcissistic scales approached significance). For the remaining categories, the patient groups either had significantly higher scores or there was no significant difference. Figure 13.4 shows the mean scale scores of the four participant groups for five of the eleven personality disorder sub-categories Board and Fritzon studied: antisocial, borderline, histrionic, narcissistic and schizotypal. One can see that the business managers' scores on the histrionic items are higher than the other groups. Board and Fritzon suggest that a business environment is not hostile to the kinds of characteristics associated with the histrionic (e.g. superficial charm, insincerity, egocentricity, manipulativeness) and possibly with the narcissistic (grandiosity, lack of empathy, exploitativeness, independence) and compulsive (perfectionism, excessive devotion to work, rigidity, stubbornness and dictatorial tendencies) sub-scales on the MMPI. However, by way of comparison, the scores on schizotypal items are much lower for the business managers, suggesting that perhaps these characteristics may be less conducive to a business environment. They note that

> In summary, the senior business manager group appears to possess, to a degree that is equivalent to and at times exceeds the PPD and MI patient groups, elements of psychopathic PD that have been referred to as the emotional components, and they closely resemble characteristics known to be beneficial to achieving in a senior management role. However, the group does not have, to a comparable degree, elements of psychopathic PD that have been referred to as the deviant lifestyle components, characteristics that perhaps reflect more of the impulsive

acting out. Nor does the senior business manager group PD profile contain, to any relatively equivalent degree, elements associated with the schizotypal, schizoid, avoidant and dependent scales.

Board and Fritzon (2005, p. 26)

Bakan (2004) argues that one could view corporations themselves as psychopathic (see, for example the revelations in the early part of the 21st century of Enron executives' greed and criminality or the actions of key figures in the financial industry that prompted the 2008 economic crisis) and, in his book, he invites Hare (a psychopathy researcher) to compare company behaviour with his checklist, finding a good match. Indeed, Elliott (2010) has called for research examining links between personality traits and embezzlement and fraud in business. In his book *The Psychopath Test* (Ronson, 2011) journalist Jon Ronson seeks out those in power to determine if they could be considered to be psychopaths. Findings like these have led the commentator George Monbiot to opine:

> [I]t seems to me that if you have psychopathic tendencies and are born to a poor family, you're likely to go to prison. If you have psychopathic tendencies and are born to a rich family, you're likely to go to business school.

(Monbiot, 2011)

These kinds of findings are a salutary reminder of the importance of the social and cultural context. However, might there be differences between ethnic groups that are not simply due to cultural bias? For example, in a US study, Combs, Penn and Fenigstein (2002) reported that African–Americans scored higher than non-Hispanic Whites on a paranoia scale. How might we understand this? Firstly, one must bear in mind that this was a research study on the normal population, not a study of personality disorder per se, but it might explain how cultural influences affect the judgements of those seeking help as well as diagnosers. Over recent years, a number of studies have indicated that a higher rate of paranoia may reflect the greater exposure of black people in the West to discrimination (Janssen et al., 2003; Read, 2004). The African American family therapist Kenneth Hardy has noted that '[w]hat is seen through one lens as psychological paranoia, in another can be seen as a logical result of discrimination and racism' (Hardy, 2001, p. 54). This has led to the development of the notion of a 'healthy cultural paranoia' which is 'an adaptive mechanism for coping with a life that is plagued by prejudice and discrimination' and which 'must be differentiated from paranoia as a functional illness' (Newhill, 1990, p. 177) and, indeed, it has received official recognition (American Psychological Association, 1993).

Gender and personality disorder

There appear to be gender differences in the rates with which men and women are given a diagnosis of one of the sub-categories of personality disorder. For instance First et al. (2002) report that:

> Paranoid, schizoid, schizotypal, antisocial, narcissistic, and compulsive personality disorders are more commonly diagnosed in males. Dependent, histrionic, and borderline personality disorders are more commonly diagnosed in women.

First et al. (2002, p. 155)

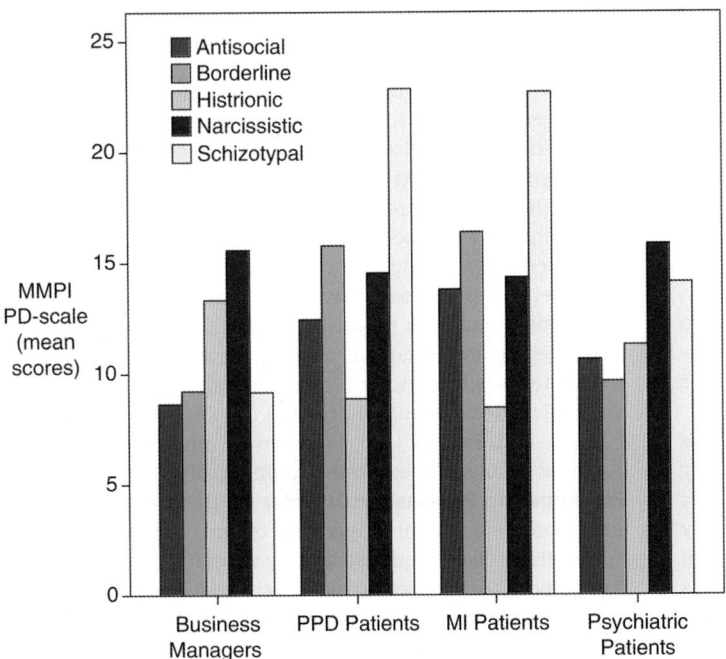

Figure 13.4 **The distribution of five selected personality disorders across the four groups of participants in Board and Fritzon's (2005) study**

According to DSM-IV (American Psychiatric Association, 2000), antisocial personality disorder is more commonly diagnosed in men, whilst 75% of those with a borderline personality disorder diagnosis are women. These findings are primarily based on those who are diagnosed in routine clinical practice. In this respect, then, Salima and Carl's diagnoses are very representative. According to Grant et al.'s large US study of the general population (2004), avoidant, dependent and paranoid personality disorders were significantly more likely to be diagnosed in women whilst antisocial personality disorder was diagnosed more in men. They reported no sex differences in obsessive–compulsive, schizoid or histrionic personality disorders. A study conducted on a normal population sample in the UK (Coid et al., 2006) indicated the prevalence rates for men and women shown in Table 13.7.

In general the prevalence rates are higher for men than for women. However, for both men and women the most prevalent categories are personality disorder not otherwise specified (with men 1.8% higher than women) and obsessive–compulsive personality disorder (with men 1.3% higher than women). Interestingly, more men met the criteria for borderline personality disorder than women. However, it is important to emphasize that though such studies may tell us about the distribution of particular experiences in the population, they do not tell us either whether they would have been diagnosed in this way by clinicians nor whether people would have sought help for these problems, and there is substantial evidence that, in general, women are much more likely to seek help in relation to mental health (Oliver, Pearson, Coe & Gunnell, 2005). This may be one of the reasons rates of referral to health professionals are different from those reported in community surveys.

How are we to understand these kinds of gender differences? One possibility is that the findings are an artefact of gender bias.

Table 13.7 **Prevalence rates for personality disorder by gender**

Prevalence (%)	Male	Female	All
Paranoid	1.2%	0.3%	0.7%
Schizoid	0.9%	0.8%	0.8%
Schizotypal	0.02%	0.1%	0.06%
Antisocial	1%	0.2%	0.6%
Borderline	1%	0.4%	0.7%
Histrionic	0%	0%	0%
Narcissistic	0%	0%	0%
Avoidant	1%	0.7%	0.8%
Dependent	0.2%	0.02%	0.1%
Obsessive–compulsive	2.6%	1.3%	1.9%
Personality disorder not otherwise specified*	4.8%	6.6%	5.7%
Any	5.4%	3.4%	4.4%

Note: ***Fulfils 10 or more personality disorder criteria but not diagnosis of any specific disorder.**

Source: **Coid et al. (2006).**

Gender bias in the diagnosis of personality disorders?

Might diagnosers be biased by stereotypical assumptions about gender and gender roles? There is substantial evidence that they are (Ali, Caplan & Fragnant, 2010; Caplan & Cosgrove, 2004; Marecek & Hare-Mustin, 2004; Russell, 1995). Widiger (1998) suggests that further research is needed to clarify the different kinds of biases at work. One key bias is in evidence when a different diagnosis is given, even when two people meet the same criteria, solely on the basis of gender. In an experimental study, Ford and Widiger (1989) found that a sample of US psychologists under-diagnosed histrionic personality disorder in men and antisocial personality disorder in women. Nuckolls (1992) develops an account of the cultural history of the antisocial and histrionic disorders. He argues that they are extreme forms of the dominant Western cultural stereotypes of the 'independent' male and the 'dependent' female. It is possible, then, that clinicians are influenced by these stereotypes when making diagnoses.

Rienzi and Scrams (1991) asked male and female university students to assign gender to six descriptions of DSM personality disorders. They reported that men tended to be diagnosed as paranoid, antisocial and compulsive whilst women tended to receive diagnoses of histrionic and dependent personality disorders. They argued, on the basis of their study, that this occurred because these diagnoses mapped onto gender-specific role expectations and stereotypes. Thus, within society in general, women are encouraged to prioritize intimate relationships and to be emotionally expressive, whilst men are 'directed to be clever and aggressive but not antisocial, to be sophisticated and suspicious but not paranoid' (Rienzi & Scrams, 1991, p. 978).

Adler, Drake and Teague (1990) asked 46 clinicians to rate personality traits and disorders in two versions of a case vignette constructed to meet DSM-III Axis II diagnoses of histrionic, narcissistic, borderline and dependent personality disorder, differing only in the sex of the patient. They reported that the clinicians were more likely to diagnose borderline personality disorder in women and antisocial personality disorder in men. Since the descriptions were identical apart from gender, this suggested a gender bias. Interestingly, the clinician's own gender had no impact on the process.

However, as Garb (2001) notes, another source of bias occurs if diagnostic criteria 'are more valid for one group than for another (e.g. if diagnostic criteria are more valid for males than for females)' (p. 2041). Kutchins and Kirk (1999) discuss two examples in which assumptions about gender appear to influence theory and practice in this area. They describe how the 1985 draft version of DSM-III-R contained a new category of 'Masochistic Personality Disorder', which was subsequently renamed and appeared in a special appendix of the manual as **'Self-Defeating Personality Disorder'** (SDPD) when it was finally published in 1987. The definition stated that it was:

> A pervasive pattern of Self-Defeating behaviour, beginning in early adulthood and present in a variety of contexts. The person may often avoid or undermine pleasurable experiences, be drawn to situations or relationships in which he or she will suffer, and prevent others from helping him or her
>
> Kutchins and Kirk (1999, p. 135)

Kutchins and Kirk note that this proposed category attracted a great deal of criticism. Feminist critics such as Caplan (1985) argued that the notion of masochism led to victim-blaming in cases of domestic violence in heterosexual couples: that responsibility would be placed on the abused woman for not leaving her partner rather than on the man for his violence. There can be very complex dynamics in such relationships (e.g. Goldner, Penn, Sheinberg & Walker, 1990) and women's relative lack of power is also a factor: for instance, many women lack the financial means to escape violent relationships.

Although SDPD (see also Box 5.1) appeared in the appendix of the DSM-III-R it did not appear in DSM-IV, published in 1994, though only following much debate. In 1989 during the DSM-IV deliberations, psychologist Paula Caplan and sociologist Margrit Eichler proposed the category of **'Delusional Dominating Personality Disorder'** (DDPD) in order to highlight how assumptions about gender influenced the development of psychiatric diagnosis – this was later elaborated on more fully in Pantony and Caplan (1991). This category included criteria like 'a tendency to feel inordinately threatened by women who fail to disguise their intelligence' (Kutchins & Kirk, 1999, p. 168). Although neither SDPD nor DDPD appeared in DSM-IV, critics point to the proposal of SDPD as evidence of how negative gender stereotypes can exert an influence on how we conceptualize distress.

So do reported associations between gender and personality disorder reflect something about how men and women are different in relation to their distress? Or, given the evidence of gender bias in the diagnosis of personality disorders, do they reflect something about the influence of gender stereotypes? Or do both explanations have some validity?

The kind of differences in early life experience we saw in Salima and Carl's stories at the start of the chapter may provide one explanation. In Castillo's (2003) small study, 73% of the men with an antisocial personality disorder diagnosis had experienced early emotional abuse and 55% early violent abuse, but only 9% reported experiences of sexual abuse. For the women with a diagnosis of borderline personality disorder, 70% reported experiences of sexual abuse whilst 87% reported early emotional abuse and 51% early violent abuse. One hypothesis is that sexual abuse may be more likely to lead to the dissociative experiences and difficulty in coping with emotions associated with borderline personality disorder, while physical and emotional abuse may lead to difficulties more associated with antisocial personality disorder.

Based on findings of apparent gender differences in prevalence rates as seen by clinicians, in particular the apparent contrast between antisocial personality disorder and borderline personality disorder, Paris (1997) has argued that antisocial personality disorder and borderline personality disorder may represent different aspects of the same disorder but that their expression is mediated by a tendency for women and girls to internalize difficulties while men and boys externalize them. The reason for this tendency is unclear but it may well be that, since violence and aggression are more socially sanctioned for men, it is more socially acceptable for them to engage in actions which may attract the antisocial personality disorder label.

Social inequality

As we saw in Chapter 6, social inequality is implicated in the development of a number of forms of mental distress. In particular, there appears to be an association between a range of social problems and countries with a bigger gap between the rich and the poor (e.g. Wilkinson & Pickett, 2009). Pickett and Wilkinson (2010) have presented material specifically showing the relationship between income inequality and mental health. It is, perhaps, no surprise, then, that those who receive a diagnosis of personality disorder are likely to have experienced social inequality.

Low socio-economic status has been reported as a causal factor by a number of studies (e.g. National Collaborating Centre for Mental Health, 2010). Prevalence studies of the general population also report a strong link between low socio-economic status and experiences associated with the diagnosis of personality disorder (Grant et al., 2004). Coid et al. (2006) reported a link between such experiences and being 'unemployed or economically inactive, of lower social class, living in rented accommodation and living in an urban area' (p. 427). In Box 13.3 we noted that Singleton et al. (1998) reported that the two most important causal factors were economic activity status and the number of stressful life events people had experienced. As we saw with Carl's and, to some extent, Salima's story, a poorer background means that one is less protected from the stresses of everyday life. Research into the link between social inequality and the kind of problems which might be seen associated with the diagnosis of personality disorder is at an early stage and hampered by problematic diagnostic constructs. One possibility is that social inequality prevents families from providing a sufficiently nurturing environment.

Family and childhood influences

I had a doctor ... do a personality test on me yeah? It was ninety questions long and it was like, 'yes, no, yes, no' questions yeah? And at the end of it he turned round and said I have a personality disorder. I said you don't even know what I went through when I was in care: I've never really had no family, I've had foster parents for nine years – very good people, yeah? But I've never really had no support in my life. I've been brought up the hard way. And I says you don't know none of that. I've never been to prison. I gave up drugs. I gave up alcohol, really. So I'm quite responsible. And you're gonna sit there and tell me I've got a personality disorder? I think I've turned out quite okay considering what I've been through.

Sam, (pseudonym) mental health service user in Taylor (2011)

Kessler et al. (2010),in their survey of over 50,000 people in a World Health Organization study, reported that childhood adversities were highly prevalent and interrelated. Adversities related to family relationships (e.g. parental mental health problems, childhood abuse and neglect) were the strongest predictors of a range of distress. They estimated that 'childhood adversities account for 29.8% of all disorders across countries' (Kessler et al., 2010, p. 378).

Both Salima and Carl experienced abuse as children – Carl experiencing physical abuse whilst Salima experienced this together with sexual abuse. Experience of childhood physical and sexual abuse, neglect and maltreatment are associated with personality disorder diagnoses. Johnson, Cohen, Brown, Smailes and Bernstein (1999) interviewed 639 youths and their mothers from two counties in the state of New York in 1975, 1983, 1985 to 1986, and 1991 to 1993. Evidence of childhood physical abuse, sexual abuse and neglect was obtained from New York State records and from participant self-reports in 1991 to 1993, when they were young adults. Personality disorders were assessed in the children between 1991 and 1993 using questions designed to focus on particular kinds of experience. Participants with documented childhood abuse or neglect were more than four times as likely to be diagnosed with a personality disorder in early adulthood as those who were not abused or neglected after age, parental education and parental psychiatric disorders were controlled statistically. Childhood physical abuse, sexual abuse and neglect were each associated with elevated symptoms linked with a variety of personality disorders during early adulthood, after other types of childhood maltreatment were controlled statistically. Of the 12 categories of DSM-IV personality disorder symptoms, ten were associated with childhood abuse or neglect.

Some types of childhood maltreatment appeared to be more related to experiences associated with the diagnosis of some personality disorders than others. Documented physical abuse was significantly associated with experiences associated with diagnoses of both antisocial and depressive personality disorders, whilst both childhood maltreatment and neglect were significantly associated with experiences associated with diagnoses of antisocial, borderline and narcissistic personality disorders. Evidence of sexual abuse (from either New York State records or self-report) was associated with elevated symptom levels of borderline, histrionic, depressive and total personality disorders after controlling for the gender of the young person, parental education, parental psychiatric disorders, physical abuse and neglect.

This study suggests that particular types of abuse may be linked to particular kinds of experience. One explanation of this is that the coping strategies called upon by children to cope with abuse may vary according to the type of abuse. For example, sexual abuse may be experienced as more psychologically invasive than physical abuse and may lead to dissociative strategies. Physical abuse may be more likely to lead to a more intense emotional response (e.g. anger). It may also lead to behavioural disinhibition, which Paris (2000) has suggested may be one of the factors explaining the trajectory from having conduct disorder-related problems as a child to having problems associated with a diagnosis of antisocial personality disorder as an adult. Behavioural disinhibition might be signified by aggressive, impulsive and irritable behaviours. Some authors have argued that, given the high proportions of people abused as children who attract a personality disorder diagnosis, their distress might be better seen as a way of coping with severe trauma rather than as a personality disorder (Castillo, 2003; Plumb, 2005; Warner, 2000, 2009; Warner & Wilkins, 2003): see Box 13.4.

Studies have indicated that the longer-term effects of childhood abuse depend to some extent on how caregivers respond (Horwitz, Widom, McLaughlin & White, 2001): we saw how, in Salima's case, her mother did not believe her and, instead, supported her abusive father. Zanarini et al. (2000) reported that people with a diagnosis of borderline personality disorder were significantly more likely than controls to report that caregivers of both sexes denied the validity of their thoughts and feelings, failed to provide them with needed protection, neglected their physical care, withdrew from them emotionally and treated them inconsistently. Linehan (1993) sees an invalidating family environment as key to the development of experiences associated with a diagnosis of borderline personality disorder. The UK National Institute for Health and Clinical Excellence (NICE – see Chapter 8) guidelines for borderline personality disorder conclude that the lack of a nurturing environment and stability may mediate between childhood

---

BOX **13.4**

Self-harm: symptom or coping strategy?

Self-harm used to be a way to get rid of the feelings inside of me. To get out all the hurt, anger and pain that I was feeling. The rush it gave, the sense of feeling better was always so short lived. So short that I was doing it many times. I've been through times when I haven't been able to get up in the morning and function during the day without self-harm. But not now. Now the longer I can manage without it the better. I'm trying to get my life 'normal' though for me self-harm is normal. Something I have always done to mask my feelings. I don't know how to release my feelings in any other way and find talking exceptionally difficult.
Mental Health Foundation (2006, p. 17)

My emotions can vary rapidly and be very intense. If in an emotionally charged situation, I will either during or shortly after harm myself. I'm not good at dealing with emotions or communicating mine to others.
Mental Health Foundation (2006, p. 22)

Many of those with a diagnosis of borderline personality disorder may attempt suicide or may injure themselves (e.g. by cutting themselves) on repeated occasions. This is obviously of concern to health professionals, who often find it bewildering that someone should do this to themselves (Hadfield, Brown, Pembroke & Hayward, 2009) and can lead to negative reactions to the person from health staff (Pembroke, 2007).

Castillo (2003) noted that, amongst the women with a borderline personality disorder diagnosis in her sample, 87% reported experiencing early emotional abuse, 70% reported early sexual abuse and 51% reported early violent abuse. In her small qualitative study, Miller (1994) reported that her participants used a variety of coping strategies, such as dissociation, which corresponded with the symptoms associated with a diagnosis of borderline personality disorder. Thus, the use of certain coping strategies may attract this kind of diagnosis. As a result of findings like this, a number of service users and professionals have argued that what are commonly regarded as 'symptoms' of personality disorder (e.g. dissociation and self-harm) may represent strategies that people used to cope with the abuse they experienced as children, when they were unable to escape and lacked control (Shaw & Proctor, 2005; Spandler & Warner, 2007; Warner, 2000, 2009; Warner & Wilkins, 2003).

As we saw in Chapter 7, service user groups like the National Self Harm Network have developed and survivors have begun to share both experiences and ways of managing self-harm (Cresswell, 2005). For example, some service users have described harm minimization strategies: ways of reducing the physical health risks (Pembroke, 2007).

abuse and experiences associated with a diagnosis of personality disorder (National Collaborating Centre for Mental Health, 2009).

As we have seen, there is considerable evidence linking childhood abuse and forms of distress associated with a diagnosis of personality disorder. We have also seen evidence that how families respond to abuse may also be a factor. However, it is clear that a range of childhood adversities can lead to mental health problems in later life. The NICE guidelines on antisocial personality disorder suggest that other family factors may also be important; in particular, antisocial behaviour by parents and harsh parenting styles have been found to be associated with this diagnosis (National Collaborating Centre for Mental Health, 2010). In both Carl and Salima's stories there was evidence of harsh parenting styles. Of course, if a child responds to a harsh parenting style with antisocial behaviour, this is likely to lead to further harsh parenting, and so on. In addition to this we saw that Salima witnessed domestic violence at home, whilst Carl saw his father committing crime and going to prison.

Researchers have indicated that the attachment relationship between children and caregivers may also be important in the development of the kinds of experiences associated with a diagnosis of borderline personality disorder. For example, Lyons-Ruth, Yellin, Melnick and Atwood (2005) suggest that an insecure attachment between caregivers and children is linked to experiences associated with a diagnosis of borderline personality disorder. We discussed attachment and its links with emotional regulation in Chapter 4.

However, the news in relation to families and childhood is not all bad. Skodol et al. (2007) investigated predictors of remission in – and recovery from – the kinds of problematic experiences associated with a diagnosis of personality disorder. They reported that, for those with diagnoses of avoidant and schizotypal personality disorders, positive experiences of achievement and of interpersonal relationships during childhood or adolescence were significantly associated with the reduction of experiences associated with this diagnosis. They concluded that the greater the number of positive experiences and the broader the developmental period they spanned, the better the prognosis.

We noted earlier that social inequality may impact on the ability of families to provide a nurturing environment. However, there is some evidence that social inequality exposes families to more – and more severe – negative life events.

Life events

Grant et al. (2004) report that key causal factors in the general population include being divorced, separated, widowed or never married. In their normal population study, Coid et al. (2006) found that being 'male, older, separated or divorced' (p. 427) was linked to experiences associated with personality disorder diagnoses. The causal relationship between these factors are unclear and, in particular, a link between age and personality disorder characteristics provides a challenge to a traditional perspective, which assumes that personality characteristics do not change over time.

Both Carl and Salima had experienced a range of negative life events; some events, such as being abused and placed into the care of the local authority, may mean one moves on a particular kind of trajectory. As we saw in Box 13.3, Singleton et al.'s (1998) study reported that a number of negative life events were associated with the kind of problematic experiences associated with a diagnosis of personality disorder, the most common being: running away from home, serious money problems, separation or the breakdown of a steady relationship and the death of a close relative or friend. In addition, a quarter of the female sentenced prisoners and a third of the male remand prisoners had been taken into the care of social services as children. Whilst this may indicate that local authority care is problematic, it is also likely that this is a proxy indicator of the effects of childhood abuse, since children are only taken into care when there is significant evidence of abuse or neglect. Vizard, Hickey and McCrory (2007) identified a number of factors common amongst juveniles who engaged in sexually abusive behaviour and who were high scorers both on a youth version of Hare's (1991) psychopathy checklist and a measure of conduct disorder. They reported that those with 'emerging severe personality disorder traits' (s27) were more likely to have had parents who had mental health problems who had themselves been abused. They were also likely to have received inconsistent parenting, been taken into care and to have been insecurely attached to their caregivers.

What kinds of psychological processes might explain the link between forms of distress seen as characteristic of personality disorders and the kind of relationship caregivers have with children? We examine this in the next section.

Psychological processes

We have already seen that parental invalidation, family instability and the lack of a nurturing environment are important in the development of the kinds of distress seen in those with a diagnosis of personality disorder. These kinds of factors may well be linked to the development of the ability to regulate emotions, a key process potentially implicated in the kinds of problems with both anger (associated with conduct disorder and antisocial personality disorder) and with other emotions (associated with self-harm and borderline personality disorder).

Once again, research which has focused on a particular process or experience has tended to be more fruitful than simply using heterogeneous diagnostic categories. One particular area of research has looked at the link between psychopathy and the ability to recognize one's own and others' emotions. Fonagy, Target, Gergely, Allen and Bateman (2003) have described one way that attachment patterns may lead to the kinds of problematic experiences seen as emblematic of borderline personality disorder. They suggest that insecure and/or disorganized attachments may lead to a failure to develop the social cognitive ability to 'mentalize': in other words, to be able to think about one's own and others' thoughts. This thinking has led to the development of an intervention called Mentalization-Based Treatment (see the next section on interventions).

Fruzzetti, Shenk and Hoffman (2005) have suggested that invalidating family environments may impair the development of the ability to identify and label emotion in oneself and others. They argue that the constant undermining of one's perceptions found in such environments means that the child does not learn to differentiate between their caregiver's thoughts and feelings and their own, thus impairing the development of mentalization.

In Lykken's (1957) classic study, 49 people with a diagnosis of psychopathy were divided into two groups based on Cleckley's

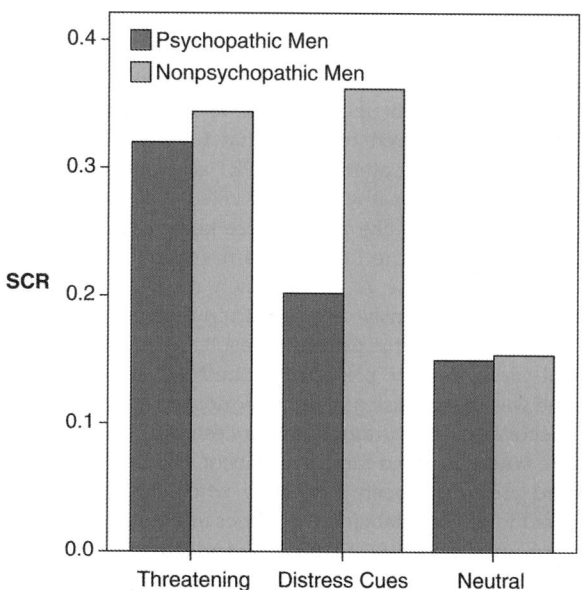

(1950) criteria. Together with a control group they were assessed with self-report instruments, had their Galvanic Skin Response (GSR) – a physiological measure of stress – measured in response to an electric current and were engaged in 'avoidance learning' (which evaluates how good a person is at learning to avoid a negative or unpleasant experience). Lykken reported that the group most closely fitting Cleckley's criteria had less anxiety according to the questionnaire, less GSR reactivity in response to the electric shock and less avoidance of punished responses in the avoidance learning task. Birbaumer et al. (2005) recently replicated these findings. Lykken's study appeared to show that psychopaths might respond differently to emotions like anxiety and fear and, it was hypothesized, this might account for their engagement in risky and illegal conduct.

A number of researchers have suggested that those who meet the criteria for psychopathy lack the ability to process the kind of emotional information necessary in order to feel empathy for someone. A classic study by Blair, Jones, Clark and Smith (1997) attempted to test this hypothesis. They selected 18 people from Broadmoor maximum security psychiatric hospital and 18 prisoners from Wormwood Scrubs prison. They reviewed their files using Hare's (1991) PCL–R criteria to ensure that the Broadmoor group were high scorers whilst the prisoners were low scorers. Each person viewed 28 slides including 10 practice slides, five slides depicting distress (e.g. a crying face), five depicting threatening images (e.g. a shark, a pointed gun, an angry face) and eight depicting neutral objects (e.g. a hairdryer, a book). Again, skin conductance was used as a measure of physiological arousal.

As we can see in Figure 13.5, the groups did not differ in their response to the neutral or threatening images, but there was a significant difference in relation to the images of distress, with the high PCL–R scorers showing less of a physiological response than the prisoner control group. This study appeared to show that psychopaths were less able to process emotional information related to the distress of others, and this was

interpreted as evidence of a lack of empathy. In a related study, Blair et al. (2004) compared 19 men who were high PCL–R scorers with 19 low scorers, all recruited from Category B prisons in the London area. They were shown images of faces which began with a neutral affect but which gradually morphed into a particular emotional expression. Participants had to signal when they recognized the emotion the face was expressing. The results indicated that the high psychopathy group showed a selective impairment for the recognition of fearful expressions.

Other psychological processes have been hypothesized as playing a role in the development of the kinds of experiences and distress associated with a diagnosis of personality disorder. Following the work of Young (1990) and others, some studies have investigated the role of **Early Maladaptive Schemas**: ways of viewing the world which develop in response to aversive experiences in early childhood. For example, in a study examining the relationship between these schemas and personality disorders in a large university sample, Reeves and Taylor reported (2007) that the 'unrelenting standards' schemas – in which people set themselves continually high standards to achieve – was related to experiences associated with a diagnosis of obsessive–compulsive personality disorder. In another study of a non-clinical sample, Carr and Francis (2010) reported that early maladaptive schemas significantly predicted all such experiences associated with personality disorder diagnoses, apart from borderline and antisocial. They also found associations between specific schemas and personality disorder sub-categories.

It might be worth considering what kinds of psychological processes you would predict in the cases of Carl and Salima.

Biological processes

As we saw in Chapter 4, investigations of genetic and biological factors in the aetiology of mental health problems have been hampered by a focus on global and heterogeneous diagnostic categories (rather than specific kinds of experience), a dualistic model of the relationship between biology and the environment (rather than an approach which sees them as inter-penetrating), a search for single gene causes, a lack of a focus on temporal specificity and the methodological flaws of genetic studies in which genetic influence is inferred from proxy indicators. Moreover, premature conclusions have often been reached about the causal primacy of biological or genetic factors. However, as we noted in Chapter 4, these factors are not best conceptualized in this manner; instead, our biology and genetic inheritance enables rather than causes (see Box 4.3 in Chapter 4).

One approach has been to investigate the neural correlates of important psychological processes. As we have seen, the ability to empathize with others is a key issue in psychopathy. However, the ability to 'read' others' minds – to mentalize (Frith & Frith, 1999) – appears to have neural correlates (Jackson, Meltzoff & Decety, 2005) which merit further investigation.

Similarly, neurotransmitters appear to be involved in the regulation of emotional state, which is a key element in a diagnosis of borderline personality disorder. As we saw in Chapter 4, there are many neurotransmitters and these also interact with each other. Serotonin is one of the most studied and it appears that reduced serotonergic activity may inhibit a person's ability to modulate or control destructive urges (National Collaborating Centre for Mental Health, 2009). Rinne,

Figure 13.5 **The mean skin conductance response scores of 'psychopathic men' and 'non-psychopathic men' when exposed to three different kinds of stimuli**

Source: **Blair et al. (1997).**

Westenberg, den Boer and van den Brink (2000) conducted a study on a small group of women, comparing them with a control group. They reported that severe and sustained traumatic stress in childhood affected the 5-HT system and especially 5-HT1A receptors. One interpretation of these results is that child abuse may lead to an impairment in this system which, in turn, may lead to a difficulty with aggression. Or, more prosaically, one could say that that traumatization of this nature may lead one to feel powerful emotions, including anger, which are hard to control.

Another line of research has examined hypothesized links between brain injury and cognitive, emotional and behavioural patterns which are consistent with a diagnosis of antisocial personality disorder. For example Brower and Price (2001) note that 'case descriptions suggest that focal orbitofrontal injury specifically impairs capacities for social judgment, risk avoidance, and empathy that inhibit inappropriate or reflexive aggression' (p. 725).

Lifelines, plasticity and specificity

As we have noted in the other chapters on particular forms of distress, all of the causal elements described so far interact with each other in complex ways. Unfortunately, research into the kinds of problematic experience related to the personality disorders has been bedevilled by the methodological and conceptual problems we have identified. For example, although a recent review claimed that many personality disorder-related traits were heritable (Livesley & Jang, 2008), it assumed that familial transmission implicated genetic transmission even though there have been no studies where DNA was directly sampled or twin adoption studies of personality disorder (although, as we saw in Chapter 4, there are methodological problems with that paradigm).

As a result, much research in this area is speculative. The most promising avenues for further research in this area seem to be to focus on particular kinds of problematic experience. For example, antisocial behaviour is a key element in antisocial personality disorder, so there has been research into its aetiology. Viding and colleagues have examined genetic influences on the influence of 'callous and unemotional traits' on the antisocial behaviour of seven-year-old twins. They concluded that genetic influences on these traits overlapped significantly with genetic influences on conduct problems (Viding, Frick & Plomin, 2007). However, here again, familial transmission was conflated with genetic transmission. Vizard and colleagues' research indicates that social factors are also implicated in developmental pathways. Indeed, a study by Sadeh et al. (2010) reported that callous-unemotional and narcissistic traits increased as socio-economic status decreased, suggesting an important relationship between the development of these traits and social inequality. Moreover, Fergusson, Boden, Horwood, Miller and Kennedy's (2011) 30-year longitudinal study in New Zealand suggested that antisocial behaviour ('offending, conduct problems and hostility') was more likely to be reported for those with the low activity variant of the Monoamine Oxidase A (MAOA) gene, but only when these participants had experienced abuse in childhood.

Apparent gender differences in experience are intriguing, but they do not necessarily point only to genetic explanations. There are differences in the prevalence of different types of mental health problem in childhood. Meltzer, Gatward, Goodman and Ford's (2000) community survey with 10,438 interviews suggested that similar proportions of boys and girls met diagnostic criteria for emotional disorders between the ages of five and ten, but that girls were slightly more likely to meet criteria for emotional problems between the ages of 11 and 15. Boys, however, were twice as likely to meet the criteria for a conduct disorder and even more likely to meet the criteria for hyperkinetic disorders across the age ranges. It is not surprising, then, that men tend to be over-represented in the latter group. We discussed earlier Paris's (1997) suggestion that men might be over-represented in externalizing problems, while women might be over-represented in relation to internalizing problems. If this is the case, and it seems possible, then this process clearly begins early in life.

There are few childhood analogues of adult personality disorders such as borderline personality disorder, but conduct disorder is considered analogous to antisocial personality disorder. Dodge and Pettit (2003) outline a comprehensive biopsychosocial model of conduct disorder problems in adolescence. Their model assumes a biological predisposition but, as in other biopsychosocial models (see Chapter 4), there is a lack of clarity about what this predisposition is and exactly how it makes the person vulnerable. Belsky and Pluess (2009) have recently called for clearer conceptual thinking about the nature of such vulnerabilities. They suggest that, rather than there being vulnerability factors, there may, instead, be 'plasticity factors' which render people differentially malleable or susceptible to both positive and negative environmental influences. We have already seen how processes such as empathy, mentalization, the response to childhood abuse and emotional regulation have biological correlates, and it is likely that how these processes develop depends on a wide variety of factors, including not only the family but the developmental stage. Hopefully, once researchers focus on particular problematic experiences rather than heterogeneous categories, there will be more progress to allow us to follow a lifelines approach more thoroughly.

An interesting example of the interplay between biological and environmental factors can be seen in the case of Emeritus Professor James Fallon, a neuroscientist at the University of California, Irvine, who was interviewed for both US National Public Radio in 2010 and BBC Radio 4's *All in the Mind* in 2011. He reported his shock upon examining a PET scan of his own brain, which appeared to show that his orbital cortex was inactive – a similar pattern to the PET scans of people with a diagnosis of psychopathy who had killed – 'If you look at the PET scan, I look just like one of those killers' (Haggerty, 2010). He also found that he had a certain version of the MAO-A (monoamine oxidase A) gene which meant that his brain would be less responsive to the calming effects of serotonin. He considered that this pattern of results –a relatively inactive orbital cortex and the presence of the MAO-A gene – meant that he was at high risk of being diagnosed with psychopathy. He discovered that amongst his ancestors there were seven people who had killed family members. Fallon explained that he had previously been somebody who had 'really strongly believed in the inevitability of genetics and not much in terms of the nurture side' (BBC Radio 4, 26 April 2011):

> Frankly I thought that you couldn't really change somebody's fundamental genetically-driven behaviours but I think with a lot, with the right kind of upbringing, that can probably actually protect you against a life of crime and psychopathy ... I was, I think, really taken care of and

loved a lot so all of this love and protection and nurturing somehow must have offset these genes ... I was clearly not a slave to my genetics and so I had to really admit that I was wrong on this.

BBC Radio 4 (26 April 2011)

Interventions

Therapeutic pessimism and negative attitudes towards those with a diagnosis of personality disorder

Although it is still something of a taboo subject, mental health professionals can have quite negative emotional reactions to service users. Within the psychodynamic model, strong emotions felt by the psychotherapist (known as the counter-transference) may indicate something of significance about the client. These feelings may occur because the client is seen as (unconsciously) enacting a previous transference relationship (i.e. they are unconsciously inviting the therapist to relate to them similarly to a previous figure in their life, often a parent or caregiver). They may also occur because the client somehow unconsciously projects their emotional state into the therapist. Donald Winnicott, later well known for his work on attachment, argued in *Hate and the Countertransference* (1958) that strong negative emotions could be understood in relation to the client's problems. Although he focused mainly on psychosis rather than personality disorder it is the latter which seems to arouse most negative reactions from clinicians today. For example, Lewis and Appleby (1988) asked psychiatrists to rate a case vignette of which there were several versions, in which most details remained the same. One version of the vignette mentioned a previous diagnosis of personality disorder. Ratings of these cases revealed that psychiatrists saw the person in the vignette 'as manipulative, attention-seeking, annoying, and in control of their suicidal urges and debts' (p. 44). They concluded that personality disorder was 'an enduring pejorative judgement rather than a clinical diagnosis' (p. 44). Similar findings have been found across a range of settings. For example, Carr-Walker, Bowers, Callaghan, Nijman and Paton (2004) found that British prison officers working in a unit for people seen as dangerous and with a severe personality disorder (DSPD) had more positive attitudes than nursing staff in maximum security hospitals. In another questionnaire study of nursing staff, Markham (2003) reported they were less optimistic and more negative about patients with a borderline personality disorder diagnosis than they were about patients with diagnoses of schizophrenia or depression. In a related study, Markham and Trower (2003) noted that nursing staff regarded those with this label as more in control of negative behaviour, and this was related to staff sympathy. It seems, then, that one possible reason for negative staff reactions is that they may see a service user's perceived negative behaviour as deliberate and intentional.

In a British study of service user views, Haigh (2002) reported that:

> many of the group had been called time-wasters, difficult, manipulative, bed-wasters or attention-seeking. Some felt that a more appropriate description would be 'attachment-

seeking'. They felt blamed for their condition and often sought basic acceptance and someone to listen to them. (p. 1)

Negative attitudes towards a person can also influence the process of diagnosis: Weinstock and Nair (1984) reported that dislike of patients or negative moral judgments about their actions frequently were involved in making a diagnosis of antisocial personality disorder. Perkins and Repper (1998) note that when faced with service users who 'upset other service users, make demands on services that are considered excessive or inappropriate and lack any apparent desire to change' (p. 36) clinicians 'may assert that "we cannot help" or "we have nothing to offer them" or "they are not mentally ill" ' (p. 37).

Recent UK government policy has recognized that negative staff attitudes and practices are problematic. In *Personality Disorder: No Longer a Diagnosis of Exclusion*, the National Institute for Mental Health in England (NIMHE, 2003), these were seen as stemming from a lack of skills and knowledge. In particular, it noted that a lack of an explanatory framework for understanding – and skills to deal with – the challenging behaviours which may be exhibited by people with these diagnoses could lead to staff responding with negative judgements and exclusionary practices. Wright, Haig and McKeown (2007) have argued that, to some extent, these exclusionary attitudes and practices are related to how people with a diagnosis of personality disorder are viewed as essentially different from others. They suggest that emphasizing characteristics which are shared with others without the diagnosis may lead to better outcomes. This seems important, as people with this diagnosis have been found to have high levels of self-reported unmet need (Hayward, Slade & Moran, 2006).

Despite such therapeutic pessimism, people with a borderline personality disorder diagnosis generally make a good recovery, with three quarters no longer meeting diagnostic criteria by the age of 40 (Paris, 2009). Given this, and the diagnostic instability noted above, it is problematic that many studies use the meeting of diagnostic criteria as the main outcome variable.

In the next section, we examine some of the interventions available for people with diagnoses of borderline personality disorder and antisocial personality disorder. Many studies use a variety of outcomes, including measures of particular problematic experiences (or 'symptoms' or 'complaints') as well as measures of service usage (e.g. hospital admission), rather than global ratings of the severity of a particular category, which would be of doubtful validity. As a result, it is possible to distil some more useful information from these studies.

Interventions: borderline personality disorder

Studies evaluating the outcome of interventions for borderline personality disorder have used a variety of assessments of personality disorder and measures of outcome. For example, the recent National Institute for Health and Clinical Excellence (NICE) report noted that studies did not use consistent outcomes that enabled easy comparison. They identified the following outcomes measured in the studies they reviewed: aggression, anger, irritability, anxiety, depression, mental distress, hopelessness, impulsivity, general functioning, quality of life, social functioning, self-harm, suicidality, abstinence from drugs, amount of use of services, the number of diagnostic criteria fulfilled and the acceptability of the treatment

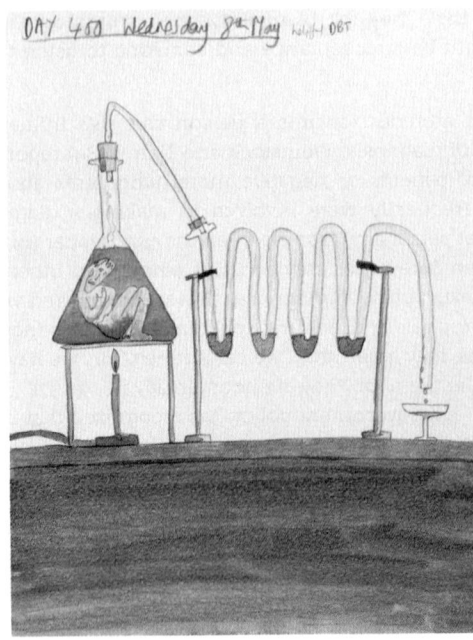

Day 400, from Baker (2010). Bobby Baker is an artist who received a diagnosis of borderline personality disorder. This is a drawing from her diary, kept during her treatment

(National Collaborating Centre for Mental Health, 2009). Many of these outcomes were assessed through self-administered questionnaires, some by clinician rating scales and some by collecting service management data. Thus, when researchers or reviewers note that an intervention has led to some benefits, this may only refer to one of a number of outcomes measured. As we will see, with both these interventions and those for people with a diagnosis of antisocial personality disorder, researchers tend to focus on particular kinds of problematic experience (e.g. impulsivity, mood stabilization) rather than global changes in the particular personality disorder.

Preventative interventions

There are few specifically preventative interventions available for borderline personality disorder and the NICE guideline does not include a review (though it does for antisocial personality disorder). However, as we saw in both Carl and Salima's cases, it may well have been possible to intervene at an earlier stage in a way that would have been accessible and acceptable to them as young people. Coid et al. (2006) note that there is clearly a need to develop preventative interventions, given that many people attracting personality disorder diagnoses have been in institutional care.

Psychological interventions

Unsurprisingly, given that much early theorizing about borderline personality disorder was conducted by psychoanalysts, traditional psychoanalysis was a common treatment for many years. In recent years, **transference-focused psychotherapy** (TFP), developed by psychoanalyst Otto Kernberg, has developed a research base. Within a psychodynamic model, a person attracting this diagnosis tends to experience 'splits' in the way they experience themselves and others, emotionally and cognitively. In other words, within this model they may see themselves as all good and others as all bad, or vice versa.

Similarly, they may idealize one person or group as all good and demonize another. The aim of this twice-weekly therapy is to help the person become aware of these strategies and learn to integrate different aspects of themselves, primarily through a focus on the transference relationship between the person and the therapist. In a recent randomized controlled trial (RCT– see Chapter 8) comparing transference-focused psychotherapy with treatment by community psychotherapists, fewer clients dropped out of treatment, attempted suicide or were admitted to hospital and there were some improvements in 'personality organization', psychosocial functioning and other experiences associated with this diagnosis but there were no changes in self harming behaviour (Doering et al., 2010).

A number of cognitive behaviour therapy approaches have been developed. Here there is a particular focus on the identification of core beliefs and on agreeing collaborative therapy goals (Davidson, 2008). In a recent trial comparing approximately 16 sessions (although they had been offered about twice as many) of cognitive therapy over a year with treatment as usual, there was some reduction in suicide, self harm and inpatient admission (Davidson et al., 2006).

In **schema-focused cognitive therapy** (SFCT), there is a concern with how maladaptive schemas may develop as a result of early life experiences (Young, 1990), and it draws on both cognitive and psychoanalytic traditions. Giesen-Bloo et al. (2006) compared this approach with transference-focused psychotherapy, offering twice-weekly sessions over three years. Whilst SFCT performed better than TFP, both achieved reduction in problematic experiences. Paris (2009) suggests that the three–year-long treatment casts doubt on its clinical utility, although a small uncontrolled study suggests a shorter period may be possible (Nordahl & Nysæter, 2005).

Cognitive analytic therapy similarly draws on ideas from cognitive and psychoanalytic approaches. A key aim is to help the client identify particular patterns of thinking, feeling and relating to others (Ryle, 1997). There are no randomized controlled trials of this approach to borderline personality disorder, and the NICE guidelines report methodological problems with the outcome studies published (National Collaborating Centre for Mental Health, 2009). However, Kerr (1999) notes how a cognitive analytic formulation can be useful not only in therapy with the client but in educating other professionals in a Community Mental Health Team (CMHT) and associated agencies about the meaning of the person's problems. This can help with the management of the complex organizational dynamics that these problems may evoke in professional systems.

The recent NICE guideline concludes that 'there is very little evidence for the efficacy of individual psychological interventions in the treatment of people with borderline personality disorder because almost all studies are uncontrolled' (National Collaborating Centre for Mental Health, 2009, p. 141). It does, however, call for more research, especially well-designed trials, to answer key questions.

In recent years, a number of integrated therapy programmes have been developed. Two of the most common are dialectical behaviour therapy and mentalization-based treatment.

Dialectical behaviour therapy (DBT) (Linehan, 1993) is a 'third-wave' therapy, drawing on cognitive behavioural theories, dialectical philosophy and Zen Buddhist practice. In DBT the importance of invalidating early environments is recognized, so therapists have to balance an overall validating approach with encouragement to make therapeutic changes.

'Thus a self-injuring behaviour might be responded to by a therapist with a validation of the need to reduce distress whilst encouraging the development of other coping strategies which might fulfil this need (Lynch, Trost, Salsman & Linehan, 2007). As initially envisaged, DBT moves through four stages: engaging in therapy and achieving control over problematic behaviours (e.g. suicide, self-injury, substance misuse or eating problems); emotionally processing the past; resolving problems in living; and learning to experience joy. However, as this may take several years, research has generally focused on the first two stages. DBT consists of individual therapy and a psychoeducational and skills training group, both taking place weekly, usually over a year. The therapists work as a team, receiving weekly supervision. A key skill taught is mindfulness, a Zen meditative practice in which one learns how to attend to one's thoughts and feelings in the present moment without moral evaluation or judgement. By learning this technique it is hoped that the client can begin to identify repetitive and destructive patterns. At the end of therapy clients may be supported in generalizing the skills they have learnt through telephone-based 'coaching calls' (Lynch et al., 2007). In a recent trial comparing DBT with treatment by experienced therapists recommended by 'local community mental health leaders', both groups showed some improvements, with the DBT group generally doing better than the other group on a number of measures (Linehan et al., 2006).

Another psychoanalytically-informed approach is mentalization-based treatment (Bateman & Fonagy, 2004). Here the focus is on increasing the person's ability to mentalize or think about the mental states both of themselves and of others. As we noted in the previous section, those attracting this diagnosis are seen within this model as having an impaired ability to mentalize as a result of poor attachment experiences in early life. Key elements again include a focus on transference but here the interventions are delivered through a day hospital programme involving weekly individual therapy, expressive therapy with psychodrama and a weekly community meeting, together with group analytic therapy three times a week. Compared with treatment as usual, outcomes include improved employment prospects, less medication and less outpatient psychiatric treatment, with many changes sustained at five-year follow-up (National Collaborating Centre for Mental Health, 2009; Paris, 2009).

NICE is more positive about these programmes:

> The RCT evidence for psychological therapy programmes showed some benefit in reducing symptoms such as anxiety and depression. They also have some benefit on rates of self-harm. Most of the evidence is of moderate quality, and the majority is of DBT, with a single study of MBT with partial hospitalisation. The non-RCT evidence provides support for the feasibility of using DBT in various settings.
>
> National Collaborating Centre for Mental Health (2009, p. 170)

Family interventions

Given that many people with a diagnosis will be in a relationship and since many of the criteria concern relational issues, it is surprising that there has not been more focus on couple- and family-based work. However, Kirby and Baucom (2007) provided group therapy for couples in which one partner had participated in a year-long DBT skills training group, reporting positive effects including a reduction in the diagnosed partner's depressive problematic experiences and emotion dysregulation, and an increase in their partners' relationship satisfaction.

Social interventions

As we saw in the previous section, a number of originally individual therapeutic modalities have evolved into broader-based integrative approaches offering, for example, a mix of individual- and group-based approaches. Until relatively recently, therapeutic communities were a well known mode of intervention. In the UK hospitals such as the Henderson and the Cassel were examples of attempts to create therapeutic environments founded on democratic principles. Here, in addition to regular therapies, there were community meetings where staff and service users were able to reflect on how they related to each other. It was thought that opportunities like this would enable residents to learn more about the way they related to others and be able to make changes. Lees, Manning and Rawlings (2004) conducted a systematic review and meta-analysis of 29 published studies of general therapeutic community effectiveness (i.e. not focusing specifically on adults with a borderline personality disorder diagnosis) using controls, including eight randomized controlled trials, and reported that therapeutic communities were effective. They noted that democratic communities appeared to be being overtaken by 'concept-based' ones like those found in drug rehabilitation programmes. Unfortunately, in the UK, changes in NHS and local authority funding arrangements have meant that fully residential therapeutic communities are few and far between. The Henderson hospital closed in 2008 and the Cassel hospital has largely changed its focus. However, in line with the therapeutic programmes such as mentalization-based treatment and dialectical behaviour therapy noted above, day hospitals are increasingly acting as a kind of therapeutic community offering, for example, a once-weekly community

Day 480: Attacked By Sharp Thoughts, from Baker (2010). Bobby Baker is an artist who received a diagnosis of borderline personality disorder. This is a drawing from her diary, kept during her treatment

environment (e.g. Hodge et al., 2010) including some of the successful elements of the earlier residential democratic communities. The NICE guideline reports some encouraging results from cohort studies but notes that these remain tentative, as there were no trials matching their criteria (National Collaborating Centre for Mental Health, 2009).

Service-level interventions

As we have mentioned already, services often feel challenged by the kinds of experiences people with this diagnosis present with, such as suicide and self-injury. The National Institute for Mental Health in England (2004) notes that people may become 'revolving door patients, attempting to obtain help from a wide range of community services that are often unable and/or unwilling to provide it' (p. 7). Community mental health teams are increasingly expected to offer therapeutic intervention for this client group but may feel challenged by this (Sampson, McCubbin & Tyrer, 2006). This is particularly the case in secure therapeutic settings, where there is a need to manage a difficult balance between two potentially contradictory aims: security and therapy (Richman, 2007). In the English Special Hospital system of maximum security psychiatric hospitals, a number of public inquiries have been held over the years, which appear to swing between advocating a more liberal therapeutic regime and more security (Pilgrim, 2007). Warner (2009) describes some of the complex dynamics that can develop between staff and service users and within staff groups, particularly in secure settings:

> In this context, splits between workers become inevitable and symptomatic behaviour associated with the diagnosis of borderline personality disorder and experiences of abuse may then become institutionalized. (p. 237)

We noted earlier how Kerr (1999) used a cognitive analytic formulation to aid team thinking, planning and decision-making about one client. This kind of case consultation has become more established, enabling teams to manage service user and staff anxieties and explain them through the use of formulations. Ramsden (2010), for example, talks of facilitating thinking in a personality disorder service, developing a 'mindful team'. This is important, since service users report that consistent long-term involvement with experienced staff can help them to manage their emotions (Fallon, 2003).

Medication

Although there are no psychotropic medications specifically targeted at personality disorders, people with the diagnosis of personality disorder may be given medication for a number of other reasons, for example because it is prescribed in relation to another diagnosis, or because the medication is deemed to help with a particular problematic experience (e.g. agitation or sleep problems). As we saw with Salima at the start of the chapter, she was prescribed a range of medications.

Baker-Glenn, Steels and Evans (2010) conducted a small survey of 113 community mental health team service users with a primary diagnosis of personality disorder. Four-fifths were prescribed at least one psychotropic medication; antidepressants were the most common, accounting for nearly half of all prescriptions. Indeed, polypharmacy with this client group is said to be 'common' (National Collaborating Centre for Mental Health, 2009). In one study reviewed, 'over 50% of the 264 patients with borderline personality disorder studied

were taking two or more drugs concurrently, over 36% were taking three or more drugs, over 19% were taking four or more and over 11% were taking five or more at six years' (National Collaborating Centre for Mental Health, 2009, p. 212).

The recent NICE guideline examined evidence for the efficacy of antipsychotics, anti-convulsants and lithium, antidepressants, omega-3 fatty acids and Naloxone (usually used to help with opioid withdrawal). It concluded that though medication might help with specific experiences (e.g. anger, anxiety, depression, hostility and impulsivity), the evidence for this was largely based on single studies (National Collaborating Centre for Mental Health, 2009). Because of the weakness of the evidence base it recommended that medication should not be used either for borderline personality disorder or for associated experiences. However, it recommended further research in the area, particularly into mood stabilizers, given that emotional instability is a key experience for those attracting this diagnosis.

A year after the NICE review appeared, Lieb, Vollm, Rucker, Timmer and Stoffers's (2010) Cochrane systematic review of randomized controlled trials of drug treatment was published. They concluded that 'the evidence does not currently support effectiveness for overall severity of borderline personality disorder' (p. 4). However, they argued that some studies reported some beneficial effects for specific problematic experiences with some mood stabilizers and second-generation antipsychotics. The authors of the NICE (2009) guideline on borderline personality disorder responded to Lieb et al. (2010) by arguing that the latter had included some studies the NICE team regarded as unreliable. Furthermore, they noted that many of their recommendations were based on 'weak and/or low quality evidence' (p. 158).

A recent survey of the first 100 referrals to a London personality disorder service revealed that, of those with a borderline personality disorder diagnosis who were prescribed psychotropic medication, only one person had a clear current indication based on the NICE guideline (Garrett et al., 2011).

The NICE guideline adds many caveats, given the problems with the diagnosis of borderline personality disorder. One major research recommendation it makes is that clear outcome criteria need to be developed and agreed between clinicians, researchers and service users so that interventions can be accurately compared.

Interventions: antisocial personality disorder

Preventative interventions

The NICE review of interventions for those with a diagnosis of antisocial personality disorder argued that, given the strong links between this diagnosis in adulthood and the development of conduct problems in childhood, there should be much more of an emphasis given to preventative interventions (National Collaborating Centre for Mental Health, 2010). It concluded that the best evidence was for early childhood interventions (i.e. in the first five years of a child's life) aimed at the family as a whole, particularly those identified as meeting a number of risk factors for the later development of problems. Effective interventions correlated with a broad range of positive outcomes including in cognitive skills, school attainment, higher earning capacity, health and mental health benefits, reduced maltreatment and lower rates of delinquency and crime (since criminal offending is highly correlated with poor educational attainment). However, the evidence for both preschool and school-based interventions on later offending appears to be modest and weaker (National Collaborating Centre for Mental Health, 2010).

Psychological interventions

In stark contrast with borderline personality disorder, there has been relatively little development of therapeutic interventions for people with these kinds of problems. Indeed, the recent NICE guideline identified only one randomized controlled trial of men with a diagnosis of antisocial personality disorder (Davidson et al., 2008). This compared a CBT intervention with treatment as usual. The men were all living in the community and all had committed an act of aggression in the previous six months. There was no significant effect of treatment, although there were some modest non-significant trends. The research team produced an account of some of the dilemmas they faced during the study (Davidson et al., 2010).

Because of this paucity of evidence, the NICE review also considered CBT interventions used in the prison and probation service to reduce offending behaviour. In these interventions, offenders are encouraged to identify beliefs and 'thinking errors' which lead them to offend. This may be combined with skills training, problem-solving and anger management. These are often delivered in a group setting. The NICE review concluded that there was some evidence that these interventions contributed to reducing offending behaviour. In addition, there have been a number of programmes developed in secure settings, which raise important ethical questions.

Antisocial personality disorder, dangerousness and treatability

As we saw in the discussion of compulsory treatment in Chapter 8, UK mental health law allows compulsory psychiatric treatment to be given to people who are considered to be dangerous and a risk to the public because of their mental health. However, under the 1983 Mental Health Act it was recognized that there was a danger that, if a person did not respond to treatment, they might be incarcerated for the rest of their life. This was felt to be disproportionate, since many of those who commit murder or violent assaults usually serve a prison sentence of a specific length, so people with mental health problems would be discriminated against and have their civil liberties curtailed. As a result, the 1983 Act required that a person's condition should be considered treatable by the psychiatrist.

In 1996 in Kent Michael Stone killed Lin and Megan Russell, a mother and her young daughter, leaving the other daughter, Josie (aged nine), severely injured. Subsequent investigations revealed that Stone had a violent past and was well known to mental health services. He had a diagnosis of antisocial personality disorder but was not considered treatable. Jack Straw, the then Home Secretary, clashed publicly with Robert Kendell, the then president of the Royal College of Psychiatrists. Straw said that it was 'time, frankly, that the psychiatric profession seriously examined their own practices and tried to modernize them in a way they have so far failed to do' (Warden, 1998b, p. 1270). The government argued that, instead of being an important safeguard of civil liberties, the treatability requirement had become a loophole, allowing people like Stone to pose a danger to the public.

In line with this, the government published a set of proposals, *Managing Dangerous People with Severe Personality Disorder* (Department of Health/Home Office, 1999). This introduced the concept of people considered to be dangerous and to have a **dangerous and severe personality disorder: DSPD**, as it became known. The notion of 'severe personality disorder' was little used at that time and is not a formalized category in diagnostic manuals. Indeed, Manning (2000, 2002) has suggested that the concept served a number of functions for disparate interest groups including policy makers, clinical academic researchers and others. The DSPD construct was controversial from the start, as many professionals were concerned that they were being called upon to fulfil an explicit social control function. John Cox, another president of the Royal College of Psychiatrists, stated:

> We are not containers of people whom we can't do anything to help. The idea that it is our job to modify unwanted behaviour brings psychiatrists too close to being agents of the state whose job is to modify behaviour the state doesn't like. We don't want to collude with the state and we don't want political interference with professional judgement.
>
> Laurance (2003a, p. 60)

Under the government's proposals, a person could potentially be detained and given compulsory treatment without having committed an offence. Some critics noted that the law would only allow detention of those with psychiatric diagnoses whereas, arguably, much more dangerous people (e.g. violent criminals) were still free to pose a danger to the public.

Despite criticisms the government's proposals became law with the 2007 amendments to the Mental Health Act. Also, following the 1999 proposals, a 10-year programme of cognitive behavioural interventions was designed and implemented in new services costing £200m. According to Tyrer et al. (2010), the programme was responsible for 240 people in two maximum security hospitals and two Category A prisons. Although evaluations of it are continuing, they note that 'it has been less effective in managing those whom it was primarily targeting and may not have been cost-effective' (p. 95). They also specifically warn of the danger of being seen to simply 'warehouse' recipients, since less than 10% of their time is spent in active treatment, which lasts, on average, for two years.

Social interventions

As we noted above, therapeutic communities (TCs) have, historically, been involved in offering interventions to those with diagnoses of personality disorder. However, the NICE review identified no trials focused on antisocial personality disorder, though they did identify a number of therapeutic communities focused on drug rehabilitation, for which they concluded there was some evidence of effectiveness.

Medication

As with borderline personality disorder, there is no medication specifically recommended for those with a diagnosis of antisocial personality disorder. However, 'multiple drugs in various combinations are used in this group either to control aberrant behaviour or in the hope that something might work' (National Collaborating Centre for Mental Health, 2010, p. 219). As we saw in Carl's case, medication was given to him primarily to help him sleep and calm him down, something often found in institutional settings like prisons or hospitals.

The NICE guideline concluded that medication 'should not be routinely used for the treatment of antisocial personality disorder or associated behaviours of aggression, anger and impulsivity' (National Collaborating Centre for Mental Health, 2010, p. 216).

In Box 8.4 we reviewed some of the criticisms of the process by which NICE guidelines are developed. One interesting factor, not considered there but noted by Pickersgill (2009) in relation to the guidelines on antisocial personality disorder, is how the developers manage the considerable uncertainties posed by the variable quality of the evidence base. Pickersgill argues that, in choosing not to emphasize this uncertainty, it risks reifying a contested category. He notes that this is of particular concern given the ethical implications for people receiving this diagnosis.

Chapter summary

In this chapter we have discussed the origins of the notion of personality disorder. We saw how its conception was very closely tied to the development of the notion of personality itself, which emerged in a particular cultural and historical context. We have noted that many of the diagnostic criteria seem to refer to infractions of culturally valued norms and rules. We reviewed some of the problems identified with the use of this diagnosis, particularly in relation to its reliability and validity but also including the views of service users, many of whom feel it is a pejorative label. In this chapter we also examined a range of theoretical frameworks, primarily categorical and continuum models, as well as causal factors linked to behaviours seen as characteristic of a form of personality disorder. We considered the cultural and gender context of distress seen as characteristic of personality disorder, including evidence of biases in diagnostic judgements. Finally, we reviewed some of the interventions suggested for two of the major sub-categories: borderline personality disorder and antisocial personality disorder. Given the substantial criticism the category of personality disorder has received, if there is to be significant therapeutic and research progress in the future it will be necessary, as we have argued in other chapters, to move away from heterogeneous and vague diagnostic categories like personality disorder which make unwarranted conceptual assumptions and are vulnerable to being used as a form of social control. Instead researchers and clinicians will need to focus on particular problematic experiences (e.g. difficulty managing intense emotions). We began the chapter by questioning whether this was a legitimate, valid and reliable category or a moral judgement of conduct which transgressed social norms. We leave it to the reader to answer this question themselves.

End of chapter questions

1   Are the kinds of problematic experiences seen as characteristic of personality disorder most helpfully viewed as disorders of personality?
2   Given the sustained criticism this diagnostic category has received, how has it survived for so long?
3   Is the concept of psychopathy useful in understanding the conduct of some people in the world of business and finance?
4   How might we draw on psychological theory to develop a formulation of why mental health staff might react negatively to some of the experiences associated with this diagnosis?
5   Since there appear to be strong links between inequality and abusive experiences as a child and the kinds of problematic experiences associated with personality disorder, would it be better to reformulate these experiences as effects of abuse rather than as disorders of personality?

Find out more

1   www.personalitydisorder.org.uk/
    This is an online portal hosted by the Department of Health. It includes short videos explaining NICE guidance in respect of both borderline and antisocial personality disorder and includes the latest guidance, news, upcoming training events and resources and information about ongoing research programmes.

2   Hagerty, B. B. (2010). A neuroscientist uncovers a dark secret. Available from www.npr.org/templates/story/story.php?storyId=127888976 (29 June).
    This is an account of the case of Emeritus Professor James Fallon, who was discussed in the lifelines section.

3   Girl, interrupted.
    This is a 1999 film starring Winona Ryder, who plays a character with a diagnosis of borderline personality disorder, and Angelina Jolie, who plays a character with a diagnosis of antisocial personality disorder. It is based on the memoir by Susanna Kaysen (1993) which gives an account of her stay in a psychiatric hospital in the 1960s.

4   The Millennium Trilogy
    This trilogy consists of the novels *The Girl with the Dragon Tattoo*, *The Girl Who Played with Fire* and *the Girl Who Kicked the Hornets' Nest*, all authored by the late Swedish author Stieg Larsson. These novels were subsequently made into three films of the same name released in 2009. The two main characters are Mikael Blomkvist, an investigative journalist, and Lisbeth Salander, a computer hacker who helps Blomkvist with his work. Lisbeth Salander has been involved with mental health and other welfare services but a psychiatric diagnosis is not given, though her behaviour shows characteristics of Asperger's syndrome, borderline personality disorder and antisocial personality disorder.

5   Baker, B. (2010). *Diary Drawings: Mental Illness and Me*. London: Profile Books/Wellcome Collection
    This book by artist Bobby Baker (2010) contains watercolour pictures produced after she was given a diagnosis of borderline personality disorder in 1996. The pictures and commentary provide an insightful, moving and evocative account of her encounter with distress and with mental health services.

APPENDIX: MENTAL HEALTH PROFESSIONS IN THE UK

Throughout this book, we will frequently refer to mental health services and to the various professionals who are involved in delivering them. Here is a very brief summary of some of these professions, and some of the main settings where they usually work. Our descriptions are based upon UK professions and services, but some of the professional roles are quite similar in other countries.

Clinical psychologist

In the UK, a clinical psychologist is someone who has the equivalent of a degree-level qualification in psychology and has gone on to complete a three-year full-time doctoral qualification in clinical psychology. Their training involves working with clients throughout the lifespan (e.g. children, young people, adults and older adults), across a range of specialisms (e.g. adult mental health and people with intellectual impairments) and at different levels (e.g. a GP's surgery, Community Mental Health Team or a specialist team like Early Intervention for Psychosis services). Clinical psychologists provide assessments and a range of therapeutic interventions, and in the UK the vast majority work in the NHS. The title 'clinical psychologist' is protected under UK law, and clinical psychologists are regulated by the Health and Care Professions Council. In 2011, the British Psychological Society's Division of Clinical Psychology had 10,202 members.

Counselling psychologist

A counselling psychologist has the equivalent of a degree-level qualification in psychology and has gone on to complete a doctoral qualification in counselling psychology. Their training tends to focus on work with adults. They provide assessment and a range of therapeutic interventions, and in the UK many counselling psychologists work in the NHS. The title 'counselling psychologist' is legally protected in the UK, and counselling psychologists are regulated by the Health and Care Professions Council. In 2010, the British Psychological Society's Division of Counselling Psychology had 2,892 members.

Psychiatrist

A psychiatrist has a medical degree, and is a medical doctor who has specialized by doing further training in psychiatry. In the past, such training was primarily focused on physical treatments but now includes some training in psychotherapy. A *Consultant Psychiatrist* has completed their training and is of the same seniority as any other medical consultant. In 2005 there were approximately 4,235 consultant psychiatrists in England, Wales and Northern Ireland. Other grades of psychiatrist include *Senior House Officers* (of whom there were about 1,875 in 2005) and *Specialist Registrars*. In the UK, psychiatrists are regulated by the General Medical Council.

Psychotherapist

A psychotherapist does not necessarily have a degree in psychology, but has undergone specialist training in psychotherapy.

Some training courses are integrative or eclectic but many are focused on a single model (e.g. humanistic, cognitive behavioural, psychoanalytic, systemic or existentialist). In the UK, some training courses are at Master's or Doctorate level. Many psychotherapists have first trained as mental health professionals (e.g. nurse, social worker or clinical psychologist) and then undergone further training in psychotherapy. The UK Council for Psychotherapy had approximately 6,600 members in 2011. A *cognitive therapist* has usually trained as a mental health professional and then undergone a course in cognitive psychotherapy. The British Association for Behavioural and Cognitive Psychotherapies has approximately 7,500 members. Currently, psychotherapists in the UK are regulated by their own professional organizations, and there are ongoing debates about future arrangements.

Counsellor

The term 'counsellor' is a very general one. A counsellor does not necessarily have a degree or previous mental health professional training, but they will have some training in counselling skills. Counsellor training varies in length and intensity. In the UK, some people are employed as counsellors (e.g. in GP surgeries), but many others draw on counselling skills as part of another job. The British Association for Counselling and Psychotherapy has approximately 32,000 members. Currently, in the UK, the field is regulated by professional organizations and there are ongoing debates about future arrangements.

Social worker

Social workers have a degree or a postgraduate diploma qualification in social work (if a person already has a degree in another subject when they choose to join the profession, they may then undertake a postgraduate qualification in social work). They work with a variety of different client groups including children and young people, adults with mental health problems, people with disabilities, older people and so on. In the UK social workers used to be regulated by the General Social Care Council which had 100,882 members in 2009–10. However, as of August 2012 they are regulated by the Health and Care Professions Council. The 2007 Mental Health Act introduced the role of the *Approved Mental Health Professional* (see Chapter 8) and, at the time of writing, most Approved Mental Health Professionals are social workers.

Mental health nurse

Mental health nurses in the UK, like other nurses, have completed a 3–4 year degree-level or diploma-level training programme, but most of their training and experience will have involved working with people with mental health problems. The majority of mental health nurses work on in-patient wards. In 2004, there were 47,000 qualified Mental Health Nurses and 31,000 support workers in the UK's National Health Service. A *Community Mental Health Nurse*

(CMHN; previously known as a Community Psychiatric Nurse or CPN) is a senior nurse (e.g. Staff Nurse or Ward Manager) with extensive experience. CMHNs visit people in their own homes and can give injections of medication outside of a hospital. White and Brooker (2001) report that there were about 7,000 CMHNs in 1996, but numbers may well have increased substantially since then (the figure of 7,000 itself represented a 70% increase on the number in 1990). In the UK, some advanced nurse practitioners have been given powers to prescribe medication independently from doctors (Wix, 2007): they may also be known as *consultant nurses*. In the UK, all nurses are regulated by the Nursing and Midwifery Council.

Occupational therapist

Occupational therapists in the UK have a degree-level qualification. As implied by their title, their focus tends to be on activity-based interventions designed to improve a person's functioning. They work with in-patients and people in the community and in a variety of specialist areas. The British Association of Occupational Therapists had 28,969 members in 2009–2010, although not all of these work in mental health. 'Occupational therapist' is a legally protected title in the UK, and the profession is regulated by the Health and Care Professions Council.

Other roles

In addition to these disciplines, there are roles in the UK that may be carried out by a number of different professionals. A *Care Manager* is someone who assesses, monitors and manages the services and care a mental health service user receives; he or she is also responsible for how money is spent on those services. A *Care Programme Co-ordinator* is a mental health service user's key worker, whose job is to co-ordinate and monitor the work of different professionals, ensuring it follows an agreed Care Programme. There are also two roles – *Responsible Clinician* and *Approved Mental Health Professional* – relating to the 2007 Mental Health Act; these are no longer discipline-specific and can be carried out by a range of professions. We will discuss these roles in Chapter 8.

Settings

These professionals might work in a variety of settings, the structure of which varies by region and country. However, there are some common features. Many people first discuss distress with their general practitioner (GP) in a *primary care* setting (like a GP surgery, health centre or other clinic). If their distress is considered to be moderate they may be referred to an in-house counsellor, psychotherapist, clinical psychologist or other psychological therapist. Alternatively, they might be referred to a psychological therapies service. For example, in the UK, there has been significant investment in *Increasing Access to Psychological Therapies* (IAPT) services, where short term interventions are available at either a low intensity (including befriending and telephone counselling) or a high intensity (e.g. cognitive behaviour therapy).

Those in more serious distress are often referred to specialist mental health services. In the UK these are often accessed via a *Community Mental Health Team (CMHT)*: a multi-disciplinary team (including most of the professionals listed here) managed by someone with a background as a mental health professional. These teams assess, make decisions about care, and offer a range of interventions from individual and group therapy to medication. Admission to hospital is usually only decided by a psychiatrist. There may also be a range of day services available, including schemes aimed at helping people back into employment and *day hospitals* (which often offer a more intensive service than treatment at home, without the service user having to be admitted to hospital).

If a person requires more specialist input than is available within the team they may be referred on to other services, such as (in the UK):

- *Psychological Therapies Services*, which usually offer a range of individual, group, couple and family therapies, with teams focusing on particular forms of distress or forms of psychotherapy such as Dialectical Behaviour Therapy
- *Drug and Alcohol Services*
- *Dual Diagnosis* teams, for those experiencing mental health or drug or alcohol problems
- *Early Intervention in Psychosis Services*, dealing with young people thought to be at risk of attracting a diagnosis of schizophrenia
- *Crisis Home Resolution Teams*, providing support to those in crisis as a way of avoiding their admission into hospital
- *Assertive Outreach Teams*, dealing with mental health service users who are hard to engage.

In addition there are *Forensic Mental Health Services* (often including both secure in-patient wards and out-patient services to those with mental health problems who are offenders or thought to be a risk to others) and *prison in-reach services* (offering interventions to those in prison). There is also a range of services available in the *voluntary sector*, run by charities, community groups and other organizations. For example, in the UK, mental health charities like Rethink and Mind, or black mental health groups, may offer day centre and other services.

GLOSSARY

acceptance and commitment therapy	a **third-wave behavioural therapy** which emphasizes the need to adopt an accepting stance towards oneself
accidie	in medieval times, a mixture of misery, boredom and disgust characterized by a loss of faith in God and a failure to perform required duties
acculturation	a process of psychological transition in which an individual moves from one culture to another; also the exchange or merging of cultural values, behaviours and features that occur when different cultural groups come into direct contact
active placebo	a drug administered to a control group which should not lead to any active improvement but which produces some subjective effects, leading participants to think they are on an active medication: this is a more methodologically rigorous comparison than wholly inert placebos
aetiology	the study of causation of medical diseases
affect synchrony	the reciprocal, mutual regulation of emotional states in two people, commonly an infant and a carer
agonists	drugs which activate neurotransmitter receptors
Alcoholics Anonymous	a self-help movement set up in the USA in 1935 by Bill Wilson and Dr Bob Smith, who had both struggled to find ways of coping with their problem drinking
alexithymia	a psychiatric term to describe individuals who seem to have difficulty recognizing and interpreting emotions
alienist	a term used to describe a doctor working in state-run asylums during the 19th century (from the French aliéné – insane)
alters	the distinct personalities displayed in persons given a diagnosis of Dissociative Identity Disorder
ameliorative	enabling people to cope better without fundamental changes in their relationship to society
amyostatic-akinetic form	a form of encephalitis lethargica, the symptoms of which included rigidity, without a real paralysis, emotions which were mentally present but not facially expressed – also termed 'Parkinsonism'
anomie	Durkheim's term for mismatches between small-group norms and those of wider society, and an absence of a distinct social ethic to unite people: in both senses, anomie refers to phenomena operating at the level of societies rather than individuals
anorexia nervosa	a psychiatric diagnosis given to people who do not maintain a healthy body weight (as defined by the **Body Mass Index**) and characterized by experiences of persistent and excessive fear of weight gain
anti-histamine	a drug used in treating allergies
anti-psychiatry	a set of disparate work, mostly published in the 1960s, which rejected the view that mental health problems are illnesses or diseases: see Chapter 1
antipsychotic	a term more recently preferred by drug companies instead of the term 'neuroleptic' or 'major tranquillizer'
Approved Mental Health Professional	in the UK a mental health professional – usually a social worker but sometimes a community mental health nurse or other qualified person – trained to implement elements of the **Mental Health Act**
arbitrary inference	drawing conclusions in the absence of appropriate evidence
assumptive framework	a worldview within which certain things are implicit and simply taken for granted
asylum	an institution for those seen as mad; the term is derived from the Latin word for refuge or sanctuary
attachment	the idea that the nature of one's early relationships can strongly influence one's mental health as an adult by providing 'templates' for the ways in which we are able as adults to relate to other people; see **attachment theory**
attachment relationship	in **attachment theory**, a relationship which, more than others, sets the conditions for the development of systems of emotional control and stress regulation
attachment theory	a psychoanalytic approach pioneered by John Bowlby which proposes that a baby's relations with its parents or carers need to constitute an 'environment of adaptiveness' that is sufficient to enable it to develop adequate life-long mechanisms for regulating emotion and coping with stress

	a reduction or decrease in numbers of participants as some participants drop out, or fail to complete a study
...ssants	drugs which increase levels of norepinephrine and dopamine, as well as raising serotonin
...tics	a varied grouping of **neuroleptic** drugs, described as atypical because they are said to cause fewer unwanted effects than the older 'typical' drugs; some nevertheless appear to act in a similar fashion to the older drugs, and have prominent dopamine-blocking properties
auditory hallucinations	a psychiatric term used to refer to a form of **hallucination** that involves perceiving sounds without auditory stimulus; a common form involves hearing one or more talking voices
behaviour therapy	a **psychotherapy** based on the principles of operant conditioning
behavioural genetic research	the study of correlations between diagnostic categories and patterns of genetic relatedness
behaviourism	a philosophy of psychology based on the proposition that psychology should focus only on observable behaviours
benzodiazepines	drugs which increase the levels of gamma-amino butyric acid or GABA; the best known of these drugs is diazepam (brand name 'Valium')
Berkson's bias	the fact that, since people with multiple symptoms are probably more likely to seek help than those with only a few symptoms, the observed correlation between symptoms is likely to be inflated in clinical samples when compared with samples drawn at random from the community
biblio-therapy	a form of self-help therapy, based on self-help books
binge eating disorder	a psychiatric diagnosis given to people who consume large quantities of food (up to 4000 calories) within a very short period (e.g. 2–3 hours). Purging and dieting does not necessarily accompany binging episodes
biological	pertaining to biology
biological disorder	an organic pathology; when something is physically wrong with the body, or causes problems with the body
biological model	a model of distress which prioritizes biological (neurological, brain structural and physiological) explanations. See biomedical
biological psychiatry	an approach to distress which emphasizes the importance of biological causation and of biological treatments
biomedical	an approach to medicine which emphasizes physical processes, such as the pathology, biochemistry and physiology of a disease. See biological model
biomedical model	a model of distress which assumes that it is caused by diseases or illnesses of the brain or mind
biopsychosocial model	an approach to distress which purports to show how biological, psychological and social influences interact, but which critics say frequently prioritizes biological influences over others; see Chapter 4
bipolar disorder	a psychiatric diagnosis given to people who experience extreme fluctuations of mood. Can be differentiated into bipolar I disorder, given to people who experience **psychosis** and extreme mania; and bipolar II disorder, given to people who experience elevated moods that are considered hypomanic and excluding anyone having psychotic experiences
bisexuality	where a person can be sexually attracted to a member of any gender
body image	an individual's perception of their body shape and size and the sexual attractiveness of their own body
body image distortion (BID)	a psychiatric term to describe a person who appears to hold an inaccurate and exaggerated view of their body weight and size
body mass index (BMI)	a measure of body fat currently used in the UK
bulimia nervosa	a psychiatric diagnosis given to people who restrict their intake of food, sometimes for long periods of time, but then eat excessively for short periods, followed by purging behaviours, such as the use of laxatives and vomiting
cannabis psychosis	a psychiatric diagnosis that may be given when a psychotic experience is thought to have been primarily caused or triggered by cannabis use
capitalism	an economic system based on the principles of the free market
Cartesian dualism	a term that means the same as **mind-body dualism** and which is drawn from the name of the philosopher René Descartes, who first formalized this view
catastrophic misinterpretation	where ordinary bodily sensations are mistaken for serious problems – for example, thinking that chest pain caused by indigestion is actually a heart attack
catecholaminic	of or relating to catecholamines: a subset of the monoamine neurotransmitters, such as epinephrine and dopamine, that have similar effects on the sympathetic nervous system
categorical models	models of distress that clearly distinguish it from mental health and assume that it falls into discrete categories (e.g. as opposed to dimensions)

causal attributions	everyday common-sense explanations for behaviour and its consequences
child sexual abuse	using a child for the purpose of sexual gratification: this can include exposure, using the child in pornography, verbal and physical contact between an adult and child, or contact between a child five years older than another child
Cialis	the commercial name for the drug tadalafil, used to treat male erectile dysfunction
circadian rhythms	the biorhythms or 'body clocks' that govern sleeping, wakefulness, and levels of energy and activity
cisgender	refers to individuals whose gender assigned at birth matches their social and personally ascribed gender role or identity
classical conditioning	the behaviourist principle of how associations can be learned by the temporal pairing of an external stimulus, such as a bell, with an involuntary reflex, such as a dog's salivation
client	a term sometimes used to describe a person who receives an intervention for distress; it is often used in the context of psychological therapies
client-centred therapy	a form of **humanistic psychotherapy** in which the therapist adopts core values of genuineness in their responses, empathy for their client, and unconditional positive regard for their client (derived from the work of Carl Rogers)
clinical psychology	a relatively young subdiscipline of psychology which emerged in the USA and UK with the Second World War, which aims to use psychological theory to reduce distress and enhance and promote well-being
coercive treatment	the non-consensual delivery of treatment or services to individuals who are either reluctant or refuse to enter treatment unless forced. See **compulsory treatment**
cognition	the act or process of knowing or thinking
Cognitive analytic therapy	a form of psychological therapy developed by Anthony Ryle in the UK in the 1980s and 1990s. It draws from both cognitive and psychoanalytic traditions, focusing on helping the client understand repetitive emotional and relational patterns in their life
cognitive–behavioural therapy (CBT)	a synthesis of both cognitive and behavioural therapies that aims to modify an individual's thought processes and behaviour
cognitive therapy	a form of **psychotherapy** in which thoughts and beliefs are seen as influencing emotion: consequently, a person's distress might be relieved by changing their thoughts and beliefs
Cold War	historically, a sustained state of political and military tension between the Eastern Bloc (i.e. the former Soviet Union and its allies) and the Western Bloc (i.e. the USA, NATO and its allies); often dated 1947–1991
collaborative empiricism	therapeutic strategies designed to exploit a client's ability to reason almost scientifically about what has happened in their life: clients are encouraged to weigh up and evaluate the evidence for distressing beliefs, propose alternative accounts of their experiences, and try simple behavioural experiments to test out their hypotheses
collectivist	societies (mainly non-industrial or developing societies) in which selfhood is largely seen to be invested in or derived from community and family activities and relations
College of Sexual and Relationship Therapists	a UK charity for sexual and relationship therapy
communication deviance (CD)	a form of vague communication associated with unfocused attention
communication theory	a theory concerning how information and meaning is conveyed and passed between people
community care	treating and caring for people in their homes rather than in an institution
Community Treatment Order (CTO)	a directive issued to those undertaking **Supervised Community Treatmen**t (e.g. to take medication, attend day centres, allow visits by mental health professionals) which they must adhere to so they can be treated at home
co-morbidity	the simultaneous diagnosis of more than one illness – e.g. a psychiatric disorder – in an individual
component studies	studies of the 'active' ingredients of **cognitive behavioural therapies**
compulsory treatment	treatment given without a person's consent. See **coercive treatment**
computerized axial tomography(CAT)	an imaging technique where a computer pictures a slice of body tissue using x-rays
conditions of possibility	the socio-culturally and historically specific conditions which make a particular experience and its interpretation possible; often identified by analysing the **discourses** commonly used to construct and situate this experience
conscientization	a term referring to the development of a critical awareness of society, whereby one understands the political roots of one's own oppression. A concept developed by Paolo Freire

consumer	a term used to refer to those who use mental health services, now seen by many activists as giving the misleading impression that they are freely choosing consumers of services when, for instance, compulsory treatment is not a choice
consumer culture	a term referring to societies in which the purchasing of material goods is driven by desire rather than need
consumerism	in individuals, the socially and economically driven desire to purchase goods and services in ever greater amounts; in a culture, the tendency to emphasize people's social role as consumers as a significant element of their identity and status, or to explain their actions largely on this basis
contingently	dependent for existence, occurrence, character and so on something not yet certain and therefore somewhat unpredictable
control group	a comparison group in an experiment, against which the efficacy of the experimental intervention can be compared; the members of this group receive either no treatment or one whose efficacy is already established
convenience samples	research participants who happened to be readily available, and whom we imagine are suitable
convergence zone	in neuroscience, a term sometimes used to refer to brain regions where information from many neural networks and systems gets collated together
conversion therapy	also termed reorientation/reassignment therapy: a therapeutic technique designed to reorient an individual from a homosexual or bisexual sexual orientation to a heterosexual orientation
correspondence bias	a tendency to make assumptions about a person's dispositions from behaviours that can be explained entirely by the situations in which they occur
cosmetic surgery	procedures designed to enhance an individual's physical appearance
cothymia	a single diagnosis that encompasses experiences of mixed sadness and worry
counter-narrative	an alternative narrative or story running counter to a more dominant narrative
couples therapy	a therapeutic approach which aims to give couples the tools to communicate more effectively, negotiate differences, problem solve and even argue in a healthier way
cross-dressing	the adoption of the dress code of the opposite gender
decompensation	the functional deterioration of a previously working structure or system in the human body; this can occur as a result of trauma, fatigue, stress, disease or ageing
degenerationist theories	theories popular in the 19th and early 20th century but now discredited, which argue that the unrestricted reproduction of people with disabilities or psychiatric diagnoses will result in hereditary degradation, i.e. a cumulative process where each subsequent generation is seen as descending further into imbecility
de-institutionalization	the closing down of large mental hospitals and the development of new forms of treatment for distress in the community
delusion	a belief sincerely held by a person (e.g. a service user) which is considered false or impossible by mental health professionals or by wider society
delusional dominating personality disorder (DDPD)	a psychiatric diagnosis proposed ironically by Caplan and Margrit as a response to **self-defeating personality disorder** to describe men who comply enthusiastically with male gender norms, and including criteria like 'a tendency to feel inordinately threatened by women who fail to disguise their intelligence'
de-personalization or de-realization	where either the self, the surrounding world, or both, are experienced as fundamentally strange or unreal and the person feels profoundly detached from things that are happening; frequently includes physiological dimensions such as palpitations, hyperventilation, heightened muscular tension, dry mouth, tight chest, difficulty breathing, frequent need to urinate, hot flushes, sweating, tremors, numbness and tingling around the mouth and in the fingers and toes
developing countries	countries of lower economic wealth, usually corresponding with less industrialization and technology
deviance model	a model of behaviour which frames that behaviour as deviant or as a criminal act
diagnostic categorizations	definitions of different categories of distress with lists of indicative symptoms
dialectical behaviour therapy (DBT)	a **third wave behavioural therapy** which draws on cognitive behavioural theories, dialectical philosophy and Zen Buddhist practice; that recognizes the significance of invalidating early environments, and in which therapists try to balance an overall validating approach with encouragement to make therapeutic changes
diathesis	a vulnerability or impairment, typically organic in character
dichotic listening	where two different audio stimuli are presented simultaneously to each ear
dimensional models	models of distress that do not presume a sharp dividing line between mental health and mental illness, instead seeing distressing experiences as existing along a continuum
Discourse	A way of looking at the world (e.g. a set of images, texts, beliefs and metaphors) that acts as a cultural resource from which people may draw to understand and represent their experiences (e.g. of distress).

For Michel Foucault, discourses are not simply narratives, rather they are embedded into institutions like the Church, the academy and so on and so he saw them as 'practices that systematically form the objects of which they speak' – in other words they construct particular versions of reality (e.g. that distress is a medical illness)

discriminant validity the extent to which a measure differentiates between two or more constructs

disease-centred model the view that psychiatric drugs work by correcting a defective or diseased brain; according to this model, drug treatment renders the brain more normal by helping to reverse an underlying biological abnormality that leads to experiences of distress

disorganized attachment relationship an **attachment relationship** in which, rather than simply being the main source of comfort and security, carers themselves become a source of fear and anxiety for their infants

dissociation a partial or complete disruption or disintegration of an individual's conscious or psychological functioning; a common response to trauma, sometimes seen as a way of coping that allows people to 'space out' or 'switch off'

dissociative identity disorder a psychiatric diagnosis give to individuals who seemingly display a number of distinct identities or personalities (sometimes known as alters or alter egos) each with its own unique perspective and ways of behaving; this diagnosis used to be called Multiple Personality Disorder

dissociative states states in which people experience **dissociation**

distress a non-medical concept, used in this book in place of terms like 'mental illness' or 'psychopathology'; a general term for all of the kinds of mental health difficulties for which people might receive clinical psychological or psychiatric interventions

divination a religious process or ritual carried out by a healer to read signs of future events, including illness and spirit possession

dose–response relationship the change in effect on an organism caused by differing levels of exposure (or doses) to an agent (e.g. a drug) or a stressor (i.e. they have a tendency to co-vary)

double-blind a clinical trial in which neither the research participant nor the health professional is aware of whether the participant is in the intervention or control (comparison) group

double-blind randomized controlled trials **double-blind** clinical trials where participants are randomly allocated to the intervention or control (comparison) group – designed to minimize the influence of things like selection and the effects of expectation; often referred to as the 'gold standard' of treatment research

drapetomania a purported (and discredited) mental disorder associated with the desire to escape from slavery

drug-centred model the view that psychiatric drugs, like all psychoactive drugs, modify the functioning of the nervous system and so produce altered mental states; this model suggests that drugs can sometimes be helpful because the features of the altered drug-induced state can be functional in some circumstances (but not in others)

DSM The Diagnostic and Statistical Manual of Mental Disorders published by the American Psychiatric Association: one of the two major works defining the diagnostic criteria used by psychiatrists (the other is the International Classification of Diseases). Each successive version until now has been denoted by a Roman numeral e.g. DSM III, but the forthcoming version is currently being referred to as DSM 5.

dual representation theory the theory that we have one memory system that stores consciously processed verbal or narrative aspects of a traumatic event, and a separate system that stores images, sounds, and feeling states or bodily reactions: in essence, all of the sensory, non-verbal aspects

dynamic pertaining to or characterized by energy or effective action; vigorously active or forceful; not fixed and stable

dysfunction when a system – whether understood as psychological or cognitive (e.g. memory), or as bodily and biological (e.g. the dopamine system) – fails to function in the normal manner

dyspareunia experience of pain during sexual penetration

dysregulates impairs the capacity for control and regulation

early maladaptive schemas in cognitive psychology, unhelpful ways of viewing the world which develop in response to aversive experiences in early childhood

eating disorders a group of psychiatric diagnoses characterized by unusual eating habits, including restrictive or excessive food intake, which may have negative consequences for mental and physical health

eating disorders not otherwise specified (EDNOS) a psychiatric diagnosis given to people whose eating patterns are considered unusual but who do not meet the criteria for the main eating disorders diagnoses; by far the most common diagnosis in this area of psychiatry

ecological model of systems Bronfenbrenner's (1979) model which conceptualizes systems as having four levels: micro, meso, exo, and macro

effectiveness the study of whether a therapy 'works' in a real-life clinical setting

efficacy the study of whether a therapy 'works' in an experimental setting

electro-convulsive therapy (ECT)	a form of therapy whereby an epileptic seizure is induced via the administration of electricity to the brain; typically given when people are experiencing profound sadness, sometimes described by psychiatrists as a 'treatment of last resort', for example when it is considered that a person is at immediate risk of committing suicide and has not responded to other treatments
electromyography	a procedure of recording the tiny electrical impulses in muscle tissue
embodied	an aspect of experience that is shaped by the character of our physical bodies
embodiment	the location and the character of our bodies within the world; those aspects of experience shaped by the location and character of our bodies in the world
emic	an approach prioritizing the meanings a person attributes to their beliefs, experiences and behaviours, using their own cultural and community reference points
emotion work	a sociological concept that refers to the ways people are sometimes expected to manage, cultivate, refine and display their emotions in line with the expectations of employers or others
empowerment	ways in which groups with less power – for example, those with little access to economic resources – attain greater power
epidemiology	a branch of medicine that involves the study of how frequently different diseases occur in different populations
epigenetics	the study of how environmental influences can produce heritable changes in offspring without changing their genes
equal environment assumption (EEA)	the assumption that environmental influence operates equally for both monozygotic (MZ) and dizygotic (DZ) twins: typically, that MZ twin pairs are treated no more similarly than DZ twin pairs
etic	an approach prioritizing a universal (as opposed to local) definition of beliefs, experiences and behaviours, offered by a scientific observer, with the aim to be culturally neutral and objective
eugenics	a movement in politics and social policy popular in the 19th and early 20th century but now discredited, which advocated the use of practices aimed at improving the genetic composition of a population, usually human; based on the idea that certain groups of people were genetically inferior and that if they were allowed to reproduce freely they would weaken the genetic composition of the general population. See **degenerationist theories**
existentialist philosophy	a philosophy derived from the view that life is essentially meaningless and that we need to strive to create meaning in our own lives
exo	level of Bronfenbrenner's ecological model of systems involving more distal systems which influence proximal systems (e.g. local authorities and school governing bodies), which impact on the micro and meso systems
experience	something that happens within the life and subjective awareness of a person
expressed emotion (EE)	the amount of emotion (usually hostile or negative) displayed in a family
external locus of control	where one believes that causal agency for events is located outside – rather than inside – oneself
external validity	the ability to generalize to the real world from the artificial circumstances of an experimental situation
externalizing attributional bias	the specific tendency to attribute events to the actions of others – e.g. when negative events are seen as caused by others rather than oneself
family blaming	holding families morally responsible for the development of the distress of a member of the family
family therapy	a form of **psychotherapy** in which individual distress is seen to arise from problems in relationships and communication between family members; the therapist therefore uses a range of strategies to help family members change the way they relate to one another
feminism	a collection of social movements with a shared aim of promoting equal rights for women
feminist	a person who upholds or proclaims the principles of feminism
feminist family therapy	uses feminist theories to explore the relationship between wider cultural messages about gender (as well as a variety of socio-political and socio-economic factors, such as race, class and disability that can impact on family life) in the generation and maintenance of family difficulties and psychological distress. The approach advocates the establishment of egalitarian relationships within the family and a non victim-blaming position
fetishism	recurrent sexual arousal from inanimate objects
first rank symptoms	a variety of hallucinations and delusions (see **Schneiderian**)
five factor model	a personality model which proposes that all human personalities contain greater or lesser degrees of the same five traits: openness to experience, conscientiousness, extraversion, agreeableness and neuroticism
flashbacks	moments where vivid memories of trauma get re-lived involuntarily, and are accompanied by severe emotional impacts
flooding	introduction of a feared stimuli in its full form in behavioural therapy, whilst the person is in a relaxed state

formulation	an individual summary of someone's difficulties, based on psychological theory; it can be seen as a kind of a story or narrative which attempts to link the person's difficulties to the relationships and events in their lives, and the sense they have made of their experiences: see Chapter 5
free association	a psychotherapeutic strategy used in psychoanalysis in which people are encouraged to say whatever words come to mind in relation to a topic
function creep	where an original goal is revised to include additional goals
functional diagnoses	psychiatric diagnoses in which behaviour is judged to be dysfunctional but no consistent organic basis for the dysfunction has been shown
functional MRI (fMRI)	an imaging technique which uses magnetic fields to generate measures of blood oxygen levels in the brain; these are thought to be consistently related to neural activity
functional redundancy	a frequent feature of complex systems where there are many possible pathways to what is, functionally, much the same outcome
fundamental attribution error	a common tendency to over-emphasize internal or dispositional factors (such as personality or motivation) in accounting for the actions of others
gamma-aminobutyric acid or GABA	an inhibitory neurotransmitter that dampens down the rate of neural firing
gay affirmative therapy	a form of **psychotherapy** that encourages gay or bisexual clients to learn to accept and celebrate their sexual orientation rather than attempt to change it to a heterosexual orientation
gender identity disorder	a psychiatric diagnostic category describing a person who views their current biological sex as contrary to their perceived gender identity (usually opposite to the one they were assigned at birth)
gender inequalities	the discrepancy between access to rights and resources as a function of one's membership of a gender category (male/female)
gender roles	the set of prescribed norms (relating to emotions, behaviour and thinking) considered to be socially and culturally appropriate for individuals of a designated gender (male/female)
gender variance	holding gender traits that are contrary to one's biological sex (according to culturally prescribed norms of gendered behaviour)
general paralysis of the insane	neurological condition, commonly diagnosed in the 19th century; subsequently found to be caused by syphilis
generalizable	the capacity to infer a general principle, trend and so on from particular facts, statistics, or the like
genome scan	an analysis of the entire genome of an individual that compares its character to established markers for diseases and disease characteristics
genome-wide association studies	molecular genetic studies which compare the prevalence of putative genetic markers between groups of unrelated individuals given a diagnosis, and control groups of similar people without a diagnosis
glial cells	brain cells which support the neuronal tissue
good enough parenting	from the work of Donald Winnicott, where parents and carers meet their child's basic needs for nutrition, warmth, and comfort; are responsive to their child's emotional needs, offering comfort and reassurance that is fairly consistent across time, communicated sufficiently clearly, pitched at the right kind of level, and arrives relatively soon after it is first needed
graded exposure	a therapeutic strategy in behavioural therapy where a person employs coping strategies as they expose themselves to feared objects or situations, working through a hierarchy from the least feared to most feared level
grandiose beliefs	when an individual seems to think that they are uniquely special in some way (e.g. that they are Jesus)
habituation	how, over time, we become used to responding to something – such as distress – in a particular way that may become somewhat familiar and even reassuring
hallucination	a general term for the perception of a stimulus that is not present
hearing voices	a form of **auditory hallucination**
heteronormativity	the view that men and women should adhere to a biologically prescribed set of gender-specific behaviours (e.g. women as exclusive care givers). Within this, heterosexuality is viewed as the only 'natural' and 'normal' form of sexual orientation
heterosexual	an individual who is sexually attracted to a member of the opposite gender
historicism	a mode of thinking that assigns a central and basic significance to a specific context, such as historical period, geographical place or local culture
holistic	a perspective which emphasizes the interrelationships between different elements of the self
homeodynamics	the striving of the body–brain system to maintain certain key variables within strict limits; the equilibria produced are always fluctuating around an optimal point; this optimal point itself fluctuates somewhat, according to environmental circumstances: sometimes called homeostasis
homicide	the act of a human killing another human

homosexual	an individual who is sexually attracted to a member of the same gender
homosexuality	sexual attraction to one's own gender
human sexual response cycle (HSRC)	a model of sexual stimulation and activity developed by sexologists William Masters and Virginia Johnson. The model involves four stages of sexual response: excitement, plateau, orgasm and resolution
humanist philosophy	a philosophy which asserts that those without religious faith can still act ethically and morally because of their faith in human values
humanistic psychotherapy	a form of **psychotherapy** based on **humanist philosophy**
hyperkinetic form	a form of encephalitis lethargica, the symptoms of which include restlessness and involuntary movements
hypervigilance	a general sensory state referring to an individual's exaggerated senses and behaviours, used to check for perceived threat, which usually results in fatigue
hypnotism	the practice whereby a person is put into a trance-like and suggestible state
hypomania	a psychiatric term to describe milder experiences of mania, in which mood is elevated, expansive or irritable but not to such an extent or for such a length of time as to meet the criteria for a **manic episode**
hypothalamic-pituitary-adrenal (HPA) axis	a term that summarizes a complex set of interactions and feedback loops between the hypothalamus and the pituitary and adrenal glands
hysteria	a purported disorder – now discredited – said to occur largely in women, supposedly signified by a wide range of symptoms including anything from anxiety and fainting to insomnia and loss of appetite for food or sex
iatrogenic problem	a problem created by the treatment itself
ICD	The International Classification of Diseases, produced by the World Health Organization, which includes a section on psychiatric diagnoses. Each successive version is numbered e.g. ICD 10
impotence	the inability to develop or maintain an erection; also called **male erectile dysfunction**
incidence	the number of new cases of something during a fixed time period (e.g. over the course of a year) and the occurrence of this within a population
individualism	a philosophical tradition which emphasizes the properties, experiences and agency of the individual
industrialization	the historical shift from a broadly agricultural and rural society to an industrial and urban society, signalling technological and economic advances
ineffable	incapable of being fully expressed or described in words
inner speech	the unspoken commentary that we experience accompanying the actions of ourselves and others; how language is part of the way that we think
insecure-ambivalent attachment relationship	an **attachment relationship** in which carers are somewhat inconsistent in their responses: sometimes they respond appropriately to their infant's needs, but at other times fail to do so; infants respond to this kind of care by coping relatively well with short periods of separation, but when the carer returns they display anger and reluctance, before eventually showing any degree of warmth
insecure-avoidant attachment relationship	an **attachment relationship** in which carers show relatively little emotional response to their infant's distress, encouraging independence and self-reliance, and infants respond by becoming relatively autonomous when separated from their carers; they show relatively little distress when left briefly alone, but relatively little joy when their carers return
institutionalization	the process whereby, over time, a person begins to structure their life according to the routines of an institution, gradually losing their independence and becoming more dependent on the institution's routines and practices
insulin coma therapy	a form of therapy in which temporary comas were induced in patients through the administration of insulin
internal validity	a characteristic of experiments that enables experimenters to be confident that any observed outcomes are produced by the experimental variables
internalized stigma	where the discriminatory attitudes of others are adopted – internalized – by service users themselves
interpenetrate	when two or more things (e.g. humans and their environments) come to include aspects of each other
interpersonal	thoughts and emotions communicated between individuals; pertaining to relationships between people
interpersonal therapy	a style of therapy that focuses on the interpersonal context in which a person lives, such as their intimate relationships and family, and concentrates on building a set of interpersonal skills with the client to enable the establishment of stronger and more fulfilling relationships and a greater sense of personal well-being
intersex	term used to describe individuals with gender characteristics that may be indistinguishable as being typically *either* male *or* female or typically *both* male *and* female

intrapersonal	thoughts and emotions taking place within the individual
introspection	the reporting by a participant of their conscious thoughts, memories, feelings and experiences
involuntary commitment	US term referring to compulsory admission to hospital (also termed civil commitment)
Kingsley Hall	a therapeutic community in the East end of London, which ran for five years from 1965 to 1970
labelling theory	the notion that mental illness is actually the end result of a series of social processes whereby 'abnormal' behaviour is subtly reinforced
leucotomy	a surgical procedure in which the connections to and from the prefrontal cortex are cut; sometimes called a **lobotomy**
liberalism	a political and economic philosophy, associated with **capitalism**, which emphasizes tolerance and equal rights
lifeline	from the work of biologist and neuroscientist Steven Rose: the trajectory of a living creature as it grows, develops and ages, as it constantly modifies, and is modified by, the various environments it occupies
lifetime prevalence	how many people would meet diagnostic criteria over the course of their lifetime
limbic kindling	where the limbic system enters into a continuously hyperactive state
linkage studies	molecular genetic studies which try to identify genetic markers associated (linked) with specific diseases, using statistical analyses to estimate whether the linkage might have occurred by chance
lobotomy	The pre-frontal **leucotomy** technique after being adapted by the American surgeon Walter Freeman
locus coeruleus-norepinephrine (LC-NE) system	a brain system that begins in the pons and radiates upward, and has close connections with the **hypothalamic-pituitary-adrenal (HPA) axis** and the sympathetic nervous system
low sexual desire or hypoactive sexual desire	the absence of sexual thoughts, fantasies or desire for sex; considered to be a sexual dysfunction in the **DSM**
macro	level of Bronfenbrenner's ecological model of systems involving large-scale systems characterized by social structures and ideologies, such as policies of governments and multinational companies, aspects of capitalism such as the maximization of profits and off-loading of costs, unemployment rates and the role of gender and religion in society
madness	an ordinary language term used in this book to collectively describe the more severe forms of distress, typically characterized by experiences such as **hallucinations** or **delusions**
magnetic resonance imaging (MRI)	an imaging technique where images of the brain or body are produced through the use of magnetic fields and radio waves
major tranquillizers	drugs marketed by pharmaceutical companies as addressing an underlying biological disorder, used when a calming effect is desired and often given to people with a diagnosis of **schizophrenia**
male erectile dysfunction (MED)	the inability to develop or maintain an erection during sexual activity, also called **impotence**
mandatory treatment	Canadian term referring to **compulsory treatment** and admission to hospital
manic episode	in psychiatry, an experience of persistently elevated, expansive or irritable mood, lasting for at least a week
mass media	the broad range of technologies used to communicate information, news and entertainment to a population (within and across countries): mostly television, the internet, newspapers, film and radio
Maudsley method	in psychiatric practice associated with the diagnosis of anorexia, involving parents in the initial phase of treatment, mainly emphasizing the restoration of weight and the regulation of dieting behaviour
medical definition of normality	a definition of normality which classes as abnormal those activities, behaviours and characteristics that are associated with danger to life or well-being or which cause harm to bodily organs or tissues
medicalization	the tendency to view problems of living and everyday difficulties and stresses as the symptoms of medical problems
melancholy (melancholia)	a state of distress believed, in Ancient Greek thought, to be caused by an excess of black bile and characterized by anguish and distress
Mental Health Act	the law in England and Wales governing the compulsory treatment of mental health difficulties
mental illness	a medical concept of distress which views it as a matter of disease or sickness
Mental Patients Union	a mental health activist group established in the UK in the 1970s
meso	level of Bronfenbrenner's ecological model of systems where links exist between an individual's proximal systems, such as between home and school
meta-analysis	a quantitative comparison of the results of a number of different trials of the same treatment or intervention
metabolite	a substance produced by the biological processes of metabolism
metacognition	'thinking about thinking' or higher cognitive functions and processes

micro	level of Bronfenbrenner's ecological model of systems involving the individual and their immediate/proximal systems, such as home, school and work
migration	when a group of people (sometimes large groups) move from one place to another, sometimes over large distances; this can be either voluntary or involuntary
mind-body dualism	a way of thinking about the relationship between mind and body which presumes that they are distinct, separate entities or substances: sometimes referred to as **Cartesian Dualism**
mindfulness-based cognitive therapy (MBCT)	monitoring and other techniques that encourage clients to develop different relationships with their negative feelings: to treat them as passing events rather than the beginning of a trend, to minimize rather than maximize their significance and import, to recognize that their feelings are not necessarily an accurate representation of their actual situation, and so on
mixed episode	in psychiatry, an experience where moods fluctuate between mania and profound misery
molecular genetic research	statistical analyses of DNA sequences
monoamine	any of various biogenic amine neurotransmitters having a single amino group: for example dopamine, epinephrine and norepinephrine
monoamine oxidase inhibitors (MAOI's)	a class of drugs usually prescribed to people given diagnoses of depression, with similar effects to stimulants
monogamous	a relationship that is exclusive, involving only two sexual or intimate partners .
motherese	a tone of voice and way of speaking specially adapted for one's infant
nasogastric feeding	treatment in which a plastic tube is inserted through the nose, past the throat and into the stomach: a medical technique used to administer food or medication when a person is unable to eat, or refuses to feed themselves. It is controversially used to force-feed individuals given a diagnosis of anorexia, who are of a very low body weight and dangerously close to death
necessary causes	influences or events that must be present for distress to arise
negative schema	a collection of interrelated beliefs about the self, negative in character and acquired in childhood, usually as a result of adverse life experiences; in cognitive theory, negative self-schemas cause individual cognitive biases toward pessimistic, negative or critical interpretations of events and experiences
negative symptoms	in people who have or might be given a diagnosis of **schizophrenia**, the presence of experiences such as apathy, or difficulty in motivating oneself to engage in activities, anhedonia (an inability to experience pleasure) and flat affect (where one's emotions seem flattened)
negative triad	in Aaron Beck's cognitive theory of depression, the notion that people given this diagnosis have negative thoughts about themselves, their experiences in the world, and the future
neurasthenia	a clinical diagnosis previously common in the West, the symptoms of which may include anxiety, low mood, muscular weakness, fatigue, dizziness, insomnia, poor appetite and a lack of energy; today in the West, people who formerly received this diagnosis might now be described as having chronic fatigue syndrome
neuroleptics	literally, 'taking hold of one's nerves'; an alternative term for the psychiatric drugs also called **major tranquillizers**; a term in common psychiatric usage in the first few decades of the use of these drugs
neurological	of or relating to the nervous system (neurological conditions are disorders of the nervous system)
neurosis	in psychiatry, a collective term for forms of distress that involve exaggerations of everyday responses (e.g. excessive worrying) but do not involve distorted perceptions or unusual beliefs
neurosurgery	see **psychosurgery**
non-monogamous	individuals who, whilst in a romantic relationship, also form emotional and/or sexual bonds and/or romantic relationships with other individuals. The arrangement is usually an open one (i.e. each partner is aware of and in agreement with the arrangement)
norm of reaction	the pattern of phenotypic expression of a single genotype across a range of environments
normalizing approach	one in which experiences are explained as within the range of normal responses, and emphasis is placed instead on the typically unusual circumstances that may have produced these experiences (e.g. sleep deprivation or social isolation)
number needed to treat	the number of persons with whom a practitioner would need to conduct an intervention before, on average, the intervention might yield more benefit than if the people treated had been in the control group
Nuremberg Code	a set of ethical principles which require that research participants give full voluntary consent, the research should be of value to society, the results not be attainable in any other way, and studies should not result in death or serious injury: introduced after World War Two and the discovery that horrific medical experiments had been carried out on inmates of the Nazi concentration camps
obesity	a medical term for excess body weight, to the extent that health and life expectancy is threatened

obsessive compulsive personality disorder (OCD)	a psychiatric diagnosis given to people who are said to be preoccupied with perfectionism and orderliness and in whom this is thought to be an enduring element of their personality. There are many sub-categories of personality disorder diagnosis, see Table 13.2.
Oedipus complex	a term from Freudian psychoanalysis to describe when a child is in love with their mother but jealous of their father
oestrogen	a hormone found in both sexes but more commonly described as a 'female' sex hormone. It is responsible for the regulation of the reproductive cycle in women and the generation of typical female sexual characteristics
open	the ability of a system to continuously respond to external, environmental influences
operant conditioning	the behaviourist principle of shaping voluntary responses by the use of reinforcement (rewards or punishments) to encourage desired responses and discourage others
organic diagnoses	diagnoses such as dementia, syphilis, and Huntington's Chorea where a biological cause of the dysfunction has been clearly demonstrated
outer speech	fragments of conversations with others that we later speak out loud to ourselves, using them to monitor and guide our actions
outpatient commitment/ assisted outpatient treatment	US term for **Community Treatment Order/Supervised Community Treatment**
over-determined	the idea that a single observed effect is determined by multiple causes at the same time (any one of which alone might be enough to account for the effect)
over-generalization	assuming that, for example, all future events will go badly because one event has
panic attacks	relatively brief but intense periods of overwhelming anxiety accompanied by pronounced physiological effects such as breathlessness and dizziness
paranoia	a term in general use to refer to an unwarranted belief that others intend to harm us – also referred to as a persecutory **delusion** in diagnostic manuals
paranoid beliefs	those characterized by a feeling of threat and the belief that others are actively conspiring to harm one – see also **paranoia**
paranoid personality disorder	a psychiatric diagnosis given to people who are said to be persistently hostile and suspicious, when this is thought to be an element of their personality. There are many sub-categories of personality disorder diagnosis, see Table 13.2.
paraphilia	a term used to describe sexual attraction to unusual objects, or sexual activities that are deemed unusual in nature
Parental Bonding Instrument	a retrospective measure of one's childhood relationships with one's parents
Parkinson's disease	a degenerative neurological disease caused by reduced activity of dopamine in a part of the brain called the basal ganglia, which controls movement and also influences thought, emotion and motivation
passing	the ability to conceal one's identity (e.g. as transgender) and 'pass' without being recognized as belonging to this category. This act of concealing may also be a source of stress for individuals – where authenticity does not exclude acknowledging one's past reality
pathologizing approach	where experiences are seen as symptoms of an illness, and are seen as lying outside of normal human experience
pathoplastic	the various influences (biological, social, cultural, psychological) on the form of a disease once it has developed
patient	someone who receives medical treatment; the term is frequently used in medical contexts to describe people experiencing distress. See **service user**
patriarchal	of or pertaining to a patriarch, the male head of a family, tribe, community, church, order, etc.; characteristic of an entity, family, church, society etc., controlled or dominated by men
perfectionism	a firmly held belief that perfection can be achieved; in relation to distress, failing to achieve perfection can be a threat to worth and esteem
persecutory delusion	the term used in psychiatric diagnostic manuals for an unwarranted belief that others intend to harm us – also known as **paranoia**
personality disorders (PD)	a group of psychiatric diagnoses in which enduring distress, problems in relating to others and engaging in behaviour which breaches social norms are seen as primarily caused by a person's personality. There are many sub-categories of personality disorder diagnosis, see Table 13.2.
personality disorder not otherwise specified	a psychiatric diagnosis given to people who meet some of the criteria for personality disorder sub-categories but may not fully meet the criteria for any single diagnosis
pharmacological revolution	a historical period beginning in the 1950s in the West, in which new and advanced medicines of all types were coming to the forefront of medical and mainstream culture

phenomenology	what an experience is like subjectively, its character; in philosophy, a form of analysis that frequently emphasizes experience and the body
phobias	intense worries that seem to be tied to very particular objects, places or situations; phobias can be triggered by creatures such as spiders or moths, activities such as flying or travelling in cars, or events such as dental appointments
placebo	a false medical intervention used in clinical trials. Patients given a placebo can sometimes experience a perceived or actual improvement in their medical condition – this is known as the placebo effect. Placebo conditions are often included in **randomized controlled trials** to assess the effects of psychological suggestion on medical intervention
plasticity	the capacity to be moulded, receive shape, or be made to assume a specific form
point prevalence	the number of people meeting diagnostic criteria at a particular point in time
political dissidents	those who question the prevailing political system under which they live
positron emission tomography(PET)	an imaging technique in which positron-emitting radioisotopes – short-lived radioactive substances – are introduced into the body in order to produce three-dimensional coloured images of their concentration in body tissue
positive symptoms	in people who have or might be given a diagnosis of **schizophrenia**, the presence of unusual experiences, notably **hallucinations** and **delusions**
post-encephalitic Parkinsonism	a condition causing nerve damage similar to Parkinson's disease, thought to be the result of a viral infection
postpsychiatry	not a new theory or therapy, but a call to open up spaces 'in which other perspectives can assume a validity previously denied them', in particular the voices of service users
post-traumatic stress disorder (PTSD)	a psychiatric diagnosis frequently given to people experiencing ongoing distress as a result of a traumatic event; for example, experiencing flashbacks of the event and avoiding situations which are reminiscent of it
predicatives	verbal terms or phrases that index or point to aspects of the current situation
prefrontal leucotomy	a surgical technique for severing the connections to and from the prefrontal cortex. See **lobotomy**
Present State Examination	a questionnaire designed in the 1960s to assess an individual's present mental state (questions refer to the past month only) in order to identify whether they have a psychiatric disorder
presentism	historical accounts written through the lens of the present, judging the past according to our current knowledge and values
prevalence	in epidemiology, the total number of cases of a disease or disorder in a population at any given time
primary prevention	targeting and ameliorating the proximal causes of distress
prodrome	in psychiatric practice, the period of time immediately before the point where somebody might reach the threshold to be given a diagnosis (for example of **schizophrenia**)
professionalization	the establishment, within a field of interest, of specific professional disciplines with their own training, rules and regulations
prolactin	a hormone involved in the regulation of lactation
prospective	a stance of anticipating events in the future: prospective studies are those in which participants are interviewed, observed or measured *before* an event occurs
pseudo-patients	people playing the role of a psychiatric patient usually in the context of a research study
psychiatric system survivor	someone who receives or uses mental health services; this term is preferred by some organizations of service users and campaigning groups, as it conveys that those in distress have to survive services, not just distress
psychoanalysis	a branch of **psychotherapy** interested in the conscious and unconscious drives that motivate people. Psychoanalysts believe that mental health difficulties and other problems with living arise as a result of unconscious conflicts that need to be brought into conscious awareness, in order to be sufficiently dealt with and disposed of. Talking freely (**free association**) under the skilled guidance of an analyst is one way to reveal these unconscious conflicts
psychogenic model	a model of distress which views its causes as arising out of the mind
psychological types	the Jungian categorization of people into primary types of psychological function
psychologize	to emphasize the individual, emotional and cognitive aspects of an experience, as opposed to its social, physical and somatic aspects
psychopathic personality disorder (PPD)	a psychiatric diagnosis given to people described as having a personality characterized by shallow emotions (in particular reduced fear), reduced empathy, superficial charm, manipulativeness, impulsivity and other antisocial behaviours. There are many sub-categories of personality disorder diagnosis, see Table 13.2. See **psychopathy**
psychopathology	a medical concept of distress which views it as a matter of disease or sickness (pathology: disease or impairment)

Psychopathy	This notion has been developed by Hervey Cleckley and Robert Hare and refers to a constellation of behavioural and personality characteristics including shallow emotions, a lack of empathy, superficial charm, manipulativeness and anti-social behaviour. Although in common parlance this term is not used in either the DSM or ICD classifications although it is similar to the categories of anti-social (DSM) and dissocial (ICD) subcategories of personality disorder (see Table 13.2)
psychosis	a term for psychiatric diagnoses in which there is an assumed loss of contact with reality, usually characterized by hearing or seeing things others cannot hear or see (**hallucinations**) or holding beliefs that others consider strange and unusual (**delusions**);in this book, called **madness**
psychosocial model	a model of distress which views the psychological processes involved as caused and maintained by adverse life events and circumstances
psychosomatic	a medical term for the effects of social, psychological and behavioural factors on bodily processes
psychosurgery	a surgical operation in which brain tissue is destroyed for the treatment of mental health problems (also known as neurosurgery for mental disorder). For example, a **lobotomy**
psychotherapy	a broad term referring to the 'talking therapies'. Its aim is to provide a person with the opportunity to explore and gain insight into their difficulties and distress. Through a greater understanding of the person's underlying difficulties, psychotherapy is said to equip the person with a set of coping skills that can lead to long-term changes in thinking, feeling and behaviour
publication bias	the trend that published literature is likely to overstate the benefits of an intervention because it is more difficult to publish studies that fail to demonstrate significant effects
purging	behaviours that serve the purpose of controlling weight, such as the removal of food from the body by vomiting, the use of laxatives, enemas, diuretics and over exercising
qualitative	qualitative research is interested in the meanings provided by individuals for their beliefs, experiences and behaviours: the aim is not to standardize or mathematically measure meaning, but to understand the meaning making process
quantitative	quantitative research adopts standardized measurements of phenomena so that the relationships between them can be measured and analysed mathematically
random allocation	in experimental method, the allocation of people by chance to either control or experimental groups
randomized controlled trial	research study involving randomly allocating study participants to experimental conditions and including a **control group** which receives a **placebo**; devised to control for a number of factors that could influence the outcome of treatment studies
rational emotive behaviour therapy	a form of **psychotherapy** which focuses on resolving emotional and behavioural problems and disturbances, based on **rationalist** principles
rationalist	pertaining to any view appealing to reason and logic as a source of knowledge or justification
recipient	a term for **service users** that emphasizes the often passive or involuntary nature of the relationship; it is preferred by some commentators who consider that terms like 'consumer' and 'client' imply a person's active consent
recovery movement	a social movement rejecting the idea that people with psychotic experiences are suffering from an irreversible or chronic condition; the model emphasizes optimism, empowerment and interpersonal support, and focuses on collaborative approaches, productive roles, peer support and stigma-reduction.
reductive	methods or ways of thinking that tend to reduce distress to a single dimension, typically the biological
rehabilitation	the process of restoration of community functioning and well-being of an individual experiencing distress
relapse rates	the extent to which, following either remission or an apparently successful intervention, persons experience a recurrence of their original difficulties
relationships	emotional, sexual or other connections, associations, or involvements between people
repressed memories	significant memories, usually of a traumatic nature, that have become unavailable for recall; also called 'motivated forgetting' in which a subject blocks out painful or traumatic times in their life
reproductive fitness	the ability to pass on genes to the next generation
response prevention	a therapeutic strategy found in behaviour therapy in which a person with a compulsion to conduct a particular behaviour (e.g. continually checking that one has switched the oven off) learns to stay relaxed and manage the fear caused by not conducting the ritual
Responsible Clinician	the mental health professional responsible for organizing a service user's care under the English and Welsh **Mental Health Act**
retrograde amnesia	impaired recall of the past
retrospective	a stance of looking back at events that have already taken place
sadomasochism	the process of administering or receiving acts of pain or humiliation for the purpose (usually) of sexual arousal and pleasure

schema-focused cognitive therapy (SFCT)	a form of cognitive **psychotherapy** that focuses on changing **maladaptive schemas** seen as developing as a result of early life experiences
schizophrenia	a psychiatric diagnosis given to people who experience **auditory hallucination**s, **paranoid** or bizarre **delusions**, chaotic or disorganized speech, and unusual emotional responses, typically accompanied by significant social or occupational dysfunction
Schneiderian	a term referring to the work of Kurt Schneider, who categorized the symptoms that make up a **schizophrenia** diagnosis into first and second rank symptoms, in order to differentiate diagnoses of schizophrenia from other psychotic diagnoses
secondary prevention	the practice of identifying and trying to ameliorate distressing experiences before they reach such a pitch that the person might be given a psychiatric diagnosis (as in early intervention services)
sectioned	an informal term used in the UK for when a person is taken into hospital without their consent for further assessment or treatment; usually occurring if the person is perceived to be a threat to themselves or others: from the relevant section of the **Mental Health Act**
secure attachment relationship	an **attachment relationship** in which carers respond to the emotional needs of infants appropriately, promptly and consistently, with the consequence that infants are better able to deal with potentially difficult situations such as being left alone for a short while
seduction theory	a hypothesis posited by Freud, who for a time believed that the origins of hysteria and obsessional neurosis lay in early childhood sexual abuse
selective abstraction	taking details out of context and magnifying them
selective placement bias	whereby the best potential adoptive parents are in a position to choose from a range of potential adoptees and may well have been put off from adopting children with a biological family history of mental health difficulties, since potential adopters are usually well-informed of any difficulties in the adoptee's family background
selective serotonin re-uptake Inhibitors (SSRI's)	a class of compounds which block the neurotransmitter serotonin, usually prescribed for people given diagnoses of depression; commonly reported effects include drowsiness, feelings of cognitive impairment, agitation (and other so-called 'activating' effects like anxiety), emotional blunting and emotional instability
self-defeating personality disorder (SDPD)	a proposed but discredited psychiatric diagnosis, purportedly characterized by a person failing to promote their own needs before those of others; often associated with experiences of domestic or childhood abuse. See **delusional dominating personality disorder**
self-esteem	a psychological concept describing an individual's overall appraisal of their self-worth. It can operate in a specific domain (I am worthless because I am fat) or be more global in presentation (I am simply worthless)
self-harm	the intentional, direct injuring of one's own body tissue, most often done without suicidal intentions; often seen by those who engage in it as a coping strategy. See Box 13.4
self-help movement	a contemporary trend for people to adopt coping strategies acquired from their own reading or from learning from others with similar problems rather than professionals
self-organizing	a system of **synergistically** co-operative elements whose patterns of global behaviour are distributed and self-limiting in nature
sensate focus	a therapeutic technique developed by **sexologists** Masters and Johnson in couples therapy. Partners are instructed to sensually touch each other without touching genitals and progressing to full sexual activity, with the aim of gradually reducing anxiety regarding sex
sensory deprivation	where a person's sensory input is reduced, for example by lying in a dark and soundproofed cubicle; after continuous isolation in this manner, participants begin to experience **hallucinations** and a degraded ability to think clearly
service user	someone who receives or uses mental health services: the most commonly used term in UK mental health policy and the term we mainly use in this book to describe people experiencing distress
service user/survivor movement	self-organized groups of mental health service users who collectively develop and promote coping strategies for distress and campaign for a more enlightened approach to distress
sex therapists	therapists who predominantly treat difficulties with having sex
Sexologist	a scientist who studies sexual behaviour in humans
sexual abuse	the coercion of an adult person (using either psychological pressure or physical force) by another to engage in sexual activity. See also **child sexual abuse**
sexual and gender identity disorder	a psychiatric diagnostic category that covers both sexual disorders (with psychological as opposed to physiological causes) and gender identity disorders
sexual arousal	sexual excitement at the thought, or anticipation, of sexual activity
sexual disorder	a general term referring to diagnoses of either **sexual dysfunction**, **paraphilia** and/or **gender identity disorder**

sexual dysfunction	a diagnostic term referring to a difficulty an individual or couple may experience with any aspect of the human sexual response cycle, including desire, arousal or orgasm
sexual functioning	the ability for the person to be able to experience desire, to be aroused, to physically engage in a sexual act and experience orgasm
sham ECT	a placebo form of **electro-convulsive therapy (ECT)** involving the participant in a clinical trial going through a procedure identical to that of ECT, including receiving anaesthetic and muscle relaxants and even having the electrodes placed on the head, but with no electric current passed through the brain
shellshock	in the First World War, a purported psychiatric illness presumed to result from injury to the nerves during combat; most people experiencing this kind of distress would probably be given a diagnosis of **post-traumatic stress disorder**
side-effects	the unintended or unwanted effects of a drug
signs	in medical diagnosis, signs are biological phenomena that can be objectively observed and verified by other people, and that can be compared to an objective norm
single blind	a clinical trial in which participants are not informed about (i.e. are 'blind' to) whether they are in the intervention or control (comparison) group
single nucleotide polymorphisms (SNPs)	in **molecular genetic research**, markers of genetic variation
single photon emission computed tomography (SPECT)	an imaging technique that produces a computerized cross-section of physical structures in the body based on their differential absorption of gamma-rays
social capital	both the number of social networks (community organizations like churches and youth groups) there are in a community, and how strong the links between them are; the social glue that binds a community together
social causation	an explanation for the higher prevalence of distress in more deprived sections of the community, which proposes that the greater stresses of such lifestyles and environments cause mental health problems to develop
social construction (social constructionism)	a paradigm within which how something is talked about produces it in a particular form or version; these versions are associated with socio-cultural norms of knowledge and understanding and often seen to be organized in **discourses**
social Darwinism	an interpretation of Darwin's notion of 'survival of the fittest' as a moral injunction to prefer the strong over the weak
social definition of normality	a definition of normality which classes as abnormal those activities, behaviours and characteristics disapproved of in a particular time and place
social distance	a measure of how comfortable people feel with members of a particular social group; used to study the extent to which members of a group may be treated differently as a result of prejudice and discrimination
social drift	an explanation for the higher prevalence of distress in more deprived sections of the community, which proposes that people experiencing distress tend to move down the social scale as their ability to cope with more highly skilled jobs diminishes, and lower salaries or unemployment force them to move to cheaper neighbourhoods
Socialist Patients' Collective (SPK)	an activist political group founded in Heidelberg in February 1970 by Wolfgang Huber, which argued that mental and physical illness was a revolt against an insane world of **capitalism**, alienation, pollution and repressive sexual morals
socio-cultural	the complex, bi-directional relationships between the organization of a society (e.g. its institutions for work, family life and education) and the production of cultural values, identities, beliefs and rituals
sociogenic model	a model of distress which views distress and disturbing conduct as the result of a person's social location (e.g. suffering, poverty and abuse), events in the world (e.g. particular negative life events), and their relationships with others
socio-therapy	treatment emphasizing modification of the environment and improvement in interpersonal relationships rather than intrapsychic factors
Socratic dialogue	in cognitive therapies, a systematic attempt to help the client to question and challenge their unhelpful beliefs about themselves
somatization	the tendency to understand psychological stress or distress in terms of bodily or physical complaints
somatogenic model	a model of distress which views it as caused by the body
somato-psychic	a medical term for the effects of the body on the mind
somnolent-opthalmoplegic form	a form of encephalitis lethargica, the symptoms of which included expressionless faces and sleepiness, often leading to coma and death
source monitoring	the skill of distinguishing between self-generated thoughts and perceptions of the external world

specificity	the quality or state of being specific, in which outcomes are much less open to fluctuation and variation
spell-binding	from the work of Peter Breggin, a term that describes how, when people are under the influence of a psychoactive substance, they may not be able to judge their actions and behaviours very well
split-brain patients	people who have had the fibres joining the two halves of their cortex (the corpus callosum) severed, usually to control intractable epilepsy which would otherwise cause brain damage
spontaneous remission	the phenomenon of improvement without any treatment over a period of time
start/stop squeeze techniques	the standard techniques used to tackle male premature ejaculation
statistical definition of normality	a definition of normality which classes as abnormal those activities, behaviours and characteristics that are numerically unusual in a given population (e.g. which lie at the extremes of a continuum)
sterotactic subcaudate tractotomy	the use of micro-surgical techniques to sever connections between areas including the basal ganglia, the caudate nucleus and the amygdala
stigma	from the work of sociologist Erving Goffman, the outcome of processes of discrimination that cast someone as deviant and link them to negative stereotypes
straitjacket	a jacket used to control persons experiencing madness, made of strong material and with overly long sleeves which were secured behind the person's back so they could not move their arms
stress-vulnerability model	assumes that we inherit varying degrees of genetic susceptibility to mental illnesses. The greater this inherited vulnerability, the smaller the amount of stress required to trigger the illness
Stroop test	an experimental procedure to assess the amount of information processing associated with different kinds of stimuli by comparing the reaction times associated with them in alternate conditions
subvocalization	a process related to voice-hearing in which one's vocal chords make minute movements accompanying **inner speech**
sufficient causes	influences or events that do not have to be present for distress to arise, but which always result in distress occurring if they are present
suffocation alarm	a theory which holds that when levels of carbon dioxide and oxygen are altered, as occurs during hyperventilation, a neural message is sent that there is a danger of suffocation, which results in panic
suicide	the act of intentionally causing one's own death
supervised community treatment	where a person no longer has to stay in hospital to be given treatment compulsorily, but may now be treated at home provided they agree to follow their **Community Treatment Order**. See **mental health act**
survivor	a term used to refer to those who use mental health services, which carries an explicit criticism of services, although what is being survived may differ (e.g. distress or psychiatric services)
symptoms	a medical term for subjective reports by the person of a departure from normal function or feeling which is seen as indicating the presence of disease or abnormality; can be contrasted with **signs**
synergistically	when one cause and its effects magnify the influence of another cause and its effects
syphilis	a sexually transmitted infection which can cause a range of physical and neurological symptoms
systematic desensitization	a strategy used in behaviour therapy in which a person with an unwarranted fear or **phobia** gradually learns to remain relaxed in the presence of an object of which they were previously frightened
systems theory	a theory which emphasizes the way in which different elements in a system – like members of a family or a society – interact with each other
tardive dyskinesia	a recognized effect of **antipsychotic** drugs, in which abnormal repetitive twitching type movements (similar to Parkinson's disease) occur, usually affecting the face; may be due to over-compensation of dopamine and other neurotransmitter systems
temporal organization	the organization of phenomena (e.g. in terms of **plasticity** and **specificity**) over time
testosterone	a hormone found in both sexes but often described as a 'male' sex hormone, and involved in the production of male sex characteristics such as enlargement of the testes and the growth of facial hair
test-retest approach	where people are assessed and then re-assessed after the passage of some period of time
the interpreter	from the work of neuroscientist Michael Gazzaniga, a collection of left hemisphere brain systems which functions to provide a continuous, running narrative upon our lives and activities
theory of mind (ToM)	the ability to understand the mental states of others
theory of shattered assumptions	the theory that the shock of trauma can be so great that it thoroughly challenges and changes pre-existing core beliefs about the basically benevolent character of the world; consequently, people who experience trauma may be left struggling to understand their relation to the world, to such an extent that they may sometimes experience both themselves and the world as somewhat unreal
therapeutic alliance	the development of a trusting relationship between a **client** and a therapist
therapeutic communities	a participative, group-based approach to treatment of long-term distress, where people live together as a community often according to a democratic philosophy

third force in psychotherapy	humanistic psychotherapy; developed as a reaction against the dominance of **psychoanalysis** and **behaviour therapy** in the mental health field during the 1960s
third wave behavioural therapies	in **psychotherapy**, a movement away from cognitivism and back toward radical behaviourism, functional analysis and behavioural models of verbal behaviour, sometimes drawing on elements of Eastern philosophy
thought disorder	where a person's thoughts are presumed to be incoherent and confused on the basis of incoherent and confusing speech
token economy	a technique in **behaviour therapy** in which the desired behaviour is rewarded with tokens which can be exchanged for desired activities or other rewards
tonic immobility	responses characterized by simultaneous sympathetic and parasympathetic nervous system activity
trans	an umbrella term to include all **transvestite**, **transgender** and **transsexual** identities
transdiagnostic approach	a perspective which acknowledges that many overlapping dimensions exist across psychiatric diagnoses, and which emphasizes these overlapping behavioural or psychological dimensions
transference	in psychoanalysis when a person acts towards their psychotherapist in a manner reminiscent of how they have been treated by or related to others: in other words, they transfer their feelings from others onto the therapist
transference-focused psychotherapy (TFP)	a psychodynamic **psychotherapy** designed especially for people given a diagnosis of borderline personality disorder (BPD: the sub-categories of personality disorder diagnosis are explained in Table 13.2).
transformative	the transforming of an individual's or community's social circumstances – more fundamental and paradigmatic than **ameliorative** change
transgender	refers to a group or groups of individuals who differ from or completely transcend culturally prescribed gender roles. This can include individuals who have undertaken gender corrective surgery to transfer from the gender they were assigned at birth to the gender which fits their personal identity
transitional form	a stage in a transformation
transsexual	the term with which most people will be familiar to describe individuals who alter their bodies to reflect a different gender than that which was assigned to them at birth
transvestic fetishism	a diagnostic term describing sexual arousal as a result of cross-dressing
transvestite	a person who cross-dresses (dressing in clothing traditionally associated with the opposite gender), whether for emotional or psychic reasons or as sexual fetish
traumagenic neurodevelopmental model	a model which emphasizes the contribution of early traumatic events in the development of **psychosis**
tricyclic antidepressants	heterocyclic chemical compounds, such as amitriptyline, which are chemically similar to early **neuroleptic** drugs, and share many of their effects: they are sedating, impair mental functioning and some have been shown to block dopamine in animal studies
triple-blinding	a clinical trial in which the participant, health professionals and the researcher are all unaware of whether the participant is in the intervention or **control** (comparison) **group**
Twelve Step programmes	an adaptation of the **Alcoholics Anonymous** model of intervention to help people cope with other kinds of problem; the term refers to the number of stages in the original programme
tyramine	a naturally-occurring monoamine
unblind	the process in which participants, professionals or researchers guess who is in the intervention group (e.g. by noticing the effects of an administered drug)
unconscious libidinal desires	sexual desires outside conscious awareness
vaginismus	diagnosis made on the basis of a reported involuntary vaginal spasm that occurs when penetration is attempted
Viagra	the commercial name for the drug sildenafil, used to treat **male erectile dysfunction**
weight control behaviours	behaviours that support the maintenance of a desired body weight, for example calorie control, food restriction and purging
withdrawal symptoms	effects that occur when a drug intervention is stopped because the drug is no longer present to oppose the adaptations the body has made to its presence
zeitgeist	'the spirit of the times'; general trend of thought or feeling characteristic of a particular period of time

REFERENCES

Abel, G. G., Becker, J. V., Mittelman, M., Cunningham-Rathner, J., Rouleau, J. L. & Murphy, W. D. (1987). Self-reported sex crimes of nonincarcerated paraphiliacs. *Journal of Interpersonal Violence*, 2, 3–25.

Abraham, K. (1907/1955). On the significance of sexual truama in childhood for the symptomatology of dementia praecox. In K. Abraham & H. Abraham (Eds), *Clinical Papers and Essays on Psychoanalysis*. New York: Brunner-Mazel.

Abrahamson, L., Seligman, M. & Teasdale, J. (1978). Learned helplessness in humans: Critique and reformulation. *Journal of Abnormal Psychology*, 78, 40–74.

Abramowitz, C. & Dokecki, P. (1977). The politics of clinical judgment: Early empirical returns. *Psychological Bulletin*, 84(3), 460–76.

Abse, D. W., Dahlstrom, W. G. & Tolley, A. G. (1960). Evaluation of tranquilizing drugs in the management of acute mental disturbance. *American Journal of Psychiatry*, 116, 973–80.

Ackard, D. M., Neumark-Sztainer, D., Story, M. & Perry, C. (2003). Overeating among adolescents: Prevalence and associations with weight-related characteristics and psychological health. *Pediatrics*, 111, 67–74.

Addlakha, R. (2008). Deconstructing Mental Illness: An Ethnography of Psychiatry, Women and the Family. New Delhi: Zubaan.

Adler, D. A., Drake, R. E. & Teague, G. B. (1990). Clinicians' practices in personality assessment: Does gender influence the use of DSM-III axis II? *Comprehensive Psychiatry*, 31, 125–33.

Advisory Council on the Misuse of Drugs (2008). *Cannabis: Classification and Public Health*. London: Home Office.

Agar, K. & Read, J. (2002). What happens when people disclose sexual or physical abuse to staff at a community mental health centre? *International Journal of Mental Health Nursing*, 11(2), 70–9.

Agar-Jacomb, K. & Read, J. (2009). Mental health crisis services: What do service users need when in crisis? *Journal of Mental Health*, 18(2), 99–110.

Agras, W. S., Crow, S. J., Halmi, K. A., Mitchell, J. E., Wilson, G. T. & Kraemer, H. C. (2000a). Outcome predictors for the cognitive behavioral treatment for bulimia nervosa: Data from a multisite study. *American Journal of Psychiatry*, 1302–8.

Agras, W. S., Rossiter, E. M., Arnow, B., Schneider, J. A., Telch, C. F., Raeburn, S. D. et al. (1992). Pharmacological and cognitive-behavioral treatment for bulimia nervosa: A controlled comparison. *American Journal of Psychiatry*, 149(l), 82–7.

Agras, W. S., Walsh, B. T., Fairburn, C. G., Wilson, G. T. & Kraemer, H. C. (2000b). A multi-center comparison of cognitive-behavior therapy and interpersonal therapy for bulimia nervosa. *Archives of General Psychiatry*, 459–66.

Ahlers, C. J., Schaefer, G. A., Mundt, I. A., Roll, S., Englert, H., Willich, S. N. et al. (2011). How unusual are the contents of paraphilias? Paraphilia-associated sexual arousal patterns in a community-based sample of men. *Journal of Sexual Medicine*, 8, 1362–70.

Aizenberg, D., Zemishlany, Z., Dorfman-Etong, P. & Weizman, A. (1995). Sexual dysfunction in male schizophrenic patients. *Journal of Clinical Psychiatry*, 56, 137–41.

Al-Adawi, S., Martin, R. G., Al-Salmi, A. & Ghassani, H. (2001). Zar: Group distress and healing. *Mental Health, Religion & Culture*, 4, 46–61.

Alanen, Y., de Chavez, M., Silver, A. & Martindale, B. (Eds). (2009). *Psychotherapeutic Approaches to Schizophrenic Psychoses: Past, Present and Future*. London: Routledge.

Alarcón, R. D. (1996). Personality disorders and culture in DdSM-IV: A critique. *Journal of Personality Disorders*, 10, 260–70.

Alarcón, R. D., Foulks, E. F. & Vakkur, M. (1998). Personality Disorders and Culture: Clinical and Conceptual Interactions. New York: Wiley.

Albee, G. (1996). Revolutions and counter-revolutions in prevention. *American Psychologist*, 51, 1130–3.

Albee, G. & Fryer, D. (2003). Towards a public health psychology. *Journal of Community and Applied Social Psychology*, 13, 71–5.

Ali, A., Caplan, P. J. & Fragnant, R. (2010). Gender stereotypes in diagnostic criteria. In J. C. Chrisler & D. R. McCreary (Eds), *Handbook of Gender Research in Psychology*. New York: Springer.

Al-Issa, I. (1995). The illusion of reality or the reality of an illusion? *British Journal of Psychiatry*, 123, 269–74.

Al-Issa, I. & Oudji, S. (1998). Culture and anxiety disorders. In S. Kazarian & D. Evans (Eds), *Cultural Clinical Psychology* (127–51). Oxford: Oxford University Press.

Al-Khalili, J. (2010). Pathfinders: The Golden Age of Arabic Science. London: Allen Lane.

Altabe, M. (1998). Ethnicity and body image: Quantitative and qualitative analysis. *International Journal of Eating Disorders*, 23, 153–9.

Altman, S. & Shankman, S. S. (2009). What is the association between obsessive-compulsive disorder and eating disorders? *Clinical Psychology Review*, 29, 638–46.

Alwin, N., Blackburn, R., Davidson, K., Hilton, M., Logan, C. & Shine, J. (2006). *Understanding Personality Disorder: A Report by the British Psychological Society*. Leicester: British Psychological Society.

American Psychiatric Association (1968). *Diagnostic and Statistical Manual of Mental Disorders* (2nd edn). Washington DC: Author.

American Psychiatric Association (1987). *Diagnostic and Statistical Manual of Mental Disorders* (3rd edn). DSM III-R. Washington DC: American Psychiatric Association.

American Psychiatric Association (1994). *Diagnostic and Statistical Manual of Mental Disorders* (4th edn). Washington DC: American Psychiatric Association. Accessed at www.behavenet.com/capsules/disorders on 20/12/06.

American Psychiatric Association (2000). *Diagnostic and Statistical Manual of Mental Disorders* (4th edn), text revision. Arlington, VA: Author.

American Psychiatric Association (2001). *The Practice of ECT: A Task Force Report*, (2nd edn). Washington, DC: APA.

American Psychiatric Association (2010). *DSM-5: The Future of Psychiatric Diagnoses* http://www.dsm5.org. Part of AmericanPsychiatricAssociation, http://www.dsm5.org/ProposedRevision/Pages/proposedrevision.aspx?rid=411#. Washington DC: AmericanPsychiatricAssociation.

American Psychological Association (1993). Guidelines for providers of psychological services to ethnic, linguistic and culturally diverse populations. *American Psychologist*, 48, 45–8.

Anda, R., Felitti, V., Bremner, J. D., Walker, J., Whitfield, C., Perry, B. (2006). The enduring effects of abuse and related adverse experiences in childhood: A convergence of evidence from neurobiology and epidemiology. *European Archives of Psychiatry and Clinical Neuroscience*, 256(3), 174–86.

Andersen, A. E. & Hay, A. B. (1985). Racial and socioeconomic: Influences in anorexia nervosa and bulimia. *International Journal of Eating Disorders*, 4, 479–85.

Anderson, S., Brownlie, J. & Given, L. (2009). Therapy culture? Attitudes towards emotional support in Britain. In A. Park, J. Curtice, K. Thomson, M. Phiollips & E. Clery (Eds), *British Social Attitudes: The 25th Report* (155–72). London: Sage/National Centre for Social Research.

Andreasen, N. C. & Olsen, S. (1982). Negative v positive schizophrenia: Definition and validation. *Archives of General Psychiatry*, 39, 789–94.

Andreasson, S., Allebeck, P., Engstrom, A. & Rydberg, U. (1987). Cannabis and schizophrenia. A longitudinal study of Swedish conscripts. *Lancet*, 26(2), 1483–6.

Andrews, G., Anderson, T., Slade, T. & Sunderland, M. (2008). Classification of anxiety and depressive disorders: Problems and solutions. *Depression and Anxiety*, 25, 274–81.

Andrijasevic, R. & Anderson, B. (2009). Conflicts of mobility: Migration, labour and political subjectivities. *Subjectivitiy*, 29, 363–6.

Angel, R. & Guarnaccia, P. J. (1989). Mind, body, and culture: Somatization among Hispanics. *Social Science & Medicine*, 28, 1229–38.

Angermeyer, M. & Dietrich, S. (2006). Public beliefs about and attitude towards people with mental illness: A review of population studies. *Acta Psychiatrica Scandinavica*, 113, 163–79.

Angermeyer, M., Hozinger, A., Carta, M. & Schomerus, G. (2012). Biogenetic explanations and public acceptance of mental illness: Systematic review of population studies. *British Journal of Psychiatry*, 199, 367–72.

Angermeyer, M. & Matschinger, H. (2003). Public beliefs about schizophrenia and depression: Similarities and differences. *Social Psychiatry and Psychiatric Epidemiology*, 38(9), 526–34.

Angermeyer, M. & Schulze, B. (2001). Reinforcing stereotypes: How the focus on forensic cases in news reporting may influence public attitudes towards the mentally ill. *International Journal of Law and Psychiatry*, 24(4–5), 469–86.

Angrist, B. M. & Gershon, S. (1970). The phenomonenology of experimentally induced amphetamine psychosis – preliminary observations. *Biological Psychiatry*, 2, 95–107.

Angst, J. (1998). The emerging epidemiology of hypomania and bipolar II disorder. *Journal of Affective Disorders*, 50, 143–51.

Annon, J. S. (1974). *The Behavioral Treatment of Sexual Problems*. Honolulu HI: Kapiolani Health Services.

Annsseau, M., Fischler, B., Dierick, M., Albert, A., Leyman, S. & Mignon, A. (2008). Socio-economic correlates of generalised anxiety disorder and major depression in primary care: The GADISII study. *Depression and Anxiety*, 25, 506–13.

Anonymous (1999). The 'personality disorder' label. Dialogue, 2, 3.

Appleby, L. (2007). Breaking down barriers. Clinical case for change. Report by Louis Appleby, National Director for Mental Health. London: Department of Health.

Archer, M. (1995). *Realist Social Theory: The Morphogenetic Approach*. Cambridge: Cambridge University Press.

Armstrong, D. (1987). Theoretical tensions in biopsychosocial medicine. *Social Science and Medicine*, 25, 1213–18.

Arseneault, L., Cannon, M., Witton, J. & Murray, R. (2004). Causal association between cannabis use and psychosis: Examination of the evidence. *British Journal of Psychiatry*, 184, 110–17.

Ash, P. (1949). The reliability of psychiatric diagnoses. *Journal of Abnormal and Social Psychology*, 4, 272–7.

Ashmore, R. & Carver, N. (2001). The pharmaceutical industry and mental health nursing. *British Journal of Nursing*, 10(21), 1396–402.

Ashton, C. (1999). Adverse effects of cannabis and cannabinoids. *British Journal of Anaesthesia*, 83(4), 637–49.

Attia, E. & Schroeder, L. (2005). Pharmacologic treatment of anorexia nervosa: Where do we go from here? *International Journal of Eating Disorders*, 37, s60–s63.

Attwood, F. (2005). Fashion and passion: Marketing sex to women. *Sexualities*, 8(4), 392–406.

Audini, B. & Lelliott, P. (2002). Age, gender and ethnicity of those detained under Part II of the Mental Health Act 1983. *British Journal of Psychiatry*, 180, 222–6.

Aust, S. (2008). *The Baader Meinhof Complex*. Revised edition. London: The Bodley Head.

Ayllon, T. & Azrin, N. (1968). *The Token Economy: A Motivational System for Therapy and Rehabilitation*. New York: Appleton Century Crofts.

Ayllon, T. & Michael, J. (1959). The psychiatric nurse as a behavioral engineer. *Journal of the Experimental Analysis of Behavior*, 2, 323–34.

Babiak, P. & Hare, R. D. (2007). *Snakes in Suits: When Psychopaths go to Work*. London: Harper Collins.

Babiak, P., Neumann, C. S. & Hare, R. D. (2010). Corporate psychopathy: Talking the walk. *Behavioral Sciences and the Law*, 28, 174–93.

Baca-Garcia, E., Perez-Rodriguez, M. M., Basurte-Villamor, I., Fernandez Del Moral, A. L., Jimenez-Arriero, M. A., Gonzalez De Rivera, J. L. et al. (2007). Diagnostic stability of psychiatric disorders in clinical practice. *British Journal of Psychiatry*, 190, 210–16.

Bacaltchuk, J. & Hay, P. (2005). Antidepressants versus placebo for people with bulimia nervosa. *Evidence-Based Mental Health*, 5, 74–5.

Bach, A. K., Wincze, J. P. & Barlow, D. H. (2001). Sexual dysfunction. In D. H. Barlow (Ed.), *Clinical Handbook of Psychological Disorders*. New York: Guildford.

Baggaley, M. (2008). Sexual dysfunction in schizophrenia: Some recent evidence. *Human Psychopharmacology: Clinical and Experimental*, 23, 201–9.

Bailey, L. & Hoffman, D. (2008). Female sexual dysfunction: A nontraditional risk factor for cardiovascular disease. *Current Sexual Health Reports*, 5, 208–12.

Bakan, J. (2004). The Corporation: The Pathological Pursuit of Profit and Power. London: Constable.

Baker, C. (2004). Female Survivors of Child Sexual Abuse: An Integrated Guide to Treatment. London: Routledge.

Baker, P. (1989). *Hearing Voices*. Manchester: The Hearing Voices Network.

Baker, P. (2009). *The Voice Inside: A Practical Guide for and About People Who Hear Voices*. Fife: P&P Press.

Baker-Glenn, E., Steels, M. & Evans, C. (2010). Use of psychotropic medication among psychiatric out-patients with personality disorder. *The Psychiatrist*, 34, 83–6.

Baldessarini, R. J., Tondo, L. & Viguera, A. C. (1999). Discontinuing lithium maintenance treatment in bipolar disorders: Risks and implications. *Bipolar Disorders*, 1, 17–24.

Baldwin, S. (1987). From communities to neighbourhoods: I. Disability, *Handicap & Society*, 2, 41–59.

Balon, R. (2007). Issues for DSM-V: Sexual dysfunction, disorder, or variation along normal distribution: Toward rethinking DSM criteria of sexual dysfunctions. *American Journal of Psychiatry*, 164, 198–200.

Bancroft, J. (1989). *Human Sexuality and Its Problems*. Oxford: Churchill Livingstone.

Bancroft, J. (Ed.) (2003). *Sexual Development in Childhood*. Bloomington IN: Indiana University Press.

Bancroft, J., Loftus, J. & Long, J. S. (2003). Distress about sex: A national survey of women in heterosexual relationships. *Archives of Sexual Behavior*, 32(3), 193–208.

Bannister, D. (1971). The logical requirements of reseach into schizophrenia. *Schizophrenia Bulletin*, 1(4), 72–7.

Barbaree, H. E. and Marshall, W. L. (1989). Treatment of the sexual offender. In R. M. Wettstein (Ed.), *Treatment of the Mentally Disordered Offender*. New York: Guilford Press.

Barbui, C., Nosè, M., Bindman, J., Schene, A., Becker, T., Mazzi, M. A. et al. (2005). Sex differences in the subjective tolerability of antipsychotic drugs. *Journal of Clinical Psychopharmacology*, 25, 521–6.

Barker, P. & Buchanan-Barker, P. (2003). The not so NICE guidelines. Critical Psychiatry Network. Accessed at www.critpsynet.freeuk. com/NICEcommentary.htm, 11/05/2011.

Barkus, E., Stirling, J., Hopkins, R., McKie, S. & Lewis, S. (2007). Cognitive and neural processes in non-clinical auditory hallucinations. *British Journal of Psychiatry*, 191(51), 76–81.

Barlow, D. H. (Ed.) (2008). Clinical Handbook of Psychological Disorders: A Step-by-Step Treatment Manual (4th edn). New York: Guilford Press.

Barnes, T., Mutsatsa, S., Hutton, S., Watt, H. & Joyce, E. (2006). Comorbid substance use and age at onset of schizophrenia. *British Journal of Psychiatry*, 188, 237–42.

Barnett, S. (2008). Bonkersfest. New Statesman, 8 July. Accessed 23 December 2011 at www.newstatesman.com/health/2008/07/became-bonkersfest-mental

Barraclough, B., Bunch, J., Nelson, B. & , Sainsbury, P., (1974)., 'A hundred cases of suicide: Cclinical aspects.', *British Journal of Psychiatry*, 125, 355–73.

Barron, D. (1994). DSM IV: Making it culturally relevant. In S. Friedman (Ed.), *Anxiety Disorders in African-Americans*, 15–39. New York: Springer.

Bateman, A. & Fonagy, P. (2004). Mentalization-based treatment of BPD. *Journal of Personality Disorders*, 18, 36–51.

Bateman, A. & Fonagy, P. (2006). Mentalisation-Based Treatment for Borderline Personality Disorder: A Practical Guide. Oxford & New York: Oxford University Press.

Bateman, A. & Holmes, J. (1995). Introduction to Psychoanalysis: Contemporary Theory and Practice. London: Routledge.

Bates, Y. (2004). Preface. In Y. Bates (Ed.), *Shouldn't I Be Feeling Better By Now? Client Views of Therapy*. London: Palgrave Macmillan.

Bateson, G., Jackson, D. D., Haley, J. & Weakland, J. (1956). Toward a theory of schizophrenia. *Behavioral Science*, 1, 251–64.

Baumeister, R. F. (2001). Social Psychology and Human Sexuality: Key Readings in Social Psychology. London: Psychology Press.

Baumeister, R. F., Catanese, K. R. and Vohs, K. D. (2001) Is there a gender difference in strength of sex drive? Theoretical views, conceptual distinctions, and a review of relevant evidence. *Personality and Social Psychology Review*, 5(3), 242–73.

BBC Radio 4 (2011). All in the Mind (first broadcast 26 April).

Beales, D. L. & Dolton, R. (2000). Eating disordered patients: Personality, alexithymia, and implications for primary care. *British Journal of General Practice*, 50, 21–6.

Bean, P. (1980). *Compulsory Admissions to Mental Hospitals*. Chichester: Wiley.

Beaumont, J. G., Kenealy, P. M. & Rogers, M. J. C. (1996). *The Blackwell Dictionary of Neuropsychology*. Oxford: Blackwells.

Beavan, V. (2011). Toward a definition of 'hearing voices': A phenomenological approach. *Psychosis: Psychological, Social and Biological Approaches*, 3, 63–73.

Beavan, V. & Read, J. (2010). Hearing voices and listening to what they say: The importance of voice content in understanding and working with distressing voices. *Journal of Nervous & Mental Disease*, 198, 201–5.

Beavan, V., Read, J. & Cartwright, C. (2011). The prevalence of voice-hearing in the general population: A literature review. *Journal of Mental Health*, 20(3), 281–92.

Bebbington, P. E., Bhugra, D., Brugha, T., Singleton, M., Farrell, M. & Jenkins, R. (2004). Psychosis, victimisation and childhood disadvantage: Evidence from the second British National Survey of Psychiatric Morbidity. *British Journal of Psychiatry*, 185, 220–6.

Beck, A. T. (1967). Depression: Clinical, Experimental and Theoretical Aspects. New York: Hoeber.

Beck, A. T. (1976). *Cognitive Therapy and the Emotional Disorders*. Oxford, UK: International Universities Press.

Beck, A. T. (1991). Cognitive Therapy and the Emotional Disorders. London: Penguin.

Beck, J. & van der Kolk, B. (1987). Reports of childhood incest and current behavior of chronically hospitalized psychotic women. *American Journal of Psychiatry*, 144, 1474–6.

Becker (1963). *Outsiders: Studies in the Sociology of Deviance*. Free Press of Glencoe: Collier-Macmillan.

Beckwith, J. & Alper, J. (2002). Genetics of human personality: Social and ethical implications. In B. Ebstein & R. Belmaker (Eds), *Molecular Genetics and the Human Personality* (315–31). Washington DC: American Psychiatric Press.

Beebe, G. (1975). Follow-up studies of World War II and Korean war prisoners. *American Journal of Epidemiology*, 101, 400–2.

Beech, A. R., Fisher, D. & Beckett, R. (1999). An Evaluation of the Prison Sex Offender Treatment Programme (UK Home Office Occasional Report). Home Office Publications.

Beers, C. W. (1917). *A Mind that Found Itself* (4th edn). London: Longmans Green & Co.

Bekelman, J., Li, Y. & Gross, C. (2003). Scope and impact of financial conflicts of interest in biomedical research. *Journal of the American Medical Association*, 289(4), 454–65.

Bell, R. (1987). *Holy Anorexia*. Chicago IL: Chicago University Press.

Bell, V. (1993). *Interrogating Incest: Feminism, Foucault and the Law*. London: Routledge.

Bellack, A. S. (1986). Schizophrenia: Behavior therapy's forgotten child. *Behavior Therapy*, 17, 199–214.

Bellamy, G. T. (2008). Women's understandings of sexuality, sex and sexual problems: An interview study. Unpublished PhD manuscript, University of Sheffield.

Bellini, M. & Merlt, M. (2004). Current drug treatment of patients with bulimia nervosa and binge-eating disorder: Selective serotonin reuptake inhibitors versus mood stabilizers. *International Journal of Psychiatry in Clinical Practice*, 8, 235–43.

Belmaker, R. H. & Wald, D. (1977). Haloperidol in normals. *British Journal of Psychiatry*, 131, 222–3.

Belsky, J. & Pluess, M. (2009). Beyond diathesis stress: Differential susceptibility to environmental influences. *Psychological Bulletin*, 135, 885–908.

Bem, S. L. (1993b). *The Lenses of Gender*. New Haven CT: Yale University Press.

Bemis, K. M. (1978). Current approaches to the etiology and treatment of anorexia nervosa. *Psychological Bulletin*, 85, 593–617.

Benjamin, Jr, L. T. (2005). A history of clinical psychology as a profession in America (and a glimpse at its future). *Annual Review of Clinical Psychology*, 1, 1–30.

Bennett, D., Sharpe, M., Freeman, C. & Carson, A. (2004). Anorexia nervosa among female secondary school students in Ghana. *The British Journal of Psychiatry*, 85, 312–17.

Bennett, M. R. & Hacker, P. M. S. (2003). *Philosophical Foundations of Neuroscience*. Oxford: Blackwells.

Bennett, P. (2003). *Abnormal and Clinical Psychology*. Buckingham: Open University Press.

Benson, H. & McCallie, D. P., Jr (1979). Angina pectoris and the placebo effect. *New England Journal of Medicine*, 300, 1424–9.

Bentall, R. (1990a). *Reconstructing Schizophrenia*. London: Routledge.

Bentall, R. (1990b). The illusion of reality: A review and integration of psychological research on hallucinations. *Psychological Bulletin*, 107, 82–95.

Bentall, R. (2004). *Madness Explained: Psychosis and Human Nature*. London: Allen Lane/Penguin (paperback version). A hardback version (Allen Lane, 2003).

Bentall, R. (2009). Doctoring the Mind: Why Psychiatric Treatments Fail. London: Allen Lane/Penguin.

Bentall, R., Baker, G. & Havers, S. (1991). Reality monitoring and psychotic hallucinations. *British Journal of Clincal Psychology*, 30, 213–22.

Bentall, R. P.& Fernyhough, C. (2008). Social predictors of psychotic experiences: specificity and psychological mechanisms. *Schizophrenia Bulletin*, 34, 1012–20.

Bentall, R., Jackson, H. F. & Pilgrim, D. (1988). Abandoning the concept of 'schizophrenia': Some implications of validity arguments for psychological research into psychotic phenomena. *British Journal of Clinical Psychology*, 27, 303–24.

Bentall, R., Kinderman, P. & Kaney, S. (1994). The attributional processes and abnormal beliefs: Towards a model of persecutory delusions. *Behaviour Research and Therapy*, 32, 331–41.

Bentall, R. & Morrison, A. (2002). More harm than good: The case against using anti-psychotic drugs to prevent severe mental illness. *Journal of Mental Health*, 11, 351–6.

Bentall, R., Rowse, G., Shyrane, N., Kinderman, P., Howard, R., Blackwood, N. et al. (2009). The cognitive and affective structure of paranoid delusions: A transdiagnostic investigation of patients with schizophrenia spectrum disorders and depression. *Archives of General Psychiatry*, 66, 236–47.

Bentall, R. & Slade, P. (1985). Reality testing and auditory hallucinations: A signal-detection analysis. *British Journal of Clincal Psychology*, 24, 159–69.

Berk, L. E. (1994). Why children talk to themselves. *Scientific American*, 61–5.

Berkman, L. F., Glass, T., Brissette, I. & Seeman, T. E. (2000). From social integration to health: Durkheim in the new millennium. *Social Science & Medicine*, 51, 843–57.

Berntson, G., Cacioppo, J. & Quigley, K. (1991). Autonomic determinism: The modes of autonomic control, the doctrine of autonomic space, and the laws of autonomic constraint. *Psychological Review*, 98, 459–87.

Berry, K., Barrowclough, C. & Wearden, A. (2008). Attachment theory: A framework for understanding symptoms and interpersonal relationships in psychosis. *Behaviour Research and Therapy*, 46(12), 1275–82.

Berzins, K., Petch, A. & Atkinson, J. M. (2003). Prevalence and experience of harassment of people with mental health problems living in the community. *British Journal of Psychiatry*, 183, 526–33.

Besley, A. C. (2002). Foucault and the return to narrative therapy. *The British Journal of Guidance and Counselling*, 30, 125–43.

Bharati, A. (1985). The self in Hindu thought and action. In A. J. Marsella, G. Devos & F. S. K. Hsu (Eds), *Culture and Self: Asian and Western Perspectives*. New York: Tavistock Publications.

Bhugra, D. (2000). Migration and schizophrenia. *Acta Psychiatrica Scandinavica*, 40, 68–73.

Bhugra, D. (2004). Migration, distress and cultural identity. *British Medical Bulletin*, 129–41.

Bhugra, D. & Becker, M. A. (2005). Migration, cultural bereavement and cultural identity. *World Psychiatry*, 4, 16–24.

Bhui, K., Abdi, A., Abdi, M., Pereira, S., Dualeh, M., Robertson, D. et al. (2003). Traumatic events, migration characteristics and psychiatric symptoms among Somali refugees: Preliminary communication. *Social Psychiatry and Psychiatric Epidemiology*, 38(1), 35–43.

Bhugra, D., Leff, J., Mallett, R., Der, G., Corridan, B. & Rudge, S. (1997). Incidence and outcome of schizophrenia in Whites, African-Caribbeans and Asians in London. *Psychological Medicine*, 27, 791–8.

Bhui, K., Bhugra, D., Goldberg, D., Dunn, G. & Desai, M. (2001). Cultural influences on the prevalence of common mental disorder, general practitioners' assessments and help-seeking among Punjabi and English people visiting their general practitioner. *Psychological Medicine*, 31, 815–82.

Bhui, K., Bhugra, D., Goldberg, D., Sauer, J. & Tylee, A. (2004). Assessing the prevalence of depression in Punjabi and English primary care attenders. *Transcultural Psychiatry*, 41,: 307–-322.

Biedel, D. & Turner, S. (1997). At risk for anxiety: I. Psychopathology in the offspring of anxious parents. *Journal of the American Academy of Child and Adolescent Psychiatry*, 36(7), 918–24.

Billig, M. (1987). *Arguing and Thinking: A Rhetorical Approach to Social Psychology*. Cambridge: Cambridge University Press.

Billig, M., Condor, S., Edwards, D., Gane, M., Middleton, D. & Radley, A. (1988). *Ideological Dilemmas: A Social Psychology of Everyday Thinking*. London: Sage Publications.

Bindman, J., Tighe, J., Thornicroft, G. & Leese, M. (2002). Poverty, poor services, and compulsory psychiatric admission in England. *Social Psychiatry and Psychiatric Epidemiology*, 37, 341–5.

Binik, Y. M. (2005). Should dyspareunia be retained as a sexual dysfunction in DSM-V? A painful classification decision. *Archives of Sexual Behavior*, 34(1), 11–21.

Binswanger, L. (1946). The existential analysis school of thought. In R. May, E. Angel & H. F. Ellenberger (Eds), *Existence*. New York: Basic Books.

Birashk, B. (2004). Psychology in Iran. In K. Pawlik and M. Rosezweig (Eds), *The Handbook of International Psychology*. London: Sage.

Birbaumer, N., Veit, R., Lotze, M., Erb, M., Hermann, C., Grodd, W. et al. (2005). Deficient fear conditioning in psychopathy: A functional magnetic resonance imaging study. *Archives of General Psychiatry*, 62, 799–805.

Birchwood, M., Mason, R., MacMillan, F. & Healy, J. (1993). Depression, demoralization and control over psychotic illness: A comparison of depressed and non-depressed patients with a chronic psychosis. *Psychological Medicine*, 23(2), 387–95.

Birtchnell, J. (2002). Relating in Psychotherapy: The Application of a New Theory. London: Brunner-Routledge.

Black, T. (2002). Clinical psychologists should care about the Mental Health Act reforms. *Clinical Psychology*, 19, 6–8.

Blackburn, R. (1988). On moral judgements and personality disorders: The myth of psychopathic personality revisited. *British Journal of Psychiatry*, 153, 505–12.

Blackless, M., Charuvastra, A., Derryck, A., Fausto-Sterling, A., Lauzanne, K. & Lee, E. (2000). How sexually dimorphic are we? Review and synthesis. *American Journal of Human Biology*, 12, 151–66.

Blair, R. J., Jones, L., Clark, F. & Smith, M. (1997). The psychopathic individual: A lack of responsiveness to distress cues? *Psychophysiology*, 34, 192–8.

Blair, R. J. R., Mitchell, D. G. V., Peschardt, K. S., Colledge, E., Leonard, R. A., Shine, J. H. et al. (2004). Reduced sensitivity to others' fearful expressions in psychopathic individuals. *Personality and Individual Differences*, 37, 1111–22.

Blais, M. & Norman, D. (1997). A psychometric evaluation of the DSM-IV personality disorder criteria. *Journal of Personality Disorders*, 11, 168–76.

Blanchard, R. (2010). The DSM diagnostic criteria for pedophilia. *Archives of Sexual Behavior*, 39, 304–16.

Blashfield, R. K. (1984). *The Classification of Psychopathology: Neo-Kraepelinian and Quantitative Approaches*. New York: Plenum.

Blazer, D. (2009). Depression in late life: Review and Commentary. *Focus*, 7, 118–36.

Blazer, D., Hughes, D. & George, L. (1987). Stressful life events and the onset of a generalized anxiety syndrome. *American Journal of Psychiatry*, 144, 1178–83.

Bleuler, E. (1911/1951). *Dementia Praecox of the Group of Schizophrenias* (J. Zinkin, Trans.). New York: International Universities Press.

Bleuler, E. (1924). *Textbook of Psychiatry* (A. Brill, Trans.). New York: Macmillan.

Bleuler, M. (1978). *The Schizophrenic Disorders: Long-Term Patient and Family Studies*. New Haven, CT: Yale University Press.

Bliss, E. L. (1980). *Multiple Personality, Allied Disorders and Hypnosis*. New York: Oxford University Press.

Block, J. (1995). A contrarian view of the five-factor approach to personality description. *Psychological Bulletin*, 117, 187–215.

Blüher, S. & Mantzoros, C. S. (2004). The role of leptin in regulating neuroendocrine function in humans. *Journal of Nutrition*, 134, 2469S–2474S.

Board, B. J. & Fritzon, K. (2005). Disordered personalities at work. *Psychology, Crime & Law*, 11, 17–32.

Boast, N. & Chesterman, P. (1995). Black people and secure psychiatric facilities. *British Journal of Criminology*, 35, 218–35.

Bockting, W. O. (2008). Psychotherapy and the real-life experience: From gender dichotomy to gender diversity. *Sexologies*, 17(4), 211–24.

Boevink, W. (2006). From being a disorder to dealing with life: An experiential exploration of the association between trauma and psychosis. *Schizophrenia Bulletin*, 32(1), 17–19.

Bohart, A. C. (2000). The client is the most important common factor: Clients' self-healing capacities and psychotherapy. *Journal of Psychotherapy Integration*, 10(2), 127–49.

Boisen, A. (1938). Types of dementia praecox. *Psychiatry*, 1, 233–6.

Bola, J., Lehtinen, K., Cullberg, J. & Ciompi, L. (2009). Psychosocial treatment, antipsychotic postponement, and low dose medication strategies in first episode psychosis: A review of the literature. *Psychosis: Psychological, Social and Integrative Approaches*, 1(1), 4–18.

Bolsover, N. (2004). Psychotherapy and evidence. *Journal of Critical Psychology, Counselling & Psychotherapy*, 4, 68–77.

Bordo, S. (1992). Anorexia-nervosa – psychopathology as the crystallization of culture. In H. Crowley & S. Himmelweit (Eds), *Knowing Women: Feminism and Knowledge*. Cambridge: Cambridge University Press.

Bordo, S. (1993). *Unbearable Weight: Feminism, Western Culture and the Body*. Berkeley CA: University of California Press.

Bordo, S. (1997). *Twilight Zones: The Hidden Life of Cultural Images from Plato to OJ. Berkley*. CA: University of California Press.

Bordo, S. (2009a). Not just a 'white girl's thing': The changing face of food and body image problems. In H. Malson & M. Burns (Eds), *Critical Feminist Approaches to Eating Dis/Orders*. London: Routledge.

Bordo, S. (2009b). Twenty years in the twilight zone. In C. J. Heyes & M. Jones (Eds), *Cosmetic Surgery: A Feminist Primer*. Farnham: Ashgate Publishing.

Borkovec, T., Hazlett-Stevens, H. & Diaz, M. (1999). The role of positive beliefs about worry in generalised anxiety disorder and its treatment. *Clinical Psychology and Psychotherapy*, 6(2), 126–38.

Borkovec, T., Lyonfields, J., Wiser, S. & Deihl, L. (1993). The role of worrisome thinking in the suppression of cardiovascular response to phobic imagery. *Behaviour Research and Therapy*, 31(3), 321–4.

Bornstein, K. (1994). *Gender Outlaw: On Men, Women, and the Rest of Us*. New York: Routledge.

Boskind-Lodahl, M. (1976). Cinderella's step-sisters: A feminist perspective on anorexia nervosa and bulimia. *Signs*, 2, 342–56.

Bostock, J. (1998). Communication and commentary: Developing coherence in community and clinical psychology: The integration of idealism and pragmatism. *Journal of Community & Applied Social Psychology*, 8, 363–71.

Bostock, J. & Diamond, R. E. (2005). The value of community psychology: Critical reflections from the NHS. *Clinical Psychology Forum*, 153, 22–5.

Bostock, J. & Noble, V. (2001). Promoting community resources. In C. Newnes, C. Dunn & G. Holmes (Eds), *This is Madness Too: A Critical Look at the Mental Health System*. Ross-On-Wye. PCCS.

Bostock, J., Noble, V. & Winter, R. (1999). Promoting community resources. In C. Newnes, G. Holmes & C. Dunn (Eds), *This is Madness: A Critical Look at Psychiatry and the Future of Mental Health Services*. Ross-on-Wye: PCCS Books.

Bourguignon, E. (1980). *A World of Women: Anthropological Studies of Women in the Societies of the World*. New York: Praeger.

Bourne, J. (2011). From 'bad character' to BPD: The medicalization of 'personality disorder'. In M. Rapley, J. Dillon & J. Moncrieff (Eds), *De-Medicalising Misery*. London: Palgrave Macmillan.

Bouwer, C. & Stein, D. (1997). Association of panic disorder with a history of traumatic suffocation. *American Journal of Psychiatry*, 154(11), 1566–70.

Bowden, C. L., Calabrese, J. R., McElroy, S. L., Gyulai, L., Wassef, A., Petty, F. et al. (2000). A randomized, placebo-controlled 12-month trial of Divalproex and Lithium in treatment of outpatients with bipolar I disorder: Divalproex maintenance study group. *Archives of General Psychiatry*, 57, 481–48.

Bowe, S. (2002). The relationship between childhood trauma and auditory hallucinations. Unpublished DClinPsy Dissertation, Leeds University, Leeds.

Bowlby, J. (1958). The nature of the child's tie to his mother. *International Journal of Psychoanalysis*, 39, 1–23.

Boydell, J., van Os, J., McKenzie, K., Allardyce, J., Goel, R., McGreadie, R.G. et al. (2001). Incidence of schizophrenia in ethnic minorities in London: Ecological study into interactions with environment. *British Medical Journal*, 323, 1336–8.

Boydell, J., van Os, J., McKenzie, K. & Murray, R. (2004). The association of inequality with the incidence of schizophrenia: An ecological study. *Social Psychiatry and Psychiatric Epidemiology*, 39(8), 597–9.

Boyle, M. (1999). Diagnosis. In C. Newnes, G. Holmes & C. Dunn (Eds), *This Is Madness: A Critical Look at Psychiatry and the Future of Mental Health Services* (53–71). Ross, UK: PCCS Books.

Boyle, M. (1990). *Schizophrenia: A Scientific Delusion?* London: Routledge.

Boyle, M. (1993). Sexual dysfunction or heterosexual dysfunction. *Feminism & Psychology*, 3(1), 73–88.

Boyle, M. (2002). *Schizophrenia: A scientific delusion?* (2nd edn). London: Routledge.

Boyle, M. (2004). Preventing a non-existent illness? Some issues in the prevention of 'schizophrenia'. *The Journal of Primary Prevention*, 24(4), 445–69.

Boyle, M. (2006). 'From schizophrenia to psychosis – paradigm shift or more of the same?' Paper presented at the annual conference of the British Psychological Society's Division of Clinical Psychology, London 14–15 December.

Bracken, P. & O'Sullivan, P. (2001). The invisibility of Irish migrants in British health research. *Irish Studies Review*, 9(1), 41–51.

Bracken, P. & Thomas, P. (1999). CBT, Cartesianism and the moral order. *European Journal of Counselling, Psychotherapy & Health*, 2, 325–44.

Bracken, P. & Thomas, P. (2001). Postpsychiatry: A new direction for mental health. *British Medical Journal*, 322, 724–7.

Bradley, B. (2005). *Psychology and Experience*. Cambridge: Cambridge University Press.

Brady, E. & Kendall, P. (1992). Comorbidity of anxiety and depression in children and adolescents. *Psychological Bulletin*, 111(2), 244–55.

Braehler, C., Holowka, D., Brunet, A., Beaulieu, S., Baptista, T., Beruille, J.-M. et al. (2005). Diurnal cortisol in schizophrenia patients with childhood trauma. *Schizophrenia Research*, 79, 353–4.

Braun, D. L., Sunday, S. R. & Halmi, K. A. (1994). Psychiatric comorbidity in patients with eating disorders. *Psychological Medicine*, 24, 859–67.

Braun, V. (2005). In search of (better) sexual pleasure: Female genital 'cosmetic' surgery. *Sexuailties*, 407–24.

Braunholtz, S., Davidson, S. & King, S. (2004). Well? What do you think? The second national Scottish survey of public attitudes to mental health, mental well-being and mental health problems. Edinburgh: Scottish Executive Social Research.

Brebion, G., Amador, X., David, A., Malaspina, D. & Sharif, Z. (2000). Positive symptomatology and source monitoring failure in schizophrenia: An analysis of symptom-specific effects. *Psychiatry Research*, 95, 119–31.

Breggin, P. R. (1983). *Psychiatric Drugs: Hazards to the Brain*. New York: Springer.

Breggin, P. R. (1991). *Toxic Psychiatry: Why Therapy, Empathy and Love Must Replace the Drugs, Electroshock, and Biochemical Theories of the 'New Psychiatry'*. New York: St. Martin's Press.

Breggin, P. R. (1993). *Toxic Psychiatry*. London: Fontana.

Breggin, P. R. (1997). *Brain Disabling Treatments in Psychiatry: Drugs, Electroshock and the Role of the FDA*. New York: Springer.

Breggin, P. R. (2001). *Talking Back to Ritalin: What Doctors Aren't Telling You About Stimulants and ADHD*. Cambridge MA: Perseus Publishing.

Breggin, P. R. (2006). Intoxication anosognosia: The spellbinding effect of psychiatric drugs. *Ethical Human Psychology & Psychiatry*, 8, 201–15.

Brekke, J., Prindle, C., Bae, S. & Long, J. (2001). Risks for individuals with schizophrenia who are living in the community. *Psychiatric Services*, 52(10), 1358–66.

Breslau, N. & Davis, G. (1985). DSM-III generalized anxiety disorder: An empirical investigation of more stringent criteria. *Psychiatry Research*, 15(3), 231–8.

Bresnahan, M., Menezes, P., Varma, V. & Susser, E. (2003). Geographical variation in incidence, course and outcome of schizophrenia: A comparison of developing and developed countries. In R. M. Murray, P. B. Jones, E. Susser, J. van Os & M. Cannon (Eds), *The Epidemiology of Schizophrenia* (18–33). New York: Cambridge University Press.

Brewer, G. (1999). The challenges of interdisciplinarity. *Policy Sciences*, 32(4), 327–37.

Brewin, C. (2001). Memory processes in post-traumatic stress disorder. *International Review of Psychiatry*, 13, 159–63.

Brewin, C. R. (1996). Theoretical foundations of cognitive-behavior therapy for anxiety and depression. *Annual Review of Psychology*, 47, 33–57.

Brezsnyak, M. & Whisman, M. (2004). Sexual desire and relationship functioning: The effects of marital satisfaction and power. *Journal of Sex and Marital Therapy*, 30, 199–217.

Briere, J. & Elliot, D. M. (2003). Prevalence and psychological sequelae of self-reported childhood physical and sexual abuse in a general population sample of men and women. *Child Abuse & Neglect*, 27, 1205–22.

Briere, J., Woo, R., McRae, B., Foltz, J. & Sitzman, R. (1997). Lifetime victimization history, demographics and clinical status in female psychiatric emergency room patients. *Journal of Nervous & Mental Disease*, 185(2), 95–101.

British Association of Psychotherapy & Counselling (BACP) (2007). *Ethical Framework for Good Practice in Counselling and Psychotherapy* (2nd edn). Lutterworth: Author.

British Psychological Society (2002). *Criteria for the Accreditation of Postgraduate Training Programs in Clinical Psychology*. Leicester: Author.

British Psychological Society (2006). *Code of Ethics and Conduct*. Leicester: Author.

British Psychological Society (2008). *Socially Inclusive Practice*. Leicester: Author.

British Psychological Society (2011). *2010 Annual report*. Leicester: Author.

Bronfenbrenner, U. (1979). *The Ecology of Human Development: Experiments by Nature and Design*. Cambridge MA: Harvard University Press.

Brower, M. C. & Price, B. H. (2001). Neuropsychiatry of frontal lobe dysfunction in violent and criminal behaviour: A critical review. *Journal of Neurology, Neurosurgery & Psychiatry*, 71, 720–6.

Brown, G. R., Wise, T. N., Costa, P. T., Herbst, J. H., Fagan, P. J. & Schmidt, C. W. (1996). Personality characteristics and sexual functioning of 188 cross-dressing men. *The Journal of Nervous and Mental Disease*, 184, 265–73.

Brown, G. W. (1996). Life events, loss and depressive disorders. In T. Heller, J. Reynolds, R. Gomm, R. Muston & S. Pattison (Eds), *Mental Health Matters: A Reader*. London: Macmillan/Open University.

Brown, G. W. & Harris, T. O. (1978). *Social Origins of Depression: A Study of Psychiatric Disorder in Women*. London: Tavistock.

Brown, G. W. & Moran, P. (1997). Single mothers, poverty and depression. *Psychological Medicine*, 27, 21–33.

Brown, G. W., Ni Bhrolchain, M. & Harris, T. (1975). Social class and psychiatric disturbance among women in an urban population. *Sociology*, 9, 225–54.

Brown, H., Stein, J. & Turk, V. (1995). The sexual abuse of adults with learning disabilities: Report of a second two-year incidence survey. *Mental Handicap Research*, 8, 3–24.

Brown, L. S. (2009). *Feminist Therapy*. Washington D.C.: American Psychological Association.

Brown, P. (1990). The name game: Towards a sociology of diagnosis. *Journal of Mind and Behaviour*, 11, 385–406.

Brown, W. A. (2002). Are antidepressants as ineffective as they look? *Prevention & Treatment*, 5(1). doi: 10.1037/1522-3736.5.1.526c

Bruce, S., Yonkers, K., Otto, M., Eisen, J., Weisberg, R., Pagano, M. et al. (2005). Influence of psychiatric comorbidity on recovery and recurrence in generalized anxiety disorder, social phobia, and panic disorder: A 12-year prospective study. *American Journal of Psychiatry*, 162, 1179–87.

Brune, M. (2005). 'Theory of mind' in schizophrenia: A review of the literature. *Schizophrenia Bulletin*, 31, 21–42.

Bulik, C. M., Devlin, B., Bacanu, S., Thornton, L., Klump, K. L., Fichter, M. M. et al. (2003). Significant linkage on chromosome 10p in families with bulimia nervosa. *American Journal of Human Genetics*, 72(1), 200–7.

Bulik, C. M., Sullivan, P. F., Fear, J. I. & Joyce, R. I. (2007). Eating disorders and antecedent anxiety disorders: A controlled study. *Acta Psychiatrica Scandinavica*, 96, 101–7.

Bullard, A. (2005). L'Oedipe Africain: A retrospective. *Transcultural Psychiatry*, 42, 171–203.

Bullimore, P. (2010). My personal experience of psychosis. *Psychosis: Psychological, Social and Biological Approaches*, 2(2), 173–77.

Bunn, G. (2011). The History of the Brain, Episode 2 'The Blood of the Gladiators', BBC Radio 4, first broadcast 8 November 2011. Accessed 25 January 2012 at www.bbc.co.uk/programmes/b016wzrd.

Burnham, J. B. (1986). *Family Therapy: First Steps Towards a Systemic Approach*. London: Tavistock.

Burns, J. K. & Esterhuizen, T. (2008). Poverty, inequality and the treated incidence of first-episode psychosis: An ecological study from South Africa. *Social Psychiatry and Psychiatric Epidemiology*, 43(4), 331–5.

Burr, J. (2002). Cultural stereotypes of women from South Asian communities: Mental health care professionals' explanations of depression and suicide. *Social Science and Medicine*, 55, 835–45.

Burr, V. (2000). *An Introduction to Social Constructionism*. London: Routledge.

Burri, A. V., Cherkas, L. M. & Spector, T. D. (2009). The genetics and epidemiology of female sexual dysfunction. *Journal of Sexual Medicine*, 6, 646–57.

Burton, M., Boyle, S., Harris, C. & Kagan, C. (2007). Community psychology in Britain. In S. Reich, M. Riemer, I. Prilleltensky & M. Montero (Eds), *International Community Psychology: History and Theories*. New York: Springer.

Burton, M. & Kagan, C. (1996). Rethinking empowerment. In I. Parker & R. Spears (Eds), *Psychology and Society: Radical Theory and Practice*. London: Pluto Press.

Burton, M. & Kagan, C. (2011). Towards a really social psychology: Liberation Psychology beyond Latin America. In M. Montero & C. C. Sonn (Eds), *The Psychology of Liberation: Theory and Applications*. New York: Springer.

Burton, N. (2006). *Psychiatry*. Oxford: Blackwells.

Busfield, J. (1996). *Men, Women and Madness: Understanding Gender and Mental Disorder*. Basingstoke: Macmillan.

Butler, C. (2006). Vagina dialogues: Catherine Butler in conversation with Lih-Mei Liao. *Lesbian & Gay Psychology Review*, 7(3), 287–91.

Butler, C. & Byrne, A. (forthcoming, 2007). Queer in practice: Therapy and queer theory. In L. Moon (Ed.), *Feeling Queer or Queer Feelings: Counselling and Sexual Cultures*. London: Routledge.

Butler, G. (1998). Clinical formulation. In A. S. Bellack & M. Hersen (Eds), *Comprehensive Clinical Psychology* (1–23). Oxford: Pergamon.

Butler, J. (1993). *Bodies That Matter*. London: Routledge.

Butzlaff, R. L. & Hooley, J. M. (1998). Expressed emotion and psychiatric relapse: A meta-analysis. *Archives of General Psychiatry*, 55, 547–52.

Bydlowski, S., Corcos, M., Jeammet, P., Paterniti, S., Berthoz, S., Laurier, C. et al. (2005). Emotion-processing deficits in eating disorders. *International Journal of Eating Disorders*, 37, 321–9.

Bynum, W. F., Porter, R. & Shepherd, M. (Eds) (1985). *The Anatomy of Madness: Essays in the History of Psychiatry, Vol. I: People and Ideas*. London: Tavistock.

Byrne, R., Davies, L. & Morrison, A. (2010). Priorites and preferences of for the outcomes of treatment of psychosis: A service user perspective. *Psychosis: Psychological, Social and Biological Approaches*, 2(3), 210–17.

Cahill, J., Barkham, M. & Stiles, W. B. (2010). Systematic review of practice based research on psychological therapies in routine clinic settings. *British Journal of Clinical Psychology*, 49, 421–53.

Caldji, C., Diorio, J. & Meaney, M. (2000). Variations in maternal care in infancy regulate the development of stress reactivity. *Biological Psychiatry*, 58, 1164–74.

Califia, P. (1997). *Sex Changes: The Politics of Transgenderism*. San Francisco: Cleis.

Calton, T., Cheetham, A., D'Silva, K. & Glazebrook, C. (2005). International schizophrenia research and the concept of patient-centredness – an analysis over two decades. Paper presented at the International Congress on Schizophrenia Research, Savannah GA, USA.

Calton, T., Ferriter, M., Huband, N. & Spandler, H. (2008). A systematic review of the Soteria paradigm for the treatment of people diagnosed with schizophrenia. *Schizophrenia Bulletin*, 34(1), 181–92.

Campbell, P. (1996). The history of the user movement in the United Kingdom. In T. Heller, J. Reynolds, R. Gomm, R. Muston & S. Pattison (Eds), *Mental Health Matters: A Reader*. Basingstoke: Macmillan /Open University.

Campbell, P. (2006). Changing the mental health system – a survivor's view. *Journal of Psychiatric and Mental Health Nursing*, 13(5), 578–80.

Cannon, T. D., Cadenhead, K., Cornblatt, B., Woods, S. W., Addington, J., Walker, E. et al. (2008). Prediction of psychosis in youth at high clinical risk: A multisite longitudinal study in North America. *Archives of General Psychiatry*, 65, 28–37.

Cantor-Graae, E. and Selten, J.-P. (2005). Schizophrenia and migration: A meta-analysis and review. *American Journal of Psychiatry*, 162, 12–24.

Caplan, P. (1985). *The Myth of Women's Masochism*. New York: Signet.

Caplan, P. J. & Cosgrove, L. (Eds) (2004). *Bias in Psychiatric Diagnosis*. Lanham, MD: Jason Aronson.

Care Quality Commission (2010). Monitoring the use of the Mental Health Act in 2009/10. London: Author. Accessed 31 May 2011 at www.cqc.org.uk/mentalhealthactannualreport2009–10/downloadthereport.cfm

Care Quality Commission (2011). *Count me in 2010: Results of the 2010 National Census of Inpatients and Patients on Supervised Community Treatment in Mental Health and Learning Disability Services in England and Wales*. London: Author. Accessed on 2 December 2011 at www.cqc.org.uk/publications.cfm?fde_id=18114

Care Services Improvement Partnership/Shift (2006). *Mind over Matter: Improving Media Reporting of Mental Health*. London: Shift.

Carr, S. N. & Francis, A. J. (2010). Early maladaptive schemas and personality disorder symptoms: An examination in a non-clinical sample. *Psychology & Psychotherapy: Theory, Research and Practice*, 83, 333–49.

Carr-Walker, P., Bowers, L., Callaghan, P., Nijman, H. & Paton, J. (2004). Attitudes towards personality disorders: Comparison between prison officers and psychiatric nurses. *Legal and Criminological Psychology*, 9, 265–77.

Carson, R.C. & Butcher, J. N. (1992). *Abnormal Psychology and Modern Life* (9th edn). New York: HarperCollins.

Carter, R., Wittchen, H. U., Pfister, H. & Kessler, R. (2001). One-year prevalence of subthreshold and threshold DSM-IV generalised anxiety disorder in a nationally representative sample. *Depression and Anxiety*, 13, 78–88.

Cartwright, N. (2007). Are RCT's the Gold Standard? *Biosocieties*, 2, 11–20.

Cartwright, S. A. (1851). Report on the diseases and physical peculiarities of the Negro race. *The New Orleans Medical and Surgical Journal*, May, 691–715. (Reprinted as: Cartwright, Dr. (1851). Diseases and peculiarities of the negro race. *Debow's review, Agricultural, Commercial, Industrial Progress and Resources*, 11(3), 331–6.)

Cascardi, M., Mueser, K., Degiralomo, J. & Murrin, M. (1996). Physical aggression against psychiatric inpatients by family members and partners. *Psychiatric Services*, 47(5), 531–3.

Casey, J. F., Bennett, I. F., Lindley, C. J., Hollister, L. E., Gordon, M. H. & Springer, N. N. (1960). Drug therapy in schizophrenia: A controlled study of the relative effectiveness of chlorpromazine, promazine, phenobarbital, and placebo. *Archives of General Psychiatry*, 2, 210–20.

Casey, J. F., Lasky, J. J., Klett, C. J. & Hollister, L. E. (1960). Treatment of schizophrenic reactions with phenothiazine derivatives: A comparative study of chlorpromazine, triflupromazine, mepazine, prochlorperazine, perphenazine, and phenobarbital. *American Journal of Psychiatry*, 117, 97–105.

Cash, T., Ancis, J. & Strachan, M. (1997). Gender attitudes, feminist identity, and body images among college women. *Sex Roles*, 36(7/8), 433–47.

Cash, T. F. & Deagle, E. A. (1997). The nature and extent of body-image disturbances in anorexia nervosa and bulimia nervosa: A meta-analysis. *International Journal of Eating Disorders*, 22, 107–26.

Caspi, A., Moffitt, T., Cannon, M., McClay, J., Murray, R., Harrington, H. et al. (2002). Moderation of the effect of adolescent-onset cannabis use on adult psychosis by a functional polymorphism in the catechol-O-methyltransferase gene: Longitudinal evidence of a gene X environment interaction. *Biological Psychiatry*, 57(10), 1117–27.

Castillo, H. (2000). Temperament or trauma? Users' views on the nature and treatment of personality disorder. *Mental Health Care*, 4(2), 53–8.

Castillo, H. (2003). *Personality Disorder: Temperament or Trauma? An Account of an Emancipatory Research Study Carried Out by Service Users Diagnosed with Personality Disorder*. London: Jessica Kingsley.

Castro, J., Gila, A., Puig, J. & Toro, J. (2004). Predictors of rehospitalisation after total weight recovery in adolescents with anorexia nervosa. *International Journal of Eating Disorders*, 36: 22–30.

Cavanagh, M.-R., Read, J. & New, B. (2004). Sexual abuse inquiry and response: A New Zealand training programme. *New Zealand Journal of Psychology*, 33(3), 137–44.

Chadwick, P. D. J. & Lowe, C. F. (1994). A cognitive approach to measuring and modifying delusions. *Behaviour Research and Therapy*, 32, 355–67.

Chakraborty, A., McManus, S., Brugha, T. S., Bebbington, P. & King, M. (2011). Mental health of the non-heterosexual population of England. *The British Journal of Psychiatry*, 198, 143–8.

Chamberlin, J. (1978). *On Our Own: Patient-Controlled Alternatives to the Mental Health System*. London: Mind.

Chamberlin, J. (1990). The ex-patients' movement: Where we've been and where we're going. *Journal of Mind and Behavior*, 11(3&4), 323–36.

Chamberlin, J. (2004). User-run services. In J. Read, L. Mosher & R. Bentall (Eds), *Models of Madness: Psychological, Social and Biological Approaches to Psychosis* (283–90). London: Routledge.

Chambless, D. L. & Ollendick, T. H. (2001). Empirically supported psychological interventions: Controversies and evidence. *Annual Review of Psychology*, 52, 685–716.

Chandra, P., Deepthivarma, S., Carey, M., Carey, K. & Shalinianant, M. (2003). A cry from the wilderness: Women with severe mental illness in India reveal their experiences with sexual coercion. *Psychiatry*, 66(4), 323–34.

Chang, W. (1985). A cross-cultural study of depressive symptomatology. *Culture, Medicine and Psychiatry*, 9, 295–317.

Charlton, B. (2000). Infostat, cargo-cult science and the policy sausage machine: NICE, CHI and the managerial take over of clinical practice. In J. R. Hampton & B. Hurwitz (Eds), *NICE, CHI and the NHS Reforms: Enabling Excellence or Imposing Control?* London. Aesculapeus Press.

Chau, P.-L. & Herring, J. (2004). Men, women, people: The definition of sex. In B. Brooks-Gordon, L. Gelsthorpe, M. Johnson & A. Bainham (for the Cambridge Socio-Legal Group) (Eds), *Sexuality Repositioned: Diversity and the Law* (187–213). Oxford: Hart.

Cheng, A. (2002). Expressed emotion: a cross-culturally valid concept? *British Journal of Psychiatry*, 181, 466–7.

Cherlin, A. J. (1999). Going to extremes: Family structure, children's well-being, and social science. *Demography*, 36, 421–8.

Cheshire, C. & Pilgrim, D. (2004). *A Short Introduction to Clinical Psychology*. London. Sage.

Chesler, P. (1972). *Women and Madness*. New York: Doubleday.

Chesler, P. (2005). *Women and Madness*. New York, NY: Palgrave Macmillan.

Chilvers, C., Dewey, M., Fielding, K., Gretton, V., Miller, P., Palmer, B. et al. (2001). Antidepressant drugs and generic counselling for treatment of major depression in primary care: Randomised trial with patient preference arms. *British Medical Journal*, 322(7289), 772–5.

Chin, J. T., Hayward, M. & Drinnan, A. (2009). 'Relating' to voices: Exploring the relevance of this concept to people who hear voices. *Psychology and Psychotherapy: Theory, Research and Practice*, 82, 1–17.

Chodorow, N. (1978). *The Reproduction of Mothering*. London: University of California Press.

Ciompi, L. (1980). The natural history of schizophrenia in the long term. *British Journal of Psychiatry*, 136, 413–20.

Ciompi, L. (1984). Is there really a schizophrenia? The long-term course of psychotic phenomena. *British Journal of Psychiatry*, 145, 636–40.

Clare, A. W. (1976). *Psychiatry in dissent: Controversial Issues in Thought and Practice*. London: Tavistock Publications.

Claridge, G. (Ed.) (1997). *Schizotypy: Implications for Illness and Health*. Oxford: Oxford University Press.

Clarke, I. (ed.) (2010). *Psychosis and Spirituality: Consolidating the New Paradigm*. Oxford: Wiley-Blackwell.

Clarke, L. (1999). *Challenging Ideas in Psychiatric Nursing*. London: Routledge.

Clark, L. A. & Harrison, J. A. (2001). Assessment instruments. In W. J. Livesley (Ed.), *Handbook of Personality Disorders: Theory, Research, and Treatment*, 277–306. New York: Guilford.

Clarke, V. & Peel, E. (Eds) (2007). *Out in Psychology: Lesbian, Gay, Bisexual, Trans & Queer Perspectives*. Chichester: Wiley & Sons.

Classen, C. C., Palesh, O. G. & Aggarwal, R. (2005). Sexual revictimization: A review of the empirical literature. *Trauma Violence Abuse*, 6(2), 103–29.

Claudino, A. M., Hay, P., Lima, M. S., Bacaltchuk, J., Schmidt, U. & Treasure, J. (2006). Antidepressants for anorexia nervosa. *Cochrane Database of Systematic Reviews*, 25(1), CD00436.

Clayton, A. H., Pradko, J. F., Croft, H. A., Montano, C. B., Leadbetter, R. A., Bolden-Watson. C. et al. (2002). Prevalence of sexual dysfunction among newer antidepressants. *Journal of Clinical Psychiatry*, 63, 357–66.

Cleckley, H. (1950). *The Mask of Sanity*. St Louis MI: C. V. Mosby.

Clements, J., Clare, I. & Ezelle, L. A. (1995). Real men, real women, real lives? Gender issues in learning disabilities and challenging behaviour. *Disability and Society*, 10, 425–35.

Clements, J. & Davies, E. (2013). Prevention of psychosis: Creating societies where more people flourish. In J. Read & J. Dillon (Eds), *Models of Madness* (2nd edn). London: Routledge.

Clements-Nolle, K., Marx, R., Katz, M. (2006). Attempted suicide among transgender persons: The influence of gender-based discrimination and victimization. *Journal of Homosexuality*, 51(3), 53–69.

Cohen, A., Patel, V., Thara, R. & Gureje, O. (2008). Questioning and axiom: Better prognosis for schizophrenia in the developing world? *Schizophrenia Bulletin*, 34, 229–44.

Cohen, F. & Densen-Gerber, J. (1982). A study of the relationship between child abuse and drug addiction in 178 patients: Preliminary results. *Child Abuse and Neglect*, 6(4), 383–7.

Coid, J., Petruckevitch, A., Feder, G., Chung, W., Richardson, J. & Moorey, S. (2001). Relation between childhood sexual and physical abuse and risk of revictimisation in women: A cross sectional survey. *Lancet*, 358, 450–4.

Coid, J., Yang, M., Tyrer, P., Roberts, A. & Ullrich, S. (2006). Prevalence and correlates of personality disorder in Great Britain. *British Journal of Psychiatry*, 188, 423–31.

Cole, M. (2005). *Cultural Psychology: A Once and Future Discipline*. Cambridge MA: Harvard University Press.

Cole, S. (2000). *'Don We Now Our Gay Apparel': Gay Men's Dress in the Twentieth Century*. Oxford: Berg.

Cole-Detke, H. & Kobak R. (1996). Attachment processes in eating disorder and depression. *Journal of Consulting and Clinical Psychology*, 64(2), 282–90.

Coleman, R. (1999). Hearing voices and the politics of oppression. In C. Newnes, G. Holmes & C. Dunn (Eds), *This is Madness Too: A Critical Look at the Mental Health System*. Ross-on-Wye, PCCS Books.

Coleman, R. (2004). *Recovery: An Alien Concept*. Fife: P&P Press.

Coleman, R. & Ellis, W. (2008). *Working with Voices: A Working to Recovery Training Manual*. Fife: P&P Press.

Coleman, R. & Smith, M. (2006). *Working with Voices: Victim to Victor*. Fife: P&P Press .

Collier , D. A. & Treasure, J. (2004). The aetiology of eating disorders. *British Journal of Psychiatry*, 185, 363–85.

Collignon, R. & Gueye, M. (1995). The interface between culture and mental illness in French-speaking West Africa. In I. Al-Issa (Ed.), *Culture and Mental Illness: An International Perspective*, 93–112. Madison WI: International Universities Press.

Colombo, A., Bendelow, G., Fulford, B., & Williams, S. (2003). Evaluating the influence of implicit models of mental disorder on processes of shared decision-making within community-based mental health teams. *Social Science and Medicine*, 56, 1557–70.

Combs, D. R., Penn, D. L. & Fenigstein, A. (2002). Ethnic differences in subclinical paranoia: An expansion of norms of the paranoia scale. *Cultural Diversity and Ethnic Minority Psychology*, 8, 248–56.

Comer, R. J. (1999). *Abnormal Psychology* (2nd edn). New York: Worth/Freeman.

Connell, R. W. (2002). *Gender*. Cambridge: Polity Press.

Connolly, W. (2002). *Neuropolitics: Thinking, Culture, Speed*. Minneapolis: University of Minnesota Press.

Connor-Greene, P. (2001). Family, friends and self: The real-life context of an abnormal psychology class. *Teaching of Psychology*, 28, 210–12.

Conrad, P. (2002). Genetics and behaviour in the news: Dilemmas of a rising paradigm. In J. Alper, C. Ard, A. Asch, J. Beckwith, P. Conrad & L. Geller (Eds), *The Double-Edged Helix: Social Implications of Genetics in a Diverse Society* (58–79). Baltimore MD: Johns Hopkins University Press.

Conus, P., Cotton, S., Schimmelmann B., Berk, M., Daglas, R., McGorry, P. et al. (2010). Pretreatment and outcome correlates of past sexual and physical trauma in 118 bipolar I disorder patients with a first episode of psychotic mania. *Bipolar Disorders*, 12(3), 244–52.

Conus, P., Cotton, S., Schimmelmann, B., McGorry, P. & Lambert, M. (2010). Pretreatment and outcome correlates of sexual and physical trauma in an epidemiological cohort of first-episode psychosis patients. *Schizophrenia Bulletin*, 36(6), 1105–14.

Cooke, A. & Hayward, M. (2010). Service users and carers as placement advisors: Part 1 – getting started. *Clinical Psychology Forum*, 209, 21–2.

Cooke, A., Kinderman, P. & Harper, D. (2002). DCP update: Criticisms and concerns. *Clinical Psychology*, 13, 43–7.

Cooke, D. J., Michie, C., Hart, S. D. & Clark, D. (2005). Assessing psychopathy in the UK: Concerns about cross-cultural generalisability. *British Journal of Psychiatry*, 186, 335–41.

Coolidge, F. L. & Segal, D. L. (1998). Evolution of personality disorder diagnosis in the *Diagnostic and Statistical Manual of Mental Disorders*. *Clinical Psychology Review*, 18, 585–99.

Coons, P. M., Bowman, E. S. & Milstein, V. (1988). Multiple personality disorder: A clinical investigation of 50 cases. *Journal of Nervous and Mental Diseases*, 176, 519–27.

Cooper, D. (1967). *Psychiatry and Anti-psychiatry*. London: Tavistock.

Cooper, I. E., Kendell, R. F., Gurland, B. J., Sartorius, N., Farkas, T. (1969). Cross-national study of diagnosis of the mental disorders: Some results from the first comparative investigation. *American. Journal of. Psychiatry*, 125, 21–9.

Cooper, M. (2003). *Existential Therapies*. London: Sage.

Cooper, M. (2008). *Essential Research Findings in Counselling and Psychotherapy*. London: Sage.

Cooper, M., Todd, G. & Wells, A. (2005). *Treating Bulimia Nervosa and Binge Eating – An Integrated Metacognitive and Cognitive Therapy Manual*. Routledge: East Sussex, UK and New York.

Cooper, M. J., Grocutt, E., Deepak, K. & Bailey, E. (2007). Metacognition in anorexia nervosa, dieting and non-dieting controls: A preliminary investigation. *British Journal of Clinical Psychology*, 46, 113–17.

Cooper, P. J., Whelan, E., Woolgar, M., Morrell J. & Murray, L. (2004). Association between childhood feeding problems and maternal eating disorder: Role of the family environment. *The British Journal of Psychiatry*, 184, 210–15.

Cooper, W. O., Arbogast, P. G., Ding, H., Hickson, G. B., Fuchs, D. C. & Ray, W. A. (2006). Trends in prescribing of antipsychotic medications for US children. *Ambulatory Pediatrics*, 6(2), 79–83.

Copeland, J., Cooper, J., Kendell, R. & Gourlay, A. (1971). Differences in usage of diagnostic labels amongst psychiatrists in the British Isles. *British Journal of Psychiatry*, 118(547), 629–40.

Copolov, D. & Crook, J. (2000). Biological markers and schizophrenia. *Australian and New Zealand Journal of Psychiatry*, 34 (suppl.), s108–12.

Coppock, V. & Hopton, J. (2000). *Critical Perspectives on Mental Health*. London: Routledge.

Corbin, J. (2007). Reactive attachment disorder: A biopsychosocial disturbance of attachment. *Child and Adolescent Social Work Journal*, 24, 539–52.

Corcoran, R., Cahill, C. & Frith, C. D. (1997). The appreciation of visual jokes in people with schizophrenia: A study of 'mentalizing' ability. *Schizophrenia Research*, 24, 319–27.

Corcoran, R., Rowse, G., Moore, R., Blackwood, N., Kinderman, P., Howard, R. et al. (2008). A transdiagnostic investigation of theory of mind and jumping to conclusions in paranoia: A comparison of schizophrenia and depression with and without delusions. *Psychological Medicine*, 38, 1577–83.

Corrigall, J. (2003). Brief psychoanalytic psychotherapy: A contradiction in terms? In L. King & R. Randall (Eds), *The Future of Pyschoanalytic Psychotherapy*. London: Wurr.

Corstens, D., Escher, S. & Romme, M. (2008). Accepting and working with voices: The Maastricht approach. In A. Moskowitz, I. Schäfer & M. J. Dorahy (Eds), *Psychosis, Trauma and Dissociation: Emerging Perspectives on Severe Psychopathology*. Oxford: Wiley-Blackwell.

Corstens, D., Longden, E. & May, R. (2012). Talking with voices. In M. Romme & S. Escher (Eds), *Psychosis as a Personal Crisis: An Experienced Based Approach*. London: ISPS Publications.

Corstens, D., May, R. & Longden, E. (2011). Talking with voices. In M. Romme & S. Escher (Eds), *Psychosis as a Personal Crisis: An Experience-based Approach* (166–78). London: Routledge.

Costa, Jr., P. T. & McCrae, R. R. (1992). *Revised NEO Personality Inventory (NEO-PI-R) and NEO Five-Factor Inventory (NEO-FFI) Manual*. Odessa, FL: Psychological Assessment Resources.

Costa, Jr., P. T., Terracciano, A. & McCrae, R. R. (2001). Gender differences in personality traits across cultures: Robust and surprising findings. *Journal of Personality & Social Psychology*, 81, 322–31.

Cove, J. & Boyle, M. (2002). Gay men's self-defined sexual problems, perceived causes and factors in remission. *Sexual and Relationship Therapy*, 17, 137–47.

Cove, J. and Petrak, J. (2004). Factors associated with sexual problems in HIV-positive gay men. *International Journal of STD & AIDS*, 15(11), 732–6.

Cowan, L. & Hart, D. (1998). Changing minds: Every family in the land: A new challenge for the future (editorial). *Psychiatric Bulletin*, 22, 593–4.

Craddock, N. & Owen, M. J. (2005). The beginning of the end for the kraepelinian dichotomy. *British Journal of Psychiatry*, 186, 364–6.

Craig, T. & Hwang, M. Y. (2000). Comorbidity in schizophrenia: Epidemiology and clinical implications. *Psychiatric Annals*, 30(1), 76–8.

Crane, G. E. (1956). Further studies on iproniazid phosphate. *Journal of Nervous & Mental Disease*, 124, 322–31.

Cresswell, M. (2005). Self-harm 'survivors' and psychiatry in England, 1988–1996. *Social Theory & Health*, 3, 259–85.

Crisp, A. H., Gelder, M. G., Rix, S. Meltzer, H. I. & Rowlands, O. J. (2000). Stigmatisation of people with mental illnesses. *British Journal of Psychiatry*, 177, 4–7.

Crisp, R. J. & Turner, R. N. (2011). Cognitive adaptation to the experience of social and cultural diversity. *Psychological Bulletin*, 137, 242–66.

Croissant, J. L. (2006). The new sexual technobody: Viagra in the hyperreal world. *Sexualities*, 9(3), 333–44.

Cromby, J. (2004). Between constructionism and neuroscience: The societal co-constitution of embodied subjectivity. *Theory and Psychology*, 14(6), 797–821.

Cromby, J. (2007). Integrating social science with neuroscience: Potentials and problems. *Biosocieties*, 2(2), 149–70.

Cromby, J., Harper, D. & Reavey, P. (2008). Mental health teaching to UK psychology undergraduates: Report of a survey. *Journal of Community & Applied Social Psychology*,18, 83–90.

Crossley, N. (2005). *Contesting Psychiatry: Social Movements in Mental Health*. London: Routledge.

Cromby, J. & Harper, D. (2009). Paranoia: A social account. *Theory and Psychology*, 19(3), 335–61.

Croudace, T., Bloom, R., Jones, P. & Harrison, G. (2000). Non-linear relationship between a measure of social deprivation, psychiatric admission prevalence and the incidence of psychosis. *Psychological Medicine*, 30, 177–85.

Crow, T. J. (1980). Molecular pathology of schizophrenia: More than one disease process? *British Medical Journal*, 280, 66–8.

Crow, T. J. (2010). The continuum of psychosis, 1986–2010. *Psychiatric Annals*, 40(2), 115–19.

Crowe, M. & Ridley, J. (2000). *Therapy with Couples: A Behavioural-Systems Approach to Couple Relationship and Sexual Problems*. Oxford: Blackwell.

Curtis, T., Dellar, R., Leslie, E. &Watson, B. (Eds) (2000). *Mad Pride: A Celebration of Mad Culture*. London: Spare Change Books.

Cushman, P. (1995). *Constructing the Self, Constructing America*. Cambridge MA: Da Capo Press.

Dain, N. (1989). Critics and dissenters: Reflections on 'anti-psychiatry' in the United States. *Journal of the History of the Behavioral Sciences*, 25, 3–25.

Dallos, S. & R. Dallos (1997). *Couples, Sex and Power: The Politics of Desire*. Maidenhead: Open University Press.

Damasio, A. R. (1994). *Descartes' Error: Emotion, Reason, and the Human Brain*. London: Picador.

Dare, C., Russell, G., Treasure, J. & Dodge, L. (2001). Psychological therapies for adults with anorexia nervosa : Randomised controlled trial of out-patient treatments. *The British Journal of Psychiatry*, 178, 216–21.

Darves-Bornoz, J.-M., Lemperiere, T., Degiovanni, A. & Gaillard, P. (1995). Sexual victimisation in women with schizophrenia and bipolar disorder. *Social Psychiatry & Psychiatric Epidemiology*, 30(2), 78–84.

Das-Munshi, J., Becares, L., Dewey, M. E., Stansfield, S. A. and Prince, M. J. (2010). Understanding the effect of ethnic density on mental health: Multi-level investigation of survey data from England. *British Medical Journal*, 341, 871.

Davey, G. (2008). *Psychopathology: Research, Assessment and Treatment in Clinical Psychology*. West Sussex: BPS Blackwell.

Davey, G. & Chapman, L. (2009). Disgust and eating disorder symptomatology in a non-clinical population: The role of trait anxiety and anxiety sensitivity. *Clinical Psychology & Psychotherapy*, 16, 268–75.

Davey, G., Tallis, F. & Capuzzo, N. (1996). Beliefs about the consequences of worrying. *Cognitive Therapy and Research*, 20, 499–518.

Davidson, K., Halford, J., Kirkwood, L., Newton Howes, G., Sharp, M. & Tata, P. (2010). CBT for violent men with antisocial personality disorder. Reflections on the experience of carrying out therapy in MASCOT, a pilot randomized controlled trial. *Personality and Mental Health*, 4, 86–95.

Davidson, K., Norrie, J., Tyrer, P., Gumley, A., Tata, P., Murray, H. et al. (2006). The effectiveness of cognitive behavior therapy for borderline personality disorder: Results from the borderline personality disorder study of cognitive therapy (BOSCOT) trial. *Journal of Personality Disorders*, 20, 450–65.

Davidson, K. M. (2008a). *Cognitive Therapy for Personality Disorders: A Guide for Clinicians* (2nd edn). London: Routledge.

Davidson, K. M., Tyrer, P., Tata, P., Cooke, D., Gumley, A., Ford, I. et al. (2008b). Cognitive behaviour therapy for violent men with antisocial personality disorder in the community: An exploratory randomized controlled trial. *Psychological Medicine*, 38, 1–9.

Davidson, L., Chinman, M., Kloos, B., Weingarten, R., Stayner, D. & Tebes, J. K. (1999). Peer support among individuals with severe mental illness: A review of the evidence. *Clinical Psychology: Science & Practice*, 6, 165–87.

Davidson, R. J. & Henriques, J. (2000). Regional brain function in sadness and depression. In J. Borod (Ed.), *The Neuropsychology of Emotion*. Oxford: Oxford University Press.

Davidson, R. J., Jackson, D. & Kalin, N. (2000). Emotion, plasticity, context and regulation: Perspectives from affective neuroscience. *Psychological Bulletin*, 126, 890–906.

Davies, D. (1997). *Counselling in Psychological Services*. Maidenhead: Open University Press.

Davies, D. & Neal, C. (1996). *Pink Therapy: Guide for Counsellors Working with Lesbian, Gay and Bisexual Clients*. London: Sage.

Davies, E. & Burdett, J. (2004). Preventing 'schizophrenia': Creating the conditions for saner societies. In J. Read, L. Mosher & R. Bentall (Eds), *Models of Madness: Psychological, Social and Biological Approaches to Schizophrenia* (271–82). London: Routledge.

Davis, C. & Claridge, G. (1998). The eating disorders as addiction: A psychobiological perspective. *Addictive Behaviors*, 23, 463–75.

Davis, J. M., Schaffer, C. B., Killian, G. A., Kinard, C. & Chan, C. (1980). Important issues in the drug treatment of schizophrenia. *Schizophrenia Bulletin*, 6(1), 70–87.

Davison, G. C., Neale, J. M. & Kring, A. M. (2004). *Abnormal Psychology* (9th edition). New York: Wiley.

Dawes, R. (1994). *House of Cards: Psychology and Psychotherapy Built on Myth*. New York: Macmillan.

Dawood, K., Kirk, K. M., Bailey, J. M., Andrews, P. W. & Martin, N. G. (2005). Genetic and environmental influences on the frequency of orgasm in women. *Twin Research and Human Genetics*, 8(1), 27–33.

De Jongh, A., Muris, P., Ter Horst, G. & Duyx, M. (1995). Acquisition and maintenance of dental anxiety: The role of conditioning experiences and cognitive factors. *Behaviour Research and Therapy*, 33(2), 205–10.

De Kruiff, M. E., Ter Kuile, M. M., Weijenborg, P. T. M. & van Larikveld, J. J. D. M. (2000). Vaginismus and dyspareunia: Is there a difference in clinical presentation? *Journal of Psychosomatic Obstetrics & Gynecology*, 21(3), 149–55.

De Raad, B., Barelds, D. P. H., Levert, E., Ostendorf, F., Mlačić, B., Blas, L. D. et al. (2010). Only three factors of personality description are fully replicable across languages: A comparison of 14 trait taxonomies. *Journal of Personality and Social Psychology*, 98, 160–73.

Dean, B. (2000). Signal transmission, rather than reception, is the underlying neurochemical abnormality in schizophrenia. *Australian and New Zealand Journal of Psychiatry*, 34, 560–69.

Dean, R., Bilsky, E. J. Luby, E. & Koval, D. (2009). *Opiate Receptors and Antagonists: From Bench to Clinic*. New York: Humana Press.

Dehue, T. (2002). A Dutch treat: Randomized controlled experimentation and the case of heroin-maintenance in the Netherlands. *History of the Human Sciences*, 15(2), 75–98.

Dein, K., Williams, P. S. & Dein, S. (2007). Ethnic bias in the application of the Mental Health Act 1983. *Advances in Psychiatric Treatment*, 13, 350–7.

Delay, J. & Deniker, P. (1952). Trent-huit cas de psychoses traités par la cure prolongée et continue de 4560 R.P. *Congrès des Médecins Aliénistes et Neurologistes de Langue Française*, 50, 503–13.

Dell, P. & O'Neil, J. (Eds) (2009). *Dissociation and the Dissociative Disorders: DSM-V and Beyond*. New York: Routledge.

Deniker, P. (1960). Experimental neurological syndromes and the new drug therapies in psychiatry. *Comprehensive Psychiatry*, 1, 92–102.

Denman, C. (2004). *Sexuality: A Biopsychosocial Approach*. London: Palgrave Macmillan.

Department of Health (1999). *National Service Framework for Mental Health*. London: Department of Health.

Department of Health (2001). *Treatment of Choice in Psychological Therapies and Counselling*. London: HMSO.

Department of Health (2001). *Safety First: Report of the National Confidential Inquiry (NCI) into Suicide and Homicide by People with Mental Illness – Annual report: England and Wales*. London: Department of Health.

Department of Health (2002). *Women's Mental Health: Into the Mainstream*. London: Department of Health.

Department of Health (2003). *Electro Convulsive Therapy: Survey Covering the Period from January 2002 to March 2002, England*. London: Author. Accessed 29 December 2011 at www.dh.gov.uk/en/Publicationsandstatistics/Publications/PublicationsStatistics/DH_4083142

Department of Health (2006a) *Forecasting Obesity 2010* by Paola Zaninotto, Heather Wardle, Emmanuel Stamatakis, Jennifer Mindell and Jenny Head.

Department of Health (2006b). *Tackling the Health and Mental Health Effects of Domestic and Sexual Violence and Abuse*. London: Department of Health.

Department of Health (2007). *Valuing People Now*. London: HMSO.

Department of Health (2008). *Implementing National Policy on Violence and Abuse. Briefing 162*. London: Department of Health.

Department of Health (2010). *Average Daily Number of Available Beds, by Sector, England, 1987–88 to 2009–10*. London: Author.

Department of Health/Home Office (1999). *Managing Dangerous People with Severe Personality Disorder*. London: HMSO.

Department of Health/National Statistics (2010). In-patients formally detained in hospitals under the Mental Health Act 1983 and patients subject to supervised community treatment, Annual figures, England 2009/10. London: The Health and Social Care Information Centre, Community and Mental Health Team.

Derksen, M. (2001). Science in the clinic: Clinical psychology at the Maudsley. In G. C. Bunn, A. D. Lovie & G. D. Richards (Eds), *Psychology in Britain: Historical Essays and Personal Reflections*. Leicester: BPS Books in association with the Science Museum.

Diamond, B. (2002). Clinical psychologists' responses to the Mental Health Act reforms: Acquiescence, ambivalence or confusion? *Clinical Psychology*, 19, 9–12.

Diamond, B. (2008). Opening up space for dissention: A questioning psychology. In A. Morgan (Ed.), *Being Human: Reflections on Mental Distress in Society*. Ross-On-Wye: PCCS.

Diaz-Guerrero, R. (1976). Test anxiety and general anxiety in Mexican and American schoolchildren. In C. Spielberger & R. Diaz-Guerrero (Eds), *Cross-Cultural Anxiety*, Vol. 1 (135–42). Washington DC: Hemisphere.

Dickerson, F. B., Tenhula, W. N. & Green-Paden, L. D. (2005). The token economy for schizophrenia: Review of the literature and recommendations for future research. *Schizophrenia Research*, 75, 405–16.

Dietrich, S., Beck, M., Bujantugs, B., Kenzine, D., Matschinger, H. & Angermeyer, M. (2004). The relationship between public causal beliefs and social distance toward mentally ill people. *Australian and New Zealand Journal of Psychiatry*, 38, 348–54.

Dietrich, S., Matschinger, H. & Angermeyer, M. (2006). The relationship between biogenetic causal explanations and social distance toward people with mental disorders: Results from a population survey in Germany. *Inernational Journal of Social Psychiatry*, 52, 166–74.

Digman, J. M. (1990). Personality structure: Emergence of the five-factor model. *Annual Review of Psychology*, 41, 417–40.

Dillon, J. (2006). Collective voices. *Open Mind*, 142, 16–18.

Dillon, J. (2010). The tale of an ordinary little girl. *Psychosis: Psychological, Social and Integrative Approaches*, 2(1), 79–83.

Dillon, J. (2011). The personal is the political. In M. Rapley, J. Moncrieff & J. Dillon (Eds), *Demedicalising Misery: Psychiatry, Psychology and the Human Condition*. Basingstoke: Palgrave Macmillan.

Dillon, J. & Longden, E. (2011). Hearing voices groups: Creating safe spaces to share taboo experiences. In M. Romme & S. Escher (Eds), *Psychosis as a Personal Crisis: An Experience-based Approach* (129–39). London: Routledge.

Dinan, T. G. (1994). Glucocorticoids and the genesis of depressive illness: A psychobiological model. *British Journal of Psychiatry*, 164, 365–71.

Dineen, T. (1999). *Manufacturing Victims: What the Psychology Industry is Doing to People*. London, Constable.

Diokno, A. C., Brown, M. B. & Herzog, A. R. (1990). Sexual function in the elderly. *Archives of Internal Medicine*, 150, 197–200.

Doane, J., West, K., Goldstein, M., Rodnick, E. H. & Jones, J. E. (1981). Parental communication deviance and affective style: Predictors of subsequent schizophrenia spectrum disorders in vulnerable adolescents. *Archives of General Psychiatry*, 38(6), 679–85.

Dodge, K. A. & Pettit, G. S. (2003). A biopsychosocial model of the development of chronic conduct problems in adolescence. *Developmental Psychology*, 39, 349–71.

Doering, S., Horz, S., Rentrop, M., Fischer-Kern, M., Schuster, P., Benecke, C. et al. (2010). Transference-focused psychotherapy v. treatment by community psychotherapists for borderline personality disorder: Randomised controlled trial. *British Journal of Psychiatry*, 196, 389–95.

Dols, M. W. (1992). *Majnun: The Madman in Medieval Islamic Society*. Oxford: Clarendon Press.

Dorahy, M. & Lewis, C. A. (2001). The relationship between dissociation and religiosity: An empirical evaluation of Schumaker's theory. *Journal for the Scientific Study of Religion*, 40, 315–22.

Dorling, D. (2008). Prime suspect: Murder in Britain. In D. Dorling, D. Gordon, P. Hillyard, C. Pantazis, S. Pemberton & S. Tombs. (Eds), *Criminal Obsessions: Why Harm Matters More Than Crime*. London: Crime and Society Foundation. Retrieved onAccessed 2 December 2011 at www.crimeandjustice.org.uk/opus912/Criminal_obsessions.pdf

Double, D. D. (Ed.) (2006). *Critical Psychiatry: The Limits of Madness*. London: Palgrave Macmillan.

Downs, J. (2005a). *Starting and Supporting Hearing Voices Groups*. Manchester: The Hearing Voices Network.

Downs, J. (2005b). *Coping with Voices and Visions*. Manchester: The Hearing Voices Network.

Dozier, M. & Lee, S. W. (1995). Discrepancies between self and other-report of psychiatric symptomatology: Effects of dismissing attachment strategies. *Development and Psychopathology*, 7, 217–26.

Dozier, M., Stevenson, A., Lee, S. & Velligan, D. (1991). Attachment organisation and familial overinvolvement for adults with serious psychopathological disorders. *Development and Psychopathology*, 3, 475–89.

Dozier, M., Stovall, K., Chase, Albus, K. E. (1999). Attachment and psychopathology in adulthood. In J. Cassidy & P. Shaver (Eds), *Handbook of Attachment: Theory, Research, and Clinical Applications*. New York: Guilford Press.

Drescher, J. (2010). Queer diagnoses: Parallels and contrasts in the history of homosexuality, gender variance, and the diagnostic and statistical manual. *Archives of Sexual Behavior*, 39, 427–60.

Drevets, W. C., Frank, E., Price, J. C., Kupfer, D. J., Holt, D., Greer, P. J. et al. (1999). Pet imaging of serotonin 1A receptor binding in depression. *Biological Psychiatry*, 46(10), 1375–87.

Drury, J. & Reicher, S. (2009). Collective psychological empowerment as a model of social change: Researching crowds and power. *Journal of Social Issues*, 65, 707–25.

Drury, V. M., Robinson, E. J. & Birchwood, M. (1998). 'Theory of mind' skills during an acute episode of psychosis and following recovery. *Psychological Medicine*, 28, 1101–12.

Dryden, W. (Ed.) (2007). *Dryden's Handbook of Individual Therapy* (5th edn). London: Sage.

Dubovsky, S. L. (1987). Unusual faces of depression: Recognizing and treating complicated and atypical depressive syndromes. *Therapeutic Strategies in Depression*, 1, 3–14.

Dubovksy, S. L., Davies, R. & Dubovsky, A. N. (2001) Mood disorders. In R. E. Hales & S. C. Yudofsky (Eds), *Textbook of Clinical Psychiatry*. Washington: American Psychiatric Association.

Dudley, R. E. & Over, D. E. (2003). People with delusions jump to conclusions: A theoretical account of research findings on the reasoning of people with delusions. *Clinical Psychology and Psychotherapy*, 10, 263–74.

Dumont, G. J., de Visser, S. J., Cohen, A. F. & van Gerven, J. M. (2005). Biomarkers for the effects of selective serotonin reuptake inhibitors SSRIs) in healthy subjects. *British Journal of Clinical Pharmacology*, 59, 495–510.

Duncombe, J. & Marsden, D. (1993). Love and intimacy: The gender division of emotion and 'emotion work'. *Sociology*, 27(2), 221–41.

Dunn, K. M., Cherkas, L. F. & Spector, T. D. (22 September 2005) Genetic influences on variation in female orgasmic function: A twin study. *Biology Letters*, 1(3), 260–3. doi:10.1098/rsbl.2005.0308 1744-957X

Dunner, D. L. (1998). The issue of co-morbidity in the treatment of panic. *International Clinical Psychopharmacology*, 13(Apr), S19–24.

Earls, C. M., Martin, A. E. & Lalumière, L. (2007). A case study of preferential bestiality. *Archives of Sexual Behaviour*, 25, 263–78.

Eaton, W. (1980). A formal theory of selection for schizophrenia. *American Journal of Sociology*, 86, 149–58.

Eaton, W. W. & Harrison, G. (2001). Life chances, life planning and schizophrenia: A review and interpretation of research on social deprivation. *International Journal of Mental Health*, 30, 58–81.

Eaton, W. W., Kessler, R. & Wittchen, H. U. (1994). Panic and panic disorder in the United States. *American Journal of Psychiatry*, 151, 413–20.

Eddy, K. T., Keel, P. K., Dorer, D. J., Delinsky, S. S., Franko, D. L. & Herzog, D. B. (2002). Longitudinal comparison of anorexia nervosa subtypes. *International Journal of Eating Disorders*, 31, 191–201.

Eells, T. D. (Ed.) (1997). *Handbook of Psychotherapy Case Formulation*. New York: Guilford Press.

Egger, G., Gangning, L., Aparicio, A. & Jones, P. (2004). Epigenetics in human disease and prospects for epigenetic therapy. *Nature*, 429, 457–63.

Ehlers, A. & Breuer, P. (1992). Increased cardiac awareness in panic disorder. *Journal of Abnormal Psychology*, 101(3), 371–82.

Eichenbaum, L. & Orbach, S. (1983). *Understanding Women: A Feminist Psychoanalytic Approach*. New York: Basic Books.

Eisler, I., Dare, C., Hodes, M., Russell, G., Dodge, E. & Le Grange, D. (2000). Family therapy for adolescent anorexia nervosa: The results of a controlled comparison of two family interventions. *Journal of Child Psychology and Psychiatry*, 41(6), 727–36.

Eisler, I., Dare, C., Russell, G., Szmukler, G., Le Grange, D., Dodge, E. (1997). A five-year follow-up of a controlled trial of family therapy in severe eating disorders. *Archives of General Psychiatry*, 54, 1025–30.

Eisler, I., Lock, J. & le Grange, D. (2009). Family based treatments for adolescents with anorexia nervosa: Single family and multifamily approaches. In C. M. Grilo & J. E. Mitchell (Eds), *The Treatment of Eating Disorders: A Clinical Handbook*. New York: Guildford Press.

Eisler, I., Simic, M., Russell, G. & Dare, C. (2007). A randomised controlled treatment trial of two forms of family therapy in adolescent anorexia nervosa: A five-year follow-up. *Journal of Child Psychology and Psychiatry*, 6, 552–60.

Eisner, D. (2000). *The Death of Psychotherapy: From Freud to Alien Abductions*. New York, Preager.

Elhai, J., Frueh, C., Gold, P., Gold, S. & Hamner, M. (2000). Clinical presentations of posttraumatic stress disorder across trauma populations. *Journal of Nervous & Mental Disease*, 188, 708–13.

Elhai, J., Frueh, C., Gold, P., Hamner, M. & Gold, S. (2003). Postraumatic stress, depression and dissociation as predictors of MMPI Scale 8 scores in combat veterans with PTSD. *Journal of Trauma and Dissociation*, 4, 51–64.

Elklit, A. & Shevlin, M. (2010). Female sexual victimization predicts psychosis: A case-control study based on the Danish registry system. *Schizophrenia Bulletin*.

Ellason, J. & Ross, C. (1995). Positive and negative symptoms in dissociative identity disorder and schizophrenia: A comparative analysis. *Journal of Nervous and Mental Disease*, 183(4), 236–41.

Elliott, R. T. (2010). Examining the relationship between personality characteristics and unethical behaviors resulting in economic crime. *Ethical Human Psychology and Psychiatry*, 12, 269–76.

Ellis, D. & Cromby, J. (2009). Inhibition and reappraisal within emotional disclosure: Embodying narration. *Counselling and Psychology Quarterly*, 22 (3), 319–31.

El-Rufaie, O. E. F., Bener, A., Abuzeid, M. S. O. & Ali, T. A. (1997). Sexual dysfunction among type II diabetic men: A controlled study. *Journal of Psychosomatic Research*, 43, 605–12.

Engel, G. (1977). The need for a new medical model. *Science*, 196, 129–36.

Entman, R. (2007). Framing bias: Media in the distribution of power. *Journal of Communication*, 57(1), 163–73.

Enzlin, P., Mathieu, C., Van den Bruel, A., Bosteels, J., Vanderschueren, D., Demyttenaere, K. (2002). Sexual dysfunction in women with type 1 diabetes: A controlled study. *Diabetes Care*, 25(4), 787–8.

Epstein, W. (1996). *The Illusion of Psychotherapy*. New York: Transaction.

Epstein, W. (2006). *The Civil Divine: Psychotherapy as Religion in America*. Reno: University of Nevada Press.

Ernst, C. (1988). Are early childhood experiences over-rated? *European Archives of Psychiatry and Clinical Neuroscience*, 237, 80–90.

Erwin, E. (1997). *Philosophy and Psychotherapy: Razing the Troubles of the Brain*. London: Sage.

Escher, S. (1993). Talking about voices. In M. Romme & S. Escher (Eds), *Accepting Voices*. London: Mind Publications.

Escher, S. (2009). Accepting voices and finding a way out. In M. Romme, S. Escher, D. Corstens, J. Dillon & M. Morris (Eds), *Living with Voices: Fifty Stories of Recovery*. Ross-on-Wye: PCCS Books.

Ewen, C. E. (1929). *Witch Hunting and Witch Trials: The Indictments for Witchcraft from the Records of 1373 Assizes Held for the Home Circuit A.D. 1559–1736*. New York: The Dial Press.

Eysenck, H. J. & Eysenck, S. B. G. (1976). *Psychoticism as a Dimension of Personality*. London: Hodder & Stoughton.

Fagan, P. J., Wise, T. N., Schmidt, C. W., Ponticas, Y. Marshall, R.A. & Costa, P.T. (1991). Comparison of five-factor personality dimensions in males with sexual dysfunction and males with paraphilia. *Journal of Personality Assessment*, 57, 434–48.

Fairburn, C. G. (1981). A cognitive behavioural approach to the treatment of bulimia. *Psychological Medicine*, 11, 707–11.

Fairburn, C. G. (2008). *Cognitive Behaviour Therapy and Eating Disorders*. New York: Guilford Press.

Fairburn, C. G. & Bohn, K. (2005) Eating disorder NOS (EDNOS): An example of the troublesome 'not otherwise specified' (NOS) category in DSM-IV. *Behaviour Research and Therapy*, 43(6), 691–701.

Fairburn, C. G., Cooper, Z. & Shafran, R. (2003). Cognitive behaviour therapy for eating disorders: A 'transdiagnostic' theory and treatment. *Behaviour Research and Therapy*, 41, 509–28.

Fairburn, C. G., Cooper, Z., Shafran, R., Wilson, G. T. (2008). Eating disorders: A transdiagnostic protocol. In D. H. Barlow (Ed.), 578–614.

Fairburn, C. G. & Harrison, P. J. (2003a). Eating disorders. *Lancet*, 361, 407–16.

Fairburn, C. G. & Harrison, P. J. (2003b). Risk factors for anorexia nervosa. *Lancet*, 361(9372), 1914–31.

Fairburn, C. G., Welch, S. L., Norman, P. A., O'Connor, M. E. and Doll, H. A. (1996). Bias and bulimia nervosa: How typical are clinic cases? *American Journal of Psychiatry*, 153, 386–91.

Fairburn, C. G. & Wilson, G. T. (Eds) (1993). *Bing Eating: Nature, Assessment, and Treatment*. New York: Guildford Press.

Fallon, P. (2003). Travelling through the system: The lived experience of people with borderline personality disorder in contact with psychiatric services. *Journal of Psychiatric and Mental Health Nursing*, 10, 393–401.

Fallon, P., Katzman, M. A. & Wooley, S. C. (1994). *Feminist Perspectives on Eating Disorders*. New York: Guilford Press.

Famularo, R., Kinscherff, R. & Fenton, T. (1992). Psychiatric diagnoses of maltreated children: Preliminary findings. *Journal of the American Academy of Child & Adolescent Psychiatry*, 31(5), 863–7.

Fan, A. P. & Eaton, W. W. (2001). Longitudinal study assessing the joint effects of socio-economic status and birth risks on adult emotional and nervous conditions. *British Journal of Psychiatry*, 178 (suppl. 40), s78–s83.

Fancher, R. (1996). *Cultures of Healing: Correcting the Image of American Health Care*. San Francisco: W. H. Freeman & Co.

Fanon, F. (1963). *The Wretched of the Earth*. Harmondsworth: Penguin.

Farber, J. (1981). The role of calcium in cell death. *Life Sciences*, 29, 1289–95.

Farber, S. (1981). *Identical Twins Reared Apart: A Re-analysis*. New York: Basic Books.

Farmer, M. A. & Meston, C. M. (2007). Predictors of genital pain in young women. *Archives of Sexual Behavior*, 36, 831–43.

Farmer, R. F. (2000). Issues in the assessment and conceptualization of personality disorders. *Clinical Psychology Review*, 20, 823–51.

Farr, D. (2010). A very personal world: Advertisement and identity of trans-persons on Craigslist' in C. Pullen & M. Cooper (Eds), *LGBT Identity and Online New Media* (87–99). New York: Routledge.

Fass, R., Fullerton, S., Naliboff, B. Hirsh T. & Mayer, E.A. (1998). Sexual dysfunction in patients with irritable bowel syndrome and non-ulcer dyspepsia. *Digestion*, 59, 79–85.

Fassino, S., Leombruni, P., Pierò, A., Abbate-Daga, G. & Rovera, G. G. (2003). Mood, eating attitudes, and anger in obese women with and without binge eating disorder. *Journal of Psychosomatic Research*, 54, 559–66.

Fausto-Sterling, A. (2000). *Sexing the Body: Gender Politics and the Construction of Sexuality*. New York: Basic Books.

Favaro, A., Ferrara, S. & Santonastaso, P. (2003). The spectrum of eating disorders in young women: A prevalence study in a general population sample. *Psychosomatic Medicine*, 65, 701–8.

Fazel, S., Langstrom, N., Hjern, A., Grann, M. & Lichtenstein, P. (2009). Schizophrenia, substance abuse, and violent crime. *Journal of the American Medical Association*, 301(19), 2016–23.

Fearon, P., Kirkbride, J. B., Morgan, C., Dazzan, P., Morgan, K., Lloyd, T. et al. (2006). Incidence of schizophrenia and other psychoses in ethnic minority groups: Results from the MRC AESOP Study. *Psychological Medicine*, 36(11), 1541–50.

Feldman, R., Greenbaum, C. & Yirimiya, N. (1999). Mother-infant affect synchrony as an antecedent of the emergence of self-control. *Developmental Psychology*, 35, 223–31.

Feltham, C. (1999). Against and beyond core theoretical models. In C. Feltham (Ed.), *Controversies in Psychotherapy and Counselling*. London: Sage.

Fer Winterkjaer, T. & Dalchow, J. (dir). (2004). 100% Human (100% Menneske). TV 2, Handy Film, and Winterlove.

Fergusson, D. M., Boden, J. M., Horwood, L. J., Miller, A. L. & Kennedy, M. A. (2011). MAOA, abuse exposure and antisocial behaviour: 30-year longitudinal study. *British Journal of Psychiatry*, 198, 457–63.

Fernández-Aranda, F. (1999). Body image in eating disorders and analysis of its relevance: A preliminary study. *Journal of Psychosomatic Research*, 47, 419–28

Fernando, S. (1991). *Mental Health, Race and Culture*. Macmillan/Mind.

Fernando, S. (2002). *Mental Health, Race and Culture* (2nd edn). Basingstoke: Palgrave.

Fernando, S. (2003). *Cultural Diversity, Mental Health and Psychiatry: The Struggle against Racism*. Hove: Brunner-Routledge.

Fernando, S. (2007). Cheering the 'deranged'. *Open Mind*, 145, 24–5.

Ferns, P. (2005). Finding a way forward: A black perspective on social approaches to mental health. In J. Tew (Ed.), *Social Perspectives in Mental Health: Developing Social Models to Understand and Work with Distress*. London: Jessica Kingsley Publishers.

Ferreday, D. & Lock, S. (2007). Computer cross-dressing: Queering the virtual subject. In K. O'Riordan & D. J. Phillips (Eds), *Queer Online: Media, Technology and Sexuality* (155–76). New York: Peter Lang.

Finkelhor, D. (1984). *Child Sexual Abuse: New Theory and Research*. New York: Free Press.

Finkelhor, D. & Browne, A. (1985). The traumatic impact of child sexual abuse: A conceptualization. *American Journal of Orthopsychiatry*, 55(4), 530–41.

Finkelhor, D. & Browne, A. (1986). Impact of child sexual abuse: A review of the research. *Psychological Bulletin*, 99, 66–77.

Finlay-Jones, R. & Brown, G. (1981). Types of stressful life event and the onset of anxiety and depressive disorders. *Psychological Medicine*, 11(4), 803–15.

First, M. B. (2009). Harmonisation of ICD–11 and DSM–V: Opportunities and challenges. *British Journal of Psychiatry*, 195, 382–90.

First, M. B., Bell, C. C., Cuthbert, B., Krystal, J. H., Malison, R., Offord, D. R. et al. (2002). Personality disorders and relational disorders: A research agenda for addressing crucial gaps in DSM. In D. J. Kupfer, M. B. First & D. A. Regier (Eds), *Research Agenda for DSM-V* (123–99). Washington DC: American Psychiatric Association.

Fisher, D., Beech, R. A. & Browne, K. (1999). Comparison of sex offenders to no-offenders on slected psychological measures. *International Journal of Offender Therapy and Comparative Criminology*, 43, 473–91.

Fisher, H. L., Craig, T. K., Fearon, P., Morgan, K., Dazzan, P., Lappin, J. et al. (2011). Reliability and comparability of psychosis patients' retrospective reports of childhood abuse. *Schizophrenia Bulletin*, 37, 546–53.

Fisher, H., Craig, T., Fearon, P., Morgan, K., Dazzan, P., Lappin, J. et al. (2011). Reliability and comparability of psychosis patients' retrospective reports of childhood abuse. *Schizophrenia Bulletin*, 37(3), 546–53.

Fisher, H., Morgan, C., Dazzan, P., Craig, T., Morgan, K., Hutchinson, G. et al. (2009). Gender differences in the association between childhood abuse and psychosis. *British Journal of Psychiatry*, 194, 319–25.

Fisher, J. & Farina, A. (1979). Consequences of beliefs about the nature of mental disorders. *Journal of Abnormal Psychology*, 88, 320–7.

Fisher, S. & Greenberg, R. P. (1993). How sound is the double-blind design for evaluating psychotropic drugs? *Journal of Nervous & Mental Disease*, 181, 345–50.

Fivush, R. (1991). The social construction of personal narratives. *Merril-Palmer Quarterly*, 37(1), 59–81.

Flanagan, E. H., Davidson, L. & Strauss, J. S. (2007). Issues for DSM-V: Incorporating patients' subjective experiences. *American Journal of Psychiatry*, 164, 391–2.

Foa, E., Steketee, G. & Rothbaum, D. (1989). Behaviour/cognitive conceptualisation of post-traumatic stress disorder. *Behavior Therapy*, 20, 155–76.

Foley, D. J., Manderscheid, R. W., Atay, J. E., Maedke, J., Sussman, J. & Cribbs, S. (2006). Highlights of organized mental health services in 2002 and major national and state trends. In R. W. Manderscheid & J. T. Berry (Eds), *Mental health, United States, 2004*. Rockville MD: Substance Abuse and Mental Health Services Administration.

Fonagy, P., Target, M., Gergely, G., Allen, J. G. & Bateman, A. (2003). The developmental roots of borderline personality disorder in early attachment relationships: A theory and some evidence. *Psychoanalytic Inquiry*, 23, 412–59.

Ford, J. M. & Mathalon, D. H. (2004). Electrophysiological evidence of corollary discharge dysfunction in schizophrenia during talking and thinking. *Journal of Psychiatric Research*, 38, 37–46.

Ford, M. R. & Widiger, T. A. (1989). Sex bias in the diagnosis of histrionic and antisocial personality disorders. *Journal of Consulting & Clinical Psychology*, 57, 301–5.

Form, A. (2000). Does old age reduce the risk of anxiety and depression? A review of epidemiological studies across the adult life span. *Psychological Medicine*, 30(1), 11–22.

Foucault, M. (1961). *Madness and Civilisation*. London: Routledge.

Foucault, M. (1971). *Madness and Civilization: A History of Insanity in the Age of Reason*. London: Tavistock.

Foucault, M. (2009). *History of Madness*. London: Routledge.

Fox, J. R. E. (2009). Eating disorders and emotions. *Clinical Psychology and Psychotherapy*, 16(4), 237–9.

Fox, J. R. E. & Harrison, A. (2008). The relation of anger to disgust: The potential role of coupled emotions within eating pathology. *Clinical Psychology and Psychotherapy*, 15(2), 86–95.

Fox, J. R. E. & Power, M. J. (2009). Eating disorders and multi-level models of emotion: An integrated model. *Clinical Psychology & Psychotherapy*, 16, 240–67.

France, A. (1988). *Consuming Psychotherapy*. London: Free Association.

Frances, A. (2010). Opening Pandora's box: The 19 worst suggestions for DSM5. *Psychiatric Times*. Accessed 8 May 2011 at www.psychiatrictimes.com/display/article/10168/1522341

Frank, J. D. and Frank, J. B. (1991). *Persuasion and Healing: A Comparative Study of Psychotherapy*. Baltimore, Johns Hopkins University Press.

Fredrickson, B., Roberts, T., Noll, S., Quinn, D. & Twenge, J. (1998). That swimsuit becomes you: Sex differences in self-objectification, restrained eating and math performance. *Journal of Personality and Social Psychology*, 75(1), 269–84.

Freeman, D., Garety, P. A., Kuipers, E., Fowler, D. & Bebbington, P. (2002). A cognitive model of persecutory delusions. *British Journal of Clinical Psychology*, 41, 331–47.

Freeman, W. (1941). Brain-damaging therapeutics. *Diseases of the Nervous System*, 2, 83.

Freidberg, N. L. & Lyddon W. J. (1996). Self-other working models and eating disorders. *Journal of Cognitive Psychotherapy: An International Quarterly*, 10, 193–203.

Freire, P. (1970). *Pedagogy of the Oppressed*. New York: Herder & Herder.

French, P., Hutton, P., Barratt, S., Parker, S., Byrne, R., Shryane, N. et al. (2011). Provision of online normalizing information to reduce stigma associated with psychosis: Can an audio podcast challenge negative appraisals of psychotic experiences. *Psychosis: Psychological, Social and Biological Approaches*, 3, 52–62.

Frese, F. J. (2010). On the impact of being diagnosed with schizophrenia. *Journal of Mental Health*, 19(4), 376–8.

Freud, S. (1917). Mourning and melancholia. In J. Strachey (Ed.), *The Standard Edition of Complete Psychological Works*. London: Hogarth Press.

Freud, S. (1917/1974). *Introductory Lectures on Psychoanalysis*. Harmondsworth: Penguin Books.

Freud, S. & Breuer, J. (1895/2004). *Studies on Hysteria* (Trans. N. Luckhurst). London: Penguin Classics.

Friedli, L. (2009). *Mental Health, Resilience and Inequalities*. Copenhagen: World Health Organization.

Friedman, S., Smith, L., Fogel, D., Paradis, C., Viswanathan, R., Ackerman, R. et al. (2002). The incidence and influence of early traumatic life events in patients with panic disorder: A comparison with other psychiatric outpatients. *Journal of Anxiety Disorders*, 16(3), 259–72.

Friendship, C., Mann, R. E. & Beech, A. R. (2003). Evaluation of a national prison-based treatment program for sexual offenders in England and Wales. *Journal of Interpersonal Violence*, 18, 744–59.

Frith, C. (1994). Theory of mind in schizophrenia. In A. S. David & J. C. Cutting (Eds), *The Neuropsychology of Schizophrenia* (147–61). Hove: Erlbaum.

Frith, C. D. & Frith, U. (1999). Interacting minds: A biological basis. *Science*, 286, 1692–5.

Fromm-Reichmann, F. (1954). Psychotherapy of schizophrenia. *The American Journal of Psychiatry*, 111, 410–19.

Frosh, S. (2009). *Hate and the Jewish Science: Anti-Semitism, Nazism and Psychoanalysis*. Revised edition. London: Palgrave Macmillan.

Fruzzetti, A. E., Shenk, C. & Hoffman, P. D. (2005). Family interaction and the development of borderline personality disorder: A transactional model. *Development and Psychopathology*, 17, 1007–30.

Fryers, T., Melzer, D., Jenkins, R. & Brugha, T. (2005). The distribution of the common mental disorders: Social inequalities in Europe. *Clinical Practice and Epidemiology in Mental Health*, 1, 14.

Fugl-Meyer, A. S., Branholm, J. B. & Fugl-Meyer, K. S. (1991). Happiness and domain-specific life satisfaction in adult northern Sweden. *American Medical Association*, 5, 25–33.

Fuller Torrey, E. (2010). Psychiatric genocide. *Schizophrenia Bulletin*, 36, 26–32.

Furnham, A. and Bower, P. (1992). A comparison of academic and lay theories of schizophrenia. *British Journal of Psychiatry*, 62, 201–10.

Furnham, A. & Rees, J. (1988). Lay theories of schizophrenia. *International Journal of Social Psychiatry*, 34, 212–20.

Gabbay, J. (1982). Asthma attacked: Tactics for the reconstruction of a disease concept. In P. Wright & A. Treacher (Eds), *The Problem of Medical Knowledge: Examining the Social Construction of Medicine* (23–48). Edinburgh: Edinburgh University Press.

Gagnon, M. & Lexchin, J. (2008). The cost of pushing pills: A new estimate of pharmaceutical promotion expenditures in the United States. *PLOS Medicine*, 5(1), 29–33.

Gaines, A. D. (1992). From DSM I to III R; Voices of self, mastery and the other: A cultural constructivist reading of US psychiatric classification. *Social Science and Medicine*, 35, 3–24.

Gaines, A. D. (1995). Culture-specific delusions: Sense and nonsense in cultural context. *The Psychiatric Clinics of North America*, 18, 281–301.

Gainetdinov, R. R., Mohn, A. R. & Caron, M. G. (2001). Genetic animal models: Focus on schizophrenia. *Trends in Neurosciences*, 24(9), 527–33.

Gamel, K. (2001). Report finds many controversial sterilization cases were voluntary. Associated Press, 28 March. Accessed 15 January 2011 at http://extras.journalnow.com/againsttheirwill/background/storybody11.html

Garb, H. N. (2001). Clinical psychology: Validity of judgment. In N. J. Smelser & P. B. Baltes (Eds), *International Encyclopedia of the Social & Behavioral Sciences*, 26, 2040–3.

Garber, M. (1997). Cross-dressing, gender and representation: Elvis Presley. In C. Belsey & J. Moore (Eds), *The Feminist Reader* (2nd edn, 164–81) (1st edn 1989). Basingstoke: Palgrave Macmillan.

Garcia-Moreno, C., Jansen, H. A. F. M., Ellsberg, M., M., Heise, L. & Watts, C. (2005). *WHO Multi-country Study on Women's Health and Domestic Violence against Women*. Geneva: World Health Organization.

Garety, P. A., Freeman, D., Jolley, S., Dunn, G., Bebbington, P. E., Fowler, D. G. et al. (2005). Reasoning, emotions and delusional convictions in psychosis. *Journal of Abnormal Psychology*, 114, 373–84.

Garety, P. A., Hemsley, D. R. & Wessely, S. (1991). Reasoning in deluded schizophrenic and paranoid patients. *Journal of Nervous and Mental Disease*, 179(4), 194–201.

Garety, P. A., Kuipers, E., Fowler, D., Freeman, D. & Bebbington, P. E. (2001). A cognitive model of the positive symptoms of psychosis. *Psychological Medicine*, 31, 189–95.

Garfield, D. & Mackler, D. (Eds) (2008). *Beyond Medication: Therapeutic Engagement and the Recovery from Psychosis*. London: Routledge.

Garfinkel, H. (1967). *Studies in Ethnomethodology*. Engelwood Cliffs NJ: Prentice Hall.

Garrett, C., Lee, T., Blackburn, S., Priestly, L. & Bhui, K. (2011). Personality disorder: Challenges in service development in the light of the new NICE guidelines. *The Psychiatrist*, 35, 22–6.

Garrett, M. & Turkington, D. (2011). CBT for psychosis in a psychoanalytic frame. *Psychosis: Psychological, Social and Biological Approaches*, 3(1), 2–13.

Gavey, N. (2005). *Just Sex? Heterosexuality and the Cultural Scaffolding of Rape*. London: Routledge.

Gazzaniga, M. S. (1988). *The Mind's Past*. Berkeley: University of California Press.

Geddes, J. R., Burgess, S., Hawton, K., Jamison, K. & Goodwin, G. M. (2004). Long-term lithium therapy for bipolar disorder: Systematic review and meta-analysis of randomized controlled trials. *American Journal of Psychiatry*, 161, 217–22.

Geddes, J., Freemantle, N., Harrison, P. & Bebbington, P. (2000). Atypical antipsychotics in the treatment of schizophrenia: Systematic overview and meta-regression analysis. *British Medical Journal*, 321(7273), 1371–6.

Geekie, J. & Read, J. (2009). *Making Sense of Madness: Contesting the Meaning of Schizophrenia*. New York: Routledge/Taylor & Francis Group.

Geertz, C. (1983). *Local Knowledge: Further Essays in Interpretive Anthropology*. New York: Basic Books.

Geertz, C. (1984). From the native's point of view: On the nature of anthropological understanding. In R. A. Shweder & R. A. Levine (Eds), *Culture Theory: Essays on Mind, Self and Emotion*. Cambridge: Cambridge University Press.

Geller, J., Cockell, S. J., Hewitt, P. L., Goldner, E. M. & Flett, G. L. (2000). Inhibited expression of negative emotions and interpersonal orientation in anorexia nervosa. *International Journal of Eating Disorders*, 28, 8–19.

Gellner, E. (1993). *The Psychoanalytic Movement: The Cunning of Unreason*. London. Fontana.

Gergen, K. J. (1990). Therapeutic professions and the diffusion of deficit. *The Journal of Mind & Behavior*, 11, 353–68.

Ghaderi, A. & Scott, B. (2003). Pure and guided self-help for full and sub-threshold bulimia nervosa and binge eating disorder. *British Journal of Clinical Psychology*, 42, 257–69.

Giesen-Bloo, J., van Dyck, R., Spinhoven, P., van Tilburg W., Dirksen C., van Asselt, T. et al. (2006). Outpatient psychotherapy for borderline personality disorder: Randomized trial of schema-focused therapy vs. transference-focused psychotherapy. *Archives of General Psychiatry*, 63, 649–58.

Gilbert, D. & Malone, P. (1995). The correspondence bias. *Psychiatric Bulletin*, 117, 21–38.

Gilbert, M. (2009). Churchill and eugenics. Accessed 15 January 2011 at www.winstonchurchill.org/support/the-churchill-centre/publications/finest-hour-online/594-churchill-and-eugenics

Gilbert, N. & Meyer, C. (2005). Fear of negative evaluation and eating attitudes: A replication and extension study. *International Journal of Eating Disorders*, 37(4), 360–3.

Gilbert, P. (2009). Moving beyond cognitive behaviour therapy. *The Psychologist*, 22, 400–3.

Gilburt, H., Rose, D. & Slade, M. (2008). The importance of relationships in mental health care: A qualitative study of service users' experiences of psychiatric hospital admission in the UK. BMC Health Services Research, 8, 92. Accessed 29 December 2011 at www.biomedcentral.com/1472-6963/8/92

Giles, D. C. (2006). Constructing identities in cyberspace: The case of eating disorders. *British Journal of Social Psychology*, 45, 463–77.

Gill, R. (2006). *Gender and the Media*. Cambridge: Polity Press.

Gillmer, B.T. & Taylor, J. L. (2011). On psychologists becoming responsible clinicians. *Clinical Psychology Forum*, 218, 7–10.

Glaser, D. (2000). Child abuse and neglect and the brain – a review. *Journal of Child Psychology and Psychiatry*, 41(1), 97–116.

Gleeson, J., Killackey, E. & Krstev, H. (2008). *Psychotherapies for the Psychoses: Theoretical, Cultural and clinical Intergration*. London: Routledge.

Goffman, E. (1961). *Asylums: Essays on the Social Situation of Mental Patients and Other Inmates*. Harmondsworth: Penguin.

Goffman, E. (1963). *Stigma: Notes on the Management of Spoiled Identity*. New York: Prentice-Hall.

Goldacre, B. (2009). *Bad Science*. London: Harper Perennial.

Goldberg, A., Allis, D. & Bernstein, E. (2007). Epigenetics: A landscape takes shape. *Cell*, 128, 635–8.

Goldberg, D. & Huxley, P. (1992). *Common Mental Disorders: A Bio-social Model*. London: Routledge.

Goldberg, L. R. (1993). The structure of phenotypic personality traits. *American Psychologist*, 48, 26–34.

Goldner, V., Penn, P., Sheinberg, M. & Walker, G. (1990). Love and violence: Gender paradoxes in volatile attachments. *Family Process*, 29, 343–64.

Goldsmith, L. P. & Moncrieff, J. (2010). The psychoactive effects of antidepressants: Evidence from an internet database. Unpublished manuscript.

Goldstein, M. (1987). The UCLA High Risk Project. *Schizophrenia Bulletin*, 13, 505–14.

Goldstein, M. J. (1985). Family factors that antedate the onset of schizophrenia and related disorders. *Acta Psychiatrica Scandinavica*, 71(suppl. 319), 7–18.

Gomm, R. (1996). Mental health and inequality. In T. Heller, J. Reynolds, R. Gomm, R. Muston and S. Pattison (Eds), *Mental Health Matters: A Reader*. London: Macmillan/Open University.

Goodman, A., Siegel, C., Craig, T. & Lin, S. (1983). The relationship between socioeconomic class and prevalence of schizophrenia, alcoholism, and affective disorders treated by inpatient care in a suburban area. *The American Journal of Psychiatry*, 140(2), 166–70.

Goodman, L., Salyers, M., Mueser, K., Rosenberg, S., Swartz, M., Essock, S. et al. (2001). Recent victimization in women and men with severe mental illness: Prevalence and correlates. *Journal of Traumatic Stress*, 14(4), 615–32.

Goodwin, F. K. & Jamison, K. R. (1990). *Manic-Depressive Illness*. Oxford: Oxford University Press.

Goodwin, F. K. & Jamison, K. R. (2007). *Manic-depressive illness: Bipolar disorders and recurrent depression* (2nd edn). New York: Oxford University Press.

Goodwin, G. M. & Geddes, J. R. (2007). What is the heartland of psychiatry? *The British Journal of Psychiatry*, 191, 189–91.

Gooren, L. (1990). The endocrinology of transsexualism: A review and commentary. *Psychoneuroendocrinology*, 15(1), 3–14.

Gordon, C. (1990). Histoire de la folie: An unknown book by Michel Foucault. *History of the Human Sciences*, 3, 3–26.

Gordon, J. (2010). Testing the glutamate hypothesis of schizophrenia. *Nature Reviews Neuroscience*, 13, 2–4.

Gordon, P. (2009). *The Hope of Therapy*. Ross-On-Wye: PCCS.

Gordon, R. (2000). *Eating Disorders: Anatomy of a Social Epidemic*. Oxford: Blackwell.

Gorman, J., Kent, J., Sullivan, G. & Coplan, J. (2000). Neuroanatomical hypothesis of panic disorder, revised. *American Journal of Psychiatry*, 157, 493–505.

Goss, K. & Allan, S. (2009). Shame, pride and eating disorders. *Clinical Psychology & Psychotherapy*, 16, 303–16.

Gottdiener, W. (2004). Psychodynamic therapy for schizophrenia: Empirical support. In J. Read, L. Mosher & R. Bentall (Eds), *Models of Madness: Psychological, Social and Biological Approaches to Schizophrenia* (307–18). London: Routledge.

Gottesman, I. (1991). *Schizophrenia Genesis*. New York: W. H. Freeman & Co.

Gould, L. N. (1948). Verbal hallucinations and activity of vocal musculature. *American Journal of Psychiatry*, 105, 367–72.

Gould, R. A., Otto, M. W. & Pollack, M. H. (1995). A meta-analysis of treatment outcome for panic disorder. *Clinical Psychology Review*, 15, 819–44.

Gould, S. J. (1981). *The Mismeasure of Man*. Harmondsworth: Penguin.

GPMH/Consortium (1988). *Treated well? A Code of Practice for Psychiatric Hospitals*. London: Good Practices in Mental Health.

Grace, V., Potts, A., Gavey, N. & Vares, T. (2006). The discursive condition of Viagra. *Sexualities*, 9(3), 295–314.

Grant, B. F., Hasin, D. S., Stinson, F. S., Dawson, D. A., Chou, S. P., Ruan, W. J. et al. (2004). Prevalence, correlates, and disability of personality disorders in the United States: Results from the national epidemiologic survey on alcohol and related conditions. *Journal of Clinical Psychiatry*, 65, 948–58.

Gray, J. A. (1979). *Pavlov*. London: Fontana.

Green, E. R. (2006). Debating trans inclusion in the feminist movement: A trans-positive analysis. *Journal of Lesbian Studies*, 10(1/2), 231–48.

Green, J. & Goldwyn, R. (2002). Annotation: Attachment disorganisation and psychopathology: New findings in attachment research and their potential implications for developmental psychopathology in childhood. *Journal of Child Psychology and Psychiatry*, 43(7), 835–46.

Green, M. F. (1998). *Schizophrenia from a Neurocognitive Perspective: Probing the Impenetrable Darkness*. Needham Heights, MA, US: Allyn & Bacon.

Green, R. & Fleming, D. T. (1990). Transexual surgery follow-up: Status in the 1990s. In J. Bancroft, C. David & D. Weinstein (Eds), *Annual Review of Sex Research I*. Society for the Scientific Study of Sexuality. Allentown.

Greenberg, J. (1964). *I Never Promised You a Rose Garden*. New York: Holt, Rinehart & Winston.

Gregory, S., Shawcross, C. & Gill, D. (1985). The Nottingham ECT study. *British Journal of Psychiatry*, 146, 520–4.

Grice, D. E., Halmi, K. A., Fichter, M. M., Strober, M., Woodside, D. B., Treasure, J. T. et al. (2002). Evidence for a susceptibility gene for anorexia nervosa on chromosome I. *The American Journal of Human Genetics*, 70, 787–92.

Grilo, C. M. (2006). *Eating and Weight Disorders*. London: Psychology Press.

Grilo, C. M., Levy, K. N. Becker, D. F., Edell, W. E. & McGlashan, T. H. (1995). Eating disorders in female inpatients with versus without substance use disorders. *Addictive Behaviors*, 20, 255–60.

Grilo, C. M. & Mitchell, J. E. (2009). *The Treatment of Eating Disorders: A Clinical Handbook*. New York: Guilford Press.

Grimby, A. (1993). Bereavement among elderly people: Grief reactions, post-bereavement hallucinations and quality of life. *Acta Psychiatrica Scandinavica*, 87, 72–80.

Groesz, L., Levine M. P. & Murnen, S. K. (2002). The effect of experimental presentation of thin media images on body satisfaction: A meta-analytic review. *International Journal of Eating Disorders*, 31, 1–16.

Grossman, D. (1995). *On Killing: The Psychological Cost of Learning to Kill in War and Society*. New York: Time Warner.

Grove, W. M. (1987). The reliability of psychiatric diagnosis. In C. G. Last & M. Hersen (Eds), *Issues in Diagnostic Research* (99–119). New York: Plenum Press.

Groza, V. (1999). Institutionalization, behavior, and international adoption. *Journal of Immigrant Health*, 1(3), 133–43.

Guilfoyle, M. (2008). CBT's integration with networks of power. In R. House & D. Loewenthal (Eds), *Against and For CBT: Towards a Constructive Dialogue*? Ross-On-Wye: PCCS.

Gumley, A., O'Grady, M., McNay, L., Reilly, J., Power, K. & Norrie, J. (2003). Early intervention for relapse in schizophrenia: Results of a 12-month randomized controlled trial of cognitive behavioural therapy. *Psychological Medicine*, 33, 419–31.

Gunnar, M. & Donzella, B. (2002). Social regulation of the cortisol levels in early human development. *Psychoneuroendocrinology*, 27, 199–220.

Gunnell, D., Saperia, J. & Ashby, D. (2005). Selective serotonin reuptake inhibitors (SSRIs) and suicide in adults: Meta-analysis of drug company data from placebo controlled, randomised controlled trials submitted to the MHRA's safety review. *British Medical Journal*, 330, 385.

Gureje, O., Simon, G. E., Ustun, T. B. & Goldberg, D. P. (1997). Somatization in cross-cultural perspective: A World Health Organization study in primary care. *American Journal of Psychiatry*, 154, 989–95.

Gutierrez, M. A., Glen, L. & Stimmel, L. (1999). Pharmacotherapy management of and counseling for psychotropic drug-induced sexual dysfunction. *Pharmacotherapy*, 19(7), 823–31.

Guy, A., Thomas, R., Stephenson, S. & Loewenthal, D. (2011). NICE under scrutiny: The impact of the National Institute for Health and Clinical Excellence guidelines on the provision of psychotherapy in the UK. London: United Kingdom Council for Psychotherapy. Accessed on 29 December 2011 at www.psychotherapy.org.uk/nice_under_scrutiny.html

Haaken, J. (1998). *Pillar of Salt: Gender, Memory and the Perils of Looking Back*. Piscataway NJ: Rutgers University Press.

Hacking, I. (1996). *Rewriting the Soul: Multiple Personality Disorder and the Sciences of Memory*. Princeton NJ: Princeton University Press.

Hadfield, J., Brown, D., Pembroke, L. & Hayward, M. (2009). Analysis of accident and emergency doctors' responses to treating people who self-harm. *Qualitative Health Research*, 19, 755–65.

Haefner, H. (2010). Comment on E. F. Torrey and R. H. Yolken: 'Psychiatric genocide: Nazi attempts to eradicate schizophrenia' and R. D. Strous: 'Psychiatric genocide: Reflections and responsibilities'. *Schizophrenia Bulletin*, 36, 450–4.

Hagan, T. & Smail, D. (1997a). Power-mapping I: Background and basic methodology. *Journal of Community and Applied Social Psychology*, 7, 257–67.

Hagan, T. & Smail, D. (1997b). Power-mapping II. Practical application: The example of child sexual abuse. *Journal of Community and Applied Social Psychology*, 7, 269–84.

Hagerty, B. B. (2010). A Neuroscientist Uncovers a Dark Secret. www.npr.org/templates/story/story.php?storyId=127888976.

Hagnell, O., Lanke, J., Rorsman, B. & Ojesjo, L. (1982). Are we entering an age of melancholy? Depressive illnesses in a prospective epidemiological study over 25 years: The Lundby Study, Sweden. *Psychological Medicine*, 12(2), 279–89.

Haigh, R. (2002). *Services for People with Personality Disorder: The Thoughts of Service Users*. London: Department of Health.

Halbarstam, J. (1998). *Female Masculinity*. Durham, NC: Duke University Press.

Hall, D. M. B. (1984). *The Child with a Handicap*. Oxford: Blackwell Scientific Publications.

Hall, G. C., Hirschman, R. & Oliver, L. L. (1995). Sexual arousal and arousability to pedophile stimuli in a community sample of normal men. *Behavior Therapy*, 26, 681–94.

Hall, J. (2007). The emergence of clinical psychology in Britain from 1943–1958 Part I: Core tasks and the professionalisation process. *History & Philosophy of Psychology*, 9, 29–55.

Hall, J., Lavender, T. & Llewelyn, S. (2002). A history of clinical psychology in Britain: Some impressions and reflections. *History & Philosophy of Psychology*, 4, 32–48.

Halpern, D. & Nazroo, J. (2000). The ethnic density effect: Results from a national community survey of England and Wales. *International Journal of Social Psychiatry*, 46(1), 34–46.

Hamilton, E., Asarnow, J. & Tompson, M. (1999). Family interaction styles of children with depressive disorders, schizophrenia-spectrum disorders, and normal controls. *Family Process*, 38(4), 463–76.

Hamilton, K. & Waller, G. (1993). Media influences on body size estimation in anorexia and bulimia. An experimental study. *The British Journal of Psychiatry*, 162, 837–40.

Hamilton, S. (2008). Schizophrenia candidate genes: Are we really coming up blank? *American Journal of Psychiatry*, 165, 420–3.

Hammen, C. (2005). *Depression*. Basingstoke: Psychology Press.

Hammersley, P., Dias, A., Todd, G., Bowen-Jones, K., Reilly, B. & Bentall, R. (2003). Childhood trauma and hallucinations in bipolar affective disorder: A preliminary investigation. *British Journal of Psychiatry*, 182, 543–7.

Hammersley, P., Read, J., Woodall, S. & Dillon. J. (2008). Childhood trauma and psychosis: The genie is out of the bottle. *The Journal of Psychological Trauma*, 6(2/3), 7–20.

Haney, C. (2006). The wages of prison overcrowding: Harmful psychological consequences and dysfunctional correctional reactions. *Washington University Journal of Law & Policy*, 22, 265–93. Available at: http://digitalcommons.law.wustl.edu/wujlp/vol22/iss1/22, accessed 24 September 2012.

Hankin, B. & Abramson, J. (1999). Development of gender differences in depression: Description and possible explanations. *Annals of Medicine*, 31, 372–9.

Haracz, J. (1982). The dopamine hypothesis. *Schizophrenia Bulletin*, 8, 438–69.

Harding, C. M., Brooks, G. W., Ashikaga, T., Strauss, J. S. & Breier, A. (1987). The Vermont longitudinal study of persons with severe mental illness: I. Methodology, study sample, and overall status 32 years later. *The American Journal of Psychiatry*, 144(6), 718–26.

Hardy, A., Fowler, D., Freeman, D., Smith, B., Steel, C. & Evans, J. (2005). Trauma and hallucinatory experience in psychosis. *Journal of Nervous and Mental Disease*, 193(8), 501–7.

Hardy, K. V. (2001). African-American experience and the healing of relationships: An interview with Kenneth V. Hardy. In D. Denborough (Ed.), *Family Therapy: Exploring the Field's Past, Present and Possible Futures*, 47–56. Adelaide: Dulwich Centre Publications.

Hare, L., Bernard, P., Sánchez, F. J., Baird, P. N., Vilain, E., Kennedy, T. et al. (2009). Androgen receptor repeat length polymorphism associated with male-to-female transsexualism. *Biological Psychiatry*, 65 (1), 93–6.

Hare, R. D. (1991). *The Hare Psychopathy Checklist* – Revised. Toronto: Multi-Health Systems.

Härkänen, T., Knekt, P., Virtala, E. & Lindfors, O. (2005). A case study in comparing therapies involving informative drop-out, non-ignorable non-compliance and repeated measurements. *Statistics In Medicine*, 24, 3773–87.

Harper, D. (2005). The critical professional and social policy: Negotiating dilemmas in the UK mental health act campaign. *International Journal of Critical Psychology*, 13, 55–75.

Harper, D. (2006). Some problems with the case for psychologists becoming clinical supervisors: A response to Pilgrim and others. *Clinical Psychology Forum*, 168, 7–12.

Harper, D. (2008). Clinical psychology. In C. Willig & W. Stainton-Rogers (Eds), *The Sage Handbook of Qualitative Research in Psychology* (430–54). London: Sage.

Harper, D. (2011). The social context of 'paranoia'. In M. Rapley, J. D. Dillon & J. Moncrief (Eds), *De-Medicalizing Misery*. Basingstoke: Palgrave Macmillan.

Harper, D., Gannon, K. N. & Robinson, M. (2013). Beyond evidence-based practice: Rethinking the relationship between research, theory and practice. In R. Bayne & G. Jinks (Eds), *Applied Psychology: Practice, Training and New Directions* (2nd revised edn). London: Sage.

Harré, R. (2002). *Cognitive Science: A Philosophical Introduction*. London: Sage.

Harré, R. & Finlay-Jones, R. (1986). Emotion talk across times. In R. Harré (Ed.), *The Social Construction of Emotions*, 220–33. Oxford: Blackwell.

Harris, B. (1979). Whatever happened to Little Albert? *American Psychologist*, 34, 151–60.

Harris, C. (2005). The family well-being project: Providing psychology services for children and families in a community regeneration context. In C. Newnes & N. Radcliffe (Eds), *Making and Breaking Children's Lives*. Ross-on-Wye: PCCS Books.

Harris, G. T., Rice1, M. E., Quinsey, V. L. & Chaplin, T. C. (1996). Viewing time as a measure of sexual interest among child molesters and normal heterosexual men. *Behaviour Research and Therapy*, 34(4), 389–94.

Harris, M., Chandran, S., Chakraborty, N. & Healy, D. (2003). Mood-stabilizers: the archeology of the concept. *Bipolar Disorders*, 5, 446–52.

Harrison, A., Sullivan, S., Tchanturia, K. & Treasure, J. (2009). Emotion recognition and regulation in anorexia nervosa. *Clinical Psychology and Psychotherapy*, 16, 348–56.

Harrison, G., Amin, S., Singh, S. P. Croudace, T. & Jones, P. (1999). Outcome of psychosis in people of African-Caribbean family origin. Population-based first-episode study. *The British Journal of Psychiatry*, 175, 43–9.

Harrison, G., Gunnell, D., Glazebrook, C., Page, K. & Kwiecinski, R. (2001). Association between schizophrenia and social inequality at birth: Case-control study. *British Journal of Psychiatry*, 179, 346–50.

Harrison, G., Hopper, K., Craig, T., Laska, E., Siegel, C., Wanderling, J. et al. (2001). Recovery from psychotic illness: A 15- and 25-year international follow-up study. *British Journal of Psychiatry*, 178, 506–17.

Harrison, G., Owens, D., Holton, A., Neilson, D. & Boot, D. (1988). A prospective study of severe mental disorder in Afro-Caribbean patients. *Psychological Medicine*, 18, 643–57.

Harrop, C. & Trower, P. (2001). Why does schizophrenia develop at late adolescence? *Clinical Psychology Review*, 21, 241–65.

Harrop, C. & Trower, P. (2003). *Why Does Schizophrenia Develop at Late Adolescence? A Cognitive Developmental Approach to Psychosis*. Chichester: Wiley-Blackwell.

Hartig, T. (2008). Green space, psychological restoration and health inequality. *Lancet*, 372, 1614–15.

Hartley, L. P. (1953). *The Go-between*. London: Hamish Hamilton.

Hawkes, G. (1996). *Sociology of Sex and Sexuality*. Buckingham: Open University Press.

Hawton, K., Gath, D. & Day, A. (1994). Sexual function in a community sample of middle-aged women with partners: Effects of age, marital, socioeconomic, psychiatric, gynecological, and menopausal factors. *Archives of sexual behaviour*, 23, 375–95.

Hay, P. & Fairburn, C. (1998). The validity of the DSM-IV scheme for classifying bulimic eating disorders. *International Journal of Eating Disorders*, 23, 7–15.

Hayes, S. C., Follette, V. M. & Linehan, M. M. (Eds) (2004). *Mindfulness and Acceptance: Expanding the Cognitive Behavioral Tradition*. New York: Guilford.

Hayward, M., Slade, M. & Moran, P. A. (2006). Personality disorders and unmet needs among psychiatric inpatients. *Psychiatric Services*, 57, 538–43.

Healthcare Commission (2007a). *Talking about Medicines: The Management of Medicines in Trusts Providing Mental Health Services*. London: Author.

Healthcare Commission (2007b). *No Voice, No Choice: A Joint Review of Adult Community Mental Health Services in England*. London: Commission for Healthcare Audit and Inspection.

Healthcare Commission (2008). *The Pathway to Recovery: A Review of NHS Acute In-Patient Mental Health Services*. London: Commission for Healthcare Audit and Inspection.

Healy, D. (1987). Rhythm and blues: Neurochemical, neuropharmacological and neuropsychological implications of a hypothesis of circadian rhythm dysfunction in the affective disorders. *Psychopharmacology*, 93, 271–85.

Healy, D. (2002). *The Creation of Psychopharmacology*. London: Harvard University Press.

Healy, D. & Farquhar, G. (1998). Immediate effects of droperidol. *Human Psychopharmacology*, 13, 113–20.

Healy, D., Savage, M., Tranter, R., Austin, R., Ljaz, Q., Hughes, J. et al. (2007). Guidelines, tramlines, and faultlines. *Ethical Human Psychology & Psychiatry*, 9, 138–44.

Healy, D., Thase, M. E., Cannon, M., McKenzie, K. & Sims, A. (2003). Is academic psychiatry for sale? *British Journal of Psychiatry*, 182(5), 388–90.

Heatherton, T. F. & Baumeister, R. F. (1991). Binge eating as escape from self-awareness. *Psychological Bulletin*, 110, 86–108.

Hebdige, D. (1979). *Subculture: The Meaning of Style*. London: Routledge.

Heiman, J. R. (2002). Sexual dysfunction: overview of prevalence, etiological factors, and treatment. *Journal of Sex Research*, 39, 73–8.

Heise, D. R. (1998). Delusions and the construction of reality. In T. F. Oltmanns & B. A. Maher (Eds), *Delusional Beliefs*. New York: Wiley.

Heins, T., Gray, A. & Tennant, M. (1990). Persisting hallucinations following childhood sexual abuse. *Australian and New Zealand Journal of Psychiatry*, 24(4), 561–5.

Held, B. (1995). *Back to Reality: A Critique of Postmodern Theory in Psychotherapy*. New York: Norton.

Helman, C. G. (2000). *Culture, Health and Illness*. London: Hodder Arnold.

Helman, C. G. (2007). *Culture, Health and Illness* (5th edn). London: Hodder Arnold.

Henderson, A., Form, A., Korten, A., Jacomb, P., Christensen, H. & Rodgers, B. (1998). Symptoms of depression and anxiety during adult life: Evidence for a decline in prevalence with age. *Psychological Medicine*, 28, 1321–8.

Hendricks, H., van Limbeek, J., Geurts, A. & Zwarts, M. (2002). Motor recovery after stroke: A systematic review of the literature. *Archives of Physical Medicine and Rehabilitation*, 83(11), 1629–37.

Henquet, C., van Os, J., Kuepper, R., Delespaul, P., Smits, M., A Campo, J. et al. (2010). Psychosis reactivity to cannabis use in daily life: An experience sampling study. *British Journal of Psychiatry*, 196, 447–53.

Hepworth, J. (1999). *The Social Construction of Anorexia*. London: Sage.

Herbert, T. & Cohen, S. (1993). Stress and immunity in humans: a meta-analytic review. *Psychosomatic Medicine*, 55(4), 364–79.

Herdt, G. H. (1997*). Same Sex, Different Cultures: Gays and Lesbians across Cultures*. Boulder CO: Westview Press.

Herman, J. (1997). *Trauma and Recovery: From Domestic Abuse to Political Terror*. New York: Basic Books.

Herman, J. & Schatzow, E. (1987). Recovery and verification of childhood sexual trauma. *Psychoanalytic Psychology*, 4(1), 1–14.

Herron, W. G., Schultz, C. L. & Welt, A. G. (1992). A comparison of 16 systems to diagnose schizophrenia. *Journal of Clinical Psychology*, 48(6), 711–21.

Hervey, N. (1986). Advocacy or folly: The alleged lunatics' friend society, 1845–63. *Medical History*, 30, 254–75.

Herzog, D. B., Dorer, D., Keel, P. K., Selwyn, S. E., Ekeblad, E. R., Flores, A. T. et al. (1999). Recovery and relapse in anorexia and bulimia nervosa: A 7.5-year follow-up study. *Journal of the American Academy of Child and Adolescent Psychiatry*, 38, 829–37.

Hewstone, M. (1989). *Causal Attribution: From Cognitive Processes to Collective Beliefs*. Oxford: Blackwell.

Heyes, C. J. & Jones, M. (Eds) (2009). *Cosmetic Surgery A Feminist Primer*. Surrey: Ashgate.

Hickling, F. W. & Rodgers-Johnson, P. (1995). The incidence of first contact schizophrenia in Jamaica. *British Journal of Psychiatry*, 167, 193–6.

Hiday V. A. (1995). The social context of mental illness and violence. *Journal of Health & Social Behavior*, 36, 122–37.

Hilsenroth, M. J., Ackerman, S. J., Blagys, M. D., Baumann, B. D., Baity, M. R., Smith, S. R. et al. (2000). Reliability and validity of DSM-IV axis V. *The American Journal of Psychiatry*, 157(11), 1858–63.

Himmelweit, S. (1998). Accounting for Caring. Accessed 10 February 2010 at www.radstats.org.uk/no070/article1.htm

Hiroeh, U., Appleby, L., Mortensen, P. B. & Dunn G. (2001). Death by homicide, suicide, and other unnatural causes in people with mental illness: A population-based study. *Lancet*, 358, 2110–2.

Hite, S. (1976). *The Hite Report: A Nationwide Survey of Female Sexuality*. New York: Macmillan.

Ho, B., Andreassen, N., Ziebell, S., Pierson, R. & Magnotta, V. (2011). Long-term antipsychotic treatment and brain volumes: A longitudinal study of first-episode schizophrenia. *Archives of General Psychiatry* 68, 128–37.

Hochschild, A. R. (1979). Emotion work, feeling rules and social structure. *American Journal of Sociology*, 85, 551–75.

Hodes, M. Timimi, S. & Robinson, P. (1997). Children of mothers with eating disorders: A preliminary study. *European Eating Disorders Review*, 5, 11–24.

Hodge, S., Barr, W., Göpfert, M., Hellin, K., Horne, A. & Kirkcaldy, A. (2010). Qualitative findings from a mixed methods evaluation of once-weekly therapeutic community day services for people with personality disorder. *Journal of Mental Health*, 19, 43–51.

Hoek, H. W. & van Hoeken, D. (2003). Review of the prevalence and incidence of eating disorders. *International Journal of Eating Disorders*, 34, 383–96.

Hofstede, G. (1980). *Culture's Consequences*. Beverley Hills CA: Sage.

Hofstede, G. (1984). *Culture's Consequences*, Abridged. Beverley Hills CA: Sage.

Holland, S. (1991). From private symptoms to public action. *Feminism & Psychology*, 1, 58–62.

Holland, S. (1992a). From social abuse to social action: A neighbourhood psychotherapy and social action project for women. In J. Ussher & P. Nicolson (Eds), *Gender Issues in Clinical Psychology*. London: Routledge.

Holland, S. (1992b). From social abuse to social action: A neighbourhood psychotherapy and social action project for women. *Changes: An International Journal of Psychology & Psychotherapy*, 10, 146–53.

Hollingshead, A. & Redlich, R. C. (1958). *Social Class and Mental Illness*. New York. Wiley.

Holmes, G. (2002). Some thoughts on why clinical psychologists should not have formal powers under the new mental health act. *Clinical Psychology*, 12, 40–3.

Holmes, G. (2005). Learning humility. *Clinical Psychology*, 45, 20–1.

Holmes, G. (2010). *Psychology in the Real World: Community-based Groupwork*. Ross-on-Wye: PCCS Books.

Holmes, G. & Gahan, L. (2007). Psychology in the real world: Understanding yourself and others: An attempt to have an impact on stigma and social inclusion. *Groupwork*, 16, 9–25.

Holmes, G., Hudson, M. & May, R. (2008). Coping with coming off. *Open Mind*, 150, 12–14.

Holmes, G. & Newnes, C. (2004). Thinking about community psychology and poverty. *Clinical Psychology*, 38, 19–22.

Home Office (2006). Home Office Crime Statistics. Accessed 6 November 2006 at www.crimestatistics.org.uk/output/Page1.asp

Honos-Webb, L. & Leitner, L. M. (2001). How using the DSM causes damage: A client's report. *Journal of Humanistic Psychology*, 41(4), 36–56.

Hopper, K. (2004). Interrogating the meaning of 'culture' in the WHO international studies of schizophrenia. In J. H. Jenkins & J Barrett (Eds), *Schizophrenia, Culture and Subjectivity*. Cambridge: Cambridge University Press.

Horn, N., Johnstone, L. & Brooke, S. (2007). Some service user perspectives on the diagnosis of borderline personality disorder. *Journal of Mental Health*, 16(2), 255–69.

Horne, R. L., Van Vactor, J. C. & Emerson, S. (1991). Disturbed body image in patients with eating disorders. *American Journal of Psychiatry*, 148, 211–15.

Hornstein, G. A. (2009). *Agnes's Jacket: A Psychologist's Search for the Meanings of Madness* (UK edn). Ross-on-Wye: PCCS.

Horwitz, A. V., Widom, C. S., McLaughlin, J. & White, H. R. (2001). The impact of childhood abuse and neglect on adult mental health: A prospective study. *Journal of Health and Social Behaviour*, 42, 184–201.

Horowitz, H. L. (2002). *Rereading Sex : Battles over Sexual Knowledge and Suppression in Nineteenth-century America*. New York: Knopf.

Horwitz, A. V., Widom, C. S., McLaughlin, J. & White (2001). The impact of childhood abuse and neglect on adult mental health: A prospective study. *Journal of Health and Social Behaviour*, 42, 184–201.

House, R. (2003). *Therapy Beyond Modernity: Deconstructing and Transcending Profession Centred Therapy*. London: Karnac.

House, R. & Bohart, A. C. (2008). Empirically supported/validated treatments as modernist ideology. In R. House & D. Loewenthal (Eds), *Against and For CBT: Towards a Constructive Dialogue?* Ross-On-Wye: PCCS.

Houston, J., Murphy, J., Adamson, G., Stringer, M. & Shevlin, M. (2008). Childhood sexual abuse, early cannabis use, and psychosis: Testing an interaction model based on the National Comorbidity Survey. *Schizophrenia Bulletin*, 34(3), 580–5.

Howard, A. (1998). *Challenges to Psychotherapy and Counselling*. London: Macmillan

Howard, A. (2000). *Philosophy for Counselling and Psychotherapy*. London: Macmillan.

Howard, A. (2005). *Identity and Counselling*. London: Palgrave Macmillan.

Howell, C., Wilson, A. D. & Waring, W. S. (2007). Cardiovascular toxicity due to venlafaxine poisoning in adults: A review of 235 consecutive cases. *British Journal of Clinical Pharmacology*, 64, 192–7.

Howitt, D. (2010). *Introduction to Qualitative Methods in Psychology*. Harlow: Pearson.

Hsu, L. (1996). Epidemiology of the eating disorders. *Psychiatric Clinics of North America*, 19, 681–700.

Hsu, L. G. (1989). The gender gap in eating disorders: Why are the eating disorders more common among women? *Clinical Psychology Review*, 9, 393–407.

Huang, Y., Kotov, R., de Girolamo, G., Preti, A., Angermeyer, M., Benjet, C. et al. (2009). DSM-IV personality disorders in the WHO World Mental Health Surveys. *British Journal of Psychiatry*, 195, 46–53.

Humphrey, L. L. (1989). Observed family interactions among subtypes of eating disorders using structural analysis of social behavior. *Journal of Consulting and Clinical Psychology*, 57, 206–14.

Hunt, C., Issakidis, C. & Andrews, G. (2002). DSM-IV generalised anxiety disorder in the Australian national survey of mental health and well-being. *Psychological Medicine*, 4, 649–59.

Hunt, W., Wittson, C. & Hunt, E. (1953). A theoretical and practical analysis of the diagnostic process. In P. Hoch & J. Zubin (Eds), *Current Problems in Psychiatric Diagnosis* (53–65). Oxford: Grune & Stratton.

Hunter, R. & Macalpine, I. (Eds) (1963). *Three Hundred Years of Psychiatry: 1535–1860*. London: Oxford University Press.

Huon, G. F., Mingyi, Q., Oliver, K. & Xiao, G. (2002). A large-scale survey of eating disorder symptomatology among female adolescents in the People's Republic of China. *International Journal of Eating Disorders*, 32, 192–205.

Hwang, M. & Bermanzohn, P. (Eds) (2001). *Schizophrenia and Comorbid Conditions: Diagnosis and Treatment*. Arlington VA.: American Psychiatric Publishing.

Hwang, W. & Wood, J. J. (2010). Acculturative Family Distancing (AFD) and depression in Chinese American families. *Journal of Consulting and Clinical Psychology*, 78, 655–7.

Hyland, M. (2002). The intelligent dody and its discontents. *Journal of Health Psychology*, 7(1), 21–32.

Iliffe, S. (2008). *From General Practice to Primary Care: The Industrialization of Family Medicine*. Oxford: Oxford University Press.

Illich, I. (1977). *Disabling Professions*. London: Boyars.

Ingleby, D. (Ed.) (1981). *Critical Psychiatry: The Politics of Mental Health*. Harmondsworth: Penguin.

Ingram, R., Bernet, C. & McLoughlin, S. (1994). Attentional allocation processes in individuals at risk for depression. *Cognitive Therapy and Research*, 18(4), 317–32.

Inouye, T. & Shimizu, A. (1970). The electromyographic study of verbal hallucination. *Journal of Nervous and Mental Disease*, 151, 415–22.

Institute of Psychiatry. (2006). *Risk of Violence to Other People*. London.

International Classification of Diseases (1993). World Health Organization. Accessed 22 December 2011 at http://who.int/classifications/icd/en/

The International Schizophrenia Consortium (2009). Common polygenic variation contributes to risk of schizophrenia and bipolar disorder. *Nature*, 460, 748–52.

Ioannidis, J. (2011). Excess significance bias in the literature on brain volume abnormalities. *Archives of General Psychiatry*, 68(8), 773–80.

Ioannou, K. & Fox, J. R. (2009). Perception of threat from emotions and its role in poor emotional expression within eating pathology. *Clinical Psychology & Psychotherapy*, 16, 336–47.

Irigaray, L. (1993). *An Ethics of Sexual Difference*. London: Athlone Press.

Jablensky, A. & Cole, S. W. (1997). Is the earlier age at onset of schizophrenia in males a confounded finding? Results from a cross-cultural investigation. *British Journal of Psychiatry*, 170, 234–40.

Jablensky, A. Sartorius, N. Enberg, G., Anker, M., Korten, A., Cooper, J. E., Day, R. et al. (1992). Schizophrenia: Manifestations, incidence and course in different cultures: A World Health Organization ten-country study. *Psychological Medicine* (Monograph Supplement), 20, 1–97.

Jablonka, E. & Lamb, M. (2002). The changing concept of epigenetics. *Annals of the New York Academy of Sciences*, 981, 82–96.

Jack, G. (2004). Child protection at the community level. *Child Abuse Review*, 13, 368–83.

Jackson, H. (1986). Is there a schizotoxin? In N. Eisenberg & D. Glasgow (Eds), *Current Issues in Clinical Psychology*. Aldershot: Gower.

Jackson, P. L., Meltzoff, A. & Decety, J. (2005). How do we perceive the pain of others? A window into the neural processes involved in empathy. *Neuroimage*, 24, 771–9.

Jacobi, C., Hayward, C., de Zwaan, M., Kraemer, H. C. & Agras, W. S. (2004). Coming to terms with risk factors for eating disorders:

Application of risk terminology and suggestions for a general taxonomy. *Psychological Bulletin*, 130, 19–65.

Jacobs, H. (2006). *The Presenting Past: The Core of Psychodynamic Counselling and Therapy* (3rd edn). London: Sage.

Jacobs, M. (1999). *Psychodynamic Counselling in Action* (2nd Edn). London: Sage.

Jacobson, N., Martell, C. & Dimidjian, S. (2001). Behavioural activation treatment for depression: Returning to conceptual roots. *Clinical Psychology: Science and Practice*, 8(3), 255–70.

Jahoda, M. (1979). The impact of unemployment in the 1930s and 1970s. *Bulletin of the British Psychological Society*, 32, 309–14.

James, A. (1998). The contribution of social anthropology to the understanding of atypical gender identity in childhood. In D. D. Ceglie & D. Freedman (Eds), *A Stranger In My Own Body: Atypical Gender Identity Development and Mental Health* (79–94). London: Karnac Books.

James, A. (2001). *Raising Our voices: An Account of the Hearing Voices Movement*. Gloucester: Handsell Publishing.

James, H. (1996). Requiem for 'schizophrenia'. *Integrative Physiological Behavioral Sciences*, 31, 148–54.

Jankowiak, W. R. (Ed.) (2008). *Intimacies: Love + Sex across Cultures*. New York: Columbia University Press.

Janoff-Bulman, R. (1992). *Shattered Assumptions: Toward a New Psychology of Trauma*. New York: Simon & Schuster.

Janowsky, D., El-Yousef, M., Davis, J. & Serkerke, H. (1972). A cholinergic-adrenergic hypothesis of mania and depression. *Lancet*, ii, 632–5.

Janssen, I., Hanssen, M., Bak, M., Bijl, R. V., de Graaf, R., Vollebergh, W. et al. (2003). Discrimination and delusional ideation. *British Journal of Psychiatry*, 182, 71–6.

Janssen, I., Krabbendam, L., Bak, M., Hanssen, M., Vollebergh, W., de Graaf, R. et al. (2004). Childhood abuse as a risk factor for psychotic experiences. *Acta Psychiatrica Scandinavica*, 109, 38–45.

Janssen, I., Versmissen, D., Campo, J. A., Myin-Germeys, I., van Os, J. & Krabbendam, L. (2006). Attributional style and psychosis: Evidence for externalizing bias in patients but not individuals at high risk. *Psychological Medicine*, 27, 1–8.

Jardine, L. (1989). The politics of impenetrability. In T. Brennan (Ed.), *Between Feminism and Psychoanalysis*. Cambridge: Cambridge University Press.

Jaynes, J. (1976). *The Origin of Consciousness in the Breakdown of the Bicameral Mind*. Boston: Houghton Mifflin.

Jehu, D. (1989). Sexual dysfunctions among women clients who were sexually abused in childhood. *Behavioural Psychotherapy*, 17, 53–70.

Jellinek, E. (1939). Some principles of psychiatric classification. *Psychiatry*, 2, 161–5.

Jenike, M. (1986). Theories of aetiology. In M. Jenike, L. Baer & W. Minichiello (Eds), *Obsessive-Compulsive Disorders*. Littleton: PSG Publishing.

Jenkins, A. H., Kleinman, A. & Good, B. (1991). Cross-cultural studies of depression. In J. Becker & A. Kleinman (Eds), *Psychosocial Aspects of Depression* (67–99). New York: Earlbaum.

Jenkins, J. H. (1992). The meaning of 'expressed emotion': Theoretical issues raised by cross-cultural research. *Special article in American Journal of Psychiatry*, 35, 357–76.

Jenkins, J. H. & Barrett, R. J. (Eds) (2004). *Schizophrenia, Culture and Subjectivity: The Edge of Experience*. Cambridge: Cambridge University Press.

Jenkins, J. H. & Karno, M. (1992). The meaning of 'expressed emotion': Theoretical issues raiused by cross-cultural research. *Special article in American Journal of Psychiatry*, 149, 9–21.

Jenkins, R., Lewis, G., Bebbington, P., Brugha, T., Farrell, M., Gill, B. et al. (1997). The national psychiatric morbidity surveys of Great Britain: Initial findings from the household survey. *Psychological Medicine*, 27, 775–89.

Jensen, P. S., Arnold, L. E., Swanson, J. M., Vitiello, B., Abikoff, H. B., Greenhill, L. L. et al. (2007). 3-year follow-up of the NIMH MTA study. *Journal of the American Academy of Child & Adolescent Psychiatry*, 46, 989–1002.

Jeste, D., Caligiuri, M. P., Paulsen, J. S., Heaton, R. K., Lacro, J., Harris, M. et al. (1995). Risk of tardive dyskinesia in older patients: A prospective longitudinal study of 266 outpatients. *Archives of General Psychiatry*, 52(9), 756–65.

Jeste, D. & Wyatt, R. (1979). In search of treatment for tardive dyskinesia. *Schizophrenia Bulletin*, 5, 251–93.

Jilek, W. (1993). Traditional medicine relevant to psychiatry. In N. Sartorius., G. de Girolamo., G. Andrews., G. A. German., L. & L. Eisenberg (Eds), *Treatment of Mental Disorders: A Review of Effectiveness*. World Health Organization. Washington DC: American Psychiatric Association Press.

Johannessen, J. (2004). The development of early intervention services. In J. Read, L. Mosher & R. Bentall (Eds), *Models of Madness: Psychological, Social and Biological Approaches to Schizophrenia*. London: Routledge.

Johannessen, J., Martindale, B. & Cullberg, J. (Eds) (2007). *Evolving Psychosis: Different Stages, Different Treatments*. London: Routledge.

Johns, L. C., Rossell, S., Frith, C., Ahmad, F., Hemsley, D., Kuipers, E. et al. (2001). Verbal self-monitoring and auditory hallucinations in people with schizophrenia. *Psychological Medicine*, 31, 705–15.

Johns, L. & van Os, J. (2001). The continuity of psychotic experiences in the general population. *Clinical Psychology Review*, 21(8), 1125–41.

Johnson, J. G., Cohen, P., Brown, J., Smailes, E. M. & Bernstein, D. P. (1999). Childhood maltreatment increases risk for personality disorders during early adulthood. *Archives of General Psychiatry*, 56, 600–6.

Johnson, K. (2007). Transsexualism: Diagnostic dilemmas, transgender politics and the future of transgender care. In V. Clarke & E. Peel (Eds), *Out in Psychology: Lesbian, Gay, Bisexual, Trans & Queer Perspectives*. West Sussex: Wiley Press.

Johnson, M. H. (2004). A biological perspective on human sexuality. In B. Brooks-Gordon, L. Gelsthorpe, M. Johnson & A. Bainham (for the Cambridge Socio-Legal Group) (Eds), *Sexuality Repositioned: Diversity and the Law* (155–85). Oxford: Hart.

Johnson, M. K., Hashtroudi, S. & Lindsay, D. S. (1993). Source monitoring. *Psychological Bulletin*, 114(1), 3–28.

Johnson, S. D., Phelps, D. L. & Cottler, L. B. (2004). The association of sexual dysfunction and substance use among a community. *Epidemiological Sample*, 33, 55–63.

Johnston, J. (1974). *Lesbian Nation: The Feminist Solution*. New York: Simon & Schuster.

Johnstone, E. C., Frith, C. D., Crow, T. J., Husband, J. & Kreel, L. (1976). Cerebral ventricular size and cognitive impairment in chronic schizophrenia. *Lancet*, 308, 924–6.

Johnstone, L. (1989). *Users and Abusers of Psychiatry: A Critical Look at Traditional Psychiatric Practice*. London: Routledge.

Johnstone, L. (1993). Family management in 'schizophrenia': Its assumptions and contradictions. *Journal of Mental Health*, 2, 255–69.

Johnstone, L. (2000). *Users and Abusers of Psychiatry: A Critical Look at Traditional Psychiatric Practice* (2nd edn). London: Routledge.

Johnstone, L. (2011). Voice hearers are people with problems, not patients with illnesses. In M. Romme & S. Escher (Eds), *Psychosis as* a Personal Crisis: An Experience-based Approach (27–36). London, England: Routledge.

Johnson, M. H. (1992). Imprinting and the development of face recognition: From chick to man. *Current Directions in Psychological Science*, 1, 52–5.

Johnstone, J., Whomsley, S., Cole, S. & Oliver, N. (2011). *Good Practice Guidelines on the Use of Psychological Formulation*. Leicester: British Psychological Society.

Johnstone, L. (1999a). Do families cause 'schizophrenia'? Revisiting a taboo subject. In C. Newnes, G. Holmes & C. Dunn (Eds), *This is Madness Too: A Critical Look at the Mental Health System*. Ross-On-Wye. PCCS.

Johnstone, L. (1999b). Adverse psychological effects of ECT. *Journal of Mental Health*, 8, 69–85.

Johnstone, L. (2000). *Users and Abusers of Psychiatry: A Critical Look at Psychiatric Practice* (2nd edn). London and Philadelphia: Routledge.

Johnstone, L. (2003). A shocking treatment? *The Psychologist*, 16, 236–9.

Johnstone, L. (2007). Can trauma cause 'psychosis'? Revisiting (another) taboo subject. *Journal of Critical Psychology, Counselling and Psychotherapy*, 7(4), 211–20.

Johnstone, L. & Dallos, R. (2013). *Formulation in Psychology and Psychotherapy: Making Sense of People's Problems*. London, New York: Routledge.

Jolley, S., Garety, P., Bebbington, P., Dunn, G., Freeman, D., Kuipers, E. et al. (2006). Attributional style in psychosis: The role of affect and belief type. *Behaviour Research and Therapy*, 44, 1597–607.

Jones, E. & Harris, V. (1967). The attribution of attitudes. *Journal of Experimental Social Psychology*, 3, 1–24.

Jones, N., Field, T., Fox, N., Davalos, M. & Malphus, J. (1997). Infants of intrusive and withdrawn mothers. *Infant Behaviour and Development*, 20, 175–86.

Jones, S. R. & Fernyhough, C. (2007). Neural correlates of inner speech and auditory verbal hallucinations: A critical review and theoretical integration. *Clinical Psychology Review*, 27, 140–54.

Jorm, A. (2000). Mental health literacy. *British Journal of Psychiatry*, 177, 396–401.

Jorm, A., Angermeyer, M. & Katschnig, H. (2000). Public knowledge of and attitudes to mental disorders: A limiting factor in the optimal use of treatment services. In G. Andrews and S. Henderson (Eds), *Unmet Need in Psychiatry: Problems, Resources, Responses* (399–413). New York: Cambridge University Press.

Jorm, A., Christensen, H. & Griffiths, K. M. (2005). Public beliefs about causes and risk factors for mental disorders. *Social Psychiatry & Psychiatric Epidemiology*, 40, 764–7.

Jorm, A., Korten, A., Jacomb, P., Christensen, H. & Henderson, S. (1999). Attitudes towards people with a mental disorder: A survey of the Australian public and health professionals. *Australian and New Zealand Journal of Psychiatry*, 33(1), 77–83.

Jorm, A. F. & Wright, A. M. (2008). Influences on young people's stigmatising attitudes towards peers with mental disorders: National survey of young Australians and their parents. *British Journal of Psychiatry*, 192, 144–9.

Joseph, J. (2003). *The Gene Illusion: Genetic Research in Psychiatry and Psychology under the Microscope*. Ross on Wye: PCCS Books.

Joseph, J. (2004). Schizophrenia and heredity: Why the emperor has no genes. In J. Read, L. Mosher & R. Bentall (Eds), *Models of Madness: Psychological, Social and Biological Approaches to Schizophrenia* (67–84). London: Routledge.

Joseph, J. (2006). *The Missing Gene: Psychiatry, Heredity and the Fruitless Search for Genes*. New York: Algora.

Joseph, J. (2010). Genetic research in psychiatry and psychology: A critical overview. In K. E. Hood, C. T. Halpern, G. Greenberg & R. M. Lerner (Eds), *Handbook of Developmental Science, Behaviour and Genetics* (557–625). Oxford: Blackwells.

Joseph, S., Williams, R. & Yule, W. (1995). Psychosocial perspectives on post-traumatic stress. *Clinical Psychology Review*, 15, 515–44.

Joukamaa, M., Heliovaara, M., Knekt, P., Aromaa, A., Raitasalo, R. & Lehtinen, V. (2006). Schizophrenia, neuroleptic medication and mortality. *British Journal of Psychiatry*, 188, 122–7.

Judd, L. L., Hubbard, B., Janowsky, D. S., Huey, L. Y. & Attewell, P. A. (1977). The effect of lithium carbonate on affect, mood, and personality of normal subjects. *Archives of General Psychiatry*, 34, 346–51.

Jung, C. (1939). On the psychogenesis of schizophrenia. *Journal of Mental Science*, 85, 999–1011.

Jung, C. (2009). *The Red Book: Liber Novus* (Trans.S. Shamdasani). New York: W. W. Norton.

Kafka, M. P. (1997). Hypersexual desire in males: An operational definition and clinical implications for males with paraphilias and paraphilia-related disorders. *Archives of Sexual Behavior*, 26(5), 505–26.

Kafka, M. P. (2010). The DSM diagnostic criteria for paraphilias not otherwise specified. *Archives of Sexual Behavior*, 39, 373–6.

Kafka, M. P. and Hennen, J. (2003). Hypersexual Desire in males: Are males with paraphilias different from males with paraphilia-related disorders? *Sexual Abuse: A Journal of Research and Treatment*, 15(4), 307–21.

Kagan, C., Burton, M., Duckett, P., Lawthom, R. & Siddiquee, A. (2011). *Critical Community Psychology: Critical Action and Social Change*. Chichester: Wiley.

Kagan, C., Sixsmith, J., Siddiquee, A., Bol, S. Lawthom, R. & Kilroy, A. (2005). Community psychology meets participatory arts: Well-being and creativity. Paper presented at Hominis, International Conference. Havana, Cuba.

Kagan, J. (1984). *The Nature of the Child*. New York: Basic Books.

Kagan, J. (1998). *Three Seductive Ideas*. Cambridge, MA: Harvard University Press.

Kaiser, A., Katz, R. & Shaw, B. (1998). Cultural issues in the management of depression. In S. Kazarian & D. Evans (Eds), *Cultural Clinical Psychology* (177–214). Oxford: Oxford University Press.

Kalikhat (2004). Paying the price for not fitting in. *Asylum: The Magazine for Democratic Psychiatry*, 14(3), 26–7.

Kamakura, T., Ando, J., Ono, Y. & Maekawa, H. (2003). A twin study of genetic and environmental influences on psychological traits of eating disorders in a Japanese female sample. *Twin Research*, 6, 292–6.

Kaplan, H. S. (1974). *The New Sex Therapy: Active Treatment of Sexual Dysfunction*. New York: Brunner/Mazel.

Kaplan, H. S. (1979). *Disorders of Sexual Desire*. New York: Brunner/Mazel.

Kaplan, H. S. (1987). *The Illustrated Manual of Sex Therapy*. New York: Brunner/Mazel.

Karasic, D. & Drescher, J. (Eds) (2007). *Sexual and Gender Diagnoses of the Diagnostic and Statistical Manual of Mental Disorders: A Re-evaluation*. New York: Haworth Press.

Karon, B. P. (2007). Trauma and schizophrenia. *Journal of Psychological Trauma*, 6(2–3), 127–44.

Karon, B. P. & VandenBos, G. R. (1994). *Psychotherapy of Schizophrenia: The Treatment of Choice*. Lanham MD: Jason Aronson.

Kaschak, E. & Tiefer, L. (2001). *A New View of Women's Sexual Problems*. New York: Haworth.

Kato, T. (2007). Molecular genetics of bipolar disorder and depression. *Psychiatry and Clinical Neurosciences*, 61(1), 3–19.

Katzman, M. A. & Lee, S. (1997). Beyond body image: The integration of feminist and transcultural theories in the understanding of self-starvation. *International Journal of Eating Disorders*, 27, 317–27.

Kaye, W., Gendall, K. & Strober, M. (1998). Serotonin neuronal function and selective serotonin reuptake inhibitor treatment in anorexia and bulimia nervosa. *Biological Psychiatry*, 44, 825–38.

Kaye, W. H., Frank, G. K., Bailer, U. F., Shannan E., Henry, S. E., Meltzer, C. C. et al. (2005). Serotonin alterations in anorexia and bulimia nervosa: New insights from imaging studies. *Physiology and Behavior*, 85, 73–81.

Kaysen, S. (1994). *Girl, Interrupted*. New York: Vintage.

Kazarian, S. S. & Evans, D. R. (Eds) (1998). *Cultural Clinical Psychology: Theory, Research and Practice*. Oxford: Oxford University Press.

Kearny, J. (1996). *Culture, Class and Politics: Undisclosed Influences in Therapy and Counselling*. Ross-On-Wye: PCCS.

Keel, P. K., Dorer, D. J., Franko, D. L., Jackson, S. C. & Herzog, D. B. (2005). Postremission predictors of relapse in women with eating disorders. *American Journal of Psychiatry*, 162, 2263–8.

Keel, P. K. & Klump, K. L. (2003). Are eating disorders culture bound syndromes? Implications for conceptualising the etiology. *Psychological Bulletin*, 129, 747–69.

Keel, P. K., Klump, K. L., Miller, K. B., McGue, M. & Iacono, W. G. (2005). Shared transmission of eating disorders and anxiety disorders. *International Journal of Eating Disorders*, 38(2), 99–105.

Keller, M., Lavori, P., Mueller, T. & Endicott, J. (1992). Time to recovery, chronicity and levels of psychopathology in major depression: A 5 year prospective follow-up of 431 subjects. *Archives of General Psychiatry*, 49, 809–16.

Kendall, K. (2004). Dangerous thinking: A critical history of correctional cognitive behaviourism. In G. Mair (Ed.), *What Matters in Probation*. Cullompton, Devon: Willan Publishing.

Kendall, T., Burbeck, R. & Bateman , A. (2010). Pharmacotherapy for borderline personality disorder: NICE guideline. *British Journal of Psychiatry*, 196, 158–9.

Kendall, T., Pilling, S., Tyrer, P., Duggan, C., Burbeck, R., Meader, N. et al. (2009). Borderline and antisocial personality disorders: summary of NICE guidance. *British Medical Journal*, 338, 293–5. Accessed 31 January 2011 at www.bmj.com/content/338/bmj.b93.full?view=long&pmid=19176682

Kendell, R. E. (1975). *The Role of Diagnosis in Psychiatry*. Oxford: Blackwell Scientific Publications.

Kendell, R. E. (1981). The present state of ECT. *British Journal of Psychiatry*, 139, 265–93.

Kendler, K. S. (2005). Towards a philosophical structure for psychiatry. *American Journal of Psychiatry*, 162, 433–40.

Kendler, K. S., Hettema, J., Butera, F., Gardner, C. & Prescott, C. (2003). Life event dimensions of loss, humiliation, entrapment, and danger in the prediction of onsets of major depression and generalized anxiety. *Archives of General Psychiatry*, 60(8), 789–96.

Kendler, K. S., McGonagle, K., Swartz, M., Blazer, D. & Nelson, C. (1993). Sex and depression in the national co-morbidity survey 1: Lifetime prevalence, recurrence and chronicity. *Journal of Affective Disorders*, 29, 85–96.

Kenrick, D., Neuberg, S. & Cialdini, R. (2010). *Social Psychology: Goals in Interaction*. London: Pearson Education.

Kent, H. & Read, J. (1998). Measuring consumer participation in mental health services: Are attitudes related to professional orientation? *International Journal of Social Psychiatry*, 44(4), 295–310.

Keown, P., Meyer, G. & Scott, J. (2008). Retrospective analysis of hospital episode statistics, involuntary admissions under mental health act, and number of psychiatric beds in England 1996–2006. *British Medical Journal*, 337, 976–8.

Kerr, I. B. (1999). Cognitive analytic therapy for borderline personality disorder in the context of a community mental health team: Individual and organizational psychodynamic implications. *British Journal of Psychotherapy*, 15, 425–38.

Kesey, K. (1962). *One Flew over the Cuckoo's Nest: A Novel*. London: Methuen & Co.

Kessler, R. C. (2002). Evidence that generalised anxiety disorder is an indepent disorder. In D. Nutt, K. Rickels & D. Stein (Eds), *Generalised Anxiety Disorder: Symptomatology, Pathogenesis and Management* (3–10). London: Martin Dunitz Ltd.

Kessler, R. C., Berglund, P., Demler, O., Jin, R., Merikangas, K. R. & Walters, E. E. (2005). Lifetime prevalence and age-of-onset distributions of DSM-IV disorders in the National Comorbidity Survey Replication. *Archives of General Psychiatry*, 62, 593–602.

Kessler, R. C., Davis, C. G. & Kendler, K. S. (1997). Childhood adversity and adult psychiatric disorder in the US National Comorbidity Survey. *Psychological Medicine*, 27(5), 1101–19.

Kessler, R. C., Demler, O., Frank, R. G., Olfson, M., Pincus, H. A., Walters, E. E. et al. (2005). Prevalence and treatment of mental disorders, 1990 to 2003. *The New England Journal of Medicine*, 32, 957–9.

Kessler, R. C., McLaughlin, K. A., Green, J. G., Gruber, M. J., Sampson, N. A., Zaslavsky, A. M. et al. (2010). Childhood adversities and adult psychopathology in the WHO World Mental Health Surveys. *British Journal of Psychiatry*, 197, 378–85.

Kessler, S. J. & McKenna, W. (2000). Gender construction in everyday life. *Transsexualism. Feminism and Psychology*, 10(1), 11–29.

Keyes, C. L. M. & Ryff, C. D. (2003). Somatization and mental health: A comparative study of the idiom of distress hypothesis. *Social Science and Medicine*, 57, 1833–45.

Kiesler, D. J. (1983). The 1982 interpersonal circle: A taxonomy for complementarity in human transactions. *Psychological Review*, 90, 185–214.

Kilcommons, A., Morrison, A., Knight, A. & Lobban, F. (2008). Psychotic experiences in people who have been sexually assaulted. *Social Psychiatry and Psychiatric Epidemiology*, 43, 602–11.

Killen, J. D., Hayward, C., Wilson, D. M., Taylor, C. B., Hammer, L. D., Litt, I. et al. (1994). Factors associated with eating disorder symptoms in a community sample of 6th and 7th grade girls. *International Journal of Eating Disorders*,15, 357–67.

Kilzieh, N., Wood, A., Erdmann, J., Raskind, M. & Tapp, A. (2003). Depression in chronic 'Kraepelinian' schizophrenia. *Comprehensive Psychiatry*, 44, 1–6.

King, D. (1996). Gender blending: Medical perspectives and technology. In R. Ekins and D. King (Eds), *Blending Genders: Social Aspects of Cross-dressing and Sex-changing* (79–98). London: Routledge.

King, M., Coker, E., Leavey, A., Hoare, A. & Johnson-Sabine, D. (1994). Incidence of psychotic illness in London: Comparison of ethnic groups. *British Medical Journal*, 309, 1115–19.

King, M., McKeown, E., Warner, J., Ramsay, A., Johnson, K., Cort, C. et al. (2003). Mental health and quality of life of gay men and lesbians in England and Wales. Controlled, cross-sectional study. *British Journal of Psychiatry*, 183, 552–8.

King, N., Clowes-Hollins, V. & Ollendick, T. (1997). The etiology of childhood dog phobia. *Behaviour Research and Therapy*, 35(1), 77.

Kingdon, D. (2009). What is normal. In D. Turkington, D. Kingdon, S. Rathod, S. Wilcock, A. Brabban, P. et al. (Eds), *Back to Life, Back to*

Normality: Cognitive Therapy, Recovery and Psychosis (23–33). New York: Cambridge University Press.

Kingdon, D. & Turkington, D. (2005). *Cognitive Therapy of Schizophrenia*. New York: Guilford Press.

Kirby, J. & Baucom, D. (2007). Treating emotion dysregulation in a couples context: A pilot study of a couples skills group intervention. *Journal of Marital and Family Therapy*, 33, 275–391.

Kirk, S. & Kutchins, H. (1992). *The Selling of DSM: The Rhetoric of Science in Psychiatry*. New York: Aldine de Gruyter.

Kirk, S. & Kutchins, H. (1994).The myth of the reliability of DSM. *Journal of Mind and Behaviour*, 15(1 and 2), 71–86.

Kirk, S. & Kutchins, H. (1997). *Making Us Crazy*. New York: Free Press.

Kirmayer, L. (2001). Cultural variation in the clinical presentation of depression and anxiety: Implications for diagnosis and treatment. *Journal of Clinical Psychiatry*, 62 [suppl. 13], 22–8.

Kirsch, I. (2009). *The Emperor's New Drugs: Exploding the Antidepressant Myth*. London: Bodley Head.

Kirsch, I., Moore, T. J., Scoboria, A. & Nicholls, S. S. (2002). The Emperor's New Drugs: An Analysis of Antidepressant Medication Data Submitted to the US Food and Drug *Administration, Prevention & Treatment*, 5.

Kitzinger, C. & Perkins, R. (1993). *Changing Our Minds: Lesbian Feminism and Psychology*. London. Onlywomen Press.

Kitzinger, J. (2002). The ultimate neighbour from hell? Stranger danger and the media framing of paedophiles. In Y. Jewkes & G. Letherby (Eds), *Criminology: A Reader*. London: Sage.

Klein, D. (1993). False suffocation alarms, spontaneous panics, and related conditions: An integrative hypothesis. *Archives of General Psychiatry*, 50(4), 306–17.

Kleinman, A. (1986). Social origins of distress and disease : Depression, neurasthenia, and pain in modern China. *Current Anthropology*, 24(5), 499–509.

Kleinman, A. (1987). Anthropology and psychiatry. The role of culture in cross-cultural research on illness. *British Journal of Psychiatry*, 151, 447–54.

Kleinman, A. (1991). *Suffering, Healing and the Human Condition. Encyclopedia of Human Biology*. New York: Academic Press.

Kleinman, A. (1997). Triumph or pyrrhic victory? The inclusion of culture in DSM-IV. Harvard *Review of Psychiatry*, 4(6), 343–4.

Kleinman, A. (2004). Culture and depression. *New England Journal of Medicine*, 351, 951–3.

Kleinman, A. (2005). *Culture and Psychiatric Diagnosis and Treatment: What Are the Necessary Therapeutic Skills?* Utrecht, Netherlands: Trimbos-instituut.

Kleinman, A. & Kleinman, J. (1985). Somatization: Interconnections among Chinese culture, depressive meanings and the experience of pain. In A. Kleinman & B. Good (Eds), *Culture and Depression* (429–90). Berkeley CA: University of California Press.

Kleinman, A. & Kleinman, J. (1995). Suffering and its transformations. In A. Kleinman (Ed.), *Writing at the Margin: Discourse between Anthropology and Medicine*. Berkeley CA: University of California Press.

Kleinplatz, P. J. (1998). Sex therapy for vaginismus: A review, critique and humanistic alternative. *Journal of Humanistic Psychology*, 38, 51–81.

Kleinplatz, P. J. (Ed.) (2001). *New Directions in Sex Therapy: Innovations and Alternatives*. Philadelphia PA: Brunner-Routledge.

Kleinplatz, P. J. (2003). What's new in sex therapy. *From stagnation to fragmentation Sex and Relationship Therapy*, 18, 95–106.

Kleinplatz, P. J. (2004). Beyond sexual mechanics and hydraulics: Humanising the discourse surrounding erectile dysfunction. *Journal of Humanistic Psychology*, 44(2), 215–42.

Klerman, G. (1988). The current age of youthful melancholia. Evidence for increase in depression among adolescents and young adults. *British Journal of Psychiatry*, 152, 4–14.

Kline, P. (1988). *Psychology Exposed: Or the Emperor's New Clothes*. London: Routledge.

Klump, K. L., Miller, K. B., Keel, P. K., McGue, M. & Iacono, W. G. (2001). Genetic and environmental influences on anorexia nervosa syndromes in a populaion-based twin sample. *Psychological Medicine*, 31, 737–40.

Klump, K. L., Suisman, B. S., Burt, A. S., McGue, M. & Iacono, W. G. (2009). Genetic and environmental influences on disordered eating: An adoption study. *Journal of Abnormal Psychology*, 118, 797–805.

Klump, K. L., Wonderlich, S., Lehoux, P., Lilenfeld, L. R. & Bulik, C. (2002). Does environment matter? A review of nonshared environment and eating disorders. *International Journal of Eating Disorders*, 31(2), 118–35.

Knapp, M., McDaid, D., Mossialos, E. & Thornicroft, G. (Eds) (2007). *Mental Health Policy and Practice across Europe: The Future Direction of Mental Health Care*. Maidenhead: Open University Press.

Knegtering, H., Blijd, C. & Boks, M. (1999). Sexual dysfunction and prolactin levels in patients using classical antipsychotic, risperidone or olanzapine. *Schizophrenia Research*, 35, 355.

Koehler, B., Silver, A. & Karon, B. (2013). Psychodynamic approaches to understanding psychosis: Defences against terror. In J. Read & J. Dillon (Eds), *Models of Madness* (2nd edn). London: Routledge.

Kohn, M. (1976). The interaction of social class and other factors in the etiology of schizophrenia. *American Journal of Psychiatry*, 133, 177–80.

Kolb, B. & Whishaw, I. (1998). Brain plasticity and behaviour. *Annual Review of Psychology*, 49, 43–64.

Kotowicz, Z. (1997). *R. D. Laing and the Paths of Anti-psychiatry*. London: Routledge.

Kovel, J. (1980). The American mental health industry. In D. Ingleby (Ed.), *Critical Psychiatry: The Politics of Mental Health*. Harmondsworth: Penguin

Koverola, C., Papas, M., Pitts, S., Murtaugh, C., Black, M. & Dubowitz, H. (2005). Longitudinal investigation of the relationship amongst maternal victimisation, depressive symptoms, social support, and children's behaviour and development. *Journal of Interpersonal Violence*, 20(12), 1523–46.

Kraepelin, E. (1904). Comparative psychiatry I. In R. Littlewood & S. Dein (Eds), *Cultural Psychiatry and Medical Anthropology*. London: Routledge.

Kraepelin, E. (1907). *Clinical psychiatry: A Textbook for Students and Physicians, Abstracted and Adapted from the 7th German Edition of Kraepelin's Lehrbuch der Psychiatrie* (new edn, rev. and augmented) by A. R. Diefendorf. London: MacMillan & Co.

Kraepelin, E. (1913/1919). *Psychiatrica* (Trans. R. Barclay, 8th edn). Melbourne, FL: Krieger.

Krafft-Ebing, R. F. (1886). *Psychopathia Sexualis*, reprinted by Bloat Books, 1999.

Krause, I. B. (1998). *Therapy across Culture: Psychotherapy and Cultural Diversity*. London: Sage.

Krause, N. & Liang, J. (1992). Cross-cultural variations in depressive symptoms in later life. *International Psychogeriatrics*, 4 (suppl 2), 185–202.

Kringlen, E. (1967). *Heredity and Environment in the Functional Psychoses: Case Histories*. Oslo: Universitetsforlaget.

Krippner, S. & Achterberg, J. (2000). Anomalous healing experiences. In E. Etzel., S. J. Lynn & S. Krippner (Eds), *Varieties of Anomalous*

Experience: Examining the Scientific Evidence (353–95). Washington DC: American Psychological Association.

Kruger, A. (2000). Schizophrenia: Recovery and hope. *Psychiatric Rehabilitation Journal*, 24(1), 29–37.

Kubin, M., Wagner, G. & Fugl-Meyer, A. R. (2003). Epidemiology of erectile dysfunction, *International Journal of Impotence Research*, 15, 63–71.

Kuch, K., Cox, B. & Evans, R. (1996). Post-traumatic stress disorder and motor vehicle accidents: A multidisciplinary overview. *Canadian Journal of Psychiatry*, 41, 429–34.

Kucharska-Pietura, K., Vasilis, N., Masiak, M. & Treasure, J. (2004). The recognition of emotion in the faces and voice of anorexia nervosa. *International Journal of Eating Disorders*, 35, 42–7.

Kuhn, T. (1970). *The Structure of Scientific Revolutions*. Chicago IL: University of Chicago Press.

Kuipers, E., Garety, P., Dunn, G., Bebbington, P., Fowler, D. & Freeman, D. (2002). Correspondence: CBT for psychosis. *British Journal of Psychiatry*, 181, 534.

Kutchins, H. & Kirk, S. (1997). *Making Us Crazy: DSM–The Psychiatric Bible and the Creation of Mental Disorders*. New York: Free Press.

Kutchins, H. & Kirk, S. (1999). *Making Us crazy: DSM–The Psychiatric Bible and the Creation of Mental Disorders*. London: Constable.

Labbatte, L., Young, P. & Arana, G. (1999). Panic disorder in schizophrenia. *Canadian Journal of Psychiatry*, 44, 488–90.

Lacasse, J. & Leo, J. (2005). Serotonin and depression: A disconnect between the advertisements and the scientific literature. *PLOS Medicine*, 2(12, e.392), 1211–16.

Lacey, H. & Price, C. (2004). Disturbed families, or families disturbed? *British Journal of Psychiatry*, 185, 195–6.

Ladouceur, R., Dugas, M. & Freeston, M. (2000). Efficacy of a cognitive-behavioural treatment for generalised anxiety disorder: Evaluation in a clinically-controlled trial. *Journal of Consulting and Clinical Psychology*, 68(6), 957–64.

Ladouceur, R., Talbot, F. & Dugas, M. J. (1997). Behavioral expressions of intolerance of uncertainty in worry. *Behavior Modification*, 21(3), 355–71.

Lafrance, M. (2009). *Women and Depression: Recovery and Resistance*. Hove: Routledge.

Laine, D. (2007). *African Gods: Contemporary Rituals and Beliefs*. Paris: Flammarion.

Laing, R. D. (1960). *The Divided Self*. London: Tavistock Press.

Laing, R. D. (1967). *The Politics of Experience and the Bird of Paradise*. Harmondsworth: Penguin.

Laing, R. D. & Esterson, A. (1964). *Sanity, Madness and the Family*. London: Tavistock Press.

Laing, R. D. & Esterson, A. (1970). Sanity, Madness and the Family. *Families of Schizophrenics*. 281.

Lake, A. J., Staiger, P. K. & Glowinski, H. (2000). Effect of Western culture on women's attitudes to eating and perceptions of body shape. *International Journal of Eating Disorders*, 27, 83–9.

Lam, D. C. K., Salkovskis, P. M. & Warwick, H. M. C. (2005). An experimental investigation of the impact of biological versus psychological explanations of the cause of 'mental illness'. *Journal of Mental Health*, 14, 453–64.

Lambert, M. J. & Ogles, B. M. (2004). The efficacy and effectiveness of psychotherapy. In A. E. Bergin & S. I. Garfield (Eds), *Handbook of Psychotherapy and Behavioural Change* (4th edn). New York: Wiley.

Lampshire, D. (2009). Lies and lessons: The ramblings of an alleged mad woman. *Psychosis: Psychological, Social and Biological Approaches*, 1(2), 178–84.

Lancelot, C. & Kaslow, N. J. (1994). Sex role orientation and disordered eating in women: A review. *Clinical Psychology Review*, 14, 139–57.

Lane, C. (2009). The surprising history of passive-aggressive personality disorder. *Theory & Psychology*, 19, 55–70.

Langdridge, D. & Barker, M. (Eds) (2005). Contemporary perspectives on sadomasochism (S/M). *Special Issue of Lesbian & Gay Psychology Review*, 6(3).

Langdridge, D. & Barker, M. (2007). *Safe, Sane and Consensual: Contemporary Perspectives on Sadomasochism*. Basingstoke: Palgrave.

Langer, E. J. & Abelson, R. P. (1974). A patient by any other name: Clinician group difference in labelling bias. *Journal of Consulting and Clinical Psychology*, 42, 4–9.

Langevin, R., Lang, R. A. & Curnoe, S. (1998). The prevalence of sex offenders with deviant fantasies. *Journal of Interpersonal Violence*, 3, 315–27.

Lapouse, R., Monk, M. & Terris, M. (1956). The drift hypothesis and socioeconomic differentials in schizophrenia. *American Journal of Public Health*, 46, 978–86.

Large, M., Smith, G. & Nielssen, O. (2009). The relationship between the rate of homicide by those with schizophrenia and the overall homicide rate: A systematic review and meta-analysis. *Schizophrenia Research*, 112, 123–9.

Large, M., Smith, G., Swinson, N., Shaw, J. & Nielssen, O. (2008). Homicide due to mental disorder in England and Wales over 50 years. *British Journal of Psychiatry*, 193, 130–3.

Larkin, W. & Morrison, A. (Eds) (2006). *Trauma and Psychosis: New Directions for Theory and Therapy*. London: Routledge.

Larkin, W. & Read, J. (2008). Childhood trauma and psychosis: Evidence, pathways and implications. *Journal of Postgraduate Medicine*, 54, 284–90.

Laruelle, M. (2000). The role of endogenous sensitisation in the pathophysiology of schizophrenia. *Brain Research Reviews*, 31, 371–84.

Laruelle, M. & Abi-Dargham, A. (1999). Dopamine as the wind of the psychotic fire: New evidence from brain imaging studies. *Journal of Psychopharmacology*, 13(4), 358–71.

Latour, B. & Woolgar, S. (1986). *Laboratory Life: The Construction of Scientific Facts*. Princeton NJ: Princeton University Press.

Lattuada, E., Serretti, A., Cusin, C., Gasperini, M. & Smeraldi, E. (1999). Symptomatologic analysis of psychotic and non-psychotic depression. *Journal of Affective Disorders*, 54, 183–7.

Laub, D. (2005). From speechlessness to narrative. *Literature and Medicine*, 24, 253–65.

Laumann, E. O., Nicolosi, D. B., Glasser, D. B., Paik, A., Gingell, C., Moreira, E. et al. (2005). Sexual problems among women and men aged 40–80y: prevalence and correlates identified in the global study of sexual attitudes and behaviours. *International Journal of Impotence Research*, 17, 39–57.

Laumann, E. O., Paik, A. & Rosen, R. C. (1999). Sexual dysfunction in the United States. *Journal of the American Medical Association*, 281, 537–44.

Laurance, J. (2003a). *Pure Madness: How Fear Drives the Mental Health System*. London: Routledge.

Laurance, J. (2003b). Life stories: Ron Coleman. In *Pure Madness: How Fear Drives the Mental Health System*. London: Routledge.

Lawrence, A. A. (2003). Factors associated with satisfaction or regret following male-to-female sex reassignment surgery. *Archives of Sexual Behavior*, 32(4), 299–315.

Laws, D. R. & Marshall, W. L. (1991). Masturbatory reconditioning with sexual deviates: An evaluative review. *Advances in Behaviour Research and Therapy*, 13, 13–25.

Laws, D. R. & O'Donohue, W. (Eds) (1997). *Sexual Deviance: Theory, Assessment and Treatment*. New York: Guilford Press.

Lawton Smith, S. (2010). Briefing Paper 2: Supervised Community Treatment. London: Mental Health Alliance.

Le Doux, J. (1999). *The Emotional Brain*. London: Phoenix.

Leahey, T. H. (1992). The mythical revolutions of American psychology. *American Psychologist*, 47, 308–18.

Learmonth, M. (2006). NICE Guidelines on Depression: A full digest for Arts Therapists. Insider Art, May. Accesssed 11 May 2011 at www.insiderart.org.uk/UserFiles/File/The%20NICE%20Guidelines%20on%20Depression,%20an%20analysis%20from%20an%20art%20therapy%20perspective.pdf.

Leary, T. (1957). *Interpersonal Diagnosis of Personality*. New York: Ronald Press.

Lebedun, M. & Collins, J. (1976). Effects of status indicators on psychiatrists' judgements of psychiatric impairment. *Social Science Research*, 60, 199–210.

Lecomte, T., Spidel, A., Leclerc, C., MacEwan, W., Greaves, C. & Bentall, R. (2008). Predictors and profiles of treatment non-adherence and engagement in service problems in early psychosis. *Schizophrenia Research*, 102, 295–302.

Lee, R. (1976). The causal priority between socio-economic status and psychiatric disorder. *Inernational Journal of Social Psychiatry*, 22, 1–8.

Lee, S. (2001). Fat phobia in anorexia nervosa. In M. Nasser, M. A. Katzman & R. A. Gordon (Eds), *Eating Disorder and Cultures in Transition*. London: Routledge.

Lees, J., Manning, N. & Rawlings, B. (2004). A culture of enquiry: Research evidence and the therapeutic community. *Psychiatric Quarterly*, 75, 279–94.

Leff, J. P. (1973). Culture and the differentiation of emotional states. *British Journal of Psychiatry*, 123, 299–306.

Leff, J. P. (1977). International variations in the diagnosis of psychiatric illness. *British Journal of Psychiatry*, 131, 329–38.

Leff, J. P. (2001). Why is community care perceived as a failure? *British Journal of Psychiatry*, 179, 381–3.

Leff, J. P. & Vaughn, C. (1985). *Expressed Emotions in Families: Its Significance for Mental Illness*. New York: Guilford Press.

Lefley, H. (1999). Mental health systems in cross-cultural context. In A. V. Horwitz & T. L. Scheid (Eds), *A Handbook for the Study of Mental Health and Illness: Social Contexts, Theories and Systems*. Cambridge: Cambridge University Press.

Legenbauer, T., Vocks, S. & Rüddel, H. (2008). Emotion recognition, emotional awareness and cognitive bias in individuals with bulimia nervosa. *Clinical Psychology*, 64, 687–702.

Leiblum, S. R. & Rose, R. C. (2000). *Principles and Practice of Sex Therapy*. New York: Guilford Press.

Leising, D., Rogers, K. & Ostner, J. (2009). The undisordered personality: Normative assumptions underlying personality disorder diagnoses. *Review of General Psychology*, 13, 230–41.

Lemert, E. M. (1967). *Human Deviance, Social Problems and Social Control*. Englewood Cliffs NJ: Prentice-Hall.

Leo, J. & Lacasse, J. (2008). The media and the chemical imbalance theory of depression. *Society*, 45(1), 35–45.

Leonard, L. M. & Follette, V. M. (2002). Sexual functioning in women reporting a history of child sexual abuse: Review of the literature and clinical implications. *Annual Review of Sex Research*, 13, 346–88.

Lerner, G. (1993). *The Creation of Feminist Consciousness*. New York: Oxford University Press.

Lester, H. (2010). Ethnic density and mental health. *British Medical Journal*, 341, 843–4.

Leucht, S., Arbter, D., Engel, R. R., Kissling, W. & Davis, J. M. (2009). How effective are second-generation antipsychotic drugs? A meta-analysis of placebo-controlled trials. *Molecular Psychiatry*, 14, 429–47.

Leudar, I. & Thomas, P. (2000). *Voices of Reason, Voices of Insanity: Studies of Verbal Hallucinations*. London: Routledge.

Lev, A. I. (2004). *Transgender Emergence: Therapeutic guidelines for working withgender-variant people and their families*. Binghamton, NY: The Haworth Press, Inc.

Lev, A. I. (2006). Disordering gender identity: Gender identity disorder in the DSM-IV-TR. *Journal of Psychology & Human Sexuality*. 17, 35–69.

Lev, A. I. (2006). Transgender communities: Developing identity through connection. In K. Bieschke, R. Perez K. & DeBord (Eds), *Handbook of Counseling and Psychotherapy with Lesbian, Gay, and Bisexual Clients* (2nd edn). Washington DC: APA.

Levack, B. P. (1987). *The Witch-hunt*. New York: Longman.

Levenson, M. R. (1992). Rethinking psychopathy. *Theory & Psychology*, 2, 51–71.

LeVay, S. & Valente, S. M. (2002). *Human Sexuality*. Sunderland, M.A.: Sinauer Associates, Inc.

Levenson, M. R., Kiehl, K. A. & Fitzpatrick, C. M. (1995). Assessing psychopathic attributes in a noninstitutionalized population. *Journal of Personality and Social Psychology*, 68, 151-8.

Levey, S. & Howells, K. (1995). Dangerousness, unpredictability and the fear of people with schizophrenia. *The Journal of Forensic Psychiatry*, 6, 19–39.

Levine, M. P. & Smolak, L. (2006). *The Prevention of Eating Problems and Eating Disorders: Theory, Research, and Practice*. Mahwah, NJ: Lawrence Earlbaum.

Levine, M. P. & Smolak, L. (2007). Prevention of negative body image, disordered eating, and eating disorders: An update. In S. Wonderlich, J. Mitchell, M., De Zwaan & H. Steiger (Eds), *Annual Review of Eating Disorders*, Part I (1–14). Oxford: Radcliffe.

Lewin, K. (1946). Action research and minority problems. *Journal of Social Issues* 2, 34–46.

Lewinsohn, P. & Hobermann, H. (1982). Depression. In A. Bellack, M. Hersen & A. Kazdin (Eds), *International Handbook of Behaviour Modification and Therapy* (397–425). New York: Plenum Press.

Lewinsohn, P., Hops, H., Roberts, R., Seeley, R. & Andrews, J. (1993). Adolescent psychopathology: I. Prevalence and incidence of depression and other DSM-III-R disorders in high school students. *Journal of Abnormal Psychology*, 102(1), 133–44.

Lewinsohn, P., Youngren, M. & Grosscup, S. (1979). Reinforcement and depression. In A. Depue (Ed.), *The Psychobiology of the Depressive Disorders*. New York: Academic Press.

Lewis, D. (1987). *Philosophical Papers*, Vol 11. Oxford: Oxford Scholarship Online.

Lewis, G. (1993). Another British Disease? A recent increase in the prevalence of psychiatric morbidity. *Journal of Epidemiology and Community Health*, 47, 358–61.

Lewis, G. & Appleby, L. (1988). Personality disorder: The patients psychiatrists dislike. *British Journal of Psychiatry*, 153, 44–9.

Lewis, G., David, A. & Andreasson, S. (1992). Schizophrenia and city life. *Lancet*, 340, 137–40.

Lewis, G. & Sloggett, A. (1998). Suicide, deprivation and unemployment: Record linkage study. *British Medical Journal*, 317, 1283–6.

Lewis, I. (1971). *Ecstatic Religion: An Anthropological Study of Spirit Possession and Shamanism*. New York: Penguin.

Lewis, K. (1995). *Lancashire County Asylum: 'A Place of Safety' 1897–1997*. Newton-le-Willows: Willow Printing.

Lexchin, J., Bero, L. & Djulbegovic, B. (2003). Pharmaceutical industry sponsorship and research outcome and quality: Systematic review. *British Medical Journal*, 326, 1167.

Liddle, P. F. (1987). The symptoms of chronic schizophrenia. A re-examination of the positive-negative dichotomy. *British Journal of Psychiatry*, 151, 145–51.

Lidz, R. W. & Lidz, T. (1949). The family environment of schizophrenic patients. *American Journal of Psychiatry*, 106, 332–45.

Lieb, R., Becker, E. & Altamura, C. (2005). The epidemiology of generalized anxiety disorder in Europe. *European Neuropsychopharmacology*, 15, 445–52.

Lieb, K., Vollm, B., Rucker, G., Timmer, A. & Stoffers, J. M. (2010). Pharmacotherapy for borderline personality disorder: Cochrane systematic review of randomised trials. *British Journal of Psychiatry*, 196, 4–12.

Lieberman, J., Stroup, T., McEvoy, J., Swartz, M., Rosenheck, R., Perkins, D. et al. (2005). Effectiveness of antipsychotic drugs in patients with chronic schizophrenia. *The New England Journal of Medicine*, 353(12), 1209–23.

Lieberman, J., Tollefson, G., Charles, C., Zipursky, R., Sharma, T., Kahn, R. et al. (2005). Antipsychotic drug effects on brain morphology in first-episode psychosis. *Archives of General Psychiatry*, 62(4), 361–70.

Lief, H. I. & Hubschman, L. (1993). Orgasm in the post operative transsexual. *Archives of Sexual Behaviour*, 22, 145–55.

Lindemann, G. (1997). The body of gender difference. In K. Davis (Ed.), *Embodied Practices: Feminist Perspectives on the Body*. London: Sage.

Lindow, V. (1992). A service user's perspective. In H. Wright & M. Goddey (Eds), *Mental Health Nursing: From First Principles to Professional Practice*. London: Chapman and Hall.

Linehan, M. M. (1993). *Cognitive-Behavioral Treatment of Borderline Personality Disorder*. New York: Guilford Press.

Linehan, M. M., Comtois, K. A., Murray, A. M., Brown, M. Z., Gallop R. J., Heard, H. L. et al. (2006). Two-year randomized controlled trial and follow-up of dialectical behavior therapy vs therapy by experts for suicidal behaviors and borderline personality disorder. *Archives of General Psychiatry*, 62, 1–10.

Liotti, G. & Gumley, A. (2008). An attachment perspective on schizophrenia: The role of disorganized attachment, dissociation and mentalization. In A. Moskowitz, I. Schafer & M. Dorahy (Eds), *Psychosis, Trauma and Dissociation: Emerging Perspectives on Severe Psychopathology* (117–33). Chichester: Wiley-Blackwell.

Lipsey, M. W. & Wilson, D. B. (1993). The efficacy of psychological, educational, and behavioural treatment: Confirmation from metaanalysis. *American Psychologist*, 48, 1181–209.

Lipsitz, J. D., Mannuzza, S., Klein, D. F., Ross, D. C. & Fyer, A. J. (1999). Specific phobia 10–16 years after treatment. *Depression and Anxiety*, 10, 105–11.

Lisak, D. (1994). The psychological impact of sexual abuse: Content analysis of interviews with male survivors. *Journal of Traumatic Stress*, 7(4), 525–48.

Littlewood, R. (1989). Community-initiated research: A study of psychiatrists' conceptualisations of 'cannabis psychosis'. *Psychiatric Bulletin*, 13, 486–8.

Littlewood, R. (1998). A religious interest questionnaire for use with psychiatric patients. *Mental Health, Religion & Culture*, 1,: 57–63.

Littlewood, R. (2002). *Pathologies of the West: An Anthropology of Mental Illness in Europe and America*. New York: Cornell University Press.

Littlewood, R. & Lipsedge, M. (1982). *Aliens and Alienists: Ethnic Minorities and Psychiatry* (1st edn). Oxford: Oxford University Press.

Littlewood, R. & Lipsedge, M. (1997). *Aliens and Alienists: Ethnic Minorities and Psychiatry* (3rd edn). London, NewYork: Routledge.

Litvinoff, S. (1992). *The Relate Guide to Sex in Loving Relationships*. London: Vermilion.

Livesley, W. J. (2001). Conceptual and taxonomic issues. In W. J. Livesley (Ed.), *Handbook of Personality Disorders: Theory, Research, and Treatment*, 3–39. New York: Guilford Press.

Livesley, W. J. & Jang, K. L. (2008). The behavioral genetics of personality disorder. *Annual Review of Clinical Psychology*, 4, 247–74.

Llorca, P., Chereau, I., Bayle, F. & Lancon, C. (2002). Tardive dyskinesias and antipsychotics: A review. *European Psychiatry: the Journal of the Association of European Psychiatrists*, 17(3), 129–38.

Lock, J., Agras, W. S., Bryson, S. & Kraemer, H. C. (2005). A comparison of short- and long-term family therapy for adolescent anorexia nervosa. *Journal of the American Academy of Child and Adolescent Psychiatry*, 44(7), 632–9.

Lock, J., Le Grange, D., Agras, W. S. & Dare, C. (2001). *Treatment Manual for Anorexia Nervosa: A Family-Based Approach*. New York: Guilford Press.

Lock, J., Le Grange, D., Agras, S., Moye, A., Bryson, S. W. & Jo, B. (2010). Randomized clinical trial comparing family-based treatment with adolescent-focused individual therapy for adolescents with Anorexia Nervosa. *Archives of General Psychiatry*, 67, 1025–32.

Lock, M. (1988). New Japanese mythologies: Faltering discipline and the ailing housewife. *American Ethnologist*, 15, 275.

Locker, D., Liddell, A., Dempster, L. & Shapiro, D. (1999). Age of onset of dental anxiety. *Journal of Dental Research*, 78(3), 790–6.

Loewenthal, K. (2007). *Religion, Culture and Mental Health*. Cambridge: Cambridge University Press.

Lomas, P. (1999). *Doing Good? Psychotherapy Out of its Depth*. Oxford: Oxford University Press.

Lomas, P. (2003). Telling it like it is. In L. King & R. Randall (Eds), *The Future of Pyschoanalytic Psychotherapy*. London: Wurr.

Longden, E. (2010). Making sense of voices: A personal story of recovery. *Psychosis: Psychological, Social and Biological Approaches*, 2(3), 255–9.

Longden, E., Corstens, D., Escher, S. & Romme, M. (2012). Voice hearing in a biographical context: A model for formulating the relationship between voices and life history. *Psychosis*, 4(3), 224–34.

Longden, E., Madill, A. & Waterman, M. G. (2012). Dissociation, trauma, and the role of lived experience: Toward a new conceptualization of voice hearing. *Psychological Bulletin*, 138, 28–76.

Longmore, R. J. & Worrell, M. (2007). Do we need to challenge thoughts in cognitive behavior therapy? *Clinical Psychology Review*, 27, 173–87.

López, S. R., Nelson Hipke, K., Polo, A. J., Jenkins, J. H., Karno, M., Vaughn, C. et al. (2004). Ethnicity, expressed emotion, attributions, and course of schizophrenia: Family warmth matters. *Journal of Abnormal Psychology*, 113(3), 428–39.

Lorber, J. (2007). *Gendered Bodies: Feminist Perspectives*. LA: Roxbury.

Lothian, J. & Read, J. (2002). Asking about abuse during mental health assessments: Clients' views and experiences. *New Zealand Journal of Psychology*, 31(2), 98–103.

Lovie, A. D. (1983). Attention and behaviourism: Fact and fiction. *British Journal of Psychology*, 74, 301–10.

Low, S. (1981). The meaning of nervios: A sociocultural analysis of symptom presentation in San Jose, Costa Rica. *Culture, Medicine and Psychiatry*, 5, 25–48.

Luborsky, L., Diguer, L., Seligman, D. A., Rosenthal, R., Krause, E. D., Johnson, S. et al. (1999). The researcher's own therapy allegiances: A 'wild card' in comparisons of treatment efficacy. *Clinical Psychology: Science & Practice*, 6, 95–106.

Luby, E. D. & Koval, D. (2009). CNS opiate receptors and eating disorders. In R. Dean, E. J. Bilsky & S. Stevens Negus (Eds), *Opiate Receptors and Antagonists: From Bench to Clinic* (407–21). Humana Press .

Luders, E., Sánchez, F. J., Gaser, C., Toga, A. W., Narr, K. L., Hamilton, L. S. et al. (2009). Regional gray matter variation in male-to-female transsexualism. *NeuroImage*, 46(4), 904–7.

Lutfey, K. E., Link, C. L., Litman, H. J., Rosen, R. C. & McKinlay, J. B. (2008) An examination of the association of abuse (physical, sexual, or emotional) and female sexual dysfunction: Results from the Boston area community health survey. *Fertility and Sterility*, 90(4), 957–64.

Lykken, D. T. (1957). A study of anxiety in the sociopathic personality. *Journal of Abnormal and Social Psychology*, 55, 6–10.

Lynam, D. R., Whiteside, S. & Jones, S. (1999). Self-reported psychopathy: A validation study. *Journal of Personality Assessment*, 73, 110–32.

Lynam, D. R. & Widiger, T. A. (2001). Using the five-factor model to represent the DSM-IV personality disorders: An expert consensus approach. *Journal of Abnormal Psychology*, 110, 401–12.

Lynch, D., Laws, K. R. & McKenna, P. J. (2010). Cognitive behavioural therapy for major psychiatric disorder: Does it really work? A meta-analytical review of well-controlled trials. *Psychological Medicine*, 40, 9–24.

Lynch, T. R., Trost, W. T., Salsman, N. & Linehan, M. M. (2007). Dialectical behavior therapy for borderline personality disorder. *Annual Review of Clinical Psychology*, 3, 181–205.

Lyons, D., Yang, C., Mobley, B., Nickerson, J. & Schatzburg, A. (2000). Stress level cortisol treatment impairs inhibitory control of behaviour in monkeys. *Journal of Neuroscience*, 20, 20.

Lyons, J. O. (1978). *The Invention of the Self: The Hinge of Consciousness in the Eighteenth Century*. Carbondale IL: Southern Illinois University Press.

Lyons-Ruth, K., Yellin, C., Melnick, S. & Atwood, G. (2005). Expanding the concept of unresolved mental states: Hostile/helpless states of mind on the adult attachment interview are associated with disrupted mother-infant communication and infant disorganization. *Development and Psychopathology*, 17, 1–23.

Lysaker, P., Yanos, P. & Roe, D. (2009). The role of insight in the process of recovery from schizophrenia: A review of three views. *Psychosis: Psychological, Social and Biological Approaches*, 1, 113–21.

Ma, S. & Teasdale, J. (2004). Mindfulness-based cognitive therapy for depression: Replication and exploration of differential relapse prevention effects. *Journal of Consulting and Clinical Psychology*, 72(1), 31–40.

MacDonald, M. (1981). *Mystical Bedlam: Madness, Anxiety, and Healing in Seventeenth–Century England*. Cambridge: Cambridge University Press.

Macgowan, M. (2008). *A Guide to Evidence-based Groupwork*. Oxford: Oxford University Press.

Machado, P. P. P., Machado, B. C., Gonçalves, S. & Hoek, H. W. (2006). The prevalence of eating disorders not otherwise specified. *International Journal of Eating Disorders*, 40, 212–17.

Mackler, D. (2008). *Take These Broken Wings: Recovery from Schizophrenia without Medication*. USA: D. Mackler.

Maercker, A. (2001). Association of cross-cultural differences in psychiatric morbidity with cultural values: A secondary data analysis. *German Journal of Psychiatry*, 4, 1433–1055.

Maguire, E., Gadian, D., Johnsrude, I., Good, C., Ashburner, J., Frackowiak, R. et al. (2000). Navigation related structural change in the hippocampi of taxi drivers. *Proceedings of the National Academy of Science (USA)*, 97(8), 4398–403.

Maher, B. A. (1992). Delusions: Contemporary etiological hypotheses. *Psychiatric Annals*, 22, 260–8.

Mair, K. (1992). The myth of therapist expertise. In W. Dryden & C. Feltham (Eds), *Psychotherapy and its Discontents*. Maidenhead: Open University Press.

Makkawi, I. (2009). Towards an emerging paradigm of critical community psychology in Palestine. Journal of Critical Psychology. *Counselling and Psychotherapy*, 9, 75–86.

Malhi, G. & Bartlett, J. (2000). Depression: A role for neurosurgery? *British Journal of Neurosurgery*, 14(5), 415–22.

Malinowski, B. (1927). *Sex and Repression in Savage Society*. London: Routledge.

Malson, H. (1998). *The Thin Woman: Feminism, Post-structuralism and the Social Psychology of Anorexia Nervosa*. London: Routledge.

Malson, H. (2009). Appearing to disappear: Postmodern femininities and self-starved subjectivities. In H. Malson & M. Burns (Eds), *Critical Feminist Approaches to Eating Dis/Orders*. London: Routledge.

Malson, H. & Ussher, J. (1996). Body poly-texts: Discourses of the anorexic body. *Journal of Community and Applied Social Psychology*, 6, 267–80.

Maltby, J., Giles, D. C., Barber, L. & McCutcheon, L. E. (2005). Intense-personal celebrity worship and body image: Evidence of a link among female adolescents. *British Journal of Health Psychology*, 10, 17–32.

Maltz, W. & Holman, B. (1987) *Incest and Sexuality: A Guide to Healing*. Lexington, MA, England: Lexington Books.

Mancini, C., Van Ameringen, M. & MacMillan, H. (1995). Relationship of childhood sexual and physical abuse to anxiety disorders. *Journal of Nervous and Mental Disease*, 183(5), 309–22.

Manning, N. (2000). Psychiatric diagnosis under conditions of uncertainty: Personality disorder, science and professional legitimacy. *Sociology of Health and Illness*, 22, 621–39.

Manning, N. (2002). Actor networks, policy networks and personality disorder. *Sociology of Health and Illness*, 24, 644–66.

Manson, S., Shore, J. & Bloom, J. (1985). The depressive experience in American Indian communities: A challenge for psychiatric theory and diagnosis. In A. Kleinman & B. Good (Eds), *Culture and Depression* (331–68). Berkeley CA: University of California Press.

Marce, V. (1860). On a form of hypochondriarcal occurring consecutive to dyspepsia and characterized by refusal of food. *Journal of Psychological Medicine and Mental Pathology*, 13, 264–6.

Marecek, J. & Hare-Mustin, R. T. (2004). Clinical psychology: The politics of madness. In D. Fox, I. Prilleltensky & S. Austin (Eds), *Critical Psychology: An Introduction* (2nd edn). London: Sage.

Margison, F. R., Barkham, M., Evans, C., McGrath, G., Mellor Clark, J., Audin, K. et al. (2000). Measurement and psychotherapy: evidence-based practice and practice-based evidence. *British Journal of Psychiatry*, 177, 123–30.

Maric, N., Myin-Germeys, I., Delespaul, P., de Graaf, R., Vollebergh, W. and Van Os, J. (2004). Is our concept of schizophrenia influenced by Berkson's bias? *Social Psychiatry and Psychiatric Epidemiology*, 39, 600–5.

Marino, R. & Cosgrove, G. (1997). Neurosurgical treatment of neuropsychiatric illness. *Psychiatric Clinics of North America*, 20(4), 933–43.

Markham, D. (2003). Attitudes towards patients with a diagnosis of 'borderline personality disorder': Social rejection and dangerousness. *Journal of Mental Health*, 12, 595–612.

Markham, D. & Trower, P. (2003). The effects of the psychiatric label borderline personality disorder on nursing staffs' perceptions and causal attributions for challenging behaviours. *British Journal of Clinical Psychology*, 42, 243–56.

Marks, D. (2002). Freedom, responsibility and power: Contrasting approaches to health psychology. *Journal of Health Psychology, 7,* 5–19.

Marks, J. (1979). *The Search for the 'Manchurian Candidate'*. London: Norton.

Markus, H. R. & Kitayama, S. (1991). Culture and the self: Implications for cognition, emotion, and motivation. *Psychological Review, 98,* 224–53.

Marlatt, G. & Gordon, J. (1985). *Relapse Prevention: Maintenance Strategies in Addictive Behavior Change*. New York: Guilford Press.

Marques, J. K., Day, D. M., Nelson, C. et al. (1991). The Sex Offender Treatment and Evaluation Project.

Marrazzi, M. A., Luby, E. D., Kinzie, J., Inam, D. Munjal, J. & Sydney Spector, S. (1997). Endogenous codeine and morphine in anorexia and bulimia nervosa. *Life Sciences, 60,* 1741–7.

Marsella, A. J. & White, G. (1982). *Cultural Conceptions of Mental Health and Therapy (Culture, Illness and Healing)*. New York: Springer.

Marshall, B. L. (2002). 'Hard Science': Gendered constructions of sexual dysfunction in the 'Viagra' age. *Sexualities, 5*(2), 131–58.

Marshall, M. & Rathbone, J. (2011). Early intervention for psychosis. Cochrane Database of Systematic Reviews CD004718.

Marshall, R. (1990). The genetics of schizophrenia: axiom or hypothesis? In R. Bentall (Ed.), *Reconstructing Schizophrenia*, 89–117. London: Routledge.

Marshall, W. L. (1989). Intimacy, loneliness and sexual offenders. *Behaviour Research and Therapy, 27,* 491–503.

Marshall, W. L. (1993). The role of attachments, intimacy, and loneliness in the etiology and maintenance of sexual offending. *Sexual and Marital Therapy, 8,* 109–21.

Marshall, W. L. (1997). Pedophilia: Psychopathology and theory. In D. R. Laws & W. O'Donohue (Eds), *Sexual Deviance: Theory, Assessment and Treatment*. New York: Guilford Press.

Marshall, W. L., Hudson, S. M. & Hodkinson, S. (1993). The importance of attachment bonds in thedevelopment of juvenile sex offending. In H. E. Barbaree,W. L. Marshall & S. M. Hudson (Eds), *The Juvenile Sex Offender* (164–81). New York: Guilford Press.

Martín-Baró, I. (1996). Toward a liberation psychology. In A. Aron & S. Corne (Eds), *Writings for a Liberation Psychology*. New York: Harvard University Press.

Marty, D. (2007). Secret detentions and illegal transfers of detainees involving Council of Europe member states: Second report. Council of Europe, doc. 11302 rev., 11 June 2007. Accessed at assembly. coe.int/Documents/WorkingDocs/Doc07/edoc11302.pdf on 15 January 2012.

Marx, K. (1858). The increase of lunacy in Great Britain. New York Tribune, 20 August.

Marzillier, J. (2004). The myth of evidence based psychotherapy. *The Psychologist 17,* 392–5.

Marzillier, J. & Hall, J. (2009). The challenge of the Layard initiative. *The Psychologist, 22,* 396–9.

Maser, J. D., Kaelber, C. & Weise, R .F. (1991). International use and attitudes toward DSM-III and DSM-III-R: Growing consensus in psychiatric classification. *Journal of Abnormal Psychology, 100,* 271–9.

Masson, J. M. (1988). *Against Therapy: Emotional Tyranny and the Myth of Psychological Healing*. New York: Athenaum.

Masters, W. H. & Johnson, V. E. (1966). *Human Sexual Response*. Boston: Little Brown.

Masters, W. H. & Johnson, V. E. (1970). *Human Sexual Inadequacy*. Boston: Little Brown.

Mauthner, N. (1995). Postnatal depression: The significance of social contacts between mothers. *Women's Studies International Forum,* 18(3), 311–23.

May, R., Hartley, J. & Knight, T. (2003). Making the personal political. *The Psychologist, 16,* 182–3. Accessed at www.thepsychologist. org.uk/archive/archive_home.cfm?volumeID=16&editionID=93&Ar ticleID=537 on 2 December 2011.

May, R. & Longden, E. (2010). Self-help approaches to hearing voices. In F. Larøi & A. Aleman (Eds), *Hallucinations: A Guide to Treatment and Management*. Oxford: Oxford University Press.

McCarthy, M. (1999). *Sexuality and Women with Learning Disabilities*. London: Jessica Kingsley Press.

McClellan, J., Susser, E. & King, M. (2006). Maternal famine, de novo mutations, and schizophrenia. *Journal of the American Medical Association, 296*(5), 582–4.

McClelland, L. & Crisp, A. (2001). Anorexia nervosa and social class. *International Journal of Eating Disorders, 29,* 150–6.

McCoy, A. W. (2006). *A Question of Torture: CIA Interrogation, from the Cold War to the War on Terror*. New York: Metropolitan Books.

McCrae, R. R. & Sutin, A. R. (2007). New frontiers for the five-factor model: A preview of the literature. *Social and Personality Psychology Compass, 1,* 423–40.

McElhiney, M. C., Moody, B. J., Steif, B. L., Prudic, J., Devanand, D. P., Nobler, M. S. et al. (1995). Autobiographical memory and mood: Effects of electroconvulsive therapy. *Neuropsychology, 9,* 501–17.

McGilloway, A., Hall, R. E., Lee, T. & Bhui, K. S. (2010). A systematic review of personality disorder, race and ethnicity: *Prevalence, Aetiology and Treatment BMC Psychiatry, 10,* 33.

McGlashan, T., Zipursky, R., Perkins, D., Addington, J., Miller, T., Woods, S. et al. (2006). Randomized, double-blind trial of olanzapine versus placebo in patients prodromally symptomatic for psychosis. *American Journal of Psychiatry, 163,* 790–9.

McGoldrick, M. (1998). *Re-visioning Family Therapy: Race, Culture, and Gender in Clinical Practice*. New York: Guilford Press.

McGorry, P., Bell, R., Dudgeon, P. & Jackson, H. (1998). The dimensional structure of first episode psychosis: An exploratory factor analysis. *Psychological Medicine: A Journal of Research in Psychiatry and the Allied Sciences, 28*(4), 935–47.

McGovern, D. & Cope, R. (1987). The compulsory detention of males of different ethnic groups, with special reference to offender patients. *British Journal of Psychiatry, 150,* 505–12.

McGruder, J. (2004). Disease models of mental illness and aftercare patient education: Critical observations from meta-analyses, cross-cultural practice and anthropological study. *The British Journal of Occupational Therapy, 67,* 310–18.

McGue, M. & Christensen, K. (2003). The heritability of depression symptoms in elderly danish twins: Occasion-specific versus general effects. *Behaviour Genetics, 33*(2), 83–93.

McGuffin, P., Katz, R., Watkins, S. & Rutherford, J. (1996). A hospital-based twin register of the heritability of DSM-IV unipolar depression. *Archives of General Psychiatry, 53*(2), 129–36.

McGuigan, F. J. (1966). Covert oral behavior and auditory hallucinations. *Psychophysiology, 3,* 73–80.

McInnis, M. & Potash, J. (2004). Psychiatric genetics: Into the 21st century. *International Review of Psychiatry, 16,* 301–10.

McIntosh, K., Jordan, V. W., Carter, J., Luty, F. A., McKenzie, S. E., Bulik, J. M. et al. (2005). Three psychotherapies for anorexia nervosa: A randomized, controlled trial. *American Journal of Psychiatry, 62,* 741–7.

McKay, R., Langdon, R. & Coltheart, M. (2007). The defensive function of persecutory delusions: An investigation using the implicit association test. *Cognitive Neuropsychiatry, 12,* 1–24.

McKie, R. (2001, 11 February 2001). Revealed: The Secret of Human Behaviour. The Observer.

Mclaren, N. (1998). A critical review of the biopsychosocial model. *Australian and New Zealand Journal of Psychiatry*, 32(1), 86–92.

McLean, A. (1995). Empowerment and the psychiatric consumer/ex-patient movement in the United States: Contradictions, crisis and change. *Social Science & Medicine*, 40, 1053–71.

Mcleish, A. & Del Ben, K. (2008). Symptoms of depression and post-traumatic stress disorder in an outpatient population before and after Hurricane Katrina. *Depression and Anxiety*, 25, 416–21.

McLeod, J. (1994). *Doing Counselling Research*. London: Sage.

McLeod, J. (2003). *An Introduction to Counselling* (3rd edn). Maidenhead: Open University Press.

McNally, R. (1995). Preparedness, phobias and the Panglossian paradigm. *Behavioral and Brain Sciences*, 18, 303–4.

McNally, R. (2009). Can we fix PTSD in DSM V? *Depression and Anxiety*, 26, 597–600.

McVey, G., Tweed, S. & Blackmore, E. (2004). Dieting among preadolescent and young adolescent females. *Canadian Medical Association Journal*, 170, 1559–61.

Mead, M. (1928). *Coming of Age in Samoa*. New York: William Morrow.

Meddings, S., Walley, L., Collins, T., Tullett, F. & McGowan, B. (2006). The voices don't like it. *Mental Health Today*, September, 26–30.

Medical Research Council (1965). Clinical trial of the treatment of depressive illness. *British Medical Journal*, 3(1), 881–6 (April).

Mehta, S. & Farina, A. (1997). Is being sick really better? Effect of the disease view of mental disorder on stigma. *Journal of Social and Clinical Psychology*, 16, 405–19.

Melander, H., Ahlqvist-Rastad, J., Meijer, G. & Beermann, B. (2003). Evidence b(i)ased medicine – selective reporting from studies sponsored by pharmaceutical industry: Review of studies in new drug applications. *British Medical Journal*, 326, 1171–3.

Melechi, A. (2003). *Fugitive Minds*. London: Arrow (Random House).

Mellsop, G., Varghese, F., Joshua, S. & Hicks, A. (1982). The reliability of axis II of DSM-III. *American Journal of Psychiatry*, 139, 1360–1.

Meltzer, H., Gatward, R., Goodman, R. & Ford, T. (2000). *Mental Health of Children and Adolescents in Great Britain*. London: HMSO.

Meltzer, H., Gill, B., Petticrew, M. & Hinds, K. (1995a). *OPCS Surveys of Psychiatric Morbidity in Great Britain, Report 1: The Prevalence of Psychiatric Morbidity among Adults Living in Private Households*. London: HMSO.

Meltzer, H., Gill, B., Petticrew, M. & Hinds, K. (1995b). *OPCS Surveys of Psychiatric Morbidity in Great Britain, Report 2: Physical Complaints, Service Use and Treatment of Adults with Psychiatric Disorders*. London: HMSO.

Meltzer, H., Gill, B., Petticrew, M. & Hinds, K. (1995c). *OPCS Surveys of Psychiatric Morbidity in Great Britain, Report 3: Economic Activity and Social Functioning of Adults with Psychiatric Disorders*. London: HMSO.

Meltzer, H., Gill, B., Petticrew, M. & Hinds, K. (1995d). *OPCS Surveys of Psychiatric Morbidity in Great Britain, Bulletin No.2: The Prevalence of Psychiatric Morbidity among Adults Living in Institutions*. OPCS: London.

Melzer, D., Fryers, T. & Jenkins, R. (2004). *Social Inequalities and the Distribution of the Common Mental Disorders*. Hove: Psychology Press.

Mental Health Act Commission (2009). Coercion and consent: Monitoring the Mental Health Act 2007–2009. The Mental Health Act Commission Thirteenth Biennial Report 2007–2009. London. Accessed at www.cqc.org.uk/_db/_documents/MHAC_Biennial_Report_0709_final.pdf on 2/12/2011.

Mental Health Foundation (2000). *Pull Yourself Together! A Survey of People's Experiences of Stigma and Discrimination as a Result of Mental Distress*. London: Author.

Mental Health Foundation (2006). *Truth Hurts: Report of the National Inquiry into Self-Harm among Young People*. London: Camelot Foundation.

Metalsky, G., Joiner, T., Hardin, T. & Abrahamson, L. (1993). Depressive reactions to failure in a naturalistic setting: A test of the hopelessness and self-esteem theories of depression. *Journal of Abnormal Psychology*, 102, 101–9.

Meyer, J. H., Houle, S., Sagrati, S., Carella, A., Hussey, D. F., Ginovart, N. et al. (2004). Brain serotonin transporter binding potential measured with carbon11–labeled DASB positron emission tomography: Effects of major depressive episodes and severity of dysfunctional attitudes. *Archives of General Psychiatry*, 61(12), 1271–9.

Meyer, S., Chrousos, G. & Gold, P. (2001). Major depression and the stress system: A life span perspective. *Developmental Psychopathology*, 13, 565–80.

Meyer-Bahlburg, H. F., Nostlinger, C., Exner, T. M., Ehrhardt, A. A., Gruen, R. S., Lorenz, G. et al. (1993). Sexual functioning in HIV+ and HIV- injected drug-using women. *Journal of Sex and Marital Therapy*,19, 56–68.

Middleton, D. & Brown, S. D. (2005). *The Social Psychology of Experience: Studies in Remembering and Forgetting*. London: Sage Publications.

Midlands Psychology Group (2010). Welcome to NICEworld. *Clinical Psychology Forum*, 212, 52–56.

Mihalopoulos, C., Harris, M., Henry, L., Harrigan, S. & McGorry, P. (2009). Is early intervention in psychosis cost-effective over the long term? *Schizophrenia Bulletin*, 35(5), 909–18.

Mikton, C. & Grounds, A. (2007). Cross-cultural clinical judgment bias in personality disorder diagnosis by forensic psychiatrists in the UK: A case-vignette study. *Journal of Personality Disorders*, 4, 400–17.

Milgram, S. (1963). Behavioral study of obedience. *Journal of Abnormal & Social Psychology*, 67, 371–8.

Miller, J. & Mclleland, L. (2006). Social inequalities formulation: Mad, bad and dangerous to know. In L. Johnstone & R. Dallos (Eds), *Formulation in Psychology and Psychotherapy: Making Sense of People's Problems*. London: Routledge.

Miller, L. J. (1997). Sexuality, reproduction, and family planning in women with schizophrenia. *Schizophrenia Bulletin*, 23, 623–35.

Miller, M. N. & Pumariega, A. J. (2001). Culture and eating disorders: A historical and cross-cultural review. Psychiatry: *Interpersonal and Biological Processes*, 64, 93–110.

Miller, S. D., Hubble, M. & Duncan, B. (2008). Supershrinks: What is the secret of their success? *Psychotherapy in Australia*, 14(4), 14–22.

Miller, P. & Rose, N. (1988). The Tavistock programme: The government of subjectivity and social life. *Sociology*, 22, 171–92.

Miller, S. G. (1994). Borderline personality disorder from the patient's perspective. *Psychiatric Services*, 45, 1215–19.

Millner, V. S. (2005). Female sexual arousal disorder and counselling deliberations. *The Family Journal: Counselling and Therapy for Couples and Families*, 13(1), 95–100.

Milos, G., Spindler, A., Schnyder, U. & Fairburn, C. G. (2005). Instability of eating disorder diagnoses: Prospective study. *The British Journal of Psychiatry*, 187, 573–8.

Milton, M. (2000). Is existential psychotherapy a lesbian and gay affirmative psychotherapy? *Journal of the Society for Existential Analysis*, 11(1), 86–102.

Mind (2000). *Counting the Cost*. London: Author.

Mind (2004). *Not Alone? Isolation and Mental Distress*. London: Author

Mind (2009). Statistics 6: The Social Context of Mental Distress. www.mind.org.uk/Information/Factsheets.Statistics/Statistics+6.htm

Minuchin, S., Rosman, B. L. & Baker, L. (1978). *Psychosomatic Families*. Cambridge MA: Harvard University Press.

Mirowsky, J. (1990). Subjective boundaries and combinations in psychiatric diagnosis. *The Journal of Mind and Behaviour*, 11(3 and 4), 407–24. Accessed at: www.brown.uk.com/brownlibrary/MIROWSKY.htm on 22 December 2011.

Mirowsky, J. & Ross, C. E. (1983). Paranoia and the structure of powerlessness. *American Sociological Review*, 48, 228–39.

Mirowsky, J. & Ross, C. E. (1989). *Social Causes of Psychological Distress*. New York: Aldine de Gruyter.

Mirowsky, J. & Ross, C. E. (2003). *Social Causes of Psychological Distress* (2nd edn). New York: Aldine de Gruyter.

Mischel, W. (1968). *Personality and Assessment*. New York: Wiley.

Mischel, W. (2009). From Personality and Assessment (1968) to personality science. *Journal of Research in Personality*, 43, 282–90.

Mitchell, J. E., Hatsukami, D., Eckert, E. D. & Pyle, R. L. (1985). Characteristics of 275 patients with bulimia. *American Journal of Psychiatry*, 142, 482–5.

Mitchell, K. (2006). Medicalising female sexual experience: The case of female orgasmic disorder. Presentation at the 2nd European Female Sexual Dysfunction Conference 'The Picture in 2006', London, 21 September 2006.

Mitchell, S. (2010). Depression and recovery. *Journal of Mental Health*, 19(4), 369–372.

Modestin, J. (1992). Multiple personality disorder in Switzerland. *American Journal of Psychiatry*, 149, 88–92.

Moffit, T., Caspi, A., Harrington, H., Milne, B., Melchior, M., Goldberg, D. et al. (2007). Generalized anxiety disorder and depression: Childhood risk factors in a birth cohort followed to age 32. *Psychological Medicine*, 37(3), 441–52.

Moffitt,T. E., Caspi, A., Taylor, A., Kokaua, J., Milne, B. J., Polanczyk, G. et al. (2010). How common are common mental disorders? Evidence that lifetime prevalence rates are doubled by prospective versus retrospective ascertainment. *Psychological Medicine*, 40(6), 899–909.

Mogg, K., Bradley, B., Williams, R. & Matthews, A. (1993). Subliminal processing of emotional information in anxiety and depression. *Journal of Abnormal Psychology*, 102(2), 695–704.

Mojtabai, R. & Nicholson, R. A. (1995). Interrater reliability of ratings of delusions and bizarre delusions. *American Journal of Psychiatry*, 152, 1804–06.

Monbiot, G. (2011). The 1% are the very best destroyers of wealth the world has ever seen. The Guardian, 7 November. Accessed at www.guardian.co.uk/commentisfree/2011/nov/07/one-per-cent-wealth-destroyers on 30 December 2011.

Moncrieff, J. (2006). Does antipsychotic withdrawal provoke psychosis? Review of the literature on rapid onset psychosis (supersensitivity psychosis) and withdrawal-related relapse. *Acta Psychiatrica Scandinavica*, 114, 3–13.

Moncrieff, J. (2007). Co-opting psychiatry: The alliance between academic psychiatry and the pharmaceutical industry. *Epidemiologia e Psichiatria Sociale*, 16(3), 192–6.

Moncrieff, J. (2008). *The Myth of the Chemical Cure: A Critique of Psychiatric Drug Treatment*. London: Palgrave.

Moncrieff, J. (2009a). *A Straight-Talking Guide to Psychiatric Drugs*. Ross-on-Wye: PCCS Books.

Moncrieff, J. (2009b). A critique of the dopamine hypothesis of schizophrenia and psychosis. *Harvard Review of Psychiatry*,17, 214–25.

Moncrieff, J. & Cohen, D. (2006). Do antidepressants cure or create abnormal brain states? *PLoS Medicine*, 3, E240.

Moncrieff, J., Cohen, D. & Mason, J. P. (2009). The subjective experience of taking antipsychotic medication: A content analysis of internet data. *Acta Psychiatrica Scandinavica*, 120, 102–11.

Moncrieff, J. & Kirsch, I. (2005). Efficacy of antidepressants in adults. *British Medical Journal*, 331, 155–7.

Moncrieff, J. & Leo, J. (2010). A systematic review of the effects of antipsychotic drugs on brain volume. *Psychological Medicine*, 1–14.

Moncrieff, J., Wessely, S. & Hardy, R. (1998). Meta-analysis of trials comparing antidepressants with active placebos. *British Journal of Psychiatry*, 172, 227–31.

Monga, M., Alexandrescu, B., Katz, S., Stein, M & Ganiats, T. (2002). Impact of infertility on quality of life, marital adjustment, and sexual function. *Urology*, 63, 126–30.

Montague, P. R., Dayan, P. & Sejnowski, T. J. (1996). A framework for mesencephalic dopamine systems based on predictive Hebbian learning. *Journal of Neuroscience*, 16, 1936–47.

Moore, S., Zammit, T., Lingford-Hughes, T., Barnes, P., Jones, M. & Burke, G. (2007). Cannabis use and risk of psychotic or affective mental health outcomes: A systematic review. *Lancet*, 370(9584), 319–28.

Morey, L. C., Gunderson, J., Quigley, B. D. & Lyons, M. (2000). Dimensions and categories: The 'Big Five' factors and the DSM personality disorders. *Assessment*, 7, 203–16.

Morgan, C. & Curran, V. (2008). Effects of cannabidiol on schizophrenia-like symptoms in people who use cannabis. *British Journal of Psychiatry*, 192, 320.

Morgan, C. & Fisher, H. (2007). Enviroment and schizophrenia: environmental factors in schizophrenia: Childhood trauma – a critical review. *Schizophrenia Bulletin*, 33, 3–10.

Morgan, C., Fisher, H., Hutchinson, G., Kirkbride, J., Craig, T., Morgan, K. et al. (2009). Ethnicity, social disadvantage and psychotic-like experiences in a healthy population based sample. *Acta Psychiatrica Scandinavica*, 119(3), 226–35.

Morgan, C., Kirkbride, J., Leff, J., Craig, T., Hutchinson, G., McKenzie, K. et al. (2007). Parental separation, loss and psychosis in different ethnic groups: A case-control study. *Psychological Medicine*, 37(4), 495–503.

Moritz, S., Werner, R. & von Collani, G. (2006). The inferiority complex in paranoia readdressed: A study with the implicit association test. *Cognitive Neuropsychiatry*, 11, 402–15.

Moritz, S. & Woodward, T. S. (2005). Jumping to conclusions in delusional and nondelusional schizophrenic patients. *British Journal of Clinical Psychology*, 44, 193–207.

Morland, R. (2003). How do people experience being part of a hearing voices group? *Voices Magazine*, Summer, 10–12.

Morrall, P. (2008). *The Trouble with Therapy: Sociology and Psychotherapy*. Maidenhead: Open University Press.

Morris, M. W., Leung, K., Ames, D. & Lickel, B. (1999). Views from inside and outside: Integrating emic and etic insights about culture and justice judgment. *The Academy of Management Review*, 24, 731–6.

Morrison, A. P. (2004). *Cognitive Therapy for Psychosis: A Formulation-Based Approach*. Hove: Brunner-Routledge.

Morrison, A. P. (2009). Cognitve behaviour therapy for first episode psychosis: Good for nothing or fit for purpose? *Psychosis: Psychological, Social and Integrative Approaches*, 1(2), 103–12.

Morrison, A. P., Byrne, R. & Bentall, R. (2010). DSM-5 and the 'psychosis risk syndrome': Whose best interests would it serve? *Psychosis: Psychological, Social and Integrative Approaches*, 2(2), 96–9.

Morrison, A. P., French, P., Walford, L., Lewis, S. W., Kilcommons, A., Green, J. et al. (2004). Cognitive therapy for the prevention of psychosis in people at ultra-high risk Randomised controlled trial. *British Journal of Psychiatry*, 185, 291–7.

Morrison, A. P. & Haddock, G. (1997). Cognitive factors in source monitoring and auditory hallucinations. *Psychological Medicine*, 27, 669–79.

Morrison, A. P., Hutton, P., Wardle, M., Spencer, H., Barratt, S., Brabban, A. et al. (2012). Cognitive therapy for people with a schizophrenia spectrum diagnosis not taking antipsychotic medication: An exploratory trial. *Psychological Medicine*, 42, 1049–56.

Mortensen, P., Pedersen, C., Westergaard, T., Wohlfahrt, J., Ewald, H., Mors, O. et al. (1999). Effects of family history and place and season of birth on the risk of schizophrenia. *New England Journal of Medicine*, 340, 603–8.

Moser, C. & Kleinplatz, P. J. (2005). DSM-IV-TR and the paraphilias: An argument for removal. *Journal of Psychology and Human Sexuality*, 17(3/4), 91–109.

Mosher, L. (1998). Letter of resignation from the American Psychiatric Association. www.moshersoteria.com/resig.htm.

Mosher, L. (2004). Non-hospital, non-drug intervention with first episode psychosis. In J. Read, L. Mosher & R. Bentall (Eds), *Models of Madness: Psychological, Social and Biological Approaches to Schizophrenia* (349–64). London: Routledge.

Mosher, L., Gosden, R. & Beder, S. (2013). Drug companies and schizophrenia: Unbridled capitalism meets madness. In J. Read & J. Dillon (Eds), *Models of Madness: Psychological, Social and Biological Approaches to Psychosis* (2nd edition). London: Routledge.

Mosher, L., Hendrix, V. & Fort, D. (2005). *Soteria: Through Madness to Deliverance*. Philadelphia PA: Xlibris.

Moskowitz, A., Read, J., Rudegeair, T., Farrely, S. & Williams, O. (2009). Are psychotic symptoms traumatic in origin and dissociative in kind? In P. Dell & J. O'Neill (Eds), *Dissociation and the Dissociative Disorders: DSM-V and Beyond* (322–51). New York: Routledge.

Moskowitz, A., Schafer , I. & Dorahy, M. J. (Eds) (2008). *Psychosis, Trauma and Dissociation: Emerging Perspectives on Severe Psychopathology*. Chichester: John Wiley and Sons.

Moutoussis, M., Williams, J., Dayan, P. & Bentall, R. P. (2007). Persecutory delusions and the conditioned avoidance paradigm: Towards an integration of the psychology and biology of paranoia. *Cognitive Neuropsychiatry*, 12, 495–510.

MTA Cooperative Group (1999). A 14-Month randomized clinical trial of treatment strategies for attention-deficit/hyperactivity disorder. The MTA cooperative group: Multimodal treatment study of children with ADHD. *Archives of General Psychiatry*, 56, 1073–86.

Mueller, T., Leon, A., Keller, M., Solomon, D., Endicott, J., Coryell, W. et al. (1999). Recurrence after recovery from major depressive disorder during 15 years of observational follow-up. *American Journal of Psychiatry*, 156, 1000–6.

Muenzenmaier, K., Castille, D. & Shelley, A. (2005). Comorbid PTSD and schizophrenia. *Psychiatr Annals*, 35, 51–6.

Mukherjee, R., Fialho, A., Wijetunge, A., Checinski, K. & Surgenor, T. (2002). The stigmatisation of psychiatric illness the attitudes of medical students and doctors in a London teaching hospital. *Psychiatric Bulletin*, 26, 178-81.

Mullen, P. E. (1997). A reassessment of the link between mental disorder and violent behaviour, and its implications for clinical practice. *Australian and New Zealand Journal of Psychiatry*, 31(1), 3–11.

Mullins-Sweatt, S. N., Glover, N. G., Derefinko, K. J., Miller, J. D. & Widiger, T. A. (2010). The search for the successful psychopath. *Journal of Research in Personality*, 44, 554–8.

Munro, R. (2002). *Dangerous Minds: Political Psychiatry in China Today and Its Origins in the Mao Era*. New York: Human Rights Watch.

Murad, M. H., Elamin, M. B., Garcia, M. Z., Mullan, R. J., Murad, A., Erwin, P. J. et al. (2010). Hormonal therapy and sex reassignment: A systematic review and meta-analysis of quality of life and psychosocial outcomes. *Clinical Endocrinology*, 72(2), 214–31.

Murnen, S. & Smolak, L. (1997). Femininity, masculinity, and disordered eating: A meta-analytic review. *International Journal of Eating Disorders*, 22, 231–42.

Murphy, R. (1995). Sociology as if nature did not matter: An ecological critique. *British Journal of Sociology*, 46(4), 688–707.

Murphy, J., Horton, N., Laird, N., Monson, R., Sobol, A. & Leighton, A. (2004). Anxiety and depression: A 40-year perspective on relationships regarding prevalence, distribution, and comorbidity. *Acta Psychiatrica Scandinavica*, 109(5), 355–75.

Murphy, J., Shevlin, M., Adamson, G. & Houston, J. (2011). Positive psychosis symptom structure in the general population: Assessing dimensional consistency and continuity from 'pathology' to 'normality'. *Psychosis: Psychological, Social and Biological Approaches*, 2, 199–209.

Murray, R. (1994). The Independent, 13 September 1994.

Murray, R., Grech, A., Phillips, P. & Johnson, S. (2003). What is the relationship between substance abuse and schizophrenia? In R. Murray, P. Jones, E. Susser & J. Van Os (Eds), *The Epidemiology of Schizophrenia* (317–42). Cambridge: Cambridge University Press.

Myers, H. (1993). Biopsychosocial perspectives on depression in African Americans. In K. Lin, R. Poland & G. Nakasaki (Eds), *Psychopharmacology and Psychobiology of Ethnicity* (201–22). Washington DC: American Psychiatric Press.

Myers, I. B. & Myers, P. B. (1995). *Gifts Differing: Understanding Personality Type* (2nd revised edn). Mountain View CA: Davies-Black Publishing.

Myhrman, A., Rantakallio, P., Isohanni, M. & Jones, P. (1996). Unwantedness of preganacy and schizophrenia in the child. *British Journal of Psychiatry*, 169, 637–40.

Nasser, M. (1997). The EAT speaks many languages: Review of the use of the EAT in eating disorders research. *Eating & Weight Disorders*, 2, 174–81.

Nasser, M., Katzman, M. A. & Gordon, R. A. (2001). *Eating Disorders and Cultures in Transition*. London: Brunner-Routledge.

Nathan, P. E. & Langenbucher, J. W. (1999). Psychopathology: Description and classification. *Annual Review of Psychology*, 50, 79–107.

National Collaborating Centre for Mental Health (2009). Borderline Personality Disorder: The NICE Guideline on Treatment and Management. National Clinical Practice Guideline Number 78. Leicester & London: British Psychological Society and Royal College of Psychiatrists.

National Collaborating Centre for Mental Health (2010). Antisocial Personality Disorder: A NICE Guideline for Treatment, Management and Prevention. National Clinical Practice Guideline Number 77. Leicester & London: British Psychological Society and Royal College of Psychiatrists.

National Confidential Inquiry into Suicide and Homicide by People with Mental Illness (NCISH) (2009). Annual Report: England and Wales. London: National Patient Safety Agency. Accessed at www.medicine.manchester.ac.uk/psychiatry/research/suicide/prevention/nci/ on 2 December 2011.

National Institute for Health & Clinical Excellence (NICE) (2002). Schizophrenia: Core Interventions in the Treatment and Management of Schizophrenia in Primary and Secondary Care. London: Author.

National Institute for Health & Clinical Excellence (NICE) (2003). Technology Appraisal 59: Guidance on the Use of Electroconvulsive Therapy. London: Author.

National Institute for Health & Clinical Excellence (NICE) (2004a). Depression: Management of Depression in Primary and Secondary Care. Clinical Practice Guideline Number 23. London: Author.

National Institute for Health & Clinical Excellence (NICE) (2004b). Anxiety: Management of Anxiety (Panic Disorder, with or without Agoraphobia, and Generalised Anxiety Disorder) in Adults in Primary, Secondary and Community Care. London: Author.

National Institute for Health & Clinical Excellence (NICE) (2005). Depression in Children and Young People. London: Author.

National Institute for Health & Clinical Excellence (NICE) (2006). Attention Deficit Hyperactivity Disorder (ADHD): Stakeholder Consultation Table. London: Author. Accessed at www.nice.org.uk/nicemedia/live/11632/34228/34228.pdf on 11 May 2011.

National Institute for Health & Clinical Excellence (NICE) (2007a). Depression: Management of Depression in Primary and Secondary Care (Clinical Guideline 23 (amended)). London: Author.

National Institute for Health & Clinical Excellence (NICE) (2007b). Anxiety: Management of Anxiety (Panic Disorder, with or without Agorophobia, and Generalised Anxiety Disorder) in Adults in Primary, Secondary and Community Care. London: Author.

National Institute for Health & Clinical Excellence (NICE) (2009a). Clinical Guideline 90: Depression: The Treatment and Management of Depression in Adults. London: Author.

National Institute for Health & Clinical Excellence (NICE) (2009b). Schizophrenia: Core Interventions in the Treatment and Management of Schizophrenia in Primary and Secondary Care (update). London: Author.

National Institute for Health & Clinical Excellence (NICE) (2009b). Depression: Treatment and Management of Depression in Adults, Including Adults with a Chronic Physical Health Problem. London: Author.

National Institute for Mental Health in England (2003). Personality Disorder: No Longer a Diagnosis of Exclusion. London: Department of Health.

Neale, J. M. & Oltmanns, T. F. (1980). *Schizophrenia*. Chichester: Wiley.

Nehls, N. (1999). Borderline personality disorder: The voice of patients. *Research in Nursing & Health*, 22, 285–93.

Neighbors, H. W., Trierweiler, S. J., Ford, B. C. & Muroff, J. R. (2003). Racial differences in dsm diagnosis using a semi-structured instrument: The importance of clinical judgment in the diagnosis of African Americans. *Journal of Health and Social Behavior*, 44(3), 237–56.

Nelson, G. & Prilleltensky, I. (Eds) (2010). *Community Psychology: In Pursuit of Liberation and Well-being* (2nd edn). Basingstoke: Palgrave MacMillan.

Nelson, G., Prilleltensky, I. & Macgillivary, H. (2001). Building value-based partnerships: toward solidarity with oppressed groups. *American Journal of Community Psychology*, 29, 649–77.

Nemeroff, C. B., Bremner, J. D., Foa, E. B., Mayberg, H. S., North, C. S. & Stein, M. B. (2006). Posttraumatic stress disorder: A state-of-the-science review. *Journal of Psychiatric Research*, 40, 1–21.

Neumark-Sztainer, D., Wall, M., Guo, J., Story, K., Haines, J. & M. Eisenberg, M. (2006). Disordered eating, and eating disorders in a longitudinal study of adolescents: How do dieters fare 5 years later? *Journal of the American Dietetic Association*, 106, 559–68.

New Jerusalem Bible (1985). London: Darton, Longman & Todd.

Newbiggin, K. (2005). Making a real difference. *Mental Health Today*. September, 27–30.

Newham IAPT (2007). Newham Improved Access to Psychological Therapies (IAPT): The First Year, Draft 3, Mental Health Matters; NHS Newham Primary Care Trust: London Borough of Newham, 21 September.

Newhill, C. E. (1990). The role of culture in the development of paranoid symptomatology. *American Journal of Orthopsychiatry*, 60, 176–85.

Newnes, C., Holmes, G. & Dunn, C. (1999). *This is Madness: A Critical Look at Psychiatry and the Future of Mental Health Services*. Ross-on-Wye: PCCS Books.

Newnes, C., Holmes, G. & Dunn, C. (2001). *This is Madness Too: Critical Perspectives on Mental Health Services*. Ross-on-Wye: PCCS Books.

Newnes, C. & Radcliffe, N. (2005). *Making and Breaking Children's Lives*. Ross-On-Wye: PCCS Books.

Newton, T. (2002). Truly embodied sociology: marrying the social and the biological. *The Sociological Review*, 51(1), 20–42.

Newton, T. (2007). *Nature and Sociology*. London: Routledge.

Newton, E., Larkin, M., Melhuish, R. & Wykes, T. (2007). More than just a place to talk: Young people's experiences of group psychological therapy as an early intervention. *Psychology and Psychotherapy: Theory, Research and Practice*, 80, 127–49.

Neylan, T. C., Canick, J. D., Hall, S. E., Reus, V. I., Sapolsky, R. M. & Wolkowitz, O. M. (2001). Cortisol levels predict cognitive impairment induced by electroconvulsive therapy. *Biological Psychiatry*, 50, 331–6.

Ng, B. (2000). Phenomenology of trance states seen at a psychiatric hospital in Singapore: A cross cultural perspective. *Transcultural Psychiatry*, 35, 560–79.

NHS Confederation (2008). *Implementing National Policy on Violence and Abuse*. London: Author.

NHS Information Centre (2011). In-patients formally detained in hospitals under the Mental Health Act, 1983 – and patients subject to supervised community treatment, Annual figures, England 2010/11. October 2011. London: Health and Social Care Information Centre.

Nichols, H. R. and Molinder, I. (1984). *The Multiphasic Sex Inventory Manual*. Tacoma: Nichols and Molinder Assessments.

Nicholls, L. (2005). Constructing female sexuality: How heterosexual women's accounts of sex and sexual difficulties correspond with contemporary classification systems for female sexual problems. Unpublished Doctoral thesis, University of East London.

Nicholls, L. (2008). Putting the new view classification scheme to an empirical test. *Feminism & Psychology*, 18, 515–26.

Nicolsi, A., Laumann, E. O., Moreira, E. D., Palik, A. & Gingell, C. (2004). Sexual behavior and sexual dysfunctions after age 40: The global study of sexual attitudes and behaviors. *Urology*, 65, 991–7.

Nicolson, P. & Burr, V. (2003). What is 'normal' about women's (hetero) sexual desire and orgasm? A report of an in-depth interview study. *Social Science and Medicine*, 57, 1735–45.

Nightingale, D. J. & Cromby, J. (2001). Critical psychology and the ideology of individualism. *Journal of Critical Psychology. Counselling and Psychotherapy*, 1(2), 117–28.

Nissen, S. E. (2006). ADHD drugs and cardiovascular risk. *New England Journal of Medicine*, 354, 1445–8.

Nobre, P. J. & Pinto-Gouveia, J. (2006). Emotions during sexual activity: Differences between sexually functional and dysfunctional men and women. *Archives of Sexual Behavior*, 35, 491–9.

Nolen-Hoeksema, S. (1990). *Sex Differences in Depression*. Stanford CA: Stanford University Press.

Nolen-Hoeksema, S. & Morrow, J. (1991). A prospective study of depression and posttraumatic stress symptoms after a natural disaster: The 1989 Loma Prieta Earthquake. *Journal of Personality and Social Psychology*, 61(1), 115–21.

Nordahl, H. M. & Nysæter, T. E. (2005). Schema therapy for patients with borderline personality disorder: A single case series. *Journal of Behavior Therapy and Experimental Psychiatry*, 36, 254–64.

NSPCC (2006). Tackle child abuse to create safer communities says NSPCC. Accessed at www.nspcc.org.uk/WhatWeDo/MediaCentre/PressReleases/05_Sep_Tackle_Child_Abuse_to_Create_Safer_Communities_Says_NSPCC_wda38464.html on 13 November 2006.

Nuckolls, C. W. (1992). Toward a cultural history of the personality disorders. *Social Science & Medicine*, 35, 37–47.

Nuechterlein, K. H. & Dawson, M. E. (1984). A heuristic vulnerability/stress model of schizophrenic episodes. *Schizophrenia Bulletin*, 10, 300–12.

Oaks, D. (2006). Letters: The evolution of the consumer movement. *Psychiatric Services*, 57, 8.

Oakley-Browne, M., Joyce, P., Wells, J., Bushnell, J. & Hornblow, A. (1995). Adverse parenting and other childhood experience as risk factors for depression in women aged 18–44 years. *Journal of Affective Disorders*, 34(1), 13–23.

Obeyesekere, G. (1985). Depression, Buddhism and the work of culture in Sri Lanka. In A. Kleinman & B. Good (Eds), *Culture and Depression: Studies in Anthropology and Cross-Cultural Psychiatry of Affect and Disorder* (134–52). Berkeley, CA: University of California Press.

O'Connor, T. & Rutter, M. (2000). Attachment disorder behavior following early severe deprivation: Extension and longitudinal follow-up. English and Romanian Adoptees Study Team. *Journal of the American Academy of Child and Adolescent Psychiatry*, 39(6), 703–12.

Oei, T., Llamas, M. & Devilly, G. (1999). The efficacy and cognitive processes of cognitive-behaviour therapy in the treatment of panic disorder with agorophobia. *Behavioural and Cognitive Psychotherapy*, 27(1), 63–88.

Oetomo, D. (2000). Masculinity in Indonesia: Genders, sexuality, and identities in a changing society. In R. Parker, R. M. Barbosa & P. Aggleton (Eds), *Framing The Sexual Subject: The Politics of Gender, Sexuality, and Power* (46–59). Berkeley: University of California Press.

Office for National Statistics (2009). Annual Survey of Hours and Earnings 2009 – Statistical Bulletin 78/2009. Accessed at wales.gov.uk/topics/statistics/headlines/econ2009/hdw200911125/?lang=en on 10/2/2010.

Office for National Statistics (2010a). Social Trends No. 40 – 2010 edition. London: Author.

Office for National Statistics (2010b). Attitudes to mental illness 2010. London: Author.

Ofori-Atta, L. & Linden, W. (1995). The effect of social change on causal beliefs of mental disorders and treatment preferences in Ghana. *Social Science & Medicine*, 40, 1231–42.

Ogden, J. (1997). The rhetoric and reality of psychosocial theories: A challenge to biomedicine. *Journal of Health Psychology*, 2, 21–9.

Ogden, J. (2009). *The Psychology of Eating: From Healthy to Disordered Behaviour* (2nd edn). Oxford: Wiley-Blackwell.

Ogden, J. & Steward, J. (2000). The role of the mother-daughter relationship in explaining weight concern. *International Journal of Eating Disorders*, 23, 78–83.

Ohman, A. & Minecka, S. (2001). Fears, phobias and preparedness: Phobic versus neutral pictures as conditioned stimuli for human autonomic responses. *Journal of Abnormal Psychology*, 84(1), 41–5.

Oliver, M. I., Pearson, N., Coe, N. & Gunnell, D. (2005). Help-seeking behaviour in men and women with common mental health problems: Cross-sectional study. *British Journal of Psychiatry*, 186, 297–301.

Orford, J. (2008). *Community Psychology: Challenges, Controversies and Emerging Consensuses*. Chichester: Wiley.

Oruc, L. & Bell, P. (1995). Multiple rape trauma followed by delusional parasitosis. *Schizophrenia Research*, 16, 173–4.

Osatuke, K., Humphreys, C. L., Glick, M. J., Graff-Reed, R. L., Mack, L. M. & Stiles, W. B. (2005). Vocal manifestations in internal multiplicity: Mary's voices. *Psychology & Psychotherapy: Theory, Research and Practice*, 78, 21–44.

Ost, L., Alm, T., Brandberg, M. & Breitholtz, E. (2001). One versus five sessions of exposure and five sessions of cognitve therapy in the treatment of claustrophobia. *Behaviour Research and Therapy*, 39(2), 167–83.

Oyewumi, L. K. & Kazarian, S. S. (1992). Abnormal eating attitudes among a group of Nigerian youths: II. Anorexic behaviour. *East African Medical Journal*, 69, 667–9.

Page, A., Morrell, S. & Taylor, R. (2002). Suicide and political regime in New South Wales and Australia during the 20th century. *Journal of Epidemiology and Community Health*, 56, 766–72.

Palace, E. M. (1995). Modification of dysfunctional patterns of sexual response through autonomic arousal and false physiological feedback. *Journal of Consulting and Clinical Psychology*, 63, 604–15.

Paley, G. & Lawton, D. (2001). Evidence-based practice: Accounting for the importance of the therapeutic relationship in UK national health service therapy provision. *Counselling and Psychotherapy Research*, 1(1), 12–17.

Paley, G. & Shapiro, D. A. (2002). Lessons from psychotherapy research for psychological interventions for people with schizophrenia. *Psychology & Psychotherapy: Theory, Research & Practice*, 75, 5–17.

Panksepp, J. (1998). *Affective Neuroscience*. Oxford: Oxford University Press.

Pantony, K. L. & Caplan, P. J. (1991). Delusional dominating personality disorder: A modest proposal for identifying some consequences of rigid masculine socialization. *Canadian Psychology*, 32, 120–35.

Paolucci, E., Genuis, M. & Violato, C. (2001). A meta-analysis of the published research on the effects of child sexual abuse. *Journal of Psychology*, 135(1), 17–36.

Paris, J. (1997). Antisocial and borderline personality disorders: Two separate diagnoses or two aspects of the same psychopathology? *Comprehensive Psychiatry*, 38, 237–42.

Paris, J. (1998). Personality disorders in sociocultural perspective. *Journal of Personality Disorders*, 12, 289–301.

Paris, J. (2000). Childhood precursors of borderline personality disorder. *Psychiatric Clinics of North America*, 23, 77–88.

Paris, J. (2009). The treatment of borderline personality disorder: Implications of research on diagnosis, etiology, and outcome. *Annual Review of Clinical Psychology*, 5, 277–90.

Parker, I. (1995). Michel Foucault, psychologist. *The Psychologist*, 8, 214–16.

Parker, I. (2007). *Revolution in Psychology: Alienation to Emancipation*. London: Pluto Press.

Parker, I., Georgaca, E., Harper, D. J., McLaughlin, T. & Stowell–Smith, M. (1995). *Deconstructing Psychopathology*. London: Sage.

Parry-Jones, W. L. (1972). *The Trade in Lunacy: A Study of Private Madhouses in England in the Eighteenth and Nineteenth Centuries*. London: Routledge & Kegan Paul.

Parsey, R. V., Oquendo, M. A., Ogden, R. T., Olvet, D. M., Simpson, N., Huang, Y.-y. et al. (2006). Altered Serotonin 1A binding in major depression: A [carbonyl-C-11]way100635 positron emission tomography study. *Biological Psychiatry*, 59(2), 106–13.

Parsons, T. (1951). Illness and the role of the physician: A sociological perspective. *American Journal of Orthopsychiatry*, 21, 452–60.

Paul, T., Schroeter, K., Dahme, B. & Nutzinger, D. O. (2002). Self-injurious behavior in women with eating disorders. *American Journal of Psychiatry*, 159, 408–11.

Paunonen, S. V. & Ashton, M. C. (2001). Big Five factors and facets and the prediction of behaviour. *Journal of Personality and Social Psychology*, 81, 524–39,

Pavlov, I. P. (1941). *Psychotherapy: Lectures on Conditioned Reflexes.* Volume Two: Conditioned Reflexes and Psychiatry (Trans. W. Horsley Gantt). London: Lawrence & Wishart.

Payne, J., Nadel, L., Britton, W. & Jacobs, W. (2004). The biopsychology of trauma and memory. In D. Reisberg & P. Hertel (Eds), *Memory and Emotion.* New York: Oxford University Press.

Payne, M. (2006). *Narrative Therapy* (2nd edn). London: Sage.

Pearson, T. & Manolio, T. (2008). How to interpret a genome-wide association study. *Journal of the American Medical Association*, 299, 1335–44.

Pembroke, L. R. (undated). Politicising Self-harm. Accessed at www.soteria.freeuk.com/pembroke-jul.htm on 11 May 2011.

Pembroke, L. R. (1995a). *Self Harm: Perspectives from Personal Experience.* London: Survivors Speak Out.

Pembroke, L. R. (1995b). National self-harm network. *Openmind*, 73, 13.

Pembroke, L. R. (2007). Harm-minimisation: Limiting the damage of self-injury. In H. Spandler & S. Warner (Eds), *Beyond Fear and Control: Working with Young People Who Self-harm.* Ross-on-Wye: PCCS books.

Perkins, R. (2001). What constitutes success? *British Journal of Psychiatry*, 179, 9–10.

Perkins, R. & Repper, J. (1998). *Dilemmas in Community Mental Health Practice: Choice or Control.* Abingdon: Radcliffe Medical Press.

Perkins, R. E. & Moodley, P. (1993). Perception of problems by psychiatric inpatients: Denial, race and service usage. *Social Psychiatry and Psychiatric Epidemiology*, 28, 189–201.

Perlis, R., Perlis, C., Be, M., Yelena Wu, B., Hwang, C., Joseph, M. et al. (2005). Industry sponsorship and financial conflict of interest in the reporting of clinical trials in psychiatry. *American Journal of Psychiatry*, 162(10), 1957–60.

Perrons, D. (2000). Care, paid work, and leisure: Rounding the triangle. *Feminist Economics*, 6(1), 105–14.

Perry, B., Pollard, R., Blakely, T., Baker, W. & Vigilante, D. (1995). Childhood trauma, the neurobiology of adaptation, and 'use dependent' development of the brain: How states become traits. *Infant Mental Health Journal*, 16, 271–91.

Perry, J. C. (1992). Problems and considerations in the valid assessment of personality disorders. *American Journal of Psychiatry*, 149, 1645–53.

Petersen, D. (1982). *A Mad People's History of Madness.* Pittsburgh PA: University of Pittsburgh Press.

Petrides, M. & Milner, B. (1982). Deficits on subject-ordered tasks after frontal and temporal lobe lesions in man. *Neuropsychologia*, 20, 249–62.

Pfeiffer, W. (1982). Culture-bound syndromes. In I. Al-Issa (Ed.), *Culture and Psychopathology*, 201–18. Baltimore MD: University Park Press.

Phillips, N., Hammen, C., Brennan, P., Najman, J. & Bor, W. (2005). Early adversity and the prospective prediction of depressive and anxiety disorders in adolescents. *Journal of Abnormal and Child Psychology*, 33(1), 13–24.

Philo, G. (1994). Media images and popular beliefs. *Psychiatric Bulletin*, 18, 173–4.

Philo, G. (Ed.) (1996). *Media and Mental Distress.* London: Longman.

Pickering, L., Simpson, J. & Bentall, R. (2008). Insecure attachment predicts proneness to paranoia but not hallucinations. *Personality and Individual Differences*, 44, 1212–14.

Pickersgill, M. (2009). NICE guidelines, clinical practice, and antisocial personality disorder: The ethical implications of ontological uncertainty. *Journal of Medical Ethics*, 35, 668–71.

Pickett, K. E. & Wilkinson, R. G. (2010). Inequality: An underacknowledged source of mental illness and distress. *British Journal of Psychiatry*, 197, 426–8.

Pierce, J. (1997). *Gender Trials: Emotional Lives in Contemporary Law Firms.* Berkeley CA: University of California Press.

Pike, K. M. (1998). Long-term course of anorexia nervosa: Response, relapse, remission and recovery. *Clinical Psychology Review*, 18, 447–75.

Pike, K. M., Dohm, F. A., Striegel-Moore, R. H., Wilfley, D. E. & Fairburn, C. G. (2001). A comparison of black and white women with binge eating disorder. *American Journal of Psychiatry*, 158, 1455–60.

Pike, K. M., Walsh, T. B., Vitousek, K., Wilson, T. G. & Bauer, J. (2003). Cognitive behavior therapy in the posthospitalization treatment of anorexia nervosa. *American Journal of Psychiatry*, 160, 2046–9.

Pilgrim, D. (1997). *Psychotherapy and Society.* London. Sage.

Pilgrim, D. (2001). Disordered personalities and disordered concepts. *Journal of Mental Health*, 10, 253–65.

Pilgrim, D. (2005). A case for psychologists becoming clinical supervisors. *Clinical Psychology Forum*, 155, 4–7.

Pilgrim, D. (Ed.) (2007). *Inside Ashworth: Professional Reflections of Institutional Life.* Abingdon: Radcliffe Medical Press.

Pilgrim, D. (2008). The eugenic legacy in psychology and psychiatry. *International Journal of Social Psychiatry*, 54, 272–84.

Pilgrim, D. (2009) *Key Concepts in Mental Health.* London: Sage.

Pilgrim, D. & Rogers, A. (2005). *A Sociology of Mental Health and Illness* (3rd edn). Maidenhead: Open University Press.

Pilgrim, P. & Rogers, A. (2002). *Mental Health and Inequality.* Basingstoke: Palgrave Macmillan.

Pilgrim, R. & Bentall, R. P. (1999). The medicalisation of misery: A critical realist analysis of the concept of depression. *Journal of Mental Health*, 8, 261–84.

Pilgrim, R. & Rogers, A. (2010). *A Sociology of Mental Health and Illness.* Buckingham: Open University Press.

Pilling, S., Bebbington, P., Kuipers, E., Garety, P., Geddes, J., Orbach, G. et al. (2002). Psychological treatments in schizophrenia: I. Meta-analysis of family intervention and cognitive behaviour therapy. *Psychological Medicine: A Journal of Research in Psychiatry and the Allied Sciences*, 32(5), 763–82.

Pineros, M., Rosselli, D. & Calderon, C. (1998). An epidemic of collective conversion and dissociation disorder in an indigenous group of Colombia: Its relation to cultural change. *Social Science and Medicine*, 46, 1425–8.

Pinfold, V. & Thornicroft, G. (2006). Influencing the public perception of mental illness. In M. Slade & S. Priebe (Eds), *Choosing Methods in Mental Health Research.* London: Routledge.

Pistrang, N., Barker, C. & Humphreys, K. (2008). Mutual help groups for mental health problems: A review of effectiveness studies. *American Journal of Community Psychology*, 42, 110–21.

Pithers, W. D., Kashima, K. M., Cumming, G. F., Beal, L. S. & Buell, M. M. (1988). Relapse prevention of sexual aggression. *Human Sexual Aggression: Current Perspectives*, 581, 244–60.

Pitt, L., Kilbride, M., Welford, M., Nothard, S. & Morrison, A. P. (2009). Impact of a diagnosis of psychosis: User-led qualitative study. *The Psychiatrist*, 33, 419–23.

Pivac, N., Kozaric-Kovacic, D. & Muck-Seler, D. (2004). Olanzapine versus fluphenazine in an open trial in patients with psychotic combat-related posttraumatic stress disorder. *Psychopharmacology*, 175, 451–6.

Playdon, Z. (2004). Intersecting oppressions: Ending discrimination against lesbians, gay men and trans people in the UK. In B. Brooks-Gordon, L. Gelsthorpe, M. Johnson & A. Bainham (for the Cambridge Socio-Legal Group) (Eds), *Sexuality Repositioned: Diversity and the Law* (131–52). Oxford: Hart.

Plumb, S. (2005). The social/trauma model: Mapping the mental health consequences of childhood sexual abuse and similar experiences. In J. Tew (Ed.), *Social Perspectives in Mental Health: Developing Social Models to Understand and Work with Mental Distress*. London: Jessica Kingsley.

Polivy, J. & Herman, P. (2002). Causes of eating disorders. *Annual Review of Psychology*, 53, 187–213.

Polusny, M. & Follette, V. (1995). Long-term correlates of child sexual abuse. *Theory and review of the empirical literature Applied and Preventive Psychology*, 4(3), 143–66.

Pope, H. G. & Hudson, J. I. (1992). Is childhood sexual abuse a risk factor for bulimia nervosa? *Psychosomatic Medicine*, 54, 59–69.

Porter, R. (1987a). *A Social History of Madness: Stories of the Insane*. London: Weidenfield.

Porter, R. (1987b). *Mind-forg'd Manacles*. London: Athlone.

Porter, R. (1996). Mental illness. In R. Porter (Ed.), *The Cambridge Illustrated History of Medicine*. Cambridge: Cambridge University Press.

Porter, R. (2002). *Madness: A Brief History*. Oxford: Oxford University Press.

Postle, D. (2007). *Regulating the Psychological Therapies: From Taxonomy to Taxidermy*. Ross-On-Wye: PCCS Books.

Potter, J. (1996). *Representing Reality: Discourse, Rhetoric and Social Construction*. London: Sage Publications.

Potts, A. (2000). 'The essence of the hard on': Hegemonic masculinity and the cultural construction of 'erectile dysfunction'. *Men and Masculinities*, 3(1), 85–103.

Potts, A. (2002). *The Science/fiction of Sex: Feminist Deconstruction and the Vocabularies of Heterosex*. London: Routledge.

Potts, A. (2005). Cyborg masculinity in the Viagra era. *Sexualities, Evolution & Gender*, 7, 3–16.

Poulton, R., Caspi, A., Moffitt, T. E., Cannon, M., Murray, R. & Harrington, H. (2000). Children's self-reported psychotic symptoms and adult schizophreniform disorder: A 15 year longitudinal study. *Archives of General Psychiatry*, 57, 1053–8.

Povey, D. (Ed.), Coleman, K., Kaiza, P. & Roe, S. (2009). Home Office Statistical Bulletin: Intimate Violence 2007/08 (Supplementary Volume 2 to Crime in England and Wales 2007/08) (3rd edn). London: Home Office. Accessed at www.homeoffice.gov.uk/rds/pdfs09/hosb0209.pdf on 29 December 2011.

Poynton, A., Bridges, P. & Bartlett, J. (1988). Resistant bipolar affective disorder treated by stereotactic subcaudate tractotomy. *British Journal of Psychiatry*, 152, 354–8.

Pratt, P., Tallis, F. & Eysenck, M. (1997). Information-processing, storage characteristics and worry. *Behaviour Research and Therapy*, 35(11), 1015–23.

Pretty, G., Bishop, B., Fisher, A. & Sonn, C. (2007). Psychological sense of community and its relevance to well-being and everyday life in Australia. *The Australian Community Psychologist*, 19, 6–25.

Price, J., Cole, V. & Goodwin, G. M. (2009). Emotional side-effects of selective serotonin reuptake inhibitors: Qualitative study. *British Journal of Psychiatry*, 195, 211–17.

Priest, P. (2006). That was then, this is now. *Clinical Psychology Forum*, 162, 25–8.

Priest, P. (2007). The healing balm effect: Using a walking group to feel better. *Journal of Health Psychology*, 12, 36–52.

Prilleltensky, I. & Nelson, G. (2002). Psychologists and the object of social change: Transforming social policy. Chapter 13 of I. Prilleltensky & G. Nelson, *Doing Psychology Critically: Making a Difference in Diverse Settings*. Basingstoke, Hampshire: Palgrave Macmillan.

Prochaska, J. O. & Norcross, J. C. (2010). *Systems of Psychotherapy: A Transtheoretical Analysis* (7th edn). Belmont, CA: Brooks/Cole, Cengage Learning.

Proctor, G. (2002). *The Dynamics of Power in Counselling and Psychotherapy: Ethics, Politics and Practice*. Ross-On-Wye: PCCS Books.

Proctor, G. (2007). Disordered boundaries? A critique of 'borderline personality disorder'. In H. Spandler & S. Warner (Eds), *Beyond Fear and Control: Working with Young People Who Self-harm* (105–20). Ross-on-Wye: PCCS Books.

Proctor, G. (2008). CBT: The obscuring of power in the name of science. In R. House & D. Loewenthal (Eds), *Against and for CBT: Towards a Constructive Dialogue*? Ross-On-Wye: PCCS Books.

Propping, P. (2005). The biography of psychiatric genetics: From early achievements to historical burden, from an anxious society to critical geneticists. *American Journal of Medical Genetics Part B (Neuropsychiatric Genetics)*, 136B(1), 2–7.

Prosser, J. (1998). *Second Skins: The Body Narratives of Transsexuality*. New York: Columbia University Press.

Puri, B., Hutton, S., Saeed, N., Oatridge, A., Hajnal, J., Duncan, L. et al. (2001). A serial longitudinal quantitative MRI study of cerebral changes in first-episode schizophrenia using image segmentation and subvoxel registration. *Psychiatry Research: Neuroimaging*, 106(2), 141–50.

Putnam, F. (2003). Ten-year research update review: Child sexual abuse. *Journal of the American Academy of Child and Adolescent Psychiatry*, 42(3), 269–78.

Pynoos, R., Steinberg, A. & Piacentini, J. (1999). A developmental psychopathology model of childhood traumatic stress and intersection with anxiety disorders. *Biological Psychiatry*, 46(11), 1542–54.

Raffi, A. R., Rondini, M., Grandi, S. & Fava, G. A. (2000). Life events and prodromal symptoms in bulimia nervosa. *Psychological Medicine: A Journal of Research in Psychiatry and the Allied Sciences*, 30, 727–31.

Raine, A., Mellingen, K., Liu, J., Venables, P. & Mednick, S. (2003). Effects of environmental enrichment at ages 3–5 years on schizotypal personality and antisocial behavior at ages 17 and 23 years. *American Journal of Psychiatry*, 160, 1627–35.

Raleigh, M. J., McGuire, M. T., Brammer, G. L. & Yuwiler, A. (1984). Social and environmental influences on blood serotonin concentrations in monkeys. *Archives of General Psychiatry*, 41(4), 405–10.

Ramsden, J. (2010). Facilitating thinking: The role of the psychologist in a specialist personality disorder service. *Clinical Psychology Forum*, 207, 21–4.

Rankin, P. & O'Carrol, P. (1995). Reality monitoring and signal detection in individuals prone to hallucinations. *British Journal of Clinical Psychology*, 34, 517–28.

Rapley, M. (2004). *The Social Construction of Intellectual Disability*. Cambridge: Cambridge University Press.

Raskin, A., Schulterbrandt, J., Reatig, N., Chase, C. & McKeon, J. (1970). Differential response to chlorpromazine, imipramine, and placebo: A study of subgroups of hospitalized depressed patients. *Archives of General Psychiatry*, 23(2), 164–73.

Raskin, N. J. (1996). Person-centred psychotherapy: Twenty historical steps. In W. Dryden (Ed.), *Developments in Psychotherapy: Historical Perspectives*. London: Sage.

Rathburn, C., DiVirgilio, J. & Waldfogel, A. (1958). A restitutive process in children following radical separation from family and culture. *American Journal of Orthopsychiatry*, 28, 408–15.

Rattehalli, R. D., Jayaram, M. B. & Smith, M. (2010). Risperidone versus placebo for schizophrenia. *Cochrane Database of Systematic Reviews*, 1, CD006918.

Ravaldi, C., Vannacci, A., Zucchi, T., Mannucci, E., Luigi, P., Cabras, L. et al. (2003). Eating disorders and body image disturbances among ballet dancers, gymnasium users and body builders. *Psychopathology*, 6, 247–54.

Read, J. (2004a). Biological psychiatry's lost cause. In J. Read, L. Mosher & R. Bentall (Eds), *Models of Madness: Psychological, Social and Biological Approaches to Schizophrenia* (1st edn, 57–66). London: Routledge.

Read J. (2004b). Electroconvulsive therapy. In J. Read, L. Mosher & R. Bentall (Eds), *Models of Madness: Psychological, Social and Biological Approaches to Schizophrenia* (85–99). London: Routledge.

Read, J. (2004c). Does 'schizophrenia exist? Reliability and validity. In J. Read, L. Mosher & R. Bentall (Eds), *Models of Madness: Psychological, Social and Biological Approaches to Schizophrenia* (1st edn, 43–56). London: Routledge.

Read, J. (2004d). A history of madness. In J. Read, L. Mosher & R. Bentall (Eds), *Models of Madness: Psychological, Biological and Social Approaches to Schizophrenia* (1st edn, 9–20). London: Routledge.

Read, J. (2004e). The invention of 'schizophrenia'. In J. Read, L. Mosher & R. Bentall (Eds), *Models of Madness: Psychological, Social and Biological Approaches to Schizophrenia* (1st edn, 21–34). London: Routledge.

Read, J. (2005a). Childhood trauma, psychosis and schizophrenia: A literature review with theoretical and clinical implications. *Acta Psychiatrica Scandinavica*, 112, 330–50.

Read, J. (2005b). The bio-bio-bio model of madness. *The Psychologist*, 18(10), 596–7.

Read, J. (2007). Why promoting biological ideology increases prejudice against people labelled 'schizophrenic'. *Australian Psychologist*, 42(2), 118–28.

Read, J. (2008). Schizophrenia, drug companies and the internet. *Social Science & Medicine*, 66(1), 99–109.

Read, J. (2010). Can poverty drive you mad? 'Schizophrenia', socio-economic status and the case for primary prevention. *New Zealand Journal of Psychology*, 39(2), 7–19.

Read, J. (2012). The subjective experience of the link between bad things happening and psychosis: Research findings. In J. Geekie, P. Randal, D. Lampshire & J. Read (Eds), *Experiencing Psychosis: Personal and Professional Perspectives* (127–36). London: Roultedge.

Read, J., Agar, K., Argyle, N. & Aderhold, V. (2003). Sexual and physical abuse during childhood and adulthood as predictors of hallucinations, delusions and thought disorder. *Psychology and Psychotherapy: Theory, Research and Practice*, 76(1), 1–22.

Read, J. & Argyle, N. (1999). Hallucinations, delusions, and thought disorder among adult psychiatric inpatients with a history of child abuse. *Psychiatric Services*, 50(11), 1467–72.

Read, J. & Baker, S. (1996). *Not Just Sticks and Stones: A Survey of the Stigma, Taboos and Discrimination Experienced by People with Mental Health Problems*. London: Mind.

Read, J. & Bentall, R. (2010a). The effectiveness of electroconvulsive therapy: A literature review. *Epidemiologia e Psichiatria Sociale*, 19, 333–47.

Read, J. & Bentall, R. (2010b). Schizophrenia and childhood adversity. *American Journal of Psychiatry*, 167(6), 717.

Read, J. & Bentall, R. (2010c). The effectiveness of electroconvulsive therapy: A literature review. *Epidemiologia e Psychiatria Sociale*, 19(4), 333–47.

Read, J. & Bentall, R. (2012). Negative childhood experiences and mental health: Theoretical, clinical and primary prevention implications. *British Journal of Psychiatry*, 200, 89–91.

Read, J., Bentall, R. & Fosse, R. (2009). Time to abandon the bio-bio-bio model of psychosis: Exploring the epigenetic and psycholgocial mechanisms by which adverse life events lead to psychotic symptoms. *Epidemiologia e Psichiatria Sociale*, 18(4), 299–317.

Read, J., Bentall, R. P. & Mosher, L. R. (Eds) (2004). *Models of Madness: Psychological, Social and Biological Approaches to Schizophrenia*. London: Brunner-Routledge/ISPS.

Read, J., & Dillon, J. (Eds) (2013). *Models of Madness: Psychological, Social and Biological Approaches to Schizophrenia* (2nd edn). London: Routledge.

Read, J., Fink, P., Rudegeair, T., Felitti, V. & Whitfield, C. (2008). Child maltreatment and psychosis: A return to a genuinely integrated bio-psycho-social model. *Clinical Schizophrenia & Related Psychoses*, 2, 235–54.

Read, J. & Fraser, A. (1998a). Abuse histories of psychiatric inpatients: To ask or not to ask? *Psychiatric Services*, 49(3), 355–9.

Read, J. & Fraser, A. (1998b). Staff response to abuse histories of psychiatric inpatients. *Australian and New Zealand Journal of Psychiatry*, 32(2), 206–13.

Read, J. & Gumley, A. (2008). Can attachment theory help explain the relationship between childhood adversity and psychosis? *Attachment: New Directions in Psychotherapy and Relational Psychoanalysis*, 2, 1–35.

Read, J., Hammersley, P. & Rudegeair, T. (2007). Why, when and how to ask about child abuse. *Adances in Psychiatric Treatment*, 13, 101–10.

Read, J. & Harré, N. (2001). The role of biological and genetic causal beliefs in the stigmatisation of 'mental patients'. *Journal of Mental Health*, 10, 223–35.

Read, J., Haslam, N. & Magliano, L. (2013). Prejudice, stigma and 'schizophrenia': The role of bio-genetic ideology. In J. Read & J. Dillon (Eds), *Models of Madness: Psychological, Social and Biological Approaches to Psychosis* (2nd edn). London: Routledge.

Read, J., Haslam, N., Sayce, L. & Davies, E. (2006). Prejudice and schizophrenia: A review of the 'Mental illness is an illness like any other' approach. *Acta Psychiatrica Scandinavica*, 114(5), 303–18.

Read, J. & Johnstone, L. (2013). Psychosis, poverty and ethnicity. In J. Read & J. Dillon (Eds), *Models of Madness: Psychological, Social and Biological Approaches to Schizophrenia* (2nd edn). London: Routledge.

Read, J., Johnstone, L. & Taitimu, M. (2013). Psychosis, poverty and ethnicity. In J. Read & J. Dillon (Eds), *Models of Madness: Psychological, Social and Biological Approaches to Psychosis* (2nd edn). London: Routledge.

Read, J. & Law, A. (1999). The relationship of causal beliefs and contact with users of mental health services to attitudes to the 'mentally ill'. *International Journal of Social Psychiatry*, 45(3), 216–29.

Read, J., Magliano, L. & Beavan, V. (2013). Public opinion: Bad things happen and can drive you crazy. In J. Read & J. Dillon (Eds), *Models of Madness: Psychological, Social and Biological Approaches to Schizophrenia* (2nd edn). London: Routledge.

Read, J. & Masson, J. (2013). Genetics, eugenics and mass murder. In J. Read & J. Dillon (Eds), *Models of Madness: Psychological, Social and Biological Approaches to Schizophrenia* (2nd edn). London: Routledge.

Read, J., Mosher, L. & Bentall, R. (2004). *Models of Madness: Psychological, Social and Biological Approaches to Schizophrenia.* London: Routledge.

Read, J., Perry, B., Moskowitz, A. & Connolly, J. (2001). The contribution of early traumatic events to schizophrenia in some patients: A traumagenic neurodevelopmental model. *Psychiatry: Interpersonal and Biological Processes*, 64(4), 319–45.

Read, J. & Sanders, P. (2010). *A Straight Talking Introduction to the Causes of Mental Health problems.* Ross, UK: PCCS Books

Read, J., van Os, J., Morrison, A. P. & Ross, C. A. (2005). Childhood trauma, psychosis and schizophrenia: A literature review with theoretical and clinical implications. *Acta Psychiatrica Scandinavica*, 112, 330–50.

Reavey, P. & Warner, S. (2003). *New Feminist Stories of Child Sexual Abuse: Sexual Scripts and Dangerous Dialogues.* London: Routledge.

Reeves, A. (1997). *Recovery: A Holistic Approach.* Gloucester: Handsell Publishing.

Reeves, M. & Taylor, J. (2007). Specific relationships between core beliefs and personality disorder symptoms in a non-clinical sample. *Clinical Psychology and Psychotherapy*, 14, 96–104.

Regan, P. C. (1999). Hormonal correlates and causes of sexual desire: A review. *Canadian Journal of Sexuality*, 8, 1–16.

Reich, S., Riemer, M., Prilleltensky, I. & Montero, M. (Eds) (2007). *International Community Psychology: History and Theories.* New York: Springer-Verlag.

Reissing, E., Binik, Y., Khalife, S., Cohen, D. & Amsel, R. (2004). Vaginal spasm, pain, and behavior: An empirical investigation of the diagnosis of vaginismus. *Archives of Sexual Behavior*, 33, 5–17.

Reivich, M., Amsterdam, J. D., Brunswick, D. J. &YannShiue, C. (2004). PET brain imaging with [11C](+)McN5652 shows increased serotonin transporter availability in major depression. *Journal of Affective Disorders*, 82(2), 321–7.

Rellini, A. H. & Meston, C. M. (2011). Sexual self-schemas, sexual dysfunction and the sexual responses of women with a history of childhood sexual abuse. *Archives of Sexual Behavior*, 40, 351–62.

Renaud, C. A. & Byers, S. (1999). Exploring the frequency, diversity and content of university students' positive and negative sexual cognitions. *The Canadian Journal of Human Sexuality*, 8, 54–73.

Repper, J., Sayce, L., Strong, S., Willmot, J. & Haines, M. (1997). *Respect: Time to End Discrimination on Mental Health Grounds. Tall Stories from the Back Yard: A Survey of 'Nimby' Opposition to Community Mental Health Facilities, Experienced by Key Service Providers in England and Wales.* London: Mind.

Rethink Mental Illness (2006). Churchill statue. Accessed at www.rethink.org/how_we_can_help/our_campaigns/ stigma_and_discrimination/time_to_change/norwich_campaign/ churchill_statue.html on 28 January 2012.

Reveley, M. (1985). CT scans in schizophrenia. *British Journal of Psychiatry*, 146, 367–71.

Rhoten, D. & Parker, A. (2004). Risks and rewards of an interdisciplinary career path. *Science*, 306, 2046.

Richard, L. D., & O' Donohue, W. T. (2008). *Sexual Deviance: Theory, Assessment, and Treatment.* New York: Guilford Press.

Richards, B. (1995). Psychotherapy and the hidden injuries of class. *BPS Psychotherapy Section Newsletter*, 17, 21–35.

Richardson, T., Gallagher, A. & Garavan, H. (2011). Cannabis use and psychotic experiences in an international sample of undergraduate students. *Psychosis: Psychological, Social and Integrative Approaches*, 3(2), 141–4.

Richman, J. (2007). The disorder of things: An ethnographer's reflections from Park Lane in the 1980s and 1990s. In D. Pilgrim (Ed.), *Inside Ashworth: Professional Reflections of Institutional Life* (39–57). Abingdon, Oxon: Radcliffe.

Rickel, A. (1987). The 1965 Swampscott conference and future topics for community psychology. *American Journal of Community Psychology*, 15, 511–13.

Ridley-Dash, M. & Bostock, J. (2007). *Influences on wellbeing in Croft and Cowpen Quay.* Northumberland Care Trust: Community Psychology Service.

Riedel-Heller, S. G., Matschinger, H. & Angermeyer, M. C. (2005). Mental disorders – who and what might help? Help-seeking and treatment preferences of the lay public. *Social Psychiatry and Psychiatric Epidemiology*, 40(2), 167–74.

Rienzi, B. M. & Scrams, D. J. (1991). Gender stereotypes for paranoid, antisocial, compulsive, dependent and histrionic personality disorders. *Psychological Reports*, 69, 976–8.

Riley, S., Rodham, K. & Gavin, J. (2009). Doing weight: Pro-ana and recovery identities in cyberspace. *Journal of Community & Applied Social Psychology*. Special Issue: *Beyond Psychopathology: Interrogating (Dis)Orders of Body Weight and Body Management*, 19, 348–59.

Rinne, T., Westenberg, H. G., den Boer, J. A. & van den Brink, W. (2000). Serotonergic blunting to meta-chlorophenylpiperazine (m-CPP) highly correlates with sustained childhood abuse in impulsive and autoaggressive female borderline patients. *Biological Psychiatry*, 47, 548–56.

Rissmiller, D. J. & Rissmiller, J. H. (2006). Evolution of the antipsychiatry movement into mental health consumerism. *Psychiatric Services*, 57, 863–6.

Ritsher, J. E. B., Warner, V., Johnson, J. G. & Dohrenwend, B. P. (2001). Inter-generational longitudinal study of social class and depression: A test of social causation and social selection models. *British Journal of Psychiatry*, 178 (suppl. 40), s84–s90.

Ritter, K., Chaudhry, H. R., Aigner, M., Zitterl, W. & Stompe, T. (2010). Mental health beliefs between culture and subjective illness experience. *Neuropsychiatry*, 24, 33–41.

Roberts, A. (2008). Mental health and survivors' movements and context. Accessed at studymore.org.uk/mpu.htm on 6 May 2008.

Roberts, R. & Itten, T. (2006). Laing and Szasz: Anti-psychiatry, capitalism and therapy. *The Psychoanalytic Review*, 93, 781–99.

Robertson, A. F. (2001). *Greed: Gut Feelings, Growth and History.* Cambridge: Polity Press.

Robertson, H. & Pryor, R. (2006). Memory and cognitive effects of ECT: Informing and assessing patients. *Advances in Psychiatric Treatment*, 12, 228–38.

Robins, L. N., Locke, B. Z. & Reiger, D. A. (1991). An overview of psychiatric disorders in America. In L. N. Robins & B. Z. Locke (Eds), *Psychiatric Disorders in America*. New York: Free Press.

Robins, L. & Regier, D. (1991). *Psychiatric Disorders in America: The Epidemiologic Catchment Area study.* New York: The Free Press.

Robinson, D., Woerner, M., McMeniman, M., Mendelowitz, A. & Bilder, R. (2004). Symptomatic and full recovery from a first episode of schizophrenia or schizoaffective disorder. *American Journal of Psychiatry*, 161, 473–9.

Roe, A. (1949). Integration of personality theory and clinical practice. *American Psychologist*, 44, 36–41.

Roenneberg, T., Kuehnle, T., Juda, M., Kantermann, T., Allebrandt, K., Gordijn, M. et al. (2007). Epidemiology of the human circadian clock. *Sleep Medicine Reviews*, 11, 429–38.

Rogers, A., Day, J. C., Williams, B., Randall, F., Wood, P., Healy, D. et al. (1998). The meaning and management of neuroleptic medication: A study of patients with a diagnosis of schizophrenia. *Social Science & Medicine*, 47, 1313–23.

Rogers, A. & Pilgrim, D. (1991). 'Pulling down churches': Accounting for the mental health users' movement. *Sociology of Health and Illness*, 13, 129–48.

Rogers, A. & Pilgrim, D. (1993). Service users' views of psychiatric treatments. *Sociology of Health & Illness*, 15, 612–31.

Rogers, A. & Pilgrim, D. (2003). *Mental Health and Inequality*. London. Palgrave.

Rogers, A., Pilgrim, D. & Lacey, R. (1993). *Experiencing Psychiatry: Users' Views of Services*. London: Macmillan.

Rogers, C. R. (1951). *Client-centered Therapy: Its Current Practice, Implications and Theory*. London: Constable.

Rogers, C. R. (1961). *On Becoming a Person*. Boston: Houghton Mifflin

Rogers, C. R. (1980). *A Way of Being*. Boston: Houghton Mifflin.

Rollin, H. R. (2000). Psychiatry at 2000: A bird's-eye view. *Psychiatric Bulletin*, 11–15.

Romme, M. (2000). Redefining hearing voices. Based on a speech given at the launch of the Hearing Voices Network, Manchester, UK, Summer 2000. Available online at: www.psychminded.co.uk/critical/marius.htm

Romme, M. (2009a). What causes hearing voices? In M. Romme, S. Escher, D. Corstens, J. Dillon & M. Morris (Eds), *Living with Voices: Fifty Stories of Recovery*. Ross-on-Wye: PCCS Books.

Romme, M. (2009b). Metaphors and emotions. In M. Romme, S. Escher, D. Corstens, J. Dillon & M. Morris (Eds), *Living with Voices: Fifty Stories of Recovery*. Ross-on-Wye: PCCS Books.

Romme, M. (2009c). Hearing voices groups. In M. Romme, S. Escher, D. Corstens, J. Dillon & M. Morris (Eds), *Living with Voices: Fifty Stories of Recovery*. Ross-on-Wye: PCCS Books.

Romme, M. & Escher, S. (1989). Hearing voices. *Schizophrenia Bulletin*, 15, 209–16.

Romme, M. & Escher, S. (Eds) (1993). *Accepting Voices*. London: Mind Publications.

Romme, M. & Escher, S. (2000). *Making Sense of Voices*. London: Mind Publications.

Romme, M. & Escher, S. (2006). Trauma and hearing voices. In W. Larkin & A. Morrison (Eds), *Trauma and Psychosis: New Directions for Theory and Therapy* (162–91). London: Routledge.

Romme, M. & Escher, S. (Eds) (2012). *Psychosis as a Personal Crisis: An Experience-Based Approach*. London: Routledge.

Romme, M., Escher, S., Dillon, J., Corstens, D. & Morris, M. (Eds) (2009). *Living with Voices: 50 Stories of Recovery*. Ross-on-Wye: PCCS Books.

Ronson, J. (2011). *The Psychopath Test*. London: Picador.

Rorty, M., Yager, J. & Rossotto, E. (1994). Childhood sexual, physical, and psychological abuse and their relationship to comorbid psychopathology in bulimia nervosa. *International Journal of Eating Disorders*, 16, 317–34.

Rose, D. (1998a). *In Our Experience: User-focused Monitoring of Mental Health Services in Kensington & Chelsea and Westminster Health Authority*. London: Sainsbury Centre for Mental Health.

Rose, D. (1998b). Television, madness and community care. *Journal of Community & Applied Social Psychology*, 8, 213–28.

Rose, D. (2001a). *Users' Voices: The Perspectives of Mental Health Service Users on Community and Hospital Care*. London: Sainsbury Centre for Mental Health.

Rose, D. (2001b). Terms of Engagement. *Openmind*, 108, 16–17.

Rose, D., Fleischmann, P. & Wykes, T. (2004). Consumers' views of electroconvulsive therapy: A qualitative analysis. *Journal of Mental Health*, 13, 285–93.

Rose, D., Thornicroft, G., Pinfold, V. & Kassam, A. (2007). 250 labels used to stigmatise people with mental illness. *BMC Health Services Research*, 7, 97.

Rose, D., Thornicroft, G. & Slade, M. (2006). Who decides what evidence is? Developing a multiple perspectives paradigm in mental health. *Acta Psychiatrica Scandinavica*, 113, 109–14.

Rose, D., Wykes, T. H., Bindman, J. P. & Fleischmann, P. S. (2005). Information, consent and perceived coercion: Patients' perspectives on electroconvulsive therapy. *British Journal of Psychiatry*, 186, 54–9.

Rose, D., Wykes, T., Leese, M., Bindman, J. & Fleischmann, P. . (2003). Patients' perspectives on electroconvulsive therapy: Systematic review. *British Medical Journal*, 326, 1363–7.

Rose, N. (1989). *Governing the Soul: The Shaping of the Private Self*. London: Routledge.

Rose, N. (1990). Psychology as a 'social' science. In I. Parker & J. Shotter (Eds), *Deconstructing Social Psychology*. London: Routledge.

Rose, N. (1998). *Inventing Our Selves: Psychology, Power, and Personhood*. Cambridge: Cambridge University Press.

Rose, N. (2004). Becoming neurochemical selves. In N. Stehr (Ed.), *Biotechnology, Commerce and Civil Society*. London: Transaction Publishers.

Rose, R. C. & Laumann, E. O. (2003). The prevalence of sexual problems in women: How valid are comparisons across studies? Commentary on Bancroft, Loftus and Long's (2003) 'Distress about sex: A national survey of women in heterosexual relationships'. *Archives of Sexual Behavior*, 32, 209–11.

Rose, S. (1997). *Lifelines: Life Beyond the Gene*. Oxford: Oxford University Press.

Rose, S. (2001). Moving on from old dichotomies: Beyond nature-nurture towards a lifeline perspective. *British Journal of Psychiatry*, 178, s3–s7.

Rose, S., Lewontin, R. & Kamin, I. (1984). *Not in Our Genes*. Harmondsworth: Penguin.

Rosen, R. C. (2007). Prevalence and risk factors of sexual dysfunction in men and women. *Current Psychiatric Reports*, 1523–645.

Rosen, R. C., Altwein, J., Boyle, P., Kirby, R. S. & Lukacs, B. (2003). Lower urinary tract symptoms and male sexual dysfunction: The multinational survey of the aging male (MSAM-7). *European Urology*, 44, 637–49.

Rosen, R. C. and Laumann, E. O. (2003). The prevalence of sexual problems in women: How valid are comparisons across studies? Commentary on Bancroft, Loftus, and Long's (2003) 'Distress about sex: A national survey of women in heterosexual relationships'. *Archives of Sexual Behavior*, 32(3), 209–11.

Rosen, R. C., Leiblum, S. R. & Spector, I. (1994). Psychologically based treatment for male erectile disorder: A cognitive-interpersonal model. *Journal of Marital Therapy*, 20, 67–85.

Rosenhan, D. (1973). On being sane in insane places. *Science*, 179(4070), 250–8.

Rosenhan, D. & Seligman, M. (1989). *Abnormal Psychology* (2nd edn). New York: W. W. Norton.

Rosenthal, D., Wender, P. H., Kety, S. S., Schulsinger, F., Welner, J., Lawlor, W. G. et al. (1975). Assessing degree of psychopathology from diagnostic statements. *Canadian Psychiatric Association Journal*, 20(1), 35–45.

Ross, C. (2010). DSM-5 and the 'psychosis risk syndrome': Eight reasons to reject it. *Psychosis: Psychological, Social and Integrative Approaches*, 2(2), 107–10.

Ross, C. & Keyes, B. (2009). Clinical features of dissociative schizophrenia in China. *Psychosis: Psychological, Social and Integrative Approaches*, 1(1), 51–60.

Ross, C. & Read, J. (2004). Antipsychotic medication: Myths and facts. In J. Read, L. Mosher & R. Bentall (Eds), *Models of Madness: Psychological, Social and Biological Approaches to Schizophrenia* (101–14). London: Routledge.

Ross, C. E. & Mirowsky, J. (2008). Age and the balance of emotions. *Social Science and Medicine*, 66, 2391–400.

Ross, L. (1977). The intuitive psychologist and his shortcomings: Distortions in the attribution process. In L. Berkowitz (Ed.), *Advances in Experimental Social Psychology* (vol. 10), 173–220. New York: Academic Press.

Roth, A. & Fonagy, P. (2005). *What Works for Whom? A Critical Review of Psychotherapy Research* (2nd edn). New York: Guilford Press.

Roth, M. & Kroll, J. (1986). *The Reality of Mental Illness*. Cambridge: Cambridge University Press.

Royal College of Psychiatrists (2010). *Information on ECT*. http://www.rcpsych.ac.uk/mentalhealthinfo/treatments/ect.aspx

Rubel, A. J. (1964). The epidemiology of a folk illness: Susto in Hispanic America. *Ethnology*, 3, 268–83.

Rubin, G. (1984). Thinking sex: Notes for a radical theory of the politics of sexuality. In C. S. Vance (Ed.), *Pleasure and Danger: Exploring Female Sexuality*, 267–319. London: Harper Collins.

Rushing, W. & Ortega, S. (1979). Socioeconomic status and mental disorder. *American Journal of Sociology*, 84, 1175–200.

Ruskay Rabinor, J. (1994). Mothers, daughters and eating disorders: Honoring the mother daughter relationship. In P. Fallon, M. A. Katzman & S. C. Wooley (Eds), *Feminist Perspectives on Eating Disorders*. New York: Guilford Press.

Russell, D. (1995). *Women, Madness and Medicine*. Cambridge MA: Oxford.

Russell, G. F. M., Szmukler, G. I., Dare, C. & Eisler, I. (1987). An evaluation of family therapy in anorexia nervosa and bulimia nervosa. *Archives of General Psychiatry*, 44, 1047–56.

Russon, L. & Alison, D. (1998). Does palliative care have a role in treatment of anorexia nervosa? Palliative care does not mean giving up. *British Medical Journal*, 317(7152), 196–7.

Ryan, W. (1971). *Blaming the Victim*. New York: Pantheon books.

Ryan, G. & Lane, S. (1997). *Juvenile Sexual Offending: Causes, Consequences, and Correction*. Chicago IL: Jossey Bass.

Ryan, G. & Miyoshi, T. (1990). Summary of a pilot follow-up study of adolescent sexual perpetrators after treatment. *Interchange*, 1, 6–8.

Ryle, A. (1997). *Cognitive Analytic Therapy of Borderline Personality Disorder: The Model and the Method*. Chichester: Wiley.

Sachs-Ericsson, N., Verona, E., Joiner, T. & Preacher, K. (2006). Parental verbal abuse and the mediating role of self-criticism in adult internalizing disorders. *Journal of Affective Disorders*, 93(1–3), 71–8.

Sackeim, H., Prudic, J., Fuller, R., Keilp, J., Lavori, P. & Olfson, M. (2007). The cognitive effects of ECT in community settings. *Neuropyschophamacology*, 32, 244–54.

Sadeh, N., Javdani, S., Jackson, J., Reynolds, E. K., Potenza, M. N., Gelernter, J. et al. (2010). Serotonin transporter gene associations with psychopathic traits in youth vary as a function of socioeconomic resources. *Journal of Abnormal Psychology*, 119, 604–9.

Sadler, J. Z. (2005). *Values and Psychiatric Diagnoses*. Oxford: Oxford University Press.

Sadow, D., Ryder, M. & Webster, D. (2002). Is education of health professionals encouraging stigma towards the mentally ill? *Journal of Mental Health*, 11, 657–65.

Saha, S., Chant, D., Welham, J. & McGrath, J. (2005). A systematic review of the prevalence of schizophrenia. *PLoS Medicine*, 2(5), e141.

Sainsbury Centre for Mental Health (1998). *Acute Problems: A Survey of the Quality of Care in Acute Psychiatric Wards*. London: Author.

Sainsbury Centre for Mental Health (2002). *Breaking the Cycles of Fear: A Review of the Relationship between Mental Health Services and the African Caribbean Community*. London: Author.

Salize, H. J. & Dressing, H. (2004). Epidemiology of involuntary placement of mentally ill people across the European Union. *British Journal of Psychiatry*, 184, 163–8.

Salter, A. C. (1988). *Treating Child Sex Offenders and Victims: A Practical Guide*. London: Sage.

Samaha, A. N., Seeman, P., Stewart, J., Rajabi, H. & Kapur, S. (2007). 'Breakthrough' dopamine supersensitivity during ongoing antipsychotic treatment leads to treatment failure over time. *Journal of Neuroscience*, 27, 2979–86.

Samele, C., van Os, J., McKenzie, K., Wright, A., Gilvarry, C., Manley et al. (2001). Does socioeconomic status predict course and outcome in patients with psychosis? *Social Psychiatry and Psychiatric Epidemiology*, 36, 573–81.

Samelson, F. (1974). History, origin myth and ideology: 'Discovery' of social psychology. *Journal for the Theory of Social Behaviour*, 4, 217-31.

Samelson, F. (1980). J. B. Watson's Little Albert, Cyril Burt's twins, and the need for a critical science. *American Psychologist*, 35, 619–25.

Sampson, M. J., McCubbin, R. A. & Tyrer, P. J. (Eds) (2006). *Personality Disorder and Community Mental Health Teams*. Chichester: Wiley.

Samuels, J., Eaton, W. W., Bienvenu, O. J., Brown, C. H., Costa, P. T. Jr & Nestadt, G. (2002). Prevalence and correlates of personality disorders in a community sample. *British Journal of Psychiatry*, 180, 536–42.

Sanders, A., Duan, J., Levinson, D., Shi, J., He, D., Hou, C. et al. (2008). No significant association of 14 candidate genes with schizophrenia in a large European ancestry sample: Implications for psychiatric genetics. *American Journal of Psychiatry*, 165, 497–506.

Sanderson, W., Rapee, R. & Barlow, D. (1989). The influence of an illusion of control on panic attacks induced via inhalation of 5.5% CO2 enriched air. *Archives of General Psychiatry*, 46(2), 157–62.

Sands, A. (2000). *Falling for Therapy*. London: Macmillan.

Sanislow, C. A., Little, T. D., Ansell, E. B., Grilo, C.M., Daversa, M., Markowitz, J.C. et al. (2009). Ten-year stability and latent structure of the DSM-IV schizotypal, borderline, avoidant, and obsessive-compulsive personality disorders. *Journal of Abnormal Psychology*, 118, 507–19.

Sapir, E. (1924). Culture, genuine and spurious. *American Journal of Sociology*, 29, 401–29.

Sarbin, T. R. & Mancuso, J. C. (1980). *Schizophrenia: Medical Diagnosis or Moral Verdict?* New York: Praeger.

Sargent, P. A., Kjaer, K. H., Bench, C. J., Rabiner, E. A., Messa, C., Meyer, J. et al. (2000). Brain serotonin1a receptor binding measured by positron emission tomography with [11c]way-100635: Effects of depression and antidepressant treatment. *Archives of General Psychiatry*, 57(2), 174–80.

Sarita, E., Janakiramiaiah, N., Gangadhar, B., Subbakrishna, D. & Rao, K. (1998). Efficacy of combined ECT after two weeks of neuroleptics in schizophrenia. *NIMHANS Journal*, 16, 243–51.

SARP-ED (2006). Protocol for the Management of Erectile Dysfunction. Guys Hospital Sex and Relationships Problems Clinic. Internal Document.

SARP-vaginismus (2006). Assessment for Vaginismus. Guys Hospital Sex and Relationships Problems Clinic. Internal Document.

Sartorious, N., Ustun, T. B., Lecrubier, Y. & Wittchen, H. U. (1996). Depression co-morbid with anxiety: Results from the WHO study on psychological disorders in primary health care. *British Journal of Psychiatry* Suppl., 30(June), 38–43.

Sarwer, D. B., Crawford, I. & Durlak, J. A. (1997). The relationship between childhood sexual abuse and adult male sexual dysfunction. *Child Abuse & Neglect*, 21, 649–55.

Satel, S. (2001). *P.C. M.D.: How Political Correctness is Corrupting Medicine*. New York: Perseus.

Satel, S. L. & Redding, R. E. (2005). Sociopolitical trends in mental health care: The consumer/survivor movement and multiculturalism. In B. J. Sadock & V. A. Sadock (Eds), *Kaplan and Sadock's Comprehensive Textbook of Psychiatry* (8th edn). Philadelphia, PA: Lippincott Williams & Wilkins.

Sayce, L. (1998). Stigma, discrimination and social exclusion: What's in a word? *Journal of Mental Health*, 7, 331–43.

Sayce, L. (2000). *From Psychiatric Patient to Citizen: Overcoming Discrimination and Stigma*. London: Palgrave Macmillan.

Sayce, L. (2003). Beyond good intentions: Making anti-discrimination strategies work. *Disability and Society*, 18(5), 625–42.

Schaaf, K. & McCanne, T. (1995). Relationship of childhood sexual, physical, and combined sexual and physical abuse to adult victimization and posttraumatic stress disorder. *Child Abuse and Neglect*, 22(11), 1119–33.

Schachter, H. M., Pham, B., King, J., Langford, S. & Moher, D. (2001). How efficacious and safe is short-acting methylphenidate for the treatment of attention-deficit disorder in children and adolescents? A meta-analysis. *Canadian Medical Association Journal*, 165, 1475–88.

Schafer, I., Ross, C. & Read, J. (2008). Childhood trauma in psychotic and dissociative disorders. In A. Moskowitz, I. Schafer, M. J. Dorahy (Eds), *Psychosis, Trauma and Dissociation: Emerging Perspectives on Severe Psychopathology* (137–50). Chichester: Wiley-Blackwell.

Schafer, M., Schnack, B. & Soyka, M. (2000). Sexual and physical abuse during early childhood or adolescence and later drug addiction. *Psychotherapie, Psychosomatik, Medizinische Psychologie*, 50(2), 38–50.

Schaffer, H. & Emerson, P. (1964). The development of social attachments in infancy. *Monographs of Social Research in Child Development*, 29(94).

Scheff, T. J. (1966). *Being Mentally Ill: A Sociological Theory*. London: Weidenfeld and Nicolson.

Scheff, T. J. (1974). The labelling theory of mental illness. *American Sociological Review*, 39, 444–52.

Schiavi, R. C., Stimmel, B. B., Mandeli, J. & White D. (1995). Chronic alcoholism and male sexual function. *American Journal of Psychiatry*, 152, 1045–51.

Schilt, K. & Westbrook, L. (2009). Doing gender, doing heteronormativity: 'Gender normals,' transgender people, and the social maintenance of heterosexuality. *Gender & Society*, 23(4), 440–64.

Schmidt, U., Lee, S., Beecham, J., Perkins, S., Treasure, J., Yi, I. et al. (2007). A randomized controlled trial of family therapy and cognitive behavior therapy guided self-care for adolescents with bulimia nervosa and related disorders. *American Journal of Psychiatry*, 164, 591–8.

Schmidt, U., Tiller, J., Blanchard, M., Andrews, B. & Treasure, J. et al. (2000). Is there a specific trauma precipitating anorexia nervosa? *Psychological Medicine*, 30, 727–31.

Schmidt, U. and Treasure J. (2006). Anorexia nervosa: valued and visible. A cognitive-interpersonal maintenance model and its implications for research and practice. *British Journal of Clinical Psychology*, 45, 343–66.

Schmidt, U., Treasure, J. & Garthe, R. (2003). Four-year follow-up of guided self-change for bulimia nervosa. *Eat Weight Disorders*, 8, 212–7.

Schneider, K. (1959). *Clinical Psychopathology* (5th edn). New York: Grune & Stratton.

Schore, A. (2001). The effects of early relational trauma on right brain development, affect regulation, and infant mental health. *Infant Mental Health Journal*, 22(1), 201–69.

Schorka, E. J., Eckerta, E. D. & Halmi, K. A. (1994). The relationship between psychopathology, eating disorder diagnosis, and clinical outcome at 10-year follow-up in anorexia nervosa. *Comprehensive Psychiatry*, 35(2), 113–23.

Schreier, A., Wolke, D., Thomas, K., Horwood, J., Hollis, C., Gunnell, D. et al. (2009). Prospective study of peer victimization in childhood and psychotic symptoms in a nonclinical population at age 12 years. *Archives of General Psychiatry*, 66, 527–36.

Schwartz, T. L., Saba, M., Hardoby, W., Virk, S. & Masand, P. S. (2002). Use of atypical antipsychotics in a veterans affairs hospital. *Progress in Neuro-Psychopharmacology and Biological Psychiatry*, 26, 1207–10.

Scott Gordon, N. (2000). Researching psychotherapy, the importance of the client's view: A methodological challenge. The Qualitative Report, 4(3). Accessed at www.nova.edu/ssss/QR/QR4–3/gordon. html on 29 December 2011.

Scottish Association of Mental Health (2004). *All You Need to Know? Scottish Survey of People's Experience of Psychiatric Drugs*. Glasgow: Scottish Association of Mental Health.

Scull, A. (1984). *Decarceration: Community Treatment and the Deviant*. Cambridge: Polity Press.

Scull, A. (1993). Museums of madness revisited. *Social History of Medicine*, 11, 3–23.

Scull, A. (2011). *Madness: A Very Short Introduction*. Oxford: Oxford University Press.

Scully, P., Quinn, J. F., Morgan, M. G., Kinsella, A., O'Callaghan, E., Owens, J. M. et al. (2002). First-episode schizophrenia, bipolar disorder and other psychoses in a rural Irish catchment area: Incidence and gender in the Cavan-Monaghan study at 5 years. *British Journal of Psychiatry*, 181 (suppl. 43), s3–s9.

Sedgwick, P. (1982). *Psychopolitics*. London: Pluto Press.

Seeman, P., Lee, T., Chau-Wong, M. & Wong, K. (1976). Antipsychotic drug dose and neuroleptic/dopamine receptors. *Nature*, 261, 717–19.

Segrin, C. (2000). Social skills deficits associated with depression. *Clinical Psychology Review*, 20(3), 379–403.

Segrin, C. & Flora, J. (2000). Poor social skills are a vulnerability factor in the development of psychosocial problems. *Human Communication Research*, 26(3), 489–514.

Seivewright, H., Tyrer, P. & Johnson, T. (1998). Prediction of outcome in neurotic disorder: A 5-year prospective study. *Psychological Medicine*, 28, 1149–57.

Seligman, M. E. P. (1975). *Helplessness: On Depression, Development and Death*. San Francisco: Freeman.

Seligman, M. E. P. (1995). The effectiveness of psychotherapy: The Consumer Reports study. *American Psychologist*, 30, 965–74.

Selten, J.-P. & Cantor-Graae, E. (2005). Social defeat: Risk factor for schizophrenia? *British Journal of Psychiatry*, 187, 101–2.

Selten, J.-P., Veen, N., Feller, W., Blom, J. D., Schols, D., Camoenie, W. et al. (2001). Incidence of psychotic disorders in immigrant groups to the Netherlands. *British Journal of Psychiatry*, 178, 367–72.

Sensky, T., Turkington, D., Kingdon, D., Scott, J. L., Scott, J., Siddle, R. et al. (2000). A randomized controlled trial of cognitive-behavioral therapy for persistent symptoms in schizophrenia resistant to medication. *Archives of General Psychiatry*, 57, 165–72.

Shafran, R. & Marshall, W. (2001). Perfectionism and psychopathology: A review of research and treatment. *Clinical Psychology Review*, 21, 879–906.

Shallice, T. (1972). The Ulster depth interrogation techniques and their relation to sensory deprivation research. *Cognition*, 1, 385–405.

Shapiro, D. A. & Paley, G. (2002). Invited rejoinder: The continuing potential relevance of equivalence and allegiance to research on psychological treatment of psychosis. *Psychology & Psychotherapy: Theory, Research & Practice*, 75, 375–9.

Sharpe, M., Hawton, K., Clements, A. & Cowen, P. J. (1997). Increased brain serotonin function in men with chronic fatigue syndrome. *British Medical Journal*, 315, 164–5.

Shaughnessy, P. (2000). Into the deep end. In T. Curtis, R. Dellar, E. Leslie & B. Watson (Eds), *Mad Pride: A Celebration of Mad Culture*. London: Spare Change Books.

Shaw, C. & Proctor, G. (2005). Women at the margins: A critique of the diagnosis of borderline personality disorder. *Feminism & Psychology*, 15, 483–90.

Shearer Underhill, C. & Marker, C. (2010). The use of the number needed to treat (NNT) in randomized clinical trials in psychological treatment. *Clinical Psychology: Science and Practice*, 17, 41–7.

Shedler, J. & Block, J. (1990). Adolescent drug use and psychological health: A longitudinal inquiry. *American Psychologist*, 45, 612–30.

Shevlin, M., Murphy, J., Houston, J. & Adamson, G. (2009). Childhood sexual abuse, early canabis use, and psychosis: Testing the effects of different temporal orderings based on the National Comorbidity Survey. *Psychosis: Psychological, Social and Integrative Approaches*, 1(1), 19–28.

Shields, J. (1954). Personality differences and neurotic traits in normal twin schoolchildren. *Eugenics Review*, 45, 213–46.

Shooter, M. (2010). What my diagnosis means to me. *Journal of Mental Health*, 19 (4), 366–8.

Shorter, E. (1997). *A History of Psychiatry: From the Era of the Asylum to the Age of Prozac*. Chichester: Wiley.

Shotter, J. (1993). *Conversational Realities: Constructing Life through Language*. London: Sage.

Shweder, R. (1990). 'X Cultural psychology: What is it?' In J. W. Stigler, R. A. Shweder & G. Herdt (Eds), *Cultural Psychology: Essays on Comparative Human Development*. Cambridge: Cambridge University Press.

Siever, M. D. (1994). Sexual orientation and gender as factors in socioculturally acquired vulnerability to body dissatisfaction and eating disorders. *Journal of Consulting and Clinical Psychology*, 62, 252–60.

Silver, A., Koehler, B. & Karon, B. (2004). Psychodynamic therapy of schizophrenia: Its history and development. In J. Read, L. Mosher & R. Bentall (Eds), *Models of Madness: Psychological, Social and Biological Approaches to Schizophrenia* (209–22). London: Routledge.

Silverstein, B. & Perlick, D. (1995). *The Cost of Competence: Why Inequality Causes Depression, Eating Disorders, and Illness in Women*. New York: Oxford University Press.

Silverstein, C. (2009). The implications of removing homosexuality from the DSM as a mental disorder. *Archives of Sexual Behavior*, 38, 161–3.

Simmons, J. P., Nelson, L. D. & Simonsohn, U. (2011). False-positive psychology. *Psychological Science*, 22(11), 1359–66.

Simons, J. S. & Carey, M. P. (2001). Prevalence of sexual dysfunctions: Results from a decade of research. *Archives of Sexual Behavior*, 30, 177–219.

Simpson, N. (2004). Untwining the transference. In Y. Bates (Ed.), *Shouldn't I Be Feeling Better by Now? Client Views of Therapy*. London: Palgrave Macmillan.

Sinfield, A. (2004). *On Sexuality and Power*. New York: Columbia University Press.

Singer, M. T. & Wynne, L. C. (1965). Thought disorder and family relations of schizophrenics: IV. Results and implications. *Archives of General Psychiatry*, 12, 201–12.

Singleton, N., Bumpstead, R., O'Brien, M., Lee, A. & Meltzer, H. (2001). Psychiatric Morbidity among Adults Living in Private Households, 2000: Summary Report. London: HMSO.

Singleton, N., Meltzer, H., Gatward, R., Coid, J. & Deasy, D. (1998). Psychiatric Morbidity among Prisoners in England and Wales: Summary Report. London: Office of National Statistics.

Skinner, B. F. (1938). *The Behavior of Organisms: An Experimental Analysis*. Oxford: Appleton-Century.

Skinner, B. F. (1974). *About Behaviourism*. London: Cape.

Skinner, R. (2007). *Ethno-psychology and Alternative Models*. Unpublished manuscript.

Skodol, A. E., Bender, D. S., Pagano, M. E., Shea, M. T., Yen, S., Sanislow, C. A. et al. (2007). Positive childhood experiences: Resilience and recovery from personality disorder in early adulthood. *Journal of Clinical Psychiatry*, 68, 1102–8.

Slade, P. D.& Bentall, R. P. (1988). *Sensory deception: A scientific analysis of hallucination*. London: Croom-Helm.

Smail, D. J. (1978). *Psychotherapy: A Personal Approach*. London: Dent.

Smail, D. J. (1990). Design for a post-behaviourist clinical psychology. *Clinical Psychology Forum*, 28, 2–10. Accessed at www.davidsmail.info/postbeh.htm on 15 January 2012.

Smail, D. J. (1993). *The Origins of Unhappiness: A New Understanding of Personal Distress*. London: HarperCollins.

Smail, D. J. (1994). Community psychology and politics. *Journal of Community and Applied Social Psychology*, 4, 3–10.

Smail, D. J. (1995). Power and the origins of unhappiness: Working with individuals. *Journal of Community & Applied Social Psychology*, 5, 347–56.

Smail, D. J. (1996). *How to Survive without Psychotherapy*. London: Constable.

Smail, D. J. (2001). Commentary. De-psychologizing community psychology. *Journal of Community and Applied Social Psychology*, 11, 159–65.

Smail, D. J. (2005). *Power, Interest and Psychology: Elements of a Social-Materialist Understanding of Distress*. Ross-On-Wye: PCCS Books.

Smail, D. J. (1984). *Illusion and Reality: The Meaning of Anxiety*. London: Dent.

Smail, D. J. (1987). *Taking Care: An Alternative to Therapy*. London: Dent.

Smail, D. J. (1993). *The Origins of Unhappiness*. London: Constable.

Smith, G., Bartlett, A. & King , M. (2004). Treatments of homosexuality in Britain since the 1950s – an oral history: The experience of patients. *British Medical Journal*, 328, 427–9.

Smith, M., Coleman, R. & Good, J. (2003). *Psychiatric First Aid in Psychosis: A Handbook for Nurses, Carers and People Distressed by Psychotic Experiences*. Fife: P&P Press.

Smith, M. L., Glass, G. V. & Miller, T. I. (1980). *The Benefits of Psychotherapy*. Baltimore MD: Johns Hopkins University Press.

Smith, Y. L., van Goozen, S. H. M., Kuiper, A. J. & Cohen-Kettenis, P. T. (2005). Sex reassignment: Outcomes and predictors of treatment for adolescent and adult transsexuals. *Psychological Medicine*, 35, 89–99.

Smith-Pickard, P. & Swynnerton, R. (2005). The body and sexuality. In E. van Deurzen & C. Arnold-Baker (Eds), *Existential Perspectives on Human Issues: A Handbook for Therapeutic Rractice* (48–57). New York: Palgrave Macmillan.

Smolak, L. & Murnen, S. (2002). A meta-analytic examination of the relationship between child sexual abuse and eating disorders. *International Journal of Eating Disorders*, 31, 136–50.

Smoller, J., Gardner-Schuster, E. & Misiaszek, M. (2008). Genetics of anxiety: Would the genome recognize the DSM? *Depression and Anxiety*, 25(4), 368–77.

Social Exclusion Unit (2004). *Mental Health and Social Exclusion*. London: Office of the Deputy Prime Minister.

Sohlberg, S. & Norring, C. (1985). A three-year prospective study of life events and course for adults with anorexia nervosa/bulimia nervosa. *The British Journal of Psychiatry*, 147, 265–71.

Sohlberg, S. S., Norring, C. A. & Rosmark, B. (1992). Prediction of the course of anorexia nervosa/bulimia nervosa over three years. *International Journal of Eating Disorders*, 12, 121–31.

Spandler, H. (1992). To make an army out of an illness: A history of the *Socialist Patients Collective* Heidelberg 1970–2. *Asylum*, 6(4), 3–16.

Spandler, H. (2006). *Asylum to Action: Paddington Day Hospital, Therapeutic Communities and Beyond*. London: Jessica Kingsley.

Spandler, H. & Warner, S. (Eds) (2007). *Beyond Fear and Control: Working with Young People Who Self-harm*. Ross-on-Wye: PCCS Books.

Spanos, N. P. (1994). Multiple identity enactments and multiple personality disorder: A sociocognitive perspective. *Psychological Bulletin*, 116, 143–65.

Speer, S. & Green, R. (2007). On passing: The interactional organization of appearance attributions in the psychiatric assessment of transsexual patients. In V. Clarke & E. Peel (Eds), *Out in Psychology Lesbian, gay, Bisexual, Trans and Queer Perspectives*. West Sussex: Wiley & Sons.

Spencer, T. J., Biederman, J., Madras, B. K., Faraone, S. V., Dougherty, D. D., Bonab, A. A. et al. (2005). In vivo neuroreceptor imaging in attention-deficit/hyperactivity disorder: A focus on the dopamine transporter. *Biological Psychiatry*, 57, 1293–300.

Spicer, J. & Chamberlain, K. (1996). Developing psychosocial theory in health psychology: Problems and prospects. *Journal of Health Psychology*, 1, 161–71.

Spitzer, R. & Fleiss, J. (1974). A re-analysis of the reliability of psychiatric diagnosis. *British Journal of Psychiatry*, 125, 341–7.

Spoor, S. T., Stice, E., Bekker, M. H., Van Strien, T., Croon, M. A. & Van Heck, G. L. (2006). Relations between dietary restraint, depressive symptoms, and binge eating: A longitudinal study. *International Journal of Eating Disorders*, 39(8), 700–7.

Squire, L. R., Judd, L. L., Janowsky, D. S. & Huey, L. Y. (1980). Effects of lithium carbonate on memory and other cognitive functions. *American Journal of Psychiatry*, 137, 1042–6.

Stahl, S. M. (2000). *Essential Psychopharmacology*. Cambridge: Cambridge University Press.

Stahl, S. M. (2001). The psychopharmacology of sex, Part 2: Effects of drugs and disease on the 3 phases of human sexual response. *The Journal of Clinical Psychiatry*, 62, 147–8.

Stainton Rogers, R., Stenner, P., Gleeson, K. & Stainton Rogers, W. (1995). *Social Psychology: A Critical Agenda*. Cambridge: Polity.

Startup, H. & Davey, G. (2003). Inflated responsibility and the use of stop rules for catastrophic worrying. *Behaviour Research and Therapy*, 41, 495–503.

Stastny, P. & Lehmann, P. (Eds) (2007). *Alternatives beyond Psychiatry*. Shrewsbury: Lehmann Publications.

Stein, D., Phillips, K., Bolton, D., Fulford, K., Sadler, J. & Kendler, K. S. (2010). What is a mental/psychiatric disorder? From DSM-IV to DSM V. *Psychological Medicine*, 40, 1759–65.

Stein, M. B. & Rauch, S. (2008). Do Syndromes Matter (DSM)? *Depression and Anxiety*, 25, 273.

Stein, M. B., Walker, J. R. & Forde, D. R. (1994). Setting diagnostic thresholds for social phobia: Considerations from a community survey of social anxiety. *American Journal of Psychiatry*, 151, 408–12.

Steiner-Adair, C. (1986). The body politic: Normal female adolescent development and the development of eating disorders. *Journal of American Academy of Psychoanalysis*, 14, 95–114.

Stenfert-Kroese, B. & Holmes, G. (2001). 'I've never said "no" to anything in my life': Helping people with learning disabilities who experience psychological problems. In C. Newnes, G. Holmes & C. Dunn (Eds), *This is Madness Too: A Critical Look at the Mental Health System*. Ross-On-Wye. PCCS.

Stephens, J. H., Richard, P. & McHugh, P. R. (1997). Long-term follow-up of patients hospitalized for schizophrenia, 1913 to 1940. *Journal of Nervous and Mental Disease*, 185(12), 715–21.

Stephenson, N. & Papadopoulos, D. (2007). *Analysing Everyday Experience: Social Research and Political Change*. London: Palgrave Macmillan.

Stern, A. M. (2005). *Eugenic Nation: Faults and Frontiers of Better Breeding in Modern America*. Berkeley CA: University of California Press.

Stevens, J. (1987). Brief psychoses: Do they contribute to the god prognosis and equal prevalence of schizophrenia in developing countries? *British Journal of Psychiatry*, 151, 393–6.

Stice, E. (1994). Review of the evidence for a sociocultural model of bulimia nervosa and an exploration of the mechanisms of action. *Clinical Psychology Review*, 14, 633–61.

Stice, E. (2002). Risk and maintenance factors for eating pathology: A meta-analytic review. *Psychological Bulletin*, 128, 825–48.

Stice, E., Schupak-Neuberg, E., Shaw, H. & Stein, R. I. (1994). Relation of media exposure to eating disorder symptomatology: An examination of mediating mechanisms. *Journal of Abnormal Psychology*, 103, 836–40.

Stiles, D. A. & Stiles, W. B. (1989). Abuse of the drug metaphor in psychotherapy process-outcome research. *Clinical Psychology Review*, 9, 521–54.

Still, A. & Velody, I. (Eds) (1992). *Rewriting the History of Madness: Studies in Foucault's 'Histoire de la folie'*. London: Routledge.

Stivers, R. (1999). *Technology as Magic: The Triumph of the Irrational*. New York: Continuum.

Stivers, R. (2004). *Shades of Loneliness: Pathologies of a Technological Society*. London: Continuum.

Stoppard, J. & McMullen, L. (Eds) (2003). *Situating Sadness: Women and Depression in Social Context*. New York: New York University Press.

Storr, A. (1989). *Churchill's Black Dog and Other Phenomena of the Human Mind*. London: HarperCollins.

Stowell-Smith, M. & McKeown, M. (1999a). Race, psychopathy and the self: A discourse analytic study. *British Journal of Medical Psychology*, 72, 459–70.

Stowell-Smith, M. & McKeown, M. (1999b). Locating mental health in black and white men: A Q-methodological study. *Journal of Health Psychology*, 4, 209–22.

Strakowski, S. M., Lonczak, H. S., Sax, K. W., West, S. A., Crist, A., Mehta, R. et al. (1995). The effects of race on diagnosis and disposition from a psychiatric emergency service. *Journal of Clinical Psychiatry*, 56(3), 101–7.

Strakowski, S. M., Shelton, R. C. & Kolbrener, M. L. (1993). The effects of race and comorbidity on clinical diagnosis in patients with psychosis. *Journal of Clinical Psychiatry*, 54(3), 96–102.

Strathearn, L. (2007). Exploring the neurobiology of attachment. In L. Mayes, P. Fonagy & M. Target (Eds), *Developmental Science and Psychoanalysis: Integration and Innovation*. London: Karnac.

Streatfield, D. (2006). *Brainwash: The Secret History of Mind Control*. London: Hodder.

Strickland, P. L., Deakin, J. F. W., Percival, C., Dixon, J., Gater, R. A. & Goldberg, D. P. (2002). Bio-social origins of depression in the community: Interactions between social adversity, cortisol and serotonin neurotransmission. *British Journal of Psychiatry*, 180, 168–73.

Striegel-Moore, R. H. (1997). Risk factors for eating disorders. *Annals of the New York Academy of Sciences*, 817, 98–109.

Striegel-Moore, R. H., Silberstein, L. R. & Rodin, J. (1986). Toward an understanding of risk factors for bulimia. *American Psychologist*, 41, 246–63.

Strober, M. (1997). Stressful life events associated with bulimia in anorexia nervosa. Empirical findings and theoretical speculations. *International Journal of Eating Disorders*, 3, 3–16.

Strober, M., Freeman, R., Lampert, C., Diamond, J. & Kaye, W. (2000). Controlled family study of anorexia nervosa and bulimia nervosa: Evidence of shared liability and transmission of partial syndromes. *American Journal of Psychiatry*, 157(3), 393–401.

Strober, M., Freeman, R. & Morrell, W. (1997) The long-term course of severe anorexia nervosa in adolescents: Survival analysis of recovery, relapse, and outcome predictors over 10–15 years in a prospective study. *International Journal of Eating Disorders*, 22(4), 339–60.

Strous, R. D. (2010). Psychiatric genocide: Reflections and responsibilities. *Schizophrenia Bulletin*, 36, 208–10.

Stuart, J. (2006). Dr Rufus May: One man and a bed. Independent on Sunday, 6 August. Accessed at www.independent.co.uk/news/people/profiles/dr-rufus-may-one-man-and-a-bed-410698.html on 23 December 2011.

Suh, E., Diener, E., Oishi, S. & Triandis, H. C. (1998). The shifting basis of life satisfaction judgments across cultures: Emotions versus norms. *Journal of Personality and Social Psychology*, 74, 482–93.

Sullivan, H. S. (1927). Tentative criteria of malignancy in schizophrenia. *American Journal of Psychiatry*, 84, 759–82.

Sullivan, H. S. (1938). Psychiatry: Introduction to the study of interpersonal relations. *Psychiatry: Journal for the Study of Interpersonal Processes*, 1, 21–134.

Sullivan, H. S. (1962). *Schizophrenia as a Human Process*. New York: W. W. Norton.

Sullivan, H. S. (1974). *Schizophrenia as a Human Process*. New York: W. W. Norton.

Summers, A. & Rosenbaum, B. (2013). Psychodynamic psychotherapy for psychosis: Empirical evidence. In J. Read & J. Dillon (Eds), *Models of Madness* (2nd edn). London: Routledge.

Summerfield, D. (1999). A critique of seven assumptions behind psychological trauma programmes in war-affected areas. *Social Science & Medicine*, 48, 1449–62.

Surowiecki, J. (2004). *The Wisdom of Crowds: Why the Many are Smarter than the Few*. London: Abacus.

Survivors History Group (2011). Survivors history group takes a critical look at historians. In M. Barnes & P. Cotterell (Eds), *Critical Perspectives on User Involvement*. Bristol: The Policy Press.

Swaggerty-Valdes, N. (2009). The impact of race and social class on clinician bias. Unpublished PhD thesis. Nova Southeastern University, USA.

Swan, S. & Andrews B. (2003). The relationship between shame, eating disorders and disclosure in treatment. *British Journal of Clinical Psychology*, 42, 367–78.

Swank, R. L. & Marchand, W. E. (1946). Combat neuroses: Development of combat exhaustion. *Archives of Neurology & Psychology*, 55, 236–47.

Swanson, J. M., Elliott, G. R., Greenhill, L. L., Wigal, T., Arnold, L. E., Vitiello, B. et al. (2007). Effects of stimulant medication on growth rates across 3 years in the MTA follow-up. *Journal of the American Academy of Child & Adolescent Psychiatry*, 46, 1015–27.

Sweeney, A., Beresford, P., Faulkner, A., Nettle, M. & Rose, D. (Eds) (2009). *This is Survivor Research*. Ross-on-Wye: PCCS Books.

Syvälahti, E., Räkköläinen, V., Aaltonen, J., Lehtinen, V. & Hietala, J. (2000). Striatal D2 dopamine receptor density and psychotic symptoms in schizophrenia: A longitudinal study. *Schizophrenia Research*, 43(2–3), 159–66.

Szabo, C. P., Berk, M. & Allwood, T. E. (1995). Eating disorder in black South African females: A series of cases. *South African Medical Journal*, 87, 524–30.

Szabo, C. P. & Le Grange, D. (2001). Eating disorders and the politics of identity: The South African experience. In M. Nasser, M. A. Katzman & R. A. Gordon (Eds), *Eating Disorder and Cultures in Transition*. London: Routledge.

Szasz, T. S. (1961). *The Myth of Mental Illness: Foundations of a Theory of Personal Conduct*. New York: Paul B. Hoeber.

Szasz, T. S. (1976a). Schizophrenia: The sacred symbol of psychiatry. *British Journal of Psychiatry*, 129, 308–16.

Szasz, T. S. (1976b). Anti-psychiatry: The paradigm of the plundered mind. *The New Review*, 3(29), 3–14.

Szasz, T. (1994). Psychiatric diagnosis, psychiatric power and psychiatric abuse. *Journal of Medical Ethics*, 20, 135–8.

Szasz, T. (2009). *Antipsychiatry: Quackery Squared*. New York: Syracuse University Press.

Szmukler, G. I., Eisler, I., Russell, G. F. & Dare, C. (1985). Anorexia nervosa, parental 'expressed emotion' and dropping out of treatment. *The British Journal of Psychiatry*, 147, 265–71.

Taitimu, M. (2007). Ngā Whakawhitinga: Standing at the crossroads. Māori ways of understanding extra-ordinary experiences and schizophrenia.Unpublished doctoral thesis, University of Auckland.

Takahashi, T. (1989). Social phobia syndrome in Japan. *Comprehensive Psychiatry*, 30, 45–52.

Tarrier, N. (1991). Some aspects of family interventions in schizophrenia: Adherence to treatment programmes. *British Journal of Psychiatry*, 159, 475–80.

Tarrier, N. (2002). Commentary: Yes, cognitive behaviour therapy may well be all you need. *British Medical Journal*, 324, 291–2.

Tarrier, N., Haddock, G., Barrowclough, C. & Wykes, T. (2002). Are all psychological treatments for psychosis equal? The need for CBT in the treatment of psychosis and not for psychodynamic psychotherapy: Invited commentary Paley and Shapiro. *Psychology & Psychotherapy: Theory, Research & Practice*, 75, 365–74.

Tarrier, N., Lewis, S., Haddock, G., Bentall, R., Drake, R., Kinderman, P. et al. (2004). Cognitive-behavioural therapy in first-episode and early schizophrenia 18-month follow-up of a randomised controlled trial. *British Journal of Psychiatry*, 184, 231–9.

Tarrier, N. & Wykes, T. (2004). Is there evidence that cognitive behaviour therapy is an effective treatment for schizophrenia? A cautious or cautionary tale? *Behaviour Research and Therapy*, 42, 1377–401.

Taylor, G. (2011). Making sense of unusual experiences: A dialogical approach to insight. Unpublished Clin Psy D thesis, Scool of Psychology, University of East London.

Taylor, L. (1984). *In the Underworld*. London: Unwin paperbacks.

Taylor, J. L., Gillmer, B. T. & Robertson, A. (2003). An alternative perspective on the proposed Mental Health Act reforms. *Clinical Psychology*, 22, 35–7.

Taylor, T., Taske, N., Swann, C., Waller, S., Barnett-Page, E. & Seymour, L. (2007). *Public Health Interventions to Promote Positive Mental Health and Prevent Mental Health Disorders among Adults*. London: National Institute for Health & Clinical Excellence.

Teggin, A., Elk, R., Ben-Arie, O. & Gillis, L. (1985). A comparison of CATEGO class 'S' schizophrenia in three ethnic groups: Psychiatric manifestations. *British Journal of Psychiatry*, 147, 683–7.

Teicher, M. H., Glod, C. & Cole, J. O. (1990). Emergence of intense suicidal preoccupation during fluoxetine treatment. *American Journal of Psychiatry*, 147, 207–10.

Tenback, D. E., van Harten, P. N., Slooff, C. J. & van Os, J. (2010). Incidence and persistence of tardive dyskinesia and extrapyramidal symptoms in schizophrenia. *Journal of Psychopharmacology*, 24, 1031–5.

Tepper, S. J. & Haas, J. F. (1979). Prevalence of tardive dyskinesia. *Journal of Clinical Psychiatry*, 40, 508–16.

Tew, J. (Ed.) (2005). *Social Perspectives in Mental Health*. London: Jessica Kingsley.

Thakker, J. & Ward, T. (1998). Culture and classification: The cross-cultural application of the DSM-IV. *Clinical Psychology Review*, 18, 501–29.

Thara, R. & Eaton, W. W. (1996). Outcome of schizophrenia: The Madras longitudinal study. *Australian and New Zealand Journal of Psychiatry*, 30(4), 516–22.

The Observer (2001). Revealed: The Secret of Human Behaviour. Sunday, 11 February.

Thewissen, V., Bentall, R., Lecomte, T., van Os, J. & Myin-Germeys, I. (2008). Fluctuations in self-esteem and paranoia in the context of everyday life. *Journal of Abnormal Psychology*, 117, 143–53.

Thewissen, V., Myin-Germeys, I., Bentall, R., De Graaf, R., vollebergh, W. & van Os, J. . (2007). Instability in self-esteem and paranoia in a general population sample. *Social Psychiatry and Psychiatric Epidemiology*, 42, 1–5.

Thiels, C., Schmidt, U., Treasure, J. & Garthe, R. (1998). Four-year follow-up of guided self-change for bulimia nervosa. *American Journal of Psychiatry*, 155, 947–53.

Thomas, P. (1997). *The Dialectics of Schizophrenia*. London: Free Association Books.

Thomas, P. & Leuder, I. (2000). *Voices of Reason, Voices of Insanity: Studies of Verbal Hallucinations*. London: Routledge.

Thompson, A., Nelson, B., McNab, C., Simmon, M., Leicester, S., McGorry, P. et al. (2010). Psychotic symptoms with sexual content in the 'ultra high risk' for psychosis population: Frequency and association with sexual trauma. *Psychiatry Research*, 177(1–2), 84–91.

Thompson, A., Stuart, H., Bland, R., Arboledo-Florez, J., Warner, R. & Dickson, R. (2002). Attitudes about schizophrenia from the pilot site of the WPA worldwide campaign against the stigma of schizophrenia. *Social Psychiatry and Psychiatric Epidemiology*, 37, 475–82.

Thomson, R. (1982). Side effects and placebo amplification. *British Journal of Psychiatry*, 140, 64–8.

Thornicroft, G. (2006). *Shunned: Discrimination against People with Mental Illness*. Oxford: Oxford University Press.

Thornicroft, G. & Goldberg, D. (1998). Has community care failed? *Maudsley Discussion Paper* No. 5. London: Institute of Psychiatry.

Tiefer, L. (1996). *Sex is Not a Natural Act*. Boulder CO: Westview Press.

Tiefer, L. (2001). A new view of women's sexual problems: Why new, why now? *The Journal of Sex Research*, 38, 89–96.

Tiefer, L. (2004). *Sex Is Not A Natural Act & Other Essays*. Boulder: Westview Press.

Tiefer, L. (2006). The viagra phenomenon. *Sexualities*, 9(3), 273–94.

Tiefer, L., Hall, M. & Tavris, C. (2002). Beyond dysfunction: A new view of women's sexual problems. *Journal of Sex & Marital Therapy*, 28(1), 225–32.

Tien, A. (1991). Distribution of hallucinations in the population. *Social Psychiatry & Psychiatric Epidemiology*, 26, 287–92.

Tien, A. & Eaton, W. W. (1992). Psychopathologic precursors and sociodemographic risk factors for the schizophrenia syndrome. *Archives of General Psychiatry*, 49, 37–46.

Tienari, P., Sorri, A., Lahti, I., Naarala, M., Wahlberg, K.-E., Moring, J. et al. (1987). Genetic and psychosocial factors in schizophrenia: The Finnish adoptive family study. *Schizophrenia Bulletin*, 13(3), 477–84.

Tienari, P., Wynne, J., Moring, I., Lahti, M, Narasala, A, Sorri, K. et al. (1994). The Finnish adoptive study of schizophrenia: Implications for family research. *British Journal of Psychiatry*, 164 (suppl. 23), 20–6.

Tiggemann, M., Gardiner, M. & Slater, A. (2000). I would rather be size 10 than have straight A's. A focus group study of adolescent girls' wish to be thinner. *Journal of Adolescence*, 23, 645–59.

Tiggemann, M. & Slater, A. (2004). Thin ideals in music television: A source of social comparison and body dissatisfaction. *International Journal of Eating Disorders*, 35, 48–58.

Tiihonen, J., Lonnqvist, J., Wahlbeck, K., Klaukka, T., Niskanen, L., Tanskanen, A. et al. (2009). 11-year follow-up of mortality in patients with schizophrenia: A population-based cohort study (Fin11 Study). *Lancet*, 374, 620–7.

Timko, C., Striegel-Moore, R. H., Silberstein, L. R. & Rodin, J. R. (1987). Feminity/masculinity and disordered eating in women: How are they related? *International Journal of Eating Disorders*, 6, 701–12.

Tohen, M., Calabrese, J. R., Sachs, G. S., Banov, M. D., Detke, H. C., Risser, R. et al. (2006). Randomized, placebo-controlled trial of olanzapine as maintenance therapy in patients with bipolar I disorder responding to acute treatment with olanzapine. *American Journal of Psychiatry*, 163, 247–56.

Tolman, C. (1994). *Psychology, Society, Subjectivity: An Introduction to German Critical Psychology*. London: Routledge.

Tomm, K. (1990). A critique of the DSM. *Dulwich Centre Newsletter*, 3, 5–8.

Tooth, J. C. & Newton, M. P. (1961). Leucotomy in England and Wales 1942–1954. Reports on public health and medical subjects. London: Ministry of Health.

Torgersen, S., Kringlen, E. & Cramer,V. (2001). The prevalence of personality disorders in a community sample. *Archives of General Psychiatry*, 58, 590–6.

Torrey, E. F. (1987). Prevalence studies in schizophrenia. *British Journal of Psychiatry*, 150, 598–608.

Torrey, E. F. & Yolken, R. H. (2010). Psychiatric genocide: Nazi attempts to eradicate schizophrenia. *Schizophrenia Bulletin*, 36, 26–32.

Totton, N. (2000). *Psychotherapy and Politics*. London: Sage.

Tozzi, F., Thornton, L. M., Klump, K. L., Fichter, M. M., Halmi, K. A. & Kaplan, A. S. et al. (2005). Symptom fluctuation in eating disorders: Correlates of diagnostic crossover. American Journal of Psychiatry, 162(4), 732–40.

Triandis, H. C. (1989). Self and social behavior in differing cultures. *Psychological Review*, 96, 269–89.

Triandis, H. C. (1995). *Individualism and Collectivism* (New Directions in Social Psychology). Boulder: Westview Press.

Triandis, H. C., Leung, K., Villareal, M. J. & Black, F. L. (1985). Allocentric versus ideocentric tendencies: Convergent and discriminant validation, *Psychological Review*, 96, 269–89.

Trierweiler, S. J., Neighbors, H. W., Munday, C., Thompson, E. E., Binion, V. J. & Gomez, J. P. (2000). Clinician attributions associated with the diagnosis of schizophrenia in African American and non-African American patients. *Journal of Consulting and Clinical Psychology*, 68(1), 171–5.

Triffleman, E., Marmar, C., Delucchi, K. & Ronfeldt, H. (1995). Childhood trauma and posttraumatic stress disorder in substance abuse inpatients. *Journal of Nervous and Mental Disease*, 183(3), 172–6.

Troisi, A., Massaroni, P. & Cuzzolaro, M. (2005). Early separation anxiety and adult attachment style in women with eating disorders. *British Journal of Clinical Psychology*, 44, 89–97.

Troop, N. A. & Treasure, J. L. (1997). Psychosocial factors in the onset of eating disorders: Responses to life-events and difficulties. *British Journal of Medical Psychology*, 70, 373–85.

Trower, P., Birchwood, M. & Meaden, A. (2010). Appraisals: Voices' power and purpose. In F. Larøi & A. Aleman (Eds), *Hallucinations: A Guide to Treatment and Management*. Oxford: Oxford University Press.

Truax, C. B. (1966). Reinforcement and nonreinforcement in Rogerian psychotherapy. *Journal of Abnormal Psychology*, 71, 1–9.

Trull, T. J. & Durrett, C. A. (2005). Categorical and dimensional models of personality disorder. *Annual Review of Clinical Psychology*, 1, 355–80.

Tseng, W. S. (2001). *Handbook of Cultural Psychiatry*. San Diego CA: Academic Press.

Tummey, R. & Tummey, F. (2008). Iatrogenic abuse. In R. Tummey & T. Turner (Eds), *Critical Issues in Mental Health*. Basingstoke: Palgrave Macmillan.

Turner, B. S. (1992). *Regulating Bodies: Essays in Medical Sociology*. London: Routledge.

Turner, V. W. (1974). *Revelation and Divination in Ndembu Ritual*. Ithaca NY: Cornell University Press.

Twenge, J. (2000). The age of anxiety? Birth cohort change in anxiety and neuroticism 1952–1993. *Journal of Personality and Social Psychology*, 79(6), 1007–21.

Tyrer, P. (Ed.) (2000). *Personality Disorders: Diagnosis, Management and Course* (2nd revised edn). Oxford: Butterworth Heinemann.

Tyrer, P. (2001). The case for cothymia: Mixed anxiety and depression as a single diagnosis. *British Journal of Psychiatry*, 179, 191–3.

Tyrer, P. & Baldwin, D. (2006). Generalised anxiety disorder. *Lancet*, 368, 2156–66.

Tyrer, P., Coombs, N., Ibrahimi, F., Mathilakath, A., Bajaj, P. & Ranger, M. (2007). Critical developments in the assessment of personality disorder. *British Journal of Psychiatry*, 190 (suppl. 49), s51–s59.

Tyrer, P., Duggan, C., Cooper, S., Crawford, M., Seivewright, H., Rutter, D. et al. (2010). The successes and failures of the DSPD experiment: The assessment and management of severe personality disorder. *Medicine, Science and the Law*, 50, 95–9.

Uhlhass, P. & Singer, W. (2010). Abnormal neural oscillations and synchrony in schizophrenia. *Nature Reviews Neuroscience* 11, 100–13.

Ujike, H., Otani, K., Nakatsuka, M., Ishii, K., Sasaki, A., Oishi, T. et al. (2009). Association study of gender identity disorder and sex hormone-related genes. *Progress in Neuro-Psychopharmacology and Biological Psychiatry*, 33(7), 1241–4.

UK Drug Policy Commission (2010). *Drugs and Diversity: Ethnic Minority Groups*. Accessed at www.ukdpc.org.uk/reports/shtml on 11 June 2011.

Ukpong, D., Makanjuola, R. & Morakinyo, O. (2002). A controlled trial of modified electroconvulsive therapy in schizophrenia in a Nigerian teaching hospital. *West African Journal of Medicine*, 21, 237–40.

United Kingdom Advocacy Network (UKAN) (2001). *A Clear Voice, a Clear Vision: An Advocacy Reader*. Sheffield: Author.

United Kingdom Advocacy Network (UKAN) (2004). *Advocacy Today and Tomorrow: The UK Advocacy Network Training Tool*. Sheffield: Author.

United Kingdom Advocacy Network/Mental Health Task Force User Group (1994). *Advocacy: A Code of Practice*. London: Department of Health.

Ussher, J. M. (1989). *The Psychology of the Female Body*. London: Routledge.

Ussher, J. M. & Baker, C. D. (1993). *Psychological Perspectives on Sexual Problems: New Directions in Theory and Practice*. New York: Routledge.

Ustun, T. B. & Sartorius, N. (1995). The background and rationale of the WHOL collaborative study on 'psychological problems in general health care'. In T. B. Ustin & N. Sartorius (Eds), *Mental Illness in General Health Care: An International Study* (347–60). Chichester: Wiley.

Vale, V. (Ed.) (2008). *Pranks!* (2nd edn). San Francisco CA: RE/Search Publications.

van der Kolk (2003). The neurobiology of childhood trauma. *Child and Adolescent Psychiatric Clinics of North* America, 12, 293–3.

van der Kolk, B. & Fisler, R. (1994). Childhood abuse and neglect and loss of self-regulation. *Bulletin of the Menninger Clinic*, 58, 145–68.

Van Deurzen, E. (1998). *Paradox & Passion in Psychotherapy: An Existential Approach to Therapy and Counselling*. Chichester: Wiley-Blackwell.

van Ijendoorn, M., Schuengel, C. & Bakermans-Kranenburg, M. (1999). Disorganised attachment in early childhood: Meta-analysis of precursors, concomitants and sequelae. *Development and Psychopathology*, 11, 225–49.

Van Os, J., Galdos, P., Lewis, G., Bourgeois, M. & Mann, A. (1993). Schizophrenia sans frontières: Concepts of schizophrenia among French and British psychiatrists. *British Medical Journal*, 307, 489.

Van Os, J., Hanssen, M., Bijl, R. & Ravelli, A. (2000). Strauss (1969) revisited: A psychosis continuum in the general population? *Schizophrenia Research*, 45, 11–20.

Van Os, J. & Kapur, S. (2009). Schizophrenia. *Lancet*, 374(9690), 635–45.

Van Os, J. & Verdoux, H. (2003). Diagnosis and classification of schizophrenia: Categories versus dimensions, distributions versus disease. In R. M. Murray, P. B. Jones, E. Susser, J. van Os & M. Cannon (Eds), *The Epidemiology of Schizophrenia* (364–410). New York: Cambridge University Press.

Van Putten, T. & Emory, W. (1973). Traumatic neuroses in Vietnam returnees: Forgotten diagnosis? *Archives of General Psychiatry*, 29, 695–8.

van Voren, R. (2010). Political abuse of psychiatry – an historical overview. *Schizophrenia Bulletin*, 36, 33–5.

Vares, T. & Braun, V. (2002). Spreading the word, but what word is that? Viagra and male sexuality in popular culture. *Sexualities*, 9(3), 315–32.

Varese, F., Smeets, F., Drukker, M., Lieverse, R., Lataster, T., Viechtbauer, W. et al. (2012). Childhood adversities increase the risk of psychosis: A meta-analysis of patient-control, prospective- and cross-sectional cohort studies. *Schizophrenia Bulletin*, 38, 661–71.

Vaughn, C. E. & Leff, J. (1976). The influence of family and social factors on the course of psychiatric illness. A comparison of schizophrenic and depressed neurotic patients. *British Journal of Psychiatry*, 129, 125–37.

Vaughn, C. E., Snyder, K. S., Jones, S., Freeman, W. B. & Falloon, I. R. (1984). Family factors in schizophrenic relapse: Replication in California of British research on expressed emotion. *Archives of General Psychiatry*, 41: 1169–77.

Verheul, R., Bartak, A. & Widiger, T. (2007). Prevalence and construct validity of personality disorder not otherwise pecified (PDNOS). *Journal of Personality Disorders*, 21, 359–70.

Viding, E., Frick, P. J. & Plomin, R. (2007). Aetiology of the relationship between callous-unemotional traits and conduct problems in childhood. *British Journal of Psychiatry*, 190(suppl. 49), S33–S38.

Viguera, A. C., Baldessarini, R. J., Hegarty, J. D., Van Kammen, D. P. & Tohen, M. (1997). Clinical risk following abrupt and gradual withdrawal of maintenance neuroleptic treatment. *Archives of General Psychiatry*, 54, 49–55.

Vita, A. & de Peri, L. (2007). The effects of anti-psychotic treatment on cerebral structure and function in schizophrenia. *International Review of Psychiatry*, 19, 431–8.

Vitousek, K. B. & Hollon, S. D. (1990). The investigation of schematic content and processing in eating disorders. *Cognitive Therapy & Research*, 14, 191–214.

Vizard, E., Hickey, N. & McCrory, E. (2007). Developmental trajectories associated with juvenile sexually abusive behaviour and emerging severe personality disorder in childhood: 3-year study. *British Journal of Psychiatry*, 190(suppl. 49), s27–s32.

Volcano, D. & Halberstam, J. (1999). *The Drag King Book*. London: Serpent's Tail.

Vygotsky, L. S. (1962). *Thought and Language* (Trans. E. Hanfmann & G. Vakar). Cambridge MA: MIT Press.

Vygotsky, L. S. (1978). *Mind in Society*. Harvard: Harvard University Press.

Waddington, J. L., O'Callaghan, E., Larkin, C. & Kinsella, A. (1993). Cognitive dysfunction in schizophrenia: Organic vulnerability factor or state marker for tardive dyskinesia? *Brain & Cognition*, 23, 56–70.

Wahl, O. (1999). Mental health consumers' experience of stigma. *Schizophrenia Bulletin*, 25, 467–78.

Wahlberg, K. E., Wynne, L. C., Oja, H., Keskitalo, P., Pykäläinen, L., Lahti, I. et al. (1997). Gene-environment interaction in vulnerability to schizophrenia: Findings from the Finnish Adoptive Family Study of Schizophrenia. *American Journal of Psychiatry*, 54, 355–62.

Wakefield, J. (1992). The concept of mental disorder: On the boundary between biological facts and social values. *American Psychologist*, 47(3), 373–88.

Walker, I. & Read, J. (2002). The differential effectiveness of psychosocial and biogenetic causal explanations in reducing negative attitudes toward 'mental illness'. *Psychiatry: Interpersonal and Biological Processes*, 65(4), 313–25.

Wallcraft, J., Read, J. & Sweeney, A. (2003). *On Our Own Terms: Users and Survivors of Mental Health Services Working Together for Support and Change*. London: Sainsbury Centre For Mental Health.

Wallcraft, J., Schrank, B. & Amering, M. (Eds) (2009). *Handbook of Service User Involvement in Mental Health Research*. Chichester: Wiley-Blackwell.

Waller, G., Hamilton, K., Rose, N., Sumra, J. & Baldwin, G. (1993). Sexual abuse and body-image distortion in the eating disorder. *British Journal of Clinical Psychology*, 32, 350–2.

Waller, G., Kennerley, H. & Ohanian, V. (2007). Schema focused cognitive-behaviour therapy with eating disorders. In L. P. Riso, P. T. du Poit & J. E. Young (Eds), *Cognitive Schemas and Core Beliefs in Psychiatric Disorders: A Scientist-Practitioner Guide* (139–75). New York: American Psychiatric Association.

Walsh, B. T., Kaplan, A. S., Attia, E., Olmsted, M., Parides, M., Carter, J. C. et al. (2006). Fluoxetine after weight restoration in anorexia nervosa. A randomized controlled trial. *The Journal of the American Medical Association* (JAMA), 295, 2605–12.

Walsh, E., Moran, P., Scott, M., McKenzie, K., Burns, T., Creed, M. et al. (2003). Prevalence of violent victimisation in severe mental illness. *British Journal of Psychiatry*, 183, 233–8.

Walsh, J. & Burns, F. (2000). Sexual maturation and control issues among sexually abused and non-abused anorexia patients. *British Journal of Clinical Psychology*, 39, 307–10.

Walter, G. (1998). The attitude of health professionals towards carers and individuals with mental illness. *Australasian Psychiatry*, 6, 70–1.

Walton, J. (1985). Casting out and bringing back in Victorian England: Pauper lunatics, 1840–1870. In W. F. Bynum, R. Porter & M. Shepherd (Eds), *The Anatomy of Madness*, Vol. 2 (132–46). London: Tavistock.

Ward, C. H., Beck, A. T., Mendelson, M., Mock, J. E. & Erbaugh, J. K. (1962). The psychiatric nomenclature: Reasons for diagnostic disagreement. *Archives of General Psychiatry*, 7, 198–205.

Ward, A., Ramsay, R., Turnbull, S., Benedettini, M. & Treasure, J. (2000). Attachment patterns in eating disorders: Past in the present. *International Journal of Eating Disorders*, 28, 370–6.

Warden, J. (1998a). England abandons care in the community for the mentally ill. *British Medical Journal*, 317, 1611.

Warden J. (1998b). Psychiatrists hit back at home secretary. *British Medical Journal*, 317, 1270.

Warner, R. (1994). *Recovery from Schizophrenia: Psychiatry and Political Economy*. London: Routledge.

Warner, R. (1996). Response to 'the role of self-help programs in the rehabilitation of persons with severe mental illness and substance use disorders'. *Community Mental Health Journal*, 32, 83–6.

Warner, R. (2003). How much of the burden of schizophrenia is alleviated by treatment? *British Journal of Psychiatry*, 183, 375–6.

Warner, R. (2004). *Recovery from Schizophrenia: Psychiatry and Political Economy*. London: Routledge.

Warner, R. (2005). Prevention in psychiatry: Some cautions. *Die Psychiatrie: Grundlagen & Perspektiven*, 2(1), 52–4.

Warner, R. (2008). Schizophrenia in the third world. In *Deviance across Cultures* (243–53). New York, NY: Oxford University Press; US.

Warner, R. (2009). Recovery from schizophrenia and the recovery model. *Current Opinion in Psychiatry*, 22(4), 374–80.

Warner, S. (2000). *Understanding Child Sexual Abuse: Making the Tactics Visible*. Gloucester: Handsell.

Warner, S. (2009). *Understanding Child Sexual Abuse: Feminist Revolutions in Theory, Research and Practice*. London: Routledge.

Warner, S. & Wilkins, T. (2003). Diagnosing distress and reproducing disorder: Women, child sexual abuse and 'borderline personality disorder'. In P. Reavey & S. Warner (Eds), *New Feminist Stories of Childhood Sexual Abuse* (167–86). London: Routledge.

Wartmann, T. (dir). (2005). Between the Lines: India's Third Gender. Filmquadrat.

Waterson, L. (2000). Dying to be thin. *Reader's Digest*, May, 26–32.

Watkins, J. (2008). *Hearing Voices: A Common Human Experience*. South Yarra, Australia: Michelle Anderson Publishing.

Watkins, M. & Shulman, H. (2008). *Toward Psychologies of Liberation*. New York: Palgrave Macmillan.

Watson, J. B. (1913). Psychology as the behaviorist views it. *Psychological Review*, 20, 158–77.

Watson, P. (1978). *War on the Mind: The Military Uses and Abuses of Psychology*. New York: Basic Books.

Weatherall, A. (2002). *Gender, Language and Discourse*. London: Routledge.

Weber, D. A. and Reynolds, C. R. (2004) Clinical perspectives on neurobiological effects of psychological trauma. *Neuropsychology Review*, 14(2), 115–29.

Webster, G. D. (2009). The person–situation interaction is increasingly outpacing the person–situation debate in the scientific literature: A 30-year analysis of publication trends, 1978–2007. *Journal of Research in Personality*, 43, 278–9.

Webster, J. J. & Palmer, R. L. (2000). The childhood and family background of women with clinical eating disorders: A comparison with women with major depression and women without psychiatric disorder. *Psychological Medicine*, 30(1), 53–60.

Weeks, J. (1985). *Sexuality and its Discontents: Meanings, Myths and Modern Sexualities*. London: Routledge.

Weeks, J. (2003). *Sexuality* (2nd edn). London: Routledge.

Weeks, J. (2011) *The Languages of Sexuality*. London: Routledge.

Weeks, J., Holland, J. & Waites, M. (Eds) (2003). *Sexualities and Society: A Reader*. Cambridge: Polity Press.

Weerasekera, P. (1996). *Multiperspective Case Formulation: A Step towards Treatment Integration*. Malabar, FL: Krieger.

Weinmann, S. & Aderhold, V. (2010). Antipsychotic medication, mortality and neurodegeneration: The need for more selective use and lower doses. *Psychosis: Psychological, Social and Integrative Approaches*, 2(1), 50–69.

Weinmann, S., Read, J. & Aderhold, V. (2009). Influence of antipsychotics on mortality in schizophrenia: Systematic review. *Schizophrenia Research*, 113(1), 1–11.

Weinstock, R. & Nair, M. (1984). Antisocial personality: Diagnosis or moral judgment? *Journal of Forensic Sciences*, 29, 557–65.

Weishaar, M. E. (1996). Developments in cognitive therapy: 1960–95. In W. Dryden (Ed.), *Developments in Psychotherapy: Historical Perspectives*. London: Sage.

Weiss, M. & Kleinman, A. (1988). Depression in cross-cultural perspective: Developing a culturally informed model. In P. Dasen, J. Berry & N. Sartorious (Eds), *Cross-cultural Psychology and Health: Toward Applications* (179–206). Newbury Park CA: Sage.

Weissman M. M., Bland R. C., Canino G. J., Faravelli C., Greenwald S., Hwu H. G. et al. (1996). Cross-national epidemiology of major depression and bipolar disorder. *Journal of the American Medical Association*, 276, 293–9.

Welch, S. L., Doll, H. A. & Fairburn, C. G. (1997). Life events and the onset of bulimia nervosa: a controlled study. *Psychological Medicine*, 27, 515–22.

Werner, S., Malaspina, D. & Rabinowitz, J. (2001). Socioeconomic status at birth is associated with risk of schizophrenia: Population-based multi-level study. *Schizophrenia Bulletin*, 33(6), 1373–8.

Wertheim, E. H., Paxton, S. J., Schutz, H. K. & Muir, S. L. (1997). Why do adolescent girls watch their weight? An interview study examining sociocultural pressures to be thin. *Journal of Psychosomatic Research*, 42, 345–55.

Wescott, P. (1979). One man's schizophrenic illness. *British Medical Journal*, 1, 989–90.

Wessely, S. (1990). Old wine in new bottles: Neurasthenia and 'ME'. *Psychological Medicine*, 20, 35–53.

Westen, D. (1997). Divergences between clinical and research methods for assessing personality disorders: Implications for research and the evolution of axis II. *American Journal of Psychiatry*, 154, 895–903.

Westen, D. & Morrison, K. (2001). A multi-dimensional meta-analysis of treatments for depression, panic and generalised anxiety disorder: An empirical examination of the status of empirically supported therapies. *Journal of Consulting and Clinical Psychology*, 69(6), 875–99.

Whaley, A. (2001). Cultural mistrust and the clinical diagnosis of paranoid schizophrenia in African American patients. *Journal of Psychopathology and Behavioral Assessment*, 23(2), 93–100.

Wheaton, B. (1978). The sociogenesis of psychiatric disorder. *American Sociological Review*, 43, 383–403.

Wheen, F. (2010). *Strange Days Indeed: The Golden Age of Paranoia*. London: Fourth Estate.

Whitaker, R. (2002). *Mad in America: Bad Science, Bad Medicine and the Enduring Mistreatment of the Mentally Ill*. Cambridge MA: Perseus.

White, E. & Brooker, C. (2001). The fourth quinquennial national community mental health nursing census of England and Wales. *International Journal of Nursing Studies*, 38, 61–70.

White, M. (2007). *Maps of Narrative Therapy*. New York: Norton.

White, M. & Epston, D. (1990). *Narrative Means to Therapeutic Ends*. London: Norton.

Whitley, R., Prince, M., McKenzie, K. & Stewart, R. (2006). Exploring the ethnic density effect: A qualitative study of a London electoral ward. *International Journal of Social Psychiatry*, 52(4), 376–91.

Whittington, C. J., Kendall, T., Fonagy, P., Cottrell, D., Cotgrove, A. & Boddington, E. (2004). Selective serotonin reuptake inhibitors in childhood depression: Systematic review of published versus unpublished data. *Lancet*, 363, 1341–5.

Whittle, S. (1998). The trans-cyberian mail way. *Social Legal Studies*, 7, 389–408.

Widiger, T. A. (1998). Invited essay: Sex biases in the diagnosis of personality disorders. *Journal of Personality Disorders*, 12, 95–118.

Widiger, T. A. & Mullins-Sweatt, S. N. (2009). Five-factor model of personality disorder: A proposal for DSM-V. *Annual Review of Clinical Psychology*, 5, 197–220.

Wiener, M. & Marcus, D. (1994). A sociocultural construction of depression. In T. R. Sarbin & J. L. Kitsuse (Eds), *Constructing the Social* (213–31). London: Sage Publications.

Wig, N. N., Mernon, H., Medi, J., Kuipers, A. Ghosh, R. D., Korten, A. et al. (1987). Expressed emotion and schizophrenia in North India. II: Distribution of expressed emotion components among relatives of schizophrenia patients in Aarhus and Chandigarh. *British Journal of Psychiatry*, 151, 160–5.

Wiggins, J. S. (1982). Circumplex models of interpersonal behavior in clinical psychology. In P. C. Kendall & J. N. Butcher (Eds), *Handbook of Research Methods in Clinical Psychology* (183–221). New York: Wiley.

Wilberg, T., Hummelen, B., Pedersen, G. & Karterud, S. (2008). A study of patients with personality disorder not otherwise specified. *Comprehensive Psychiatry*, 49, 460–8.

Wilkinson, R. (1996). *Unhealthy Societies: The Afflictions of Inequality*. London: Routledge.

Wilkinson, R. (2005). *The Impact of Inequality: How to Make Sick Societies Healthier*. London. Routledge.

Wilkinson, R. & Pickett, K. (2009). *The Spirit Level: Why More Equal Societies Almost Always Do Better*. London: Allen Lane.

Williams, J. (1999). Social inequalities and mental health. In C. Newnes, C. Dunn & G. Holmes (Eds), *This is Madness: A Critical Look at Psychiatry and the Future of Mental Health Services*. Ross-On-Wye: PCCS.

Willoughby, C. (2001). Waiting for the penny to drop. *The Journal of Critical Psychology, Counselling & Psychotherapy*, 2, 108–17.

Wilson, D. (2011). F.D.A. Panel Is Split on Electroshock Risks. *New York Times*, 28 January.

Wilson, E. (2003). *Adorned in Dreams: Fashion and Modernity*. London: I.B. Taurus.

Wilson, G., Grilo, C. M. & Vitousek, K. M. (2007). Psychological treatment of eating disorders. *American Psychologist*, 62, 199–216.

Wilson, G., Loeb, K. & Walsh, B. T. (1999). Psychological versus pharmacological treatments of bulimia nervosa: Predictors and processes of change. *Journal of Consulting and Clinical Psychology*, 67, 451–7.

Wilson, G. & Shafran, R. (2005). Eating disorders guidelines from NICE. *Lancet*, 365, 79–81.

Wilson, M. (1993). DSM III and the transformation of American psychiatry: A history. *American Journal of Psychiatry*, 150, 399–410.

Wilson, T. E., Jean-Louis, G., Schwartz, R., Golub, E. T., Cohen, M. H., Maki, P. et al. (2010). HIV infection and women's sexual functioning. *Journal of Acquired Immune Deficiency Syndrome*, 54(4), 360–7.

Wincze, J. P., Bach, A. K. & Barlow, D. H. (2008). Sexual dysfunction In Barlow, D. H. (Ed.), *Clinical Handbook of Psychological Disorders: A Step-by-step Treatment Manual*. NewYork: The Guildford Press.

Wincze, J. P. & Carey, M. P. (2001). *Sexual Dysfunction: A Guide for Assessment and Treatment*. New York: Guilford Press.

Winnicott, D.W. (1958). Hate in the countertransference. In D.W. Winnicott (Ed.), *Collected Papers: Through Pediatrics to Psycho-analysis* (chapter XV, 194–203). New York : Basic Books.

Winnicott, D. W. (1987). *Babies and Their Mothers*. London: Free Association Books.

Winter, D. (2008). Cognitive behaviour therapy: From rationalism to constructivism? *European Journal of Psychotherapy & Counselling*, 10, 221–30.

Winter, D. (2010). Editorial for special issue: Researcher allegiance in the psychological therapies. *European Journal of Psychotherapy & Counselling*, 12, 3–9.

Winters, K. (2007). Issues of GID reform for transsexual women and men. Accessed at www.gidreform.org.

Winters, K. (2008). *Gender Madness in Modern Psychiatry: Essays from the Struggle for Dignity*. Dillon CO: GID Reform Advocates.

Winton, M. A. (2001). The medicalization of male sexual dysfunctions: An analysis of sex therapy journals. *Journal of Sex Education and Therapy*, 25, 231–9.

Wiseman, C. V., Gray, J. J., Mossiman, J. E. & Ahrens, A. H. (1992). Cultural expectations of thinness in women: An update. *International Journal of Eating Disorders*, 11, 85–9.

Witztum, E., Grisaru, N. & Budowski, D. (1996). The 'Zar' possession syndrome among Ethiopian immigrants to Israel: Cultural and clinical aspects. *British Journal of Medical Psychology*, 69, 207–25.

Wix, S. (2007). Independent nurse prescribing in the mental health setting. *Nursing Times*, 103(44), 30–1.

Woerner, M. G., Kane, J. M., Lieberman, J. A., Alvir, J., Bergmann, K. J., Borenstein, M. et al. (1991). The prevalence of tardive dyskinesia. *Journal of Clinical Psychopharmacology*, 11, 34–42.

Wolkowitz, O. M. & Pickar, D. (1991). Benzodiazepines in the treatment of schizophrenia: A review and reappraisal. *American Journal of Psychiatry*, 148, 714–26.

Wonderlich, S. A., Brewerton, T., Jocic, Z., Dansky, B. & Abbot, D. (1997). Relationship of childhood sexual abuse and eating disorders. *Journal of the American Academy of Child and Adolescent Psychiatry*, 36, 1107–15.

Woodruff, P., Wright, I., Bullmore, E., Brammer, M., Howard, R., Williams, S. et al. (1997). Auditory hallucinations and the temporal cortical response to speech in schizophrenia: A functional magnetic resonance imaging study. *American Journal of Psychiatry*, 154, 1676–82.

World Health Organization (1973). *The International Pilot Study of Schizophrenia*. Geneva: Author.

World Health Organization (1992). *The ICD-10 Classification of Mental and Behavioural Disorders: Diagnostic Criteria for Research*. Geneva: Author.

World Health Organization Office for Europe (2009). *Mental Health, Resilience and Inequalities*. Copenhagen: Author.

Wright, K., Haigh, K. & McKeown, M. (2007). Reclaiming the humanity in personality disorder. *International Journal of Mental Health Nursing*, 16, 236–46.

Wundt, W. V. (1888). Volkerpsychologie.

Wykes, T., Parr, A. & Landau, S. (1999). Group treatment of auditory hallucinations: Exploratory study of effectiveness. *British Journal of Psychiatry*, 175, 180–5.

Wykes, T., Steel, C., Everitt, B. S. & Tarrier, N. (2008). Cognitive behavior therapy for schizophrenia: Effect sizes, clinical models, and methodological rigor. *Schizophrenia Bulletin*, 34, 523–7.

Yamada, H., Sadato, N., Konishi, Y., Muramoto, S., Kimura, K., Tanaka, M. et al. (2000). A milestone for normal development of the infantile brain detected by functional MRI. *Neurology*, 55(2), 218–23.

Yen, S., Robins, C. J. & Lin, N. (2000). A cross-cultural comparison of depressive symptom manifestation: China and the United States. *Journal of Consulting and Clinical Psychology*, 68, 993–9.

Yonkers, K., Dyck, I., Warshaw, M. & Keller, M. (2000). Factors predicting the clinical course of generalised anxiety disorder. *British Journal of Psychiatry*, 176, 544–9.

Young, E., Abelson, J., Curtis, G. & Nesse, R. (1997). Childhood adversity and vulnerability to mood and anxiety disorders. *Depression and Anxiety*, 5, 66–72.

Young, J. (1990). *Cognitive Therapy for Personality Disorders: A Schema-focused Approach*. Saratosa FL: Professional Resource Exchange.

Young, M., Read, J., Barker-Collo, S. & Harrison, R. (2001). Evaluating and overcoming barriers to taking abuse histories. *Professional Psychology: Research and Practice*, 32(4), 407–14.

Yung, A. R., Killackey, E., Nelson, B. & McGorry, P. (2010). The impact of early intervention in schizophrenia. In W. F. Gattaz & G. Busatto (Eds), *Advances in Schizophrenia Research* (299–316). New York: Springer Science + Business Media.

Yung, A. R., Phillips, L. J., McGorry, P. D., McFarlane, C. A., Francey, S., Harrigan, S. et al. (1998). Prediction of psychosis: A step towards indicated prevention of schizophrenia. *British Journal of Psychiatry* Suppl, 172, 14–20.

Yung, A. R., Phillips, L. J., Nelson, B., Francey, S., PanYuen, H., Simmons, M. et al. (2011). Randomized controlled trial of interventions for young people at ultra high risk for psychosis: 6-month analysis. *Journal of Clinical Psychiatry*, 72(4), 430–40.

Yung, A. R., Stanford, C., Cosgrave, E., Killackey, E., Phillips, L., Nelson, B. et al. (2006). Testing the ultra high risk (prodromal) criteria for the prediction of psychosis in a clinical sample of young people. *Schizophrenia Research*, 84, 57–66.

Zanarini, M. C., Frankenburg, F. R., Dubo, E. D., Sickel, A. E., Trikha, A., Levin, A. et al. (1998). Axis I comorbidity of borderline personality disorder. *American Journal of Psychiatry*, 155, 1733–9.

Zanarini, M. C., Frankenburg, F. R., Reich, D. B., Marino, M. F., Lewis, R. E., Williams, A. A. et al. (2000). Biparental failure in the childhood experiences of borderline patients. *Journal of Personality Disorders*, 14, 264–73.

Zanarini, M. C., Skodol, A. E., Bender, D., Dolan, R., Sanislow, C., Schaefer, E. et al. (2000). The collaborative longitudinal personality disorders study: Reliability of axis I and II diagnoses. *Journal of Personality Disorders*, 14, 291–9.

Zeiss, A. M., Davies, H. D., Wood, M. & Tinklenberg, J. R. (1990). The incidence and correlates of erectile problems in patients with Alzheimer's disease. *Archives of Sexual Behavior*, 19, 325–31.

Zimmerman, M. (1994). Diagnosing personality disorders: A review of issues and research methods. *Archives of General Psychiatry*, 51, 225–45.

Zimmerman, M., Francione-Witt, C., Chelminski, I., Young, D. & Tortolani C. (2008). Problems applying the DSM-IV eating disorders diagnostic criteria in a general psychiatric outpatient practice. *Journal of Clinical Psychiatry*, 69, 381–4.

Zimmerman, M., Rothschild, L. & Chelminski, I. (2005). The prevalence of DSM-IV personality disorders in psychiatric outpatients. *American Journal of Psychiatry*, 162, 1911–18.

Zlotowitz, S., Alcock, C. & Barker, C. (2010). Music and change: The psychological impact of a community music project for marginalised young people. Paper presented at British Psychological Society Annual Conference, Holiday Inn, Stratford-upon-Avon 14–16 April.

Zuardi, A., Crippa, J., Hallak, J., Moriera, F. & Guimaraes, F. (2006). Cannabidiol, a cannabis sativa constituent, as an antipsychotic drug. *Brazilian Journal of Medical and Biological Research*, 39, 421–9.

Zubin, J. & Spring, B. (1977). Vulnerability: A new view of schizophrenia. *Journal of Abnormal Psychology*, 86, 103–26.

Zuercher, J. N., Cumella, E. J., Woods, B. K., Eberly, M. & Carr, J. K. (2003). Efficacy of voluntary nasogastric tube feeding in female inpatients with anorexia nervosa. *Journal of Parenteral and Enteral Nutrition*, 27, 268–76.

INDEX

Note: Page numbers in **bold** refer to definition/concept; Page numbers in *italics* refer to figures; Page numbers followed by "b" indicate boxed material; Page numbers followed by "t" indicate tables.